STATISTICS USING SPSS: AN INTEGRATIVE APPROACH
SECOND EDITION

This is an introductory applied statistics text that can be used for a one- or two-semester course at either the undergraduate or graduate level. Central features are its hands-on approach; the use of real data; the wealth of exercises and illustrated examples using these data; the complete set of detailed answers to exercises in an appendix; the presentation of statistical methods with a clear, conceptual emphasis that includes an historical account of each method; and the integration of SPSS in a way that reflects statistical practice. Step-by-step instructions for using SPSS are provided as each new analytic procedure is introduced. A data CD is included with the text so that students may conduct their own statistical analyses and learn firsthand how statistics is used in practice.

Sharon Lawner Weinberg is Professor of Quantitative Methods and Psychology and former Vice Provost for Faculty Affairs at New York University. She is widely published, with more than 50 publications in her field, including books, book chapters, journal articles, and major reports. She is the recipient of numerous grants and author with Kenneth P. Goldberg of *Statistics for the Behavioral Sciences* (Cambridge, 1990).

Sarah Knapp Abramowitz is Associate Professor of Mathematics and Computer Science at Drew University. She received her Ph.D. from New York University and is an Associate Editor of the *Journal of Statistics Education*.

Statistics Using SPSS

AN INTEGRATIVE APPROACH
Second Edition

SHARON LAWNER WEINBERG

New York University

SARAH KNAPP ABRAMOWITZ

Drew University

CAMBRIDGE
UNIVERSITY PRESS

CAMBRIDGE UNIVERSITY PRESS
Cambridge, New York, Melbourne, Madrid, Cape Town, Singapore,
São Paulo, Delhi, Dubai, Tokyo

Cambridge University Press
32 Avenue of the Americas, New York, NY 10013-2473, USA

www.cambridge.org
Information on this title: www.cambridge.org/9780521676373

First published 2008
Reprinted 2010

Printed in the United States of America

A catalog record for this publication is available from the British Library.

Library of Congress Cataloging in Publication Data

Weinberg, Sharon L.
    Statistics using SPSS 2nd ed. / Sharon L. Weinberg, Sarah Knapp Abramowitz. –
    p.   cm.
    Includes bibliographical references and index.
    ISBN-13: 978-0-521-89922-2 (hardback)
    ISBN-13: 978-0-521-67637-3 (pbk.)
    ISBN-10: 0-521-67637-1 (pbk.)
    1. Mathematical statistics – Data processing. 2. SPSS (Computer file)
I. Abramowitz, Sarah Knapp, 1967– II. Title.
QA276.W4423   2008
519.50285–dc22

                                                        2007031423

ISBN 978-0-521-89922-2 Hardback
ISBN 978-0-521-67637-3 Paperback

Contents

Preface

Although based loosely on *Basic Statistics for Education and the Behavioral Sciences* by Sharon Lawner Weinberg and Kenneth P. Goldberg, published by Cambridge University Press (1990), this text, in its second edition, capitalizes on the widespread availability of menu-driven software packages to create a course of study that links good statistical practice to the analysis of real data. Several important guiding principles continue to motivate our presentation.

First, and perhaps most importantly, we believe that a good data analytic plan must serve to uncover the story behind the numbers, what the data tell us about the phenomenon under study. To begin, a good data analyst must know his data well and have confidence in it. Accordingly, we emphasize the usefulness of diagnostics in both graphical and statistical form to expose anomalous cases, which might unduly influence results, and to help in the selection of appropriate assumption-satisfying transformations so that ultimately we may have confidence in our findings. We also emphasize the importance of using more than one method of analysis to answer fully the question posed. Seeing a three-dimensional sculpture in its entirety requires viewing that sculpture from many vantage points. Likewise, fully understanding the phenomenon under study often requires delving into data from more than one vantage point via the application of more than one method of analysis.

Second, because we believe that data are central to the study of good statistical practice, this text comes with an accompanying disk that contains several data sets used throughout the text. One is a large set of real data containing 48 variables and 500 cases that we make repeated use of in both worked-out examples and end-of-chapter exercises. By posing interesting questions about variables in this large, real data set (e.g., Is there a gender difference in expected income at age 30 of eighth graders?), we are able to employ a more meaningful and contextual approach to the introduction of statistical methods and to engage students more actively in the learning process. The repeated use of this data set also contributes to creating a more cohesive presentation of statistics, one that links different methods of analysis to each other and avoids the perception that statistics is an often-confusing array of so many separate and distinct methods of analysis with no bearing or relationship to one another.

Third, we believe that the result of a null hypothesis test (to determine whether an effect is real or merely apparent) is only a means to an end (to determine whether the effect being studied is important or useful), rather than an end in itself. Accordingly, in our presentation of null hypothesis testing, we stress the importance of evaluating the magnitude of the effect if it is deemed to be real, and of drawing clear distinctions between statistically significant and substantively significant results. Toward this end, we introduce the computation of standardized measures of effect size as common practice following a statistically significant result. While we provide guidelines for evaluating, in general, the magnitude of an effect, we encourage readers to think more subjectively about the magnitude of an effect, bringing into the evaluation their own knowledge and expertise in a particular area.

Fourth, a course in applied statistics should not only provide students with a sound statistical knowledge base but also with a set of data analytic skills. Accordingly, we have incorporated SPSS, a popularly used statistical software package, into the presentation of statistical material using a highly integrative approach. SPSS is used to provide students with a platform for actively engaging in the learning process associated with what it means to be a good data analyst by allowing them to apply their newly learned knowledge to the real world of applications. This approach serves also to enhance the conceptual understanding of material and the ability to interpret output and communicate findings.

Finally, we believe that a key ingredient of an introductory statistics text is a clear, conceptual, yet rigorous approach. We emphasize conceptual understanding through an exploration of both the mathematical principles underlying statistical methods and real-world applications. We use an easygoing, informal style of writing that we have found gives readers the impression that they are involved in a personal conversation with the authors. And we sequence concepts with concern for student readiness, reintroducing topics in a spiraling manner to provide reinforcement and promote transfer of learning.

New to the second edition are a description of each statistical method within a historical context so that students can appreciate the development of this relatively new field of study as a twentieth-century phenomenon; the inclusion of Fisher's Exact Test; the updating of all SPSS commands to be consistent with SPSS version 15; a bibliography of references to relevant books and journal articles; several new real data sets from a variety of fields, including health; an expanded appendix of SPSS syntax programs for generating simulated data; and many more end-of-chapter exercises along with detailed answers in an appendix.

The book is intended for use in a one- or two-semester introductory applied statistics course for the behavioral, social, or health sciences at either the graduate or undergraduate level, or as a reference text as well. It is not intended for readers who wish to acquire a more theoretical understanding of mathematical statistics. The book consists of 16 chapters. In addition to topics traditionally found in introductory applied statistics texts in the behavioral, social, or health sciences, the book covers such topics as data transformations, diagnostic tools for the analysis of model fit, the logic of null hypothesis testing, assessing the magnitude of effects, interaction and its interpretation in two-way analysis of variance and multiple regression, and non-parametric statistics. This broad coverage of topics gives the instructor flexibility in curriculum planning and provides students with more advanced material for future work in statistics.

Acknowledgments

Each of the editions of our book has benefited from the many helpful comments of our New York University and Drew University students. Each also has benefited from the insights and suggestions of several colleagues. For their help in improving the first edition, we would like to thank (in alphabetical order) Chris Apelian, John Daws, Linda Lesniak, Kathleen Madden, Robert Norman, and Eileen Rodriguez; for their help on the second edition, we would like to thank Gabriella Belli, Patricia Busk, Ellie Buteau, Michael Karchmer, Steve Kass, and Jon Kettenring. Of course, any errors or shortcomings in the second edition remain the responsibility of the authors.

Finally, and most importantly, we would like to thank our families, Martha Lawner; Steve, Allison, and Carolyn Weinberg; Jason and Danielle Barro; Philip Korn; Susan and Tony Knapp; and Dave, Michelle, and Scott Abramowitz for their enduring love, patience, and support.

CHAPTER ONE

Introduction

Welcome to the study of statistics! It has been our experience that many students face the prospect of taking a course in statistics with a great deal of anxiety, apprehension, and even dread. They fear not having the extensive mathematical background that they assume is required, and they fear that the contents of such a course will be irrelevant to the work in their fields of concentration.

Although it is true that an extensive mathematical background is required at more advanced levels of statistical study, it is not required for the introductory level of statistics presented in this book. Greater reliance is placed on the use of the computer for calculation and graphical display so that we may focus on issues of conceptual understanding and interpretation. Although hand computation is de-emphasized, we believe that a basic mathematical background – including the understanding of fractions, decimals, percentages, signed (positive and negative) numbers, exponents, linear equations, and graphs – is essential for an enhanced conceptual understanding of the material.

As for the issue of relevance, we have found that students better comprehend the power and purpose of statistics when statistics is presented in the context of a substantive problem with real data. In this information age, data are available on a myriad of topics. Whether our interests are in health, education, psychology, business, the environment, or another subject, numerical data may be accessed readily to address our questions of interest. The purpose of statistics is to allow us to analyze these data to extract the information that they contain in a meaningful way and to write a story about the numbers that is both compelling and accurate.

Throughout this course of study we make use of a series of real data sets that are contained in the data disk attached to this book. We will pose relevant questions and learn the appropriate methods of analysis for answering such questions. You will learn that more than one statistic or method of analysis typically is needed to fully address a question. You will learn also that a detailed description of the data, including possible anomalies, and an ample characterization of results are critical components of any data analytic plan. Through this process we hope that you will come to view statistics as an integrated set of data analytic tools that when used together in a meaningful way will serve to uncover the story contained in the numbers.

THE ROLE OF THE COMPUTER IN DATA ANALYSIS

From our own experience, we have found that the use of a computer statistics package to carry out computations and create graphs not only enables a greater emphasis on conceptual understanding and interpretation but also allows students to study statistics in a way that reflects statistical practice. We have selected the latest version of SPSS for Windows available to us at the time of writing, version 15.0, for use with this text. We have selected SPSS because it is a well-established package that is widely used by behavioral and social scientists. Also, because it is menu-driven, it is easily learned. SPSS is a computational package, like MINITAB, JMP, Data Desk, Systat, Stata, and SPlus, that is powerful enough to quickly handle the analysis of large data sets. By the end of the course, you will have obtained a conceptual understanding of statistics as well as an applied, practical skill in how to carry out statistical operations. SPSS version 14.0 operates in a Windows environment.

STATISTICS: DESCRIPTIVE AND INFERENTIAL

The subject of statistics may be divided into two general branches: descriptive and inferential. *Descriptive statistics* is used when the purpose of an investigation is to *describe* the data that have been (or will be) collected. Suppose, for example, that a third-grade elementary school teacher is interested in determining the proportion of children who are firstborn in her class of 30 children. In this case, the focus of the teacher's question is her own class of 30 children and she will be able to collect data on all of the students about whom she would like to draw a conclusion. The data collection operation involves noting whether each child in the classroom is firstborn or not; the statistical operations involve counting the number who are firstborn and dividing that number by 30, the total number of students in the class, to obtain the proportion sought. Because the teacher is using statistical methods merely to describe the data she collected, this is an example of descriptive statistics.

Suppose, on the other hand, that the teacher is interested in determining the proportion of children who are firstborn in *all* third-grade classes in the city where she teaches. It is highly unlikely that she will be able to (or even want to) collect the relevant data on all individuals about whom she would like to draw a conclusion. She will probably have to limit the data collection to some randomly selected smaller group and use *inferential statistics* to generalize to the larger group the conclusions obtained from the smaller group. *Inferential statistics* is used when the purpose of the research is not to describe the data that have been collected, but to generalize or make inferences based on it. The smaller group on which she collects data is called the *sample*, whereas the larger group to whom conclusions are generalized (or inferred) is called the *population*. In general, two major factors influence the teacher's confidence that what holds true for the sample also holds true for the population at large. These two factors are the method of sample selection and the size of the sample. Only when data are collected on *all* individuals about whom a conclusion is to be drawn (when the sample *is* the population and we are therefore in the realm of descriptive statistics) can the conclusion be drawn with 100 percent certainty. Thus, one of the major goals of inferential statistics is to assess the degree of certainty of inferences when such inferences are drawn from sample data. Although this text is divided roughly into two parts, the first on descriptive statistics and the second on inferential statistics, the second part draws heavily on the first.

VARIABLES AND CONSTANTS

In the preceding section, we discussed a teacher's interest in determining the proportion of students who are firstborn in the third grade of the city where she teaches. What made this question worth asking was the fact that she did not expect everyone in the third grade to be firstborn. Rather, she quite naturally expected that, in the population under study, birth order would vary, or differ, from individual to individual and that only in certain individuals would it be first.

Characteristics of persons or objects that vary from person to person or object to object are called *variables*, whereas characteristics that remain constant from person to person or object to object are called *constants*. Whether a characteristic is designated as a variable or a constant depends, of course, on the study in question. In the study of birth order, birth order is a variable: it can be expected to vary from person to person in the given population. In that same study, grade level is a constant; all persons in the population under study are in the third grade.

. . . .

EXAMPLE 1.1. Identify some of the variables and constants in a study comparing the math achievement of tenth-grade boys and girls in the southern United States.

Solution. *Constants:*   Grade level; Region of the United States
  Variables: Math achievement; Sex

. . . .

EXAMPLE 1.2. Identify some of the variables and constants in a study of math achievement of secondary-school boys in the southern United States.

Solution. *Constants:*   Sex; Region of the United States
  Variables: Math achievement; Grade level

Note that grade level is a constant in Example 1.1 and a variable in Example 1.2. Because constants are characteristics that do not vary in a given population, the study of constants is neither interesting nor informative. The major focus of any statistical study is therefore on the variables rather than the constants. Before variables can be the subject of statistical study, however, they need to be given numerical values. The next section describes the process of measuring variables so as to achieve that goal.

THE MEASUREMENT OF VARIABLES

Measurement involves the observation of characteristics on persons or objects, and the assignment of numbers to those persons or objects so that the numbers represent the amounts of the characteristics possessed. As introduced by S. S. (Stanley Smith) Stevens (1946) in the paper "On the Theory of Scales of Measurement," and later described by him (1951) in a chapter "Mathematics, Measurement, and Psychophysics" in the *Handbook of Experimental Psychology*, we describe four levels of measurement in this text. Each of the four levels is defined by the nature of the observation and the way in which the numbers assigned correspond to the amount of the underlying characteristic that has been observed. The level of measurement of a variable determines which numerical operations (e.g., addition, subtraction, multiplication, or division) are permissible to be performed on that variable. If other than the permissible numerical operations are used on a variable given its level of measurement, one can expect the statistical conclusions drawn with respect to that variable to be questionable.

Nominal Level. The nominal level of measurement is based on the simplest form of observation – whether two objects are similar or dissimilar (e.g., whether they are short versus nonshort, male versus female, or college student versus non–college student). Objects observed to be similar in some characteristic (e.g., college student) are assigned to the same class or category, whereas objects observed to be dissimilar in that characteristic are assigned to different classes or categories. In the nominal level of measurement, classes or categories are *not* compared as, say, taller or shorter, better or worse, or more educated or less educated. Emphasis is strictly on observing whether the objects are similar or dissimilar. As befitting its label, classes or categories are merely named, but not compared, in the *nominal* level of measurement.

Given the nature of observation for this level of measurement, numbers are assigned to objects using the following simple rule: if objects are dissimilar, they are assigned different numbers; if objects are similar, they are assigned the same number. For example, all persons who are college students would be assigned the same number (say, 1); all persons who are non–college students also would be assigned a number that is different from 1 (say, 2) to distinguish them from college students. Because the focus is on distinction and not comparison, in this level of measurement, the fact that the number 2 is larger than the number 1 is irrelevant in terms of the underlying characteristic being measured (whether or not the person is a college student). Accordingly, the number 1 could have been assigned, instead, to all persons who are non–college students and the number 2 to all persons who are college students. Any numbers other than 1 and 2 also could have been used.

Although the examples in this section (e.g., college student versus non–college student) may be called *dichotomous* in that they have only two categories, nominal variables also may have more than two categories (e.g., car manufacturers – Toyota, Honda, General Motors, Ford, Chrysler, etc.).

Ordinal Level. The ordinal level of measurement is based not only on observing objects as similar or dissimilar but also on ordering those observations in terms of an underlying characteristic. Suppose, for example, we were not interested simply in whether a person was a college student, but rather in ordering college students in terms of the degree of their success in college (e.g., whether the college student was below average, average, or above average). We would, therefore, need to observe such ordered differences among these college students in terms of their success in college, and we would choose numbers to assign to the categories that corresponded to that ordering. For this example, we might assign the number 1 to the below-average category, the number 2 to the average category, and the number 3 to the above-average category. Unlike in the nominal level of measurement, in the ordinal level of measurement it is relevant that 3 is greater than 2, which, in turn, is greater than 1, because this ordering conveys in a meaningful way the ordered nature of the categories relative to the underlying characteristic of interest. That is, comparisons among the numbers correspond to comparisons among the categories in terms of the underlying characteristic of success in college. In summary, the ordinal level of measurement applies two rules for assigning numbers to categories: (1) different numbers are assigned to persons or objects that possess different amounts of the underlying characteristic, and (2) the higher the number assigned to a person or object, the less (or more) of the underlying characteristic that person or object is observed to possess. From these two rules it does *not* follow, however, that equal numerical differences along the number scale correspond to equal increments in the underlying measured characteristic in the ordinal level of measurement. Although the differences between 3 and 2 and between 2 and 1 in our college student success example are both equal to 1, we cannot infer that the difference in success between above-average college students and average college students equals the difference in success between average college students and below-average college students.

We consider another example that may more clearly convey the idea of the ordinal level of measurement. Suppose we line ten people up according to their size place and assign a number from 1 to 10, respectively, to each person so that each number corresponds to the person's size place in line. We could assign the number 1 to the shortest person, the number 2 to the next shortest person, and so forth, ending by assigning the number 10 to the tallest person. According to this method, the numbers assigned to each pair of adjacent people in line will differ from each other by the same value (i.e., 1), but clearly the heights of each pair of adjacent people will not necessarily also differ by the same value. Some adjacent pairs will differ in height by only a fraction of an inch, whereas other adjacent pairs will differ in height by several inches. Accordingly, only some of the features of this size place ranking are reflected or modeled by the numerical scale. In particular, whereas in this case the numerical scale can be used to judge the relative order of one person's height compared to another's, differences between numbers on the numerical scale cannot be used to judge how much taller one person is than another. As a result, statistical conclusions made about variables that are measured on the ordinal level and are based on some aspect other than an ordering or ranking of the numbers (including taking sums or differences) are not expected to be meaningful.

Interval Level. An ordinal level of measurement can be developed into a higher level of measurement if it is possible to assess how near to each other the persons or objects are in the underlying characteristic being observed. If numbers can be assigned in such a way that equal numerical differences along the scale correspond to equal increments in the underlying characteristic, we have what is called an *interval level of measurement.* As an example of an interval level of measurement, consider the assignment of yearly dates – the chronological scale. Because one year is defined as the amount of time necessary for the earth to revolve once around the sun, the yearly date may be thought of as a measure of the number of revolutions of the earth around the sun up to and including that year. Hence, the assignment of numbers to the property *number of revolutions of the earth around the sun* is on an interval level of measurement. Specifically, this means that equal numerical differences for intervals (such as A.D. 1800 to 1850 and A.D. 1925 to 1975) represent equal differences in the number of revolutions of the earth around the sun (in this case, 50). In the interval level of measurement, therefore, we may make meaningful statements about the amount of *difference* between any two points along the scale. As such, the numerical operations of addition and subtraction (but not multiplication and division) lead to meaningful conclusions at the interval level and are therefore permissible at that level. For conclusions based on the numerical operations of multiplication and division to be meaningful, we require the ratio level of measurement.

Ratio Level. An interval level of measurement can be developed into a higher level of measurement if the number zero on the numeric scale corresponds to zero or "not any" of the underlying characteristic being observed. With the addition of this property (called an *absolute zero*), ratio comparisons are meaningful, and we have what is called the *ratio level of measurement.* Consider once again the chronological scale and, in particular, the years labeled A.D. 2000 and 1000. Even though 2000 is numerically twice as large as 1000, it does not follow that the number of revolutions represented by the year 2000 is twice the number of revolutions represented by the year 1000. This is because, on the chronological scale, the number zero (A.D. 0) does not correspond to zero revolutions of the earth around the sun (i.e., the earth had made revolutions around the sun many times prior to the year A.D. 0). To make meaningful multiplicative or ratio comparisons of this type between points on our number scale, the number zero on the numeric scale must correspond to zero (none) of the underlying characteristic being observed.

In measuring height, not by size place but with a standard ruler, for example, we would typically assign a value of 0 on the number scale to "not any" height and assign the other numbers according to the rules of the interval scale. The scale that would be produced in this case would be a ratio scale of measurement, and ratio or multiplicative statements (such as "John, who is 5 feet tall, is *twice* as tall as Jimmy, who is 2.5 feet tall") would be meaningful. It should be pointed out that, for variables to be considered to be measured on a ratio level, "not any" of the underlying characteristic only needs to be theoretically meaningful. Clearly, no one has zero height, yet using zero as an anchor value for this scale to connote "not any" height is theoretically meaningful.

Choosing a Scale of Measurement. Why is it important to categorize the scales of measurement as nominal, ordinal, interval, or ratio? If we consider college students and assign a 1 to students who are male college students, a 2 to female college students, and a 3 to those who are not college students at all, it would not be meaningful to add these numbers or even to compare their sizes. For example, two male college students together do not suddenly become a female college student, even though their numbers add up to the number of a female college student ($1 + 1 = 2$). And a female college student who is attending school only half-time is not suddenly a male college student, even though half of her number is the number of a male college student ($2/2 = 1$). On the other hand, if we were dealing with a ratio-leveled height scale, it would be possible to add, subtract, multiply, or divide the numbers on the scale and obtain results that are meaningful in terms of the underlying trait, height. In general, and as noted earlier, the scale of measurement determines which numerical operations, when applied to the numbers of the scale, can be expected to yield results that are meaningful in terms of the underlying trait being measured. *Any numerical operation can be performed on any set of numbers; whether the resulting numbers are meaningful, however, depends on the particular level of measurement being used.*

Note that the four scales of measurement exhibit a natural hierarchy, or ordering, in the sense that each level exhibits all the properties of the level below it (see Table 1.1). Any characteristic that can be measured on one scale listed in Table 1.1 can also be measured on any scale below it in that list. Given a precise measuring instrument such as a perfect ruler, we can measure a person's height, for example, as a ratio-scaled variable, in which case we could say that a person whose height is 5 feet has twice the height of a person whose height is 2.5 feet. Suppose, however, that no measuring instrument were available. In this situation, we could, as we have done before, "measure" a person's height according to size place or by categorizing a person as tall, average, or short. By assigning numbers to these three categories (such as 5, 3, and 1, respectively), we would create an ordinal level of measurement for height.

Table 1.1. Hierarchy of scales of measurement

1. Ratio
2. Interval
3. Ordinal
4. Nominal

In general, it may be possible to measure a variable on more than one level. The level that is ultimately used to measure a variable should be the highest level possible, given the precision of the measuring instrument used. A perfect ruler allows us to measure heights on a ratio level, whereas the eye of an observer allows us to measure height only on an ordinal level. If we are able to use a higher level of measurement but decide to use a lower level instead, some of the information that would have been available on the higher level would be lost. We would also be restricting ourselves to a lower level of permissible numerical operations.

EXAMPLE 1.3. Identify the level of measurement (nominal, ordinal, interval, or ratio) most likely to be used to measure the following variables:

1. Ice cream flavors
2. The speed of five runners in a 1-mile race, as measured by the runners' order of finish: first, second, third, and so on
3. Temperature measured in degrees Centigrade
4. The annual salary of individuals

Solution.

1. The variable ice cream flavors is most likely measured at the nominal level of measurement because the flavors themselves may be categorized simply as being the same or different and there is nothing inherent to them that would lend themselves to a ranking. Any ranking would have to depend on some extraneous property such as, say, taste preference. If numbers were assigned to the flavors as follows,

Flavor	Number
Vanilla	0
Chocolate	1
Strawberry	2
etc.	etc.

   meaningful numerical comparisons would be restricted to whether the numbers assigned to two ice cream flavors are the same or different. The fact that one number on this scale may be larger than another is irrelevant.

2. This variable is measured at the ordinal level because it is the order of finish (first, second, third, and so forth) that is being observed and not the specific time to finish. In this example, the smaller the number the greater the speed of the runner. As in the case of measuring height via a size place ranking, it is not necessarily true that the difference in speed between the runners who finished first and second is the same as the difference in speed between the runners who finished third and fourth. Hence, this variable is not measured at the interval level. If time to finish had been used to measure the speed of the runners, the level of measurement would have been ratio for the same reasons that height, measured by a ruler, is ratio-leveled.

3. Temperature measured in degrees Centigrade is at the interval level of measurement because each degree increment, no matter if it is from 3 to 4 degrees Centigrade or from 22 to 23 degrees Centigrade, has the same physical meaning in terms of the underlying characteristic, heat. In particular, it takes 100 calories to raise the temperature of 1 mL of water by 1 degree Centigrade, no matter what the initial temperature reading on the Centigrade scale. Thus, equal differences along the Centigrade scale correspond to equal

increments in heat, making this scale interval-leveled. The reason this scale is not ratio-scaled is because 0 degrees Centigrade does not correspond to "not any" heat. The 0 degree point on the Centigrade scale is the point at which water freezes, but even frozen water contains plenty of heat. The point of "not any" heat is at -273 degrees Centigrade. Accordingly, we cannot make meaningful ratio comparisons with respect to amounts of heat on the Centigrade scale and say, for example, that at 20 degrees Centigrade there is twice the heat than at 10 degrees Centigrade.

4. The most likely level of measurement for annual salary is the ratio level because each additional unit increase in annual salary along the numerical scale corresponds to an equal additional dollar earned no matter where on the scale one starts (e.g., whether it be at $10,000 or at $100,000), and furthermore, because the numerical value of 0 on the scale corresponds to "not any" annual salary, giving the scale a true or absolute zero. Consequently, it is appropriate to make multiplicative comparisons on this scale, such as "Sally's annual salary of $100,000 is twice Jim's annual salary of $50,000."

DISCRETE AND CONTINUOUS VARIABLES

As we saw in the preceding section, any variable that is not intrinsically numerically valued, such as the ice cream flavors in Example 1.3, may be converted to a numerically valued variable. Once a variable is numerically valued, it may be classified as either discrete or continuous.

Although there is really no exact statistical definition of a discrete or a continuous variable, the following usage generally applies. A numerically valued variable is said to be *discrete* (or *categorical* or *qualitative*) if the values it takes on are integers or can be thought of in some unit of measurement in which they are integers. A numerically valued variable is said to be *continuous* if, in any unit of measurement, whenever it can take on the values *a* and *b*, it can also theoretically take on all the values between *a* and *b*. The limitations of the measuring instrument are not considered when discriminating between discrete and continuous variables. Instead, it is the nature of the underlying variable that distinguishes between the two types.

☞ **Remark.** As we have said, there is really no hard and fast definition of discrete and continuous variables for use in practice. However, the words discrete and continuous do have precise mathematical meanings, and in more advanced statistical work, where more mathematics and mathematical theory are employed, the words are used in their strict mathematical sense. In this text, where our emphasis is on statistical practice, the usage of the terms discrete and continuous is not usually helpful in guiding our selection of appropriate statistical methods or graphical displays. Rather, we generally use the particular level of measurement of the variable, whether it is nominal, ordinal, interval, or ratio.

EXAMPLE 1.4. Let our population consist of all eighth-grade students in the United States, and let X represent the region of the country in which the student lives. X is a variable, because there will be different regions for different students. X is not naturally numerically valued, but because X represents a finite number of distinct categories, we can assign numbers to these categories in the following simple way: 1 = Northeast, 2 = North Central, 3 = South, and 4 = West. X is a discrete variable, because it can take on only four values.

Furthermore, because X is a nominal-leveled variable, the assignment of 1, 2, 3, and 4 to Northeast, North Central, South, and West, respectively, is arbitrary. Any other assignment rule would have been just as meaningful in differentiating one region from another.

EXAMPLE 1.5. Consider that we repeatedly toss a coin 100 times and let X represent the number of heads obtained for each set of 100 tosses. X is naturally numerically valued and may be considered discrete because the only values it can take on are the integer values 0, 1, 2, 3, and so forth. We may note that X is ratio-leveled in this example because 0 on the numerical scale represents "not any" heads.

EXAMPLE 1.6. Consider a certain hospital with 100 beds. Let X represent the percentage of occupied beds for different days of the year. X is naturally numerically valued as a proportion of the number of occupied beds. Although X takes on fractional values, it is considered discrete because the proportions are based on a count of the number of beds occupied, which is an integer value.

EXAMPLE 1.7. Let our population consist of all college freshmen in the United States, and let X represent their heights, measured in inches. X is numerically valued and is continuous because all possible values of height are theoretically possible. Between any two heights exists another theoretically possible height. For example, between 70 and 71 inches in height exists a height of 70.5 inches, and between 70 and 70.5 exists a height of 70.25 inches, and so on.

☞ **Remark.** Even if height in Example 1.7 were reported to the nearest inch (as an integer), it would still be considered a continuous variable because all possible values of height are theoretically possible. Reporting values of continuous variables to the nearest integer is usually due to the lack of precision of our measuring instruments. We would need a perfect ruler to measure the exact values of height. Such a measuring instrument does not, and probably cannot, exist. When height is reported to the nearest inch, a height of 68 inches is considered to represent all heights between 67.5 and 68.5 inches. Although the precision of the measuring instrument determines the accuracy with which a variable is measured, it does not determine whether the variable is discrete or continuous. For that we need only consider the theoretically possible values that a variable can assume.

☞ **Remark.** In addition to the problem of not being able to precisely measure variables, another problem that often confronts the behavioral scientist is the measurement of traits, such as intelligence, that are not directly observable. Instead of measuring intelligence directly, tests have been developed that measure it indirectly, such as the IQ test. Whereas such tests report IQ as an integer value, IQ is considered to be a continuous trait or variable, and an IQ score of 109, for example, is thought of as theoretically representing all IQ scores between 108.5 and 109.5.

Another issue, albeit more controversial, related to the measurement of traits that are not directly observable is the level of measurement employed. Whereas some scientists would argue that IQ scores are only ordinal (given a good test of intelligence, a person whose IQ score is higher than another's on that test is said to have greater intelligence), others would argue that they are interval. Even though equal intervals along the IQ scale (say, between 105 and 110 and between 110 and 115) may not necessarily imply equal amounts of change in intelligence, a person who has an IQ score of 105 is likely to be closer in intelligence to a person who has an IQ score of 100 rather than to a person who has an IQ score of 115. By considering an IQ scale and other such psychosocial scales as ordinal only, one would lose such information that is contained in the data and the ability to make use of statistical operations based on sums and differences, rather than merely on rankings.

Another type of scale, widely used in attitude measurement, is the Likert scale, which consists of a small number of values, usually five or seven, ordered along a continuum representing agreement. The values themselves are labeled typically from strongly disagree to strongly agree. A respondent selects a score on the scale that corresponds to his or her level of agreement with a statement associated with that scale. For the same reasons noted earlier with respect to the IQ scale, for example, the Likert scale is considered by many to be interval rather than strictly ordinal.

· ·

EXAMPLE 1.9. For each variable listed, describe whether the variable is discrete or continuous. Also, describe the level of measurement for each variable. Use the following data set excerpted from data analyzed by Tomasi and Weinberg (1999). The original study was carried out on 105 elementary school children from an urban area who were classified as learning disabled and who, as a result, were receiving special education services for at least three years. In this example, we use only the four variables described in the following table.

Variable Name	What the Variable Measures	How It Is Measured
SEX		0 = Male 1 = Female
GRADE	Grade level	1, 2, 3, 4, or 5
AGE	Age in years	Ages ranged from 6 to 14
MATHCOMP	Mathematical comprehension	Higher scores associate with greater mathematical comprehension; scores could range from 0 to 200

Solution. The variable SEX is discrete because the underlying construct represents a finite number of distinct categories (male or female). Furthermore, individuals may be classified as either male or female, but nothing in between. The level of measurement for SEX is nominal because the two categories are merely different from one another.

The variable GRADE is discrete because the underlying construct represents a finite number of distinct categories (five) and individuals in this study may only be in one of the five grades. The level of measurement for GRADE is interval because the grades are ordered and equal numerical differences along the grade scale represent equal increments in grade.

The variable AGE is continuous even though the reported values are rounded to the nearest integer. AGE is continuous because the underlying construct can theoretically take on any value between 5.5 and 14.5 for study participants. The level of measurement for AGE is ratio because higher numerical values correspond to greater age, equal numerical differences along the scale represent equal increments in age within rounding, and the value of zero is a theoretically meaningful anchor point on the scale representing "not any" age.

The variable MATHCOMP, like AGE, is continuous. The underlying construct, mathematical comprehension, theoretically can take on any value between 0 and 200. The level of measurement is at least ordinal because the higher the numerical value, the greater the comprehension in math; it is also considered to be interval because equal numerical differences along the scale are thought to represent equal or nearly equal increments in math comprehension. Because individuals who score zero on this scale do not possess a total absence of math comprehension, the scale does not have an absolute zero and is, therefore, not ratio-leveled.

SETTING A CONTEXT WITH REAL DATA

We turn now to some real data and gain familiarity with SPSS. For this example and for others throughout the book, we have selected data from the National Educational Longitudinal Study begun in 1988, which we will refer to as the NELS data set.

In response to pressure from federal and state agencies to monitor school effectiveness in the United States, the National Center of Education Statistics (NCES) of the U.S. Department of Education conducted a survey in the spring of 1988. The participants consisted of a nationally representative sample of approximately 25,000 eighth graders that was used to measure achievement outcomes in four core subject areas (English, history, mathematics, and science), in addition to personal, familial, social, institutional, and cultural factors that might relate to these outcomes. Details on the design and initial analysis of this survey may be referenced in Horn, Hafner, and Owings (1992). A follow-up of these students was conducted during tenth grade in the spring of 1990; a second follow-up was conducted during the twelfth grade in the spring of 1992; and, finally, a third follow-up was conducted in the spring of 1994.

For this book, we have selected a subsample of 500 cases and 48 variables. The cases were sampled randomly from the approximately 5,000 students who responded to all four administrations of the survey, who were always at grade level (neither repeated nor skipped a grade), and who pursued some form of post-secondary education. The particular variables were selected to explore the relationships between student and home-background variables, self-concept, educational and income aspirations, academic motivation, risk-taking behavior, and academic achievement.

Some of the questions that we are able to address using these data include the following: Do boys perform better on math achievement tests than girls? Does socioeconomic status relate to educational and/or income aspirations? To what extent does enrollment in advanced math in eighth grade predict twelfth-grade math achievement scores? Can we distinguish between students who use marijuana and those who don't in terms of self-concept? Does owning a computer vary as a function of geographical region of residence (Northeast, North Central, South, and West)? As you become familiar with this data set, perhaps you will want to generate questions that are of particular interest to you and explore ways to answer them.

SPSS uses several different windows to help navigate between information about the data set itself and statistical summaries of analyses that have been carried out on that data set. Upon opening the SPSS program, the first window to appear is the Data View window, which contains the values on each of the variables for each of the individuals or objects in the data set. In the Data View window, columns represent variables and rows represent individuals or objects. A second window that relates to the data is the Variable View window, which contains information about the variables themselves, such as their levels of measurement. Statistical summaries of SPSS calculations appear in an Output window, which is introduced in Chapter 2 of this text. Two other SPSS windows, the Chart Editor window and the Syntax window, are introduced in Chapters 2 and 13, respectively.

Exercises 1.9 through 1.13 introduce some of the variables in the NELS data set, including how their levels of measurement and missing values are defined in SPSS. Exercise 1.15 elaborates on data entry and definition in SPSS.

☞ **Remark.** Although we have described four levels of measurement in this chapter, SPSS distinguishes among only three levels of measurement: nominal, ordinal, and scale. The scale level of measurement includes both interval and ratio levels of measurement, as the two are defined in this chapter. Whereas, for analysis purposes, SPSS does not distinguish between these two levels of measurement, distinctions must be kept in mind when interpreting results.

A more complete description of the NELS data set may be found in Appendix A. Descriptions of the other real data sets used throughout this text are also found in Appendix A.

☞ **Remark.** There is an important distinction to be drawn between the numerical results of a statistical analysis and the *interpretation* of these results given by the researcher. Methods involved in the interpretation of results, such as researcher judgment, are not statistical operations. They are extrastatistical. For instance, to determine on the basis of having administered the same standardized test to a group of boys and girls that the girls attain higher scores on average than the boys is a statistical conclusion. However, to add that the reason for this difference is that the test is biased toward the girls is a researcher-based, not a statistically based, conclusion. In offering such an interpretation, the researcher is drawing on nonstatistical information. It is important to be able to separate statistical conclusions from researcher-inferred conclusions. The latter may not justifiably follow from the former; and unfortunately the latter are the ones that are usually remembered and cited.

EXERCISES

1.1. Suppose you are a researcher who is gathering information on the yearly income and number of years of experience of all female doctors practicing in the United States. Identify each of the following as either a constant or a variable in this study. If your answer is variable, identify its most likely level of measurement (nominal, ordinal, interval, or ratio).
  a) Sex
  b) Yearly income as reported on one's tax return
  c) Ethnicity
  d) Profession (not specialty)
  e) Number of years of experience

1.2. Given the population of all clowns in the Ringling Brothers, Barnum and Bailey Circus, identify the following as either constant or variable. If your answer is variable, identify its most likely level of measurement (nominal, ordinal, interval, or ratio).
  a) Height
  b) Profession
  c) Age
  d) Eye color

1.3. Identify each of the following numerical variables as either discrete or continuous and identify their most likely levels of measurement (nominal, ordinal, interval, or ratio).
  a) Percentage of high school seniors each year who report that they have never smoked cigarettes

b) Annual rainfall in Savannah, Georgia, to the nearest inch
c) Number of runs scored in a baseball game
d) Weight
e) Verbal aptitude as measured by SAT verbal score
f) Salary of individual government officials

1.4. Identify the following numerical variables as either discrete or continuous and identify their most likely levels of measurement (nominal, ordinal, interval, or ratio).
   a) Number of students enrolled at Ohio State University in any particular term
   b) Distance an individual can run in five minutes
   c) Hair length
   d) Number of hot dogs sold at baseball games
   e) Self-concept as measured by the degree of agreement with the statement "I feel good about myself," on a five-point scale where 1 represents strongly disagree, 2 represents disagree, 3 represents neutral, 4 represents agree, and 5 represents strongly agree
   f) Lack of coordination as measured by the length of time it takes an individual to assemble a certain puzzle

1.5. Identify the following numerical variables as either discrete or continuous and identify their most likely levels of measurement (nominal, ordinal, interval, or ratio):
   a) Baseball jersey numbers
   b) Number of faculty with Ph.D.s at an institution
   c) Knowledge of the material taught as measured by grade in course
   d) Number of siblings
   e) Temperature as measured on the Fahrenheit scale
   f) Confidence in one's ability in statistics as measured by a yes or no response to the statement, "I am going to do very well in my statistics class this semester"

1.6. A survey was administered to college students to learn about student participation in university-sponsored extracurricular activities. Identify the most likely level of measurement of each of the following variables, taking into account the coding used.

Variable Name	Question Asked	Coding (if any)
AGE	How old are you in years?	
EXTRAC	At which type of extracurricular activity do you spend most of your time?	1 = Sports 2 = Student government 3 = Clubs and organizations 4 = None
TIME	How much time do you spend weekly on university-sponsored extracurricular activities?	0 = None 1 = 1–2 hours 2 = 3–5 hours 3 = 6–10 hours 4 = 10–20 hours 5 = More than 20 hours

   a) AGE
   b) EXTRAC
   c) TIME

1.7. The Campus Survey of Alcohol and Other Drug Norms is administered to college students to collect information about drug and alcohol use on campus. Identify the most likely level of measurement of each of the following variables from that survey, taking into account the coding used.

Variable Name	Question Asked	Coding (if any)
ABSTAIN	Overall, what percentage of students at this college do you think consume no alcoholic beverages at all?	
LIVING	Living arrangements	1 = House/apartment/etc. 2 = Residence hall 3 = Other
STATUS	Student status	1 = Full-time (12+ credits) 2 = Part-time (1–11 credits)
ATTITUDE	Which statement about drinking alcoholic beverages do you feel best represents your own attitude?	1 = Drinking is never a good thing to do. 2 = Drinking is all right but a person should not get drunk. 3 = Occasionally getting drunk is okay as long as it doesn't interfere with academics or other responsibilities. 4 = Occasionally getting drunk is okay even if it does interfere with academics or other responsibilities. 5 = Frequently getting drunk is okay if that's what the individual wants to do.
DRINK	How often do you typically consume alcohol (including beer, wine, wine coolers, liquor, and mixed drinks)?	0 = Never 1 = 1–2 times/year 2 = 6 times/year 3 = Once/month 4 = Twice/month 5 = Once/week 6 = 3 times/week 7 = 5 times/week 8 = Every day

    a) ABSTAIN
    b) LIVING
    c) STATUS
    d) ATTITUDE
    e) DRINK

Exercise 1.8 includes descriptions of some of the variables in the Framingham data set. The Framingham data set is based on a longitudinal study investigating factors relating to coronary heart disease. A more complete description of the Framingham data set may be found in Appendix A.

1.8. For each variable described from the Framingham data set, indicate the level of measurement.

a) CURSMOKE1 indicates whether or not the individual smoked cigarettes in 1956. It is coded so that 0 represents no and 1 represents yes.

b) CIGPDAY1 indicates the number of cigarettes the individual smoked per day, on average, in 1956.

c) BMI1 indicates the body mass index of the individual in 1956. BMI can be calculated as follows:

$$BMI = \left(\frac{Weight\_in\_Pounds}{(Height\_in\_inches) \times (Height\_in\_inches)} \right) \times 703$$

d) SYSBP1 and DIABP1 indicate the systolic and diastolic blood pressures, respectively, of the individuals in 1956. Blood is carried from the heart to all parts of your body in vessels called arteries. Blood pressure is the force of the blood pushing against the walls of the arteries. Each time the heart beats (about 60–70 times a minute at rest), it pumps out blood into the arteries. Your blood pressure is at its highest when the heart beats, pumping the blood. This is called systolic pressure. When the heart is at rest, between beats, your blood pressure falls; this is the diastolic pressure.

Blood pressure is always given as these two numbers, the systolic and diastolic pressures. Both are important. Usually they are written with the systolic above or before the diastolic, such as 120/80 mmHg. If your blood pressure is 120/80, you say that it is "120 over 80." Blood pressure changes during the day. It is lowest when you sleep and rises when you get up. It also can rise when you are excited, nervous, or active. Still, for most of your waking hours, your blood pressure stays pretty much the same when you are sitting or standing still. Normal values of blood pressure should be lower than 120/80. When the level remains too high, for example, 140/90 or higher, the individual is said to have high blood pressure. With high blood pressure, the heart works harder, your arteries take a beating, and your chances of a stroke, heart attack, and kidney problems are greater.

Exercise 1.9 includes descriptions of some of the variables in the NELS data set. The NELS data set is a subset of a data set collected by the NCES, which conducted a longitudinal study investigating factors relating to educational outcomes. A more complete description of the NELS data set may be found in Appendix A.

1.9. Read the description of the following variables from the NELS data set. Then classify them as either discrete or continuous and specify their levels of measurement (nominal, ordinal, interval, or ratio). The variable names are given in capital letters.

a) GENDER. Classifies the student as either male or female, where 0 = "male" and 1 = "female."

b) URBAN. Classifies the type of environment in which each student lives, where 1 = "urban," 2 = "suburban," and 3 = "rural."

c) SCHTYP8. Classifies the type of school each student attended in eighth grade, where 1 = "public," 2 = "private, religious," and 3 = "private, nonreligious."

d) TCHERINT. Classifies student agreement with the statement "My teachers are interested in students" using the Likert scale 1 = "strongly agree," 2 = "agree," 3 = "disagree," and 4 = "strongly disagree."

e) NUMINST. Gives the number of post-secondary institutions the student attended.

f) ACHRDG08. Gives a score for the student's performance in eighth grade on a standardized test of reading achievement. Actual values range from 36.61 to 77.2, from low to high achievement.

g) SES. Gives a score representing the socioeconomic status (SES) of the student, which is a composite of father's education level, mother's education level, father's occupation, mother's occupation, and family income. Values range from 0 to 35, from low to high SES.

h) SLFCNC12. Gives a score for student self-concept in twelfth grade. Values range from 0 to 43. Self-concept is defined as a person's self-perceptions, or how a person feels about himself or herself. Four items comprise the self-concept scale in the NELS questionnaire: I feel good about myself; I feel I am a person of worth, the equal of other people; I am able to do things as well as most other people; and, on the whole, I am satisfied with myself. A self-concept score, based on the sum of scores on each of these items, is used to measure self-concept in the NELS study. Higher scores associate with higher self-concept and lower scores associate with lower self-concept.

i) SCHATTRT. Gives the average daily attendance rate for the school.

j) ABSENT12. Classifies the number of times the student missed school: 0 = never, 1 = 1–2 times, 2 = 3–6 times, and so on.

Exercises 1.10–1.13 require the use of SPSS and the NELS data set.

1.10. Use the instructions that follow to access the NELS data set from the CD that comes with this text. If it is not already selected, click the "Variable View" tag on the bottom left-hand side of the Data Editor. As noted in the text, the Variable View window gives a listing of the variables and their properties, including variable labels, variable type, and level of measurement. Use the Variable View window in the SPSS Data Editor to answer the following questions about the variables in the NELS data set.

To open the NELS data set, click on **File** on the main menu bar, and **Open**. Place the CD that comes with your text into the D: drive. Change the "Look in" box to D:. Double-click on **NELS**. A spreadsheet containing the NELS data set will appear. Open SPSS and the NELS data set. To view the NELS data set, you may find it helpful to change the preferences as follows: Click on **Edit**, **Options**. On the top right of the "General" screen, in the Variable Lists box, click on the circles next to **Display names** and **Alphabetical**. Click on **OK**. After you change this setting, the variables will be displayed in alphabetical order by name in the SPSS menus. It will not change the order of the variables in the data set.

a) What is the first variable in the NELS data set?

b) What is the second variable in the data set and what is its variable label?

c) What are the value labels for this variable? That is, how is the variable coded?

d) What is the level of measurement entered for this variable in SPSS?

e) What is the variable label for the variable FAMSIZE?

f) Why are there no value labels for this variable?

g) What is the level of measurement entered for this variable in SPSS?

h) How many variables are there in the NELS data set?

1.11. If it is not already selected, click the **Data View** tag on the bottom left-hand side of the Data Editor. Use the Data View window in the SPSS Data Editor to answer the following questions about the particular values that different individual students attain in the NELS data set.

a) How many people are in the family (FAMSIZE) of the first student (ID = 1) in the NELS data set?

b) Did the first student in the NELS data set (ID = 1) take advanced math in eighth grade (ADVMATH8)?

c) Did the second student in the NELS data set (ID = 2) take advanced math in eighth grade (ADVMATH8)?

d) How many people are in the NELS data set?

1.12. The variable LATE12 gives the number of times a student was late for school in twelfth grade using the following coding: 0 = never, 1 = 1–2 times, 2 = 3–6 times, 3 = 7–9 times, 4 = 10–15 times, and 5 = more than 15 times. Although a code of 0 indicates that the student was never late, LATE12 is not measured on a ratio scale. Explain. Identify the level of measurement used. Describe how the variable might have been measured using a higher level of measurement.

1.13. The variable EXPINC30 gives, for each student in the NELS, the expected income at age 30 in dollars. Identify the level of measurement used. Describe how the variable might have been measured using a lower level of measurement.

Exercise 1.14 requires the use of SPSS and the States data set. The States data set contains educational information for the 50 states and Washington, DC. A more complete description of the States data set may be found in Appendix A.

1.14. In this exercise, we introduce the notion of Type in the Variable View window and review some of the other information that may be obtained through the SPSS Data Editor. Open the States data set in SPSS.

a) Verify that the variable type for STATE is String (alpha-numeric), for the variable STUTEACH it is Numeric, and for TEACHPAY it is Dollar (currency). What is the variable type for ENROLLMT?

b) Labels are typically used for variables at the nominal and ordinal levels to document the values assigned to the different categories of the variable. For the variable REGION, which category or region of the country is coded 3?

To verify that the value labels for REGION indicate the values associated with each of the four regions, click on **Variable View** in the bottom left-hand corner of the Data Editor window. The second row corresponds to REGION and the values are given in the sixth column. Click on the cell at the intersection of the second row and the sixth column, where it is written

{**1, Northeast,**. . . . Notice that the periods are highlighted. If you click on the periods the complete list of value labels will appear. When you are finished looking at the value labels, click **OK**.

---

  c) What is the difference between Variable Labels and Values?
  d) Why does the variable REGION have no label?
  e) In what region is Arizona?

Exercise 1.15 provides a tutorial on data entry and requires the use of SPSS.

1.15. In this exercise, we will enter data on 12 statisticians who each have contributed significantly to the field of modern statistics. We have provided a table of variable descriptions and a table of data values and detailed instructions on how to proceed.

  a) Set up the data set in SPSS. For each of the five variables, enter the variable Name, Type, Label, and, where appropriate, Values.

Name	Type	Label	Values
Statistician	String		
Gender	Numeric		1 = Female
			2 = Male
Birth	Numeric	Year of birth	
Death	Numeric	Year of death	
AmStat	Numeric	Number of references in *The American Statistician*, 1995–2005	

To enter the variable information into SPSS, make a new "spreadsheet" appear on the monitor either by restarting SPSS or by selecting **File** from the main menu bar, and then **New** and **Data**. Click **Variable View** in the bottom left-hand corner of the Data Editor window. In the first row, under Name, type **Statistician**. Click the next cell in that row. The SPSS defaults will appear. Under the Type column, click the three highlighted dots next to **Numeric** and click the circle next to **String**. Change the Characters from 8 to **28**, because the longest name in the list (Prasanta Chandra Mahalanobis) has 28 characters. Click **OK**. Verify that the Measurement is Nominal. You have finished defining the variable STATISTICIAN. Move to the second row to define the variable GENDER. In the second row, under Name, type **Gender**. Click the next cell in that row. The SPSS defaults will appear. Leave the Type as **Numeric**. Keep the width **8**, but change the decimal places to **0** (if necessary). In the Values column, click **None**, and then the three highlighted dots. In the Value Labels box, type **1** for the Value and **Female** for the Value Label. Click **Add**. Type **2** for the Value and **Male** for the Value Label. Click **Add**. Click **OK**. Change the level of Measurement to **Nominal**. You have finished defining the variable GENDER. Move to the third row to define the variable BIRTH. In the third row, under Name, type **Birth**. Click the next cell in that row. The SPSS defaults will appear. Leave the Type as **Numeric**. Keep the width **8**, but change the decimal places to **0** (if necessary). Verify that the Measurement is **Scale**. You have finished defining the variable BIRTH. Complete the assignment by using this approach to enter the variables DEATH and AMSTAT.

b) Enter the data. The data set is provided in the following table. Click on the Data View tab on the bottom left of the SPSS Data Editor and enter the following values into the spreadsheet, cell by cell.

Statistician	Gender	Birth	Death	AmStat
Sir Francis Galton	2	1822	1911	7
Karl Pearson	2	1857	1936	16
William Sealy Gosset	2	1876	1937	0
Ronald Aylmer Fisher	2	1890	1962	5
Harald Cramer	2	1893	1985	0
Prasanta Chandra Mahalanobis	2	1893	1972	0
Jerzy Neyman	2	1894	1981	7
Egon S. Pearson	2	1895	1980	1
Gertrude Cox	1	1900	1978	6
Samuel S. Wilks	2	1906	1964	1
Florence Nightingale David	1	1909	1995	0
John Tukey	2	1915	2000	12

c) Save the data set on a CD or on your computer hard drive in a file called *Statisticians.sav*.

CHAPTER TWO

Examining Univariate Distributions

As noted in Chapter 1, the function of descriptive statistics is to describe data. A first step in this process is to explore how the collection of values for each variable is distributed across the array of possible values. Because our concern is with each variable taken separately, we say that we are exploring *univariate distributions*. Tools for examining such distributions, including tabular and graphical representations, are presented in this chapter.

COUNTING THE OCCURRENCE OF DATA VALUES

We again make use of the NELS data set (introduced in Chapter 1) by looking at the various univariate distributions it includes. To begin our exploration, we ask the following questions about two of them: How many students in our sample are from each of the four regions of the country (Northeast, North Central, South, and West)? How are the students distributed across the range of values on socioeconomic status (SES)? By counting the number of students who live within a region, or who score within a particular score interval on the SES scale, we obtain the *frequency* of that region or score interval. When expanded to include all regions or all score intervals that define the variable, we have a *frequency distribution*. Frequency distributions may be represented by tables and graphs. The type of table or graph that is appropriate for displaying the frequency distribution of a particular variable depends, in part, on whether the variable is discrete or continuous.

WHEN VARIABLES ARE MEASURED AT THE NOMINAL LEVEL

The variable REGION in the NELS data set is an example of a discrete variable with four possible values or categories: Northeast, North Central, South, and West. To display the number of student respondents who are from each of these regions, we may use frequency and percent tables as well as bar and pie graphs.

Frequency and Percent Distribution Tables

To create frequency and percent distribution tables, click **Analyze** on the main menu bar, **Descriptive Statistics**, and then **Frequencies**. From the list of variables that appears on the left-hand side of the screen, click the variable, REGION, then click the arrow facing to the right to move REGION into the box of variables that will be analyzed. Click **OK**.

Table 2.1. Frequency distribution for region

Geographic Region of School

		Frequency	Percent	Valid Percent	Cumulative Percent
Valid	Northeast	106	21.2	21.2	21.2
	North Central	151	30.2	30.2	51.4
	South	150	30.0	30.0	81.4
	West	93	18.6	18.6	100.0
	Total	500	100.0	100.0	

The result, as given in Table 2.1, should appear in the Output Viewer on your screen.

In Table 2.1, the first column lists the four possible categories of this variable. The second column, labeled Frequency, presents the number of respondents from each region. From this column, we may note that the fewest number of respondents, 93, are from the West. Note that if we sum the frequency column we obtain 500, which represents the total number of respondents in our data set. This is the value we should obtain if an appropriate category is listed for each student and all students respond to one and only one category. If an appropriate category is listed for each student and all students respond to one and only one category, we say the categories are *mutually exclusive and exhaustive*. This is a desirable, though not essential, property of frequency distributions.

In addition to the frequency of a category, the *relative frequency* of the category – that is, the frequency of the category relative to (divided by) the total number of individuals responding – is also important. The relative frequency represents the *proportion* of the total number of responses that are in the category. The relative frequency of student respondents from the West, for example, is 93/500 or .186.

Relative frequencies can also be converted easily to *percents* by multiplying the relative frequency by 100. Making this conversion, we find that 18.6 percent (.186 $\times$ 100), or close to 20 percent of our sample is from the West. The full percent distribution relative to all four regions may be found in the third column of Table 2.1. Note that the sum of values in this column equals 100 percent, as one would expect. In some cases, however, when a round-off error is incurred in converting fractions to percents, a sum slightly different from 100 percent may be obtained.

Column four of Table 2.1, labeled "Valid Percent," is useful as an adjunct to the percent column when there are missing data (when some students in our sample have not answered this question). In this case, the Percent and Valid Percent columns contain identical values because there are no missing data. The last column, Cumulative Percent, is described later in this chapter in the section on accumulating data. For reasons that will be discussed at that time, the Cumulative Percent column in this case is meaningless because the region data are nominal.

Bar Graphs

In addition to a tabular format, frequency and percent distributions of nominal data may be represented visually in the form of a bar graph. Figure 2.1 contains an interactive bar graph depicting the frequency of each region.

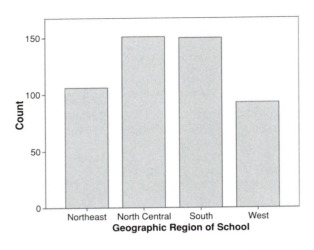

Figure 2.1   Bar graph of frequency distribution for REGION.

To generate a bar graph, click **Graphs** on the main menu bar, **Legacy Dialogs, Bar, Define**. Move REGION into the Category Axis box and click **OK**.

As depicted in Figure 2.1, the values of the variable REGION are represented by points along the category (or horizontal) axis, whereas the frequencies are represented by points along the vertical axis, labeled Count. In other cases, relative frequencies or percents are represented along the vertical axis. The ordering of the categories along the category axis follows the ordering of the numerical values assigned to the categories when the data were entered originally. Recall that, as noted in Example 1.4 in Chapter 1, a 1 is assigned to the category Northeast, 2 to North Central, and so on. Because REGION is a nominal-leveled variable, this assignment of numbers to region categories is arbitrary.

Accordingly, in the case of Figure 2.1, the ordering of the regions along the category axis is arbitrary. For ordinal-, interval-, or ratio-leveled variables, however, the inherent ordering of the variable itself dictates the ordering of categories along the horizontal axis. The importance of this distinction becomes clear when we discuss cumulative distributions.

A bar graph is characterized by *unconnected* bars or rectangles of equal width, where the height of each bar reflects the frequency of the category it represents. For example, the height of the bar labeled South reaches a count of 150, indicating that the frequency of that category is 150. Furthermore, because the heights of the bars labeled North Central and South are approximately equal, we may infer that the frequencies for those two categories are approximately equal as well.

☞ **Remark.** A nice property of this graph is that the vertical axis starts at zero. As discussed in Chapter 1, frequency, like height, may be considered to be a ratio-leveled variable. As a ratio-leveled variable, we may make multiplicative or ratio comparisons between different values along the frequency scale. Because height, as another ratio-leveled variable, is used to represent frequency in a bar graph, for such ratio comparisons to be meaningful using the heights of the bars, a bar with zero height should represent a category with zero frequency. Fortunately, this is the case in Figure 2.1. Before using the heights of the bars alone in a bar graph to make ratio comparisons between categories along the horizontal axis, check that the vertical axis actually begins at the value zero – that a bar of zero height would represent a category with zero frequency.

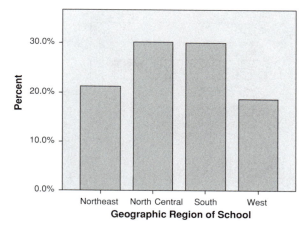

Figure 2.2 Bar graph of percent distribution for REGION.

Although we have illustrated the use of bar graphs to depict frequency distributions, we may also use bar graphs to depict percent distributions.

To generate a bar graph by percents instead of counts, click **Graphs** on the main menu bar, **Legacy Dialogs, Bar, Define**. Move REGION into the Category Axis box and click the circle so that the bars represent % of cases. Click **OK**.

Notice that the relative standing of the heights of the bars in Figure 2.2 is the same as that in the graph in Figure 2.1. This is because the percent scale differs from the count scale in terms of a constant of proportionality only. To obtain each percent value, recall that we divide each frequency value by the sample size (500 in this case) and then multiply by 100. Effectively, then, each frequency value is multiplied by the constant of proportionality (one-fifth, or 100/500 in this case) to obtain the corresponding percent value.

Pie Graphs

Pie graphs may be used to depict frequency and percent distributions in the discrete variable case as long as the categories are exhaustive. Pie graphs are particularly useful for depicting each category relative to the entire set of categories. A pie graph of the frequency distribution for REGION is given in Figure 2.3.

To create a pie graph, click **Graphs** from the main menu bar, **Legacy Dialogs, Pie, Define**. Move REGION into the Define Slices by box. Click **OK**.

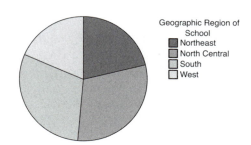

Figure 2.3 Pie graph of frequency distribution for REGION.

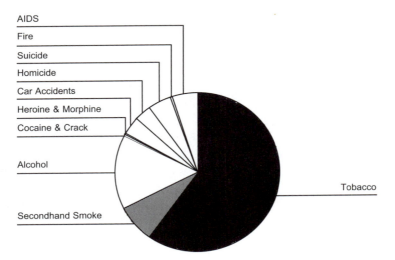

Figure 2.4   Annual number of deaths in New York City for different causes.

In a pie graph, the larger frequencies are indicated by larger slices. Notice that the two regions of approximately equal numbers of students, South and North Central, are represented by approximately equal-sized slices and that together these two regions account for more than half of the students who are in our sample. Just as bar graphs may be misleading if their vertical axes do not start at zero, pie graphs may be misleading if the categories they depict are not exhaustive. Consider the case illustrated in Figure 2.4 depicting the annual number of deaths in New York City: Tobacco vs. Other.

Notice that this pie graph misleads the viewer into thinking that tobacco is the greatest cause of death. However, not included in the list of causes considered are, for example, heart disease and cancer unrelated to tobacco use, which are known leading causes of death. In this example, the categories are not exhaustive, and clearly for a reason. This pie graph was created as part of an anti-smoking campaign.

WHEN VARIABLES ARE MEASURED AT THE ORDINAL, INTERVAL, OR RATIO LEVEL

In the preceding section we discussed ways to explore univariate distributions of variables that are measured at the nominal level. In this section, we present analogous tools for variables that are measured at the ordinal, interval, or ratio level.

Frequency and Percent Distribution Tables

Because a variable often has many distinct values in its distribution, a frequency distribution table where each category represents one value is often too unwieldy to be informative. Table 2.2 contains such a table generated by SPSS for SES, a variable that is part of the NELS data set. SES ranges from 0 to 35 with higher scores associated with higher SES. SES is a composite of parents' education level, occupation, and family income. Notice that, although we have not lost any information contained in the original data set with this tabular representation, the number of categories is too large for easy interpretation.

In Table 2.3, the data have been grouped into categories defined by intervals of values, and the number of categories, therefore, has been reduced. Notice that unlike the fre-

Table 2.2. Frequency distribution for socioeconomic status (SES)

Socio-Economic Status

		Frequency	Percent	Valid Percent	Cumulative Percent
Valid	0	1	.2	.2	.2
	1	1	.2	.2	.4
	2	2	.4	.4	.8
	3	2	.4	.4	1.2
	4	4	.8	.8	2.0
	5	1	.2	.2	2.2
	6	12	2.4	2.4	4.6
	7	7	1.4	1.4	6.0
	8	15	3.0	3.0	9.0
	9	9	1.8	1.8	10.8
	10	18	3.6	3.6	14.4
	11	22	4.4	4.4	18.8
	12	16	3.2	3.2	22.0
	13	15	3.0	3.0	25.0
	14	19	3.8	3.8	28.8
	15	24	4.8	4.8	33.6
	16	18	3.6	3.6	37.2
	17	33	6.6	6.6	43.8
	18	28	5.6	5.6	49.4
	19	39	7.8	7.8	57.2
	20	24	4.8	4.8	62.0
	21	22	4.4	4.4	66.4
	22	19	3.8	3.8	70.2
	23	22	4.4	4.4	74.6
	24	14	2.8	2.8	77.4
	25	21	4.2	4.2	81.6
	26	20	4.0	4.0	85.6
	27	16	3.2	3.2	88.8
	28	16	3.2	3.2	92.0
	29	12	2.4	2.4	94.4
	30	16	3.2	3.2	97.6
	31	8	1.6	1.6	99.2
	32	3	.6	.6	99.8
	35	1	.2	.2	100.0
	Total	500	100.0	100.0	

quency distribution for region, where each of the small number of categories contains a single value (Northeast, North Central, South, and West), each category for SES is actually a range of SES values represented by its midpoint. For example, the first category, represented by its midpoint 1.5, contains all values from 0 to 3. Six students, representing 1.2 percent, have SES values within this range. Because the SES scale is constructed so that a lower score corresponds to a lower socioeconomic status, these students are the most socioeconomically disadvantaged in our sample.

Each SES category defines an interval of values in Table 2.3; the values are said to be grouped together. Accordingly, this type of frequency distribution is often referred to as a *grouped frequency distribution*. Unfortunately, grouped frequency distributions are not

Table 2.3. Grouped frequency distribution of socioeconomic status (SES)

		Frequency	Percent	Valid Percent	Cumulative Percent
Valid	1.50	6	1.2	1.2	1.2
	4.50	17	3.4	3.4	4.6
	7.50	31	6.2	6.2	10.8
	10.50	56	11.2	11.2	22.0
	13.50	58	11.6	11.6	33.6
	16.50	79	15.8	15.8	49.4
	19.50	85	17.0	17.0	66.4
	22.50	55	11.0	11.0	77.4
	25.50	57	11.4	11.4	88.8
	28.50	44	8.8	8.8	97.6
	31.50	11	2.2	2.2	99.8
	34.50	1	.2	.2	100.0
Total			500	100.0	100.0
Total		500	100.0		

obtained easily using SPSS, and so their construction is de-emphasized in this text. Good alternatives to grouped frequency distributions are the histogram and the stem-and-leaf display, which are described in this chapter.

The following general advice is offered for creating grouped frequency tables. For variables that are at least ordinal and have many distinct values, grouped frequency tables should be created so that

1. The number of categories is sufficiently small to reduce the data and make them more understandable, yet sufficiently large so as to retain much of the specific information contained in the data. Considering both clarity and retention of information, the number of categories typically is from six to twelve.
2. The categories are mutually exclusive and exhaustive (i.e., each piece of data must fall into one and only one category).
3. The categories are all of equal size so as to achieve a clear picture of the data.

Note that in Table 2.3 there are twelve mutually exclusive and exhaustive categories defined by intervals of equal size (0–3, 3–6, 6–9, and so forth).

☞ **Remark.** To uphold the principle that all categories should be mutually exclusive, one must decide whether an endpoint common to two successive categories, such as 3 in this example, is to be included in the numerically lower or higher category. The decision is arbitrary, but once made, one must adhere to it. Throughout this text, we always consider the common endpoint of two successive categories as belonging to the numerically lower category. Hence, for example, the interval 3–6 in Table 2.3 includes 6 but not 3.

Stem-and-Leaf Displays

An alternative technique for describing data that are at least ordinal is the stem-and-leaf display. In this display, the digits of each data value are separated into two parts, called a stem and a leaf. For distributions of values between 0 and 100, the stem contains all but the units (rightmost) digit of each data value, and the leaf contains only the units (rightmost) digit. The stems are ordered numerically in a column from smallest to largest and the leaves are listed to the right of their associated stems, also in increasing order from left to right.

Our first example of a stem and leaf relates to the States data set, which includes different educational measures of the 50 states. In this case, we will create a stem-and-leaf plot of PERTAK, a variable that gives, for each state, the percentage of high school seniors who took the SAT in that state in 2005. These data are from *The 2006 World Almanac and Book of Facts*.

To obtain the stem-and-leaf display, click **Analyze** from the main menu bar, then **Descriptive Statistics** and then **Explore**. Move PERTAK to the **Dependent List**. (If you want to make it so that no extra output is provided, under Display, click the circle next to Plots, click the gray Plots box, and under Boxplots, click the circle next to None.) Click **OK**.

Table 2.4 contains a stem-and-leaf display of the variable PERTAK, including a column of frequencies on the left-hand side.

This stem-and-leaf display sorts the 50 values into nine groupings. The first grouping consists of the values from 0 to 9 only, the second grouping consists of values from 10 to 19, the third grouping consists of values from 20 to 29, and so on. We know this to be the case because the "Stem width" (at the bottom of the display) is 10, indicating that we must multiply each value in the display by 10 to obtain its true value. Accordingly, we multiply the lowest value of 0.4 by 10 to obtain its true value of 4, we multiply the highest value of 9.2 by 10 to obtain its true value of 92, and so on. We see that there are three instances of 7, indicating that three states have only 7 percent of their high school seniors taking the SAT tests.

Because of the relatively small size of this data set (50 cases), there is only one line per stem. The first line contains the leaves for those states whose stem is 0, that is, where the percentage of high school seniors taking the SAT is less than 10. From the frequency column, we see that there are twelve such states. The second line contains the leaves for those states whose stem is 1, that is, where the percentage of high school seniors taking the SAT

Table 2.4. Stem-and-leaf display of PERTAK

```
Percentage of Eligible Students Taking
the SAT, 2005 Stem-and-Leaf Plot

Frequency          Stem &  Leaf
  12.00              0   .  445566777889
   8.00              1   .  00012236
   4.00              2   .  0169
   3.00              3   .  139
    .00              4   .
   5.00              5   .  02459
   5.00              6   .  14567
   9.00              7   .  123445559
   4.00              8   .  1666
   1.00              9   .  2

Stem width:         10
Each leaf:           1 case(s)
```

is greater than or equal to 10 but less than 20. From the frequency column, we see that there are eight such states.

Because the length of each row in the leaf part of the display represents the frequency of occurrence of its associated stem, the stem-and-leaf display may be used to graphically represent the pattern of frequencies contained in the data. The most frequently occurring PERTAK values in our display are those values less than 10 because they comprise the longest row of leaves. As we shall see in a later section, such patterns of frequency are useful for describing and understanding the characteristics of a distribution.

Another stem-and-leaf display is presented to exemplify a situation in which the values are not between 0 and 100. This example also comes from the States data set. In this case, we create a stem-and-leaf plot of SATM, a variable that gives, for each state, the average math SAT score of high school seniors in that state. Table 2.5 contains this stem and leaf.

In Table 2.5, the stem represents the hundreds place and the leaf represents the tens place. For example, 60 represents the value 600, the highest SATM average of all 50 states.

If we review the original data, we see that the value of 600 is actually 608. The stem-and-leaf display drops the units digit in this case.

With larger data sets, such as the NELS, the stem-and-leaf displays can be more complicated. To show this, Table 2.6 contains a stem-and-leaf display of the variable SES from the NELS data set.

Notice that at the bottom of Table 2.6, the stem width is 10, indicating that each display value must be multiplied by 10 to return it to its correct magnitude. For example, the values 0.2 and 0.3 located in the second line of the display are to be multiplied by 10 and read as 2 and 3, respectively. Also, because each leaf represents two cases (see bottom of Table 2.6), there are two students in our data set with an SES value of 2 and two students with a value of 3. The ampersand symbol (&) represents a "fractional leaf," that is, a leaf value that occurs only once, as opposed to twice. Because fractional leaves take on greater importance, proportionally speaking, when frequencies are relatively low, the ampersands occur only in the tails of the distribution.

Each stem in Table 2.6 occupies five lines to accommodate the many values in our large data set. Each of the five lines contains one-fifth, or two, of the possible leaf values per stem in the display. In our example, the top line of each stem contains the leaves between 0 and 1, the second line contains the leaves between 2 and 3, and so forth. Stem-and-leaf displays of smaller data sets often consist of only one line per stem.

Table 2.5. Stem-and-leaf display of SATM

```
Average SAT Math in 2005 Stem-and-Leaf Plot

Frequency          Stem & Leaf
   4.00            4 . 7999
  28.00            5 . 0000001111111111122223344444
  16.00            5 . 5555566667788899
   3.00            6 . 000

Stem width: 100
Each leaf:   1 case(s)
```

Table 2.6. Stem-and-leaf display of SES

```
Socio-Economic Status Stem-and-Leaf Plot

Frequency        Stem &    Leaf
    2.00           0  .    &
    4.00           0  .    23
    5.00           0  .    44&
   19.00           0  .    666666777
   24.00           0  .    88888889999
   40.00           1  .    00000000011111111111
   31.00           1  .    222222223333333
   43.00           1  .    4444444445555555555555
   51.00           1  .    66666666677777777777777777
   67.00           1  .    8888888888888899999999999999999999
   46.00           2  .    00000000000011111111111
   41.00           2  .    22222222233333333333
   35.00           2  .    44444445555555555
   36.00           2  .    666666666677777777
   28.00           2  .    88888888999999
   24.00           3  .    000000001111
    3.00           3  .    2
    1.00           3  .    &

Stem width:      10
Each leaf:        2 case(s)
& denotes fractional leaves.
```

Histograms

Another graphic for representing data that are at least ordinal is the *histogram*. Figure 2.5 illustrates the use of a histogram to represent SES data from our NELS data set. Along the horizontal axis of Figure 2.5 are the midpoints of the intervals whose frequencies are represented by the heights of the bars. The histogram differs from a bar graph in that no spaces appear between the bars unless categories with zero frequency occur. Eliminating the spaces

Figure 2.5   Default histogram of SES.

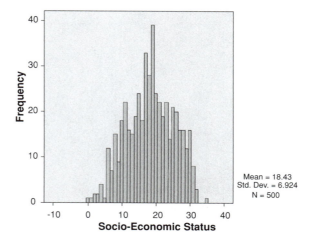

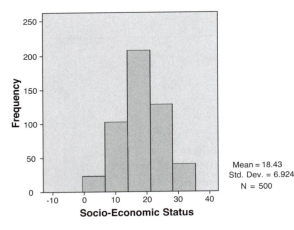

Figure 2.6   Histogram with 5 intervals.

between bars in a histogram makes the graph convey a feeling of continuity that reflects the ordinal nature of the variable. Bar graphs, on the other hand, include spaces between the bars to avoid the interpretation of a trend in the case of nominal-level data. The ordering of categories from nominal-level data would be arbitrary along the horizontal axis.

To obtain the histogram, click **Graphs** from the main menu bar, **Legacy Dialogs, Histogram**. Move SES to the **Variable** box, and click **OK**.

The legend on the right-hand side provides numerical summary statistics for the histogram that is discussed in Chapter 3.

We note that a histogram is affected by the number of bars (or bins) chosen. Figure 2.5 has 21 bins by default, whereas Figures 2.6 and 2.7 have 5 and 30 bins, respectively. The default setting, creating Figure 2.5, appears to provide a good balance between summarizing the data and providing details about the distribution.

To edit the scale of the horizontal axis of a histogram, click twice on the graph to put it in the Chart Editor. Then click twice on the bars themselves and the Properties box will appear. Click

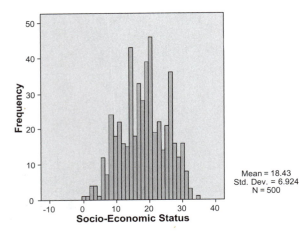

Figure 2.7   Histogram with 30 intervals.

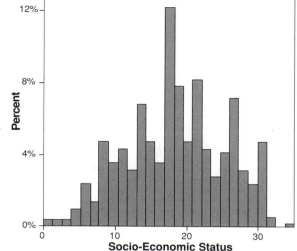

Figure 2.8 Histogram of SES by percentages.

the Scale tab in the Properties box. Verify that the Binning tab is selected. To obtain Figure 2.6, click the circle next to Custom and then click the circle next to number of intervals under Custom and type in the value 5. Click Apply and Close. To obtain Figure 2.7, change the number of intervals to 30.

To obtain percents and other options for the vertical axis for a histogram one should use Interactive Graphs in SPSS.

To obtain a Histogram with percents represented by the vertical axis, click **Graphs**, **Interactive**, and **Histogram**. Under the Assign Variables tab, replace Count [$Count] in the box on the vertical axis by Percent [$Pct]. (Note that both $Count and $Pct are temporary variables that appear in the variables list.) Drag the variable, SES, into the box for the box on the horizontal axis and click **OK**.

The resulting graph is depicted in Figure 2.8. The shape of the histogram by percentages is identical to that of the default histogram depicted in Figure 2.5.

A histogram differs from a stem-and-leaf display in that the latter uses the leaf values themselves to create the bars of the display. As a result, the stem-and-leaf display provides more information about the original data set than the histogram.

Line Graphs

Another type of graph that is often used to represent data that are at least ordinal is the *line graph* or *polygon*. Figure 2.9 illustrates a frequency polygon for our SES variable.

To create a one-variable line graph, click **Graphs** from the main menu bar, **Interactive**, **Line**. Drag SES into the Horizontal Axis box and click **OK**.

As one would expect, the stem-and-leaf display, the histogram, and the line graph all bear strong resemblance to each other in their depiction of SES frequencies. Although, as

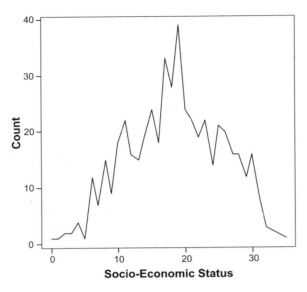

Figure 2.9   Line graph of SES.

noted, there may be some advantages of one type of display over another, the ultimate choice of display method belongs to the researcher.

Most often, line graphs are used when two variables are involved and one of them is time. An example is given in Figure 2.10 that is taken from the Marijuana data set. The figure shows, for the years 1987–2004, the percentage of high school seniors who said that they had ever used marijuana. These data are from *The 2006 World Almanac and Book of Facts*.

To create a two-variable line graph, click **Graphs** from the main menu bar, **Interactive**, **Line**. Drag YEAR into the Horizontal Axis box and replace $count with MARIJ in the Vertical Axis box. Click **OK**.

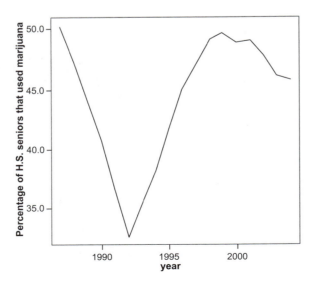

Figure 2.10   Line graph of marijuana use by high school seniors.

If you were to create this line graph using the SPSS Graphs procedure instead of the Interactive Graphs procedure, you would notice a difference in treatment of the year variable. In the case of a regular line graph, YEAR is treated by SPSS as though it were ordinal, with the different years listed in order, but without necessarily an equal spacing of years along the axis. If, for example, a year is missing in the data set, SPSS will space the two years on either side of that year as though they were only one year apart, without regard to the missing value.

Many graphs can be created using either the regular Graphs or the Interactive Graphs procedures. In general, the advantage of interactive graphs is that the user has more control over the way the variable is treated. The disadvantage of the interactive graph is that it takes longer to create and uses more computer memory. Unless the graph calls for a specific feature that is available only through interactive graphs, the regular graph option is used in this text.

DESCRIBING THE SHAPE OF A DISTRIBUTION

A curve is said to be *symmetric* if, when folded from left to right along its vertical axis of symmetry (its middle), one-half of the curve overlaps the other. Two symmetric curves are shown in Figure 2.11 and differ because the graph on the left is single-peaked and the one on the right is double-peaked. In Chapter 3, we introduce other words to describe the shape of the curve based on its peaks. If, on the other hand, overlapping does not result, the curve is said to be *asymmetric.*

Another characteristic often used to describe the shape of a frequency or percent distribution graph is the *skewness.* For our purposes, the term skewness refers to the distribution of the graph's area about its mean. For example, the histogram for self-concept in grade 12 (SLFCNC12) from our NELS data set (Figure 2.12) is asymmetric. The bulk of its scores ranges from 25 to 45 and its tail is to the left of this bulk (or in a negative direction).

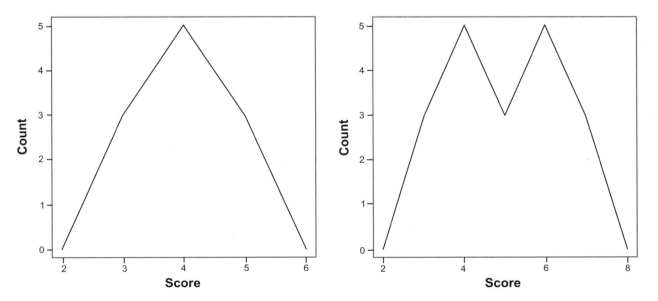

Figure 2.11   Symmetric curves.

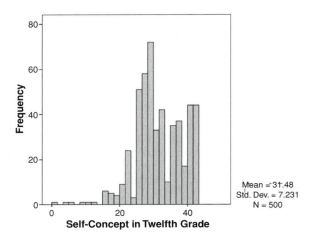

Figure 2.12   Histogram of SLFCNC12.

That is, the bulk of the data consists of relatively high scores, yet there are a few relatively low scores. Accordingly, we say that these data are *skewed to the left*, or *skewed negatively*. Thus, most students in our sample have higher values of self-concept and only relatively few have lower values of self-concept.

If the graph looked like Figure 2.13 instead, with its tail to the right of the main bulk (or in a positive direction from the main bulk), we would say that the graph is *skewed to the right*, or *skewed positively*. The skewness of a graph is the direction in which its tail lies relative to its main bulk. Figure 2.13 depicts for our sample the frequency distribution of responses to the question: "What annual income do you expect to have at the age of thirty?" Clearly, the bulk of students expect incomes less than or equal to $150,000 per year, whereas only a relative few expect incomes in excess of $150,000; one student, in fact, expects an income of $1,000,000. Where would your response fit within this depiction: within the bulk of the responses, or in the tail?

☞ **Remark.** Extreme values, such as the $1,000,000 expected income, are called *outliers*. For reasons that become clear in the next chapter, one of the key jobs of a data analyst is to learn how to identify and handle such outliers.

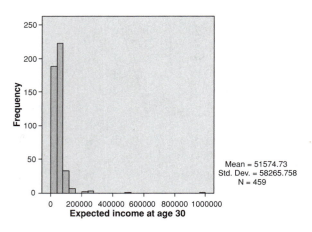

Figure 2.13   Histogram of EXPINC30.

☞ **Remark.** Figure 2.13 is noticeably more skewed than Figure 2.12.

It is possible for a graph to be asymmetric without being noticeably skewed either to the left or to the right. In this case, we would simply say that the graph is asymmetric and leave it at that.

ACCUMULATING DATA

When data are at least ordinal, the inherent ordering of the values allows us to accumulate the data in ways that make sense. We can look at the percentage (or number) of scores below a given score. For example, we can find the percentage of students in the NELS data set who have SES ratings of 9 or lower. We can also look at the score below which a certain percentage of scores fall. For example, we can ask, "What is the SES score below which 25 percent of the students in the NELS data set fall?"

CUMULATIVE PERCENT DISTRIBUTIONS

Until now, the vertical axis has represented either frequency or percent, but there are other possibilities to be considered. Referring once again to the grouped frequency distribution of SES (Table 2.3), suppose we want to know at a glance the percent of students in our sample who have SES ratings of 9 or lower. Although we could sum the percents associated with the categories 0–3, 3–6, and 6–9, respectively, to obtain the sum 10.8 percent (1.2, 3.4, and 6.2 percent), a more direct solution is available from the column labeled *Cumulative Percent* in Table 2.3. This column contains the cumulative percent distribution for SES and may be used to obtain the percent of students whose SES values fall *at or below* a certain point in the distribution.

Table 2.3 is useful in finding the cumulative percent of a value of 9, because 9 is the uppermost value of one of the categories (6–9) contained in this table. Had we been interested in the cumulative percent of a value of 8, on the other hand, Table 2.3 would not have been useful because we do not know from this table how many of the 31 students with SES between 6 and 9 actually have an SES value at or below 8. By grouping the data into larger than unit intervals, we lose the specific information needed to exactly answer this question. Therefore, based on Table 2.3 alone, we do not know whether all, none, or some of the 31 students have SES values between 8 and 9 and should not be counted in answering this question. Because there is no way to determine the true situation from only the grouped distribution given in Table 2.3 – to determine the percent of students with SES values at or below 8, for example – we make use of the ungrouped percent distribution found in Table 2.2. In so doing, we find that 9 percent of the students have SES values at or below 8 in this distribution.

OGIVE CURVES

A line graph representing a cumulative frequency or percent distribution is called an *ogive curve* (the g is pronounced as a j) or *S curve* because the curve often looks like an elongated S. Ogive curves are always nondecreasing, because they represent accumulated values. The graph of the cumulative percent SES distribution appears in Figure 2.14. As noted, the curve does take on the appearance of an elongated S.

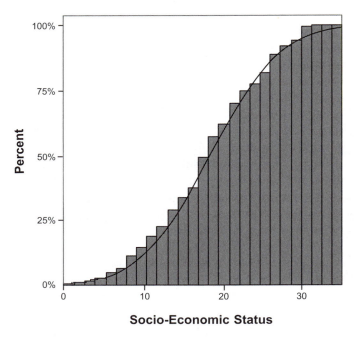

Figure 2.14   Cumulative percent distribution of SES.

To obtain the ogive graph, click **Graphs** from the main menu bar, then **Interactive**, then **Histogram**. Drag the continuous variable, SES, over to the box on the horizontal axis; remove the $count variable from the box on the vertical axis, and drag the $pct variable into that box. Click the Cumulative Histogram checkbox. Click the Histogram tab and then the checkbox labeled Normal Curve to include the added line curve above the histogram. Click **OK**.

☞ **Remark.** Like many continuous variables, SES is measured using a scale of integer values. Hence, anyone with SES greater than or equal to 24.5 but less than 25.5 will be recorded to have SES equal to 25. If the measure had been more precise – for example, if it had been recorded to two decimal places – the cumulative SES distribution would probably have been a straight line, because no two people would have had exactly the same SES.

PERCENTILE RANKS

The *percentile rank* of a given raw score is the percent of scores that fall below that raw score in a specified distribution. As discussed previously, the cumulative percent of a given raw score is the percent of scores falling at or below that raw score in a specified distribution. The difference between these two statistics, that one reports the percent *below* a given raw score, whereas the other reports the percent *at or below* a given raw score, rests in the distinction between continuous and discrete variables. Technically the percentile rank is more appropriate for variables that are continuous, and the cumulative percent is more appropriate for variables that are discrete.

However, because many discrete variables (such as income, property value, and frequency data) share many of the properties of a continuous variable, the percentile rank and the cumulative percent, when applied to such variables, provide similar results. Likewise, when applied to continuous variables, in practice, the cumulative percent and the percentile rank provide similar results. Given their respective definitions, the cumulative percent value will generally be larger than the percentile rank. In this book, for simplicity, we do not compute the exact values of percentile ranks; rather we estimate them using cumulative percents based on an ungrouped frequency distribution such as the one in Table 2.2.

· ·

EXAMPLE 2.1. Use the cumulative percent to estimate the percentile rank of an SES value of 13 for the sample of 500 students under study.

Solution. We obtain an estimate of the percentile rank of 13 by using the cumulative percent distribution in Table 2.2. We find that one-fourth (25 percent) of the students in our sample have SES scores equal to or below 13; therefore, an estimate of the percentile rank of an SES score of 13 is 25th.

As the example illustrates, the percentile rank makes raw score data more meaningful by allowing us to know the relative standing of a single score within a set of scores. From another viewpoint, knowing that your raw score on an exam is 90, for example, has little meaning, because the exam could have been out of 100 points or it could have been out of 500 points. Knowing that your percentile rank on an exam is 90, however, means that 90 percent of the people taking the exam received scores below yours.

Often, we seek to know an individual's raw score corresponding to a particular percentile rank. For example, suppose you were told that your percentile rank on an exam was 90, and you wanted to find your raw score. In so doing, you would be finding the 90th percentile, or that raw score corresponding to the 90th percentile rank (the raw score with 90 percent of the scores below it).

PERCENTILES

In general, a percentile is the theoretical raw score that corresponds to a given percentile rank in a specified distribution. From Example 2.1, we know that approximately one-fourth of these students' SES values are below the value of 13 – that the value of 13 is at the 25th percentile in the SES distribution. Just as the value of 13 has approximately one-fourth of the distribution below it, it also has approximately three-fourths (75 percent) of the distribution above it. Accordingly, the value of 13 may be said to divide the SES distribution into two groups of students: one group that contains 25 percent or 125 students, and the other group that contain 75 percent or 375 students.

☞ **Remark.** The percentile is often referred to as a centile and is denoted by the letter C. The 25th percentile, therefore, is denoted as C_{25}.

For a fuller understanding of what centiles represent in terms of an underlying distribution, we examine the set of centiles $C_1, C_2, C_3, \ldots, C_{99}$. These percentiles are the 99 theoretically possible raw scores that divide a distribution into 100 equal parts. That is, between any two consecutive centiles there will be 1 percent of all the scores in the distribution. For example, if, as in our SES distribution, there are 500 raw scores, then between any two consecutive centiles there is 1 percent of the 500 scores, or $(0.01)(500) = 5$ scores.

☞ **Remark.** C_{100} is not necessary because only 99 points are needed to divide a set of scores into 100 intervals with equal frequencies. The scores from C_{99} to the maximum value in the distribution define the 100th interval.

. . . .

EXAMPLE 2.2. How many of the raw scores in a distribution made up of 500 raw scores will fall:

a. Between C_{40} and C_{41}?
b. Between C_{40} and C_{50}?
c. Below C_{25}?
d. Below C_{10}?

Solution.

a. Because C_{40} and C_{41} are consecutive percentiles, there will be 1% of the total number of scores in the distribution, or $(0.01)(500) = 5$ scores between them.

b. Because C_{40} and C_{50} differ by 10 percentiles ($50 - 40 = 10$ percentiles), there will be $(10)(1\%) = 10\%$ of the total number of scores in the distribution between them. This would be $(0.10)(500) = 50$ scores.

c. Because C_{25} is by definition the raw score that has 25% of the total number of scores in the distribution below it, C_{25} has $(0.25)(500) = 125$ scores below it. C_{25} is commonly referred to as the *1st quartile* and denoted by the symbol Q_1. C_{50} is commonly referred to as the *2nd quartile* and denoted by the symbol Q_2, and C_{75} is commonly referred to as the *3rd quartile* and denoted by the symbol Q_3. Therefore, $Q_1 = C_{25}$, $Q_2 = C_{50}$, and $Q_3 = C_{75}$. Because no reference is made to a 100th percentile, C_{100}, we likewise make no reference to a 4th quartile, Q_4.

d. Because C_{10} is by definition the raw score that has 10% of the total number of scores in the distribution below it, C_{10} would have $(0.10)(500) = 50$ scores below it. C_{10} is commonly referred to as the *1st decile* and denoted by the symbol D_1. Similarly, C_{20} is commonly referred to as the *2nd decile* and denoted by the symbol D_2, and so on. Therefore, $D_1 = C_{10}$, $D_2 = C_{20}$, $D_3 = C_{30}$, $D_4 = C_{40}$, $D_5 = C_{50}$, $D_6 = C_{60}$, $D_7 = C_{70}$, $D_8 = C_{80}$, and $D_9 = C_{90}$. Because no reference is made to a 100th percentile, C_{100}, we likewise make no reference to a 10th decile, D_{10}.

☞ **Remark.** We will make most use of quartiles. Another way of thinking of quartiles is that Q_2 divides the entire distribution in half, Q_1 divides the bottom half in half, and Q_3 divides the top half in half.

☞ **Remark.** Like percentile ranks, percentiles are appropriately defined on distributions of continuous variables and may be thought of as cut points that divide a distribution into a given number of groups of equal frequency. The set of three quartiles represents the three cut points that divide a distribution into four groups of equal frequency; the set of nine deciles represents the nine cut points that divide a distribution into ten groups of equal frequency, and so on. To divide a distribution into a given number of groups of equal frequency, each cut point or percentile, by definition, is a theoretically possible value, which may or may not be one of the actual values from the scale of measurement used to measure the variable. However, because estimates of percentiles suffice for most applications, SPSS does not calculate percentiles exactly; it only estimates them. As a result, the groups defined by these estimated percentiles do not necessarily have equal frequencies, although their frequencies are approximately equal.

☞ **Remark.** Be careful not to confuse the raw score with the percentile. For example, a person who gets a 75 percent on a test is probably not at the 75th percentile. For example, if 10 people took the test and 9 people get 100 percent and one person gets 75 percent, the percentile rank of the score of 75 percent is 0.

. . . .

EXAMPLE 2.3. Using SPSS, find the three quartiles of the SES distribution – those values that divide the distribution into four (approximately) equal groups. Because there are 500 values in the SES distribution, each group should contain approximately 125 values. Use Table 2.2 to determine how many values are actually in each of the four groups.

Solution.

To find the quartiles of the SES distribution, click **Analyze** from the main menu bar, **Descriptive Statistics**, **Frequencies**. Move the variable SES to the **Variables** box. Click **Statistics** at the bottom of the screen. Click **Quartiles** (alternatively, click percentiles, 25, add, 50, add, and 75, add; the percentiles option may be used to find any percentile, the 14th, for example), **Continue**. To get rid of extra output, click off the box next to Display Frequency Tables. Click **OK.**

The 25th, 50th, and 75th percentiles, corresponding to the first, second, and third quartiles, are given as 13.25, 19, and 24, respectively. If these percentiles were exact, then exactly 25 percent of the distribution (or 125 scores) would fall below 13.25, exactly 25 percent would fall between 13.25 and 19, exactly 25 percent would fall between 19 and 24, and, exactly 25 percent would fall at or above 24. But, these percentiles are not exact, and, as we shall see, the four groupings are only approximately equal to each other.

Statistics

Socio-Economic Status		
N	Valid	500
	Missing	0
Percentiles	25	13.25
	50	19.00
	75	24.00

☞ **Remark.** By SPSS convention, to determine how many scores fall between two percentiles, we include the frequency of the lower percentile but not the frequency of the upper percentile.

Using Table 2.2 we find that 125 students (1 + 1 + 2 + 2 + 4 + 1 + 12 + 6 + 16 + 9 + 18 + 22 + 16 + 15) have SES ratings in the first quartile (below a score of 13.25), 122 students have SES ratings between the first and second quartiles (greater than or equal to 13.25 but less than 19), 126 students have SES ratings between the second and third quartiles (greater than or equal to 19 but less than 24), and, finally, 127 students have SES ratings at or above a score of 24.

Notice that, just as the three quartiles, as a set, divide the SES distribution into (approximately) equal quarters, the second quartile, labeled as the 50th percentile, divides the SES distribution into (approximately) equal halves. There are 247 scores below 19 and 253 scores at 19 or above. As such, the score of 19 is the middle score in the distribution – the score that locates the distribution's center.

Notice also that the middle 50 percent of the distribution is contained between the first and third quartiles, 13.25 and 24. Said differently, the middle 50 percent of this distribution lies between 13.25 and 24 and, therefore, extends over 10.75 SES values (24 − 13.25). If the distribution were such that the value of 19 were again at its center, but the first and third quartiles were at 8 and 29, respectively, then the middle 50 percent of this distribution would extend over 21 SES values (29 − 8). In this case, we would say that, relative to the first distribution, the second distribution has a greater spread about its center, or a greater *interquartile range* or *midspread*. We could say, equivalently, that the second distribution is less densely concentrated about its middle than the first distribution.

As the preceding example illustrates, a lot can be learned about the location, shape, and form of a distribution by finding the quartiles of that distribution. The second quartile tells us something about its location, and the first and third quartiles tell us something about its spread. With the addition of two more points, the distribution's lowest value (its *minimum*) and its highest value (its *maximum*), a more complete picture may be obtained.

FIVE-NUMBER SUMMARIES AND BOXPLOTS

A five-number summary of a distribution includes the three quartiles, Q_1, Q_2, and Q_3, as well as the minimum and maximum values. While the three quartiles summarize distributional characteristics about the center, the minimum and maximum characterize the tails of the distribution. We may obtain the five-number summary from a cumulative percent distribution (e.g., Table 2.2), from a stem-and-leaf display (e.g., Table 2.4), or we may use a software package like SPSS to obtain it for us. Whenever you do obtain the values from a software package, you should check that the values obtained are reasonable; in this case, consult either a cumulative percent distribution or a stem-and-leaf display.

To obtain the five-number summary of the SES distribution, click **Analyze** from the main menu bar, **Descriptive Statistics**, **Frequencies**. Move the variable SES to the **Variables** box. Click **Statistics** at the bottom of the screen. Click **Quartiles**, **Minimum** and **Maximum**, **Continue**. To get rid of extra output, click off the box next to Display Frequency Tables. Click **OK**.

In so doing, we obtain Table 2.7 in the Output Navigator.

From the five-number summary in Table 2.7, we know that the SES distribution extends from a minimum value of zero to a maximum value of 35, with its center at 19 and its center bulk of 50 percent situated over the interval 13.25 to 24.

Table 2.7. Five-number summary for SES

Statistics

Socio-Economic Status

N	Valid	500
	Missing	0
Minimum		0
Maximum		35
Percentiles	25	13.25
	50	19.00
	75	24.00

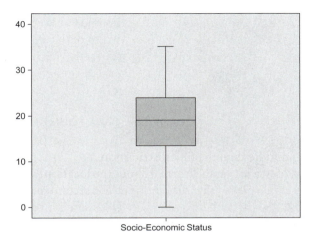

Figure 2.15 Boxplot of SES.

A graphical representation of the five-number summary is given by a *boxplot*, also called a *box-and-whiskers plot*. Figure 2.15 is a boxplot for our SES data. The box depicts the middle 50 percent of the distribution, which ranges from $Q_1 = 13.25$ to $Q_3 = 24$. The middle line in the box represents Q_2, the middle score of the distribution, which is equal to 19. The whiskers extend out from the box on both ends. From the end representing lower values, the whisker extends to the minimum value of 0; from the end representing higher values, it extends to the maximum value of 35. Notice in this representation that the distance from Q_3 to Q_2 approximately equals the distance from Q_2 to Q_1, and that the whiskers are of about equal length, suggesting that this distribution is reasonably symmetric, as we know it to be.

To obtain a boxplot for SES, click **Graphs**, **Legacy Dialogs**, **Boxplot.** Click the circle next to Summaries of separate variables, and **Define**. Move SES to the box labeled **Boxes Represent** and click **OK.**

In comparing the boxplot to either the stem-and-leaf display (Table 2.4) or the histogram (Figure 2.6) of these data, we observe that, with only five numbers, the boxplot captures well the important features of this distribution. Characterizations that summarize data well with only a small number of values are called *parsimonious.* As you will learn, one of the goals of statistics is parsimony.

It is instructive to examine the boxplots for both self-concept in twelfth grade and expected income at age 30 that appear in Figures 2.16 and 2.17, respectively, and to compare these boxplots to the corresponding histograms of these variables that appear in Figures 2.12 and 2.13. In SPSS, extreme values in the boxplots are provided and identified by case number. We modify the boxplot to identify the extreme values by ID instead, because the case numbers can change during certain procedures, but the ID does not.

To create a boxplot for which outliers are identified by a variable such as ID rather than by the case number, follow the steps outlined for the boxplot and, in addition, move ID into the Label Cases by box.

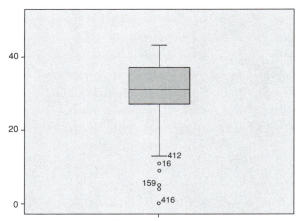

Figure 2.16 Boxplot of SLFCNC12.

Self-Concept in Twelfth Grade

Notice first, like the boxplot of SES depicted in Figure 2.15, that the boxplots of self-concept and expected income capture the essential features of their corresponding histograms. By looking at these boxplots alone, we should have no problem visualizing the complete distributions of these variables. In Figure 2.16, the several outliers, or extreme values, at the bottom of the plot (the lower tail of the distribution) suggest negative skewness. Add the fact that the distance between the end of the top whisker and Q_2 is smaller than the distance between the end of the bottom whisker and Q_2 – that is, that the bulk of the distribution of self-concept is relatively high – and we have a rather full picture of the shape of the distribution of this variable.

There are four ways that the boxplot can indicate skewness of the distribution, listed from least serious to most serious skew. First, the middle line, or 50th percentile, can be unevenly spaced within the box. Second, the box can be unevenly spaced between the whiskers. Third, there are asymmetric outliers, that is, points that lie beyond the whiskers on one side of the distribution, indicated by a circle on the boxplot. Fourth, there are asymmetric outliers indicated by a star on the boxplot.

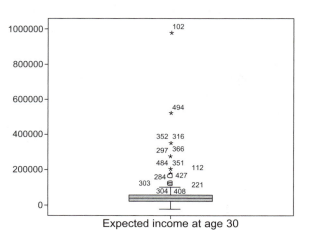

Figure 2.17 Boxplot of EXPINC30.

Expected income at age 30

Expected income at age 30 is more extremely skewed than self-concept. The greater concentration of values between 0 and 150,000, coupled with the larger number of more extreme outliers located in the more positive direction, characterize this distribution as highly positively skewed. In fact, case number 102 is highly optimistic. He (this person actually is male) expects to earn $1 million! Exercise 2.23 asks you to determine this individual's self-concept relative to the sample. Once again, we may notice that this boxplot summarizes well the histogram depicted in Figure 2.13.

☞ **Remark.** Although there are no set conventions for defining an extreme value or outlier, SPSS uses the following convention in relation to boxplots. Recall that the interquartile range or midspread is the length of the box in the boxplot. SPSS uses a circle to denote outliers that are farther than 1.5 interquartile ranges, yet closer than 3 interquartile ranges, from the nearer edge of the box, and a star to denote outliers that are farther than 3 interquartile ranges from the nearer edge of the box. Thus, the skew of the distributions of expected incomes (Figure 2.17) is considered to be more extreme than the skew of the distributions of self-concept (Figure 2.16).

☞ **Remark.** To allow the full range of values to be displayed in the boxplot of Figure 2.17, the vertical scale must extend from the minimum of 0 to the maximum of 1,000,000, thanks to our optimist. Because of the presence of outliers in this case, the bulk of the distribution, as depicted by the box, appears to be quite compact relative to the full range. To alleviate the influence of outliers on the graph, we may delete these cases from consideration, or we may change the scale of measurement from dollars to some other unit that preserves the ordinality of the data. Ordinality is an essential feature of these data that makes the boxplot meaningful. Changing from one scale of measurement to another is called *transforming* or *re-expressing* the data. More will be said about this in Chapter 4.

☞ **Remark.** A distribution can be skewed even though no outliers are present, when the box is not centered between the whiskers, or when the middle line is unevenly spaced within the box. In such cases, skewness tends not to be severe. We illustrate in Figure 2.18 with the variable teacher's pay, TEACHPAY, from the States data, which gives the mean teacher salary by state. TEACHPAY is slightly positively skewed.

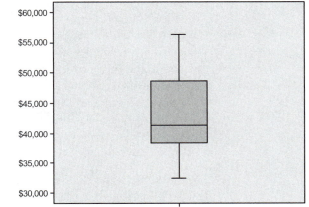

Figure 2.18   Boxplot of TEACHPAY.

Average Annual Salary for Public School Teachers, Fall 2002

EXAMPLE 2.4. Use SPSS to construct four side-by-side boxplots based on the States data set showing the states' average educational expenditure per pupil by region. Use the graph to determine (1) whether there are differences in the level of educational expenditures by region, (2) whether there are differences in the spread of the educational expenditures by region, and (3) whether there are differences in the shape of the educational expenditures by region.

Solution.

To obtain a single graph giving boxplots of educational expenditure by region, go to **Graphs**, **Legacy Dialogs, Boxplot, Define**. Move EDUCEXP into the Variable box and REGION into the Category Axis box. Click **OK**.

The result is the following boxplots:

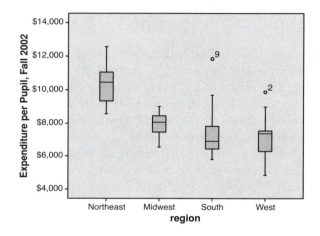

1. According to the heights of the 50th percentiles for the four regions, the Northeast has the highest overall level of educational expenditures per pupil, followed by the Midwest, the West, and the South.
2. According to the interquartile ranges, the educational expenditures are most spread out in the Northeast, followed by the West, the South, and the Midwest.
3. The distributions of educational expenditures are fairly symmetric in the Midwest and the Northeast, because there are no outliers and the boxes are fairly evenly spaced between the whiskers. Because the 50th percentile line is not evenly spaced in the box for the Northeast, but it is for the Midwest, the distribution is slightly more skewed in the Northeast, but it is not severely skewed. The distributions for the South and West are positively skewed, because although most states in these regions have relatively low educational expenditures, there are a few states with extremely high educational expenditures. The distribution is more severely skewed in the South because it has the more serious type of outlier.

☞ **Remark.** Both the stem-and-leaf display and the boxplot are inventions of John Tukey (1915–2000), which he described, along with other such novel and ingenious methods of data analysis, in his highly influential work *Exploratory Data Analysis* (1977). In this book and elsewhere, Tukey promoted a very practical approach to data analysis, one that emphasizes an examination of the data themselves, rather than prior assumptions about the data, as the starting point for choosing an appropriate data analytic model. Because of Tukey's creative genius and versatility, demonstrated over a long and active career in statistics, Salsburg quite appropriately calls him the "Picasso of Statistics" (2001, p. 229).

EXERCISES

Exercises 2.1 through 2.3 involve questions about frequency and percent distribution tables of variables in the NELS data set.

2.1. Create a frequency distribution table of the variable ABSENT12, which gives the number of times a student was absent in twelfth grade. Use the frequency distribution to answer the following questions.
   a) How many students in the NELS data set were absent 3–6 times in twelfth grade?
   b) How many students in the NELS data set were absent exactly 3 times in twelfth grade?
   c) What percentage of students in the NELS data set was absent 3–6 times in twelfth grade?
   d) What percentage of students in the NELS data set was absent 6 or fewer times in twelfth grade?
   e) How would you describe the shape of the distribution of absences in twelfth grade – positively skewed, negatively skewed, or reasonably symmetric? Explain.

2.2. Create a frequency distribution table of the variable PARMARL8, which gives the marital status of the parents when the student was in eighth grade. Use it and the Data View window to answer the following questions.
   a) What does a score of 3 indicate on the variable PARMARL8?
   b) For how many students in the NELS data set was PARMARL8 equal to 3?
   c) For what percent of students in the NELS data set was PARMARL8 equal to 3? Interpret the values from both the percent and the valid percent columns.
   d) Why is the cumulative percent column of PARMARL8 not meaningful?
   e) What is the most frequently occurring marital status for parents of students in the NELS?

2.3. Create a frequency distribution table of the variable FAMSIZE, which represents the number of people in a student's household when the student was in eighth grade. Use the frequency distribution table to answer the following questions.
   a) What was the greatest number of people in a household for all the students in the NELS data set?
   b) How many students lived in households with only three members?
   c) How many students lived in households with at most three members?
   d) What percentage of the students lived in households with only three members?
   e) What percentage of the students lived in households with at most three members?
   f) Estimate Q_2 for FAMSIZE.

Exercises 2.4 through 2.7 involve questions about bar graphs of variables in the NELS data set.

2.4. Create a bar graph summarizing the variable GENDER. Use it to answer the following questions.

To edit the bar graph so the bars are labeled with their respective frequencies, click twice on the graph to bring it to the Chart Editor. Click **Elements** from the main menu bar, **Show Data Labels**.

a) Why is a bar graph an appropriate display in this case?

b) Are there more males or females in the NELS?

c) What percentage of students is female?

d) Would a pie graph be appropriate to depict these data?

2.5. In this exercise, we will make separate bar graphs for males and females of the variable ALCBINGE, which indicates whether a student has ever binged on alcohol.

To create separate graphs or analyses by a grouping variable, click **Data** on the main menu bar, **Split File**. Click the circle next to **Compare Groups** and move GENDER into the box. Click **OK**. Then create a bar graph of ALCBINGE in the usual way.

When your grouped analyses are complete, return to **Data, Split File**. Click the circle next to **Analyze all cases and do not create groups** and click **OK**.

---

a) What percentage of males in the NELS data set has ever binged on alcohol? What percentage of females?

b) Given the two frequency bar graphs, why are the scales on the vertical axes different for the two graphs?

2.6. Create a bar graph for average daily school attendance rate given by the variable SCHATTRT in the NELS data set. Use the bar graph to answer the following questions.

a) What appears to be problematic with the way in which the values are set along the *X*-axis of the bar graph?

b) What is a type of graph that could be selected to display SCHATTRT that does not have that problem?

c) What is the shape of the distribution of SCHATTRT?

2.7. This exercise is based on the Statisticians data set created in Exercise 1.15.

a) Create a bar graph indicating the number of recent citations for each of the statisticians.

To generate a bar graph based on the values of individual cases, click **Graphs** on the main menu bar and then **Legacy Dialogs, Bar**. Click the circle next to **Values of individual cases**. Click **Define**. Let the bars represent AMSTAT and label categories STATISTICIAN. Click **OK**.

---

b) How did SPSS determine the ordering of categories along the *X*-axis?

c) Use the bar graph to approximate the number of citations of Ronald A. Fisher.

d) Construct a new bar graph with statisticians ordered on the *X*-axis according to their respective number of citations.

There are at least two ways to create an ordered bar graph in SPSS:

(1) Go to **Data, Sort Cases,** and move AMSTAT into the Sort by box. Click **OK**. Create the bar graph as in part (a).

(2) Go to **Graphs** in the Main Menu, then **Legacy Dialogs, Bar**. Click the circle next to **Data in Chart are: Summaries for groups of cases**. Click **Define** then the circle next to **Other Statistic** and put AMSTAT in the variable box (the default is that the other statistic is the mean). Put STATISTICIAN in the Category Axis box and click **OK**. The graph will have the statisticians in alphabetical order as in part (a). To place them in order of their ascending number of citations, click on the chart to get into the Chart Editor, then click anywhere on the *X*-axis and a **Properties** window will appear. Choose the **Categories** tab and then **Sort by Statistic** and then

Direction: Ascending and then **Apply**. The graph will now show statisticians in ascending order by their respective number of recent AMSTAT citations.

e) What is a useful feature of this ordered graph?
f) Of the twelve statisticians, where in the ranking (from the top) is Ronald A. Fisher?
g) The bar graphs constructed in parts (a) and (d) of this exercise depict the number of recent citations considered individually for each statistician listed separately. Construct a different type of bar graph that depicts the shape, location, and spread of the number of recent citations considered collectively across all 12 statisticians. To obtain a pleasing graph, use Interactive graphs and edit the graph so that the bar width is 50%. What variable is represented by the *X*-axis in this graph? Why is it appropriate to continue to use a bar graph for this depiction?
h) Describe the shape of this distribution. Where does the center of this distribution appear to be located and what is its spread, from the minimum to the maximum value?

Exercise 2.8 involves questions about a pie graph of a variable in the NELS data set.

2.8. Construct a pie graph of the variable URBAN, which indicates whether the student lived in an urban, suburban, or rural area in the United States in eighth grade.
a) Edit the graph so the slices are labeled by counts (values) and by percents.

To edit the pie graph, click twice on the graph to get it into the Chart Editor. Assuming that you created the graph in regular, not interactive, graph mode, the following instructions indicate how to label the graph. To label the slices, click **Elements**, **Add Data Labels**. Click the up arrow to move percent to the Displayed box. Count is already there. Click **Apply, Close**.

b) How many students come from an urban area? What percentage of students comes from an urban area?
c) Use SPSS to construct the associated bar graph.
d) Compare the two graphs. Which do you prefer? Why?
e) What have you learned about the distribution of students in this sample across urban, suburban, and rural areas?

Exercises 2.9 through 2.14 involve questions about stem-and-leaf graphs of variables from different data sets.

2.9. Create a stem-and-leaf graph of the variable MATHCOMP from the learndis data set. Use it to answer the following questions.
a) What is another type of graph that could be used to depict these data?
b) What is the total number of scores in this distribution?
c) How many scores are in the seventies?
d) Are there any outliers (i.e., extreme values) in this distribution?
e) How would you describe the shape of this distribution? Explain.
f) What is the 50th percentile?
g) What is/are the most frequently occurring score(s) in this distribution? How many times does it/do they occur?
h) What is the highest score in this distribution?
i) Can we use this stem-and-leaf graph to obtain the original set of values for this variable?

2.10. Create a stem-and-leaf graph of the variable BIRTH from the Statisticians data set that you entered in Exercise 1.15. Use it to answer the following questions.
   a) How many people in the data set were born in 1900?
   b) Are there any outliers (i.e., extreme values) in this distribution?
   c) How would you describe the shape of this distribution? Explain.
   d) What is/are the most frequently occurring score(s) in this distribution? How many times does it/do they occur?
   e) What is the highest score in this distribution?
   f) Can we use this stem-and-leaf graph to obtain the original set of values for this variable?

2.11. Create a stem-and-leaf of the variable AMSTAT from the Statisticians data set that you entered in Exercise 1.15. Use it to answer the following questions.
   a) How many statisticians in the data set had 7 citations?
   b) How would you describe the shape of this distribution? Explain.
   c) What is the most frequent number of citations for statisticians in this data set?
   d) What is the 50th percentile for this data set?

2.12. Create a stem-and-leaf graph of the variable total cholesterol, given by the variable TOTCHOL1 found in the Framingham data set. Use it to answer the following questions.
   a) What is the lowest score in this distribution?
   b) Are there any outliers (i.e., extreme values) in this distribution? Describe them.
   c) How would you describe the shape of this distribution? Explain.
   d) What is the 50th percentile of these data?
   e) What is the highest score in this distribution?
   f) Can we use this stem-and-leaf graph to obtain the complete set of original values for this variable?

2.13. Create a stem-and-leaf graph of eighth-grade math achievement scores given by the variable ACHMAT08 in the NELS data set. Use the stem-and-leaf graph to answer the following questions.
   a) According to the stem-and-leaf plot, what is the lowest eighth-grade math achievement score?
   b) According to the stem-and-leaf graph, approximately how many students received the lowest eighth-grade math achievement score?
   c) According to the stem-and-leaf plot, are there any outliers (extreme values) in this distribution?
   d) According to the stem-and-leaf plot, how would you characterize the shape of this distribution – negatively skewed, approximately symmetric, or positively skewed?
   e) According to the stem-and-leaf plot, which eighth-grade math achievement score occurs most often?
   f) What type of question is better answered with a stem-and-leaf graph and what type of question is better answered by a frequency distribution table?

2.14. Follow the instructions to create separate stem-and-leaf graphs of SYSBP1 (systolic blood pressure) for men and women (SEX) using the Framingham data set.

To obtain separate stem-and-leaf displays for different values of a grouping variable, click **Analyze** from the main menu bar, then **Descriptive Statistics** and then **Explore**. Move SYSBP1 to the **Dependent List** and SEX into the **Factor List**. Click **OK**.

a) In which distribution (male or female) do we find the lowest systolic blood pressure value? Explain.

b) In which distribution is the most frequently occurring systolic blood pressure value higher? Explain.

c) In which, if either, distribution does systolic blood pressure have a greater spread? Explain.

d) In which, if either, distribution is systolic blood pressure more skewed? Explain.

Exercises 2.15 through 2.17 involve questions about histograms of variables in the NELS data set.

2.15. Create a histogram of twelfth-grade math achievement given by the variable ACHMAT12 in the NELS data set. Use the histogram to answer the following questions.

a) According to the histogram, what is the smallest twelfth-grade math achievement score in the NELS data set? Approximately how many times does that score occur?

b) According to the histogram, what is the most frequently occurring twelfth-grade math achievement score interval?

c) According to the histogram, what is the shape of the distribution? Explain.

2.16. Follow the instructions to create two side-by-side histograms for SES, given by the variable SES in the NELS data set. Let one histogram represent those students who did not own a computer in eighth grade and the other histogram represent those who did own a computer in eighth grade (COMPUTER). Use the histograms to answer the following questions.

To create side-by-side histograms, click **Graphs**, **Legacy Dialogs**, **Population Pyramid**. Move SES into the **Show Distribution** over box and COMPUTER into the **Split by** box. Click **OK**.

a) Which computer group has the single highest SES score?

b) Would you say that SES is higher for the group that owns a computer? Why or why not?

c) Do the SES values have more spread for one group over another?

2.17. Create two histograms, one for a student's self-concept in eighth grade as given by the variable SLFCNC08 in the NELS data set and the other for a student's self-concept in twelfth grade as given by the variable SLFCNC12 in the NELS data set. Edit the histograms so that they each have the same scale and range of values on both the horizontal and vertical axes, and use them to answer the following questions.

a) For which grade (eighth or twelfth) is the overall level of self-concept higher?

b) For which grade is the spread of self-concept scores less?

c) For which grade is self-concept more skewed, and in which direction?

Exercises 2.18 through 2.20 involve questions about line graphs of variables in the NELS data set.

2.18. Create regular and interactive line graphs for average daily attendance rate per school as given by the variable SCHATTRT in the NELS data set. Use the graphs to answer the following questions.

a) In which line graph does SCATTRT appear more negatively skewed?

b) Which graph gives the more accurate portrayal of skewness in this case and why?

2.19. Create an ogive or cumulative line graph for the distribution of SCHATTRT. Use it to answer the following questions.

a) Approximately how many students attend schools where the average daily attendance rate is less than 90 percent?

b) Based on the ogive or cumulative line graph, would you describe the distribution as positively skewed, negatively skewed, or symmetric?

2.20. In this exercise we will see that the interpretation of a line graph can change with a change in the scale of the vertical and horizontal axes.

a) Use the Marijuana data set and SPSS to construct an interactive line graph of the percentage of students who have ever tried marijuana by year.

b) Use the following instructions to compress the scale on the vertical axis.

Double click on the graph to put it into the Chart Editor. Double click on any value on the vertical axis to bring up the **Scale Axis** box. Unclick **Auto for Minimum, Maximum, and Tick Interval**. Type the value 0 for the minimum, 60 for the maximum, and 10 for the tick interval. Click **OK**.

What is the effect of this change on the interpretation of the graph?

c) Use the following instructions to restrict the range of values on the horizontal axis to 1992 through 1999 in the uncompressed graph. Provide an interpretation of the graph.

To select cases, click **Window** on the main menu bar. Have the data set showing. Click **Data, Select Cases**. Click the circle next to **If Condition is Satisfied**. Click **If**. Type YEAR ≥ 1992 & YEAR ≤ 1999. Click **Continue, OK**. Now when you make the line graph, it will show the years from 1992 through 2002 only.

Exercises 2.21 through 2.23 involve questions about percentiles and percentile ranks of variables in the NELS data set. In these exercises, we use the cumulative percent to estimate the percentile rank.

2.21. Find the following values for a student's expected income at age 30 given by the variable EXPINC30 in the NELS data set.

a) What is the exact value of the 15th percentile, according to SPSS?

b) What is the exact value of the 50th percentile, according to SPSS?

c) What is the approximate percentile rank of an expected income of $50,000?

2.22. Why is the calculation of percentiles not appropriate for the variable PARMARL8.

2.23. This question relates to the optimist who is expecting to earn $1,000,000 per year at age 30 (EXPINC30 = 1,000,000).

a) What is this student's ID?

b) What was this student's eighth-grade self-concept score (SLFCNC08)?

c) What is the percentile rank of his eighth-grade self-concept score? Is it what you expected?

d) Use percentile ranks to determine the grade (eighth, tenth, or twelfth) in which this student was least self-confident relative to his peers.

Exercise 2.24 deals with questions about a boxplot of a single variable from the NELS data set.

2.24. Create a boxplot that shows the number of times a student in twelfth grade was recorded late for school as given by the variable LATE12. Use the boxplot to answer the following questions.

a) What is the level of measurement of LATE12?
b) Estimate and interpret the value of the 50th percentile for LATE12, represented by the line in the middle of the box.
c) What is the shape of this distribution? Explain by referring to the boxplot.
d) What is the significance of the fact that the graph has no bottom whisker?

Exercise 2.25 deals with questions about boxplots of more than one ordinal or scale variable constructed on the same axes.

2.25. Create one graph that has three boxplots, one for each of the distributions of self-concept scores for eighth, tenth, and twelfth grades, respectively. Use this graph to answer the following questions.

To obtain a boxplot for SLFCNC08, SLFCNC10, and SLFCNC12, click **Graphs**, **Legacy Dialogs**, **Boxplot**, **Summaries of separate variables**, and **Define**. Move SLFCNC08, SLFCNC10, and SLFCNC12 to the box labeled **Boxes Represent** and click **OK**.

a) How would you describe the shape of the distribution of self-concept in eighth grade?
b) For which grade is the self-concept distribution most nearly symmetric?
c) Overall, which of the three grades has the highest level of self-concept?
d) Which of the three grades contains the highest single self-concept score? And what is your estimate of that score?
e) Based on the interquartile range, which distribution appears to have the highest spread?

Exercises 2.26 and 2.27 involve boxplots of a single variable for different subgroups.

2.26. Create four boxplots on the same axis, one for each REGION, that plot the number of years of math taken in high school as given by the variable UNITMATH of the NELS data set. Use the graph to answer the following questions.

To create a boxplot of UNITMATH by REGION, click **Graphs**, **Legacy Dialogs**, **Boxplot**, **Summaries for Groups of Cases**, and **Define**. Move UNITMATH into the box labeled **Variable** and REGION into the box labeled **Category Axis**. Click **OK**.

a) Which region is most symmetric with respect to the distribution of units (years) of math taken in high school?
b) In which of the four regions is the overall level of UNITMATH lowest?
c) Which of the four regions contains the student with the single lowest number of units of math taken in high school? And what is that number?
d) In which region, if any, is the spread of UNITMATH smallest?
e) How many of the 106 students in the Northeast have UNITMATH scores between Q_1 and Q_2? Is this number confined to UNITMATH scores or does it generalize to all variables in this data set?

2.27. Construct four side-by-side boxplots of the number of AP classes offered at a student's school (APOFFER), one for each of the four types of high school programs (HSPROG) represented in the NELS data set.

a) How might one explain that there are academic program schools that offer many AP courses, but not any rigorous academic program schools that offer more than 20?

b) What would be a better way to represent AP course offerings other than by their number per school?

Exercise 2.28 involves boxplots of more than one ordinal, interval, or ratio variable broken down by a grouping variable.

2.28. Make four side-by-side boxplots showing the distributions of SLFCNC08, SLFCNC10, and SLFCNC12, the self-concept scores in eighth, tenth, and twelfth grades, respectively, by GENDER.

To obtain a boxplot for SLFCNC08, SLFCNC10, and SLFCNC12 separated by gender, click **Graphs, Legacy Dialogs, Boxplot, Clustered, Summaries of separate variables**, and **Define**. Move SLFCNC08, SLFCNC10, and SLFCNC12 to the box labeled **Boxes Represent** and GENDER to the box labeled **Category axis** and click **OK**.

---

a) Does self-concept generally appear to be increasing from eighth to twelfth grade for both sexes?

b) What is most noticeable about these boxplots when comparing males to females?

c) If not for the female outliers in 11th grade, would you say that males and females are comparable in their homogeneity of self-concept in 11th grade?

Exercises 2.29 through 2.31 involve a variety of boxplots.

2.29. In this exercise, we review the construction of the four different types of boxplots using the NELS data set.

a) Construct a boxplot of eighth-grade reading achievement (ACHRDG08).

b) Construct, within one set of axes, two boxplots of eighth-grade reading achievement, one for males and the other for females, using the variable GENDER.

c) Construct, within one set of axes, three boxplots, respectively, of eighth-, tenth-, and twelfth-grade reading achievement.

d) Construct, within one set of axes, boxplots of eighth-, tenth-, and twelfth-grade reading achievement, separately for males and females.

2.30. Describe the shape of each the following distributions denoted a, b, c, d, e, and f.

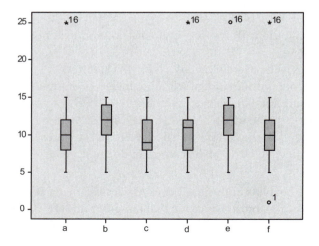

2.31. The boxplots below show, for each of the four regions, the average educational expenditure for the states in that region. The four stem-and-leaf displays, labeled A, B, C, and D, show the same. For each stem-and-leaf graph, the stem width is 1,000 and each leaf represents one case. Match the letter associated with each stem-and-leaf graph to the appropriate boxplot.

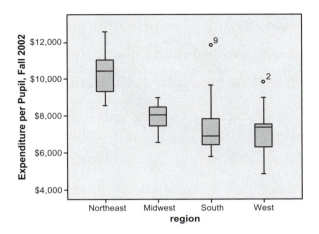

a)

```
Expenditure per Pupil, Fall 2002 Stem-and-Leaf
Plot for region = A

  Frequency      Stem & Leaf
      1.00          5 . 7
      8.00          6 . 01344569
      4.00          7 . 0178
      1.00          8 . 3
      2.00          9 . 16
      1.00 Extremes     (>=11847)
 Stem width:   1000
 Each leaf:    1 case(s)
```

b)

```
Expenditure per Pupil, Fall 2002 Stem-and-Leaf
Plot for region = B

  Frequency      Stem & Leaf
      1.00          4 . 8
       .00          5 .
      3.00          6 . 002
      6.00          7 . 123445
      2.00          8 . 19
      1.00 Extremes    (>=9870)
 Stem width:   1000
 Each leaf:    1 case(s)
```

c)

```
Expenditure per Pupil, Fall 2002 Stem-and-Leaf
Plot for region = C

  Frequency      Stem &  Leaf
     2.00            6 .  58
     3.00            7 .  445
     6.00            8 .  001267
     1.00            9 .  0
 Stem width:    1000
 Each leaf:     1 case(s)
```

d)

```
Expenditure per Pupil, Fall 2002 Stem-and-Leaf
Plot for region = D

  Frequency      Stem &  Leaf
     2.00            8 .  59
     1.00            9 .  3
     3.00           10 .  344
     2.00           11 .  09
     1.00           12 .  5
 Stem width:    1000
 Each leaf:     1 case(s)
```

Exercise 2.32 involves questions about selection of appropriate graphical displays.

2.32. For the following variables in the NELS data set, indicate whether the most appropriate types of graphical displays are (1) bar graph or pie graph, or (2) histogram, interactive line graph, stem-and-leaf plot, or boxplot.

a) GENDER
b) URBAN
c) SCHTYP8
d) TCHERINT
e) NUMINST
f) ACHRDG08
g) SCHATTRT
h) ABSENT12

Exercises 2.33 and 2.34 involve a number of different topics.

2.33. The following questions pertain to the tenth-grade social studies achievement score for students as given by the variable ACHSLS10 in the NELS data set.

a) What is the highest tenth-grade social studies achievement score in the NELS data set?
b) How many students obtained the highest score?
c) What is the most frequently occurring score in this distribution?
d) What is the 50th percentile of the distribution?
e) What is the 67th percentile?

f) What percentage of students scored 70 or below?

g) What is the shape of the distribution?

2.34. The following questions pertain to the amount of time spent weekly on extracurricular activities in twelfth grade as given by EXCURR12 in the NELS data set.

a) What does the value 2 represent?

b) How many students in the NELS data set answered EXCURR12 that they spent 1 to 4 hours per week on extracurricular activities?

c) What is the value at the 50th percentile?

d) What is the shape of this distribution?

Exercises 2.35 through 2.39 involve reading and interpreting graphs.

2.35. The line graphs below show approval rating and gasoline prices for different U.S. presidents. The graph comes from the News Analysis and Commentary section of *Business Week* from May 15, 2006. The large graph across the top covers George W. Bush's time in office. At the left is a scale for gas prices in dollars; at the right is a scale for job approval in percent. Answer the following questions.

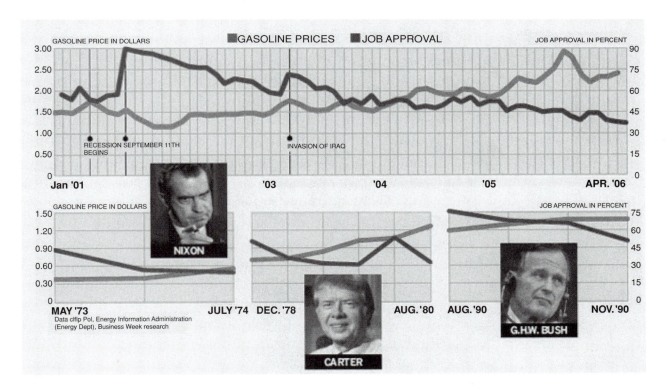

a) The vertical line above '03 represents what month?

b) What was the month and year of the invasion of Iraq?

c) Give the month and year of George W. Bush's highest approval rating. What was that rating?

d) Give the month and year of the lowest price of gasoline during George W. Bush's presidency. What was that price?

e) Give the month and year of George W. Bush's lowest approval rating. What was that rating?

f) Give the month and year of the highest price of gasoline during George W. Bush's presidency. What was that price?

g) Based on this graph, is it fair to say that for President George W. Bush higher gasoline prices are associated with lower job approval ratings?

2.36. According to the *Advertising Age* website, in 2004 Procter & Gamble was the second leading national advertiser (after General Motors), spending approximately $3,919,680,000 on advertising in the United States alone. The bar graph below shows the amount spent on advertising by Procter & Gamble on a select number of its products.

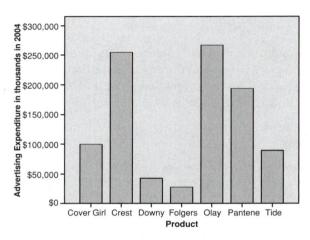

a) Estimate the advertising expenditure for Cover Girl.

b) Estimate the proportion or percentage of Proctor & Gamble's U.S. advertising expenditure spent on these seven products.

c) In the above bar graph, the products are ordered alphabetically on the *X*-axis. Below, the graph is redone so that the products are now ordered in ascending order according to their respective advertising expenditures. Instructions for creating the ordered bar graph are given in Exercise 2.6.

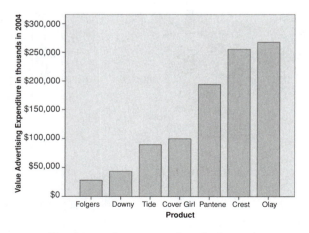

Do the products, so ordered, cluster in some meaningful fashion along the *X*-axis?

d) What is the drawback of representing these products by a pie chart?

2.37. The *Washington Post* published the information in the following pie graph indicating that Americans would rather be rich than good looking. The results were based on a *Washington Post* telephone survey of 1,011 randomly selected adults and was conducted in early June 2006.

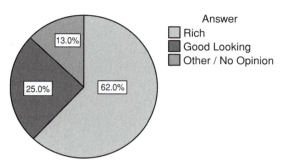

Answer
☐ Rich
■ Good Looking
▨ Other / No Opinion

Q: If you had to choose, which would you rather be: physically good looking or rich?

a) What percentage of people responded that they would rather be rich?
b) How many people responded that they would rather be rich?
c) Had the question been changed to, "If you had to choose, which would you rather be: extremely attractive or rich?" how might the graph have changed? What does this imply about the importance of knowing the phrasing of the question in interpreting a result?

2.38. Consider the following cartoon of Dilbert and his dog, Dogbert.

a) What defines the horizontal axis in the graph Dilbert is showing his dog?
b) Draw a picture of what the graph will probably look like after Dogbert makes his next remark.

2.39. The following graph is from the *Washington Post* on July 4, 2006. It describes the popularity of bottled water.

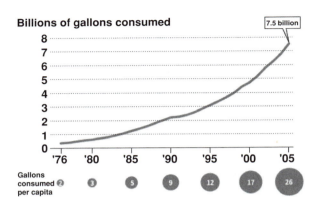

a) Approximately how many billions of gallons of water were consumed in 1980? How many billions of gallons of water were consumed in 2005?
b) From 1980 to 1985, what is the percentage increase in gallons consumed per capita?
c) From 2000 to 2005, what is the percentage increase in gallons consumed per capita?
d) Based on your answers to (b) and (c), would you say that consumption of water on a per capita basis is decreasing in growth, increasing in growth, or staying the same?

Exercises 2.40 through 2.50 check your conceptual understanding of the material in this chapter, without the use of SPSS.

2.40. Assuming the statistics are all calculated on the same set of data, rank the following from numerically smallest to numerically largest: C_{50}, C_4, D_1, D_3, Q_1, Q_3.

2.41. Determine what, if anything, is wrong with the following statement: A raw score of 75 is always surpassed by 25 percent of the scores in the distribution from which it comes.

2.42. Determine what, if anything, is wrong with the following statement: A 90-item test was scored by giving one point for each correct answer so that possible scores ranged from 0 to 90. On this test, the highest percentile rank possible is 90.

2.43. Determine what, if anything, is wrong with the following statement: On a certain English exam, Alice's score is twice as high as Ellen's. Therefore, Alice's percentile rank on the exam must be twice Ellen's percentile rank.

2.44. Determine what, if anything, is wrong with the following statement: If it takes 10 raw score points to go from a percentile rank of 50 to a percentile rank of 58, then it must also take 10 raw score points to go from a percentile rank of 90 to a percentile rank of 98.

2.45. Determine what, if anything, is wrong with the following statement: A student who scores at the 85th percentile in a math achievement test given to everyone in her or his school, and at the 95th percentile in a science test given to all students in the city in which the school is located, is doing better in science than in math.

2.46. Determine what, if anything, is wrong with the following statement: In a recent door-to-door survey, only five of the people questioned said they were opposed to a proposed school bond issue. The local school board publicized the results of this survey as evidence of tacit approval of the proposal.

2.47. Are the following possible values for percentiles: 50, −2, 512? Are they possible values for percentile ranks?

2.48. Explain how a symmetric distribution can have outliers in its boxplot.

2.49. Explain how a boxplot could have only one whisker.

2.50. Draw a picture of two side-by-side boxplots so that
   a) The one on the left clearly has scores that are typically at a higher level and the one on the right has scores that are clearly less consistent. The graphs you create indicate that higher scores do not necessarily mean more spread.
   b) The one on the left is clearly less spread out and the one on the right is clearly less skewed. The graphs you create indicate that more skew does not necessarily mean more spread.

CHAPTER THREE

Measures of Location, Spread, and Skewness

In our examination of univariate distributions in Chapter 2, three summarizing characteristics of a distribution were discussed: first, its shape (as denoted by its skewness or its symmetry, by how many peaks and/or outliers it has, and so on); second, its location (as denoted by its middle score, Q_2); and third, its spread (as denoted by both the range of values and by the interquartile range (IQR) or the range of values within which its middle 50 percent falls). In this chapter, we expand on that discussion by introducing other summary statistics for characterizing the location, spread, and shape of a distribution.

CHARACTERIZING THE LOCATION OF A DISTRIBUTION

When we speak of the location of a univariate distribution, we mean the point or number between the smallest and largest values of the distribution that best represents the distribution's "center." That point is a single value that connotes the typical or "average" value in the distribution, the point around which most values are centered. For this reason, measures of location are also known as measures of *central tendency*. In this section, we discuss three commonly used measures of location: mode, median, and mean. These measures can be used to answer questions like: "Do seniors typically have higher grade point averages than freshmen?" "Do union workers have a higher overall income than nonunion workers?" "Does female self-concept change, on average, from eighth grade to twelfth grade?"

THE MODE

The *mode* is that data value that occurs most often in a distribution and can be found for any distribution. The mode is easy to compute and simple to interpret. The mode of the distribution for HOMELANG (home language background) for the 500 students in our NELS

Table 3.1. Frequency distribution of home language background

Home Language Background

		Frequency	Percent	Valid Percent	Cumulative Percent
Valid	Non-English Only	15	3.0	3.0	3.0
	Non-English Dominant	35	7.0	7.0	10.0
	English Dominant	47	9.4	9.4	19.4
	English Only	403	80.6	80.6	100.0
	Total	500	100.0	100.0	

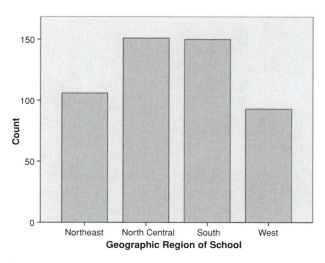

Figure 3.1   Bar graph of frequencies for REGION.

sample (see Table 3.1 for the frequency distribution) is English Only because that category occurs more often than any other in the distribution. That is, most students in our sample come from home backgrounds in which English is the only language spoken. Because relatively few students come from different home language backgrounds, the mode, English Only, best describes the typical home language background for this sample. As such, the category English Only is an effective measure of location for this distribution. In other situations, however, the mode is not so effective as a measure of a distribution's location.

Consider the frequency distribution of REGION presented in Table 2.1 of Chapter 2 and represented here as the bar graph of Figure 3.1. Notice that the frequencies of the categories North Central and South are approximately equal; North Central outnumbers South by only one case. Accordingly, it would be misleading to report North Central as the only mode of this distribution. A more appropriate characterization would be to report both North Central and South as modes in this case. Distributions that have two modes are called *bimodal*.

In Figure 3.1, the two peaks, one above each mode, are adjacent to each other. Because REGION is a nominal-leveled variable, and the order of categories in the distribution is arbitrary; the fact that the two modes are adjacent to each other is arbitrary as well.

When variables are ordinal-leveled or higher, however, and the order of categories in the distribution is not arbitrary, bimodal frequency distributions typically contain two peaks that are separated from each other by a gap in between. Figure 3.2 is an example of a bimodal distribution of 100 scores on a test of Spanish fluency.

Notice that most students speak Spanish either fluently (and receive very high scores on the test) or hardly at all (and receive very low scores on the test); a small number of students can speak some Spanish (and receive scores in the middle range). Another distribution that has been suggested as being bimodal is that of the intelligence quotients (IQs) of viewers of the television show *Court TV*. Viewers of *Court TV* are purported to have either very high IQs or very low IQs; a small number of viewers are reported as having IQs in the middle range. Can you think of other examples of bimodal distributions?

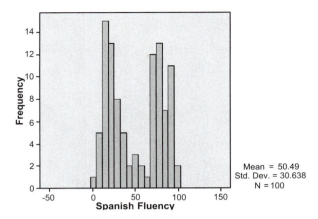

Figure 3.2 A bimodal distribution of test scores of Spanish fluency.

Some distributions are trimodal (three modes), and by extension it is possible to have a distribution in which every category has the same, and therefore the largest, frequency. Such distributions are called *uniform* or *rectangular* distributions and are not well characterized by the mode. Figure 3.3 is an example of a rectangular distribution. In this distribution, each score category contains exactly five cases.

While HOMELANG was at least ordinal and REGION was nominal, and both had fewer than five categories, we could obtain the mode of a distribution of a variable that takes on any number of possible values and is measured at any level of measurement. As in the previous cases, however, the effectiveness of a mode as a measure of a distribution's location depends on the shape of the distribution itself. Where distributions are skewed or contain gaps in the middle, the effectiveness of the mode as a measure of location is diminished. Where the distribution is reasonably symmetric, and *unimodal* (one mode, or *single-peaked*), however, the mode is useful in characterizing the location, or center, of a distribution.

Recall that the frequency distribution of socioeconomic status (SES), presented in Table 2.2 of Chapter 2 and reproduced here as Figure 3.4 in its histogram form, is reasonably symmetric and unimodal. From the histogram, the mode of this distribution

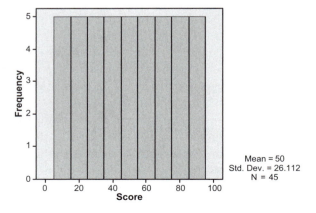

Figure 3.3 A rectangular distribution.

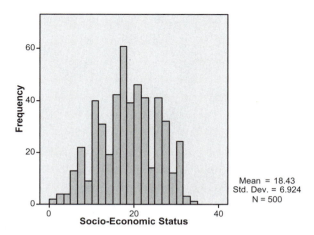

Figure 3.4 Histogram of SES.

appears to be contained in the category with midpoint value 20 since that category occurs most often among the students in our sample of 500. Notice that, because the distribution is reasonably symmetric and single-peaked, the mode is an effective numerical summary of the location of the SES distribution on the continuum from lowest to highest possible values.

The mode of a variable also may be obtained directly from SPSS.

To find the mode of SES, click **Analyze** in the main menu bar, **Descriptive Statistics**, and **Frequencies**. Move SES into the **Variables box**, click **Statistics, Mode, Continue**, and **OK**.

In so doing, we find the actual mode to be 19, because 19 is the single value that occurs most frequently in the SES distribution.

When a distribution has more than one mode, SPSS indicates that and reports the smallest mode.

THE MEDIAN

The *median* is defined as any theoretically possible data value in a distribution of a continuous variable below which 50 percent of all data values fall. Intuitively, then, the median may be thought of as the middle point in a distribution or as the point that divides a distribution into two equal halves. Because Q_2 (the second quartile, or, equivalently, the 50th percentile) also is defined as the middle point in a distribution, the median is another name for Q_2.

To approximate the median of a variable in a small data set, order the values in magnitude from lowest to highest. If the data set contains an odd number of values, the median is simply the middle value. If, on the other hand, the data set contains an even number of values, the median is the average of the two middle values obtained by summing the two middle values and dividing by 2.

EXAMPLE 3.1. National data for the United States on the number of home accident deaths from firearms for years 1997 to 2003 are given in the *2006 World Almanac and Book of*

Facts. Approximations to these data are given here by year. What is the median number of deaths?

Year	Number of accidental deaths due to firearms
1997	981
1998	866
1999	824
2000	776
2001	802
2002	800
2003	700

Solution. To find the median number of home accident deaths in the United States due to firearms during the period from 1997 to 2003, we order the data from its lowest to highest values as follows:

$$700 \quad 776 \quad 800 \quad 802 \quad 824 \quad 866 \quad 981$$
$$\wedge$$
$$\text{median}$$

Given that there are an odd number of values in this distribution, the median is simply the middle value, or 802. Notice that on each side of this middle value there is an equal number of values.

To find the median of a variable in a large data set, like SES, for example, we make use of a software package, like SPSS, and obtain Q_2 as shown in Chapter 2.

We may also find the median using SPSS by clicking on **Analyze** in the main menu bar, **Descriptive Statistics**, and **Frequencies**. In the case of SES, we move SES into the **Variables box**, click **Statistics**, **Median**, **Continue**, and then **OK**.

In so doing, we find that, like the mode, the median of SES is 19.

Recall that the median is defined as that point below which are half the values in the distribution and above which also are half the values in the distribution. As a result, the median is meaningful only when it makes sense to order the values in a data set from low to high, that is, when the variable is at least ordinal-leveled. A median is not meaningful for data that are nominal-leveled because such data would be ordered arbitrarily and different orderings would give rise to different medians. For nominal-leveled data, the mode, therefore, is the only appropriate measure of location.

Suppose we are interested in knowing the incomes of three individuals, and we are told that one of these individuals has an income of $0, another has an income of $5,000, and the median income for all three individuals is also $5,000. Because the median can be thought of as the middle or central point in a distribution, it might seem reasonable to suppose that the third individual has an income of $10,000. In reality, the third individual's income could be any value above $5,000 and still be consistent with the given information. The third individual's income could, for example, be $1,000,000, and the three incomes of $0, $5,000, and $1,000,000 would still have a median of $5,000. Thus, because the total number of values above the median equals the total number of values below the median, the median is not particularly sensitive to the exact values in a distribution. Changing one of the data values may or may not have any effect on the value of the median.

THE ARITHMETIC MEAN

The *arithmetic mean* (or simply the *mean*) is the most frequently used measure of location and is especially useful in inferential statistics. If we denote the ith observation of the variable X by X_i, the mean (denoted $\overline{X}$) is the sum of all the data values of the distribution (denoted $\sum X_i$, where the upper-case Greek letter sigma (Σ) represents the operation of summation) divided by N, the total number of data values in the distribution. The definition of the mean may be translated into the following mathematical equation:

$$\overline{X} = \frac{\sum X_i}{N}$$

(3.1)

• •

EXAMPLE 3.2. Find the mean number of home accident deaths due to firearms in the United States from the years 1997 to 2003.

Solution. Following Equation 3.1, we obtain

$$\frac{700 + 776 + 800 + 802 + 824 + 866 + 981}{7} = \frac{5749}{7} = 821.29$$

The mean for these data equals approximately 821 deaths.

To find the mean using SPSS, we can use the Frequencies procedures as before, or use the Descriptives procedure as follows.

To find the mean SES value for our sample of 500 students using SPSS, click **Analyze** in the main menu bar, **Descriptive Statistics**, and **Descriptives**. Move SES into the **Variables** box, and click **OK**.

The resulting output is as follows:

Descriptive Statistics

	N	Minimum	Maximum	Mean	Std. Deviation
Socio-Economic Status	500	0	35	18.43	6.924
Valid N (listwise)	500				

We find the mean SES to be 18.43. Recall that the median and mode for these data were both equal to 19.

Unlike the mode and the median, the mean is sensitive to any change in the data values of the distribution. Thus, if one value in the distribution is increased (or decreased), the mean of the distribution increases (or decreases), but not by the same amount. If, for example, we increase one of the values in the SES distribution by 25 points, the new mean will equal 18.93, an increase of 0.5. Try it on your data, using any one of the values in the

SES distribution. Be sure to replace the altered value by the original one once you have finished this check.

Of course, if more than one data value in a distribution is changed with some values increased and some values decreased, the changes can cancel out each other's effects on the mean and leave the mean unchanged.

There is another property of the mean worth mentioning. If for each X value in the distribution, X_i, we calculate its difference from the mean, $X_i - \overline{X}$, then these differences, summed across all data values, are equal to zero. The difference, $X_i - \overline{X}$, may also be thought of as the deviation or distance of the value from the mean. This property may be expressed in terms of the following equation:

$$\sum (X_i - \overline{X}) = 0 \tag{3.2}$$

Equation 3.2 shows that, when distance is measured from the mean, the total distance of points above the mean equals the total distance of points below the mean. As a result, a point that is far from the others in a distribution (e.g., an outlier) would pull the mean closer to it so as to balance the negative and positive differences about the mean. Furthermore, because the mean relies on distances to find a distribution's center, means should be computed only on variables that are at least interval-leveled. A mean of REGION or HOMELANG (home language background), for example, would be meaningless.

. . . .

EXAMPLE 3.3. Verify that $\sum (X_i - \overline{X}) = 0$ for the deaths due to firearms data.

Solution.

$(700 - 821.29) + (776 - 821.29) + (800 - 821.29) + (802 - 821.29) + (824 - 821.29) + (866 - 821.29) + (981 - 821.29) = (-121.29) + (-45.29) + (-21.29) + (-19.29) + (2.71) + (44.71) + (159.71) = -207.16 + 207.13 = -0.03.$

This value is within rounding of 0.

☞ **Remark.** Most statistical software packages compute any measure of location on any set of numerical values, regardless of how meaningful or meaningless these values are in measuring the underlying trait in question. SPSS, for example, readily computes a mean of the variable REGION in the NELS data set because numerical values have been assigned to the variable REGION's different categories. Using the SPSS Descriptive Statistics procedure, we see that the mean of REGION is 2.46, which is the average of all 500 of the values that REGION assumes, where each value is between 1 and 4. The value 2.46 does not have a meaningful interpretation because the variable REGION is measured at the nominal level with more than two categories. The onus is on the researcher, then, to know which summary measures are appropriate in which circumstances. Without good judgment and thought in data analysis, interpretations of results may often be meaningless.

Although the mean is usually meaningless when calculated on a nominal-leveled variable, it has an interpretation when calculated on a dichotomous variable for which the categories are coded as 0 and 1. In Chapter 1 we defined a dichotomous variable as a variable that has two categories. When those categories are assigned numerical values of 0 and 1, respectively, the mean of the variable is equal to the proportion of cases in the category assigned the value of 1.

EXAMPLE 3.4. Find the mean of GENDER in our NELS data set of 500 cases.

Solution. Recall that GENDER is a dichotomous variable with the two categories, male and female. In the NELS data set, the category female is assigned the value of 1 whereas the category male is assigned the value of 0.

To find the mean of GENDER, together with a frequency distribution table, click **Analyze**, **Descriptive Statistics**, **Frequencies**. Move GENDER into the **Variables** box. Click **Statistics**, **Mean**. Click **Continue**, **OK**.

We obtain the following result:

Statistics

Gender

N	Valid	500
	Missing	0
Mean		.55

Gender

		Frequency	Percent	Valid Percent	Cumulative Percent
Valid	Male	227	45.4	45.4	45.4
	Female	273	54.6	54.6	100.0
	Total	500	100.0	100.0	

Notice that the mean of GENDER equals .55 (rounded to two decimal places), which is equal to the proportion of females in our sample of 500 cases.

COMPARING THE MODE, MEDIAN, AND MEAN

As we have noted in earlier sections of this chapter, the mode, median, and mean measure different aspects of the location of a distribution of data values. Depending on the particular shape of a distribution, the numerical values of these three measures may be the same or different. Conversely, knowing the values of these three measures relative to one another can often provide a better understanding of the shape of the underlying distribution.

When a distribution is symmetric, the mean is equal to the median (see Distributions A and B in Figure 3.5). When a distribution, such as Distribution B, is symmetric and also unimodal, the mode equals the mean and the median as well. The distribution of our data on home accident deaths due to firearms in Example 3.1 is symmetric and unimodal, which explains why the mode, median, and mean were all equal to each other.

If a distribution is highly negatively skewed, the mean will generally be smaller than the median, because the value of the mean is more influenced than the value of the median by the extreme low values present in such a distribution. Analogously, for a distribution that is highly positively skewed, the mean will generally be larger than the median, because it is more influenced than the median by the extreme high values present in such a distribution. Because of the differential influence of extreme scores on the mean and median, the mean of a highly skewed distribution lies in the direction of skewness (the direction of the tail) relative to the median. This relationship between the mean and the median is illustrated in Figures 3.6 and 3.7, which depict unimodal continuous distributions. Exercise 3.6

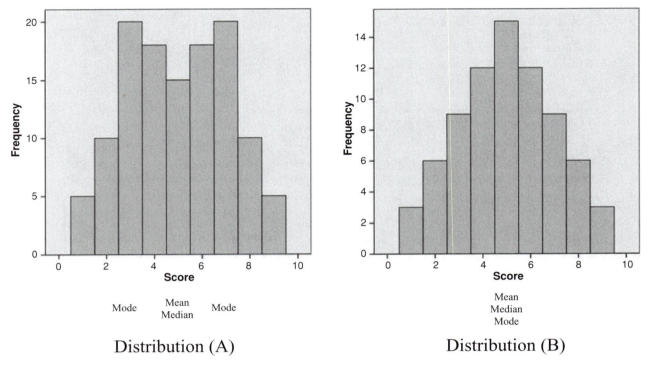

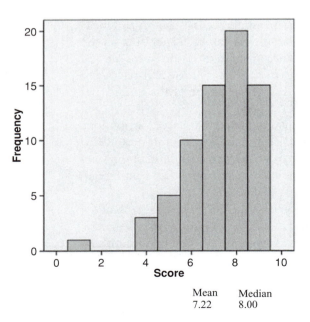

Distribution (A)   Distribution (B)

Figure 3.5   Histograms of two symmetric distributions.

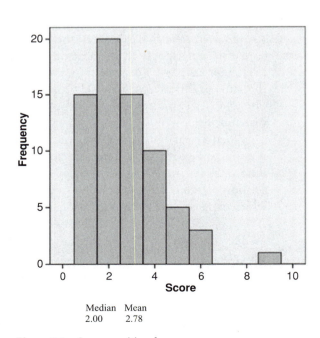

Figure 3.6   Severe negative skew.   **Figure 3.7**   Severe positive skew.

illustrates that, in the case of discrete distributions or multimodal continuous distributions, counter-examples exist and are not, in fact, uncommon in those circumstances. However, when a distribution is severely skewed and unimodal continuous, we can expect the mean and median to differ in a predictable way.

☞ **Remark.** The converse is not true, however. That is, if the mean and the median are different from each other, the distribution need not be skewed. Analogously, if the mean is equal to the median, the distribution need not be symmetric.

· ·

EXAMPLE 3.5. Compare the values of the mode, median, and mean for (a) SES, (b) EXPINC30 (expected income at age 30), (c) SCHATTRT (school attendance rate, which measures the average daily attendance rate of the high school that each student attended), and (d) SLFCNC08 (self-concept score in eighth grade). Explain the direction of difference that exists among these three measures of location. Note that, by calculating the mean of these variables, we are treating them as at least interval-leveled.

Solution.

To generate a single table with summary statistics for each of the three variables, click **Analyze**, **Descriptive Statistics**, **Frequencies**. Move SES, EXPINC30, SCHATTRT, and SLFCNC08 into the **Variables** box. Click **Statistics**, **Mean**, **Median**, **Mode**, **Continue**. Click the box next to **Display frequency tables** so that it is not selected. Click **OK**.

The resulting SPSS output is reproduced below. Note that the order in which the variables are displayed is the order in which they are moved to the Variables box.

Statistics

		Socio-Economic Status	Expected Income at Age 30	School Average Daily Attendance Rate
N	Valid	500	459	417
	Missing	0	41	83
Mean		18.43	51574.73	93.65
Median		19.00	40000.00	95.00
Mode		19	50000	95

Recall that the distribution of SES is reasonably symmetric. We see that the three measures of location (central tendency) are approximately equal. On the other hand, we know from our earlier work that expected income at age 30 is highly positively skewed. Not surprisingly, the value of the mean is quite a bit higher than the value of the median. From Exercise 2.15(c) we know that average daily school attendance rate is highly negatively skewed, which explains why the mean is smaller than the median in this case.

CHARACTERIZING THE SPREAD OF A DISTRIBUTION

When we speak of the spread of a univariate distribution, we mean the extent to which the values in the distribution vary from its "average" and from one another. Instead of the word *spread*, we may equivalently use the words *variability, dispersion, heterogeneity, inconsistency*, and *unpredictability*. Several different summary statistics exist to measure spread: the range, the IQR, the variance, and the standard deviation. As we shall see, each of these summary statistics taps a different aspect of spread. Measures of spread may be used to answer the following sample questions: "Are females more variable than males in their self-concept?" "Are reading scores more homogeneous in private schools than in public schools?" "Are home insurance fees more consistent in California than in New York?"

We present a variation of an example from Burrill and Hopfensperger (1993) to illustrate more clearly what it is that measures of spread capture about a set of numbers, as opposed to, for example, measures of location.

. . . .

EXAMPLE 3.6. Congratulations! You have just won a trip to one of two cities in the United States that have similar average annual temperatures (approximately 57 degrees): San Francisco, CA, or Springfield, MO. The prize also includes a wardrobe of clothes that would be suitable, from the point of view of warmth, for visiting the city of your choice any time during the year.

Would the same clothes be suitable for both cities at any time during the year? For which city would the wardrobe of clothing necessarily be more extensive? The average monthly temperatures (in Fahrenheit) for the two cities are given in Table 3.2 and are saved on your data CD in the TEMP data set.

Solution. Because a more extensive wardrobe would be required by the city that has a greater variability in temperature across the months of the year, we explore the relative variability in monthly temperature for the two cities using boxplots.

☞ **Remark.** There are two ways to enter these data as two variables. First, we could use two variables, CITY and TEMP. CITY is a dichotomous variable with two categories

Table 3.2. Average monthly temperature of Springfield and San Francisco

Month	Springfield Temperature	San Francisco Temperature
Jan	32	49
Feb	36	52
Mar	45	53
Apr	56	55
May	65	58
Jun	73	61
Jul	78	62
Aug	77	63
Sep	70	64
Oct	58	61
Nov	45	55
Dec	36	49

(Springfield, assigned the value of 1, and San Francisco, assigned the value of 2) whereas TEMP is a continuous variable of temperature in degrees Fahrenheit for each month. This is the way the data are displayed in the Temp data set on the data disk. An excerpt of the data file is presented.

CITY	TEMP
1	32
2	49
1	36
2	52
1	45
2	53
etc.	etc.

Second, we could use two variables, SPRING and SANFRAN. The first gives the Springfield temperature and the second the San Francisco temperature. The resulting graphs and statistics are the same regardless of the format of the data, but, because the methods for obtaining them differ slightly, both are presented.

There are two ways to create side-by-side boxplots that give the temperatures for the two cities. The first is based on the first layout for the data.

Boxplots comparing distributions of a single variable from different subgroups may be obtained using SPSS by clicking **Graphs**, **Legacy Dialogs**, **Boxplot**, and **Define**. Move the variable TEMP to the **Variable** box and CITY to the **Category Axis** box. Click **OK**.

Boxplots comparing distributions from two different variables may be obtained using SPSS by clicking **Graphs**, **Legacy Dialogs**, **Boxplot**, the circle next to **Summaries of separate variables**, and **Define**. Move the variables SPRING and SANFRAN to the **Boxes represent** box. Click **OK**.

The result, using either of the two procedures, is the following boxplot.

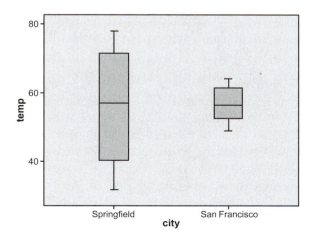

From the boxplot display, we may observe that, although the cities share the same typical or "average" temperature across the 12 months of the year (the median is approximately 57 degrees), they differ quite markedly in terms of the temperature spread. For Springfield, the temperature varies from a low of 32 to a high of 78, whereas for San Francisco the temperature varies only from a low of 48 to a high of 64. What this suggests is that, while middle-weight clothes would be suitable for all months of the year for San Francisco, for Springfield, light-, middle-, and heavy-weight clothes are necessary. Said differently, Springfield requires the more extensive wardrobe of the two cities.

More formally, we may characterize the variability in temperature using one of several numeric summaries of spread.

THE RANGE AND INTERQUARTILE RANGE

The *range* of a distribution is simply the difference between the highest and lowest values in the distribution. The range is easy to compute and simple to interpret. For San Francisco, the range is $64 - 49$ or 15 degrees Fahrenheit, whereas for Springfield, the range is $78 - 32$ or 46 degrees Fahrenheit. Because 46 degrees is greater than 15 degrees, the range correctly captures the relative spread for the data of these two distributions. However, because the range depends on the highest and lowest values of a distribution, and because these values tend to be the least stable values of a distribution, the range is not usually the best measure of a distribution's spread.

For example, the IQR, introduced in Chapter 2, is less sensitive than the range to changes in the extreme values, or, more generally, to changes in the shape of the tails of a distribution. The *IQR* is the difference between the third quartile, Q_3, and the first quartile, Q_1, and as such equals the distance covered by the middle 50 percent of the distribution.

Because the IQR is based on the values near the center of the distribution, it is not sensitive to the small number of values in the tails. Statistics, such as the IQR, that are not sensitive to changes in a small number of values within a distribution are called *resistant statistics*. The median is another example of a resistant statistic because, unlike the mean, the median is not sensitive to extreme values in either tail of the distribution.

To estimate the IQR for both cities, we first order the 12 temperature values from lowest to highest for each city.

For Springfield, the ordered temperature values are:

32   36   36   45   45   56   58   65   70   73   77   78

                        ∧

Therefore, the median is 57. Because we may think of Q_1 as the value that divides the lower half of the distribution in half, a good estimate for Q_1 is the middle value of the six lowest values (32, 36, 36, 45, 45, 56) or that value that has three values below it and three values above it. An estimate of that value is halfway between 36 and 45, or 40.5. Likewise, a good estimate for Q_3 is the value halfway between 70 and 73, or 71.5. An estimate of the IQR is therefore $Q_3 - Q_1 = 71.5 - 40.5 = 31$.

For San Francisco, the ordered temperature values are:

49   49   52   53   55   55   58   61   61   62   63   64

                        ∧

The median for these data is 56.5, an estimate of $Q_1 = 52.5$, and an estimate of $Q_3 = 61.5$. Therefore, an estimate of the IQR is $Q_3 - Q_1 = 61.5 - 52.5 = 9$.

We may use SPSS to obtain an estimate of the IQR that is based on a somewhat different set of assumptions about the data. The IQR from SPSS is not necessarily equal to the value obtained by our estimation procedure.

To obtain the IQRs for distributions of a single variable for different subgroups using SPSS, click **Analyze, Descriptive Statistics,** and **Explore.** Move the variable TEMP to the **Dependent List** box and CITY to the **Factor List** box. Click **Statistics,** and then **OK.**

To obtain the IQRs for two different variables using SPSS, click **Analyze, Descriptive Statistics,** and **Explore.** Move the variable SPRING and SANFRAN to the **Dependent List** box. Click **Statistics,** and then **OK.**

The results are given in the table that follows. Notice that, whereas the medians agree with our own estimates, the IQRs differ. For all practical purposes, we may estimate the IQR using the procedure outlined in this section. Notice that, regardless of the estimation procedures used, the IQR values are ordered in a way that we would expect based on our visual examination of the data using the boxplot.

Descriptives

	city				Statistic	Std. Error
temp	Springfield	Mean			55.92	4.856
		95% Confidence	Lower Bound		45.23	
		Interval for Mean	Upper Bound		66.61	
		5% Trimmed Mean			56.02	
		Median			57.00	
		Variance			282.992	
		Std. Deviation			16.822	
		Minimum			32	
		Maximum			78	
		Range			46	
		Interquartile Range			34	
		Skewness			−.078	.637
		Kurtosis			−1.599	1.232
	San Francisco	Mean			56.83	1.556
		95% Confidence	Lower Bound		53.41	
		Interval for Mean	Upper Bound		60.26	
		5% Trimmed Mean			56.87	
		Median			56.50	
		Variance			29.061	
		Std. Deviation			5.391	
		Minimum			49	
		Maximum			64	
		Range			15	
		Interquartile Range			10	
		Skewness			−.178	.637
		Kurtosis			−1.474	1.232

THE VARIANCE

If we conceptualize the spread of a distribution as the extent to which the values in the distribution differ from the mean and from each other, then a reasonable measure of spread might be the average deviation, or difference, of the values from the mean. In notation form, this may be expressed as follows:

$$\frac{1}{N}\sum(X_i - \overline{X}) \tag{3.3}$$

Although at first glance this might seem reasonable, using Equation 3.2, this expression always equals zero regardless of the actual spread of the data values in the distribution. Recall that this occurs because the negative deviations about the mean always cancel out the positive deviations about the mean, producing a sum or average of 0.

To avoid this cancellation effect, one may simply drop any negative signs from the deviation values before averaging. In mathematical terminology, dropping the negative sign of a number is called taking that number's absolute value. The mean of the absolute values of the deviations is called the mean deviation. Although the mean deviation is a good measure for describing the spread of a given set of data, it is not often used because the concept of absolute value does not lend itself to the kind of advanced mathematical manipulation necessary for the development of inferential statistical equations.

The usual method for avoiding such cancellation is, therefore, to square the deviations rather than taking their absolute values. In so doing, we obtain a measure that is sensitive to differences in spread and is easy to work with mathematically in the development of inferential statistical equations. The average of the squared deviations about the mean is called the *variance*. It is denoted by the symbol SD^2 and is given by Equation 3.4:

$$SD^2 = \frac{\sum(X_i - \overline{X})^2}{N} \tag{3.4}$$

The variance of the distribution of Springfield temperatures is 259.41 whereas the variance of San Francisco temperatures is 26.64. These values are consistent with our observation that Springfield has a larger temperature spread than San Francisco, or that the distribution of Springfield temperatures is more variable (less homogeneous, or more heterogeneous) than the distribution of San Francisco temperatures.

Although this book has a noncomputational focus, we believe that seeing a worked-out example for computing the variance using Equation 3.4 will aid in conceptualizing this statistic.

EXAMPLE 3.7. Use Equation 3.4 to find the mean and variance of the San Francisco monthly temperature. (Recall that these values are approximately 56.83 and 26.64, respectively.)

Solution. We denote the temperature variable as X.

X	$X - \overline{X}$	$(X - \overline{X})^2$
49	−7.83	61.31
52	−4.83	23.33
53	−3.83	14.67
55	−1.83	3.35
58	1.17	1.37

X	$X - \overline{X}$	$(X - \overline{X})^2$
61	4.17	17.39
62	5.17	26.73
63	6.17	38.07
64	7.17	51.41
61	4.17	17.39
55	−1.83	3.35
49	−7.83	61.31
Total: 682		**Total: 319.67**

$$\text{Mean} = \overline{X} = \frac{\sum X_i}{N} = \frac{682}{12} = 56.83$$

$$\text{Sum of Squares} = SS = \sum(X_i - \overline{X})^2 = 319.67$$

$$\text{Variance} = SD^2 = \frac{SS}{N} = \frac{\sum(X_i - \overline{X})^2}{N} = \frac{319.67}{12} = 26.64$$

According to Equation 3.4, the more the values of the distribution tend to differ from the mean, the larger the variance. But how large is a large variance? Unfortunately, there is no simple answer. Variances, like other measures of spread, are used primarily to compare the spread of one distribution to the spread of another and not to judge, offhand, whether or not a single distribution has a large spread. However, a variance of zero, the smallest possible value, indicates that there is no spread; that is, that all of the scores are the same.

The numerical value of a variance of a distribution also depends on the unit of measurement used. As we formalize in the next chapter, the variance of a distribution of heights measured in inches, for example, is considerably larger than the variance of the same distribution of heights measured in feet. Therefore, when comparing the variances of two or more distributions, for comparability the unit of measurement should be the same for all distributions.

The results from the SPSS Explore procedure given in the previous Descriptives table contain the variance of temperature values for each city as computed by SPSS. For San Francisco, the variance is 29.06. This value is different from the value of 26.64 that we obtained by hand.

☞ **Remark.** A problem with SPSS is that it does not calculate the variance as it is defined in Equation 3.4. Rather than calculating it as the sum of squared deviations about the mean divided by N, it calculates it as the sum of squared deviations about the mean divided by $N - 1$. Although dividing by $N - 1$ makes sense in the context of inferential statistics, when we seek to obtain a variance estimate based on sample data, in the context of descriptive statistics it does not. To obtain the variance, as it is defined, you need only to multiply the value obtained from SPSS by $(N - 1)/N$. Alternatively you may reason that, especially when N is large, the value obtained from SPSS should be close enough to the correct value to forego making this adjustment. For descriptive purposes, we adjust the value obtained from SPSS by multiplying by $(N - 1)/N$ whenever N is less than 30. With an N of 30 or more, the adjustment factor $(N - 1)/N$ is close enough to 1 not to matter in practice.

Based on this remark, to obtain the value of the variance as defined by Equation 3.4, we simply multiply 29.06 by $(N - 1)/N$, or in this case 11/12, to obtain 26.64.

☞ **Remark.** Although the range and IQR for our temperature example are in terms of degrees Fahrenheit, the original units of measurement, this is not the case for the variance. The variance is expressed in terms of squared units as opposed to the original units of measurement. This means that, for this example, the variance is expressed in terms of squared degrees Fahrenheit, rather than degrees Fahrenheit. To see that this is the case we need only to review Example 3.7, in which the variance of the distribution of San Francisco temperatures is calculated. In Example 3.7, the mean (in degrees Fahrenheit) is subtracted from the value of each temperature to obtain a deviation, $X - \overline{X}$, in degrees Fahrenheit for each month. But then these deviations are squared. The squared deviations are in squared degrees Fahrenheit rather than in degrees Fahrenheit. The variance, which is the average of these squared deviations, is then also in squared degrees Fahrenheit.

THE STANDARD DEVIATION

Because the variance is expressed in squared units rather than in the original units of measurement, the variance value cannot meaningfully be related to the original set of data. However, the variance may be expressed in terms of the original units of measurement if we take the positive square root of the variance. This new measure is called the *standard deviation*, is denoted by the symbols *SD* or *S*, and is given by the following equation:

$$SD = +\sqrt{SD^2} \qquad\qquad (3.5)$$

Because the standard deviation is a measure of spread in terms of the original units of measurement, it may be directly related to the original set of data. The standard deviation of the San Francisco temperatures is 5.16. If we order the temperatures from lowest to highest, we have the following: 49, 49, 52, 53, 55, 55, 58, 61, 61, 62, 63, 64.

The values within 57 ± 5.16 are the values within the interval 51.84 to 62.16. These are the values 52, 53, 55, 55, 58, 61, 61, and 62. Hence, 8 of the 12 values, or 67 percent, fall within one standard deviation of the mean. All values fall within two standard deviations of the mean for this distribution. The number of values that fall within one standard deviation of the mean in a distribution vary somewhat from distribution to distribution; so do the number of standard deviations needed to capture all the values of a distribution.

☞ **Remark.** One may also describe the standard deviation as that distance from the mean (in both directions) within which the majority of values of a distribution fall. The distance is shorter in distributions that are clustered tightly about the mean and longer in distributions that are not clustered so tightly about the mean.

☞ **Remark.** Whereas the IQR is a resistant statistic, as noted earlier, the variance and standard deviation are not. The variance is conceptualized as the average of squared deviations about the mean and the standard deviation as the square root of that. Cases with extreme deviations, therefore, are highly influential because they enter the calculation as the deviation squared rather than as the deviation itself. Because a deviation of 10 adds 100 points to the calculation whereas a deviation of 20 adds 400 points, for example, the more extreme the deviation, the greater the increase in its influence on the variance and standard deviation. As a result, the variance and standard deviation are especially sensitive to the influence of extreme values and are considered to be highly nonresistant statistics.

☞ **Remark.** The standard deviation obtained from SPSS is also not consistent with the convention used in this text. Whereas the SPSS variance is off by a factor of $(N-1)/N$, the SPSS standard deviation is off by a factor of $\sqrt{(N-1)/N}$. Thus, SPSS reports the standard deviation of the San Francisco temperatures as 5.39 rather than 5.16.

CHARACTERIZING THE SKEWNESS OF A DISTRIBUTION

In the preceding chapter we described the shape of a distribution as symmetric, or as positively or negatively skewed. Our description was based on visually "eyeballing" the represented data. Often one may be interested in a numerical summary of skewness for the purpose of comparing the skewness of two or more distributions or for evaluating the degree to which a single distribution is skewed. The *skewness statistic* is such a numerical summary. Equation 3.6 gives the expression for the skewness statistic:

$$\text{Skewness} = \frac{N}{(N-1)(N-2)}\frac{\sum(X_i - \overline{X})^3}{(SD)^3} \tag{3.6}$$

where SD is defined as the standard deviation computed with $N-1$ in the denominator.

$$\text{Standard Error Skewness} = \sqrt{\frac{6N(N-1)}{(N-2)(N+1)(N+3)}}$$

Whereas the variance is based on the sum of squared deviations about the mean, the skewness statistic is based on the sum of cubed deviations about the mean. And although the variance can only be positive or zero (because it is based on the sum of *squared* deviations), the skewness statistic may be positive, zero, or negative (because it is based on the sum of *cubed* deviations). The skewness statistic is positive when the distribution is skewed positively and it is negative when the distribution is skewed negatively. If the distribution is perfectly symmetric, the skewness statistic equals zero. The more severe the skew, the more the skewness statistic departs from zero.

· ·

EXAMPLE 3.8. Use Equation 3.6 to calculate the skewness and standard error of the skew for the San Francisco monthly temperature. (Recall that, according to the Descriptives table obtained using the SPSS Explore procedure, these values are −.178 and .637, respectively.)

Solution. We denote the temperature variable as X. Recall that, according to the Descriptives table obtained using the SPSS Explore procedure, $\overline{X} = 56.83$ and $SD = 5.39$ for San Francisco.

X	$X - \overline{X}$	$(X - \overline{X})^3$
49	−7.83	−480.05
52	−4.83	−112.68
53	−3.83	−56.18
55	−1.83	−6.13
58	1.17	1.60
61	4.17	72.51
62	5.17	138.19

X	$X - \overline{X}$	$(X - \overline{X})^3$
63	6.17	234.89
64	7.17	368.60
61	4.17	72.51
55	−1.83	−6.13
49	−7.83	−480.05
	Total: −256.08	

$$\text{The skewness} = \frac{N}{(N-1)(N-2)} \frac{\sum (X_i - \overline{X})^3}{(SD)^3} = \frac{12}{(11)(10)} \times \frac{-256.08}{5.39^3} = -.178$$

$$\text{The standard error of the skewness} = \sqrt{\frac{6N(N-1)}{(N-2)(N+1)(N+3)}} = \sqrt{\frac{6(12)(11)}{(10)(13)(15)}}$$

To compare the skewness of two distributions of relatively equal size, one may use the skewness values themselves. To compare the skewness of two distributions that are quite unequal in size, or to evaluate the severity of skewness for a particular distribution when that distribution is small or moderate in size, one should compute a ratio. The skewness ratio is obtained as the skewness statistic divided by the standard error of the skewness statistic. The meaning of the standard error is discussed in Chapter 9. For now, we use it to perform a computation and note that it is a function of the sample size.

According to the Explore procedure results given in the previous Descriptives table, the skewness statistic for the Springfield temperature values is −.178 with standard error of .637, and for San Francisco these values are −.078 and .637, respectively. To evaluate the severity of the skew of these distributions we calculate the skewness ratio for each distribution. For Springfield, the skewness ratio is −.178/.637 = −.279; for San Francisco, the skewness ratio is −.078/.637 = −.122. By convention, when this ratio exceeds 2.00 for small- and moderate-sized samples, one should consider the distribution to be severely skewed. In our case, these statistics corroborate our impressions from the boxplot that these distributions are not skewed.

Because many summary statistics are sensitive to extreme values, and because skewed distributions often contain extreme values, one should routinely check a distribution for the severity of its skewness. It is often possible to reduce the skewness of a distribution by expressing the data of that distribution in an alternative form. Ways for doing so are covered in the next chapter.

SELECTING MEASURES OF LOCATION AND SPREAD

Table 3.4 provides a summary of the relationship between the level of measurement of a variable and the generally appropriate measures of central tendency and spread. In the case of interval- or ratio-leveled variables, the shape of the distribution influences whether one chooses a resistant measure (i.e., median and IQR) or a nonresistant measure (i.e., mean, standard deviation, and range) to summarize the data. If a distribution is not severely skewed, either measure may be appropriate. If the distribution is severely skewed, however, resistant measures are generally more appropriate. As discussed in this chapter, resistant measures are not as influenced by outliers as nonresistant measures and, therefore, provide better summary characterizations of the data when data are severely skewed.

Table 3.4. Guidelines for selecting appropriate measures of location and spread based on a variable's level of measurement

Level of measurement	Appropriate measures of	
	Location	Spread
Nominal	Mode	None
Ordinal	Median	IQR
Interval	Mean or Median	SD or IQR
Ratio	Mean or Median	SD or IQR

APPLYING WHAT WE HAVE LEARNED

Suppose we wish to know the extent to which eighth-grade males expect larger incomes at age 30 than eighth-grade females, and the extent to which there is lack of consensus among twelfth-grade males in their expectations of income at age 30 relative to females. We make use of the statistics presented thus far to find answers to our questions.

Although quick answers might be obtained by comparing the numerical summaries of location and spread for EXPINC30 for both males and females, to be confident of their accuracy we first need to examine the data that are being summarized. A good way to do so is with the help of two side-by-side boxplots, one for males and one for females. The Explore procedure in SPSS can be used to generate both summary statistics and associated graphs and is especially useful when comparing two or more groups on the same variable.

To obtain these boxplots and summary statistics, click **Analyze**, **Descriptive Statistics**, and **Explore**; move the variable EXPINC30 to the **Dependent List** box and GENDER to the **Factor List** box; click **OK**.

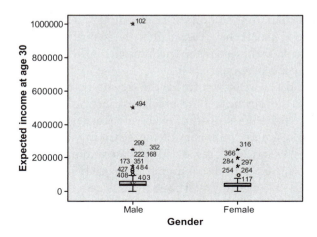

Descriptives

	Gender				Statistic	Std. Error
Expected income at age 30	Male	Mean			60720.93	5405.410
		95% Confidence Interval for Mean	Lower Bound		50066.27	
			Upper Bound		71375.60	
		5% Trimmed Mean			50596.90	
		Median			45000.00	
		Variance			6E + 09	
		Std. Deviation			79258.866	
		Minimum			1	
		Maximum			1000000	
		Range			999999	
		Interquartile Range			25000	
		Skewness			8.863	.166
		Kurtosis			96.801	.330
	Female	Mean			43515.57	1726.263
		95% Confidence Interval for Mean	Lower Bound		40115.23	
			Upper Bound		46915.92	
		5% Trimmed Mean			40837.89	
		Median			40000.00	
		Variance			7E + 008	
		Std. Deviation			26965.088	
		Minimum			0	
		Maximum			250000	
		Range			250000	
		Interquartile Range			20000	
		Skewness			3.816	.156
		Kurtosis			22.694	.310

From the boxplots we notice that, with the exception of two outliers (cases 102 and 494), the distributions of EXPINC30 are similar in shape for males and females. Because of these outliers, however, and the fact that the male distribution is much more positively skewed than the female distribution, we expect that different summary statistics should result in different interpretations. In particular, for the nonresistant summary statistics (e.g., the mean, range, and standard deviation), males have considerably higher values than females; for the more resistant summary statistics (e.g., the median and IQR), the differences between males and females will be less pronounced.

From the table of summary statistics we may note that the skewness of the male distribution is approximately 8.9 whereas the skewness of the female distribution is approximately 3.8. Because the NELS data set has different numbers of males and females, we compute the skewness ratios and use them to compare the shapes of the distributions. The skewness ratios for males and females are 53.39 and 24.46, respectively. These summary statistics corroborate our graphical impressions that both distributions are severely positively skewed and that the male distribution is far more positively skewed than the female distribution.

Notice that, as expected, the male mean is considerably higher than the female mean. On average, the 215 males who responded to this question expect an income at age 30 of $60,721, whereas the 244 females who responded to this question expect an income at age

30 of only $43,516. Notice also that the male median is $45,000 whereas the female median is $40,000. Thus, whether one uses the mean or the median, males are shown to have higher expected incomes at age 30 than females. However, the magnitude of difference is considerably greater between the sexes when one uses the mean rather than the median as a measure of location. This attests more to the fact that the distribution of EXPINC30 is more positively skewed for males than for females than to some essential truth about the difference in expected income between the majority of males and females.

Comparing the spread of the male and female distributions, we find again that different summary statistics lead to different interpretations. The difference in expected income variability between males and females is most pronounced when nonresistant measures are used (e.g., the range, variance, and standard deviation) and less pronounced when more resistant measures of spread are used (e.g., the IQR). When a nonresistant statistic, like the standard deviation, is used to compare the spreads of the male and female distributions, males, with $SD = 79,259$, are shown to have a much greater lack of consensus than females with $SD = 26,965$. When a resistant statistic like the IQR is used, the degree of discrepancy between the genders is diminished. Although males (with IQR $= 25,000$) are again shown to have a greater lack of consensus than females (IQR $= 20,000$), the degree of difference in consensus is far smaller.

☞ **Remark.** Note that, because the values of the variance are large for the two distributions, scientific notation was used by SPSS to express these values. This is often the case when values are either very large or very small. To understand this format, we translate the value of the variance for males from scientific to standard notation. The value in scientific notation is 6.3E + 09. This is equivalent to 6.3×10^9 or 6,300,000,000.

Because of the extreme outliers in the male distribution, the more resistant statistics, not being so influenced by these two extreme cases, are more accurate in describing the extent of difference between males and females relative to the bulk of the cases in our data set. Had we not examined the data initially, we might have characterized the magnitude of the difference between the bulk of males and females as being greater than it actually is, both in terms of level and spread.

We might also explore the extent to which our summary statistics would change if these two male outliers were removed from the analysis. By eliminating these two outliers, we can expect our numerical summaries to represent with greater accuracy the bulk of cases in our sample. The following table on next page contains the new statistics calculated for the male group without cases 102 and 494.

Notice that the skewness of this "new" male distribution is now quite similar to the skewness of the original female distribution. Notice also that the resistant statistics have not changed at all, and that the nonresistant statistics all have moved quite a bit closer to the resistant statistics. In short, by eliminating 2 of the 500 cases, we have convergence in our results. We know now the extent to which males have higher expected incomes at age 30 and the extent to which they have less consensus on their income expectations relative to females. The reason why we know the extent of outlier influence in this example is because two separate analyses were carried out, one with and one without the outliers. Before eliminating outliers from a data set, the standard practice should be to carry out one analysis on all data points, including outliers, and another analysis on the subset of data points excluding outliers. Then the results of the original analyses can be reported along with the extent to which these results have been influenced by the outliers.

Descriptives

	Gender				Statistic	Std. Error
Expected income at age 30	Male	Mean			54248.83	2400.503
		95% Confidence Interval for Mean	Lower Bound		49516.92	
			Upper Bound		58980.74	
		5% Trimmed Mean			50061.29	
		Median			45000.00	
		Variance			1E + 009	
		Std. Deviation			35034.195	
		Minimum			1	
		Maximum			250000	
		Range			249999	
		Interquartile Range			25000	
		Skewness			3.020	.167
		Kurtosis			12.829	.332
	Female	Mean			43515.57	1726.263
		95% Confidence Interval for Mean	Lower Bound		40115.23	
			Upper Bound		46915.92	
		5% Trimmed Mean			40837.89	
		Median			40000.00	
		Variance			7E + 008	
		Std. Deviation			26965.088	
		Minimum			0	
		Maximum			250000	
		Range			250000	
		Interquartile Range			20000	
		Skewness			3.816	.156
		Kurtosis			22.694	.310

In practice, one should not eliminate data points indiscriminately to achieve a "better" result. One should not report that "the average expected income for the males in this sample is $54,248" without adding that "two subjects with extremely high expected incomes were excluded."

If outliers are present, one needs to understand why they are there. Perhaps they represent errors in data entry, or perhaps they belong to persons who are not part of the population identified for study. Additionally, it may be that they represent a segment of the population underrepresented in your study and that through further sampling these cases would longer be extreme. Besides eliminating the two outliers in this example, other ways for reducing the effects of outliers are presented in the next chapter.

EXERCISES

Exercises 3.1 through 3.6 involve measures of central tendency and require the use of SPSS.

3.1. For the following variables from the NELS data set, what are the appropriate measures of central tendency (mean, median, mode) and why? Use SPSS to calculate the values of these measures and interpret the results.

a) GENDER

b) URBAN

   c) SCHTYP8
   d) TCHERINT
   e) NUMINST
   f) ACHRDG08
   g) SCHATTRT
   h) ABSENT12

3.2. These questions involve the variable LATE12 from the NELS data set.
   a) How many students in the data set were never late to school?
   b) How often was the first person in the data set late to school?
   c) What is a typical number of times students were late to school?

3.3. For the following variables in the NELS data set, indicate the most appropriate set of summary statistics for summarizing the distribution: (1) frequencies or percentages and mode; (2) median and IQR; (3) median, IQR, and skewness ratio; or (4) mean, standard deviation, and skewness ratio. Your answers should depend on the level of measurement of the variable as well as the extent to which extreme values are present in the distribution to unduly influence the value of these summary statistics.
   a) GENDER
   b) URBAN
   c) SCHTYP8
   d) TCHERINT
   e) NUMINST
   f) ACHRDG08
   g) SCHATTRT
   h) ABSENT12

3.4. CIGARETT is a dichotomous variable coded 0 for people who have not smoked and 1 for those who have.
   a) Compute the proportion of people that ever smoked based on the number from the frequency distribution.
   b) Compute the mean of CIGARETT. Interpret the mean in view of the result of part (a).
   c) Do a greater proportion of males or females report having ever smoked?

3.5. In this exercise, we examine the gender difference in the number of cigarettes smoked per day in the Framingham data set, taking into account the presence of one extreme male outlier.
   a) Create a boxplot showing the distribution of the number of cigarettes smoked per day (CIGPDAY1) by gender (SEX). Comment on the presence of outliers in the two distributions.
   b) Are there gender differences in the number of cigarettes smoked per day? Provide statistical support for your answer.

3.6. It was noted in this chapter that, when a unimodal continuous distribution is positively skewed, the mean is generally larger than the median given that extreme values influence the value of the mean more than they do the value of the median. Whereas there are rare exceptions to this rule in the case when a variable is many-valued, in other cases, as exemplified by this exercise, exceptions are more common.
   a) Create a histogram of the variable TCHERINT from the NELS data set, which contains only four possible values. According to the histogram, what is the shape of the distribution?
   b) Which is larger, the mean of TCHERINT, or the median?

Exercise 3.7 involves measures of dispersion and the NELS data set.

3.7. Which measure(s) of dispersion or variability (range, IQR, standard deviation, or variance), if any, may be used appropriately to measure the spread of the following variables from the NELS data set? In stating your answer, take into account both the level of measurement of the variable and whether there are extreme values in its distribution that could unduly influence the value of certain dispersion statistics, making them less representative of the distribution as a whole.

   a) GENDER
   b) URBAN
   c) NUMINST
   d) ACHRDG08
   e) SCHATTRT
   f) ABSENT12

Exercises 3.8 through 3.13 involve selecting a relevant SPSS procedure and calculating and interpreting a variety of appropriate summary statistics using variables from the NELS data set.

3.8. Use SPSS to find the following summary descriptive statistics for a student's self-concept in eighth grade (SLFCNC08).

   a) Minimum
   b) Maximum
   c) 40th percentile
   d) 25th percentile
   e) Mean
   f) Median
   g) Mode
   h) Range
   i) IQR
   j) Variance
   k) Standard deviation
   l) Skewness
  m) Standard error of the skewness

3.9. The following questions investigate how, among the students in the NELS data set, tenth-grade math achievement (ACHMAT10) is related to whether or not the student's family owned a computer when he or she was in eighth grade (COMPUTER).

   a) Compare the shape of the distributions of ACHMAT10 for students whose family did and those who did not own a computer in eighth grade. Begin by constructing boxplots of ACHMAT10, one for each value of COMPUTER.
   b) Is tenth-grade math achievement typically higher or lower for students whose families owned a computer when they were in eighth grade than for students whose families did not own a computer when they were in eighth grade?
   c) Among students in the NELS data set, is tenth-grade math achievement more or less variable for students whose families owned a computer when they were in eighth grade? Explain and support your answer with the value of at least one appropriate descriptive statistic, indicating if any other statistics contradict your conclusion.

3.10. This exercise addresses differences in SES by urbanicity (URBAN) for students in the NELS data set. Use the Explore procedure to generate the descriptive statistics to be used for answering the following questions.

  a) Describe the shape of SES for each of the three levels of URBAN.

  b) What type of student has the highest typical SES: those from urban, suburban, or rural settings? Support your answer with appropriate descriptive statistics, indicating whether all such statistics support your conclusion.

  c) For what type of setting is the SES of the students most dispersed: urban, suburban, or rural settings? Support your answer with appropriate descriptive statistics, indicating whether all such statistics support your conclusion.

  d) In what type of setting does the person with the highest SES live: urban, suburban, or rural?

3.11. Answer the following questions to compare eighth-grade self-concept (SLFCNC08) to twelfth-grade self-concept (SLFCNC12) for students in the NELS data set.

  a) Is the distribution of twelfth-grade reading achievement scores severely skewed for either students who attended nursery school or those who did not? Explain and support your answer using the value(s) of at least one appropriate statistic. Is the distribution of self-concept scores in the NELS data set severely skewed in either eighth or twelfth grade? If the distribution is severely skewed, indicate the direction of the skew. If the distributions are severely skewed, indicate which is more skewed. Explain and support your answer using the value(s) of at least one appropriate statistic.

  b) Do students in the NELS data set typically have higher self-concept scores in eighth or twelfth grade? Explain and support your answer with the value(s) of at least one appropriate statistic.

  c) Are the self-concept scores of students in the NELS data set more heterogeneous in eighth or twelfth grade? Explain and support your answer with the value(s) of at least one appropriate statistic.

3.12. In this exercise, we explore differences between males and females on three variables in the NELS data set, one affective, another cognitive, and the third behavioral.

  a) Are males and females similar in terms of the extent to which they believe teachers show an interest in them (TCHERINT)? Begin by considering similarities in their distributions by constructing histograms, one for each gender, using the Interactive mode. (Note: Because there are an unequal number of males and females in the sample (227 males, 273 females), percents should represent the heights of the bars, not frequencies. The regular graphs option with the panel variables option does not give the correct percent values on the vertical axis.)

To obtain the correct percents on the axis, relative to each gender, Interactive Graphs must be used as follows: Click **Graphs, Interactive, Histogram**. In the **Assign Variable** tab, assign $pct to the vertical axis, TCHERINT to the horizontal axis, and GENDER to panel variables. Click the **Histogram** tab and unclick **Set interval size automatically**; set **Number of intervals** equal to 4. Click **OK**.

---

  b) Do males and females display similar patterns of change in achievement in reading across eighth (ACHRDG08), tenth (ACHRDG10), and twelfth grades (ACHRDG12)? Begin with boxplots, and then use the Explore procedure (**Analyze, Compare Means, Means**) to obtain a comparison of means for these achievement scores across grades.

c) Do males and females have similar patterns of school attendance in grade 12 as measured by ABSENT12, CUTS12, and LATE12? Does one gender report greater incidents of absenteeism than the other? Begin by constructing boxplots. Given the ordinal nature of these three variables, follow up with EXPLORE to calculate medians, IQRs, and skewness for all three variables by gender.

3.13. Taking advanced math in eighth grade is often thought to be a proxy for being a more serious student who is on a college-bound track. In this exercise we explore differences on a number of academic and nonacademic variables between those who did and did not take advanced math in eighth grade (ADVMATH8).

a) Do those students who took advanced math in eighth grade report having spent more time per week on homework outside of school in twelfth grade (HWKOUT12) than those who did not take advanced math in eighth grade? Construct a boxplot for each group and follow up with appropriate descriptive statistics for this ordinal variable.

b) Do those students who took advanced math in eighth grade report typically fewer incidents of absenteeism in twelfth grade (ABSENT12) than those who did not take math in eighth grade?

c) Is there a difference between those students who took advanced math in eighth grade and those who did not in terms of the number of post-secondary institutions they attended (NUMINST)? Recall the NUMINST is a ratio-leveled variable. Begin by constructing histograms using Interactive Graphs as described in Exercise 3.12(a) and then follow up with descriptive statistics using Explore.

Exercises 3.14 and 3.15 are based on data sets other than the NELS and relate to a variety of summary statistics.

3.14. Create a stem-and-leaf plot of the variable READCOMP from the Learndis data set. Use it to answer the following questions.

a) What term best describes the shape of this distribution: positively skewed, negatively skewed, or symmetric?

b) What is the mode reading comprehension score for these students? If there is more than one mode, report them all.

c) What is the maximum reading comprehension score for these students?

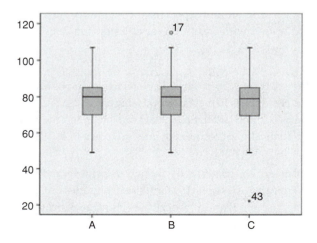

d) Without calculating, which is probably larger for these students, the mean reading comprehension score or the median comprehension score? Explain.

e) Without calculating it, which statistic would probably be best to summarize the spread of this distribution? Explain.

f) Which boxplot below (A, B, or C) best describes the data in the stem-and-leaf plot?

3.15. This question explores variables from the Framingham data set. Provide a demographic assessment by sex of this sample of individuals at baseline with respect to the following variables.

a) Age (AGE1)

b) Total serum cholesterol (TOTCHOL1)

c) Blood pressure (systolic and diastolic) (SYSBP1 and DIASBP1)

d) BMI (BMI1)

e) Current cigarette smoker (CURSMOKE1)

f) Number of cigarettes smoked per day (CIGPDAY1)

Exercises 3.16 through 3.18 require some computation by hand to reinforce your understanding of how the values provided by SPSS are derived. In so doing, we believe that your conceptual understanding of these descriptive statistics should be enhanced.

3.16. Use the Statisticians data set in this exercise.

a) Calculate the mean, median, mode, range, IQR, variance, and standard deviation of the variable AMSTAT by hand.

b) Use SPSS to check your answers to part (a).

c) Demonstrate that the sum of the deviations about the mean equals zero.

3.17. The following distribution of initial blood pressure values comes from the Blood data set.

| 107 | 110 | 123 | 129 | 112 | 111 | 107 | 112 | 135 | 102 | 123 |
| 109 | 112 | 102 | 98 | 114 | 119 | 112 | 110 | 117 | 130 | |

a) Calculate the mean, median, mode, range, IQR, variance, and standard deviation of the distribution by hand.

b) Calculate the mean, median, mode, range, IQR, variance, and standard deviation of the distribution using SPSS.

3.18. Create a frequency distribution table of the variable IQ from the Learndis data set. Use it to answer the following questions.

a) Estimate Q_1, Q_2, and Q_3 for this distribution based on the frequency distribution table.

b) Estimate the IQR for this distribution.

c) Suppose an error was found in the data, and two of the cases classified as 6 years old were really 5 years old. After the data are corrected, which of the mode, median, and mean will have changed, and in which direction?

Exercises 3.19 through 3.37 test your conceptual understanding and do not require the use of SPSS.

3.19. For a sample of size 12, the mean is 4, the median is 5, and the mode is 6. Is it true that the sum of the raw scores is 36?

3.20. For each of parts (a)−(f), create a (possibly different) data set with five numbers from −5 to 5 (with repeats allowed) for which

a) The mean, median, and mode are all equal.

b) The mean is greater than the median.

c) The mode is higher than the median or mean.

d) The mean is zero.

e) The standard deviation is as small as possible.

f) The distribution is negatively skewed.

3.21. Three different people correctly report the typical wage of a group of five wage earners to be $5,000, $7,000, and $10,000. Explain how this is possible. Find a set of five wages that can correctly be said to have these three measures of location.

3.22. Show that a distribution with a higher mean does not necessarily have a higher standard deviation. Construct two distributions, X and Y, with two scores each, so that X has the larger mean and Y has the larger standard deviation.

3.23. Show that a distribution with a higher mean does not necessarily have a higher median. Construct two distributions, X and Y, so that X has the larger mean and Y has the larger median.

3.24. Show that a distribution with more values does not necessarily have a higher standard deviation. Construct two distributions, X and Y, so that X has more values in its distribution, but Y has the larger standard deviation.

3.25. Construct a distribution X for which the mode is not the majority response.

3.26. Is it possible for the standard deviation of a distribution to be more than half the range? Explain.

3.27. Show that a symmetric distribution exists for which the mean does not equal the mode, by sketching the graph of such a distribution.

3.28. Show that a distribution can have outliers and still be symmetric, by sketching the graph of such a distribution.

3.29. Show that a distribution with a higher maximum does not necessarily have a higher mean. Construct two distributions, X and Y, so that X has a higher maximum value, but Y has a higher mean.

3.30. Show that a skewed distribution can be consistent. Construct two distributions, X and Y, so that X is less skewed, but Y is more consistent.

3.31. Show that a skewed distribution can contain low typical scores. Construct two distributions, X and Y, so that X is more skewed, but Y has a larger mean.

3.32. According to *USA Today* on July 6, 1998, the average NBA player earns $2.24 million, with 139 of 411 players topping the average.

a) According to the statement, which is higher, the mean or the median? Explain.

b) What is the probable shape of the distribution of NBA player salaries and how do you know?

3.33. Consider the distribution, for all children in the United States, of the ages at which they enter kindergarten. Do you think that the standard deviation of this distribution is closer to 5 years or 5 months? Explain.

3.34. Assume that on a final exam the raw scores for student performance were severely negatively skewed.

a) What is probably true about the performances of the students in the class on the exam?

b) If the exam were to be curved, which is preferable from a student perspective, that the median be set to a B− or that the mean be set to a B−?

3.35. Match each set of summary statistics (A, B, C, D, E) with the corresponding histogram (X1, X2, X3, X4, X5) below. Computations are not necessary to complete this exercise.

	A	B	C	D	E
Mean	4.5	5	5	5.5	6
Standard Deviation	1.96	1.22	.82	1.96	1.22

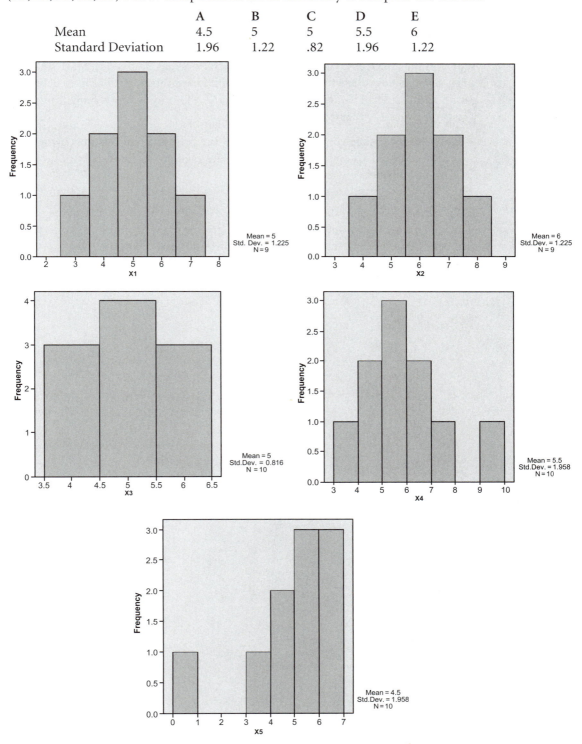

3.36. The following excerpt was taken from an editorial by Paul Krugman in the *New York Times* on January 21, 2003 (p. 23):

"On Saturday, in his weekly radio address, George W. Bush declared that 'the tax relief I propose will give 23 million small-business owners an average tax cut of $2,042 this year.' That remark is intended to give the impression that the typical small-business owner will get $2,000. But as the Center on Budget and Policy Priorities points out, most small businesses will get a tax break of less than $500; about 5 million of those 23 million small businesses will get no break at all. The average is more than $2,000 only because a small number of very wealthy businessmen will get huge tax cuts."

a) What is the shape of the distribution of tax cuts for small-business owners?
b) What would you guess is the value of the median of the distribution of tax cuts for small-business owners?
c) Would you suppose that the standard deviation is smaller or larger than $500? Explain.

3.37. Among women in the United States aged 40−49, would you expect the mean number of living children per woman to be less than, greater than, or about the same as the median number of living children per woman? Explain your answer.

CHAPTER FOUR

Re-expressing Variables

Often, variables in their original form do not lend themselves well to comparison with other variables or to certain types of analysis. In addition, often we may obtain greater insight by expressing a variable in a different form. For these and other reasons, in this chapter we discuss four different ways to re-express or transform variables: applying linear transformations, applying nonlinear transformations, recoding, and combining.

LINEAR AND NONLINEAR TRANSFORMATIONS

In Chapter 1 we discussed measurement as the assignment of numbers to objects to reflect the amount of a particular trait such objects possess. For example, a number in inches may be assigned to a person to reflect how tall that person is. Of course, without loss of information, a number in feet or even in meters can be assigned instead.

What we draw upon in this section is the notion that the numbers themselves used to measure a particular trait, whether they be in inches, feet, or meters, for example, are not intrinsic to the trait itself. Rather they are mere devices for helping us to understand the trait or other phenomenon we are studying. Accordingly, if an alternative numeric system, or *metric* (as a numeric system is called), can be used more effectively than the original one, then this metric should be substituted as long as it retains whatever properties of the original system we believe are important. In making this change on a univariate basis, each number in the new system corresponds on a one-to-one basis to each number in the original system. That is, each number in the new system can be matched uniquely to one and only one number in the original system.

The rule that defines the one-to-one correspondence between the numeric systems is called the *transformation*. Transformations may be classified according to the properties they retain of the original system. When transformations retain the order of data points in the original system, they are called *monotonic transformations*. In this chapter, we confine the discussion of transformations to monotonic transformations because, in the work we do in the behavioral and social sciences, ordinality is an important feature of a data set and is worth retaining. This section is devoted to two types of monotonic transformation: *linear* and *nonlinear*. In short, a linear transformation preserves or reflects the shape of the original distribution, whereas a nonlinear transformation is often used to change the shape of the original distribution.

LINEAR TRANSFORMATIONS: ADDITION, SUBTRACTION, MULTIPLICATION, AND DIVISION

Linear transformations are defined by rules that include only a combination of multiplication, division, addition, and subtraction to set up the one-to-one correspondence between numeric systems. For example, suppose we are interested in studying the relative heights of professional basketball players in the United States and Italy. If we used the original numbers for measuring the players' heights in both countries, the numbers would not be comparable because of the different measurement systems used in the two countries. (In the United States, height is measured in inches or feet; in Italy, it is measured in centimeters or meters.) *To obtain comparability of measures*, a more appropriate approach might be to express the heights of the U.S. players in centimeters rather than in inches. To do so, we need only multiply the values of height in inches by 2.54 because there are 2.54 centimeters per inch.

EXAMPLE 4.1. Re-express in centimeters the heights of the 20 scoring leaders, 10 each from the U.S. Women's and Men's National Basketball Association, for the 2006 season. Use the following arithmetic operation to do so.

Height (in centimeters) = height (in inches) * 2.54

Solution. The heights in inches and the heights re-expressed in centimeters are presented below.

NAME	HEIGHTIN	HEIGHTCM
Diana Taurasi	72	183
Seimone Augustus	72	183
Lisa Leslie	77	196
Cappie Pondexter	69	175
Lauren Jackson	77	196
Alana Beard	71	180
Tina Thompson	74	188
Katie Douglas	72	183
Tamika Whitmore	74	188
Chamique Holdsclaw	74	188
Gilbert Arenas	76	193
LeBron James	80	203
Vince Carter	78	198
Dwyane Wade	76	193
Kobe Bryant	78	198
Michael Redd	78	198
Dirk Nowitzki	84	213
Tim Duncan	83	211
Elton Brand	80	203
Bonzi Wells	77	196

We may use SPSS to perform the computation to re-express the original values of height.

To transform height in inches to height in centimeters using SPSS, open the basket data set. The variable HEIGHTIN contains the heights in inches of these scoring leaders. Click **Transform** on the main menu bar, and **Compute**. In the box labeled **Target Variable** type a name for the new variable that is to be created (e.g., HEIGHTCM) and move the variable HEIGHTIN into the box labeled **Numeric Expression**. Type ***2.54** and then **OK**. (The asterisk before the number 2.54 represents the operation of multiplication.) The variable HEIGHTCM will be added to your data set as the last variable. You should verify that this is the case.

Because the rule for re-expressing inches as centimeters involves multiplying every value in the distribution by a positive constant, it is an example of a *linear transformation*.

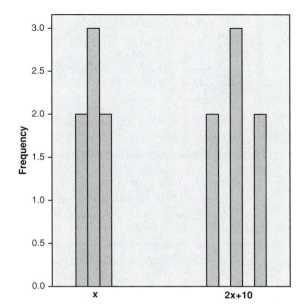

Figure 4.1   Histograms of original values and linearly transformed values ($2X + 10$).

Notice that the order of data points has been retained under this transformation. Lisa Leslie is taller than Diana Taurasi regardless of whether their heights are measured in inches or in centimeters.

Whereas this linear transformation involves multiplication only, linear transformations may involve multiplication, addition, or a combination of multiplication and addition. The general form of a linear transformation may be expressed as

$$X_{new} = K * X_{old} + C \qquad\qquad (4.1)$$

where K and C are constants and $K \neq 0$. It is worth pointing out that K represents both multiplication and division. For example, when $K = 1/2$, multiplication by K is equivalent to division by 2. Also, C represents both addition and subtraction. For example, when $C = -4$, adding C units is equivalent to subtracting 4 units. K changes the scale of the original values, either by stretching (when K is less than -1 or greater than 1) or compressing (when K is between -1 and $+1$) the horizontal axis, whereas C translates the location of the original values either up (when C is positive) or down (when C is negative) along the horizontal axis. Figure 4.1 illustrates a linear transformation where $K = 2$ and $C = 10$. Notice that the scale of the new values is doubled (with each unit increase in X, there is a two-unit increase in $2X + 10$) and the location of the new values is shifted in a positive direction along the horizontal axis from 2 to 14 ($2 * 2 + 10$).

Linear transformations are so named because, as Equation 4.1 suggests, the new values are a linear function of the original values.

THE EFFECT ON THE SHAPE OF A DISTRIBUTION

Linear transformations retain not only the order of points in a distribution, but also the relative distance between points in a distribution. That is, two points that are far from one another under the original numeric system will be as far from one another to the same relative extent under the new system. In our example, Diana Taurasi's height is closer to Cappie Pondexter's height than to Lisa Leslie's height to the same relative extent in both inches and centimeters. Because relative distance does not change under linear transformation, neither does the general shape of a distribution under linear transformation.

EXAMPLE 4.2. Construct histograms of both distributions of height (in inches and in centimeters). For each histogram divide the range of the distribution into five intervals. Comment on the shape of these two distributions as represented by the histograms.

Solution. Create histograms of HEIGHTIN and HEIGHTCM using SPSS. To get an accurate comparison of the distributions, we custom edit the histograms to have comparable scales, bin sizes, and anchor values as noted in the box below.

To edit the histogram for HEIGHTCM as noted above, double click each histogram in turn to open the Chart Editor. Double click the values on the horizontal axis to open the **Properties** box within the Chart Editor. Click the **Scale** tab and make the following changes: for HEIGHTIN, we set Minimum = 65, Maximum = 90, Major Increment = 5, and Origin = 0; and for HEIGHTCM, we set Minimum = 160, Maximum = 230, Major Increment = 10, and Origin = 0. Click the **Histogram Options** tab and make the following changes: for HEIGHTIN, we set Custom Value for Anchor = 68 (the minimum data value in this data set) and Custom Number of Intervals = 5; and for HEIGHTCM, we set Custom Value for Anchor = 172.5 (the minimum data value in this data set) and Custom Number of Intervals = 5. Click **Apply, Close**.

After performing a similar procedure on the histogram for HEIGHTCM, the histograms appear as in Figures 4.2 and 4.3. Clearly, the two histograms have the same shape. By transforming the data linearly from inches to centimeters, the general shape of a distribution remains the same.

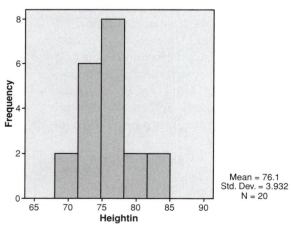

Mean = 76.1
Std. Dev. = 3.932
N = 20

Figure 4.2   Histogram of height (in).

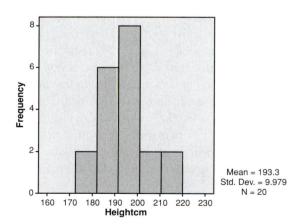

Mean = 193.3
Std. Dev. = 9.979
N = 20

Figure 4.3   Histogram of height (cm).

THE EFFECT ON SUMMARY STATISTICS OF A DISTRIBUTION

While under linear transformation, the general shape of a distribution remains the same, but the summary characteristics of a distribution do not. Notice the difference in mean and standard deviation values for the two histograms pictured in Figures 4.2 and 4.3. More specifically, the mean height in centimeters (193.29) equals the mean height in inches (76.10) multiplied by 2.54, and the standard deviation of the height in centimeters (9.99) equals the standard deviation of the height in inches (3.93) multiplied by 2.54. In other words, both the mean and standard deviation are multiplied by 2.54, the value by which the heights themselves were multiplied.

While the new standard deviation is larger than the original standard deviation by a factor of 2.54, the new variance will be larger than the original variance by a factor of 2.54^2, or 6.45. Because the old variance was 3.93^2 or 15.46, the new variance equals 6.45*15.46 or 99.76.

More generally, the effects on the mean, median, mode, standard deviation, range, interquartile range (IQR), and variance of a distribution of multiplying (or dividing) all the values in a distribution by a constant, K, are summarized as follows.

When every data value in a distribution is multiplied (or divided) by a constant, K,

1. the new mean, median, and mode are equal to the old mean, median, and mode multiplied (or divided) by the constant.
2. the new standard deviation, range, and IQR are equal to the old standard deviation, range, and IQR multiplied (or divided) by the absolute value of that constant, |K|.
3. the new variance is equal to the old variance multiplied (or divided) by the square of the constant, K^2.
4. if K is positive, the new skewness and skewness ratio are equal to the old skewness and skewness ratio; if K is negative, the new skewness and skewness ratio are equal to −1 times the old skewness and skewness ratio.

Recall that another type of linear transformation involves adding a constant, C, to all values in a distribution. The effects on summary statistics of this type of transformation are summarized as follows.

When a constant, C, is added to (or subtracted from) every data value in a distribution,

1. the new mean, median, and mode are equal to the old mean plus (or minus) the constant.
2. the new standard deviation, range, and IQR are equal to the old standard deviation, range, and IQR.
3. the new variance is equal to the old variance.
4. the new skewness and skewness ratio are equal to the old skewness and skewness ratio.

COMMON LINEAR TRANSFORMATIONS

In this section we present examples of three common types of linear transformation: translation, reflection, and standard scores. Among standard scores, we make the most use of z-scores.

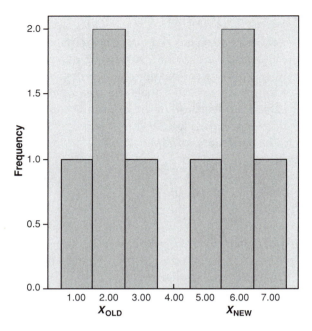

Figure 4.4   The effect of adding the value   [Au1] 4 to each data point in a distribution.

EXAMPLE 4.3. Using the data set 1, 2, 2, 3, show graphically and numerically the effects of adding 4 to all points in this data set.

Solution. Let X_{OLD} = 1, 2, 2, 3 and X_{NEW} = 5, 6, 6, 7. A graphical representation of the distributions of X_{OLD} and X_{NEW} are given in Figure 4.4.

Notice that the distributions are identical but for their location. In particular, the standard deviation, range, IQR, and variance of X_{NEW} equal the respective standard deviation and variance of X_{OLD}, but the mean, median, and mode of X_{NEW} are 4 points higher than the respective mean, median, and mode of X_{OLD}. In other words, X_{NEW} is X_{OLD} shifted along the axis 4 points to the right.

A linear transformation that shifts a distribution along the horizontal axis is called a *translation*. One type of translation that we make use of in Chapter 15 is called *centering*, in which the mean of the distribution is subtracted from each of the scores.

EXAMPLE 4.4. Assume that the following item appears on a scale that measures assertiveness:

Circle one value along the five-point scale below to indicate your degree of agreement with the statement: "I have the ability to stand up for my own rights without denying the rights of others."

strongly agree	agree	neutral	disagree	strongly disagree
1	2	3	4	5

Notice that, on this scale, high scores are associated with low levels of assertiveness. This scoring could be considered to be illogical. Find a linear transformation that reverses the scores on this scale so that, instead, high scores associate with high levels of assertiveness and low scores associate with low levels of assertiveness. Keep the range of values from 1 to 5.

Solution. Multiplying all values in the distribution by −1 will convert the scale scores from 1 to 5 to −5 to −1 so that, now, the higher (the less negative) the value, the more assertive the response. Adding 6 to each value shifts the scale along the horizontal axis from −5 to −1 to 1 to 5, as desired. On this new scale, a value of 5 now corresponds to the response "strongly agree" and a response of 1 now corresponds to a response of "strongly disagree." On this new scale, the higher the score, the greater the assertiveness. Alternatively, we could have achieved the same result by subtracting each value in the scale from the value 6.

To use SPSS to reflect the variable ASSERT, click on **Transform** from the main menu bar, then **Compute**. Place a new variable name in the **target variable** box, like ASSERTRE, to stand for reflected assertiveness. Type −1*ASSERT+6, assuming ASSERT was the name of this response variable in the original data set. Click **OK**. Alternatively, instead of typing −1*ASSERT+6 we could have typed more simply 6−ASSERT and then clicked **OK** to achieve the same result.

☞ **Remark.** Any time the values of a scale are multiplied by −1, the new values on the scale will be mirror images of the original values. As a result, this type of transformation is called a *reflection*. Values that were low on the original scale are now high on the new scale and values that were high on the original scale are now low on the new scale. Because the values on the new scale are based on a reversed direction of scoring, caution must be exercised when interpreting results based on scales that have been reflected.

STANDARD SCORES

In addition to enhancing the comparability of values measured in different units, data are often linearly transformed to give meaning to individual scores within a distribution. For example, an SAT verbal score of 750 carries with it its own meaning relative to the distribution of individuals who have taken this test. Said differently, if you were told that on a recently administered SAT test you scored 750, you would not ask, "Is that a good score?" You would know already, by the score itself, that you performed better than the vast majority of other SAT test-takers. You would know this because SAT scores are an example of what are called *standard scores*. By contrast to raw scores that reveal nothing about the relative standing of a score within a distribution, standard scores convey meaning about relative standing because they are linked directly to the mean and standard deviation of the distribution of which they are a part.

In short, a standard score conveys how far above or below a raw score is from the mean of its distribution relative to the standard deviation of that distribution. Because the vast majority of scores of most distributions are clustered within two standard deviations of their means, scores that are approximately two standard deviations above the mean in a distribution are considered to be extremely high. Analogously, scores that are approximately two standard deviations below the mean in a distribution are considered to be extremely low. Scores that are at the mean fall zero standard deviations from the mean and are considered to be average, or typical scores in a distribution, and scores that fall between zero and two standard deviations away from the mean are considered to be somewhere between average and extreme.

Table 4.1. Means and standard deviations of commonly used standard score systems

Standard Score System	Mean	Standard Deviation
Graduate Record Exam (GRE)	500	100
Intelligence Quotient (IQ)	100	15
Scholastic Aptitude Test (SAT)	500	100
T Scores	50	10
z-Scores	0	1

Standard score systems, like the SAT, each have a specified mean and standard deviation. Table 4.1 provides the mean and standard deviation of each of several commonly used standard score systems.

To determine how many standard deviations from the mean the SAT score of 750 actually falls, we need to transform the SAT score linearly by performing a simple arithmetic operation. That is, we need to first subtract 500, the mean of the SAT score distribution, from 750 to find out how many SAT score units the score of 750 falls from the mean of 500. We then need to divide that difference by 100, the standard deviation of the SAT distribution, to determine how many standard deviations from the mean the score falls. This arithmetic operation is expressed as

$$\frac{750 - 500}{100} = \frac{250}{100} = 2.5 \tag{4.2}$$

According to Equation 4.2, an SAT verbal score of 750 is 2.5 standard deviations above the SAT verbal mean. A score that is 2.5 standard deviations above its mean surpasses the vast majority of scores in its distribution and is considered to be extremely high. This explains why, of course, a score of 750 would make some SAT test-taker quite happy.

z-SCORES

Knowing the number of standard deviation distances a score is from the mean is quite informative and useful for locating a score within its distribution. Scores that have been re-expressed in terms of standard deviation distances from the mean are given a special name: *z-scores*. Because z-scores themselves convey the number of standard deviations a score is from the mean, a distribution of z-scores has, as Table 4.1 indicates, a mean of 0 and a standard deviation of 1. Any score may be re-expressed as a z-score by using Equation 4.3:

$$z = \frac{X - \overline{X}}{S} \tag{4.3}$$

A comparison of Equation 4.3 with that of 4.2 suggests that in Equation 4.2 we converted the SAT verbal score of 750 to a z-score so that we could obtain the number of standard deviations the score was from the mean of 500. To convert an individual raw score to a z-score, one only needs the mean and standard deviation of the distribution of which the raw score is a part.

EXAMPLE 4.5. Determine the number of standard deviations away from the mean the following standard scores are: (a) an IQ score of 110; (b) a GRE score of 450; (c) a z-score of −2.

Solution.

a) From Table 4.1, we know that the mean and standard deviation of an IQ scale are 100 and 15, respectively. We use Equation 4.3 to find that the z-score of an IQ score of 110 is

$$z = \frac{110 - 100}{15} = 0.67.$$

In other words, an IQ score of 110 is .67 standard deviations above the IQ mean.

b) From Table 4.1, we know that the mean and standard deviation of the GRE scale are 500 and 100, respectively. We use Equation 4.3 to find that the z-score of a GRE score of 450 is

$$z = \frac{450 - 500}{100} = -0.50.$$

In other words, a GRE score of 450 is one-half standard deviations below the GRE mean.

c) A z-score of −2 may be interpreted directly as being two standard deviations below the mean.

. . . .

EXAMPLE 4.6. Determine the number of standard deviations away from the mean the following scores are: (a) a score of 90 on a test of Spanish fluency that has a mean of 85 and a standard deviation of 10; (b) a score of 30 on the socioeconomic status (SES) scale from the NELS data set; (c) all scores on the SES scale from the NELS data set; (d) verify that the z-score distribution has mean 0 and standard deviation 1.

Solution.

a) To find the number of standard deviations away from the mean a score of 90 is on a Spanish fluency test, we use Equation 4.3.

$$z = \frac{90 - 85}{10} = 0.50$$

A score of 90 on this test is one-half of a standard deviation above the mean in the distribution of Spanish fluency test scores.

b) Using SPSS, we compute the mean and standard deviation of the SES distribution to be 18.43 and 6.92, respectively, when rounded to two decimal places. From Equation 4.3, we find the z-score equivalent of an SES score of 30 to be

$$z = \frac{30 - 18.43}{6.92} = 1.67$$

c) There are two ways to transform all scores in the SES distribution to z-scores using SPSS.

The easiest way to create standardized variables is to go to **Analyze** on the main menu bar, **Descriptive Statistics**, **Descriptives**. Move SES into the **Variable(s)** box. Click the box next to **Save Standardized Values as Variables**. Click **OK**. The new variable, zses, ought to appear as the last column in the NELS data set. (You may have to change to the data editor to see this new column.)

Alternatively, to create a standardized version of the SES variable, you could click **Transform** on the main menu bar, and then **Compute**. Provide a name for the Target Variable, say, ZSES. Move the cursor to the **Numeric Expression** field and type in the following expression: (SES–18.43)/6.92
Click **OK**. The new variable, ZSES, ought to appear as the last column in the NELS data set.

d) To verify that ZSES has mean 0 and standard deviation 1, we click **Statistics** on the main menu bar, **Summarize**, and then one of the following: **Frequencies**, **Descriptive**, or **Explore**. In each of these, the mean is given as 5.78E−04, which is scientific notation for the number 0.000578, which is equal to zero when rounded to two decimal places. Also, the standard deviation is 1.0006, which is equal to 1 when rounded to two decimal places.

Thus, by linearly transforming the scores of a distribution into z-scores, we gain knowledge of the placement of each score in that distribution relative to the mean and standard deviation of the scores in that distribution. Because conversion to z-scores involves a linear transformation, and because all linear transformations are monotonic, the order of scores in the original distribution is preserved in the z-score distribution. If Carolyn's score is higher than Allison's in the original distribution, it will still be higher than Allison's in the z-score distribution. In addition, because linear transformations preserve the relative distance between points in a distribution, the shape of a z-score distribution is the same as that of the original distribution, except for possible stretching or shrinking along the horizontal axis.

Just as we can transform raw (or standard) scores to z-scores when the mean and standard deviation of the original distribution are known, we also can use Equation 4.3 to transform z-scores to raw (or standard scores) when the mean and standard deviation of the new distribution are known. Equation 4.3 can also be re-expressed so that it can be used directly to convert any z-score to its corresponding original score. Thus, any z-score may be converted to its corresponding raw score by using Equation 4.4:

$$X = Sz + \overline{X} \tag{4.4}$$

EXAMPLE 4.7. Transform the following z-scores to raw scores within a distribution with a given mean and standard deviation: (a) a z-score of −2.5 on a test of Spanish fluency with mean 85 and standard deviation 10; (b) a z-score of −3 on the SES scale from the NELS data set; (c) a z-score of 0 on the SES scale from the NELS data set.

Solution.

a) We use Equation 4.4 to find the Spanish fluency raw score equivalent of a z-score of −2.5 in a distribution with mean and standard deviation 85 and 10, respectively.

$$X = 10(-2.5) + 85$$
$$X = 60$$

b) We use Equation 4.4 to find the NELS SES raw score equivalent to a z-score of −3. Recall that the mean and standard deviation of the NELS SES distribution are 18.43 and 6.92, respectively.

$$X = 6.92(-3) + 18.43$$
$$X = -2.33$$

c) A z-score of 0 is at the mean of the z-score distribution. Therefore, the equivalent raw SES score would be equal to the mean of the SES distribution, 18.43. Of course, we could use Equation 4.4 to verify that this is the case.

Using z-Scores to Detect Outliers

In our discussion of boxplots in Chapter 2, we noted that SPSS defines an outlier as a score that falls more than 1.5 IQRs beyond the 75th or 25th percentile. Because boxplots are

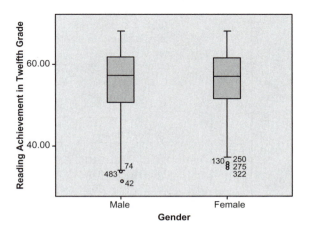

Figure 4.5 Boxplot of twelfth-grade reading achievement by gender.

based on resistant statistics, including the median, it makes sense to measure outliers in terms of IQR distances. In other contexts, when the location of a distribution is measured in terms of the mean, it makes sense to measure outliers in terms of standard deviation distances. Again, although there are no set conventions for defining outliers in terms of standard deviations, a reasonable approach is to call a score an outlier if it falls more than two standard deviations away from its distribution's mean; that is, if its z-score is greater than 2 in magnitude.

Using z-Scores to Compare Scores in Different Distributions

In addition to using z-scores to determine the relative standing of a raw score within its own distribution, z-scores are often used to compare raw scores from different distributions. For such comparisons to be meaningful, however, the underlying raw score distributions must have similar shapes.

The boxplots in Figure 4.5 show the distributions of twelfth-grade reading achievement by gender. Notice both distributions are negatively skewed.

To find the means and standard deviations of a distribution broken down by subgroups using SPSS, we could use Explore as before, or alternatively Compare Means.

To find means and standard deviations by subgroups using Compare Means, go to **Analyze**, **Compare Means**, **Means**. Put ACHRDG12 in the **Dependent List** box and GENDER in the **Independent List** box. Click **OK**.

The output is given in Table 4.2.

Consider Pat, who scored 65. Did Pat score better relative to the males or the females in the data set? Pat scored above the mean in both groups, and scored more points above the male mean than the female mean. However, when deciding in which group the score is further above the mean *relative to the scores in the group*, we should take into consideration the spread of the scores in the distributions. One way to do so is to calculate z-scores.

$$\text{Relative to the males: } z = \frac{65 - 55.3104}{8.5601} = 1.13$$

$$\text{Relative to the females: } z = \frac{65 - 55.8443}{7.4804} = 1.22$$

Table 4.2. Means and standard deviations of twelfth-grade reading achievement by gender.

Report
Reading Achievement in
Twelfth Grade

Gender	Mean	N	Std. Deviation
Male	55.3104	227	8.56015
Female	55.8443	273	7.48037
Total	55.6019	500	7.98492

Because 1.22 exceeds 1.13, we see that Pat performed better relative to the females. The score of 65 is 1.22 standard deviations above the mean for the females and only 1.13 standard deviations above the mean for the males.

Relating z-Scores to Percentile Ranks

In the preceding section, we looked at the use of z-scores in comparing scores in different distributions. Recall that for such comparisons to be meaningful, however, the underlying raw score distributions must have similar shapes. It is not even enough, as the following example illustrates, for the two raw score distributions to have the same mean and standard deviation. If the raw score distributions do not have similar shapes, the same z-scores may correspond to different percentile ranks, which undermines the utility of z-scores in comparing raw scores from different distributions. Consider that two tests, math and English, have been administered to the same individuals and that their score distributions are as in Table 4.3.

These two distributions do not have similar shapes. The math distribution is positively skewed; the English distribution is negatively skewed. (You might want to construct a histogram for each distribution to convince yourself of this.) Both math and English distributions have means of 5 and standard deviations of 2.72. (You may want to convince yourself of this as well.) Therefore, in each distribution, a raw score of 8 corresponds to a z-score of

$$z = \frac{X - \overline{X}}{S} = \frac{8 - 5}{2.72} = \frac{3}{2.72} = 1.10$$

But, in the math distribution, the percentile rank of a score of 8 is 70 (as estimated by the cumulative percent), whereas in the English distribution the percentile rank of a score of 8 is 90. Although a comparison based on z-scores suggests that an individual with a raw score of 8 on both math and English tests has the same performance on these exams relative to the two distributions, this is not the case. Because these two distributions are dissimilar in shape, the more appropriate comparison of performance is based on percentile ranks. Based on percentile ranks, a score of 8 represents a higher score in English than in math for this group of students.

Table 4.3. Distributions of Math and English achievement

Math Achievement	English Achievement
2 3 3 3 4 4 4 8 9 10	0 1 2 6 6 6 7 7 7 8

In sum, when the shapes of distributions are not known to be similar, percentile ranks are a better scoring system than z-scores for comparing scores between distributions.

NONLINEAR TRANSFORMATIONS: SQUARE ROOTS AND LOGARITHMS

As we have seen, statistics, like the mean and standard deviation, do not characterize well the bulk of values in a highly skewed distribution. To remedy this situation, in the preceding chapter we eliminated the two extreme values in the right tail of the distribution of expected income at age 30. In so doing, we shortened the long right tail and made this once highly positively skewed distribution more symmetric. As a result, the mean and standard deviation corroborated with the other, more resistant numeric summaries of location and spread, making the job of describing the bulk of our data easier and more accurate.

By making a distribution more symmetric, we avoid the problem of a small number of extreme values highly influencing the numeric summaries that characterize a data set. For this reason and others, it is advantageous to symmetrize distributions. But, as we have observed previously, we are often not justified in making distributions more symmetric by merely eliminating extreme values.

An approach that is preferred, because it does not entail the elimination of points from a distribution, is the *monotonic nonlinear transformation*. Like the linear transformation, the monotonic nonlinear transformation retains the order of values in a distribution. Unlike the linear transformation, however, the monotonic nonlinear transformation changes the relative distances between the values in a distribution and, in so doing, effects a desired change in the shape of the distribution. Two commonly used monotonic nonlinear transformations are the square root and logarithm base 10.

☞ **Remark**. Logarithms are defined by exponents. The logarithm of the value 8 using the base 2 equals 3 since $2^3 = 8$. This statement can be expressed as $\log_2 8 = 3$. Likewise, the logarithm of 16 base 2 equals 4 since $2^4 = 16$ (i.e., $\log_2 16 = 4$). And, the logarithm of 100 base 10 equals 2 since $10^2 = 100$ (i.e., $\log_{10} 100 = 2$). What is $\log_{10} 1,000,000$?

☞ **Remark**. Examples of logarithmic scales used in practice are the Richter scale to measure the motion of the ground due to earthquakes, decibels to measure the energy intensity of sound, and pH to measure the acidity of a substance. For example, an earthquake that measures 4 on the Richter scale is 10 times more powerful than one that measures 3 and 100 times more powerful than one that measures 2. In other words, an increase in the Richter scale of k units indicates that the earthquake is more powerful by a factor of 10^k. Decibels compare the level of pressure from a sound (represented by p_1) to the level of pressure from the smallest noise audible to a person with normal hearing (represented by p_0). The decibel is then given by $D = 10 \log \left(\dfrac{p_1}{p_0} \right)$. Finally, the acidity, or pH, of a substance is found by the formula $pH = -\log(H^+)$, where (H^+) represents the concentration of the hydrogen ion. If the pH is less than 7, the solution is said to be acidic. If the pH equals 7, the solution is said to be neutral. If the pH is greater than 7, the solution is said to be basic.

Example 4.8 illustrates how a monotonic nonlinear transformation changes the relative distance between the values in a distribution and, in so doing, changes the shape of the distribution.

EXAMPLE 4.8. Given the following set of data points: 1 4 16 64 256

a) Compute the distances between the adjacent points in the data set. Would you say the distribution is skewed? Why? Compute the skewness of these data using SPSS.

b) Transform the data set linearly by multiplying each value by 1/2. Compute the distances between the adjacent points in the data set. Compare the distances and skewness of the distribution to those obtained in part (a). What does this result imply about the effect of a linear transformation on the skewness and relative distances between points in a distribution?

c) Transform the data set nonlinearly by taking the square root of each value.

d) Compute the distances between the adjacent points in the data set. Have the relative distances between adjacent points changed? In what way? Is the square root-transformed data set less positively skewed than the original data set?

e) Transform the data set nonlinearly by taking the logarithm (using base 2) of each value.

f) Compute the distances between the adjacent points in the data set. Have the relative distances between adjacent points changed? In what way? Is the logarithmic-transformed data set less positively skewed than the original data set? Is it less positively skewed than the square root-transformed data set?

Solution.

a) The original values along with their adjacent distances are

Values:	1		4		16		64		256
		∨		∨		∨		∨	
Adjacent distances:		3		12		48		192	

Because these distances between adjacent points increase as the values themselves increase, the distribution appears to be skewed positively. Using SPSS, we find that the distribution is positively skewed with skew = 1.96.

b) The new values, linearly transformed from multiplication by 1/2, along with their adjacent distances, are

Values:	.5		2		8		32		128
		∨		∨		∨		∨	
Adjacent distances:		1.5		6		24		96	

Notice that the transformed scores and their adjacent distances are both half as large as the original scores and their adjacent distances. Relative to the new scale, the distances between points remain the same and the skewness, therefore, remains the same. Using SPSS, we find that the linearly transformed distribution has skew = 1.96, as before. What this implies is that linear transformations do not change the relative distances between points and, hence, do not change the shape of the distribution, including its skew.

c) The original distribution, transformed by its square root, is as follows: 1 2 4 8 16.

d) The transformed values from part (c) along with their adjacent distances are

Values:	1		2		4		8		16
		∨		∨		∨		∨	
Adjacent distances:		1		2		4		8	

The relative distances between the values have changed as a result of this square root transformation. In particular, the square root transformation has reduced the distances between adjacent values in a nonuniform way. The higher the value, the more the distance between it and its adjacent points is reduced. The most extreme distance of 192 units in the original distribution is reduced to a distance of only 8 units after square roots are taken; the next most extreme distance of 48 units in the original distribution is reduced to a distance of 4 units after square roots are taken. Because a nonlinear transformation, such as the square root transformation, differentially reduces the distances between points in a distribution, with the greatest reduction occurring in the right tail, the shape of the distribution changes. Such a transformation has the effect of "bringing in" the right tail and making the distribution more symmetric, as indicated by the new skew value of 1.33 (obtained from SPSS).

e) The original distribution, transformed by the logarithm base 2, is 0 2 4 6 8.

f) The log-transformed values along with their adjacent distances are

Values:	0	2	4	6	8
		∨	∨	∨	∨
Adjacent distances:		2	2	2	2

Notice that, in contrast to the other cases in this example, the log-transformed distribution is symmetric about the value of 4 and the adjacent distances are all equal to one another. Using SPSS, we find that the skew value for these log-transformed values is, in fact, zero. A log transformation does not usually make a distribution perfectly symmetric. Because the log transformation has a greater impact on extreme scores than does the square root transformation, it is often the case that, for highly skewed data, the log transformation is more effective than the square root transformation for making a distribution more symmetric. It is often a good idea to try both types of transformation to see which of the two produces more symmetric results and to use the one that does.

☞ **Remark.** Whereas we used a base 2 logarithm in Example 4.8, other positive values except 1 may be used as bases. A logarithmic transformation, whether its base is 2.7, 3, 4, 5, or 10, for example, reduces the skewness of a distribution by the same amount and changes the shape of the distribution to the same extent. Two commonly used logarithmic bases are e (approximated by 2.7), associated with what is called the natural logarithm, and 10, associated with what is called the common logarithm. SPSS denotes these two logarithm systems as LN and LG10, respectively. In this text, we make use of LG10.

☞ **Remark.** For the type of data we encounter in the behavioral and social sciences, square roots are defined only on values greater than or equal to zero, whereas logarithms are defined only on values greater than zero. Thus, to apply a square root transformation to data that range from −12 to 5, we would first add 12, for example, to all values in the distribution, so that the values are all greater than or equal to zero. Likewise, to apply a logarithmic transformation to data that range from −12 to 5, we would first need to add 13, for example, to all values in the distribution so that the values are all greater than zero.

In Example 4.9, we illustrate with NELS data the effects on the shape and skewness of a distribution of using the natural and common logarithms. Through this example, you will learn that we may often need to apply a combination of transformations in our efforts to reduce the skew of a distribution. In this example, the square root and log transformations are used in conjunction with a reflection and a translation.

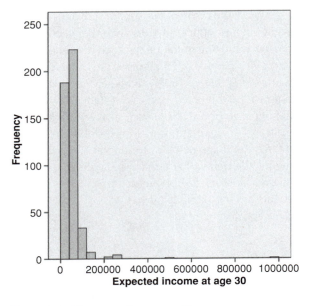

Figure 4.6   Histogram for expected income.

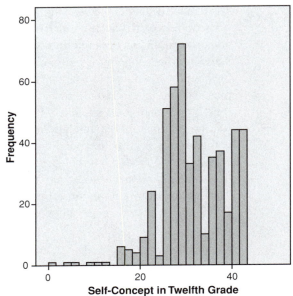

Figure 4.7   Histogram for self-concept.

EXAMPLE 4.9. As we have observed, and as indicated in Figures 4.6 and 4.7, the distribution of expected income at age 30 is positively skewed and the distribution of self-concept in grade 12 is negatively skewed. Use appropriate transformations to make both distributions more symmetric.

Solution. The descriptive statistics for these two variables are as follows.

Descriptive Statistics

	N	Range	Minimum	Maximum	Mean	Std.	Skewness	
	Statistic	Statistic	Statistic	Statistic	Statistic	Statistic	Statistic	Std. Error
Expected income at age 30	459	1000000	0	1000000	51574.73	58265.758	10.934	.114
Self-Concept in Twelfth Grade	500	43	0	43	31.48	7.231	−.384	.109
Valid N (listwise)	459							

In symmetrizing the distribution of income at age 30, which is positively skewed, we try both the square root and logarithm (base 10) transformations. Because the minimum value of expected income is 0, and because the logarithm of 0 is undefined, we first add some small quantity, like 1, to each value, and then we take the logarithm of each value. The numeric expression for carrying out the logarithm transformation is LG10 (EXPINC30 + 1). Although it would be meaningful to take the square root of 0, for consistency, we also compute the square root of the translated expected income.

To create the transformed variables of EXPINC30, we use the **Compute** function under the **Transform** option. In this case, the **Numeric Expression** is defined as SQRT(EXPINC30 + 1). We may label the **Target Variable** as EXPINCSQ (to stand for the square root transformation of expected income). Click **OK**. Repeat to create the log transformation with the **Numeric Expression** LG10(EXPINC30 + 1) and **Target Variable** EXPINCLG.

Descriptive statistics for the transformed variables are as follows.

Descriptive Statistics

	N	Range	Minimum	Maximum	Mean	Std.	Skewness	
	Statistic	Statistic	Statistic	Statistic	Statistic	Statistic	Statistic	Std. Error
expincsq	459	1000	0	1000	214.52	74.619	3.732	.114
expincig	459	6	0	6	4.59	.526	−6.889	.114
Valid N (listwise)	459							

Notice that the log transformation overcompensates for the positive skew because it results in a highly negatively skewed distribution. In this case, the square root transformation is the better of the two, as Figure 4.8 illustrates.

As we have seen, the logarithm and square root transformations may be used to symmetrize a positively skewed distribution. If the logarithm or square root transformation is

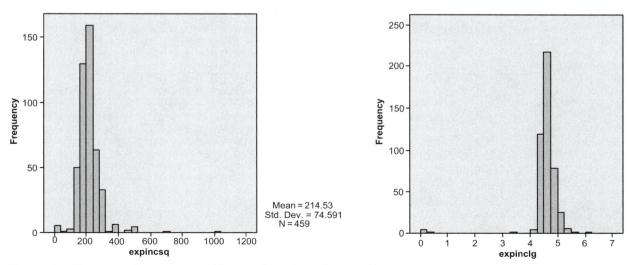

Figure 4.8 Histograms of square root and log transformations of expected income at age 30.

applied to a negatively skewed distribution, however, the effect is to make that distribution even more negatively skewed. Accordingly, when a distribution is negatively skewed, a first step in symmetrizing such a distribution would be to reflect it so that it becomes positively skewed. Because the square root is not defined on negative values and the logarithm is not defined on negative or zero values, if there are negative or zero values in the distribution, the next step would be to add a constant to each value in the distribution to eliminate such negative or zero values. The third step would be to apply the logarithm or square root transformation as before.

Self-concept in grade 12 (SLFCNC12) is an example of a negatively skewed distribution.

To reflect self-concept, we simply multiply each self-concept value by −1. To do so using SPSS, we use the **Compute** function under the **Transform** option. In this case, the **Numeric Expression** is defined as −1*SLFCNC12. We may label the **Target Variable** as SLFCNCF1 (to stand for self-concept, reflected).

We now translate SLFCNCF1 by adding 44 to each value so that all values will be greater than 0 and appropriate for square root and logarithm transformation. (Note that 44 equals the maximum esteem value plus 1.)

Using SPSS, we can effect this translation by using the **Compute** function under the **Transform** option and creating a new variable, SLFCNCF2, using the following **Numeric Expression**: 44 + SLFCNCF1.

☞ **Remark.** Through this numeric operation, scores that were originally high are now low on this scale, and scores that were originally low are now high on this scale. As a consequence, high self-concept is associated with low scores and low self-concept is associated with high scores.

The distribution of SLFCNC12 is presented in Figure 4.9(a). Following the outlined procedure, we first reflect SLFCNC12 and obtain the distribution of SLFCNCF1 presented in Figure 4.9(b). We then translate and obtain the distribution of SLFCNCF2 presented in Figure 4.9(c). When we take both the square root and the logarithm transformations, we obtain the results presented in Figures 4.10 and 4.11, respectively. The summary statistics are also presented.

Descriptive Statistics

	N	Minimum	Maximum	Mean	Std.	Skewness	
	Statistic	Statistic	Statistic	Statistic	Statistic	Statistic	Std. Error
Self-Concept in Twelth Grade	500	0	43	31.48	7.231	−.384	.109
SLFCNCF1	500	−43	0	−31.48	7.231	.384	.109
SLFCNCF2	500	1	44	12.52	7.231	.384	.109
slfcncsq	500	1	7	3.35	1.152	−.497	.109
slfcnclg	500	0	2	.98	.389	−1.324	.109
Valid N (listwise)	500						

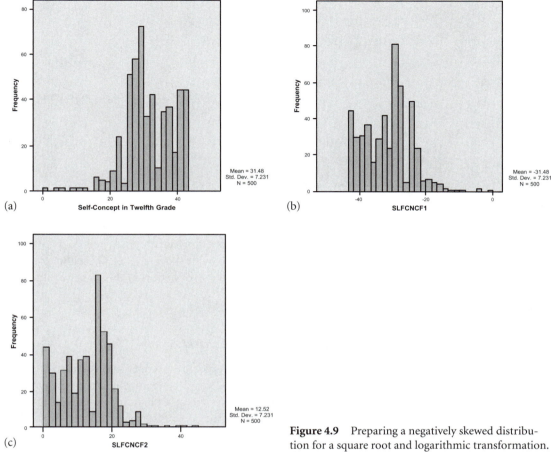

(a)

(b)

(c)

Figure 4.9 Preparing a negatively skewed distribution for a square root and logarithmic transformation.

Figure 4.10 The square root transformation.

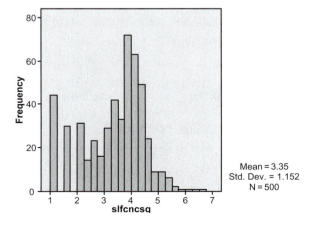

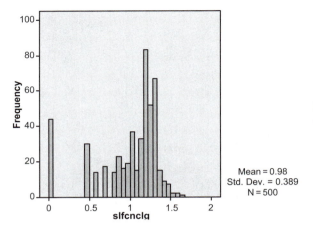

Figure 4.11   The logarithmic transformation.

Because both transformations, after reflection, make the twelfth-grade self-concept distribution more negatively skewed than it was originally (with skew $= -.384$), neither transformation improves symmetry. Accordingly, the best course of action in this case would be to leave SLFCNC12 in its original form.

NONLINEAR TRANSFORMATIONS: RANKING VARIABLES

Sometimes we may be interested in knowing the ranking of scores in a distribution and working with those rather than the scores themselves. For example, although we may have information on each student's grade point average in a particular graduating class, we also may be interested in their class ranking; that is, whether they placed first, 50th, or in some other position. To transform scores to ranks, we shall assign a 1 to the highest score, a 2 to the next highest, and so on. In the case of tied scores, each score is assigned the mean of the ranks that would have been assigned those scores had they not been tied. We illustrate the ranking procedure in Example 4.10 with the Hamburger data from McDonald's on the number of grams of fat and calories contained in each of five types of hamburger sold.

EXAMPLE 4.10. Rank the five hamburgers by their (a) fat content and (b) calorie content using SPSS. In both instances, assign the value 1 to the hamburger with the highest value. Assign the mean ranking in the case of ties.

Solution.

To rank the cases, click **Transform** on the main menu bar and **Rank Cases**. Move FAT and CALORIES into the **Variables** box. Under the heading **Assign Rank 1 to**, click the circle next to **Largest Value**. Click **OK**.

The two new ranked variables, named RFAT and RCALORIES, should appear in your data editor as shown below. Notice that in the case of FAT, where there are no ties (each hamburger has a unique fat content), the rankings are the whole numbers 1 to 5. From this ranking we know, for example, that a Quarter Pounder with Cheese ranks number 1 in fat relative to the other hamburgers and that a Hamburger ranks last. In the case of CALORIES, there is a tie between the Quarter Pounder with Cheese and the Big Mac. Accordingly, these two types of hamburger share the first- and second-place ranks and so are assigned the mean of 1 and 2, which is, of course, 1.5.

name	fat	calories	rfat	rcalories
Hamburger	10	270	5.0	5.0
Cheeseburger	14	320	4.0	4.0
Quarter Pounder	21	430	3.0	3.0
Quarter P. w/c	30	530	1.0	1.5
Big Mac	28	530	2.0	1.5

We may note that a rank transformation preserves the ordinality of the values, but that is all. The interval or ratio properties that might have existed in the original data are now lost.

☞ **Remark.** Rankings provide the ordinal position of a value in a distribution. From rankings we may know, for example, that a value is 100th in a distribution, but from that rank alone, we do not know how many other, or what percentage of, values are below that value. For this information, we use the percentile ranking introduced in Chapter 2.

OTHER TRANSFORMATIONS: RECODING AND COMBINING VARIABLES

RECODING VARIABLES

Variables may be recoded for at least two reasons: to transform variables and to collapse or combine categories. In Example 4.4, we reflected the Likert scale used to measure assertiveness so that lower scores no longer associated with agreement, but rather with disagreement, and higher scores no longer associated with disagreement, but rather with agreement. In particular, we applied the linear transformation 6 − ASSERT to achieve the desired transformation of this five-point scale. In Example 4.11 we provide another way to achieve this same result using the Recode procedure in SPSS.

EXAMPLE 4.11. Reflect the variable ASSERT that is scored using the five-point Likert scale shown below:

strongly agree	agree	neutral	disagree	strongly disagree
1	2	3	4	5

Solution.

To use the Recode procedure in SPSS to reflect ASSERT, click **Transform** from the main menu bar, **Recode**, and **Into Different Variables**. Click ASSERT and move it into the **Input Variable** box. Under the **Output Variable Name**, type in ASSERTRE and click **Change**. Click **Old and New Values**. Next to **Old Value** type in 1 and next to **New Value** type in 5. Click **Add**. Again, next to **Old Value** type in 2 and next to **New Value** type in 4. Click **Add**. Continue until all the old values 1 through 5 have been recoded. Click **Continue** and **OK**.

The next example uses Recode to collapse categories of a variable.

EXAMPLE 4.12. In the frequency distribution of eighth-grade school type, SCHTYP8 given below, we may note that school type is described as: 1 = public, 2 = private (religious), and 3 = private (nonreligious). If we are interested in distinguishing between 1 = public and 2 = private types only, then we may use the Recode procedure to collapse these three categories into two in the following way.

Solution.

To use SPSS to collapse the three categories of SCHTYP8 into two (public and private), click **Transform** from the main menu bar, **Recode**, and **Into Different Variables**. Click **SCHTYP8** and move it into the **Input Variable** box. Under the **Output Variable Name**, type in SCHTYPRE and click **Change**. Click **Old and New Values**. Next to **Old Value** type in 1 and next to **New Value** type in 1. Click **Add**. Again, next to **Old Value** type in 2 and next to **New Value** type in 2. Click **Add**. Finally, next to **Old Value** type in 3 and next to **New Value** type in 2. Click **Add**. Click **Continue** and **OK**.

Whenever a variable is treated as if it were continuous, it is preferable to retain as much of the variability in the scores as possible, which implies continuing to measure the variable on a many-valued scale. Sometimes, however, researchers choose to dichotomize such variables to simplify interpretation, among other reasons, using a *median split*. The Bem Sex-Role Inventory (1977), for example, uses two median splits, one on each of two continuous variables, Masculinity and Femininity, to divide the scores for each into two categories: low and high Masculinity and low and high Femininity. The low Femininity–low Masculinity category is labeled Undifferentiated, the low Femininity–high Masculinity category is labeled Masculine, the high Femininity–low Masculinity category is labeled Feminine, and the high Femininity–high Masculinity category is labeled Androgynous.

Simply stated, a median split transforms a many-valued variable into two categories: one includes all scores above the median and the other includes all scores below the median. The scores at the median typically are assigned arbitrarily to one of the two categories. Note that if the variable is skewed originally, in taking a median split, the new variable is symmetric. Although we do not recommend the median split, the next example describes how to split a variable at its median to create a dichotomous variable from one that is originally continuous.

EXAMPLE 4.13. Find the median of self-concept in eighth grade (SLFCNC08) and transform this variable using a median split procedure.

Solution. We find the median of SLFCNC08 using the SPSS Frequencies or Explore procedures to be 21.

To use SPSS to take a median split of SCHTYP8 we click **Transform** from the main menu bar, **Recode**, and **Into Different Variables**. Click **SLFCNC08** and move it into the **Input Variable** box. Under the **Output Variable Name**, type in SLFCN8MS and click **Change**. Click **Old and**

New Values. Click the circle next to **Range lowest through** and type 21 in the box. Under **New Value**, type 1. Click **Add**. Click the circle next to **Range through highest** and type in 22. Under **New Value,** type 2. Click **Add**. Click **Continue** and **OK**.

The frequency distribution of SLFCN8MS is given below.

SLFCNC8MS

		Frequency	Percent	Valid Percent	Cumulative Percent
Valid	1	266	53.2	53.2	53.2
	2	234	46.8	46.8	100.0
	Total	500	100.0	100.0	

The decision whether to lump all scores that equal the median value in the lower or upper category needs to be made by the researcher. Because there are 30 individuals who scored at the median of 21, the two categories do not each constitute 50 percent of the distribution. In this case, the median value of 21 was placed in the lower category. The upper category started at 22 because the distribution takes on only integer values.

☞ **Remark.** When recoding a distribution with missing values, it is important to assign old missing values to new missing values. This type of assignment is utilized in Exercise 4.26.

COMBINING VARIABLES

Although variables may be combined in a variety of ways, in this book we are concerned with combining variables using the operations of addition, subtraction, multiplication, and division. For example, using the NELS data set, suppose we wished to construct a variable that represented the combined number of years of math and English courses the student took in high school. The NELS data set has two variables that are relevant: the number of years of math taken, UNITMATH, and the number of years of English taken, UNITENGL. In Example 4.14, we construct a new variable that represents the combined number of years of math and English.

EXAMPLE 4.14. Construct a new variable, SUMUNITS, which represents the combined number of years of math and English taken in high school.

Solution.

Click **Transform** from the main menu bar, then **Compute**. Type SUMUNITS in the **Target Variable** box and move the variable UNITMATH into the **Numeric Expressions** box, type or click the + sign and then move the second variable, UNITENGL, into the **Numeric Expressions** box. Click **OK**. The new variable SUMUNITS will appear as the last variable in the data set.

EXERCISES

Exercises 4.1 through 4.8 involve the effects of linear transformations on the summary statistics of a distribution.

4.1. In this series of exercises, we find the summary statistics of distributions that are linear transformations of original distributions. These exercises do not require the use of SPSS.

a) If each value in a distribution with mean equal to 5 has been tripled, what is the new mean?

b) If each value in a distribution with standard deviation equal to 5 has been tripled, what is the new standard deviation?

c) If each value in a distribution with skewness equal to 1.14 has been tripled, what is the new skewness?

d) If each value in a distribution with mean equal to 5 has the constant 6 added to it, what is the new mean?

e) If each value in a distribution with standard deviation equal to 5 has the constant 6 added to it, what is the new standard deviation?

f) If each value in a distribution with skewness equal to 1.14 has the constant 6 added to it, what is the new skewness?

g) If each value in a distribution with mean equal to 5 has been multiplied by –2, what is the new mean?

h) If each value in a distribution with standard deviation equal to 5 has been multiplied by –2, what is the new standard deviation?

i) If each value in a distribution with skewness equal to 1.14 has been multiplied by –2, what is the new skewness?

j) If each value in a distribution with mean equal to 5 has had a constant equal to 6 subtracted from it, what is the new mean?

k) If each value in a distribution with standard deviation equal to 5 has had a constant equal to 6 subtracted from it, what is the new standard deviation?

l) If each value in a distribution with skewness equal to 1.14 has had a constant equal to 6 subtracted from it, what is the new skewness?

4.2. Consider a situation in which you would like to measure the amount of time it takes children in grades 4 and 6 to complete a task. This exercise does not require SPSS.

a) The fourth-grade teacher found that the average time to complete a task was 20 minutes with a standard deviation of 7 minutes. The sixth-grade teacher found that the average time was 0.25 hours to complete a task with a standard deviation of 0.09 hours. In which grade were the students faster? In which grade were the students more similar in the amount of time taken to complete the task?

b) The fourth-grade teacher found that the average time was 20 minutes with a standard deviation of 7 minutes and the sixth-grade teacher found that the average time was 22 minutes with a standard deviation of 5 minutes. If the sixth-grade teacher had included reading the instructions, which took 4 minutes, in his calculation of the time to complete the task, after adjusting for this additional time to make the two classes comparable, in which grade were the students faster? In which grade were the students more similar in the amount of time taken to complete the task?

4.3. Assume that you are studying college students and have measured a variable called CREDITS that gives the number of credits taken by a part-time or full-time student during the current semester. For the individuals you are studying, the number of credits taken ranges from 4 to 26, with a mean of 16.26, a standard deviation of 2.40, and a skewness ratio of −12.05. This exercise does not require SPSS.

    a) Assuming that, on average, each class is worth 3 credits, define an SPSS Compute statement to create a variable called CLASSES as a linear transformation of CREDITS that estimates the average number of classes taken during the current semester.

    b) What is the mean of CLASSES?

    c) What is the standard deviation of CLASSES?

    d) What is the shape of the distribution of CLASSES? Explain and support your answer with an appropriate descriptive statistic. Be sure to indicate whether or not the distribution is *severely* skewed.

    e) Why do you suppose the skewness is so severe in the negative direction?

4.4. The variable SCHATTRT in the NELS data set gives the average daily attendance rate for the school that the student attends.

    a) What are the mean, median, standard deviation, variance, range, IQR, and skewness of SCHATTRT?

    b) Compute a new variable SCHATTPP that expresses the average daily attendance as a decimal instead of as a percentage, that is, a variable that gives the average daily attendance proportion for the school that the student attends. What is the numeric expression you used?

    c) Based on the summary statistics for SCHATTRT that you generated in part (a), find the mean, median, standard deviation, variance, IQR, and skewness of SCHATTPP.

    d) Use SPSS to calculate the mean, median, standard deviation, variance, range, IQR, and skewness of SCHATTPP.

4.5. The variable EXPINC30 in the NELS data set measures the expected annual income at age 30 of students in the eighth grade.

    a) What are the mean, median, standard deviation, variance, range, IQR, and skewness of EXPINC30?

    b) Compute a new variable, EXPCENTS, which gives the expected income at age 30 in terms of pennies, not dollars. What is the numeric expression you used?

    c) Based on the summary statistics for EXPINC30 that you generated in part (a), find the mean, median, standard deviation, variance, IQR, and skewness of EXPCENTS.

    d) Use SPSS to calculate the mean, median, standard deviation, variance, range, IQR, and skewness of EXPCENTS.

4.6. The variable COMPUTER in the NELS data set indicates whether the student's family owned a computer when the student was in eighth grade. The variable is coded so that $0 =$ No and $1 =$ Yes.

    a) Verify that, in using this coding, the mean equals the proportion of Yes responses, or, in this case, 1s. What is that value?

    b) Use SPSS to compute the standard deviation of the variable COMPUTER.

    c) What is the linear transformation to convert COMPUTER into COMP1, which is coded 1 for No and 2 for Yes?

    d) What is the linear transformation to convert COMPUTER into COMP2, which is coded 0 for Yes and 1 for No?

    e) Use the rules for the effects of linear transformations on summary statistics to determine the means and standard deviations of the variables COMP1 and COMP2.

4.7. The variable CIGPDAY1 from the Framingham data set gives the number of cigarettes smoked per day by the respondents at first examination in 1956. Assume that the values of CIGPDAY1 are then multiplied by −2 and then 3 is added to each value to create the variable CIGTRANS.

   a) What are the values of the mean, standard deviation, and skewness ratio of CIGPDAY1?
   b) What is the value of the mean of CIGTRANS?
   c) What is the value of the new standard deviation?
   d) What is the value of the new skewness statistic?

4.8. In the Framingham data set, SEX is coded so that 1 = Men and 2 = Women. What is the mean of SEX? Apply appropriate linear transformations to interpret the mean of SEX as a proportion of women.

Exercises 4.9 through 4.17 involve z-scores.

4.9. Consider the variable representing number of members in a student's household, given by the NELS variable FAMSIZE (family size).

   a) If a student has a z-score of −1.28, how many members are in her household?
   b) What is the z-score for a student with 6 members in her household?
   c) Using the z-score criteria for outliers – that a score is an outlier if its associated z-score is less than −2 or greater than 2 – how many outliers are in this distribution?

4.10. Consider the variable for self-concept in eighth grade, given by the NELS variable SLFCNC08.

   a) Find the mean and standard deviation of SLFCNC08.
   b) Write down an SPSS Compute statement to calculate the z-score distribution for SLFCNC08. Use the SPSS Compute procedure to calculate ZSCORE, the z-score distribution for SLFCNC08.
   c) Use the SPSS Descriptives procedure to verify your calculated z-scores for SLFCNC08. The name given to this variable by SPSS is ZSLFCNC0.
   d) Without computing, what are the means and standard deviations of ZSCORE and ZSLFCNC0?
   e) If a new variable, SLF08P5, were created by adding 5 points to the eighth-grade self-concept score for each student in the NELS data set, what would be the mean and standard deviation of SLF08P5?

4.11. The variable UNITENGL in the NELS data set gives the number of years of English taken in high school. The variable UNITMATH gives the number of years of math taken in high school. Advanced course work enabled some of the the recorded values of these two variables in the data set to exceed 4.

   a) What is the z-score of a student who took 5.5 years of high school English?
   b) How many years of high school English did a student with a z-score of −1.71 take?
   c) Using the z-score criteria for outliers – that a score is an outlier if its associated z-score is less than −2 or greater than 2 – how many outliers are in the distribution UNITENGL?
   d) According to cumulative percentages, if a student took 5.5 years of both math and English, is that more unusual for English or math, relative to his classmates?
   e) According to z-scores, if a student took 5.5 years of both math and English, is that more unusual for English or math, relative to his classmates?

4.12. The variables SLFCNC08, SLFCNC10, and SLFCNC12 in the NELS data set measure self-concept in eighth, tenth, and twelfth grade, respectively. A self-concept score of 25 is relatively highest in which of these distributions?

a) Base your answer on cumulative percentages.

b) Base your answer on z-scores.

4.13. Does an eighth-grade self-concept (SLFCNC08) score of 25 represent a higher level of eighth-grade self-concept for males or for females? Use as criteria (a) cumulative percentages and (b) z-scores. Use Split File to create separate frequency distributions for males and female students in the NELS.

To get separate frequency distribution tables for males and females, first split the file. Go to **Data, Split File**. Click the circle next to **Compare Groups** and move GENDER into the box for **Groups Based on**. Click **OK**. All subsequent commands will be performed separately for males and females. After getting the frequency distributions, turn off the split file by going to **Data, Split File**. Click the circle next to **Analyze all cases**.

4.14. Who scores higher in science achievement in eighth grade (ACHSCI08) relative to his or her gender, a female who scores 58, or a male who scores 63? Use as criteria (a) cumulative percentages and (b) z-scores. Use Split File to create separate frequency distributions for males and female students in the *NELS*.

4.15. Determine the number of standard deviations away from the mean a score of 89 is on a test with mean 92 and variance 4.

4.16. If Steve's z-score on a test is $+1.5$, what is his raw score if the mean of the test is 75 and the standard deviation is 10?

4.17. Given a unimodal, symmetric distribution, rank from numerically smallest to numerically largest the following values from that distribution:

$$z = +1 \qquad \overline{X} \qquad Q_1$$

Exercises 4.18 through 4.20 involve a mixture of topics about linear transformations and some review topics.

4.18. The following questions involve the variable GRADE from the Learndis data set.

a   What are the mean and standard deviation of the variable GRADE?

b) Assume that students start first grade at age 6 and go up one grade each year. Use a linear transformation to convert GRADE to AGE, the approximate age of the student in that grade.

c) Use the information about the distribution GRADE to find the mean age for students in the data set.

d) Use the information about the distribution GRADE to find the standard deviation for AGE.

e) Examine the shape of the GRADE distribution. How would you describe the shape of the AGE distribution?

4.19. Compare the distribution of reading comprehension scores (READCOMP) in the Learndis data set by whether the student was assigned part time to the resource room for additional instruction (PLACEMEN $= 0$) or full time in a self-contained classroom (PLACEMEN $= 1$).

a) Is either of the two distributions severely skewed? If so, which one(s) and what is the direction of the skew? Explain and support your answer with appropriate descriptive statistics.

b) In which type of placement do these students have a higher overall level of reading comprehension? Explain and support your answer with an appropriate descriptive statistic, taking into account the varying degrees of skewness in the two distributions. Is there another statistic that suggests an alternative conclusion?

c) For which type of placement are the reading comprehension scores more consistent? Explain and support your answer with an appropriate descriptive statistic, taking into account the varying degrees of skewness in the two distributions. Is there another statistic that suggests an alternative conclusion?

d) Does the student with the highest reading comprehension score in the data set have a resource room or a self-contained classroom placement? Provide statistical support your answer.

e) What is the z-score corresponding to a reading comprehension score of 75 for a student with a resource room placement?

f) What is the reading comprehension score corresponding to a z-score of 2 for a student with a resource room placement?

g) Would a student with a reading comprehension score of 75 be more unusual (further from the bulk of the scores in standard deviation units) relative to the resource room students or to the self-contained classroom students? Explain and support your answer.

h) Can a percentile in the distribution of reading comprehension scores for the students with a resource room placement have the value 103? Explain.

4.20. Consider the variable AGE1 in the Framingham data set, which gives a respondent's age in 1956, the first year of the study.

a) How many people in the data set were 40 years old in 1956?

b) What percentage of people in the data set were younger than or equal to 40 in 1956?

c) Is 40 years old above or below the median in this data set? Explain.

d) Is 40 years old above or below the mean in this data set? How many standard deviations is 40 years old above or below the mean?

e) If we consider a score to be an outlier if its associated z-score is less than -2 or greater than 2, how many outliers are there in the AGE1 distribution?

f) What is the breakdown of outliers by men and women?

g) Write the formula for linearly transforming the variable AGE1 to the new variable BIRTHYR, which gives the year in which the person was born.

h) What is the median of the variable BIRTHYR?

i) What is the standard deviation of the BIRTHYR?

Exercises 4.21 through 4.23 involve square root and logarithmic transformations.

4.21. Consider the four achievement measures in the tenth grade, ACHMAT10, ACHRDG10, ACHHIS10, and ACHSCI10. Determine their skewness and a nonlinear transformation (e.g., log, square root) that will be useful in symmetrizing the variable if it is highly skewed.

4.22. For each of the following variables from the NELS data set, determine whether the variable is skewed and, if so, whether a log or square root transformation is effective in symmetrizing the variable.

a) APOFFER

b) FAMSIZE

c) SCHATTRT

d) What would be the effect, if any, of a nonlinear transformation on a dichotomous variable such as CIGARETT?

4.23. For each of the following variables from the Learndis data set, determine whether the variable is skewed and, if so, whether a log or square root transformation is effective in symmetrizing the variable.

a) GRADE

b) MATHCOMP

c) READCOMP

Exercises 4.24 through 4.28 involve recoding and combining variables.

4.24. In the NELS data set, UNITMATH represents the total number of units (in years) of mathematics taken in high school, and UNITCALC represents the number of units (in years) of calculus taken.

a) Create the variable UNITMNC to represent the number of units of noncalculus mathematics taken.

b) What is the largest number of units of noncalculus math taken by a student in the NELS data set? How many student(s) took that amount of noncalculus math?

4.25. There are four variables in the NELS data set that describe different types of achievement in twelfth grade: ACHMATH12, ACHRDG12, ACHSCI12, and ACHSLS12.

a) Create a composite variable, ACHTOT12, that represents the sum of a student's achievement on all four tests.

b) Describe the shape of the distribution of ACHTOT12.

c) On average, do boys score higher on ACHTOT12 than girls? Support your answer with appropriate descriptive statistics and indicate if different statistics lead to different conclusions.

4.26. The variable APOFFER gives the number of Advanced Placement (AP) courses offered by the school that the student attends.

a) Create a new variable, APOFFYN, that indicates whether or not the school offers any AP courses, where 0 = No and 1 = Yes. Make sure to record missing data on APOFFER as missing data on APOFFYN.

b) How many schools in the NELS data set do not offer AP courses?

c) How may we interpret the mean of this 0–1 coded dichotomous variable APOFFYN?

4.27. In Exercise 1.15, you created the Statisticians data set. Using the variables in that data set, compute the following new variables and answer related questions about them.

a) Create the variable ALIVE, representing how long they each lived. Who lived the longest?

b) Create the variable OLD, which indicates how old they would be now if they were still living. Who is the "youngest" statistician in the data set?

4.28. Use the Framingham data set to determine if, after experiencing a coronary heart disease (CHD) event, individuals reduce their weight (as measured by BMI) and cigarette smoking (as measured by CIGDAY). Consider the initial period as period 1 (1956) and the final period as period 3 (1968). The variable ANYCHD4 indicates whether a person in the study experienced a CHD event during the study.

a) Compute two new variables that reflect the difference in BMI and CIGDAY from period 1 to period 3; for example, BMIDIFF = BMI3 – BMI1 and CIGPDIFF = CIGDAY3 – CIGDAY1. Looking at the frequency distribution of these two variables, how many individuals lost weight? How many reduced their cigarette smoking?

b) What is the change in BMI, on average, from period 1 to period 3 for those who experienced a CHD event during this time period compared to those who did not experience a CHD event during this time period?

c) What is the change in CIGDAY, on average, from period 1 to period 3 for those who experienced a CHD event during this time period compared to those who did not experience a CHD event during this time period?

CHAPTER FIVE

Exploring Relationships Between Two Variables

Up to this point, we have been examining data univariately, that is, one variable at a time. We have examined the location, spread, and shape of several variables in the NELS data set, such as socioeconomic status, mathematics achievement, expected income at age 30, and self-concept. Interesting questions often arise, however, that involve the relationship between two variables. For example, using the NELS data set we may be interested in knowing if self-concept relates to socioeconomic status; if gender relates to science achievement in twelfth grade; if sex relates to nursery school attendance; or if math achievement in twelfth grade relates to geographical region of residence.

When we ask whether one variable relates to another, we are really asking about the shape, direction, and strength of the relationship between the two variables. We also find it useful to distinguish among the nature of the variables themselves; that is, whether the two variables in question are both measured at least at the interval level, are both dichotomous, or are a combination of the two. For example, when we ask about the relationship between socioeconomic status and self-concept, we are asking about the relationship between two at least interval-leveled variables. When we ask about whether sex relates to nursery school attendance, we are asking about the relationship between two dichotomous variables. And, when we ask about whether sex relates to twelfth-grade science achievement, we are asking about the relationship between one dichotomous variable and a variable that is at least interval-leveled.

WHEN BOTH VARIABLES ARE AT LEAST INTERVAL-LEVELED

Although the questions posed in the introductory paragraph of this chapter are motivated by our familiarity with the NELS data set, for heuristic reasons we have chosen much smaller, yet real, data sets, to introduce the important ideas associated with the concept of a relationship between two continuous variables.

Do hamburgers that have more fat tend to have more calories? Table 5.1 contains the fat grams and calories associated with the different types of hamburger sold by McDonald's.

Table 5.1. Fat grams and calories by type of McDonald's hamburgers

Type of McDonald's hamburger	Grams of fat (X)	Calories (Y)
Hamburger	10	270
Cheeseburger	14	320
Quarter Pounder	21	430
Quarter Pounder w/cheese	30	530
Big Mac	28	530

Table 5.2. Value and total circulation of U.S. currency

Denomination	Total circulation ($)	Number in circulation
$1	8,397,526,319	8397526319
$2	1,428,842,156	714421078
$5	9,715,702,340	1943140468
$10	14,810,410,070	1481041007
$20	110,116,823,780	5505841189
$50	60,189,902,300	1203798046
$100	524,467,735,200	5244677352

The data are from McDonald's Nutrition Information Center and are saved in the Hamburg data set.

Does a state's average SAT verbal score relate to the percentage of students who have taken the SAT in that state? Data on the percentage of students who took the SAT in 2005 in each state along with the average SAT verbal score are taken from the States data set. The source for these data is *The World Almanac and Book of Facts 2006*.

For bills of $100 or lower, is there an association between the value of the bill and the total number in circulation? Table 5.2 contains, for the smaller bill denominations, the value of the bill and the total circulation in dollars. These values are saved in the Currency data set. We use the methods of Chapter 4 to calculate the total number of bills in circulation by dividing the total circulation in dollars by the bill value, given as the last column in Table 5.2. The source for these data is *The World Almanac and Book of Facts 2006*.

Finally, what is the pattern of marijuana use by twelfth graders from 1987 through 1996? We answer this question by using data from the Marijuana data set, which gives the year and the percentage of twelfth graders who report that they have ever used marijuana. The source for these data is *The World Almanac and Book of Facts 2006*.

SCATTERPLOTS

With any of these data sets, a natural question is, how may we describe the relationship between the two variables? Although the relationship may often be grasped by inspecting the table of pairs of data values, a better approach is to use a graphic that depicts each pair of (X,Y) values as a separate point in an (X,Y) coordinate plane. Such a graphic is called a *scatterplot*. The scatterplots for the data in our four examples are given in Figures 5.1 through 5.4, respectively.

To obtain the scatterplot in Figure 5.1, for example, using SPSS, go to **Graphs** on the main menu bar, **Legacy Dialogs**, and then **Scatter**. Click **Define**. Put CALORIES into the box labeled **Y-axis** and FAT into the box labeled **X-axis** and click **OK**.

An important feature of a relationship is its *shape*. Notice that, in the scatterplots of Figures 5.1 and 5.2, although all points do not fall exactly along a single straight line, the points are represented well by a straight line. Accordingly, the relationships between fat content and calories and between the percentage of students taking the SAT exam and the average SAT math score for states in the western United States are said to be linear. By contrast, the variables of the scatterplot of Figure 5.3 are not systematically related because the

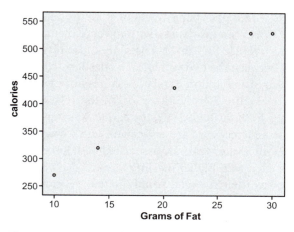

Figure 5.1   McDonald's hamburgers.

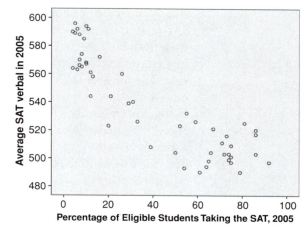

Figure 5.2   The SAT in the United States.

points follow neither a single straight line nor a simple curve. We say that there is no relationship between the denomination of the bill and the number of such bills in circulation.
In Figure 5.4, on the other hand, the variables are systematically related because the points
of this scatterplot are best represented by a simple curve, not by a single straight line.
Marijuana use is relatively high in the late 1980s and early 1990s, decreases until 1992, and
then increases again through 1996. This particular type of curvilinear relationship is called
quadratic because it has an approximately parabolic shape and parabolic curves are represented by quadratic functions.

   Another important feature of a relationship is its *direction*. Because the straight line
representing the points of Figure 5.1 has a positive slope, the linear relationship is said to
be positive; that is, the higher the fat content, the higher the number of calories (and the
lower the fat content, the lower the number of calories). On the other hand, because the
straight line representing the points of Figure 5.2 has a negative slope, the linear relation-

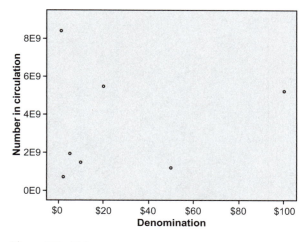

Figure 5.3   U.S. currency.

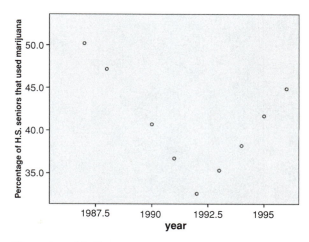

Figure 5.4   Marijuana use.

ship is said to be negative. That is, the states with higher percentages of students taking the SAT tend to have lower average SAT math scores (and the states with lower percentages of students taking the SAT tend to have higher average SAT math scores). Because Figure 5.3 suggests no simple systematic relationship between the two variables in question (currency value and number in circulation), the notion of a direction of relationship is not meaningful. Finally, in the quadratic relationship of Figure 5.4, the direction of the relationship changes from negative to positive. For years 1988 through 1992, the earlier years are associated with higher marijuana use whereas the later years are associated with lower marijuana use. For the years 1992 through 1996, the earlier years are associated with lower marijuana use whereas the later years are associated with higher marijuana use.

Relationships also may be characterized by their *strength*. Simply stated, the closer the points in the scatterplot are to the straight line (or curve) that best represents the points, the stronger the relationship between the two variables. If all the points in the scatterplot fall exactly on the line (or curve) that best represents the points, we would say that a perfect linear (or nonlinear) relationship exists between the two variables. The farther the points in the scatterplot are from the line (or curve), the weaker the linear (or nonlinear) relationship between the two variables.

Figures 5.5(a) through (i) provide a series of scatterplots varying in the direction and strength of the linear relationships they depict. Axes are labeled with the possible pair of variables that might be so related. Panels (a) through (d) depict increasingly weaker negative linear relationships because the points in these figures depart increasingly from the straight line that best represents them. Whereas Figure 5.5(a) represents a perfect negative linear relationship because all points fall exactly on the straight line, Figures 5.5(b) through (d) do not. Figure 5.5(e) depicts no relationship between the two variables and Figures 5.5(f) through (i) depict increasingly stronger positive linear relationships.

A scatterplot may be used to depict the shape, direction, and to a lesser extent the strength of the relationship between two variables, but summary statistics may also be used to quantify the strength and direction of relationships. In the case of two continuous variables, when both are on at least interval scales of measurement, the direction and strength

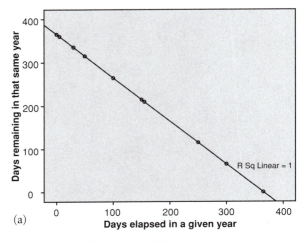

(a)

Figure 5.5 (a)   The passage of time.

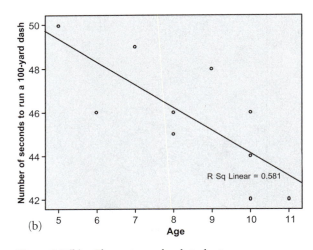

(b)

Figure 5.5 (b)   Elementary school students.

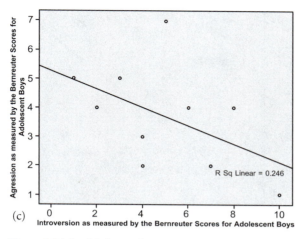

Figure 5.5 (c)   Adolescent boys.

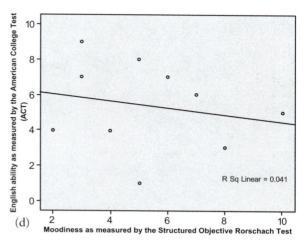

Figure 5.5 (d)   College freshmen.

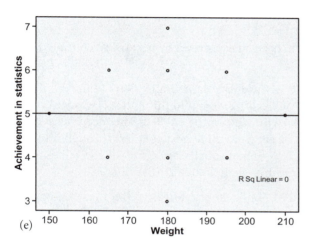

Figure 5.5 (e)   Male college students.

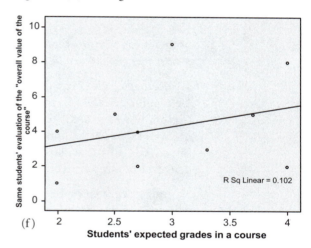

Figure 5.5 (f)   College students.

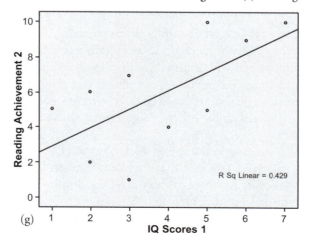

Figure 5.5 (g)   Children in grades K–3.

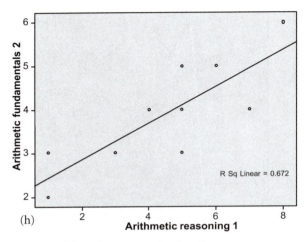

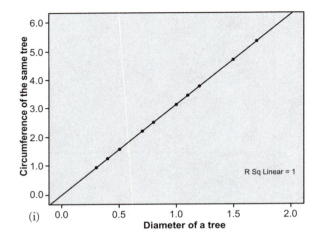

Figure 5.5 (h)   Elementary school students.   **Figure 5.5 (i)**   Dimensions of a tree.

of the linear relationship between them may be characterized by what is called the *Pearson Product Moment Correlation Coefficient.*

☞   **Remark.** The Pearson Correlation Coefficient is named after Karl Pearson, who in 1896 published the first mathematically rigorous treatment of this index. It was Sir Francis Galton, however, a cousin of Charles Darwin, who in the 1870s first conceptualized the notion of correlation and regression (to be covered in the next chapter) through his work in genetics, in particular by examining two-dimensional scatterplots of the relationship between the sizes of sweet pea plants of mother–daughter pairs (Stanton, 2001).

Indices exist to represent the strength of nonlinear relationships, but these are beyond the scope of our discussion, which in this section is confined to linear relationships only. For a more advanced treatment of correlation, including nonlinear relationships, the interested reader is referred to Cohen, Cohen, West, and Aiken (2003).

THE PEARSON PRODUCT MOMENT CORRELATION COEFFICIENT

The strength of a linear relationship is characterized by the extent to which a straight line fits the data points. That is, strength is characterized by the extent to which high scores on one variable are paired with high scores on the other and low scores on one variable are paired with low scores on the other, in the case of a *positive*, or *direct*, linear relationship. Or strength can also be characterized by the extent to which high scores on one variable are paired with low scores on the other and vice versa, in the case of a *negative*, or *indirect*, linear relationship.

To illustrate, we refer to the values for fat content (X) and calories (Y) of the five types of hamburger given in Table 5.1 that we have observed to have a positive linear relationship. For convenience, as shown in Table 5.3, we index the values by a subscript letter rather than by the type of hamburger itself.

We may determine whether high scores on fat content are paired with high scores on calories and whether low scores on fat content are paired with low scores on calories by first determining if each type of hamburger's fat content value is high or low *within the set*

Table 5.3. Fat content and calories of five hamburger types

Type of McDonald's hamburger (indexed)	Grams of fat (X)	Calories (Y)
1	$X_1 = 10$	$Y_1 = 270$
2	$X_2 = 14$	$Y_2 = 320$
3	$X_3 = 21$	$Y_3 = 430$
4	$X_4 = 30$	$Y_4 = 530$
5	$X_5 = 28$	$Y_5 = 530$

of fat content values. And we can do likewise for each type of hamburger's value in calories. Once we have labeled each fat content value and calorie value as either high or low within its own distribution, we can compare one to the other for each type of hamburger. In so doing, we may determine the extent to which high fat content values tend to be paired with high calorie values and low fat content values tend to be paired with low calorie values.

To label a particular fat content value as either high or low within its own distribution, we calculate the *z*-scores for each fat and calorie value within its own distribution. These *z*-scores, as calculated using the SPSS Descriptives procedure, are shown in Table 5.4 for both X and Y.

To determine whether a high fat content is paired with a high calorie count, and whether a low fat content is paired with a low calorie count, we form the product of the two *z*-scores for each hamburger type. If both X *and* Y scores are high with regard to their respective distributions, then both terms in the product are positive and the product itself is positive. Likewise, if both X *and* Y scores are low with regard to their respective distributions, then both terms in the product are negative and the product is again positive.

Notice that all the products in Table 5.5 are positive. A positive product results when either both terms are positive or both terms are negative.

☞ **Remark.** When one (but not both) of the differences is negative, signifying either a high X value paired with a low Y value or a low X value paired with a high Y value, a negative product results.

To obtain a summary measure that incorporates all types of hamburger and all types of fat content and calorie count values, we can approximate the *average* tendency of the values to have positive (or negative) products by dividing the sum of the products by $N - 1$.

$$r = \frac{\sum z_x z_y}{N - 1} \tag{5.1a}$$

Table 5.4. Difference about the mean for fat content and calories

Type of McDonald's hamburger (indexed)	Grams of fat (X)	Calories (Y)	zfat	zcalories
1	$X_1 = 10$	$Y_1 = 270$	-1.226	-1.226
2	$X_2 = 14$	$Y_2 = 320$	$-.763$	$-.806$
3	$X_3 = 21$	$Y_3 = 430$	$.046$	$.118$
4	$X_4 = 30$	$Y_4 = 530$	1.087	$.957$
5	$X_5 = 28$	$Y_5 = 530$	$.856$	$.957$

Table 5.5. Taking the product of the difference terms

Fat (X)	Calories (Y)	z_x	z_y	$z_x z_y$
$X_1 = 10$	$Y_1 = 270$	-1.226	-1.226	1.503
$X_2 = 14$	$Y_2 = 320$	$-.763$	$-.806$	$.615$
$X_3 = 21$	$Y_3 = 430$	$.046$	$.118$	$.005$
$X_4 = 30$	$Y_4 = 530$	1.087	$.957$	1.041
$X_5 = 28$	$Y_5 = 530$	$.856$	$.957$	$.819$

Equation 5.1a is called the *Pearson Product Moment Correlation Coefficient*, denoted by the symbol r_{xy} or the letter r. N represents the number of pairs of fat content and calorie count values in the data set. In the McDonald's example, N equals 5 because there are five pairs of values. For these data, $r = .996$.

Had we not used SPSS to calculate the z-scores, it is likely that we would have divided by N in calculating the standard deviation values upon which the z-scores are based. In this case, the Pearson Product Moment Correlation Coefficient is expressed as follows:

$$r = \frac{\sum z_x z_y}{N} \tag{5.1b}$$

When N is large, results from Equations 5.1a and 5.1b are only negligibly different.

The sign of the correlation indicates the direction of the relationship; the magnitude of the correlation indicates the strength. The correlation is bounded between -1.00 and $+1.00$ inclusive. A correlation value of -1.00 indicates a *perfect negative linear relationship*, whereas a Pearson Correlation value of $+1.00$ indicates a *perfect positive linear relationship*. A correlation value of 0 indicates no linear relationship.

As expected, the sign of the correlation between fat and calories is positive, suggesting that hamburgers with low fat content tend to have low calorie counts and hamburgers with high fat content tend to have high calorie counts. Furthermore, because the magnitude of this correlation is so close to 1.00, we may infer that the relationship between fat content and calorie count is very strong.

☞ **Remark.** The calculation of z-scores in Equations 5.1a and 5.1b requires that we divide by both S_x and S_y. Because division by 0 is not defined, we must impose the restriction that, whenever either $S_x = 0$ or $S_y = 0$ (all the X values are the same or all the Y values are the same) or both, the Pearson Correlation Coefficient is undefined. Conceptually, the Pearson Correlation Coefficient should not be defined in this case. For example, suppose we wanted to determine the relationship between age rounded to the nearest year (X) and income (Y), and the data consisted only of 25-year-olds. Because there is no variability on age for such data, the standard deviation of age would be zero, and there would be no way to determine whether in fact income varies with age.

To use SPSS to obtain the correlation coefficient between these two variables, click **Analyze** on the main menu bar, **Correlate**, and **Bivariate**. Move the two variables, CALORIES and FAT, in that order, into the **Variables** box and click **OK**.

The output from SPSS is reproduced below.

Correlations

		Calories	Grams of Fat
calories	Pearson Correlation	1	.996**
	Sig. (2-tailed)		.000
	N	5	5
Grams of Fat	Pearson Correlation	.996**	1
	Sig. (2-tailed)	.000	
	N	5	5

** Correlation is significant at the 0.01 level
(2-tailed).

The output is formatted as a two-by-two table called a matrix. The upper-left and bottom-right cells form what is called the *main diagonal* of the matrix. The cells in the main diagonal contain the correlations of each variable with itself. Because a variable is always perfectly positively correlated with itself, these correlations (the first value in each cell) equal 1.00. The lower-left and upper-right cells form what is called the *off-diagonal* of the matrix. The correlation in the upper-right cell is the correlation between CALORIES and FAT whereas the correlation in the lower-left cell is the correlation between FAT and CALORIES. Notice that in both cells this correlation equals .996. These correlations are equal because the bivariate correlation is a symmetric measure of a linear relationship; that is, $r_{xy} = r_{yx}$.

EXAMPLE 5.1. Given the data corresponding to Figures 5.2 through 5.4, find and interpret the correlations between (a) the percentage of students taking the SAT and the average verbal SAT score in the United States; (b) the currency value of a bill and the total number of such bills in circulation; (c) percentage marijuana use among twelfth graders and year from 1987 through 1996.

Solution. Using SPSS we obtain the following results.

(a) $r = -.88$, suggesting that states with larger percentages of students taking the SAT tend to have lower average verbal SAT scores, and vice versa.

(b) $r = .11$, suggesting that the currency value of a bill is only weakly negatively linearly related to the total number of such bills in circulation. From the scatterplot of Figure 5.3, we may conclude further that knowing the currency value of a bill tells us almost nothing about how many such bills are in circulation.

(c) $r = -.42$, suggesting that percentage of marijuana use is negatively linearly related to the year of observation, from 1987 to 1996. However, we know from looking at the scatterplot of Figure 5.4 that this correlation, which measures the strength and direction of the linear relationship, is not a good statistic to use to describe the relationship between these two variables. Over the entire span of years measured, the relationship is better described as quadratic, not linear. Alternatively, one could compute two correlations, one based on the data from 1992 and earlier, and the other on the data from 1992 and later. These two correlations would better reflect the strong relationship between marijuana use and year of use, negative before 1992 and positive after 1992.

EXAMPLE 5.2. The following table gives the correlation coefficient for each of the scatter-plots depicted in Figures 5.5(a) through (i). Do the magnitude and direction of these relationships corroborate the impressions obtained from the scatterplots?

Figure letter	Correlation, r
a	-1.00
b	$-.76$
c	$-.50$
d	$-.20$
e	0
f	$+.32$
g	$+.65$
h	$+.82$
i	$+1.00$

Solution. The correlations (a) through (d) are increasingly less negative and corroborate the fact that the points in these figures depart increasingly from the negatively sloped straight line that best represents them. As expected, the correlation of Figure 5.5(e) is zero, and the correlations of Figures 5.5(f) through (i) are increasingly more positive.

Interpreting the Pearson Correlation Coefficient

Judging the Strength of the Linear Relationship. Whether a Pearson Correlation Coefficient value r is to be judged unusually strong or unusually weak depends on the situation in which the correlation has been computed.

For example, if we administered the Stanford-Binet Intelligence Test to a group of elementary school children and then re-administered the test to these same children a week later, the correlation value we would expect to obtain between the two testings is approximately $r = .90$. Under these circumstances, the correlation value of $r = .90$ would not be considered unusually strong; it would be considered typical. This is because, given the relatively short time between testings, it is unlikely that anything has happened to substantially alter the responses to the test.

Under different circumstances, a correlation value of $r = .90$ might be considered unusually strong. If, for example, two different tests had been used instead of only one (a test of intelligence and a test of creativity, for example), then a correlation of $r = .90$ might be considered unusually strong. Thus, the terms *strong* and *weak* are used to compare descriptively the obtained correlation value to the value we would expect under the given circumstances.

Within an applied psychology framework, specific criteria for categorizing the magnitude of linear relationships as strong, moderate, and weak were first introduced by Cohen (1969) and are now widely used in behavioral science research.

According to an often-cited publication by Cohen (1988), Pearson correlation values of $r = \pm.50$ are considered strong, $r = \pm.30$ are considered moderate, and $r = \pm.10$ are considered weak. Cohen's classification of a correlation of $\pm.50$ as strong comes from his assertion that "workers in personality-social psychology, both pure and applied (i.e., clinical, educational, personnel), normally encounter correlation coefficients above the .50–.60 range only when the correlations are measurement reliability coefficients" (1969, p. 75).

Based on these criteria, case (h) of Example 5.2 ($r = .82$) indicates a *very strong* linear relationship between the two variables, whereas case (f) ($r_{xy} = .32$) indicates only a

Table 5.6. Correlation coefficients for selected variables

Variables	Correlation Coefficient
Heights of identical twins	.95
Intelligence test scores of identical twins	.88
Reading test scores grade 3 versus grade 6	.80
Rank in high school class versus teachers' rating of work habits	.73
Height versus weight of 10-year-olds	.60
Arithmetic computation test versus nonverbal intelligence test (grade 8)	.54
Height of brothers, adjusted for age	.50
Intelligence test score versus parental occupational level	.30
Strength of grip versus speed of running	.16
Height versus Binet IQ	.06
Ratio of head length to width versus intelligence	.01
Armed Forces Qualification Test scores of recruits versus number of school grades repeated	−.27
Artist interest versus banker interest	−.64

moderate linear relationship between the two variables. However, both are examples of typical correlation values within their respective contexts.

Because the sign of the correlation value indicates only the nature of the relationship between the two variables (whether it is positive or negative) and not its magnitude, a Pearson Correlation Coefficient value of $+.50$ indicates a linear relationship of the same strength as a Pearson Correlation Coefficient value of $-.50$. Likewise, a correlation of $-.76$ represents a stronger linear relationship than a correlation of .65.

To get a sense of some of the correlation values that appear in the literature, Table 5.6 gives correlation coefficients for selected variables (Thorndike and Hagen, 1977).

The Correlation Scale Itself Is Ordinal. One may ask whether an increase in correlation values of 0.10 units represents a constant increase in the strength of the relationship regardless of the values of the correlations themselves. Because the Pearson Correlation Coefficient as a measure of linear relationship is on an ordinal level of measurement, it does not. Whereas a correlation value of $+.50$ represents a stronger relationship between two variables than a correlation value of $+.30$, and a correlation value of $+.30$ represents a stronger relationship between two variables than a correlation value of $+.10$, the increase in strength from $+.10$ to $+.30$ is not the same as (and is actually smaller than) the increase in strength from $+.30$ to $+.50$.

Correlation Does Not Imply Causation. Another important consideration in interpreting a Pearson Correlation Coefficient value is that, in general, the existence of a correlation between two variables does not necessarily imply the existence of a causal link between these two variables.

For example, suppose we obtain a correlation of $r = +.60$ between the number of television sets in various countries at a particular time and the number of telephones in the same countries at the same time. This correlation does not necessarily imply that a causal relationship exists between the number of televisions and the number of telephones in a country. For example, importing a million television sets into a country does not automatically increase that country's number of telephones. Similarly, importing a million telephones into a country does not automatically increase that country's number of television sets.

It is possible that the values of both of these variables are due to a common third variable (such as the industrial level of the country or its gross national product) and that this third variable causes both of the other two variables. If this is true, an artificial increase in either the number of television sets or the number of telephones does not cause a change in the other variable, because the real cause of normal changes, the third variable, has remained the same. In general, causal links cannot be deduced merely from the existence of a correlation between two variables. All that can justifiably be said is that the two variables are related. We need more information than the existence of a correlation to establish a cause-and-effect relationship.

The Effect of Linear Transformations

Another important point in interpreting a Pearson Correlation Coefficient relates to the units of measurement employed. Suppose you compared the heights of individuals measured in inches to the weights of the same individuals measured in pounds and found a Pearson correlation value of $r = .30$. Would you expect the correlation value to change if you re-computed the correlation, measuring the heights of the individuals in feet and the weights of the individuals in ounces, and could get all measurements perfectly? We do not suppose you would. If a person's height is high relative to that of others in the group when the heights are measured in inches, it should be just as high relative to the others when the heights are measured in feet. That is, the position of an individual relative to his or her group remains the same, despite the fact that the scores of the group are transformed into some other scale or frame of reference. In this example, each original height score, measured in inches, was converted to feet by dividing by 12. In addition, each original weight score, measured in pounds, was converted to ounces by multiplying by 16.

Had a constant value been added to either height or weight or both, in addition to the multiplication or division that was done, the relative standing of individuals within each group would still have been the same, and the correlation value would have remained the same. Thus, linear transformations of the X variable and/or Y variable do not change the magnitude (size) of the Pearson Correlation Coefficient. The sign of the coefficient is reversed only if one but not both of the sets of scores (X or Y) is multiplied or divided by a negative number. For example, if the correlation between X and Y is $r_{XY} = .70$ and if all the X scores are multiplied by -2, the new correlation coefficient has the same magnitude but a reversed sign. That is, the new correlation coefficient value is $r_{XY} = -.70$.

Restriction of Range

When a correlation is computed on a subset of the natural range of one or both variables, the magnitude of the correlation may be either smaller or larger than the correlation computed on the entire range.

Suppose, for example, that we are interested in the correlation coefficient between Age X and Weight Y for a group of individuals whose ages range from 1 to 15 years. A correlation coefficient calculated on only the very youngest and the very oldest of the individuals (say, only those individuals who are 3 or younger or 12 or older) results in a stronger correlation than one based on the entire set of data. This is because, in this subset, there is a greater tendency for the younger group to have lower weight and for the older group to have higher weight than for the entire set of individuals taken as a whole.

Analogously, if we calculate the correlation coefficient on a restricted, more homogeneous subset of the entire range (such as only those individuals with ages between $X = 9$ and $X = 11$

years of age), then we can expect the correlation to be weaker (closer to 0) than if it were calculated on the entire set of data. This is because, with all the individuals in this subset being so similar to each other in age relative to the entire group, there is less of a tendency for differences in age among the individuals to correspond to systematic differences in weight.

We present another example of restriction of range which involves the elimination of the middle values of the distribution. The Brainsz data set, taken from the Data and Story Library website, is based on a study by Willerman et al. (1991) in which such a method was used. The purpose of the study was to examine the relationships among brain size, gender, and intelligence. The research participants consisted of 40 introductory psychology students who were selected from a larger pool of psychology students with total SAT scores higher than 1350 or lower than 940, where these scores were used to measure intelligence. In other words, students with moderate intelligence scores were omitted from the study. The result was that the correlations between gender and intelligence and brain size and intelligence were inflated.

The conclusion to be drawn from this discussion is that you should not expect the correlation between two variables to be the same for a large group as it is for a subset of that group if the subset is either more or less homogeneous than the larger group in one or both of the variables under study. By eliminating the middle group, the subset becomes less homogeneous than the original, larger group.

The Shape of the Underlying Distributions

Another factor that affects the size of a correlation is the relative similarity or dissimilarity of the shapes of the X and Y distributions. Simply stated, a perfect positive correlation between X and Y ($r = +1$) can only occur when the X and Y distributions have exactly the same shape. For example, if X were positively skewed and Y were negatively skewed, we would expect this difference in shape to result in a weaker positive correlation than if the two distributions had the same shape. If one or both of the variables is skewed, one should consider applying a nonlinear transformation (e.g., square root or logarithm) to symmetrize the distribution(s) prior to calculating r.

The Reliability of the Data

A third factor that affects the size of r concerns the reliability of the X and Y values or, in other words, the extent to which the X and Y values consistently reflect the amounts of the characteristics they are supposed to represent. The less reliable a measure, the greater the amount of error in each of its observed values. Because error, by definition, is random and does not correlate with anything, the more error a variable contains, the less we can expect that variable to correlate with any other variable. Consequently, it is important to check the reliability of any measuring instruments used and to employ those instruments with a high reliability. A more complete discussion of reliability is beyond the scope of this book. The interested reader should consult a text on tests and measurement. One such example is Cohen and Swerdlik (2005).

WHEN AT LEAST ONE VARIABLE IS ORDINAL AND THE OTHER IS AT LEAST ORDINAL: THE SPEARMAN RANK CORRELATION COEFFICIENT

The Spearman Rank Correlation Coefficient measures the strength of the linear relationship between two variables when the values of each variable are rank-ordered from 1 to N, where N is the number of pairs of values. The formula for the Spearman Correlation

Coefficient, given as Equation 5.4, and denoted by r_s, ρ, or rho, may be obtained as a special case of the Pearson Correlation Coefficient when the N cases of each variable are assigned the integer values from 1 to N inclusive and no two cases share the same value.

$$r_s = 1 - \frac{6 \sum d_i^2}{N^3 - N} \tag{5.4}$$

where d_i represents the difference between ranks for each case. As a special case of the Pearson Correlation Coefficient, r_s is interpreted in the same way as the Pearson. For example, notice that, when the ranks for the two variables being correlated are identical, the differences between them are zero and the Spearman Correlation Coefficient is 1.00, indicating a perfect positive correlation between the variables.

· ·

EXAMPLE 5.3. Consider the McDonald's hamburger data. Suppose we are not convinced that our measure of fat is interval-leveled. That is, although we believe that the Quarter Pounder™, with 21 grams of fat, has more fat than the Cheeseburger, with 14 grams of fat, and less fat than the Big Mac™, with 28 grams of fat, we are not convinced that, in terms of fat, the Quarter Pounder™ is midway between the other two types of hamburger. Accordingly, we decide to consider the fat scale as ordinal, and we transform the original data to ranked data. To find the relationship between fat and calories, we compute the Spearman Correlation Coefficient on the ranked data instead of the Pearson Correlation Coefficient on the original data.

☞ **Remark.** The formula for the Spearman Coefficient is derived as a special case of the Pearson Coefficient formula by taking advantage of the fact that the data are rankings from 1 to N. We may note that the Spearman Correlation Coefficient on the ranked data gives the identical result as the Pearson Correlation Coefficient on the ranked data.

Solution. To obtain the ranked data by hand, we simply rank order the five types of hamburger in terms of fat and assign a value from 1 to 5 to each hamburger to denote its place in that ranking. Then we assign ranked values to the five types of hamburger in terms of calories. The original data, together with their rankings, are provided in the first five columns of Table 5.7. The last two columns contain the difference and squared difference between the ranks for each hamburger, respectively.

Notice that the Quarter Pounder with Cheese™ and the Big Mac™ have the same original calorie count of 530. Accordingly, they are tied for first and second place in the rankings. Therefore, we assign the average of these two ranks, 1.5, to each of them. The same procedure is used whenever ties occur.

Table 5.7. Original and ranked data for hamburger fat and calories

Hamburger type	Grams of fat (X)	Ranked fat	Calories (Y)	Ranked calories	d_i	d_i^2
Hamburger	$X_1 = 10$	5	$Y_1 = 270$	5	0	0
Cheeseburger	$X_2 = 14$	4	$Y_2 = 320$	4	0	0
Quarter Pounder™	$X_3 = 21$	3	$Y_3 = 430$	3	0	0
Quarter Pounder w/Cheese™	$X_4 = 30$	1	$Y_4 = 530$	1.5	−.5	.25
Big Mac™	$X_5 = 28$	2	$Y_5 = 530$	1.5	.5	.25

The Spearman Correlation Coefficient equals, in this case, $r_s = 1 - 6(.50)/(125 - 5) = .975$, suggesting that there is a very strong linear relationship between fat and calories expressed in ranked form. Notice that this value is slightly different from the Pearson Correlation Coefficient of $r = .996$, because the Quarter Pounder with Cheese™ and the Big Mac™ are tied in their numbers of calories.

To use SPSS to find the Spearman Correlation Coefficient, click **Analyze**, **Correlate**, **Bivariate**. Move the variables FAT and CALORIES into the **Variables** box. Click **Spearman** and click off **Pearson** in the **Correlation Coefficients** box. Click **OK**. Note that when using SPSS we do not need to transform the data to rankings to obtain the Spearman Correlation Coefficient; SPSS does this transformation for us.

☞ **Remark.** The Pearson Correlation Coefficient measures the direction and strength of the linear relationship between the *numerical values* assigned to the variables in question. Because these numerical values may take on many forms, including rankings and dichotomies, we need to be sensitive to the nature of these numerical values when interpretations are made.

WHEN AT LEAST ONE VARIABLE IS DICHOTOMOUS: OTHER SPECIAL CASES OF THE PEARSON CORRELATION COEFFICIENT

In measuring the correlation between two variables when one is at least interval and the other is dichotomous or when both are dichotomous, we may use the Pearson Correlation Coefficient. In these cases, however, the Pearson Correlation Coefficient is often given a different name to reflect the type of data being analyzed.

The *Point Biserial Correlation Coefficient* is the name given to the special case of the Pearson Coefficient for measuring the direction and strength of the linear relationship between two variables when one is dichotomous and the other is at least interval. The *Phi Coefficient* is the name given to the special case of the Pearson Coefficient for measuring the direction and strength of the linear relationship between two dichotomous variables.

THE POINT BISERIAL CORRELATION COEFFICIENT: THE CASE OF ONE AT-LEAST-INTERVAL AND ONE DICHOTOMOUS VARIABLE

EXAMPLE 5.4. Use the Hamburg data set to perform a correlation analysis to determine whether there is a relationship between the calorie count of a burger and whether or not it comes with cheese and if there is a correlation, to describe it. In other words, we perform a correlation analysis to determine whether there is a difference in the average number of calories between those hamburgers with and those without cheese. Table 5.8 contains, for each of the five types of hamburger, the calories and whether or not the burger has cheese.

Solution. CHEESE is a dichotomous variable because it takes on two values (No, Yes) whereas the variable CALORIES is measured at the ratio level. We use SPSS to obtain the Pearson Correlation Coefficient because we know that the Pearson Coefficient gives a numerical result identical to the Point Biserial Correlation Coefficient, the special case of the Pearson Coefficient when one variable is at least interval and the other is dichotomous.

Table 5.8. Calories and cheese for McDonald's hamburgers

Hamburger type	Calories (Y)	Cheese (0 = "No", 1 = "Yes")
Hamburger	270	0
Cheeseburger	320	1
Quarter Pounder™	430	0
Quarter Pounder w/Cheese™	530	1
Big Mac™	530	1

As in the case of two at-least-interval variables, we first depict the relationship between these two variables using a scatterplot. If we proceed as shown earlier to obtain the scatterplot with CHEESE as the X variable and CALORIES as the Y variable, the result appears as in Figure 5.6. Recall that, for these data, hamburgers without cheese are assigned the value 0 on CHEESE and hamburgers with cheese are assigned the value 1.

Because CHEESE is dichotomous, the scatterplot does not appear as a cloud of points as it does in Figures 5.1 through 5.4, but rather as two vertical columns of points centered, respectively, over 0 (for no cheese) and 1 (for cheese). By inspecting the scatterplot and, in particular, the locations of the two vertical columns relative to the calorie scale (the Y axis), we may infer that, for these McDonald's hamburgers, hamburgers with cheese have more calories on average than those without cheese.

Furthermore, because hamburgers without cheese are assigned a value of 0 and hamburgers with cheese a value of 1, we may note that low scores on CHEESE (no cheese) associate with low scores on CALORIES and high scores on CHEESE (cheese) associate with high scores on CALORIES. Given the coding of our variables, we should expect to obtain a positive correlation between calorie and cheese content for these hamburgers. Using SPSS, we find that the correlation between CHEESE and CALORIES is $r = .51$, a strong positive correlation.

☞ **Remark.** Had the coding scheme been reversed for the variable CHEESE so that hamburgers with no cheese were assigned a 1 and hamburgers with cheese a 0, the sign of the correlation coefficient would have changed from positive to negative, leaving the interpre-

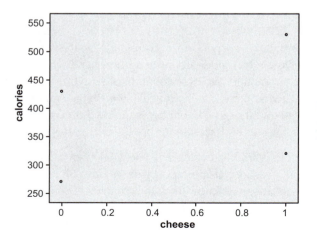

Figure 5.6 Scatterplot of calorie and cheese content for McDonald's hamburgers.

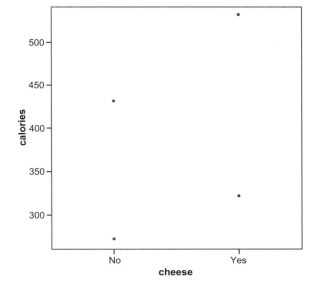

Figure 5.7 Interactive scatterplot of calorie and cheese content for McDonald's hamburgers.

tation of the direction of the relationship unchanged. Although the coding reversal changes the sign of the correlation, it does not affect the magnitude.

Notice that the horizontal axis of the scatterplot given in Figure 5.6 treats CHEESE as if it were continuous. It makes more sense to have a discrete horizontal axis with two categories representing the two types of cheese content. Such a graph is obtained using the SPSS Interactive Graphs procedure and is provided as Figure 5.7.

To create a scatterplot when one of the variables is at the nominal level, use interactive graphs. Go to **Graphs**, **Interactive**, **Scatterplot**. Put CALORIES in the **Vertical Axis** box and CHEESE in the **Horizontal Axis** box. Click **OK**.

· ·

EXAMPLE 5.5. Use the NELS data set to determine the correlation for students in the West between (1) gender and achievement in science in twelfth grade and (2) gender and achievement in reading in twelfth grade. Our focus on the students in the West in this example is for heuristic reasons.

Solution.

1) Gender is a dichotomous variable because it takes on two values (male, female), whereas achievement in science in twelfth grade is a continuous variable. We use SPSS to obtain the Pearson Correlation Coefficient because we know that the Pearson Coefficient gives a numerical result identical to the Point Biserial Correlation Coefficient, the special case of the Pearson Coefficient when one variable is continuous and the other is dichotomous.

Given our question, we first need to select the students in the West so that our analysis is confined only to those students.

To select the students in the West using SPSS, we first click **Data** on the main menu bar, **Select Cases**, **If**, and type within the large box "REGION = 4" (for West). Click **Continue**, **OK**.

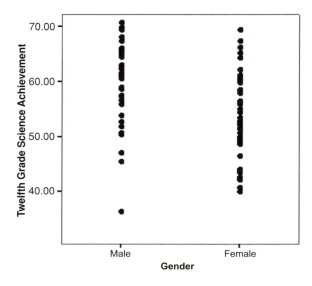

Figure 5.8 Interactive scatterplot of gender and twelfth-grade science achievement for students in the West.

NOTE: To have access to the full data set once this analysis is complete, return to the **Select Cases** command and click **All Cases.**

As in the case of two continuous variables, we first depict the relationship between these two variables using a scatterplot created using the SPSS Interactive Graphs procedure. The result may be found in Figure 5.8.

By inspecting the scatterplot and, in particular, the locations of the two vertical columns relative to the achievement-in-science scale (the Y axis), we may infer that, for students in the West, males do slightly better in science achievement in twelfth grade than females.

Furthermore, because males are assigned a value of 0 and females a value of 1, we may note that low scores on GENDER (males) associate with high scores on achievement in science and high scores on GENDER (females) associate with low scores on achievement in science. Therefore, given the coding of our variables, we should expect to obtain a negative correlation between gender and achievement in science in twelfth grade. Using SPSS we find that, for the 93 students in the West, the correlation between gender and achievement in science in twelfth grade is $r = -.395$, a moderately strong negative correlation.

☞ **Remark.** Notice the outlier in the distribution of male science achievement scores in Figure 5.8. Checking further, we find that this outlier score belongs to case number 194. (The series of steps needed to obtain this case number is the focus of Exercise 5.5.) To see to what extent score 194 influences the result, we re-compute the correlation between gender and achievement in science on these data, but without the score for this individual. The result is $r = -.443$, suggesting an even stronger relationship between gender and science achievement in twelfth grade for students in the West without this outlier.

2) The interactive scatterplot for GENDER and ACHRDG12 for students in the West is given in Figure 5.9.

Notice that in Figure 5.9 the locations of the two vertical columns relative to the achievement-in-reading scale (Y axis) are not as different from one another as they are in

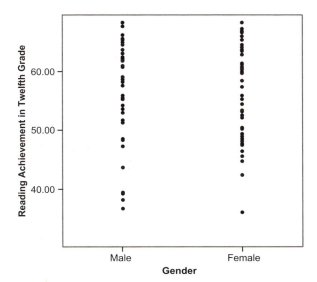

Figure 5.9 Interactive scatterplot of gender and reading achievement in twelfth grade for students in the West.

Figure 5.8 (relative to science achievement). In fact, they are hardly different from one another at all, suggesting that there is little or no relationship between gender and achievement in reading in twelfth grade for students in the West. That is, boys do not appear to do better or worse than girls in reading achievement in the twelfth grade. Using SPSS we find that, for the 93 students in the West, the Pearson Correlation Coefficient between sex and reading achievement in the twelfth grade is $r = -.021$, confirming our impressions of little or no relationship.

☞ **Remark.** From the preceding two results, we may infer that the stronger the correlation between a dichotomous variable and a continuous one, the greater the separation between the two groups, designated by the dichotomous variable, in terms of the values on the continuous measure. On average, the reading achievement distributions for boys and girls were quite similar, whereas the science achievement distributions for boys and girls were not. Conceptually, therefore, it should make sense that a point biserial correlation reflects the degree to which the means of the two groups on the continuous measure are different. The formula for the point biserial correlation coefficient, given as Equation 5.5, makes this interpretation clear:

$$r_{pb} = \frac{(\overline{Y}_1 - \overline{Y}_0)S_X}{S_Y} \tag{5.5}$$

where $\overline{Y}_1$ and $\overline{Y}_0$ are the Y means of the groups designated by the dichotomous variable. S_X and S_Y represent the standard deviations of X and Y, respectively. Note that, because X is dichotomous and takes on the values 0 and 1, S_X can be expressed as $\sqrt{pq}$, where p and q are the respective proportions of the total for each of the two groups. From Equation 5.5 we realize that, when there is no separation between the two groups on the continuous measure Y, (i.e., when $\overline{Y}_1 = \overline{Y}_0$), r_{pb} equals zero. Likewise, the larger the separation between the two groups relative to the spread (i.e., the more discrepant 1 and 0 relative to the spread), the stronger is the correlation, r_{pb}.

THE PHI COEFFICIENT: THE CASE OF TWO DICHOTOMOUS VARIABLES

As noted earlier, when both variables are dichotomous the Pearson Correlation Coefficient may be expressed in a simplified, numerically equivalent form called the Phi Coefficient.

• •

EXAMPLE 5.6. Use the NELS data to determine the correlation between (1) nursery school attendance and gender for students in the South and (2) nursery school attendance and computer ownership for students in the West.

Solution. 1) To select students from the South only, we use the Select Cases option in the Data menu and choose REGION = 3 in SPSS. We then proceed with the solution to the problem.

Although interactive scatterplots were useful in depicting the types of bivariate relationship discussed earlier in this chapter, they are not useful when the two variables in question are both dichotomous, as Figure 5.10 illustrates.

If there was a relationship between gender and nursery school attendance, then the pattern of frequencies of the four cells, represented by the four points in Figure 5.10, would vary in a systematic way. That is, a relationship would be suggested if, for example, the relative frequency of girls who attended nursery school was different from the relative frequency of boys who attended nursery school. Said differently, if the likelihood of attending nursery school varied as a function of gender, then a relationship between the two variables would be said to exist. To obtain information on the frequencies, an alternative graphic is the clustered bar graph. For these data the clustered bar graph appears in Figure 5.11.

To obtain a clustered bar graph using SPSS for the data of Figure 5.10 click **Graphs** on the main menu bar, **Legacy Dialogs**, and **Bar**. Change from **Simple** to **Clustered** and click **Define**. Put NURSERY in the **Category Axis** box and GENDER in the **Define Clusters By** box. Click **OK**.

Notice that each bar represents one of the four points of the scatterplot depicted in Figure 5.10 and that the heights of the bars represent the corresponding point frequencies. The rel-

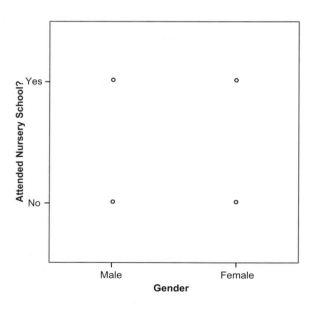

Figure 5.10   Interactive scatterplot of gender by nursery school attendance for students in the South.

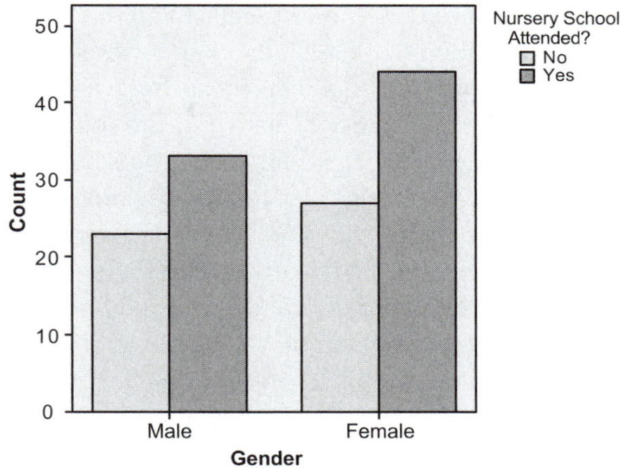

Figure 5.11 Clustered bar graph of gender by nursery school attendance for students in the South.

ative difference in bar heights between students who have attended nursery school and those who have not is similar for males and females in both direction and magnitude. This similarity in profiles suggests little or no relationship between nursery school attendance and gender for these students in the South. As an alternative to reading the four cell frequencies from the heights of the bars, we may obtain the frequencies directly in tabular form using the Crosstabs option in SPSS.

To obtain the frequencies of each of the four cells represented by the four points (a contingency table or cross-tabulation), click **Analyze** on the main menu bar, **Descriptive Statistics**, **Crosstabs**. Put NURSERY in the **Row(s)** box and GENDER in the **Column(s)** box. Click **OK**.

The result is given in Figure 5.12.

To understand whether nursery school attendance varies as a function of gender, we may compare the pattern of the total counts either for gender or for nursery school to the pattern of cell counts by either row or column. The total counts are called *marginals* because they appear in the margins of the Crosstabs table. The nursery school (or row) marginals are 77 and 50 while the gender (or column) marginals are 56 and 71.

Figure 5.12 Cross-tabulation of gender by nursery school attended for students in the South.

gender Gender * nursery Nursery School Attended? Crosstabulation

Count

		nursery Nursery School Attended?		
		0 No	1 Yes	Total
gender Gender	0 Male	23	33	56
	1 Female	27	44	71
Total		50	77	127

The proportion of males who did attend nursery school relative to the total number of individuals who did attend nursery school is 33/77 = .43. That is, 43 percent of the individuals who did attend nursery school are males. Analogously, the proportion of males who did not attend nursery relative to the total number of individuals who did not attend nursery school is 23/50 = .46. That is, 46 percent of the individuals who did not attend nursery school are males. Because these proportions are nearly equal, we may conclude that there is little or no relationship between gender and nursery school attendance. An analysis based on a comparison between students who did and did not attend nursery school for males and females separately would have led to the same result.

An alternative analysis of the relationship may be based on a comparison of the ratio of frequencies that appears in the column marginals (e.g., 56 to 71) to the ratio of frequencies that appears in the columns within each row of the table. That is, we would expect the same ratio of column marginals between males and females (e.g., 56 to 71) to be replicated in each row if there were no relationship. The ratio of males to females overall is 56 to 71 (equivalently, 1 to 1.27), the ratio of males to females for those who attended nursery school is 33 to 44 (equivalently, 1 to 1.33), and the ratio of males to females for those who did not attend nursery school is 23 to 27 (equivalently, 1 to 1.17). These ratios are not identical, but they are close in value, suggesting, once again, little or no relationship between gender and nursery school attendance.

We may measure the magnitude of this relationship by computing the Phi Coefficient. To do so, we calculate the Pearson Correlation Coefficient as before, because the Phi Coefficient is a special case of the Pearson Coefficient. The result of this calculation is that $r = .031$, suggesting that, as expected, little or no relationship exists between these variables. Based on our earlier interpretation of the results of the Crosstabs table, you should be able to justify the positive sign associated with this correlation value.

☞ **Remark.** The table produced by the Crosstabs procedure is called a *contingency table* because the entries in each cell are contingent upon the row and column of each cell. It is also called a cross-tabulation.

☞ **Remark.** The Phi Coefficient may be expressed as a special case of the Pearson Correlation Coefficient that relates to the entries in the contingency table. In particular, if we label the cells

A	B
C	D

then the Phi Coefficient is given by Equation 5.6:

$$\phi = \frac{AD - BC}{\sqrt{(A + B)(C + D)(A + C)(B + D)}} \tag{5.6}$$

In the case of the data of Figure 5.9, we obtain the following result:

$$\phi = \frac{44 \times 23 - 33 \times 27}{\sqrt{77 \times 50 \times 56 \times 71}} = \frac{121}{3{,}912.5} = 0.031$$

which agrees with our earlier result when using the Pearson Correlation Coefficient. We now return to solving the second part of Example 5.6.

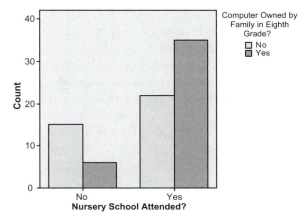

Figure 5.13 Clustered bar graph of nursery school attendance and computer ownership for students in the West.

Solution. 2) To select students from the West only, we use the **Select Cases** option and choose REGION = 4 in SPSS. We then proceed with the solution to the problem.

The frequencies of each of the four cells defined by the two dichotomous variables are given as a clustered bar graph and contingency table in Figures 5.13 and 5.14, respectively.

The bar graph of Figure 5.13 suggests a relationship between eighth-grade computer ownership and past nursery school attendance. The relative difference in bar heights between students who owned computers in eighth grade and those who did not is strikingly different in both magnitude and direction for those who attended nursery school and those who did not. In particular, those who attended nursery school were more likely to own a computer in eighth grade whereas those who did not attend nursery school were more likely not to own a computer in eighth grade.

As one would expect, Figure 5.14 also suggests a relationship between these two variables. Among students who had attended nursery school, 39 percent did not own a computer, whereas, among students who had not attended nursery school, 71 percent did not own a computer.

Alternatively, the ratio of noncomputer ownership to computer ownership for those who attended nursery school is 22 to 35 (equivalently, 1 to 1.59), whereas the ratio for those who

Figure 5.14 Cross-tabulation of nursery school attendance by computer ownership for students in the West.

nursery Nursery School Attended? * computer Computer Owned by Family in Eighth Grade? Crosstabulation

Count

		computer Computer Owned by Family in Eighth Grade?		Total
		0 No	1 Yes	
nursery Nursery School Attended?	0 No	15	6	21
	1 Yes	22	35	57
Total		37	41	78

did not attend nursery school is 15 to 6 (equivalently, 1 to 0.4). Because the individual row ratios differ from the marginal ratio of 1 to 1.11 (and from each other), a systematic relationship appears to exist between these two dichotomous variables. In particular, the likelihood of computer ownership is greater for those families who sent their children to nursery school (1.59 versus 1.11) than for those who did not (0.4 versus 1.11).

To measure the magnitude of this relationship using a single summary statistic, we compute the Pearson Correlation Coefficient using SPSS and find the correlation to be moderate in size ($r = .292$). The positive direction of the correlation tells us that low values on computer ownership (response of no) associate with low values on attended nursery school (response of no) and vice versa, thus corroborating our conclusions based on either the clustered bar graph of Figure 5.13 or the contingency table of Figure 5.14.

OTHER VISUAL DISPLAYS OF BIVARIATE RELATIONSHIPS

In the foregoing sections of this chapter, we discussed the quantification of linear relationships between two variables in the case where (1) both variables are at least interval, (2) both are dichotomous, (3) one is at least interval and the other is dichotomous, and (4) both are ranked. We also discussed ways to visually represent the relationships contained within these four cases. In this section we revisit the boxplot and clustered bar graph and show their versatility in representing relationships that arise from (2) and (3) and variations of (2) and (3) that involve nominal- and ordinal-leveled variables that are not necessarily dichotomous. We present these graphics without corresponding indices for quantifying the nature and magnitude of the relationships represented.

EXAMPLE 5.7. Use a boxplot to depict the relationships between (1) gender and achievement in science and (2) gender and achievement in reading for students in the West. This question was addressed earlier in Example 5.5.

Solution. Notice that the boxplot in Figure 5.15 resembles closely the scatterplot of Figure 5.8 and offers the same interpretation – males tend to score higher than females on science achievement in twelfth grade for students in the West.

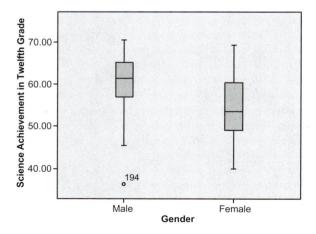

Figure 5.15   Boxplot of science achievement in twelfth grade by gender for students in the West.

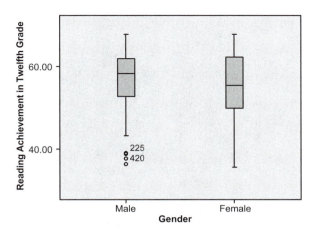

Figure 5.16 Boxplot of reading achievement in twelfth grade by gender for students in the West.

The boxplot depicting reading achievement in twelfth grade by gender appears in Figure 5.16 and also closely resembles the scatterplot of Figure 5.9.

Although we have used the boxplot to compare the distributions of a continuous measure for two groups, we may also use boxplots to compare the distributions of a continuous measure for any (reasonably small) number of groups, and in so doing look for a relationship between group membership and the continuous measure.

☞ **Remark.** Because group membership typically is nominal-leveled, with more than two groups, the relationship between group membership and a continuous measure cannot be described meaningfully as a linear one. Therefore, it follows that one would not want to compute a Pearson Correlation Coefficient on nominal data with more than two categories because its interpretation, as a measure of linear relationship, would be meaningless. The type of relationship that can be explored with such data is simply whether the groups, on average, differ from one another on the continuous measure. An index for measuring the strength of this type of relationship is discussed in a later chapter.

EXAMPLE 5.8. Construct a boxplot of twelfth-grade math achievement by region and use it to determine whether there appears to be a relationship between the two variables.

Solution. Because region is a nominal-leveled variable, the order of the four region categories (Northeast, North Central, South, and West) on the X-axis is arbitrary. As a result, it would not be meaningful to attempt to interpret the relationship between region and mathematics achievement in twelfth grade as linear. The best we can do is to define a relationship between these two variables in terms of the extent to which the four regions, on average, differ from one another on mathematics achievement in twelfth grade.

Given that the medians for the four groups are different from one another, we say that there appears to be a relationship between region and twelfth-grade math achievement for the students in our NELS data set. The highest level of math achievement is in the West, he lowest is in the South, and the other regions are intermediate. When both variables are dichotomous, an appropriate visual display is the *clustered bar graph* and an appropriate

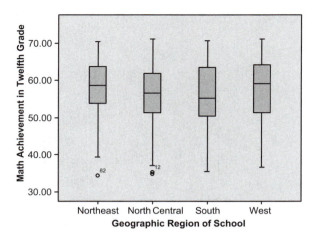

Figure 5.17   Boxplot of twelfth-grade math achievement by region.

statistical indicator of the relationship is the contingency table and the associated percentages. The clustered bar graph, the contingency table, and percentages may be used also when one or both variables have more than two, yet a reasonably small number, of categories.

· ·

EXAMPLE 5.9. Do families in the NELS data set differ on computer ownership by the region of the country in which they reside?

Solution. The contingency table is reproduced below.

**computer Computer Owned by Family in Eighth Grade?
* region Geographic Region of School
Crosstabulation**

Count

		region Geographic Region of School				
		1 Northeast	2 North Central	3 South	4 West	Total
computer Computer Owned by Family in Eighth Grade?	0 No	46	89	86	42	263
	1 Yes	60	62	64	51	237
Total		106	151	150	93	500

The results in the contingency table indicate that there is a relationship between computer ownership and region. Students in the Northeast and West were more likely to own a computer than not, with 56.6 and 54.8 percent, respectively, owning a computer. Students in the North Central and South were less likely to own a computer than not, with 41.1 and 42.7 percent, respectively, owning a computer.

The clustered bar graph is an appropriate graphical display to illustrate this relationship.

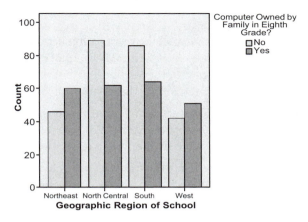

SELECTION OF APPROPRIATE STATISTIC/GRAPH TO SUMMARIZE A RELATIONSHIP

The table provides guidelines. Other choices may be correct.

Level of measurement	Nominal with two categories (dichotomous)	Non-dichotomous nominal or ordinal with more than two categories, but not more than approx. five, categories	Ordinal with more than approx. five categories	Interval or ratio
Nominal with two categories (dichotomous)	Pearson Correlation; percentages from cross-tabulation; clustered bar graph	Percentages from cross-tabulation; clustered bar graph	Spearman Correlation; interactive scatterplot; boxplot	Pearson Correlation; interactive scatterplot; boxplot
Non-dicthotomous nominal or ordinal with more than two, but not more than approx. five, categories	Percentages from cross-tabulation; clustered bar graph	Percentages from cross-tabulation; clustered bar graph	Medians; Spearman Correlation; interactive scatterplot; boxplot	Means or medians (depending on the shape of the scale variable); interactive scatterplot; boxplot
Ordinal with more than approx. five categories	Spearman Correlation; Interactive scatterplot; Boxplot	Median; Spearman Correlation; interactive scatterplot; Boxplot	Spearman Correlation; scatterplot	Spearman Correlation; scatterplot
Interval or ratio	Pearson Correlation; interactive scatterplot; boxplot	Means or medians (depending on the shape of the scale variable); interactive scatterplot; boxplot	Spearman Correlation; scatterplot	Pearson Correlation; scatterplot. Correlation should not be used unless scatterplot is well represented by a line.

EXERCISES

Exercises 5.1 through 5.5 involve scatterplots.

5.1. Use the States data set to create a scatterplot to depict the relationship between the percentage of students taking the SAT (PERTAK) and the expenditure per pupil (EDUCEXPE). Use it to explain why a correlation captures one aspect of the relationship, but that it is probably not the most appropriate technique to use for measuring this relationship.

5.2. Use the States data set to create a scatterplot to depict the relationship between the average teacher salary (TEACHPAY) and the graduation rate (GRADRATE). Use it to determine whether states that pay their teachers better tend to have higher graduation rates.

5.3. Use the States data set and scatterplots to investigate the relationships between the average SAT verbal score for the state (SATV) and the following three variables: average SAT math score for the state (SATM), average expenditure per pupil for the state (EDUCEXPE), and the average student-to-teacher ratio for the state (STUTEACH). Use the graphs that you create to answer the following questions.
   a) Rank these linear relationships from strongest to weakest.
   b) Describe the nature of the linear relationship, or indicate that little or no linear relationship exists, between the SATV and the SATM.
   c) Describe the nature of the linear relationship, or indicate that little or no linear relationship exists, between the SATV and the average expenditure per pupil for the state.
   d) Describe the nature of the linear relationship, or indicate that little or no linear relationship exists, between the SATV and the student-to-teacher ratio for the state.

5.4. Use the States data set to create a scatterplot to depict the relationship between the average teacher's salary (TEACHPAY) and the expenditure per pupil (EDUCEXPE). Label the points by state. Use your scatterplot to answer the following questions.
   a) Describe the nature of the linear relationship, or indicate that little or no linear relationship exists, between the expenditure per pupil and the average annual salary for public school teachers.
   b) Name a state that appears to be unusual relative to this trend. How can you tell? In what way is this state unusual?
   c) Do the mid-Atlantic states (NY, NJ, CT) appear to cluster together? Do other clusters by geographical location appear to exist? Why do you suppose such geographical clusters exist?

5.5. In Example 5.5, using the NELS data set, we identified the outlier for the relationship between ACHSCI12 and GENDER as ID number 194. This exercise takes you through the steps that enabled that determination and then asks you to perform a similar analysis using the Framingham data set.
   Start by selecting those cases in the West.

To label the scatterplot by ID using SPSS, go to **Graphs** on the main menu bar, **Legacy Dialogs, Scatter**, click **Define**. Put ACHSCI12 as the **Y Variable** and GENDER as the **X Variable**. Put ID into the **Label Cases By** box. Click **OK**. Click twice on the graph to get it into edit mode. Click **Elements, Show Data Labels**.

---

a) Where is case number 194?

b) For the Framingham data set, report and interpret the correlation between the initial body mass index (BMI1) and the initial total cholesterol (TOTCHOL1).

c) Create the scatterplot between these two variables. Which person is most unusual in terms of this trend? What is his or her ID number? Is this person a male or a female? How old was this person when the study began?

d) Calculate the correlation between these two variables without this person in the data set. Does the correlation value change as a result of omitting this person from the data set?

In addition to labeling points on scatterplots by an identifying variable, as in Exercise 5.5, points on scatterplots can also be labeled to differentiate between subgroups. This option is illustrated in Exercise 5.26.

Exercises 5.6 through 5.8 involve Pearson Correlation between two scale variables.

5.6. Conduct a correlation analysis using the States data set to determine whether various factors are associated with EDUCEXPE, the average educational expenditure per pupil. These factors are STUTEACH, student-to-teacher ratio; SATV, average verbal SAT score for the state; and TEACHPAY, the average salary of public school teachers in the state.

a) Create a matrix scatterplot of the variables and determine whether a linear model is an appropriate representation of the relationships between all pairs of these variables.

b) Calculate the correlation matrix between all pairs of these variables.

c) Do states in which expenditures per pupil are higher tend to pay their teachers more?

d) Do states in which expenditures per pupil are higher tend to have higher verbal SAT scores, on average?

e) Do states in which expenditures per pupil are higher tend to have lower pupil-to-teacher ratios?

f) Of the three variables – pupils per teacher, average SAT verbal scores, and teacher salary – which is most strongly correlated with expenditure per pupil?

5.7. For each of the following variables in the NELS data set, indicate whether you think their correlations with mathematics achievement in grade 12 (ACHMAT12) is positive, negative, or near zero. Use SPSS to determine if your thinking is correct.

a) Socioeconomic status (SES).

b) The extent to which students agree with the statement "My teachers are interested in their students" (TCHERINT), where 1 represents "Strongly Agree" and 4 represents "Strongly Disagree."

c) Family size (FAMSIZ).

5.8. The following questions, using the NELS data set, show how nonlinear transformations can affect the value of a correlation coefficient.

a) Find and interpret the correlation between SCHATTRT, the average daily school attendance rate (as a percentage) of the school the student attends, and SLFCNC08, the student's eighth-grade self-concept score.

b) In Exercise 4.4(b), the variable SCHATTPP was created to give the average daily school attendance rate as a proportion (rather than as a percentage) for the school that the student attends. Based only on your answer to Exercise 5.8(a), and without using SPSS, what is the correlation between SCHATTPP and SLFCNC08?

c) In general, do children who have higher SES expect to have greater incomes by age 30? Construct the scatterplot and determine the correlation coefficient between EXPINC30 and SES. Interpret the results.

d) Rather than simply eliminating the most extreme value in the scatterplot, we reduce its undue influence on the value of the correlation by following the methods in Chapter 4 and creating a new variable that represents the square root of EXPINC30. Label this new variable EXPINCSQ. Construct the scatterplot and determine the correlation coefficient between EXPINCSQ and SES. Do children who have higher SES expect to have higher incomes by age 30?

e) What is the correlation between EXPINCSQ and EXPINC30? Under what circumstance would the correlation be equal to 1.00?

f) For students in the Northeast, find the Pearson Correlation Coefficient between SLFCNC12 and EXPINC30.

g) Using the procedures described in Chapter 4, create two new variables: the square root of expected income and the logarithm of the reflection of the self-esteem variable. For students in the Northeast, find the Pearson Correlation Coefficient between the transformed versions of esteem and expected income.

h) Which is stronger, the correlation between the original or the reflected variables?

i) Why are the signs of the correlations between the transformed and untransformed variables different?

j) Has the general interpretation of the relationship changed now that the sign is negative?

Exercises 5.9 through 5.14 involve using the Pearson Correlation when at least one of the variables is dichotomous.

5.9. In this exercise, we use the NELS data set to look at the relationship of SES with eighth-grade computer ownership (COMPUTER), a dichotomous variable. Do students whose families owned a computer when they were in eighth grade tend to have a higher SES than those whose families did not own a computer when they were in eighth grade?

a) Create a scatterplot between COMPUTER and SES. Use it to describe whether students whose families owned a computer when they were in eighth grade tend to have a higher SES than those whose families did not own a computer when they were in eighth grade.

b) Calculate the correlation between these variables to determine the extent to which there is a relationship as described.

5.10. Use the Learndis data set to investigate whether different variables are associated with reading achievement. Determine the correlations between all pairs of the following variables: reading achievement (READCOMP), grade level (GRADE), intellectual ability (IQ), and whether the student was placed in the resource room for part of the day or in a full-time self-contained classroom (PLACEMEN, where 0 = resource room and 1 = self-contained classroom).

a) Interpret the correlation between reading comprehension and intellectual ability.

b) Based on the correlation table, which group has higher reading comprehension on average: those in the resource room or those in a self-contained classroom? Explain.

c) Interpret the correlation between type of placement and grade level.

d) Interpret the correlation between grade level and reading comprehension for these students.

5.11. In this exercise, you are asked about the relationship between pairs of variables in the Framingham data set.
   a) Compute the correlation (r) between the initial diastolic blood pressure at time 1 (DIABP1) and whether or not the person was taking anti-hypertensive (blood pressure) medication at time 1 (BPMEDS1). Interpret your result.
   b) What is another name for the special case of the Pearson Correlation Coefficient calculated between DIABP1 and BPMEDS1?
   c) In part (a), a positive yet weak correlation was noted between the taking of blood pressure medication and blood pressure level. That is, those people who take blood pressure medication have higher blood pressure levels, on average, than those who don't. What is a likely explanation for this relationship?
   d) Which gender (SEX) is more likely to have developed coronary heart disease (CHD) by the end of the study (ANYCHD4)? Explain and support your answer with appropriate statistic(s).
   e) What is another name for the special case of the Pearson Correlation Coefficient calculated between SEX and ANYCHD4?
   f) Explain why correlation is not the most appropriate way to statistically describe the relationship between the initial casual glucose level (GLUCOSE1) and the initial number of cigarettes smoked per day (CIGPDAY1).

5.12. What evidence is there in these data to suggest that HDL is "good" cholesterol and LDL is "bad" cholesterol? [HINT: Compute the correlation between HDL3 and ANYCHD4 and between LDL3 and ANYCHD4.]

5.13. In the NELS data set, the variable COMPUTER indicates whether the student's family owned a computer when the student was in eighth grade. In this question we look at the effect that the coding of this variable has on the correlation.
   a) Compute and interpret the correlation between SES and COMPUTER.
   b) Recode the variable COMPUTER into COMP1 so that 1 = No and 2 = Yes. Write the equation representing this linear transformation. Does this transformation include a reflection of the original variable COMPUTER? Recall that the original coding is 0 = No and 1 = Yes.
   c) What is the correlation between COMPUTER and COMP1?
   d) Recode the variable COMPUTER into COMP2 so that 0 = Yes and 1 = No. Write the equation representing this linear transformation. Does this transformation include a reflection of the original variable COMPUTER?
   e) What is the correlation between COMPUTER and COMP2?
   f) Without using SPSS, what is the correlation between SES and COMP1? Between SES and COMP2?

5.14. The median split, discussed in Chapter 4, is a type of nonlinear transformation that serves to symmetrize the distribution of a continuous variable into two equal halves. The resulting variable is dichotomous because all values below the median are assigned one code and all values above the median are assigned a different code. Depending on the nature of the underlying distribution of the continuous variable, the correlation between the newly formed dichotomous variable (via the median split transformation) and another variable may be stronger or weaker in magnitude than the correlation based on the original continuous variable and that other variable. This example illustrates the case, using the NELS data set, in which the resulting correlation becomes weaker in magnitude.

a) Find and interpret the correlation between SES and SLFCNC12.
b) Create new variables SESDI and SLF12DI that are the median splits of SES and SLFCNC12, respectively. Find and interpret the correlation between SESDI and SLFCNC12.
c) Comment on the effect of using the median split transformation in this case given that one of the continuous variables (SLFCNC12) is skewed negatively.

Exercise 5.15 involves the Spearman Correlation.

5.15. In this exercise, we investigate the relationship of two variables with EXCURR12 (participation in extracurricular activities in twelfth grade). Note that this variable is measured using an ordinal level of measurement.

a) Is there a correlation between smoking cigarettes (CIGARETT) and participation in extracurricular activities in twelfth grade (EXCURR12)? If so, describe the nature of the correlation. Provide statistical support for your answer.
b) Is there a correlation between missing school in twelfth grade (ABSENT12) and participation in extracurricular activities in twelfth grade (EXCURR12)? If so, describe the nature of the correlation. Provide statistical support for your answer.
c) Is there a correlation between SES and participation in extracurricular activities in twelfth grade (EXCURR12)? If so, describe the nature of the correlation. Provide statistical support for your answer.

Exercises 5.16 through 5.18 involve contingency tables (cross-tabulation).

5.16. Use Crosstabs applied to two variables from the NELS data set (ADVMATH8 and URBAN) to obtain a summary of who took advanced math in eighth grade by type of environment. Use the resulting summary to answer the following related questions.

a) What proportion of students took advanced math in eighth grade from each of the three environments: urban, suburban, and rural?
b) What proportion of students took advanced math in eighth grade over all environments?
c) Which environment has the largest proportion of advanced math takers: urban, suburban, or rural?
d) Is there a relationship between urbanicity and enrollment in advanced math in eighth grade? Explain.

5.17. In this exercise, we make use of the Framingham data set to explore the relationship between gender and cigarette use at time 1 and at time 3.

a) Create a contingency table of cigarette use at time 1 (CURSMOKE1) by sex and use it to determine whether the two variables are related.
b) Create a contingency table on cigarette use at time 3 (12 years into the study; CURSMOKE3) by sex and use it to determine whether the two variables are related.
c) Calculate the correlation between cigarette use at time 1 (CURSMOKE1) and sex and use it to confirm that the two variables are not related.
d) Calculate the correlation between cigarette use 12 years into the study (CURSMOKE3) and sex and use it to determine whether the two are related.

5.18. The body mass index (BMI) is a tool for indicating weight status in adults. It is a measure of weight for height; for adults over 20 years old, the BMI falls into one of three weight status categories: below 18.5, underweight; 18.5 to 24.9, normal; 25.0 to 29.9, overweight; and above 30.0, obese. In this exercise, we make use of these categories. [HINT: To create this new categorical variable, use **Transform**, **Recode into Different Variable** on BMI1.]

    a) Initially, at time 1, what is the distribution of men and women in this sample across these categories? [HINT: Use Crosstabs.] According to this distribution, what percentage of men is categorized as overweight or obese versus women?

    b) Are there differences in weight category by gender? Explain.

    c) Compare the relative proportions of people who did not experience a CHD event over the course of this study versus those who did (ANYCHD4) for men and for women. Use the obtained ratio of proportions within sex as the basis for comparison.

    d) How are these ratios affected if we restrict the samples of men and women only to those who are obese?

Exercise 5.19 requires you to select an appropriate statistic for answering the question asked and to analyze the NELS data set using that statistic.

5.19. Select an appropriate statistic that conveys the magnitude and nature of the relationship that exists between pairs of variables in the NELS data set. When describing that relationship, use terms that someone who has not taken statistics could understand (for example, positive correlation is not sufficient).

    a) Is there a relationship between years of math taken in high school (UNITMATH) and math achievement in twelfth grade (ACHMAT12)? If so, describe that relationship.

    b) Is there a relationship between the number of times the student is late to school in twelfth grade (LATE12) and the number of times the student skipped/cut classes in twelfth grade (CUTS12)? If so, describe that relationship.

    c) Is there a relationship between the school type attended in eighth grade (SCHTYP8) and whether or not the student took any Advanced Placement classes in high school (APPROG)? If so, describe that relationship.

    d) Is there a relationship between family size (FAMSIZE) and self-concept in twelfth grade (SLFCNC12)? If so, describe that relationship.

    e) Is there a relationship between SES and science achievement in twelfth grade (ACHSCI12)? If so, describe that relationship.

    f) Is there a relationship between region of the country (REGION) and whether or not a student took advanced math in eighth grade (ADVMATH8)? If so, describe that relationship.

    g) Is there a relationship between number of classes cut in twelfth grade (CUTS12) and whether or not the student took advanced math in eighth grade (ADVMATH8)? If so, describe that relationship.

    h) Is there a relationship between cigarette use (CIGARETT) and urbanicity (URBAN)? If so, describe that relationship.

    i) Is there a relationship between whether or not students took advanced math in eighth grade (ADVMATH8) and whether or not they took an AP class (APPROG) in high school? If so, describe that relationship.

j)   Is there a relationship between the frequency of cutting class in twelfth grade (CUTS12) and being absent from school in twelfth grade (ABSENT12)? If so, describe that relationship.

k)   Is there a relationship between twelfth-grade self-esteem (SLFCNC12) and SES? If so, describe that relationship.

l)   Is there a relationship between SES and nursery school attendance (NURSERY)? If so, describe that relationship.

m)   Is there a relationship between SES and urbanicity (URBAN)? If so, describe that relationship.

Exercises 5.20 through 5.25 include a variety of topics. These exercises are based on the Impeach data set, created by Professor Alan Reifman of Texas Tech University in response to a U.S. Senate vote taken on February 12, 1999, on whether to remove a president from office, based on impeachment articles passed by the U.S. House of Representatives. This was only the second time in U.S. history that such a vote took place. The data contain descriptions of each senator as a way to try to understand each senator's voting behavior.

5.20. The questions in this exercise relate to a correlation analysis carried out between all pairs of the following variables: the vote on perjury (VOTE1), the degree of conservatism of the senator (CONSERVA), the state voter support for Clinton (SUPPORTC), and whether or not it was the senator's first term (NEWBIE).

a)   Was it appropriate to compute a correlation between CONSERVA and SUPPORTC? Why or why not?

b)   Describe the magnitude and nature of the linear relationship between these two variables: the degree of conservatism of the senator and the state voter support for Clinton.

c)   Based on the results of the correlation analysis, can you determine whether conservative senators are more likely to vote guilty or not guilty on perjury? Explain.

d)   Based on the results of the correlation analysis, can you determine whether senators from states that supported Clinton in 1996 were more likely to vote guilty or not guilty on perjury? Explain.

e)   Based on the results of the correlation analysis, can you determine whether first-term senators were more likely to vote guilty or not guilty on perjury? Explain.

f)   If you were looking for one variable to statistically discriminate between those senators who voted guilty and those who voted not guilty on perjury, which variable (CONSERV, SUPPORTC, NEWBIE) would you choose? Explain.

g)   Explain why it would not be appropriate to calculate the correlation between the region of the country that the senator is from (REGION, where 1 = Northeast, 2 = Midwest, 3 = South, and 4 = West) and the vote on perjury. Give the name of an alternative analysis that could be used to analyze the relationship between the two variables.

5.21. Create two interactive scatterplots, one to depict the relationship between conservatism and the vote on perjury and the other to depict the relationship between conservatism and the vote on obstruction of justice. Use them to answer the following questions.

a)   Describe the nature of the relationship between the vote on obstruction of justice and conservatism. Use language that could be understood by someone who has never taken statistics.

b) Based on your political knowledge, explain why your answer to part (a) makes sense.

c) According to the scatterplots, which pair of variables has the stronger correlation? Explain.

5.22. Create a contingency table that gives the breakdown of the vote on perjury by region. Use it to answer the following questions.

a) How many senators voted not guilty on perjury?

b) What percentage of senators voted not guilty on perjury?

c) Of all not guilty votes, what percentage (or proportion) came from the South?

d) Of all votes from the South, what percentage (or proportion) were not guilty votes?

e) According to the contingency table, are there differences in the vote on perjury depending on the region the senator is from? Explain in a way that someone with no background in statistics could understand and support your answer with the values of relevant statistics.

f) What type of graph is best used to display the relationship between the vote on perjury and region? Create this graph.

g) Explain why a contingency table should not be used to analyze the relationship between region and conservatism.

5.23. Create a clustered bar graph that gives the number of guilty and not guilty votes on perjury (VOTE1) for both first-term and more senior senators (NEWBIE). Use it to answer the following questions.

a) Is there a relationship between the vote on perjury and whether or not it is the senator's first term? Explain.

b) Without calculating, what is the sign of the Pearson Correlation between VOTE1 and NEWBIE? Explain.

5.24. Create two clustered bar graphs that depict the relationships between whether or not it was the senator's first term (NEWBIE) and how the senator voted on obstruction of justice (VOTE2). Let one graph represent those senators who were up for re-election in 2000 and the other graph represent those who were up for re-election in 2002. Use them to answer the following questions.

a) For those senators up for re-election in 2000, describe the nature of the relationship between seniority status as a senator (whether the senator was first-term or not) and voting behavior on the issue of obstruction of justice. Explain.

b) Is the Pearson Correlation Coefficient that may be calculated to describe the relationship noted in part (a) positive, negative, or near zero? Explain.

c) According to these clustered bar graphs, is the correlation between whether or not it was the senator's first term and his or her vote on obstruction of justice stronger for senators up for re-election in 2000 or in 2002? Explain.

5.25. To determine whether the relationship between state voter support for Clinton (SUPPORTC) and conservatism (CONSERVA) varies as a function of how the senator voted on perjury (VOTE1), create a scatterplot of SUPPORTC by CONSERVA and Set Markers by VOTE1. Use your scatterplot to answer the following questions.

a) Describe the nature of the relationship, or indicate that there is not one, between state voter support for Clinton and conservatism for those senators who voted guilty on perjury.

b) Describe the nature of the relationship, or indicate that there is not one, between state voter support for Clinton and conservatism for those senators who voted not guilty on perjury.

Exercises 5.26 through 5.35 test conceptual understanding and do not require the use of SPSS.

5.26. The correlation between manual dexterity (X) and age from 2 to 80 years (Y) is $r = .08$. Nevertheless, the investigator was able to make reasonably accurate predictions of a person's manual dexterity score on the basis of his or her age. Explain how this could be possible.

5.27. What (if anything) is wrong with the following statement: "A Pearson Correlation Coefficient value of $r = .8$ between two variables represents twice the linear relationship that a Pearson Correlation Coefficient value of $r = .4$ represents."

5.28. Consider the following statements made by U.S. Education Secretary Richard Riley (1998) in an address to the American Mathematical Society: "A recent U.S. Department of Education report demonstrates that a challenging mathematics education can build real opportunities for students who might not otherwise have them. It found, for example, that young people who have taken gateway courses like Algebra I and Geometry go on to college at much higher rates than those who do not – 83 percent to 36 percent." Is it fair to conclude, based on this information, that we can increase the proportion of students who go to college by requiring all students to take these gateway courses?

5.29. What (if anything) is wrong with the following statements that appeared in *USA Today* online on October 9, 1998: "The number of American youths taking up smoking as a daily habit jumped 73 percent between Joe Camel's debut in 1988 and 1996, the government said Thursday. The Centers for Disease Control and Prevention said tobacco ads that rely heavily on giveaways and kid-friendly cartoons are partly to blame."

5.30. What (if anything) is wrong with the following statement: "A Pearson Correlation Coefficient value of $r = 1.05$ was found between two variables X and Y. This represents a very strong linear relationship between the two variables."

5.31. What (if anything) is wrong with the following statement about the NELS data: "The correlation between region and the number of Advanced Placement classes offered is $r = .11$, indicating that the higher the region, the more Advanced Placement courses offered, on average."

5.32. What (if anything) is wrong with the following statement: "If the correlation between X and Y is $r = .50$, then you can perform any linear transformation on the variable X and the correlation between the transformed X and Y is still $r = .50$."

5.33. What (if anything) is wrong with the following statement: "If the correlation between average math SAT and average verbal SAT for all 50 states is $r = .97$, it can be implied that the scores on the verbal portion are higher than the scores on the math portion."

5.34. Draw a scatterplot for which the Pearson Product Moment Correlation would not capture the true magnitude and nature of the relationship between the two variables.

5.35. The following questions relate to the scatterplot below, which shows the relationship between X and Y for four different subgroups. For each subgroup, select the Pearson Correlation Coefficient r, from the column at right, that best represents the relationship between X and Y for the subgroup. You may select a value more than once.

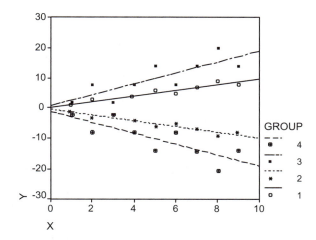

Group 1: _____   a) $r = 1.25$
                       b) $r = -1.25$
Group 2: _____   c) $r = .95$
                       d) $r = -.95$
Group 3: _____   e) $r = .82$
                       f) $r = -.82$
Group 4: _____   g) $r = 0$

(Exercise 5.35 continued)

CHAPTER SIX

Simple Linear Regression

In the preceding chapter, we remarked that, even when a strong linear correlation exists between two variables X and Y, it may not be possible to talk about either one of them as the cause of the other. Even so, there is nothing to keep us from using one of the variables to *predict* the other. In making predictions from one variable to another, the variable being predicted is called the *dependent variable* and the variable predicting the dependent variable is called the *independent variable*. The dependent variable may also be referred to as the *criterion* or *outcome*; the independent variable may also be referred to as the *predictor* or *regressor*. One way of facilitating such predictions is to obtain a linear equation that somehow fits, or represents, the available data. This equation can then be used to predict the variable Y from the variable X. It can also be used to *explain* the relationship between Y and X in more detail than correlation alone provides. In particular, the equation can be used to study how a change in one variable, X, relates to a change in the other variable, Y.

In this chapter, we introduce a technique for finding such a linear equation, called the *regression equation*, and measuring the extent to which it describes the data. As we will see, the stronger the correlation between X and Y, the more accurately Y can be predicted from X; the weaker the correlation, the less accurately Y can be predicted from X.

THE "BEST-FITTING" LINEAR EQUATION

If the linear relationship between X and Y were perfect, so that all points of the data set fell along a single straight line, the task of finding a linear equation that fits the given data exactly would be quite straightforward. With the help of some coordinate geometry, we could find the equation of the single straight line that passes through all the points.

In behavioral and social research, however, it is extremely unlikely to encounter data that are perfectly linearly related. The question we would like to investigate in this section is: "How do we find the best-fitting line to predict one variable from another when the two variables are not perfectly linearly related?" Let us return to the data from our McDonald's example reproduced here as Table 6.1. Recall that the Pearson Correlation Coefficient between fat and calories for these is .996.

Although $r = .996$ implies an extremely strong positive linear relationship between fat and calories, the fact that it is not a perfect linear relationship means that no one line passes exactly through all five points of the scatterplot. However, because such a strong correlation value implies that the relationship between fat (X) and calories (Y) is *almost* perfectly linear, there should be many lines that almost work. Three such lines are illustrated in Figure 6.1 with the scatterplot of our data.

Table 6.1. Fat grams and calories by type of McDonald's hamburgers

Type of McDonald's hamburger	Grams of fat (X)	Calories (Y)
Hamburger	10	270
Cheeseburger	14	320
Quarter Pounder	21	430
Quarter Pounder w/ Cheese	30	530
Big Mac	28	530

Because all three lines in Figure 6.1 (as well as many others) almost fit the data of Table 6.1, it would seem reasonable to use any one of them for prediction purposes. But which one is the best-fitting line, and how do we find its equation? The question of which line is best fitting is subjective and depends to a large extent on what we mean by "best." We might, for example, select the line that actually goes through as many of the points of the scatterplot as possible. But if we do this, the line might turn out to be very far from the points it does not pass through. The usual way of choosing a best-fitting line, and the one we use, is to take one that, on average, comes "closest" in terms of squared deviations to *all* the points of the scatterplot. Such a line is called a (least squares) *regression line* or

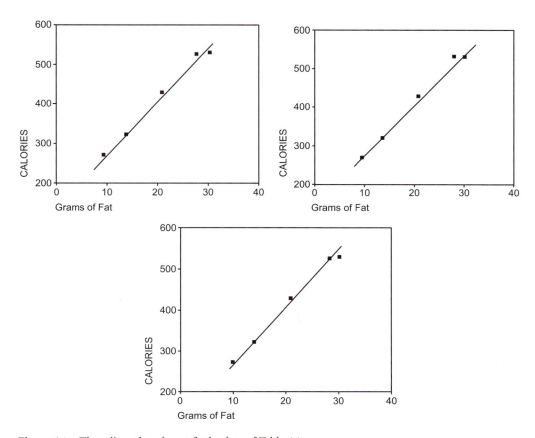

Figure 6.1   Three lines that almost fit the data of Table 6.1.

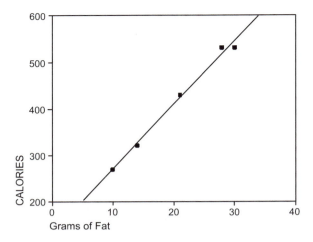

Figure 6.2 The regression line for the data of Table 6.1.

(least squares) *prediction line*, and its equation is called a (least squares) *linear regression equation*. Let us now see what is meant by a *deviation* and how we find the equation of the best-fitting line.

Suppose we have a line L that we think of using to predict calories (Y) from fat (X) for the data of Table 6.1 (see Figure 6.2). For each of our given X_i values ($i = 1, 2, 3, 4, 5$), let $\hat{Y}_i$ be the Y value that the equation of line L predicts from X_i (i.e., the value that is obtained when X_i is substituted into the equation of line L; or, equivalently, the value that when paired with X_i gives a point X_i, Y_i on line L). Then, because Y_i is the actual Y value paired with X_i, and $\hat{Y}_i$ is the Y value predicted by L to pair with X_i, their difference (or deviation) $d_i = Y_i - \hat{Y}_i$ is just the error of prediction (or error of estimate) at X_i when using L. Although we have been referring to errors of prediction as deviations, they are also more commonly referred to as *residuals*. Figure 6.3 zooms in on three pairs of X, Y values to provide a magnified view of their residuals.

Note that, for the three points of Figure 6.3, two residuals (d_i) are positive, whereas one is negative. Positive residuals indicate that the predicted Y value, $\hat{Y}$, is less than the actual

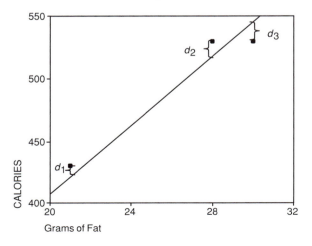

Figure 6.3 Residuals from the regression line: a magnified view using three points.

Y value, whereas negative residuals indicate that the predicted Y value, $\hat{Y}$, is greater than the actual Y value. If we obtained the sum of the residuals for all five pairs of values in our data set based on the regression line, the negative residuals would cancel out the positive residuals, resulting in the false impression that there is no error of prediction. To obtain a valid measure of error of prediction (one that avoids cancellation of positive with negative error terms), we could either take the absolute value of each term before summing, or we could square each error term before summing. These are exactly the two alternatives we faced in Chapter 3 when defining a measure of variability. As before, we choose to square each of the individual error terms d_i to obtain d_i^2 before summing. To make this squared index of error independent of the number of pairs of data values, we divide the sum of the d_i^2 by N to obtain what is called the *average squared deviation* (or *average squared* error) D^2 Finally, to bring the measure back to the original units of the data, we take the square root of D^2 and obtain D, the *standard error of estimate* or *prediction*:

$$D = \sqrt{\frac{\sum di^2}{N}} \tag{6.1}$$

We see that D is approximately the average vertical distance to the regression line in the same way that the standard deviation is approximately the average distance to the mean. We use D as our index of error of prediction for a given prediction line on a given set of data.

We now can define what we mean by the best-fitting line for a given set of data. The best-fitting line is the line that minimizes (or gives the smallest possible number for) the value of D for the given data. It is called the (least squares) *regression line* or (least squares) *prediction line*. The equation of the regression line is called the *linear regression equation*, and the criterion we use to define it (that of minimizing the value of D) is called the *least squares criterion*. Although the actual derivation of the equation for the regression line is beyond the scope of this book, the equation itself is really quite simple. Given a set of paired data (X, Y) with N pairs, the equation of the regression line (the linear regression equation) for predicting Y from X is

$$\hat{Y} = bX + a \tag{6.2}$$

where

$$b = r\frac{S_Y}{S_X} \tag{6.3}$$

$$a = \overline{Y} - b\overline{X} \tag{6.4}$$

In Equation 6.2, $\hat{Y}$ represents the predicted value for Y. The value of b for use in the linear regression equation to predict Y from X is called the *regression coefficient*. In Equation 6.2 the regression coefficient b represents the slope of the linear regression equation, and the constant a represents the Y-intercept.

While the regression equation, Equation 6.2, can be used to find the predicted Y for a given value of X, the values of b and a can be used to explain the relationship between X and Y.

Equation 6.3 shows the relationship between the slope of the regression equation, b, and the value of the Pearson Correlation Coefficient, r. Because standard deviation is always positive, we see that b and r always have the same sign. That is, if b is positive, then

Y increases with an increase in *X*, whereas if *b* is negative, *Y* decreases with an increase in *X*. Moreover, *b* can always be interpreted as the amount of change in $\hat{Y}$, on average, for each unit increase in *X*.

Equation 6.4 shows the relationship between the *Y*-intercept of the regression line, *a*, and the means of both *X* and *Y*. In particular, *a* is defined so that an *X* value equal to the mean of *X* would be predicted to have a *Y* value equal to the mean of *Y* – so that $(\overline{X}, \overline{Y})$ lies on the regression line. The value of *a* can be interpreted as the predicted *Y* for the value *X* = 0. Such an interpretation makes sense only when 0 is a reasonable value for the variable *X* and when data close to *X* = 0 have been collected.

☞ **Remark.** According to Equation 6.3, when *r* = 0 (i.e., the two variables are not linearly associated), *b* = 0 In this case, we see that $\hat{Y}$ is just the constant, $\overline{Y}$. Said differently, if *X* and *Y* are not linearly related, then, given any *X* value, the predicted *Y* value is simply the mean of *Y*.

☞ **Remark.** Suppose you were told that the mean height of ten-year-old girls is 4 feet 1 inch and that the mean weight for ten-year-old girls is 82 pounds. Alice is a ten-year-old girl who is 4 feet 1 inch tall. Based on this information alone, what would you predict Alice's weight to be? If you said 82 pounds, the mean weight for ten-year-old girls, you would agree with the prediction that would be obtained from the linear regression equation for predicting weight from height for ten-year-old girls.

EXAMPLE 6.1. Given the data of Table 6.1, use SPSS to obtain the linear regression equation for predicting calories (*Y*) from fat content (*X*) in two ways. (1) Derive the regression equation from Equations 6.2 through 6.4 using SPSS to obtain the required values. (2) Derive the equation directly using SPSS. (3) Interpret the slope and, if meaningful, the intercept of the regression equation. (4) Create a scatterplot and edit it in SPSS to include the regression line. (5) Use the regression line found in parts (1) and (2) and the graph of the regression line found in part (4) to find the predicted number of calories for a McDonald's hamburger with fat content of 28 grams.

Solution.

1) Using SPSS Descriptives and Correlation procedures, we find that $\overline{X}$ = 20.6 grams, S_X = 8.65 grams, $\overline{Y}$ = 416 calories, S_Y = 119.08 calories, and r_{XY} = .996. We need to use these values to find *a* and *b*.

   Using Equation 6.3, we find that $b = r\dfrac{S_Y}{S_X} = .996\,\dfrac{119.08}{8.65} = 13.71$

   Using Equation 6.4, we find that $a = \overline{Y} - b\overline{X} = 416 - (13.71)(20.6) = 133.57$
   Equation 6.2 gives the general form of the regression equation: $\hat{Y} = bX + a$.
   Substituting for *a* and *b*, we have

   $$\hat{Y} = 13.71X + 133.57 \quad \text{or} \quad \hat{Y} = 13.71(\text{FAT}) + 133.57.$$

2)

To perform a regression analysis using SPSS, go to **Analyze** on the main menu bar, **Regression**, **Linear**. Put CALORIES in the box for the **Dependent variable** and FAT in the box for the **Independent variable**. Click **OK**.

Coefficientsᵃ

Model	Unstandardized Coefficients		Standardized Coefficients		
	B	Std. Error	Beta	t	Sig.
1 (Constant) fat	133.576	16.125		8.284	.004
Grams of Fat	13.170	.733	.996	18.709	.000

ᵃDependent Variable: calories.

Figure 6.4 Coefficient information for the simple linear regression equation.

The part of the output relevant for finding the regression equation is reproduced in Figure 6.4.

Note that b is given as the "Unstandardized Coefficient" for FAT, which equals approximately 13.71, and a is given as the "Unstandardized Coefficient" for the "Constant," which equals approximately 133.58. These agree, within rounding, with the values obtained in part (1).

As before, we write the regression equation using Equation 6.2:

$$\hat{Y} = 13.71X + 133.58 \quad \text{or} \quad \hat{Y} = 13.71(\text{FAT}) + 133.58.$$

3) The slope of 13.71 tells us that each additional gram of fat is associated with 13.71 additional calories on average. The intercept of 133.57 is not meaningful because none of the hamburgers in the data set had close to 0 grams of fat, so that the value $X = 0$ is beyond the range of the data.

4)

To use SPSS to edit the scatterplot to include the regression line, obtain a scatterplot using **Graphs** on the main menu bar, **Scatter**, and **Define**. Put CALORIES in the box for the **Y-Axis** and FAT in the box for the **X-Axis**. Click **OK**. Once the graph appears in the Output Navigator, click it twice to go into Edit Mode. Click **Chart** on the edit menu bar, **Options**. In the box marked "Fit Line," click the box next to **Total**. Click **OK**.

The regression line should appear as it does in Figure 6.2.

5) To find the predicted calorie content of a hamburger with 28 grams of fat using the regression equation, we substitute the value $X = 28$ into $13.71X + 133.57$:

$$\hat{Y} = (13.71)(28) + 133.57 = 517.45.$$

Thus, we predict that a hamburger with 28 grams of fat has approximately 517 calories. To estimate the predicted calorie content of a hamburger with 28 grams of fat using the scatterplot of the regression equation, we approximate the location of $X = 28$ on the horizontal axis, read up to the regression line, and then read across to the predicted number of calories. We get the less accurate estimate of approximately 520 calories.

Note in Table 6.1 that there actually *was* a hamburger in our original data set for which the fat content was 28 grams, and for that amount of fat there is 530 calories. According to Example 6.1, however, we would predict the number of calories to be approximately 517. Because of this discrepancy between actual and predicted *Y* values, a question arises. In which of these two values (517 or 530) can we place more confidence when making predictions about different types of hamburger at McDonald's for which the fat content is 28 grams?

Recall that our interest was in developing a *general* prediction model based on the available data – a model that could then be used to make predictions in similar situations occurring in the future. By making the simplifying assumption that our prediction model should be linear and by *making use of all the available data*, we were able to develop the linear regression equation that is just such a general prediction model. Clearly, predictions made using the linear regression equation (which is based on *all* the available data) can be made with more confidence than predictions made using other prediction systems that are *not* based on all the available data. Therefore, it follows that we can place more confidence in a prediction based on the linear regression equation than on a prediction based on a single observation.

THE ACCURACY OF PREDICTION USING THE LINEAR REGRESSION MODEL

Our goal in this section is to show the relationship between the Pearson Correlation Coefficient *r* and the standard error of estimate or prediction, *D*.

Recall that *r* was introduced in Chapter 5 as a measure of the linear relationship between two variables and that the more the points of the scatterplot conform to a straight line, the closer the value of *r* is to a perfect correlation of either -1 or $+1$. Recall further that *D* was introduced as a measure of how well a given linear equation fits a set of data and that the linear regression equation was defined as the particular linear equation that minimized *D*. From now on we reserve the symbol *D* to indicate the standard error of estimate based on the linear regression equation, not just any linear equation. Because the linear regression equation is the best-fitting line for the points of the scatterplot and *D* is the measure of error of fit for this best-fitting line, it is clear that, when *r* is close to a perfect correlation value of $+1$ or -1, the regression line should fit the scatterplot almost perfectly and consequently the value of *D* should be close to zero. Thus, an inverse relationship between *D* and the magnitude of *r* is suggested. Namely, when the magnitude of *r* is small (*r* near 0), *D* should be large; when the magnitude of *r* is large (*r* near $+1$ or -1, *D* should be small. Because it is the magnitude (not the sign) of *r* that is apparently inversely related to *D*, we might obtain a better indication of this relationship by comparing *D* with r^2 rather than with *r*. There is, in fact, a simple equation that relates the values of *D* and r^2 for a given set of *X*, *Y* data pairs:

$$D = \sqrt{S_Y^2(1 - r_{XY}^2)} \tag{6.5}$$

where S_Y^2 is the variance of the given *Y* values.

From Equation 6.5, it should now be clear that, in general, the closer *r* is to a perfect correlation, the more accurate the prediction equation is for the data on which it is based. It is tempting to infer that the more accurate the prediction equation is for the data on which it is based (the closer *r* is to a perfect correlation), the more accurate we can expect it to be when we are using it to make predictions in the future under similar circumstances. Although this inference is usually a valid one, many factors (such as the number of pairs of data values on which the linear regression equation is based) influence the relationship between the magnitude of r and the accuracy of prediction in the future. These factors involve an understanding that we have not as yet acquired of the basic concepts of inferential statistics. We must therefore postpone a more complete discussion of linear regression analysis until Chapter 14.

THE STANDARDIZED REGRESSION EQUATION

When the regression analysis is computed on the standardized variables z_X and z_Y (the z-score transformations of X and Y), the resulting equation takes the form

$$\hat{z}_Y = rz_X \tag{6.6}$$

Equation 6.6 is a simplification of Equation 6.2 because, for standard scores, $\bar{z}_X = \bar{z}_Y$ $z = 0$ and $S_{z_X} = S_{z_Y} = 1$. The slope of the standardized regression equation is denoted as β, the Greek letter beta.

As shown in Equation 6.6, $\beta = r$ in the case where there is only one independent variable (simple linear regression). Not surprisingly, therefore, the value of β is given as .996 in Figure 6.4. The value of r between X and Y is also .996.

The standard score regression equation is not particularly useful for making predictions, because scores are generally given in raw form. When we study multiple regression in Chapter 15, we see how β may be used to assess the relative importance of the independent variables in the equation.

R AS A MEASURE OF THE OVERALL FIT OF THE LINEAR REGRESSION MODEL

As part of the regression output, SPSS provides a model summary. For now, we limit our discussion of that summary to the value of R, which is the correlation between the actual and predicted values of Y. For the McDonald's example, the summary is provided in Figure 6.5.

In the McDonald's example, $R = r$. That is, in this example, the correlation between Y and $\hat{Y}$ is the same as the correlation between Y and X. This is also the case in Example 6.4.

Figure 6.5   Model summary for simple linear regression.

Model Summary

Model	R	R Square	Adjusted R Square	Std. Error of the Estimate
1	.996[a]	.992	.989	12.676

[a]Predictors: (Constant), fat Grams of Fat.

Model Summary

Model	R	R Square	Adjusted R Square	Std. Error of the Estimate
1	.996[a]	.992	.989	12.68

[a]Predictors: (Constant), Grams of Fat.

However, as we shall see in Example 6.3, it is not generally true in simple linear regression that $R = r$. Because R is always positive, $R = r$ only when r is positive. When r is negative, then $R = -r$. In general, we may say that $R = |r|$, the absolute value of r.

EXAMPLE 6.2. (1) Use SPSS to find the predicted values, $\hat{Y}$, for the McDonald's example. (2) Find the correlation between predicted calories ($\hat{Y}$) and calories (Y) and compare this value to the correlation between fat content (X) and calories (Y). (3) Construct a scatterplot of Y and $\hat{Y}$ and of X and $\hat{Y}$.

Solution.

1)

To use SPSS to find the predicted values we use the Regression procedure. Go to **Analyze** on the main menu bar, **Regression**, **Linear**. Put CALORIES in the box for the **Dependent variable** and FAT in the box for the **Independent variable**. Click **Save** and in the box labeled **Predicted Values**, click the box next to **Unstandardized**. Click **Continue**, and **OK**. In the data window, you will see that a new variable, PRE_1, has been created that gives predicted calories for each hamburger.

These values are provided in Table 6.2.

2) Using the SPSS Correlation procedure, we find that the correlation between fat and calories $r_{XY} = .996$ and that the correlation between predicted calories and calories $r_{Y\hat{Y}} = .996$.

☞ **Remark.** In the McDonald's example, the correlation between fat content (X) and calories (Y) is equal to the correlation between predicted calories ($\hat{Y}$) and calories (Y). In general, that is not true. Because, in simple linear regression, $R = |r|$, R and r have the same magnitude, but they may not have the same sign.

3) The scatterplot between Y and $\hat{Y}$ is given below.

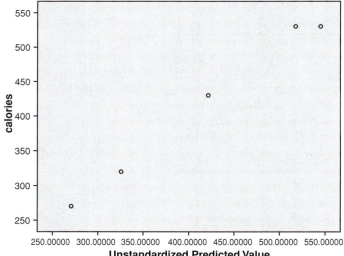

Table 6.2. Predicted values for the McDonald's example

Type	Fat	Calories	Pre_1
Hamburger	10	270	270.67513
Cheeseburger	14	320	325.51471
Quarter Pounder™	21	430	421.48396
Quarter Pounder with Cheese™	30	530	544.87299
Big Mac™	28	530	517.45321

Conceptually, it makes sense that the correlation between the actual and predicted values of Y is always positive. It is desirable for high actual values to be associated with high predicted values and for low actual values to be associated with low predicted values. Hence, the correlation between Y and $\hat{Y}$ is always be positive.

The scatterplot of X and $\hat{Y}$ is given below.

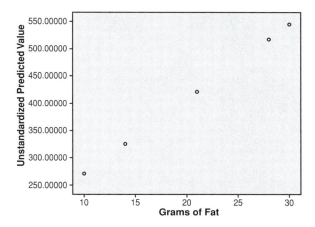

Notice that the points fall along a perfect straight line with positive slope, indicating that the correlation between X and $\hat{Y}$ is +1. This is because $\hat{Y}$ is defined as a linear transformation of X ($bX + a$) for which b is positive. If b were negative, the line would have a negative slope and the correlation would be −1.

R does not enhance our understanding of the overall fit of the regression equation to our data over and above r in the case of simple regression. The situation is different in multiple regression, as discussed in Chapter 15.

EXAMPLE 6.3. In Chapter 5, we performed a correlation analysis to determine that, in the United States, the average SAT verbal score of a state (SATV) is inversely related to the percentage of students who have taken the SAT in that state (PERTAK). In this example, we perform a regression analysis to predict the average SAT verbal score for these states, and use it to answer the following questions.

1) Why is a regression analysis appropriate for these data?
2) Write down the regression equation for predicting the SAT math score from the percentage of students who have taken the SAT in the state.

3) What is the value of the intercept of this regression equation and what is its interpretation within the context of this problem?
4) What is the value of the slope of this regression equation and what is its interpretation within the context of this problem?
5) Use the regression equation to predict the average SAT math score for a state where 25 percent of the students take the SAT.
6) Construct a scatterplot of Y and $\hat{Y}$ and compare that scatterplot to the scatterplot constructed in part (1). What does this comparison imply about the relationship between R and r?

Solution.

1) To determine whether regression analysis is appropriate, we construct the scatterplot, add the fit line, and note that the pattern of the points is linear, confirming that regression analysis is appropriate for these data. The scatterplot is produced below.

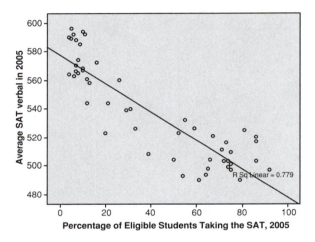

2) We use the SPSS regression procedure. We see from the coefficients table, reproduced below, that the regression equation is $\hat{Y} = -.995\,(\text{PERTAK}) + 577.725$, where $\hat{Y} =$ predicted SATV.

Coefficients[a]

Model	Unstandardized Coefficients		Standaridized Coefficients		
	B	Std. Error	Beta	t	Sig.
1 (Constant) pertak	577.725	3.819		151.291	.000
Percentage of Eligible Students Taking the SAT, 2005	−.995	.076	−.883	−13.147	.000

[a]Dependent Variable: satv Average SAT verbal in 2005.

3) The value of the intercept is 577.73. The intercept indicates the predicted average SATV score when a state has no students taking the SAT. In this case, it is impossible for a state to have an average if no students take the SAT, and so the intercept is not meaningful.

4) The value of the slope is $-.995$. The slope indicates that every additional 1-point increase in the percentage of students taking the SAT in the state is associated with a .995-point decrease in the average SATV score for the state.

5) $\hat{Y} = -.995(25) + 577.726 = 522.851$

6) The scatterplot of Y and $\hat{Y}$ is given below. It suggests a positive relationship between Y and $\hat{Y}$ in contrast to the scatterplot given in part (1), which suggests a negative relationship between X and Y. Hence, whereas R, a measure of the relationship between Y and $\hat{Y}$, is positive, r, a measure of the relationship between X and Y is negative in this case. Because we know from the coefficients table in part (2) that $\beta = -.883$ and we know that $\beta = r$, we know that $r = -.883$. Because $R = |r|$, we know that $R = .883$, as expected from the positive linear shape of the scatterplot.

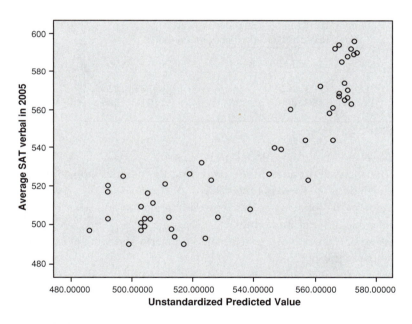

SIMPLE LINEAR REGRESSION WHEN THE INDEPENDENT VARIABLE IS DICHOTOMOUS

In this section we present an example of simple linear regression when the independent variable is dichotomous and we highlight the connection between the strength of a correlation and the difference between the means on the continuous variable of the two groups represented by the dichotomy.

EXAMPLE 6.4. In Example 6.1 we were concerned with obtaining a regression equation that predicts calories from fat content. In this example, we wish to predict calories from whether or not the hamburger contains cheese. Table 6.3 contains the data for our example. Notice that variable X, representing the presence of cheese, equals 1 when cheese is present and 0 otherwise. Variable X is therefore a dichotomous variable.

Table 6.3. Calories and cheese content by type of McDonald's hamburgers		
Type of McDonald's hamburger	Cheese? (X)	Calories (Y)
Hamburger	0	270
Cheeseburger	1	320
Quarter Pounder	0	430
Quarter Pounder w/ Cheese	1	530
Big Mac	1	530

A regression analysis is performed to predict the number of calories based on whether or not the hamburger contains cheese. The coefficients table from the SPSS output is provided below. Use it to respond to the following items.

Coefficients[a]

Model		Unstandardized Coefficients		Standardized Coefficients	t	Sig.
		B	Std. Error	Beta		
1	(Constant)	350.000	83.865		4.173	.025
	cheese	110.000	108.269	.506	1.016	.384

[a]Dependent Variable: calories.

1) What is the correlation between calories and cheese?
2) Write down the regression equation for predicting the calories from the presence of cheese. How well does the model fit the data?
3) What is the value of the intercept of this regression equation and what is its interpretation within the context of this problem?
4) What is the value of the slope of this regression equation and what is its interpretation within the context of this problem?
5) Compute the mean number of calories for hamburgers with cheese.
6) Use the regression equation to predict the calorie content of a burger with cheese.
7) Compute the mean number of calories for hamburgers without cheese.
8) Use the regression equation to predict the calorie content of a burger without cheese.
9) What is the difference in calorie content between a burger with cheese and one without cheese? How is this reflected in the regression equation?
10) Construct a scatterplot with the names of the different hamburgers as case labels and superimpose the regression fit line on the total plot.
11) Use the graph you constructed in part (10) to determine the sign of the residual for the cheeseburger.

Solution.

1) $r = .506$.
2) $\hat{Y} = 110$ (CHEESE) $+350$, where $\hat{Y} =$ predicted calories. Note that CHEESE takes on the values 0 and 1. The correlation of $r = .506$ is strong, indicating that the model fits the data well.

3) The value of the intercept is 350. The intercept indicates the predicted Y value when $X = 0$. In this case it indicates that when CHEESE = 0, that is, when the burger does not have cheese, the predicted number of calories is 350.

4) The value of the slope is 110. The slope indicates the change in the predicted Y value for a unit increase in the X value. In this case, it indicates that a unit increase in the value of CHEESE is associated with a 110-calorie increase; that is, a burger with cheese is predicted to have 110 more calories than a burger without cheese.

5) The mean number of calories for hamburgers with cheese may be found using the regression equation. A burger with cheese has the value CHEESE = 1. Substituting that into the regression equation, we obtain $\hat{Y} = 110(1) + 350 = 460$.

6) The predicted number of calories for hamburgers is 460, the mean number of calories for hamburgers with cheese.

7) The mean number of calories for hamburgers without cheese is found using the regression equation. A burger without cheese has the value CHEESE = 0. Substituting that into the regression equation, we obtain $\hat{Y} = 110(0) + 350 = 350$.

8) The predicted number of calories for hamburgers without cheese equals 350, the mean number of calories for hamburgers without cheese.

9) The difference in calories between a burger with cheese and one without is $460 - 350 = 110$. This is the value of the slope of the regression equation as explained in part (4).

10) To obtain the graph using SPSS:

Select **Graphs**, **Legacy Dialogs, Scatterplot, Define**. Assign CALORIES to the **Y-axis** and CHEESE to the **X-axis** and NAME to **Label Cases by**. Click **OK**. Once the Graph appears double click on it to get into the Chart Editor. Click **Elements**, **Fit Line at Total,** and **Elements, Show Data Labels**. Close the Chart Editor. The following graph should appear.

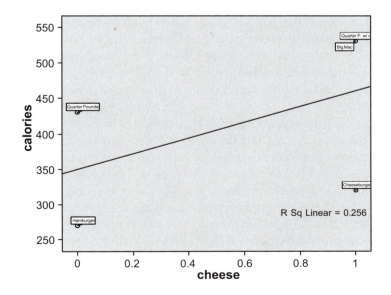

11) The actual number of calories for a cheeseburger is lower than the value that is predicted by the model, so the residual is negative.

☞ **Remark.** We should point out that, as reflected by the equation for the point biserial correlation coefficient (Equation 5.5), the stronger the correlation between the dichotomous variable (CHEESE, in this case) and the dependent variable (CALORIES, in this case), the greater the separation between the means on the dependent variable for the two groups represented by the dichotomous variable (relative to the spread). Here the means of the two groups are 460 and 350. If the spread of the calories in each group stayed the same, but the mean of 460 was now 500, the correlation between CHEESE and CALORIES would be even stronger than what it is now.

USING *r* AND *R* AS MEASURES OF EFFECT SIZE

The *effect size* of the simple linear regression model refers to the strength of the linear relationship between the two variables. As we have seen, one measure of effect size for the linear relationship is r, the Pearson Correlation Coefficient between the variables, and we have used Cohen's scale to evaluate the size of the effect. We also have noted that, when the independent variable is dichotomous, the difference between means on the continuous dependent variable relative to the spread may be expressed as a correlation coefficient. Accordingly, the correlation coefficient is a good measure of effect size for simple linear regression, whether it is used to assess the strength of a linear relationship between two variables or the difference between the means of two groups relative to spread. Because r and R always have the same magnitude, either may be used to express the size of the effect.

EMPHASIZING THE IMPORTANCE OF THE SCATTERPLOT

Throughout this book we have made the point that summary statistics may be misleading if the data they are purported to characterize are anomalous (if, for example, they contain outliers or are skewed in other ways). The linear regression model is no exception. Because the regression model serves to characterize, in summary form, the linear relationship between two variables as a line with intercept and slope, it too may be misleading or in some way may fail to capture the salient features of the data. The use of graphical displays is critical in the process of assessing how appropriate a given model is for describing a set of data.

To illustrate, we consider the four panels of X, Y pairs located in Table 6.4 (Anscombe, 1973). For all panels, the respective X and Y means, X and Y standard deviations, and correlations, slopes, intercepts, and standard errors of estimate are equal. In particular, for each of the four panels, $\overline{X} = 9.0$, $\overline{Y} = 7.5$, $S_X = 3.17$, $S_Y = 1.94$ (according to our formula, not SPSS), the equation of regression line is $\hat{Y} = 0.5X + 3$, the standard error of the estimate is 1.12, and $r_{XY} = .82$. Accordingly, without a visual representation of these four panels, one might assume that the statistics from all four panels summarize the same data set. Yet, if we look at the four scatterplots of Figures 6.6(a) through (d), we see to what extent these data sets are different from one another.

Table 6.4. Anscombe's data in four panels

I		II		III		IV	
X	Y	X	Y	X	Y	X	Y
10.0	8.04	10.0	9.14	10.0	7.46	8.0	6.58
8.0	6.95	8.0	8.14	8.0	6.77	8.0	5.76
13.0	7.58	13.0	8.74	13.0	12.74	8.0	7.71
9.0	8.81	9.0	8.77	9.0	7.11	8.0	8.84
11.0	8.33	11.0	9.26	11.0	7.81	8.0	8.47
14.0	9.96	14.0	8.10	14.0	8.84	8.0	7.04
6.0	7.24	6.0	6.13	6.0	6.08	8.0	5.25
4.0	4.26	4.0	3.10	4.0	5.39	19.0	12.50
12.0	10.84	12.0	9.13	12.0	8.15	8.0	5.56
7.0	4.82	7.0	7.26	7.0	6.42	8.0	7.91
5.0	5.68	5.0	4.74	5.0	5.73	8.0	6.89

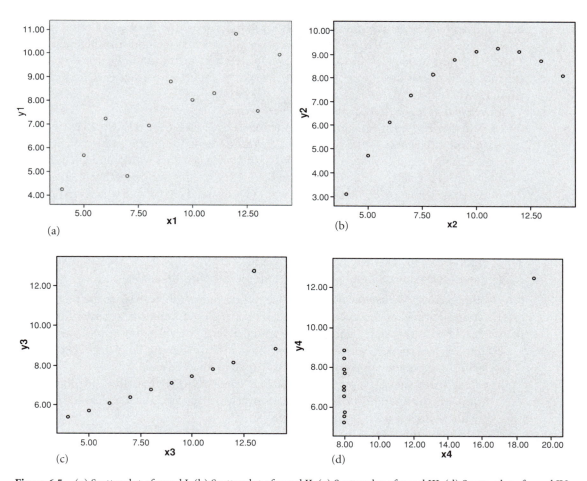

(a) (b) (c) (d)

Figure 6.5 (a) Scatterplot of panel I. (b) Scatterplot of panel II. (c) Scatterplot of panel III. (d) Scatterplot of panel IV.

In only one case, that of panel (a), is the linear model a good characterization of the underlying data. In panel (b) nonlinearity is a salient feature, yet that feature is not captured by the linear regression model. In panel (c), the presence of the outlier, perhaps due to an error in data entry, unduly influences the result of the analysis and, in so doing, compromises what otherwise would have been a perfectly fitting model. Finally, the regression model in panel (d) exists only because of the single outlier. Without this outlier, we would have been unable to fit a nonvertical line to these data at all.

Although the correlation coefficient in all four panels is $r = .82$, which by itself suggests a strong linear relationship between the X,Y pairs and a good-fitting linear model, our visual displays tell us otherwise. The moral of this story is to beware of summary statistics without accompanying visual representations!

EXERCISES

Exercises 6.1 through 6.7 involve simple linear regression models between variables that are interval- or ratio-level.

6.1. In Exercise 5.6, we used the States data set to determine that there was a positive linear relationship between EDUCEXPE, the average educational expenditure per pupil, and TEACHPAY, the average salary of public school teachers in the state. In this exercise, we expand on that relationship to create and interpret a model to predict EDUCEXPE from TEACHPAY.

a) Verify that regression is appropriate in this case.

b) Find the regression equation for predicting EDUCEXPE from TEACHPAY.

c) Interpret the value of the slope of the regression equation in the context of this exercise using language that someone who hasn't taken statistics would understand.

d) Interpret the value of the intercept in the context of this exercise using language that someone who hasn't taken statistics would understand or indicate why it is not meaningful.

e) What is the predicted educational expenditure for a state with teacher pay of $40,000?

f) Is it appropriate to use the regression equation to find the predicted educational expenditure for a state with teacher pay of $70,000?

g) Report the value of R and interpret it in the context of this analysis.

6.2. In this exercise, we use the States data set to find the variables that are the best predictors, in a linear sense, of the variable TEACHPAY, which gives the average salary of public school teachers in the state. The possible independent variables are pupils per teacher (STUTEACH), average SAT verbal (SATV), and expenditure per pupil (EDUCEXPE).

a) Is linear regression appropriate for these three models? Explain.

b) Of the three variables, pupils per teacher, average SAT verbal, and expenditure per pupil, which would be the best predictor of teacher salary using the technique of simple linear regression?

c) Would it be appropriate to perform a simple linear regression analysis to create a model to predict the average teacher pay for the state from the pupils per teacher? Explain.

d) Explain why it would not be appropriate to use REGION as an independent variable for the prediction of TEACHPAY.

6.3. Using the NELS data set, can twelfth-grade math achievement (ACHMAT12) be predicted by eighth-grade socioeconomic status (SES) for students in the NELS data set? Perform a regression analysis using SPSS and use the results to answer the questions that follow.

a) Create a scatterplot of ACHMAT12 by SES. Edit the graph to include the regression line. Determine that regression is an appropriate technique to use for predicting ACHMAT12 from SES.

b) What is the regression equation for predicting ACHMAT12 from SES?

c) Is there a way to interpret the slope that is meaningful in the context of this analysis? If so, explain what additional information it provides.

d) Is there a way to interpret the Y-intercept that is meaningful in the context of this analysis? If so, explain what additional information it provides.

e) What is the predicted twelfth-grade math achievement score of a student with SES = 20?

f) For the first student in the NELS data set (ID = 1), what is the value of the actual twelfth-grade math achievement score?

g) For the first student in the NELS data set (ID = 1), what is the value of the predicted twelfth-grade math achievement score?

6.4. Use the Impeach data set to perform a simple linear regression analysis to predict the conservatism of the senator (CONSERVA) based on his or her state's voter support for Clinton (SUPPORTC). Use it to answer the following questions.

a) Create a scatterplot and use it to verify that the data have an approximately linear shape.

b) What is the correlation, r, between conservatism and state voter support for Clinton?

c) What is the value of R, a measure of the goodness of fit of the regression model to the data? Describe the goodness of fit for this example.

d) Write down the linear regression equation for predicting conservatism (Y) from the state voter support for Clinton (X).

e) What is the interpretation of the slope of the regression equation in the context of this analysis?

f) Interpret the Y-intercept or constant within the context of this analysis, or explain why it is not meaningful.

g) Use the regression equation to predict the conservatism score for a senator with voter support (the percent of the vote Clinton received in the 1996 presidential election in the senator's state) of 50.

6.5. The following scatterplot, created using variables from the Framingham data set, shows the relationship between initial body mass index (BMI1) and initial diastolic blood pressure (DIABP1). The points are labeled by the ID number of the person. Use the scatterplot to answer the following questions.

a) Is linear regression appropriate to analyze the relationship between these variables? Explain.

b) Is the slope of the regression line positive, negative, or near zero? What does that tell you about the relationship between the variables involved?

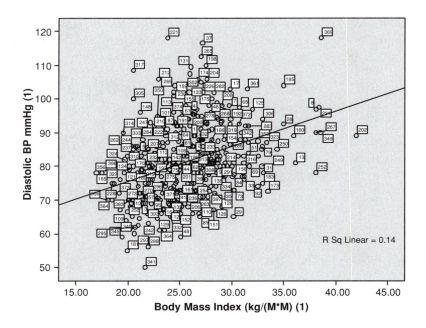

c) Use the regression line in the scatterplot to estimate the initial diastolic blood pressure of a person with an initial body mass index of 19.

d) Explain why the regression model should not be used to estimate the initial diastolic blood pressure of a person with an initial body mass index of 50.

6.6. In this exercise, we use scatterplots created using the Framingham data set to compare the relationship between initial body mass index (BMI1) with initial diastolic blood pressure (DIABP1) to the relationship between initial body mass index (BMI1) with initial heart rate (HEARTRTE1).

a) Create two scatterplots, one depicting the relationship between BMI1 and DIABP1 and the other depicting the relationship between BMI1 and HEARTRTE1. Add the regression line to both scatterplots.

b) Based on the scatterplots, which relationship with BMI has the stronger Pearsons r value, diastolic blood pressure or heart rate? Explain.

c) On average, is a one-unit increase in BMI associated with a greater increase in diastolic blood pressure or heart rate?

6.7. Select those people in the Framingham data set who are not on blood pressure medication at period 1 (BPMEDS1 = 0).

a) Construct a scatterplot of SYSBP1 by AGE1 and set markers by SEX. Super-impose fit lines at subgroups.

b) Construct, for each sex, a regression equation to predict systolic blood pressure (SYSBP1) from age (AGE1).

c) Interpret results.

d) Comment on the goodness of fit of each regression line.

e) Use the respective regression lines to predict the systolic blood pressure for a man and a woman who are each 50 years old.

Exercises 6.8 and 6.9 involve residual analysis for simple linear regression.

6.8. In Exercise 6.1, we used the States data set to create and interpret a model to predict EDUC-EXPE from TEACHPAY. In this exercise, we examine and interpret some of the residuals.

    a) For Alabama, the first state in the data set, what is the predicted average educational expenditure for the state?

    b) For Alabama, the first state in the data set, what is the actual average educational expenditure for the state?

    c) For Alabama, the first state in the data set, what is the value of the residual?

    d) Does the model over- or underpredict the value of EDUCEXPE for Alabama?

    e) What state deviates the most from the model?

    f) What is the value of the largest positive residual in the data set? To what state does it correspond? Does the model over- or underpredict the value of EDUCEXPE for this state?

    g) Was there a larger residual (in magnitude) for the first or second state in the data set?

6.9. In this exercise, we use the Framingham data set to create and interpret the residuals from a scatterplot of the linear regression equation to predict the initial total cholesterol (TOTCHOL1) from the initial body mass index (BMI1).

    a) Create the scatterplot between these two variables. Label the scatterplot by ID number and superimpose the regression line.

    b) Would you say that linear regression is appropriate in this case? Explain.

    c) Based on the scatterplot, approximate the predicted serum cholesterol for the person with ID = 165.

    d) Based on the scatterplot, approximate the actual serum cholesterol for the person with ID = 165.

    e) Based on the scatterplot, approximate the residual serum cholesterol for the person with ID = 165.

    f) According to the scatterplot, which person is most unusual in terms of the linear trend between serum cholesterol and BMI? What is his or her ID number? Looking at the data set, is this person male or female? How old was this person when the study began?

    g) With all people included in the data set, what is the slope of the regression line?

    h) With the bivariate outlier identified in part (f) omitted, what is the slope of the regression line? Does the b-value change as a result of omitting this person from the data set?

Exercises 6.10 and 6.11 involve the use of linear transformations.

6.10. Perform a simple linear regression analysis using the Learndis data set with reading comprehension score (READCOMP) as the dependent variable and grade level (GRADE) as the independent variable.

    a) What is the regression equation to predict the reading comprehension score from the grade level of the student?

    b) Recall that in Exercise 4.18(b) you created a linear transformation to convert GRADE to AGE. Use it to find the regression equation to predict the reading comprehension score from the age of the student.

    c) Why do you suppose that the slope of the regression line does not change, in this case?

    d) Why do you suppose that the intercept is 16.725 points larger for the model with AGE as the independent variable?

6.11. The variable SCHATTRT in the NELS data set gives the average daily attendance percentage for the school that the student attends.

   a) Find the regression equation to predict SLFCNC08 from SCHATTRT. Find also the means and standard deviations of SLFCNC08 and SCHATTRT.

   b) If we were to transform SCHATTRT by dividing its values by 100 we would create a variable SCHATTPP that gives the average daily attendance proportion for the school that the student attends. Using the information obtained in part (a), find the regression equation to predict SLFCNC08 from SCHATTPP.

Exercise 6.12 involves the use of nonlinear transformations in simple linear regression.

6.12. In this exercise, we create a model to predict SES from expected income at age 30 (EXPINC30).

   a) Conduct initial univariate and bivariate analyses of the variables involved in the multiple regression model.

   b) Use the square root and log transformations to diminish the severe negative skew in the variable EXPINC30. Which, if any, are effective?

   c) Perform a correlation analysis to determine the variable that is most highly correlated with SES, the untransformed expected income or the log or square root transformation of the variable.

   d) Of the three expected income variables correlated with SES in part (c), select the one that gives the best-fitting regression model for predicting SES and construct that model.

   e) Use your regression equation to predict the SES of a student who predicted that he or she would earn $75,000 a year at age 30.

Exercises 6.13 and 6.14 involve simple linear regression when the independent variable is dichotomous.

6.13. In this exercise, we use the NELS data set to create a model to predict SES from eighth-grade computer ownership (COMPUTER), a dichotomous variable.

   a) Create the scatterplot between SES and COMPUTER, using an Interactive scatterplot so the COMPUTER axis is nicely labeled.

   b) What is the regression equation for predicting SES from computer ownership?

   c) Interpret the slope of the regression equation in the context of this analysis.

   d) Interpret the intercept of the regression equation in the context of this analysis or indicate why it would not be meaningful to do so.

   e) Use the regression equation to predict the SES of students who owned a computer in eighth grade.

   f) Use the regression equation to predict the SES of students who did not own a computer in eighth grade.

   g) Use SPSS to find the mean SES of students who did and those who did not own a computer in eighth grade.

   h) If the coding of COMPUTER had been changed into the variable COMP1, with 1 representing students that did not own a computer and 2 representing those that did, what would be the regression equation for predicting SES from COMP1?

   i) If the coding of COMPUTER had been changed into the variable COMP2, with 1 representing students that did not own a computer and 0 representing those that did, what would be the regression equation for predicting SES from COMP2?

   j) Is it ever not meaningful to interpret the intercept of the regression equation in the case of an independent dichotomous variable?

6.14. Students in an introductory college statistics course took the Survey of Attitudes Toward Statistics (Schau et al., 1995), a regression model was conducted to predict VALUE (attitudes about the usefulness, relevance, and worth of statistics in personal and professional life, rated on the average of several 1–7 Likert-scale items) from GENDER (coded with 1 representing male and 2 representing female). The regression equation is $\hat{Y} = .573(\text{GENDER}) + 4.059$. You do not have this data set, so you must use the given regression equation and the coding to answer the following questions.

    a) What is the sign of the correlation between GENDER and VALUE?

    b) Which gender tended to give a higher rating to the value of the course?

    c) What is the predicted VALUE score for females?

    d) What is the average VALUE score for males?

Exercises 6.15 through 6.25 involve a variety of regression topics. For each question, select the most appropriate answer from among the response alternatives.

6.15. If $r = 0$, and one were asked to predict Y for a given value of X, the best prediction of Y, in a least squares sense, would be:

    a) The mean of all the X values

    b) The mean of all the Y values

    c) The given X value

    d) None of the above

6.16. If there is a positive linear correlation between X and Y, then we know that the regression equation for predicting Y from X has a

    a) positive slope

    b) negative slope

    c) positive Y-intercept

    d) negative Y-intercept

6.17. The degree to which the points of a scatterplot cluster about the regression line predicting Y from X is reflected by

    a) The correlation between X and Y

    b) The standard error of prediction

    c) The slope of the regression equation, b

    d) Both (a) and (b)

    e) Both (a) and (c)

    f) Both (b) and (c)

    g) (a), (b), and (c)

6.18. A regression line for predicting Y from X always

    a) Passes through the origin (0,0)

    b) Passes through $(\overline{X}, \overline{Y})$

    c) Has a positive slope, b

    d) Has a positive Y-intercept, a

6.19. If the correlation coefficient between X and Y is $r = .60$, and the standard deviations of the Y scores and the X scores are 8 and 4, respectively, then the slope of the regression line for predicting Y from X must be

    a) 1.20

    b) 0.60

    c) 0.30

    d) 1.00

    e) One cannot determine from the data

6.20. During the semester, the students in a statistics class provided their average weekly study time and their course grade (on a scale from 0.0 to 4.0) for purposes of analysis. The regression equation for predicting grade from the number of hours studied was found to be $\hat{Y} = 1.2X + 0.3$. If a student studies 3 hours per week on average, what is her predicted numerical grade in the course?

    a) 2.25

    b) 3.90

    c) 3.60

    d) One cannot determine from the data

6.21. Given the scenario in Exercise 6.20 which of the following conclusions is warranted?

    a) For each additional hour of study per week, the predicted grade increases by 1.2 on average.

    b) For each additional hour of study per week, the predicted grade increases by 0.3 on average.

    c) For each additional hour of study per week, the predicted grade decreases by 1.2 on average.

    d) For each additional hour of study per week, the predicted grade decreases by 0.3 on average.

6.22. The correlation between exhaustion level and performance on an essay exam was found to be $r = -.90$. If Alejandro scores below the mean on exhaustion level, it is likely that he will score

    a) above the mean on the essay exam

    b) below the mean on the essay exam

    c) on the mean on the essay exam

    d) in an unpredictable way on the essay exam

6.23. We know that, unless certain restrictions are placed on a regression model, such models may not be used to make causative claims. Give a concrete example to illustrate a situation in which prediction makes sense, but causation does not.

6.24. The following questions relate to the scatterplot below, which shows the relationship between X and Y for four different subgroups.

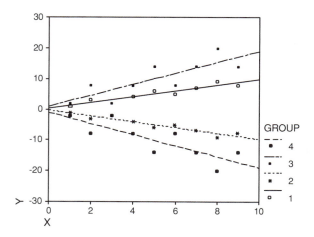

For each subgroup, select the slope of the regression line, b, from the column at right that best represents the relationship between X and Y for the subgroup. You may select a value more than once.

Group 1: _____   a) $b = .95$
                    b) $b = -.95$
Group 2: _____   c) $b = 1.80$
                    d) $b = -1.80$
Group 3: _____   e) $b = 0$

Group 4: _____

6.25. It is known that the correlation between X and Y is $r = -.46$.
   a) Find the correlation between X and X.
   b) Find the correlation between Y and $\hat{Y}$.
   c) Find the correlation between X and $\hat{Y}$.

Exercises 6.26 through 6.29 involve the use of formulas to enhance understanding of regression analysis.

6.26. Use Equations 6.2 and 6.4 to show that the regression line always passes through the point $(\overline{X}, \overline{Y})$.

6.27. Use Equations 6.3 and 5.5 to show that in the case where one variable is dichotomous and one is continuous that $b = \overline{Y}_0 - \overline{Y}_1$. [HINT: You need to use the fact that $S_X = \sqrt{pq}$, assuming that X is the dichotomous variable.]

6.28. Use Equation 6.2 to show that the mean of the predicted values is $\overline{Y}$.

6.29. Use the regression equation to show that $R = |r|$.

Exercise 6.30 relates to different ways of obtaining D, the standard error of the estimate.

6.30. Given the data in Table 6.1, the Hamburg data set, use SPSS to obtain D, the standard error of the estimate in three ways.
   a) Calculate D from Equation 6.1 using SPSS to obtain the values required by this equation.
   b) Calculate D from Equation 6.5 using SPSS to obtain the values required by this equation.
   c) Use SPSS to obtain D directly from the regression output.
   d) Compare these three values of D to one another.

CHAPTER SEVEN

Probability Fundamentals

In Chapter 1, we made a distinction between descriptive and inferential statistics. We said that when the purpose of the research is to describe the data that have been (or will be) collected, we are in the realm of descriptive statistics. In descriptive statistics, because the data are collected on *all* the individuals about whom a conclusion is to be drawn, conclusions can be drawn with 100 percent certainty. In inferential statistics, on the other hand, the purpose of the research is not to describe the set of data that have been collected, but to generalize or make inferences based on them to a larger group called the *population*. Because data are not available on the entire population, however, we cannot draw conclusions about the population with 100 percent certainty. One of the questions that confronts us in inferential statistics is therefore: "What degree of certainty do we have that our inferred conclusions about the population are correct, and how can we quantify this degree of certainty?" The quantification of degree of certainty is defined in terms of basic probability.

While the concepts of probability apply to variables that are either discrete or continuous, for ease of understanding in this chapter we illustrate our discussion of probability with examples based only on variables that are discrete. In the next chapter, we introduce the continuous case and describe how the fundamentals introduced in this chapter are modified for the continuous case.

THE DISCRETE CASE

We begin the topic of basic probability with the definition of a (*simple*) *experiment*. A simple experiment is defined as any action (such as tossing a coin or answering an item on a test) that leads to an observable outcome. The observable outcomes of any experiment, or any combinations of observable outcomes, are called *events*. If our experiment is to take a die and roll it once, we can observe six possible outcomes {1, 2, 3, 4, 5, 6}, and any one or any combination of these six outcomes can be classified as an event. For example, "the die comes up 6" is an event; "the die comes up 4 or 6" is also an event; and "the die comes up odd" is a third example of an event.

• •

EXAMPLE 7.1. Take a fair coin and toss it once.

a. List all the possible outcomes of this simple experiment.

b. State some examples of events for this simple experiment.

Solution.

a. The outcomes of this simple experiment are: {Head (H), Tail (T)}

b. Some examples of events for this simple experiment are
"the coin comes up heads" or "the coin comes up tails."

EXAMPLE 7.2. Take a fair coin and toss it twice.

a. List all the possible outcomes of this simple experiment.

b. State some examples of events for this simple experiment.

Solution.

a. The possible outcomes of this experiment are {HH, HT, TH, TT}.

b. Some examples of events for this experiment are "the coin comes up first H and then T," "the coin comes up HH," "the coin comes up with an H and a T in any order," or "the coin comes up TT."

How can we determine the *probability*, or degree of certainty, that a particular event will occur when an experiment is actually carried out. *If we assume that all outcomes of an experiment are equally likely* (that they all have the same chance of occurring), then we can define the probability of an event E, P(E), as the number of outcomes that satisfy event E divided by the total number of outcomes of the experiment:

$$P(E) = \frac{\text{Number of Outcomes Satisfying E}}{\text{Total Number of Outcomes of the Experiment}} \quad (7.1)$$

For example, in terms of the die experiment mentioned at the beginning of this section, we obtain the probability of event E – "the die comes up 6" – as $P(E) = \frac{1}{6}$, because only one outcome of the six possible outcomes (the outcome "6") satisfies event E.

EXAMPLE 7.3. In the experiment of taking a fair coin and tossing it twice, what is the probability of the event E: "HH"? (Said differently, "What is the probability of obtaining two heads?")

Solution. Because there are four possible equally likely outcomes for this experiment {HH, HT, TH, TT} and only of them, HH, satisfies event E, Equation 7.1 gives $P(E) = \frac{1}{4}$.

EXAMPLE 7.4. In the NELS data set, there are 227 males and 273 females. If the experiment consists of selecting one individual from this data set at random,

a. What is the probability that the individual is a female?

b. What is the probability that the individual is a male?

c. What is the probability that the individual is a toddler?

d. What is the probability that the individual is either a female or a male?

Solution. There are 500 possible outcomes for this experiment: 227 outcomes are male and 273 outcomes are female. Because we are selecting one of these individuals at random, we can assume that all 500 possible outcomes are equally likely. Therefore, we use Equation 7.1.

a. P(individual is a female) $= \frac{273}{500} = 0.546$

b. P(individual is a male) $= \frac{227}{500} = 0.454$

c. P(individual is a toddler) $= \dfrac{0}{500} = 0.00$, because there are no toddlers in the NELS data set.

d. P(individual is either a female or a male) $= \dfrac{500}{500} = 1.00$, because all 500 individuals are either female or male.

☞ **Remark.** From part (c) of Example 7.4, we note that the probability of an event that has no chance of occurring in the given experiment is 0, whereas from part (d) we note that the probability of an event that occurs with certainty in the given experiment is 1.00. In general, the probability of an event is a number between 0 and 1 inclusive. We may also note from parts (a) and (b) that events that are more likely to occur have higher probabilities. If you were asked to bet on whether a randomly sampled individual from the NELS data set were male or female, the better choice would be female because there is a greater probability of selecting a female from this data set than a male. Keep in mind that only within the context of a well-defined experiment are events and their probabilities of occurrence defined.

☞ **Remark.** Notice that the probability of an event is its relative frequency. As such, probability values are often reported as percentages.

THE COMPLEMENT RULE OF PROBABILITY

Let us take another look at parts (a) and (b) of Example 7.4. Because males and females have no possible outcomes in common (in other words, a female individual cannot also be male and vice versa), we call these two events *mutually exclusive* or *disjoint*. In addition, because there are only two categories, the event "the individual selected is male" may be described as well as "the individual selected is *not* female." Accordingly, we say that the event "the individual selected is male" is the *complement* of the event "the individual selected is female."

Complement Rule of Probability. If two events E_1 and E_2 are complements of each other, then

$$P(E_1) = 1 - P(E_2) \tag{7.2}$$

Given that the probability is 0.546 that the individual selected is a female, we could have obtained the answer to part (b) of Example 7.4 as $1 - 0.546 = 0.454$.

THE ADDITIVE RULES OF PROBABILITY

In part (d) of Example 7.4, we sought the probability of occurrence for the event "the individual selected is *either* male *or* female," which in this case equals 1.00 because all individuals in our sample are either male or female. We can approach the solution to this problem in a slightly different way. Because this event consists of a combination of two types of outcome (selecting a male, selecting a female), we can consider each of these types of outcome as separate events and recast the problem as *finding the compound probability of the two events*: E_1, "the person selected is a male," and E_2, "the person selected is a female." We are now seeking the probability of the combined event "E_1 *or* E_2," labeled $P(E_1 \text{ } or \text{ } E_2)$. Because E_1 and E_2 have no possible outcomes in common (in other words, the outcomes that satisfy E_1 do not also satisfy E_2, and vice versa, because a male cannot also be a female), we call these two events *mutually exclusive* or *disjoint*. In this case, we can find $P(E_1 \text{ } or \text{ } E_2)$ by simply adding together the simple probabilities $P(E_1)$ and $P(E_2)$. Using this new approach, we find that for Example 7.4(d) that P(individual is female) + P(individual is male) =

$$P(\text{individual is either a female or a male}) = \frac{273}{500} + \frac{227}{500} = \frac{500}{500} = 1.00.$$

We may state this more formally as the *First Additive Rule of Probability*.

FIRST ADDITIVE RULE OF PROBABILITY

First Additive Rule of Probability. When two events, E_1 and E_2, of the same experiment are mutually exclusive (or disjoint) and we seek to find the probability of the event "E_1 *or* E_2," we can do so by adding $P(E_1)$ and $P(E_2)$ together. In other words,

$$P(E_1 \text{ or } E_2) = P(E_1) + P(E_2) \tag{7.3}$$

This rule also holds for more than two events if they are all *pairwise disjoint*, which means that no two of them can occur at the same time.

EXAMPLE 7.5. The number of students in the NELS data set by region is given below. If a student is selected at random from this data set, find the probability that:

Geographic Region of School

		Frequency	Percent	Valid Percent	Cumulative Percent
Valid	Northeast	106	21.2	21.2	21.2
	North Central	151	30.2	30.2	51.4
	South	150	30.0	30.0	81.4
	West	93	18.6	18.6	100.0
	Total	500	100.0	100.0	

a. The student is from the Northeast.
b. The student is from the South.
c. The student is from either the Northeast or South.
d. The student is not from the South.

Solution. Because we are randomly selecting one of the students from the data set, we can reasonably assume that all 500 students are equally likely to be chosen.

a. $P(\text{Northeast}) = \dfrac{106}{500} = .21$

b. $P(\text{South}) = \dfrac{150}{500} = .30$

c. If we define the events, E_1 and E_2 as follows:
   E_1, "the student is from the Northeast"
   E_2, "the student is from the South"
   then E_1 and E_2 are mutually exclusive events – they cannot both occur at the same time. Therefore, we can use the First Additive Rule of Probability. Accordingly, P(Northeast or South) = $P(E_1 \text{ or } E_2) = P(E_1) + P(E_2) = .21 + .30 = .51$.

d. We may calculate the probability of the event E, "the student is not from the South," in two ways, either through the First Additive Rule or through the Complement Rule. Using the First Additive Rule,
P(E) = P(Northeast or North Central or West)
= P(Northeast) + P(North Central) + P(West) = .21 + .30 + .19 = .70.
Using the Complement Rule,
P(E) = 1 − P(South) = 1 − .30 = .70.

In part (c) of Example 7.5, we were able to determine the probability of the event "the student is from the Northeast *or* South" as the sum of the probabilities of the two mutually disjoint events "the student is from the Northeast" and "the student is from the South." If, however, the two were *not* mutually exclusive, we would not have been able to use the First Additive Rule of Probability to find the answer. A more general rule is the *Second Additive Rule of Probability,* which applies to whether the events are either mutually exclusive or not.

SECOND ADDITIVE RULE OF PROBABILITY

Second Additive Rule of Probability. Given two events E_1 and E_2 of the same experiment, if we seek to find the probability of the event "E_1 *or* E_2," we can do so by using the equation:

$$P(E_1 \ or \ E_2) = P(E_1) + P(E_2) - P(E_1 \ and \ E_2) \tag{7.4}$$

where $P(E_1 \ and \ E_2)$ represents the probability of the outcomes that E_1 and E_2 have in common.

☞ **Remark.** If, in the Second Additive Rule of Probability, the events E_1 and E_2 are disjoint, then they have no outcomes in common and $P(E_1 \ and \ E_2) = 0$. Consequently, when the events are mutually disjoint, the Second Additive Rule gives the same answer as the First Additive Rule. The Second Additive Rule may, therefore, be considered the more general of the two and may be used in either case.

· ·

EXAMPLE 7.6. A cross-tabulation of the number of students in the NELS data set by region and whether or not the family owned a computer when the student was in eighth grade is given below. If a student is selected at random from this data set, determine the probability of selecting a student who is from the South or whose family owned a computer.

Computer Owned by Family in Eighth Grade?
* Geographic Region of School Crosstabulation

Count

		Northeast	North Central	South	West	Total
		\multicolumn{4}{c	}{Geographic Region of School}	
Computer Owned by Family in Eighth Grade?	No	46	89	86	42	263
	Yes	60	62	64	51	237
Total		106	151	150	93	500

Solution. The events "student is from the South" and "student's family owned a computer" are not mutually exclusive because they have 64 outcomes in common: students who are from the South and who attended nursery school. Therefore, we use the more general Second Additive Rule with E_1 = "student is from the South" and E_2 = "student's family owned a computer" to find:

$$P(E_1 \ or \ E_2) = P(E_1) + P(E_2) - P(E_1 \ and \ E_2) = \frac{150}{500} + \frac{237}{500} - \frac{64}{500} = \frac{323}{500} = .65.$$

THE MULTIPLICATIVE RULE OF PROBABILITY

Suppose, in an experiment involving two tosses of single fair coin, we are interested in finding the probability of obtaining a head on the first toss and a head on the second toss. That is, we want the probability that the events E_1, "head on first toss," and E_2, "head on second toss," will both occur. This is denoted by $P(E_1 \ and \ E_2)$. One way of proceeding is simply to enumerate all possible outcomes of the experiment and then find the desired probability by inspection. The possible outcomes of this experiment are {HH, HT, TH, TT}.

The only outcome of this experiment that satisfies *both* E_1 and E_2 is {HH}. Accordingly,

$$P(E_1 \ and \ E_2) = P(HH) = \frac{1}{4} = .25.$$

In more complex situations, the job of enumerating such probabilities becomes rather tedious. In some problems, it may actually be impossible to enumerate a set of equally likely outcomes. In such cases, the following rule, called the *Multiplicative Rule of Probability*, can sometimes be used.

Multiplicative Rule of Probability. Suppose E_1 and E_2 are independent events of the same experiment. (E_1 and E_2 are said to be *independent* events if they have no effect on each other; that is, the occurrence of E_1 has no effect on the probability of E_2.) Then

$$P(E_1 \ and \ E_2) = P(E_1) \cdot P(E_2) \tag{7.5}$$

This result also holds for more than two events if they are mutually independent.

We can use the Multiplicative Rule of Probability to obtain the answer to our last problem of finding $P(E_1$ and $E_2)$ where E_1 is "head on first toss" and E_2 is "head on second toss" because, in this case, E_1 and E_2 are independent events. Simply,

$$P(E_1 \ and \ E_2) = P(E_1) \cdot P(E_2) = P(\text{head on first toss}) \cdot P(\text{head on second toss})$$

$$= \frac{1}{2} \cdot \frac{1}{2} = \frac{1}{4} = .25$$

· ·

EXAMPLE 7.7. We select, at random, a student from the entire NELS data set and note whether that student ever smoked marijuana. Then we select again, at random, from the entire NELS data set and note again whether the newly selected student (which, according to our sampling scheme, may be the same student that was selected first) ever smoked marijuana. What is the probability that neither student smoked marijuana?

☞ **Remark.** The type of sampling scheme used in Example 7.7 is called *sampling with replacement* because the student selected on the first draw was replaced before the second draw was made. When sampling with replacement, the entire data set is available for selection at each draw and, therefore, the probability of drawing any student from the data set (e.g., one who has ever smoked marijuana) remains constant from one draw to the next. The topic of sampling is covered in more detail later in this chapter.

Solution. We first obtain the frequency distribution for marijuana use by students in the NELS data set using SPSS.

Smoked Marijuana Ever?

		Frequency	Percent	Valid Percent	Cumulative Percent
Valid	Never	408	81.6	81.6	81.6
	Yes	92	18.4	18.4	100.0
	Total	500	100.0	100.0	

We define E_1 as "the first student selected never smoked marijuana" and E_2 as "the second student selected never smoked marijuana." We want the probability of the event (E_1 and E_2). At each stage of the selection process, the probability of selecting a student who never smoked is $\frac{408}{500} = .816$. In addition, because we used sampling with replacement, E_1 and E_2 are independent of each other. Therefore, we can use the Multiplicative Rule of Probability.

P(neither student ever smoked marijuana) = P(first student never smoked marijuana and the second student never smoked marijuana) = P(E_1 and E_2) = P(E_1) • P(E_2) = .816 • .816 = .67.

....

EXAMPLE 7.8. Three students are randomly selected with replacement from the NELS data set. What is the probability that
a. the first two students never smoked marijuana whereas the third student did?
b. the first and third students never smoked marijuana whereas the second student did?
c. the second and third students never smoked marijuana whereas the first student did?
d. exactly two of the three students never smoked marijuana?

Solution.
a. Let the events E_1, E_2, and E_3 be defined as follows.

   E_1: "The first student never smoked marijuana."
   E_2: "The second student never smoked marijuana."
   E_3: "The third student smoked marijuana."

   We are looking for the probability of the event "E_1 and E_2 and E_3." For each student selected, the probability that the student never smoked marijuana is .816, and the probability that the student smoked marijuana is .184. Furthermore, because E_1, E_2, and E_3 all refer to a different stage of the selection process and because sampling is with replacement, the student selected at any one stage does not affect who is selected at any other stage; these three events are independent of each other. Therefore, we can use the Multiplicative Rule of Probability:

   P(E_1 and E_2 and E_3) = P(E_1) • P(E_2) • P(E_3) = .816 • .816 • .184 = .1225

b. Let the events E_1, E_2, and E_3 be defined as follows.

E_1: "The first student never smoked marijuana."
E_2: "The second student smoked marijuana."
E_3: "The third student never smoked marijuana."

Once again, we are looking for the probability of the event "E_1 and E_2 and E_3" and we can use the Multiplicative Rule of Probability:

$$P(E_1 \text{ and } E_2 \text{ and } E_3) = P(E_1) \bullet P(E_2) \bullet P(E_3) = .816 \bullet .184 \bullet .816 = .1225$$

c. Let the events E_1, E_2, and E_3 be defined as follows.

E1: "The first student smoked marijuana."
E2: "The second student never smoked marijuana."
E3: "The third student never smoked marijuana."

Once again, we are looking for the probability of the event "E_1 and E_2 and E_3" and we can use the Multiplicative Rule of Probability:

$$P(E_1 \text{ and } E_2 \text{ and } E_3) = P(E_1) \bullet P(E_2) \bullet P(E_3) = .184 \bullet .816 \bullet .816 = .1225$$

d. If we define the events F, G, and H as
F: "The first two students never smoked marijuana whereas the third student did."
G: "The first and third students never smoked marijuana whereas the second student did."
H: "The second and third students never smoked marijuana whereas the first student did."
then we can think of the event "exactly two of the three students never smoked marijuana" as F or G or H because these three combinations are the only ways in which the event "exactly two of the three students never smoked marijuana" can occur. As we have seen in parts (a), (b), and (c) of this example, P(F) = .1225, P(G) = .1225, and P(H) = .1225. The three events, F, G, and H, are mutually disjoint, because no two of them can occur at the same time. Therefore, we can use the First Additive Rule of Probability.
P(exactly two of the three students never smoked marijuana)
= P(F or G or H)
= P(F) + P(G) + P(H)
= .1225 + .1225 + .1225
= .3675

THE RELATIONSHIP BETWEEN INDEPENDENCE AND MUTUAL EXCLUSIVITY

The Multiplicative Rule of Probability can be used only when the two events, E_1 and E_2, are independent of one another, whereas the First Additive Rule of Probability can be used only when the two events, E_1 and E_2, are mutually exclusive of, or disjoint from, one another. Because confusion often arises over the distinction between independence and mutual exclusivity, we include the following statement to clarify the relationship between these two concepts.

Given two events, E_1 and E_2, of the same experiment, E_1 and E_2 cannot be both independent of one another and mutually exclusive of one another. However, they can be (1) independent and not mutually exclusive, (2) not independent and mutually exclusive, or (3) not independent and not mutually exclusive. We return to this point in Exercises 7.9 through 7.11.

CONDITIONAL PROBABILITY

As already mentioned, when two events E_1 and E_2 are independent, they have no effect on each other, and the probability of each event does not depend on whether or not the other event has occurred. When two events are not independent, however, the probability of one event does depend on whether or not the other has occurred. To denote the probability of an event E_1 given that an event E_2 has occurred, we write $P(E_1|E_2)$.

. . . .

EXAMPLE 7.9. We know from Example 7.7 that the probability that a randomly selected student from the NELS data set has never smoked marijuana is .816 $\left(\dfrac{408}{500}\right)$. Is this probability the same for males and females? That is, is the probability of never having smoked marijuana *given* that the student is male equal to the probability of never having smoked marijuana *given* that the student is female?

Solution. We obtain, as shown in Table 7.1, the cross-tabulation of gender by marijuana use for the NELS data set using SPSS.

Gender * Smoked Marijuana Ever? Crosstabulation

Count

		Smoked Marijuana Ever?		Total
		Never	Yes	
Gender	Male	185	42	227
	Female	223	50	273
Total		408	92	500

a. To find the probability that a randomly selected student from the NELS data set never smoked marijuana *given that the student is male*, we need only consult the first row of the table because that row contains all the information we need to solve this problem. From the first row, we find that

$$P(\text{student never smoked marijuana} \mid \text{student is male}) = \frac{185}{227} = .815.$$

b. To find the probability that a randomly selected student from the NELS data set never smoked marijuana *given that the student is female*, we need only consult the second row of the table because that row contains all the information we need to solve this problem. From the second row, we find that

$$P(\text{student never smoked marijuana} \mid \text{student is female}) = \frac{223}{273} = .817.$$

According to these results, the probability of never smoking marijuana is effectively the same for males and females.

EXAMPLE 7.10. Find the probability that a randomly selected student is male given that the student never smoked marijuana.

Solution. Using the table associated with Example 7.9, we refer to the first column to find that

$$P(\text{student is male} \mid \text{student never smoked marijuana}) = \frac{185}{408} = .453.$$

☞ **Remark.** Because P(student never smoked marijuana | student is male) does not equal P(student is male | student never smoked marijuana), we may note that $P(E_1|E_2)$ and $P(E_2|E_1)$ do not have to be equal to each other. In fact, they are equal to each other only when $P(E_1) = P(E_2)$.

To find a conditional probability, as we have done in Examples 7.9 and 7.10, we may use Equation 7.6 as an alternative approach:

$$P(E_1|E_2) = \frac{P(E_1 \text{ and } E_2)}{P(E_2)} \tag{7.6}$$

In applying Equation 7.6 to the problem of Example 7.9(a), we let E_1 = "the student never smoked marijuana" and E_2 = "the student is male." Then, $P(E_1 \text{ and } E_2) = \frac{185}{500} = .370$, $P(E_2) = \frac{227}{500} = .454$. Substituting these values into Equation 7.6, we obtain

$$P(E_1|E_2) = \frac{P(E_1 \text{ and } E_2)}{P(E_2)} = \frac{.370}{.454} = .815,$$

the same result as before.

☞ **Remark.** By the Multiplicative Rule of Probability, if events E_1 and E_2 are independent, then $P(E_1 \text{ and } E_2) = P(E_1) \times P(E_2)$. Consequently, by Equation 7.6,

$$P(E_1|E_2) = \frac{P(E_1 \text{ and } E_2)}{P(E_2)} = \frac{P(E_1) \times P(E_2)}{P(E_2)} = P(E_2)$$

In other words, if E_1 and E_2 are independent, the probability of E_1 is the same whether or not we know that E_2 has occurred, which goes back to the definition of independence.

THE LAW OF LARGE NUMBERS

So far we have been interested in probabilities simply as a way of determining the likelihood of events when an experiment is performed once. The theory of probability is even more useful, however, when an experiment is repeated several times. This fact is illustrated by the following law, which provides the basic link between the theoretical notion of probability and the applied, empirical one. It is known as the *Law of Large Numbers*.

Law of Large Numbers. Suppose E is an event in an experiment and the probability of E is p ($P(E) = p$). If the experiment is repeated n independent and identical times (each repetition may be called a trial), then the relative frequency of E occurring in these n trials is approximately equal to p. In general, the larger the number of trials, the better p is as an approximation of the relative frequency of E actually obtained.

☞ **Remark.** We can therefore think of p, the probability of event E, as the relative frequency with which E will occur "in the long run" (i.e., for an infinite number of trials). A value of $p = .75$ would then mean in the long run that event E will occur 75 percent of the time. Because we never actually do any of our experiments an infinite number of times, all we can expect, as stated in the Law of Large Numbers, is for p to approximate the relative frequency of E, with the approximation generally becoming better as the number of trials, n, increases.

EXERCISES

Exercises 7.1 through 7.5 relate to the NELS data set.

7.1. Create a frequency and percent distribution table of the variable EDEXPECT, which indicates the highest level of education the students in eighth grade expect to achieve eventually. If one student is selected at random from the NELS data set, what is the probability that:
   a) The student anticipates earning a bachelor's degree?
   b) The student anticipates earning a master's degree?
   c) The student anticipates earning either a bachelor's or master's degree?
   d) The student anticipates earning something other than a bachelor's degree?

7.2. Create a cross-tabulation of EDEXPECT by GENDER. Use it to find the following probabilities if one student is selected at random from the NELS data set:
   a) The student expects to earn less than a college degree.
   b) The student is female.
   c) The student expects to earn less than a college degree and is female.
   d) The student expects to earn less than a college degree or is female.
   e) The student does not expect to earn less than a college degree.
   f) The student is female given that the student expects to earn less than a college degree.
   g) The student expects to earn less than a college degree given that the student is female.
   h) The student is female given that the student does not expect to earn less than a college degree.

7.3. Use the frequency and percent distribution table you created in Exercise 7.1 to find the following probabilities. One student is selected at random from those in the NELS data set. This student is then replaced and a second student is selected at random. What is the probability that
   a) The first student anticipates earning a bachelor's degree?
   b) The second student anticipates earning a master's degree?
   c) The first student anticipates earning a bachelor's degree and the second student anticipates earning a master's degree?
   d) Can you use the Multiplicative Rule of Probability to answer part (c) of this exercise? Explain why or why not.

7.4. Use the frequency and percent distribution table you created in Exercise 7.1 to find the following probabilities. One student is selected at random from those in the NELS data set. Without replacement, a second student is selected at random. What is the probability that

a) The first student anticipates earning a bachelor's degree?

b) The first student anticipates earning a bachelor's degree and the second student anticipates earning a master's degree?

c) Can you use the Multiplicative Rule of Probability to answer part (b) of this exercise? Explain why or why not.

7.5. Use the frequency and percent distribution table you created in Exercise 7.1 to find the following probabilities. One student is selected at random from those in the NELS data set. If this experiment is repeated 1,000 times, approximately how many times of the 1,000 do you expect to select

a) A student who anticipates earning a bachelor's degree?

b) A student who anticipates earning a master's degree?

c) A student who anticipates earning either a bachelor's or a master's degree?

d) A student who anticipates earning something other than a bachelor's degree?

7.6. The numbers 1–10 inclusive are written on pieces of paper and the pieces of paper are put in a bowl. If one of them is drawn at random, what is the probability that the number selected is

a) even?

b) odd?

c) either even or odd?

d) either less than 5 or even?

e) either greater than 2 or odd?

7.7. What (if anything) is wrong with the following statement? Consider the events

E_1: "before finishing this book you will inherit $1 million."

E_2: "before finishing this book you will not inherit $1 million."

Because these two events are mutually exclusive and exhaustive (one of them must occur and both of them cannot occur at the same time), $\text{Prob}(E_1) = \text{Prob}(E_2) = \frac{1}{2}$.

7.8. What (if anything) is wrong with the following statement? "We are given an urn containing white and black marbles in equal numbers. It is impossible to determine the probability that one marble selected at random from this urn is white, because we do not know how many marbles there are in the urn to begin with."

7.9. In this exercise, we see that two events of the same experiment, E_1 and E_2, can be independent and not mutually exclusive. Suppose we toss a fair coin twice. Let E_1 and E_2 be defined as follows.

E_1: "the first toss is a head."

E_2: "the second toss is a head."

a) Show that E_1 and E_2 are *not* mutually exclusive.

b) Show that E_1 and E_2 are independent of each other.

[HINT for part (b): To show that E_2 is independent of E_1, show that the probability of E_2 occurring is not influenced by whether or not E_1 occurs. This can be done in three steps. First, find the probability of E_2 assuming we have no information about whether E_1 occurred. Second, determine the probability of E_2 assuming we know that E_1 has occurred. Third, determine the probability of E_2 assuming we know that E_1 has not occurred. Because these three values are equal, we may conclude that the occurrence or nonoccurrence of E_1 has no effect on the probability of E_2 and thus that E_2 is independent of E_1.]

7.10. In this exercise, we see that two events of the same experiment, E_1 and E_2, can be dependent and mutually exclusive. Suppose we toss a fair coin once. If it comes up heads, we stop. If it comes up tails, we toss it again. Let E_1 and E_2 be defined as follows.

E_1: "the first toss is a head."
E_2: "the second toss is a head."

   a) Show that E_1 and E_2 are mutually exclusive.
   b) Show that E_1 and E_2 are dependent.

7.11. In this exercise, we see that two events of the same experiment, E_1 and E_2, can be dependent and not mutually exclusive. Suppose we toss a fair coin once. If it comes up heads, we stop. If it comes up tails, we toss it again. Let E_1 and E_2 be defined as follows.

E_1: "the first toss is a tail."
E_2: "the second toss is a tail."

   a) Show that E_1 and E_2 are not mutually exclusive.
   b) Show that E_1 and E_2 are dependent.

CHAPTER EIGHT

Theoretical Probability Models

A theoretical probability model is a mathematical representation of a class of experiments having certain specified characteristics in common, from which we may derive the probabilities of outcomes of any experiment in the class. The extent to which the probabilities derived from the theoretical model are correct for a particular experiment depends on the extent to which the particular experiment possesses the characteristics required by the model. In most cases, the match between the theoretical model and a specific experiment is not perfect, and the answer we obtain using the model is only an approximation of the true answer. The advantage of using a theoretical model, however, is that it enables us to answer questions about all the experiments that have the specified characteristics of the model without having to treat each experiment as a completely new and unique situation. Theoretical probability models are applicable when all possible outcomes of an experiment, taken together, follow a pattern of regularity that may be described by the model. As a result, the models enable us to obtain the probability of any single outcome or combination of outcomes for that experiment.

In this chapter we present two theoretical probability models that have widespread applicability: the binomial probability model and the normal probability model. The binomial probability model answers questions about a particular type of discrete variable, whereas the normal probability model answers questions about a particular type of continuous model. Of the two models, the normal model is more widely used. In fact, the normal model is perhaps the most widely used of all theoretical probability models.

THE BINOMIAL PROBABILITY MODEL AND DISTRIBUTION

In general, the binomial probability model applies to experiments that consist of *independent* and *identical* trials, the outcomes of which on any one trial may be thought of as *dichotomous* (as either success or failure). This dichotomy is the reason for the name *binomial* – there are two outcomes (such as head/tail, pass/fail, or absent/present).

Recall Example 7.8(d), in which we sought the probability that exactly two of three students selected randomly with replacement from the NELS data set never smoked marijuana. Using the language of the binomial model, we define a trial as the selection of one student from the data set, and recognize that, for this example, there are three trials. As we shall see, the three trials satisfy the assumptions of the binomial probability model in that they are independent and identical and the outcomes of each are dichotomous.

The trials are *independent* because each student is selected at random with replacement; knowing who is selected in one trial tells us nothing about who will be selected in subsequent trials. The trials are *identical* because each and every trial consists of selecting one student at random from the 500 students of the NELS data set. And finally, because the outcome of each trial may be categorized as either "student has smoked marijuana" or "student has never smoked marijuana," each outcome is *dichotomous*.

In Example 7.8(d), we are interested in the probability that two of the three students never smoked marijuana. In the language of the binomial model, we may say that we are interested in the probability of obtaining two "successes" in three trials. A *success*, in this case, therefore means, *the student never smoked marijuana*.

Of course, given that there are three trials in this example, a *complete* description of the probabilities associated with each possible result would include knowing the probabilities of observing 0 successes, 1 success, 2 successes, and 3 successes in the three trials. These probabilities, obtained "by hand" using the approach of Example 7.8(d), are given in Table 8.1 and displayed as a bar graph in Figure 8.1. Taken together, these probabilities define what is called the *binomial probability distribution* for this case. That is, the number of trials (denoted by n) equals 3, the probability of a success on any one trial (denoted by p) equals .816, and the number of successes (denoted by k) takes on the values 0, 1, 2, and 3, in turn. Then the binomial probability distribution consists of the probabilities associated with each possible number of successes (given numerically in Table 8.1 and graphically in Figure 8.1).

Notice that the probabilities associated with obtaining either 2 or 3 successes are much greater than the probabilities associated with obtaining either 0 or 1 success. In other words, this discrete distribution is skewed negatively. Can you explain why this distribution is skewed negatively? [HINT: Recall that it is quite likely (with probability .816) that a randomly selected student never smoked marijuana.]

☞ **Remark.** In defining a complete binomial probability distribution, we need to specify the values of n and p and allow k, the number of successes, to vary from 0 (no successes) to n (all successes). If we do this, we can evaluate the probability for each possible value of k individually and construct a corresponding probability distribution and probability bar graph for the given experiment.

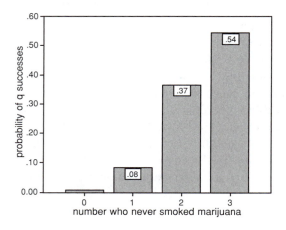

Figure 8.1 Bar graph of binomial probability distribution for $n = 3$ and $p = .816$.

Table 8.1. Binomial probability distribution for $n = 3$ and $p = .816$

k	Probability of k Successes
0	.006
1	.083
2	.368
3	.543

☞ **Remark.** Two interesting observations may be made concerning the bars in the binomial distribution bar graph of Figure 8.1. First, the probability of each of the individual events (0 students never smoked marijuana, 1 student never smoked marijuana, 2 students never smoked marijuana, 3 students never smoked marijuana) is just the height of the corresponding bar in the bar graph. Therefore, we can obtain any desired probability by summing the heights of the appropriate bars in the bar graph. Moreover, because each bar has the same width, and the sum of the areas of all the bars is 1, we can also obtain any desired probability by summing the areas of the appropriate bars in the bar graph. In general, whenever we use a probability distribution in which the total area of the graph is 1, we can obtain the probability of any event by finding the proportion of the area under the graph corresponding to that event. Thinking of probabilities as proportions of area under the relevant probability graph (or curve) is extremely useful in solving problems for situations in which only areas are available, such as those involving continuous, as opposed to discrete, variables.

Although we computed the probabilities in Table 8.1 by hand, using the approach of Example 7.8(d), there are three other approaches we can take. We can use an SPSS compute statement; we can use Table 3 in Appendix C, which summarizes the binomial distribution to approximate this particular binomial distribution; or we can use Equation 8.2.

SPSS, Version 15, offers a simple, direct solution using the probability distribution function (PDF) for the binomial, or PDF.BINOM(*quant*, *n*, *prob*). Given a binomial distribution, this function gives the probability of obtaining *quant* successes in *n* trials where *prob* is the probability of success on each trial. We now use this function in Example 8.1 to find the probability of exactly *k* successes in *n* trials.

· ·

EXAMPLE 8.1. Use SPSS to obtain the probability that exactly 2 students out of 3, who are randomly selected from the NELS data set, never smoked marijuana.

Solution Using SPSS. Using the language of the binomial probability model we may rephrase this problem in terms of the probability of obtaining $k = 2$ successes in $n = 3$ trials, where a success is defined as "the student never smoked marijuana" and $p = .816$, the probability of a success on any one trial.

Open a new Data Editor screen in SPSS. You will be in the **Data View** window. Define the variable *k* to be numeric (*k* is always an integer because it represents a whole number of successes) and enter the values 0, 1, 2, and 3 as the first four lines of variable *k*. Click on **Transform** and then **Compute**. Type the variable name **probability** in the **Target Variable** box. Use the down arrow in the **Function group** box to find and click on the category **PDF & Noncentral PDF**. Then in the **Functions and Special Variables** box (below the **Function group** box) locate and click on **Pdf.Binom**. Highlight this function and move it to the **Numerical Expression** box. The **Numerical Expression** box should contain the following:

PDF.BINOM(?,?,?)

The question marks represent *k*, *n*, and *prob*, respectively. (Note that in SPSS *k* is referred to as *quant*.) The set of question marks should be replaced by *k*, 3, and .816 so that we now have the following in the **Numerical Expression** box:

PDF.BINOM(*k*,3,.816)

Click **OK**. The **Data View** window in the SPSS Data Editor should now contain the values for **probability** in the second column, to two decimal places. To increase to three decimal places, click on the **Variable View** tab at the bottom left of the screen and increase the number of decimals from 2 to 3. Return to the **Data View** window and you should see the following:

k	probability
.00	.006
1.00	.083
2.00	.368
3.00	.543

The values in this output are the same as those in Table 8.1, computed by hand. The probability of obtaining two students who never smoked marijuana in a random sample of three students selected from the NELS data set is .368, as before.

Solution Using Table 3 in Appendix C. To obtain this distribution using Table 3, we have $n = 3$ and $p = .816$. The box associated with $n = 3$ contains many columns, each representing the binomial distribution for fixed values of p. Note that the highest value of p given is $p = .5$. In our case, we have defined "success" to be "the student never smoked marijuana," and for a single randomly selected student the probability of success is .816. However, because the table is made to approximate distributions with $p \leq .5$, we redefine success as "the student smoked marijuana at least once." Because the probability is .816 that the student never smoked marijuana, then $1 - .816$, or .184, is the probability that the student smoked marijuana at least once. Also, because $n = 3$, the event "0 students never smoked marijuana" is equivalent to the event "3 students smoked marijuana at least once."

Because there is no value of p exactly equal to .184, we use the closest tabled value, which is $p = .20$. From the table, we see that the probability that 0 students smoked marijuana is approximately .512, that 1 student smoked marijuana is approximately .384, that 2 students smoked marijuana is approximately .096, and that 3 students smoked marijuana is approximately .008. Accordingly, the probability that 0 students never smoked marijuana is approximately .008, the probability that 1 student never smoked marijuana is .096, and so on. These values are close to the ones provided by SPSS in Table 1 based on the more precise $p = .816$.

Solution Using Equation 8.2. The binomial formula, which gives the probability of obtaining k successes in n trials, where p is the probability of success and q is the probability of failure, involves notation that we have not used before. Before presenting the binomial equation itself, we provide a discussion of factorial notation and combinations.

We introduce the new notation, *factorial notation*, to help us more conveniently denote the operation of sequential multiplication. The mathematical symbol $n!$ (read "n factorial") is defined, for the positive integer n, as the ordered product of all the positive integers from 1 up to and including n: $n! = 1 \times 2 \times 3 \times \ldots \times (n - 1) \times (n)$

For example, $5! = 1 \times 2 \times 3 \times 4 \times 5 = 120$.

☞ **Remark.** It would be meaningless to try to use the equation $n! = 1 \times 2 \times 3 \times \ldots \times (n - 1) \times (n)$ to evaluate $0!$; we could not start at 1 and multiply "up to" 0, because 0 is less than 1. Because there are formulas involving factorial notation in which we may want to use this notation for all the nonnegative integers including 0, we now define the symbol $0!$ as $0! = 1$.

We also introduce combination notation. Given n objects, the number of ways in which k of these objects (k between 0 and n inclusive) can be combined, or selected, without regard to order of selection is denoted by either the symbol $_nC_k$ or the symbol $\binom{n}{k}$ and is given by Equation 8.1:

$$\binom{n}{k} = \frac{n!}{k!(n-k)!} \tag{8.1}$$

We can now express the binomial equation that gives the probability of obtaining k successes in n trials, where p is the probability of success and q is the probability of failure:

$$P(k \text{ successes in } n \text{ trials}) = \binom{n}{k}p^k q^{n-k} \tag{8.2}$$

Applying Equation 8.2 to the example at hand, we have $n = 3$, $p = .816$, and $q = 1 - .816 = .184$.

For $k = 0$, P(0 students ever smoked marijuana) $= \binom{3}{0}.816^0.184^3 = .006$.

For $k = 1$, P(1 student ever smoked marijuana) $= \binom{3}{1}.816^1.184^2 = .083$.

For $k = 2$, P(2 students ever smoked marijuana) $= \binom{3}{2}.816^2.184^1 = .368$.

For $k = 3$, P(3 students ever smoked marijuana) $= \binom{3}{3}.816^3.184^0 = .543$.

☞ **Remark.** Of course, we did not need to generate the complete distribution to answer the particular question of Example 8.1. We did so to describe how to generate an entire binomial distribution. With that knowledge in hand, we can suggest a simpler and more straightforward solution to Example 8.1.

More Direct Solution Using SPSS. A more direct solution may be obtained using the SPSS Compute procedure. (If you are not already in a data set open a new Data Editor screen in SPSS, define the variable k to be numeric, and enter the value 2 as the first line of variable k.)

To obtain the individual binomial probability value, click on **Transform** and then **Compute**. Adapt the earlier procedure to place PDF.Binom(2,3,.816) in the **Numeric Expression** box. Designate **probability** as the Target Variable. Click **OK**.

The individual probability value of .368 appears in the **Data View** window once you have changed the number of decimal places of **probability** to three by going into the **Variable View** window.

The individual probability also may be estimated using Table 3 in Appendix C by looking up $n = 3$, $k = 1$, and $p = .20$. We use $k = 1$ because the probability that 2 students of 3 never smoked marijuana is the same as the probability that 1 student of 3 smoked marijuana at least once. The individual value is .384.

☞ **Remark.** The complete binomial distribution may be described in summary statistic form like any other distribution. Fairly simple equations are available for both the mean and the standard deviation. For the case of the binomial, these summary statistics are presented in terms of number of successes. The equations, presented without derivation, are as follows:

$$\text{Mean} = np; \quad \text{Standard deviation} = \sqrt{npq} \tag{8.3}$$

where n = number of trials, p = probability of success on any one trial, and q = probability of failure on any one trial. Note that for Example 8.1 the mean and standard deviation of the binomial distribution are $(3)(.816) = 2.45$ and $\sqrt{(3)(.816)(.184)} = .67$, respectively. Both Table 8.1 and Figure 8.1 indicate that these values are reasonable for this distribution. Notice that this binomial distribution is negatively skewed. Because the probability of a success, p, on any one trial is large ($p = .816$), it is unlikely that we would observe a relatively small number (near zero) of successes and likely that we would observe a relatively large number of successes. In general, when $p > .5$, the binomial distribution is skewed negatively; when $p < .5$, it is skewed positively; and when $p = .5$, it is symmetric.

THE APPLICABILITY OF THE BINOMIAL PROBABILITY MODEL

We were able to use the binomial probability model to solve the problem of Example 8.1 because, as we noted, this problem satisfied the assumptions of this model. In this section we seek to clarify the criteria an experiment must meet to be considered a binomial experiment by examining situations for which the model does and does not apply.

To review, the criteria an experiment must meet to be considered a binomial experiment are as follows:

1. The experiment consists of n identical trials ($n \geq 1$).
2. The trials are independent of each other.
3. On each trial, the outcomes can be thought of in a dichotomous manner as Success and Failure, so that the two events, Success and Failure, are mutually exclusive (cannot both happen at the same time) and exhaustive (each trial must result in either a Success or a Failure).
4. If P(Success) = p and P(Failure) = q, then p and q do not change their values from trial to trial, and (by criterion 3)$p + q = 1$ on each trial.

· ·

EXAMPLE 8.2. Does the binomial model apply to the following situation: In random sampling with replacement of 10 students from the NELS data set, what is the probability that 5 are from the Northeast, 3 from the South, 1 from the West, and 1 from the North Central regions?

Solution. No, the binomial model does not apply to this situation because the outcomes of the experiment on any one trial are not dichotomous. In particular, four events are specified on each trial: obtaining a student from the Northeast, obtaining a student from the South, obtaining a student from the West, and obtaining a student from the North Central region.

EXAMPLE 8.3. Does the binomial model apply to the following situation: In random sampling with replacement of 10 students from the NELS data set, what is the probability that 5 are from the Northeast, and 5 from the South?

Solution. No, the binomial model does not apply to this situation. Although only two events are specified on each trial, the sum of the probabilities, p and q, for these two events does not equal 1.00. The probability of obtaining a student from the Northeast, p, is 106/500 = .21 and the probability of obtaining a student from the South, q, is 150/500 = .30. Therefore, $p + q =$ .51, not 1.00. The reason $p + q$ is not equal to 1 in this example is that the events "the student is from the Northeast" and "the student is from the South" are not exhaustive. That is, it is possible for an outcome of a trial to be neither a student from the Northeast nor a student from the South; for example, the student could be from the West.

EXAMPLE 8.4. Does the binomial model apply to the following situation: Ten students are randomly selected from the NELS data set *without* replacement. What is the probability that exactly ten students are from the South?

Solution. No, the binomial model does not apply to this situation because by sampling without replacement we caused the values of p and q to change from one trial to the next. On the first trial, the probability that the student is from the South, p, is 150/500 or .30 and the probability that the student is not from the South, q, is 350/500 or .70. On the second trial, however, the probabilities of p and q depend on the outcome of the first trial. If, in the first trial, the student selected is from the South, then on the second trial the probability of selecting a student from the South is 149/499 or .299. On the other hand, if, in the first trial, the student selected is not from the South, then on the second trial the probability of selecting a student from the South is 150/499 or .301. In either case, the values of p and q will have changed from the first trial to the second (and will continue to change in each subsequent trial). Because p and q change from one trial to the next, these trials may not be considered to be either identical or independent.

EXAMPLE 8.5. Does the binomial model apply to the following situation: Ten students are randomly selected from the NELS data set *with* replacement. What is the probability that exactly 5 students are from the South?

Solution. Yes! The binomial model does apply to this situation. Because we are explicitly interested in obtaining students from the South, we can define Success as "selecting a student from the South" and Failure as "not selecting a student from the South." In each trial, the probability of Success is .30, whereas the probability of Failure is .70 and p and q do not change from trial to trial. Because the events defined as Success and Failure are mutually exclusive and exhaustive, $p + q = 1.00$.

Given that this example satisfies the binomial probability model, let's find the answer to the question posed using SPSS, approximate it using Table 3 in Appendix C, and calculate it using Equation 8.2.

Following our earlier procedure using SPSS, we compute PDF.Binom (5, 10, .30) = .103.

Following our earlier procedure using Table 3, we look up $n = 10$, $k = 5$, and $p = .30$. We find that the probability is .1029 or .103 when rounded to three decimal places.

Following our earlier procedure for using Equation 8.2, we calculate P(5 successes in 10

trials) $= \binom{10}{5}.30^5.70^5 = .103$

That is, the probability of obtaining 5 students from the South in a sample of 10 students randomly selected with replacement from the NELS data set is .103.

By the Law of Large Numbers we may interpret this result to mean that, if we repeated this experiment 1,000 times, then our sample of 10 will contain exactly 5 students from the South approximately 103 times.

Following are some other examples to which the binomial model applies and that do not rely on the NELS data set.

• •

EXAMPLE 8.6. Jill is taking a 10-question multiple-choice examination on which there are 4 possible answers to each question. Assuming that Jill just *guesses* the answer to each question, what is the probability of her getting exactly 4 of the questions correct?

Solution. Let Success on each question (or trial) be "getting the correct answer" and Failure be "getting an incorrect answer." Because these two events are mutually exclusive and exhaustive on each trial, and because Jill is *guessing* on each question, so that $p = 1/4$ and $q = 3/4$ (there are four possible answers to each question and only one of them is correct), the binomial model is applicable to this situation ($k = 4$, $n = 10$, $p = .25$).

Using SPSS, the answer, obtained through the use of the numeric expression PDF.Binom(4,10,.25), is .1460.

Using Table 3 in Appendix C we find also that the probability is .1460.

Using Equation 8.2, we find also that P(4 successes in 10 trials) $= \binom{10}{4}.25^4.75^6 = .146$

By the Law of Large Numbers, we can interpret this result in the following way: If a large number of people take this 10-question exam and guess on each of the questions, then about 14 or 15 percent of these people will get exactly 4 of the 10 questions correct.

• •

EXAMPLE 8.7. Erie Pharmaceutical Company manufactures a drug for treatment of a specific type of ear infection. They claim that the drug has probability .40 of curing people who suffer from this ailment. Assuming their claim to be true, if the treatment is applied to 50 people suffering from this ailment, what is the probability that exactly 25 of these 50 people will be cured?

Solution. If we consider the treatment of each person with this ailment to be a trial, we can define Success and Failure on each trial as "the person's ailment is cured" and "the person's ailment is not cured," respectively. These two events are mutually exclusive and exhaustive for each trial (each person being treated). Because the claim is that the long-run probability of this treatment working is .40 (and we are accepting this claim as true), we can take this value as the probability of success on each trial. Therefore, the binomial probability model is applicable to this situation ($k = 25$, $n = 50$, $p = .40$).

Using SPSS, the answer obtained through the use of the numeric expression PDF.Binom(25,50,.40) is .0405.

Because the maximum value of *n* given in Table 3 is 20, we cannot use Table 3 to find a solution to this problem. For interested readers, an alternative approach is discussed in Exercise 8.27 using the normal distribution to approximate the binomial.

Using Equation 8.2, we obtain P(25 successes in 50 trials) $= \binom{50}{25}.4^{25}.6^{25} = .0405$

Note that this value is difficult to compute unless your calculator has a built-in combination calculation routine.

In other words, if the company's claim is true, and a large number of groups of 50 people each are treated with this drug, then we should expect approximately 4 percent of these groups to have exactly 25 people cured.

. . . .

EXAMPLE 8.8. Using the same situation as in Example 8.7, what is the probability of obtaining:

(a) at most 10 Successes (cures)?
(b) at least 20 Successes (cures)?

Solution. As we saw in Example 8.7, the binomial model is applicable to this situation with $n = 50$ and $p = .40$.

a. "At most 10 Successes" is the same as "10 or fewer Successes" and can be expressed as $k \le 10$. The answer may be obtained directly using another binomial function available in SPSS, called the cumulative distribution function (CDF).

To obtain a cumulative (rather than an individual) binomial probability value (i.e., the probability that the number of successes is less than or equal to some value, say *k*), click on **Transform** and then **Compute**. In the **Function group** box, locate and click on **CDF & Noncentral CDF**. Click on and move CDF.Binom into the **Numeric Expression** box and replace the question marks to obtain CDF.Binom(2,3,.816). Designate **probability** as the Target Variable. Click **OK**.

Following this procedure, the answer obtained from the numeric expression CDF.Binom(10,50,.40) is .0955. In other words, if many groups of 50 people each are treated with this drug, then we should expect approximately 10 percent of all the groups to have at most 10 people cured.

b. "At least 20 Successes" is the same as "20 or more Successes" and can be expressed as $k \ge 20$. The answer may be obtained using the Complement Rule of Probability in conjunction with the CDF for the binomial in SPSS. The answer obtained from the numeric expression CDF.Binom(19,50,.40) is .4465. This gives us the probability that at most 19 of the 50 will be cured. To find the probability that at least 20 of the 50 will be cured, we take the complement of .4465 (which is 1.00 − .4465) and obtain .5535. In other words, if large numbers of groups of 50 people each are treated with this drug, then we should expect approximately 55 percent of these groups to exhibit at least 20 people cured.

In summary, in a binomial experiment with *n* trials, where *p* equals the probability of success on a single trial,

PDF.Binom(k, n, p) = the probability of exactly *k* successes

CDF.Binom(k, n, p) = the probability of at most *k* successes = the probability of *k* or fewer successes

$1 - \text{CDF.Binomial}(k-1, n, p)$ = the probability of at least k successes = the probability of k or more successes

THE NORMAL PROBABILITY MODEL AND DISTRIBUTION

The importance of the normal probability model lies in the fact that in the real world many traits – such as height, weight, IQ scores, and the like – have relative frequency curves that are closely approximated by this model. Moreover, as we shall see throughout the course of this book, many problems in mathematical statistics either are solved, or can be solved, by using the normal probability model or a probability model based on the normal.

The normal probability model was developed by one of the greatest mathematicians of all time, Johann Friedrich Carl Gauss (1777–1855). Most mathematicians of Gauss' period were interested in applying mathematics to real-world problems, such as in astronomy and navigation. Knowing that data obtained through observation and measurement contained errors due to the imprecision of the measuring instruments, Gauss studied many different sets of such data and noticed that they all possessed certain common characteristics. In general, each set of observations was symmetric about some central value and the farther from this central value, the fewer and fewer such observations there were. Based on such studies, Gauss was able to develop a mathematical model that could be used to describe the distribution of errors contained in these sets of data. Gauss called the mathematical model the *normal probability model*, and the distribution of errors the normal probability distribution.

We will use the normal probability model descriptively, to describe real variables. Furthermore, we will use it when we introduce inferential statistics to describe the sampling distribution of the mean when the standard deviation of the population is known.

Although the normal probability model is given by a mathematical equation, we do not present that equation here. Instead, we list three characteristics of the distributions described by the normal probability model. The model is used to find the probabilities of certain score ranges by finding the corresponding areas under the normal curve.

1. A normal distribution is symmetric about its mean, $\overline{X}$.
2. A normal distribution extends indefinitely to the right and to the left of the mean, always getting closer and closer to the horizontal axis but never quite reaching it. (That is, observations that are farther from the mean have smaller relative frequencies than observations that are closer to the mean.)
3. The total area under the normal distribution is 1. By symmetry, this means that one-half of the area is to the right of the mean and one-half is to the left.

In general, all normal distributions have the same bell-shaped appearance and differ from each other only in their particular mean and standard deviation values. The mean indicates where the distribution is located on the horizontal axis, whereas the standard deviation indicates the extent to which the scores tend to cluster about the mean. Figure 8.2 shows a general normal distribution curve with mean $\overline{X}$ and standard deviation S and indicates what proportion of the distribution can be expected to lie within one and two standard deviations of the mean.

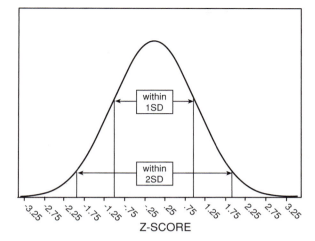

Figure 8.2 The general normal distribution curve.

The normal probability model describes the entire family of normal probability distributions, each with its own mean and standard deviation. The particular normal distribution with mean 0 and standard deviation 1 is called the *standard normal distribution.*

The family of normal probability distributions may be used to answer probability questions about sets of data that are either known, or assumed, to be normally distributed. Probabilities generally can be obtained as proportions of area under the appropriate normal curve.

Because the probabilities are found as areas, all probability values in the continuous case are between 0 and 1 inclusive.

The probability that a single randomly selected score is lower than a particular score *x* is found by calculating the area under the normal distribution curve to the left of *x*. The probability that a single randomly selected score is higher than a particular score *x* is found by calculating the area under the normal distribution curve to the right of *x*.

Alternatively, by the Complement Rule, the probability that a single score selected at random from a normal distribution is higher than the score *x* may be calculated as 1 minus the probability that the score selected is lower than the score *x*.

Because the normal distribution is symmetric, with area under the curve equal to 1, the probability that a single randomly selected score is above the mean equals .5 and the probability that the score is below the mean equals .5.

Because the distribution is continuous rather than discrete, the probability that a randomly selected score has a particular value is zero. As a result, the probability that a single randomly selected score is greater than a particular value *x* is the same as the probability that the single randomly selected score is greater than or equal to *x*.

We illustrate the method of finding probabilities under the normal curve using SPSS and Table 1 in Appendix C, which contains areas under the standard normal curve.

Recall the histogram of the socioeconomic status (SES) distribution illustrated in Chapter 2 as Figure 2.6 and reproduced here as Figure 8.3. Note that in Figure 8.3 a normal curve is superimposed on the histogram.

Although the SES distribution is not normally distributed, it may be considered to be approximately so with mean 18.40 and standard deviation 6.92 and we may use the normal probability distribution to estimate areas under the SES curve.

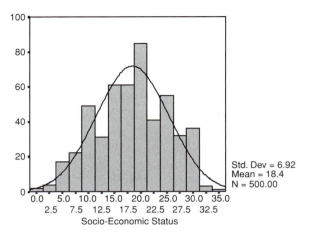

Figure 8.3   SES distribution with normal-curve overlay.

EXAMPLE 8.9. Use the normal distribution with mean 18.40 and standard deviation 6.92 to approximate the proportion of students in the NELS data set with SES values *less than or equal to* 26.

Solution (Based on SPSS Compute Statement). To find the area under the normal curve to the left of $x = 26$ (see Figure 8.4), there are two CDFs available to use in SPSS. First we use the CDF for which we must provide the mean and standard deviation. Then we use the one for the standard normal curve.

First, we use the CDF for the normal curve in SPSS (CDF.NORMAL).

(If you are not already in a data set, open a new Data Editor screen in SPSS and enter a single value in the top-left cell. We do so because a data set is required to activate the Compute procedure in SPSS.)

Click on **Transform** and then **Compute**. Type the variable name PROB (for probability) in the **Target Variable** box. Use the down arrow in the **Functions group** box to locate and click on **CDF & Noncentral CDF** and then locate and find in the **Functions and Special Variables** box **CDF.Normal**.

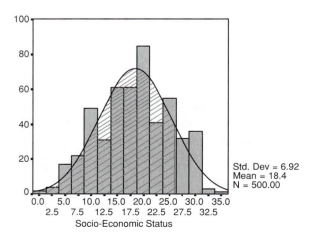

Figure 8.4   The area under the normal curve with $\overline{X} = 18.40$ and $S = 6.92$ to the left of 26.

Highlight this function and move it to the **Numerical Expression** box. The **Numerical Expression** box should contain the following:

CDF.Normal(?,?,?)

The question marks represent *X*, mean, and standard deviation, respectively. This set of question marks should be replaced by 26, 18.40, and 6.92 so that we now have the following in the **Numerical Expression** box:

CDF.Normal(26,18.40,6.92)

Click **OK**. The **Data View** window should contain the value .86 in the column labeled prob. This means that the area under this normal curve to the left of the value 26 equals .86, or that, if you randomly select a score from a normal distribution with mean 18.4 and standard deviation 6.92, the probability that it falls below the value 26 is .86. In the context of our example, this means that approximately 86 percent of the individuals in our NELS data set have SES scores at or below 26.

If you prefer to use the cumulative distribution for the standard normal curve, you must first calculate the *z*-score corresponding to an SES score of 26 using Equation 4.3. We find that z = 1.10, approximately. Click on **Transform** and then **Compute**. Type the variable name PROB (for probability) in the **Target Variable** box. Use the down arrow in the **Functions group** box to locate and click on **CDF & Noncentral CDF** and then in the **Functions and Special Variables** box locate and click on **CDFNorm**.

Highlight this function and move it to the **Numerical Expression** box. The **Numerical Expression** box should contain the following:

CDFNorm(?)

The question mark represents the *z*-score. Replace it with 1.10 so that we now have the following in the **Numerical Expression** box:

CDFNorm(1.10)

Click **OK**. The Data Editor screen should now contain the values for prob in the second column, to two decimal places. The Data Editor screen should contain the value .86 in the column labeled PROB, as it did when we used the CDF.Normal function.

Solution (Based on Table 1 in Appendix C). To use Table 1 in Appendix C to find the proportion of students in the NELS data set with SES values less than or equal to 26 in a distribution with mean 18.40 and standard deviation 6.92, we first need to convert the value 26 to a *z*-score using Equation 4.3. We need to do so because Table 1 gives areas under the standard normal curve with mean 0 and standard deviation 1.

$$z = \frac{X - \overline{X}}{S_X} = \frac{26 - 18.40}{6.92} = 1.10$$

This *z*-score may be decomposed as 1.1 + .00. According to Table 1, the area to the right of this *z*-score is .1357. To find the area to the left of the *z*-score, we use the complement rule and compute 1 − .1357 = .8643, which is the proportion we seek.

We may see how far this estimate departs from the actual percentage of cases at or below an SES score of 26 to assess the accuracy of our approximation. To do so, we use

SPSS to find the percentile rank of 26, estimated from the cumulative percent column obtained from Frequencies. According to the output, the cumulative percent of scores at or below a score of 26 is 85.6, suggesting that the approximation using the normal curve is a good one in this case.

☞ **Remark.** Because SES is a continuous variable, when we ask about the proportion of cases at or below an SES value of 26, it is equivalent to ask about the proportion of cases below an SES value of 26. This is because, for truly continuous variables, the value of exactly 26 has zero probability of occurring.

In inferential statistics, for reasons that become clear in the next chapter, we focus on the upper and lower tails of a probability distribution, as opposed to its middle area. Hence, the next example has as its focus the area in the right tail of a normal distribution.

. . . .

EXAMPLE 8.10. Determine how likely it is to select a value at random from a set of scores known to be normally distributed that is two or more standard deviations above the mean.

Solution (Based on SPSS Compute Statement). This problem is equivalent to finding the area under the normal curve to the right of a z-score of 2. This area is shaded in Figure 8.5. We use the SPSS Compute procedure applied to a standard normal distribution. Because we want the area to the *right* of the z-score and the CDF provides us with areas to the left, we need to use the Complement Rule to find the area we want. In particular, in the **Numerical Expression** box we type the following:

$1 - CDF.Normal (2,0,1)$

or

$1 - CDFNorm(2).$

In so doing, we obtain the area to the right of a z-score of 2 to be .023.

Solution (Based on Table 1 in Appendix C). To use Table 1 in Appendix C to find the area under the standard normal curve to the right of $z = 2.00$, we decompose 2.00 as 2.0 + .00 and find the area under the curve to the right of this value to be .0228.

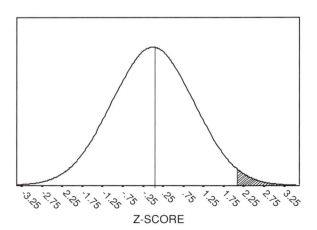

Figure 8.5 Area under the standard normal curve to the right of a z-score of 2.

Z-SCORE

That is, the probability of selecting a score at random from a set of scores known to be normally distributed that is two or more standard deviations above the mean is only .023. Said differently, only 2.3 percent of scores fall in this range.

. . . .

EXAMPLE 8.11. Assuming that SES has a normal distribution with mean 18.4 and standard deviation 6.92, find the SES value that has an area of .025 to its right.

Solution (Based on SPSS Compute Statement). In contrast to the two earlier problems where we sought an area corresponding to a given score, in this problem we seek a score corresponding to a given area. To do so, we make use of the inverse density function (IDF) for the normal curve available in SPSS. (If you are not already in a data set, open a new Data Editor screen in SPSS, and enter a single value in the top-left cell.) Click on **Transform** and then **Compute**. Type the variable name rawscore in the **Target Variable** box. Use the down arrow in the **Functions** box to find **IDF.Normal(p, mean, standard deviation)**.

Highlight this function and move it to the **Numerical Expression** box. The **Numerical Expression** box should contain the following:

IDF.Normal(?,?,?).

The question marks represent the area to the left of the score we are seeking: the distribution mean and standard deviation, respectively. For this example, this set of question marks should be replaced by .975, 18.4, and 6.92 so that we now have the following in the **Numerical Expression** box:

IDF.Normal(.975,0,1).

Click **OK**. The Data Editor screen should now contain the SES value of 31.96 in the column labeled rawscore. This means that .025 of the area under a normal curve falls to the right of the SES score 31.96.

As will be seen in Chapter 10, the z-score with area of .025 to its right is an important value, so we present an alternative solution to the example. To find the z-score with area .025 to its left, we use the same procedure except that we replace the variable name with zscore and the set of question marks in the IDF.Normal expression with .025, 0, 1.

We see that the Data Editor screen now contains the z-score value of 1.96 in the column labeled z-score. This means that .025 of the area under a normal curve falls to the left of 1.96 standard deviations below the mean. By symmetry, the z-score value of 1.96 marks off .025 of the area to its right.

To convert 1.96 to a value within the SES metric, we use Equation 4.4 as follows:

$$X = Sz + \overline{X} = (6.92)(1.96) + 18.4 = 31.96.$$

Solution (Based on Table 1 in Appendix C). To use Table 1 in Appendix C to find the z-score that has an area under the standard normal curve of .025 to its right, we look for .0250 in the body of the table and see what its corresponding z-score is. We find .0250 in the row labeled 1.9 and column labeled .06. Accordingly, the z-score we seek is 1.9 + .06 = 1.96. To convert 1.96 to a value within the SES metric, we use Equation 4.4 as follows:

$$X = Sz + \overline{X} = (6.92)(1.96) + 18.4 = 31.96.$$

EXAMPLE 8.12. Find the left-tailed area corresponding to a z-score of -2.45.

Solution (Based on SPSS Compute Statement). We find CDF.NORMAL(-2.45, 0, 1) or CDFNORM(-2.45) and obtain the value .007.

Solution (Based on Table 1 in Appendix C). To use Table 1 in Appendix C to find the area to the left of $z = -2.45$, we use symmetry to see that it is the same as the right-tailed area for $z = 2.45$. The right-tailed area corresponding to $z = 2.45$ is .0071. Thus, the left-tailed area corresponding to $z = -2.45$ is .0071.

USING THE NORMAL DISTRIBUTION TO APPROXIMATE THE BINOMIAL DISTRIBUTION

As the number of trials in a binomial experiment, n, increases, the binomial distribution more closely resembles, or approaches, the normal distribution. In fact, as long as both products np and nq are greater than or equal to 5, the approximation of the binomial by the normal is quite good. The values p and q, in addition to n, are important conditions for this approximation because a larger value of n is needed to compensate for the skewness introduced whenever $p \neq q$. Exercise 8.28 illustrates how to compute an approximation of a binomial probability using the normal distribution.

EXERCISES

Exercises 8.1 through 8.13 involve the binomial probability model. In Exercises 8.1 through 8.8, decide whether the given problem satisfies the conditions of a binomial experiment; solve the exercise only if it satisfies this requirement.

8.1. A person taking a 15-item true/false examination has studied the material to be covered on the exam. What is the probability that this person will get exactly 10 of the 15 items correct?

8.2. A new drug is being tested, and the results of treatment with this drug are being categorized as full recovery, partial recovery, and additional treatment required. The probabilities of these three possible outcomes are 1/3, 1/3, and 1/3, respectively. If this drug is used on 100 patients, what is the probability that exactly 40 of the patients will have full recovery, 20 will have partial recovery, and 40 will need further treatment?

8.3. It is known that the toys produced by a certain toy manufacturer have a 1-in-10 chance of containing imperfections. What is the probability that, in a day's production of 500 of these toys, exactly 50 have imperfections?

8.4. Suppose giving birth to a girl and giving birth to a boy are equally likely, and Mrs. Fecund is due to give birth to triplets. What is the probability that exactly one of the three children born is a girl?

8.5. A 10-item multiple-choice test is given with 4 possible answers on each item. If a student guesses on each item, what is the probability that she will get
   a) none of the 10 items correct?
   b) exactly 3 of the 10 items correct?
   c) all of the 10 items correct?

    d) at least 8 of the 10 items correct?

    e) at most 4 of the 10 items correct?

    f) between 2 and 5 (inclusive) of the 10 items correct?

8.6. Use the frequency and percent distribution table provided in Exercise 7.1 to find the probability that if 10 schools are selected at random from this data set with replacement that exactly 5 are from the Northeast.

8.7. Suppose that a certain automobile manufacturing company has a problem installing airbags. Usually, these are installed correctly 95 percent of the time. However, on Friday afternoons, these are installed correctly only 90 percent of the time. Assuming that the company manufactures 1,000 cars per week, what is the probability that exactly 950 of these have correctly installed airbags?

8.8. Women over 50 are advised to get a mammogram every year, so there is a need to be aware of the prevalence of false-positive results. A false-positive is defined as a mammogram that is interpreted as indicative of cancer, indeterminate, or prompts recommendations for additional tests in a woman who is not diagnosed with breast cancer within a year. Assuming that the risk of a false-positive result is constant from year to year, the probability of a false-positive result from a single mammogram is $p = .0653$. Given that, find the probability of at least 1 false-positive result in 10 mammograms. The information in this exercise is based on Elmore et al. (1998).

Exercise 8.9 requires the use of SPSS, the NELS data set, and the binomial distribution.

8.9. If one student is selected at random from the NELS data set, use the variable URBAN to determine the probability that

    a) the student is from an urban environment.

    b) the student is from a suburban environment.

    c) the student is not from a rural environment.

    d) the student is from a rural or a suburban environment.

If five students are selected at random with replacement from the NELS data set, determine the probability that

    e) at most 3 of them are from urban environments.

    f) exactly 3 of them are from urban environments.

    g) at least 3 of them are from urban environments.

    h) no more than 3 of them are from urban environments.

8.10. An individual tosses a fair coin 10 times. Find the probability of getting

    a) heads on the first 5 tosses and tails on the second 5 tosses.

    b) 5 heads and 5 tails in any order.

8.11. Suppose you are going to toss a fair coin 3 times and want to determine the probability of obtaining exactly 2 heads in the 3 tosses. Why do the following two methods of solving this problem give different answers?

> **Solution 1.** In terms of numbers of heads obtained, the possible outcomes of the experiment are
>
>   0 heads   1 head   2 heads   3 heads

Because only one of the four outcomes listed satisfies the given condition (2 heads), the probability of this event is 1/4 = .25.

Solution 2. In terms of the way each toss comes out, the possible outcomes of the experiment are

HHH   HTH   HTT   TTH
HHT   THH   THT   TTT

Because three of the eight outcomes listed satisfy the given condition (HHT, HTH, THH), the probability of this event is 3/8=.375.

8.12. Is the following statement true or false? "By the Law of Large Numbers, you are much more likely to obtain 5 heads in 10 tosses of a fair coin than to obtain 2 heads in 4 tosses of a fair coin."

8.13. Given a binomial experiment with $n = 6$ and $p = .5$:
   a) Determine the probability distribution for this experiment.
   b) Construct the corresponding probability bar graph and describe the shape of the distribution.
   c) Use Equation 8.3 to find the mean and the standard deviation of the binomial distribution.

Exercises 8.14 through 8.18 involve the standard normal probability model.

8.14. If a single score is selected at random from a standard normal distribution, find the probability that
   a) the score is above $z = 1.36$.
   b) the score is above $z = -2.08$.
   c) the score is below $z = 1.36$.
   d) the score is below $z = -2.08$
   e) the score is between $z = -2.08$ and $z = 1.36$.
   f) the score is between $z = .40$ and $z = 1.36$.
   g) the score is between $z = -.40$ and $z = -1.36$.
   h) the score is less than $z = -.40$ or greater than $z = .40$.

8.15. If a single score is selected at random from a standard normal distribution,
   a) What is the value of the score, z, such that the probability of selecting a score greater than or equal to z is approximately 30 percent?
   b) What is the value of the score, z, such that the probability of selecting a score greater than or equal to z is approximately 65 percent?
   c) What is the value of the score, z, such that the probability of selecting a score less than or equal to z is approximately 30 percent?
   d) What is the value of the score, z, such that the probability of selecting a score less than or equal to z is approximately 65 percent?

8.16. If a distribution is normally distributed, what proportion of the scores fall
   a) at least two standard deviations below the mean?
   b) at least two standard deviations above the mean?
   c) at least two standard deviations away from the mean?
   d) between $z = -2$ and $z = 2$?

8.17. Find the area under the standard normal curve and
   a) to the right of $z = 2.15$.
   b) more extreme than $z = \pm.85$, that is, more than .85 standard deviations away from the mean.

c) to the left of $z = -1.63$.

d) to the left of $z = 1.3$.

8.18. Find the following z-scores:

a) What z-score on the standard normal curve has an area of .1151 to its right?

b) What z-score on the standard normal curve has an area of .6446 to its right?

c) What z-score on the standard normal curve has an area of .3372 to its left?

Exercises 8.19 through 8.31 involve the use of the normal probability model. In some cases, we assume a normal distribution and find probabilities related to that distribution. In other cases, we look to see the extent to which the normal distribution gives a good approximation to the distribution of the observed data

8.19. If a single score is selected at random from a normal distribution with mean 50 and standard deviation 10, find the probability that

a) the score is above 70.

b) the score is above 40.

c) the score is below 70.

d) the score is below 40.

e) the score is between 40 and 70.

f) the score is between 60 and 70.

g) the score is between 30 and 40.

h) the score is 10 or more points away from the mean.

8.20. A single score is selected at random from a normal distribution with mean 50 and standard deviation 10:

a) What is the value of the score, X, such that the probability of selecting a score greater than or equal to X is 10 percent?

b) What is the value of the score, X, such that the probability of selecting a score greater than or equal to X is 90 percent?

c) What is the value of the score, X, such that the probability of selecting a score less than or equal to X is 90 percent?

d) What is the value of the score, X, such that the probability of selecting a score less than or equal to X is 10 percent?

8.21. Suppose a distribution is normally distributed with mean 75 and standard deviation 10:

a) What is the value of the score, X, such that the probability of selecting a score less than or equal to X is 5 percent?

b) What is the value of the score, X, such that the probability of selecting a score greater than or equal to X is 5 percent?

c) If a single score is selected at random from the distribution, what is the probability that the score falls above 90?

d) If a single score is selected at random from the distribution, what is the probability that the score falls at 90 or above?

e) If a single score is selected at random from the distribution, what is the probability that the score falls between 70 and 80?

f) If a single score is selected at random from the distribution, what is the probability that the score falls below 50?

g) If a single score is selected at random from the distribution, what is the probability that the score falls between 70 and 90?

8.22. Find the *z*-score that has the following percentages of area under the standard normal curve contained between $-z$ and z:

  a) 90 percent.
  b) 95 percent.
  c) 99 percent.

8.23. Given a set of scores that is normally distributed with mean 90 and standard deviation 8, what proportion of individuals will score

  a) between 92 and 96 inclusive?
  b) at least 94?
  c) at most 98?

8.24. One way to qualify to join Mensa, a high IQ society, is to score in the top 2 percent on a standardized IQ test such as the Wechsler Adult Intelligence Scales Full Scale IQ test. The scores on the Full Scale IQ test are normally distributed and standardized to have a mean of 100 and a standard deviation of 15. What score is necessary on this test to qualify for Mensa?

8.25. Suppose the distribution of maximum daily temperatures for a 1,000-day period in a certain tropical area is normal in shape with a mean of 87 degrees Fahrenheit and a standard deviation of 3 degrees Fahrenheit.

  a) How many of these days had maximum daily temperatures above 80 degrees Fahrenheit?
  b) What would be the percentile rank in this distribution for a day that had a maximum temperature of 80 degrees Fahrenheit?

8.26. Suppose you are told that 1,000 scores from a nationally administered achievement test are normally distributed with mean 50 and standard deviation 5.

  a) How many people would you expect to score greater than 57?
  b) What is the percentile rank of a score of 52?
  c) What raw score would you expect 10 percent of the scores to fall above?

8.27. Suppose you are told that the distribution of weights for all 12-month-old males in the United States is normally distributed with a mean of 18 pounds and a standard deviation of 3 pounds. If your son is 12 months old and weighs 22.5 pounds:

  a) What proportion of the 12-month-old male population weighs less than your son?
  b) What is your son's percentile rank relative to this population?

Exercises 8.28 through 8.30 involve the NELS data set and require the use of SPSS.

8.28. Use the normal distribution to approximate the percentage of students in the NELS data set with eighth-grade math achievement scores less than or equal to 72. Then find the actual percentile rank of a score of 72. How do these two values compare and what does this comparison suggest about the appropriateness of using the normal curve to approximate the distribution of eighth-grade math achievement scores?

8.29. Use the normal distribution to approximate the number of students in the NELS data set with eighth-grade math achievement scores (ACHMAT08) that are within one standard deviation of the mean. How does the estimate based on the normal probability model compare to the actual number of scores in the NELS data set that are so extreme?

8.30. Although some distributions of observed data, especially those based on the sum or average of many items, are approximately normal, others are not. In this exercise, we look at an instance where the normal distribution does not give a good approximation of a distribution. Use the normal distribution to approximate the number of students in the NELS data set coming from a school in which 6 or more Advanced Placement (AP) classes are offered (APOFFER). Compare the estimate based on normal distribution to the actual number of students coming from a school in which 6 or more AP classes are offered. Speculate on the reason for the discrepancy.

Exercise 8.31 involves the Impeach data set and requires the use of SPSS.

8.31. Consider the variable SUPPORTC, which gives the distribution of the percentages of the voter support for Clinton. Unless otherwise specified, use the *normal curve* to approximate the distribution of SUPPORTC in order to answer the following questions.

a) Create a histogram with a normal-curve overlay of the variable SUPPORTC. Describe the shape of the distribution.

b) What SUPPORTC score has $z = 1.3$?

c) If SUPPORTC $= 35$ percent, what is z?

d) Use the normal curve to estimate the proportion of states with voter support for Clinton at or below 35 percent.

e) Use a frequency distribution table to find the actual proportion of states with voter support for Clinton at or below 35 percent.

f) What is the approximate percentile rank of a score of 35 percent in SUPPORTC?

g) What proportion or percent of senators score above SUPPORTC $= 55$ percent for their states?

h) What proportion or percent of senators score below SUPPORTC $= 55$ percent for their states?

i) What proportion or percent of senators score between SUPPORTC $= 35$ percent and SUPPORTC $= 55$ percent for their states?

j) What SUPPORTC score cuts off the bottom 30 percent of SUPPORTC values?

k) What SUPPORTC score would place you in the top 5 percent of scores?

l) Use the normal curve to estimate the percentage state voter support for Clinton that would place a state at the 50th percentile for these states.

Exercise 8.28 involves normal approximations to the binomial.

8.32. Given a binomial experiment with number of trials, n, probability of success, p, and probability of failure, q, if both of the products np and nq are greater than or equal to 5, we may use a normal curve with mean $\overline{X} = np$ and standard deviation $SD = \sqrt{npq}$ to approximate the binomial distribution, demonstrated in this exercise.

a) We take a fair coin and toss it 20 times. What is the probability of obtaining between 10 and 15 heads inclusive? Answer this question using the binomial distribution.

b) Demonstrate that the criterion for a normal approximation to the binomial is satisfied.

c) What are the mean and standard deviation of the normal distribution that we use to approximate this binomial distribution?

d) It is not quite so simple as approximating the area under this normal curve between 10 and 15 because the normal distribution is continuous and the binomial distribution is discrete. We need to use a continuity correction. We accomplish this by thinking of the binomial distribution as if it were really continuous with all scores being reported to the nearest integer value. Therefore, the event "between 10 and 15 successes inclusive" should be thought of as if it were really "between 9.5 and 15.5 inclusive." Note that all we have done is to extend the original interval (10 to 15 inclusive) by 0.5 in each direction. This extension of the real interval by 0.5 in each direction is called a correction for continuity and is employed whenever a (continuous) normal distribution is used to approximate a (discrete) binomial distribution for calculating binomial probabilities. Find the area under the normal curve with mean and standard deviation specified in part (c) between 9.5 and 15.5 inclusive. This number is the normal approximation to the answer you obtained in part (a).

CHAPTER NINE

The Role of Sampling in Inferential Statistics

As noted at the beginning of Chapter 7, a distinction exists between descriptive and inferential statistics. Whereas descriptive statistics is used to describe the data at hand, inferential statistics is used to draw inferences from results based on the data at hand to a larger *population* from which the data at hand have been selected. The data at hand form what is called a *sample*. In this chapter we discuss some fundamental components of inferential statistics, including sampling, sampling distributions, and characteristics of estimators.

SAMPLES AND POPULATIONS

Why, you may ask, should we study a sample at all if what we are really interested in is the population? Why not just study the population itself and be done with it? The answer to this question is that in actual research situations it is often not possible, in terms of both time and resources, to obtain the desired data from the entire population.

For example, suppose we wanted to know, in a particular election year, how people were going to vote in the upcoming presidential election. The population, in this case, consists of all the people eligible to vote in the general election. Clearly, it would be enormously expensive and time-consuming to gather and tabulate data from each person in the population. Instead, we would select a sample that is somehow representative of the entire population, poll the sample on how they will vote, and then draw conclusions about the population from the sample. Though we are studying the sample, our real interest in inferential statistics is the population, and the conclusions we draw are always about the population.

We can describe measures taken of populations of things in the same ways that we can describe measures taken of samples of things. For example, if we could get data from the entire population, we could compute all measures of location, variability, and relationship (e.g., the mean, standard deviation, and correlation) just as we can on a sample taken from that population. When computed for populations, the values of such descriptive measures are called *parameters*; when computed for samples, they are called *statistics*. In inferential statistics, we use statistics computed on a sample to draw conclusions about unknown parameters in the population. To make it clear whether we are talking about a measure taken of a sample or of a population, we denote statistics by Roman letters and parameters by Greek letters. Table 9.1 contains examples of these symbols.

As another example, consider that we want to find the mean (average) number of hours eighth graders in the United States spend watching television per week. To find exactly

Table 9.1. Symbols for common statistics and parameters

Statistics	Parameters
$\overline{X}$ = M = Sample Mean	μ = Population Mean
S^2 = Sample Variance	σ^2 = Population Variance
S = Sample Standard Deviation	σ = Population Standard Deviation
r = Sample Correlation	ρ = Population Correlation

what we want (the population mean, μ), we would somehow have to obtain the number of hours of television viewing for each member of the population. This is obviously impractical. Instead we might pick a sample of, say, 1,000 eighth graders in the New York metropolitan area, find the mean number of hours of television watched in the sample, and then use our calculated value of the sample mean, $\overline{X}$, as an estimate of the unknown population mean μ.

Do you think the procedure we have just outlined is a good one for estimating the mean number of hours of television viewing, μ, of the population described? Actually, there are several things wrong with it. First, we have not explained how our sample is to be picked or why we want it to be of size $N = 1,000$. Do we just walk into the nearest middle school and pick the first 1,000 eighth graders we see? If we are going to draw valid conclusions about the population from calculations made on the sample, we want the sample to be representative of the population. Second, can we expect the sample mean $\overline{X}$ to be a good estimator of the population mean μ? Analogously, can we expect the sample mode to be a good estimator of the population mode and the sample variance to be good estimator of the population variance? After all, the sample size N is not a good estimator of the population size, is it? Considerations like these are crucial for the correct use and understanding of inferential statistics. Before proceeding, let us take a closer look at them.

RANDOM SAMPLES

For conclusions about our population to be accurate, the sample we use must be a subset of the population. For example, if we were interested in estimating the median income for all practicing attorneys in the United States (the population), it would make no sense to select a sample of medical doctors on which to base the estimate. Obviously, our sample should comprise attorneys from the population. That is, we would in some way select a sample of attorneys from our population of all practicing attorneys in the United States and compute the median income of the sample. We might then be able to use this sample median as an estimator of the median of the population. Many samples could be picked from this population; however, each sample would differ somewhat from all the other samples, even though they all come from the same population. Therefore, the accuracy of our estimate depends, among other things, on how representative our sample is of the population. If our sample is truly representative of the population, we can expect our estimate of the population median to be accurate. On the other hand, if our sample deviates to some extent from being truly representative of the population, we would expect our estimate to be inaccurate to some extent.

The question that naturally arises in this connection is whether it is possible to determine just how representative is a particular sample, and therefore how accurate is the corresponding estimate. The answer to this question is that in most cases we cannot make such a determination with a particular sample, but we can do so in the long run if we use specific sampling procedures in selecting our sample, called *probability sampling*. If we follow the procedure known as *simple random sampling* (or just *random sampling)* to select our sample, we can often determine probabilistically just how representative or nonrepresentative our sample can be expected to be. This is not possible or feasible with many other types of sampling procedures, which is why much of inferential statistics is based on the assumptions of random sampling from populations.

Suppose, for example, we wish to estimate the proportion of students enrolled in fifth grade throughout the state of Idaho who are female. Suppose too that somehow we are able to determine that, if we use simple random sampling to select a sample of size $N = 25$, the probability of selecting a representative sample is high. We then go ahead and select a random sample of 25 fifth graders in Idaho and find that our sample consists of 25 males and no females. Our estimate of the proportion of students enrolled in the fifth grade who are female would therefore be 0/25, or 0.

In this example, we know enough about the characteristics of the population under study (all fifth graders in Idaho) to realize that the sample we have selected, by virtue of the fact that it contains no females, is not representative of the population. In most cases, however, we simply do not know enough about the characteristics of the population to determine whether the sample actually selected is representative. (If we knew so much about the population, we probably would not be using inferential statistics on it in the first place.) *Before selecting our sample*, we know only what the *chances* are of obtaining a sample with a given degree of representativeness. All we can do is set up our sampling procedures so as to ensure that the probabilities of obtaining representative samples are large and the probabilities of obtaining nonrepresentative samples are small. And we must be aware that either type of sample *could* occur. We should then be able to answer such questions as: "What is the probability that a random sample of 200 practicing lawyers in the United States will have a median income that differs from the median income of all practicing lawyers in the United States by less than $1,000?" If that probability is high and the sample median turns out to be $25,000, we can be reasonably sure that the population median is somewhere between $24,000 ($25,000 − $1,000) and $26,000 ($25,000 + $1,000). With this introduction, we turn to a discussion of simple random sampling.

OBTAINING A SIMPLE RANDOM SAMPLE

Once we have decided we want to use random sampling, the question becomes: "What is a random sample and how do we get one?" Simply stated, a simple *random sample* is a sample chosen from a given population in such a way as to ensure that each person or thing in the population has an equal and independent chance of being picked for the sample. To understand what we mean by the words *equal and independent*, think of the selection of a sample as picking a first object from the population to be in the sample, then picking a second object from those remaining in the population, and so on. *Equal* means that at each stage of the selection process all the objects remaining in the population are equally likely to be picked for the sample. *Independent* means that no pick has any effect on any other pick. Violating either one of these conditions results in a nonrandom sample.

Let us illustrate what can go wrong in selecting a random sample. Suppose you are the president of the local Democratic Club and you want to get some indication of how the registered Democrats in your district feel about a certain bill. You plan to select a random sample of size 20 from the population of registered Democrats in your district and ask the people in the sample their opinion of the bill. After randomly selecting 19 registered Democrats, you suddenly notice that all 19 are female, so you decide to pick your 20th member of the sample from among the male registered Democrats only. Is your sample a random one? It is not, because at the last stage (the 20th selection), all the people remaining in the population *did not have an equal chance of being picked*. In fact, the women remaining at the last stage had no chance of being picked.

As another example, suppose you want some information about all the students in the local high school. To save time, you are going to select a random sample of 25 students from this population, find out from the sample what you want to know, and then infer from the sample to the population. You also decide, however, that you do not want more than one student from any one family in the sample. Is this a random sample of your population? It is not if the population contains any brother–brother, sister–sister, or brother–sister pairs. If such pairs exist, the different stages of the selection process *might not be independent of each other*. In other words, each selection of a member of the sample disqualifies all that student's brothers and sisters from selection in later stages of the selection process.

The actual selection of a random sample can be accomplished through the use of a uniform random-number generator available in most statistical software packages, including SPSS. The important properties of a uniform random-number generator are that (1) each digit generated is independent of all other digits and (2) in the long run each digit occurs with equal frequency. For example, one million digits generated by a uniform random-number generator should contain approximately one hundred thousand 0s, one hundred thousand 1s, . . . , and one hundred thousand 9s.

Suppose you have 5,000 cases in your population from which you would like to select a simple random sample of size 50 and collect data on these 50. Number the objects in your population from 1 to 5,000. We may perform the selection using SPSS by opening a new data file and by defining, for example, a variable ID that has values, ordered consecutively, from 1 to 75, the size of the desired sample plus 25 to take into account the generation of possible duplicate values. The 75 values may be entered manually or, for the more sophisticated reader, may be entered using the syntax window with the program *idgener.sps* and instructions given in item (1) of Appendix B. Once the variable ID is defined with all 75 values, click **Transform**, **Compute**. Type RANDM as the target variable, and in the **Function Group** box, locate and click **Random Numbers**. Next, in the **Functions and Special Variables** box, locate and click RV.UNIFORM and move it into the **Numerical Expression** box. It should appear as RV.UNIFORM(?,?). The question marks represent, respectively, the minimum and maximum value of the uniform distribution from which the 75 random digits are selected. Substitute 1 and 5,000 for min and max, respectively. Click **OK**. Seventy-five uniform random numbers ranging from 1 to 5,000 should appear in the **Data View** window under the variable RANDM. These values each contain two decimal places. Round each to the nearest whole integer by moving to the **Variable View** window and decreasing the number of decimals for this variable from two to zero. Read down the list, one number at a time, and select that case from your population that corresponds to that random number in the list. If the random number in the list duplicates an earlier number, discard it and move on to the next random number.

SAMPLING WITH AND WITHOUT REPLACEMENT

Simple random sampling is an example of what is called *sampling without replacement*. That is, once an object from the population has been selected to be included in the sample, it is removed from consideration in all remaining stages of the selection process. (Although the same number may be *picked* more than once, it is never *used* more than once in obtaining the sample.) In *sampling with replacement*, *every* object in the population is available for selection to the sample at every stage of the selection process, regardless of whether it has already been selected. Note that one consequence of sampling with replacement is that the same object may be picked more than once. Because simple random sampling is sampling without replacement, this cannot happen in our sampling procedure. The following example illustrates some of the differences between these two sampling procedures.

EXAMPLE 9.1. We have a deck of 52 playing cards (consisting of 4 suits, clubs, diamonds, hearts, spades, with 13 cards per suit, ace, 2, 3, 4, 5, 6, 7, 8, 9, 10, Jack, Queen, and King), and we want to select a sample of size 2 from this population. Describe both sampling with and sampling without replacement in this context and the probabilities of selection associated with each.

Solution

1. *With replacement.* One of the 52 cards is selected to be in the sample. Then this card is replaced in the deck and a second card is selected to complete the sample. Because the card that is picked first is replaced before the second card is selected, the same card can be selected both times, and the probability of any particular card being picked does not change from the first selection to the second. (The probability of any particular card being picked is 1/52 on the first selection and 1/52 on the second selection.)

2. *Without replacement.* One of the 52 cards is selected to be in the sample. Then, without this card being replaced, a second card is selected from the remaining 51 to complete the sample. In this case, the same card *cannot* be selected both times, and the probability of any particular card being picked *does* change from the first selection to the second. (For the first selection, each card has a probability of 1/52 of being picked. For the second selection, the card that was picked the first time has a probability of 0 of being picked, and all the other cards have a probability of 1/51 of being picked.)

Why have we gone to the trouble of discussing and comparing these two types of sampling? Although random sampling is sampling *without* replacement, many of the techniques we want to use in inferential statistics hold only when sampling with replacement is being used. Somehow we must reconcile this apparent conflict of interest. We can do this by introducing the concept of an infinite population.

A population is said to be *infinite* if it has at least as many objects in it as there are positive integers (1, 2, 3, . . .). If we draw a finite sample from an infinite population, then

Table 9.2. Probabilities of selecting the second card (population size = 52; sample size = 2)

	With replacement	Without replacement
Probability of ace of hearts	$\frac{1}{52} = .0192307$	$\frac{0}{52} = .0$
Probability of all other cards	$\frac{1}{52} = .0192307$	$\frac{1}{51} = .0196078$

sampling with and without replacement are essentially the same because discarding a few objects does not appreciably alter the relative occurrence of objects in the population. Most realistic applications of inferential statistics involve very large, but still finite, populations. When our population size is very large relative to the sample size N, then *for all practical purposes* it can be thought of as an infinite population, in which case sampling with and without replacement are essentially the same. For most statistical purposes, this is the case when the population size *is at least 100 times* as large as the sample size. To illustrate, let us return to the example of selecting a sample of size 2 from a deck of playing cards. If the first card selected were the ace of hearts, the probabilities for selecting the second card are as given in Table 9.2.

Note how different the probabilities are with and without replacement. This is because the population is only 26 times as large as the sample being drawn from it (52 compared to 2). If, on the other hand, we take 100 decks of cards as our population, the proportions are still the same (each type of card makes up 100/5,200 or 1/52 of the population), but now the population is 2,600 times as large as the sample (5,200 compared to 2). If we again assume that the first card selected was an ace of hearts, the probabilities for selecting the second card are as given in Table 9.3.

The probabilities for sampling with and without replacement are much closer to each other in Table 9.3 than in Table 9.2. In other words, when the population is at least 100 times as large as the sample being drawn from it, we can assume that, for all practical purposes, sampling with and without replacement are essentially the same.

☞ **Remark.** The inferential statistical techniques we present from this point on are really appropriate only for sampling with replacement. However, by assuming that all populations are at least 100 times as large as the samples being drawn from them, we are able to use sampling without replacement and obtain quite accurate results.

Table 9.3. Probabilities of selecting the second card (population size = 5,200; sample size = 2)

	With Replacement	Without Replacement
Probability of ace of hearts	$\frac{100}{5,200} = .0192307$	$\frac{99}{5,199} = .0190421$
Probability of all other cards	$\frac{100}{5,200} = .0192307$	$\frac{100}{5,199} = .0192344$

SAMPLING DISTRIBUTIONS

Now that we are somewhat more familiar with what a random sample is and how one is selected, we turn to the question of how it is used in inferential statistics. As mentioned previously, the basic idea in inferential statistics is to use a statistic calculated on a sample to estimate a parameter of a population. This procedure is made difficult by the unavoidable fact that in most cases the value we get for any statistic varies somewhat from sample to sample, even when all the samples are randomly selected from the same "parent" population.

DESCRIBING THE SAMPLING DISTRIBUTION OF MEANS EMPIRICALLY

Imagine the process of deciding on a particular sample size N to use, randomly choosing and listing all possible samples of size N from the parent population, and, for each sample, recording the value of the statistic we are interested in. (Of course, each *sample* of size N is replaced in the population before the next sample of size N is selected.) If we then take all the values we have obtained for this statistic, we can construct a frequency distribution of them just as we can construct a frequency distribution of any collection of numbers. Such a distribution is called an *empirical* (or observed) *sampling distribution* for the given statistic.

EXAMPLE 9.2. Use the following population of 10 scores and compute by hand the *sampling distribution of means* for samples of size $N = 2$ drawn from it. Use the sampling distribution of means to determine the probability that, when a single sample of size $N = 2$ is selected from the population, its mean is within 2 points of the actual population mean.

(We really should not use a population that is only five times as large as the sample being drawn from it, but doing so makes the sampling distribution easier to enumerate.)

Population: 0 1 3 3 5 7 7 7 8 10

Note that, according to SPSS, the population mean is 5.1 and the population standard deviation is 3.25.

Solution. In the following table, we list all possible random samples of size $N = 2$ that could possibly be drawn from this population and for each one calculate its sample mean $\overline{X}$.

Sample	Mean	Sample	Mean	Sample	Mean	Sample	Mean	Sample	Mean
0,0	0.0	3,0	1.5	5,0	2.5	7,0	3.5	8,0	4.0
0,1	0.5	3,1	2.0	5,1	3.0	7,1	4.0	8,1	4.5
0,3	1.5	3,3	3.0	5,3	4.0	7,3	5.0	8,3	5.5
0,3	1.5	3,3	3.0	5,3	4.0	7,3	5.0	8,3	5.5
0,5	2.5	3,5	4.0	5,5	5.0	7,5	6.0	8,5	6.5
0,7	3.5	3,7	5.0	5,7	6.0	7,7	7.0	8,7	7.5
0,7	3.5	3,7	5.0	5,7	6.0	7,7	7.0	8,7	7.5
0,7	3.5	3,7	5.0	5,7	6.0	7,7	7.0	8,7	7.5
0,8	4.0	3,8	5.5	5,8	6.5	7,8	7.5	8,8	8.0
0,10	5.0	3,10	6.5	5,10	7.5	7,10	8.5	8,10	9.0

Sample	Mean	Sample	Mean	Sample	Mean	Sample	Mean	Sample	Mean
1,0	0.5	3,0	1.5	7,0	3.5	7,0	3.5	10,0	5.0
1,1	1.0	3,1	2.0	7,1	4.0	7,1	4.0	10,1	5.5
1,3	2.0	3,3	3.0	7,3	5.0	7,3	5.0	10,3	6.5
1,3	2.0	3,3	3.0	7,3	5.0	7,3	5.0	10,3	6.5
1,5	3.0	3,5	4.0	7,5	6.0	7,5	6.0	10,5	7.5
1,7	4.0	3,7	5.0	7,7	7.0	7,7	7.0	10,7	8.5
1,7	4.0	3,7	5.0	7,7	7.0	7,7	7.0	10,7	8.5
1,7	4.0	3,7	5.0	7,7	7.0	7,7	7.0	10,7	8.5
1,8	4.5	3,8	5.5	7,8	7.5	7,8	7.5	10,8	9.0
1,10	5.5	3,10	6.5	7,10	8.5	7,10	8.5	10,10	10.0

For example, the first pair listed in the table (0,0) represents the sample of size 2 containing the values 0 and 0. Its corresponding sample mean is (0 + 0)/2 = 0.0.

We can now enter these sample mean values into SPSS and create a frequency distribution table and a corresponding frequency histogram, shown in Table 9.4 and Figure 9.1, respectively.

The histogram depicts the way in which the process of sampling at random from a population produces a distribution of mean values. It is an example of what we have called an empirical sampling distribution-in this case, a sampling distribution of means from samples of size $N = 2$.

means

		Frequency	Percent	Valid Percent	Cumulative Percent
Valid	.00	1	1.0	1.0	1.0
	.50	2	2.0	2.0	3.0
	1.00	1	1.0	1.0	4.0
	1.50	4	4.0	4.0	8.0
	2.00	4	4.0	4.0	12.0
	2.50	2	2.0	2.0	14.0
	3.00	6	6.0	6.0	20.0
	3.50	6	6.0	6.0	26.0
	4.00	12	12.0	12.0	38.0
	4.50	2	2.0	2.0	40.0
	5.00	15	15.0	15.0	55.0
	5.50	6	6.0	6.0	61.0
	6.00	6	6.0	6.0	67.0
	6.50	6	6.0	6.0	73.0
	7.00	9	9.0	9.0	82.0
	7.50	8	8.0	8.0	90.0
	8.00	1	1.0	1.0	91.0
	8.50	6	6.0	6.0	97.0
	9.00	2	2.0	2.0	99.0
	10.00	1	1.0	1.0	100.0
	Total	100	100.0	100.0	

Table 9.4. Frequency and percent distribution table for the sampling distribution of means for samples of size $N = 2$

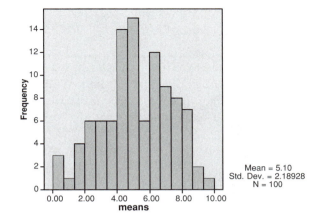

Figure 9.1 Histogram of sampling distribution of means for samples of size $N = 2$.

To use the sampling distribution of means to determine the probability that a sample mean selected at random is within 2 points of the actual population mean, we find the proportion of sample means that are between 3.5 and 7 inclusive. According to the frequency distribution table, 62 of the 100 equally likely sample means fall within that range, so we conclude that the probability that a randomly selected sample mean is within 2 points of the actual population mean is .62.

EXAMPLE 9.3. Compare the graph of Figure 9.2, the sampling distribution of means from the population {0, 1, 3, 3, 5, 7, 7, 7, 8, 10} based on 50,000 samples of size 8 randomly selected with replacement from this population of 10 scores, with that of Figure 9.1.

☞ **Remark.** The data for Figure 9.2 were generated via a program called a macro, written in the SPSS syntax language, that generates the sampling distribution of means from the population given in Example 9.2, based on samples of size 8. The macro is provided in Appendix B, Section 2, along with additional instructions on how to run it. It is also available on the CD included with your text in the file labeled *sampdis.sps*. Unfortunately, the student version of SPSS does not come with a syntax window and so

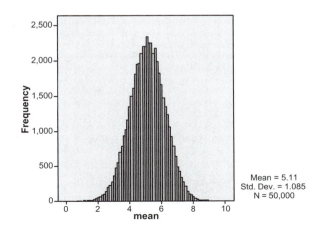

Figure 9.2 Sampling distribution of means, $N = 8$.

readers of this text who only have access to a student version will not be able open or execute this syntax file.

To use the SPSS macro *sampdis.sps*, open the file in the SPSS syntax window from the CD that accompanies the text. Click **Run, All.** Results appear under the variable labeled Mean in the data editor. The file is called *bootmean.sav*. Construct a histogram of these data. You should obtain a figure similar, but not necessary exactly equal to, Figure 9.2.

Solution. We can use Figures 9.1 and 9.2 to compare how much we can expect our sample statistic value to vary from sample to sample depending on the size of the sample. For example, Figure 9.1 reveals that if we were to select a sample of size $N = 2$ at random with replacement from the given population, the mean value for this sample would most likely fall somewhere between 3 and 8. Notice that sample mean values down to 0.0 and up to 10 would also be possible but less likely. Figure 9.2 reveals that, if we were to select at random, and with replacement, a sample of size $N = 8$ from the given population, the mean value for this sample would most likely fall somewhere between the narrower interval of 4.0 to 6.5. Sample mean values below 2 and above 8 would also be possible, but far less likely.

Based on this comparison, we find that the range of mean values *most likely* to be obtained decreases as the sample size increases. We also note that the population mean for our 10 scores is $\mu = 5.1$, which falls within both intervals, 3 and 8, and 4.5 and 6.0, the sample mean values most likely to be obtained in each of the two cases, respectively. Thus, we find that as we increase the size of our sample we can expect to obtain a more accurate estimate of the population mean. As a general rule, when we use sample statistics to estimate population parameters, the larger the sample we use, the more accurate an estimate we can expect.

Figures 9.1 and 9.2 illustrate not only that the larger the sample size, the more accurate the population parameter estimate, but also that the larger the sample size, the more the shape of the sampling distribution resembles the normal distribution. Notice that Figure 9.2 looks much more like a normal distribution than Figure 9.1. The population we used in these examples (Examples 9.2 and 9.3) consists of a particular set of ten scores with a particular distribution. However, it can be shown that, if we had begun with a different population of scores with a different distribution (and, of course, there are an infinite number of distributions that we could have chosen), we would have obtained a similar result. That is, regardless of the population distribution of scores, as the sample size increases, the estimate of the population mean becomes more accurate and the shape of the sampling distribution of means becomes much more like that of a normal distribution. This is what is called the *Central Limit Theorem* (CLT), which is more formally stated in the next section.

DESCRIBING THE SAMPLING DISTRIBUTION OF MEANS THEORETICALLY: THE CENTRAL LIMIT THEOREM

Using the methods of mathematical statistics, it is often possible to determine *theoretically* what the sampling distribution of a particular sample statistic should look like. Whereas the previous example was concerned with the mean, theoretical sampling distributions may be obtained for other common sample statistics as well, including, for example, the variance and correlation coefficient. As noted in the preceding section, the sampling distribution of means becomes more normal in shape as the sample size increases. As discussed in later chapters, the theoretical sampling distributions of many of the other common statistics covered in this book (e.g., the variance) approach a different set of shapes as the sample size increases. Regardless of their eventual shape, however, these theoretical sampling distributions provide the foundation for drawing inferences about the population by making explicit the relationship that exists between the parameters of that population and those of the sampling distribution.

We now present a more formal statement of the CLT, which specifies the shape, mean, and standard deviation of a sampling distribution of means in terms of the parameters, μ and σ, of the population from which these samples have been derived.

CENTRAL LIMIT THEOREM (CLT)

Given a population of values with no specified distribution, and a sample of size N that is sufficiently large, the *sampling distribution of means* for samples drawn from this population with replacement can be described as follows:

1. Its shape is *approximately* normally distributed.
2. Its mean, $\mu_{\bar{X}}$, is equal to μ.
3. Its standard deviation, $\sigma_{\bar{x}}$, is equal to $\sigma/\sqrt{N}$.

☞ **Remark.** Notice that we denote the mean of the sampling distribution of means as $\mu_{\bar{X}}$ because it is the mean of means. Furthermore, we denote the standard deviation of the sampling distribution of means as $\sigma_{\bar{x}}$ because it is the standard deviation of means. The standard deviation of the sampling distribution of means, $\sigma_{\bar{x}}$, is also referred to as the *standard error of the mean*.

Note that the CLT requires that the samples be drawn from the population with replacement. However, as long as the population being considered is relatively large compared to the sample being drawn from it (for our purposes, at least 100 times as large), sampling with or without replacement gives approximately equivalent results, so the CLT holds approximately. One of the statements in the CLT is that if the sample size N being used is sufficiently large, then certain results will be true. Just what is meant here by "sufficiently large"? This is a subjective question. The answer varies from one situation to another and from one researcher to another. In general, the larger the sample size N being used, the closer the approximation, and it is up to the researcher to decide just how good an approximation is desired. By empirical observation, for our purposes in this book we consider that the distribution of means based on samples of N greater than or equal to 30 ($N \geq 30$) gives a good enough approximation to a normal distribution.

☞ **Remark.** Notice that Figure 9.2 looks quite normal in shape despite the fact that the conditions of the CLT are not met. That is, the parent population is not normally distributed and $N = 8$. It is likely that Figure 9.2 looks quite normal in shape because the distribution of the population from which the samples have been randomly selected is approximately symmetric. When distributions are known to be symmetric or approximately so, a minimum value of $N = 30$ is rather conservative. When distributions are known to be nearly normal, sample sizes as low as 10 or even 8 may be appropriate, and when distributions are known to be exactly normal, a sample of any size yields a normally distributed sampling distribution.

The CLT was first proved by Abraham de Moivre in connection with his interest in developing techniques for the calculation of gamblers' odds that emerged from his frequent visits to London coffeehouses. The proof, along with the techniques he developed, was first published in 1738 in his book, *The Doctrine of Chances* (Salsburg, 2001; Stigler, 1986).

The CLT is a powerful and extremely useful statement of probability theory that underlies why the normal distribution is commonly used to model (or approximate the distribution of) observed data.

Let us look at some examples of how to use the CLT to determine, for given populations and sample sizes, what sampling distributions of means should look like.

EXAMPLE 9.4. Suppose we are given a normally distributed population of 5,000 scores with mean equal to 15 and standard deviation equal to 3. (a) What does the corresponding sampling distribution of means for samples of size $N = 16$ (with replacement) look like? (b) If we were to select a single sample of size $N = 16$ at random from this population of scores, what is the probability that the mean for this sample falls between 13 and 17?

Solution.

1. Because the parent population is normally distributed, the sampling distribution of means is also normally distributed; its mean, $\mu_{\bar{x}}$, is equal to the mean of the population, 15, and its standard deviation, $\sigma_{\bar{x}}$, is given by $\sigma_{\bar{x}} = \sigma/\sqrt{N} = 3/4 = .75$. The parent population and the corresponding sampling distribution of means based on 1,000 samples, each of size 16, randomly drawn from the population with replacement are shown in Figures 9.3 and 9.4, respectively. Notice that even though the means are the same in both figures, the range of scores on the horizontal axis in Figure 9.3 is from 6 to 24, whereas in Figure 9.4 it is only from 12 to 18.

2. Because we are making a statement about the sampling distribution of means, which is known to be normally distributed with mean 15 and standard deviation .75, we use the CDF.Normal function with these values. To find the area between 13 and 17, we find the area below 17 and subtract the area below 13. To do that, we use the SPSS COMPUTE statement with the following numeric expression:

CDF.Normal(17,15,.75) − CDF.Normal(13,15,.75).

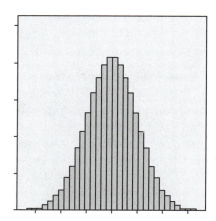

Figure 9.3   Normally distributed population, 1,000 scores; $\mu = 15, \sigma = 3$.

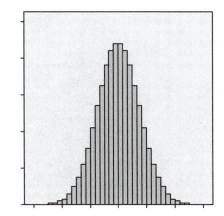

Figure 9.4 Sampling distribution of means, $N = 16$, $\mu_{\bar{X}} = 15$, $\sigma_{\bar{X}} = .75$.

The value obtained is .99, indicating that almost all such sample means fall within the specified range.

EXAMPLE 9.5. Suppose we are given an arbitrarily distributed (say, positively skewed) population of 1,000 scores with mean equal to 8 and standard deviation equal to 4. What does the corresponding sampling distribution of means for samples of size $N = 100$ (with replacement) look like?

Solution. Because the sample size ($N = 100$) is sufficiently large, we know from the CLT that the sampling distribution of means is approximately normally distributed; that its standard deviation is equal to $\sigma_{\bar{x}} = \sigma/\sqrt{N} = 4/10 = 0.4$; and that its mean $\mu_{\bar{X}}$ is equal to the mean of the parent population, 8. Figure 9.5 shows what the parent population might look like and Figure 9.6 shows what the corresponding sampling distribution of means based on 10,000 samples, each of size 100, randomly selected from the positively skewed parent population with replacement will look like. The means and histogram are generated by the syntax program SAMPDISVER2.SPS described in Appendix B, Section 6. Because the means are generated by this program through a random process, one that relies on randomly selecting samples from the positively skewed parent population, the histogram you obtain on re-running this program is similar, but not identical, to the histogram of Figure 9.6.

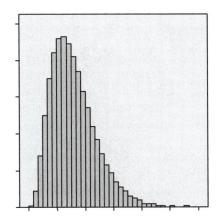

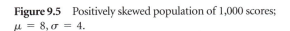

Figure 9.5 Positively skewed population of 1,000 scores; $\mu = 8$, $\sigma = 4$.

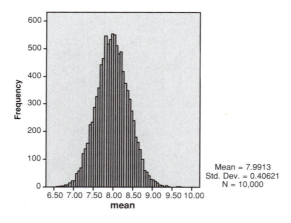

Figure 9.6 Sampling distribution of 10,000 means, each of size 100; $\mu_{\overline{X}} = 8, \sigma_{\overline{X}} = 0.4$.

One of the things the CLT tells us is that, as long as sampling with replacement is used and the other conditions specified are satisfied, the sampling distribution of means will have its mean equal to the mean of the parent population. As a matter of fact, this result is exactly true even if sampling is without replacement, if the sample size is not sufficiently large, and if the population is not at least 100 times as large as the sample being drawn from it. In other words, given any size population and any sample size N, and whether we are sampling with or without replacement, the sampling distribution of means of size N from this population will have its mean equal to the mean of the parent population. We use this fact in the next section on estimators and bias.

Another immediate consequence of the CLT is that whenever its conditions are satisfied we can, by increasing sample size N, make the sampling distribution of means cluster as closely as we want around its mean μ. (Look again at the formula for the standard deviation of the sampling distribution given in the CLT. Because the denominator is just the square root of N, we can make $\sigma_{\overline{x}}$ as small as we like by making N sufficiently large, and a small standard deviation implies that the scores are all clustered about the distribution's mean.) Because the mean of the sampling distribution is also the mean of the parent population, we can conclude once again that as the sample size we are using increases we can expect our sample means $\overline{X}$ to become more and more accurate as estimators of the population mean μ.

ESTIMATORS AND BIAS

Suppose that we have a population with an unknown mean μ and that we want to use a random sample to estimate μ. It seems reasonable to expect that the sample mean $\overline{X}$ should be a better estimator of μ than either the sample mode or sample median. But just what is it that makes an estimator good or bad? One important property, and the one we discuss in this section, is what is called "unbiasedness."

A sample statistic is said to be an *unbiased estimator* for a population parameter if the sampling distribution for this statistic has a mean value equal to the parameter being estimated. In other words, the statistic is an unbiased estimator if the values of the statistic obtained from sampling are, on average, equal to the parameter.

As we mentioned earlier, the sample mean $\overline{X}$ has exactly this property as an estimator of the population mean μ. Therefore, we can say that $\overline{X}$ is an unbiased estimator of μ. The sample variance, however, when computed using the usual variance formula, $S^2 = \dfrac{\sum(X_i - \overline{X})^2}{N}$, is *not* an unbiased estimator of the population variance σ^2. It is a biased estimator. In particular, the mean of all the S^2 for a given sample size is always smaller than the value of σ^2. If the N in the denominator of the variance formula were replaced by $N - 1$, however, it can be shown mathematically that the resulting formula would be an unbiased estimator of σ^2. For the purpose of estimating the variance of the population, we therefore define a new sample statistic, $\hat{\sigma}^2$, called the *variance estimator*, which is given by Equation 9.1:

$$\hat{\sigma}^2 = \frac{\sum(X_i - \overline{X})^2}{N - 1}.$$ (9.1)

Recall that SPSS calls this variance estimator the "variance." When our aim is to describe the "spread" of scores in the sample for its own sake and not to estimate the variance of the population, we seek the sample variance and therefore need to adjust the variance value that SPSS provides by multiplying that value by $(N - 1)/N$. When the purpose is to estimate the population variance σ^2, however, we seek the variance estimator provided directly by SPSS.

If we take the positive square root of the variance estimator, we obtain $\hat{\sigma}$, which is referred to as the *square root* of the variance estimator. We do not call $\hat{\sigma}$ the standard deviation estimator because, even though $\hat{\sigma}^2$ is an unbiased estimator of σ^2, $\hat{\sigma}^2$ is *not* an unbiased estimator of σ.

EXERCISES

9.1. Given the following population of values: {0, 1, 2, 3, 4, 5, 6, 7, 8, 9}.
   a) Describe the shape of the distribution of the population scores.
   b) Make a list of all the samples of size $N = 2$ that could be selected with replacement from this population.
   c) Enter the list of the means of these samples into a new SPSS data set. Create a frequency and percent distribution table.
   d) Construct a histogram for the distribution of sample means found in part (b). This graph depicts the sampling distribution of means for samples of size $N = 2$ from our population. Describe the shape of this distribution.
   e) Find the mean and standard deviation of both the population and the sampling distribution of means. How do they compare?
   f) If we were to use the mean of a randomly selected sample of size $N = 2$ to estimate the population mean in this exercise, what would be the probability of getting an estimate within two points of the exact answer?

9.2. Use the computer and the syntax instructions located in Appendix B to generate an approximation to the sampling distributions of means from the population {0, 1, 2, 3, 4, 5, 6, 7, 8, 9} based on 10,000 samples of size 36. Construct a histogram of the distribution.

Compare the actual mean and standard deviation for the sampling distribution of means to those based on the CLT.

9.3.

a) Describe how one obtains the sampling distribution of means for samples of size $N = 8$.

b) If a certain population is normally distributed with mean 70 and standard deviation of 2.5, give the mean and the standard deviation of the sampling distribution of means of size $N = 8$.

c) Describe the effect on your answer to part (b) of increasing the sample size.

d) If we were to select a single sample of size $N = 8$, what is the probability that the mean of this sample is two or more points higher than the actual population mean?

9.4. Suppose we are given a normally distributed population of scores with mean equal to 500 and standard deviation equal to 100.

a) Describe the shape of the sampling distribution of means of size $N = 30$ (with replacement).

b) What is the mean of the sampling distribution of means of size $N = 30$ (with replacement)?

c) What is the standard deviation of the sampling distribution of means of size $N = 30$ (with replacement), also called the standard error of the mean?

d) If we were to select a single sample of size $N = 30$ at random from this population of scores, what is the probability that the mean for this sample is more than two standard errors away from the actual population mean?

e) What does the sampling distribution of means of size $N = 9$ (with replacement) look like?

9.5. Suppose we are given a uniformly distributed population of scores with mean equal to 500 and standard deviation equal to 100.

a) Describe the shape of the sampling distribution of means of size $N = 50$ (with replacement).

b) What is the mean of the sampling distribution of means of size $N = 50$ (with replacement)?

c) What is the standard deviation of the sampling distribution of means of size $N = 50$ (with replacement), also called the standard error of the mean?

d) If we were to select a single sample of size $N = 50$ at random from this population of scores, what is the probability that the mean for this sample will be more than two standard errors away from the actual population mean?

e) What does the sampling distribution of means of size $N = 9$ (with replacement) look like?

9.6. Use the RV.UNIFORM function to select 10 random numbers between 1 and 50 inclusive.

9.7. To get some idea of what television programs are watched by people in New York City, we hand out a questionnaire to the members of all statistics classes at New York University and then tabulate the answers we receive. Is this a random sample of the population in which we are interested? Why or why not?

9.8. What (if anything) is wrong with the following statement: "A sampling distribution of means is always normally distributed."

9.9. What (if anything) is wrong with the following statement: "In order to obtain a sampling distribution of means for use in inferential statistics, one must empirically draw many samples of size N from the population of interest and record the corresponding sample mean values obtained."

9.10. Suppose researchers want to estimate the IQ of children who have a twin brother or twin sister. Assume that 100 children (50 pairs of twins) constitute the available population and that the researchers can administer intelligence tests to 30 children. Each time the researchers choose a child at random, they also select that child's twin. Using this procedure, will the researchers obtain a simple random sample of children who have a twin brother or twin sister? Why or why not?

9.11. Given the population of 5,000 scores with $\mu = 8$ and $\sigma = 4$ as shown below:

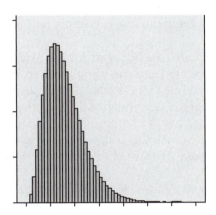

a) If a researcher randomly draws a single sample of 300 values from this population, what is the likely shape of the distribution of sample scores: negatively skewed, positively skewed, approximately normal, or exactly normal?

b) If a researcher randomly draws 200 samples, each containing 300 values, from this population and computes the sample mean for each of the 200 samples, what is the likely shape of the distribution of sample means: negatively skewed, positively skewed, approximately normal, or exactly normal?

c) What is an appropriate label for the horizontal axis of the distribution described in part (a)?

d) What is an appropriate label for the horizontal axis of the distribution described in part (b)?

CHAPTER TEN

Inferences Involving the Mean of a Single Population when σ Is Known

One population parameter that is of particular interest to the behavioral scientist is the mean of a population, μ. In this chapter, we discuss two approaches to statistical inference involving the mean of a population: interval estimation and hypothesis testing. Although these approaches are both carried out using samples and they give essentially equivalent results, there is a basic difference between them and it is important to recognize this difference.

In interval estimation of the population mean μ, we begin with no a priori belief about the value of μ. We select at random a sample from the population of interest, compute its sample mean $\overline{X}$, and then use this sample value $\overline{X}$ to construct an interval centered at $\overline{X}$ that contains μ with a known degree of confidence. In hypothesis testing, we start with an a priori belief about the value of the population mean μ. We select at random a sample from the population of interest, compute its sample mean $\overline{X}$, and then use this sample value $\overline{X}$ to decide whether this belief about the value of μ is plausible.

For example, inference concerning the average amount of some trait possessed by the people or objects of a particular population, where "average" is generally construed to be the arithmetic mean, could be concerned with the mean height of all American males, the mean number of cavities of all children aged 7–8 years in Los Angeles in a particular year, or the mean annual rainfall in inches in Chicago for each year since 1925. Although our discussion of statistical inference in this chapter is confined to examples concerning the mean μ, it applies equally well to many of the other parameters we encounter later in the book.

ESTIMATING THE POPULATION MEAN μ WHEN THE POPULATION STANDARD DEVIATION σ IS KNOWN

The use of a single sample value such as $\overline{X}$ to estimate a population value is known as *point estimation*, because the single value $\overline{X}$ represents one point (or one number) on the real-number line. In the task of trying to estimate the mean height of all American males, we might select a random sample of 25 American males, calculate the sample mean height $\overline{X}$, and then use this sample-mean value as our *point estimate* of the population mean μ.

Although the technique of point estimation is often employed in inferential statistics, it has some serious drawbacks that we should know. One of the drawbacks is illustrated by Example 9.1 in the preceding chapter in the section on sampling distributions. In this example, we were given the following population of 10 values: {0, 1, 3, 3, 5, 7, 7, 7, 8, 10}.

Table 10.1. Intervals of length 6 constructed about sample means

Sample mean value $\overline{X}$	Frequency of $\overline{X}$	Interval of length 6 Centered around $\overline{X}$	Contains $\mu = 5.1$?
0.0	1	$(-3.0, 3.0)$	No
0.5	2	$(-2.5, 3.5)$	No
1.0	1	$(-2.0, 4.0)$	No
1.5	4	$(-1.5, 4.5)$	No
2.0	4	$(-1.0, 5.0)$	No
2.5	2	$(-0.5, 5.5)$	Yes
3.0	6	$(0.0, 6.0)$	Yes
3.5	6	$(0.5, 6.5)$	Yes
4.0	12	$(1.0, 7.0)$	Yes
4.5	2	$(1.5, 7.5)$	Yes
5.0	15	$(2.0, 8.0)$	Yes
5.5	6	$(2.5, 8.5)$	Yes
6.0	6	$(3.0, 9.0)$	Yes
6.5	6	$(3.5, 9.5)$	Yes
7.0	9	$(4.0, 10.0)$	Yes
7.5	8	$(4.5, 10.5)$	Yes
8.0	1	$(5.0, 11.0)$	Yes
8.5	6	$(5.5, 11.5)$	No
9.0	2	$(6.0, 12.0)$	No
10.0	1	$(7.0, 13.0)$	No

From this population, we constructed the sampling distribution of means for all possible samples of size $N = 2$. If we look at the list of all possible sample means that could occur from samples of this size taken from this population, we see that the only values $\overline{X}$ could take on are the following:

0.0	0.5	1.0	1.5	2.0	2.5	3.0	3.5	4.0	4.5
5.0	5.5	6.0	6.5	7.0	7.5	8.0	8.5	9.0	10.0

But the real mean of this population is $\mu = 5.1$, and none of the sample means listed is exactly equal to 5.1. In other words, in this example it would have been impossible, using point estimation with samples of size 2, to obtain a perfectly accurate estimate of μ.

However, suppose that, around each sample mean $\overline{X}$ on the list, we had constructed an interval of length 6 centered at the sample mean. Considering the intervals rather than just the sample points themselves, we find from Table 10.1 that 79 of the 100 intervals (or 79 percent) actually contain the population mean 5.1.

This result leads us to consider using intervals centered at the sample statistic, rather than just the sample statistic points themselves, to estimate the population parameter. Although for this example we chose an interval length of 6, as we see later in this chapter it is always possible to choose an interval length for which some nonzero percent of intervals contain ("capture") the population mean μ. Furthermore, in most cases it is possible to determine just what length interval should be used to give exactly any desired percent of intervals that "work" (capture μ.)

INTERVAL ESTIMATION

Interval estimation involves the estimation of a population parameter by means of a line segment (or interval) on the real-number line within which the value of the parameter is thought to fall. For example, we might estimate the mean height (to the nearest inch) of all American males by using the interval 65–71 inches centered at the sample-mean value $\overline{X} = 68$ inches rather than by using the sample-mean value itself, $\overline{X} = 68$ inches. We could then say we believe μ to be one of the numbers within the interval 65–71 or, equivalently, that we believe the interval 65–71 contains μ. Of course, this is not as precise a statement as saying that we believe $\mu = 68$ inches exactly. But because both statements are statements of belief, we may ask: "In which of the two statements (the interval statement or the point statement) do we have more confidence that our belief is true?"

In general we can place more confidence in interval estimations than in point estimations and, by extension, more confidence in interval estimation using longer intervals than in interval estimation using shorter intervals. There is a trade-off between the precision of an estimate and our confidence that the estimate is true.

If we develop a procedure for constructing intervals of estimation that has a prescribed probability of giving an interval that contains μ, then we can use this probability as our measure of confidence that the population mean falls within the interval. Such a procedure is based on the Central Limit Theorem (CLT).

Recall that under the conditions of the CLT, the sampling distribution of means calculated on samples of size N drawn at random from a population with mean μ and standard deviation σ is either exactly or approximately normally distributed, with mean μ and standard error $\sigma_{\overline{x}} = \sigma/\sqrt{N}$. Also recall from Example 8.11 that 95 percent of the area under any normal curve lies within 1.96 standard deviations of its mean (within $z = \pm 1.96$ of its mean). Using these two pieces of information, as Figure 10.1 illustrates, 95 percent of the sample means fall within 1.96 standard errors of the population mean; that is, from $\mu - 1.96\sigma_{\overline{x}}$ to $\mu + 1.96\sigma_{\overline{x}}$. Said differently, the probability of selecting at random a sample of size N whose mean $\overline{X}$ lies between $\mu - 1.96\sigma_{\overline{x}}$ and $\mu + 1.96\sigma_{\overline{x}}$ is .95, or the probability that $\overline{X}$ lies within a distance of $1.96\sigma_{\overline{x}}$ from μ is .95.

But, if $\overline{X}$ lies within a distance of $1.96\sigma_{\overline{x}}$ from μ, then μ must lie within a distance of $1.96\sigma_{\overline{x}}$ from $\overline{X}$, and μ must lie within the interval $\overline{X} - 1.96\sigma_{\overline{x}}$ to $\overline{X} + 1.96\sigma_{\overline{x}}$. Because

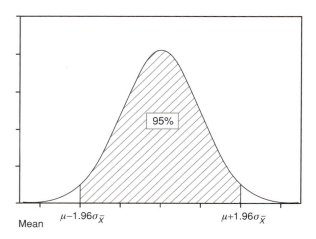

Figure 10.1   Sampling distribution of means: 95 percent of the sample means fall between the points $\mu - 1.96\sigma_{\overline{X}}$ and $\mu + 1.96\sigma_{\overline{X}}$.

95 percent of all sample means *do* fall within a distance $1.96\sigma_{\overline{X}}$ from μ, it follows that 95 percent of all intervals $\overline{X} - 1.96\sigma_{\overline{x}}$ to $\overline{X} + 1.96\sigma_{\overline{x}}$ capture μ.

Figure 10.2 shows graphically that, when $\overline{X}$ is within $1.96\sigma_{\overline{x}}$ of μ (which happens 95 percent of the time), the resulting interval around $\overline{X}$ captures μ. Figure 10.3 shows graphically that when $\overline{X}$ is farther than $1.96\sigma_{\overline{x}}$ from μ (which happens 5 percent of the time), the resulting interval around $\overline{X}$ does not capture μ.

The interval $(\overline{X} - 1.96\sigma_{\overline{x}}, \overline{X} + 1.96\sigma_{\overline{x}})$ is called a *confidence interval* (CI) *for* μ, and its confidence level is defined as the proportion of such intervals that can be expected to capture μ, in this case .95, or 95 percent. Although any level of confidence may be used, the three that are most common are 90, 95, and 99 percent. A general equation for the CI for estimating μ is as follows:

$$\text{Upper Limit} = \overline{X} + z_c\sigma_{\overline{X}} = \overline{X} + z_c\frac{\sigma}{\sqrt{N}}$$

$$\text{Lower Limit} = \overline{X} - z_c\sigma_{\overline{X}} = \overline{X} - z_c\frac{\sigma}{\sqrt{N}} \tag{10.1}$$

$$\text{or, equivalently, } \overline{X} - z_c\frac{\sigma}{\sqrt{N}} \le \mu \le \overline{X} + z_c\frac{\sigma}{\sqrt{N}}$$

$$\text{or, equivalently, } \overline{X} \pm z_c \text{ (s.e.)}$$

where

$z_c = 1.645$ for a 90 percent CI.
$ 1.960$ for a 95 percent CI.
$ 2.576$ for a 99 percent CI.

☞ **Remark.** Because these CIs require the value of $\sigma/\sqrt{N}$ in their construction, they are based on the assumption that σ, the population standard deviation, is known and does not need to be estimated. In practice, this assumption is not tenable and one would normally need to estimate σ. We make this assumption here for heuristic reasons and present a more realistic approach in the next chapter.

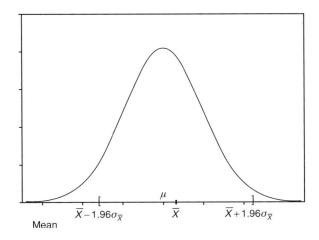

Figure 10.2 $\overline{X}$ falls within $1.96\sigma_{\overline{X}}$ of μ.

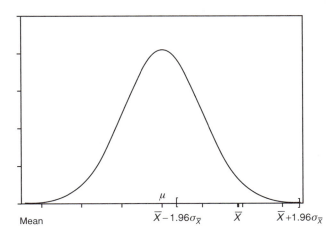

Figure 10.3 $\overline{X}$ does not fall within $1.96\sigma_{\overline{X}}$ of μ.

EXAMPLE 10.1. Never Ready Flashlight Company has just invented a new, longer-lasting flashlight. Company analysts believe the life expectancy of this new model to have the same variance as the old model, $\sigma^2 = 16$, but they do not know the mean life expectancy, μ. (Keep in mind that μ represents the *population* mean, and in this example the population consists of *all* these new flashlights.) To estimate μ, they take a random sample of size $N = 100$ flashlights and run them until they die out. If the sample mean turns out to be $\bar{X} = 150$ *hours*, find a 95 percent CI for μ.

Solution. Because $N = 100$ is large enough to permit us to use the CLT and we know that $\sigma = \sqrt{16} = 4$, we can use Equation 10.1 with $\bar{X} = 150$, $\sigma_{\bar{x}} = \sigma/\sqrt{N} = 4/10 = .4$, and $z_c = 1.960$.

Thus, our 95 percent CI for μ is (149.216, 150.784) hours.

☞ **Remark.** Keep in mind that the procedure and equation given in this chapter for the construction of CIs rests on the assumption that the sampling distribution of means is normally or approximately normally distributed. If this were not true, the z-values provided in Equation 10.1 would not be accurate. Thus, either the population must be known to be normally distributed or the sample must be large enough ($N \geq 30$ to invoke the CLT to be sure that the sampling distribution of means is normally or approximately normally distributed.

☞ **Remark.** Contrary to what you might believe, the CI constructed in Example 10.1 does not have a 95 percent chance of containing the true average lifetime of these new flashlights, μ. Said differently, we are not 95 percent confident or certain that the true average lifetime of these new flashlights is between 149 and 151 hours. Once we have selected our sample, calculated $\bar{X}$, and found the corresponding CI, either μ, the true average lifetime of these new flashlights, is in this interval or it is not, and the probability that the interval contains that true mean is either 1 (if it contains μ) or 0 (if it does not contain μ), not .95. What we can say about Example 10.1 is that if we repeated the *process* of sampling 100 flashlights randomly and computing their average lifetimes, then 95 percent of all the intervals we would construct about these sample means would contain μ. The particular interval that we have constructed (149, 151) may be either one of the 95 percent that do contain the true average lifetime of these new flashlights or one of the 5 percent that do not. However, because such a large proportion of all the intervals would contain μ, the true average lifetime of these new flashlights, we cannot help but believe that this particular interval is one of those that does.

☞ **Remark.** Based on the preceding discussion, the reader should convince him- or herself that the 95 percent CI (149, 151) also does NOT imply, for example, that 95 percent of all such new flashlights last between 142 and 151 hours, nor that 95 percent of the particular new flashlights in our sample of 100 flashlights last between 142 and 151 hours, nor that there is a 95 percent probability that each of the flashlights in our sample of 100 lasts between 142 and 151 hours. Said simply, the level of confidence (in this case 95 percent) is a statement about the likely true average lifetime of such flashlights, not about the lifetime of individual flashlights themselves.

☞ **Remark.** The notion of the CI was first introduced by Jerzy Neyman, another giant in the development of the history of modern statistics, in 1934 in a talk before the Royal

Statistical Society, entitled "On the Two Different Aspects of the Representative Method" (Salsburg, 2001, p. 120).

RELATING THE LENGTH OF A CONFIDENCE INTERVAL, THE LEVEL OF CONFIDENCE, AND THE SAMPLE SIZE

Based on Equation 10.1, we may note the following:

1. If we increase the confidence level, say from 90 to 95 percent, and keep the sample size the same, the resulting CI is longer. Our estimate of μ is then less precise, but we can be more confident that it is accurate.
2. If we increase the sample size N and keep the confidence level the same, the resulting CI is shorter.
3. If we decrease the length of the CI and keep sample size N the same then the confidence level decreases.

In actual research situations employing interval estimation, it is often possible to specify a desired precision of estimation (i.e., a desired CI length). Because a direct relationship exists between the precision of estimation and sample size N, as we discuss in a later section on power, it should be possible to obtain any desired precision of estimation by simply selecting an appropriate sample size N.

HYPOTHESIS TESTING

In contrast with interval estimation, where we do not need to begin with an a priori belief about the population parameter of interest (e.g., μ), in hypothesis testing we do. We usually make hypotheses based on our own past experiences and any other available information and then act on these hypotheses. To take an example from everyday life, we take aspirin when we have a headache because we hypothesize, from what we read, from what other people say, and from our own experiences that aspirin helps to relieve headaches. But, if the headache gets better some of the time and other times it gets worse, then these experiences are inconsistent with our original hypothesis, and so we may decide that our original hypothesis is not plausible. As another example, we pay for the privilege of using certain credit cards because we hypothesize, from their advertisements, that using them makes our shopping and traveling easier. If it turns out, however, that many of the stores in which we shop do not honor these credit cards, then these experiences are inconsistent with our original hypothesis, and so we may decide that our hypothesis is not plausible. How then do we decide whether data we have obtained are consistent or inconsistent with our hypothesis; that is, whether a hypothesis we have made is plausible? One way is to use the method of hypothesis testing.

Suppose, based on past observation and theory, you believe that the average mathematics aptitude of first-year college students in California is better than that of the country at large and you would like to test your belief. You decide to use the Scholastic Aptitude Test in Mathematics (SAT-M) to measure mathematics aptitude. You know that the mean score for the national population on which the test was standardized is known to be 500, but you believe that the mean score for California students is higher. Because you have limited funds, you are able to collect data on only a sample of students from the population of

160,000 first-year college students in California and you randomly select a sample of 1,600 from this population. For the time being, assume that you do not have any reason to believe that the variability of the population of California students is different from that of the national standardization population for which the standard deviation is known to be 100.

When stated formally, your belief (that, on average, California students perform better than the country at large on the SAT-M) is called a *hypothesis*. Because your hypothesis challenges conventional wisdom, that California students do not score higher than the country at large in terms of mathematics aptitude, your hypothesis is called the *alternative hypothesis*, denoted in this book by the symbol H_1. The hypothesis that represents current thinking and that is believed true until you demonstrate that it is implausible (or nullifies it) is called the *null hypothesis*, denoted in this book by the symbol H_0. By contrast, the alternative hypothesis is the statement we would switch to if, through your experiment or study, H_0 were shown to be implausible and H_1 plausible; that is, if the observed results were inconsistent with H_0.

The null hypothesis, in this case, states that the mean of the population of California first-year college students is 500 and may be expressed symbolically as

$$H_0: \mu = 500.$$

The alternative hypothesis, in this case, states that the mean of the population of California first-year college students is *greater than* 500 and may be expressed symbolically as

$$H_1: \mu > 500.$$

In sum, the null hypothesis is the hypothesis of no effect (that, in this case, California is no different from the rest of the country in its SAT-M performance); it is also the hypothesis we would like to nullify, or cast doubt on. The alternative hypothesis, on the other hand, is the hypothesis of an effect; it is the hypothesis that we would like to support. H_0 and H_1 represent two different statements about the state of the California population in this case. The purpose of hypothesis testing is to determine which one of the two is the more plausible.

The outcome of the hypothesis test is determined by the data you obtain on your random sample of size $N = 1,600$. In particular, if your data are consistent with H_0 (i.e., if $\overline{X}$ is close to 500), then you should conclude that H_0 is a plausible hypothesis. If, on the other hand, your data are not consistent with H_0 (i.e., if $\overline{X}$ is far larger than 500), then you should conclude that H_0 is an implausible hypothesis and H_1 is a plausible one. Notice that, as constructed, the focus of the hypothesis test is on H_0, the null hypothesis, because this is the hypothesis that represents what is believed currently and what will be believed in the future unless something or someone casts doubt upon it through some experiment or study.

In determining which sample outcomes are likely and which are not we assume that H_0 is true (that $\mu = 500$) and use the CLT to provide us with information concerning the distribution of all possible sample means that could be obtained. In this example, we know from the CLT that the sampling distribution of means is approximately normally distributed, with mean $\mu_{\overline{X}} = 500$ and standard deviation $\sigma_{\overline{x}} = \sigma/\sqrt{N} = 100/\sqrt{1,600} = 100/40 = 2.5$. From this information we can assess, given that H_0 is true, the probabilities of obtaining all possible sample means. Let's consider two possible sample means, $\overline{X} = 505$ and $\overline{X} = 502$, and find the probabilities associated with them given that H_0 is true. The shaded areas of Figures 10.4 and 10.5 represent these respective probabilities.

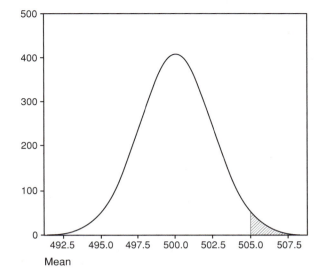

Figure 10.4 The p-value associated with $\overline{X} \geq 505$ or $z \geq 2.0$.

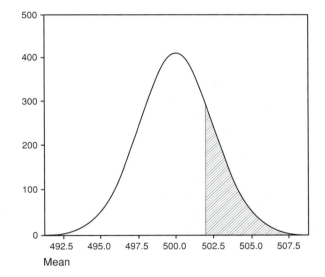

Figure 10.5 The p-value associated with $\overline{X} \geq 502$ or $z \geq 0.8$.

The shaded area in both cases represents the probability of obtaining a result (e.g., sample mean) that is as or more extreme than the actual result (e.g., sample mean) observed, given that the null hypothesis is true. This probability is called the *p-value* of the test.

First we consider the case where $\overline{X} = 505$. To obtain the p-value, or probability of obtaining a mean of 505 or more, we may use either the CDF.Normal function within the Compute procedure in SPSS or Table 1 in Appendix C. To use SPSS, we simply input the following as the numerical expression: $1 - $ CDF.Normal (505, 500, 2.5). To use Table 1, we need to first convert the mean of 505 to a z-score to find the number of standard errors $\overline{X} = 505$ is away from $\mu = 500$. To do so we adapt Equation 4.3, the z-score formula, as Equation 10.2. Equation 10.2 gives the number of standard errors ($\sigma_{\overline{x}}$) the observed mean

$(\overline{X})$ is away from the null hypothesized mean (μ) under the sampling distribution of means.

$$z = \frac{\overline{X} - \mu}{\sigma_{\overline{X}}} \tag{10.2}$$

According to Equation 10.2, the obtained z-statistic is $z = \dfrac{505 - 500}{2.5} = 2.0$. We may then consult Table 1 to find the area under the curve to the right of $z = 2.0$. Whether we use SPSS or Table 1, we find that the p-value associated with $\overline{X} \geq 505$ is .023.

Given that this probability of occurrence is so small, if the null hypothesis were true, we could hardly expect to obtain a sample of 1,600 first-year college students with a mean mathematics aptitude score that would be so much greater than 500. Accordingly, we would have to question the truth of the null hypothesis. In fact, if we were to obtain a sample with such a large mean value, we would have evidence to support our belief in the alternative hypothesis. Based on this evidence we would decide to reject the null hypothesis in favor of the alternative.

☞ **Remark.** Because this test is based on a variation of the z-score formula (Equation 10.2), in general a hypothesis test of the parameter μ when σ is known is called a *z-test*.

Now we consider the case where $\overline{X} = 502$. To obtain the p-value, or probability of obtaining a mean of 502 or more, we may once again use either the CDF.Normal function within SPSS or Table 1 in Appendix C. Either we input $1 - \text{CDF.Normal}\,(502, 500, 2.5)$ or we calculate a z-value using Equation 10.2 ($z = .8$) and consult Table 1 in Appendix C. In either case, we find the p-value to be approximately .21.

Given that, in this case, the probability is so large (there is one chance in five of obtaining 502 or more), the result is consistent with the null hypothesis, casting doubt on our belief in the alternative hypothesis. Based on this result we would decide not to reject the null as implausible.

☞ **Remark.** The p-value may be viewed as the degree to which the observed result is consistent with the null hypothesis. The less consistent the observed result is with the null hypothesis, the lower the p-value. In our example, a result of 505 or more is less consistent with a true population mean of 500 than is a result of 502 or more. Accordingly, p-values provide an indication of the strength of evidence to reject or not to reject the null hypothesis in favor of the alternative.

Although we have categorized .023 as a probability associated with an unlikely event and .21 as a probability associated with a likely one, it is up to the researcher to decide, *when setting up the hypothesis test*, the probability level that distinguishes between likely and unlikely outcomes. The probability level that the researcher chooses to distinguish an unlikely outcome from a likely one is called the *significance level* of the test and is denoted by α. Whereas p-values depend on the particular result observed, significance levels do not. A significance level may be considered a standard or criterion from which to judge the strength of evidence against the null hypothesis. Commonly used significance levels are $\alpha = .10, \alpha = .05$, and $\alpha = .01$. When a significance level is set at .01, for example, stronger evidence is required to reject the null hypothesis than when either .05 or .10 is used. Accordingly, $\alpha = .01$ is considered to be a more stringent criterion than $\alpha = .05$ or .10.

Although the commonly used significance levels in the behavioral and social sciences are .10, .05, and .01, a range of reasonable values should be considered before one is chosen. Significance levels greater than .10, however, are generally not used because they allow too great a chance of incorrectly rejecting H_0. Significance levels less than .01 are also generally not used because they tend to make the test so conservative that we run a large risk of retaining H_0 when we should not have done so (more is discussed about this type of error later in this chapter). The significance level α is set as the largest risk of incorrectly rejecting the null hypothesis that the researcher is willing to make in a particular situation. According to Fisher (1959), the individual who introduced the hypothesis testing procedure in the 1920s, "no scientific worker has a fixed level of significance at which, from year to year, and in all circumstances, he rejects [null] hypotheses; he rather gives his mind to each particular case in the light of his evidence and his ideas" (p. 42).

In our example, we implicitly used .05 as our significance level, and as a result we judged the p-value of .023 as providing sufficiently strong evidence to reject the null hypothesis in favor of the alternative. Therefore, in the first case we concluded that, on average, first-year college students in California score statistically significantly higher on the SAT-M than the country as a whole ($\overline{X} = 505, \sigma = 100, p = .023$). Analogously, using a .05 significance level, or even a .10 significance level, a p-value of .21 does not provide sufficiently strong evidence to reject the null hypothesis in favor of the alternative. In the second case, therefore, we concluded that, on average, first-year college students in California do not score statistically significantly higher on the SAT-M than the country as a whole ($\overline{X} = 502, \sigma = 100, p = .21$).

In general, if the p-value is less than α we reject the null hypothesis as implausible in favor of the alternative and say that the result is statistically significant. Alternatively, if the p-value is greater than α we retain the null hypothesis as plausible and say that the result is not statistically significant.

We remarked at the beginning of Chapter 9 that when we work in the area of inferential statistics we can never be 100 percent certain of our conclusions. Whenever a hypothesis is tested, the decision to reject or not to reject H_0 is always made with some degree of uncertainty. In other words, the possibility always exists that the decision made is, in fact, the wrong decision.

Suppose that, with respect to our example, we did observe a mean of 505. Although the p-value of .023 associated with a mean of 505 or greater renders this event *unlikely* if H_0 is true, it does not render this event *impossible*. There is still a possibility, albeit small ($p = .023$), that we would have observed a mean of 505 or greater in a sample selected randomly from a population whose true mean is 500.

Analogously, suppose we did observe a mean of 502. Although the p-value of .21 associated with a mean of 502 or greater renders this event likely if H_0 is true, this p-value does not prove that H_0 is true. There is still an unknown possibility that we would have observed a mean of 502 or greater in a sample selected randomly from a population whose true mean is greater than 500.

Thus, while rejection of a null hypothesis does not, by itself, say a lot about the truth of that null hypothesis, neither does nonrejection. By failing to reject a null hypothesis, one cannot conclude that the null hypothesis is true; all that one can conclude is that one cannot conclude that the null hypothesis is false (Cohen, 1990). However, the null hypothesis testing procedure provides a way to make sense of the observed result in terms of whether it is real or merely apparent (due to sampling error).

☞ **Remark.** As mentioned earlier, Sir Ronald A. Fisher introduced the null hypothesis testing procedure in the 1920s. In his approach, one states a hypothesis that describes in null form the state of affairs in a population with regard to the value of some parameter, such as a mean. Through the collection of data, randomly sampled from that population, one seeks to nullify that hypothesis with some degree of probability and, in so doing, to engage in a scientific process of proof through disproof. Jerzy Neyman and Egon Pearson, Karl Pearson's son, later expanded Fisher's approach by incorporating an alternative hypothesis and by forcing a choice between the null and its alternate. In the Neyman and Pearson approach, which is the one currently used today, one does not simply reject the null hypothesis, but rather rejects the null *in favor of the alternative*. The Neyman and Pearson null hypothesis testing procedure is further illustrated in Example 10.2.

EXAMPLE 10.2. Suppose Write-On Pen Company manufactures a pen that has a mean and a standard deviation, measured in hours of continuous writing, of $\mu = 100$ and $\sigma = 9$, respectively. To increase its sales, the company has slightly modified the manufacturing process to produce a pen that it claims will last longer than the old pens. It has no reason to believe, however, that the new process alters the variability of these pens in terms of hours of continuous writing. To test this claim, the company selects at random $N = 400$ pens manufactured under the new process and uses them continuously until they no longer work. If the sample mean in terms of hours of continuous writing turns out to be $\overline{X} = 101$ and the significance level selected is $\alpha = .05$, what conclusion can the company draw about this new pen?

Solution. The company would like to claim that its new pen is an improvement (in terms of hours of continuous writing) over its old pen – that the mean writing time of the new pen is greater than that of the old pen. However, until evidence is provided to the contrary, the company must assume that the mean writing time of the new pen is 100 hours, the same as the mean writing time of the old pen. These hypotheses may be stated symbolically as follows:

$$H_0: \ \mu = 100$$
$$H_1: \ \mu > 100$$

where μ represents the mean continuous writing time (in hours) of the population of all pens manufactured using the new process.

☞ **Remark.** Although expressed as $H_0: \mu = 100$ versus $H_1: \mu > 100$, there are two reasons why a more logical rendition of these hypotheses would be $H_0: \mu \leq 100$ versus $H_1\}: \mu > 100$. First, it would be in the company's best interests to nullify the hypothesis that the mean writing time of its new pen is *at most* 100 hours (not simply *equals* 100 hours) in favor of the hypothesis that the mean writing time of its new pen is greater than 100 hours. Second, the hypotheses, $H_0: \mu \leq 100$ versus $H_1: \mu > 100$, account for *all* possible values of μ, not just those equal to or greater than 100. Why then do we express the hypotheses as $H_0: \mu = 100$ versus $H_1: \mu > 100$? Simply stated, the CLT requires a single-valued null hypothesis (e.g., $H_0: \mu = 100$) to describe the sampling distribution of means upon which the hypothesis test rests; the single value used (100 in this case) is most reasonable because

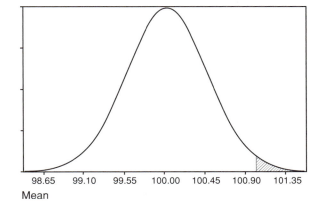

Figure 10.6   The p-value associated with $\overline{X} \geq 101$.

any sample result that would cause us to reject H_0: $\mu = 100$ in favor of H_1: $\mu > 100$ would also cause us to reject any other single value of μ that is less than 100.

Because the null hypothesis specifies a particular (single) value for μ (i.e., 100), we can use the CLT to describe the sampling distribution of means. If we assume H_0 is true, the sampling distribution of means for samples of size $N = 400$ from this population should be approximately normal, with mean $\mu_{\overline{X}} = \mu - 100$ and standard deviation $\sigma_{\overline{X}} = \sigma/\sqrt{N} = 100/\sqrt{400} = 9/20 = 0.45$. Using the CDF.Normal function in SPSS or Table 1 in Appendix C we determine the p-value, the probability of observing a mean of 101 hours or greater given the null hypothesis is true, to be $p = .013$ (see Figure 10.6).

Because the significance level for this test has been set at $\alpha = .05$, and because p is less than α in this case, we reject the null hypothesis as implausible in favor of the alternative. That is, the new pen lasts statistically significantly longer than the old pen ($\overline{X} = 101$, $\sigma = 9$, $p = .013$).

☞ **Remark.** In our example, we were able to reject the null in favor of the alternative that the new pen lasts longer than the old pen because the observed sample mean was sufficiently *greater than* 100. Had the sample mean been *less than* 100, no matter how much less, logically, we would not have been able to reject the null hypothesis in favor of the alternative because under this circumstance the alternative would have been even less plausible than the null. Because the alternative hypothesis stipulates a direction of difference from the null, as illustrated in Figure 10.6, only one tail under the normal curve would yield an appropriate p-value. As illustrated in Figure 10.6, for this example, the one tail that yields an appropriate p-value is the right tail. Had the alternative hypothesis been of the form H_1: $\mu < 100$, the left tail would have been the one to yield an appropriate p-value. Directional alternative hypotheses always give rise to *one-tailed tests*.

The alternative hypotheses in both the SAT-M and Write-On Pen situations were directional and hence required one-tailed tests. In the next example we present an example where the alternative hypothesis is nondirectional and the hypothesis test is *two-tailed*.

• •

EXAMPLE 10.3. P. Ahjay, a well-known researcher in learning theory, would like to determine whether a particular type of preconditioning affects the time it takes individuals to solve a given set of anagram problems. In the past, individuals without such preconditioning have solved the set of problems in an average of 280 seconds with a standard deviation of 20 seconds. For her study, Ms. Ahjay selects a random sample of $N = 100$ individuals, gives them the preconditioning, and then computes the time it takes them to solve the set of problems. Although she expects the preconditioning to affect mean performance, she has no reason to believe that it will affect performance variability. Accordingly, she assumes that the standard deviation of the population with preconditioning is the same as the standard deviation of the population without preconditioning: $\sigma = 20$ seconds. (In the next chapter, we discuss more fully the reasonableness of this assumption about the standard deviation, but for the time being we need to make such an assumption to use the CLT.) If she finds the mean time for solving this set of problems for her sample to be $\bar{X} = 276$ seconds, determine, using the null hypothesis testing procedure and $\alpha = .05$, whether preconditioning affects the mean time for solving this set of problems.

Solution. Because preconditioning may have the effect of increasing or decreasing the time it takes to solve the set of anagram problems, P. Ahjay would like to support the hypothesis that mean time to complete the set of anagrams is *different* (either more or less) with preconditioning than without. However, until evidence is provided to the contrary, she must assume that the mean time to solve this set of problems is 280 seconds, the same as without preconditioning. Therefore, our null and alternative hypotheses are

$$H_0: \mu = 280$$
$$H_1: \mu \neq 280$$

where μ represents the mean time (in seconds) for the population to solve the anagram task with preconditioning.

Because the null hypothesis specifies a particular value for μ (i.e., 280), we can use the CLT to describe the sampling distribution of means. If we assume H_0 is true, the sampling distribution of means for samples of size $N = 100$ from this population should be approximately normal, with mean $\mu_{\bar{X}} = \mu = 280$ and standard deviation $\sigma_{\bar{x}} = \sigma/\sqrt{N} = 20/\sqrt{100} = 20/10 = 2$.

☞ **Remark.** Recall that when the alternative hypothesis is directional, and we are using a one-tailed test, we find the *p*-value by finding the probability of obtaining the observed result or one that is more extreme in the direction of the tail that allows us to reject the null in favor of the alternative. If the alternative hypothesis is of the form $H_1: \mu >$ some value, then the appropriate tail is on the right. On the other hand, if the alternative hypothesis is of the form $H_1: \mu <$ some value, then the appropriate tail is on the left. In the case of a nondirectional alternative hypothesis, we find the *p*-value by finding the probability of obtaining the observed result or one that is more extreme in the direction of *both tails* because an extreme value in either tail would logically allow us to reject the null hypothesis in favor of the alternative.

Because the observed result in our example is 276 seconds, a difference of 4 from the hypothesized population mean μ of 280 seconds, a result more extreme than 276 seconds is defined as 276 or fewer seconds *or* 284 or more seconds. Figure 10.7 illustrates the two areas under the normal curve that when combined yield the *p*-value we seek; that is, the probability of observing a mean result of 276 seconds or one more extreme given the null

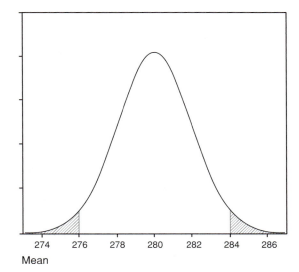

Figure 10.7 The p-value associated with $\overline{X} \leq 276$ or $\overline{X} \geq 284$.

hypothesis is true. Using the CDF.Normal function in SPSS we determine this p-value to be $.023 + .023 = .046$.

Alternatively, we could have found the p-value associated with $\overline{X} \leq 276$ or $\overline{X} \geq 284$ relative to a mean of 280 and a standard error of 2 as the area associated with $z \leq -2$ or $z \geq 2$ relative to a mean of 0 and a standard deviation of 1 using Table 1 in Appendix C. (Note that $z = \dfrac{276 - 280}{2} = -2$ from Equation 10.3, and that $z = \dfrac{284 - 280}{2} = 2$). In this case as well, the p-value equals .046.

Because the significance level for this test has been set at $\alpha = .05$, and because p is less than α in this case, we reject the null hypothesis as implausible in favor of the alternative. That is, the preconditioning statistically significantly affects the time it takes to complete the anagram task. Furthermore, because the observed result of 276 seconds is below 280 seconds, we may conclude that preconditioning statistically significantly decreases the amount of time it takes to complete the anagram task ($\overline{X} = 276$, $\sigma = 20$, $p = .046$).

THE RELATIONSHIP BETWEEN HYPOTHESIS TESTING AND INTERVAL ESTIMATION

In the introduction to this chapter, we noted that interval estimation and hypothesis testing of the mean μ give essentially equivalent results. We explore this more closely in relation to Example 10.3.

Recall that P. Ahjay hypothesized in Example 10.3 that a certain type of preconditioning affects the time it takes individuals to solve a given set of anagram problems. In particular, she hypothesized that with preconditioning the population mean time to complete the anagram task would be different from 280 seconds, the known time to complete this task without preconditioning. Using a random sample of $N = 100$ individuals, she found the mean time with preconditioning to be $\overline{X} = 276$ seconds. She set $\alpha = .05$ and found the probability to be only $p = .046$ of observing this mean, or one more extreme in either direction, in a random sample selected from a population whose true mean is $\mu = 280$. Accordingly, she concluded that preconditioning statistically significantly affects the mean time for solving this set of problems and, in fact, decreases it.

Suppose that, instead of running a hypothesis test of H_0: $\mu = 280$ versus H_1: $\mu \neq 280$, P. Ahjay decided to use her sample result to construct a 95 percent CI for μ. Using Equation 10.1, the 95 percent CI she would have constructed is $(276 - 1.96(2), 276 + 1.96(2))$, or equivalently $(272.08, 279.92)$. Given this interval, she would have confidence that μ is equal to one of the values within the interval 272.08–279.92, and that μ is *not* equal to any of the values outside the interval 272.08–279.92.

Because $\mu = 280$ is *not* within the CI, she would conclude that it is unlikely that 280 is a plausible value of μ. In hypothesis test terms this implies a rejection of H_0: $\mu = 280$ in favor of H_1: $\mu \neq 280$. Because in this case $\mu = 280$ falls above the upper limit of the CI, she would conclude that preconditioning statistically significantly decreases the mean time for solving this set of problems, which is exactly the conclusion she reached on the basis of her earlier hypothesis test.

In general, given a $(1 - \alpha) \times 100$ percent CI estimate of μ:

1. *the values that fall within the CI are exactly those values of μ that would be retained as plausible in a nondirectional hypothesis test at significance level α.*
2. *the values that fall outside the CI are exactly those values of μ that would be rejected as implausible in a nondirectional hypothesis test at significance level α.*

Constructing a $(1 - \alpha) \times 100$ percent CI estimate of μ may be viewed as the equivalent of running nondirectional hypothesis tests at significance level α simultaneously on all possible values of μ from negative infinity to positive infinity. Because confidence intervals capture the magnitude of the difference between the observed and null hypothesized values, they provide more meaningful information about the magnitude of the treatment effect than just whether the difference is likely to be zero in the population.

EFFECT SIZE

From Equation 10.2, we may note that the size of the z-value, representing the degree to which the observed mean deviates from the null hypothesized mean, depends not only on $\overline{X}$, μ, and σ but also on the sample size N. When N is large, even when the difference between $\overline{X}$ and μ is small, z will be large because the standard error of the mean, $\sigma_{\overline{x}} = \sigma/\sqrt{N}$, the denominator of the z-ratio, is small. As a result, even trivially small deviations from the null hypothesized mean can be statistically significant. Although the hypothesis test tells us the likelihood of the observed sample result given that the null hypothesis is true, it tells us nothing about *the degree to which* the null hypothesis is false -that is, the degree to which the observed result departs from the value of the null hypothesis. To be useful in helping us discover truths about phenomena of interest, the null hypothesis test must be supplemented by other forms of analysis that are independent of sample size to determine the nature and magnitude of the obtained result. Knowing the magnitude of the obtained result, called the *effect size*, allows us to determine whether our statistically significant result is also *practically significant.*

In Example 10.3, the test result was statistically significant, indicating that H_1: $\mu \neq 280$ was a more plausible statement about the true value of the population mean μ than

H_0: $\mu = 280$. Taking this result literally, all we have shown is that there is reason to believe that μ differs from 280. The amount by which μ differs from 280 is not specified by our conclusion. That is, our conclusion could imply that μ differs from 280 by a great deal or by a trivially small amount. If trivially small, the difference is likely not to have practical significance or importance and would render inconsequential the fact of having achieved statistical significance.

In our example, preconditioning resulted in a 4-second reduction in the solution time for the sample. Whether this reduction is deemed to be trivially small must rely on the content area experience and best judgment of the researcher carrying out the study. Of course, the researcher may gain insight into the importance of her finding by constructing a CI to consider the range of plausible values for μ so that she can determine how close the boundaries of the interval are to the null hypothesized value of 280, in this case. That the upper limit to the CI in this case is 279.92 suggests a potential population mean difference of only .08 seconds (from 280), which one could assume is small. She may also gain insight by computing Cohen's (1988) d, one of many possible measures of effect size that are independent of sample size.

In this situation, d is computed by taking the difference between the observed mean and null hypothesized mean μ and dividing that difference by the population standard deviation σ, which is assumed to be known. An algebraic expression for Cohen's d is given by Equation 10.3:

$$d = \frac{\overline{X} - \mu}{\sigma}. \tag{10.3}$$

For Example 10.2, $d = \dfrac{276 - 280}{20} = \dfrac{-4}{20} = -.20$. The sign indicates the direction of the effect (it is negative in this example because the observed mean falls below the null hypothesized mean), whereas the absolute value indicates the magnitude of the effect (.20 standard deviations). Thus, Cohen's d tells our researcher that the observed result falls only .20 standard deviations below the null hypothesized mean of 280. This finding would appear to corroborate the CI estimate of a small effect and suggest that preconditioning has limited utility in altering the time to solve such anagram problems. In the final analysis, however, judgments about the magnitude of effect size are subjective and must be based ultimately on the content area knowledge of the researcher. In the absence of such knowledge, Cohen (1988) offers the following guidelines for evaluating effect sizes in terms of d:

$d = .20$ represents a "small" effect size
$d = .50$ represents a "medium" effect size
$d = .80$ represents a "large" effect size.

These guidelines suggest the effect of preconditioning to be small in the case of these anagrams.

TYPE II ERROR AND THE CONCEPT OF POWER

When a decision is made based on a hypothesis test, four different situations can result:

1. H_0 is true but we reject it.
2. H_0 is true and we retain it.

3. H_0 is false and we reject it.
4. H_0 is false but we retain it.

These outcomes and their probabilities of occurrence are displayed in Figure 10.8. Notice that situations 1 and 4 represent incorrect decisions, and situations 2 and 3 represent correct decisions.

The incorrect decision of situation 1 is what we have called a Type I error. The risk of committing a Type I error equals the α level of the test, the level at which we would regard an observation to be unlikely to occur by chance. The incorrect decision of situation 4 is what is called a Type II error. The risk of committing a Type II error equals the β (beta) level of the test.

When we conduct a hypothesis test, we want to minimize the probability of making either a Type I or a Type II error. Unfortunately, these two types of errors are, in a sense, inversely related. The typical research situation of concern in this book is one in which H_0 represents some established procedure and H_1 represents a deviation from it. A decision to reject H_0 in favor of H_1 might therefore result in further expenditures, further testing, and possibly even in some basic changes in the established procedure.

Accordingly, if we are to reject H_0, we certainly do not want to reject it falsely (commit a Type I error), so we generally try to set our test so that the significance level α is the one that is kept small at the possible expense of having a relatively large β.

The correct decision of situation 2 arises when the test does not detect a difference from the null hypothesis when the null hypothesis is in fact true. The probability of this correct decision is represented by the complement of α, $1 - \alpha$. Finally, the correct decision of situation 3 arises when the test does detect a difference from the null hypothesis when the null hypothesis is in fact false (when the alternative hypothesis is true). The probability of this correct decision is represented by the complement of β, $1 - \beta$, and because of its importance within the null hypothesis test procedure this probability is called the *power* of the test.

The power of a hypothesis test may be likened to the power of magnification used to view a cell under a microscope (Hays, 1973). Suppose, for example, a particular cell in which we are interested has a break in its cell wall that we cannot observe with the naked eye. If we place the cell under the microscope and use a low-power setting, we still do not detect the break in the cell wall. In this case, we say that the microscope lacks sufficient power to detect the difference or break that exists in the cell wall. When we increase the microscope power setting to high we detect the difference in the cell wall. In this case, the power of the microscope is sufficiently high to detect the break in the cell wall.

	Reject H_0	Retain H_0
H_0 is true	Incorrect decision: Type I error Probability = α	Correct decision Probability = $1 - \alpha$
H_0 is false	Correct decision Probability = $1 - \beta$	Incorrect decision: Type II error Probability = β

Figure 10.8   The four possible outcomes of a hypothesis test.

Without sufficient power in the microscope, we are not likely to detect the difference that exists in the cell wall; it is the same for the hypothesis test. Without sufficient power in the hypothesis test, we are not likely to detect a difference from the null hypothesis even when such a difference exists. Hence, when we set up a hypothesis test, we want to maximize the power of the test, $1 - \beta$. We also want to minimize the risk of making a Type I error, α. As noted earlier, an α level greater than .10 is seldom used. Likewise, a power level less than .80 is also seldom used. When conducting a hypothesis test, researchers like to have a probability of at least .80 of detecting a difference where one exists. In that case, if no difference were detected and the null hypothesis were retained, the researcher would be reasonably confident that a difference did *not* exist rather than that a difference did exist and that the test had insufficient power to detect it.

A good way to understand power is through its graphic representation as shown in Figure 10.9. In Figure 10.9, the curve labeled "H_0 true" represents the sampling distribution of means given that H_0 is true. We know by the CLT that this curve is normal in shape. We also know by the CLT that the mean of the means, $\mu_{\overline{X}}$, under this distribution equals μ and that the standard deviation of the means, $\sigma_{\overline{x}}$, under this distribution equals $\sigma/\sqrt{N}$, where N equals the size of the sample randomly selected from the population of interest. The shaded area under the curve in the right tail depicts α; that is, if $\alpha = .05$, for example, the shaded area represents 5 percent of the area under that curve. The z-value that marks off this shaded area to its right is labeled z_c. Whenever the observed sample mean $\overline{X}$ exceeds z_c, our decision is to reject H_0 as implausible. Hence, the shaded area (to the right of z_c) represents the probability of rejecting H_0 as implausible when in fact H_0 is true.

The curve labeled "H_0 false (H_1 true)" represents the sampling distribution of means given that H_0 is false by a difference of δ units. Once again, we know by the CLT that this curve is normal in shape. We also know by the CLT and the rules of transformation that the mean of the means under this distribution, $\mu_{\overline{X}}$, equals $\mu + \delta$ and that the standard deviation of the means under this distribution, $\sigma_{\overline{x}}$, equals $\sigma/\sqrt{N}$, where N equals the size of the sample randomly selected from the population of interest. (We assume that the curves differ only in their means, by an amount δ, and that their standard deviations are the same.) The cross-hatched area under this curve depicts $1 - \beta$, the power of the test, because in this area H_0 is false and our decision is to reject H_0 as implausible because the observed $\overline{X}$ exceeds z_c in this area. If $1 - \beta = .80$, for example, then the shaded area represents 80 percent of the area under that curve.

☞ **Remark.** By separating the two curves by an amount equal to δ units, we indicate that we wish to find the power associated with this hypothesis test for detecting a difference of δ units from the null hypothesized mean μ. When units are expressed in terms of standard deviation units, the difference of δ units is the effect size. In practice if the effect size is set equal to the minimum-sized difference that the researcher would like to detect as meaningful, and if the power of the hypothesis test is adjusted to detect that effect size as statistically significant, then only meaningful or important effects, as judged by the researcher, should be declared statistically significant. In general, such practice avoids the problem of detecting trivially important effects as statistically significant. Effects that are trivially important are just that, even in the face of statistical significance. Hence, effects that are statistically significant but trivially important should not be declared significant in the broad sense of the term. To be truly significant, an effect should be both statistically and practically significant.

If we wish to adjust power to detect differences that are deemed to be important, we must understand the factors that influence power. Using Figures 10.10 through 10.12 in conjunction with Figure 10.9 we illustrate that the size of the cross-hatched area, the area that represents the power of the test, varies as a function of α, δ, and $\sigma_{\bar{x}}$. That is, we illustrate that, all things being equal, if the value of any one of the parameters α, δ, or $\sigma_{\bar{x}}$ changes, the result will be a change in the proportion of the cross-hatched area under the curve – the power of the test.

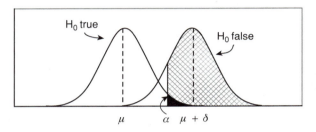

Figure 10.9   Sampling distributions of means under H_0 true and H_0 false with α, δ, and $\sigma_{\bar{x}}$ shown.

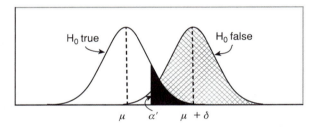

Figure 10.10   Sampling distributions of means under H_0 true and H_0 false with $\alpha' > \alpha$, δ, and $\sigma_{\bar{x}}$.

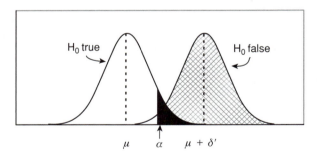

Figure 10.11   Sampling distributions of means under H_0 true and H_0 false with α, $\delta' > \delta$, and $\sigma_{\bar{x}}$.

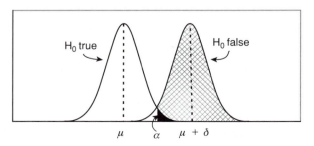

Figure 10.12   Sampling distributions of means under H_0 true and H_0 false with α, δ, and $\sigma'_{\bar{x}} < \sigma_{\bar{x}}$.

INCREASING THE LEVEL OF SIGNIFICANCE, α

If we hold δ and $\sigma_{\bar{x}}$ to be the same as in Figure 10.9 but we increase α, the level of significance, to α', then the shaded area associated with the level of significance in Figure 10.10 exceeds that of Figure 10.9. If we compare Figures 10.9 and 10.10, we may note that an increase in the level of significance, while keeping δ and $\sigma_{\bar{x}}$ the same, increases the proportion of cross-hatched area under the H_0 false curve. Said differently, *an increase in the level of significance of a hypothesis test, with δ and $\sigma_{\bar{x}}$ held constant, increases the power of that test.* However, as noted earlier, because levels of significance greater than 0.10 are seldom used, an increase in α to achieve greater power is self-limiting.

INCREASING THE EFFECT SIZE, δ

If we hold α and $\sigma_{\bar{x}}$ to be the same as in Figure 10.9 but we increase δ, the effect size, to δ', then in Figure 10.11 the cross-hatched area associated with the power of the test increases. Said differently, *an increase in the minimum effect size – the minimum difference in population means that we would like to detect by a hypothesis test – with α and $\sigma_{\bar{x}}$ held constant increases the power of that test.* Because there are specific, minimum-sized differences in population means that a researcher would like to detect as meaningful, the effect size, like the level of significance, cannot be set to be arbitrarily large for the sake of increasing power.

DECREASING THE STANDARD ERROR OF THE MEAN, $\sigma_{\bar{x}}$

If we hold α and δ to be the same as in Figure 10.9 but decrease $\sigma_{\bar{x}}$, the standard error of the means, to $\sigma_{\bar{x}}'$, then in Figure 10.12 the cross-hatched area associated with the power of the test increases. Said differently, *an increase in the standard error of the means, $\sigma_{\bar{x}}$, with α and δ held constant, decreases the power of the test.* Furthermore, because $\sigma_{\bar{x}} = \sigma/\sqrt{N}$, a simple way to decrease $\sigma_{\bar{x}}$ is by increasing sample size N. Thus, *an increase in sample size N, with α and δ held constant, increases the power of the test.*

Of the three factors shown to affect the power of a test – the level of significance α, the effect size δ, and the standard error of the means, $\sigma_{\bar{x}} = \sigma/\sqrt{N}$ – an increase in sample size N is usually the most viable way of producing an increase in power.

In practice, given a specified α-value, one should set the power of the test to detect a difference from the null hypothesis that is of practical importance. As noted earlier, this approach can avoid detecting trivially small departures from the null hypothesis as statistically significant. The usual procedure is to set α, to decide on the appropriate effect size worth detecting, and to find the sample size N that decreases the standard error of the means sufficiently to achieve the desired power. A number of computer programs are available both commercially and from the Internet that are designed to help researchers find the sample size required to achieve a desired power with specified α and δ. Alternatively, one may use a book of power tables, such as the one by Cohen (1988), to make this determination.

To give some perspective on the sample size required to obtain a power of .80 to detect a small, medium, and large effect given $\alpha = .05$, two-tailed, we present Table 10.2.

☞ **Remark.** For other values of Cohen's d, when $\alpha = .05$ and the alternative hypothesis is nondirectional, we may use the following equation to find N to achieve a power of .80:

$$\sqrt{N} = \frac{2.80}{d}. \tag{10.4}$$

Table 10.2. Approximate sample sizes required to obtain a power of .80 for different effect sizes when $\alpha = .05$

Effect Size (Cohen's d)	Sample Size (N)
.20	196
.50	31
.80	12

CLOSING REMARKS

This chapter has been concerned with inferences involving the population mean based on interval estimation and the null hypothesis testing procedure. For some time now, and with greater recent frequency, the null hypothesis testing procedure has been the subject of much scrutiny and public debate (Bakan, 1966; Carver, 1978; Cohen, 1990, 1994; Falk & Greenbaum, 1995; Hagen, 1997; Harlow, Mulaik, & Steiger, 1997; Kaplan, 1964; Kirk, 1996; Lykken, 1968; Meehl, 1967; Rosnow & Rosenthal, 1989; Rozeboom, 1960; Thompson, 1994, 1996).

Intended as a method of ruling out chance as an explanation of observed results, the null hypothesis testing procedure has become, since its introduction by Fisher in the 1920s, a ubiquitous technique in the behavioral sciences. Not only is it "identified with 'scientific method,' but it is so mechanically applied that it undermines the very spirit of scientific inquiry" (Kaplan, 1964, p. 29). For this reason, in this chapter we have taken care to point out some of the pitfalls associated with using the null hypothesis testing procedure in so purely a mechanical way.

We reiterate that statistical significance without practical significance does not advance our knowledge regarding the truths concerning phenomena of interest; practical significance may be established only through an interplay of strong theories, critical thinking, and subjective judgment. To have the greatest impact on a field of inquiry, the research process must be a process in the true sense of the word. It must rely on scientific principles and formulations, but it must also engage the researcher with all his good judgment, creative energies, and content area expertise. As Kaplan (1964) suggests, "Electronic computers, game-theoretic models, and statistical formulas are but instruments after all; it is not *they* [emphasis in original] that produce scientific results but the investigator who uses them scientifically" (p. 29).

In the remainder of this book we present some of the instruments of scientific inquiry and rely upon you, our reader, to provide your own good judgment, creative energies, and content area expertise to use these instruments scientifically.

EXERCISES

10.1. Suppose we want to estimate the mean height μ for American males and we know that the standard deviation σ for the entire population is 3 inches. We take a random sample of American males of sample size $N = 100$ from this population and find that its sample mean is $\overline{X} = 68$.

  a) Explain why the normal curve gives a good approximation of the sampling distribution of means.

  b) Use this information to construct a 90 percent CI for μ.

c) To what does the 90 percent refer?

d) Can we conclude that 90 percent of the males from this population have heights within the interval of values obtained in part (b)?

e) Would the 95 percent CI be longer or shorter?

10.2. Suppose we know that the standard deviation for the IQ of all Americans is $\sigma = 15$ but we do not know the mean IQ score μ. To estimate μ we select a random sample of size $N = 225$ and find that the sample has mean $\overline{X} = 105$.

a) Use this information to construct a 99 percent CI for μ.

b) To what does the 99 percent refer?

c) Can we conclude that 99 percent of the 225 individuals from this sample have IQs within the interval of values obtained in part (b)?

d) Can we conclude that we are 95 percent certain that each individual from this population of Americans has an IQ within the interval of values obtained in part (b)?

10.3. Given that $N = 100$, $\sigma = 15$, and $\overline{X} = 92$ for a random sample selected from a given population of values:

a) Construct a 90 percent CI for the population mean μ.

b) Using the result of part (a), what would your decision be if you were to run the following hypothesis test at $\alpha = .10$?

H_0: $\mu = 96$

H_1: $\mu \neq 96$

c) Using the result of part (a), what would your decision be if you were to run the following hypothesis test at $\alpha = .10$?

H_0: $\mu = 91.5$

H_1: $\mu \neq 91.5$

10.4. To estimate the mean air-pollution index μ for Pittsburgh, Pennsylvania, over the past five years, we randomly select a sample of $N = 64$ of those days and compute the mean air-pollution index for this sample. Assuming that the sample mean is found to be $\overline{X} = 15$ and the population is known to have a standard deviation of $\sigma = 4$, find a 95 percent CI for μ. Use the CI to determine whether the air-pollution index for the past five years is statistically significantly different from 14.

10.5. The Weston, Massachusetts Postal Service is thinking of introducing a training program for their employees on how to sort mail by zip code number in order to increase sorting speed. They know that without any such training their employees sort an average of 600 letters per hour with a standard deviation of 20. A random sample of $N = 400$ postal employees is selected and given the training program. Their average mail-sorting speed at the end of training is recorded as 603. Assume that the standard deviation is no different with training from without training.

a) State the null and alternative hypotheses in terms of specific values for the population mean for determining whether the training program increases the sorting speed.

b) Explain why the z-distribution may be used as a basis of the hypothesis test, in this instance, by explaining why the sampling distribution of means is normally or approximately normally distributed.

c) Calculate the observed z-statistic.

d) Is the test one- or two-tailed?

e) Find the *p*-value for conducting a hypothesis test at significance level .10 on whether training increases mail-sorting speed.

f) What can you conclude based on your results in part (e)?

g) If the result of the hypothesis test is statistically significant, find and interpret an appropriate effect size.

h) Would you recommend that the town endorse such training? Why or why not?

i) Could a 90 percent CI have been used to determine whether training increases mail-sorting speed?

10.6. Children graduating from a particular high school district in a disadvantaged area of New York City have on the average scored 55 on a standard college-readiness test with a standard deviation of 12. A random sample of 36 students from this district is selected to participate in Project Advance, a special program to help high school students prepare for college. At the end of the project, the 36 students are given the college-readiness test. They obtain a sample mean of $\overline{X} = 56$. Assume that the standard deviation for the population of all students in this district who might participate in Project Advance is no different from that for all those who would not participate ($\sigma = 12$). Conduct a hypothesis test at significance level $\alpha = .05$ to determine whether students in this district who participate in Project Advance generally score *higher* on the college-readiness test than those who do not participate. State your conclusions clearly in the context of the problem.

10.7. The average cholesterol level for adults in the United States is known to be 200 mg per dl. A group of 50 randomly selected adults in the United States participated in a study on the efficacy of diet in reducing cholesterol. They ate a low-fat diet (less than 30 percent of their total daily calories came from fat) for six months. After six months their average serum cholesterol level was 185 mg per dl. Assume that the standard deviation for the population of cholesterol levels for adults in the United States following the diet is the same as it is for all adults in the United States, $\sigma = 50$, and that the distribution of cholesterol levels for the population of adults in the United States following the diet is normally distributed.

a) Conduct a hypothesis test at significance level $\alpha = .05$ to determine whether adults following the diet have significantly *lower* cholesterol levels than 200 mg per dl, on average. State your conclusions clearly in the context of the problem.

b) If the result in part (a) is statistically significant, find and interpret the effect size, classifying its magnitude according to Cohen's scale. Does the effect size support the results of the hypothesis test?

10.8. You are dean of a college that has just admitted 1,000 first-year students, and you want to know whether these students have a scholastic aptitude (as measured on a standard scholastic aptitude test) *different* from that of previous first-year classes. You pick a random sample of size $N = 81$ from the new class and give them the scholastic aptitude test on which previous first-year classes scored a mean of 100. Assume that this entire first-year class would have a standard deviation of $\sigma = 9$ on this test if they all took it.

a) Construct a 95 percent CI for the mean scholastic aptitude for all 1,000 current first-year students if the sample mean is 101.5.

b) Use the CI to determine whether the current first-year students, on average, have a scholastic aptitude *different* from that of previous first-year classes. If their average is statistically significantly different from that of previous first-year classes, determine whether it is statistically significantly higher or lower.

c) If the result is statistically significant, approximate and describe the effect size.

d) The 90 percent CI for the mean scholastic aptitude for all 1,000 current first-year students would be
   (1) longer (wider) than the 95 percent CI.
   (2) shorter (narrower) than the 95 percent CI.
   (3) the same as the 95 percent CI.

e) If the sample selected had been smaller, but with the same mean and standard deviation as in the original analysis, the 95 percent CI for the mean scholastic aptitude for all 1,000 current first-year students would be
   (1) longer.
   (2) shorter.
   (3) the same.

f) If everything had been the same as in the original analysis except that the standard deviation had been 10 instead of 9, then the 95 percent CI for the mean scholastic aptitude for all 1,000 current first-year students would have been
   (1) longer.
   (2) shorter.
   (3) the same.

10.9. A test of general intelligence is known to have a mean of 100 and a standard deviation of 15 for the population at large. You believe that students at the university where you teach have a *different* mean on this test. To test this belief, you randomly select a sample of 36 students at your university and give them this test of general intelligence. Assume that the standard deviation of your university's students is no different from that of the population at large and that your sample result is $\overline{X} = 106$. Construct a 90 percent CI and use it to test your belief. State your conclusions clearly in the context of the problem. If the result is statistically significant, calculate and interpret the effect size.

10.10. Curriculum planners decided to determine whether a curriculum change should be instituted to increase the reading comprehension of eighth graders in Seattle, Washington. The mean reading-comprehension score under the old curriculum was 92 on the Stanford Secondary School Comprehension Test. After the new curriculum was used for one term, the mean of a sample of 400 students was 95. Assume that the standard deviation for the entire population of eighth graders in Seattle is the same under the new curriculum as under the old ($\sigma = 10$). Test at significance level .01 whether there would be an *improvement* in reading comprehension in general if the entire population of eighth graders in Seattle were taught using the new curriculum. State your conclusions clearly in the context of the problem. If the result is statistically significant, calculate and interpret the effect size. Could a CI have been used to answer the research question? Explain.

10.11. A publishing company has just published a new college textbook. Before the company decides to charge $79 for the textbook, it wants to know the average price of all such textbooks in the market to determine whether it is statistically significantly different from $79. The research department at the company takes a random sample of 40 such textbooks and collects information on their prices. This information produced a mean price of $76.40 for the sample. Assume that the standard deviation of the prices of all such textbooks is $7.50.

Test at a significance level of .05 whether the mean price of all such textbooks is different from $79. State your conclusions clearly in the context of the problem. If the result is statistically significant, calculate and interpret the effect size.

10.12. Explain why $z_c = 1.96$ for a 95 percent CI.

10.13. Given the scenario of Exercise 10.9, assume that the students at the university where you teach have a higher mean on this test. Would the *power* of the test have been less, the same, or greater had you wanted to determine whether the students had a higher mean on this test, instead of whether the students had a different mean on this test? Explain.

Inferences Involving the Mean When σ Is Not Known: One- and Two-Sample Designs

In the preceding chapter we presented a statistical model for answering questions about a single population mean μ when σ was known. Because σ usually is not known in practice, we present in this chapter a statistical model that is appropriate for answering questions about a single population mean when σ is not known. We also present two other statistical models that are appropriate for answering questions about the equality of two population means. In one model the groups representing the two populations are related and in the other they are not. In later chapters we consider different research questions that involve different designs and different parameters of interest (including the mean, variance, correlation, and so on) and we present statistical models appropriate to each situation. In general, you will find that by knowing the features of a particular design as well as the parameter of interest you should be able to make sense of the array of statistical models presented and choose one or more that are appropriate to a given situation.

SINGLE SAMPLE DESIGNS WHEN THE PARAMETER OF INTEREST IS THE MEAN AND σ IS NOT KNOWN

As you should have noted in Chapter 10, which dealt in part with questions about the mean of a single population, a wide range of questions may be addressed by studies that are carried out to estimate or test the value of a single population mean. Whereas the type of questions we address in this section are like those addressed in Chapter 10, different and more realistic assumptions are made in this section about the nature of our data. These different assumptions change the procedures for estimating or testing the value of the single population mean.

In Chapter 10 we assumed that σ, the standard deviation of the population, was known so that we could use the Central Limit Theorem to justify the use of the normal distribution of the sampling distribution of means and to compute the standard error, $\sigma_{\overline{X}} = \dfrac{\sigma}{\sqrt{N}}$. We used the z-test, $z = \dfrac{\overline{X} - \mu}{\dfrac{\sigma}{\sqrt{N}}}$, provided in Equation 10.2 of Chapter 10 to determine how deviant a particular sample mean $\overline{X}$ is from the population mean μ. Because in most cases, however, the value of σ is not known, in this chapter we introduce another way to describe the sampling distribution of means – one that does not rely on knowledge of σ. As we shall see, when the parent population is normally distributed, but when σ is not known, we can use what is called the *Student's t-* (or just *t-*) *distribution* to describe the sampling distribution of means.

In this section we use the t-distribution to determine whether adult African-American males, on average, have a systolic blood pressure that is different from the general population of adult American males; whether college-bound females from the South who have always been at grade level take three years of mathematics in high school on average; and whether college-bound males from the South who have always been at grade level take more than three years of mathematics in high school on average.

For all questions regarding a single population mean, we can represent the null and alternative hypotheses as follows:

$H_0: \mu = c$

$H_1: \mu \neq c$ or $H_1: \mu < c$ or $H_1: \mu > c$

where c is a specified number.

THE t-DISTRIBUTION

From Chapter 9 we know that $\hat{\sigma}^2$ calculated from sample data is an unbiased estimator of σ^2. If we substitute $\hat{\sigma}$ for σ in the z-test equation, we obtain a new statistic called Student's t, or simply t, as our measure of sample mean deviation from μ. Equation 11.1 displays the equation for the t-statistic for the one sample t-test:

$$t = \frac{\overline{X} - \mu}{\dfrac{\hat{\sigma}}{\sqrt{N}}} = \frac{\overline{X} - \mu}{\hat{\sigma}_{\overline{X}}}. \tag{11.1}$$

Although the t-statistic resembles the z-statistic in form, there is an important difference between them. In the z-statistic, the numerator $\overline{X} - \mu$ depends on the particular sample selected, because $\overline{X}$ is the sample mean. Hence, the value of $\overline{X} - \mu$ generally varies from one sample to another. The denominator $\dfrac{\sigma}{\sqrt{N}}$ of the z-statistic, however, depends only on the population parameter σ and the sample size N and, therefore, stays constant from sample to sample. By contrast, both numerator $\overline{X} - \mu$ *and* denominator $\dfrac{\hat{\sigma}}{\sqrt{N}}$ of the t-statistic depend on the particular sample selected and, therefore, both generally vary from sample to sample.

Because the t-statistic appears to be a reasonable measure of sample-mean deviation that may be used in place of the z-statistic when σ is not known, we should be interested in knowing the shape of the t-distribution. Because of the differences between the z- and t-statistics, we should not expect the t-distribution to have exactly the same shape as the z-distribution. In fact, as discovered by a young chemist named William Sealy Gossett in the early twentieth century, they do not. His results appeared in a short paper entitled "The Probable Error of the Mean," published in the journal *Biometrika* in 1908 (Salsburg, 2001). Because the company he worked for, the Guiness Brewing Company of Dublin, Ireland, prohibited its employees from publishing, Gossett published under the pseudonym Student. He chose that pseudonym because he considered himself to be a student of statistics—hence, the name given to this distribution.

Gossett set up a normal parent population, empirically selected random samples of size N from this population, and computed a t-statistic as given in Equation 11.1 for each sample selected. He then constructed a distribution of these t-statistics and found it to be generally similar in shape to the standard normal curve distribution but flatter at its center and taller in its tails. When different sample sizes N were used, he obtained distributions with slightly different shapes, indicating that there are really many t-distributions, one for each sample size N. He also found that the family of t-distributions varies not by their sample size N but rather as a function of their sample size, called the degrees of freedom, symbolized by df or by the Greek letter ν (nu).

DEGREES OF FREEDOM FOR THE ONE-SAMPLE t-TEST

The number of degrees of freedom of a statistic not only depends on the number of observations in the sample (N) but also considers other factors that tend to affect the sampling distribution.

The number of degrees of freedom of a statistic is the number of *independent pieces* of data used in computing that statistic.

The t-statistic, as given in Equation 11.1, relies on the square root of the variance estimator, $\hat{\sigma}$, which may be computed from Equation 9.1 in Chapter 9; it is reproduced here as Equation 11.2:

$$\hat{\sigma} = \sqrt{\frac{\sum (X_i - \overline{X})^2}{N - 1}}. \tag{11.2}$$

From Equation 11.2 it appears at first glance that the value of $\hat{\sigma}$ depends on N independent pieces of data: $d_1 = X_1 - \overline{X}, d_2 = X_2 - \overline{X}, d_3 = X_3 - \overline{X}, \ldots, d_N = X_N - \overline{X}$. Recall, however, that the sum of all deviations about the mean must equal 0 ($\sum d_i = 0$), so that if we know $N - 1$ of the d_is, then the Nth, or last one, must be completely determined by them.

For example, suppose you are told to make up a set of five scores using any numbers you desire, provided that the scores have a mean of 3. Suppose for your first four numbers you freely and arbitrarily select the numbers 4, 2, 7, and 1. Accordingly, $d_1 = X_1 - \overline{X} = 4 - 3 = 1; d_2 = -1; d_3 = 4; d_4 = -2$. Do you now have the same freedom of choice in selecting the fifth score to complete the set? Clearly you do not. The only score consistent with $\sum d_i = 0$ is $X_5 = 1$, making $d_5 = -2$. In short, you had no freedom in selecting the fifth or last score; the choice was determined by the fact that the mean had been specified. Thus, with a specified mean, required for the estimation of the variance, there are only four degrees of freedom for selecting a set of five scores. In general, with a specified mean, there are only $N - 1$ degrees of freedom for selecting a set of N scores.

When σ is not known, the number of degrees of freedom associated with the one-sample t-statistic for μ is $df = N - 1$ when either constructing a confidence interval (CI) or carrying out a hypothesis test.

☞ **Remark.** In general, t-distribution curves resemble the standard normal curve in that they are symmetric and unimodal, but they are flatter at the middle and taller in the tails. The mean of a t-distribution with any number of degrees of freedom, df, is 0, the same mean as in the standard normal curve. The variance of the t-distribution, however, is not

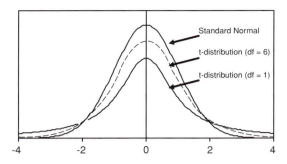

Figure 11.1   Comparison of two *t*-curves with the standard normal curve.

always 1 as it is in the standard normal curve. For a *t*-distribution with more than two degrees of freedom ($df > 2$), the variance is $\dfrac{df}{df - 2}$. The smaller the value of *df*, the larger the variance; as *df* becomes large, the variance of the *t*-distribution approaches 1 (the variance of the standard normal curve). As a matter of fact, as the number of degrees of freedom *df* increases, the *t*-distribution itself approaches the standard normal curve; that is, the *t*-distribution has the standard normal curve as a limiting curve (see Figure 11.1).

In addition to SPSS, we may use Table 2 in Appendix C to obtain *t*-distribution values for right-tail areas. That is, the *t*-value that has .05 of the area to its right under a distribution with 10 degrees of freedom, for example, may be found in Table 2 at the intersection of the row labeled $df = 10$ and the column labeled .05; this *t*-value is 1.812. With an infinite number of *df*, the *t*-value with .05 of the area to its right is 1.645, which, as you may recall, equals the *z*-value with .05 of the area to its right under the standard normal distribution. This confirms that, as the degrees of freedom increase, the *t*-distribution approaches the standard normal distribution. Table 2 may also be used to find approximate *p*-values corresponding to approximate *t*-values.

VIOLATING THE ASSUMPTION OF A NORMALLY DISTRIBUTED PARENT POPULATION IN THE ONE-SAMPLE *t*-TEST

The *t*-distribution defines a sampling distribution of means when the parent population is normally distributed and when σ needs to be estimated from sample data. If Gossett had not placed a restriction of normality on the parent population, however, he would not have been able to determine the distribution of *t*-statistics in a simple form. Although the requirement of normality in the parent population may seem too limiting to be useful in practice, it is often actually a reasonable assumption to make. As we mentioned in our discussion of normal curves, many natural occurrences due to chance give rise to normally distributed probability curves. In addition, even when the parent population is not normally distributed, it can be shown mathematically that, for a sufficiently large sample size *N*, the *t*-distribution is not affected appreciably by violations of the normality assumption.

In general, the more the parent population deviates from normality, the larger the sample size must be to apply the *t*-distribution to determine sample-mean deviation. For this reason, there is no specific sample size above which deviation from normality in the parent population can always be ignored. It has been found, however, that unless the parent population deviates radically from normality, a sample of size 30 or larger is sufficient to compensate for the lack of normality in the parent population. Therefore, it is generally a good idea to use samples of size 30 or larger. In practice, however, this is not a real restriction because the sample size necessary to obtain reasonably high power when using the null hypothesis test procedure almost always exceeds 30, as does the sample size necessary to obtain reasonably high precision when constructing a CI.

CONFIDENCE INTERVALS FOR THE ONE-SAMPLE *t*-TEST

We may construct CIs about μ using the *t*-distribution when the parent population is known to be normally distributed (or the sample size is sufficiently large) and when σ needs to be estimated using sample data. We could use Equation 11.3 to find the CIs by hand.

☞ **Remark.** The CI based on the *t*-distribution is obtained by hand using Equation 11.3 instead of Equation 10.1. Note that, in contrast to Equation 10.1, Equation 11.3 uses t_c instead of z_c and $\hat{\sigma}_{\overline{X}}$ instead of $\sigma_{\overline{X}}$:

$$\text{Upper limit} = \overline{X} + t_c \hat{\sigma}_{\overline{X}}.$$

$$\text{Lower limit} = \overline{X} - t_c \hat{\sigma}_{\overline{X}}.$$

(11.3)

To find the value of t_c using SPSS we follow the procedure outlined in Chapter 8 with respect to finding z_c except that we use either the IDF.T instead of the IDF.NORMAL function in SPSS or Table 2 in Appendix C. To use the IDF.T distribution we need to specify the *p*-value and the degrees of freedom as shown in Example 11.1.

. . . .

EXAMPLE 11.1. Construct a 95 percent CI using the following data to determine whether adult African–American males, on average, have a systolic blood pressure that is different from the general population of adult American males, which is known to be 120. The data are based on a sample of 21 African–American adult males selected randomly from the population of African–American adult males. These data come from the Data and Story Library website.

Systolic blood pressure (mm per Hg):

107	110	123	129	112	111	107	112	135	102	123
109	112	102	98	114	119	112	110	117	130	

Solution. If we knew σ, the standard deviation of the parent population, we would use the Central Limit Theorem and proceed as we did in Chapter 10, using Equation 10.1 to construct the desired 95 percent CI. Because we do not know σ, however, we estimate it as $\hat{\sigma}$ using Equation 11.2. We then construct the 95 percent CI based on the *t*-distribution using Equation 11.3.

For these data,

$$\overline{X} = (107 + 110 + 123 + 129 + 112 + 111 + 107 + 112 + 135 + 102 + 123$$

$$109 + 112 + 102 + 98 + 114 + 119 + 112 + 110 + 117 + 130)/21 = 114$$

$$\hat{\sigma}^2 = [(107 - 114)^2 + (110 - 114)^2 + (123 - 114)^2 + (129 - 114)^2 + \cdots +$$

$$(112 - 114)^2 + (110 - 114)^2 + (117 - 114)^2 + (130 - 114)^2]/(21 - 1) = 92.16$$

$$\hat{\sigma} = \sqrt{92.16} = 9.60; \quad \hat{\sigma}_{\overline{X}} = \frac{\hat{\sigma}}{\sqrt{N}} = \frac{9.60}{\sqrt{21}} = 2.10$$

To find the critical t-value, t_c, we make use of either SPSS or Table 2 from Appendix C.

To use SPSS, we use the IDF.T(p, df) function under Compute where p is the proportion of area to the left of the t-value. Because we want the 95 percent CI, we need the t-values that mark off .025 area in each of the two tails. The t-value with .025 area to its left is IDF.T(.025, 20) $= -2.086$; the t-value with .975 area to its left is IDF.T(.975, 20) $=$ 2.086.

To use Table 2 in Appendix C to find the critical t-value, we refer to the value at the intersection of the row labeled $df = 20$ and the column labeled .025. By contrast to the IDF.T function in SPSS, the p-value in Table 2 marks off that proportion of area under the t-distribution to its right. The t-value from Table 2 that marks off .025 area to its right is 2.086, which agrees with the value obtained from SPSS. Because of symmetry we know that the t-value that marks off .025 of the area under the t-distribution to its left is -2.086. To calculate upper and lower limits we use only the positive t-value:

$$\text{Lower limit} = \bar{X} - t_c\hat{\sigma}_{\bar{X}} = 114 - t_c(2.10) = 114 - (2.086)(2.10) = 114 - 4.38 = 109.62$$

$$\text{Upper limit} = \bar{X} + t_c\hat{\sigma}_{\bar{X}} = 114 + t_c(2.10) = 114 + (2.086)(2.10) = 114 + 4.38 = 118.38$$

Accordingly, the 95 percent CI for μ in this case is (109.62, 118.38). Because $\mu = 120$ does not fall within this interval, it is not a plausible value of the population mean systolic blood pressure for adult African–American males. Based on the interval, plausible population mean values fall in the range of 109.62 to 118.38 and suggest that the mean systolic blood pressure for adult African–American males is statistically significantly lower than 120.

Alternatively, we may use SPSS to obtain the confidence interval directly. These data may be found in the Blood data set.

First, we click **Analyze, Descriptive Statistics**, and **Descriptives including skewness** to get a sense of the SYSTOLC1 data.

Descriptive Statistics

	N	Minimum	Maximum	Mean	Std.	Skewness	
	Statistic	Statistic	Statistic	Statistic	Statistic	Statistic	Std. Error
Initial blood pressure	21	98	135	114.00	9.597	.612	.501
Valid N (listwise)	21						

As expected, the mean and standard deviation values are the same as calculated by hand. The skewness ratio of .612/.501 $= 1.22$ is less than 2 in magnitude, suggesting that the normality assumption is tenable.

To construct the 95 percent CI for μ when σ is not known, click **Analyze**, **Compare Means**, and **One-Sample *t*-test**. Move SYSTOLC1 into the **Test Variable** box. Verify that test Value = 0 and click **OK**.

The use of the one-sample test is dictated by the fact that our design contains only one sample in this case. The relevant portion of the output is reproduced in the following table.

One-Sample Test

	Test value = 0	
	95% Confidence Interval of the Difference	
	Lower	Upper
Initial blood pressure	109.63	118.37

The 95 percent CI from SPSS agrees within rounding error with the interval we obtained by hand.

EXAMPLE 11.2. Use SPSS to construct a 95 percent CI to estimate the population mean number of units (years) of mathematics taken in high school by females who live in the South. Recall that the population of such students is defined as those who responded to all four administrations of the NELS survey, who were always at grade level, and who pursued some form of post-secondary education. Assume that σ is not known and that it needs to be estimated from the sample data. Note that the data on math units taken were collected originally by the National Assessment of Educational Progress (NAEP) and then incorporated into the NELS data set.

Solution. If we knew σ, the standard deviation of the parent population, we would use the Central Limit Theorem and proceed as we did in Chapter 10, using Equation 10.1 to construct the desired 95 percent CI. Because we do not know σ, however, we construct the 95 percent CI based on the *t*-distribution. This construction is readily performed using SPSS.

Because our focus for this example is on girls from the South only, we start by selecting this subgroup from the data set.

To select the subgroup of the NELS, females from the south, we click **Data;** we **Select Cases** if GENDER = 1 & REGION = 3. After the test has been conducted, we return and click the circle next to **Analyze all cases**.

To get a sense of our data, we next click **Analyze**, **Descriptive Statistics**, and **Descriptives including skewness** and obtain the following statistics for UNITMATH.

Descriptive Statistics

	N	Minimum	Maximum	Mean	Std.	Skewness	
	Statistic	Statistic	Statistic	Statistic	Statistic	Statistic	Std. Error
Units in Mathematics (NAEP)	84	2.0	6.0	3.664	.7226	.122	.263
Valid N (listwise)	84						

Recall that the standard deviation given in the SPSS output is actually $\hat{\sigma}$. Thus, we know that $N = 84$, $\overline{X} = 3.66$, $\hat{\sigma} = .72$, skewness $= .12$, and the skewness ratio $= \dfrac{.122}{.263} = .46$.

The skewness ratio suggests that our population of UNITMATH scores does not deviate radically from normality. Furthermore, the sample of size 84 is sufficiently large to warrant the use of the t-distribution in this case.

We use SPSS to construct the 95 percent CI as before. Once again, the use of the one-sample test is dictated by the fact that our design contains only one sample in this case. In addition to some sample statistics, we obtain the following output:

One-Sample Test

	Test Value = 0	
	95% Confidence Interval of the Difference	
	Lower	Upper
Units in Mathematics (NAEP)	3.507	3.821

Of interest in this example is the 95 percent CI, (3.51, 3.82). In other words, it is plausible that the mean number of years of math taken in high school for the population of Southern girls represented by our sample falls between 3.51 and 3.82. Said differently, this result means that if we were to construct an interval estimate of μ for all possible random samples of size 84 from this population, exactly 95 percent of all these interval estimates would in fact contain μ and only 5 percent would not. Does this estimate surprise you? Would you have expected college-bound females from the South to take fewer or more years of math in high school?

EXAMPLE 11.3. Use the same data as in Example 11.2 to construct a 99 percent CI about μ.

Solution. We may bypass the need to select cases and the need to determine N and skewness ratio to assess the impact they may have on the validity of the t-distribution because we have already done so in connection with the preceding example.

To obtain the 99 percent CI, click **Analyze**, **Compare Means**, and **One-Sample *t*-test** and leave UNITMATH as the Test Variable. To change the confidence level, click **Options** and replace the default value of 95% with 99%.

In so doing, we obtain the following results.

One-Sample Test

	Test Value = 0	
	99% Confidence Interval of the Difference	
	Lower	Upper
Units in Mathematics (NAEP)	3.456	3.872

Notice that the 99 percent CI (3.46, 3.87) is longer than the 95 percent CI. As noted in the previous chapter, if we increase the confidence level, say from 95 to 99 percent, and keep the sample size the same, the resulting CI is longer. Our estimate of μ is then less precise, but we can be more confident that it is accurate.

HYPOTHESIS TESTS: THE ONE-SAMPLE *t*-TEST

When the parent population is known to be normally distributed (or the sample size is sufficiently large) and when σ is not known and needs to be estimated using sample data, we may conduct hypothesis tests of μ by carrying out a *t*-test (as opposed to a *z*-test). A *t*-test is based on the *t*-distribution whereas the *z*-test is based on the normal distribution. We may ask, as we have done previously, whether adult African-American males, on average, have a systolic blood pressure that is different from the general population of adult American males, which is known to be 120. In reference to our NELS data, we may ask, for example, whether college-bound females from the South who have always been at grade level take an average of three years of math in high school. We may also ask, among other questions, whether college-bound males from the South who have always been at grade level take an average of more than three years of math in high school. We use SPSS to carry out these tests, but we also carry out the systolic analysis by hand.

EXAMPLE 11.4. Use the same data as in Example 11.1 to test, using a one-sample *t*-test, whether adult African-American males have, on average, a systolic blood pressure that is different from the general population of adult American males, which is known to be 120. Use $\alpha = .05$. Carry out the analysis by hand and also with SPSS.

Solution. If we knew σ, the standard deviation of the parent population, we would use the Central Limit Theorem and proceed as we did in Chapter 10 to test these hypotheses. Because we do not know σ, however, we use the *t*-distribution as the basis for the null hypothesis testing procedure in this case. We are warranted to do so because from Example 11.1 we know that our sample is sufficiently symmetric to make the assumption of normality a reasonable one.

The null and alternative hypotheses are $H_0: \mu = 120$ versus $H_1: \mu \neq 120$.

Based on our earlier calculations in connection with Example 11.1, we know that

$$\bar{X} = 114; \hat{\sigma}^2 = 92.16; \hat{\sigma} = \sqrt{92.16} = 9.60; \hat{\sigma}_{\bar{X}} = \frac{\hat{\sigma}}{\sqrt{N}} = \frac{9.60}{\sqrt{21}} = 2.10.$$

Using the t-ratio of Equation 11.1, we may determine the number of standard errors the observed sample mean of 114 is from the population mean of 120 as follows:

$$t = \frac{\bar{X} - \mu}{\frac{\hat{\sigma}}{\sqrt{N}}} = \frac{\bar{X} - \mu}{\hat{\sigma}_{\bar{X}}} = \frac{114 - 120}{2.10} = -2.86.$$

The t-ratio tells us that the observed mean of 114 is 2.86 standard errors below the hypothesized mean of 120.

To find the p-value associated with this t-ratio, we use SPSS and Table 2 in Appendix C. In both cases we need the value of the t-ratio and its associated degrees of freedom. We have $t = -2.86$. Given that this is a one-sample t-test, $df = N - 1 = 21 - 1 = 20$.

To use SPSS, we use the following numerical expression in the Compute statement to find the one-tailed p-value: $1 - \text{CDF.T}(t, df) = 1 - \text{CDF.T}(2.86, 20)$. Because of symmetry, we may also find the one-tailed p-value by using $\text{CDF.T}(-2.86, 20)$. In both cases, the one-tailed p-value is .0048. The two-tailed p-value is obtained by multiplying .0048 by 2, so that $p = .0048 * 2 = .0096$, which may be rounded to .010.

To use Table 2, we make use of the symmetry of the t-distribution. Because the t-distribution is symmetric, we may ignore the negative sign and look for the printed value closest to 2.86 in Table 2 to approximate the obtained p-value. We scan the row labeled $df = 20$ in Table 2 and find that the closest printed t-value to 2.86 is 2.845. This value has .005 of the area under the t-distribution to its right. Because the alternative hypothesis is nondirectional ($H_1: \mu \neq 120$), we multiply this value by 2 to obtain the approximate two-tailed p-value, which is $p = .005 * 2 = .010$.

That is, the probability that we have observed a mean as extreme as, or more extreme than, 114 that comes from a population with mean equal to 120 is only .01. Because this probability is so small (it is smaller than .05), we conclude that it is likely that the population mean is not equal to 120 and we reject the null hypothesis in favor of the alternative. Because the sample mean of 114 is smaller than the null hypothesized value of 120, we conclude that the systolic blood pressure of African-American males ($M = 114$, $SD = 9.6$) is statistically significantly lower than 120, the mean for the general population of adult American males, $t(20) = -2.86$, $p = .01$.

We now carry out the analysis for this example using SPSS.

To find the p-value associated with a one-sample t-test, click **Analyze**, **Compare Means**, and **One-Sample t-test**. Move SYSTOLC1 into the **Test Variable** box, replace the default Test Value of 0 with the null hypothesized value of 120, and click **OK**.

We obtain the following results.

One-Sample Test

					95% Confidence Interval of the Difference	
					Test Value = 120	
	t	df	Sig. (2-tailed)	Mean Difference	Lower	Upper
Initial blood pressure	−2.865	20	.010	−6.000	−10.37	−1.63

Notice that the obtained t-value of −2.87 matches the one we obtained by hand within rounding error and the two-tailed p-value also agrees with our earlier result.

☞ **Remark.** As the default, SPSS includes a 95% CI for μ – Test Value with all one-sample tests. For the preceding output we have the 95% CI:

$$-10.37 \leq \mu - 120 \leq -1.63.$$

If we prefer to have the CI expressed in terms of μ, there are two equivalent approaches. First, we could re-run the one-sample test using SPSS with Test Value = 0. Alternatively, we could add 120 to each of the inequalities in the expression for the 95% CI for μ–Test Value:

$$-10.37 + 120 \leq \mu - 120 + 120 \leq -1.63 + 120$$
$$109.63120 \leq \mu \leq 118.37$$

EFFECT SIZE FOR THE ONE-SAMPLE t-TEST

In terms of d, the effect size for a one-sample t-test equals

$$d = \frac{\overline{X} - \mu}{\hat{\sigma}} \tag{11.4}$$

The effect size for the result in Example 11.4 is $d = \dfrac{114 - 120}{9.60} = -.625$, which indicates

that the mean systolic blood pressure of adult African-American males is .625 standard deviations below 120. This is a moderate-to-large effect in this case according to Cohen's rule-of-thumb guidelines.

EXAMPLE 11.5. Suppose that a recent survey conducted in the southern region of the United States indicates that college-bound females who have always been at grade level take an average of three years of math in high school. Based on your own personal knowledge and what you have read in the literature, you believe that this is not the case, although you do not know whether the number of years is more or less than 3. Accordingly, you wish to carry out a test to nullify the hypothesis that $H_0: \mu = 3$ in favor of the alternative hypothesis that $H_1: \mu \neq 3$. Use the NELS data set and set $\alpha = .05$.

Solution. If we knew σ, the standard deviation of the parent population, we would use the Central Limit Theorem and proceed as we did in Chapter 10 to test these hypotheses. Because we do not know σ, however, we use the t-distribution as the basis for the null hypothesis testing procedure in this case. We are warranted to do so because of the size of our sample ($N = 84$) and the fact that, from Example 11.2, we know that our sample is sufficiently symmetric to make the assumption of normality a reasonable one.

We select cases as in Example 11.2. Because the data set is large, we do not carry out the computations by hand; we use SPSS.

To find the p-value associated with the t-test in SPSS, we click **Analyze**, **Compare Means**, and **One-Sample t-test**. Follow the method of Example 11.4 to find the p-value, replacing the default Test Value of 0 with the null hypothesized value of 3 and click **OK**.

We obtain the following results.

One-Sample Statistics

	N	Mean	Std. Deviation	Std. Error Mean
Units in Mathematics (NAEP)	84	3.664	.7226	.0788

One-Sample Test

	Test Value = 3					
					95% Confidence Interval of the Difference	
	t	df	Sig. (2-tailed)	Mean Difference	Lower	Upper
Units in Mathematics (NAEP)	8.423	83	.000	.6640	.507	.821

The t-value is 8.42 with 83 degrees of freedom ($df = N - 1 = 84 - 1 = 83$, in this case) and the p-value is given in the Sig. (2-tailed) column ($p = .000$). By default the test is conducted as two-tailed, which in this case is appropriate because our alternative hypothesis is nondirectional. Our conclusion then is to reject the null hypothesis in favor of the alternative: that the mean number of units of math taken in high school by southern females is indeed different from 3.

Furthermore, because the obtained sample mean is $\overline{X} = 3.66$, we may conclude that the mean number of units of math taken in high school is statistically significantly *higher* than 3.

In terms of d, the effect size is given by $d = \dfrac{\overline{X} - \mu}{\hat{\sigma}} = \dfrac{3.66 - 3}{.72} = .92$, which indicates that the mean number of years of math taken by college-bound females from the South who have always stayed at grade level is .92 standard deviations larger than 3, suggesting a large effect in this case according to Cohen's rule-of-thumb guidelines.

☞ **Remark.** Note that we should not interpret $p = .000$ as if p were identically equal to zero. The reason that p is reported as .000 is because SPSS reports results to three significant digits. Our result is highly unlikely given that the null hypothesis is true, but it is not impossible, which would be the case if p were truly identically equal to zero. To indicate that p is not identically equal to zero, we write $p < .0005$ when reporting such results.

☞ **Remark.** If we had used the 95 percent CI that we constructed in Example 11.2 to test $H_0: \mu = 3$ versus $H_1: \mu \neq 3$, we would have arrived at the same conclusion that we did in Example 11.5: to reject H_0 in favor of H_1. That 95 percent CI so constructed in Example 11.2 equals (3.51, 3.82). By the definition of a CI we know that the values falling within the CI (from 3.51 to 3.82) are exactly those values of μ that would *not* be rejected as implausible in a nondirectional hypothesis test at significance level .05. We also know that the values of μ falling outside the CI are the ones that would be rejected in a nondirectional hypothesis test at significance level .05. Because the null hypothesized value of 3 does not fall within the CI, it is not considered to be a plausible value of μ and so must be rejected in the context of a hypothesis test.

☞ **Remark.** In the one-sample t-test, CIs are given for μ minus the test value. In this case the test value was set at 3; hence, the 95 percent CI for $\mu - 3$ is (.507, .821). We may infer, therefore, that plausible population mean differences (from 3) in this case range from .507 to .821. In Example 11.2, to create the CI for μ, we set the test value at 0 and obtain the 95 percent CI as (3.507, 3.821).

· ·

EXAMPLE 11.6. Suppose that a recent survey conducted in the southern region of the United States indicates that college-bound males who have always been at grade level take an average of three years of math in high school. Based on your own personal knowledge and what you have read in the literature, you believe that this is not the case – that, in fact, they take more than 3 years of math in high school. Accordingly, you wish to carry out a test to nullify the hypothesis that $H_0: \mu = 3$ in favor of the alternative hypothesis that $H_1: \mu > 3$. You use the NELS data set and set $\alpha = .05$.

Solution. The descriptive statistics given for NELS data set males from the South show that $N = 66$ and the skewness ratio $= \dfrac{.148}{.295} = .50$ and these statistics suggest that the data set is sufficiently large and symmetric to justify our use of the t-distribution to test the null hypothesis of interest.

Descriptive Statistics

	N	Minimum	Maximum	Mean	Std.	Skewness	
	Statistic	Statistic	Statistic	Statistic	Statistic	Statistic	Std. Error
Units in Mathematics (NAEP)	66	2.0	6.0	3.917	.7369	.148	.295
Valid N (listwise)	66						

We do not use the z-test because σ is not known and needs to be estimated from the data. We carry out the test to determine whether the amount by which 3.9 exceeds 3 is indicative of a real significant difference or is due only to sampling error. Had the obtained value been less than 3, there would have no reason to carry out the hypothesis test at all because the null hypothesis would be more plausible than the alternative.

We proceed as in Example 11.5 to find the p-value associated with the t-test and obtain the following results:

One-Sample Test

	Test Value = 3					
					95% Confidence Interval of the Difference	
	t	df	Sig. (2-tailed)	Mean Difference	Lower	Upper
Units in Mathematics (NAEP)	10.107	65	.000	.9167	.736	1.098

For this example, we expect the degrees of freedom to be $N - 1 = 66 - 1 = 65$, which is the value reported in the output. The t-value of 10.11 with 65 degrees of freedom has an associated two-tailed p-value of .000 ($p < .0005$). Because the alternative hypothesis in this case is directional, a one-tailed p-value is appropriate. Accordingly, we must divide the two-tailed p-value by 2 to obtain the desired p-value result. In so doing, we obtain $p < .00025$, suggesting that the result is statistically significant–that the population of college-bound males in the southern region of the United States takes more than three years of math in high school on average.

We could not have used a CI to determine whether college-bound males from the South take more than three years of high school math because, as formulated in this text, CIs can be used only in the case of nondirectional research questions.

Given that the results of the one-sample t-test are statistically significant, they should be further analyzed for practical significance, using a measure of the magnitude of the effect.

In terms of d, the effect size is $\dfrac{\overline{X} - \mu}{\hat{\sigma}} = \dfrac{3.92 - 3}{.74} = 1.24$, which indicates that the mean number of years of math taken by college-bound males from the South who have always stayed at grade level is approximately 1.24 standard deviations larger than 3, a very large effect according to Cohen's rule-of-thumb guidelines.

TWO-SAMPLE DESIGNS WHEN THE PARAMETER OF INTEREST IS μ, AND σ IS NOT KNOWN

In this section we expand the number of groups in the design from one to two and in so doing allow for the possibility of answering a whole different set of questions. As related to the various populations represented by the NELS data set, we may ask, for example, whether

1. college-bound males from the South who have always been at grade level differ on average in the number of years of math taken in high school from females from the South?
2. college-bound females from the Northeast who have always been at grade level who own a computer score higher on average in twelfth-grade math achievement than those who do not own a computer?
3. college-bound females from the South who have always been at grade level change on average in self-esteem from eighth to twelfth grade?

Each of these questions is concerned with estimating the means of two populations, μ_1 and μ_2, for the purpose of comparing them to each other. In question 1, we may define μ_1 as the mean number of years of math taken in high school by females from the South and μ_2 as the mean number of years of math taken in high school by males from the South. In question 2, we may define μ_1 as the mean math achievement score in twelfth grade for students who own a computer and μ_2 as the mean math achievement score in twelfth grade for those who do not own a computer. Finally, in question 3, we may define μ_1 as the mean self-esteem score of females in eighth grade and μ_2 as the mean self-esteem scores of the same females, now in twelfth grade. In each case, we are concerned with knowing whether a difference between the two population means exists; that is, whether it is plausible that the difference between population means is zero. If the difference is not zero, then we would be interested in knowing the magnitude of the difference that exists.

To test whether the two population means, μ_1 and μ_2, in fact differ from each other, we begin by estimating μ_1 and μ_2 by $\overline{X}_1$ and $\overline{X}_2$, respectively, where we calculate each sample mean on a sample randomly selected from the appropriate population. We then compute the difference between $\overline{X}_1$ and $\overline{X}_2$. Because our interest is not with the sample mean difference per se but rather with the population mean difference, we need a procedure for judging whether the sample mean difference is real or merely apparent (due to sampling error). In the preceding section, when the design involved only one sample and σ was unknown, we used the one-sample t-distribution (the sampling distribution of means when σ is unknown) to determine whether the observed sample mean was statistically significantly different from the hypothesized value, μ. In the present case, our design involves two samples and we assume that $\sigma_1 = \sigma_2 = \sigma$ and that σ is not known. By analogy, we turn to the sampling distribution of differences between means $\overline{X}_1$ and $\overline{X}_2$ calculated on samples of size N_1 and N_2, respectively, to determine whether the observed difference between sample means is statistically significantly different from the hypothesized difference $\mu_1 - \mu_2$.

INDEPENDENT (OR UNRELATED) AND DEPENDENT (OR RELATED) SAMPLES

To determine whether an observed difference in sample means is large enough to cause us to infer a difference in population means, we need first to consider another aspect of study design: the degree to which factors extraneous to the main variable of interest are controlled. We may think of the observed difference in sample means as comprising two components: a *signal* component that reflects the true difference between sample means in terms of the variable under study (e.g., the number of years of math taken during high school) and a *noise* component that reflects the difference between sample means due to extraneous and random factors (e.g., educational aspirations, academic interests, and career goals). By analogy, we may think of the signal as a radio broadcast and the noise as static in the airwaves. Just as our ability to detect a particular radio signal depends on the amount of static present, so our ability to detect a statistical difference depends on the degree to which extraneous and random factors have not been controlled.

In the preceding question 1, if all variables that might affect the number of years of math taken in high school were the same for males and females (e.g., educational aspirations, academic interests, career goals, and so on), we would say that the system contained little or no noise. In this case, we would have little difficulty detecting the signal – the true difference – no matter how small. On the other hand, if none of the variables that might affect the number of years of math taken in high school were controlled, we would say that the system contained a great deal of noise. In this case, we might have great difficulty detecting the signal, no matter how large. In general, the more control we exercise over extraneous factors, the smaller the difference between $\overline{X}_1$ and $\overline{X}_2$ that we are able to detect as statistically significant, that is, as significant of a difference between population means.

If, with respect to question 1, a random sample of males was selected and a random sample of females was selected *independently*, extraneous factors such as educational aspirations, academic interests, career goals, and the like would not be explicitly controlled for. Any or all of these factors would be considered noise in the system and they could contribute to the observed difference between $\overline{X}_1$ and $\overline{X}_2$. Explicit control over extraneous factors may be achieved if a random sample of males was selected and a sample of females was then selected in such a way that each female *matched* each male on a one-to-one, pairwise basis with respect to as many of the extraneous factors as possible. A result of such control is a reduction in the noise component and a consequent expectation of smaller differences between means. Accordingly, decisions as to whether a statistical difference is real or apparent (merely due to sampling error) must depend, at least, in part, on whether the study design controls for extraneous factors or not. When the selection of subjects for one sample has no effect whatsoever on the selection of subjects for the second sample (as when the females were selected independently of the males), the two samples are said to be *independent*, or *unrelated*. When the samples are selected in such a way as to allow individual matching into pairs on extraneous factors across samples (such as when individuals are matched on educational aspirations, academic interests, career goals, etc.), the two samples are said to be *dependent, paired,* or *related*.

A particular case of related samples arises when *the same individuals* are tested twice with an intervening treatment or interval of time (as in question 3 at the beginning of the chapter). Because measures are taken repeatedly on the same individuals, this type of design is often called a *repeated-measures design*. Although repeated-measures designs do generally afford more control than unrelated-samples designs, repeated-measures designs are usually employed to comply with the theoretical framework of the research problem rather than for explicit control.

Because the size of sample mean differences, $\overline{X}_1 - \overline{X}_2$, depends in part on whether the design controls for extraneous factors or not (i.e., whether it is based on related or unrelated samples), we must treat the cases of related and unrelated samples separately in our discussion of sampling distributions. We first consider designs that use independent samples.

INDEPENDENT SAMPLES t-TEST AND CONFIDENCE INTERVAL

In the earlier section on the one-sample t-test, we determined that southern U.S. college-bound males and females who have always been at grade level each take an average of more than three years of math in high school. But does the population of males differ from the population of females in terms of the number of years of math taken in high school? Questions like these imply a comparison of one group mean to the other rather than a separate comparison of each group mean to a specified value – three in this case. Furthermore, because the males and females are each selected independently of each other, the appropriate test to answer this question is the independent samples t-test.

The sample means and standard deviations of the number of years of high school mathematics taken by both males and females from the South obtained using the compare means procedure are given in Table 11.1.

As with the one-group t-test, our question concerns whether the observed mean difference between males and females ($3.92 - 3.66 = .26$) is large enough to conclude that a real difference exists between males and females in the population. To determine whether it is large enough, we need to extend the procedure we used in relation to the one-sample t-test to incorporate the fact that we are now interested in making judgments about differences between means rather than about means alone. Recall that the one-sample t-ratio is described by Equation 11.1 as

$$t = \frac{(\overline{X} - \mu)}{\hat{\sigma}_{\overline{X}}}.$$

Table 11.1. Descriptive statistics for units of math taken by males and females in the southern region

Report

Units in Mathematics (NAEP)

Gender	Mean	N	Std. Deviation
Male	3.917	66	.7369
Female	3.664	84	.7226
Total	3.775	150	.7372

In extending this ratio to the case of mean differences, we simply substitute a mean difference quantity for every instance of a mean. Thus, we obtain Equation 11.5 as the t-ratio that is used to test hypotheses about mean differences on independent samples:

$$t = \frac{(\overline{X}_1 - \overline{X}_2) - (\mu_1 - \mu_2)}{\hat{\sigma}_{\overline{X}_1 - \overline{X}_2}} \tag{11.5}$$

Whereas the computation of the numerator of this ratio contains no new notation, the denominator requires some explanation. In short, $\hat{\sigma}_{\overline{X}_1 - \overline{X}_2}$ is the standard deviation of the sampling distribution of sample mean differences, also called the *standard error of mean differences*. The equation for determining $\hat{\sigma}_{\overline{X}_1 - \overline{X}_2}$ when the variances for the two populations from which the samples are drawn are equal is given as

$$\hat{\sigma}_{\overline{X}_1 - \overline{X}_2} = \sqrt{\frac{(N_1 - 1)\hat{\sigma}_1^2 + (N_2 - 1)\hat{\sigma}_2^2}{N_1 + N_2 - 2} \left(\frac{1}{N_1} + \frac{1}{N_2}\right)}, \tag{11.6}$$

which is based on a weighted average of the two variance estimators, $\hat{\sigma}_1^2$ and $\hat{\sigma}_2^2$. Notice that $\hat{\sigma}_1^2$ is weighted by the degrees of freedom of sample one, $N_1 - 1$, and σ_2^2 is weighted by the degrees of freedom of sample two, $N_2 - 1$. The degrees of freedom for each group, $N_1 - 1$ and $N_2 - 1$, respectively, are a function of the group's size. Because estimators from larger samples are generally more accurate, Equation 11.6 weights more heavily the estimate that comes from the larger sample.

Substituting Equation 11.6 into Equation 11.5, we present an alternate version of the t-statistic for the two-population, unrelated-samples case with homogeneous variances as

$$t = \frac{(\overline{X}_1 - \overline{X}_2) - (\mu_1 - \mu_2)}{\sqrt{\frac{(N_1 - 1)\hat{\sigma}_1^2 + (N_2 - 1)\hat{\sigma}_2^2}{N_1 + N_2 - 2} \left(\frac{1}{N_1} + \frac{1}{N_2}\right)}}. \tag{11.7}$$

The number of degrees of freedom for this t-statistic may be determined by recalling that we are using both sample variance estimators, $\hat{\sigma}_1^2$ and $\hat{\sigma}_2^2$, to obtain the denominator of this statistic and that $\hat{\sigma}_1^2$ has $N_1 - 1$ degrees of freedom associated with it, whereas $\hat{\sigma}_2^2$ has $N_2 - 1$ degrees of freedom associated with it. Because $\hat{\sigma}_1^2$ and $\hat{\sigma}_2^2$ come from independent samples, the total number of independent pieces of information contained in the data, and therefore the number of degrees of freedom for this t-statistic, is

$$\nu = \nu_1 + \nu_2 = (N_1 - 1) + (N_2 - 1) = N_1 + N_2 - 2 \tag{11.8}$$

To estimate the mean difference between populations, we construct a CI:

$$\text{Upper limit} = (\overline{X}_1 - \overline{X}_2) + (t_{crit})(\hat{\sigma}_{\overline{X}_1 - \overline{X}_2})$$

$$\text{Lower limit} = (\overline{X}_1 - \overline{X}_2) + (t_{crit})(\hat{\sigma}_{\overline{X}_1 - \overline{X}_2}) \tag{11.9}$$

where $\hat{\sigma}_{\overline{X}_1 - \overline{X}_2}$, the standard error of the mean difference, is given in Equation 11.6 and t_{crit} is found as before using IDF.T with df equal to $N_1 + N_2 - 2$.

Notice that Equation 11.9 is an extension of Equation 11.3 for constructing CIs in the one-sample design when σ is not known.

THE ASSUMPTIONS OF THE INDEPENDENT SAMPLES t-TEST

Although the t-test procedure just outlined results in a sample statistic, there is in general no guarantee that this procedure yields a t-statistic with a corresponding t-distribution. If certain conditions are satisfied by our two populations, however, then the statistic is a t-statistic. The conditions are as follows:

1. The null hypothesis is true.
2. Both parent populations are normally distributed.
3. The two populations have equal variances (which is called homogeneity of variance).

If any of these three conditions is not met, then the statistic obtained may not be distributed as a t-distribution with hypothesized mean difference $\mu_1 - \mu_2$ and estimated variance $\hat{\sigma}^2_{\overline{X}_1 - \overline{X}_2}$, so that the p-values calculated based on this distribution would be invalid.

In testing the difference between population means, if conditions 2 and 3 are known to be satisfied and an unusual sample outcome is observed, then the plausibility of the remaining condition, condition 1, becomes questionable and one would decide to reject H_0 as implausible.

Thus, it appears that conditions 2 and 3 need to be satisfied to test condition 1, that H_0 is true, using the t-statistic provided in Equation 11.7. For this reason, conditions 2 and 3 are usually referred to as the underlying assumptions of this t-test. In actual research situations, we cannot always be certain that either or both conditions 2 and 3 hold and we must expend some effort to investigate the tenability of these assumptions.

Violations of the first underlying assumption, normality of the two parent populations, may be assessed qualitatively by constructing either boxplots or histograms and quantitatively by the skewness ratio. Sometimes violations of the normality assumption may be corrected using nonlinear transformations as discussed in Chapter 4. Violations of the second underlying assumption, equality of the two parent population variances, may be assessed by Levene's test. As we shall see, results from this test are provided routinely in SPSS in the output of an independent samples t-test.

For now, it is enough to know that the null hypothesis tested by Levene's test is that the two population variances are equal (H_0: $\sigma_1^2 = \sigma_2^2$) and the alternative hypothesis is that the two population variances are not equal (H_1: $\sigma_1^2 \neq \sigma_2^2$). If the p-value associated with Levene's test is less than α, following usual procedure we reject H_0 in favor of H_1, that the two population variances are not equal, and conclude that the third assumption is not tenable. On the other hand, if the p-value associated with Levene's test is greater than α, we conclude that the homogeneity of variance assumption is tenable.

Because the t-distribution is based on the assumptions of normality and homogeneity of variance, there has been much research on the effect of violations of these assumptions on the t-test. Based on the results of such research, we know that, under certain conditions, the t-test can withstand a great deal of deviation from its underlying assumptions. In statistical terms, we say that the t-test is *robust*. For an extensive review of research related to the consequences of violating the assumptions of the t-test on the probability statements of the t-test, the interested reader is referred to Glass, Peckham, and Sanders (1972).

Violations of the normality assumption may be essentially ignored if the sample from the nonnormal parent population is sufficiently large (30 or larger usually suffices, as in the statement of the Central Limit Theorem) or, if the sample cannot be large, then if the distribution of the nonnormal parent population is approximately symmetric.

Violations of the homogeneity of variance assumption may be essentially ignored as long as the samples being used have equal or approximately equal sizes. If, however, Levene's test indicates that the assumption of equal population variances is not tenable, and the samples are of unequal size, it would be incorrect to pool the two variance estimates using Equation 11.5. The assumption of equal variances can be avoided by using an estimate of variance proposed by Satterthwaite (1946):

$$\hat{\sigma}_s^2 = \frac{\hat{\sigma}_1^2}{N_1} + \frac{\hat{\sigma}_2^2}{N_2}. \tag{11.10}$$

The degrees of freedom associated with Equation 11.10 are not $N_1 + N_2 - 2$ but are given by the following, much more complicated expression that does not necessarily result in an integer value:

$$df = \nu = \frac{\left(\dfrac{\hat{\sigma}_1^2}{N_1} + \dfrac{\hat{\sigma}_2^2}{N_2}\right)^2}{\left(\dfrac{1}{N_1 - 1}\right)\left(\dfrac{\hat{\sigma}_1^2}{N_1}\right)^2 + \left(\dfrac{1}{N_2 - 1}\right)\left(\dfrac{\hat{\sigma}_2^2}{N_2}\right)^2}. \tag{11.11}$$

A good rule of thumb, therefore, is that if both sample sizes are large and equal (or approximately equal), then violations of either or both underlying assumptions, normality and homogeneity of variance, do not seriously affect the applicability of the t-test for unrelated samples. If the samples are not equal, then Levene's test should be used to test for the assumption of homogeneity of variance. If according to Levene's test we find that the homogeneity of variance assumption is not tenable, we should use the t-statistic based on separate sample variances to estimate the two different population variances with degrees of freedom given by Equation 11.11.

For heuristic reasons, we begin with illustrating by hand the tests of inference described in this section using an extended data set from Example 11.1 that incorporates another feature of this study.

EXAMPLE 11.7. To determine whether an increase in calcium intake reduces blood pressure, 10 of the 21 men in Example 11.1 were randomly assigned to a treatment condition that required them to take a calcium supplement for 12 weeks. The remaining 11 men received a placebo for the 12 weeks. Conduct an analysis to determine whether there is a mean difference in the initial systolic blood pressure readings between the men assigned to the treatment and placebo conditions before they begin the experimental protocol. The data are provided in the following table. Patients in the treatment condition are coded 1;

those in the placebo condition are coded 0. SYSTOLIC has been renamed SYSTOLC1 to underscore the fact that these data are *initial*, pretreatment measures of systolic blood pressure. Use $\alpha = .05$.

Treatment Condition	Systolic blood pressure (mmHg)
1	107
1	110
1	123
1	129
1	112
1	111
1	107
1	112
1	136
1	102
0	123
0	109
0	112
0	102
0	98
0	114
0	119
0	112
0	110
0	117
0	130

Solution. In statistical terms, the null and alternative hypotheses for this test are as follows:

$$H_0: \mu_T = \mu_P, \quad \text{or equivalently,} \quad H_0: \mu_T - \mu_P = 0$$

$$H_1: \mu_T \neq \mu_P, \quad \text{or equivalently,} \quad H_1: \mu_T - \mu_P \neq 0.$$

As usual, we begin the analysis by reviewing the descriptive statistics for each group.

To obtain the table of descriptive statistics for both groups simultaneously using SPSS, we could have used the Selected Cases command as in Examples 11.2, 11.3, 11.5, and 11.6 or we could have used the SPSS Explore procedure. We demonstrate a third possibility here. When there is more than one group, we may use the SPSS Split Files command located in the Data menu. Split file treats the data as two separate data files and computes whatever statistics are requested on each group separately.

To split the file using SPSS, click **Data**, **Split File**. Click the circle next to **Compare Groups** and move the variable of interest, in this case, TREATMEN, into the **Groups Based On** box. Click **OK**.

Descriptive statistics requested for SYSTOLC1 will be printed for each of the separate groups.

Descriptive Statistics

Treatment		N	Minimum	Maximum	Mean	Std.	Skewness	
		Statistic	Statistic	Statistic	Statistic	Statistic	Statistic	Std. Error
Placebo	Initial blood pressure	11	98	130	113.27	9.023	.121	.661
	Valid N (listwise)	11						
Calcium	Initial blood pressure	10	102	135	114.80	10.623	.973	.687
	Valid N (listwise)	10						

To reverse the procedure to be able to carry out analyses on the entire data set, return to the **Split Files** command and click **Analyze All Cases**.

We use these descriptive statistics to provide an initial review of *t*-test assumptions. The skewness ratio for each group is low, suggesting that the normality assumption is reasonable. The sample standard deviations, however, are not equal, leaving open the possibility that the population variances are not equal either and that the assumption of homogeneity of variances is not met for these data. For now we assume that this assumption is met and continue with the independent samples *t*-test by hand to determine whether initial systolic blood pressure differs, on average, between those assigned to the calcium condition and those assigned to the placebo condition. We use SPSS in a later analysis to formally test the homogeneity of variance assumption and we see that it is a reasonable assumption. While we already know the descriptive statistics for each group from SPSS, for instructional purposes we determine them by hand. We arbitrarily label the Calcium Group as Group 1 and the Placebo Group as Group 2.

For the calcium condition (Group 1):

$$N_1 = 10$$

$$\bar{X}_1 = (107 + 110 + 123 + 129 + 112 + 111 + 107$$
$$+ 112 + 136 + 102)/10 = 114.8$$

$$\hat{\sigma}_1^2 = [(107 - 114.8)^2 + (110 - 114.8)^2 + (123 - 114.8)^2 + \cdots + (112 - 114.8)^2$$
$$+ (136 - 114.8)^2 + (102 - 114.8)^2]/(10 - 1) = 112.78$$

$$\hat{\sigma}_1 = \sqrt{112.78} = 10.62$$

For the placebo condition (Group 2):

$$N_2 = 11$$

$$\bar{X}_2 = (123 + 109 + 112 + 102 + 98 + 114 + 119$$
$$+ 112 + 110 + 117 + 130)/11 = 113.27$$

$$\hat{\sigma}_2^2 = [(123 - 113.27)^2 + (109 - 113.27)^2 + (112 - 113.27)^2 + \cdots + (110$$
$$- 113.27)^2 + (117 - 113.27)^2 + (130 - 113.27)^2]/(11 - 1) = 81.36$$

$$\hat{\sigma}_2 = \sqrt{81.36} = 9.02$$

Substituting these values into Equation 11.7, we obtain the following result:

$$t = \frac{(\bar{X}_1 - \bar{X}_2) - (\mu_1 - \mu_2)}{\sqrt{\dfrac{(N_1 - 1)\hat{\sigma}_1^2 + (N_2 - 1)\hat{\sigma}_2^2}{N_1 + N_2 - 2}\left(\dfrac{1}{N_1} + \dfrac{1}{N_2}\right)}}$$

$$= \frac{114.80 - 113.27}{\sqrt{\dfrac{(10 - 1)(112.78) + (11 - 1)(81.36)}{10 + 11 - 2}\left(\dfrac{1}{10} + \dfrac{1}{11}\right)}}$$

$$= \frac{1.53}{\sqrt{\dfrac{9(112.78) + 10(81.36)}{19}(.10 + .09)}}$$

$$= \frac{1.53}{4.29} = .356$$

To find the p-value associated with this t-ratio, we use SPSS and Table 2 in Appendix C. In both cases we need the value of the t-ratio and its associated degrees of freedom. We have $t = .356$ and, given that this t-value is from an independent samples t-test, $df = N_1 + N_2 - 2 = 10 + 11 - 2 = 19$.

To use SPSS, we use the following numerical expression in the Compute statement to find the one-tailed p-value of .363: $1 - \text{CDF.T}(t,df) = 1 - \text{CDF.T}(.356,19)$. The two-tailed p-value is obtained by multiplying .363 by 2, so that $p = .726$.

We may use Table 2 to approximate the obtained p-value. In this case, we scan the row labeled $df = 19$ to find that the closest printed t-value to .356 is .688. From this poor approximation, we can say that the area to the right of .356 is greater than .25. We multiply .25 by 2, because the null hypothesis is nondirectional, and obtain the result that $p > .5$. The large discrepancy between $p = .726$ and $p > .5$ is due to the fact that Table 2 provides only a limited set of p-values relative to the t-distribution. The p-values provided are only those associated with the commonly used definitions of statistical significance. The t-distribution given by SPSS, however, is complete and may be relied upon to provide accurate estimates of p-values for associated t-values.

From the more accurate SPSS p-value we know that the probability of observing a mean difference as, or more, extreme than 1.53 coming from two populations with a mean difference of zero is .726. Because this probability is so large, we conclude that the obtained result is consistent with the statement of the null hypothesis that $\mu_P - \mu_C$. We therefore do not reject the null hypothesis in favor of the alternative hypothesis and conclude, based on this p-value, that the men assigned to the calcium condition are no different, on average, from those assigned to the clacebo condition in terms of their initial, pretreatment systolic blood pressure.

To estimate the population mean difference in initial systolic blood pressure between Groups 1 and 2, we may construct a 95 percent CI for $\mu_P - \mu_C$. To do so we substitute the earlier values we calculated by hand for this example into Equation 11.9.

To find the t_c value we may use either SPSS or Table 2 in Appendix C.

To find t_c using SPSS, we compute IDF(.975,19) and obtain $t_c = 2.09$.

To find t_c using Table 2, we find the value at the intersection of the row labeled $df = 19$ and the column labeled .025. The t-value that has area .025 to its right is 2.09.

$$\text{Upper limit} = (\overline{X}_1 - \overline{X}_2) + (t_c)(\hat{\sigma}_{\overline{X}_1 - \overline{X}_2}) = (114.80 - 113.27) + t_c(4.29)$$

$$= 1.53 + 2.09(4.29) = 1.53 + 8.97 = 10.50$$

$$\text{Lower limit} = (\overline{X}_1 - \overline{X}_2) + (t_c)(\hat{\sigma}_{\overline{X}_1 - \overline{X}_2}) = (114.80 - 113.27) - t_c(4.29)$$

$$= 1.53 - 2.09(4.29) = 1.53 - 8.97 = -7.45$$

Accordingly, we estimate the mean difference in systolic blood pressure between the calcium and placebo populations to be between -7.45 and 10.50. Because zero falls within this interval it is plausible that the mean difference between populations is zero – that the null hypothesis of a zero population mean difference is true, which is the conclusion we reached from the earlier t-test.

We now carry out the analysis for this example using SPSS.

To use SPSS to perform an independent samples t-test, click **Analyze, Compare Means, Independent Samples t-test**. Move SYSTOLC1 into the **Test Variable(s)** box and TREATMEN into the **Grouping Variable** box. Define the range of TREATMEN to be 0 and 1. Click **Continue** and **OK**.

We obtain the results shown in the following table.

Independent Samples Test

| | | Levene's Test for Equality of Variances | | t-test for Equality of Means | | | | | | |
| | | | | | | | | | 95% Confidence Interval of the Difference | |
		F	Sig.	t	df	Sig. (2-tailed)	Mean Difference	Std. Error Difference	Lower	Upper
Initial blood pressure	Equal Variances assumed	.558	.464	−.356	19	.726	−1.527	4.288	−10.502	7.447
	Equal variances not assumed			−.353	17.790	.728	−1.527	4.323	−10.617	7.562

Notice that the results of Levene's test for equality of variances are provided in the first two columns of the table of output. Because $p = .464$ and $\alpha = .05$ for this example, we conclude that the population variances are not different and that the assumption of homogeneity of variance is met for these data. Accordingly, we use the results of the independent samples t-test given on the top row, labeled "Equal variances assumed," to determine whether initial mean systolic blood pressure differs between the calcium and placebo groups.

According to these results, $t(19) = .356$ and $p = .726$, suggesting that there is no difference in mean initial systolic blood pressure between the calcium and placebo groups. These are the hypothesis tests results we obtained in our hand calculation. The mean difference and standard error of the mean difference (1.53 and 4.29, respectively) are given as well. These also agree with our hand calculations, as does the 95 percent CI of the population mean difference given as -7.45 to 10.50.

· ·

EXAMPLE 11.8. Does the population of college-bound males from the southern United States who have always been at grade level differ from the corresponding population of females in terms of the number of years of math in high school? Conduct the significance test at $\alpha = .05$.

Solution. In statistical terms, the null hypothesis for this test is $H_0: \mu_M = \mu_F$, or equivalently, $H_0: \mu_M - \mu_F = 0$; the alternative hypothesis is $H_1: \mu_M \neq \mu_F$ or, equivalently, $H_1: \mu_M - \mu_F \neq 0$. As before, we begin with an evaluation of the underlying assumptions of this t-test. From the earlier descriptive statistics given for females and males, in Examples 11.2 and 11.3, respectively, we know that the assumptions of both normality and homogeneity of variance appear to have been met. Boxplots of the variable "number of years in math in high school" for males and females from the South visually confirm these impressions. Note that the boxplots suggest a trivially small difference between the two groups.

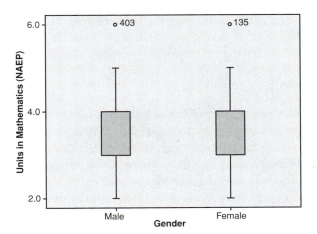

The output of the *t*-test follows.

Group Statistics

	gender Gender	N	Mean	Std. Deviation	Std. Error Mean
unitmath Units in Mathematics (NAEP)	0 Male	66	3.917	.7369	.0907
	1 Female	84	3.664	.7226	.0788

Independent Samples Test

		Levene's Test for Equality of Variances		t-test for Equality of Means						
									95% Confidence Interval of the Difference	
		F	Sig.	t	df	Sig. (2-tailed)	Mean Difference	Std. Error Difference	Lower	Upper
unitmath Units in Mathematics (NAEP)	Equal Variances assumed	1.109	.294	2.107	148	.037	.2526	.1199	.0157	.4895
	Equal variances not assumed			2.102	138.437	.037	.2526	.1202	.0150	.4902

Notice that the output of the *t*-test contains the results of two different tests, one in which the assumption of homogeneity of variance is met (equal variances assumed) and one in which it is not met (equal variances not assumed). In our example, because $p = .294$ is greater than $\alpha = .05$, the results of Levene's test corroborate our visual impressions that the two samples are from populations with equal variances. Hence, we use the results relevant to the *t*-test with equal variances assumed to test our hypothesis. In this case, $t(148) = 2.107$, $p = .04$.

Because $p < .05$, we reject the null hypothesis in favor of the alternative and conclude that there is a statistically significant difference in terms of the mean number of years of math taken in high school between college-bound males and females from the South who have always stayed on track. Based on the means given in the group statistics output, we may further conclude that this population of males appears to take statistically significantly more years in math in high school than this population of females.

☞ **Remark.** To reconcile the inconsistency between our impressions based on the boxplot and the results of the independent samples *t*-test, we generate a population pyramid to explore the distributions of this variable for both males and females. Notice that the shapes of these distributions are quite different. For males, there appear to be four groups of students who enroll in math: those who take two years of high school math, those who take three, those who take four, and those who take five. For females, on the other hand, there appear to be only three groups: those who take two years of high school math, those who take three, and those who take four. Thus, while the median equals four for both males and females, the histograms tell us that the median is more centrally located in the male distribution, whereas it is located closer to the top in the female distribution.

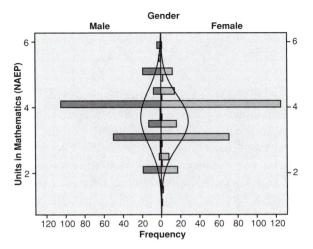

We could have calculated the t-value by substituting the descriptive statistics given in the SPSS output into Equation 11.6 as follows:

$$t = \frac{(\overline{X}_1 - \overline{X}_2) - (\mu_1 - \mu_2)}{\hat{\sigma}_{\overline{X}_1 - \overline{X}_2}} = \frac{\text{Mean Difference}}{\text{Standard Error of the Difference}} = \frac{.253}{.120} = 2.107$$

with $df = N_M + N_F - 2 = 66 + 84 - 2 = 148$. Then use an SPSS compute statement or Table 2 to find the associated p-value of .037.

The 95 percent CI can also be used to determine whether the population of college-bound males from the southern United States who have always been at grade level differ from the corresponding population of females in terms of the number of years of math in high school. Because zero is not contained in the 95 percent CI, (.02, .49), we may conclude that the difference $\mu_M - \mu_F$ is not likely to be zero and may be as great as one-half year. That is, as observed in connection with the null hypothesis test, the two group means are statistically significantly different from each other. Based on the means given in the group statistics output, we may further conclude that this population of males appears to take statistically significantly more years in math in high school than this population of females.

Note that, in the case of a nondirectional alternative hypothesis, we can base our conclusion on either a p-value or a CI.

Effect Size for the Independent Samples t-Test

In addition to the CI, we may extend Cohen's index of effect size, d, to the present case to obtain another estimate of the magnitude of the difference between population means.

Assuming the null hypothesis to be H_0: $\mu_1 = \mu_2$, Cohen's d, expressed as the difference between the two group means relative to the common standard deviation, is given by

$$d = \frac{(\overline{X}_1 - \overline{X}_2)}{\sqrt{\dfrac{(N_1 - 1)\hat{\sigma}_1^2 + (N_2 - 1)\hat{\sigma}_2^2}{N_1 + N_2 - 2}}} \tag{11.12}$$

The effect size, d, for the case of Example 11.8 is equal to

$$d = \frac{3.917 - 3.664}{\sqrt{\dfrac{(65)(.737)^2 + (83)(.723)^2}{66 + 84 - 2}}} = \frac{.253}{.729} = 0.35.$$

That is, the number of years of math, on average, taken by college-bound southern males exceeds that for college-bound southern females by .35 standard deviations, a small-to-moderate size effect, further corroborating the results supported by the CI.

Finally, we present the point biserial correlation coefficient as another measure of effect size that may be used in connection with the independent samples t-test. The point biserial correlation coefficient may be obtained as the correlation between group membership (males or females, in this case) and the variable of interest (years of math taken in high school, in this case). The greater the magnitude of the correlation, the greater the difference between group means relative to the common standard deviation. For example, if the difference in means between the two groups is zero, the point biserial correlation coefficient also is zero. Likewise, the larger the difference between group means relative to the common standard deviation, the closer the magnitude of the point biserial correlation coefficient is to 1.

The scatterplot depicting differences in number of years of math taken in high school for males (GENDER = 0) and females (GENDER = 1) is given here.

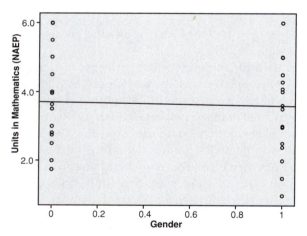

Notice that the best-fitting line, which passes through the means of the two groups, is nearly horizontal, indicating once again that the difference between the two group means is small. Based on what we have learned about correlation and regression, the nearly horizontal orientation of the line suggests a near-zero correlation between GENDER and UNITMATH. In fact, using SPSS, we find the correlation between GENDER and UNITMATH to be $r = -.171$, a small-to-moderate effect that further supports the results of the CI and hypothesis test that there is a difference between the gender groups.

☞ **Remark.** The independent samples t-test of whether the population mean difference equals zero is mathematically equivalent to the test of whether the population point biserial correlation coefficient equals zero. In a later chapter, we discuss inferential tests involving correlation coefficients.

EXAMPLE 11.9. Among college-bound students in the northeast United States who have always been at grade level, do those who own a computer score higher in math achievement in twelfth grade than those who do not? Conduct the significance test at $\alpha = .05$.

Solution. For this question, the null and alternative hypotheses are, respectively, $H_0: \mu_C = \mu_{NC}$ and $H_1: \mu_C > \mu_{NC}$. To visually inspect the math achievement distributions for both groups, we obtain the following boxplot. We also obtain the corresponding descriptive statistics for each group separately.

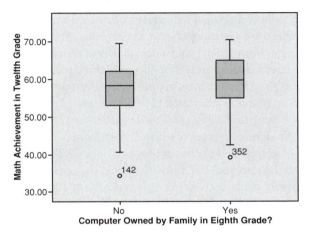

Both distributions have outliers, suggesting some negative skew for each; however, the samples are large enough to ignore the normality assumption. According to the boxplot, the variances appear to be homogeneous. Because the two samples are not equal in size ($N_C = 60$ and $N_{NC} = 46$), we rely on Levene's test to evaluate the tenability of this assumption.

Descriptive Statistics

Computer Owned by Family in Eighth Grade?		N Statistic	Minimum Statistic	Maximum Statistic	Mean Statistic	Std. Statistic	Skewness Statistic	Std. Error
No	Math Achievement in Twelfth Grade	46	34.36	69.37	57.3346	7.15603	−.895	.350
	Valid N (listwise)	46						
Yes	Math Achievement in Twelfth Grade	60	39.28	70.42	58.9440	7.79804	−.723	.309
	Valid N (listwise)	60						

The descriptive statistics for both groups corroborate our visual impressions regarding skewness and homogeneity of variance. We may note also that the students in the NELS data set who own a computer score higher on the math achievement test than the students who do not. Because the direction of difference is as hypothesized, we proceed with the t-test on means to determine whether the observed difference represents a significant difference in the population.

Because Levene's test is not statistically significant ($p = .38$), the homogeneity of variance assumption is tenable for these data. The t-test results suggest that the observed difference in means is not statistically significant (note that we adjust the p-value by dividing by

2 to obtain the one-tailed test result: $p = .278/2 = .139$). Hence, we conclude that students who own a computer do not score statistically significantly higher in twelfth-grade math achievement than those who do not ($t(104) = -1.091, p = .139$).

PAIRED SAMPLES t-TEST AND CONFIDENCE INTERVAL

Earlier in this chapter we posed three questions, each involving a comparison of two means. We asked whether, on average, males and females from the South differ in the number of math courses taken in college; whether, on average, those who own computers from the Northeast show greater achievement in twelfth-grade math than those who do not; and whether, on average, college-bound females from the South change in self-esteem from eighth to twelfth grade. Although the first two questions make use of an independent or unrelated samples design, the third question makes use of a dependent or related groups design because the same individuals are measured twice, in eighth grade and again in twelfth. Because the same individuals are measured twice, this design controls for several factors including socioeconomic status, peer group, physical appearance, and so on that may be related to self-concept.

The name *repeated measures* or *longitudinal* is used to describe the type of design in which observations are taken on the same objects across time. With only two sets of observations, one at time 1 and the other at time 2, we have, in this case, what is also called a *pre-post* design. Had we chosen instead to answer the third question using a *cross-sectional* design, we would have simultaneously studied a sample of females from eighth grade and an independently selected sample of females from twelfth grade, and we would have used the independent samples t-test to analyze our data. Because the scores in our two groups of data are matched pairwise, we select a method of analysis that exploits the particular paired or dependent structure of the data: the paired samples t-test.

The paired samples t-test capitalizes on the dependent structure of the data by basing its calculations on the difference scores computed for each matched pair. As such, the paired samples t-test may be viewed simply as a one-sample t-test on the difference scores, D, calculated on each matched pair and may be expressed as Equation 11.13, which is an adaptation of Equation 11.1, the one-sample t-test:

$$t = \frac{\overline{D} - \mu_D}{\hat{\sigma}_{\overline{D}}} \tag{11.13}$$

$df = N - 1 =$ Number of pairs $- 1$.

The standard error of the mean difference, $\hat{\sigma}_{\overline{D}}$, is given by Equation 11.14:

$$\hat{\sigma}_{\overline{D}} = \frac{\hat{\sigma}_D}{\sqrt{N}}. \tag{11.14}$$

Because difference scores form the basis of the paired samples t-test, the null hypothesis for this test is expressed as $H_0: \mu_D = 0$, which is equivalent to $H_0: \mu_1 - \mu_2 = 0$ because the difference of the sample means, $\overline{X}_1 - \overline{X}_2$, equals the mean of the paired differences, $\overline{D}$.

To estimate the mean difference between populations in a paired samples design, we construct a CI using Equation 11.15:

$$\text{Upper limit} = \overline{D} + (t_c)(\hat{\sigma}_{\overline{D}})$$
$$\text{Lower limit} = \overline{D} - (t_c)(\hat{\sigma}_{\overline{D}}) \tag{11.15}$$

where $\hat{\sigma}_{\bar{D}}$, the standard error of the mean difference, is given by Equation 11.14 and t_c is found as before using an SPSS Compute statement with IDF.T or by using Table 2 in Appendix C, both with df equal to $N - 1$.

THE ASSUMPTIONS OF THE PAIRED SAMPLES t-TEST

The underlying assumptions of the paired samples t-test and CI are the same as those for the independent samples t-test: normality and homogeneity of variance of the two parent populations. Although the normality assumption requires some investigation in the case of the paired samples t-test, the homogeneity of variance assumption does not. The two groups are, by design, equal in size; as noted earlier with respect to the independent samples t-test, violations of the homogeneity of variance assumption may be ignored when this is the case. Hence, whereas SPSS conducts the Levene's test of homogeneity of variance for the independent samples t-test, it does not for the paired samples t-test.

For heuristic reasons, we extend the situation described in Example 11.7 to illustrate how a paired samples t-test may be carried out by hand.

EXAMPLE 11.10. The 10 men in the calcium condition are given calcium supplements for the next 12 weeks, while the 11 men in the placebo condition are given a placebo for the next 12 weeks. At the end of this time period, systolic blood pressure readings of all men are recorded. Use the paired samples t-test to test whether there is a mean reduction in blood pressure from pretest to posttest based on the entire group of 21 men. Use $\alpha = .05$. The data occupy the first three columns of the table that follows. SYSTOLC2 contains the posttest measures of systolic blood pressure.

Treatment Condition	SYSTOLC1 (mmHg)	SYSTOLC2 (mmHg)	D = SYSTOLC1 − SYSTOLC2
1	107	100	7
1	110	114	−4
1	123	105	18
1	129	112	17
1	112	115	−3
1	111	116	−5
1	107	106	1
1	112	102	10
1	135	125	10
1	102	104	−2
0	123	124	−1
0	109	97	12
0	112	113	−1
0	102	105	−3
0	98	95	3
0	114	119	−5
0	119	114	5
0	112	114	−2
0	110	121	−11
0	117	118	−1
0	130	133	−3

Solution. The null and alternative hypotheses for this test are

$$H_0: \mu_{\overline{D}} = 0 \quad \text{and} \quad H_1: \mu_{\overline{D}} = 0.$$

Because we wish to test whether there is a reduction in blood pressure, we expect the mean of the difference scores, assuming we subtract SYSTOLC2 from SYSTOLC1, to be positive. Hence, this test is a directional, one-tailed paired samples t-test.

We compute the difference scores: $D =$ SYSTOLC1 − SYSTOLC2. These appear in the fourth column of the preceding table. The descriptive statistics for D, SYSTOLC1 and SYSTOLC2, are provided in the following table.

Descriptive Statistics

	N	Minimum	Maximum	Mean	Std.	Skewness	
	Statistic	Statistic	Statistic	Statistic	Statistic	Statistic	Std. Error
D	21	−11	18	2.00	7.688	.725	.501
Initial blood pressure	21	98	135	114.00	9.597	.612	.501
Final blood pressure	21	95	133	112.00	9.783	.128	.501
Valid N (listwise)	21						

Because the skewness ratios are low, we may assume that the normality assumption is tenable for these data. Notice from the table that the difference of blood pressure means $(114 − 112)$ equals the mean of the difference (2). Notice also that the standard deviation of the difference, D, is lower than the standard deviation of either SYSTOLC1 or SYSTOLC2. This is because the two samples are paired and SYSTOLC1 and SYSTOLC2 are positively related. The paired samples design, in this case, provides a more powerful hypothesis test than would an independent samples test carried out on the same data. Can you figure out why?

Given the D values, which are, incidentally, easily computed by hand, we now compute $\overline{D}$ and $\hat{\sigma}_{\overline{D}}$.

$$\overline{D} = (7 − 4 + 18 + 17 − 3 − 5 + 1 + 10 + 10 − 2 − 1 + 12 − 1 − 3$$
$$+ 3 − 5 + 5 − 2 + 11 − 1 − 3)/21 = 42/21 = 2$$

$$\hat{\sigma}_D = \sqrt{\frac{(7 − 2)^2 + (−4 − 2)^2 + (18 − 2)^2 + \cdots + (11 − 2)^2 + (−1 − 2)^2 + (−3 − 2)^2}{21 − 1}}$$

$$= \sqrt{\frac{1182}{20}} = \sqrt{59.1} = 7.69$$

$$\hat{\sigma}_{\overline{D}} = \frac{\hat{\sigma}_D}{\sqrt{N}} = \frac{7.69}{\sqrt{21}} = \frac{7.69}{4.58} = 1.68.$$

Substituting these values into Equation 11.13, we obtain

$$t = \frac{\overline{D} − \mu_D}{\hat{\sigma}_D} = \frac{2 − 0}{1.68} = 1.19$$

and $df = N - 1 = $ Number of pairs $- 1 = 21 - 1 = 20$.

We find p either by using SPSS or by using Table 2 in Appendix C. To use SPSS, we compute $p = 1 - $ CDF.T(1.19, 20) and obtain $p = .12$. To use Table 2, we look at the row with $df = 20$ and find that the closest t-value is 1.064. The associated p-value, located at the top of the column, is $p = .15$, which we use as our estimate.

We conclude that there is not a mean reduction in blood pressure from pretest to posttest: $t(20) = 1.19, p = .12$.

Whereas ordinarily we would not compute a 95 percent CI for this one-tailed test, we do so here for heuristic purposes. Substituting the values calculated by hand into Equation 11.15, we obtain the following:

$$\text{Upper limit} = \overline{D} + (t_c)(\sigma_{\overline{D}}) = 2 + t_c(1.68) = 2 + 2.086(1.68) = 2 + 3.47 = 5.47$$

$$\text{Lower limit} = \overline{D} - (t_c)(\hat{\sigma}_{\overline{D}}) = 2 - t_c(1.68) = 2 - 2.086(1.68) = 2 - 3.47 = -1.47$$

The critical t-value ($t_c = 2.086$) was obtained either by computing IDF.T(.975, 20) or from Table 2 in the row labeled $df = 20$ and column labeled .025.

Accordingly, the 95 percent CI ranges from -1.47 to 5.47. We obtain the same results using the paired samples t-test in SPSS (within rounding error).

To use SPSS to perform a paired samples t-test, click **Analyze, Compare Means, Paired Samples** **t-test**. Click **SYSTOLC1** and **SYSTOLC2** so that both are highlighted and move them into the **Paired Variables** box. Click **Continue** and **OK**.

Paired Samples Test

				95% Confidence Interval of the Difference				
		Paired Differences						
	Mean	Std. Deviation	Std. Error Mean	Lower	Upper	t	df	Sig. (2-tailed)
Pair 1 Initial blood pressure – Final blood pressure	2.000	7.688	1.678	-1.499	5.499	1.192	20	.247

We employ the paired samples t-test in Example 11.11 to answer the third question posed in this section, which is related to self-esteem.

EXAMPLE 11.11. Do college-bound females from the South who have always been at grade level change in self-esteem from eighth grade to twelfth grade on average? Conduct the significance test at $\alpha = .05$.

Solution. In statistical terms, the null hypothesis for this test is $H_0: \mu_D = 0$ and the alternative hypothesis is $H_1: \mu_D \neq 0$. We begin with an evaluation of the underlying assumption of normality using a boxplot and accompanying descriptive statistics.

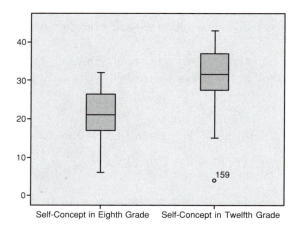

Descriptive Statistics

	N	Minimum	Maximum	Mean	Std.	Skewness	
	Statistic	Statistic	Statistic	Statistic	Statistic	Statistic	Std. Error
Self-Concept in Eighth Grade	84	6	32	21.30	6.558	−.074	.263
Self-Concept in Twelfth Grade	84	4	43	31.81	7.193	−.847	.263
Valid N (listwise)	84						

Whereas the eighth-grade distribution of self-concept is approximately symmetric, the twelfth-grade distribution is negatively skewed. Because the sample size of $N = 84$ for each sample is large, however, we are not concerned about the possible deviation of the population distributions from normality. We may note also the large increase in female self-concept from eighth to twelfth grade among the students in the data set.

Results of this t-test are given in the following tables.

Paired Samples Statistics

		Mean	N	Std. Deviation	Std. Error Mean
Pair 1	Self-Concept in Eighth Grade	21.30	84	6.558	.716
	Self-Concept in Twelfth Grade	31.81	84	7.193	.785

Paired Samples Correlations

		N	Correlation	Sig.
Pair 1	Self-Concept in Eighth Grade & Self-Concept in Twelfth Grade	84	.542	000

Paired Samples Test

		Paired Differences							
					95% Confidence Interval of the Difference				Sig.
		Mean	Std. Deviation	Std. Error Mean	Lower	Upper	t	df	(2-tailed)
Pair 1	Self-Concept in Eighth Grade – Self-Concept in Twelfth Grade	−10.512	6.605	.721	−11.945	−9.079	−14.586	83	.000

From the first of the three tables we learn that descriptively, in eighth grade, females from the South have, on average, a self-concept score of 21.30 with standard deviation 6.56; in twelfth grade they have, on average, a self-concept score of 31.81 with standard deviation 7.19. These descriptive statistics indicate higher self-concept for the sample in twelfth grade.

The third table contains the results of the hypothesis test. From these results, we see that the difference of 10.51 points in self-concept may not be attributable to chance – that it indicates a statistically significant increase in self-concept in the population ($t = −14.59, p < .0005$).

Alternatively, the third table also contains the CI, which informs us that it is likely that the self-concept mean difference between grades 8 and 12 falls between −11.95 and −9.08. Because zero is not contained in this interval, it is indicative of a statistically significant increase in self-concept in the population.

EFFECT SIZE FOR THE PAIRED SAMPLES t-TEST

In the situation of the paired samples t-test, the effect size is measured relative to the standard deviation of the paired differences, $\hat{\sigma}_D$, and is given by Equation 11.16:

$$d = \frac{\overline{D}}{\hat{\sigma}_D},$$
(11.16)

where $\hat{\sigma}_D$ is provided by SPSS in the paired samples t-test output. In this example, $\hat{\sigma}_D$ equals 6.61.

For the situation of Example 11.11, $d = \dfrac{31.81 − 21.30}{6.61} = \dfrac{10.51}{6.61} = 1.59$, suggesting that twelfth-grade self-concept among females in the South is 1.59 standard deviations (of the paired differences) higher than it was in eighth grade – a large effect.

Given the paired nature of the data, we may compute the correlation between self-concept scores measured in eighth and twelfth grades to determine to what extent those who score low on self-concept in eighth grade tend to score low on self-concept in twelfth grade, and so forth. In an independent groups design we would expect this correlation to be 0. If, by matching, one or more sources of variability have been controlled as intended, then we would expect a positive correlation between pairs. The positive correlation represents the degree to which the matched pairs design improves the power of the analysis. In contrast, a negative correlation implies that we have compromised the power of our analysis by matching on the particular values we have. Although negative correlations typically do not arise in the context of repeated measures designs, they sometimes do arise when subjects are sampled in pairs (e.g., husbands and wives, fathers and sons) or when subjects are matched by pairs on some basis by the researcher (e.g., on age and education level).

The correlation value of .542 given in the second of the three tables of output is positive and moderately strong. It suggests that by utilizing before–after matching we have removed one or more sources of variability related to self-concept and thereby improved the power of our analysis relative to a cross-sectional, independent samples design.

SUMMARY

Table 11.2 contains a summary of the equations for the different hypothesis tests based on the t-distribution given in this chapter. Table 11.3 contains a summary of the equations for the CIs based on the t-distribution given in this chapter. Table 11.4 contains a summary of the equations for the effect sizes for the different hypothesis tests given in this chapter. Figures 11.2 through 11.4 contain flow charts for the one sample, independent samples, and paired samples t-tests, respectively.

Table 11.2. Equations for obtaining observed t-test values

Test	Obtained statistic using the notation in the Book	Obtained statistic using the Notation from the SPSS output
One-sample t-test	$t = \dfrac{\bar{X} - \mu}{\dfrac{\hat{\sigma}}{\sqrt{N}}} = \dfrac{\bar{X} - \mu}{\hat{\sigma}_{\bar{X}}}$ $df = N - 1$	$t = \dfrac{\text{Mean} - \text{Test Value}}{\text{Std. Error Mean}}$ $df = N - 1$ The test value is the null hypothesized value for the population mean
Independent samples t-test	$t = \dfrac{(\bar{X}_1 - \bar{X}_2) - (\mu_1 - \mu_2)}{\sqrt{\dfrac{(N_1 - 1)\hat{\sigma}_1^2 + (N_2 - 1)\hat{\sigma}_2^2}{N_1 + N_2 - 2}\left(\dfrac{1}{N_1} + \dfrac{1}{N_2}\right)}}$ $df = N_1 + N_2 - 2$	$t = \dfrac{\text{Mean Difference}}{\text{Std. Error Difference}}$ $df = N_1 + N_2 - 2$
Paired samples t-test	$t = \dfrac{\bar{D} - \mu_D}{\hat{\sigma}_{\bar{D}}}$ $df = N - 1$	$t = \dfrac{\text{Paired Differences Mean}}{\text{Paired Differences Std. Error Mean}}$ $df = N - 1$

Table 11.3. Equations for obtaining CIs based on the *t*-distribution. To find t_c, use the equations for the degrees of freedom found in Table 11.2.

Test	Confidence interval using the Notation in the Book	Confidence interval using the Notation from the SPSS Output
One-sample *t*-test	Upper limit $= \overline{X} + t_c\hat{\sigma}_{\overline{X}}$ Lower limit $= \overline{X} - t_c\hat{\sigma}_{\overline{X}}$	U.L. = Mean + (t_c)(Std. Error Mean) L.L. = Mean − (t_c)(Std. Error Mean)
Independent samples *t*-test	Upper limit $= (\overline{X}_1 - \overline{X}_2) + t_c\cdot\hat{\sigma}_{\overline{X}_1-\overline{X}_2}$ Lower limit $= (\overline{X}_1 - \overline{X}_2) - t_c\cdot\hat{\sigma}_{\overline{X}_1-\overline{X}_2}$	U.L. = Mean Difference + (t_c)(Std. Error Difference) L.L. = Mean Difference − (t_c)(Std. Error Difference)
Paired samples *t*-test	Upper limit $= \overline{D} + t_c\cdot\hat{\sigma}_{\overline{D}}$ Lower limit $= \overline{D} - t_c\cdot\hat{\sigma}_{\overline{D}}$	U.L. = Paired Differences Mean + (t_c) (Paired Differences Std. Error Mean) L.L. = Paired Differences Mean − (t_c) (Paired Differences Std. Error Mean)

Table 11.4. Effect size equations associated with *t*-tests

Test	Approximate effect size using the Notation in the book	Approximate effect size using the Notation from the SPSS output
One-sample *t*-test	$d = \dfrac{\overline{X} - \mu}{\hat{\sigma}}$	$d = \dfrac{\text{Mean} - \text{Test Value}}{\text{Std. Deviation}}$
Independent samples *t*-test	$d = \dfrac{(\overline{X}_1 - \overline{X}_2)}{\sqrt{\dfrac{(N_1-1)\hat{\sigma}_1^2 + (N_2-1)\hat{\sigma}_2^2}{N_1 + N_2 - 2}}}$	$d = \dfrac{\text{Mean Difference}}{\sqrt{\dfrac{(N_1-1)SD_1^2 + (N_2-1)SD_2^2}{N_1 + N_2 - 2}}}$
Paired samples *t*-test	$d = \dfrac{\overline{D}}{\hat{\sigma}_D}$	$t = \dfrac{\text{Paired Differences Mean}}{\text{Paired Differences Std. Deviation}}$

THE STANDARD ERROR OF THE MEAN DIFFERENCE FOR INDEPENDENT SAMPLES: A MORE COMPLETE ACCOUNT (OPTIONAL)

Although, as noted earlier, it is unrealistic to expect σ to be known, for heuristic reasons we describe the shape of the sampling distribution of sample-mean differences when σ is known, but we do not expand on this case. We then consider in detail the case when σ is not known.

CASE 1: σ KNOWN

Suppose we have two normally distributed populations with equal variances σ^2 and with population means μ_1 and μ_2, respectively. If we intend to select random samples of size N_1 and N_2 from these two populations, respectively, then the sampling distribution of all

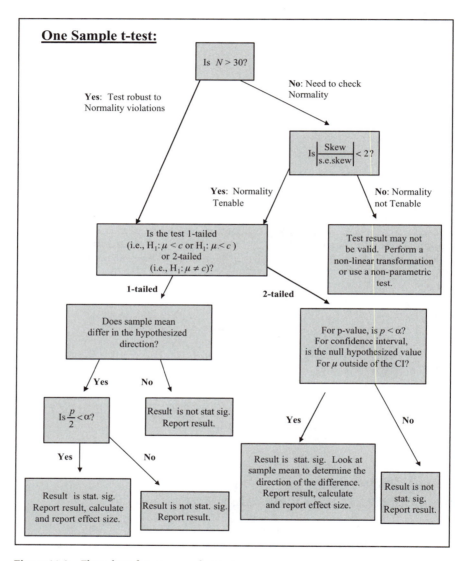

Figure 11.2   Flow chart for one-sample *t*-test.

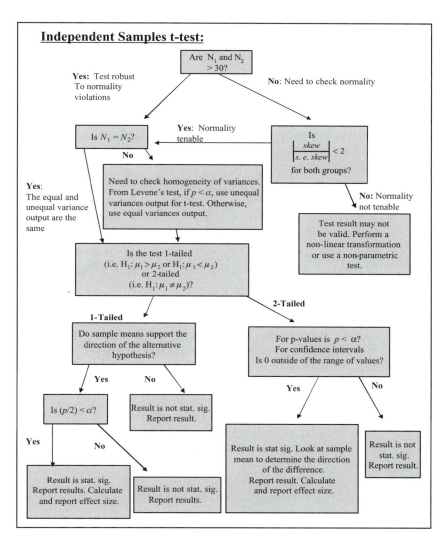

Figure 11.3   Flow chart for independent samples *t*-test.

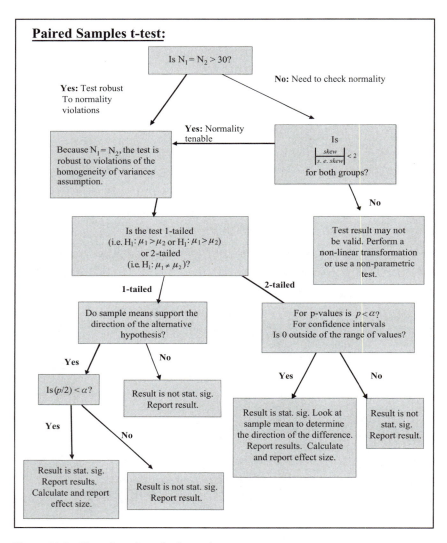

Figure 11.4 Flow chart for paired samples *t*-test.

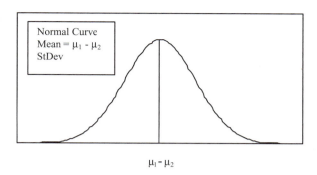

Figure 11.5   The sampling distribution of $\overline{X}_1 - \overline{X}_2$ when σ is known.

possible sample-mean differences $\overline{X}_1 - \overline{X}_2$, as shown in Figure 11.5, are normally distributed with mean $\mu_1 - \mu_2$ and standard deviation

$$\sigma_{\overline{X}_1 - \overline{X}_2} = \sqrt{\sigma^2\left(\frac{1}{N_1} + \frac{1}{N_2}\right)}.$$

Note that we can compute $\sigma_{\overline{X}_1 - \overline{X}_2}$, the standard deviation of the sampling distribution of sample-mean differences, only if we know σ. When σ is *not* known an alternative procedure is needed, just as an alternative procedure was needed when σ was not known in the one-sample case.

CASE 2: σ NOT KNOWN

Suppose we again assume that we have two normally distributed populations with equal variances σ^2 and that their population means are μ_1 and μ_2, respectively. But now assume that the value of σ is not known. Because, as noted in case 1, σ^2 is necessary for computing $\sigma_{\overline{X}_1 - \overline{X}_2}$, it is tempting to try to approximate the value of σ^2 by using the variance estimators $\hat{\sigma}_1^2$ and $\hat{\sigma}_2^2$ from our two samples. As we saw in the one-sample situation, however, the resulting sampling distribution when such an estimation procedure is used need not be normal. By using a standardization procedure, however, we were able to obtain a new statistic whose sampling distribution could be described in a simple mathematical way as a t-distribution. We again obtain a statistic that has a t-distribution using this same step-by-step procedure, as in the previous section.

Step 1: Estimating σ^2 Using the Variance Estimators $\hat{\sigma}_1^2$ and $\hat{\sigma}_2^2$

In the one-group case of the preceding section, we simply used $\hat{\sigma}^2$ to estimate σ^2, because $\hat{\sigma}^2$ is known to be an unbiased estimator of σ^2. Here we have two unbiased estimators of σ^2, one from each sample, and we would like to know the best way to use both to obtain an estimate of σ^2. Should we use $\hat{\sigma}_1^2$ alone, or $\hat{\sigma}_2^2$ alone, or should we combine the two variance estimators in some way and obtain our estimate of σ^2 from both? Because our estimate would be more accurate if it is based on a larger sample size, it makes sense to use both samples (both variance estimators) instead of either one alone.

The question we face is *how* to combine $\hat{\sigma}_1^2$ and $\hat{\sigma}_2^2$ to obtain an estimate. Clearly we would like the estimator that we expect to be more accurate to weigh more heavily in the estimation process, and we would generally believe that the estimator from a larger sample is the more accurate. But as we saw earlier, it is not the sample size that determines the accuracy of a variance estimator. Rather it is the number of independent pieces of data contained in the sample – that is, the degrees of freedom, ν. Therefore, we weight the individual variance estimators $\hat{\sigma}_1^2$ and $\hat{\sigma}_2^2$ not by their sample sizes N_1 and N_2, respectively, but by their degrees of freedom $\nu_1 = N_1 - 1$ and $\nu_2 = N_2 - 1$, respectively. The equation for pooling and using the weights $\nu_1 = N_1 - 1$ and $\nu_2 = N_2 - 1$ is

$$
\begin{aligned}
\text{Estimated } \sigma^2 &= \left(\frac{N_1 - 1}{N_1 + N_2 - 2} \right) \hat{\sigma}^2 + \left(\frac{N_2 - 1}{N_1 + N_2 - 2} \right) \hat{\sigma}^2 \\
&= \frac{(N_1 - 1)\hat{\sigma}_1^2 + (N_2 - 1)\hat{\sigma}_2^2}{N_1 + N_2 - 2}
\end{aligned}
\tag{11.17}
$$

Step 2: Estimating the Standard Error of the Mean Difference, $\sigma_{\overline{X}_1 - \overline{X}_2}$ Using σ^2

From the equation for $\sigma_{\overline{X}_1 - \overline{X}_2}$ presented in case 1 for known σ,

$$
\sigma_{\overline{X}_1 - \overline{X}_2} = \sqrt{\sigma^2 \left(\frac{1}{N_1} + \frac{1}{N_2} \right)}.
$$

Using the estimated σ^2 derived in step 1 in place of the unknown σ^2 in this equation, we obtain

$$
\text{Estimated } \sigma_{\overline{X}_1 - \overline{X}_2} = \sqrt{\text{Estimated } \sigma^2 \left(\frac{1}{N_1} + \frac{1}{N_2} \right)}.
$$

As in the one-sample t-statistic situation, we denote estimated $\sigma_{\overline{X}_1 - \overline{X}_2}$ as $\hat{\sigma}_{\overline{X}_1 - \overline{X}_2}$ for simplicity. Using the equation for estimated σ^2 obtained in step 1, we can write the complete equation for determining $\hat{\sigma}_{\overline{X}_1 - \overline{X}_2}$.

$$
\hat{\sigma}_{\overline{X}_1 - \overline{X}_2} = \sqrt{\frac{(N_1 - 1)\hat{\sigma}_1^2 + (N_2 - 1)\hat{\sigma}_2^2}{N_1 + N_2 - 2} \left(\frac{1}{N_1} + \frac{1}{N_2} \right)},
\tag{11.18}
$$

which is the denominator of the two-population, unrelated samples t-statistic with equal variances assumed.

The number of degrees of freedom for this t-statistic may be determined by recalling that we are using both sample variance estimators, $\hat{\sigma}_1^2$ and $\hat{\sigma}_2^2$, to obtain the denominator of this statistic and that $\hat{\sigma}_1^2$ has $N_1 - 1$ degrees of freedom associated with it, whereas $\hat{\sigma}_2^2$ has $N_2 - 1$ degrees of freedom associated with it. Because $\hat{\sigma}_1^2$ and $\hat{\sigma}_2^2$ come from independent samples, the total number of independent pieces of information contained in the data and, therefore, the number of degrees of freedom for this t-statistic, is $df = df_1 + df_2 = (N_1 - 1) + (N_2 - 1) = N_1 + N_2 - 2$.

EXERCISES

Exercises 11.1 and 11.2 involve one-sample t-tests using variables from the Learndis data set. For inferential purposes, we consider the children in the data set to be a random sample of all *children attending public elementary school in a certain city who have been diagnosed with learning disabilities. Use $\alpha = .05$ for all significance tests.*

11.1. The mean intellectual ability (IQ) score for all children attending public elementary school in the city is 100 with standard deviation $\sigma = 15$. The children in our sample are a random subset of the population of all children attending public elementary school in this city who are diagnosed with learning disabilities. Use SPSS to construct a 95 percent CI to estimate the mean IQ score for this population. We do not want to assume that the standard deviation of the population of learning disabled children is the same as for all children attending public elementary school in this city, but instead we want to use the sample to obtain an estimate of the standard deviation. Answer the related questions.

  a) Address the reason for choosing a *t*-test over a *z*-test in this case.
  b) Evaluate the tenability of the normality assumption or indicate why the assumption is not an issue for this analysis, that the results of the *t*-test would not be compromised by a failure to meet this assumption.
  c) What is the 95 percent CI for the mean IQ score of all children attending public elementary school in this city who have been diagnosed with learning disabilities?
  d) State the null and alternative hypotheses for determining whether or not children attending public elementary school in this city who are diagnosed with learning disabilities have a mean IQ score of 100.
  e) Using the results of the 95 percent CI, can the null hypothesis be rejected? Why or why not?
  f) State the results of the hypothesis test in context.

11.2. Find the *p*-value associated with the one-sample *t*-test to determine whether the mean reading comprehension score (READCOMP) of children attending public elementary school in this city who are diagnosed with learning disabilities is 75. Answer the related questions.

  a) Evaluate the tenability of the normality assumption or indicate why the assumption is not an issue for this analysis – that the results of the *t*-test would not be compromised by a failure to meet this assumption.
  b) What are the null and alternative hypotheses?
  c) What is the *p*-value associated with the one-sample *t*-test for testing these null and alternative hypotheses?
  d) Use the *p*-value to determine whether or not the null hypothesis can be rejected in favor of the alternative.
  e) State the results of the hypothesis test in context.
  f) What is the 95 percent CI for the mean reading comprehension score of children attending public elementary school in this city who are diagnosed with learning disabilities?
  g) Using the results of the 95 percent CI, can the null hypothesis be rejected? Why or why not?
  h) Would the test have been more or less powerful if the sample size had been larger than 76, say 300? Explain.

Exercises 11.3 and 11.4 involve one-sample t-tests using variables from the Framingham data set. For inferential purposes, we consider the people in the Framingham data set to be a random sample of the population of all noninstitutionalized adults. Use $\alpha = .05$ for all significance tests.

11.3. A person with body mass index higher than 25 is classified as overweight. In this exercise, we determine whether the mean body mass index of the population of noninstitutionalized adults as measured during the first examination (BMI1) is greater than 25.

    a) Evaluate the tenability of the normality assumption or indicate why the assumption is not an issue for this analysis – that the results of the test would not be compromised by a failure to meet this assumption.

    b) State the null and alternative hypotheses for determining whether the mean body mass index of the population of noninstitutionalized adults as measured during the first examination is greater than 25.

    c) Conduct the one-sample *t*-test and determine, based on the resulting *p*-value, whether the mean body mass index of the population of noninstitutionalized adults as measured during the first examination is greater than 25?

    d) Calculate and interpret Cohen's *d* as a measure of effect size for the analysis.

    e) Why is the CI provided in the one-sample *t*-test output not appropriate for determining whether the mean body mass index of noninstitutionalized adults at first examination is greater than 25?

11.4. Normal systolic blood pressure is less than 120 mmHg. In this exercise we determine whether the mean systolic blood pressure of noninstitutionalized adults at first examination (SYSBP1) is less than 120 mmHg.

    a) State the null and alternative hypotheses for determining whether the mean systolic blood pressure of the population of noninstitutionalized adults as measured during the first examination is less than 120 mmHg.

    b) Explain why it is not necessary to carry out a test of these hypotheses in this case.

Exercises 11.5 through 11.11 involve one-sample t-tests using variables from the NELS data set. For inferential purposes, we consider the students in the data set to be a random sample of the population of all college-bound students who have always been at grade level. Use $\alpha = .05$ for all significance tests.

11.5. Use the variable FAMSIZE, which gives the number of people in a household, to determine whether the average family size is 4.5 (2 parents and 2.5 kids) for college-bound high school students who are always at grade level.

    a) Evaluate the tenability of the normality assumption or indicate why the assumption is not an issue for this analysis – that the results of the *t*-test would not be compromised by a failure to meet this assumption.

    b) What is the 95 percent CI for the average family size?

    c) Use the CI to determine whether the average family size for this population is 4.5. If it is not 4.5, indicate whether it is higher or lower than 4.5.

    d) Calculate and interpret the value of Cohen's *d* as a measure of the effect size.

11.6. Use a 95 percent CI to estimate the average twelfth-grade self-concept score (SLFCNC12) of the population of college-bound students who have always been at grade level. Use this interval to determine whether the average twelfth-grade self-concept score is different from 32 for the population of college-bound students who have always been at grade level.

11.7. Use the *p*-value derived from an appropriate test of inference to determine whether the average twelfth-grade self-concept score (SLFCNC12) is different from 32 for the population of college-bound students who have always been at grade level.

11.8. Use the *p*-value derived from an appropriate test of inference to determine whether the population of college-bound students who have always been at grade level take on average more than 3.6 units of mathematics in high school (UNITMATH).

11.9. For the population of college-bound students from the Northeast (REGION = 1) who have always been at grade level, use a 95 percent CI to estimate the average number of years of English taken in high school (UNITENGL).

   a) Restrict the sample to students from the Northeast.
   b) Evaluate the tenability of the normality assumption or indicate why the assumption is not an issue for this analysis – that the results of the t-test would not be compromised by a failure to meet this assumption.
   c) What is the 95 percent CI for the average number of years of English taken in high school?
   d) According to the 95 percent CI, is the estimate for the average number of years of English taken in high school by this population of college-bound students from the Northeast 3?
   e) Calculate and interpret the value of Cohen's d as a measure of the effect size.
   f) Reset SPSS to analyze all students in NELS, not just those from the Northeast.

11.10. Does the population of college-bound twelfth graders who have always been at grade level and who attend rigorous academic schools (HSPROG = 1) have a mean social studies achievement score (ACHSLS12) larger than 55?

   a) Evaluate the tenability of the normality assumption or indicate why the assumption is not an issue for this analysis – that the results of the test would not be compromised by a failure to meet this assumption.
   b) State the null and alternative hypotheses.
   c) Verify that the sample mean supports the hypothesized direction of the difference.
   d) Find the p-value associated with the appropriate test of inference for determining whether the mean social studies achievement score for this population is greater than 55.
   e) Is this result statistically significant?
   f) State the conclusion in context.
   g) Calculate and interpret the value of Cohen's d as a measure of the effect size.
   h) Conceptually, not computationally, what is the difference between what the standard deviation value of 8.56 represents and what the standard error of the mean value of .70 represents?
   i) If the standard deviation had been 20 instead of 8.56, and the mean and sample size remained the same, would the p-value have been smaller or larger? Explain.

11.11. For the population of college-bound students who were always at grade level and whose parents were divorced when they were in eighth grade (PARMARL 8 = 1), use a 95 percent CI to estimate the mean twelfth grade self-concept score (SLFCNC12).

   a) Evaluate the tenability of the normality assumption or indicate why the assumption is not an issue for this analysis – that the results of the test would not be compromised by a failure to meet this assumption.
   b) What is the 95 percent CI for the mean twelfth-grade self-concept score for college-bound students who were always at grade level and whose parents were divorced when they were in eighth grade?

Exercises 11.12 and 11.13 involve independent samples t-tests using variables from the Learndis data set. For inferential purposes, we consider the children in the data set to be a random sample of all children attending public elementary school in a certain city who have been diagnosed with learning disabilities. Unless otherwise specified, use $\alpha = .05$ for all significance tests.

11.12. Conduct an independent samples *t*-test to determine whether there are gender (GENDER) differences in average math comprehension (MATHCOMP) among children attending public elementary school in a certain city who have been diagnosed with learning disabilities. Answer the following related questions.

   a) Evaluate the tenability of the normality assumption or indicate why the assumption is not an issue for this analysis – that the results of the test would not be compromised by a failure to meet this assumption.
   b) According to Levene's test of equality of variances, should the *t*-ratio be calculated using equal or unequal variances in this case?
   c) State the null and alternative hypotheses.
   d) According to the *p*-value associated with this test, are there statistically significant gender differences in average math comprehension for this type of student? If so, describe the nature of the differences.
   e) Calculate and interpret the value of Cohen's *d* as a measure of the effect size.

11.13. Conduct an independent samples *t*-test to determine whether there are differences in mean intellectual ability (IQ) by the type of placement (PLACEMEN, self-contained classroom or resource room) among children attending public elementary school in a certain city who have been diagnosed with learning disabilities Answer the following related questions.

   a) Evaluate the tenability of the normality assumption or indicate why the assumption is not an issue for this analysis – that the results of the test would not be compromised by a failure to meet this assumption.
   b) According to Levene's test of equality of variances, should the *t*-ratio be calculated using equal or unequal variances in this case?
   c) According to the 95 percent CI, are there statistically significant differences in mean intellectual ability by type of placement? If so, describe the nature of the differences.
   d) Calculate and interpret the value of Cohen's *d* as a measure of the effect size.

Exercises 11.14 through 11.18 involve independent samples t-tests using variables from the Framingham data set. For inferential purposes, we consider the people in the Framingham data set to be a random sample of the population of all noninstitutionalized adults. Use α = .05 for all significance tests.

11.14. Use the independent samples *t*-test to investigate whether on average there are initial differences in age (AGE1) between the sexes (SEX) for the population of noninstitutionalized adults represented in the Framingham data set.

   a) Based on the boxplots, do the assumptions underlying the independent samples *t*-test appear tenable? What do you anticipate as the result of the independent samples *t*-test? Explain.
   b) Evaluate further the tenability of the normality assumption or indicate why the assumption is not an issue for this analysis – that the results of the test would not be compromised by a failure to meet this assumption.
   c) According to Levene's test of equality of variances, should the *t*-ratio be calculated using equal or unequal variances in this case?
   d) According to the *p*-value, are there initial differences in age on average between the sexes of all noninstitutionalized adults? If so, describe the nature of the differences.

e) Use the 95 percent CI to estimate the average difference in age between males and females at initial examination, which we know from the hypothesis is not statistically significant.

f) Under what circumstances can we expect the test of inference on two independent groups and the CI to be consistent as they relate to a test of the hypotheses?

11.15. Is the mean body mass index (BMI3) of smokers (CURSMOKE3) lower than that for non-smokers as measured at the third and final examination time 3 (1968) among the population of non-institutionalized adults? Assume that both the normality and equality of variance assumptions are tenable.

a) What is the p-value derived from the independent samples t-test for determining whether, on average, the body mass index of smokers is lower than that for nonsmokers among the population represented by the Framingham data and what does it convey?

b) If the question had been whether among the population of noninstitutionalized adults the mean BMI of smokers is different (instead of lower) than it is for nonsmokers, would the independent samples t-test have been more or less powerful?

11.16. While one can expect initial differences in body mass index (BMI1) between males and females, we may question whether there are differences between males and females in their changes in BMI from 1956 to 1968 (BMI3 – BMI1). In this exercise, we investigate the change in BMI for both males and females. You will need to compute a new variable that captures these change values.

a) Create a new variable, BMIDIFF, that captures the change in BMI. Report and interpret BMIDIFF for the first person in the data set (ID = 1).

b) Create an associated boxplot, one for males and one females on the same axes. Describe the nature of this new variable for the two groups.

c) Evaluate the tenability of the normality assumption or indicate why the assumption is not an issue for this analysis – that the results of the test would not be compromised by a failure to meet this assumption.

d) According to Levene's test of equality of variances, should the t-ratio be calculated using equal or unequal variances in this case?

e) According to the p-value derived from the appropriate test of inference, are there differences, on average, in the change in BMI between males and females for this population of noninstitutionalized adults? If so, describe the nature of the differences.

f) Calculate and interpret the value of Cohen's d as a measure of the effect size.

11.17. In this exercise, we use a nonlinear transformation in conjunction with the independent samples t-test to determine, using the Framingham data set, whether there are differences in average systolic blood pressure (SYSBP3) between people who were and those who were not taking anti-hypertensive (blood pressure) medication at time 3 (BPMEDS3).

a) Evaluate the tenability of the normality assumption or indicate why the assumption is not an issue for this analysis – that the results of the test would not be compromised by a failure to meet this assumption.

b) Demonstrate that the log transformation is effective in normalizing the distribution of SYSBP3 for both groups.

c) Conduct an independent samples t-test on the log-transformed systolic blood pressure at time 3 between those who did and did not take anti-hypertensive medication at time 3. Report and interpret the results.

d) Is it fair to conclude that taking anti-hypertensive medication appears to increase systolic blood pressure? Explain.

11.18. Use an independent samples t-test to determine whether, among the population of noninstitutionalized adults, there are differences in total serum cholesterol (TOTCHOL3) by sex (SEX). Be sure to address the underlying assumptions. Interpret the results using either a p-value (with $\alpha = .05$) or a 95 percent CI. If the result is statistically significant, report and interpret a measure of effect size.

Exercises 11.19 and 11.20 involve independent samples t-tests using variables from the NELS data set. For inferential purposes, we consider the students in the data set to be a random sample of the population of all college-bound students who have always been at grade level. Use $\alpha = .05$ for all significance tests.

11.19. Among the population of college-bound students who have always been at grade level, do students whose families owned a computer in eighth grade (COMPUTER) score differently in twelfth-grade math achievement (ACHMAT12), on average, than those whose families did not own a computer?

a) Explain why an independent samples t-test is more appropriate than a one-sample or paired samples test to answer this question.

b) Evaluate the tenability of the normality assumption or indicate why the assumption is not an issue for this analysis – that the results of the test would not be compromised by a failure to meet this assumption.

c) According to Levene's test of equality of variances, is there reason to believe that a violation of the homogeneity of variances assumption would compromise the validity of the t-test results?

d) State the null and alternative hypotheses regarding whether, among this population, students whose families owned a computer in eighth grade score differently on average in twelfth-grade math achievement than those whose families did not own a computer.

e) Find the p-value for determining whether, among the population of college-bound students who have always been at grade level, students whose families owned a computer in eighth grade score differently in twelfth-grade math achievement, on average, from those whose families did not own a computer.

f) Interpret the results of the hypothesis test using the context of the problem.

g) Find the 95 percent CI for the mean difference in twelfth-grade math achievement between those whose families owned a computer in eighth grade and those whose families did not.

h) According to the 95 percent CI, among the population of college-bound students who have always been at grade level, do students whose families owned a computer in eighth grade score differently in twelfth-grade math achievement, on average, from those whose families did not own a computer?

i) Calculate and interpret the value of Cohen's d as a measure of the effect size.

j) Which is longer, the 99 percent CI of the difference or the 95 percent CI of the difference? Use SPSS to confirm your answer.

11.20. Use an independent samples t-test to answer the following questions or indicate why it is not appropriate to do so. In each case, the population comprises college-bound students who have always been at grade level and the data are from the NELS data set. Be sure to address the underlying assumptions. Interpret the results using either a hypothesis test with $\alpha = .05$ or a 95 percent CI. If the result is statistically significant, report and interpret a measure of effect size.

a) Among college-bound students who are always at grade level, is the average twelfth-grade self-concept score (SLFCNC12) different for smokers and nonsmokers (CIGARETT)?
b) Among college-bound students who are always at grade level, do students who take advanced math in eighth grade (ADVMATH8) have different expectations for future income (EXPINC30) than students who do not?
c) Among college-bound students who are always at grade level, do students who take advanced math in eighth grade (ADVMATH8) have better eighth-grade self-concepts (SLFCNC08) than students who do not?
d) Among college-bound students who are always at grade level, do females (GENDER) have a better self-concept (SLFCNC12) than males in twelfth grade?
e) Among college-bound students who are always at grade level, do females (GENDER) do better on twelfth-grade reading achievement tests (ACHRDG12) than males?
f) Among college-bound students who are always at grade level, do those who attended nursery school (NURSERY) tend to have smaller families (FAMSIZE) than those who did not?
g) Among college-bound students who are always at grade level, do those who live in the Northeast (REGION = 1) have mean SES that is higher than that of those who live in the West (REGION = 4)?

Exercise 11.21 relates to the Blood data set. The creation of a new variable is necessary to perform the independent samples t-test in this example.

11.21. Ten randomly selected African-American males are given calcium supplements for 12 weeks, while 11 randomly selected African-American males are given a placebo for 12 weeks. At both the beginning and the end of this time period, systolic blood pressure readings of all men were recorded. Compute a new variable, REDUCT; that is, SYSTOLC1–SYSTOLC2. This variable represents the reduction in blood pressure over the 12 weeks. Conduct an independent samples *t*-test to determine whether there is a difference in the average blood pressure reduction between the calcium and the placebo groups. Use $\alpha = .05$.

Exercise 11.22 involves paired samples t-tests using variables from the Learndis data set. For inferential purposes, we consider the children in the data set to be a random sample of all children attending public elementary school in a certain city who have been diagnosed with learning disabilities. Use $\alpha = .05$ for all significance tests.

11.22. Answer the following questions about using a paired samples *t*-test to determine whether public elementary school children diagnosed with learning disabilities in a certain city perform better in math comprehension (MATHCOMP) or in reading comprehension (READCOMP).
a) Evaluate the tenability of the normality assumption or indicate why the assumption is not an issue for this analysis – that the results of the test would not be compromised by a failure to meet this assumption.
b) Explain why failure to meet the homogeneity of variances assumption for the paired samples *t*-test would not compromise the results of this test.

c) State the null and alternative hypotheses when determining whether public elementary school children in the city diagnosed with learning disabilities perform better in math comprehension or in reading comprehension.

d) Use the results of the paired samples hypothesis test to determine whether public elementary school children diagnosed with learning disabilities in the city perform better in math comprehension or in reading comprehension.

e) Use the results of the 95 percent CI to determine whether public elementary school children diagnosed with learning disabilities in the city perform better in math comprehension or in reading comprehension.

f) Report and interpret Cohen's *d* as a measure of effect size as a way to measure the practical significance of the test result.

Exercises 11.23 and 11.24 involve paired samples t-tests using variables from the Framingham data set. For inferential purposes, we consider the people in the Framingham data set to be a random sample of the population of all noninstitutionalized adults. Use $\alpha = .05$ for all significance tests.

11.23. Answer the following questions about using a paired samples *t*-test to determine whether systolic blood pressure (SYSBP1, SYSBP2) increases over time, on average, in noninstitutionalized adults. Assume that the normality and equality of variance assumptions are tenable.

a) What is the *p*-value associated with the paired *t*-test for determining whether, among the population of noninstitutionalized adults, systolic blood pressure increases on average over time?

b) According to the *p*-value, does systolic blood pressure increase on average over time among noninstitutionalized adults?

c) Report and interpret Cohen's *d* as a measure of effect size (a measure of the magnitude of practical significance).

11.24. In this exercise, we investigate whether diastolic blood pressure decreases over time (DIABP1, DIABP3). What is the best way to demonstrate that among noninstitutionalized adults the diastolic blood pressure does not does decrease significantly on average from time 1 (1956) to time 3 (1968)?

11.25. In this exercise, we investigate whether noninstitutionalized adults smoke fewer cigarettes over time (CIGPDAY1, CIGPDAY3).

a) What is the best way to demonstrate that, among noninstitutionalized adults, the number of cigarettes smoked per day on average does decrease significantly from time 1 (1956) to time 3 (1968)?

b) What explanations can be offered to support the average decline in cigarette smoking over this time period for the sample of noninstitutionalized adults in the Framingham data set?

Exercises 11.26 and 11.27 involve paired samples t-tests using variables from the NELS data set. For inferential purposes, we consider the students in the data set to be a random sample of the population of all college-bound students who have always been at grade level. Use $\alpha = .05$ for all significance tests.

11.26. Among the population of college-bound students who have always been at grade level, does the level of science achievement on average change from eighth (ACHSCI08) to twelfth grade (ACHSCI12) relative to all students in the grade?

a) Explain why a paired samples t-test is more appropriate than a one-sample or independent samples test to determine whether the level of science achievement, relative to all students in the grade, changes from eighth to twelfth grade.

b) Evaluate the tenability of the normality assumption or indicate why the assumption is not an issue for this analysis – that the results of the test would not be compromised by a failure to meet this assumption.

c) State the null and alternative hypotheses.

d) Find the p-value associated with the paired samples t-test to determine whether the level of science achievement changes on average from eighth- to twelfth-grade achievement among the population of college-bound students who have always been at grade level.

e) According to this p-value, does the level of science achievement change from eighth to twelfth grade among this population of college-bound students?

f) Find the 95 percent CI for the mean difference in science achievement between eighth and twelfth grade.

g) According to the 95 percent CI, does the level of science achievement change from eighth to twelfth grade for this population?

11.27. Use a paired samples t-test to determine whether, among the population of college-bound students who have always been at grade level, the level of self-concept relative to that of all students in the grade increases from eighth (SLFCNC08) to twelfth grade (SLFCNC12). Be sure to address the underlying assumptions. Interpret the results using either a hypothesis test with $\alpha = .05$ or a 95 percent CI. If the result is statistically significant, report and interpret a measure of effect size.

Exercises 11.28 through 11.32 involve the selection of appropriate tests.

11.28. A study was undertaken to determine different sources of stress among college students. A sample of 1,000 college students was asked to rate different potential sources of stress such as parents, roommates, partners, and final exams. They were also asked to provide demographic information including number of enrolled credits and gender. For each of the following questions relative to this data set, select an appropriate statistical procedure from the following list for answering this question. Assume for now that the underlying assumptions for these tests have been met.

Procedures:
(1) One-tailed, one-sample t-test.
(2) Two-tailed, one-sample t-test.
(3) One-tailed, independent samples t-test.
(4) Two-tailed, independent samples t-test.
(5) One-tailed, paired samples t-test.
(6) Two-tailed, paired samples t-test.

Questions:
a) Are undergraduates at large urban universities more stressed by their parents or their roommates?
b) Are undergraduates at large urban universities more stressed by their parents than their roommates?

c) Do undergraduates at large urban universities in the Northeast typically take 15 credits per semester?

d) Are there gender differences in the stress level due to final exams among undergraduates at large urban universities?

e) Among undergraduates at large urban universities, are males more stressed than females by their partners?

11.29. For each of the following questions based on the NELS data set, select an appropriate statistical procedure to use to answer it from the list that follows. Then use SPSS to conduct the appropriate hypothesis test in cases where the underlying assumptions are tenable. If the result of a hypothesis test is statistically significant, report and interpret an appropriate measure of effect size.

Procedures:

(1) One-tailed, one-sample t-test.

(2) Two-tailed, one-sample t-test.

(3) One-tailed, independent samples t-test.

(4) Two-tailed, independent samples t-test.

(5) One-tailed, paired samples t-test.

(6) Two-tailed, paired samples t-test.

Questions:

a) Among college-bound students who are always at grade level, do those who attended nursery school (NURSERY) tend to have higher SES than those who did not?

b) Among college-bound students who are always at grade level, does self-concept differ in eighth (SLFCNC08) and tenth (SLFCNC10) grades?

c) Among college-bound students who are always at grade level, do those who attend public school (SCHTYP8) perform differently in twelfth-grade math achievement (ACHMATH12) from those who attend private school? (Note that to answer this question the variable SCHTYP8 has to be *recoded* to be dichotomous as described in Chapter 4.)

d) Among college-bound students who are always at grade level, do families typically have four members (FAMSIZE)?

e) Among college-bound students who are always at grade level, do students tend to take more years of English (UNITENGL) than math (UNITMATH)?

11.30. In this exercise we demonstrate, by example using the NELS data set, that the paired samples t-test is equivalent to a one-sample t-test of the difference scores. For college-bound students who are always at grade level, does relative math achievement change from eighth (ACHMAT08) to twelfth grades (ACHMAT12)? Follow the steps below to use both a paired samples and a one-sample t-test to answer the question.

a) Use a graphical display of your choice to anticipate the answer to the question posed.

b) Answer the question by using a paired samples t-test. Use $\alpha = .05$.

c) Use SPSS to verify that the paired samples t-test results are the same as those from a one-sample t-test on the difference scores. First use the SPSS Compute statement to create a new variable that represents the difference between eighth- and twelfth-grade math achievement. Then use a one-sample t-test on this new variable to answer the question. Use $\alpha = .05$.

d) How do your answers to parts (b) and (c) compare?

e) Would the results have been the same as those for the paired t-test had we ignored the pairing of scores and conducted an independent samples t-test on the eighth- and twelfth-grade math achievement scores? Explain.

11.31. Explain why a one-sample t-test should not be used with the NELS data set to determine whether the average number of times late for school in twelfth grade (LATE12) is 4 (LATE12 = 4).

11.32. In this exercise based on the NELS data set, we contrast a descriptive and inferential approach for determining the relationship, if any, between high school cigarette use and twelfth-grade math achievement.
  a) For the students in the NELS data set, is there a difference in twelfth-grade math achievement (ACHMATH12) between those students who do and do not smoke cigarettes (CIGARETT)?
  b) For college-bound students who are always at grade level, is there a difference in twelfth-grade math achievement (ACHMATH12) between those students who do and do not smoke cigarettes (CIGARETT)? Use $\alpha = .05$.

Exercises 11.33 through 11.43 include calculations by hand and small data sets.

11.33. Given $t = 2.364$ and $df = 100$ for a one-sample t-test, calculate p or indicate that the result is not statistically significant under the following conditions:
  a) $H_0: \mu = 30$ versus $H_1: \mu \neq 30$.
  b) $H_0: \mu = 30$ and $H_1: \mu < 30$.
  c) $H_0: \mu = 30$ and $H_1: \mu > 30$.

11.34. Given $t = 1.283$ and $df = 500$ for an independent samples t-test, calculate p or indicate that the result is not statistically significant under the following conditions:
  a) $H_0: \mu = 30$ and $H_1: \mu \neq 30$.
  b) $H_0: \mu = 30$ and $H_1: \mu < 30$.
  c) $H_0: \mu = 30$ and $H_1: \mu > 30$.

11.35. Given $t = -1.23$ and $df = 100$ for a paired samples t-test, calculate p or indicate that the result is not statistically significant under the following conditions:
  a) $H_0: \mu = 30$ and $H_1: \mu \neq 30$.
  b) $H_0: \mu = 30$ and $H_1: \mu < 30$.
  c) $H_0: \mu = 30$ and $H_1: \mu > 30$.

11.36. Given $t = 1.8$ and $df = 800$ for a one-sample t-test, calculate p or indicate that the result is not statistically significant under the following conditions:
  a) $H_0: \mu = 30$ and $H_1: \mu \neq 30$.
  b) $H_0: \mu = 30$ and $H_1: \mu < 30$.
  c) $H_0: \mu = 30$ and $H_1: \mu > 30$.

11.37. A one-sample t-test, based on the Learndis data set, was conducted to determine whether the mean intellectual ability score for all children attending public elementary school in the city who have been diagnosed with learning disabilities is 85. Partial results, with test value equal to 85, are reproduced below. Use the available information and SPSS or Table 2 to find the mean difference, t, df, and p (Sig.). Then indicate whether the mean intellectual ability score for all children attending public elementary school in the city who have been diagnosed with learning disabilities differs from 85.

One-Sample Statistics

	N	Mean	Std. Deviation
Intellectual Ability	105	81.50	10.941

One-Sample Test

	Test Value = 85			
	t	df	Sig. (2-tailed)	Mean Difference
Intellectual Ability	_	_	_	_

11.38. A one-sample *t*-test, based on the Learndis data set, was conducted to determine whether the mean intellectual ability score for all children attending public elementary school in the city who are diagnosed with learning disabilities is 85. Partial results, with test value equal to 0, are reproduced in the following tables. Use the available information and SPSS or Table 2 to find the 95 percent CI for the mean IQ. Then indicate whether the mean intellectual ability score for all children attending public elementary school in the city who are diagnosed with learning disabilities differs from 85.

One-Sample Statistics

	N	Mean	Std. Deviation
Intellectual Ability	105	81.50	10.941

One-Sample Test

	Test Value = 0	
	95% Confidence Interval of the Difference	
	Lower	Upper
Intellectual Ability	_	_

11.39. An independent samples *t*-test, based on the Learndis data set, was conducted to determine whether there are gender differences in average math comprehension among children attending public elementary school in a certain city who have been diagnosed with learning disabilities. Partial results are reproduced in the following tables. Use the available information and SPSS or Table 2 to obtain the mean difference, *t*, *df*, and *p* (Sig.), and the 95 percent CI. Then indicate whether there are gender differences in average math comprehension among children attending public elementary school in a certain city who have been diagnosed with learning disabilities.

Group Statistics

	Gender	N	Mean	Std. Deviation	Std. Error Mean
Math Comprehension	Male	60	84.05	12.958	1.673
	Female	34	90.21	14.422	2.473

Independent Samples Test

		t-test for Equality of Means						
							95% Confidence Interval of the Difference	
		t	df	Sig. (2-tailed)	Mean Difference	Std. Error Difference	Lower	Upper
Math Comprehensio	Equal Variances assumed	_	_	_	_	2.898	_	_

11.40. A paired samples *t*-test, based on the Learndis data set, was conducted to determine whether public school elementary school children in a certain city diagnosed with learning disabilities score differently, on average, in math and reading comprehension. Partial results are reproduced in the following tables. Use the available information and SPSS or Table 2 to obtain the mean difference, *t*, *df*, and *p* (Sig.) and the 95 percent CI to answer the question.

Paired Samples Statistics

		Mean	N	Std. Deviation	Std. Error Mean
Pair 1	Math Comprehension	86.41	74	14.592	1.696
	Reading Comprehension	77.78	74	13.138	1.527

Paired Samples Test

		Paired Differences							
				95% Confidence Interval of the Difference					
		Mean	Std. Error Mean	Lower	Upper		t	df	Sig. (2-tailed)
Pair 1	Math Comprehension – Reading Comprehension	_	1.627	_	_		_	_	_

11.41. From a normally distributed population, the following sample is randomly selected:

| 25 | 27 | 22 | 20 | 27 | 26 | 24 | 25 |
| 20 | 30 | 27 | 25 | 29 | 26 | 22 | 25 |

a) Use this sample to construct a 95 percent CI for μ. Use your CI to estimate μ and to see whether 27 is one of the plausible values for μ.

b) Find and interpret the p-value associated with a one-sample t-test on H_0: $\mu = 27$ versus H_1: $\mu \neq 27$ at the significance level $\alpha = .05$.

11.42. To test whether a new drug for individuals who suffer from high blood pressure affects mental alertness, a random sample of 12 patients suffering from high blood pressure is selected from a large number of such patients who regularly visit an outpatient clinic. Tests of mental alertness are administered to these patients both before and after they receive the drug. Their scores are shown in the following table. Is there evidence of a decrease in mental alertness, on average, after receipt of the drug for the population of all such patients at this outpatient clinic? Assume that the mental alertness scores are normally distributed, both before and after treatment, in the population of all such patients at this outpatient clinic and that the variances are equal in the populations. Use $\alpha = .05$.

| Before | 10 | 14 | 5 | 6 | 9 | 15 | 1 | 20 | 10 | 2 | 7 | 10 |
| After | 5 | 9 | 7 | 3 | 10 | 15 | 4 | 16 | 12 | 5 | 3 | 6 |

11.43. Eight 1-year-olds and eight 2-year olds took the same test. Scores were compared (on the average, not on an individual paired basis) to determine whether there is an age difference in the skill measured for the populations from which these two samples were randomly selected, at a significance level of $\alpha = .05$. Assume that the test scores are normally distributed for both age groups in the population and that the variances are equal in the populations. Complete the analysis using the following data and draw your conclusion:

| 1-year olds | 7 | 7 | 0 | 1 | 9 | 3 | 8 | 5 |
| 2-year olds | 13 | 13 | 9 | 9 | 13 | 5 | 5 | 5 |

Exercises 11.44 through 11.49 are conceptual and do not require the use of SPSS.

11.44. Explain why it is impossible for p to be identically equal to zero for any hypothesis test using the t-distribution.

11.45. As the sample size increases, what happens to the magnitude of t_c in a one-sample t-test?

11.46. As the sample size increases, what happens to the standard error of the mean in a one-sample t-test?

11.47. A researcher conducted a one-tailed, one-sample t-test for which the results were not statistically significant. Should she then conduct a two-tailed test? Explain.

11.48. A researcher conducted a two-tailed independent samples t-test, the results of which were statistically significant. Should she then conduct two one-tailed tests to determine the nature of the mean difference? Explain.

11.49. Give conditions under which SPSS would report a statistically significant result (i.e., a two-tailed p-value less than α or .05) for a one-sample t-test and yet the result would not be statistically significant.

CHAPTER TWELVE

One-Way Analysis of Variance

In the preceding chapter we presented statistical models for answering questions about population means when the design involves either one or two groups and when the population standard deviation is not known. In the case of two groups, we distinguished between paired and independent group designs and presented statistical models tailored to each. In this chapter we extend the model involving two independent groups to handle questions about population means of three or more groups.

When there are more than two groups in our design, we test the null hypothesis that *all* populations have the same mean versus the nondirectional alternative that not all populations have the same mean. For example, using the NELS data set, we may be interested in comparing (1) the mean number of years of math taken in high school for the populations of students from the Northeast, North Central, South, and West; (2) twelfth-grade self-concept by type of high school program (rigorous academic, academic, vocational and other); or (3) school attendance rate by region.

If there are K populations, we can represent these hypotheses as follows:

$H_0: \mu_1 = \mu_2 = \mu_3 = \cdots = \mu_K$
$H_1:$ not H_0.

The null hypothesis is true only if *all* the population means are equal to one another, and false if any two are not equal to each other.

THE DISADVANTAGE OF MULTIPLE *t*-TESTS

A question that you might be thinking at this point is why must we introduce a new model for testing H_0 against H_1? Why can't we simply use the independent groups *t*-test introduced in the preceding chapter to test H_0 against H_1 by making all possible pairwise comparisons of means?

For example, if $K = 3$ and the null and alternative hypotheses are

$H_0: \mu_1 = \mu_2 = \mu_3$
$H_1:$ not H_0,

a set of t-tests, one on each pair of samples, would produce the following three hypothesis tests:

$H_0: \mu_1 = \mu_2$ $H_0: \mu_1 = \mu_3$ $H_0: \mu_2 = \mu_3$
versus   versus   versus
$H_1: \mu_1 \neq \mu_2$ $H_1: \mu_1 \neq \mu_3$ $H_1: \mu_2 \neq \mu_3$

Following this approach, we would reject H_0: $\mu_1 = \mu_2 = \mu_3$ if at least one of the three pairwise tests in the set is statistically significant at $\alpha = .05$.

Although intuitively appealing, there is a problem that arises in connection with this approach: the probability of making a Type I error and falsely rejecting the null hypothesis (H_0: $\mu_1 = \mu_2 = \mu_3$) *exceeds* the chosen level of significance, .05.

Two definitions of Type I error rate are implied here: a Type I error rate attached to each pairwise test (called a *per-comparison error rate* (α)) and a Type I error rate attached to the *complete set* of pairwise tests related to the original null hypothesis (called a *family-wise error rate* (α_{FW})). A "family" of comparisons is a set of comparisons that are logically and conceptually linked.

A family may consist either of multiple comparisons conducted on a single dependent variable in a design consisting of more than two groups or of multiple comparisons conducted on separate dependent variables in a design consisting of two or more groups. A series of three pairwise *t*-tests for testing H_0: $\mu_1 = \mu_2 = \mu_3$ in terms of, say, twelfth-grade math achievement is an example of the first type of family. A series of four *t*-tests that compares males and females in terms of twelfth-grade math achievement, reading achievement, science achievement, and social studies achievement is an example of the second type of family.

As implied, when several logically linked comparisons are conducted, each at α, the overall family-wise error rate, α_{FW}, exceeds α. The amount by which α_{FW} exceeds α may be obtained from Equation 12.1, which expresses the relationship between these two Type I errors.

The probability of making at least one Type I error in conducting a set of K conceptually linked tests, α_{FW}, is approximated by

$$\alpha_{FW} = 1 - (1 - \alpha)^K. \tag{12.1}$$

If the number of tests carried out to test H_0: $\mu_1 = \mu_2 = \mu_3$ is $K = 3$, then α_{FW} equals approximately $1 - (.95)(.95)(.95) = 1 - .95^3 = 1 - .8574 = .1426$.

That is, for every 100 times we tested H_0: $\mu_1 = \mu_2 = \mu_3$ using a set of $K = 3$ mutually independent tests (e.g., a combination of pairwise and more complex comparisons), we would make a Type I error (i.e., reject the H_0 falsely) approximately 14 times on average, instead of 5.

A simpler expression of the relationship between α_{FW} and α is given by Equation 12.2:

$$\alpha_{FW} \leq K\alpha. \tag{12.2}$$

This relationship, proven by Bonferroni, an Italian mathematician, states that the family-wise Type I error rate is always be less than or equal to the per-comparison Type I error rate times the number of comparisons conducted.

When $K = 3$ and $\alpha = .05$, as in the current illustration, Equation 12.2 suggests that

$$\alpha_{FM} \leq (3)(.05) = .15,$$

which is consistent with our result from Equation 12.1 that $\alpha_{FW} = .1426$.

Equations 12.1 and 12.2 make amply clear the fact that as the number of comparisons in a set increases so does the family-wise error rate relative to α.

To control the family-wise Type I error at the chosen level α regardless of how many comparisons are conducted, we present two possible approaches: the one-way analysis of variance (ANOVA) and the Bonferroni adjustment.

THE ONE-WAY ANALYSIS OF VARIANCE

One-way ANOVA is a nondirectional procedure that tests the equality among two or more population means using independent groups while controlling the family-wise Type I error rate at the chosen level α regardless of the number of groups in the design. When applied to only two groups, the one-way ANOVA is exactly identical to the nondirectional t-test for independent groups. Simply stated, one-way ANOVA may be thought of as an extension of the independent two-group t-test to two or more groups.

☞ **Remark.** The name given to a procedure to test the equality of population means, analysis of variance, may seem like a misnomer. Actually, the name comes from the method that is used to test for the equality of means. As we shall see, not unlike the two independent groups t-test, ANOVA tests hypotheses about the equality of means by analyzing variances defined in different ways relative to the groups in the design.

☞ **Remark.** The ANOVA method was developed by Ronald Aylmer Fisher, one of the giants in the history of the development of modern statistics, as a way to evaluate the separate effects of various treatments (e.g., fertilizer, soil type, weather, crop variety) on crop production. Hired in 1919 to work at the Rothamsted Agricultural Experimental Station in Harpenden, a rural area north of London, he was to examine and make sense of the enormous body of data collected in connection with the agricultural experiments that had been conducted to date at that time. R.A. Fisher introduced the ANOVA in an article published in 1923; it was the second in a series of six papers entitled "Studies in Crop Variation" (Salsburg, 2001). As written by Salsburg (2001), "[t]hese papers show a brilliant originality and are filled with fascinating implications that kept theoreticians busy for the rest of the twentieth century, and will probably continue to inspire more work in the years that follow" (p. 43).

A GRAPHICAL ILLUSTRATION OF THE ROLE OF VARIANCE IN TESTS ON MEANS

Suppose the director of a drug rehabilitation center is interested in comparing the effects of three methods of therapeutic treatment on manual dexterity. Accordingly, she selects at random a sample of individuals from the population of applicants to her program and randomly assigns each to one of the three treatments, labeled Treatment 1, Treatment 2, and Treatment 3. After five weeks in the treatment programs, the participants are administered the Stanford Test of Manual Dexterity.

Suppose the three score distributions on this test, for Treatments 1, 2, and 3, are given in Figure 12.1 with means $\overline{X}_1 = -3, \overline{X}_2 = 0, \overline{X}_3 = 3$, respectively. Based on the differences in these means, can the director conclude that the three treatments differ in their effects on the mean levels of manual dexterity for the population of potential participants from whom the sample was drawn? The answer depends on whether the score distributions are separate enough to suggest that each resulted from a different treatment. Because there is no observed overlap among the different group score distributions in Figure 12.1, the

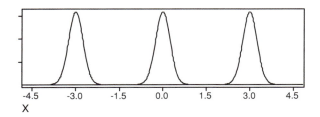

Figure 12.1   Nonoverlapping score distributions with means −3, 0, and 3, respectively.

groups may be separate enough to suggest that the treatments have an effect on manual dexterity for the population of participants from whom the sample was drawn.

Figure 12.2 offers a contrasting scenario to Figure 12.1. While the three means remain the same as in Figure 12.1 ($\overline{X}_1 = -3, \overline{X}_2 = 0, \overline{X}_3 = 3$), considerable overlap exists in Figure 12.2 among the score distributions. Accordingly, in contrast to Figure 12.1, the groups may not be separate enough to suggest that the treatments have a differential effect on manual dexterity for this population. Although an individual in Figure 12.1 with a manual dexterity score of 1.00 clearly received Treatment 2, there is a good chance that an individual with the same score in Figure 12.2 received Treatment 2, or to a lesser extent Treatment 3. There is even a small chance that the individual received Treatment 1.

Clearly, because Figures 12.1 and 12.2 display the same group means, more than mean differences determine the degree of overlap, or separation, between groups. As we make more explicit in the next section, we have already measured group separation as more than merely a difference between means in our use of the independent group t-test.

ANOVA AS AN EXTENSION OF THE INDEPENDENT SAMPLES t-TEST

In the two independent groups t-test, the t-ratio of the hypotheses $H_0: \mu_1 = \mu_2$ versus $H_1: \mu_1 \neq \mu_2$ is given as follows:

$$t = \frac{(\overline{X}_1 - \overline{X}_2) - (\mu_1 - \mu_2)}{\sqrt{\dfrac{(N_1 - 1)\hat{\sigma}_1^2 + (N_2 - 1)\hat{\sigma}_2^2}{N_1 + N_2 - 2}\left(\dfrac{1}{N_1} + \dfrac{1}{N_2}\right)}}$$

We may note that with $H_0: \mu_1 - \mu_2 = 0$ the numerator of this ratio equals the difference between groups, as represented by the respective group means $(\overline{X}_1 - \overline{X}_2)$, and the denominator of this ratio equals (a function of) the weighted average of the two variance estimators, $\hat{\sigma}_1^2$ and $\hat{\sigma}_2^2$, computed respectively within each group.

More generally, we may say that the t-ratio describes the *variability between groups*, expressed as a difference between means, relative to the *variability within groups*, which is

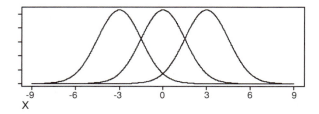

Figure 12.2   Overlapping score distributions with means −3, 0, and 3, respectively.

expressed as a weighted average of within-group variances. When there are only two groups, the variability between groups may be expressed simply as a difference between means; however, when there are more than two groups, the variability between groups may not be expressed so simply. To express the variability between groups in the case of more than two groups, we instead compute the *variance* (or variance estimator) of the group means; that is, we compute a variance on a set of mean values. If the group means are all equal, the variance of the means is zero. On the other hand, if the group means are quite distinct, the variance of the means are correspondingly large.

Thus, we may conceptualize the *t*-test as a test of the relative size of two different variances – a between-group variance and a within-group variance – for the purpose of judging hypotheses about two independent group means. Like the *t*-test, the one-way ANOVA, as discussed in this book, is by extension a test of the relative size of a between-group variance and a within-group variance for the purpose of judging hypotheses about *more than two independent* group means.

☞ **Remark.** A form of ANOVA, called repeated measures ANOVA, may be used to test hypotheses about more than two *paired* group means. This procedure is beyond the scope of this book.

DEVELOPING AN INDEX OF SEPARATION FOR THE ANALYSIS OF VARIANCE

To determine whether the groups displayed in Figures 12.1 and 12.2 are in fact separate enough to suggest differential treatment effects, we use a single measure of group separation based on the between- and within-group variances. The *between-group variance*, or spread of the means between groups, represents the degree to which the different treatments separate or pull apart individuals (on the test of manual dexterity) by virtue of their exposure to different treatments. The *within-group variance*, or spread of scores within each group, represents the naturally occurring variability that exists (in manual dexterity) among individuals who have received the same treatment and may be due to such factors as natural ability, skill, motivation, age, gender, and so on. Such naturally occurring variability among individuals who have received the same treatment is said to be due to *individual differences*. These are differences that are left unexplained by treatment effects and for this reason are referred to not only as within-group variance, but also *residual variance*.

In Figure 12.1 we may note that the between-group variance, as measured by the distance of each group mean from another, is quite large relative to the within-group variance, as measured by the spread of scores within each group. In Figure 12.2, however, the between-group variance is quite small relative to the within-group variance. The ratio of these two measures of variance (between to within) may be used to reflect the degree of separation among groups. As in the *t*-test, this ratio helps to determine whether the observed separation among score distributions is sufficiently large to suggest a real difference in the respective population means.

CARRYING OUT THE ANOVA COMPUTATION

Suppose the director of the drug rehabilitation center had selected 30 individuals from the population of applicants to her program and had randomly assigned 10 to Treatment 1, 10 to Treatment 2, and 10 to Treatment 3. After five weeks of treatment, a manual dexterity test is administered for which a higher score indicates greater manual dexterity. Suppose the scores on the manual dexterity test are as follows (these data can be found in the file *Mandex.sav*):

Treatment 1	Treatment 2	Treatment 3
6	4	6
10	2	2
8	3	2
6	5	6
9	1	4
8	3	5
7	2	3
5	2	5
6	4	3
5	4	4
$\overline{X}_1 = 7$	$\overline{X}_2 = 3$	$\overline{X}_3 = 4$

Does the variation in treatment group means suggest a real difference in treatment means for the population, using $\alpha = .05$? We compute the ratio of between-group variance to within-group variance to find out.

Because both between- and within-group variances are variance estimators, we define each as the sum of squared deviations about its respective mean divided by the appropriate degrees of freedom (SS/df). In the context of ANOVA, variance estimators are called *mean squares*, which is short for mean or average sum of squares, and are denoted by the letters MS. Thus, we say $MS = SS/df$.

To form the ratio of between-group variance to within-group variance we compute both the mean square between (MS_B) and the mean square within (MS_W). This ratio, MS_B/MS_W, is our index of separation in the one-way ANOVA.

☞ **Remark.** With one group of N values, we may recall that the degrees of freedom of a variance estimator are $N - 1$. With two groups of N values ($N = N_1 + N_2$), the degrees of freedom are $N_1 + N_2 - 2 = N - 2$ (as in the independent groups t-test). And, therefore, with K groups of N values ($N = N_1 + N_2 + N_3 + \cdots + N_K$), the degrees of freedom are $N - K$. We use this information in presenting the equations for MS_B and MS_W.

The Between-Group Variance (MS_B)

MS_B is computed as a variance on the group means and is given by Equation 12.3:

$$MS_B = \frac{SS_B}{df} = \frac{\sum_{j=1}^{K} N_j(\overline{X}_j - \overline{\overline{X}})^2}{K - 1} \tag{12.3}$$

where N_j equals the number of values in group j, $\overline{X}_j$ equals the mean of the values in group j, $\overline{\overline{X}}$ equals the overall or grand mean of all values in all groups (equivalently, the mean of the group means), and K is the total number of groups in the design.

☞ **Remark.** The between-group variance is based on a collection of K mean values. Its degrees of freedom, therefore, are $K - 1$. Because each of the means represents a different group of values, and not all groups are of the same size, we include a weighting factor, N_j, in Equation 12.3. The weighting factor N_j weights each squared deviation from the grand mean by the size of the corresponding group j so that deviations of large-sized groups are weighted more heavily than deviations of small-sized groups.

Using Equation 12.3, we compute the MS_B for the data from our example:

$$N_1 = N_2 = N_3 = 10; \bar{X}_1 = 7, \bar{X}_2 = 3, \bar{X}_3 = 4; \bar{\bar{X}} = 4.67; K = 3$$

$$SS_B = 10(7 - 4.67)^2 + 10(3 - 4.67)^2 + 10(4 - 4.67)^2 = 54.29 + 27.89 + 4.49 = 86.67$$

$$MS_B = 86.67/(3 - 1) = 86.67/2 = 43.34$$

The Within-Group Variance (MS_W)

The MS_W is computed as the sum of the separate sums of squares computed on each group divided by the appropriate degrees of freedom. It is given by Equation 12.4:

$$MS_W = \frac{SS_W}{df} = \frac{\sum_{i,j}(X_{i,j} - \bar{X}_j)^2}{N - K} \tag{12.4}$$

where $X_{i,j}$ represents the score of individual i in group j (e.g., $X_{1,3}$ represents the score of individual 1 in group 3; $X_{3,1}$ represents the score of individual 3 in group 1).

☞ **Remark.** The within-group variance is based on K groups of N values total. Its degrees of freedom are, therefore, $N - K$.

Using Equation 12.4, we compute the MS_W for the data from our example:

$$
\begin{aligned}
SS_W &= [(6 - 7)^2 + (10 - 7)^2 + (8 - 7)^2 + (6 - 7)^2 + (9 - 7)^2 + (8 - 7)^2 \\
&\quad + (7 - 7)^2 + (5 - 7)^2 + (6 - 7)^2 + (5 - 7)^2] + [(4 - 3)^2 + (2 - 3)^2 \\
&\quad + (3 - 3)^2 + (5 - 3)^2 + (1 - 3)^2 + (3 - 3)^2 + (2 - 3)^2 + (2 - 3)^2 \\
&\quad + (4 - 3)^2 + (4 - 4)^2] + [(6 - 4)^2 + (2 - 4)^2 + (2 - 4)^2 + (6 - 4)^2 \\
&\quad + (4 - 4)^2 + (5 - 4)^2 + (3 - 4)^2 + (5 - 4)^2 + (3 - 4)^2 + (4 - 4)^2] \\
&= 1 + 9 + 1 + 1 + 4 + 1 + 0 + 4 + 1 + 4 + 1 + 1 + 0 + 4 + 4 \\
&\quad + 0 + 1 + 1 + 1 + 0 + 4 + 4 + 4 + 4 + 0 + 1 + 1 + 1 + 1 + 1 + 0 \\
&= 60 \\
MS_W &= 60/(30 - 3) = 60/27 = 2.22.
\end{aligned}
$$

The index of separation, MS_B/MS_W, is called the F-ratio. If certain assumptions are satisfied by our K populations, then the distribution of all possible F-ratios, called an F-distribution, has a particular shape. We use the F-distribution in much the same way we used the t-distribution, to judge whether our observed statistic – in this case, the observed F-ratio – may be attributable to chance.

THE ASSUMPTIONS OF THE ONE-WAY ANOVA

We make the following assumptions in the one-way ANOVA:

1. The null hypothesis is true.
2. The scores are independent of each other.
3. The parent populations are normally distributed for all groups under study.
4. The parent populations have equal variances (called homogeneity of variance) for all groups under study.

Scores are independent if they are randomly selected from their respective parent population; therefore, the selection of scores from one population has no bearing on the selection of scores from any other population. Independence may be achieved if each score is from a separate individual who has been randomly assigned to one of the treatment conditions of the design.

If any of these four conditions is not met, then the statistic obtained may not be distributed as an F-distribution with hypothesized mean difference zero. In testing the equality of population means, if conditions 2, 3, and 4 are known to be satisfied and an unusual sample outcome is observed, then the plausibility of the remaining condition, condition 1, becomes questionable and one would decide to reject H_0 as implausible.

Thus, it appears that conditions 2, 3, and 4 need to be satisfied in order to test condition 1 using the F-ratio. For this reason, conditions 2, 3, and 4 are usually referred to as the underlying assumptions of the one-way ANOVA.

In actual research situations, we cannot always be certain whether either or both conditions 3 and 4 hold and we must expend some effort to investigate the tenability of these assumptions.

Violations of the assumption of normality do not affect, or only minimally affect, the validity of the ANOVA. That is, ANOVA has been shown to produce correct results even when the data are not normally distributed in the population as long as there are at least 30 subjects in each cell. In statistical terms, we say that ANOVA is *robust* to violations of the assumption of normality (see Glass, Peckham, & Sanders, 1972, for a review of studies on the empirical consequences of failing to meet ANOVA assumptions). In the case of a small data set, however, we recommend checking within cell distributions for outliers and other evidence of nonnormality to ensure that a small set of values does not unduly influence the results of the analysis.

Violations of the assumption of homogeneity of variance do not affect, or only minimally affect, the validity of the ANOVA when cell sizes are large and equal. When sample sizes are unequal and small, however, and when populations have heterogeneous variances, the Type I error rate associated with the F-test is actually greater than what is reported. For example, under such conditions, a reported p-value of .05 may actually be .10. When samples are larger, yet still unequal in size, and when variances are unequal, there is less distortion in Type I error. That is, reported Type I error levels come closer to actual levels and the effect of unequal variances is reduced when samples are larger.

In the face of heterogeneity of variance, when sample sizes are neither equal nor large, we recommend that the researcher transform scores nonlinearly to reduce heterogeneity. We recommend also that a more stringent Type I error rate (e.g., 0.01 instead of 0.05) be employed under conditions of heterogeneity to compensate for the tendency of the F-test to report p-values in excess of what they truly are.

TESTING THE EQUALITY OF POPULATION MEANS: THE F-RATIO

If the underlying assumptions are satisfied, then the distribution of all possible ratios MS_B/MS_W that could be observed from these populations form what is called an *F-distribution with $K - 1$, $N - K$ degrees of freedom*. The $K - 1$ degrees of freedom are associated with MS_B in the numerator, and the $N - K$ degrees of freedom are associated with MS_W in the denominator:

$$F(K - 1, N - K) = MS_B/MS_W \tag{12.5}$$

We use Equation 12.5 to determine whether the ratio MS_B/MS_W based on our sample data is likely to be observed when the null hypothesis of equal population means is true. Because we would reject the null hypothesis in favor of the alternative only when MS_B exceeds MS_W (as in Figure 12.1), we are only interested in situations in which MS_B exceeds MS_W, and consider areas only in the right tail of the F-distribution. Whenever the observed F-ratio is large enough to be considered unlikely to have occurred by chance (when p is small – say, less than 0.05), we would reject the null hypothesis that all population means are equal in favor of the alternative hypothesis that not all population means are equal.

Like the t-distribution, the F-distribution consists of a family of curves. Unlike the t-distribution, however, F is defined by two degrees of freedom, one related to the numerator and the other related to the denominator. Equation 12.5 refers to the particular F-distribution that has $K - 1$ degrees of freedom in its numerator and $N - K$ degrees of freedom in its denominator. Figures 12.3(a) to 12.3(d) illustrate four F-distributions,

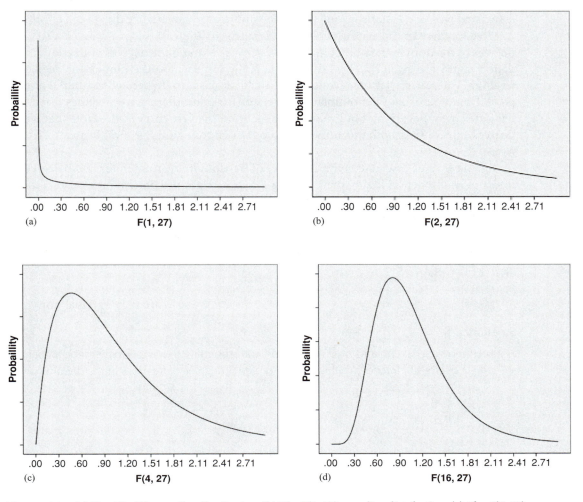

Figure 12.3   (a) The $F(1, 27)$ sampling distribution. (b) The $F(2, 27)$ sampling distribution. (c) The $F(4, 27)$ sampling distribution. (d) The $F(16, 27)$ sampling distribution.

each with 27 degrees of freedom in the denominator (as in our example) but with different numbers of degrees of freedom in the numerator; namely, 1, 2, 4, and 16, respectively. The lowest tick on the vertical axis of all four figures represents the probability value of zero.

☞ **Remark.** Notice that as the degrees of freedom increase in the numerator, the shape of the F-distribution changes considerably and becomes more symmetric. We may note without illustration that the shape of the F-distribution remains relatively constant if we change the degrees of freedom in the denominator but keep the degrees of freedom in the numerator the same.

HOW TO READ THE TABLES AND TO USE THE SPSS COMPUTE STATEMENT FOR THE F-DISTRIBUTION

Table 3 in Appendix C contains an F-distribution summary table that can be used to estimate p-values and F-values that cut off a given area. Two sets of degrees of freedom are associated with the F-statistic, one set for the numerator, or variance due to the effect, and one set for the denominator, or within variance. In the case of one-way ANOVA, the degrees of freedom in the numerator are given by $K - 1$ and the degrees of freedom in the denominator are given by $N - K$. In Table 3, the top row has the numerator degrees of freedom, whereas the leftmost column has the denominator degrees of freedom. For each pair of numerator and denominator degrees of freedom, there are 6 F-values listed that have area α to their right. For example, we see from the first entry in the table that with 1 degree of freedom in both the numerator and the denominator, $F = 5.83$ has area .25 to its right.

So, the F-value associated with 2 degrees of freedom in the numerator and 3 degrees of freedom in the denominator that has area .05 to its right is 9.55. We may express the F-value 9.55 associated with 2 degrees of freedom in the numerator and 3 degrees of freedom in the denominator as $F(2, 3) = 9.55$.

EXAMPLE 12.1. Use Table 3 to estimate the p-value associated with the following F-values:

a) $F(2, 3) = 8.66$.
b) $F(2, 3) = 1.56$.
c) $F(2, 50) = 3.5$.

Solution.

a) The following list contains the F-values and corresponding α or areas to the right, associated with 2 degrees of freedom in the numerator and 3 degrees of freedom in the denominator:

F	α
2.28	.25
5.46	.10
9.55	.05
16.04	.03
30.82	.01
148.49	.001

We find that the F-values that are closest to $F = 8.66$ are $F = 5.46$ and $F = 9.55$. The area to the right of $F = 5.46$ is .10 and the area to the right of $F = 9.55$ is .05. The p-value, or the area to the right of $F = 8.66$, is less than .10 but larger than .05. We have the estimate $.05 < p < .10$.

b) We find that the F-value that is closest to $F = 1.56$ is $F = 2.28$. The area to the right of $F = 2.28$ is .25. The p-value, or the area to the right of $F = 1.56$, is greater than .25. We have the estimate $p > .25$.

c) Because the table contains no entry for 50 degrees of freedom in the denominator, we take a conservative approach and use the closest value that is smaller than 50, or $df = 40$. We find the estimate $.03 < p < .05$. We may also get a better estimate of these areas by using the SPSS Compute statement. CDF.F(q, df_1, df_2) returns the area to the left of $F(df_1, df_2) = q$.

Returning to the data of our example, $F(2, 27) = MS_B/MS_W = 43.34/2.22 = 19.52$, which from Figure 12.3(b) appears to fall far into the right tail of the distribution. We estimate the p-value "by hand" in two ways. First, we estimate the p-value using Table 3. Then we get a better estimate using the SPSS Compute statement.

To find the proportion of the area to the right of 19.52 (that is, the p-value associated with this $F(2, 27)$) using Table 3, we estimate the denominator degrees of freedom by 26 and see that the closest F-value with 2 degrees of freedom in the numerator and 26 degrees of freedom in the denominator is $F = 9.12$, which has area .001. Because our observed F-value, 19.52, has less area to its right, we obtain the estimate $p < .001$.

To find the p-value associated with $F(2, 27)$ using the SPSS Compute statement, we make use of the numeric expression 1-CDF.F(q, df_1, df_2) and substitute 19.52 for q, 2 for df_1, and 27 for df_2. The value that is returned is $p < .000006$, which equals the area under the curve to right of 19.52. The p-value suggests that the probability of observing an F-ratio of 19.52 by chance given that the null hypothesis is true (that all population means are equal) is quite small. The value of α adopted in this instance is $\alpha = .05$. Accordingly, we reject the null hypothesis in favor of the alternative that not all population means are equal.

Our conclusion is that there are differences in average manual dexterity scores between at least two of the treatments.

For heuristic reasons, we carried out the computations associated with this example by hand. We now show how to use SPSS to provide these same results. We assume these data have been input into a data file with two variables: TREATMEN, which signifies the treatment group to which an individual has been assigned, and SCORE, which signifies the score on the manual dexterity test.

To use SPSS to carry out a one-way ANOVA, click on **Analyze, Compare Means, One-Way ANOVA**. Move SCORE to the **Dependent List** box; move TREATMEN to the **Factor** box. Click **Options**. Under Statistics, click the box next to **Descriptives and Homogeneity of Variance**. Click **Continue, OK**.

We obtain the following three sets of results: descriptive statistics, including 95 percent confidence intervals about each of the individual group means that are based on the *t*-distribution; Levene's test of homogeneity of variance; and the ANOVA summary table. We turn attention to the last two sets of results.

Descriptives

Manual Dexterity

	N	Mean	Std. Deviation	Std. Error	95% Confidence Interval for Mean Lower Bound	Upper Bound	Minimum	Maximum
1.00	10	7.0000	1.69967	.53748	5.7841	8.2159	5.00	10.00
2.00	10	3.0000	1.24722	.39441	2.1078	3.8922	1.00	5.00
3.00	10	4.0000	1.49071	.47140	2.9336	5.0664	2.00	6.00
Total	30	4.6667	2.24888	.41059	3.8269	5.5064	1.00	10.00

Test of Homogeneity of Variances

Manual Dexterity

Levene Statistic	df1	df2	Sig.
.675	2	27	.518

ANOVA

Manual Dexterity

	Sum of Squares	df	Mean Square	F	Sig.
Between Groups	86.667	2	43.333	19.500	.000
Within Groups	60.000	27	2.222		
Total	146.667	29			

Recall that, when we introduced the *F*-ratio, we assumed that all parent populations under study were normally distributed and had equal variances. However, like the independent groups *t*-test, the ANOVA test has been found to be quite insensitive to violations of normality and to violations of the assumption of equal variances as long as relatively large and equal or approximately equal sample sizes are used.

Because these sample sizes are not large, we evaluate the normality assumption by calculating the skewness ratio for each group. There are several ways to find the skewness values. You can Select Cases, as we did in Examples 11.1 and 11.3, or you can use the SPSS Explore procedure. An alternative, to generate statistics when there is more than one group, is to use the SPSS Split Files procedure obtained through the Data menu. Split File treats the data as two separate data files and separately computes whatever statistics are desired on each group.

To split the file using SPSS, go to **Data**, **Split File**. Click on the circle next to **Compare Groups** and move the variable of interest, in this case, TREATMEN, into the **Groups Based On** box. Click **OK**. Proceed to obtain any desired statistics on the separate groups. Before carrying out the ANOVA on the whole data set, click **Analyze All Cases** under the **Split Files** command.

Descriptive Statistics

treatment		N	Skewness	
		Statistic	Statistic	Std. Error
1.00	Manual Dexterity	10	.509	.687
	Valid N (listwise)	10		
2.00	Manual Dexterity	10	.000	.687
	Valid N (listwise)	10		
3.00	Manual Dexterity	10	.000	.687
	Valid N (listwise)	10		

We see that all of the skewness ratios are less than 2 so that the normality assumption is tenable.

The ANOVA output includes a test of the underlying assumption of equal (or homogeneous) variances in all cases, even when samples are equal in size. The Levene's statistic, upon which the test is based, relies on the F-distribution to provide a p-value (noted under the column labeled Sig.) to test the null hypothesis that all populations have equal variances. Because $p = .518$ ($p < .05$) in this case, we may conclude that the homogeneity of variance assumption is met for these data. In the event that Levene's test is statistically significant, we should take this as a warning to check our data for possible outliers and skewness and to think through why one or more group variances would be so different from the others. Of course, as we have argued throughout this text, one should explore the distributional properties of one's sample data before placing confidence in one's summary statistics and using them in tests of inference.

ANOVA SUMMARY TABLE

The ANOVA summary table provides, in a neatly organized way, the results we obtained by hand. Notice that the F-ratio of 19.5 is reported to have a p-value of .000. Of course, the p-value is not identically equal to zero, but rather equals zero to three decimal places. From our previous computation, we know that the p-value is more closely equal to .000006.

We may note the addition of a row labeled Total in the summary table that contains the sum of SS_B and SS_W as well as the sum of their respective degrees of freedom. The total of these sums of squares, denoted SS_T, has its own meaning. It is simply the total variability contained in the entire set of scores when one ignores group membership. As such, it reflects the distance of each individual score from the overall mean and may be calculated using Equation 12.6. If there are N total scores total in the data set, then the degrees of freedom associated with SS_T are simply $N - 1$.

$$SS_T = \sum (X_{i,j} - \overline{\overline{X}} B^2. \tag{12.6}$$

Using some elementary algebra, it can be shown that the total sum of squares is in fact equal to the sum of the sum of squares between and the sum of squares within:

$$SS_T = SS_B + SS_W. \tag{12.7}$$

MEASURING THE EFFECT SIZE

Equation 12.7 offers additional insight into ANOVA. Beginning with a data set that contains total variability SS_T, Equation 12.6 implies that ANOVA divides or partitions SS_T into two separate components, SS_B and SS_W. SS_B is that part of SS_T that is accounted for, or explained by, group differences; SS_W is that part of SS_T that is left over, or unexplained, after accounting for such group differences.

Figures 12.4 and 12.5 illustrate the partitioning of SS_T into these two components under two scenarios. Figure 12.4 corresponds to the scenario depicted in Figure 12.1 in which between-group variance is large relative to within-group variance, implying that SS_B accounts for a large proportion of the variability represented by SS_T. Figure 12.5, on the other hand, corresponds to the scenario depicted in Figure 12.2 in which between-group variance is small relative to within-group variance, implying that SS_B accounts for a small proportion of the variability represented by SS_T. In Figure 12.5 there is much leftover, or *residual*, variability yet to be explained. We see in the next chapter that in an attempt to account for or explain this residual variability one may include another factor (variable) in the design in addition to, say, treatment group, and analyze the degree to which it does account for the residual variance.

Because the ratio SS_B/SS_T reflects the magnitude of the effect of the between-group factor (e.g., treatment group), it is useful as a descriptive measure of effect size, expressed as the degree of association between the dependent variable and grouping variable in the sample. Because the measure is independent of sample size and, as a proportion, ranges from 0 to 1, it provides a useful adjunct to the *F*-test for statistical significance. It should be noted that SS_B/SS_T provides an overestimate of the proportion of dependent variable variance accounted for by the grouping variable in the population.

Applying this ratio to the data from our example, we find that the proportion of manual dexterity variance explained by treatment is $SS_B/SS_T = 86.67/146.67 = .59$. This proportion may also be expressed as a percentage: 59 percent of the variance in manual dexterity is explained by treatment.

☞ **Remark.** From here on we shall refer to SS_B/SS_T as R^2. Following effect size conventions set forth by Cohen (1988), we offer the following scale for evaluating R^2:

$R^2 = .01$ represents a "small" effect.
$R^2 = .09$ represents a "medium" effect.
$R^2 = .25$ represents a "large" effect.

EXAMPLE 12.2. Determine whether there are differences in the mean number of years of mathematics studied in high school among the four regions of the country (Northeast, North Central, South, and West) using the NELS data. Let $\alpha = .01$.

Figure 12.4 SS_B/SS_T is large.   **Figure 12.5** SS_B/SS_T is small.

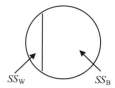

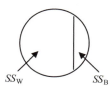

Solution. Because we have *one* grouping variable, or factor, and a dependent variable that is ratio-leveled, we use *one-way* ANOVA to find a solution to this problem. Prior to carrying out the ANOVA, we explore our data using boxplots. Despite the presence of some outliers, these distributions appear to be relatively homogeneous in their variances. Furthermore, given the large number of cases per category, departures for normality, resulting from the outliers, would not pose a problem to the validity of the *F*-statistic.

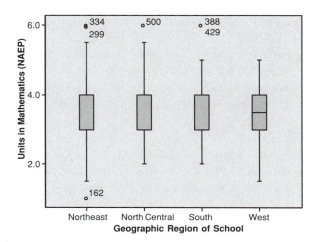

Following the procedure outlined earlier, we move UNITMATH to the **Dependent List** box and REGION to the **Factor** box. We obtain the following results.

Descriptives

Units in Mathematics (NAEP)

	N	Mean	Std. Deviation	Std. Error	95% Confidence Interval for Mean Lower Bound	95% Confidence Interval for Mean Upper Bound	Minimum	Maximum
Northeast	106	3.792	.8876	.0862	3.621	3.963	1.0	6.0
North-Central	151	3.532	.8078	.0657	3.402	3.662	2.0	6.0
South	150	3.775	.7372	.0602	3.656	3.894	2.0	6.0
West	93	3.409	.7523	.0780	3.255	3.564	1.5	5.0
Total	500	3.637	.8077	.0361	3.566	3.708	1.0	6.0

Test of Homogeneity of Variances

Units in Mathematics (NAEP)

Levene Statistic	df1	df2	Sig.
.861	3	496	.461

ANOVA

Units in Mathematics (NAEP)

	Sum of Squares	df	Mean Square	F	Sig.
Between Groups	11.886	3	3.962	6.265	.000
Within Groups	313.653	496	.632		
Total	325.539	499			

From the table of Descriptives, we may note that some variation in sample means appears to exist, especially when the Northeast and South are compared to the North Central and West. Students in the West appear to enroll for the fewest number of years of math in high school. We also note that the standard deviations of this variable appear rather homogeneous for all four regions of the country. Levene's test corroborates this impression regarding homogeneity of variance because $p = .461$ for this test. Given the large sample size, very small deviations from equality would have been detected. Hence, we can place confidence in Levene's test that for these data the assumption of homogeneity of variance is met.

According to the ANOVA summary table, we may note that the obtained $F(3, 496) = 6.265$ with $p < .0005$, suggesting that it is highly unlikely that the null hypothesis (H_0: $\mu_1 = \mu_2 = \mu_3 = \mu_4 = 0$) is true. Our data are more consistent with the alternative hypothesis that a difference exists among means. Hence, we reject the null in favor of the alternative.

We note, however, that $SS_B/SS_T = 11.89/325.54 = 3.7$ percent, suggesting that REGION by itself accounts for a very small proportion of UNITMATH variance. Clearly, other factors need to be considered in addition to REGION to explain the residual variance in number of years taken in high school (that is, the variance that remains after REGION has been accounted for).

In both examples – the effects of various treatments on manual dexterity and the relationship between region and number of years of math taken in high school – we obtained a statistically significant F-test result, indicating that differences exist among the population means. A natural question that follows a statistically significant F-test is which specific means are different from which others?

Unfortunately, the F-test tells us nothing about which means are different, only that not all of them are equal. To find out where specific mean differences exist based on our observation of the data, we use what are called, *post-hoc* tests. Post-hoc refers to the fact that we are using the data to decide which comparisons to make; that our decisions are made *after the fact* of obtaining a statistically significant result from the ANOVA and knowing, therefore, that not all population means are equal.

POST-HOC MULTIPLE COMPARISON TESTS

Our goal in conducting post-hoc tests is to extract as much meaningful information from our data as possible while still maintaining the family-wise error rate at a reasonable level. A large number of post-hoc tests exist and recommendations for choosing among them are plentiful. In this book we present two post-hoc tests that are appropriate when one is interested in making only pairwise comparisons between means. We do so because we believe that most applied research that employs an ANOVA-type design is concerned ultimately with ordering the means of the K groups on the dependent variable; a series of pairwise comparisons is useful for this purpose.

The first test, Tukey's Honestly Significant Difference (HSD), developed in 1953, directly maintains the family-wise error rate at the chosen level regardless of how many pairwise comparisons are made. The sampling distribution for the HSD is called the *studentized range distribution*. This distribution is based on the expectation that

(1) for random samples drawn from a normal population, the larger the size of the sample, the larger the difference should be between the extreme values in the sample (i.e., the range of the sample); and (2) when K samples are selected from a normal population, the larger K is, the larger the difference should be between the extreme sample means.

Accordingly, when K is greater than 2 (which it is in an ANOVA-type design), we would expect a larger difference between the two extreme means than if K were only 2. The HSD takes this into account by increasing the size of the critical values (or equivalently by reducing the size of the critical regions, α) associated with statistical significance. In so doing, the HSD makes it more difficult to obtain statistical significance for each comparison and maintains the overall family-wise error rate at the chosen value, say .05.

The formula for the Tukey test for comparing the means of treatment groups j and k is given by Equation 12.8 where q, called the *studentized range statistic*, represents a value in the studentized range distribution and the sample sizes for groups j and k are equal:

$$q = \frac{\overline{X}_j - \overline{X}_k}{\sqrt{\dfrac{MS_w}{n}}} \qquad (12.8)$$

where $\overline{X}_j$ and $\overline{X}_k$ are the sample means from treatment groups j and k, respectively, and $\overline{X}_j > \overline{X}_k$. The value of the mean square within from the original ANOVA is MS_W; and n is the common sample size for all treatment groups.

When the treatment groups do not all have a common sample size, an approximate Tukey HSD test statistic can be computed by substituting n' for n, where n' is the harmonic mean of the sample sizes of all the treatment groups. The equation for computing the harmonic mean is

$$n' = \frac{K}{\left[\dfrac{1}{n_1} + \dfrac{1}{n_2} + \cdots + \dfrac{1}{n_K} \right]}. \qquad (12.9)$$

Critical values of the studentized range statistic are provided in Table 6 of Appendix C. Like the F-test associated with the original ANOVA, the Tukey HSD is a test of a nondirectional alternative hypothesis but uses only the right tail of the sampling distribution for the rejection region. To use Table 6, one needs both the degrees of freedom associated with the number of treatment groups in the original ANOVA design, K, and the MS_W term from the original ANOVA, df_W.

The second test, Fisher's Least Significant Difference (LSD), developed in 1935 and known also as the protected t-test, is not as effective in maintaining the overall family-wise error at the chosen value. The sampling distribution for the LSD is the t-distribution. That is, given a statistically significant F-test associated with the original ANOVA (called the *omnibus F-test*), the LSD follows with a series of t-tests to compare means pairwise. If the original F-test is not statistically significant and the original null hypothesis is not rejected, no further testing would be performed.

The difference between the LSD and a series of t-tests is the requirement of a rejection of the original null hypothesis at the chosen levelof α. Because the risk of a Type I error in conjunction with the omnibus test is maintained at α, the series of t-tests following a statistically significant ANOVA would be carried out mistakenly (when all population means are truly equal) only 5 times in 100 (if $\alpha = .05$). In this way, a statistically significant omnibus ANOVA protects the subsequent t-tests. However, statisticians have pointed out that under certain circumstances such protection is not enough; the LSD family-wise Type I error may exceed α by some unknown extent that depends, in part, on the number of pairwise comparisons made.

The choice between HSD and LSD must depend on the philosophies and beliefs of the researcher. As we demonstrate in our examples, the LSD is generally more powerful than the HSD because, for each pairwise comparison, the LSD uses α whereas the HSD uses a reduced α so as to maintain the overall family-wise error rate. Thus, the LSD is able to detect true differences with greater power. On the other hand, the LSD runs a greater risk of committing a Type I error – of declaring a difference between means where there truly is none. Thus, as a researcher, one must consider the number of pairwise comparisons to be made and weigh the risks of both types of error, Type I and Type II, in deciding which procedure makes sense in a particular case.

Alternatively, one could use both procedures and draw conclusions based on the results of both. If results are consistent for the two approaches, then the conclusions to be drawn are clear. If they do not agree, then careful thinking must be done to balance the relative risks of Type I and Type II errors, taking into account the number of comparisons made and other relevant factors particular to the issue being studied. Such thinking should be made public in, say, a report of final results so that a reader or listener can understand the researcher's process in reaching the reported conclusions. With this information, the reader can then decide whether to agree or disagree with these conclusions and to suggest others of his own.

EXAMPLE 12.3. Use the LSD and HSD post-hoc tests to determine which methods of therapeutic treatment on manual dexterity for the drug rehabilitation center population are different from which others. Let $\alpha = 0.05$.

Solution. We recall that a statistically significant omnibus F-test was obtained in connection with this example, indicating that not all three population means are equal. From the table of Descriptives, we note that the three treatment group means are $\bar{X}_1 = 7, \bar{X}_2 = 3, \bar{X}_3 = 4$. Accordingly, the mean difference between groups 1 and 2 is 4; between groups 1 and 3 is 3; and between groups 2 and 3 is -1.

To carry out the Tukey HSD test by hand, we compute Equation 12.8 for each pair of treatment means because in this case $n_1 = n_2 = n_3 = 10$. From the original ANOVA, we note that $MS_W = 2.22$, and $df_W = 27$, and $K = 3$.

(1) Comparing μ_1 and μ_2:

$$q = \frac{7 - 3}{\sqrt{\dfrac{2.22}{10}}} = \frac{4}{0.47} = 8.49.$$

Table 6 in Appendix C does not list $df_W = 27$ exactly, and so we use the more conservative values associated with $df_W = 28$. In doing so, we find that 8.49 exceeds 7.19, the critical value associated with $p = .001$ when $K = 3$. Hence, we conclude that $\mu_1 \neq \mu_2$ and $p < .001$.

(2) Comparing μ_1 and μ_3:

$$q = \frac{7 - 4}{\sqrt{\dfrac{2.22}{10}}} = \frac{3}{0.47} = 6.38.$$

As in the preceding case, 6.38 exceeds 4.57, the critical value associated with $p = .01$ when $K = 3$ and $df_W = 28$. Hence, we conclude that $\mu_1 \neq \mu_3$ and $p < .01$.

(3) Comparing μ_2 and μ_3:

$$q = \frac{4 - 3}{\sqrt{\dfrac{2.22}{10}}} = \frac{1}{0.47} = 2.13.$$

The value of 2.13 is less than 2.29, the critical value associated with $p = .10$ when $K = 3$ and $df_W = 28$. Hence, we conclude that $\mu_2 = \mu_3$ and $p > .10$.

Because we already have computed the independent groups t-test by hand, we do not carry out the LSD post-hoc test by hand. Rather, we rely solely on SPSS to carry out this protected t-test.

To use SPSS to carry out the HSD and LSD post-hoc tests in connection with the one-way ANOVA, click on **Analyze, Compare Means, One-Way ANOVA**. Move SCORE to the **Dependent List** box; move TREATMEN to the **Factor** box. Click **Post Hoc**. Check **Tukey** and **LSD**. Click **Continue** and then **OK**.

The results in the following table inform us that according to the HSD the mean difference of 4 between groups 1 and 2 is statistically significant ($p > .0005$), as is the mean difference between groups 1 and 3 ($p < .0005$). (The p-values are found in the column labeled Sig. and have been written as "$<.0005$" instead of "$=.000$" to reflect that they are not exactly equal to zero.) However, the mean difference between groups 2 and 3 is not statistically significant ($p = .307$). The same conclusions may be drawn from the results of the LSD. We may notice, however, that the LSD p-value of .145 associated with the test of the mean difference between groups 2 and 3 is smaller than the HSD p-value of .307 associated with the same mean comparison, suggesting that the LSD is the more powerful procedure of the two. Of course, as noted earlier, this added power is at an increased risk of making a Type I error. From the observed sample means, we may conclude that group 1 performs significantly better than groups 2 and 3.

Multiple Comparisons

Dependent Variable: score Manual Dexterity

	(I) treatmen	(J) treatmen	Mean Difference (I-J)	Std. Error	Sig.	95% Confidence Interval Lower Bound	Upper Bound
Tukey HSD	1.00	2.00	4.00000*	.66667	.000	2.3471	5.6529
		3.00	3.00000*	.66667	.000	1.3471	4.6529
	2.00	1.00	−4.00000*	.66667	.000	−5.6529	−2.3471
		3.00	−1.00000	.66667	.307	−2.6529	.6529
	3.00	1.00	−3.00000*	.66667	.000	−4.6529	−1.3471
		2.00	1.00000	.66667	.307	−.6529	2.6529
LSD	1.00	2.00	4.00000*	.66667	.000	2.6321	5.3679
		3.00	3.00000*	.66667	.000	1.6321	4.3679
	2.00	1.00	−4.00000*	.66667	.000	−5.3679	−2.6321
		3.00	−1.00000	.66667	.145	−2.3679	.3679
	3.00	1.00	−3.00000*	.66667	.000	−4.3679	−1.6321
		2.00	1.00000	.66667	.145	−.3679	2.3679

*The mean difference is significant at the .05 level.

☞ **Remark.** The standard error given in the pairwise comparisons table is simply the standard error of the mean difference given by Equation 11.6. As such, it is *not* the value of the standard error SPSS uses in calculating the significance of the post-hoc test that appears in the pairwise comparison table. Because the standard error is simply the standard error of the mean difference, you should notice that its value is the same (.667) regardless of the post-hoc test used.

• •

EXAMPLE 12.4. Use the LSD and HSD post-hoc tests to determine which specific regions of the country are different from which others in terms of the mean numbers of years of math taken in high school. Let $\alpha = 0.05$.

Solution. We recall that a statistically significant omnibus F-test was obtained in connection with this example, indicating that the observed sample mean differences are not attributable to random sampling error. From the table of descriptive statistics, we note that the four treatment group means are $\bar{X}_{NE} = 3.79$, $\bar{X}_{NC} = 3.53$, $\bar{X}_{S} = 3.78$, $\bar{X}_{W} = 3.41$. The mean differences between groups, along with their respective statistical significance values, are given in the Multiple Comparisons table obtained from SPSS using the procedure detailed earlier.

According to the HSD, the Northeast differs statistically significantly from the North Central and West, the North Central differs from the Northeast and South, the South differs from the North Central and West, and the West differs from the Northeast and South. While the LSD gives uniformly smaller p-values because of its greater power, the conclusions reached from the LSD results concur with those from the HSD. The Northeast and South do not differ from each on the dependent variable, nor do the North Central and West. Accordingly, there appear to be two different internally consistent or homogeneous groupings

Multiple Comparisons

Dependent Variable: unitmath Units in Mathematics (NAEP)

	(I) region Geographic Region of School	(J) region Geographic Region of School	Mean Difference (I-J)	Std. Error	Sig.	95% Confidence Interval	
						Lower Bound	Upper Bound
Tukey HSD	1 Northeast	2 North Central	.2598*	.1008	.050	.000	.520
		3 South	.0169	.1009	.998	−.243	.277
		4 West	.3826*	.1130	.004	.091	.674
	2 North Central	1 Northeast	−.2598*	.1008	.050	−.520	.000
		3 South	−.2429*	.0917	.041	−.479	−.007
		4 West	.1228	.1048	.645	−.147	.393
	3 South	1 Northeast	−.0169	.1009	.998	−.277	.243
		2 North Central	.2429*	.0917	.041	.007	.479
		4 West	.3657*	.1050	.003	.095	.636
	4 West	1 Northeast	−.3826*	.1130	.004	−.674	−.091
		2 North Central	−.1228	.1048	.645	−.393	.147
		3 South	−.3657*	.1050	.003	−.636	−.095
LSD	1 Northeast	2 North Central	.2598*	.1008	.010	.062	.458
		3 South	.0169	.1009	.867	−.181	.215
		4 West	.3826*	.1130	.001	.161	.605
	2 North Central	1 Northeast	−.2598*	.1008	.010	−.458	−.062
		3 South	−.2429*	.0917	.008	−.423	−.063
		4 West	.1228	.1048	.242	−.083	.329
	3 South	1 Northeast	−.0169	.1009	.867	−.215	.181
		2 North Central	.2429*	.0917	.008	.063	.423
		4 West	.3657*	.1050	.001	.160	.572
	4 West	1 Northeast	−.3826*	.1130	.001	−.605	−.161
		2 North Central	−.1228	.1048	.242	−.329	.083
		3 South	−.3657*	.1050	.001	−.572	−.160

*The mean difference is significant at the .05 level.

of regions: the Northeast and South and the North Central and West. Each grouping differs from the other. In this case the Northeast and South are statistically significantly higher than the North Central and West.

. . . .

EXAMPLE 12.5. Does twelfth-grade self-concept vary as a function of one of three types of high school program (rigorous academic, academic, vocational, and other)? Notice that for this example the variable HSPROG was recoded so that the categories Some Vocational and Other form a single category. Use the NELS data set and let $\alpha = 0.01$.

Solution. Given that type of high school program represents groups or categories and the dependent variable, twelfth-grade self-concept, may be considered to be interval-leveled, we use one-way ANOVA to find a solution to the question. To check assumptions and get a sense of what our data look like, we obtain the following boxplots.

According to the boxplots, aside from the five cases of relatively low self-concept in the academic program category, the distributions appear relatively homogeneous in their variances.

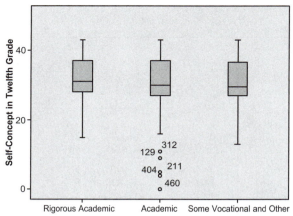

Furthermore, given the large number of cases per category, departures from normality resulting, for example, from the five cases of low self-concept in the academic category would not pose a problem to the validity of the *F*-statistic. We may also note that based on the boxplots alone twelfth-grade self-concept does not appear to vary as a function of high school program type.

We turn to the one-way ANOVA to see whether these sample results are upheld in the population.

Descriptives

slfcnc12 Self-Concept in Twelfth Grade

	N	Mean	Std. Deviation	Std. Error	95% Confidence Interval for Mean		Minimum	Maximum
					Lower Bound	Upper Bound		
1 Rigorous Academic	149	31.97	6.438	.527	30.93	33.02	15	43
2 Academic	279	31.33	7.557	.452	30.44	32.22	0	43
3 Some Vocational and Other	72	31.06	7.532	888	29.29	32.83	13	43
Total	500	31.48	7.231	.323	30.84	32.12	0	43

Test of Homogeneity of Variances

slfcnc12 Self-Concept in Twelfth Grade

Levene Statistic	df1	df2	Sig.
1.371	2	497	255

ANOVA

slfcnc12 Self-Concept in Twelfth Grade

	Sum of Squares	df	Mean Square	F	Sig.
Between Groups	55.811	2	27.905	533	587
Within Groups	26036.989	497	52.388		
Total	26092.800	499			

Like the boxplot medians, the means are quite homogeneous, suggesting that it is unlikely that self-concept varies with type of high school program. We may note that, as expected, Levene's test is nonsignificant, and the homogeneity of variance assumption is met for these data. The obtained $F = .533$ is nonsignificant ($p = .587$), confirming the impression that the means are not statistically significantly different.

Because there are no differences among self-concept means ($p = .587$), no further testing is warranted. Our conclusion is simply that a student's self-concept does not appear to be linked to the type of high school program in which that student is enrolled. Although self-concept does vary from individual to individual ($SS_T = 26,093$ units), the amount of that variability due to the type of high school program in which that individual is enrolled is quite low ($SS_B = 56$ units). Other factors need to be considered if we are to understand why there is variability among students in self-concept. Ways to consider these other factors analytically are discussed in the next chapter.

• •

EXAMPLE 12.6. Is there a relationship between school attendance rate and region? Said differently, does school attendance rate depend on the location of the school-whether it is in the Northeast, North Central, South, or West? Let $\alpha = 0.05$.

Solution. Given that there is one grouping variable, region, and that the dependent variable, school attendance rate, is ratio-leveled, a one-way ANOVA is appropriate for answering this question. Following a logical sequence of steps in the analysis, we first examine the data using a boxplot.

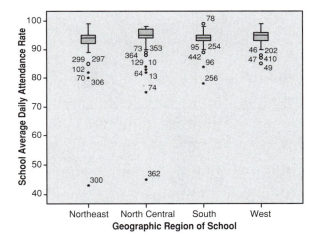

Although there are a number of extreme values per region to suggest skewness, there are two cases of particular concern: ID #64 and ID #396. From the NELS data set itself, we see that the schools that these students attended had average daily attendance rates of 45 and 43, respectively.

We have discussed two ways of handling such outliers. First, if the values are suspicious, it may make sense to eliminate them and report results based on two analyses, one with outliers excluded and another with outliers included. Second, a nonlinear transformation may be applied to reduce the influence of the outliers while using all of the available data in the analysis. Because secondary school attendance rates of 45 and 43 percent are suspiciously low, we have chosen here to conduct the analysis without these two cases.

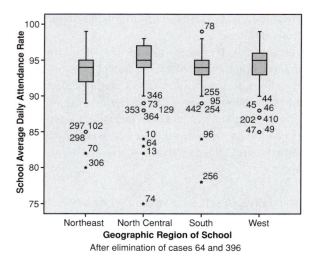

After elimination of cases 64 and 396

Once these two outliers are eliminated, the variances of the four regions appear to be reasonably homogeneous. Furthermore, the number of cases per region is sufficiently high for us not to be concerned about violations of the normality assumption. We note that although the vast majority of schools have a daily attendance rate in excess of 90 percent, there does appear to be some waiver in the actual levels of attendance by region. We turn to the ANOVA to determine whether this observed waiver is significant of differences among the respective population means or whether it may be attributable to random sampling error.

Descriptives

schattrt School Average Daily Attendance Rate

	N	Mean	Std. Deviation	Std. Error	95% Confidence Interval for Mean Lower Bound	95% Confidence Interval for Mean Upper Bound	Minimum	Maximum
1 Northeast	88	92.95	3.328	.355	92.25	93.66	80	99
2 North Central	129	94.40	3.372	.297	93.82	94.99	75	98
3 South	127	93.91	2.826	.251	93.42	94.41	78	99
4 West	71	94.07	3.067	.364	93.34	94.80	85	99
Total	415	93.89	3.184	.156	93.58	94.20	75	99

Test of Homogeneity of Variances

schattrt School Average Daily Attendance Rate

Levene Statistic	df1	df2	Sig.
.724	3	411	.538

ANOVA

schattrt School Average Daily Attendance Rate

	Sum of Squares	df	Mean Square	F	Sig.
Between Groups	113.349	3	37.783	3.803	.010
Within Groups	4083.552	411	9.936		
Total	4196.901	414			

Results suggest that, as expected, population variances are homogeneous, and there is a statistically significant difference among school mean daily attendance rates ($F(3,411) = 3.80$, $p = .01$). We note that, while the result is statistically significant, $R^2 = 113/4197 = .027$, indicating that only 3 percent of the variance in average daily attendance rate can be explained by region, a small-to-medium effect. Because the omnibus F-test is statistically significant, we seek to continue our analysis to find which specific means are statistically significantly different from which others. That is, starting with a global analysis of all four means considered simultaneously, we proceed to a local analysis that deals with comparisons between specific means taken pairwise. The results of the LSD and Tukey HSD post-hoc comparisons are provided in the following table.

Multiple Comparisons

Dependent Variable: schattrt School Average Daily Attendance Rate

	(I) region Geographic Region of School	(J) region Geographic Region of School	Mean Difference (I-J)	Std. Error	Sig.	95% Confidence Interval	
						Lower Bound	Upper Bound
Tukey HSD	1 Northeast	2 North Central	−1.449*	.436	.005	−2.57	−.32
		3 South	−.959	.437	.127	−2.09	.17
		4 West	−1.116	.503	.120	−2.41	.18
	2 North Central	1 Northeast	1.449*	.436	.005	.32	2.57
		3 South	.490	.394	.600	−.53	1.51
		4 West	.333	.466	.891	−.87	1.53
	3 South	1 Northeast	.959	.437	.127	−.17	2.09
		2 North Central	−.490	.394	.600	−1.51	.53
		4 West	−.157	.467	.987	−1.36	1.05
	4 West	1 Northeast	1.116	.503	.120	−.18	2.41
		2 North Central	−.333	.466	.891	−1.53	.87
		3 South	.157	.467	.987	−1.05	1.36
LSD	1 Northeast	2 North Central	−1.449*	.436	.001	−2.31	−.59
		3 South	−.959*	.437	.029	−1.82	−.10
		4 West	−1.116*	.503	.027	−2.10	−.13
	2 North Central	1 Northeast	1.449*	.436	.001	.59	2.31
		3 South	.490	.394	.215	−.28	1.26
		4 West	.333	.466	.475	−.58	1.25
	3 South	1 Northeast	.959*	.437	.029	.10	1.82
		2 North Central	−.490	.394	.215	−1.26	.28
		4 West	−.157	.467	.737	−1.08	.76
	4 West	1 Northeast	1.116*	.503	.027	.13	2.10
		2 North Central	−.333	.466	.475	−1.25	.58
		3 South	.157	.467	.737	−.76	1.08

*The mean difference is significant at the 0.5 level.

Notice that the HSD and LSD give different results. The HSD suggests that differences in school mean daily attendance rate are limited to the Northeast and North Central, and that the North Central, South, and West are not different from each other in this respect nor are the Northeast, South, and West. By contrast, the LSD, having greater power, suggests that not only is school attendance rate in the Northeast different from that in the North Central, but that it is also different from that in the West and South. In the HSD analysis, the Northeast stands apart from only the North Central; in the LSD analysis, the Northeast stands apart from all other regions, which cluster together in terms of mean school daily attendance rates. Which of these situations represents the truth?

Clearly, we can conclude that the school daily attendance rate in the Northeast is different from that in the North Central. Notice that these two regions occupy the extremes in a ranking of regions based on mean school daily attendance rates and that the difference between them equals a little bit more than one percentage point. Given that the difference between the North Central and South is only 0.5 percentage points, and the difference between the North Central and West is even less than that, we recommend following the more conservative HSD result – that there are no differences between these two pairs of regions. Whether this result represents the actual truth or not, our recommendation is based on a decision to be more rather than less conservative in our risk of committing a Type I error. It also takes into account the size of the effect – on how meaningful such differences are in substantive terms.

We note only small, nonsubstantive differences between the ANOVA results based on all values, including the two outliers that were eliminated from this analysis and on the set of values without the two outliers. By eliminating these outliers, we gained in variance stability without compromising the substantive conclusions of our findings.

☞ **Remark.** It sometimes happens that although the omnibus F-test is statistically significant, none of the post-hoc pairwise comparisons is statistically significant. Such contradictory results are due to the fact that our inferential estimates are subject to sampling error and that the omnibus F-test is more powerful than the multiple comparison tests that follow. Results based on the F-distribution, the sampling distribution of means for testing the null hypothesis that all K population means are equal, may not agree with results based on an appropriate, yet different, sampling distribution of means based on particular pairwise comparisons. To reduce the probability of such logically contradictory results, we need to reduce the effects of sampling error so that our estimates are more precise and our tests are more powerful. A natural way to do so is through the use of larger samples.

☞ **Remark.** Other logical inconsistencies arise from the presence of random sampling error, which would not arise if we were able to compute the population parameters directly from the entire population rather than from a random sample of that population. For example, we may observe, based on our sample data, that $\overline{X}_1 \neq \overline{X}_2 \neq \overline{X}_3$. After taking into account sampling error through the inferential process, we may conclude that $\mu_1 = \mu_2$ and that $\mu_2 = \mu_3$, but that $\mu_1 \neq \mu_3$. That is, the observed differences between $\overline{X}_1$ and $\overline{X}_2$, and between $\overline{X}_2$ and $\overline{X}_3$, are close enough to be attributable to random sampling error, whereas the observed difference between $\overline{X}_1$ and $\overline{X}_3$ is not. We may note that the inferred pattern of population mean differences appears to contradict the rule of transitivity: that things equal to the same thing are equal to each other. While μ_1 and μ_3 are both equal to μ_2, μ_1 and μ_3 are not equal to each other. The point simply is that, in the presence of sampling error, such logical inconsistencies are possible!

THE BONFERRONI ADJUSTMENT: TESTING PLANNED COMPARISONS

In each of the examples presented in this chapter, an ANOVA was used to test a *global hypothesis* about the equality of means. Following a significant omnibus F-test, and a review of the data obtained, post-hoc multiple comparison tests were then conducted to investigate whether any of the observed mean differences were statistically significant. Sometimes, however, *specific hypotheses* motivate a researcher to plan and conduct a particular study.

In our drug rehabilitation example, Treatments 1, 2, and 3 were described merely as different types of treatment that were suspected of having a differential effect on manual dexterity. Accordingly, the purpose of the study was to test a general hypothesis about the equality of population means associated with Treatments 1, 2, and 3. If, on the other hand, Treatment 3 had been designed as a control or placebo condition, our interest might naturally have focused on conducting only two specific comparisons – that of Treatments 1 and 2 against the control Treatment 3. In fact, in the initial planning of the design for this study, we might have designated Treatment 3 as the control or placebo so as to draw conclusions about these specific and presumably meaningful comparisons.

Specific comparisons that derive directly from the questions that motivate a researcher to plan a study in the first place are called *planned comparisons*. The use of planned comparisons is an alternative to the ANOVA that is made without regard to an omnibus *F*-test. Although the method of planned comparisons offers a direct method for testing the specific questions posed, its limitation is that it does not allow for other unanticipated questions to be addressed. For that, one requires the more general approach of the one-way ANOVA.

To carry out a test of planned comparisons, we must recognize the fact that planned comparisons are another form of multiple comparisons and, as such, give rise to an inflated family-wise Type I error rate. Without adjustment, α_{FW} for these two planned comparisons (Treatment 1 versus Treatment 3 and Treatment 2 versus Treatment 3) approximately equals $1 - (1 - .05)^2 = .0975$. A similar result is obtained from Equation 12.2, which states that α_{FW} is approximately equal to, albeit less than, $K\alpha$, where K is the number of planned comparisons. In this example, $K\alpha = 2(.05) = .10$.

Thus, we may use Equation 12.2 to adjust the overall family-wise Type I error to be equal to the desired level, say .05, by dividing .05 by K. We would then conduct each of the K planned comparisons at the new per-comparison error rate, α_{FW}/K, so as to maintain the overall α_{FW} at .05. For a comparison to be called statistically significant, the obtained *p*-value associated with this comparison must be less than α_{FW}/K. If $K = 3$ and we wish to maintain α_{FW} at .05, then each per-comparison α level must be set at $.05/3 = .017$. This adjustment to the per-comparison α level is called the *Bonferroni adjustment* because it is based on the equation developed by Bonferroni.

Clearly, the greater the number of planned comparisons, the smaller each per-comparison α must be to maintain α_{FW} at .05. Because the smaller the per-comparison α, the lower the power of each test, Bonferroni adjustments should be reserved for situations in which K is relatively small.

• •

EXAMPLE 12.7. Suppose that a series of recent publications in demography indicated that rural areas have lower socioeconomic status than either suburban or urban areas. Use planned comparisons to test whether this result is replicated in the NELS data set. Control the family-wise Type I error rate at 0.05.

Solution. To answer this question, we need to draw comparisons: rural SES with suburban SES, and rural SES with urban SES. These comparisons form a family of comparisons and each comparison may be tested using an independent group t-test. To control α_{FW} at 0.05, we use the Bonferroni adjustment and divide .05 by 2. Each pairwise comparison is conducted at 0.025. The results of the two t-tests are given in the following tables.

Group Statistics

	urban Urbanicity	N	Mean	Std. Deviation	Std. Error Mean
ses Socio-Economic Status	1 Urban	109	20.32	6.546	.627
	3 Rural	133	16.02	6.481	.562

Group Statistics

	urban Urbanicity	N	Mean	Std. Deviation	Std. Error Mean
ses Socio-Economic Status	2 Suburban	173	19.60	6.575	.500
	3 Rural	133	16.02	6.481	.562

Independent Samples Test

		Levene's Test for Equality of Variances		t-test for Equality of Means					95% Confidence Interval of the Difference	
		F	Sig.	t	df	Sig. (2-tailed)	Mean Difference	Std. Error Difference	Lower	Upper
ses Socio-Economic Status	Equal variances assumed	.009	.923	5.119	240	.000	4.306	.841	2.649	5.963
	Equal variances not assumed			5.114	229.851	.000	4.306	.842	2.647	5.965

Independent Samples Test

		Levene's Test for Equality of Variances		t-test for Equality of Means					95% Confidence Interval of the Difference	
		F	Sig.	t	df	Sig. (2-tailed)	Mean Difference	Std. Error Difference	Lower	Upper
ses Socio-Economic Status	Equal variances assumed	.191	.662	4.751	304	.000	3.580	.754	2.098	5.063
	Equal variances not assumed			4.760	286.084	.000	3.580	.752	2.100	5.061

Because both two-tailed p-values are $p < .0005$, the two corresponding one-tailed p-values are $p < .00025$. Because both observed p-values are less than $\dfrac{a}{2} = \dfrac{.05}{2} = .025$, the results reported in the literature are replicated using our NELS data set.

THE BONFERRONI TESTS ON MULTIPLE MEASURES

Another situation that calls for a Bonferroni adjustment to control the family-wise Type I error rate at a chosen value, say 0.05, arises when groups are compared on multiple measures. The following example illustrates the use of the Bonferroni adjustment in such contexts.

• •

EXAMPLE 12.8. Do males and females differ in twelfth-grade achievement in any of the four core areas: math, science, reading, and social studies? Use $\alpha = .05$.

Solution. Because the intent of this example is to compare males and females on these four core measures considered separately, a series of four independent group t-tests is appropriate. To avoid an inflated Type I error rate that would result if we were to conduct each of these multiple t-tests at $\alpha = 0.05$, we consider the four tests to be a family of tests and use a Bonferroni adjustment to maintain the family-wise error rate at 0.05. In particular, we conduct each of the four tests at $\alpha = \alpha_{FW}/4 = .05/4 = .0125$.

To check assumptions and get a sense of what our data look like, we obtain the following boxplots.

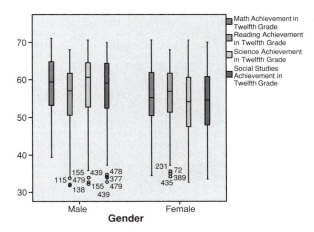

According to the boxplots, there are a few extremely low achievement scores. Given the large number of cases per group, however, such apparent departures from normality cannot be expected to compromise the validity of the t-statistic. The distributions also appear relatively homogeneous in their variances, despite the presence of extreme values in some of the groups. According to these boxplots, males generally score higher than females. The sample means and results are provided in the following tables.

Descriptives

		N	Mean	Std. Deviation	Std. Error
achmat12 Math Achievement in Twelfth Grade	0 Male	227	58.6333	7.42705	.49295
	1 Female	273	55.4709	7.97766	.48283
	Total	500	56.9066	7.88403	.35258
achrdg 12 Reading Achievement in Twelfth Grade	0 Male	227	55.3104	8.56015	.56816
	1 Female	273	55.8443	7.48037	.45273
	Total	500	55.6019	7.98492	.35710
achsci 12 Science Achievement in Twelfth Grade	0 Male	226	58.4203	8.08641	.53790
	1 Female	272	53.5605	8.33653	.50548
	Total	498	55.7659	8.56529	.38382
achsis 12 Social Studies Achievement in Twelfth Grade	0 Male	225	57.7460	8.34707	.55647
	1 Female	272	53.9483	8.39688	.50914
	Total	497	55.6676	8.57726	.38474

Independent Samples Test

		Levene's Test for Equality of Variances		t-test for Equality of Means						95% Confidence Interval of the Difference	
		F	Sig.	t	df	Sig. (2-tailed)	Mean Difference	Std. Error Difference	Lower	Upper
achmat 12 Math Achievement in Twelfth Grade	Equal variances assumed	.543	.462	4.553	498	.000	3.16234	.69457	1.79769	4.52700
	Equal variances not assumed			4.583	491.656	.000	3.16234	.69002	1.80660	4.51809
achrdg 12 Reading Achievement in Twelfth Grade	Equal variances assumed	4.127	.043	−.744	498	.457	−.53393	.71756	−1.94374	.87588
	Equal variances not assumed			−.735	452.527	.463	−.53393	.72648	−1.96162	.89375
achsci 12 Science Achievement in Twelfth Grade	Equal variances assumed	1.020	.313	6.565	496	.000	4.85983	.74022	3.40548	6.31418
	Equal variances not assumed			6.584	484.289	.000	4.85983	.73813	3.40949	6.31017
achsls 12 Social Studies Achievement in Twelfth Grade	Equal variances assumed	.214	.643	5.032	495	.000	3.79769	.75467	2.31495	5.28044
	Equal variances not assumed			5.035	478.713	.000	3.79769	.75424	2.31566	5.27972

According to results, males perform statistically significantly better than females in math $(t(498) = 4.55, p < .0005)$, science $(t(496) = 6.57, p < .0005)$, and social studies $(t(495) = 5.03, p < .0005)$. Statistically significant gender differences were not detected in reading achievement $(t(498) = .351, p = .73)$.

Figure 12.6 contains a flow chart for the one-way ANOVA.

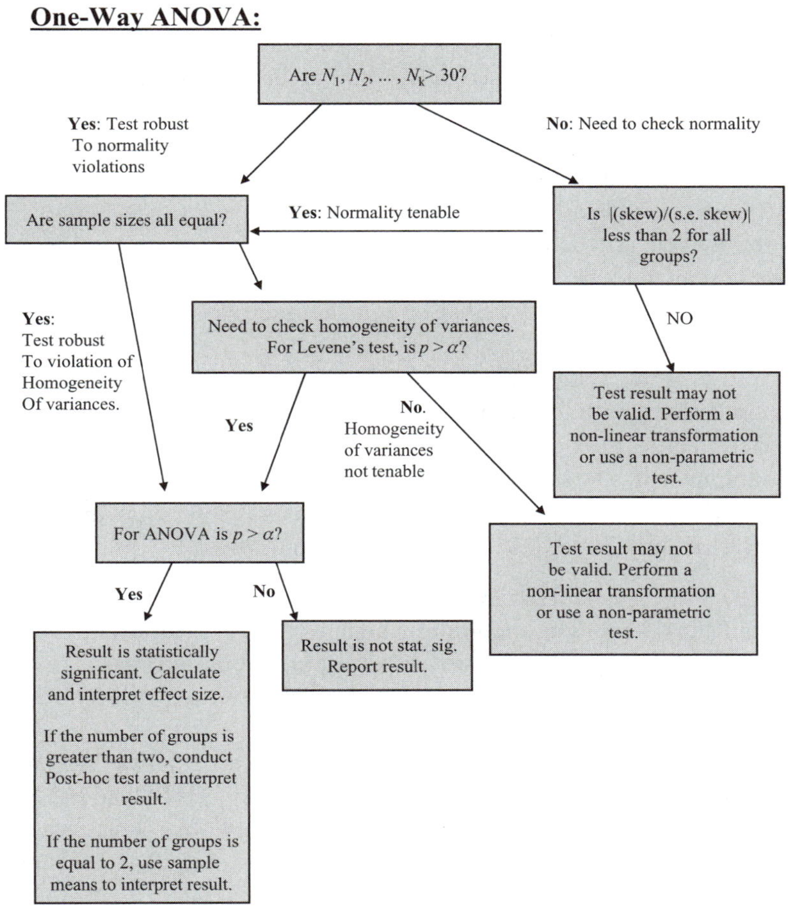

One-Way ANOVA:

Figure 12.6 Flow chart for one-way ANOVA.

EXERCISES

Exercises 12.1 through 12.7 involve one-way ANOVA using variables from the NELS data set. For inferential purposes, we consider the students in the data set to be a random sample of the population of all college-bound students who have always been at grade level. Use $\alpha = .05$ for all significance tests.

12.1. Does the average math achievement in eighth grade (ACHMAT08) of college-bound students who have always been at grade level vary as a function of whether they are enrolled in a rigorous academic, academic, or vocational and other high school program (HSPROG)? Use the following questions to guide your analysis.

a) Why is a one-way ANOVA appropriate to use to answer the question posed?

b) Based on the boxplots, do the assumptions underlying the one-way ANOVA appear tenable? What do you anticipate the results of the one-way ANOVA to be? Explain.

c) Evaluate the tenability of the normality assumption or indicate why the assumption is not an issue for this analysis – that the results of the test would not be compromised by a failure to meet this assumption.

d) Use Levene's test to evaluate the tenability of the homogeneity of variance assumption or indicate why the assumption is not an issue for this analysis – that the results of the ANOVA would not be compromised by a failure to meet this assumption.

e) State the null and alternative hypotheses for determining whether or not the average math achievement in eighth grade of college-bound students who always have been at grade level varies as a function of whether they are enrolled in a rigorous academic, academic, or vocational and other high school program.

f) What is the p-value associated with the one-way ANOVA for testing these null and alternative hypotheses?

g) Use the p-value to determine whether or not the null hypothesis can be rejected in favor of the alternative.

h) State the results of the ANOVA in context. That is, do the ANOVA results suggest that for this population, math achievement in eighth grade varies as a function of high school program type?

i) Calculate and interpret R^2 as a measure of effect size for the analysis.

j) Is it necessary to conduct a post-hoc test in this case? If so, report and interpret the results of the LSD and Tukey HSD tests. If not, explain why.

12.2. Does eighth-grade self-concept (SLFCNC08) of college-bound students who have always been at grade level vary as a function of whether they live in an urban, suburban, or rural setting (URBAN)? Use the following questions to guide your analysis.

a) Address the reason for choosing a one-way ANOVA over an independent samples t-test in this case.

b) Based on the boxplots, do the assumptions underlying the one-way ANOVA appear tenable? What do you anticipate the results of the one-way ANOVA to be? Explain.

c) Evaluate the tenability of the normality and homogeneity of variance assumption or indicate why these assumptions are not an issue for this analysis – that the results of the test would not be compromised by a failure to meet these assumptions.

d) Conduct the ANOVA and interpret your results in context.

e) Calculate and interpret R^2 as a measure of effect size for the analysis.

f) Is it necessary to conduct a post-hoc test in this case? If so, report and interpret the results of the LSD and Tukey HSD tests. If not, explain why.

g) Conduct the analysis based on a series of t-tests using the Bonferroni adjustment. Is the result obtained different from the one obtained through post-hoc testing?

12.3. Does the twelfth-grade math achievement (ACHMAT12) of college-bound students who have always been at grade level vary as a function of whether or not they ever tried cigarettes (CIGARETT)? Use the following questions to guide your analysis.

a) Based on the boxplots, do the assumptions underlying the one-way ANOVA appear tenable? What do you anticipate the results of the one-way ANOVA to be? Explain.

b) Evaluate the tenability of the underlying assumptions or indicate why these assumptions are not an issue for this analysis – that the results of the test would not be compromised by a failure to meet these assumptions.

c) Conduct the ANOVA and interpret your results in context.

d) Calculate and interpret R^2 as a measure of effect size for the analysis.

e) Is it necessary to conduct a post-hoc test in this case? If so, report and interpret the results of the LSD and Tukey HSD tests. If not, explain why.

f) Compare the results of the ANOVA to those of an independent samples *t*-test. Are they consistent? Is that what you would expect?

g) Could the one-way ANOVA have been used to determine whether, among college-bound students who are always at grade level, those who never smoked cigarettes have *better* twelfth-grade math achievement than those who smoked cigarettes at least once? Explain.

12.4. Perform a one-way ANOVA to determine whether for college-bound students who have always been at grade level the number of units of mathematics taken (UNITMATH) varies as a function of the highest degree the student anticipates earning (EDEXPECT).

a) Based on the boxplots, do the assumptions underlying the one-way ANOVA appear tenable? What do you anticipate the results of the one-way ANOVA to be? Explain.

b) Evaluate the tenability of the underlying assumptions or indicate why these assumptions are not an issue for this analysis – that the results of the test would not be compromised by a failure to meet these assumptions.

c) Conduct the ANOVA and interpret your results in context.

d) Calculate and interpret R^2 as a measure of effect size for the analysis.

e) Is it necessary to conduct a post-hoc test in this case? If so, report and interpret the results of the LSD and Tukey HSD tests. If not, explain why.

12.5. Perform a one-way ANOVA to determine whether, for college-bound students who have always been at grade level, there are differences in the average daily attendance rates (SCHATTRT) of the schools that smokers attended and those that nonsmokers attended (CIGARETT).

a) Based on the boxplots, do the assumptions underlying the one-way ANOVA appear tenable? What do you anticipate the results of the one-way ANOVA to be? Explain.

b) Evaluate the tenability of the underlying assumptions or indicate why these assumptions are not an issue for this analysis – that the results of the test would not be compromised by a failure to meet these assumptions.

c) Conduct the ANOVA and interpret your results in context.

d) Is it necessary to conduct a post-hoc test in this case? If so, report and interpret the results of the LSD and Tukey HSD tests. If not, explain why.

e) If a *t*-test had been carried out instead with a directional alternative hypothesis (that smokers have a lower school attendance rate than nonsmokers), would results have been statistically significant?

12.6. For each of the following questions based on the NELS data set, conduct a one-way ANOVA or explain why a different analysis should be used to answer the research question posed.

a) Among college-bound students who are always at grade level, do those who attended nursery school (NURSERY) tend to have higher SES, on average, than those who did not?

b) Among college-bound students who are always at grade level, does twelfth-grade reading achievement (ACHRDG12) vary by home language background (HOMELANG)?

c) Among college-bound students who are always at grade level, do students tend to take more years of English (UNITENGL) or math (UNITMATH)?

d) Among college-bound students who are always at grade level, does computer ownership (COMPUTER) vary by home language background (HOMELANG)?

e) Among college-bound students who are always at grade level, do those who take advanced math in eighth grade (ADVMAT08) tend to have better attendance in twelfth grade (ABSENT12) than those who do not?

f) Among college-bound students who are always at grade level, are there regional differences (REGION) in the size of the family (FAMSIZE), on average?

g) Does the average twelfth-grade self-concept (SLFCNC12) of college-bound students who have always been at grade level vary as a function of the population density of their environment (URBAN)?

12.7. At the end of Chapter 3, a descriptive analysis was performed to determine the extent to which eighth-grade males expect larger incomes at age 30 (EXPINC30) than eighth-grade females. Explain why an inferential analysis based on the one-way ANOVA would not be appropriate to answer this question, by indicating which underlying assumptions are violated.

Exercise 12.8 involves selection of appropriate tests of means.

12.8. For each of the following questions based on the Learndis data set, select a statistical procedure from the folowing list that would be appropriate for answering that question. For inferential purposes, we consider the children in the data set to be a random sample of all children attending public elementary school in a certain city who have been diagnosed with learning disabilities.

(1) One-tailed, one-sample *t*-test.
(2) Two-tailed, one-sample *t*-test.
(3) One-tailed, independent samples *t*-test.
(4) Two-tailed, independent samples *t*-test.
(5) One-tailed, paired samples *t*-test.
(6) Two-tailed, paired samples *t*-test.
(7) One-way ANOVA.

a) Do public elementary school females diagnosed with learning disabilities in New York City perform better in reading comprehension than males drawn from the same population of children with learning disabilities?

b) Is the average IQ of public school children with learning disabilities in New York City equal to 100?

c) Do public school children with learning disabilities in New York City have higher math comprehension scores or reading comprehension scores?

d) Are there differences in math comprehension by grade?

e) Do public school children with learning disabilities in New York City have higher math comprehension scores than reading comprehension scores?

Exercises 12.9 and 12.10 may be used to practice calculations by hand.

12.9. A recent study was conducted on levels of tryptophan, a naturally occurring amino acid that is used by the body to produce serotonin, a mood and appetite-regulating chemical in the brain. The study sought to determine whether bulimics, recovering bulimics, and a control group of people without bulimia differed in their levels of this amino acid. Suppose that 40 individuals from each of the three populations were randomly selected and that the observed group means were 20, 28, and 30, respectively. Complete the ANOVA summary table. Interpret results as best as can be expected with the information available.

ANOVA

	Sum of Squares	df	Mean Square	F	Sig.
Between groups	2,240				
Within groups	26,208				
Total					

12.10. In an effort to improve their program for teaching students how to speak French, Western Ohio University language instructors conducted the following experiment. They randomly selected 20 students from all those who registered to take first-term spoken French and randomly divided them into four groups of five students each. Group 1 is taught French the traditional, lecture-recitation way; Group 2 is taught French from a programmed text; Group 3 is taught French from tape-recorded lessons; and Group 4 is taught French from films of people and life in France. At the end of the semester, all 20 students are given the same oral final examination on ability to speak French. The following scores are recorded.

Group 1	Group 2	Group 3	Group 4
75	68	80	87
70	73	65	90
90	70	70	85
80	60	68	75
75	65	72	80

a) Use these data to perform a test at $\alpha = .05$ to determine whether, in general, these four teaching methods have differential mean effects on ability to speak French.

b) Is it appropriate now to perform a Tukey test to determine specific differences between means? If so, perform the Tukey test and describe the results.

CHAPTER THIRTEEN

Two-Way Analysis of Variance

In Chapter 12 we introduced a method for analyzing mean differences on a single dependent variable between two or more independent groups while controlling the risk of making a Type I error at some specified α level. We explained the connection between the method and its name, analysis of variance (ANOVA), and showed how the method was a generalization of the independent group t-test.

The examples presented were concerned with determining whether the observed variance of the dependent variable (e.g., manual dexterity variance or self-concept variance) was related to a single grouping variable (e.g., gender or type of high school program). The examples were also concerned with determining the proportion of the dependent variable variance that was explained by that grouping variable.

Because, in practice, a single grouping variable is not sufficient to explain all dependent-variable variance, we can expect some unexplained portion of dependent-variable variance to remain after taking into account the grouping variable. A second grouping variable is often included in a design in an attempt to explain additional residual dependent-variable variance and to gain further insight into the nature of the dependent variable.

In this chapter we introduce a method called two-way ANOVA that is an extension of one-way ANOVA to designs that contain two grouping or independent variables. The two-way ANOVA is used to assess mean differences through an analysis of dependent-variable variance explained by the two grouping variables. The method also assesses the amount of variance explained by each of the two grouping variables and by something called the interaction between the two grouping variables. The concept of interaction is an important one and is explained in some detail later in this chapter.

THE TWO-FACTOR DESIGN

In the introductory example of Chapter 12, we were interested in comparing the effects of three methods of therapeutic treatment on manual dexterity for a specified population. Thirty individuals were selected randomly from the specified population. Each was then assigned randomly to one of the three treatments, resulting in 10 individuals per treatment. After five weeks in the treatment, all 30 were administered the Stanford Test of Manual Dexterity. The scores obtained on this measure are reproduced in Table 13.1.

Under the assumption that all three populations were normally distributed and had equal variances, we used a one-way ANOVA to test the equality of all three population means and obtained $F(2,27) = 19.5$, $p < .0005$. Given this result we concluded that not all population means were equal. We also described the effect size for treatment. Treatment accounted for 59 percent of manual dexterity variance. But although treatment accounted for an extremely large proportion of manual dexterity variance, it left 41 percent of this variance unexplained.

In this chapter we consider the importance of a second variable, gender, in explaining additional residual manual dexterity variance. Accordingly, we note which of the 30 individuals in our data set are male and which are female and reorganize the 30 scores into a two-dimensional table (gender by treatment) as shown in Figure 13.1.

Figure 13.1 has two rows and three columns. The row dimension represents the grouping variable (or *factor*), gender,

Table 13.1. Scores on the Stanford Test of Manual Dexterity by treatment group

Treatment 1	Treatment 2	Treatment 3
6	4	6
10	2	2
8	3	2
6	5	6
9	1	4
8	3	5
7	2	3
5	2	5
6	4	3
5	4	4

and the column dimension represents the grouping variable (or factor), treatment. Each row represents a category, or *level*, of gender and each column represents a category, or level, of treatment. Each of the six cells in the design represents a unique combination of a level of the gender factor and a level of the treatment factor. For example, the upper left-hand cell represents all subjects in the sample who are male and who received Treatment 1.

Because all unique combinations of factor levels are represented in this design (males receive all levels of treatment, 1, 2, and 3, as do all females), we call such designs *crossed*. In crossed designs, we may multiply the number of levels of one factor by the number of levels of the second factor to determine the total number of cells in the design. In this example, we multiply 2 by 3 to obtain 6 cells. Because each dimension in the design is defined by a separate factor, such designs also are referred to as *factorial designs*. Taken together, we may say that Figure 13.1 represents a 2×3 (read as "two by three") *crossed factorial design*, where 2 refers to the number of levels of the row factor (gender) and 3 refers to the number of levels of the column factor (treatment). We may say also that Figure 13.1 represents a *two-way ANOVA design*.

We assume for simplicity that each treatment group of 10 individuals contains 5 males and 5 females and that the reorganized raw scores and means are shown in Table 13.2.

☞ **Remark.** We have assumed for simplicity that there are equal numbers of males and females in each treatment. In reality, however, if we were interested in using gender as a second factor, we would design the study so that equal numbers of males and females would be assigned to each treatment. In particular, we would randomly select equal numbers of males and females from their respective populations and then randomly assign equal numbers of each to each treatment condition. Such designs are called *randomized blocks designs*. In this case, each gender defines a block. For additional information on such designs, the interested reader is referred to Keppel (1991).

Figure 13.1 A schematic of a 2×3 factorial design.

	Treatment 1	Treatment 2	Treatment 3
Male			
Female			

Table 13.2. A 2 × 3 crossed factorial design using the data of Table 13.1

	Treatment 1	Treatment 2	Treatment 3	
Male	10, 9, 8, 8, 7 $\overline{X}_{11} = 8.4$	5, 4, 3, 2, 1 $\overline{X}_{12} = 3$	4, 3, 3, 2, 2 $\overline{X}_{13} = 2.8$	Row 1 Mean = 4.73
Female	6, 6, 6, 5, 5 $\overline{X}_{21} = 5.6$	4, 4, 3, 2, 2 $\overline{X}_{22} = 3$	6, 6, 5, 5, 4 $\overline{X}_{23} = 5.2$	Row 2 Mean = 4.60
	Col. 1 Mean = 7.0	Col. 2 Mean = 3.0	Col. 3 Mean = 4.0	Overall Mean = 4.67

To enter the data into SPSS, we require three variables, or columns: one for treatment, one for gender, and one for score. The data as they are displayed by SPSS are given in Table 13.3. We call the treatment variable TREATMEN. For the variable GENDER, 1 represents male and 2 represents female.

Table 13.3. SPSS representation of the data set of Table 13.2 (for GENDER, 1 represents male and 2 represents female)

TREATMEN	GENDER	SCORE
1	1	10
1	1	9
1	1	8
1	1	8
1	1	7
1	2	6
1	2	6
1	2	6
1	2	5
1	2	5
2	1	5
2	1	4
2	1	3
2	1	2
2	1	1
2	2	4
2	2	4
2	2	3
2	2	2
2	2	2
3	1	4
3	1	3
3	1	3
3	1	2
3	1	2
3	2	6
3	2	6
3	2	5
3	2	5
3	2	4

To calculate the six individual cell means, the two row means, the three column means, and the overall mean using SPSS, click on **Analyze**, **Compare Means**, **Means**. Put SCORE in the **Dependent List** box and TREATMEN in the **Independent List** box. Click **Next**. Put GENDER in the **Independent List** box. Click **OK**.

The resulting output is reproduced as Table 13.4.

There are six individual cell means in Table 13.2 (8.4, 3.0, 2.8, 5.6, 3.0, and 5.2). There are also two row means (4.7 and 4.6), three column means (7.0, 3.0, and 4.0), and an overall or *grand mean* (4.65).

Each of the six individual cell means equals the mean on the manual dexterity test of the five subjects in that particular cell. For example, 8.4 equals the manual dexterity mean of the five male subjects who received Treatment 1.

Each row mean, also called a *row marginal mean* because it appears in the row margin of the table, equals the mean on the manual dexterity test of those subjects in that particular row. For example, the row marginal mean of 4.7 equals the manual dexterity mean of the 15 male subjects. Alternatively, it equals the mean of the three cell means for males. In computing the row mean, we ignore the treatment the subjects received and consider only the row they are in.

Table 13.4. Summary statistics associated with the data set of Table 13.2

Report

Manual Dexterity Score

Treatment	Gender	Mean	N	Std. Deviation
Treatment 1	Male	7.80	5	1.789
	Female	6.20	5	1.304
	Total	7.00	10	1.700
Treatment 2	Male	3.00	5	1.581
	Female	3.00	5	1.000
	Total	3.00	10	1.247
Treatment 3	Male	4.00	5	2.000
	Female	4.00	5	1.000
	Total	4.00	10	1.491
Total	Male	4.93	15	2.712
	Female	4.40	15	1.724
	Total	4.67	30	2.249

Analogously, each column marginal mean equals the mean on the manual dexterity test of those subjects in that particular column. For example, the column marginal mean of 7.0 equals the manual dexterity mean of the 10 subjects who received Treatment 1. In computing the column mean, we ignore the sex of the subject and consider only the column they are in.

Finally, the overall or grand mean equals the mean on the manual dexterity test of all subjects in the study. In this example, it is the manual dexterity mean based on the 30 subjects.

If we ignore row distinctions and consider only the columns, we have all the information necessary to conduct a one-way ANOVA on manual dexterity to evaluate the effect due to treatment. Analogously, if we ignore column distinctions, and consider only the rows, we have all the information necessary to conduct a one-way ANOVA on gender to evaluate the effect due to gender. In the context of two-way ANOVA, the effects due to treatment and gender are called *main effects* because each is evaluated "in the main," ignoring the effect of the other factor. Thus, a two-factor design contains all the information necessary to conduct two separate one-way ANOVAs on the two different factors, respectively. It also contains additional information that tells how the two factors interact with each other in terms of the dependent variable.

THE CONCEPT OF INTERACTION

We note that the row marginal mean for males is 4.7 and the row marginal mean for females is 4.6. A comparison of these two values suggests that the mean manual dexterity score for males is similar to the mean manual dexterity score for females; that is, there is no main effect for gender. Because row marginal means represent averaged effects, averaged over all columns in that row, they do not reflect the variation in means contained in that row. By extension, a comparison of row marginal means does not reflect the variation in male–female mean comparisons by treatment. Whereas males and females may be quite similar on average in terms of manual dexterity, it may be that males do better than females under some treatments and worse under others or it may be that their relative performance is constant for all treatments. Only by making such treatment-by-treatment comparisons between males and females can we gain access to this important information that is carried by the individual cells of the table.

Based on the cell means of Table 13.2, we observe for Treatment 1 that males have a substantially higher mean than females (8.4 versus 5.6); for Treatment 2, males and females have the same mean (3.0 versus 3.0); and for Treatment 3, males have a substantially lower mean than females (2.8 versus 5.2). To show the situation more clearly, we present a line graph of these six means in Figure 13.2. The vertical axis of the graph contains a scale of manual dexterity means; the horizontal axis represents the levels of treatment and each line represents a gender type.

To create a line graph of means to illustrate the two-way ANOVA, click **Graphs**, **Legacy Dialogs, Line**, and click **Multiple**, but leave the data in the chart as summaries for groups of cases. Click **Define**. In the **Lines represent** box, click the circle next to **Other summary function** and move the variable SCORE into the box. Put TREATMEN as the **Category** axis and **Define Lines by** GENDER. Click **OK**. Alternatively, you can put GENDER as the **Category** axis and **Define Lines by** TREATMEN, if you prefer that representation of the data.

From Figure 13.2 it is clear that *treatments do not have a constant effect on manual dexterity performance for males and females*. If an individual were to be assigned to a particular treatment (1, 2, or 3) for optimal manual dexterity, one would want to know the gender of the individual before making that assignment. Said differently, if one were to ask, "To which treatment should we assign an individual?" the answer would be "It depends on whether the individual is male or female." If male, the individual would be assigned to

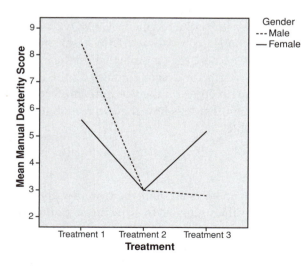

Figure 13.2 Male and female performance by treatment level: an example of a disordinal interaction.

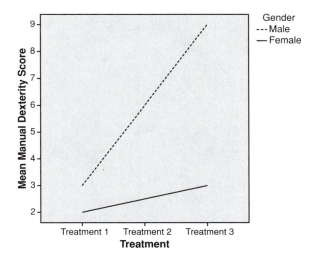

Figure 13.3 Male and female performance by treatment level: an example of an ordinal interaction.

Treatment 1; if female, the individual would be assigned to Treatment 1 or, perhaps, Treatment 3.

Whenever the relative effects of one factor (e.g., Treatment) change across the levels of the other factor (e.g., males and females), we have what is called an *interaction* between the two factors. The particular type of interaction illustrated in Figure 13.2 is called a *disordinal interaction* because the lines actually cross in the graph. That is, relative to females, males do better under Treatment 1, they do the same under Treatment 2, and they do worse under Treatment 3. If we computed the difference between the male and female manual dexterity means for each treatment, we would find that these differences change from positive $(8.4 - 5.6 = 2.8)$ to zero $(3.0 - 3.0 = 0)$ to negative $(2.8 - 5.2 = -2.4)$. Mean differences between levels of one factor computed at each level of the second factor always change sign when interactions are disordinal.

Not all interactions are disordinal, however. Figure 13.3 depicts a different set of sample means that illustrates what is called an *ordinal* interaction. In this case, while the relative effects of one factor change across the levels of the other factor, the lines maintain their ordinality; that is, one line remains higher than the other line across all levels of the second factor; the lines do not cross in the graph. As shown in Figure 13.3, males perform better than females under all treatments and their relative superiority on the manual dexterity test increases as treatments change from Treatment 1 to 2 to 3.

☞ **Remark.** In describing the interactions of Figures 13.2 and 13.3 we may say that *there is an interaction between gender and treatment on manual dexterity*. In so doing, we recognize the role of three variables in defining a two-way interaction: the two independent variables or factors (e.g., gender and treatment) and the dependent variable (e.g., manual dexterity).

If, on the other hand, the relative effects of one factor are constant across the levels of the other factor, then we say that there is no interaction between the two factors. Figures 13.4(a) through (d) illustrate four possible scenarios of no interaction in the context of our 2 × 3 factorial design. Assume that these scenarios represent population

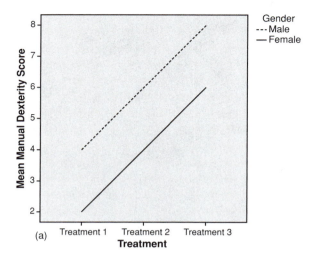

Figure 13.4(a)   Line graph depicting no interaction.

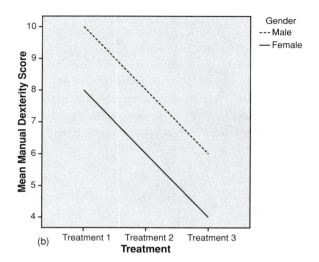

Figure 13.4(b)   Line graph depicting no interaction.

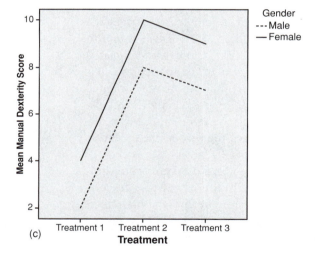

Figure 13.4(c)   Line graph depicting no interaction.

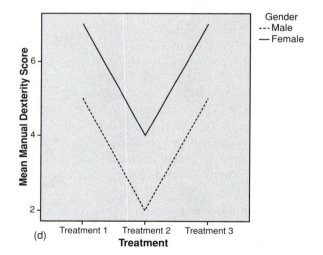

Figure 13.4(d)   Line graph depicting no interaction.

means that are, therefore, not subject to sampling error. We may observe that Figures 13.4(a) through (d) share a common feature: all line segments are equidistant from each other; that is, they are parallel.

Notice that, in the absence of an interaction, we would *not* need to take into account gender before assigning an individual to a particular treatment because the pattern of manual dexterity performance remains the same for males and females across all treatments. Figure 13.4(a) illustrates the situation in which males perform better than females across all treatments. Also, males and females have the same pattern of performance across all levels of treatment. Figures 13.4(b) through (d) illustrate other possible outcomes. The point is that, in the absence of an interaction, we do not need to qualify the relative effectiveness of treatments by gender or qualify the relative performance of males and females by the treatment they received. Effects are constant in both directions.

The distances between line segments may be expressed as mean differences in terms of manual dexterity between males and females at Treatment 1 as $\overline{X}_{11} - \overline{X}_{21}$, at Treatment 2 as $\overline{X}_{12} - \overline{X}_{22}$, and at Treatment 3 as $\overline{X}_{13} - \overline{X}_{23}$. When these differences are all equal, all line segments are parallel and there is no interaction. When any two are not equal, all line segments are not parallel and there is an interaction. Thus, a two-way interaction may be observed when the mean differences computed between the levels of one factor for each level of the second factor are not all equal. Alternatively, when there is an interaction between factors, differences between the mean differences are different!

☞ **Remark.** We have used line graphs to depict interaction effects. Although this is standard practice because the horizontal axis reflects a nominal-leveled variable (i.e., Treatment), one should be cautioned against reading a trend into the result. For example, in Figure 13.4(a) one might be tempted to conclude that manual dexterity increases at a constant rate across treatments for males and females because of the use of line segments in the graph. To avoid possible misinterpretations of this kind, researchers sometimes use clustered bar graphs to display interaction effects involving nominal-leveled variables. Figure 13.5 displays a clustered bar graph as an alternative to Figure 13.4(a). The equal distances between line segments in Figure 13.4(a), characteristic of no interaction, are represented as equal differences between bar heights within clusters in Figure 13.5. By analogy, when an interaction is present, a clustered bar graph would show unequal differences between bar heights within clusters. The decision to use line graphs or clustered bar graphs to display interactions is entirely up to the researcher.

Our discussion thus far has assumed no sampling variability; in particular, a difference in sample means implies a difference in population means as well. When sampling variability is present, however, lines do not need to be perfectly parallel to imply no interaction, and marginal means do not need to be perfectly equal to imply no main effects. Deviation

Figure 13.5 A clustered bar graph alternative to Figure 13.4(a).

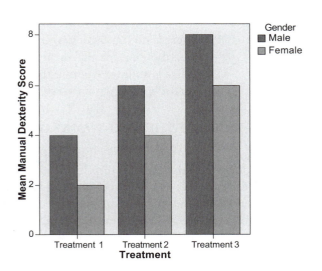

from parallelism and marginal mean equality due to sampling variability may be present. To determine whether an observed interaction between factors or an observed difference between marginal means is large enough in practice to rule out sampling variability and to suggest, therefore, an interaction or main effect in the population, we rely on the two-way ANOVA procedure.

THE HYPOTHESES THAT ARE TESTED BY A TWO-WAY ANALYSIS OF VARIANCE

Three separate hypotheses are tested by a two-way ANOVA: a row main effect, a column main effect, and an interaction between the two factors, each at significance level α.

The test of the row main effect is a test of the equality of row marginal means in the population. In our example, it is a test of whether the mean manual dexterity score for males equals that for females in the population. The null and alternative hypotheses for this example are

$$H_0: {}_R\mu_1 = {}_R\mu_2,$$
$$H_1: {}_R\mu_1 \neq {}_R\mu_2$$

where R represents row, ${}_R\mu_1$ represents the row marginal mean for row 1 (males), and ${}_R\mu_2$ represents the row marginal mean for row 2 (females).

The test of the column main effect is a test of the equality of column marginal means in the population. In our example, it is a test of whether the mean manual dexterity score for Treatment 1 equals that for Treatment 2, which in turn equals that for Treatment 3. The null and alternative hypotheses are

$$H_0: {}_C\mu_1 = {}_C\mu_2 = {}_C\mu_3$$
$$H_1: \text{not } H_0,$$

where C represents column, ${}_C\mu_1$ represents the column marginal mean for column 1 (Treatment 1), and so on.

The null and alternative hypotheses for the test of the 2×3 (Gender $\times$ Treatment) interaction may be expressed simply as follows:

> H_0: There is no interaction in the population between the effects of Gender and Treatment on manual dexterity.
> H_1: There is an interaction in the population between the effects of Gender and Treatment on manual dexterity.

ASSUMPTIONS OF THE TWO-WAY ANOVA

As in the one-way ANOVA model of Chapter 12, in this chapter the two-way ANOVA model is based on the assumption that the scores are independent. Scores are independent if, for example, each score is from a separate individual who has been randomly assigned to one of the treatment conditions of the design. In addition, like the one-way ANOVA, the two-way ANOVA model makes distributional assumptions about the scores within each group. In a one-way ANOVA, within-group distributions consist of the sample of scores within each level of the single factor (e.g., scores within Treatment 1, scores within

Treatment 2, and scores within Treatment 3). By extension, in a two-way ANOVA, within-group distributions consist of the sample of scores within each combination of factors (i.e., within each cell of the two-way design). The six within-cell distributions in our working example are the distributions of male scores within Treatment 1, male scores within Treatment 2, male scores within Treatment 3, female scores within Treatment 1, female scores within Treatment 2, and female scores within Treatment 3. In the two-way ANOVA, all within-cell samples of scores are assumed to come from populations that are normally distributed with equal variances. Considerations that deal with violations of these assumptions are discussed in Chapter 12 and also apply to the two-way ANOVA.

Prior to conducting a two-way ANOVA on the data in Table 13.2, an evaluation of the underlying assumptions of the analysis is performed.

The scores are independent because each score is from a separate individual who has been randomly assigned to one of the treatment conditions of the design.

Because we have fewer than 30 subjects in each cell, we evaluate the viability of the assumption that the within-cell samples of scores come from populations that are normally distributed.

To test the within-cell normality assumption using SPSS, we split the file and compare groups by GENDER and by TREATMEN. Then we use the Descriptives procedure to find the skewness of the manual dexterity scores. The resulting output is reproduced in the table that follows.

Descriptive Statistics

| | | | N | Skewness | |
			Statistic	Statistic	Std. Error
Treatment	Gender				
Treatment 1	Male	Manual Dexterity Score	5	.405	.913
		Valid N (listwise)	5		
	Female	Manual Dexterity Score	5	−.609	.913
		Valid N (listwise)	5		
Treatment 2	Male	Manual Dexterity Score	5	.000	.913
		Valid N (listwise)	5		
	Female	Manual Dexterity Score	5	.000	.913
		Valid N (listwise)	5		
Treatment 3	Male	Manual Dexterity Score	5	.512	.913
		Valid N (listwise)	5		
	Female	Manual Dexterity Score	5	−.512	.913
		Valid N (listwise)	5		

Looking at the skewness divided by the standard error for each of the cells, we see that all ratios are less than 2 in magnitude, indicating that the normality assumption is tenable.

Because the cell sizes are equal (there are 5 research participants in each cell), the two-way ANOVA is robust to violations of the homogeneity of variance assumption, so the assumption is not evaluated.

BALANCED VERSUS UNBALANCED FACTORIAL DESIGNS

In the one-way ANOVA, no restriction was placed on the relative sizes of the samples that comprised each level of the factor studied. The model, as described, allowed for either equal or unequal cell sizes. The model presented in this chapter for two-way ANOVA is based on the assumption that the number of subjects in each cell is equal; this is to ensure that the design is *balanced* (or *orthogonal*). An advantage of balanced designs is that they allow us to consider the two main effects as separate entities, which may be tested without regard to each other. For example, the results pertaining to one main effect may be interpreted without regard to the results pertaining to the other main effect. Said differently, the sum of squares due to each main effect in a two-way balanced design equals the sum of squares due to each main effect if each main effect were analyzed separately in a one-way design.

Analytical approaches different from those presented in this chapter are required when applying the two-way ANOVA to nonorthogonal or unbalanced designs. We touch on some of the more complicated issues that arise in connection with unbalanced designs in Chapter 15 when we discuss multiple regression.

PARTITIONING THE TOTAL SUM OF SQUARES

In Chapter 12, we pointed out that one-way ANOVA partitions the total variability (SS_T) of our dependent variable into two unrelated (orthogonal) components: variability due to the between-group effect (SS_B) and variability that remains unexplained within group after the between-group effect is accounted for (SS_W). Equation 13.1 uses the context of our working example to express the partitioning of the total manual dexterity sum of squares in a one-way design into a sum of squares due to Treatment and a sum of squares due to what remains within the group once Treatment is accounted for:

$$SS_T = SS_{TREAT} + SS_{WITHIN-GROUP}$$
$$146.67 = 86.67 + 60.00. \tag{13.1}$$

In an analogous way, two-way ANOVA also partitions the total sum of squares into unrelated (orthogonal) component parts. In the case of the two-way design of our working example, these components of variability are due to Treatment, Gender, the Gender-by-Treatment interaction, and what remains unexplained within cell after all these sources of variation are accounted for. Equation 13.2 expresses this breakdown of variability for the two-way design:

$$SS_T = SS_{TREAT} + \underbrace{SS_{GENDER} + SS_{INTER} + SS_{WITHIN-CELL}}$$
$$146.67 = 86.67 \quad + \qquad\qquad 60 \tag{13.2}$$

Notice that, because in both models the SS_T is equal to the sum of squares based on the whole set of 30 manual dexterity scores without regard to any grouping variable, the value of SS_T remains the same in both models (146.67). Analogously, because SS_{TREAT} in the two-way ANOVA continues to equal the sum of squared deviations of the three treatment means about the grand mean without regard to gender, its value in the two-way ANOVA is the same as in the one-way ANOVA (86.67).

In the two-way design, the addition of the second factor – Gender – allows for the opportunity to explain more of the 60 units of residual variability that is left unexplained in the one-way design. According to Equation 13.2, the sum of SS_{GENDER}, SS_{INTER} and $SS_{WITHIN-CELL}$ equals 60. If neither Gender nor the interaction between Gender and Treatment accounts for any additional residual variability, then SS_W remains at 60, and there is nothing gained by using the two-way design. In general, the degree to which we gain in explanatory power from using the two-way design relates to the amount by which the residual variability left unexplained in the one-way design can be reduced by the additional sources of variation, Gender and Gender by Treatment, in the two-way design.

USING THE *F*-RATIO TO TEST THE EFFECTS IN TWO-WAY ANOVA

To test whether each of the three sources of variation (main effect due to Treatment, main effect due to Gender, and interaction effect due to Gender and Treatment) explains a statistically significant proportion of total variance (that is, a proportion that is not attributable to chance), we carry out a series of three *F*-tests as shown in Table 13.5, each at a specified α-level. As in the one-way ANOVA, the denominator of each *F*-test is based on the leftover, residual variance, denoted MS_W, and the numerator of each *F*-test is based on one of the three between-group variances defined by its respective source of variation. As before, the degrees of freedom for a main effect equals one less than the number of groups for that main effect (e.g., $R - 1$ for the row main effect). The degrees of freedom for the interaction effect equals the product of $R - 1$ and $C - 1$. The degrees of freedom for the error or within-cell effect equals $N - RC$, the total sample size less the total number of cells in the design represented as the product of the number of rows by the number of columns (RC). Finally, the total degrees of freedom equals $N - 1$. We may note that the degrees of freedom for the separate effects in the design sum to the total degrees of freedom for the design (that is, $R - 1 + C - 1 + (R - 1)(C - 1) + N - RC = N - 1$).

Table 13.5 shows how the *F*-ratios are formed to construct the respective *F*-tests beginning with the *SS* terms. In the next section, we describe within a conceptual framework how these *SS* terms are generated and we carry out the two-way ANOVA by hand using our manual dexterity example.

Table 13.5. Forming *F*-ratios in a two-way ANOVA design with a row and column factor

Source of Variation	SS	df	MS	F-Ratio
Factor R	SS_R	$R - 1$	$MS_R = SS_R/(R - 1)$	MS_R/MS_W
Factor C	SS_C	$C - 1$	$MS_C = SS_C/(C - 1)$	MS_C/MS_W
$R \times C$ Interaction	$SS_{R \times C}$	$(R - 1)(C - 1)$	$MS_{R \times C} = SS_{R \times C}/(R - 1)(C - 1)$	$MS_{R \times C}/MS_W$
Within cells	SS_W	$N - RC$		
Total	SS_T	$N - 1$		

CARRYING OUT THE TWO-WAY ANOVA COMPUTATION BY HAND

The manual dexterity scores of the 30 individuals, organized by the two factors of the two-way design, are given again as Table 13.6.

The sum of squares associated with the row effect, SS_R, is given by Equation 13.3:

$$SS_R = \sum_{i=1}^{r} {}_RN_i\left({}_R\overline{X}_i - \overline{\overline{X}}^2\right) \tag{13.3}$$

where r represents the number of levels of the row factor, ${}_RN_i$ equals the number of values in row i, ${}_R\overline{X}_i$ equals the mean of the values in row i, and $\overline{\overline{X}}$ equals the overall or grand mean of all values in the sample.

Using Equation 13.3, we compute SS_R for the manual dexterity example:

$${}_RN_1 = {}_RN_2 = 15; \; {}_R\overline{X}_1 = 4.73, \; {}_R\overline{X}_2 = 4.60; \overline{\overline{X}} = 4.67; r = 2.$$

$$SS_R = 15(4.6 - 4.67)^2 + 15(4.7 - 4.67)^2 = 0.13.$$

The sum of squares associated with the column effect, SS_C, is given by Equation 13.4:

$$SS_C = \sum_{j=1}^{c} {}_CN_j({}_C\overline{X}_j - \overline{\overline{X}})^2, \tag{13.4}$$

where c represents the number of levels of the column factor, ${}_CN_j$ equals the number of values in column j, ${}_C\overline{X}_j$ equals the mean of the values in column j, and $\overline{\overline{X}}$ equals the overall or grand mean of all values in the sample.

Using Equation 13.4, we compute SS_C for the manual dexterity example:

$${}_CN_1 = {}_CN_2 = {}_CN_3 = 10; \; {}_C\overline{X}_1 = 7.0, \; {}_C\overline{X}_2 = 3.0, \; {}_C\overline{X}_3 = 4.0; \overline{\overline{X}} = 4.67; c = 3.$$

$$SS_C = 10(7 - 4.67)^2 + 10(3 - 4.67)^2 + 10(4 - 4.67)^2 = 86.67.$$

The sum of squares associated with the interaction effect, $SS_{R \times C}$, is given by Equation 13.5:

$$SS_{R \times C} = \sum_{i=1}^{r}\sum_{j=1}^{c} N_{i,j}(\overline{X}_{i,j} - {}_R\overline{X}_i - {}_C\overline{X}_j + \overline{\overline{X}})^2, \tag{13.5}$$

where $N_{i,j}$ equals the number of values in cell i,j; $\overline{X}_{i,j}$ equals the mean of the values in cell i,j; ${}_R\overline{X}_i$ equals the mean of the values in row i; ${}_C\overline{X}_j$ equals the mean of the values in column j; and $\overline{\overline{X}}$ equals the overall or grand mean of all values in the sample.

Table 13.6. A 2×3 crossed factorial design using the data of Table 13.2

	Treatment 1	Treatment 2	Treatment 3	
Male	10, 9, 8, 8, 7	5, 4, 3, 2, 1	4, 3, 3, 2, 2	${}_R\overline{X}_1 = 4.73$
	$\overline{X}_{11} = 8.4$	$\overline{X}_{12} = 3$	$\overline{X}_{13} = 2.8$	
Female	6, 6, 6, 5, 5	4, 4, 3, 2, 2	6, 6, 5, 5, 4	${}_R\overline{X}_2 = 4.60$
	$\overline{X}_{21} = 5.6$	$\overline{X}_{22} = 3$	$\overline{X}_{23} = 5.2$	
	${}_C\overline{X}_1 = 7.0$	${}_C\overline{X}_2 = 3.0$	${}_C\overline{X}_2 = 4.0$	Overall Mean = 4.67

Using Equation 13.5, we compute $SS_{R \times C}$ for the manual dexterity example:

$$N_{11} = N_{12} = N_{13} = N_{21} = N_{22} = N_{23} = 5;$$

$$\overline{X}_{11} = 8.4, \overline{X}_{12} = 3.0, \overline{X}_{13} = 2.8, \overline{X}_{21} = 5.6, \overline{X}_{22} = 3.0, \overline{X}_{23} = 5.2;$$

$$_R\overline{X}_1 = 4.73, {}_R\overline{X}_2 = 4.60; {}_C\overline{X}_1 = 7.0, {}_C\overline{X}_2 = 3.0, {}_C\overline{X}_3 = 4.0; \overline{\overline{X}} = 4.67.$$

$$
\begin{aligned}
SS_{R \times C} = {} & 5(8.4 - 4.73 - 7.0 + 4.67)^2 + 5(3.0 - 4.73 - 3.0 + 4.67)^2 \\
& + 5(2.8 - 4.73 - 4.0 + 4.67)^2 + 5(5.6 - 4.60 - 7.0 + 4.67)^2 \\
& + 5(3.0 - 4.60 - 3.0 + 4.67)^2 + 5(5.2 - 4.60 - 4.0 + 4.67)^2 \\
= {} & 33.87.
\end{aligned}
$$

The sum of squares associated with the remaining within-cell variation, SS_W, is given by Equation 13.6:

$$SS_W = \sum_{i,j,k} (X_{i,j,k} - \overline{X}_{i,j})^2, \tag{13.6}$$

where $X_{i,j,k}$ represents the kth score in row i and column j, and $\overline{X}_{i,j}$ represents the mean of the scores in row i and column j.

Using Equation 13.6, we compute SS_W for the manual dexterity example:

$$
\begin{aligned}
SS_W = {} & (10-8.4)^2 + (9-8.4)^2 + (8-8.4)^2 + (8-8.4)^2 + (7-8.4)^2 + (5-3)^2 = (4-3)^2 \\
& + (3-3)^2 + (2-3)^2 + (1-3)^2 + (4-2.8)^2 + (3-2.8)^2 + (3-2.8)^2 + (2-2.8)^2 \\
& + (2-2.8)^2 + (6-5.6)^2 + (6-5.6)^2 + (6-5.6)^2 + (5-5.6)^2 + (5-5.6)^2 + (4-3)^2 \\
& + (4-3)^2 + (3-3)^2 + (2-3)^2 + (2-3)^2 + (6-5.2)^2 + (6-5.2)^2 + (5-5.2)^2 \\
& + (5-5.2)^2 + (4-5.2)^2 = 2.56 + .36 + .16 + .16 + 1.96 + 4 + 1 + 0 + 1 + 4 + 1.44 \\
& + .04 + .04 + .64 + .64 + .16 + .16 + .16 + .36 + .36 + 1 + 1 + 0 + 1 + 1 + .64 + .64 \\
& + .04 + .04 + 1.44 = 26.00.
\end{aligned}
$$

Finally, the sum of squares associated with the total variability, SS_T, is given by Equation 13.7:

$$SS_T = \sum (X_{ijk} - \overline{\overline{X}})^2 \tag{13.7}$$

Using Equation 13.7, we compute SS_T for the manual dexterity example:

$$
\begin{aligned}
SS_T = {} & (10 - 4.67)^2 + (9 - 4.67)^2 + (8 - 4.67)^2 + (8 - 4.67)^2 + (7 - 4.67)^2 \\
& + (5 - 4.67)^2 + (4 - 4.67)^2 + (3 - 4.67)^2 + (2 - 4.67)^2 + (1 - 4.67)^2 \\
& + (4 - 4.67)^2 + (3 - 4.67)^2 + (3 - 4.67)^2 + (2 - 4.67)^2 + (2 - 4.67)^2 \\
& + (6 - 4.67)^2 + (6 - 4.67)^2 + (6 - 4.67)^2 + (5 - 4.67)^2 + (5 - 4.67)^2 \\
& + (4 - 4.67)^2 + (4 - 4.67)^2 + (3 - 4.67)^2 + (2 - 4.67)^2 + (2 - 4.67)^2 \\
& + (6 - 4.67)^2 + (6 - 4.67)^2 + (5 - 4.67)^2 + (5 - 4.67)^2 + (4 - 4.67)^2 \\
= {} & 146.67.
\end{aligned}
$$

Substituting these values for their respective sum of squares, we obtain the second column of Table 13.5.

We then calculate the values of df, MS, and F, following the formulas given in the ANOVA summary in Table 13.3.

We first find these within-cell values:

$$df_W = N - RC = 30 - 6 = 24, MS_W = SS_W/df_W = 26/24 = 1.08.$$

For the main effect of gender, we obtain the following values:

$$df_R = R - 1 = 2 - 1 = 1, MS_R = SS_R/df_R = 0.13/1 = 0.13$$
$$F = MS_R/MS_W = 0.13/1.08 = 0.12.$$

For the main effect of treatment, we obtain the following values:

$$df_C = C - 1 = 3 - 1 = 2, MS_C = SS_C/df_C = 86.76/2 = 43.34.$$
$$F = MS_C/MS_W = 43.34/1.08 = 40.13.$$

For the interaction effect, we obtain the following values:

$$df_{R \times C} = (R - 1)(C - 1) = 1 \times 2 = 2, MS_{R \times C} = SS_{R \times C}/df_{R \times C} = 33.87/2 = 16.93.$$
$$F = MS_{R \times C}/MS_W = 16.93/1.08 = 15.69.$$

The three Sig. values (or significance values, or p-values) are obtained either by using Table 3 in Appendix C or by using an SPSS Compute statement. Both approaches are described.

Table 3 in Appendix C may be used to approximate the associated p-values.

To find the p-value for the main effect of gender, we want an estimate of the area to the right of $F = .12$ with numerator degrees of freedom 1 and denominator degrees of free-dom 24. To do so, we find all of the α-values associated with df for numerator $= 1$ and df for denominator $= 24$. We see that the F-value 1.39 cuts off an area of .25 to its right, that 2.93 cuts off an area of .10 to its right, and so on. Because $F = .12$ is less than 1.39, we con-clude that the area to the right of $F = .12$ is greater than .25, that is, $p > .25$.

To find the p-value for the main effect of treatment, we want an estimate of the area to the right of $F = 40.13$ with numerator degrees of freedom 2 and denominator degrees of freedom 24. To do so, we find all of the α-values associated with df for numerator $= 2$ and df for denominator $= 24$. We find the closest value that is smaller than 40.13. In this case, the F-value 9.34 cuts off an area of .001 to its right. Because $F = 40.13$ is greater than 9.24, it must cut off even less area, so that we conclude that the area to the right of $F = 40.13$ is less than .001, that is, $p < .001$.

To find the p-value for the interaction effect, we want an estimate of the area to the right of $F = 15.69$ with numerator degrees of freedom 2 and denominator degrees of freedom 24. As with the main effect of treatment, because $F = 15.69$ is greater than 9.24, $p < .001$.

SPSS Compute statements may be used to find the associated p-values. These values are obtained using the following expressions: 1-CDF.F(0.12,1,24) for Gender, 1-CDF.F(40.13,2,24) for Treatment, and 1-CDF.F(15.69,2,24) for the Gender-by-Treatment interaction.

These results are summarized in Table 13.7. Note that the values for Sig. are those obtained using the SPSS Compute statement and are rounded to two decimal places.

Table 13.7. Summary table of results of the two-way ANOVA on manual dexterity

Source of variation	SS	df	MS	F-ratio	Sig.
Gender	0.13	1	0.14	0.12	.72
Treatment	86.67	2	43.34	40.13	.00
Gender × Treatment	33.87	2	16.93	15.69	.00
Within cells	26.00	24	1.08		
Total	146.67	29			

When interpreting the results of the two-way ANOVA, we compare each of the p-values (found in the Sig. column) to the α-level, which in this case is $\alpha = .05$. The results of the two-way ANOVA indicate that there is a statistically significant main effect of treatment, $F(2, 24) = 40.13$ ($p < .005$), and a statistically significant interaction effect $F(2, 24) = 40.13$ ($p < .005$). Because the presence of a statistically significant interaction indicates that the best treatment depends on the gender, we focus on the interaction instead of the main effect of treatment. To understand the nature of the interaction effect – that is, the way in which the best treatment depends on the gender – we conduct post-hoc multiple comparison tests. These are discussed in a later section.

Several comparisons with the one-way ANOVA results are worthwhile. First, we notice that, as expected, SS_T and $SS_{TREATMENT}$ remain the same at 146.67 and 86.67, respectively. Second, we notice that $SS_{GENDER} + SS_{INTER} + SS_W = 0.13 + 33.87 + 26.0 = 60$, as we also had expected. Third, we notice that $SS_T = SS_{TREATMENT} + SS_{GENDER} + SS_{INTER} + SS_W$, suggesting that this two-way ANOVA does partition the total variability of manual dexterity values into these four independent (orthogonal) components.

Finally, we notice that the denominator of the F-ratios, the MS_W term, is smaller in the two-way ANOVA than in the one-way ANOVA, suggesting that we have explained additional residual variance by the inclusion of Gender and the interaction between Gender and Treatment in the design. Because the denominator of the F-ratio in the two-way design is smaller than in the one-way design, we say that the two-way design is more *precise* than the one-way ANOVA in that it exacts greater control over variation due to individual differences. In the one-way ANOVA, the F-ratio for testing the Treatment effect is only 19.52, whereas in the two-way design, because of the smaller denominator, the F-ratio for testing the Treatment effect is 40.13. More precise designs give rise to larger F-ratios and, therefore, provide a greater chance of detecting significant differences where they exist. Accordingly, more precise designs are also known as more powerful designs.

Thus, we include additional variables in a design not only because we may be interested in testing the relationships between these variables and the dependent variable, but also because we are interested in enhancing the power of our design by controlling the effects of these other variables. In our example, we have reduced the within-group variance by controlling for individual differences in manual dexterity due to the interaction between Gender and Treatment.

Suppose, instead, we had added a different variable other than Gender – say, preference for ice cream or yogurt, which has nothing to do with manual dexterity – as either a main or interaction effect. In this case, the variable preference would not have helped to control for additional individual differences in manual dexterity and the design would not have been more precise than the one-way design. Accordingly, the power of the two-way ANOVA in testing the Treatment effect would not have improved. In fact, by adding a variable to a design that is not related to the dependent variable, either individually or through interaction, the power of the test diminishes as Example 13.1 illustrates.

• •

EXAMPLE 13.1. Show that the two-way design including Preference for ice cream or yogurt and Treatment has lower power for testing the Treatment effect than the one-way design with only Treatment.

Solution. Because we believe that preference for ice cream or yogurt has nothing (zero) to do with manual dexterity as a main or interaction effect, we set SS_{PREF} and $SS_{PREF\times TREAT}$ to zero in Table 13.3. We leave the degrees of freedom as they are because like Gender, Preference has only two levels: Ice cream and Yogurt. We compute a new, revised SS_W and obtain the following results.

Source of Variation	SS	df	MS	F-ratio
Preference	0	1	0/1 = 0	0/2.5 = 0
Treatment	86.67	2	86.76/2 = 43.34	43.34/2.5 = 17.34
Preference × Treatment	0	2	0/2 = 0	0/2.5 = 0
Within cells	60	24	60/24 = 2.5	
Total	146.67	29		

Notice that the *F*-ratio for Treatment decreases from a value of 19.52 in the one-way design to a value of 17.34 in the two-way design. Simply stated, adding the variable Preference to our one-way design compromises the power of our test of the Treatment effect. Preference used up one degree of freedom as a main effect and another degree of freedom as an interaction effect without explaining additional residual variance. Variables such as these, which cannot be expected to "pull their own weight" in a design context, are best excluded. Alternatively, variables that are theoretically or otherwise known to relate strongly to the dependent variable as a main or interaction effect ought to be included.

DECOMPOSING SCORE DEVIATIONS ABOUT THE GRAND MEAN

Each of the *SS* terms used to test for the main and interaction effects in a two-way design derives from a simple mathematical identity that expresses a score's total deviation from the grand mean $\left(X_{ijk} - \overline{\overline{X}}\right)$ as a sum of its component parts. In particular, we may express this identity as

$$X_{ijk} - \overline{\overline{X}} = \left(_R\overline{X}_i - \overline{\overline{X}}\right) + \left(_C\overline{X}_j - \overline{\overline{X}}\right) + \left(\overline{X}_{ij} - _R\overline{X}_i - _C\overline{X}_j + \overline{\overline{X}}\right) + \left(X_{ijk} - \overline{X}_{ij}\right). \text{ (13.8)}$$

Equation 13.8 makes explicit the notion that each score deviation about the grand mean is represented in two-way ANOVA as a sum of (1) the row deviation about the grand mean; (2) the column deviation about the grand mean; (3) the interaction between the row and column factors; and (4) an individual difference, called error, measured as the difference between an individual's score and the mean of the group for that individual.

☞ **Remark.** What makes Equation 13.8 a mathematical identity is the fact that we find, after simplifying the expression by removing parentheses and rearranging terms, as shown in (13.9), that the value to the left of the equal sign is identical to the value to the right of the equal sign:

$$X_{ijk} - \overline{\overline{X}} = \left({}_R\overline{X}_i - \overline{\overline{X}}\right) + \left({}_C\overline{X}_j - \overline{\overline{X}}\right) + \left(\overline{X}_{ij} - {}_R\overline{X}_i - {}_C\overline{X}_j + \overline{\overline{X}}\right) + \left(X_{ijk} - \overline{X}_{ij}\right)$$

$$= X_{ijk} + {}_R\overline{X}_i + {}_C\overline{X}_j - {}_R\overline{X}_i - {}_C\overline{X}_j - \overline{\overline{X}} - \overline{\overline{X}} + \overline{\overline{X}} + \overline{\overline{X}} + \overline{X}_{ij} - \overline{X}_{ij}$$

$$= X_{ijk} - \overline{\overline{X}}. \tag{13.9}$$

The importance of breaking down $X_{ijk} - \overline{\overline{X}}$ into its component parts is that it facilitates our understanding of where the *SS* terms used for testing the main and interaction effects come from. In short, Equation 13.8 makes explicit the connection between the breakdown of the total score deviation into its component parts and the partition of the total *SS* into its component parts. The total *SS* associated with the score deviation about the grand mean is also called the *corrected total SS*.

In particular, each score deviation in Equation 13.8 corresponds to a different *SS* term in Equation 13.2. In particular, the score deviation about the grand mean gives rise to SS_T; the row deviation about the grand mean gives rise to SS_{ROW}; the column deviation about the grand mean gives rise to SS_{COL}; the interaction term gives rise to SS_{INTER}; and the error term gives rise to SS_W.

MODELING EACH SCORE AS A SUM OF COMPONENT PARTS

If we add $\overline{\overline{X}}$ to both sides of Equation 13.8, we obtain Equation 13.10, which suggests that each score in ANOVA comprises of a sum of five parts: (1) the grand mean, (2) the effect due to the row factor, (3) the effect due to the column factor, (4) the effect due to the interaction between row and column factors, and (5) the within-cell deviations that represent the leftover, unexplained individual differences (the error). The grand mean may be thought of as a baseline value to which the value of each effect (row, column, interaction, and error) is added to obtain the score itself.

$$X_{ijk} = \overline{\overline{X}} + \left({}_R\overline{X}_i - \overline{\overline{X}}\right) + \left({}_C\overline{X}_j - \overline{\overline{X}}\right) + \left(\overline{X}_{ij} - {}_R\overline{X}_i - {}_C\overline{X}_j + \overline{\overline{X}}\right) + \left(X_{ijk} - \overline{X}_{ij}\right). \tag{13.10}$$

In the context of our working example, Equation 13.10 suggests that two-way ANOVA models the manual dexterity score of each individual as the sum of the grand mean (which may be viewed as a baseline value), plus the effect of the individual's gender, plus the effect of which treatment the individual received, plus the joint effect of the individual's gender and treatment, plus an unexplained amount, called error. The *SS* associated with the original raw scores are called *raw total SS*.

EXPLAINING THE INTERACTION AS A JOINT (OR MULTIPLICATIVE) EFFECT

We have referred to the interaction between the row and column factors as a joint effect. A joint effect appropriately suggests that the combination of factors produces an effect that is more than the sum of its parts (that is, more than the sum of the effects of the two separate factors). Hays (1973) likened an interaction to what happens when two parts of hydrogen combine with one part of oxygen to produce water. Clearly that combination of hydrogen and oxygen produces an effect that is more than the sum of its parts.

We use a subset of Equation 13.8 to show that the interaction effect is in fact more than the sum of its parts. Equation 13.8 describes the total score deviation as a sum of its component parts. These parts may be classified broadly as the between-group effects and the within-group effect. In this section we consider only between-group effects, which are based on the difference between each group mean $(\overline{X}_{ij})$ and the grand mean $(\overline{\overline{X}})$. This difference is defined in Equation 13.11 as the sum of the component score deviations representing the two main effects and the interaction:

$$\overline{X}_{ij} - \overline{\overline{X}} = \left({}_R\overline{X}_i - \overline{\overline{X}} \right) + \left({}_C\overline{X}_j - \overline{\overline{X}} \right) + \left(\overline{X}_{ij} - {}_R\overline{X}_i - {}_C\overline{X}_j + \overline{\overline{X}} \right). \tag{13.11}$$

By rearranging the terms we may show that Equation 13.11, like Equation 13.8, is a mathematical identity that simplifies to $\overline{X}_{ij} - \overline{\overline{X}} = \overline{X}_{ij} - \overline{\overline{X}}$. We may isolate the term representing the interaction effect on the right-hand side of the equation by subtracting the row and column effects from both sides of the equation. In so doing, we obtain

$$\left(\overline{X}_{ij} - \overline{\overline{X}} \right) - \left({}_R\overline{X}_i - \overline{\overline{X}} \right) - \left({}_C\overline{X}_j - \overline{\overline{X}} \right) = \left(\overline{X}_{ij} - {}_R\overline{X}_i - {}_C\overline{X}_j + \overline{\overline{X}} \right) \tag{13.12}$$

According to Equation 13.12, the interaction is that part of the between-group effect that remains after subtracting out the sum of the separate row and column effects. Said differently, the interaction is what remains after the additive effects of the row and column factors are removed. As such, the interaction effect may be thought of as representing the joint or multiplicative effect of both row and column factors.

MEASURING EFFECT SIZE

In Chapter 12 we measured the size of an effect (e.g., Treatment) as the ratio of the SS due to that effect divided by the SS_T. As such, this ratio represents the proportion of total variance explained by or accounted for by that effect. We extend this notion to the case of two-way ANOVA, where interest is in measuring the magnitude of not one but rather three effects: the two main effects and the interaction.

By extension, the proportion of total variance explained by the row main effect, denoted as R^2_{ROW} is given by Equation 13.13:

$$R^2_{ROW} = \frac{SS_{ROW}}{SS_T}. \tag{13.13}$$

The proportion of total variance explained by the column main effect, denoted as R^2_{COL}, is given by Equation 13.14:

$$R^2_{COL} = \frac{SS_{COL}}{SS_T}. \tag{13.14}$$

The proportion of total variance explained by the interaction effect, denoted as R^2_{INTER}, is given by Equation 13.15:

$$R^2_{INTER} = \frac{SS_{INTER}}{SS_T}.$$ (13.15)

Applying these ratios to the data from our manual dexterity example, we find that the proportion of manual dexterity variance due to Gender is 0.13/146.67 = .0009 = .09 percent, that proportion due to Treatment is 86.67/146.67 = .59 = 59 percent, and the proportion due to the Gender-by-Treatment interaction is 33.87/146.67 = .23 = 23 percent. Based on the guidelines given in Chapter 10, both the main effect due to Treatment and the Gender-by-Treatment interaction are very large whereas the main effect due to Gender is miniscule. The variable Gender contributes to this analysis not as a main effect but in combination with Treatment as an interaction. Collectively, the three effects account for approximately 82 percent of the total manual dexterity variance, leaving approximately 18 percent unexplained.

An alternative measure of effect size is the ratio of SS due to that effect divided by the sum of the SS due to that effect plus the SS due to the unexplained error after controlling for all other effects. As such, this measure of effect size may be thought of as the proportion of variance due to an effect after controlling for all other effects in the design. These measures of effect size are called *partial eta squared* terms because they are based on controlling for or partialing out the other effects in the design. The expressions of partial eta squared, denoted η^2, for the row and column main effects and the interaction effect are given in Equations 13.6 through 13.18, respectively. In general, for any given effect, η^2 is larger than the corresponding R^2 for that effect.

$$\eta^2_{ROW} = \frac{SS_{ROW}}{SS_{ROW} + SS_W}$$ (13.16)

$$\eta^2_{COL} = \frac{SS_{COL}}{SS_{COL} + SS_W}$$ (13.17)

$$\eta^2_{INTER} = \frac{SS_{INTER}}{SS_{INTER} + SS_W}.$$ (13.18)

EXAMPLE 13.2. Use SPSS to conduct a two-way ANOVA on the manual dexterity data. Verify that the answers from SPSS are the same as those we obtained by hand computation.

Solution. The data file we used to conduct the one-way ANOVA consisted of two variables, GROUP and SCORE. GROUP contains the value of the treatment group to which an individual has been assigned (1, 2, or 3), and SCORE contains an individual's score on the manual dexterity test. To avoid confusion with our second grouping variable, Gender, we rename GROUP as TREATMEN and we add another variable, GENDER, which represents the gender of an individual.

To use SPSS to carry out a two-way ANOVA, click **Analyze**, **General Linear Model**, and **Univariate**. Move SCORE into the **Dependent Variable** box; move GENDER and

TREATMEN into the **Fixed Factor(s)** box. Click **Options**. Under Display, click on the boxes next to **Descriptive Statistics**, **Homogeneity Tests**, and **Estimates of Effect Size**. Click **Continue, OK**.

We obtain the following three sets of results: descriptive statistics, Levene's test of homogeneity of variance, and the ANOVA summary table.

Descriptive Statistics
Dependent Variable: Manual Dexterity Score

Treatment	Gender	Mean	Std. Deviation	N
Treatment 1	Male	8.40	1.140	5
	Female	5.60	.548	5
	Total	7.00	1.700	10
Treatment 2	Male	3.00	1.581	5
	Female	3.00	1.000	5
	Total	3.00	1.247	10
Treatment 3	Male	2.80	.837	5
	Female	5.20	.837	5
	Total	4.00	1.491	10
Total	Male	4.73	2.915	15
	Female	4.60	1.404	15
	Total	4.67	2.249	30

The descriptive statistics provides cell and marginal means, standard deviations, and sample sizes. The last row contains the grand mean and standard deviation based on all 30 scores without regard to grouping variables. These results corroborate with those based on our hand computations.

Levene's Test of Equality of Error Variances[a]
Dependent Variable: Manual Dexterity Score

F	df1	df2	Sig.
1.169	5	24	.353

Tests the null hypothesis that the error variance of the dependent variable is equal across groups.
[a]Design: Intercept + Treatment + Gender + Treatment *Gender

Levene's test of homogeneity of variance is not statistically significant ($p = .35$), suggesting that the six populations from which the cell scores are sampled have equal variances. The assumption of homogeneity of variance is therefore tenable for these data.

☞ **Remark.** According to the SPSS output, Levene's test is based on testing "the null hypothesis that the error variance of the dependent variable is equal across groups." Rather than asking whether the original score distributions for all groups are homogeneous, Levene's test asks whether the error or residual score distributions for all groups are homogeneous. Because the residual scores contain all the information of the original scores minus the row, column, and interaction effects, tests on the error variance of the dependent variable are equivalent to tests on the original score variance of the dependent variable. This applies to tests for homogeneity of variance as well as normality.

Tests of Between-Subjects Effects
Dependent Variable: Manual Dexterity Score

Source	Type III Sum of Squares	df	Mean Square	F	Sig.	Partial Eta Squared
Corrected Model	120.667[a]	5	24.133	22.277	.000	.823
Intercept	653.333	1	653.333	603.077	.000	.962
Treatment	86.667	2	43.333	40.000	.000	.769
Gender	.133	1	.133	.123	.729	.005
Treatment * Gender	33.867	2	16.933	15.631	.000	.566
Error	26.000	24	1.083			
Total	800.000	30				
Corrected Total	146.667	29				

[a]R Squared = .823(Adjusted R Squared = .786).

We notice, as expected, that the model for the two-way design, as described in the Tests of Between-Subjects Effects table, contains an intercept, a gender effect, a treatment effect, and an interaction effect. The intercept is the grand mean. We notice also that the interaction term is represented as the product of Gender and Treatment (GENDER*TREATMNT). This reflects the fact that, as noted earlier, the interaction term represents a joint, multiplicative effect.

In the two-way ANOVA summary table, each of the main, interaction, and within-cell (labeled as error) values agree with those obtained through our hand computation.

We note that SPSS labels what we have been calling SS_T as $SS_{CORRECTED\ TOTAL}$. In addition it includes other effects that we have not discussed explicitly: SS for the Corrected Model, Intercept, and Total.

The SS for the Corrected Model is simply the sum of the SS terms associated with the three model effects: Gender, Treatment, and Gender by Treatment. If we divide $SS_{CORRMODEL}$ by SS_T we obtain an overall measure of model effect as a proportion of total variance explained by the model. Because this measure of effect is analogous to the measures of effect presented in Equations 13.13 through 13.15, it too is denoted by R^2. For our working example, we have

$$R_{CORRMODEL}^2 = \frac{SS_{CORRMODEL}}{SS_{TOTAL}}$$
$$= \frac{120.667}{146.667}$$
$$= .823$$

(13.19)

which is the same value we obtained from our hand computation. Because 82.3 percent of the total manual dexterity variance is accounted for by all three model effects taken collectively, we know that approximately 18 percent of this total variance remains unexplained. What other variables might we include in the model to account for some of this additional unexplained variance?

The SS due to (Raw) Total equals 800, which is the sum of the SS for all effects including the Intercept. Equation 13.20 gives the formula for the intercept SS:

$$SS_{\text{INTERCEPT}} = N\bar{\bar{X}}^2 \qquad\qquad (13.20)$$
$$= 30(4.667)^2$$
$$= 653.33.$$

Because $SS_{\text{INTERCEPT}}$ is based solely on the grand mean, a test of this source of variation is tantamount to a test of whether the grand mean in the population equals zero. In the behavioral and social sciences, measuring instruments typically are scaled arbitrarily as positive values (i.e., the scores of our test on manual dexterity are all positive). As a result, we can expect the grand mean to differ from zero and, in fact, to be greater than zero. Accordingly, we can expect the F-test of the intercept (grand mean) in the two-way ANOVA to be statistically significant. Because the significance of this F-test tells us nothing more than that the values of our measuring instrument are positive, it is not elucidating and may be ignored.

In sum, of the eight SS terms presented in the ANOVA summary table, only six are useful for interpreting our results: SS(Corrected Model), SS(Gender), SS(Treatment), SS(Gender*Treatment), SS(Error), and SS(Corrected Total). The SS(Intercept) and SS(Raw Total) are not useful in this regard.

FIXED VERSUS RANDOM FACTORS

In setting up the two-way ANOVA in SPSS, recall that we moved Gender and Treatment into the Fixed Factor(s) box. You may have noticed that another box in this procedure was labeled Random Factor(s).

A *fixed factor* is a factor whose levels have been fixed or specified by the researcher because he or she has interest in those particular levels. Because these are the levels about which the researcher would like to draw conclusions, if a replication were planned, these same levels would be present in the replication as well. ANOVA models appropriate for analyzing designs containing only fixed factors are called *fixed-effects models*. We moved both Gender and Treatment into the Fixed Factor(s) box in our example because our researcher was interested in drawing conclusions specifically about the particular Treatments 1, 2, and 3 and about Males and Females.

If, on the other hand, the researcher was not interested in the particular Treatments 1, 2, and 3, but only in these treatments as a random sampling from the whole population of possible drug rehabilitation treatments, then Treatment would have been considered a *random factor*. A random factor is a factor whose levels have been selected randomly from the population of all possible levels. If a replication were planned, the levels used in the first study would not necessarily be present in the replication study because in each study the levels are based on a random selection from the population of all possible levels. ANOVA models appropriate for analyzing designs containing only random factors are called *random-effects models*. ANOVA models appropriate for analyzing designs containing both fixed and random factors are called *mixed-effects models*.

In this book we restrict our discussion of ANOVA to fixed-effects models. For information regarding the other two models, the interested reader is referred to *Designing Experiments and Analyzing Data* by Maxwell and Delaney (2004) and *Design and Analysis: A Researcher's Handbook* by Keppel (1991).

POST-HOC MULTIPLE COMPARISON TESTS

In Chapter 12, following a statistically significant omnibus *F*-test in the one-way ANOVA, we conducted a series of post-hoc tests to determine which specific means differed from which others. We shall do the same in the two-way ANOVA, but there is a slight difference. In the one-way ANOVA, there is only one omnibus *F*-test. In the two-way ANOVA, there are three: one for the row main effect, another for the column main effect, and a third for the interaction. Hence, in the two-way ANOVA we conduct a post-hoc test for each statistically significant effect with one caveat. If an interaction effect is found to be statistically significant, then we first conduct the post-hoc test associated with the interaction and then decide whether it is meaningful to conduct the post-hoc tests in connection with any statistically significant main effects.

In the presence of an interaction, we know that the relationship between the two factors and the dependent variable is more complex than is suggested by either of the two main effects alone. Accordingly, in the presence of an interaction effect we postpone an in-depth analysis of main effects until we understand the more complex nature of the interaction. As we shall see, main effects are often not meaningful in the presence of an interaction effect. In such cases, we carry out post-hoc analyses on the interaction effect only and interpret accordingly.

As we have discussed, a main effect due to a factor is simply the average effect of that factor across all levels of the other factor and is reflected by differences among the population marginal means associated with that factor.

In our working example, there is a statistically significant main effect due to Treatment. This implies that the population means of the manual dexterity scores for Treatments 1, 2, and 3, averaged across males and females, are not all equal. If there were no interaction, we could simply ignore Gender and conduct the Least Significant Difference (LSD) and Tukey Honestly Significant Difference (HSD) post-hoc tests as described in Chapter 12 to determine which treatment means are different from which others. However, there is an interaction, as suggested by the nonparallel lines of Figure 13.6, reproduced from Figure 13.2.

According to the interaction of Figure 13.6, Treatment 1 appears to be more effective for males, Treatment 2 appears to be equally effective for both genders, and Treatment 3 appears to be more effective for females. Because the main effect estimates the average effect of Treatment across both males and females, it does not convey the

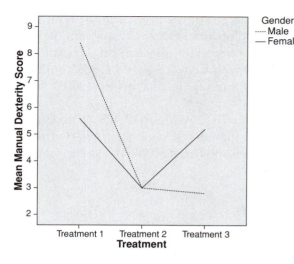

Figure 13.6   Interaction between gender and treatment on manual dexterity.

complexities that exist in the relationship among Treatment, Gender, and manual dexterity. To convey these complexities, we must analyze the effect due to Treatment for each gender separately. That is, we analyze the differences in treatment means (represented by the solid line segments) separately from the differences in treatment means (represented by the dashed line segments). In so doing, we are analyzing what are called *simple effects*.

A simple effect is the effect of one factor at a given level of the other factor. There are as many simple effects of one factor as there are levels of the other factor.

In our working example, there are two simple effects due to Treatment because there are two levels of Gender. There are the Treatment effect for males (represented by the solid line segments) and the Treatment effect for females (represented by the dashed line segments). Given the interaction between Treatment and Gender, we need to analyze these two distinct simple effects to understand the true nature of the Treatment effect.

In testing for simple effects we increase the number of statistical tests conducted and potentially increase the probability of a family-wise Type I error. To control the family-wise error a popular approach is to use the Bonferroni adjustment for simple effects. To test the simple effects associated with the Row factor (e.g., Gender), use $\alpha = \alpha_{FW}/C$, where C is the number of levels of the column factor. Likewise, to test for simple effects associated with the Column factor (e.g., Treatment), use $\alpha = \alpha_{FW}/R$, where R is the number of levels of the row factor.

To carry out the simple effects using SPSS, we use the EMMEANS COMPARE option. In particular, if we were to specify the following,

/EMMEANS(Gender*Treatment) COMPARE(Treatment),

we would get a test of the two treatment simple effects for each gender. That is, we would get the omnibus test for Treatment for males and females separately.

To use SPSS to obtain the two tests of simple effects due to Treatment, one for males and one for females, return to the two-way ANOVA procedure. Click **Options**. Under the heading

Estimated Marginal Means, in the box labeled **Factor(s) and Factor Interactions**, move the OVERALL, Gender, Treatmen, and Gender by Treatmen effects into the box labeled **Display Means for**. Click **Continue**. Click **Paste** located on the bottom of the **GLM-General Factorial** window.

The syntax window will appear with the following commands:

```
UNIANOVA
score BY gender treatmen
/METHOD = SSTYPE(3)
/INTERCEPT = INCLUDE
/PLOT = PROFILE( treatmen*gender gender*treatmen )
/EMMEANS = TABLES(OVERALL)
/EMMEANS = TABLES(gender)
/EMMEANS = TABLES(treatmen)
/EMMEANS = TABLES(gender*treatmen)
/PRINT = DESCRIPTIVE ETASQ HOMOGENEITY
/CRITERIA = ALPHA(.05)
/DESIGN = gender treatmen gender*treatmen.
```

To obtain the omnibus test for treatment for each gender, type the words COMPARE(treatment) in the command line indicated below. The changes are noted in bold.

```
UNIANOVA
score BY gender treatmen
/METHOD = SSTYPE(3)
/INTERCEPT = INCLUDE
/PLOT = PROFILE( treatmen*gender gender*treatmen)
/EMMEANS = TABLES(OVERALL)
/EMMEANS = TABLES(gender)
/EMMEANS = TABLES(treatmen)
/EMMEANS = TABLES(gender*treatmen) COMPARE(treatmen)
/PRINT = DESCRIPTIVE ETASQ HOMOGENEITY
/CRITERIA = ALPHA(.05)
/DESIGN = gender treatmen gender*treatmen.
```

To perform the modified analysis, Click **Run**, **All**. Alternatively, you can click on the right-pointing arrow head in the menu bar.

In addition to the output relative to simple effects, the commands in the syntax window provide all pairwise multiple comparisons.

As noted by the caption below the table of univariate tests, each *F*-test tests the simple effect of Treatment within each level of Gender. According to these results, both *F*-tests are statistically significant using the Bonferroni adjustment α-level (.05/2 = .025). From the eta squared values, however, we may note that the differences in treatment means are substantially greater for males than for females. This result corroborates the plot of Figure 13.6. Thus, we know that there are statistically significant treatment mean differences for both males and females.

Univariate Tests

Dependent Variable: Manual Dexterity Score

Gender		Sum of Squares	df	Mean Square	F	Sig.	Partial Eta Squared
Male	Contrast	100.933	2	50.467	46.585	.000	.795
	Error	26.000	24	1.083			
Female	Contrast	19.600	2	9.800	9.046	.001	.430
	Error	26.000	24	1.083			

Each F tests the simple effects of Treatment within each level combination of the other effects shown. These tests are based on the linearly independent pairwise comparisons among the estimated marginal means.

☞ **Remark.** Conceptually, we may think of the two tests of simple effects as two one-way ANOVAs: a one-way ANOVA on treatment mean differences based only on males and another one-way ANOVA on treatment mean differences based only on females. Although they are conceptually similar, in actuality they are different because the one-way ANOVAs and the tests for simple effects use different error terms. The one-way ANOVA on males, for example, uses an error term based only on males. Likewise, the one-way ANOVA on females uses an error term based only on females. These error terms are likely to be different because they are based on different groups. By contrast, the simple effect within males uses the error term from the two-way ANOVA and therefore is based on the data from both males and females combined. Likewise, the simple effect within females also uses the error term from the two-way ANOVA and is based on the data from both males and females combined. Hence, the error terms for both simple effects are equal, as we may note in the output above (they both equal 26.00). Use of this error term based on data from males and females combined is most appropriate when the homogeneity of variance assumption is met. We should point out as well that, when all relevant data are combined to form the estimate of the error term, the statistical power of the test is maximized.

To find out which means are different from which others, we use pairwise multiple comparison as we have done in the one-way ANOVA. Such pairwise comparisons for each gender are provided along with the tests for simple effects.

Pairwise Comparisons

Dependent Variable: Manual Dexterity Score

Gender	(I) Treatment	(J) Treatment	Mean Difference (I-J)	Std. Error	Sig.[a]	95% Confidence Interval for Difference[a]	
						Lower Bound	Upper Bound
Male	Treatment 1	Treatment 2	5.400*	.658	.000	4.041	6.759
		Treatment 3	5.600*	.658	.000	4.241	6.959
	Treatment 2	Treatment 1	−5.400*	.658	.000	−6.759	−4.041
		Treatment 3	.200	.658	.764	−1.159	1.559
	Treatment 3	Treatment 1	−5.600*	.658	.000	−6.959	−4.241
		Treatment 2	−.200	.658	.764	−1.559	1.159
Female	Treatment 1	Treatment 2	2.600*	.658	.001	1.241	3.959
		Treatment 3	.400	.658	.549	−.959	1.759
	Treatment 2	Treatment 1	−2.600*	.658	.001	−3.959	−1.241
		Treatment 3	−2.200*	.658	.003	−3.559	−.841
	Treatment 3	Treatment 1	−400	.658	.549	−1.759	.959
		Treatment 2	2.200*	.658	.003	.841	3.559

Based on estimated marginal means

*The mean difference is significant at the .05 level.

[a]Adjustment for multiple comparisons: Least Significant Difference (equivalent to no adjustments).

According to these results, for males we may note that Treatments 1 and 2 are different from each other and Treatment 1 is different from Treatment 3, but Treatment 2 is no different from Treatment 3. For females we may note that Treatment 1 is different from Treatment 2, and Treatment 2 is different from Treatment 3, but Treatment 1 is no different from Treatment 3. The difference in the pattern of treatment differences for males and females follows from the fact that there is an interaction between gender and treatment on manual dexterity.

Following a statistically significant simple effect, we would want to conduct all pairwise comparisons among the treatment levels at each level of Gender. The pairwise comparisons are unadjusted (LSD) by default, but we may use the ADJ keyword on the EMMEANS sub-command to request Bonferroni (ADJ(Bonferroni)) or Sidak (ADJ(Sidak)) corrected comparisons and confidence intervals.

The analysis we carried out investigated simple effects of treatment for each level of gender. Accordingly, we compared treatment effects for males and females separately. If, in addition, we wished to say something about the manual dexterity of males compared to females for each treatment condition, we would reverse the procedure and conduct simple effects for gender for each level of treatment. To do so, we simply use the same command as earlier, substituting the word Gender for Treatment following the command Compare, as shown. For these tests, the Bonferroni adjusted α is .05/3 = .017.

/EMMEANS(Gender*Treatmnt) **COMPARE(Gender)**.

In doing so, we obtain three simple effects (one for each treatment level) and all pair-wise comparisons, which are given in the following table.

Univariate Tests

Dependent Variable: Manual Dexterity Score

Treatment		Sum of Squares	df	Mean Square	F	Sig.	Partial Eta Squared
Treatment 1	Contrast	19.600	1	19.600	18.092	.000	.430
	Error	26.000	24	1.083			
Treatment 2	Contrast	4.93E−031	1	4.93E−031	.000	1.000	.000
	Error	26.000	24	1.083			
Treatment 3	Contrast	14.400	1	14.400	13.292	.001	.356
	Error	26.000	24	1.083			

Each F tests the simple effects of Gender within each level combination of the other effects shown. These tests are based on the linearly independent pairwise comparisons among the estimated marginal means.

The simple-effect results tell us that males and females score differently on manual dexterity under Treatments 1 and 3, but not under Treatment 2.

Pairwise Comparisons

Dependent Variable: Manual Dexterity Score

Treatment	(I) Gender	(J) Gender	Mean Difference (I−J)	Std. Error	Sig.[a]	95% Confidence Interval for Difference[a]	
						Lower Bound	Upper Bound
Treatment 1	Male	Female	−2.800*	.658	.000	1.441	4.159
	Female	Male	−2.800*	.658	.000	−4.159	−1.441
Treatment 2	Male	Female	−4.44E-0.16	.658	1.000	−1.359	1.359
	Female	Male	4.44E-0.16	.658	1.000	−1.359	1.359
Treatment 3	Male	Female	−2.400*	.658	.001	−3.759	−1.041
	Female	Male	2.400*	.658	.001	1.041	3.759

Based on estimated marginal means

*The mean difference is significant at the .05 level.

[a]Adjustment for multiple comparisions: Least Significant Difference (equivalent to no adjustments).

Notice that the results of these pairwise comparisons are no different from those of the simple effects. That is, like the simple effects, the pairwise comparisons inform us that males score differently (higher) than females in Treatment 1, they score differently (lower) than females in Treatment 3, and they score no different from females in Treatment 2. The results are the same in this case because Gender has only two levels (male and female).

SUMMARY OF STEPS TO BE TAKEN IN A TWO-WAY ANOVA PROCEDURE

In summary, we may express the sequence of tests in a two-way ANOVA as follows.

1. Conduct the two-way ANOVA using the General Linear Model (GLM) procedure and the given α-level.
2. If the interaction term and both main effects are not statistically significant, do not proceed with post-hoc testing.
3. If the interaction term is not statistically significant, but one or both main effects are statistically significant, conduct pairwise comparisons on the marginal means for each main effect that is statistically significant.
4. If the interaction term is statistically significant:
   a) Test for simple effects of the row factor within the column factor and, if desired, test for simple effects of the column factor within the row factor as well. To control the family-wise Type I error for testing simple effects associated with the row factor, use $\alpha = \alpha_{FW}/C$; for testing simple effects associated with the column factor use $\alpha = \alpha_{FW}/R$.
   b) Follow all tests of simple effects that are statistically significant with tests of pairwise comparisons on the individual group means within each simple effect.
   c) Finally, if meaningful, conduct all pairwise comparisons on the marginal means for each main effect that is statistically significant.

EXAMPLE 13.3. You are given a sample of 100 males and 100 females randomly selected from the 534 cases that make up the 1985 Current Population Survey in a way that controls for highest education level attained. The sample of 200 contains 20 males and 20 females with less than a high school diploma, 20 males and 20 females with a high school diploma, 20 males and 20 females with some college training, 20 males and 20 females with a college diploma, and 20 males and 20 females with some graduate school training. As such, the study may be described as a 2 × 5 (gender-by-education level) factorial design. Use the two-way ANOVA procedure to explore the relationship between gender (male, female), highest education level attained, and hourly wage. Specifically, investigate whether (a) there are differences in hourly wage by gender, (b) there are differences from highest education level attained, and (c) there is an interaction between gender and highest education level attained on hourly wage. The data are contained in the file *Wages.sav*.

Solution. Using the GLM procedure, with the variables Gender and Education as fixed factors and Wages as the dependent variable, we obtain the following descriptive statistics, Levene's test of homogeneity of variance, and omnibus *F*-test results.

Descriptive Statistics

Dependent Variable: Wage (dollars per hour)

Sex	Highest education level	Mean	Std. Deviation	N
Male	Less than h.s. degree	7.3315	3.92879	40
	High school degree	8.3235	3.91590	40
	Some college	10.2400	4.99963	40
	College degree	12.3235	5.39584	40
	Graduate school	13.1465	6.99735	40
	Total	10.2730	5.58918	200
Female	Less than h.s. degree	5.6145	2.47675	40
	High school degree	6.0470	2.86449	40
	Some college	7.8100	2.80764	40
	College degree	10.0610	4.40414	40
	Graduate school	12.3790	5.69452	40
	Total	8.3823	4.58156	200
Total	Less than h.s. degree	6.4730	3.37560	80
	High school degree	7.1853	3.59622	80
	Some college	9.0250	4.21027	80
	College degree	11.1923	5.02440	80
	Graduate school	12.7628	6.35053	80
	Total	9.3277	5.19088	400

We may note that males earn more than females (mean hourly wage for males is $10.26 whereas that for females is $8.38) and that education level varies directly with hourly wage (as education level increases so does hourly wage, from $6.47, to $7.18, to $9.03, to $11.19, and to $12.76). Furthermore, we may note that the relationship between education level and hourly wage appears to be the same for males and females, suggesting that there is no interaction between gender and education level on hourly wage. The following plot of mean values presents a visual account of these tentative conclusions.

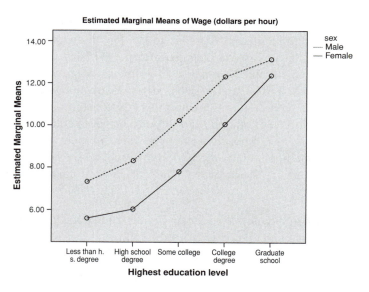

In particular, the mean hourly wage for males averaged across education level is higher than the mean hourly wage for females averaged across education level. Also, the mean hourly wage for each level of education averaged across males and females increases as education level increases. Finally, although not exactly parallel, these two sets of line segments, one for males and one for females, are almost parallel, suggesting the absence of an interaction between gender and education level on hourly wage.

Before looking at the results of the two-way ANOVA, we need to evaluate the tenability of the independence, equal cell sizes, normality, and homogeneity-of-variance assumptions. The wages are independent because individuals were randomly selected separately for each cell. Each cell has size $n = 40$ so that the cell sizes are equal. The two-way ANOVA is robust to violations of the normality assumption because each cell contains more than 30 subjects. The results of Levene's test are reproduced in the following table.

Levene's Test of Equality of Error Variances[a]
Dependent Variable: Wage (dollars per hour)

F	df1	df2	Sig.
10.335	9	390	.000

Tests the null hypothesis that the error variance of the dependent variable is equal across groups.
[a]Design: Intercept + sex + ed + sex*ed

Levene's test is statistically significant, suggesting that the homogeneity-of-variance assumption is not met for these data. Because the sample sizes in each group are equal, however, the validity of the F-test is not compromised and we may proceed with the ANOVA to determine whether our observed results are significant of differences in the population.

The results of the two-way ANOVA are given in the following table. As expected, these results indicate that although both main effects due to gender and education level are statistically significant, the interaction is not. We use post-hoc comparisons to determine which specific means are different from which others. Because the interaction effect is not statistically significant, we are only interested in comparing the marginal means relative to education level and gender.

Tests of Between-Subjects Effects
Dependent Variable: Wage (dollars per hour)

Source	Type III Sum of Squares	df	Mean Square	F	Sig.	Partial Eta Squared
Corrected Model	2643.440[a]	9	293.716	14.128	.000	.246
Intercept	34802.022	1	34802.022	1674.057	.000	.811
ed	2248.572	4	562.143	27.040	.000	.217
sex	357.475	1	357.475	17.195	.000	.042
ed* sex	37.393	4	9.348	.450	.773	.005
Error	8107.722	390	20.789			
Total	45553.184	400				
Corrected Total	10751.162	399				

[a]R Squared = .246 (Adjusted R Squared = .228)

To conduct post-hoc tests on the marginal means, we click **Options** in the GLM procedure and make use of the Estimated Marginal Means command. We move the ED and SEX factors into the box labeled **Display Means for** and click on the box next to **Compare Main Effects**.

The resulting pairwise comparisons are given in the following tables for the marginal means related to education level and gender, respectively.

Pairwise Comparisons

Dependent Variable: Wage (dollars per hour)

(I) Highest education level	(J) Highest education level	Mean Difference (I-J)	Std. Error	Sig.[a]	95% Confidence Interval for Difference[a]	
					Lower Bound	Upper Bound
Less than h.s. degree	High school degree	−.712	.721	.324	−2.130	.705
	Some college	−2.552*	.721	.000	−3.969	−1.135
	College degree	−4.719*	.721	.000	−6.137	−3.302
	Graduate school	−6.290*	.721	.000	−7.707	−4.872
High school degree	Less than h.s. degree	.712	.721	.324	−.705	2.130
	Some college	−1.840*	.721	.011	−3.257	−.422
	College degree	−4.007*	.721	.000	−5.424	−2.590
	Graduate school	−5.578*	.721	.000	−6.995	−4.160
Some college	Less than h.s. degree	2.552*	.721	.000	1.135	3.969
	High school degree	1.840*	.721	.011	.422	3.257
	College degree	−2.167*	.721	.003	−3.585	−.750
	Graduate school	−3.738*	.721	.000	−5.155	−2.320
College degree	Less than h.s. degree	4.719*	.721	.000	3.302	6.137
	High school degree	4.007*	.721	.000	2.590	5.424
	Some college	2.167*	.721	.003	.750	3.585
	Graduate school	−1.571*	.721	.030	−2.988	−.153
Graduate school	Less than h.s. degree	6.290*	.721	.000	4.872	7.707
	High school degree	5.578*	.721	.000	4.160	6.995
	Some college	3.738*	.721	.000	2.320	5.155
	College degree	1.571*	.721	.030	.153	2.988

Based on estimated marginal means
*The mean difference is significant at the .05 level.
[a]Adjustment for multiple comparisons: Least Significant Difference (equivalent to no adjustments).

Pairwise Comparisons

Dependent Variable: Wage (dollars per hour)

(I) sex	(J) sex	Mean Difference (I-J)	Std. Error	Sig.[a]	95% Confidence Interval for Difference[a]	
					Lower Bound	Upper Bound
Male	Female	1.891*	.456	.000	.994	2.787
Female	Male	−1.891*	.456	.000	−2.787	−.994

Based on estimated marginal means
*The mean difference is significant at the .05 level.
[a]Adjustment for multiple comparisons: Least Significant Difference (equivalent to no adjustments).

According to these results, the population mean hourly wage for those with a high school diploma is no different from either the population mean hourly wage for those without a high school diploma or the population mean hourly wage for those with some college. In addition, the population mean hourly wage for those with a college diploma is no different from that of those with graduate school training. All other differences are statistically significant. With the regard to gender differences, there really is no new information gained from the post-hoc comparisons because gender consists of only two levels. Based on the results, males exceed females in their population mean hourly wage.

EXERCISES

13.1. The following illustrations are of population means and are, therefore, not subject to sampling error. They are based on the results of a fictional study to determine whether there is a relationship between gender, teaching method, and achievement in reading. Assume that each illustration represents a 2 × 3 between-subjects factorial design with equal cell sizes. Use the line graphs to answer the following questions.

For each graph:
a) Is there a main effect due to gender? What mean values are compared to make this assessment?
b) Is there a main effect due to teaching method? What mean values are compared to make this assessment?
c) Is there an interaction effect? What mean values or differences in mean values are compared to make this assessment?
d) Interpret the relative effectiveness of teaching method for males and females.

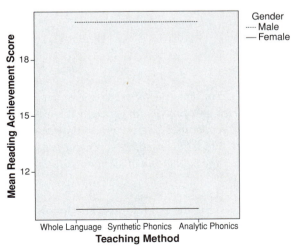

Graph 1

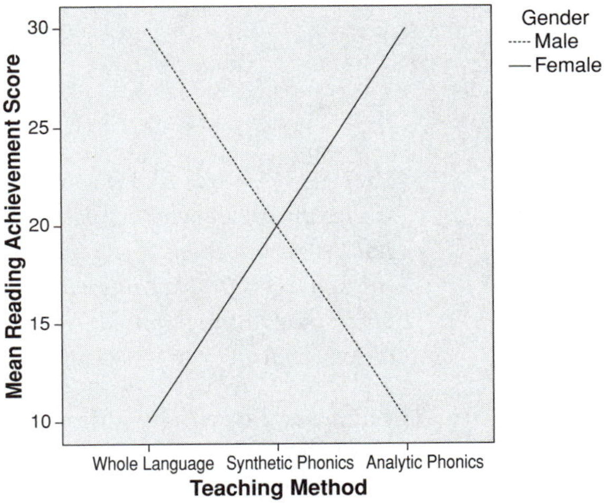

Graph 2

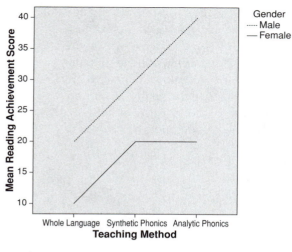

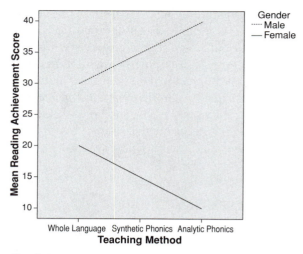

Graph 3   Graph 4

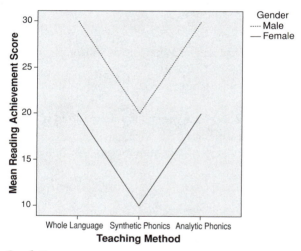

Graph 5

Exercises 13.2 and 13.3 involve the Framingham data set. In this series of exercises, we respectively investigate whether body mass index and age varied as a function of gender, whether or not the person smoked cigarettes, and the interaction of gender and whether or not the person smoked cigarettes. For inferential purposes, as described in the study itself, we consider the people in the Framingham data set to be a random sample of the population of all noninstitutionalized adults. Use $\alpha = .05$ for all significance tests.

13.2. The body mass index is a tool for indicating weight status in adults. The following questions relate to using a two-way ANOVA to determine whether at the beginning of the Framingham study body mass index (BMI1) varied as a function of gender (SEX), whether the person smoked (CURSMOKE1), and the interaction of gender and smoking status.

a) State the null and alternative hypotheses for each of the three tests associated with the ANOVA.

b) Create a multiple line graph of the sample means. Based on this graph, does there appear to be a statistically significant interaction effect? A statistically significant main effect due to gender? A statistically significant main effect due to cigarette use?

c) Evaluate the tenability of the normality assumption for these data or indicate why the assumption is not an issue for this analysis.

d) Evaluate the tenability of the homogeneity of variance assumption for these data or indicate why the assumption is not an issue for this analysis.

e) According to the ANOVA results, is there a statistically significant interaction effect? Is there a statistically significant main effect due to gender? Is there a statistically significant main effect due to cigarette use? Provide statistical support for your answer.

f) Is post-hoc testing necessary in this case? Why or why not? Interpret results.

g) Calculate and interpret the effect sizes of the statistically significant effects.

13.3. The following questions relate to using a two-way ANOVA to determine whether, at the beginning of the Framingham study, age (AGE1) varied as a function of gender (SEX), whether a person smoked (CURSMOKE1), and the interaction of gender and smoking status. Given the nature of the study design, the ANOVA in this case is considered to be robust to both normality and homogeneity of variance assumptions.

a) Create a multiple line graph of the sample means. Based on this graph, does there appear to be a statistically significant interaction effect? A statistically significant main effect due to gender? A statistically significant main effect due to cigarette use?

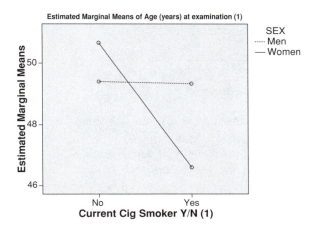

b) According to the ANOVA results, is there a statistically significant interaction effect? A statistically significant main effect due to gender? A statistically significant main effect due to cigarette use? Provide statistical support for your answer.

c) Given the statistically significant interaction, conduct and interpret simple effects, holding constant, in turn, cigarette use and then gender. If appropriate, conduct additional post-hoc tests as well. Note that, in the presence of this statistically significant interaction, main effects are not meaningful and should not be interpreted per se.

d) Calculate and interpret the effect sizes of the statistically significant effects.

Exercise 13.4 makes use of the Wages data set. In this exercise we are interested in whether number of years of work experience as of 1985 varies as a function of education level and gender. For inferential purposes, we consider the people in the Wages data set to be a random sample of the population of all adults living in America in 1985. Use α = .05 throughout this example.

13.4. The following questions relate to using a two-way ANOVA to determine whether the number of years of work experience as of 1985 varies as a function of gender (SEX), education level (ED), or the interaction between gender and education level.

    a) Create a multiple line graph of the sample means. Based on this graph, does there appear to be a statistically significant interaction effect? A statistically significant main effect due to gender? A statistically significant main effect due to education level?

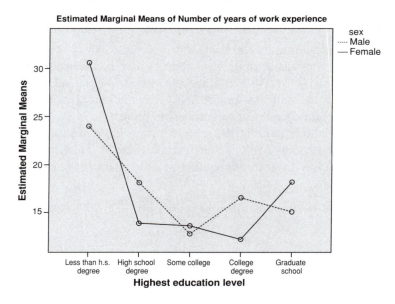

    b) Evaluate the tenability of the normality assumption for these data or indicate why the assumption is not an issue for this analysis.

    c) Evaluate the tenability of the homogeneity of variance assumption for these data or indicate why the assumption is not an issue for this analysis.

    d) According to the ANOVA results, is there a statistically significant interaction effect? A statistically significant main effect due to gender? A statistically significant main effect due to education? Provide statistical support for your answer.

    e) Given the statistically significant disordinal interaction, conduct and interpret a test of simple effects, and additional post-hoc tests, if necessary.

    f) Calculate and interpret the effect sizes of the statistically significant effects.

Exercises 13.5 and 13.6 require that you first enter the given data into SPSS. Use α = .05 for all significance tests.

13.5 Professor Dani teaches an undergraduate introductory statistics course. She teaches students from all four academic years in both morning and afternoon classes. She has reason to believe that either the grade level of the students or the time of the course or both may affect how well undergraduate students at her college do in her course. To test her conjecture, she randomly selects 40 of the students who register for her introductory statistics course the following term, 10 from each academic year, with 20 of those registered for the morning and 20 for the afternoon. At the end of the semester, she gives both classes the same final exam and arranges their final exam scores in a two-way ANOVA design, as shown in the following table. Use it to answer the following questions.

Factor B: Academic Year

		Freshmen	Sophomores	Juniors	Seniors
Factor A:	**Morning**	80	85	93	100
Time of		80	80	90	98
Course		75	80	89	95
		70	83	87	93
		70	82	87	90
	Afternoon	70	75	85	88
		70	71	84	83
		65	70	80	80
		60	69	73	79
		60	65	72	75

a) Create a table of cell and marginal means and standard deviations.

b) Evaluate the tenability of the underlying normality and homogeneity of variance assumptions or indicate why the assumptions are not an issue for this analysis.

c) Are any of the effects statistically significant? If so, which ones? Provide statistical support for your answer.

d) What is the proportion of variance explained by each of the statistically significant effects?

e) Create a line graph of the cell means to illustrate the effects. Explain how the line graph corroborates the results of the significance tests.

f) Describe the nature of the main effect due to time and explain why a Tukey post-hoc test is not necessary in this case.

g) Carry out a Tukey HSD post-hoc test on the main effect due to academic year to determine exactly which academic levels are different from which others with respect to final exam performance.

13.6. The data for this exercise are taken from the following website: http://lib.stat.cmu.edu/DASL/Datafiles/Stepping.html.

Students at Ohio State University conducted an experiment in the fall of 1993 to explore the nature of the relationship between a person's heart rate and the frequency at which that person stepped up and down on steps of various heights. The response variable, heart rate, was measured in beats per minute. For each person, the resting heart rate was measured before a trial (RestHR) and after stepping (HR). There were two different step heights (HEIGHT): 5.75 inches (coded as 0) and 11.5 inches (coded as 1). There were three rates of stepping (FREQUENCY): 14 steps/min. (coded as 0), 21 steps/min. (coded as 1), and 28 steps/min. (coded as 2). This resulted in six possible height/frequency combinations. Each subject performed the activity for three minutes. Subjects were kept on pace by the beat of an electric metronome. One experimenter counted the subject's heart rate, in beats per minute, for 20 seconds before and after each trial. The subject always rested between trials until her or his heart rate returned to close to the beginning rate. Another experimenter kept track of the time spent stepping. Each subject was always measured and timed by the same pair of experimenters to reduce variability in the experiment.

The data are saved as *Stepping.sav* on your CD. The following questions relate to using a two-way ANOVA to determine whether final heart rate varies by stepping rate, step height, and the interaction between the two.

Height	Frequency	RestHR	HR
0	0	60	75
0	1	63	84
1	2	69	135
1	0	69	108
0	2	69	93
1	1	96	141
1	0	87	120
0	0	90	99
1	2	93	153
0	2	87	129
1	1	72	99
0	1	69	93
1	0	78	93
0	2	72	99
1	2	78	129
0	0	87	93
1	1	87	111
1	2	81	120
0	2	75	123
0	1	81	96
1	0	84	99
1	0	84	99
1	1	90	129
0	1	75	90
0	0	78	87
0	0	84	84
0	1	90	108
0	2	78	96
1	1	84	90
1	2	90	147

a) Evaluate the tenability of the underlying normality and homogeneity of variance assumptions or indicate why the assumptions are not an issue for this analysis.

b) Is there a statistically significant interaction effect? Provide statistical support for your answer.

c) Is there a statistically significant main effect due to stepping rate? Provide statistical support for your answer.

d) Describe the nature of the main effect due to stepping rate.

e) Is there a statistically significant main effect due to step height? Provide statistical support for your answer.

f) Describe the nature of the main effect due to step height.

13.7. Three methods of dieting are compared for effectiveness in terms of pounds lost. Because it is believed that a person's gender may influence the relative effectiveness of the three methods, a two-way ANOVA balanced design with equal cell sizes is employed and the summary table is provided.

Tests of Between-Subjects Effects
Dependent Variable: Weight Loss

Source	Type III Sum of Squares	df	Mean Square	F	Sig.
Corrected Model	626.400[a]	5	125.280	18.514	.000
Intercept	4177.200	1	4177.200	617.320	.000
GENDER	48.133	1	48.133	7.113	.013
TREATMEN	453.800	2	226.900	33.532	.000
GENDER * TREATMEN	124.467	2	62.233	9.197	.001
Error	162.400	24	6.767		
Total	4966.000	30			
Corrected Total	788.800	29			

[a]R Squared = .794 (Adjusted R Squared = .751)

a) Describe the design by filling in the blanks in the following sentence: The design is a _____ × _____ balanced ANOVA with _____ participants per cell.

b) Complete the following table by filling in the values of the shaded boxes.

Weight Loss by Treatment

	Sum of Squares	df	Mean Square	F	Sig.
Between groups					
Within groups					
Total					

c) Which of the two types of design, the one-way or two-way, is the more powerful test of treatment, in this case? Explain.

13.8. A hypothetical study was conducted to determine whether weight differs by incidence of coronary heart disease (CHD) and cigarette use. One hundred people were randomly selected from among each of the four conditions: no-CHD nonsmokers, no-CHD smokers, CHD nonsmokers, and CHD smokers. The following line graph represents the results of the study.

a) Does the line graph suggest a main effect due to cigarette use? If so, describe the nature of the effect.

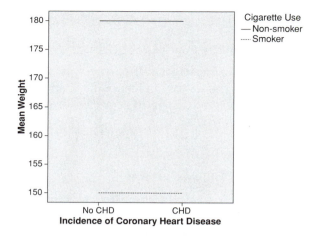

b) Does the line graph suggest a main effect due to incidence of CHD? If so, describe the nature of the effect.

c) Does the line graph suggest an interaction effect? If so, describe the nature of the effect.

d) The factorial ANOVA design in this situation is orthogonal (or balanced) because
   (i)   the lines representing the mean weights of the cells are parallel.
   (ii) the cell sizes are all equal.
   (iii) there are two factors represented (Cigarette Use and Incidence of Coronary Heart Disease (CHD)) in a 2 × 2 configuration.
   (iv) none of the above.

e) Based on the results depicted in the line graph, complete the two-way ANOVA table by filling in the values of the shaded boxes.

Source of Variation	SS	df	MS	F-value	p-value
CHD					
Cigarette Use					
Interaction					
Error	35,000				
Total	76,000				

13.9. Is the number of sources of variance in a 2 × 3 ANOVA design different from the number of sources of variance in a 3 × 5 ANOVA design? What are these sources of variance?

13.10. Under what conditions is the two-way ANOVA generally more powerful than the one-way ANOVA?

CHAPTER FOURTEEN

Correlation and Simple Regression as Inferential Techniques

In Chapter 5, we discussed the Pearson Product Moment Correlation Coefficient used to assess the degree of linear relationship between two variables. Recall that in Chapter 5 we assessed the degree of linear relationship between fat grams and calories by type of McDonald's hamburger as one example. In Chapter 6, we discussed how this linear relationship could be used to develop a linear prediction system (a linear regression equation) to predict the value of one variable when the value of the other variable is known. Recall that in Chapter 6 we developed a linear regression equation for predicting the number of calories in a McDonald's hamburger from its fat grams.

In both situations, our discussions were limited to descriptive settings. That is, our measures of linear relationship and accuracy of prediction were confined to the data at hand. In this chapter, we discuss inferential techniques applicable to measures of relationship and linear regression that enable us to generalize our results from a sample to the population from which that sample was randomly selected.

As with other inferential techniques described in this text, the inferential techniques described in this chapter are based on certain assumptions about the distribution of the parent population. Because the parent population relevant to measuring the linear relationship between two variables is comprised of *pairs of values*, the distribution of this parent population is described as a *joint distribution* and, in particular, as a *bivariate distribution*. Extending the assumption of population normality in the case of inferential tests based on univariate distributions (e.g., tests of means), the major assumption underlying the inferential test of a linear relationship between two variables is that of *bivariate normality* in the population. That is, the parent population from which the sample of pairs of values has been randomly selected is assumed in this case to have a bivariate normal distribution.

THE BIVARIATE NORMAL DISTRIBUTION

A bivariate distribution is a special case of a joint distribution in which exactly two variables are considered simultaneously or jointly. If we call one variable X and the other variable Y, we can depict a bivariate distribution graphically by using a scatterplot with the two axes labeled X and Y, respectively. Figure 14.1 shows a bivariate distribution and its corresponding scatterplot.

Whereas each pair of values in Figure 14.1 occurs with frequency of 1, in other situations, some of the pairs of values, if not all, can occur with frequency greater than 1. To represent these different frequencies, we introduce a third axis perpendicular to the X and Y

X	Y
2	3
3	3
3	4
5	7
5	3
5	5
6	7
6	6
6	9
7	5
7	7
7	8
7	10
8	9
10	8

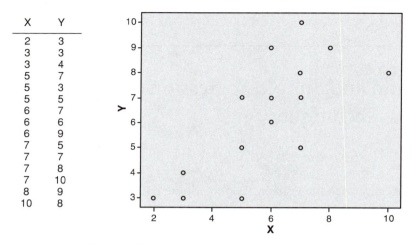

Figure 14.1   A bivariate distribution and its corresponding scatterplot.

axes. Figure 14.2 shows a bivariate distribution with some frequencies of pairs of values greater than 1 along with its scatterplot.

If X and Y are both continuous and they assume all possible values with varied frequencies, we can represent the bivariate frequency distribution of X and Y graphically as a continuous surface (kind of like a tent) sitting on top of the X,Y plane. In this chapter, we are interested in a specific type of bivariate distribution: a *bivariate normal distribution*. Such a distribution has the following seven characteristics:

1. Taken separately, the X and Y variables are both normally distributed.
2. When X is held constant at any value (for example, $X = a$), the distribution of all the Y values corresponding to this value of X (called the conditional distribution of Y given $X = a$) is normally distributed.

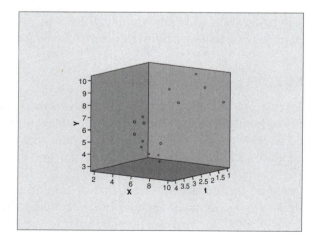

X	Y	f
2	3	1
3	3	1
3	4	2
5	7	3
5	3	2
5	5	3
6	7	4
6	6	4
6	9	2
7	5	3
7	7	4
7	8	2
7	10	1
8	9	1
10	8	1

Figure 14.2   A bivariate distribution and scatterplot with some frequencies greater than 1.

3. When Y is held constant at any value (for example, $Y = b$), the distribution of all the X values corresponding to this value of Y (called the conditional distribution of X given $Y = b$) is normally distributed.

4. All the conditional distributions of Y given X have the same standard deviation $\sigma_{Y|X}$.

5. All the conditional distributions of X given Y have the same standard deviation $\sigma_{X|Y}$.

6. The means of all the conditional distributions of Y given X fall along a straight line.

7. The means of all the conditional distributions of X given Y fall along a straight line.

We may cluster the seven characteristics of the bivariate normal distribution into the following three properties:

Normality – Characteristics 1, 2, and 3
Homoscedasticity – Characteristics 4 and 5
Linearity – Characteristics 6 and 7

As we would expect from our experience with univariate normal distributions (normal distributions of one variable), all bivariate normal distributions give rise to frequency or relative frequency curves of a particular shape. This shape is often described as a bell that has been stretched in one direction sitting above the X, Y plane. Figure 14.3 shows a typical bivariate normal distribution curve when there is no stretching in either direction; that is, when the correlation between X and Y is zero. The bivariate normal distribution of Figure 14.3 may be described as a Hershey kiss with its top licked down a bit!

Figure 14.4 shows the same bivariate normal distribution curve composed of a series of cross sections or slices at particular values of X. Each slice is a conditional distribution of Y given X. Notice that all slices satisfy the conditional distribution characteristics of a bivariate normal distribution. They are normally distributed (*normality*) with the same standard deviation $\sigma_{Y|X}$ (*homoscedasticity*) and their means all fall along a straight line (*linearity*).

The assumption of bivariate normality (defined by the characteristics of linearity, homoscedasticity, and normality) in the population is required for the tests of inference introduced in this chapter regarding the Pearson Product Moment Correlation Coefficient. In this chapter we discuss methods to evaluate these assumptions. Correlation is a symmetric index. That is, the value of the correlation indicates the degree to which X relates to Y and the degree to which Y relates to X.

☞ **Remark.** Less restrictive assumptions are required for tests of inference regarding (simple) linear regression. The assumptions of linearity, homoscedasticity, and normality are still required, but as they concern the population conditional Y distributions given X

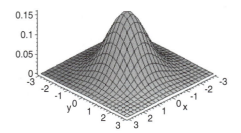

Figure 14.3 A typical bivariate normal distribution.

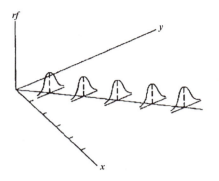

Figure 14.4   Cross sections or slices of a typical bivariate normal distribution curve.

(the slices illustrated in Figure 14.4) and not the conditional *X* distributions given *Y* as well. Less restrictive assumptions are appropriate in simple linear regression because it is based on an asymmetric relationship between *X* and *Y*. The asymmetric relationship is created by the necessity of designating *Y* as the dependent variable and, in so doing, emphasizing the importance of *Y* over *X*.

TESTING WHETHER THE POPULATION PEARSON PRODUCT MOMENT CORRELATION EQUALS ZERO

Suppose you are making extra money one summer by selling ice cream on the beach and notice that a positive trend exists between the daily highest temperature and the number of ice cream bars you sell that day. Suppose also that you are an astute businessperson and do not want to have to carry and refrigerate more ice cream than you will be able to sell. Accordingly, you check the weather forecast each morning, and the higher the temperature is expected to be, the more ice cream bars you take out with you. In other words, you use the temperature to *predict* your ice cream sales.

But, we can be even more systematic than this in making our predictions. Table 14.1 contains the temperature and ice cream sales for 30 days randomly selected between May 15 and September 6. It is saved as the file *Icecream.sav*.

Figure 14.5 presents the scatterplot of the bivariate distribution given in Table 14.1. The regression line for predicting sales from temperature is included in the plot as well.

To obtain a scatterplot with a regression line superimposed as in Figure 14.5 using SPSS, click **Graphs** in the main menu bar, **Legacy Dialogs, Scatter**, and **Define**. Move the variable TEMP to the **Y-axis** box and the variable BARSOLD to the **X-axis** box. Click **Continue**. To have the regression line included in the scatterplot, double click anywhere on the scatterplot that appears in the Output Navigator. You will now be in the Chart Editor. Click **Elements, Fit Line Total**. Click **OK**.

According to Figure 14.5, we may surmise that the linear relationship is a strong one because the points hug the regression line rather well. Furthermore, the nature of the relationship is positive – with each unit increase in temperature along the horizontal axis, there is a corresponding increase in sales along the vertical axis.

Although this relationship appears to be a strong one, it is based only on 30 randomly selected days. Our question of true interest is whether this relationship based on

Table 14.1. Temperature and ice cream sales for 30 randomly selected summer days

TEMP	BARSOLD	TEMP	BARSOLD
75	170	59	143
70	160	86	173
65	155	88	176
60	150	85	177
72	153	90	185
60	142	74	163
63	145	73	160
68	156	71	162
78	170	68	148
77	172	70	160
75	165	73	154
75	167	85	169
80	175	90	178
82	180	70	175
85	180	81	164

30 randomly selected days holds for all summer days during the time period sampled. In this context, we consider the sample correlation (r) as an estimate of the population correlation coefficient (*rho* or ρ) and apply an inferential test to determine whether the correlation between temperature and sales is greater than zero in the population – that is, whether the observed correlation coefficient r based on the sample data is greater enough than zero to infer that the corresponding population parameter ρ based on all summer days during the time period sampled is greater than zero as well.

Because our hypothesis is directional in this case, our null and alternative hypotheses are

$$H_0: \rho = 0$$
$$H_1: \rho > 0.$$

Figure 14.5 Scatterplot of bivariate distribution relating temperature to number of ice creams bars sold.

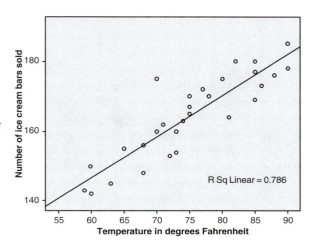

We assume that the parent population from which we have randomly sampled our 30 pairs of values has a bivariate normal distribution (as defined in the preceding section). If the null hypothesis, H_0: $\rho = 0$, is true, then it can be shown mathematically that the appropriate sampling distribution is the t-distribution presented earlier in connection with tests on means, and the appropriate t statistic is

$$t = \frac{r - 0}{\sqrt{(1 - r^2)/(N - 2)}}$$

$$df = N - 2,$$

(14.1)

where r represents the sample Pearson Product Moment Correlation Coefficient and $N - 2$ equals the number of degrees of freedom - two less than the number of pairs of values in the sample.

As we have done in Chapter 5, we use SPSS to calculate the Pearson Product Moment Correlation. Before proceeding, however, we use the scatterplot of the small data set represented in Figure 14.5 to check informally whether the assumptions of linearity, homoscedasticity, and normality are viable. According to Figure 14.5, violations of these assumptions do not appear to exist. The points conform reasonably well to a linear pattern supporting the assumption of linearity; the spread of ice cream sales for each temperature value (the conditional distributions of ice cream sales given temperature) and the spread of temperature given ice cream sales (the conditional distributions of temperature given ice cream sales) appear similar, supporting the assumption of homoscedasticity. Overall there do not appear to be severe outliers either in the univariate or conditional distributions, supporting the assumption of normality.

To obtain the Pearson Product Moment Correlation using SPSS, along with its p-value, click **Analyze** from the main menu bar, **Correlate**, **Bivariate**. Move TEMP and BARSOLD into the **Variables** box. Click **One-Tailed** for the Test of Significance in this case.

We obtain the following output:

Correlations

		barsold Number of ice cream bars sold	temp Temperature in degrees Fahrenheit
barsold Number of ice cream bars sold	Pearson Correlation	1	.887**
	Sig. (1-tailed)		.000
	N	30	30
temp Temperatue in degrees Fahrenheit	Pearson Correlation	.887**	1
	Sig. (1-tailed)	.000	
	N	30	30

**Correlation is significant at the 0.01 level (1-tailed).

The correlation between number of ice cream bars sold and temperature in degrees. Fahrenheit is .887 based on $N = 30$ pairs of values. The double asterisk indicates that the correlation is significant at the .01 level (one-tailed). A more exact p-value (.000) is given in the correlation matrix itself, suggesting that in fact $p < .0005$.

The significance (p-value) of the correlation that is provided in the output is based on the t-statistic given as Equation 14.1, but the t-value itself is not provided. We may calculate it, however, as follows:

$$t = \frac{r - 0}{\sqrt{(1 - r^2)/(N - 2)}} = \frac{.887 - 0}{\sqrt{(1 - .887^2)/(30 - 2)}} = \frac{.887}{\sqrt{.213/28}} = \frac{.887}{.087} = 10.20.$$

We may also note that the degrees of freedom for this example are $N - 2 = 30 - 2 = 28$.

If we wish, we may use the obtained t-value and corresponding degrees of freedom to find the p-value from the CDF.T(q,df) function in SPSS or from Table 2 in Appendix C. Using SPSS, we find that $1 - $ CDF.T(10.1,28) $= .0000000000386$, justifying the value provided in the correlation matrix. Using Table 2, we obtain the estimate $p < .0005$.

USING A CONFIDENCE INTERVAL TO ESTIMATE THE SIZE OF THE POPULATION CORRELATION COEFFICIENT, ρ

We may construct by hand confidence intervals (CIs) around r to estimate ρ using a method developed by R.A. Fisher. We construct these by hand because such intervals are not available through SPSS. The method for constructing such CIs is based on a transformation (called Fisher's Z-transformation) that converts r to Z values using Equation 14.2:

$$Z_r = .5 \ln \frac{1 + r}{1 - r} \tag{14.2}$$

A plot of the r-to-Z relationship is given in Figure 14.6.

Notice that from $r = -.50$ to $r = +.50$ the relationship is linear. Because this portion of the graph has slope equal to 1.00 and it passes through the origin, the transformation does not change correlation values that are originally between $-.50$ and $+.50$. The more the

Figure 14.6 Relationship between r and Fisher's Z.

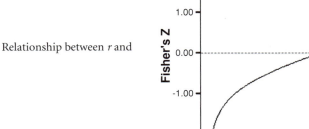

correlation diverges from zero, the greater the difference between r and Z. The net result of the Fisher r-to-Z transformation is to transform r-values from an ordinal scale to an interval one.

Assuming that the population has a bivariate normal distribution, the equation for the upper and lower limits of the CI estimate of ρ in terms of the Z-transformed values is

$$UpperLimit = Z_r + (z_{\text{critical}})\left(\frac{1}{\sqrt{N-3}}\right)$$

$$LowerLimit = Z_r - (z_{\text{critical}})\left(\frac{1}{\sqrt{N-3}}\right) \qquad (14.3)$$

where

$$\begin{aligned} z_{\text{critical}} &= 1.645 \text{ for a } 90 \text{ percent CI} \\ &= 1.960 \text{ for a } 95 \text{ percent CI} \\ &= 2.576 \text{ for a } 99 \text{ percent CI} \end{aligned}$$

Using this method, we construct a 95 percent CI for ρ, the correlation between temperature in degrees Fahrenheit and ice cream sales in the population, in terms of Z-transformed values.

1. Transform $r = .887$ to Z using the transform feature of SPSS. The Z-value obtained is 1.408.

To use SPSS to transform $r = .887$ to Z, click on **Transform** on the main menu bar, and **Compute**. Type the variable name Z in the **Target Variable** box and type the following expression in the **Numeric Expression** box: .5*LN((1 + .887)/(1 − .887)).

---

2. Compute the upper limit as: $1.408 + 1.96\left(\dfrac{1}{\sqrt{27}}\right) = 1.408 + 1.96(.192) = 1.785$.

3. Compute the lower limit as: $1.408 - 1.96\left(\dfrac{1}{\sqrt{27}}\right) = 1.408 - 1.96(.192) = 1.031$.

Therefore, the 95 percent CI for ρ in terms of the Fisher Z values is $1.031 \leq Z_\rho \leq 1.785$.

To make this estimate more meaningful, we transform these upper and lower limits back into correlation values. To do so, we use Equation 14.4:

$$r = \frac{e^{2Z} - 1}{e^{2Z} + 1}, \qquad (14.4)$$

where the letter e represents a constant approximately equal to 2.718.

Using Equation 14.4 the r-values corresponding to the Z-values of 1.031 and 1.785 are, respectively:

$$r = \frac{e^{2(1.031)} - 1}{e^{2(1.031)} + 1} = \frac{e^{2.062} - 1}{e^{2.062} + 1} = \frac{7.86 - 1}{7.86 + 1} = \frac{6.86}{8.86} = .774$$

$$r = \frac{e^{2(1.785)} - 1}{e^{2(1.785)} + 1} = \frac{e^{3.570} - 1}{e^{3.570} + 1} = \frac{35.52 - 1}{35.52 + 1} = \frac{34.52}{36.52} = .945.$$

To use SPSS to transform $Z = 1.031$ to r, click on **Transform** from the main menu bar and then **Compute**. Type a variable name (e.g., lower) in the **Target Variable** box. Type the expression $(Exp(2*1.031) - 1)/(Exp(2*1.031) + 1)$. Click **OK**. The result, lower = .774, may be found in the last column of the data editor. Follow the same procedure to transform $Z = 1.785$ to r to find the upper limit in terms of r. Note that Exp is the name used by SPSS to denote the constant e.

That is, the 95 percent CI for ρ centered about r is $.774 \leq \rho \leq .945$, suggesting that the correlation between temperature and ice cream sales in the population from which our 30 days were randomly selected is very high and positive. We are using this CI to estimate ρ, not to test the set of directional hypotheses given earlier. CIs may be used to test nondirectional hypotheses only.

☞ **Remark.** Although CIs for means are symmetric about the sample mean, $\overline{X}$, CIs for correlations are not symmetric about the sample correlation r.

. . . .

EXAMPLE 14.1. Use the NELS data set to determine whether there is a correlation between reading achievement and math achievement in twelfth grade in the population. Estimate the size of the population correlation by constructing a 95 percent CI about ρ.

Solution. Using the SPSS Correlate Bivariate procedure we find that the Pearson Product Moment Correlation Coefficient, r, between ACHMAT12 and ACHRDG12 equals .636. Because our question is whether the correlation is different from zero, a two-tailed test of significance is appropriate. According to our output, the correlation is statistically significantly different from zero ($p < .0005$), and we observe from the sign of the correlation that the relationship is positive. Using our definitions of effect size, we may also note that the relationship is a strong one.

To find the 95 percent CI about r, we follow the procedure detailed earlier.

We click on **Transform** on the main menu bar, and **Compute**. We type the variable name Z in the **Target Variable** box and type the following expression in the **Numeric Expression** box: $.5*LN((1 + .636)/(1 - .636))$. In so doing, we obtain $Z = .7514$.

We compute the upper limit in terms of the transformed Z-score as

$$.7514 + 1.96\left(\frac{1}{\sqrt{497}}\right) = .7514 + 1.96(.045) = .8396.$$

We next compute the lower limit in terms of the transformed Z-score as

$$.7514 - 1.96\left(\frac{1}{\sqrt{497}}\right) = .7514 - 1.96(.045) = .6632.$$

Finally, we transform the upper and lower limits in terms of Z-values into upper and uower uimits in terms of r-values using Equation 14.4 and the following SPSS commands.

We click **Transform** from the main menu bar and then **Compute**. We type a variable name (e.g., upper) in the **Target Variable** box and type the expression $(Exp (2*.8396) - 1)/(Exp (2*.8396) + 1)$. The upper limit in terms of r equals .69.

In following the same procedure, we obtain the lower limit in terms of r as $r = .58$. Accordingly, the 95 percent CI for r is $.58 \leq \rho \leq .69$, suggesting that the population correlation is likely to fall between .58 and .69. Because zero does not fall within this interval, we know once again that the correlation is statistically significantly different from zero. Because the range is in the positive region, we know also that the relationship is positive. Furthermore, because .58 is substantially greater than zero, we can be confident that the effect size for this result is large.

REVISITING SIMPLE LINEAR REGRESSION FOR PREDICTION

The discovery of a linear relationship between highest daily temperature and ice cream sales (the higher the temperature, the greater the number of ice cream sales) is an important aspect of the process of setting up a linear regression equation to predict number of ice cream sales from temperature. The linear prediction equation for this example has number of ice cream sales as the dependent variable (otherwise called a *criterion variable*) and highest daily temperature as the independent variable (otherwise called a *predictor variable*).

Because there is only one independent variable, this type of regression is called *simple linear regression*. When there is more than one independent variable in the equation (for example, when we use both highest daily temperature *and* humidity to predict ice cream sales) we have what is called *multiple linear regression*. In the next chapter we discuss multiple linear regression and related issues.

Recall that in Chapter 6 we introduced simple linear regression for prediction in a descriptive context. In this chapter we introduce tests of inference in connection with simple linear prediction.

As we recall from Chapter 6, the linear regression (prediction) equation is

$$\hat{Y} = bX + a, \tag{14.5}$$

where

$$b = r\frac{S_Y}{S_X} \tag{14.6}$$

$$a = \overline{Y} - b\overline{X}. \tag{14.7}$$

Equation 14.5 may be represented by a line that has slope b and intercept a. The slope b is also called the *regression coefficient* and is interpreted as the amount of change in Y, on average, for each unit increase in X. In short, b represents the *effect* that X has on Y. The intercept a is interpreted as the predicted value of Y associated with $X = 0$. The intercept a is defined to allow the regression line to pass through the center of the bivariate distribution or scatterplot, $(\overline{X}, \overline{Y})$. If you are average on the X variable, you are predicted to be average on the Y variable.

ESTIMATING THE POPULATION STANDARD ERROR OF PREDICTION, $\sigma_{Y|X}$

If the linear regression equation is based on a sample of values randomly selected from a bivariate normal population, then $\hat{Y}$ is an unbiased estimate of the mean of the conditional distribution of Y given X for all values of X within the sampling frame. That is, given that the population has a bivariate normal distribution as shown in Figure 14.4, the slices of the bivariate distribution for each X value are normally distributed in the population with mean $\overline{Y} = \hat{Y}$ and standard deviation $\sigma_{Y|X}$. Thus, if Carolyn has a value of $X = X_1$, then the linear regression equation predicts Carolyn's Y value to be equal to the mean of all the Y values for the individuals in the sample who, like Carolyn, have $X = X_1$.

This is a reasonable prediction because, among other things, the mean of any normal distribution is the value that has the largest frequency. Although the prediction is reasonable, the possibility still exists that Carolyn's actual Y score is one of the other Y scores corresponding to $X = X_1$. The accuracy of the prediction depends on how closely the Y scores for all individuals who have $X = X_1$ are to one another and to their mean or, in other words, on the spread of the Y distribution for all individuals who have $X = X_1$. The spread of this conditional Y distribution given X_1 is measured by the standard deviation of this conditional Y distribution given X_1 and is denoted as $\sigma_{Y|X_1}$. The less the Y values deviate from their mean for all individuals with $X = X_1$, the smaller the error of prediction that can be expected. The better the linear model fits the data, the closer $\hat{Y}$ will be to $\bar{Y}$ given $X = X_1$ and the smaller the expected error of prediction for $X = X_1$.

We may generalize from the case of $X = X_1$ to all values of X because of the bivariate normal distribution property of homoscedasticity. This property tells us that *all* the conditional distributions of Y given X have the same standard deviation as the Y distribution corresponding to $X = X_1$. Accordingly, we do not have to link the standard deviation of the conditional Y value given X to any particular X value, such as X_1. We may use a more generic measure for the spread of the conditional Y distributions given X for the population at large. This measure is called the *standard error of prediction* (also called the *standard error of estimate*), denoted by $\sigma_{Y|X}$.

We may use the sample data on which the linear regression equation was developed to obtain an estimate of $\sigma_{Y|X}$. This estimate is denoted by $\hat{\sigma}_{Y|X}$ and is given by Equation 14.8:

$$\hat{\sigma}_{Y|X} = \sqrt{\frac{\sum (Y_i - \hat{Y}_i)^2}{N - 2}}, \tag{14.8}$$

where Y_i is the actual Y score of individual i in the sample, $\hat{Y}_i$ is the predicted Y score of individual i in the sample using the linear regression equation, and N is the number of pairs of values in the sample.

TESTING THE b-WEIGHT FOR STATISTICAL SIGNIFICANCE

$\hat{Y}$ is an unbiased estimate of the mean of the conditional distribution of Y given X for all values of X. In addition, the slope b of the regression (prediction) line is an unbiased estimate of the slope of the population regression line.

To test whether there is a relationship in the population between Y and the single predictor X, we may test the regression coefficient b for significance. As we shall see, this test is equivalent to the test for the significance of the correlation coefficient r presented earlier in this chapter.

The test of the regression coefficient b is

$$t = \frac{b - 0}{\hat{\sigma}_b} \tag{14.9}$$
$$df = N - 2,$$

where $\hat{\sigma}_b$ represents the standard error of b, the standard deviation of the sampling distribution of b-weights based on random samples of the same size randomly drawn from the same population. This t-value tests whether the b-coefficient differs from 0 in the population. It has $N-2$ degrees of freedom-two less than the number of pairs of scores.

As we shall see, the t-value, including the b-coefficient and the standard error of the b-coefficient, along with its two-tailed level of significance are given as part of the SPSS regression output.

For completeness, the equation of the standard error of b is

$$\hat{\sigma}_b = \sqrt{\frac{\frac{1}{N-2}\sum(Y_i - \hat{Y}_i)^2}{(N-1)\hat{\sigma}_X^2}}. \tag{14.10}$$

Thus, the standard error of b is a function of the accuracy of the regression equation as measured by $\frac{1}{N-2}\sum(Y - \hat{Y})^2$ relative to (a function of) the variance estimate of X, $\hat{\sigma}_X^2$. In general, then, the standard error of the b-coefficient of X in Equation 14.5 is smaller when X has a larger variance.

. . . .

EXAMPLE 14.2. Construct the linear regression equation for predicting number of ice cream bars sold (BARSOLD) from highest daily temperature (TEMP) for the whole summer. Interpret the equation as well as the various tests of significance reported in the output.

Solution.

To perform a regression analysis using SPSS, click **Analyze** on the main menu bar, **Regression**, **Linear**. Move BARSOLD to the **Dependent** box and TEMP to the **Independent** box. Click the gray **Statistics** box. In addition to **Estimates** and **Model Fit**, click **Confidence Intervals** and **Descriptives**. Click **Continue, OK.**

Parts of the SPSS output are reproduced in the tables that follow.

Descriptive Statistics

	Mean	Std. Deviation	N
barsold Number of ice cream bars sold	164.23	11.907	30
temp Temperature in degrees Fahrenheit	74.93	8.944	30

From the table labeled Descriptives, we may verify that this analysis is based on a sample of size $N = 30$. The mean and standard deviation of number of ice cream bars sold for the 30 days captured by the sample is approximately 164 and 12, respectively. The mean and standard deviation of highest daily temperature for the 30 days captured by the sample is approximately 75 and 9, respectively.

Correlations

		barsold Number of ice cream bars sold	temp Temperature in degrees Fahrenheit
Pearson Correlation	barsold Number of ice cream bars sold	1.000	.887
	temp Temperature in degrees Fahrenheit	.887	1.000
Sig. (1-tailed)	barsold Number of ice cream bars sold	.	.000
	temp Temperature in degrees Fahrenheit	.000	.
N	barsold Number of ice cream bars sold	30	30
	temp Temperature in degrees Fahrenheit	30	30

From the table labeled Correlations, we verify that the correlation between temperature and ice cream sales is .877 with two-tailed level of significance $p < .001$.

Coefficients[a]

Model		Unstandardized Coefficients		Standardized Coefficients	t	Sig.	95% Confidence Interval for B	
		B	Std. Error	Beta			Lower Bound	Upper Bound
1	(Constant)	75.779	8.775		8.635	.000	57.803	93.755
	temp Temperature in degrees Fahrenheit	1.180	.116	.887	10.149	.000	.942	1.419

[a]Dependent Variable: barsold Number of ice cream bars sold

From the table labeled Coefficients we learn that the simple linear regression equation for predicting ice cream sales from highest daily temperature is:

Predicted BARSOLD = 1.18*TEMP + 75.78.

The *b*-coefficient for TEMP is 1.18, indicating that, for every one degree rise in temperature, 1.18 more ice cream bars are sold on average. The constant or intercept is 75.78. That is, when TEMP = 0, the number of ice creams that are predicted to be sold equals 75.78. Although in some contexts the constant has a meaningful interpretation, in this one it does not because 0 degrees Fahrenheit is not a plausible or realistic temperature reading for the summer, the time period under study.

Recall that the intercept equals the value that allows the regression line to pass through the center of the scatterplot, $\bar{X}, \bar{Y}$. In this case, the center of the scatterplot is at 74.93, 164.23.

When the highest daily temperature is equal to the mean temperature for the days sampled (74.93), the number of bars sold is predicted to equal the mean number of bars sold for the days sampled (164.23).

To determine whether the slope (or b-coefficient or b-weight) is statistically significantly different from zero, we refer to the t-test with $N - 2$ degrees of freedom and its corresponding two-tailed significance level, or p-value, from the Coefficients table. In our example, $t(28) = 10.15$, $p < .001$, suggesting that in fact the regression weight is statistically significantly different from zero. Looking at the sign of b in this case of simple linear regression, the relationship may be inferred to be positive. That is, the observed positive relationship between ice cream sales and temperature holds for the population of all summer days, not just for the 30 days that comprised our random sample.

We may calculate by hand the standard error of b using Equation 14.10:

$\hat{\sigma}_b = \sqrt{\dfrac{\dfrac{1}{N-2}\sum(Y_i - \hat{Y}_i)^2}{(N-1)\hat{\sigma}_X^2}}$. To do so, we first compute $\dfrac{1}{N-2}\sum(Y_i - \hat{Y}_i)^2$, the mean

squared residual, MS_{RES}. In particular, we obtain the predicted Y values from SPSS using the procedure described in Chapter 6 in Example 6.2, part (1).

$$\begin{aligned} MS_{RES} &= \frac{1}{28}\big((170 - 164.31)^2 + (160 - 158.41)^2 + (155 - 152.51)^2 + \cdots \\ &\quad + (178 - 182.02)^2 + (175 - 158.41)^2 + (164 - 171.39)^2 \big) \\ &= 31.385. \end{aligned}$$

From the table of Descriptive Statistics, we have the values for both N (30) and the standard deviation of X, temperature in degrees Fahrenheit (8.94). Substituting these values and the

value for MS_{RES} into Equation 14.10, we obtain $\hat{\sigma}_b = \sqrt{\dfrac{31.385}{(30 - 1)(8.94)^2}} = .116$, which is

the value printed in the Coefficients table for the standard error of b.

We may also verify that the t-value of 10.15 is obtained from Equation 14.8-the ratio of the b-coefficient divided by its standard error, $1.18/.116 = 10.15$.

Finally, we may note that, in the case of simple regression, the test of significance for the regression coefficient b is equivalent to the test of significance for the correlation coefficient r. We may do so by noting that the t-values based on Equations 14.1 and 14.8 are the same ($t = 10.15$).

The t-test of the b-coefficient tells us whether the b-coefficient in the population is statistically significantly different from zero. The 95 percent CI about b gives us an estimate of the likely values of the b-coefficient in the population. From the printout we may note that reasonable estimates of the b-weight are between .942 and 1.419. That the interval does not include zero corroborates the result of the t-test-that the b-coefficient is different from zero in the population. That the CI includes only positive values suggests that the b-coefficient in the population is positive and that increases in daily temperature associate with increases in ice cream sales and decreases in daily temperature associate with decreases in ice cream sales.

We turn now to another explanation of simple regression that is based on a decomposition of total sums of squares about the mean. This explanation links simple regression to the analysis of variance (ANOVA) framework and enables us to understand additional regression output provided by SPSS and other computer programs.

EXPLAINING SIMPLE REGRESSION USING AN ANALYSIS OF VARIANCE FRAMEWORK

Recall that in one-way ANOVA the total variability (SS_T) of the dependent variable may be decomposed in into two unrelated (orthogonal) components: variability due to the between-group effect (SS_B) and variability due to a within-group effect (SS_W). In the context of regression, SS_B is referred to as SS_{REG} (sum of squares due to regression) and SS_W is referred to as SS_{RES}, the sum of squares due to residual or error. Analogously, we may decompose or partition the total variability of the dependent variable in simple regression. We begin with $Y - \overline{Y}$, which is the error in predicting Y if we were to use $\overline{Y}$ to predict Y. The questions is: How much closer can we get to Y by predicting Y from a new variable X using a regression equation?

As shown in Figure 14.7, $Y - \overline{Y}$, the total difference between an actual Y value and its mean may be expressed as the sum of the two nonoverlapping components, $\hat{Y} - \overline{Y}$ and $Y - \overline{Y}$:

$$Y - \overline{Y} = (\hat{Y} - \overline{Y}) + (Y - \hat{Y}) \tag{14.11}$$

The first component represents that part of the total difference that is explained or accounted for by the relationship of Y with X; the other component represents that part of the total difference that remains after accounting for the relationship of Y with X.

If both sides of Equation 14.10 are squared, summed, and then simplified using properties of the regression equation, we obtain Equation 14.12:

$$\sum(Y - \overline{Y})^2 = \sum(\hat{Y} - \overline{Y})^2 + \sum(Y - \hat{Y})^2. \tag{14.12}$$

The term on the left-hand side of Equation 14.12 equals the sum of squared deviations of the actual (as opposed to predicted) values of Y about its mean and is what we have called the *total sum of squares* (SS_T) of Y. The first term on the right-hand side of Equation 14.12 equals the sum of squared deviations of the predicted values of Y, $\hat{Y}$, about the mean of the actual values of Y. Because it represents that part of Y's variability that is due to Y's relation to X (symbolized by $\hat{Y}$), this term is called the *sum of squares due to the regression* (SS_{REG}). The second term on the right-hand side of Equation 14.12 is the sum of the squared deviations between the actual and predicted values of Y. Because it represents that part of Y's variability that is left over after accounting for Y's relation to X (symbolized by $\hat{Y}$), this term is called the sum of squares due to residual (SS_{RES}). We may note that the sum of squares due

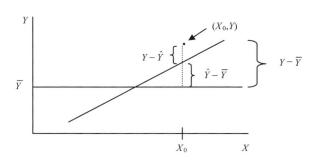

Figure 14.7 Decomposing the difference of the dependent variable from its mean.

to residual is related to the standard error of prediction because they are both based on the sum of the squared differences between the actual and predicted Y values.

In diagram form we may illustrate this decomposition as follows:

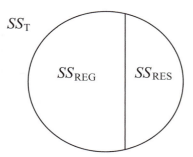

And we may rewrite Equation 14.12 as follows:

$$SS_T = SS_{REG} + SS_{RES}. \tag{14.13}$$

In like manner, the degrees of freedom associated with SS_T (df_T) may be decomposed as the sum of df_{REG} and df_{RES} as follows:

$$df_T = df_{REG} + df_{RES} \tag{14.14}$$

$$N - 1 = P + N - P - 1,$$

where P is the number of predictors in the regression equation. In the case of simple regression, $P = 1$.

We are now in a position to understand an ANOVA summary table for regression that is part of an SPSS regression analysis printout. This summary table provides a test of the statistical significance of the overall fit of the regression model. The table from the temperature/ice cream sales example is given.

ANOVA[b]

Model		Sum of Squares	df	Mean Square	F	Sig.
1	Regression	3232.599	1	3232.599	103.000	.000[a]
	Residual	878.767	28	31.385		
	Total	4111.367	29			

[a]Predictors: (Constant), temp Temperature in degrees Fahrenheit
[b]Department Variable: barsold Number of ice cream bars sold

Notice that the sum of SS_{REG} (3232.599) and SS_{RES} (878.767) equals SS_T (4111.367). Notice also that the sum of df_{REG} ($P = 1$) and df_{RES} ($N - P - 1 = 30 - 1 - 1 = 28$) equals df_T ($N - 1 = 29$). As discussed in Chapters 12 and 13 on the ANOVA, each mean square term equals the ratio of the corresponding sum of squares term to its corresponding degrees of freedom, and the F-ratio is obtained as MS_{REG}/MS_{RES}.

In the case of simple regression, when $P = 1$, the F-ratio for the regression equals the t-ratio for the b-coefficient squared (i.e., $F = t^2$ when the numerator degrees of freedom for the F-ratio equals 1). In our example, we may note that $103 = 10.15^2$.

In summary, for the case of simple regression, the t-test of the significance of r is equivalent to the t-test of the significance of b, and these two t-tests are equivalent to the F-test of the overall regression model. Hence, in the case of simple regression, when r is not statistically significant, b is not statistically significant, nor is the overall regression equation statistically significant.

MEASURING THE FIT OF THE OVERALL REGRESSION EQUATION: USING R AND R^2

A measure of the fit of the overall regression equation is given by R, the correlation between the actual values of the dependent variable and the values of the dependent variable predicted from the linear model-the correlation between Y and $\hat{Y}$. This information is provided by SPSS in the Model Summary table as part of the regression printout.

Model Summary

Model	R	R Square	Adjusted R Square	Std. Error of the Estimate
1	.887[a]	.786	.779	5.602

[a]Predictors: (Constant), temp Temperature in degrees Fahrenheit

The *standard error of estimate*, given in the Model Summary table, was defined earlier in Equation 14.8. Its value for this example is 5.60 according to the Model Summary table entry. We may also find it from the ANOVA table as the square root of MS_{RES}, the mean square due to residual or error. That is,

$$\sqrt{MS_{RES}} = \sqrt{SS_{RES}/(N-2)} = \sqrt{\sum (Y - \hat{Y})^2/(N-2)}$$
$$= \hat{\sigma}_{Y|X} = \sqrt{31.385} = 5.60.$$

Recall that in Chapter 6 we defined the effect size for regression in terms of the Pearson Product Moment Correlation Coefficient, r, and in terms of the correlation between the actual and predicted values for R. An alternative measure of effect size, or overall fit of the regression equation, is r^2 or R^2. In the case of simple regression, these two measures are equivalent.

We may link the measure of overall fit, R^2, to the ANOVA framework and, in so doing, explain R^2 as the proportion of Y variance accounted for by X. To do so we divide Equation 14.12 through by SS_T and obtain Equation 14.15:

$$1 = \frac{SS_{REG}}{SS_{TOT}} + \frac{SS_{RES}}{SS_{TOT}}. \tag{14.15}$$

The total variability of Y, represented by the whole value 1, is decomposed into two nonoverlapping components: the proportion due to the regression equation (i.e., that proportion explained by X) and the proportion due to the residual (i.e., that proportion unexplained by X). For our example,

$$1 = \frac{3232.599}{4111.367} + \frac{878.767}{4111.367}$$
$$= .786 + .214$$
$$= R^2 + (1 - R^2).$$

This result is true not only for our example, but in general as well. That is,

$$R^2 = \frac{SS_{\text{REG}}}{SS_{\text{TOT}}} \tag{14.16}$$

$$1 - R^2 = \frac{SS_{\text{RES}}}{SS_{\text{TOT}}}. \tag{14.17}$$

RELATING R^2 TO $\sigma^2_{Y|X}$

Given the assumption of homoscedasticity, we may express the relationship in the population between R^2, the proportion of Y variance explained by X, and $\sigma^2_{Y|X}$, the common variance of all the conditional Y distributions. In particular, when all conditional Y distributions have the same variance in the population, then it can be shown, from Equation 14.17, that

$$\sigma^2_{Y|X} = \sigma^2_Y(1 - R^2_{\text{POP}}), \tag{14.18}$$

where $\sigma^2_{Y|X}$ is the common variance of all conditional Y distributions in the population, σ^2_Y is the variance of the Y values in the population, and R^2_{POP} is the population squared correlation coefficient between X and Y.

We illustrate Equation 14.18 with a concrete situation. For simplicity, assume that X represents gender, a dichotomous variable, and Y represents mathematics achievement. Suppose the scores on the test of mathematical achievement are known to range from 20 to 90 with a variance of 100 in the population. Suppose also that we separate these scores into two distinct groups, male and female, and find that the scores for females range only from 50 to 90 with a variance of 51 and that the scores for males range only from 20 to 60 with a variance of 51. By controlling for gender, we obtain a consequent reduction in the variance of math scores from $\sigma^2_Y = 100$ to $\sigma^2_{Y|X} = 51$, almost half of what it was originally. Said differently, each of the two cross sections or slices of the bivariate distribution, one for males and the other for females, has a variance of 51. Taken together, however, the total variance of math scores is almost doubled.

To find what the correlation between gender and math achievement must be in order to observe such a dramatic reduction in variance, we use Equation 14.18:

$$51 = 100(1 - R^2) \rightarrow 51 = 100 - 100R^2 \rightarrow 49 = 100R^2 \rightarrow R^2 = .49 \rightarrow R = .70.$$

Thus, in order to explain or account for 49 percent of the total variance of a variable by another variable, the two variables must correlate to .70.

In the ice cream example, because $R^2 = .786$, we know that highest daily temperature accounts for 78.6 percent of the variance in ice cream sales. This implies that 21.4 percent of ice cream sales variance remains unexplained by highest daily temperature. In the next chapter, we discuss an approach called multiple regression that allows us to include other independent variables in the equation (e.g., humidity). Such other variables may account for some of the variance in Y that remains unexplained and, in so doing, may allow us to more accurately predict daily ice cream sales.

TESTING R^2 FOR STATISTICAL SIGNIFICANCE

In the case of simple regression, we have described three different, yet equivalent, ways to test the statistical significance of the regression model: the t-test of the significance of r, the t-test of the significance of b, and the ANOVA F-test of the overall regression model. A fourth, equivalent test is the test of the significance of R^2. Conceptually this makes sense because in the case of simple regression the magnitude of r, the correlation between the single predictor and Y, equals the magnitude of R, the correlation between the actual and predicted values of Y.

The equation for testing R^2 for statistical significance is

$$F_{P,N-P-1} = \frac{R^2/P}{(1 - R^2)/(N - P - 1)}, \tag{14.19}$$

where P is the number of predictors in the regression equation (note that in the case of simple regression, $P = 1$; in the next chapter, P is greater than 1), N is the sample size, and P and $N - P - 1$ are the F numerator and denominator degrees of freedom, respectively. In the case of simple regression, these are 1 and $N - 2$, respectively.

For the ice cream sales example, we may note that $F = \dfrac{.786/1}{.214/28} = \dfrac{.786}{.0076} = 103.00$.

This is the same value that appears in the ANOVA table and suggests that R^2 is statistically greater than zero in the population or, equivalently, that the fit of the overall regression model to the data is statistically significant.

☞ **Remark.** For the interested reader we provide the algebraic link between the F-test of R^2 as given by Equation 14.15 and the F-test in the ANOVA table:

$$F = \frac{MS_{REG}}{MS_{RES}} = \frac{SS_{REG}/P}{SS_{RES}/(N - P - 1)} = \frac{SS_{REG}/P}{SS_{RES}/(N - P - 1)} \times \frac{SS_{TOT}}{SS_{TOT}}$$

$$= \frac{\dfrac{SS_{REG}/SS_{TOT}}{P}}{\dfrac{SS_{RES}/SS_{TOT}}{N - P - 1}} = \frac{R^2/P}{(1 - R^2)/(N - P - 1)}$$

with numerator and denominator degrees of freedom equal to P and $N - P - 1$, respectively.

ESTIMATING THE TRUE POPULATION R^2: THE ADJUSTED R^2

Although the slope of the regression (prediction) line, b, was described as an unbiased estimate of the slope of the population regression line, the sample R^2 is not an unbiased estimate of the true population R^2, denoted R^2_{POP}. Rather, its biased upward; that is, the sample R^2 overestimates the population R^2, R^2_{POP}.

Said differently, when $R^2_{POP} = 0$, then on average the sample R^2 will be greater than 0 − it will be equal to $P/(N = 1)$.

For example, given $R^2_{POP} = 0$, if $P = 1$ and $N = 9$, then on average the sample R^2 equals $1/8 = 125$; if $P = 1$ and $N = 5$, then on average the sample R^2 equals $1/4 = .25$.

The degree to which the sample R^2 overestimates the population R^2 depends on both the number of predictors in the equation, P, and the size of the sample, N. The larger P is relative to N, the more the sample R^2 overestimates the population R^2; the smaller P is relative to N, the less the sample R^2 overestimates the population R^2.

☞ **Remark.** When $P = N - 1$, the sample R^2 is equal to 1, regardless of the size of the population R^2. That is, if you constructed a regression equation with the number of predictors equal to one less than the total sample size (e.g., if $P = 1$ and $N = 2$), the sample R^2 would equal 1, indicating perfect fit in the population! But certainly this would not be the case. With $P = 1$ and $N = 2$, the scatterplot consists of only two (X, Y) points, and a line can always be drawn connecting the two, or passing through both. Therefore, your result of $R^2 = 1$ should be taken merely as a reminder of just how upwardly biased the sample R^2 can be when the number of variables is large relative to the sample size.

A more accurate estimate of the population R^2 may be obtained by adjusting the sample R^2 using the following equation:

$$R^2_{\mathrm{ADJ}} = 1 - (1 - R^2)\frac{(N - 1)}{N - P - 1} \qquad (14.20)$$

For the ice cream sales example, we have

$$R^2_{\mathrm{ADJ}} = 1 - (1 - R^2)\frac{(N - 1)}{N - P - 1} = 1 - (1 - .786)\frac{30 - 1}{30 - 1 - 1}$$

$$= 1 - .214\frac{29}{28} = 1 - .221 = .779.$$

This is the *adjusted* R^2 value, given in the Model Summary table presented earlier, and represents a more accurate estimate of the population R^2 than the original, unadjusted R^2. Because in this case, however, the ratio of predictors to sample size is relatively large ($P{:}N$ is 1:30), .786 is trivially different from .779.

☞ **Remark.** As a general rule of thumb, when the ratio $P{:}N$ is greater than or equal to 1:30, there is little difference between the adjusted and unadjusted R^2. However, when the ratio $P{:}N$ is less than or equal to 1:10, the difference between the adjusted and unadjusted R^2 tends to be large.

☞ **Remark.** The adjusted R^2 is used to provide a more accurate estimate of the population R^2. The original, unadjusted R^2, however, is used in Equation 14.20 for testing R^2 for statistical significance.

EXPLORING THE GOODNESS OF FIT OF THE REGRESSION EQUATION: USING REGRESSION DIAGNOSTICS

Throughout this book we have made the point that summary statistics may be misleading if the data they are purported to characterize are anomalous – if, for example, they contain outliers or do not in other ways satisfy the explicit or implicit distributional assumptions upon which these statistics are based. Because the simple regression model serves to characterize, in summary form, the linear relationship between two variables as a line with intercept and slope, it too may be misleading or in some way fail to capture the salient features of

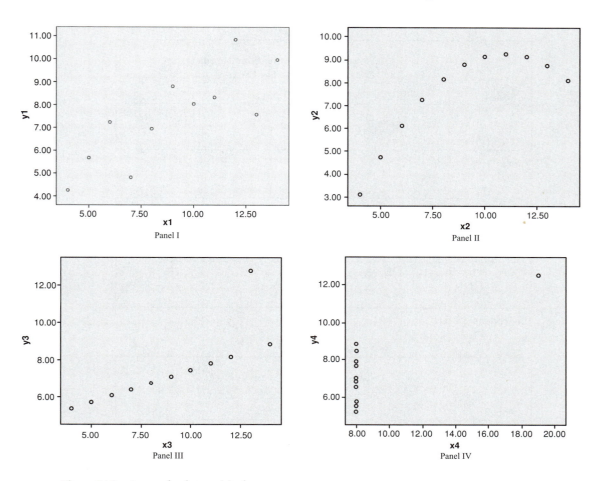

Figure 14.8 Anscombe data revisited.

the data. To be convinced that the resulting intercept and slope are not distorted by outliers and other influential observations contained in the sample, we need to explore ways to validate our linear regression model. To do so, we return to the Anscombe data presented in Chapter 6.

Consider the four panels of Anscombe data reproduced here as Figure 14.8 along with their associated summary statistics. Notice that, for all panels, the slope, intercept, correlation,

Coefficients[a]

Model		Unstandardized Coefficients		Standardized Coefficients		
		B	Std. Error	Beta	t	Sig.
1	(Constant)	3.000	1.125		2.667	.026
	x1	.500	.118	.816	4.241	.002

[a]Dependent Variable: y1

Coefficients[a]

Model		Unstandardized Coefficients		Standardized Coefficients		
		B	Std. Error	Beta	t	Sig.
1	(Constant)	3.001	1.125		2.667	.026
	x2	.500	.118	.816	4.239	.002

[a]Dependent Variable: y2

Coefficients[a]

Model		Unstandardized Coefficients		Standardized Coefficients		
		B	Std. Error	Beta	t	Sig.
1	(Constant)	3.002	1.124		2.670	.026
	x3	.500	.118	.816	4.239	.002

[a]Dependent Variable: y3

Coefficients[a]

Model		Unstandardized Coefficients		Standardized Coefficients		
		B	Std. Error	Beta	t	Sig.
1	(Constant)	3.002	1.124		2.671	.026
	x4	.500	.118	.817	4.243	.002

[a]Dependent Variable: y4

standard error, and *t*-value are the same. Yet if we look at the four scatterplots that visually represent these four panels of data, we see to what extent they are different from one another.

Notice that in only one case, in Panel I, does the linear model provide a good characterization of the underlying data. In Panel II, the data show a nonlinear relationship, yet the model that is used to characterize these data is not nonlinear – it is linear. In Panel III, the outlier gives rise to a linear regression model that is quite different from the perfectly fitting regression line that would have been created in the absence of the outlier. In Panel IV, the outlier creates a systematic relationship between the dependent and independent variables and allows a line to be fit to the data that otherwise would not have been able to be fit in the absence of the outlier. That the linear regression models in Panels III and IV are the direct result of a single outlier raises questions about the confidence we may place in these models.

Regression diagnostics are tools with which to explore our data to uncover such anomalies. As we shall see, these tools are useful for determining whether our regression models are in fact meaningful and appropriate characterizations of our data and for suggesting ways to modify our models to improve them if necessary.

Residual Plots: Evaluating the Assumptions Underlying Regression

From our work on regression, we know that error (also called residual error) is defined for each individual (or more generally, for each case) as the difference between an individual's actual value on the dependent variable, Y, and his or her predicted value, $\hat{Y}$, predicted from the linear regression model. As such, $Y - \hat{Y}$ represents that part of Y that is left over after its linear association with X has been removed.

If the assumptions underlying the linear regression model are met, then the plot of residual values along the vertical axis versus the original values of X along the horizontal axis are rectangular in shape. A rectangular scatterplot suggests that the relationship between X and Y is a wholly linear one; after the linear relationship between X and Y is removed, no systematic relationship between X and Y remains. If the relationship between X and Y is not wholly linear, then the scatterplot of the residual values is not rectangular in shape. An examination of the scatterplot may reveal the presence of a nonlinear relationship between X and Y or the violation of one or more of the other assumptions underlying the linear regression model (normality and homoscedasticity).

Residual plots for the four panels of Anscombe's data (I through IV), which appear in Figure 14.8, are given in Figure 14.9.

To obtain a residual plot using SPSS, click **Unstandardized Residual** under the **Save** option of SPSS within the regression analysis. The unstandardized residual values will be saved as a new variable labeled res_1 in the data set. Click **Graphs** from the main menu bar, **Legacy Dialogs,** and **Scatter.** Move res_1 into the **Y Axis** box and X into the **X Axis** box. Click **OK.**

Notice that in Panel I the points in the scatterplot are rectangular in shape, indicating that once the linear relationship between X and Y is removed there is no other systematic relationship between these two variables.

The situation for Panel II is quite different. In this case, after the linear relationship between X and Y is removed, a clearly discernible nonlinear relationship remains between X and Y. The nature of the nonlinear relationship is quadratic: the part of Y that remains after accounting for Y's linear association with X is a function of X^2. What this implies is that, in addition to an X term, an X^2 term should be included in the regression model to obtain a more accurate model for predicting Y. We shall see how this may be done in the next chapter, on multiple regression.

The residual plot of Panel III highlights the existence of the outlier, which, if removed, would make the relationship between X and Y perfect. The residual plot of Panel IV highlights the existence of the outlier which, if removed, would make the concept of a relationship between X and Y meaningless because, without the outlier, X would be a constant.

Figure 14.10 contains a scatterplot of X versus Y from a fabricated data set. Notice that although there is a systematic linear relationship between X and Y ($r_{X,Y} = 0.83$), the variances of the conditional Y distributions given X are not constant as stipulated by the assumption of homoscedasticity, a condition of bivariate normality. In particular, the conditional Y distributions of Figure 14.10 increase with increasing values of X. For example, the variance of the three Y values corresponding to $X = 1$ is smaller than the variance of the five Y values corresponding to $X = 2$, and so on. This funnel shape in the residual plot is indicative of heteroscedasticity.

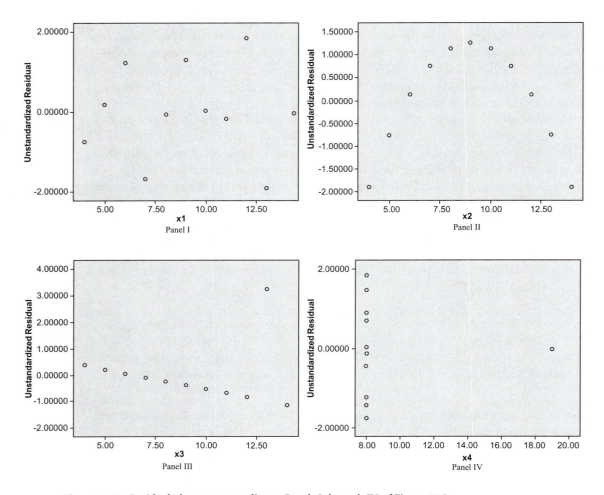

Figure 14.9   Residual plots corresponding to Panels I through IV of Figure 14.8.

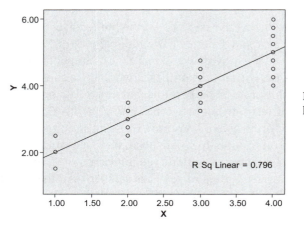

Figure 14.10   Scatterplot with heteroscedasticity.

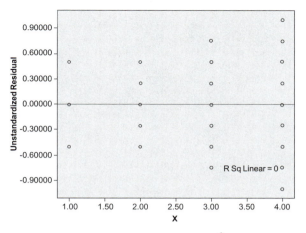

Figure 14.11 Scatterplot of X versus $Y - \hat{Y}$.

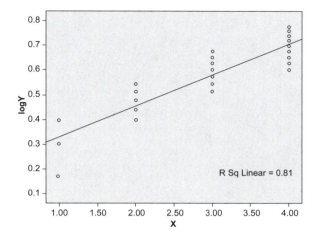

Figure 14.12 Scatterplot of X versus $\log(Y)$.

Figure 14.11 contains the scatterplot of the unstandardized residual plot X versus $Y - \hat{Y}$ corresponding to the data of Figure 14.10.

Notice that, once the part of X that is linearly related to Y is removed, no relationship remains ($r = 0$). Thus, although the assumption of linearity appears to be met by these data, the assumption of homoscedasticity is quite clearly violated.

We may transform our data nonlinearly to rectify violations of the assumptions of bivariate normality and to achieve a better fitting model. In this case, the type of transformation we want is one that produces a constant residual variance. The logarithmic transformation of Y does the trick as shown in Figure 14.12. Not only are the conditional Y distributions of Figure 14.12 homoscedastic, but the linear regression model now provides a better fit to the data ($r_{X,\log(Y)} = 0.87$).

In addition to residual plots, other diagnostic tools are available for helping to improve the fit of a regression model to data.

Detecting Influential Observations: Discrepancy and Leverage

In Chapters 2 and 4, we discussed the importance of identifying univariate outliers through the use of boxplots or z-scores. In this section, we expand that discussion to the case of bivariate distributions and introduce ways to identify bivariate outliers in a regression context. For this discussion, a bivariate outlier is a point in the scatterplot that behaves differently from the other points.

Outliers that unduly influence the slope and/or intercept of our regression model are called *influential observations*. Not all outliers are influential observations. Figures 14.13 and 14.14 each contain an outlier, yet in neither case does the outlier unduly influence the parameters of the regression equation.

In Figure 14.13, because the regression outlier is near the mean of $\overline{X}$, it does not affect the slope of the regression line at all and affects the intercept only slightly. The presence of the outlier raises the regression line to be slightly closer to the points $(1, 3)$, $(2, 4)$, $(4, 6)$, and $(5, 7)$ than it would otherwise. In Figure 14.14, the regression outlier, although far from $\overline{X}$, does not affect the slope or the intercept of the regression line because it falls directly in line with the regression line.

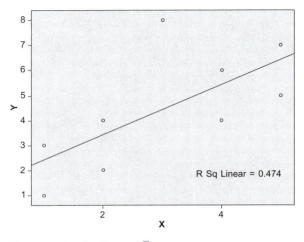

Figure 14.13   Outlier near $\overline{X}$.

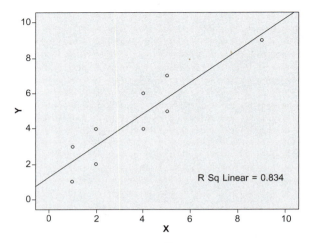

Figure 14.14   Outlier far from $\overline{X}$.

Thus, although the vertical distance of the outlier from the regression line in Figure 14.13 and the horizontal distance of the outlier from $\overline{X}$ in Figure 14.14 characterize both points as outliers, in neither case are these outliers influential observations; in neither case do these points actually influence the slope and/or intercept of the regression model.

The vertical distance of a point from a regression line is called its *residual, discrepancy,* or *deviation.* A function of the horizontal distance of a point from the X mean is called its *leverage.* In general, only when a point has both discrepancy and leverage, as noted in Figure 14.15, does a point influence the slope of a regression equation.

We may express the influence of a point on the slope of a regression equation as a function of discrepancy and leverage as shown in Equation 14.21:

$$\text{Influence} \approx \text{Discrepancy} \times \text{Leverage}. \tag{14.21}$$

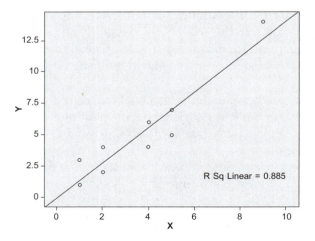

Figure 14.15   An influential point: discrepancy *and* leverage.

Several diagnostic tools are available in SPSS to measure the degree to which each point in a data set influences the coefficients of a regression equation.

Using SPSS to Obtain Leverage

The leverage of a point is the distance of a point from $\overline{X}$ in simple regression. Mathematically it is computed as the squared distance of the point from $\overline{X}$ relative to the sum of squared deviations of all points in the data set from $\overline{X}$.

To obtain the leverage of a point in SPSS, click **Leverage**, under the **Save** option of regression program. The leverage values will appear as a new variable in the data set labeled lev_1.

Table 14.2 contains the leverage of all nine points of Figure 14.15. Not surprisingly, the leverage of the last point (9, 14) is the highest because this point is farthest from $\overline{X}$ in this data set.

Using SPSS to Obtain Discrepancy

The discrepancy of a point is the vertical distance of the point from the regression line. Whereas discrepancy may be measured as a residual value, for reasons we do not explore here, a better approach is to measure discrepancy as a *Studentized residual value*. The Studentized residual value of a point is the residual value of the point relative to an estimate of the standard deviation of all residual values for the entire data set. Studentized residual values follow a *t*-distribution with $N - P - 2$ degrees of freedom.

To obtain the Studentized residual value of a point using SPSS, click residual values for **Studentized** under the **Residual** box in the **Save** option for regression analysis. The Studentized residual values will appear in your data set as a new variable labeled sres_1.

Table 14.3 contains the Studentized residual values of all nine points of Figure 14.15.

Once again, the Studentized residual value of the last point (9, 14) is highest because this point has the greatest vertical distance from the regression line. Given that this point has both the highest leverage value and highest Studentized residual value in the data set, we should investigate this point for its influence on the regression equation.

Table 14.2. Leverage values for the nine points of Figure 14.15

X, Y values	Leverage
1,1	.1368
1,3	.1368
2,2	.0534
2,4	.0534
4,4	.0021
4,6	.0021
5,5	.0342
5,7	.0342
9,14	.5470

Table 14.3. Studentized residual values for the nine points of Figure 14.14

X, Y values	Studentized Residual
1,1	−.2913
1,3	1.3712
2,2	−.6000
2,4	.9774
4,4	−1.210
4,6	.3206
5,5	−1.553
5,7	.0067
9,14	1.686

Using SPSS to Obtain Influence

The influence of a point is the amount by which the slope of the regression line (the regression coefficient) changes when that point is removed from the data set and we compute a new slope. The amount of change may be scaled by an index developed by Cook, based loosely on the *F*-statistic, so that we may evaluate which changes are relatively small, moderate, or large.

Many researchers treat cases with Cook's influence scores that are larger than 1 as outliers. We will make particular note of such cases in our analyses.

To obtain Cook's influence value for a point, click **Cook's** under the **Distances** box under the **Save** option in the regression program. Cook's influence values will appear in the data set as a new variable labeled coo_1.

Table 14.4 contains Cook's influence values of all nine points of Figure 14.15. As expected, the last value in the data set (9, 14) has the highest value of Cook's influence (called Cook's distance by SPSS), indicating that this point influences the slope of the regression equation more than any other point in the data set. It also has a Cook's value that is well larger than one so that it is classified as an outlier.

Table 14.5 presents the results of the regression analysis based on the total set of nine points in the data set and on the nine subsets of size eight, each with one point removed. Notice that Cook's influence is zero for point (5, 7). Notice also that the regression line based on the sample without this point is identical to the regression line based on the sample that includes this point. Hence, as Cook's influence value suggests, the analysis is not at all influenced by the presence of this point. With or without this point, the results are the same. Note that, however, as Cook's influence value also suggests, the point with the greatest influence on the equation is point (9, 14). The equation based on the subsample with point (9, 14) removed is quite different from all other equations that are based on samples that include point (9, 14) as one of the points in the sample.

Other measures of influence exist and are called in SPSS, Dfl3eta(s), Standardized DfBeta(s), DfFit, Standardized DfFit, and Covariance ratio. The use of Cook's distance alone is usually sufficient to measure influence.

In summary, anomalies in our data may distort the results of our regression analyses. Whereas some anomalies may be corrected easily (e.g., they are the result of data entry mistakes), others may not. Several outliers may be found to cluster together in a data set, in which case a separate regression line fit to those points may be warranted. In other cases, transformations of the data may be used to reduce the influence of the outliers. Because the particular course of action taken with regard to outliers varies with the circumstance of the problem, it is incumbent upon the researcher to provide a clear justification of whatever course of action he or she chooses to use in a particular case.

Table 14.4. Cook's influence values for the nine points of Figure 14.14

X,Y values	Cook's influence
1,1	.0140
1,3	.3098
2,2	.0354
2,4	.0941
4,4	.0936
4,6	.0066
5,5	.2050
5,7	.0000
9,14	2.7360

Table 14.5. Regression results based on all nine points and on all subsets of eight points, eliminating one point each time

Analysis	Point removed	Sample size	Regression equation
1	1,1	8	$\hat{Y} = 1.386X - .080$
2	1,3	8	$\hat{Y} = 1.523X - .720$
3	2,2	8	$\hat{Y} = 1.381X + .148$
4	2,4	8	$\hat{Y} = 1.458X - .399$
5	4,4	8	$\hat{Y} = 1.422X - .096$
6	4,6	8	$\hat{Y} = 1.407X - .101$
7	5,5	8	$\hat{Y} = 1.470X - .020$
8	5,7	8	$\hat{Y} = 1.410X - .060$
9	9,14	8	$\hat{Y} = 1.000X - 1.00$
10	none	9	$\hat{Y} = 1.410X - .060$

Using Diagnostics to Evaluate the Ice Cream Sales Example

We complete the ice cream example with an examination of our data for possible anomalies that may compromise the utility of our regression model. We begin with a scatterplot of X (TEMP) by Y (BARSOLD) with case ID numbers listed (see Figure 14.16).

To create a scatterplot that is labeled by ID numbers, go to **Graphs**, **Legacy Dialogs**, **Scatter.** Put TEMP in the **Y Axis** box, BARSOLD in the **X Axis** box, and ID in the **Label Cases by** box. Double click the scatterplot in the Output viewer to bring it into the Chart Editor. Go to **Elements**, **Show Data Labels.**

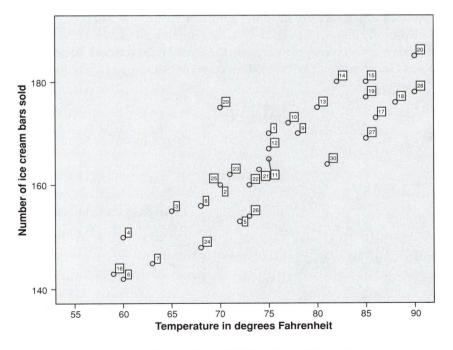

Figure 14.16 Scatterplot of TEMP by BARSOLD with case ID numbers.

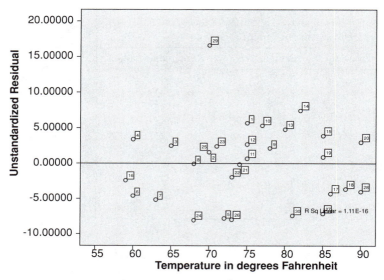

Figure 14.17   Residual plot of X versus $Y - \hat{Y}$.

With the exception of case number 29, all points fall fairly close to the regression line and the residual plot, $Y - \hat{Y}$ versus X, given in Figure 14.17 is fairly rectangular in shape, suggesting that the assumptions of linear regression are met and that transformations of the variables are not needed. Case number 29 warrants further attention (Fig. 14.17).

Accordingly, we investigate the vertical discrepancy (as measured by the Studentized residuals), the horizontal leverage, and finally the influence of all cases in this analysis. Boxplots of these statistics are provided in Figures 14.18 through 14.20, respectively.

As expected from Figures 14.16 and 14.17, case number 29 has the greatest vertical distance from the regression line as measured by the Studentized residual. Because case number 29 is close to the mean temperature value, it does not show up as an outlier with respect

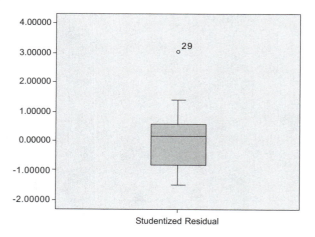

Figure 14.18   Boxplot of Studentized residuals.

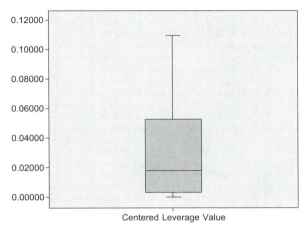

Figure 14.19 Boxplot of leverage values.

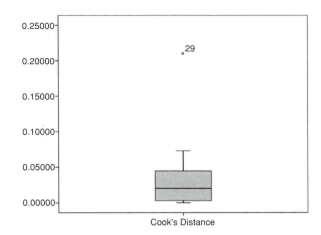

Figure 14.20 Boxplot of Cook's influence values.

to leverage or horizontal distance from the *X* mean. Although it does show up as an outlier with respect to influence, the influence value itself is close to 0 (at .2) and suggests negligible influence on the regression slope. To confirm this, however, we redo the regression analysis without case number 29 and obtain the following result.

Coefficients[a]

Model		Unstandardized Coefficients		Standardized Coefficients		
		B	Std. Error	Beta	t	Sig.
1	(Constant)	72.436	7.386		9.807	.000
	temp Temperature in degree Fahrenheit	1.217	.098	.923	12.465	.000

[a]Dependent Variable: barsold Number of ice cream bars sold

That is, without case number 29, the linear regression equation for predicting BAR-SOLD from TEMP is Predicted BARSOLD = 1.22(TEMP) + 72.44, which has a *b*-weight that is negligibly different from the *b*-weight of the original equation obtained with case number 29 included: Predicted BARSOLD = 1.18(TEMP) + 75.78.

Notice that the intercept is lower without case number 29 than with case number 29. This is to be expected because of where case number 29 sits relative to the other points in the sample. Case number 29 is near the *X* mean, indicating that it will not affect the *b*-weight by very much, but it is high above the regression line, indicating that it will raise the level of the regression line and increase the *Y*-intercept as shown.

As one might expect, without case number 29 in the sample, the fit of the regression line to the points is improved (from $R^2 = .786$ with case number 29 to $R^2 = .852$ without case number 29). However, because there is no compelling reason to eliminate case number 29 from the analysis, we leave it in and acknowledge its influence, albeit small, on our results.

USING THE PREDICTION MODEL TO PREDICT ICE CREAM SALES

Now that we have shown that our model was appropriately fit to our data using diagnostics and that the result was statistically significant, we can be confident in using our regression equation to predict ice cream sales from temperature. Simply stated, to predict the number of ice cream sales on a particular day with a given forecasted highest daily temperature, we use

$$\text{Predicted BARSOLD} = 1.18(\text{TEMP}) + 75.78.$$

Thus, if the highest daily temperature is forecasted to be 78 for a particular day, we would take Predicted BARSOLD = 1.18(78) + 75.78 = 167.82, or 168 bars, to the beach.

Given how well our model fits our data ($R^2 = .786$), we can expect our equation to yield reasonably accurate estimates of ice cream sales given particular daily highest temperatures. However, the accuracy of a particular prediction (that we will sell exactly 168 ice cream bars when the daily highest temperature is forecast to reach 78 degrees, for example) depends on several factors. One factor is the distance between the given forecasted daily high (e.g., 78 in this case) and the mean daily highest temperature for our sample of data (e.g., 75 for these data). Simply stated, the accuracy of our prediction is better the closer the particular X value is to $\overline{X}$. Thus, in the context of our example, we can expect our prediction of ice cream sales to be more accurate on days when the highest daily temperature is forecast to be around 75 than far from 75.

SIMPLE REGRESSION WHEN THE PREDICTOR IS DICHOTOMOUS

In Example 11.8 (in Chapter 11) we used the independent samples t-test on the NELS data set to determine whether gender differences exist in the number of units of mathematics taken in high school among college-bound students from the southern United States. In this problem, gender, a dichotomous variable, may be considered the independent variable and number of units of mathematics taken in high school the dependent variable. In this section we compare the result of the independent samples t-test to that of the t-test on the b-weight for predicting units of math taken in high school from gender and show that they are equivalent.

The SPSS result of the independent samples t-test for this example is reproduced in the following tables.

Group Statistics

	gender Gender	N	Mean	Std. Deviation	Std. Error Mean
unitmath Units in Mathematics (NAEP)	0 Male	66	3.917	.7369	.0907
	1 Female	84	3.664	.7226	.0788

Independent Samples Test

		Levene's Test for Equality of Variances		t-test for Equality of Means						
									95% Confidence Interval of the Difference	
		F	Sig.	t	df	Sig. (2-tailed)	Mean Difference	Std. Error Difference	Lower	Upper
unitmath Units in Mathematics (NAEP)	Equal variances assumed	1.109	.294	2.107	148	.037	.2526	.1199	.0157	.4895
	Equal variances not assumed			2.102	138.437	.037	.2526	.1202	.0150	.4902

As discussed in Chapter 11, and as noted in the preceding tables, the mean gender difference in math courses taken, .25, is statistically significant, indicating that males in the South take statistically significantly more math than females in the South ($t(148) = 2.11$, $p = .04$).

The Coefficients table from the simple linear regression analysis to predict units of math taken from gender is given here.

Coefficients[a]

Model		Unstandardized Coefficients		Standardized Coefficients		
		B	Std. Error	Beta	t	Sig.
1	(Constant)	3.917	.090		43.655	.000
	gender Gender	−.253	.120	−.171	−2.107	.037

[a]Dependent Variable: unitmath Units in Mathematics (NAEP)

Notice that the t-test of the b-weight is identical (except for the sign) to the t-test of the mean difference ($t = -2.11$, $p = .04$). The sign change in the t-value simply reflects the fact that, in one approach, the mean units of math taken by males is subtracted from the mean units of math taken by females, whereas in the other approach the reverse is the case. Notice that the b-weight of $-.253$ equals the difference in means between males and females, once again allowing for a sign change due to the way the subtraction is carried out.

Whenever a dichotomous independent variable is coded 0 for one group (e.g., males) and 1 for the other (e.g., females), the b-weight reflects the difference in means on the dependent variable between the two groups. Furthermore, the constant (3.917 in this case) equals the mean on the dependent variable of the group coded 0. Hence, we can learn from the regression equation alone that the mean number of math units taken by males is 3.917 and by females is $3.917 - .253$, or 3.664, which we know to be the case from the descriptive statistics associated with the t-test on means of independent samples. Because X takes only two values, $\hat{Y}$ also takes only two.

We already have pointed out that the *t*-test of the *b*-weight is equivalent to the *t*-test of the correlation between independent and dependent variables. The SPSS correlation output corroborates that fact.

Notice that the correlation between gender and units of math taken is $r = -.17$, which is statistically significant. The *t*-test on the correlation (note that the *t*-value is not reported) has a one-tailed *p*-value of $p = .018$. As we know, by doubling a one-tailed *p*-value, it converts to a two-tailed *p*-value. In this case, therefore, the two-tailed *p*-value is $p = .036$, which is exactly the value given in connection with the *t*-test on the *b*-weight and the *t*-test on the means of the two independent groups.

EXERCISES

Exercises 14.1 and 14.2 involve correlation and simple linear regression analyses with interval- or ratio-leveled independent variables from the Learndis data set. For inferential purposes, we consider the children in the data set to be a random sample of all children attending public elementary school in a certain city who have been diagnosed with learning disabilities. Use $\alpha = .05$ for all significance tests.

14.1. Perform correlation analyses to investigate whether grade level (GRADE), intellectual ability (IQ), placement type (PLACEMEN, where 0 = Part time resource room and 1 = Full-time self-contained classroom) are statistically significantly associated with reading achievement (READCOMP). For now, assume that the underlying assumptions have been verified.
   a) What are the null and alternative hypotheses for testing the linear relationship between reading comprehension and intellectual ability?
   b) Is the linear relationship between reading comprehension and intellectual ability statistically significant? If so, describe its nature and magnitude.
   c) Is the linear relationship between reading comprehension and grade level statistically significant? If so, describe its nature and magnitude.
   d) Is there a statistically significant difference in reading comprehension scores, on average, between the two placement types? If so, describe the nature and magnitude of the difference.
   e) Although data were collected on 105 children attending public school in the urban area who had been diagnosed with learning disabilities, reading comprehension scores were not available for 29 of the students. By using the SPSS default of listwise deletion of missing data, the scores of only 76 children were included in the analyses. Describe how this method of dealing with missing data might impact the obtained results. Because a discussion of the many possible ways of handling missing data is beyond the scope of this text, all solutions to problems with missing data are handled as if the data did not have missing values.

14.2. Perform a correlation and simple linear regression analysis to understand how mathematics comprehension (MATHCOMP) may be explained by intellectual ability (IQ).
   a) Find the 95 percent CI for ρ.
   b) Find the 95 percent CI for the population *b*.
   c) Is the regression model statistically significant? Explain.
   d) Describe, to the extent possible, the nature of the linear relationship between reading comprehension and math comprehension.

e) Describe, to the extent possible, the strength of the linear relationship between reading comprehension and math comprehension, using Cohen's scale as a guide.

Exercises 14.3 and 14.4 involve correlation and simple linear regression analyses with interval- or ratio-leveled independent variables from the NELS data set. For inferential purposes, we consider the students in the data set to be a random sample of the population of all college-bound students who have always been at grade level. Use $\alpha = .05$ for all significance tests.

14.3. Among college-bound students in an urban setting, what is the relationship between family size (FAMSIZE) and twelfth-grade self-concept (SLFCNC12)?
  a) Select cases so that URBAN = 1 (students included in the analysis are from an urban setting only). Create a scatterplot between family size (FAMSIZE) and twelfth-grade self-concept (SLFCNC12). Use it to comment on the appropriateness of a correlation analysis.
  b) Find the correlation between FAMSIZE and SLFCNC12 and indicate whether or not it is statistically significant.
  c) Find the 95 percent CI for the correlation between FAMSIZE and SLFCNC12. Use it to determine whether or not the correlation between FAMSIZE and SLFCNC12 is statistically significant.
  d) According to Cohen's scale, what is the strength of the linear relationship between FAMSIZE and SLFCNC12 in the population? Which is more useful for making the determination, the correlation or the CI?

14.4. Construct a regression model to predict twelfth-grade math achievement (ACHMAT12) from socioeconomic status (SES), reported in eighth grade?
  a) Is the regression model statistically significant?
  b) What is the regression equation for predicting ACHMAT12 (Y) from SES (X).
  c) What is the interpretation of the slope of the regression equation in the context of this analysis?
  d) Interpret the Y-intercept or constant within the context of this analysis, or explain why it would not be meaningful to do so.
  e) Report and interpret a measure of effect size for the relationship.

Exercises 14.5 and 14.6 involve simple linear regression analyses with dichotomous independent variables from the Learndis data set. For inferential purposes, we consider the children in the data set to be a random sample of all children attending public elementary school in a certain city who have been diagnosed with learning disabilities. Use $\alpha = .05$ for all significance tests.

14.5. Perform a simple linear regression analysis to understand how intellectual ability (IQ) may be predicted from gender. Use it to answer the following questions.
  a) Is the regression model statistically significant? Explain and indicate what part of the output you used to determine the significance of the model.
  b) Explain why, in this case, it is not appropriate to report the regression equation and its components.

14.6. Perform a simple linear regression analysis to determine the proportion of reading comprehension (READCOMP) variance explained by type of placement (PLACEMEN). For these data, there are two types of placement, part-time resource room, coded 0, and full-time self-contained classroom, coded 1. Use your analysis to answer the following questions.

a) Is the regression model statistically significant? Explain and indicate what part of the output you used to determine the significance of the model.

b) What is the regression equation for predicting reading comprehension scores (Y) from the type of placement (X)?

c) What is the interpretation of the slope of the regression equation in the context of this analysis?

d) Interpret the Y-intercept or constant within the context of this analysis, or explain why it would not be meaningful to do so.

e) Based on the regression model, what would you predict the reading comprehension score to be for a student within the resource room? Can the predicted score be interpreted as the mean reading comprehension score for all students within the resource room?

f) Use the regression model to predict the reading comprehension score for a student within the self-contained classroom.

g) What percentage of the variance in reading comprehension scores is explained by placement type? Explain and indicate what part of the output you used to determine this effect size.

h) What other inferential test could have been performed to determine how reading comprehension may be predicted from type of placement?

Exercise 14.7 involves simple linear regression analyses with dichotomous independent variables from the NELS data set. For inferential purposes, we consider the students in the data set to be a random sample of the population of all college-bound students who have always been at grade level. Use $\alpha = .05$ for all significance tests.

14.7. Develop a regression model to predict twelfth-grade math achievement (ACHMAT12) from computer ownership (COMPUTER), as reported in eighth grade.

a) Is the regression model statistically significant?

b) Report the regression equation for predicting ACHMAT12 (Y) from COMPUTER (X).

c) What is the interpretation of the slope of the regression equation in the context of this analysis?

d) Interpret the Y-intercept or constant within the context of this analysis, or explain why it is not meaningful.

e) Report and interpret two different measures of effect size for the relationship.

Exercise 14.8 involves correlation and simple linear regression analyses with variables from the Brainsz data set. Recall that the population of students for this study consisted only of those with either extremely high or extremely low intelligence. For inferential purposes, we consider the students in the data set to be a random sample of all college students with extremely low or high intelligence. Use $\alpha = .05$ for all significance tests.

14.8. Perform correlation analyses to investigate whether gender and brain size (MRI) are statistically significantly associated with intelligence as measured by the Full-Scale IQ (FSIQ) score of the WAIS-R test. Use these analyses to answer the following questions.

a) Is the linear relationship between intelligence and brain size statistically significant? If so, describe its nature and magnitude.

b) Is there a statistically significant relationship between intelligence and gender? If so, describe its nature and magnitude.

c) Comment on the effect of the sampling design on the correlation computed in part (a).

d) Construct a scatterplot of these two variables with FSIQ on the vertical axis and brain size as measured by the MRI on the horizontal axis.

e) Explain why there are two clouds of points in the scatterplot.

f) Regress FSIQ on MRI using a single regression model for the entire sample. Comment on the significance and fit of this model.

g) Regress FSIQ on MRI using two regression models, one fit to extremely high FSIQ group and the other fit to the extremely low FSIQ group. Comment on the fit of each model and compare these values to the fit of the model developed on the entire sample and obtained in part (f).

Exercises 14.9 through 14.12 focus on regression diagnostics using the Learndis data set. For inferential purposes, we consider the children in the data set to be a random sample of all children attending public elementary school in a certain city who have been diagnosed with learning disabilities. Use $\alpha = .05$ for all significance tests.

14.9. Create a scatterplot that depicts the relationship between reading comprehension (READCOMP) and grade level (GRADE) for the students in the data set, labeling the points by the case numbers. Use the scatterplot to answer the following questions.

a) Do any of the assumptions (normality, homoscedasticity, and linearity) underlying the correlation analysis between reading comprehension and grade level appear to be violated? Explain.

b) Which case number has the data point with the largest residual (in magnitude)? Is that residual negative or positive? That is, is that case over- or underpredicted by the model? Note that, if you used any SPSS procedures that re-sorted the data set, your case numbers may not be the same as those given in the scatterplot.

c) Give an example of a case number with relatively large leverage.

d) Give an example of a case number with relatively large discrepancy (in magnitude).

e) Give an example of a case number with relatively large influence.

14.10. Perform a simple linear regression analysis with reading comprehension (READCOMP) as the dependent variable and grade (GRADE) as the independent variable. Create a residual plot that gives the residuals associated with that analysis by grade, labeling the points by their case numbers. Use the residual plot to answer the following questions.

a) Do any of the assumptions (normality, homoscedasticity, and linearity) underlying the correlation analysis between reading comprehension and grade level appear to be violated? Explain.

b) Which case number has the data point with the largest residual (in magnitude)? Is that residual negative or positive? That is, is that case over- or underpredicted by the model? Note that, if you used any SPSS procedures that re-sorted the data set, your case numbers may not be the same as those given in the scatterplot.

c) Give an example of a case number with relatively large leverage.

d) Give an example of a case number with relatively large discrepancy (in magnitude).

e) Give an example of a case number with relatively large influence.

f) Compare the residual plot of Exercise 14.3 to the scatterplot of Exercise 14.2. In your opinion, which more clearly depicts the appropriateness of the regression model?

14.11. Perform a simple linear regression analysis with math comprehension (MATHCOMP) as the dependent variable and reading comprehension (READCOMP) as the independent variable. Create a residual plot for the analysis that is labeled by case number. Use the residual plot to answer the following questions.

    a) Do any of the assumptions (normality, homoscedasticity, and linearity) underlying the regression analysis between the dependent variable math comprehension and the independent variable reading comprehension appear to be violated? Explain.

    b) Which case number has the data point with the largest residual (in magnitude)? Is that residual negative or positive? That is, is that case over- or underpredicted by the model?

    c) Give an example of a case number with relatively large influence.

14.12. In Exercise 14.12, we identified case number 43 as being potentially influential in the model predicting math comprehension from reading comprehension. In this exercise, we compare the models with and without that case number. This type of analysis is called a sensitivity analysis.

    a) What is the regression equation for predicting math comprehension scores (Y) from reading comprehension scores (X) according to the model without case number 43? What is the regression equation for predicting math comprehension scores (Y) from reading comprehension scores (X) according to the model with all cases? How different are the parameter estimates?

    b) Are the regression models with and without case number 43 statistically significant (i.e., are both b-weights statistically significantly different from zero)?

    c) Compare the fit of each model to the underlying, respective data sets, with and without case 43.

    d) Is the Y-intercept or constant meaningful within the context of this analysis?.

    e) Interpret the b-weights in each model.

    f) Use both models to predict the math comprehension score for a student with a reading comprehension score of 75.

    f) Which model should one ultimately report and use?

    g) Where should one look in the regression output to find the number of scores used in the analysis?

    i) Compare the value for R^2 to the value for the adjusted R^2 using the model based on all cases. Why are these two values so similar?

Exercises 14.13 and 14.14 involve regression diagnostics with variables from the NELS data set. For inferential purposes, we consider the students in the data set to be a random sample of the population of all college-bound students who have always been at grade level. Use $\alpha = .05$ for all significance tests.

14.13. Comment on the appropriateness of using simple linear regression for predicting ACHMAT12 from COMPUTER, as we did in Exercise 14.7.

14.14. In Exercise 14.4, we developed a simple regression model to predict ACHMAT12 from SES. In this exercise, we follow up with some regression diagnostics to verify the appropriateness of the model.

a) Create a scatterplot of the regression for predicting ACHMAT12 from SES. Does the scatterplot suggest a linear relationship between these two variables with no apparent violation of underlying assumptions?

b) Calculate the Studentized residuals and create a residual scatterplot and frequency distribution. What are the lowest and highest values of the Studentized residuals? What do these values indicate about the appropriateness of the model?

c) Calculate Cook's influence scores and create a boxplot of the distribution. What are the lowest and highest values of Cook's influence scores? What do these values indicate about the appropriateness of the model?

d) Using the obtained regression model, what is the value of the predicted twelfth-grade math achievement score for the first person in the data set (with ID = 1)?

e) Using the obtained regression model, what is the unstandardized residual value of the twelfth-grade math achievement score for the first person in the data set (with ID = 1)?

f) Which unstandardized residual value has the greatest magnitude? What is its associated ID number?

Exercise 14.15 involves a small data set.

14.15. A research pediatrician is interested in predicting the birth weight of first-born infants (Y) from the amount of weight gained by the mother during her pregnancy (X) for the population of middle-class individuals. She therefore randomly selects 15 middle-class mothers, pregnant for the first time, and follows them through pregnancy. After the mothers give birth, she records their weight gains in pounds and the birth weights of their offspring in pounds. The data are given in the following table. Use them to answer the associated questions.

X Weight Gain of Mother (pounds)	Y Birth Weight of Infant (pounds)
14	6.2
23	6.8
28	7.5
27	7.3
12	6.0
19	6.2
25	7.0
24	6.3
34	8.0
21	6.0
30	8.0
32	8.2
26	7.5
27	7.5
23	6.8

a) Create a scatterplot and, if necessary, a diagnostic analysis, and use them to show that a correlation and simple linear regression analysis is appropriate for these data.

b) Construct a 95 percent CI for the population correlation, ρ, between the birth weight of the infant and the weight gain of the mother. According to the CI, is the correlation statistically significant? If so, describe its nature and strength.

c) Construct the linear regression equation for predicting the birth weight of the infant (Y) from the weight gain of the mother (X).

d) Is the linear regression model statistically significant? Use $\alpha = .05$. Explain.

e) What is the predicted birth weight of a first-born infant whose mother gained 25 pounds during her pregnancy?

f) Calculate the overall standard error of estimate when using the linear regression equation to predict Y from X in the population.

g) Interpret the standard error of estimate and estimate with approximately 95 percent accuracy the weight of an infant whose mother gained 25 pounds during pregnancy.

Exercises 14.17 through 14.32 are conceptual in nature and do not require the use of SPSS.

14.16. The b-weight for predicting Y from X is computed in a sample of size 200 drawn randomly from a bivariate population. If this process is repeated 2,000 times, the standard deviation of the 2,000 b-weights is approximately equal to

a) the standard deviation of X.

b) the standard deviation of Y.

c) the standard error of b for $N = 200$.

d) the standard error of b for $N = 2,000$.

e) none of the above.

14.17. Given a simple regression equation for predicting Y from X, $\hat{Y} = bX + a$. When does Var(Y) equal Var(residual)? [HINT: The residual is that part of Y that remains after accounting for X, or $Y - \hat{Y}$.]

a) When the correlation between X and Y is equal to zero.

b) When the correlation between X and Y is not equal to zero.

c) When the correlation between X and Y is positive, but not when it's negative.

d) Always.

e) Never.

f) None of the above.

14.18. Given a simple regression equation for predicting Y from X, $\hat{Y} = bX + a$. When is Var(Y) less than Var(residual)?

a) When the correlation between X and Y is equal to zero.

b) When the correlation between X and Y is not equal to zero.

c) When the correlation between X and Y is positive, but not when it's negative.

d) Always.

e) Never.

f) None of the above.

Exercises 14.20 through 14.24 relate to the following scatterplot. The regression line has been added and the points are labeled by their case numbers.

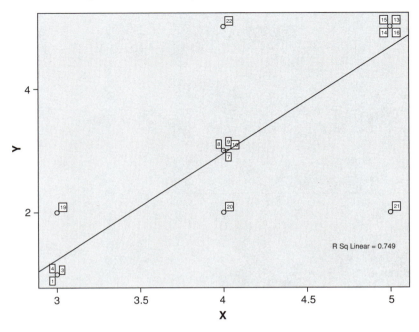

14.19. The value 3 may be described most closely as
a) $\overline{X}$, the mean of X.
b) $\overline{Y}$, the mean of Y.
c) both (a) and (b).
d) neither (a) nor (b).

14.20. The point with the greatest residual corresponds to which case number?
a) 19
b) 20
c) 21
d) 22

14.21. The point with the greatest influence corresponds to which case number?
a) 19
b) 20
c) 21
d) 22

14.22. The slope of the regression equation in this case is
a) positive.
b) negative.
c) zero.

14.23. The Y-intercept of the regression equation in this case is
a) positive.
b) negative.
c) zero.

14.24. Which regression assumption is most likely violated in the following scatterplot?

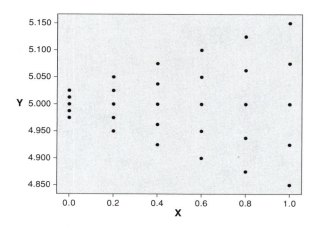

a) linearity
b) normality
c) homoscedasticity

14.25. Which regression assumption is most likely violated in the following scatterplot?

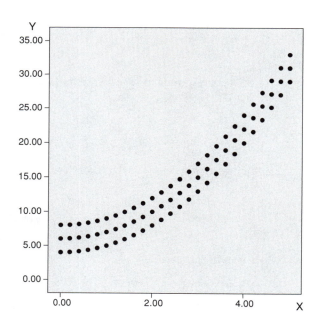

a) linearity
b) normality
c) homoscedasticity

14.26. Which regression assumption is most likely violated in the following scatterplot?

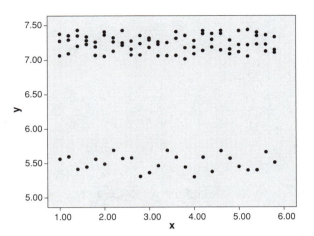

a) linearity
b) normality
c) homoscedasticity

14.27. Which regression assumption is most likely violated in the following scatterplot that depicts the Y scores of 300 boys and 300 girls?

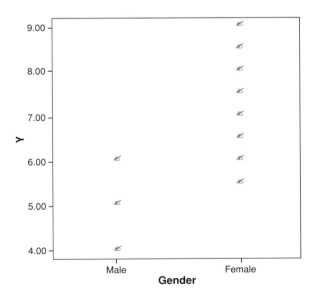

a) linearity
b) normality
c) homoscedasticity

Exercises 14.28 through 14.31 come from Becker and Kennedy (1992). Use the following graph to determine the most correct response to the multiple-choice questions.

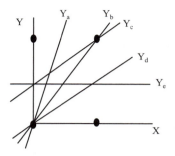

14.28. For the four sample points, which line best represents the average of the Y data? (Note that the point $(0, 0)$ is one of the observations.)

   a) Y_a b) Y_b c) Y_c d) Y_d e) Y_e

14.29. For the four sample points, which line best represents the regression line?

   a) Y_a b) Y_b c) Y_c d) Y_d e) Y_e

14.30. The value of R^2 for the regression line is

   a) less than 0.

   b) 0.

   c) between 0 and .5.

   d) .5.

   e) greater than .5.

14.31. Verify that the mean of the residuals is zero for any simple linear regression analysis.

CHAPTER FIFTEEN

An Introduction to Multiple Regression

In Chapter 12, we were concerned with predicting the number of ice cream bars we could expect to sell at the beach from the daily highest temperature. Our goal was to predict that number as accurately as possible so that we would take neither too much ice cream to the beach nor too little. Because of the linear shape depicted in the scatterplot and the strong relationship between number of ice cream sales and daily highest temperature ($r = .887$), we were able to construct a reasonably accurate simple linear regression equation for prediction with $R^2 = .78$. But, we can try to do even better. That is, we can consider ways to predict ice cream sales even more accurately.

Alternatively, we can shift our focus away from prediction and consider ways to *explain* the observed variability in ice cream sales. That is, rather than use multiple regression for prediction, we may use it to understand and explain phenomena of interest to us and to study the effects that individual independent variables have on these phenomena. That is, we can use multiple regression to understand the factors that contribute to ice cream sales at the beach rather than to predict the number of ice cream sales we can expect on a particular day at the beach. Clearly, we have already defined temperature as one explanatory factor. We now seek to identify another factor, in addition to temperature, that explains why people buy ice cream at the beach.

Assuming that our beach example takes place in the northeastern part of the United States, another factor might be relative humidity. Like increases in temperature, increases in relative humidity make us feel more uncomfortably hot. Yet, because relative humidity does not correlate highly with temperature when we consider only the summer months in the northeast, relative humidity offers the potential for tapping a set of reasons related to ice cream sales that is different from temperature. Because temperature and humidity are not highly correlated, we say that they are not *redundant* of each other. In general, to optimize the explanatory power of a multiple regression equation, we seek to add new variables to the equation that do not highly correlate with the other independent variables already in the equation and that do highly correlate with the dependent variable.

Although multiple regression, in general, allows for the inclusion of many independent variables in the equation, we shall restrict our discussion to the case of only two independent variables. We do so for simplicity and because the principles and concepts that apply in the case of only two independent variables in the equation generalize easily to the case of more than two independent variables in the equation. Whereas five or six or more independent variables are not uncommon in a regression equation, in practice it is often difficult to identify more than three independent variables that each contribute new explanatory information over and above the others. Said differently, R generally tends not to increase dramatically as the number of independent variables increases beyond even a few because the new variables tend to be redundant with those already in the equation.

THE BASIC EQUATION WITH TWO PREDICTORS

When there are two independent variables (for example, temperature and humidity) and a dependent variable (for example, ice cream sales) in a multiple regression equation, the equation has the following form:

$$\hat{Y} = b_1 X_1 + b_2 X_2 + a. \tag{15.1}$$

As in the simple linear regression case, the b is a coefficient of the X variable and a is an additive constant. The right-hand side of Equation 15.1 is called a *linear composite of the X variables*. As Equation 15.1 suggests, the linear composite is obtained by multiplying X_1 by b_1 and X_2 by b_2 and by adding these two products together with the additive constant a to obtain $\hat{Y}$, the predicted value of Y.

Coefficients b of Equation 15.1 are determined to produce the largest possible correlation between the actual value of Y and the linear composite $\hat{Y}$. Once the coefficients b are determined, the constant a is determined so that, on average, the predicted value of Y is equal to the actual value of Y – that is, so that the mean of $\hat{Y}$ equals the mean of Y, $\bar{\hat{Y}} = \bar{Y}$. The additive constant a has the following equation:

$$a = \bar{Y} - (b_1 \bar{X}_1 + b_2 \bar{X}_2). \tag{15.2}$$

The linear composite and additive constant of Equations 15.1 and 15.2 are based on raw or unstandardized scores. When, on the other hand, the independent variables are standardized to have mean zero and standard deviation 1 (when they are in z-score form), we may re-express Equation 15.1 as Equation 15.3:

$$\hat{z}_Y = \beta_1 z_1 + \beta_2 z_2. \tag{15.3}$$

β (Greek beta) as opposed to b is used in Equation 15.3 to indicate that the linear composite is based on z-scores as opposed to raw scores. Because this equation is based on z-scores, the additive constant, a, is zero.

☞ **Remark.** Because z_Y, z_1, and z_2 are in standardized form, $\bar{z}_Y = \bar{z}_1 = \bar{z}_2 = 0$. If we substitute these means of zero into Equation 15.2 we find that $a = 0$. Regression equations based on z-scores, or standardized scores, all have additive constants equal to zero.

If the independent X variables are converted to z-scores, then the linear composite of the z-scores, $z_{\hat{Y}}$, may be obtained using Equation 15.3. One simply multiplies β_1 and β_2 by z_1 and z_2, respectively, and computes the sum of these two products.

As in simple linear regression, the correlation between Y and $\hat{Y}$, or between z_Y and $z_{\hat{Y}}$, is denoted by R. In the context of multiple regression, however, R is called a *multiple correlation*. R is also denoted as $R_{Y,\hat{Y}}$ or as $R_{Y.12}$. The latter notation explicitly conveys the fact that $\hat{Y}$ is estimated from an equation that contains two predictor variables, X_1 and X_2.

In the next two sections we give the equations for b, β and R. In the first of these sections we consider the case when the two predictors are not correlated. In the second, we consider the more general case, when the two predictors are correlated.

EQUATIONS FOR b, β, AND $R_{Y.12}$ WHEN THE PREDICTORS ARE NOT CORRELATED

When the two predictors in the regression equation are not correlated (i.e., when $r_{X_1,X_2} = 0$), then b_1 and b_2 are expressed simply as

$$b_1 = r_{Y,X_1}\frac{S_Y}{S_{X_1}}$$
$$b_2 = r_{Y,X_2}\frac{S_Y}{S_{X_2}}. \tag{15.4}$$

Notice that, as Equation 15.4 suggests, when the two predictors are uncorrelated, the b-weight for each predictor is simply the b-weight that would be obtained if that predictor were the only one in the equation. That is, the b-weight of a predictor in an equation with two (or more) uncorrelated predictors is obtained simply by ignoring the remaining predictor(s) and calculating the b-weight as though that predictor were the only one in the equation (as in the case of simple linear regression).

The same, of course, applies when the two predictors are uncorrelated and all variables are standardized. The Equations for β_1 and β_2 are given by Equation 15.5:

$$\beta_1 = r_{Y,X_1}$$
$$\beta_2 = r_{Y,X_2}. \tag{15.5}$$

Here again, each β-weight is determined as if its corresponding predictor were the only one in the equation, as in the case of simple linear regression.

We may find $R_{Y.12}$ by taking the square root of $R^2_{Y.12}$ using Equation 15.6:

$$R^2_{Y.12} = r^2_{Y,X_1} + r^2_{Y,X_2}. \tag{15.6}$$

As Equation 15.6 suggests, when the two predictors are uncorrelated, the squared multiple correlation, $R^2_{Y.12}$, is simply equal to the sum of the squared correlations between each predictor and the dependent variable.

☞ **Remark.** The correlations r_{Y,X_1} and r_{Y,X_2} are called *zero-order correlations* to distinguish them from the other types of correlation we encounter in multiple regression. For notational simplicity, we follow common procedure and express r_{Y,X_1} as r_{Y1} and r_{Y,X_2} as r_{Y2}. Likewise, we also express the correlation between predictors, r_{X_1,X_2}, as r_{12} and the standard deviation of X_1, S_{X_1}, as S_{X_1}, and so on for S_{X_2}.

In previous work we have noted that R^2 (or r^2) is a measure of the overall fit of the regression model to the data and is interpreted more specifically as the proportion of Y variance explained by the regression. Accordingly, we may use Figure 15.1 to illustrate Equation 15.6.

In Figure 15.1, each circle represents the variance of one of the variables in the equation, Y, X_1, or X_2, and the amount of overlap between two circles represents their squared correlation. Because X_1 and X_2 are uncorrelated, their circles are nonoverlapping. By contrast, X_1 overlaps with Y, and X_2 overlaps with Y, indicating that these two pairs of variables are correlated. The two overlapping areas are shaded and labeled appropriately, r^2_{Y1} and r^2_{Y2}. When X_1 and X_2 are uncorrelated, we may observe quite clearly that the sum of the shaded

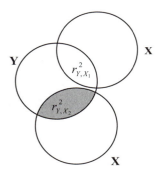

Figure 15.1   The proportion of Y variance explained by the regression when predictors are uncorrelated.

areas, r_{Y1}^2 and r_{Y2}^2, represents the overlap between Y and the two variables taken together, and as such equals $R_{Y.12}^2$, the proportion of Y variance that is explained by the regression containing X_1 and X_2.

EQUATIONS FOR b, β, AND $R_{Y.12}$ WHEN THE PREDICTORS ARE CORRELATED

When the predictors are correlated, one cannot ignore the other predictor in the equation when calculating a regression coefficient or the multiple correlation as was the case in the preceding section. As a result, the equations for the b-weights and $R_{Y.12}$ are a bit more complex than those given earlier. The equation for the b-weights is given in Equation 15.7:

$$
\begin{aligned}
b_1 &= \frac{r_{Y1} - r_{Y2}r_{12}}{1 - r_{12}^2} \times \frac{S_Y}{S_1} \\
b_2 &= \frac{r_{Y2} - r_{Y1}r_{12}}{1 - r_{12}^2} \times \frac{S_Y}{S_2}
\end{aligned}
\tag{15.7}
$$

Equation 15.7 tells us that, when the two predictors are correlated, the value of b_1 (both its magnitude and sign) depends on the correlation between X_1 and Y, r_{Y1}, the correlation between X_2 and Y, r_{Y2}, and the intercorrelation between X_1 and X_2, r_{12}. The same is true for b_2.

☞ **Remark.** When the two predictors are not correlated (when $r_{12} = 0$), Equation 15.7 reduces to Equation 15.4.

Thus, when the predictors of a multiple regression equation are correlated, we do not have the luxury of ignoring the second predictor in the equation when interpreting the importance of the first predictor, and vice versa.

Equation 15.7 reduces to Equation 15.8 when all variables are in standardized form. Once again, β is used in place of b:

$$
\begin{aligned}
\beta_1 &= \frac{r_{Y1} - r_{Y2}r_{12}}{1 - r_{12}^2} \\
\beta_2 &= \frac{r_{Y2} - r_{Y1}r_{12}}{1 - r_{12}^2}
\end{aligned}
\tag{15.8}
$$

To help conceptualize the equation for R^2, we present Figure 15.2(a) and 15.2(b), which each illustrate the relationships between the correlated independent variables and the

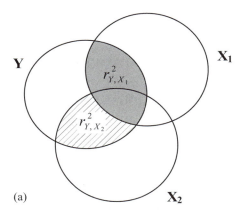

Figure 15.2(a) The proportion of Y variance explained by X_1 (shaded part) and that part of X_2 unrelated to X_1 (cross-hatched part).

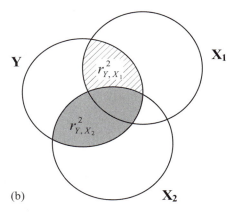

Figure 15.2(b) The proportion of Y variance explained by X_2 (shaded part) and that part of X_1 unrelated to X_2 (cross-hatched part).

dependent variable. In Figure 15.2(a), the proportion of Y variance is expressed as the sum of what is due to X_1 (the shaded part) plus what is due to that part of X_2 unrelated to X_1 (the cross-hatched part). In Figure 15.2 (b), the proportion of Y variance is expressed as the sum of what is due to X_2 (the shaded part) plus what is due to that part of X_1 unrelated to X_2 (the cross-hatched part).

Equations 15.9a and 15.9b translate what is illustrated, respectively, in Figures 15.2(a) and 15.2(b) into an equation for $R_{Y.12}^2$. Equation 15.9a is a direct translation of Figure 15.2(a) and Equation 15.9b is a direct translation of Figure 15.2(b). For both equations, $R_{Y.12}$ is obtained by simply taking the square root.

$$R_{Y.12}^2 = r_{Y1}^2 + r_{Y,2(1)}^2, \tag{15.9a}$$

where r_{Y1}^2 is the proportion of Y variance explained by X_1, and $r_{Y,2(1)}^2$ is the proportion of Y variance explained by X_2 beyond that explained by X_1.

$$R_{Y.12}^2 = r_{Y2}^2 + r_{Y,1(2)}^2, \tag{15.9b}$$

where r_{Y2}^2 is the proportion of Y variance explained by X_2, and $r_{Y,1(2)}^2$ is the proportion of Y variance explained by X_1 beyond that explained by X_2.

☞ **Remark.** Both $r_{Y,1(2)}$ and $r_{Y,2(1)}$ are called *semi-partial (or part) correlations*. In particular, $r_{Y,1(2)}^2$ is the semi-partial or (part) correlation of X_1 squared and may be interpreted as the amount R^2 would drop if X_1 were removed from the equation. Likewise, $r_{Y,2(1)}^2$ is the semi-partial (or part) correlation of X_2 squared and may be interpreted as the amount R^2 would drop if X_2 were removed from the equation. The semi-partial (or part) correlation squared is a highly useful measure of the importance of a predictor variable in an equation and we use it as such in our examples in this chapter.

☞ **Remark.** The semi-partial (or part) correlation of X_1 squared may also be thought of as the *unique contribution* of X_1 to R^2 in the context of the remaining variable in the equation, X_2. An analogous statement may be made for X_2.

SUMMARIZING AND EXPANDING ON SOME IMPORTANT PRINCIPLES OF MULTIPLE REGRESSION

1. R is high when the independent variables are each highly correlated with the dependent variable.

2. R is not less than the highest correlation between any of the independent variables and the dependent variable.

3. R is larger when the independent variables are not redundant of one another – when their intercorrelations are relatively low.

4. R is difficult to estimate from eyeballing the simple, zero-order correlation matrix when the number of independent variables is large.

5. R does not increase dramatically in practice as the number of independent variables increases because the independent variables tend to become redundant of one another as they increase in number.

6. R based on sample data tends to overestimate the population R. Said differently, the sample R is upwardly biased. The smaller the sample size relative to the number of independent variables, the more R is inflated. In situations of prediction, the best way to estimate the extent of inflation is to cross-validate results on a new sample randomly selected from the same population. When there are more than 30 subjects for each independent variable in the equation, the difference between the sample R and cross-validated R tends to be small. When there are fewer than 10 subjects for each independent variable in the equation, the difference between the sample and cross-validated R tends to be large.

7. The importance of an independent variable in an equation is best measured by the amount R^2 would drop if that variable were removed from the equation. This amount may be measured by the squared semi-partial (or part) correlation of that variable.

8. The importance of an independent variable in an equation depends on what other variables are included in the equation along with that variable. When other variables are included in the equation that correlate strongly with that variable, these other variables "rob" that variable of some of its unique contribution. As a result, that variable does not appear to be so important in the equation. Of course, if all independent variables in an equation are highly intercorrelated, none of them appear to be so important in that equation because they each rob one another of its unique contribution.

9. b_1 measures the *net effect* of X_1 partialling out or holding X_2 constant. Likewise, b_2 measures the net effect of X_2 partialling out or holding X_1 constant. Accordingly, these coefficients are called *partial regression coefficients*. Said differently, the net effect of X_1 equals the *average effect* of X_1 for any given value of X_2; the net effect of X_2 equals the *average effect* of X_1 for any given value of X_1.

10. Coefficients b_1 and b_2 are calculated on unstandardized values. As a result, the net effects associated with them are measured in terms of the original units of measure for the variables (e.g., in degrees Fahrenheit, in percentage points of relative humidity).

11. β_1 is a standardized partial regression coefficient and measures the net effect of z_1 partialling out or holding z_2 constant. Likewise, β_2 is also a standardized partial regression coefficient and measures the net effect of z_2 partialling out or holding z_1 constant.

12. Coefficients β_1 and β_2 are calculated on standardized values. As a result, the net effects associated with them are measured in standard deviation units rather than in the original units of measure for the variables.

13. In multiple regression, both b and β can be greater than 1 or less than -1, even though in the case of simple linear regression, when there is only one independent variable, β must be between -1 and 1.

Example 15.1 illustrates the points we have made thus far in this chapter using our ice cream sales example with humidity included as an independent variable in addition to temperature.

· ·

EXAMPLE 15.1. Given the scenario described in Chapter 14 and the data in the following table (saved as *Icecream* on the data CD), construct a regression equation with both temperature and relative humidity as independent variables and ice cream sales as the dependent variable. Said differently, construct an equation that regresses ice cream sales on both temperature and relative humidity. The following data contain relative humidity values in addition to daily highest temperature and number of bars sold for each of the 30 days sampled. Interpret the equation as well as the various tests of significance reported in the output.

BARSOLD	TEMP	RELHUMID
170	75	70
160	70	72
155	65	73
150	60	72
153	72	70
142	60	72
145	63	60
156	68	70
170	78	73
172	77	85
165	75	70
167	75	70
175	80	89
180	82	95
180	85	98
143	59	75
173	86	82
176	88	88
177	85	93
185	90	97
163	74	70
160	73	75
162	71	73
148	68	68
160	70	78
154	73	72
169	85	72
178	90	95
175	70	88
164	81	65

Solution.

To perform a multiple regression analysis using SPSS, click **Analyze** on the Main Menu Bar, **Regression**, **Linear**. Move BARSOLD to the **Dependent** box and TEMP and RELHUMID to the **Independent** box. Click the gray **Statistics** box. In addition to **Estimates** and **Model Fit**, click **Confidence Intervals**, **Descriptives**, and **Part and partial correlations**. Click **Continue**, **OK**.

Parts of the SPSS output are reproduced and described in the following tables.

Descriptive Statistics

	Mean	Std. Deviation	N
barsold Number of ice cream bars sold	164.23	11.907	30
temp Temperature in degrees Fahrenheit	74.93	8.944	30
relhumid	77.67	10.499	30

Once again, from the table labeled Descriptive Statistics, we may note that, as expected, the analysis is based on a sample of size $N = 30$. The mean number of ice cream bars sold is approximately 164 with standard deviation 12, the mean temperature is approximately 75 degrees Fahrenheit with standard deviation 9, and the mean relative humidity is approximately 78 with standard deviation 10.5.

From the table labeled Correlations, we note that the correlations between the dependent variable BARSOLD and the two independent variables, TEMP and RELHUMID, are .887 and .778, respectively; $p < .0005$, indicating that these relationships are statistically significant. Thus, we may conclude that both independent variables relate strongly to BARSOLD.

Correlations

		barsold Number of ice cream bars sold	temp Temperature in degrees Fahrenheit	relhumid
Pearson Correlation	barsold Number of ice cream bars sold	1.000	.887	.778
	temp Temperature in degrees Fahrenheit	.887	1.000	.649
	relhumid	.778	.649	1.000
Sig. (1-tailed)	barsold Number of ice cream bars sold	.	.000	.000
	temp Temperature in degrees Fahrenheit	.000	.	.000
	relhumid	.000	.000	.
N	barsold Number of ice cream bars sold	30	30	30
	temp Temperature in degrees Fahrenheit	30	30	30
	relhumid	30	30	30

We may also conclude from this table that TEMP and RELHUMID are not uncorrelated because the correlation between TEMP and RELHUMID is .649. If we square .649, we find that approximately 42 percent of the variance of each these variables is explained by the other.

We can, therefore, expect R to be no smaller than .887, the higher of the two correlations with the dependent variable. And, because the two independent variables are only moderately correlated, we can expect R to exceed .887 by a nonnegligible amount.

Model Summary

Model	R	R Square	Adjusted R Square	Std. Error of the Estimate
1	.926[a]	.857	.847	4.664

[a]Predictors: (Constant), relhumid, temp
Temperature in degrees Fahrenheit

According to the Model Summary, $R = .926$ and $R^2 = .857$. Thus, temperature and relative humidity *collectively* account for 85.7 percent of ice cream sales variance. While the sample R^2 value is .857, we may note that the adjusted R^2 value is .847. The small amount of shrinkage from sample to adjusted R^2 is due to the fact that the ratio of subjects to independent variables exceeds 10:1. For this example, this ratio is 30:2 or 15:1.

ANOVA[b]

Model		Sum of Squares	df	Mean Square	F	Sig.
1	Regression	3523.953	2	1761.976	80.988	.000[a]
	Residual	587.414	27	21.756		
	Total	4111.367	29			

[a]Predictors: (Constant), relhumid, temp Temperature in degrees Fahrenheit
[b]Dependent Variable: barsold Number of ice cream bars sold

According to the ANOVA table, the overall regression model with both independent variables included is statistically significant ($F(2, 27) = 80.988$, $p < .0005$). The degrees of freedom of 2 and 27 represent, respectively, the number of independent variables in the equation ($P = 2$) and the sample size minus the number of independent variables minus 1 ($N - P - 1 = 30 - 2 - 1 = 27$).

Coefficients[a]

		Unstandardized Coefficients		Standardized Coefficients			95% Confidence Interval for B		Correlations		
Model		B	Std. Error	Beta	t	Sig.	Lower Bound	Upper Bound	Zero-order	Partial	Part
1	(Constant)	67.622	7.639		8.852	.000	51.948	83.295			
	temp Temperature in degrees Fahrenheit	.878	.127	.659	6.894	.000	.617	1.139	.887	.799	.501
	relhumid	.397	.108	.350	3.659	.001	.174	.620	.778	.576	.266

[a]Dependent Variable: barsold Number of ice cream bars sold

From the table labeled Coefficients, we find that the multiple regression equation for predicting ice cream sales from both temperature and relative humidity is as follows:

Estimated BARSOLD = .878 (TEMP) + .397 (RELHUMID) + 67.622.

We may interpret $b_1 = .878$ as follows: For days with a given or specified relative humidity (X_2), each increase in temperature by one degree Fahrenheit is associated with an average increase of .878 ice cream bars sold. In this sense, b_1 represents the net effect of X_1 (temperature) when X_2 (relative humidity) is held constant.

Analogously, we may interpret $b_2 = .397$ as follows: For days with a given or specified temperature (X_1), each increase in relative humidity by one percentage point is associated with an average increase of .397 ice cream bars sold. In this sense, b_2 represents the net effect of X_2 (relative humidity) when X_1 (temperature) is held constant.

From Equation 15.7, we may note that the relative values of the coefficients b are a function of the relative values of the standard deviations of X_1 and X_2. Accordingly, the coefficients b are not a pure measure of the relative importance of the variables in an equation and cannot be used as such. To assess the relative importance of variables in an equation, β-weights are usually more useful because they are based on the standardized values, with each variable having an equal standard deviation of 1.00.

From the Coefficients table, we may note that the standardized form of the multiple regression equation is $z_{\hat{y}} = .660z_1 + .360z_2$. According to this equation, we may note that temperature is relatively more important than relative humidity in predicting ice cream sales because it receives a higher β-weight.

☞ **Remark.** In general, when there are more than two predictors, the β-weights are not the best measure of relative importance of the variables. The β-weights are not so easily interpreted when the independent variables are correlated.

☞ **Remark.** Note that for this example the same general conclusion regarding the relative importance of the independent variables may be obtained from either a comparison of either the b-weights or the β-weights. This is because, in this example, the standard deviation of temperature (11.94) is similar in value to the standard deviation of relative humidity (10.50). That is, the ratio of the two standard deviations is approximately 1:1.

TESTING THE b-WEIGHTS FOR STATISTICAL SIGNIFICANCE

Following the same procedures described in Chapter 14, we may test each of the partial regression coefficients for statistical significance by way of the t-ratio:

$$t = \frac{b}{\hat{\sigma}_b}, \tag{15.10}$$

where $\hat{\sigma}_b$ equals the standard error of b (the standard deviation of the sampling distribution of b-weights based on random samples of the same size randomly drawn from the same population). This t-ratio tests whether the b-coefficient differs from 0 in the population. With P independent variables in the equation, the t-test has $N - P - 1$ degrees of freedom. (In Chapter 14, we considered the case of only one independent variable in the equation. Thus, P equaled 1 and the degrees of freedom for the t-test of the b-weight were noted as being $N - 2$). If a b-coefficient differs significantly from 0, the variable associated with that b contributes significantly to the prediction over and above the contribution of the other variables.

We may obtain the t-ratios for b_1 and b_2 from the table of coefficients in Example 15.1. The t-ratio for b_1 is 6.894 (derived from the t-ratio $.878/.127$), is statistically significant ($p < .0005$), and suggests that b_1 is different from zero in the population. We conclude that the temperature is a statistically significant predictor of the number of ice cream bars sold over what is predicted by relative humidity. Likewise, the t-ratio for b_2 is 3.659 (derived from the t-ratio $.397/.108$), is statistically significant ($p = .001$), and suggests that b_2 is different from zero in the population. We conclude that the relative humidity is a statistically significant predictor of the number of ice cream bars sold over what is predicted by temperature.

From the results of the ANOVA, we noted that the overall regression equation containing both temperature and relative humidity is statistically significant and that, therefore, temperature and relative humidity *collectively* predict ice cream sales. From the t-test results, we now know that *individually* temperature and relative humidity each contribute uniquely to the prediction of ice cream sales.

To estimate the respective values of the b-coefficients in the population we may use confidence intervals as described in Chapter 14. The interested reader may refer back to Equation 14.3 in Chapter 14 for the equations of the upper and lower limits of the confidence interval for b.

The two-tailed 95 percent confidence intervals for b_1 and b_2 in Example 15.1 may be obtained from the Coefficients table. We note that reasonable estimates of b_1 in the population are between $.617$ and 1.139, whereas reasonable estimates of b_2 in the population are between $.174$ and $.620$. Although there is some overlap between the two estimates, b_1 is likely to be the larger of the two weights in the population.

ASSESSING THE RELATIVE IMPORTANCE OF THE INDEPENDENT VARIABLES IN THE EQUATION

As noted earlier, while the β-weights are often useful in assessing the relative importance of the independent variables in an equation, a preferred approach is to use the amount that R^2 will decrease when that variable is removed from the equation, or equivalently the amount R^2 will increase when that variable is added to the equation last.

The amount R^2 will decrease when X_2, for example, is removed from an equation that contains both X_1 and X_2 equals the cross-hatched area of Figure 15.2(a). Likewise, the amount R^2 will decrease when X_1 is removed from the equation that contains both X_1 and X_2 equals the cross-hatched area of Figure 15.2(b).

Without X_2, R^2 would only be equal to r_{Y1}^2 because it would no longer include the cross-hatched area of Figure 15.2(a). Without X_1, R^2 would only be equal to r_{Y2}^2 because it would no longer include the cross-hatched area of Figure 15.2(b).

From Equation 15.9a, we know that the cross-hatched area of Figure 15.2(a) may be expressed directly as $r_{Y,2(1)}^2$, defined earlier as the square of the semi-partial (or part) correlation of X_2. From Equation 15.9b, we know that the cross-hatched area of Figure 15.2(b) may be expressed directly as $r_{Y,1(2)}^2$, defined earlier as the square of the semi-partial (or part) correlation of X_1.

☞ **Remark.** As the cross-hatched area of Figure 15.2(a) suggests, the square of the semi-partial (or part) correlation of X_2 may be defined more explicitly as the square of the correlation between Y and that part of X_2 uncorrelated with (or orthogonal to) X_1. The part of X_2 uncorrelated with (or orthogonal to) X_1 is the part of X_2 that remains after removing all linear relationship with X_1, likewise for the semi-partial correlation of X_1.

Thus, to assess the relative importance of temperature and relative humidity in Example 15.1, we may use the values of the part correlations given in the Coefficients table for this example. The part correlations of temperature (X_1) and relative humidity are, respectively, .501 and .266. If we square these values, we obtain .251 and .071, respectively. Therefore, the amount that the total R^2 of .857 would drop if temperature were removed from the equation is .251 and the amount that the total R^2 of .857 would drop if relative humidity were removed from the equation is .071. From these statistics, it is clear that temperature is the more important variable of the two.

☞ **Remark.** In addition to the part correlation, the Coefficients table includes the zero-order correlation coefficients that also appear in the correlation table of the output. The Coefficients table also includes an index called the partial correlation. Partial correlations are closely related to part correlations and provide the same rank order of variables in terms of their importance. However, because part correlations are useful in the regression context in that they can be interpreted directly in terms of a drop in R^2, whereas partial correlations cannot, we confine our discussion to part correlations in this text. The interested reader is referred to a more advanced treatment of regression to learn more about partial correlations (Cohen, Cohen, West, & Aiken, 2003).

MEASURING THE DECREASE IN R^2 DIRECTLY: AN ALTERNATIVE TO THE SQUARED PART CORRELATION

If we so choose, we may carry out a series of regression analyses to obtain the amount that R^2 will decrease when a variable is removed from the equation. In particular, to find the amount that R^2 will decrease when temperature is removed from the equation with both temperature and humidity, we construct one regression equation with both temperature and humidity to obtain $R^2_{Y.12}$. We then construct another equation without temperature to obtain $R^2_{Y.2}$. The difference, $R^2_{Y.12} - R^2_{Y.2}$, is the amount by which R^2 will decrease when temperature is removed from the equation.

For our example, we find that $R^2_{Y.12} = .857$ and $R^2_{Y.2} = .605$; therefore, $R^2_{Y.12} - R^2_{Y.2} = .252$, which is the amount R^2 drops when temperature is removed from the equation. Notice that, within rounding error, this amount equals $(.501)^2$, the square of the part correlation for temperature.

We may use an analogous procedure to find $R^2_{Y.12} - R^2_{Y.1}$, the decrease in R^2 when humidity is removed from the equation. As before, this amount equals the part correlation of humidity squared.

EVALUATING THE STATISTICAL SIGNIFICANCE OF THE CHANGE IN R^2

Intuitively, it should make sense that whenever the b-weight of an independent variable is statistically significant, the increase in R^2 obtained when that variable is the last to be added to the equation is also statistically significant. It can be shown that the t-test of the statistical significance of the b-weight of an independent variable is equivalent to the corresponding F-test associated with the increase in R^2 when that variable is the last to be added to the equation.

Consider the following two equations, the first with only X_1 and the second with both X_1 and X_2:

$$\hat{Y} = b_1 X_1 + a_0$$
$$\hat{Y} = b_1 X_1 + b_2 X_2 + a_0 \qquad (15.11)$$

Given that the two models represented in Equation 15.11 are different, we would expect, in general, that the b_1-weights and a_0-values would also be different in the two equations.

The squared multiple correlations of the first and second equations are designated $R^2_{Y.1}$ and $R^2_{Y.12}$, respectively. As discussed earlier, a test of whether the effect of X_2, controlling for X_1, is statistically significant is given by the t-test of b_2 that appears in the Coefficients table ($t(27) = 3.659$, $p = .001$). Alternatively, it is given by the following associated F-test on the increment in R^2 due to X_2:

$$F_{(1,N-2-1)} = \frac{(R^2_{Y.12} - R^2_{Y.1})/1}{(1 - R^2_{Y.12})/(N - 2 - 1)}. \qquad (15.12)$$

For our ice cream example, we have $R^2_{Y.12} = .857$, $R^2_{Y.1} = .787$ and $N = 30$. Substituting these values into Equation 15.12 and simplifying we find that $F_{(1,27)} = \dfrac{.07}{.143/27} = \dfrac{.07}{.00529} =$ 13.22, which is within rounding error $t^2 = 3.659^2 = 13.39$.

Likewise, the t-test on the b-weight of temperature, b_1 in our equation, is equivalent to the F-test associated with the increase in R^2 when temperature is the last variable to be added to the equation (when it is added to the equation that already includes relative humidity).

To evaluate the statistical significance of the change in R^2 for our ice cream example using SPSS, click **Analyze, Regression, Linear**. Put BARSOLD in the **Dependent** box and TEMP in the **Independent(s)** box. Click **Next**. Put RELHUMID in the **Independent(s)** box. Click **Statistics**. Select **R square change**. Click **Continue, OK**.

The part of the SPSS output that tests the significance of the change in R^2 is reproduced in the following table.

Model Summary

Model	R	R Square	Adjusted R Square	Std. Error of the Estimate	R Square Change	F Change	df1	df2	Sig. F Change
						Change Statistics			
1	.887[a]	.786	.779	5.602	.786	103.000	1	28	.000
2	.926[b]	.857	.847	4.664	.071	13.392	1	27	.001

[a]Predictors: (Constant), temp Temperature in degrees Fahrenheit
[b]Predictors: (Constant), temp Temperature in degrees Fahrenheit, relhumid

The R^2 values in the Model Summary table for models 1 and 2 correspond to the values that we computed as $R_{Y.1}^2 = .786$ and $R_{Y.12}^2 = .857$. That is, we see that R^2 for model 1 is .786, so that we may conclude that 78.6 percent of the variance in ice cream sales can be explained by temperature. The R^2 for model 2 is .857, so that we may conclude that 85.7 percent of the variance in ice cream sales can be explained by both temperature and relative humidity. According to the value of the R^2 change statistic for model 2 (.071), we see that relative humidity explains 7.1 percent of the variance in ice cream sales over and above the percentage of variance explained by temperature.

The change statistics for model 2 contain the results of the significance test on the change in R^2 between the model that contains only temperature and the model that contains both temperature and relative humidity. We have $F(1, 27) = 13.39$ with $p = .001$. We conclude that relative humidity explains a statistically significant proportion of variance in ice cream sales over and above what was explained by temperature.

THE b-WEIGHT AS A PARTIAL SLOPE IN MULTIPLE REGRESSION

Recall that, in the case of simple regression, the single b-weight or regression coefficient is interpreted as a slope that signifies the expected change in the dependent variable, Y, for each unit increase in the independent variable, X. Just as b is the slope of the line that relates Y to X, we can also describe b_1 and b_2 as slopes, or more precisely, as *partial slopes*. In particular, b_1 can be described as the slope of the line that relates Y to X_1 after X_2 is *partialled from X_1*. Likewise, b_2 can be described as the slope of the line that relates Y to X_2 after X_1 is *partialled from X_2*. X_1 with X_2 partialled from it may be represented graphically as the shaded area of Figure 15.3(a). Likewise, X_2 with X_1 partialled from it may be represented graphically as the shaded area of Figure 15.3(b). As Figures 15.3(a) and 15.3(b) indicate, what remains of X_1 after X_2 is partialled from it is the part of X_1 that is unrelated (or orthogonal) to X_2, and what remains of X_2 after X_1 is partialled from it is the part of X_2 that is unrelated (or orthogonal) to X_1.

If we wanted to create a new variable that represents the shaded part of Figure 15.3(a), for example, we may do so by setting up a simple regression equation to predict X_1 from X_2,

$$\hat{X}_1 = bX_2 + a, \tag{15.3}$$

and then computing $X_1 - \hat{X}_1$. Recall that $X_1 - \hat{X}_1$ is also called the residual of X_1 after accounting for X_2 and may be denoted as $X_{1.2}$. To find $X_{2.1}$ we compute $X_2 - \hat{X}_2$, where $\hat{X}_2$ is obtained from

$$\hat{X}_2 = bX_1 + a. \tag{15.4}$$

Relating this discussion to our ice cream example, X_1 represents temperature and X_2 represents relative humidity. We may create the new variables $X_{1.2}$ and $X_{2.1}$ by constructing

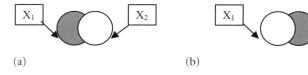

(a)   (b)

Figure 15.3(a) That part of X_1 unrelated (orthogonal) to X_2.

Figure 15.3(b) That part of X_2 unrelated (orthogonal) to X_1.

the respective simple regression equations (15.3 and 15.4) and obtaining the two respective residuals, $X_1 - \hat{X}_1$ and $X_2 - \hat{X}_2$. In so doing we create that part of temperature unrelated to humidity ($X_{1.2}$) and that part of humidity unrelated to temperature ($X_{2.1}$). Note that the correlation between $X_{1.2}$ and $X_{2.1}$ is 0.

We shall use SPSS to create the new variable $X_{1.2}$ and show that b_1, which equals .878, is simply the slope of the regression line that predicts Y from $X_{1.2}$. In Exercise 15.12 you will show that b_2, which equals .397, is simply the slope of the regression line that predicts Y from $X_{2.1}$.

To use SPSS to create this new variable $X_{1.2}$, we choose the linear regression procedure, move X_1 into the **Dependent Variable** box, and move X_2 into the **Independent Variable** box. Under **Save**, click the box next to **Unstandardized Residuals**. ($X_{1.2}$ equals the unstandardized residuals.)

Table 15.2 contains the results of the SPSS analysis that we use to show that b_1, which is .878, equals the b-weight in the simple regression equation that predicts ice cream sales

Table 15.2. Data to illustrate that b_1 is a partial slope

Ice cream bars sold (Y)	Temperature (X_1)	That part of temperature unrelated to humidity ($X_{1.2} = X_1 - \hat{X}_1$)
170	75	4.30772
160	70	−1.79864
155	65	−7.35182
150	60	−11.79864
153	72	1.30772
142	60	−11.79864
145	63	−2.16048
156	68	−2.69228
170	78	5.64818
172	77	−1.98999
165	75	4.30772
167	75	4.30772
175	80	−1.20271
180	82	−2.52179
180	85	−1.18133
143	59	−14.45819
173	86	8.66955
176	88	7.35047
177	85	1.58457
185	90	4.37185
163	74	3.30772
160	73	−.45819
162	71	−1.35182
148	68	−1.58592
160	70	−5.11773
154	73	1.20136
169	85	13.20136
178	90	5.47821
175	70	−10.64953
164	81	13.07362

(Y) from that part of temperature unrelated to humidity ($X_{1.2}$). In so doing, we can begin to appreciate why b_1 is described as a partial slope.

. . . .

EXAMPLE 15.2. Use the data of Table 15.2 to predict ice cream sales (Y) from that part of temperature unrelated to humidity ($X_{1.2}$) and show that the b-weight of $X_{1.2}$ is equal to b_1, the b-weight associated with temperature in the regression equation containing both temperature and humidity. For this to be the case, the simple b-weight from this analysis should equal .878.

Solution. To find the slope, b, of the simple regression equation that predicts number of ice cream sales from that part of temperature unrelated to humidity, we use the linear regression procedure with ice cream sales as the dependent variable and $X_{1.2}$, the unstandardized residual, as the independent variable. The following Coefficients table is obtained as part of our results.

Coefficients*

Model		Unstandardized Coefficients		Standardized Coefficients	t	Sig.
		B	Std. Error	Beta		
1	(Constant)	164.233	1.914		85.803	.000
	RES_1 Unstandardized Residual	.878	.286	.501	3.067	.005

[a]Dependent Variable: barsold Number of ice cream bars sold

Notice that, as expected, $b = .878$.

MULTIPLE REGRESSION WHEN ONE OF THE TWO INDEPENDENT VARIABLES IS DICHOTOMOUS

In the examples presented thus far in this chapter, the independent variables, temperature and relative humidity, were at least interval-leveled. We consider in Example 15.3 the situation in which one of the two independent variables is dichotomous.

. . . .

EXAMPLE 15.3. Using the NELS data set, regress twelfth-grade self-concept (SLFCNC12) on both eighth-grade self-concept (SLFCNC08) and gender. In doing so, determine the extent to which twelfth-grade self-concept variance is explained collectively by eighth-grade self-concept and gender. In addition, determine whether eighth-grade self-concept has an effect on twelfth-grade self-concept after gender is controlled and whether gender has an effect on twelfth-grade self-concept after eighth-grade self-concept is controlled.

Solution. Using the SPSS regression procedure as in Example 15.1, we obtain the following results.

Descriptive Statistics

	Mean	Std. Deviation	N
slfcnc12 Self-Concept in Twelfth Grade	31.48	7.231	500
slfcnc08 Self-Concept in Eighth Grade	21.06	5.971	500
gender Gender	.55	.498	500

From the Descriptive Statistics table, we note that the mean and standard deviation of self-concept for twelfth graders are 31.48 and 7.23, respectively, and for eighth graders they are 21.06 and 5.97, respectively. Gender has a mean of .55, which implies that 55 percent of the sample is female because females are coded 1 and males are coded 0.

Correlations

		slfcnc12 Self-Concept in Twelfth Grade	slfcnc08 Self-Concept in Eighth Grade	gender Gender
Pearson Correlation	slfcnc12 Self-Concept in Twelfth Grade	1.000	.444	−.161
	slfcnc08 Self-Concept in Eighth Grade	.444	1.000	−.191
	gender Gender	−.161	−.191	1.000
Sig. (1-tailed)	slfcnc12 Self-Concept in Twelfth Grade	.	.000	.000
	slfcnc08 Self-Concept in Eighth Grade	.000	.	.000
	gender Gender	.000	.000	.
N	slfcnc12 Self-Concept in Twelfth Grade	500	500	500
	slfcnc08 Self-Concept in Eighth Grade	500	500	500
	gender Gender	500	500	500

The Correlations table suggests a statistically significant moderate positive correlation between twelfth- and eighth-grade self-concept ($r = .444, p < .001$) and a statistically significant, yet low, correlation between twelfth-grade self-concept and gender

($r = -.161, p < .001$). The first correlation indicates that students who had relatively low self-concept in eighth grade tended also to have relatively low self-concept in twelfth grade and that students who had relatively high self-concept in eighth grade tended also to have relatively high self-concept in twelfth grade. Given the coding for gender, the negative correlation implies that on average males have higher self-concept scores than females in twelfth grade. The statistically significant intercorrelation between the two independent variables is also low ($r = -.191$) and implies, as before, that on average males have higher scores than girls in eighth grade.

The Model Summary informs us that a linear composite of gender and eighth-grade self-concept maximally correlates ($R = .450$) with twelfth-grade self-concept. Because .450 is only marginally greater than .444 – the simple, zero-order correlation between twelfth- and eighth-grade self-concept – we can infer that gender is likely to be contributing little, if anything at all, to the equation over and above eighth-grade self-concept. Said differently, gender does not appear to relate to twelfth-grade self-concept after eighth-grade self-concept is accounted for.

Model Summary

Model	R	R Square	Adjusted R Square	Std. Error of the Estimate
1	.450[a]	.203	.200	6.470

[a]Predictors: (Constant), gender Gender, slfcnc08 Self-Concept in Eighth Grade

ANOVA[b]

Model		Sum of Squares	df	Mean Square	F	Sig.
1	Regression	5290.030	2	2645.015	63.192	.000[a]
	Residual	20802.770	497	41.857		
	Total	26092.800	499			

[a]Predictors: (Constant), gender Gender, slfcnc08 Self-Concept in Eighth Grade
[b]Dependent Variable: slfcnc12 Self-Concept in Twelfth Grade

We may determine the proportion of variance accounted for by gender over and above eighth-grade self-concept by examining the R^2 values. From the Model Summary, we know that the overall R^2 with both eighth-grade self-concept and gender in the equation is .203. Thus, collectively, eighth-grade self-concept and gender account for 20.3 percent of twelfth-grade self-concept variation. (We may also obtain this measure of effect size by dividing the SS due to Regression by SS Total: $5,290/26,093.8 = .203$.) From the Correlations table, we know that eighth-grade self-concept, by itself, accounts for $r^2 = .444^2 = .197$ of twelfth-grade self-concept variance. The difference between .203 and .197 is the proportion of twelfth-grade self-concept variance due to gender after eighth-grade self-concept is accounted for. This difference, at .006, is certainly negligible, suggesting again that gender does not have much explanatory power over and above eighth-grade self-concept.

To assess the statistical significance of the individual, unique contribution of each variable and to obtain the regression equation itself, we consult the Coefficients table.

Coefficients[a]

Model		Unstandardized Coefficients		Standardized Coefficients		
		B	Std. Error	Beta	t	Sig.
1	(Constant)	21.174	1.183		17.895	.000
	slfcnc08 Self-Concept in Eighth Grade	.519	.049	.429	10.501	.000
	gender Gender	−1.143	.592	−.079	−1.931	.054

[a]Dependent Variable: slfcnc12 Self-Concept in Twelfth Grade

The unstandardized regression equation is

Estimated SLFCNC12 = (.519) (SLFCNC08) − (1.143) (GENDER) + 21.174.

Likewise, the standardized regression equation is

Estimated SLFCNC12 = (.429) $(z_{SLFCNC08})$ − (.079) (z_{GENDER}).

According to the significance values associated with the t-tests on the regression coefficients, we may note that whereas eighth-grade self-concept is statistically significant, gender is not. This result is consistent with what our earlier analysis based on the correlations showed.

According to the standardized regression equation, we may note that SLFCNC08 receives the higher β-weight because it is more important than GENDER in predicting SLFCNC12.

Because the b-weight associated with eighth-grade self-concept is statistically significant, we may say that, when controlling for gender, every one-point increase in eighth-grade self-concept associates on average with a .519-point increase in twelfth-grade self-concept. Because the b-weight associated with gender is not statistically significant, we know that after controlling for eighth-grade self-concept the magnitude of the difference in twelfth-grade self-concept between males and females is not likely to be different from zero. That is, the gender difference in twelfth-grade self-concept represented by the statistically significant zero-order correlation coefficient between gender and twelfth-grade self-concept appears to be explained by the difference in self-concept in eighth grade. Said differently, gender differences in twelfth-grade self-concept do not exist after partialling out or controlling for eighth-grade self-concept.

We may use the unstandardized regression equation to estimate the overall twelfth-grade self-concept mean as well as the separate means for males and females by substituting the relevant independent variable mean values into the equation.

The overall twelfth-grade mean is obtained by substituting the respective eighth-grade self-concept and gender means into the equation as follows:

Estimated twelfth-grade self-concept mean = (.519) (21.06) − (1.143) (.55) + 21.174 = 31.48.

Note that this is the twelfth-grade self-concept mean value printed in the Descriptive Statistics table.

The twelfth-grade self-concept mean for males may be obtained by substituting into the equation the eighth-grade self-concept mean and the value of 0 for gender (because males are coded 0) as follows:

Estimated twelfth-grade self-concept mean for males = (.519) (21.06) − (1.143) (0) + 21.174 = 32.104.

Likewise, the twelfth-grade self-concept mean for females is obtained as follows:

Estimated twelfth-grade self-concept mean for females = (.519) (21.06) − (1.143) (1) + 21.174 = 30.961.

☞ **Remark.** Notice that if we subtract the male mean from the female mean we obtain −1.143, the value of the *b*-weight associated with gender. Hence, as noted earlier, the *b*-weight associated with the dichotomous variable equals the difference between the dependent variable means for the two groups represented by the dichotomy. In our example, it equals the difference between the twelfth-grade self-concept means for males and females (30.961 − 32.104 = −1.143). Because the *b*-weight associated with gender is not statistically significant, we know that, after controlling for eighth-grade self-concept, the populations of males and females are not different on average in terms of twelfth-grade self-concept.

THE CONCEPT OF INTERACTION BETWEEN TWO VARIABLES THAT ARE AT LEAST INTERVAL-LEVELED

Thus far we have considered temperature and humidity as variables that individually and collectively affect ice cream sales at the beach. Suppose we notice, however, that when the temperature is low, the humidity influences ice cream sales to a greater extent than when the temperature is high. That is, when temperature is relatively low, ice cream sales are much stronger when humidity is relatively high rather than when it is relatively low. When temperature is relatively high, however, ice cream sales are reasonably strong regardless of whether humidity is relatively low or relatively high. Figure 15.4 illustrates this sales scenario.

As Figure 15.4 shows, the increase in ice cream sales as temperature increases is more dramatic under conditions of relatively low humidity than under conditions of relatively high humidity. Thus, the relationship between temperature and ice cream sales varies as a function of humidity. When humidity is relatively low, the relationship between temperature and ice cream sales is stronger than when humidity is relatively high. Based on our discussion of interaction in Chapter 11 in connection with two-way analysis of variance (ANOVA), we may note that Figure 15.4 depicts an interaction between temperature and humidity that affects ice cream sales – that humidity *moderates* the relationship between temperature and ice cream sales. When a variable, such as humidity, moderates the relationship between two other variables, that variable is said to be a *moderator*. The moderator variable and the variable whose relationship it moderates with the dependent variable are also called *interacting* variables.

In a multiple regression equation, interactions involving two variables (two-way interactions) are represented as the product of the two interacting variables. Thus, if the two

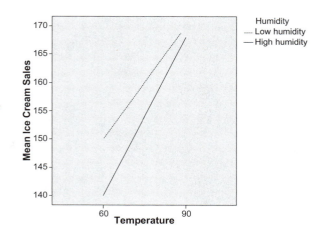

Figure 15.4 The relationship between ice cream sales and temperature varies with humidity.

variables in the equation are X_1 and X_2, the interaction between X_1 and X_2 is represented as $X_1 \cdot X_2$. The multiple regression model that includes X_1 and X_2 and their interaction is given in Equation 15.12:

$$\hat{Y} = b_1 X_1 + b_2 X_2 + b_3 X_1 \cdot X_2 + a. \tag{15.12}$$

By rearranging terms in Equation 15.12, we can show how the product term in Equation 15.12 represents situations such as that in Figure 15.4, where the slope of the line relating X_1 (temperature) to Y (ice cream sales) varies with the value of X_2 (humidity):

$$\hat{Y} = b_1 X_1 + b_2 X_2 + b_3 X_1 \cdot X_2 + a$$
$$= b_1 X_1 + b_3 X_1 \cdot X_2 + b_2 X_2 + a. \tag{15.13}$$
$$= (b_1 + b_3 X_2) X_1 + b_2 X_2 + a$$

In Equation 15.13, the slope of X_1 (temperature) is not simply b_1, but rather it is $b_1 + b_3 X_2$. If it were simply b_1 then we would know that the slope of the line relating X_1 to Y would remain constant regardless of the value of X_2 (humidity). Because the slope is $b_1 + b_3 X_2$, we know that the slope of the line relating X_1 to Y depends on the value of X_2. Figure 15.4 gives an example of this situation.

From Equation 15.13, we know that when $b_3 = 0$ the slope of the line relating X_1 to Y remains constant regardless of the value of X_2. An illustration of this situation is given in Figure 15.5.

The parallel lines in Figure 15.5, depicting a constant relationship between X_1 and Y regardless of the value of X_2, imply no interaction between X_1 and X_2. In Figure 15.4, there is an interaction between X_1 and X_2 and $b_3 = 0$. In Figure 15.5, there is no interaction between X_1 and X_2 and $b_3 = 0$. In short, therefore, an interaction exists in the population if and only if $b_3 = 0$ in the population. As before, we use the t-ratio to test whether b_3 is different from zero in the population. This t-ratio is given in Equation 15.10.

☞ **Remark.** We may interpret b_1 and b_2 in Equation 15.12 as follows: b_1 represents the slope of the line that describes the relationship between Y and X_1 when X_2 is zero; b_2 represents the slope of the line that describes the relationship between Y and X_2 when X_1 is zero. *If an interaction term is in the equation, b_1 and b_2 are easily interpreted as long as the value of*

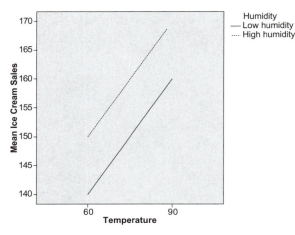

Figure 15.5 The relationship between ice cream sales and temperature does not vary with humidity ($b_3 = 0$).

zero is a meaningful one for X_1 and X_2. If an interaction term is *not* in the equation, b_1 represents the average effect of X_1 averaged across the full range of values (levels) of X_2 and b_2 represents the average effect of X_2 averaged across the full range of values (levels) of X_1.

☞ **Remark.** We may interpret b_3 in Equation 15.12 as follows: For every unit change in X_1, the slope of the line that describes the relationship between Y and X_2 changes by b_3 units. Likewise, for every unit change in X_2, the slope of the line that describes the relationship between Y and X_1 changes by b_3 units.

TESTING THE STATISTICAL SIGNIFICANCE OF AN INTERACTION USING SPSS

EXAMPLE 15.4. Test whether there is an interaction between temperature and humidity on ice cream sales. If there is an interaction, what proportion of ice cream sales variance does it explain?

Solution. Use the SPSS Compute procedure within Transform to compute a new variable called PRODUCT (note that any variable name would do as well), which is the product of temperature and relative humidity (TEMP*RELHUMID). This new variable carries the interaction term between Temperature and Relative Humidity. Once the product term is computed, click **Regression, Linear,** and move TEMP (X_1), RELHUMID (X_2), and PRODUCT (X_1X_2) into the **Independent(s) Variable** box and BARSOLD (Y) into the **Dependent Variable** Box. Click **Statistics** and within this option click **Descriptives**. The following output is obtained.

Descriptive Statistics

	Mean	Std. Deviation	N
barsold Number of ice cream bars sold	164.23	11.907	30
relhumid	77.67	10.499	30
temp Temperature in degrees Fahrenheit	74.93	8.944	30
Product	5878.77	1392.111	30

☞ **Remark.** It should not come as a surprise that the mean and standard deviation of Product are both very large, because the variable PRODUCT is formed by multiplying the values of TEMP (temperature) and RELHUMID (relative humidity).

Correlations

		barsold Number of ice cream bars sold	relhumid	temp Temperature in degrees Fahrenheit	Product
Pearson Correlation	barsold Number of ice cream bars sold	1.000	.778	.887	.899
	relhumid	.778	1.000	.649	.926
	temp Temperature in degrees Fahrenheit	.887	.649	1.000	.886
	Product	.899	.926	.886	1.000
Sig. (1-tailed)	barsold Number of ice cream bars sold	.	.000	.000	.000
	relhumid	.000	.	.000	.000
	temp Temperature in degrees Fahrenheit	.000	.000	.	.000
	Product	.000	.000	.000	.
N	barsold Number of ice cream bars sold	30	30	30	30
	relhumid	30	30	30	30
	temp Temperature in degrees Fahrenheit	30	30	30	30
	Product	30	30	30	30

☞ **Remark.** We may note that the correlations (in the Correlations table) between the product term and its component parts are both very high. The correlation between PRODUCT and TEMP is $r = .886$; the correlation between PRODUCT and RELHUMID is $r = .926$. Accordingly, PRODUCT carries within it some of the main (or *first-order*) effects due to its component parts (temperature and relative humidity). For this reason, the interaction is not the product term itself; it is the product term with its component parts removed or partialled out. As such, authors have referred to the interaction as a *partialled product*. In the case of two independent variables, the partialled product is simply obtained by entering the product term into an equation that already contains its two component, first-order effects. The test of the *b*-weight associated with the product term is then a test of the unique contribution of the product term after controlling for the two first-order effects that are already in the equation. In the context of this problem, a test of the *b*-weight associated with the product term is a test of the interaction between temperature and relative humidity on ice cream sales *as long as both first-order component terms are already in the equation.*

Coefficients[a]

Model		Unstandardized Coefficients		Standardized Coefficients		
		B	Std. Error	Beta	t	Sig.
1	(Constant)	−98.675	64.677	−	−1.526	.139
	relhumid	2.583	.851	2.278	3.035	.005
	temp Temperature in degrees Fahrenheit	2.968	.816	2.229	3.635	.001
	Product	−.027	.011	−3.185	−2.586	.016

[a]Dependent Variable: barsold Number of ice cream bars sold

The unstandardized regression equation for estimating ice cream sales (Y) from temperature (TEMP), relative humidity (RELHUMID), and their interaction (PRODUCT = TEMP*RELHUMID) is

$$\hat{Y} = 2.968 \, (TEMP) + 2.583 \, (RELHUMID) - .0272 \, (PRODUCT) - 98.675.$$

The b-weight associated with the product term is statistically significant ($p = .016$), suggesting that there is an interaction between temperature and relative humidity on ice cream sales; that the relationship between temperature and ice cream sales varies as a function of relative humidity; or that the relationship between relative humidity and ice cream sales varies as a function of temperature.

ANOVA[b]

Model		Sum of Squares	df	Mean Square	F	Sig.
1	Regression	3644.141	3	1214.714	67.596	.000[a]
	Residual	467.226	26	17.970		
	Total	4111.367	29			

[a]Predictors: (Constant), Product, temp Temperature in degrees Fahrenheit, relhumid
[b]Dependent Variable: barsold Number of ice cream bars sold

We may consult the ANOVA summary table to determine the overall goodness of fit of the model that contains the two main effects and the interaction term. By dividing $SS_{\text{Regression}}$ by SS_{Total} (3,644/4,111), we find that approximately 89 percent of the ice cream sales variance is accounted for by temperature, relative humidity, and their interaction.

We may also refer to the Model Summary table to obtain this same information.

Model Summary

Model	R	R Square	Adjusted R Square	Std. Error of the Estimate
1	.941[a]	.886	.873	4.239

[a]Predictors: (Constant), prod, temp Temperature in degrees Fahrenheit, relhumid

Alternatively, we may use the hierarchical multiple regression approach to test the statistical significance of the interaction term by evaluating the statistical significance of the change in R^2 when the interaction term is introduced to the model. In this approach, the main effects of TEMP and RELHUMID are entered simultaneously in the first block and then the interaction term PRODUCT is entered in the second block.

To evaluate the statistical significance of the interaction term by evaluating the change in R^2 when the interaction term is added using SPSS, click **Analyze**, **Regression**, **Linear**. Put BARSOLD in the **Dependent** box and TEMP and RELHUMID in the **Independent(s)** box. Click **Next**. Put PRODUCT in the **Independent(s)** box. Click **Statistics**. Click the circle next to **R square change**. Click **Continue, OK**.

For comparison, we look at the results in the Model Summary table.

Model Summary

Model	R	R Square	Adjusted R Square	Std. Error of the Estimate	Change Statistics				
					R Square Change	F Change	df1	df2	Sig. F Change
1	.926[a]	.857	.847	4.664	.857	80.988	2	27	.000
2	.941[b]	.886	.873	4.239	.029	6.688	1	26	.016

[a]Predictors: (Constant), relhumid, temp Temperature in degrees Fahrenheit
[b]Predictors: (Constant), relhumid, temp Temperature in degrees Fahrenheit, prod

The change in R^2 associated with introducing the interaction term into the equation is $R^2_{Change} = .029$, which is statistically significant ($F(1, 26) = 6.69, p = .016$). Thus, as we noted before from the t-test value associated with the product term, there is an interaction between temperature and relative humidity that affects ice cream sales. The R^2_{Change} statistic informs us that the interaction accounts for approximately 3 percent of ice cream sales variance over and above first-order effects. We emphasize the fact that the F-test on R^2_{Change} is identical to the t-test of the b-weight associated with the product term. Note that both have p-values equal to .016 and by squaring the t-value of -2.586 we obtain the F-value of 6.688. Recall that, with one degree of freedom in the numerator, $F = t^2$. Finally, we note once again that the overall R^2 equals .886, suggesting that approximately 89 percent of the ice cream sales variance is accounted for by all three terms in the equation – temperature, relative humidity, and their interaction.

☞ **Remark.** When the interaction term is not statistically significant, the regression analysis should be rerun without the product term and the resulting regression equation with only main effects reported. If the analysis is carried out using blocks, as in this example, the regression equation on the main effects may be obtained simply as the equation based on the variables in the first block only. Analyses that are carried out using blocks are called *hierarchical analyses* because they rely on a hierarchy or order of entry of terms into the equation. In this example, that order was main effects entered as the first block, followed by the interaction or product term entered as the second block.

CENTERING FIRST-ORDER EFFECTS TO ACHIEVE MEANINGFUL INTERPRETATIONS OF *b*-WEIGHTS

If an equation contains a product term, the interpretation of the *b*-weights associated with the first-order effect variables is a bit more complicated than if the equation does not contain a product term. In our example, the *b*-weight associated with temperature represents the slope of the line that describes the relationship between ice cream sales and temperature when relative humidity is 0; the *b*-weight associated with relative humidity represents the slope of the line that describes the relationship between ice cream sales and relative humidity when temperature is 0. Because both zero temperature and zero relative humidity are not meaningful in the context of this problem set in the Northeast during the summer months, the interpretation of these *b*-weights is also not meaningful.

To impart meaning to the *b*-weights of first-order-effect variables in an equation that contains a product term, we may rescale each of the first-order-effect variables to make the value of zero in each variable correspond to something meaningful. A reasonable choice is to set the mean of each rescaled variable at zero by subtracting the mean from each variable value. Such rescaling is called *centering* and the newly rescaled variables are called *centered variables*. Another advantage to centering is that it allows us to test the interaction term with greater power than if we had not centered the variables (Cohen, Cohen, West, & Aiken, 2003). In general, a product term that is based on centered first-order-effect variables correlates less strongly with each of the centered first-order variables already in the equation than a product term that is not based on centered first-order variables correlates with each of the uncentered first-order-effect variables already in the equation. As a result, the product term has a greater unique contribution to make over and above the first-order-effect variables, and we are able to test the interaction with greater power. To find the centered temperature variable, we subtract the mean temperature (74.93) from each temperature value in the distribution; to find the centered relative humidity variable, we subtract the mean relative humidity (77.67) from each relative humidity value in the distribution. The product term would then be the product of each centered variable. The analysis of the interaction from Example 15.4 using the centered temperature and relative humidity variables is left for the reader to complete as Exercise 15.17.

UNDERSTANDING THE NATURE OF A STATISTICALLY SIGNIFICANT TWO-WAY INTERACTION

A statistically significant two-way interaction informs us that the effect of X_1 (temperature) is not the same across all levels of X_2 (relative humidity) and likewise the effect of X_2 is not the same across all levels of X_1. But, beyond that, the significant *t*-ratio tells us nothing about the nature of the interaction. There are at least two ways to determine the nature of the interaction: by plotting discrete predicted values and by computing simple slopes. The first method, which is the only one that we describe in this text, does not incorporate the use of significance testing. The interested reader is referred to Aiken and West (1991) or

Darlington (1990) for a discussion of simple slopes that incorporates significance testing on the nature of the interaction.

A good way to describe the interaction is to plot it. To do so, we need to examine the estimated Y-values for each combination of meaningful X_1- and X_2-values. The estimated Y-values are the equivalent of cell means that we use to obtain a plot like Figure 15.4. To obtain a 2×2 array of cell means, we often identify as meaningful values those considered to be low and high for each of the two variables X_1 and X_2. These values are often interpreted to be at one standard deviation below the mean and at one standard deviation above the mean.

For example, with respect to our ice cream data, we may ask, "What is the average number of ice cream sales for days with low and high humidity and low and high temperature?" To answer this question, we compute $\hat{Y}$ for each combination of low and high values of our independent variables using the regression equation obtained from the solution to Example 15.3:

$$\text{Estimated Sales} = -98.68 + 2.97(\text{Temp}) + 2.58(\text{Humid}) \\ - .027(\text{Temp} \times \text{Humidity}).$$

To clarify the nature of the interaction, estimated ice cream sales at one standard deviation below the mean and at one standard deviation above the mean are obtained as follows and are plotted in Figure 15.6.

Based on calculations using the means and standard deviations obtained from the Descriptives table, we obtain the values at one standard deviation below the mean and at one standard deviation above the mean for temperature and humidity.

Variable	Mean	StDev	One SD below (low)	One SD above (high)
Temperature	74.93	8.94	65.99	83.87
Humidity	77.67	10.50	67.17	88.17
Interaction	5878.77	1392.11		

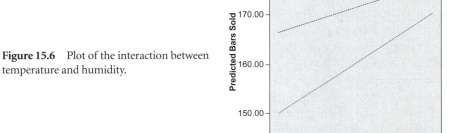

Figure 15.6 Plot of the interaction between temperature and humidity.

Substituting each combination of low and high values for these variables into the regression equation produces the following 2×2 table of cell means that givesvalues for $\hat{Y}$ at each of the four pairs of temperature and humidity values.

Humidity

		Low	High
Temperature	High	170.32	176.59
	Low	149.97	166.46

A plot of these values is given in Figure 15.6. Creating this plot is a two-step process. First, the summary data must be entered as an SPSS data set. Second, the graph must be created from the summary data.

To create an SPSS data file with the summary data, you need three columns. Create the variable TEMP with Variable Label Temperature and Value Labels 1 = Low and 2 = High. Create the variable HUMID with Variable Label Humidity and Value Labels 1 = Low and 2 = High. Create the variable SALES with Variable Label Predicted Ice Cream Sales. Type in the data as follows:

TEMP	HUMID	SALES
1	1	149.97
1	2	166.46
2	1	170.32
2	2	176.59

To create the line graph, go to **Graphs, Legacy Dialogs, Line**. Click **Multiple, Define**. Put TEMP in the **Category Axis** and **Define Lines by** HUMID. In the **Lines Represent** box, click the circle next to **Other Statistic** and put SALES in the adjacent box. Click **OK**.

Alternatively, one could plot humidity on the *X*-axis and have separate lines for high and low temperatures.

The results of our analysis of ice cream sales suggest that both temperature and humidity influence summer ice cream sales at the beach in the Northeast and that relative humidity moderates the influence that temperature has on ice cream sales. The pattern for the predicted values depicted in the line graph suggests that the relationship between ice cream sales and temperature is greater when humidity is relatively low rather than when it is relatively high. Ice cream sales on days with relatively high temperature and relatively low humidity are similar to ice cream sales on days with relatively high temperature and relatively high humidity; on such days, ice cream sales are strong. However, on days with relatively low temperature, ice cream sales are much stronger when humidity is relatively high than when it is relatively low.

In completing this analysis, we should also have paid attention to the diagnostics we discussed in the previous chapter to verify that our model was not unduly influenced by outliers and that the assumptions underlying the procedure are met. Often, to determine to what extent outliers influence the results of a regression analysis, the analysis is carried out both with and without outliers, and changes in results are noted and evaluated. Such analyses are called "sensitivity analyses" because they are measuring the sensitivity of the results to what appear to be critical changes in the data set. We ask you to complete this aspect of the analysis in Exercise 15.18.

INTERACTION WHEN ONE OF THE INDEPENDENT VARIABLES IS DICHOTOMOUS AND THE OTHER IS CONTINUOUS

In Example 15.3, we examined the extent to which eighth-grade self-concept and gender collectively and individually explained twelfth-grade self-concept. In this section we extend Example 15.3 and examine whether there is an interaction between eighth-grade self-concept and gender on twelfth-grade self-concept – that is, whether the relationship between eighth-grade self-concept and twelfth-grade self-concept varies as a function of gender.

EXAMPLE 15.5. Determine whether there is an interaction between eighth-grade self-concept and gender that affects twelfth-grade self-concept. Construct a plot to facilitate the interpretation of the interaction, if one exists.

Solution. In the solution to this example we center the eighth-grade self-concept variable to have a mean of zero to illustrate how to carry out an analysis of interactions using centered variables. By centering, the value of zero on the self-concept scale becomes a meaningful quantity for interpretation purposes. We do not need to center gender because the value of zero on the gender scale is already meaningful because it is the code for males.

Prior to conducting the regression analysis, we center the interval-leveled variable and we form the product term to represent the interaction. To center eighth-grade self-concept, we click **Transform**, **Compute** to create a new variable which we call CTRSLF08, with CTRSLF08 = SLFCNC08 − 21.06 (the mean of SLFCNC08). We then use the **Compute** command again to form the product term PRODUCT = CTRSLF08*GENDER.

To conduct the regression analysis, we select **Analyze**, **Regression**, **Linear** and move the three variables GENDER, CTRSLF08, and PRODUCT into the **Independent Variable(s)** box. The dependent variable is SLFCNC12. Click the gray **Statistics** box. Select **Descriptives**. Click **Continue**, **OK**.

The results of the regression analysis are reproduced and analyzed in the following tables.

Descriptive Statistics

	Mean	Std. Deviation	N
slfcnc12 Self-Concept in Twelfth Grade	31.48	7.231	500
Ctrslf08	.00	5.971	500
gender Gender	.55	.498	500
Product	−.57	4.752	500

Correlations

		slfcnc12 Self-Concept in Twelfth Grade	Ctrslf08	gender Gender	product
Pearson Correlation	slfcnc 12 Self-Concept in Twelfth Grade	1.000	.444	−.161	.401
	Ctrslf08	.444	1.000	−.191	.807
	gender Gender	−.161	−.191	1.000	−.109
	product	.401	.807	−.109	1.000
Sig. (1-tailed)	slfcnc12 Self-Concept in Twelfth Grade	.	.000	.000	.000
	Ctrslf08	.000	.	.000	.000
	gender Gender	.000	.000	.	.007
	product	.000	.000	.007	.
N	slfcnc 12 Self-Concept in Twelfth Grade	500	500	500	500
	Ctrslf08	500	500	500	500
	gender Gender	500	500	500	500
	product	500	500	500	500

Notice that, as expected, the mean of the centered eighth-grade self-concept variable is virtually zero. The means of the gender and twelfth-grade self-concept are the same as they were earlier because neither of these variables was centered.

Because centering is a translation – a form of linear transformation that does not involve reflection – the correlations between the first-order-effect variables remain the same. The correlations of PRODUCT with its component parts are nonzero, suggesting once again that the product term is not the interaction. Rather, the interaction is the *partialled product* – the product with its component parts removed or partialled out.

Model Summary

Model	R	R Square	Adjusted R Square	Std. Error of the Estimate
1	.457[a]	.209	.204	6.451

[a] Predictors: (Constant), product, gender Gender, Ctrslf08

ANOVA[b]

Model		Sum of Squares	df	Mean Square	F	Sig.
1	Regression	5453.098	3	1817.699	43.682	.000[a]
	Residual	20639.702	496	41.612		
	Total	26092.800	499			

[a] Predictors: (Constant), product, gender Gender, Ctrslf08
[b] Dependent Variable: slfcnc12 Self-Concept in Twelfth Grade

The ANOVA table informs us that the overall model, consisting of the product, gender, and centered eighth-grade self-concept variables, is statistically significant ($p < .0005$). Both the ANOVA table, through the ratio SS_{REG}/SS_T and the Model Summary inform us that 20.9 percent of twelfth-grade self-concept variance is explained by this model.

Coefficients[a]

Model		Unstandardized Coefficients		Standardized Coefficients		
		B	Std. Error	Beta	t	Sig.
1	(Constant)	32.270	.441		73.229	.000
	Ctrslf08	.386	.083	.319	4.639	.000
	gender Gender	−1.235	.592	−.085	−2.086	.037
	product	.204	.103	.134	1.980	.048

[a]Dependent Variable: slfcnc12 Self-Concept in Twelfth Grade

Given that the overall model is statistically significant, we look to the Coefficients table to construct the unstandardized regression equation and to determine whether the interaction is statistically significant.

The unstandardized regression equation for $\hat{Y} =$ predicted twelfth-grade self-concept (SLFCNC12) is

$$\hat{Y} = .386(CTRSLF08) - 1.235(GENDER) + .204(PRODUCT) + 32.27$$

or equivalently

$$\hat{Y} = .386(CTRSLF08) - 1.235(GENDER) + .204(CTRSLF08*GENDER) + 32.27.$$

Because the *b*-weight associated with the product term is statistically significant ($p = .048$), the interaction is statistically significant. Therefore, the relationship between eighth- and twelfth-grade self-concept is not constant for males and females; rather, it varies as a function of gender. Because the relationship between eighth-grade self-concept and twelfth-grade self-concept is different for males and females in the population, we can create two separate regression equations, one for each gender.

To find the regression equation for males, we substitute GENDER $= 0$ into the following:

$$\hat{Y} = .386(CTRSLF08) - 1.235(GENDER) + .204(CTRSLF08*GENDER) + 32.27$$

$$\hat{Y} = .386(CTRSLF08) - 1.235(0) + .204(CTRSLF08*0) + 32.27$$

$$\hat{Y} = .386(CTRSLF08) + 32.27.$$

To find the regression equation for females, we substitute GENDER $= 1$ into the following:

$$\hat{Y} = .386(CTRSLF08) - 1.235(GENDER) + .204(CTRSLF08*GENDER) + 32.27$$

$$\hat{Y} = .386(CTRSLF08) - 1.235(1) + .204(CTRSLF08*1) + 32.27$$

$$\hat{Y} = .386(CTRSLF08) - 1.235 + .204(CTRSLF08) + 32.27$$

$$\hat{Y} = .590(CTRSLF08) + 31.0.35.$$

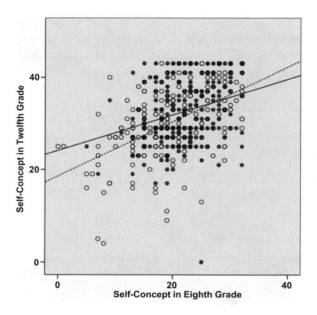

Figure 15.7   Plot of the interaction between eighth-grade self-concept and gender.

Looking at the two slopes, we see that for males, every one-point increase in eighth-grade self-concept is associated with a .386-point increase in twelfth-grade self-concept, whereas for females, every one-point increase in eighth-grade self-concept is associated with a .590-point increase in twelfth-grade self-concept. The statistical significance of the interaction term tells us that these two slopes are significantly different. That the slope for females (.591) is greater than the slope for males (.386) suggests that females exhibit greater growth in self-concept than males between grades 8 and 12.

To plot the interaction in this case, we form a composite of two scatterplots of twelfth-grade self-concept by eighth-grade self-concept, one for each gender. The plot of these values is given in Figure 15.7.

To plot the interaction of gender by eighth-grade self-concept on twelfth-grade self-concept, we go to **Graphs**, **Legacy Dialogs**, **Scatter**, and click **Define**. Put SLFCNC12 on the Y-axis, SLFCNC08 on the X-axis, and set markers by GENDER. Click **OK**. Double click the graph to put it in the Chart Editor. Click **Elements, Fit line at subgroups**.

The results of these analyses suggest that, whereas females have lower self-concept than males on average in eighth grade, by twelfth grade they appear to catch up. Thus, females appear to sustain a greater increase in self-concept across the grades than males. If there was no interaction, the rate of growth across the grades would have been the same for both males and females.

PUTTING IT ALL TOGETHER: A STUDENT PROJECT REPRINTED

The following is a project submitted by a student that uses the NELS data set to examine the relationship between mathematics achievement in twelfth grade and several independent variables. Although more than two independent variables are studied, this project shows to what extent the two-independent-variable case is easily generalized to more than two variables. The project is a good example of the kind of analysis and writing required by this type of investigation.

Responding to mounting pressure from federal and state agencies to monitor the success of schools in the United States, the National Center of Education Statistics of the U.S. Department of Education conducted a survey in the Spring of 1988 on a nationally representative sample of approximately 25,000 eighth graders to measure achievement outcomes in English, history, mathematics, and science, in addition to personal, familial, social, institutional, and cultural factors that might relate to these outcomes. A follow-up of these students was conducted during tenth grade in the spring of 1990; a second follow-up was conducted during the twelfth grade in the spring of 1992; and, finally, a third follow-up was conducted in the spring of 1994.

Approximately 5,000 students who responded to all four administrations of the survey were always at grade level (neither repeated nor skipped a grade) and pursued some form of post-secondary education. Using a random sample of 500 of these 5,000 students, this project seeks to model the relationship between mathematics achievement in twelfth grade, as measured by a standardized test of mathematics achievement, and a number of variables purported to influence such achievement, including student and home background variables (gender, socioeconomic status [SES]), self-concept, educational aspirations, enrollment in advanced math in eighth grade, and computer ownership.

MEASURING THE VARIABLES

According to the *NELS:88* handbook, the development of the survey "was guided by the research objectives of this longitudinal study. Items were chosen based on their utility in predicting or explaining future outcomes as measured in later survey waves. Questions were framed to provide consistency and continuity with earlier education longitudinal studies, as well as to address new areas of policy concern and to reflect recent advances in theory."

The variables used in this study were measured as follows:

Mathematics achievement in twelfth grade was assessed using a standardized test of mathematics achievement. The actual range of scores is 39.28 through 71.12, from low to high achievement.

SES is a composite of father's education level, mother's education level, father's occupation, mother's occupation, and family income. Each component was standardized to a mean of zero and a standard deviation of 1 and then averaged to yield the socioeconomic composite. After linear transformation to avoid negative values, the actual range for SES is 2 through 32, from low to high SES.

Sex is a dichotomous variable coded 0 for males and 1 for females.

In advanced math is a dichotomous variable that measures whether the student was enrolled in an advanced, enriched, or accelerated math class in eighth grade. The variable was coded 1 if the student was enrolled and 2 if the student was not enrolled.

Does family have a computer is a dichotomous variable coded 1 if the family owns a computer and 2 otherwise.

Self-esteem is a composite score based on responses to the following four items: I feel good about myself; I feel I am a person of worth, the equal of other people; I am able to do things as well as most other people; on the whole, I am satisfied with myself. Each of these four items was standardized separately to a mean of zero and standard deviation of 1. After linear transformation to avoid negative scores, the actual range is 0 through 43, from low to high esteem.

Educational aspiration measures how far in school the student expects to go. Coding is as follows: 1 = Some high school; 2 = finish/earn high school equivalency; 3 = vocational/trade, less than 2 yrs; 4 = vocational/trade, 2 + yrs; 5 = college, less than 2 yrs; 6 = college/2+yrs, Assoc; 7 = college/Bachelor's; 8 = College/Master's degree; 9 = College program, Ph.D.; 10 = M.D., L.L.B., J.D., D.D.S., or equivalent.

All variables, other than the three described earlier as measured dichotomously, are treated in this study as if they were continuous.

EXAMINING THE VARIABLES INDIVIDUALLY AND IN PAIRS

The sample of 500 cases consists of 227 males and 273 females. Numeric summaries of each of the variables under study are presented in Table 1 for the total group of 500.

Table 1.   Numeric summaries of all variables for total group of 500 cases

	N	Minimum	Maximum	Mean	Std.	Skewness	
	Statistic	Statistic	Statistic	Statistic	Statistic	Statistic	Std. Error
MATHEMATICS STANDARDIZED SCORE	500	34.36	71.12	56.9066	7.8840	−.423	.109
IN ADVANCED, ENRICHED, ACCELERATED MATH	491	1	2	1.54	.50	−.160	.110
DOES FAMILY HAVE A COMPUTER	500	1	2	1.53	.50	−.104	.109
Highest level of education expected	500	3	10	7.68	1.28	−.901	.109
ESTEEM	500	.00	43.00	31.4800	7.2312	−.384	.109
SES	500	.00	35.00	18.4340	6.9243	−.112	.109
Valid N (listwise)	491						

According to Table 1, none of the variables appear to be sufficiently skewed to warrant the use of symmetrizing transformations. To verify this impression, the distribution of the worst-case scenario, that of highest level of education expected (skewness = −.901), is graphed in Figure 1. Figure 1 visually corroborates the notion that symmetrizing transformations are not necessary in this case, because the normal curve describes reasonably well the shape of the histogram.

Table 2 presents numeric summaries of all variables by gender, and Table 3 presents the matrix of intercorrelations between all pairs of variables. According to Table 2, males and females have similar profiles in terms of these variables.

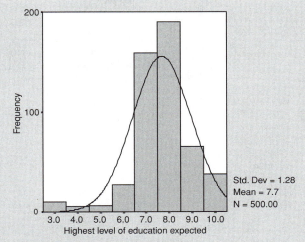

Figure 1 Histogram of highest level of education expected.

Table 2. Numeric summaries of selected variables by gender

COMPOSITE SEX		N	Minimum	Maximum	Mean	Std.	Skewness	
		Statistic	Statistic	Statistic	Statistic	Statistic	Statistic	Std. Error
MALE	MATHEMATICS STANDARDIZED SCORE	227	39.28	71.12	58.6333	7.4270	−.469	.162
	IN ADVANCED, ENRICHED, ACCELERATED MATH	224	1	2	1.54	.50	−.180	.163
	DOES FAMILY HAVE COMPUTER	227	1	2	1.46	.50	.098	.162
	Highest level of education expected	227	3	10	7.69	1.35	−.945	.162
	ESTEEM	227	.00	43.00	32.7533	7.1266	−.399	.162
	SES	227	2.00	32.00	19.1057	7.0772	−.243	.162
	Valid N (listwise)	224						
FEMALE	MATHEMATICS STANDARDIZED SCORE	273	34.36	70.69	55.4709	7.9777	−.368	.147
	IN ADVANCED, ENRICHED, ACCELERATED MATH	267	1	2	1.54	.50	−.143	.149
	DOES FAMILY HAVE COMPUTER	273	1	2	1.57	.50	−.275	.147
	Highest level of education expected	273	3	10	7.67	1.22	−.855	.147
	ESTEEM	273	4.00	43.00	30.4212	7.1591	−.398	.147
	SES	273	.00	35.00	17.8755	6.7567	−.015	.147
	Valid N (listwise)	267						

Table 3. Matrix of intercorrelations between all pairs of variables

		MATHEMATICS STANDARDIZED SCORE	DOES FAMILY HAVE A COMPUTER	Highest level of education expected	ESTEEM	SES	COMPOSITE SEX	IN ADVANCED, ENRICHED, ACCELERATED MATH
Pearson Correlation	MATHEMATICS STANDARDIZED SCORE	1.000	−.175**	.373**	.373**	146**	.323**	.263**
	DOES FAMILY HAVE A COMPUTER	−.175**	1.000	−.144**	−.079	−.349**	092*	.092*
	Highest level of education expected	.373**	−.144**	1.000	.071	.307**	−.008	−.106*
	ESTEEM	.146**	.079	.071	1.000	.114*	.161**	−.095*
	SES	323**	−.349**	307**	.114*	1.000	−.089*	−.034
	COMPOSITE SEX	−.200**	.092*	−.008	−.161**	−.089*	1.000	−.009
	IN ADVANCED, ENRICHED, ACCELERATED MATH	−.263**	.092*	−.106*	−.095*	−.034	−.009	1.000
Sig. (2-tailed)	MATHEMATICS STANDARDIZED SCORE	.	.000	.000	.001	.000	.000	.000
	DOES FAMILY HAVE A COMPUTER	.000	.	.001	.076	.000	.040	.042
	Highest level of education expected	.000	.001	.	.111	.000	.853	.019
	ESTEEM	.001	.076	111	.	.011	.000	.036
	SES	.000	.000	.000	.011	.	.048	.450
	COMPOSITE SEX	.000	.040	.853	.000	.048	.	.841
	IN ADVANCED, ENRICHED, ACCELERATED MATH	.000	.042	.019	.036	.450	.841	.
N	MATHEMATICS STANDARDIZED SCORE	500	500	500	500	500	500	491
	DOES FAMILY HAVE A COMPUTER	500	500	500	500	500	500	491
	Highest level of education expected	500	500	500	500	500	500	491
	ESTEEM	500	500	500	500	500	500	491
	SES	500	500	500	500	500	500	491
	COMPOSITE SEX	500	500	500	500	500	500	491
	IN ADVANCED, ENRICHED, ACCELERATED MATH	491	491	491	491	491	491	491

**Correlation is significant at the 0.01 level (2-tailed).
*Correlation is significant at the 0.05 level (2-tailed).

According to Table 3, each of the six regressors – owning a computer, educational aspirations, self-esteem, SES, sex, and enrolled in advanced math in eighth grade – is statistically significantly related to the criterion "mathematics achievement in twelfth grade." Moreover, both highest level of education expected and SES account for between 10 and 14 percent of the variance of the criterion. Yet, the intercorrelations between regressors are sufficiently low to suggest that redundancy of regressors is not a problem.

The results of Table 3 suggest that an individual with higher mathematics achievement in twelfth grade tends to be a male with higher self esteem, higher SES, and a higher level of expected education. In addition, the individual tends to have taken advanced math in eighth grade and owns a computer. Not surprisingly, individuals with higher SES tend also to be those who own a computer and expect to complete a higher level of education.

Scatterplots between all pairs of continuous variables were examined and confirm that the relationships depicted are linear and that the correlations reported in Table 3 are appropriate measures of relationship in this case.

EXAMINING THE VARIABLES MULTIVARIATELY WITH MATHEMATICS ACHIEVEMENT AS THE CRITERION

Multiple regression analysis was used to fit a full model that included all main effects and two-way interactions. The statistical significance of the set of 15 interaction terms (six regressors taken pairwise) is tested by the significance of the *F-change* statistic in Table 4. According to the results of Table 4, the *F-change* statistic is not significant ($F(15,469) = 1.487$, $p = .105$), suggesting that the .033 increase in R^2 is not statistically significant and that the set of two-way interactions does not contribute to explaining mathematics achievement variance. Therefore, the set of two-way interactions was removed from the model.

Table 4. Test for the significance of the set of two-way interactions

Model	R	R Square	Adjusted R Square	Std. Error of the Estimate	Change Statistics R Square Change	F Change	df1	df2	Sig. F Change
1	.522[a]	.273	.264	6.7737	.273	30.234	6	484	.00
2	.553[b]	.306	.275	6.7231	.033	1.487	15	469	.10

[a]Predictors: (Constant), SEX, IN ADVANCED, ENRICHED, ACCELERATED MATH, SES, ESTEEM, Highest level education expected, DOES FAMILY HAVE A COMPUTER
[b]Predictors: (Constant), SEX, IN ADVANCED, ENRICHED, ACCELERATED MATH, SES, ESTEEM, Highest level education expected, DOES FAMILY HAVE A COMPUTER, SESSEX, ADVSEX, COMPSES, COMPSEX, ADVSES, ESTSE, ADVCOMP, ADVEST, COMPEST, SESEST, EDEXSEX, COM-PEDEX, ADVEDEX, SESEDEX
[c]Dependent Variable: MATHEMATICS STANDARDIZED SCORE

The reduced model with only the set of six main effects is statistically significant according to Table 4 (F(6,484) = 30.234, $p = .000$). Furthermore, the proportion of mathematics achievement variance explained is .273. That is, more than one-fourth of the

Table 5. Regression coefficients and their significance in predicting math achievement

Model		Unstandardized Coefficients		Standardized Coefficients		
		B	Std. Error	Beta	t	Sig.
1	(Constant)	45.636	2.907		15.697	.000
	IN ADVANCED, ENRICHED, ACCELERATED MATH	−3.487	.621	−.220	−5.611	.000
	DOES FAMILY HAVE A COMPUTER	−.527	.659	−.033	−.799	.425
	Highest level of education expected	1.698	.251	.277	6.762	.000
	ESTEEM	5.499E-02	.043	.050	1.271	.204
	SES	.228	.050	.200	4.602	.000
	SEX	−2.620	.626	−.166	−4.186	.000

[a]Dependent Variable: MATHEMATICS STANDARDIZED SCORE

variance of mathematics achievement in twelfth grade is explained by these six variables taken collectively. An analysis of which variables contribute individually to explaining mathematics achievement may be found in Table 5.

According to Table 5, when all variables are considered simultaneously, neither self-esteem nor owning a computer contribute significantly to the model. In the case of owning a computer, it is likely that the relationship between owning a computer and mathematics achievement became zero after controlling for SES. A further reduced model, which does not include owning a computer and self-esteem, is presented in Table 6. Note that dropping both variables at once might have a surprising effect, especially if they are highly correlated.

According to Table 6, a negligible loss of explained variance resulted from eliminating the two nonsignificant variables, owning a computer and self-esteem. With the four regressors remaining, the reduced model accounts for .269 of mathematics achievement variance. This reduced model accounts for virtually the same amount of math achievement variance with two fewer variables. The interaction terms were not retested.

Table 6. Model summary and regression coefficients with four regressors

Model	R	R Square	Adjusted R Square	Std. Error of the Estimate	Change Statistics				
					R Square Change	F Change	df1	df2	Sig. F Change
1	.519[a]	.269	.263	6.7758	.269	44.752	4	486	.000

[a]Predictors: (Constant), SEX, IN ADVANCED, ENRICHED, ACCELERATED MATH, SES, Highest level of educatic

Coefficients[a]

Model		Unstandardized Coefficients		Standardized Coefficients		
		B	Std. Error	Beta	t	Sig.
1	(Constant)	46.369	2.227		20.821	.000
	IN ADVANCED, ENRICHED, ACCELERATED MATH	−3.600	.617	−.228	−5.834	.000
	Highest level of education expected	1.715	.251	.280	6.831	.000
	SES	.246	.047	.215	5.261	.000
	SEX	−2.783	.617	−.176	−4.512	.000

[a]Dependent Variable: MATHEMATICS STANDARDIZED SCORE

Based on a review of the regression coefficients in Table 6, controlling for whether an individual enrolled in advanced math in eighth grade, as well as for SES and sex, the greatest single predictor of twelfth-grade mathematics achievement is an individual's highest expected level of education. Having high educational aspirations, while controlling for other relevant factors, appears to associate with achievement in mathematics. Although one cannot say, based on this analysis, that strong mathematics achievement in twelfth grade results from having high educational aspirations, we can conclude that these two variables, after controlling for other relevant factors, are related significantly.

In addition, we may conclude that, controlling for SES, sex, and educational aspirations, whether or not one enrolls in advanced math in eighth grade is a strong predictor of mathematics achievement in twelfth grade. Those who enroll tend to achieve better in math in twelfth grade than those who do not, suggesting that achievement in math for both males and females is a stable trait across the years.

Finally, SES and sex, controlling for the other two variables and each other, are both related to math achievement in twelfth grade. Controlling for all other variables in the equation, boys tend to achieve better in math than girls and individuals with higher SES tend to achieve better in math than those with lower SES. That boys tend to surpass girls in math is a well-known yet unfortunate fact. That those who are more privileged economically tend to achieve better than those who are less privileged is also not a surprising finding.

A series of residual analyses was carried out to examine more closely the fit of the model to these data. In particular, partial plots between the residual scores and each of the two continuous regressors were examined for evidence of possible nonlinearity. These plots appear as Figures 2 and 3 and suggest that all association between mathematics achievement in twelfth grade and each of the significant regressors is accounted for by the regression model in Table 6.

In addition, boxplots of Cook's distance and leverage values, as depicted in Figure 4, suggest that no point or set of points unduly influences the results of the analysis and distorting the results obtained as all distance and leverage values cluster near zero.

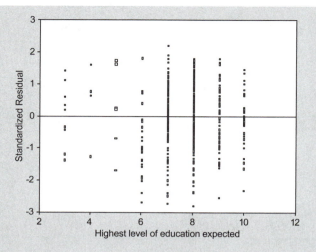

Figure 2   Partial residual plot: Ed aspirations.

Thus, according to these diagnostics, the regression model, fit to these 500 cases, is appropriate.

In conclusion, the results of this analysis based on 500 randomly selected cases from 5,000 nationally sampled students who continued to post-secondary education are interesting for at least two reasons. First, they suggest that a large portion (greater than 25 percent) of the variance due to mathematics achievement in twelfth grade can be attributable to four variables: educational aspirations, enrollment in advanced math in eighth grade, SES, and sex, taken collectively. Second, they support the notion that each variable contributes uniquely to explaining twelfth-grade math achievement over and above the contributions made by each of the other variables in the equation.

While the results of this study do not support causal inference, the relationships observed suggest a direction of study to examine ways to promote achievement in mathematics in twelfth grade and to look for other variables that have the potential to explain the remaining 75 percent of mathematics achievement variance left unexplained by the variables in this study.

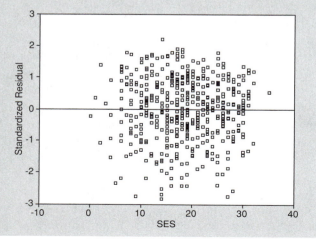

Figure 3   Partial residual plot: SES.

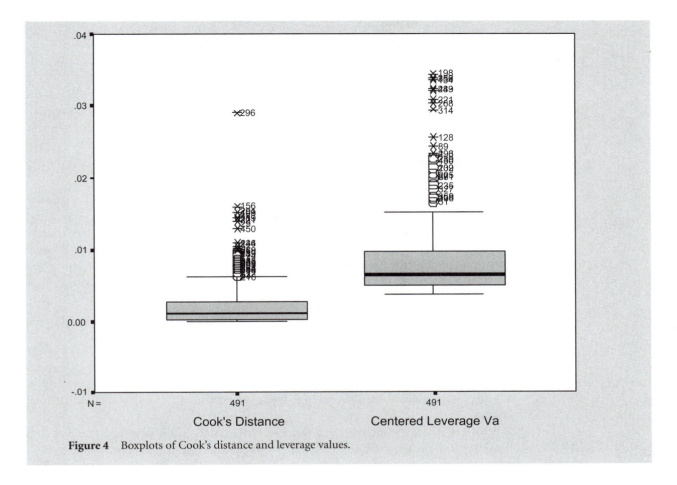

Figure 4 Boxplots of Cook's distance and leverage values.

EXERCISES

Exercises 15.1 and 15.2 make use of the NELS data set. For inferential purposes, we consider the students in the data set to be a random sample of the population of all college-bound students who have always been at grade level. Use $\alpha = .05$ for all significance tests.

15.1. In this exercise, we use multiple regression to determine whether there is a gender (GENDER) difference in twelfth-grade math achievement (ACHMAT12) after controlling for amount of math taken (UNITMATH) and to investigate related questions.

a) Conduct initial univariate and bivariate analyses of the variables involved in the multiple regression model.

b) Is the regression model for predicting ACHMAT12 from GENDER and UNITMATH statistically significant? Provide statistical support for your answer.

c) Report and interpret the value of R^2.

d) Write down the regression equation for predicting ACHMAT12 from GENDER and UNITMATH.

e) Use the regression equation to predict the twelfth-grade math achievement score of a male who took 4 National Assessment of Educational Progress (NAEP) units of math in high school.

f) Which of the two independent variables makes a greater unique contribution to the regression model? Explain and provide statistical support for your answer.

g) Interpret the value of the Y-intercept or indicate why it would not be appropriate to do so.

h) Interpret the value of the coefficient (slope) of UNITMATH in the regression equation.

i) Interpret the value of the coefficient (slope) of GENDER in the regression equation.

j) After controlling for number of years of math taken, is there a gender difference in twelfth-grade math achievement among college-bound students who are always at grade level? If so, what is the nature of the gender difference? Explain and provide statistical support for your answer.

15.2. In this exercise, we see that independent variables each by themselves may be statistically significantly correlated to the dependent variable in the bivariate sense, but, when examined together in the same regression equation, both may not be statistically significant. Perform a multiple regression analysis to determine whether twelfth-grade self-concept (SLFCNC12) is related to mathematics achievement as measured by both twelfth-grade math achievement (ACHMAT12) and the number of units of mathematics taken in high school (UNITMATH).

a) Conduct initial univariate and bivariate analyses of the variables involved in the multiple regression model.

b) Perform a multiple regression analysis with SLFCNC12 as the dependent variable and ACHMAT12 and UNITMATH as independent variables. Is the regression model statistically significant? Provide statistical support for your answer.

c) What proportion of variance in SLFCNC12 is explained by both independent variables?

d) Which, if any, of the independent variables make a statistically significant unique contribution to the regression model? Provide statistical support for your response.

e) Interpret the value of the Y-intercept or indicate why it would not be appropriate to do so.

f) Interpret the value of the statistically significant b-weight coefficient (slope) of ACHMAT12 in the regression equation.

Exercises 15.3 and 15.4 make use the Learndis data set. For inferential purposes, we consider the children in the data set to be a random sample of all children attending public school in the urban area who have been diagnosed with learning disabilities. Many students in the data set have missing values for either math or reading comprehension, or both. Such omissions can lead to problems when generalizing results. There are statistical remedies for missing data that are beyond the scope of this text. For these exercises, we assume that there is no pattern to the missing values and that our sample is representative of the population. Use $\alpha = .05$ for all significance tests.

15.3. Recall that students diagnosed with learning disabilities in this urban area are placed in one of two classroom situations: resource room for part of the day (coded as 0) or in a full-time self-contained classroom (coded as 1). Use multiple regression analysis to determine whether reading comprehension (READCOMP) variance can be explained by math comprehension (MATHCOMP) and type of placement (PLACEMEN).

a) Conduct initial univariate and bivariate analyses of the variables involved in the multiple regression model.

b) Is the regression model for predicting READCOMP from MATHCOMP and PLACE-MEN statistically significant? Are the independent variables statistically significant in the equation? Provide statistical support for your response.

c) Report and interpret the value of $R^2_{adjusted}$.

d) Compare the values of R^2 and $R^2_{adjusted}$. Explain why they are similar or different.

e) What is the regression equation for predicting READCOMP from IQ and PLACE-MEN?

f) Interpret value of the Y-intercept or indicate why it would not be meaningful to do so.

g) Controlling for type of placement, are higher math comprehension scores associated with higher or lower reading comprehension scores? Provide statistical support for your response.

h) Interpret the value of the slope of MATHCOMP.

i) Controlling for math comprehension, does reading comprehension statistically significantly differ for children attending public school in the urban area who have been diagnosed with learning disabilities depending on placement type? Provide statistical support for your response. If there is a difference, describe its nature.

j) Interpret the value of the slope of PLACEMEN.

k) Use your regression equation to predict the reading comprehension score of a student in a resource room placement who has a MATHCOMP score of 84.

l) Explain why you should not use the regression equation to predict the reading comprehension score of a student in a resource room placement who has a MATHCOMP score of 40.

15.4. In this exercise, we look at the individual and unique contributions of MATHCOMP and IQ in explaining READCOMP variance.

a) What proportion of the variance in reading comprehension scores can be explained by intellectual ability? Is this proportion statistically significant? Explain and provide statistical support for your response.

b) What proportion of the variance in reading comprehension scores can be explained by math comprehension? Is this proportion statistically significant? Explain and provide statistical support for your response.

c) What is the intercorrelation between IQ and MATHCOMP? Is it statistically significant?

d) What proportion of the variance in reading comprehension scores can be explained by math comprehension after controlling for intellectual ability? Said differently, what proportion of reading comprehension variance can be explained uniquely by math comprehension? Is this proportion statistically significant? Explain and provide statistical support for your response.

e) What proportion of the variance in reading comprehension scores can be explained by intellectual ability controlling for math ability? Said differently, what proportion of reading comprehension variance can be explained uniquely by intellectual ability? Is this proportion statistically significant? Explain and provide statistical support for your response.

f) What is another way to determine whether the proportion of variance in reading comprehension scores that can be explained by intellectual ability controlling for math ability is statistically significant?

g) Why is it that the proportion of variance in reading comprehension that can be explained by intellectual ability is larger than the proportion of variance in reading comprehension that can be explained by intellectual ability after *controlling for math comprehension*?

h) Explain why R^2 for the model with both independent variables is less than $r^2_{\text{Readng Comprehension, IQ}} + r^2_{\text{Reading Comprehension, Math Comprehension}}$.

Exercise 15.5 makes use of the Framingham data set. For inferential purposes, we consider the people in the Framingham data set to be a random sample of the population of all noninstitutionalized adults. Use $\alpha = .05$ for all significance tests.

15.5. In this exercise we use regression to model total serum cholesterol at time 3 (TOTCHOL3) using initial systolic blood pressure at time 1 (SYSBP1) and diastolic blood pressure at time 1 (DIABP1).

a) Conduct initial univariate and bivariate analyses of the variables involved in the multiple regression model.

b) Is the regression model for predicting TOTCHOL3 from SYSBP1 and DIABP1 statistically significant? Is the individual contribution of any of the variables statistically significant?

c) Why do you suppose the model is statistically significant, but none of the independent variables is?

d) What is an appropriate model for predicting TOTCHOL3?

e) Compare the proportion of variance in TOTCHOL3 explained by DIABP1 alone to that explained by the combination of DIABP1 and SYSBP1.

Exercises 15.6 through 15.8 involve regression diagnostics and nonlinear transformations using the NELS data set. For inferential purposes, we consider the students in the data set to be a random sample of the population of all college-bound students who have always been at grade level. Use $\alpha = .05$ for all significance tests.

15.6. In Exercise 15.1, we created a model to predict twelfth-grade math achievement (ACHMAT12) from GENDER and the number of NAEP units of math taken in high school (UNITMATH). In this exercise, we conduct a series of residual analyses to examine more closely the fit of the model to these data.

a) Create a partial plot between the residual scores and the continuous regressor. Examine this plot for evidence of nonlinearity.

b) Name two cases that have relatively high positive residuals and two cases that have relatively high negative residuals. What do the residuals say about these four cases?

c) Create boxplots of Cook's distance and leverage values. What do they tell you about the appropriateness of the regression model?

d) Based on these diagnostic analyses, comment on the appropriateness of this regression equation.

15.7. In Exercise 15.2, we created a model to predict twelfth-grade self-concept (SLFCNC12) from twelfth-grade math achievement (ACHMAT12) and NAEP units of math taken in high school (UNITMATH). In this exercise, we perform regression diagnostics on the model to determine whether it can be improved.

a) Create partial plots between the residual scores and the two continuous regressors. Examine these plots for evidence of nonlinearity.

b) Determine whether there are any bivariate outliers in the model, that is, points whose standardized residual is greater than 2 in magnitude. Indicate the number of such points and give their case numbers.

c) Create boxplots of Cook's distance and leverage values. What do they tell you about the appropriateness of the regression model?

d) Based on these diagnostic analyses, comment on the appropriateness of this regression equation.

15.8. In this exercise, we create a multiple regression model to determine how expected income at age 30 (EXPINC30) can be explained by GENDER and socioeconomic status (SES).

a) Conduct initial univariate and bivariate analyses of the variables involved in the multiple regression model.

b) Because of its severe positive skew, transform EXPINC30 using both the square root and log transformations to try to reduce that skew. Which of the two transformations is more effective in symmetrizing EXPINC30?

c) Conduct bivariate analyses using the square root of expected income at age 30.

d) Conduct the multiple regression analysis with the square root of EXPINC30 as the dependent variable and SES and GENDER as the independent variables. Is the model statistically significant? Provide statistical support for your response.

e) Compare the proportion of variance explained with the untransformed and the transformed EXPINC30.

f) Write down the regression for predicting EXPINC30 from SES and GENDER.

g) Use your model to predict the expected income at age 30 of a male with SES 15.

Exercise 15.9 involves regression diagnostics and nonlinear transformations using the Learndis data set. In this chapter, we consider the children in the data set to be a random sample of all children attending public school in the urban area who have been diagnosed with learning disabilities. Use $\alpha = .05$ for all significance tests.

15.9. In Exercise 15.3, we created a model to predict READCOMP from MATHCOMP and PLACEMEN. In this exercise, we perform regression diagnostics on the model to determine whether it can be improved.

a) Create a partial plot between the residual scores and the continuous regressor. Examine this plot for evidence of nonlinearity.

b) What is the numerical expression for creating the variable MATHCOMPCTRDSQD, which is the square of the centered MATHCOMP? Create this new variable.

c) What is the regression equation for predicting READCOMP from PLACEMEN, MATHCOMPCTRD, and MATHCOMPCTRDSQD?

d) Overall, is the regression model for predicting READCOMP from PLACEMEN, MATHCOMPCTRD, and MATHCOMPCTRDSQD statistically significant? In particular, is the squared term statistically significant? Provide statistical support for your responses.

e) What proportion of the variance in READCOMP is explained by the squared term over and above that explained by the other variables?

f) Construct a residual plot and boxplots of Cook's distance and leverage values for the model including the squared term. What do they tell you about the appropriateness of the regression model?

Exercises 15.10 through 15.14 involve interactions in the NELS data set. For inferential purposes, we consider the students in the data set to be a random sample of the population of all college-bound students who have always been at grade level. Use $\alpha = .05$ for all significance tests.

15.10. Predict twelfth-grade math achievement (ACHMAT12) from whether or not the student attended public school (SCHTYPDI), whether or not the student took advanced math in eighth grade (ADVMATH8), and the interaction of the two.

a) Use the Recode procedure in Transform to create SCHTYPDI, a variable with 0 = Public and 1 = Private (both religious and nonreligious) from the variable SCHTYP8. How many students attended private school?

b) Create a multiple line graph depicting the predicted twelfth-grade math achievement by school type and whether or not advanced math was taken in eighth grade and use it to anticipate the results.

c) Create the product term of the two independent variables. Report the mean of the product term to verify that you did it correctly.

d) Is the model that predicts ACHMAT12 from SCHTYPDI, ADVMAT8, and their interaction statistically significant?

e) Is the interaction statistically significant?

f) What percentage of the variance in twelfth-grade math achievement can be explained by the two main effects and the interaction effect? What percentage can be explained by the interaction alone?

g) What is the regression equation?

h) Describe the nature of the interaction by writing down and interpreting separate regression equations for predicting twelfth-grade math achievement from school type for those who did not take advanced math in eighth grade and for those who did.

i) Interpret the slopes of these two equations.

15.11. In this exercise, we expand on Exercise 15.1 by investigating whether there is an interaction between GENDER and UNITMATH on ACHMAT12.

a) Center the variable UNITMATH by computing a new variable, UNITMATC (UNITMATC = UNITMATH − 3.637, where 3.637 is the mean of UNITMATH for those values included in the analysis). Verify that the mean of the centered variable is zero.

b) Create the interaction term, PRODUCT, as UNITMATCGENDER. What is the mean of this product term?

c) To determine if there is an interaction, conduct a hierarchical multiple regression analysis with ACHMAT12 as the dependent variable, UNITMATC and GENDER in the first block, and PRODUCT in the second block. Click the blue **Statistics** box at the bottom of the **Linear Regression** command box and select the box next to **R squared change**. Is there a statistically significant interaction between gender and number of years of math taken on achievement in math? Explain.

d) What can you conclude from the results of the test of significance of the interaction?

15.12. In Exercise 15.8, we constructed a regression model to predict the square root of expected income at age 30 plus 1 (SQRT(EXPINC 30 + 1) from GENDER and SES. In this exercise, we investigate whether it is appropriate to include an interaction term in the model.

a) Create a scatterplot that summarizes the analysis. Superimpose two fit lines, one for males and the other for females. Based on the scatterplot, do you anticipate that there is a statistically significant interaction between the two independent variables on the dependent variable? Explain.

b) Is the interaction statistically significant? Provide statistical support for your answer using both the relevant *b*-weight and the *F*-change statistic.

15.13. In this exercise, we use multiple regression to determine if expected income at age 30 (EXPINC30) can be explained by eighth-grade self-concept (SLFCNC08), SES, and their interaction.

a) Conduct initial univariate and bivariate analyses of the variables involved in the multiple regression model.

b) Center the variable SLFCNC08 by computing a new variable, SLFC8C, that is defined as SLFCNC08 − 20.94 (where 20.94 is the mean of SLFCNC08 for those values included in the analysis). Center the variable SES by computing a new variable, SESC, that is defined as SES − 18.52 (where 18.52 is the mean of SES for those values included in the analysis). Create the product term that carries the interaction term, PRODUCT, as SLFC8C*SESC. Conduct a hierarchical multiple regression analysis with EXPINC30 as the dependent variable, SLFC8C and SESC in the first block, and PRODUCT in the second block. Click on the *F*-change option. Is the interaction represented by PRODUCT statistically significant? Provide statistical support for your response.

c) What is the regression equation for the full model, including the interaction?

d) Clarify the nature of the interaction by using the regression equation to estimate the expected income at age 30 at one standard deviation above and one standard deviation below zero (where zero is the mean because the variables have been centered) for both SLFC8C and SESC.

e) Create a line graph like that of Figure 15.6, which is a summary of the interaction based on the four estimates obtained in part (f).

f) Describe the nature of the interaction.

15.14. Perform a multiple regression analysis to determine whether SES can be explained by the NAEP units of mathematics taken in high school (UNITMATH), nursery school attendance (NURSERY), and their interaction.

a) Center UNITMATH. Create the product term of UNITMATH with NURSERY and conduct a simultaneous regression analysis with the three independent variables. Is the full regression model including the interaction term statistically significant? Is the interaction term statistically significant? Provide statistical support for your answer.

b) What is the regression equation for the full model, including the interaction?

c) For those who attended nursery school, what is the regression equation for predicting SES from UNITMATH?

d) For those who did not attend nursery school, what is the regression equation for predicting SES from UNITMATH?

e) Are the regression equations given in parts (c) and (d) statistically significantly different? How can you tell?

f) Describe the nature of the interaction.

g) Create a graph that depicts the interaction.

h) What does it mean that the interaction term is statistically significant, but that the *b*-weight for units of math taken in high school is not statistically significant

Exercises 15.15 and 15.16 involve interactions in the Learndis data set. In this chapter, we consider the children in the data set to be a random sample of all children attending public school in the urban area who have been diagnosed with learning disabilities. Use α = .05 for all significance tests.

15.15. Perform a multiple regression analysis to determine whether reading comprehension (READCOMP) can be explained by a combination of math comprehension (MATHCOMP), grade level (GRADE), and their interaction. Prior to the analysis, center the variables math comprehension and grade level. Create the variable PRODUCT as the product of centered math comprehension and centered grade, to facilitate the evaluation of the interaction between the independent variables.

   a) What is the average reading comprehension score for public school students diagnosed with learning disabilities in this urban area?
   b) Is the standard deviation of the centered math comprehension variable (14.59) different from the standard deviation of the original noncentered math comprehension variable? Explain.
   c) Is the interaction effect statistically significant? Explain.
   d) What is the regression equation with main effects only? Are these main effects statistically significant? Why is the regression equation that includes only main effects a better model for these data?
   e) Using the equation with main effects only, interpret b_1, the b-weight for centered math comprehension, within the context of the problem.
   f) Using the equation with main effects only, interpret b_2, the b-weight for centered grade, within the context of the problem.
   g) What is the proportion of dependent-variable variance explained by these two variables?
   h) What is the proportion of dependent-variable variance explained by math comprehension, controlling for grade?
   i) What is the proportion of dependent-variable variance explained by grade, controlling for math comprehension?
   k) What is the relative importance of the two regressors? Support your answer.
   l) Why is the F-value of 11.09 associated with model 2 in the ANOVA summary table different from the F-value of .556 associated with model 2 in the Model Summary table?

Exercises 15.16 and 15.18 relate to examples from the chapter.

15.16. In the section entitled "The b-Weight as a Partial Slope in Multiple Regression," we used SPSS to create the new variable $X_{1.2}$ and showed that b_1, which equals .878, is simply the slope of the regression line that predicts Y from $X_{1.2}$. For this exercise, show that b_2, which equals .397, is simply the slope of the regression line that predicts Y from $X_{2.1}$.

15.17. In this chapter, we analyzed the relationship among ice cream sales, temperature, humidity, and the interaction between temperature and relative humidity. We did not center the variables before conducting our analysis. For this exercise, rerun the analysis using the centered variables and compare these results to those obtained in the chapter based on the noncentered variables.

   a) Enter the data contained in Example 15.1 into SPSS. Center TEMP. Center RELHUMID. Create the PRODUCT term to represent the interaction. Using the centered variables, test whether there is an interaction between temperature and relative humidity that affects ice cream sales. What proportion of variance in ice cream sales is explained by the model including the interaction term? How do your results compare to those obtained in Example 15.4 based on noncentered variables?

b) Interpret the coefficient of centered temperature in the regression equation.

c) Interpret the coefficient of centered relative humidity in the regression equation.

d) Explain why the plot of the interaction between temperature and relative humidity, given in Figure 15.6, is the same for the two analyses.

15.18. In completing the analysis of the relationship among ice cream sales, temperature, relative humidity, and the interaction between temperature and relative humidity, we should also have paid attention to the diagnostics we discussed in the preceding chapter to verify that our model was not unduly influenced by outliers and that the assumptions underlying the procedure are met. We ask you to complete this aspect of the analysis in this exercise. Use the centered variables that you created in Exercise 15.17.

a) As part of the regression analysis, save the standardized residuals and Cook's distances. Are any of the standardized residuals less than -2 or greater than 2? Are any of the values for Cook's distance greater than 1?

b) Construct two scatterplots, one with centered TEMP versus the standardized residuals and one with centered RELHUMID versus the standardized residuals. Place the residuals on the vertical axis. Do any of the assumptions (normality, homoscedasticity, and linearity) underlying the multiple regression analysis appear to be violated? Explain.

The following exercises are conceptual and are not based on a specific data set.

15.19. Given the regression equation, $\hat{Y} = 1.2X_1 + .6X_2 + 10$:

a) X_1 is more important than X_2.

b) X_1 is less important than X_2.

c) X_1 is equally as important as X_2.

d) One cannot tell the relative importance of X_1 and X_2 from the information given.

15.20. In general, higher R^2 values arise when the correlation between each regressor and Y is _____ and the intercorrelation between the regressors is _____.

a) high, high

b) high, low

c) low, high

d) low, low

15.21. Given a regression equation with two regressors, $\hat{Y} = b_1X_1 + b_2X_2 + a$. If b_1 is *not* statistically significant, then _____ is also *not* statistically significant.

a) R

b) r_{Y1}

c) $r_{Y1(2)}$

d) none of the above

15.22. Given a regression equation with two regressors, $\hat{Y} = b_1X_1 + b_2X_2 + a$. The largest discrepancy between R^2 and $R^2_{adjusted}$ occurs when

a) $N = 100$.

b) $N = 10$.

c) $N = 5$.

d) Cannot tell from the information given.

15.23. Given Y and two different X variables, X_1 and X_2, with the following two different scatterplots, A and B. Assume the Y Sum of Squares equals 100 ($SS_Y = 100$) in both situations.

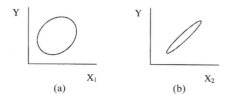

(a)   (b)

If we construct two regression equations, one for predicting Y from X_1 and anotherfor predicting Y from X_2, which is most descriptive of situations A and B?

a) For A, $SS_{REG} = 90$ and $SS_{ERROR} = 10$; for B, $SS_{REG} = 60$ and $SS_{ERROR} = 40$.
b) For A, $SS_{REG} = 60$ and $SS_{ERROR} = 40$; for B, $SS_{REG} = 90$ and $SS_{ERROR} = 10$.
c) For A, $SS_{REG} = 50$ and $SS_{ERROR} = 50$; for B, $SS_{REG} = 50$ and $SS_{ERROR} = 50$.
d) For A, $SS_{REG} = 90$ and $SS_{ERROR} = 60$; for B, $SS_{REG} = 10$ and $SS_{ERROR} = 40$.

15.24. Under what circumstances would the weights for variables X_1 and X_2 not change when a third variable X_3 is added to the multiple regression equation?

CHAPTER SIXTEEN

Nonparametric Methods

In the situations of statistical inference that we have discussed regarding the mean and the variance, the dependent variable Y was tacitly assumed to be at the interval level of measurement. In addition, the statistical tests (e.g., t and F) required the assumptions of normality and homogeneity of variance of the parent population distributions. In the situations of statistical inference regarding correlation and regression, both variables X and Y were tacitly assumed to be at the interval level of measurement and the statistical tests required the assumption of homogeneous variances and bivariate normality of the parent population distribution. When one or more of these assumptions regarding the population distributions and parameters are not reasonable, alternative methods of statistical inference must be employed. The focus of this chapter is on the development and use of such alternative methods.

PARAMETRIC VERSUS NONPARAMETRIC METHODS

Because the validity of the inferential tests we have discussed so far in this book relies on explicit assumptions about population distributions and parameters, they are called "parametric" or "distribution-tied" methods. There are occasions, however, when the use of parametric methods is not warranted. One such instance occurs when the dependent variable is not at the interval level of measurement but rather at the nominal or ordinal level of measurement, as in the case of categorical or ranked data. Another instance occurs when one or more of the required assumptions regarding the parent population distributions are not reasonable, as in the case of studying the mean of a nonnormal population using a small sample of data.

In situations where the use of parametric or distribution-tied methods is inappropriate, alternative methods, called "nonparametric" or "distribution-free" methods, may be employed. In this chapter, we first present nonparametric techniques that can be used for nominal-leveled variables and then we present techniques that can be used for ordinal-leveled variables.

Although nonparametric methods have the advantage of being relatively free from assumptions about population distributions and parameters, they have the disadvantage of generally having lower power than comparable parametric methods when these parametric methods do apply. It should also be pointed out that the hypotheses tested using nonparametric methods are not exactly the same as the hypotheses tested using parametric methods. For example, although the parametric two-group t-test specifically tests a hypothesis about the equality of two population means, the comparable nonparametric alternative (to be discussed later in this chapter) tests a hypothesis about the equality of two population distributions, providing information about the equality of the two medians as a by-product.

NONPARAMETRIC METHODS WHEN THE DEPENDENT VARIABLE IS AT THE NOMINAL LEVEL

In this section, we present two commonly used nonparametric techniques of statistical inference based on the chi-square distribution, which are applicable when the dependent variable is at the nominal level of measurement. The first method, the chi-square goodness-of-fit test, can be used to analyze the distribution of subjects among the categories of a nominal-leveled variable. For example, it can be used to answer questions such as, "Is the distribution of car sales in the eastern United States in the current year for Nissans, Mazdas, Toyotas, and Hondas the same as the known distribution of the previous year?" and "Are college-bound students who are always at grade level equally divided among the four regions of the United States?" The second method, the chi-square test of independence, can be used to determine whether two at-most ordinal-leveled variables are related. For example, it can be used to answer questions such as, "Is there a relationship between gender and political party affiliation in the United States?" "Among college-bound students in the South who are always at grade level, is there a relationship between nursery school attendance and gender?" and "Among college-bound students who are always at grade level, does computer ownership differ by region of residence?"

THE CHI-SQUARE DISTRIBUTION (χ^2)

Given a *normal* distribution with mean μ and variance σ^2, we select at random a value X from this population. We then form the corresponding z-score and square it to obtain z^2, as follows:

$$z^2 = \left(\frac{X - \mu}{\sigma}\right)^2 = \frac{(X - \mu)^2}{\sigma^2}.$$

The distribution of all z^2 values that could be obtained in this way is shown in Figure 16.1. This distribution is called a chi-square distribution with one degree of freedom, and it is denoted by the symbol $\chi^2_{(1)}$.

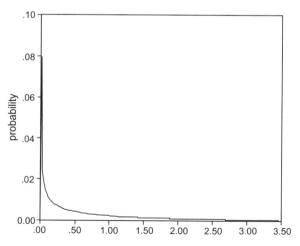

Figure 16.1 The chi-square distribution with 1 *df.*

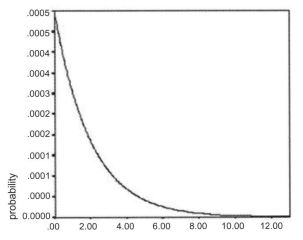

Figure 16.2 The chi-square distribution with 2 *df.*

If, instead of drawing a single value at random from the population, we select two values at random from the population and for each value compute the corresponding z^2, we obtain

$$z_1^2 = \frac{(X_1 - \mu)^2}{\sigma^2} \qquad \text{and} \qquad z_2^2 = \frac{(X_2 - \mu)^2}{\sigma^2}.$$

If we now add these two z^2 values together and plot the distribution of all such sums that could be obtained in this way (from the given population), we have what is called a chi-square distribution with two degrees of freedom. It is denoted by the symbol $\chi_{(2)}^2$. This distribution is shown in Figure 16.2. Note that, as before, all $\chi_{(2)}^2$ values are nonnegative, because the $\chi_{(2)}^2$ values are sums of z^2 values, and all squared values are nonnegative.

In general, the values of a chi-square distribution with N degrees of freedom are of the form

$$\chi_{(N)}^2 = \sum_{i=1}^{N} z_i^2 = \sum_{i=1}^{N} \frac{(X_i - \mu)^2}{\sigma^2},$$

where $X_1, X_2, X_3, \ldots, X_N$ is a random sample of size N drawn from a given normally distributed population with mean μ and variance σ^2.

Figure 16.3 illustrates two chi-square distributions with 4 and 9 degrees of freedom, respectively.

In terms of summary statistics, the mean, mode, and standard deviation of the chi-square distribution are all functions of its degrees of freedom (*df*). The chi-square distribution has mean equal to *df*, mode equal to $df - 2$ (as long as $df > 2$), and standard deviation of $\sqrt{2(df)}$.

At this point, we turn to the question of how to use this chi-square distribution (really a family of distributions, just like the *t*-distributions) to find *p*-values. To do so, we may use either an SPSS Compute statement or Table 5 in Appendix C, which gives the chi-square distribution for right-tailed areas.

EXAMPLE 16.1. Estimate the *p*-value associated with $\chi_3^2 = 23.18$, first using an SPSS Compute statement and then using Table 5 in Appendix C.

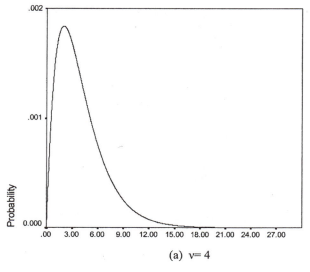

(a) $v = 4$

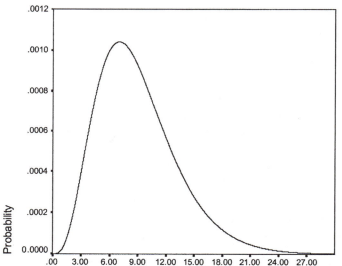

Figure 16.3   Two chi-square distributions.

Solution. Typing in 1-CDF.CHISQ(23.18,3) for the numeric expression in the SPSS Compute statement leads to the estimate $p = .00004$.

Turning to Table 5 in Appendix C, we see that the degrees of freedom are listed down the leftmost column and that they range from 1 to 100 inclusive. Listed across the top row of Table 5 are selected probability values corresponding to the right tails of the curve; these probability values refer to the amount of area located under the chi-square distribution curve that falls to the right of the chi-square value listed in the table. In our example, we look at the row with $df = 3$. To find the p-value associated with $\chi^2_3 = 23.18$, we find that the closest χ^2 value to 23.18 is 16.27 and we conclude that $p < .001$. Note that the two methods, using SPSS and the table, lead to consistent answers, but that the value obtained from SPSS is a more precise estimate.

If the number of degrees of freedom is not listed in the table, the conservative approach is to take the chi-square value closest to, but lower than, the desired degrees of freedom value. Alternately, an SPSS Compute statement may be used.

THE CHI-SQUARE GOODNESS-OF-FIT TEST

Consider the problem of determining whether the distribution of car sales in the eastern United States in the current year for Nissans, Mazdas, Toyotas, and Hondas is the same as the known distribution of the previous year, which is given hypothetically in Table 16.1.

Setting this question up as a hypothesis test, we have the following as our null and alternative hypotheses:

H_0: The current year's sales distribution is the same as that of the previous year
(Nissan: 18 percent, Mazda: 10 percent, Toyota: 35 percent, Honda: 37 percent).
H_1: The current year's sales distribution is not the same as that of the previous year.

From Motor Vehicle Bureau records, we select a random sample of 1,000 families residing in the eastern United States who have purchased one of these four types of foreign cars in the current year, and we note which type of car was purchased. From this information, we arrive at the sample distribution given in Table 16.2.

If H_0 is true, we would *expect* approximately 18 percent of this sample to have bought Nissans (18 percent of $1,000 = .18 \times 1,000 = 180$); approximately 10 percent to have bought Mazdas (10 percent of $1,000 = 0.10 \times 1,000 = 100$); approximately 35 percent to have bought Toyotas (35 percent of $1,000 = 0.35 \times 1,000 = 350$); and approximately 37 percent to have bought Hondas (37 percent of $1,000 = 0.37 \times 1,000 = 370$). We create Table 16.3 to compare the sales frequencies *observed* in this sample of 1,000 (as given in Table 16.2) to the sales frequencies *expected* if the hypothesis is true.

Table 16.1. Previous year's sales distribution of selected foreign cars in the eastern United States

Type of Car	Percentage
Nissan	18
Mazda	10
Toyota	35
Honda	37

Table 16.2. Current sales distribution of selected foreign cars in the eastern United States (sample size = 1,000)

Type of Car	Frequency
Nissan	150
Mazda	65
Toyota	385
Honda	400

Table 16.3. Comparison of observed and expected car sales in our sample of 1,000

Type of car	Observed frequency (O_i)	Expected frequency (E_i)
Nissan	150	180
Mazda	65	100
Toyota	385	350
Honda	400	370

Making use of a procedure developed by Karl Pearson in 1900 (Pearson, 1900), we may now determine how unlikely it is for the observed values (O_i) to differ as much as they do from the expected values (E_i), given that the null hypothesis is true. If we compare the observed and expected frequencies shown in Table 16.3 according to the equation

$$\chi^2_{K-1} = \sum_{i=1}^{K} \frac{(O_i - E_i)^2}{E_i}, \tag{16.1}$$

the obtained value is distributed as a chi-square with $df = K - 1$ degrees of freedom, where K is the number of cells (or categories). We can then use the chi-square distribution to calculate the associated p-value to decide whether to retain the null hypothesis that the current year's sales distribution is the same as that of the previous year. The test is always a one-tailed (and in particular a right-tailed) test, because only large, positive values of χ^2 indicate a significant discrepancy between observed and expected values.

Using the data given in Table 16.3 and Equation 16.1, we test our hypothesis that the current year's distribution of foreign car sales is the same as the previous year's distribution of foreign car sales at significance level $\alpha = .05$.

We calculate the observed chi-square as follows:

$$
\begin{aligned}
\chi^2_3 &= \sum_{i=1}^{4} \frac{(O_i - E_i)^2}{E_i} = \frac{(O_1 - E_1)^2}{E_1} + \frac{(O_2 - E_2)^2}{E_2} + \frac{(O_3 - E_3)^2}{E_3} + \frac{(O_4 - E_4)^2}{E_4} \\
&= \frac{(150 - 180)^2}{180} + \frac{(65 - 100)^2}{100} + \frac{(385 - 350)^2}{350} + \frac{(400 - 370)^2}{370} \\
&= \frac{(-30)^2}{180} + \frac{(-35)^2}{100} + \frac{(35)^2}{350} + \frac{(30)^2}{370} = \frac{900}{180} + \frac{1225}{100} + \frac{1225}{350} + \frac{900}{370} \\
&= 5.00 + 12.25 + 3.50 + 2.43 = 23.18.
\end{aligned}
$$

To find the associated p-value, we use an SPSS compute statement or Table 5 in Appendix C as illustrated in Example 16.1. In this case, the SPSS compute statement provides that $p = .00004$. That is, if the distribution of sales is the same as in the previous year, the probability of obtaining the observed sample distribution is approximately .00004. Thus, our decision is to reject H_0 and switch to H_1. We conclude that the current year's distribution of foreign car sales for these selected types is not the same as that of the previous year.

We carried out the hypothesis test by hand for heuristic reasons. We now use SPSS. We assume that the data are in tabulated summary form, as in Table 16.2. If the data are in raw form instead, consisting of 1,000 lines in this case, one for each car produced, the following instructions for entering and weighting the data are unnecessary.

To enter the tabulated data open a new SPSS Data Editor. Click the **Variable View** tab at the bottom of the screen. Put TYPE as the first Variable Name. Under **Values**, type Value 1 and Value Label Nissan. Click **Add**. Then type Value 2 and Value Label Mazda. Click **Add**. Then type Value 3 and Value Label Toyota. Click **Add**. Then type Value 4 and Value Label Honda. Click **Add**. Click **OK**. Change the Measurement of the variable to Nominal. Put FREQ as the Variable Name for the second variable. Click the **Data View** tab at the bottom of the screen and type in the data as they appear in Table 16.4. This table shows how the tabulated data set of the

Table 16.4. The tabulated data set associated with the data of Table 16.2

Type	Freq.
1	150
2	65
3	385
4	400

current sales distribution of selected foreign cars in the eastern United States should appear in SPSS.

To instruct SPSS to treat the data as tabulated data, click **Data**, **Weight Cases**. Click the circle next to **Weight cases by** and move FREQ into the **Frequency Variable** box. Click **OK**.

To perform the chi-square goodness-of-fit test using SPSS, go to **Analyze**, **Nonparametric Tests**, **Chi-Square**. Move TYPE into the **Test Variable** list. In the **Expected Values** box, click the circle next to **Values**. Type 18, click **Add**. Type 10, click **Add**. Type 35, click **Add**. Type 37, click **Add**. Click **OK**. Note: Although these values are in terms of percentages, frequencies could have been used as well.

The first part of the output gives the observed and expected frequencies and agrees with the results of Table 16.3.

TYPE

	Observed N	Expected N	Residual
Nissan	150	180.0	−30.0
Mazda	65	100.0	−35.0
Toyota	385	350.0	35.0
Honda	400	370.0	30.0
Total	1000		

Test Statistics

	TYPE
Chi-Square[a]	23.182
df	3
Asymp. Sig.	.000

[a]0 cells (.0%) have expected frequencies less than 5. The minimum expected cell frequency is 100.0.

The second part reports the observed χ^2 value, its associated degrees of freedom, and its associated p-value.

These values also agree with those obtained by hand and we conclude, as before, that the current year's distribution of foreign car sales for these selected types is not the same as that of the previous year.

Note that we rejected the null hypothesis in favor of the alternative because the fit between the observed and the expected cell values was not good enough. For this reason, this type of chi-square test is known as the *chi-square goodness-of-fit test*.

As discussed previously, because the chi-square goodness-of-fit test is a nonparametric method, its validity does not rely on assumptions about the population from which the sample is selected. The validity of the test, however, does rely on several assumptions about the sample and the treatment of the sample data. First, the cells must be mutually exclusive and exhaustive; that is, each observed piece of information must fit into one and only one of the cells. Second, the observations must be independent of each other; that is, the result of any one observation must tell us nothing about the result of any other observation. Third, the *expected* frequency in each cell must be at least 5. Fourth and last, the sum of the expected frequencies must equal the sum of the observed frequencies. To justify the use of $K - 1$ degrees of freedom rather than K, the number of cells, we note that the sum of the observed cell frequencies must be equal to the sample size, so that once the first $K - 1$ observed frequencies are known, the Kth is completely determined.

In the special case where the number of degrees of freedom is 1 (when there are two cells), the distribution of values obtained from Equation 16.1 departs markedly from a chi-square distribution. A correction called Yates' correction is used when $df = 1$ to enhance the validity of the test. When $df = 1$, the equation for the observed chi-square value is

$$\chi^2_{(1)} = \frac{(|O_1 - E_1| - .5)^2}{E_1} + \frac{(|O_2 - E_2| - .5)^2}{E_2}. \tag{16.2}$$

Note that the absolute value of the difference $O_i - E_i$ is taken *before* subtracting 0.5 and squaring.

· ·

EXAMPLE 16.2. Are college-bound high school students who have always been at grade level in the United States equally divided among the four census regions? That is, do the students in the NELS data set come from a population in which 25 percent of the students are in each region? Use $\alpha = .05$.

Solution. In this case, we solve using SPSS only.
The null and alternative hypotheses in this problem are

H$_0$: The distribution by region is uniform (25 percent in each region).
H$_1$: The distribution by region is not uniform.

To perform the chi-square goodness-of-fit test using SPSS with raw data, go to **Analyze**, **Nonparametric Tests**, **Chi-Square**. Move REGION into the **Test Variable** list and click **OK**. Note that the expected frequencies did not have to be specified because the SPSS default is that all categories are expected to be equal.

We obtain the following table with observed and expected frequencies. The observed frequencies are based on the 500 students in the NELS data set. The expected frequencies for each region are found by multiplying the proportion (or percentage) expected for that region by the total sample size. In this example, each of the four regions has an expected percentage of 25 percent (or 0.25). To find the expected frequency for each region, we multiply 0.25 by the sample size 500 to obtain $0.25 \times 500 = 125$.

Geographic Region of School

	Observed N	Expected N	Residual
Northeast	106	125.0	−19.0
North Central	151	125.0	26.0
South	150	125.0	25.0
West	93	125.0	−32.0
Total	500		

The next table gives the results of the chi-square goodness-of-fit test. Note that because there are four regions, the degrees of freedom equal 4 − 1 or 3.

Test Statistics

	Geographic Region of School
Chi-Square[a]	21.488
df	3
Asymp. Sig.	.000

[a]0 cells (.0%) have expected frequencies less than 5. The minimum expected cell frequency is 125.0.

Table 16.5. Political party affiliation by gender

	Democrat	Republican	Neither
Male	40	10	50
Female	60	20	20

We see that in this case our obtained chi-square value is $\chi^2_3 = 21.49$, which has an associated $p < .0005$. Because $p < \alpha$, we conclude that such students in the United States are not uniformly distributed among the four regions.

THE CHI-SQUARE TEST OF INDEPENDENCE

In this section, we present another application of the Pearson chi-square distribution, one that enables us to determine whether two categorical variables are related. For example, suppose we were interested in determining whether the GENDER (Male, Female) and PPA (Political Party Affiliation [Democrat, Republican, Neither]) are related (dependent). If they are related, then knowing the gender of an individual would predict the individual's political party affiliation, otherwise not.

Suppose that a random sample of 200 individuals drawn from a population of interest produces the following observed frequencies, organized in Table 16.5 as what is called a bivariate contingency table or cross-tabulation.

If we can determine the expected frequency in each cell given that the two variables are mutually independent, then, as in the chi-square goodness-of-fit test, we can compare observed and expected cell frequencies. We do so by using Equation 16.3:

$$\chi^2_{(C-1)(R-1)} = \sum_{i,j} \frac{(0_{ij} - E_{ij})^2}{E_{ij}}, \tag{16.3}$$

Table 16.6. Cross-tabulation of political party affiliation by gender with marginal frequencies

| GENDER | PPA | | | |
	Democrat	Republican	Neither	Total
Male	40	10	50	100
Female	60	20	20	100
Total	100	30	70	

which gives values that are distributed as a chi-square with $(C - 1)(R - 1)$ degrees of freedom, where C is the number of columns and R is the number of rows in the contingency table. In Table 16.5, there are three columns and two rows, so the number of degrees of freedom is $df = (C - 1)(R - 1) = (3 - 1)(2 - 1) = (2 \times 1) = 2$. We compute p based on this chi-square value to determine how unlikely it is for the observed frequencies (O_{ij}) to differ as much as they do from the expected frequencies (E_{ij}), given that the null hypothesis is true and the two variables are mutually independent.

The p-value is the area to the right of the observed chi-square value. If the fit between observed and expected values is poor, then the observed chi-square value is large and we reject the hypothesis of independence. We show how to determine the expected cell frequencies for all cells using the data (observed cell frequencies) of Table 16.5.

We first sum all the frequencies in each row to find the row marginal frequencies. We also sum all the frequencies in each column to find the column marginal frequencies. The marginal frequencies are given in Table 16.6. The marginal frequency for the first row (Males) is $40 + 10 + 50 = 100$, the marginal frequency for the second row (Females) is $60 + 20 + 20 = 100$, the marginal frequency for the first column (Democrat) is $40 + 60 = 100$, the marginal frequency of the second column (Republican) is $10 + 20 = 30$, and the marginal frequency of the third column (Neither) is $50 + 20 = 70$. The marginal frequencies tell us that there are 100 males and 100 females in the entire sample of 200 individuals and that there are 100 Democrats, 30 Republicans, and 70 of neither party in the same sample of 200 individuals.

If the two variables GENDER and Political Party Affiliation truly are independent of each other, because we have the same number of males and females in the sample we would expect the number of male Democrats to equal the number of female Democrats, the number of male Republicans to equal the number of female Republicans, and the number of males of neither party to equal the number of females of neither party. That is, because there are a total of 100 Democrats, we would expect 50 of them to be male and 50 of them to be female. Because there are a total of 30 Republicans, we would expect 15 of them to be male and 15 of them to be female. And because there are a total of 70 of neither party we would expect 35 of them to be male and 35 of them to be female.

These expected frequencies, along with the observed frequencies, are given in Table 16.7.

A more formal method for finding the expected frequency of a given cell is simply to multiply the marginal frequency of the row the cell is in by the marginal frequency of the column the cell is in and divide by the total sample size N.

For example, to find the expected frequency for "Male Democrats," the cell in row 1 and column 1 of Table 16.6, we multiply the marginal frequency of row 1 (100) by the marginal

Table 16.7. Observed and expected frequencies for political party affiliation by gender

	Democrat	Republican	Neither
Male	$O = 40$	$O = 10$	$O = 50$
	$E = 50$	$E = 15$	$E = 35$
Female	$O = 60$	$O = 20$	$O = 20$
	$E = 50$	$E = 15$	$E = 35$

frequency of column 1 (100) to obtain $100 \times 100 = 10,000$. We then divide this product by the total sample size $N = 200$ to obtain an expected frequency of $10,000/200 = 50$, the value we obtained earlier in Table 16.7. Similarly, to find the expected frequency for "Male Republicans," the cell in row 1 and column 2 in Table 16.6, we multiply the marginal frequency of row 1 (100) by the marginal frequency of column 2 (30) to obtain $100 \times 30 = 3,000$. We then divide this product by the total sample size $N = 200$ to obtain an expected frequency of $3,000/200 = 15$, the value we obtained earlier in Table 16.7.

Given these expected frequencies, we now test the null and alternative hypotheses:

H_0: Gender and political party affiliation are independent.
H_1: Gender and political party affiliation are dependent.

Because there are two rows and three columns in this example, the number of degrees of freedom is $df = (C - 1)(R - 1) = (3 - 1)(2 - 1) = (2 \times 1) = 2$.

Using Equation 16.3, we obtain the following observed chi-square value:

$$
\begin{aligned}
\chi^2_{(2)} &= \sum_{i,j} \frac{(O_{ij} - E_{ij})^2}{E_{ij}} \\
&= \frac{(40 - 50)^2}{50} + \frac{(10 - 15)^2}{15} + \frac{(50 - 35)^2}{35} + \frac{(60 - 50)^2}{50} + \frac{(20 - 15)^2}{15} + \frac{(20 - 35)^2}{35} \\
&= \frac{100}{50} + \frac{25}{15} + \frac{225}{35} + \frac{100}{50} + \frac{25}{15} + \frac{225}{35} = \frac{200}{50} + \frac{50}{15} + \frac{450}{35} = 4 + 3.33 + 12.86 \\
&= 20.19.
\end{aligned}
$$

To find the associated p-value, we use an SPSS compute statement and the chi-square table in Appendix C. In this case, the SPSS compute statement $p = 1 - \text{CDF.CHISQ}(20.19, 2)$ gives $p = .00004$. Alternatively, the estimated p-value from Table 5 in Appendix C is $p < .001$.

Thus, if there were no relationship between political party affiliation and gender, the probability of obtaining the observed sample data is approximately .00004. Accordingly, we reject H_0 in favor of H_1, that gender and political party affiliation are related, for the population under study. Said differently, the distribution of political party affiliation for males is different from that for females. The data of Table 16.5 indicate that whereas females tend to be Democrats, males are more evenly split between Democrats and neither political party.

We now illustrate how to perform the chi-square test of independence using SPSS.

We assume that the data are in tabulated summary form; that is, that the data are given as they appear in Table 16.5. If the data are in raw form instead, consisting of 200 lines, in this case one for each person, the following instructions for entering and weighting the tabulated data are unnecessary.

Table 16.8. The tabulated data set associated with the data of Table 16.5

Gender	PPA	FREQ
1	1	40
2	1	60
1	2	10
2	2	20
1	3	50
2	3	20

To enter the tabulated data open a new SPSS Data Editor. Click the **Variable View** tab at the bottom of the screen. Put GENDER as the first Variable Name. Under **Values**, type Value 1 and Value Label Male. Click **Add**. Then type Value 2 and Value Label Female. Click **Add**. Click **OK**. Change the Measurement of the variable to Nominal. Put PPA as the Variable Name for the second variable. Under **Labels**, type Political Party Affiliation as the Variable Label. Under **Values**, type Value 1 and Value Label Democrat. Click **Add**. Then type Value 2 and Value Label Republican. Click **Add**. Then type Value 3 and Value Label Neither. Click **Add**. Click **OK**. Put FREQ as the Variable Name for the third variable. Click the **Data View** tab at the bottom of the screen and type in the data as they appear in Table 16.8. This table shows how the cross-tabulation between gender and political party affiliation should appear in SPSS.

To weight the tabulated data, click **Data**, **Weight Cases**. Click the circle next to **Weight cases by** and move FREQ into the **Frequency Variable** box. Click **OK**.

To perform the chi-square test of independence using SPSS, go to **Analyze, Descriptive Statistics, Crosstabs**. You need to move GENDER and PPA into the Row and Column boxes, with one variable in each box. Although the choice does not affect the results of the test, the presentation is more compact if you put the variable with more categories (assuming there is a difference) into the **Column** box. In this case, we move GENDER into the **Row** box and PPA into the **Column** box. Click **Statistics**. Click the box next to **Chi-square**. Click **OK**.

The first part of the output gives the contingency table or cross-tabulation with marginal frequencies.

GENDER*Political Party Affiliation Crosstabultion

Count

		Political Party Affiliation			
		Democrat	Republican	Neither	Total
GENDER	Male	40	10	50	100
	Female	60	20	20	100
Total		100	30	70	200

The second part of the output gives the results of the Chi-square test of independence.

Chi-Square Tests

	Value	df	Asymp. Sig. (2-sided)
Pearson Chi-Square	20.190[a]	2	.000
Likelihood Ratio	20.708	2	.000
Linear-by-Linear Association	15.030	1	.000
N of Valid Cases	200		

[a]0 cells (.0%) have expected count less than 5. The minimum expected count is 15.00.

The Pearson chi-square results from SPSS are consistent with those obtained by hand in that $\chi^2_{(2)} = 20.19$ with $p < .0005$. As before, we conclude that the distribution of political party affiliation for males is different from that for females.

Assumptions of the Chi-Square Test of Independence

The basic assumptions underlying the use of the chi-square test of independence are as follows:

1. The individual observations are independent of each other (no observation has any effect on any other observation).
2. The expected cell frequencies are not too small (the minimum expected cell frequency required in a particular problem depends on the significance level α and how similar in size the expected cell frequencies are to each other). In general, however, a good minimum expected cell frequency is 5; that is, each cell should have an expected frequency of 5 or more.

For the analysis of the relationship between gender and political party affiliation, we see that the first assumption was met by the sampling design. The SPSS output for the test indicates that the second assumption was met as well. Following the results of the hypothesis test there is a note about the minimum expected cell frequency.

EXAMPLE 16.3. Is there a relationship between nursery school attendance and gender among college-bound high school students from the South who are always at grade level?

Solution. Note that in Example 5.6(1), we asked whether there is a relationship between nursery school attendance and gender among students in the NELS data set. To answer this descriptively, we used both the correlation (phi coefficient, in this case) and the contingency table. We now answer this question inferentially and draw conclusions for the larger population from which the students in the NELS data set have been selected.

The null and alternative hypotheses are

H_0: There is no relationship between nursery school attendance and gender in the population (they are independent).

H_1: There is a relationship between nursery school attendance and gender in the population (they are dependent).

To perform the chi-square test of independence using SPSS with raw data, go to **Analyze, Descriptive Statistics, Crosstabs**. Move GENDER into the **Column** box and NURSERY into the **Row** box. Click **Statistics**. Click the box next to **Chi-square**. Click **OK**.

The first part of the output gives the contingency table.

Attended Nursery School?* Gender Crosstabulation

Count

		Gender		Total
		Male	Female	
Attended Nursery School?	No	62	77	139
	Yes	134	147	281
Total		196	224	420

The second part of the output gives the results of the Pearson chi-square test of independence on the first line. In this case, $\chi^2_{(1)} = .36$, $p = .55$, indicating that we should retain the null hypothesis. We conclude that there is no relationship between gender and nursery school attendance among college-bound high school students from the South who are always at grade level.

Chi-Square Tests

	Value	df	Asymptoic Significance	Exact Signficance (2-sided)	Exact Significance (1-sided)
Pearson Chi-Square	.355[b]	1	.551		
Continuity Correction[a]	.242	1	.623		
Likelihood Ratio	.355	1	.551		
Fisher's Exact Test				.604	.312
Linear-by-Linear Association	.354	1	.552		
N of Valid Cases	420				

[a]Computed only for a 2 ×2 table
[b]0 cells (.0%) expf < 5. Min exp = 64.87. . .

In this case, there is an alternative approach to determine whether there is a relationship between nursery school attendance and gender among college-bound high school students from the South who are always at grade level. We can use the Pearson Correlation Coefficient, because both variables are dichotomous.

To obtain the output of the chi-square test of independence with the correlation included, go to **Analyze, Descriptive Statistics, Crosstabs**. Move GENDER into the **Column** box and

NURSERY into the **Row** box. Click **Statistics**. Click the box next to **Chi-square** and next to **correlations**. Click **OK**.

The following table is included with the aforementioned output:

Symmetric Measures

		Value	Asymptotic Std. Error[a]	Approximate T[b]	Approximate Significance
Interval by Interval	Pearson's R	−.029	.049	−.595	.552[c]
Ordinal by Ordinal	Spearman Correlation	−.029	.049	−.595	.552[c]
N of Valid Cases		420			

[a]Assuming the alternate hypothesis
[b]Using the asym std. error...
[c]Based on normal approximation

We see that $r = -.029$ with $p = .55$, corroborating the results of the chi-square test of independence.

FISHER'S EXACT TEST

The p-values obtained through the chi-square test of independence are only approximations to the true or exact p-values. In the case of a 2×2 contingency table, an approach that does provide exact p-values is Fisher's Exact Test. The approximate p-values depart from the true or exact p-values especially when sample sizes are small.

In Example 16.3, we notice a line in the SPSS output labeled "Fisher's Exact Test," with an associated "Exact Significance (2-sided)" value of .604. By contrast, the p-value associated with the Pearson chi-square test is .551. Given the large sample size of this example, in both rows and columns and overall, it is not surprising that the two different p-values give rise to consistent results in this case – that there is no relationship between gender and nursery school attendance. In contrast, when sample sizes are small, results from these two tests may lead to different conclusions regarding the null hypothesis being tested. In such cases, the Fisher's Exact Test result should be used because it provides the more accurate result. This test was first proposed in 1934 by R.A. Fisher (Fisher, 1934) and makes use of a probability distribution called the hypergeometric probability distribution for obtaining the exact probability values associated with the observed outcome or an outcome that is more extreme than the observed outcome, given that the null hypothesis is true.

In contrast to the Pearson chi-square test, the calculation of exact probabilities using the hypergeometric probability distribution is quite laborious even when sample sizes are small. We illustrate this fact with an example that makes use of the same variables as in Example 16.3, but with a far smaller sample size. In practice, however, we simply may rely on the computer to obtain these Fisher's exact probability values using SPSS.

EXAMPLE 16.3a. Is there a relationship between nursery school attendance and gender given a sample of size $N = 12$, randomly selected without replacement from a relatively small population of college-bound high school students from one particular area in the South?

In Example 16.3, notice that the ratio of students who attended nursery school to those who did not is approximately 2:1. Likewise, the ratio of males to females is approximately 1:1. For comparability, these same ratios are used in the current example. That is, for this example we assume that, of the 12 students randomly selected, 8 have attended nursery school and 4 have not, and that 6 are male and 6 are female. Accordingly, the marginal values of our 2×2 contingency table are as follows:

	Male	Female	Total
Nursery School – No			8
Nursery School – Yes			4
Total	6	6	12

Given these marginal values, Fisher's Exact Test provides the exact probability of whether the observed, or even more extreme, distribution of the proportion of males and females who attend nursery school is consistent with the null hypothesis that there is no difference between the proportion of males and females who attend nursery school.

Assume that we have observed the following number of males and females to have attended nursery school or not:

Table 16.A

	Male	Female	Total
Nursery School – No	2	6	8
Nursery School – Yes	4	0	4
Total	6	6	12

The following SPSS procedure may be used to perform Fisher's Exact Test.

To perform the Fisher's Exact Test using SPSS, go to **Analyze**, **Descriptives**, **Crosstabs**. Move Nursery and Gender into the **Row** and **Column** boxes, with one variable in each box. Click **Exact** and then click **Statistics** and the box next to **Chi-square**. Click **OK**.

Using this procedure, we obtain the following results:

Nursery School Attendance * Gender Crosstabulation

Count

		Gender		Total
		Male	Female	
Nursery School Attendance	No	2	6	8
	Yes	4	0	4
Total		6	6	12

Chi-Square Tests

	Value	df	Asymp. Sig. (2-sided)	Exact Sig. (2-sided)	Exact Sig. (1-sided)
Pearson Chi-Square	6.000[b]	1	.014		
Continuity Correction[a]	3.375	1	.066		
Likelihood Ratio	7.638	1	.006		
Fisher's Exact Test				.061	.030
Linear-by-Linear Association	5.500	1	.019		
N of Valid Cases	12				

[a]Computed only for a 2×2 table
[b]4 cells (100.0%) have expected Count less than 5. The minimum expected count is 2.00.

For this example, while the (asymptotic or approximate) two-sided probability associated with the Pearson chi-square test is $p = .014$, resulting in the rejection of the null hypothesis that there is no relationship between gender and nursery school attendance in favor of the alternative that there is a relationship between these two variables, Fisher's Exact Test two-sided probability is $p = .061$, resulting in the opposite conclusion not to reject the null hypothesis. As noted earlier, the result of the Fisher Exact Test is the more accurate of the two and should be the one used.

☞ **Remark.** The second line of the SPSS output contains a p-value ($p = .066$) obtained by applying a continuity correction to the Pearson chi-square. This continuity correction is applicable when a contingency table is of order 2×2. The p-value obtained using this correction is more precise than the one given by the Pearson chi-square without a correction, yet not as precise as the exact p-value given by the Fisher Exact Test.

Calculating the Fisher Exact Test by Hand Using the Hypergeometric Distribution

For those interested, in this section we provide the general form of the Fisher Exact Test for the 2×2 case using the hypergeometric distribution.

Given N subjects categorized into a 2×2 contingency table as follows:

	A_1	A_2	
B_1	a	b	$+ b$
B_2	c	d	$c + d$
	$a + c$	$b + d$	N

If the marginal values are considered fixed, and sampling is without replacement from a relatively small population, the one-sided exact probability of observing the relative frequencies, a, b, c, and d in the 2×2 table, is given by the hypergeometric distribution as follows:

$$\frac{\binom{a + c}{a}\binom{b + d}{b}}{\binom{N}{a + b}} = \frac{(a + b)!(c + d)!(a + c)!(b + d)}{N!a!b!c!d!} \tag{16.4}$$

Given the observed nursery school/gender results provided by Table 16.A, using Equation 16.4, we find that the one-sided exact probability of obtaining this particular set of frequencies, with the marginal values considered fixed, is

$$\frac{8!4!6!6!}{12!2!6!4!0!} = \frac{1}{33} = 0.0303.$$

Doubling this value, we obtain the two-sided exact probability to be .0606, or .061 as given by SPSS in its rounded form.

This is the exact probability of obtaining by chance the observed outcome or an outcome more extreme, given the null hypothesis is true. Accordingly, because .0606 exceeds the .05 significance level, we cannot reject the null hypothesis in favor of the alternative. We conclude that there appears to be no relationship between nursery school attendance and sex based on this example.

☞ **Remark.** Because the observed result given in Table 16.A is as extreme as possible in one direction (we know this to be the case because of the presence of the 0 in one of the cells), we needed only to compute the hypergeometric probability for this one case. Given that a test of the null hypothesis addresses the generic question: "What is the probability, given the null hypothesis is true, of obtaining the result observed or results even less consistent with the null hypothesis (i.e., more extreme)?," the calculation of the exact probability in question must consider not only the result observed but also all possible results that are more extreme (or more disproportionate) than the result observed (if the result is not already most extreme, as it was in our example). Simply stated, the calculation of the exact probability in question must be based not only on the result observed but also on all possible results that may be observed that are increasingly more extreme (increasingly less consistent with the null hypothesis of no relationship) than the result observed, until the smallest cell frequency is zero; the exact probability equals the sum of the hypergeometric probabilities of all such possible increasingly more extreme results, beginning with the result observed. We illustrate by assuming that the observed result is given in Table 16.B, rather than in Table 16.A.

Table 16.B			
	Male	Female	Total
Nursery School – No	3	5	8
Nursery School – Yes	3	1	4
Total	6	6	12

Given the marginal values of 8 and 4, and 6 and 6, respectively, we may note that the cell frequencies of Table 16.B are more consistent with the null hypothesis of no relationship between nursery school attendance and sex (and therefore less extreme) than those of Table 16.A.

Using Equation 16.4, we find that the one-sided exact probability of obtaining the particular set of cell frequencies given in Table 16.B, with the marginal values considered fixed, is

$$\frac{8!4!6!6!}{12!3!5!3!1!} = \frac{8}{33} = 0.2424.$$

Adding this probability value to the probability value associated with the more extreme result given in Table 16.A yields the following one-sided exact probability value $p = .2424 + .0303 = .2727$. Doubling this value, we find the two-sided exact probability value to be $p = .5454$, which is the value given by the following SPSS output.

Nursery School Attendance * Gender Crosstabulation

Count

		Gender		
		Male	Female	Total
Nursery School Attendance	No	3	5	8
	Yes	3	1	4
Total		6	6	12

Chi-Square Tests

	Value	df	Asymp. Sig. (2-sided)	Exact Sig. (2-sided)	Exact Sig. (1-sided)
Pearson Chi-Square	1.500[b]	1	.221		
Continuity Correction[a]	.375	1	.540		
Likelihood Ratio	1.552	1	.213		
Fisher's Exact Test				.545	.273
Linear-by-Linear Association	1.375	1	.241		
N of Valid Cases	12				

[a] Comptued only for a 2 × 2 table
[b] 4 cells (100.0%) have expected count less than 5. The minimum expected count is 2.00.

Because the exact probability ($p = .545$) of obtaining by chance the observed outcome of Table 16.B, or an outcome more extreme given the null hypothesis is true, exceeds the .05 significance level, we cannot reject the null hypothesis in favor of the alternative in this case. We conclude, therefore, that there appears to be no relationship between nursery school attendance and sex based on the observed result given in this example.

EXAMPLE 16.4. Do families of eighth graders who are college bound and always at grade level differ on computer ownership according to the region of the country in which they reside?

Solution. Note that we answered this question descriptively in Example 5.9, confining our conclusions to the 500 individuals in our NELS data set. We now answer this question inferentially and draw inferences to the larger population from which the students in the NELS data set have been selected.

The null and alternative hypotheses are

H_0: There is no relationship between region and computer ownership in the population (they are independent).

H_1: There is a relationship between region and computer ownership in the population (they are dependent).

To perform the chi-square test of independence using SPSS with raw data, go to **Analyze, Descriptive Statistics, Crosstabs**. Move REGION into the **Column** box and COMPUTER into the **Row** box. Click **Statistics**. Click the box next to **chi-square**. Click **OK**.

The first part of the output gives the contingency table.

Family Owns a Computer? * Geographic Region of School Crosstabulation

Count

| | | Geographic Region of School | | | | Total |
		Northeast	North Central	South	West	
Family Owns a Computer?	No	46	89	86	42	263
	Yes	60	62	64	51	237
Total		106	151	150	93	500

The second part of the output gives the results of the Pearson chi-square test of independence. In this case, $\chi^2_{(3)} = 9.45$, $p = .02$, indicating that we should reject the null hypothesis as implausible in favor of the alternative. We conclude that there is a relationship between region and computer ownership among college-bound high school students from the South who are always at grade level. According to the contingency table, we see that whereas in the Northeast and West, students are more likely than not to own a computer, in the North Central and South the opposite is true.

Chi-Square Tests

	Value	df	Asymptotic Significance
Pearson Chi-Square	9.448[a]	3	.024
Likelihood Ratio	9.466	3	.024
Linear-by-Linear Association	.070	1	.791
N of Valid Cases	500		

[a] 0 cells (.0%) expf < 5. Min exp = 44.08 . . .

☞ **Remark.** Although it is too advanced for inclusion in this book, we should mention the existence of a general technique called log-linear analysis that can be used to estimate and test complex models involving dependent variables measured at the nominal level. The model for log-linear analysis is similar to the model for analysis of variance in that it allows for the estimation and testing of both main and interaction effects. The interested reader should consult a more advanced book that covers this topic in detail (Marascuilo & Busk, 1987; Marascuilo & Serlin, 1988).

NONPARAMETRIC METHODS WHEN THE DEPENDENT VARIABLE IS ORDINAL-LEVELED

In this section, we present a few commonly used nonparametric techniques that are applicable when the dependent variable is at the ordinal level of measurement. In particular, we present the Wilcoxon sign test for matched pairs, the nonparametric analog to the *t*-test on means for dependent groups; the Mann–Whitney *U*-test, the nonparametric analog to the *t*-test on means for independent groups; and the Kruskal – Wallis "Analysis of Variance," the nonparametric analog of the one-way ANOVA. These tests were first introduced in the mid to late 1940s.

☞ **Remark.** Frank Wilcoxon, then a chemist at American Cyanimid, published a revolutionary paper in 1945, "Individual Comparisons by Ranking Methods" (Wilcoxon, 1945), that introduced the notion that statistical hypothesis tests do not necessarily need to be based on estimates of distribution parameters (e.g., the mean, variance, or correlation), but rather could be based more simply on assigning ranks to the observed data and comparing those ranks to ranks that would be expected randomly, or by chance. As noted earlier, because such tests do not require the estimation of a parameter, they are called *nonparametric* tests. Working independently, and in the same vein, Henry B. Mann, an economist, and D. Ransom Whitney, a graduate student in statistics at Ohio State University, published a paper two years later that served to continue a focus on nonparametric tests (Mann & Whitney, 1947). As noted by Salsburg (2001, p. 164), "[t]he work of Wilcoxon and Mann and Whitney had opened a new window of mathematical investigation by directing attention to the underlying nature of ordered ranks." One such later example is the paper by Kruskal and Wallis (1952).

A nonparametric measure of association between two variables, each in rank order form, is the Spearman Rank Correlation Coefficient. Recall that this measure of association was discussed and illustrated in Chapter 5 as a special case of the Pearson Correlation Coefficient. Consequently, although the Spearman Rank Correlation Coefficient is a nonparametric technique, it is not presented in this chapter.

WILCOXON SIGN TEST

Perhaps the simplest nonparametric procedure is the sign test for matched pairs. The sign test tests the null hypothesis that two population distributions are identical. It is used with pairwise matched (or related) samples to determine whether or not two conditions (or treatments) have identical population distributions for the dependent variable. The proportion in the population is denoted π.

The sign test assumes that there is no difference between conditions and consequently that chance alone determines whether the difference between scores on the dependent variable for each sample pair is positive or negative. If the signs of the pairwise differences are due to chance alone, then the probability that any particular pairwise difference is positive (or negative) is .50, and the probabilities of all possible outcomes of the experiment (i.e., the number of positive pairwise differences, *Pos*) may be represented by a binomial model with $p = .50$ and N equal to the number of matched pairs. In the event of ties (i.e., pairwise differences of zero), the procedure is to drop the tied pairs from the sample and to reduce the sample size accordingly. The null hypothesis of equal treatment effects in the population (H_0: $\pi = .50$) is tested using the binomial distribution. We carry out the sign test procedure by hand and then by using SPSS in Example 16.5.

• •

EXAMPLE 16.5. In a study to determine if weights recorded on packaged snack food items (muffins, cookies, cakes, candy bars, potato chips, and pretzels) are accurate, two of each item type was randomly selected, removed from its packaging, and weighed on a high-precision scale. Recorded package weights and obtained (actual) weights in ounces are given pairwise below.

> Sample 1 (recorded weights): 11.5, 10.0, 17.0, 16.0, 12.5, 9.0, 8.75, 6.0, 8.0,
>   20.5, 5.75, 16.0
> Sample 2 (actual weights): 11.8, 10.0, 16.5, 16.0, 13.0, 9.5, 9.00, 6.0, 8.2, 1
>   19.5, 6.20, 16.2

Because the data are ratio-leveled, the paired samples *t*-test could be appropriate in this case. We assume, for the purposes of this example, that at least one of the assumptions underlying the paired samples *t*-test is not tenable (namely, that either the two parent populations are not normally distributed or that they do not have equal variances). Accordingly, we employ instead its nonparametric analog, the sign test. We use a .05 level of significance. Because a direction of difference is not specified, the test is two-tailed.

Solution. The data are reproduced and the signs of the differences between the recorded and actual weights are noted as well.

> Sample 1 (recorded weights): 11.5, 10.0, 17.0, 16.0, 12.5, 9.0, 8.75, 6.0, 8.0, 20.5,
>   5.75, 16.0
> Sample 2 (actual weights): 11.8, 10.0, 16.5, 16.0, 13.0, 9.5, 9.00, 6.0, 8.2, 19.5,
>   6.20, 16.2
> Sign of difference (recorded minus actual): − 0 + 0 − − − 0 − + − −

Because there are three tied pairs (sign of difference = 0), we eliminate these pairs and reduce the sample size from $N = 12$ to $N = 9$. Using Table 2 of the binomial probability distribution with $N = 9$ and $p = .50$, we find the two-tailed rejection region to be 0, 1, 8, or 9 positive differences. We observe the number of positive pairwise differences to be $Pos = 2$. Because 2 is not in the rejection region, we cannot reject the null hypothesis of equal weights and we conclude that weights recorded on such packaged snack food items are accurate; they are not statistically significantly different from actual weights.

We may note also from the binomial distribution table with $N = 9$ and $p = .50$ that the probability of obtaining 2 or more extreme positive differences is

> Prob(0 or 1 or 2 or 7 or 8 or 9)
> = Prob(0) + Prob(1) + Prob(2) + Prob(7) + Prob(8) + Prob(9)
> = .002 + .0176 + .0703 + .0703 + .0176 + .002 = .1798 or .18.

Because.18 exceeds .05, our conclusion once again is not to reject the null hypothesis in favor of the alternative.

We may use SPSS to carry out the sign test. Once the data are entered as twelve records of two variables each (RECORDWT and ACTUALWT), select **Analyze** from the main menu bar, then

Nonparametric Tests, then **2 Related Samples**. Click the names of the two variables and move them into the **Test Pair(s) List** box. Check **Sign** as Test Type and then click **OK**.

Using SPSS, we obtain the following results, which corroborate with those just obtained:

Frequencies

		N
RECORDWT − ACTUALWT	Negative Differences[a]	7
	Positive Differences[b]	2
	Ties[c]	3
	Total	12

[a] RECORDWT < ACTUALWT
[b] RECORDWT > ACTUALWT
[c] RECORDWT = ACTUALWT

Test Statistics[b]

	RECORDWT − ACTUALWT
Exact Sig. (2-tailed)	.180[a]

[a] Binomial distribution used.
[b] Sign Test

As mentioned earlier, the *t*-test on related samples is the parametric alternative to the sign test. When the parametric assumptions underlying the *t*-test are true, the power of the *t*-test is greater than that of the corresponding nonparametric sign test. Consequently, if the underlying assumptions of the parametric test are satisfied, we should use the more powerful parametric procedure in this case, the *t*-test on related groups. If one or more of the assumptions are not satisfied, however, then the nonparametric procedure – the sign test for matched pairs, in this case – is the best available alternative.

☞ **Remark.** As noted in Chapter 8, when Np and Nq both exceed 5, the binomial distribution is well approximated by the normal. Because $p = .50$ for the sign test, N must exceed 10 to use the normal as an approximation of the binomial. In this case, the normal distribution has mean and standard deviation given by Equation 16.5:

$$\text{Mean} = \mu_{\text{Pos}} = Np = N(.5) = \frac{N}{2}. \tag{16.5}$$

$$\text{Standard Deviation} = \sigma_{\text{Pos}} = \sqrt{Npq} = \sqrt{N(.5)(.5)} = \sqrt{N}(.5) = \frac{\sqrt{N}}{2}$$

We may determine the significance of an observed value of *Pos* by transforming it to a *z*-value using Equation 16.6:

$$z = \frac{2Pos - N + C}{\sqrt{N}}, \tag{16.6}$$

where $C = +1$ if $(2Pos - N) < 0$ and $C = -1$ if $(2Pos - N) > 0$.

The *z*-value obtained in Equation 16.5 may be compared to an appropriate critical *z*-value to determine its statistical significance. The letter *C* in this equation is a correction for continuity factor, which is included to enhance the fit between the binomial model (which is discrete) and the normal model (which is continuous).

THE MANN-WHITNEY U-TEST

Like the sign test, the Mann–Whitney U-test tests the null hypothesis that two population distributions are identical. Unlike the sign test, however, the Mann–Whitney U-test is designed for use with unrelated or independent samples and uses the ranks of the sample scores rather than the scores themselves.

The Mann–Whitney U-test assumes that there is no difference between populations and, consequently, if both populations were combined into one large group, there would be a complete intermingling of scores. If we select a random sample from each population and combine both samples into one large group, we would expect a complete intermingling of sample scores similar to that of the population scores, but with some separation due to sampling error. The question is whether the observed separation between samples is significant of a true separation in the population or can be accounted for by chance factors alone.

What we need is a measure of the extent to which the two groups are not completely intermingled; that is, the extent to which the scores of one group are generally smaller than, equal to, or larger than the scores of the other group. What is also needed is a sampling distribution against which to compare this measure to determine if the difference between the two groups is statistically significant. Such a measure is provided by the U-statistic, which is defined as the number of times a score from one group is smaller than a score from the other group. For simplicity, we assume that all scores are unique and that there are no ties. For situations in which there are tie scores, the interested reader is referred to Siegel, Sidney, and Castellan (1988), a more advanced book on this topic. We illustrate with an example.

- -

EXAMPLE 16.6. Use the Mann–Whitney U-test to determine whether a random sample of four boys and a random sample of five girls who participate in varsity college soccer come from identical populations when one considers the number of injuries sustained in a season of play. Use a .05 level of significance. The data are as follows:

    Boys: 14   17   18   25
    Girls: 7   13   15   16   12

Solution. We compute U as the number of times a value in the sample of boys is smaller than a value in the sample of girls. Looking at the data, we see that 14 is smaller than two values in the sample of girls; 17 is smaller than none of the five values in the sample of girls; 18 is smaller than none of the five values, and likewise for 25. Consequently, $U = 2 + 0 + 0 + 0 = 2$.

☞ **Remark.** It may be noted that the value of U is always between zero and $(N_1)(N_2)$. A value of U near zero indicates that the values in the first group are generally larger than the values in the second group. A value of U near the middle of the range, $(N_1)(N_2)/2$, indicates that the values in the first group are generally intermingled with the values in the second group. A value of U near $(N_1)(N_2)$ indicates that the values in the first group are generally smaller than the values in the second group.

In this example, U can range between 0 and $(N_1)(N_2) = (4)(5) = 20$, so the obtained U-value of 2 suggests that the number of injuries sustained by the sample of boys is generally larger than the number of injuries sustained by the sample of girls.

To determine whether the sample data are consistent with the null hypothesis that the two population distributions are identical, we compare the obtained value of U to an appropriate sampling distribution of U-values. We reject the null hypothesis of identical population distributions if the obtained value of U is in the rejection region, otherwise we do not.

A table of critical U-values, organized by rows and columns, is given in Table 6 of Appendix C. The rows are indexed by N_1, the size of sample 1, and the columns are indexed by N_2, the size of sample 2.

In this example, $N_1 = 4$ and $N_2 = 5$. Therefore, the critical values, contained in the column labeled $N_1 = 4$ and the row labeled $N_2 = 5$, for $\alpha = .05$, two-tailed, are 1 and 19 and the rejection region for U is 0, 1, 19, 20. Because the obtained U-value of 18 is not in the rejection region, we retain belief in the null hypothesis that the two population distributions are identical.

An alternative method for obtaining the U-statistic that is based on the ranks of the scores is given in Equation 16.7:

$$U = N_1 N_2 + \frac{N_1(N_1 + 1)}{2} - R_1, \tag{16.7}$$

where N_1 is the size of sample 1, N_2 is the size of sample 2, and R_1 is the sum of the ranks of sample 1 when all scores from both samples are combined and rank ordered from smallest (assigned a rank of 1) to largest (assigned a rank of $N_1 + N_2$).

We illustrate the use of Equation 16.6 using the data of Example 16.7.

The nine scores rank ordered from smallest to largest are as follows:

Raw Score:	7	12	13	14	15	16	17	18	25
Rank:	1	2	3	4	5	6	7	8	9

The sum of sample 1 ranks is: $R_1 = 4 + 7 + 8 + 9 = 28$. Substituting the relevant values into Equation 16.6, we obtain

$$U = (4)(5) + \frac{(4)(4 + 1)}{2} - 28 = 2,$$

the same value obtained in connection with the approach presented earlier.

Our conclusion, once again, is not to reject the null hypothesis in favor of the alternative.

We may use SPSS to carry out the Mann–Whitney U-test. Once the data are entered as two variables SAMPLE (a dichotomous variable that distinguishes sample 1 from sample 2) and SCORE, select **Analyze** from the main menu bar, then **Nonparametric Tests**, then **2 Independent Samples**. Move SAMPLE into the **Grouping Variable** box and Define Groups as coded 1 and 2. Click **Continue**. Move SCORE into the **Test Variable** list box. Click **OK**.

Using SPSS, we obtain the following results, which corroborate with those obtained earlier.

Ranks

	Sample	N	Mean Rank	Sum of Ranks
Score Boys	4	7.00	28.00
Girls	5	3.40	17.00
Total	9		

Test Statistics[b]

	Score
Mann-Whitney U	2.000
Wilcoxon W	17.000
Z	−1.960
Asymp. Sig. (2-tailed)	.050
Exact Sig. [2* (1-tailed Sig.)]	.063[a]

[a]Not corrected for ties.
[b]Grouping Variable: Sample

Notice that SPSS agrees with our results (the sum of the ranks for sample 1 is 28 and $U = 2$). The exact significance value is given as .063, which exceeds our level of significance, $\alpha = .05$, and suggests the conclusion obtained earlier: we do not reject the null hypothesis that the two population distributions are identical.

☞ **Remark.** Asymp. Sig. test refers to the significance value that would be obtained if the normal distribution were used to approximate the U-distribution (Asymp. is an abbreviation of the word asymptotic). Notice that the p-value using the normal approximation (.05) is quite different from the p-value based on the exact test of significance (.063), suggesting that the approximation is a poor one in this case. The normal approximation is recommended as appropriate when N_1 or N_2 exceeds 20. Because $N_1 = 4$ and $N_2 = 5$, we have used the Exact Sig. value.

When N_1 or N_2 do exceed 20 and the normal distribution is used to approximate U, the mean and standard deviation of the normal distribution may be expressed by Equation 16.8:

$$\text{Mean} = \mu_U = \frac{(N_1)(N_2)}{2} \tag{16.8}$$

$$\text{Standard Deviation} = \sigma_U = \sqrt{\frac{(N_1)(N_2)(N_1 + N_2 + 1)}{12}},$$

and the observed z-value is calculated using Equation 16.9:

$$z = \frac{U - \mu_U}{\sigma_U}. \tag{16.9}$$

EXAMPLE 16.7. In a small study to determine whether boys have a more positive attitude than girls toward organized baseball at a co-ed summer camp, eight boys and five girls of the same age were randomly selected from a particular summer camp and given an attitude questionnaire on this topic. The following data were obtained. Higher scores indicate more positive attitudes.

Boys	25	32	16	11	29	31	22	15
Girls	9	10	12	26	24			

Use a Mann–Whitney U-test with the stated hypothesis at $\alpha = .05$.

Solution. The null hypothesis is that the distributions of boys' attitude scores and girls' attitude scores are identical in the population. Because the alternative hypothesis is directional, we use a one-tailed test. Arbitrarily, we let the boys be sample 1 and the girls sample 2. Because the value of U measures the degree to which the scores in Sample 1 are smaller than the scores in Sample 2 (that is, higher values of U suggest that boys score lower than girls, in this case), the one-tailed test for this example is left-tailed.

A combined ranking for all 13 participants is as follows:

Score	9	10	11	12	15	16	22	24	25	26	29	31	32
Rank	1	2	3	4	5	6	7	8	9	10	11	12	13

$R_1 = 3 + 5 + 6 + 7 + 9 + 11 + 12 + 13 = 66$. Substituting the relevant values into Equation 16.3, we obtain

$$U = (8)(5) + \frac{(8)(9)}{2} - 66 = 40 + 36 - 66 = 10.$$

Because the range of possible values of U in this example is from 0 to $(8)(5) = 40$, with midpoint 20, the obtained U-value of 10 indicates that, for these data in general, boys' attitude scores are higher than girls' attitude scores. We consult Table 7 in Appendix C to determine whether the obtained U-value is statistically significant at the chosen level of alpha.

From column $N_1 = 8$ and $N_2 = 5$, we find the left critical value for $\alpha = .05$ to be 6 and the rejection region is $U \le 6$. Hence, our obtained value of U, $U = 10$, does not fall in the rejection region and our conclusion is not to reject the null hypothesis that the boys' and girls' attitude distributions in the population are identical.

Using SPSS, we may obtain the more precise one-tailed p-value (exact sig. $= .171/2 = .085$) as shown in the following tables.

Ranks

	Sample	N	Mean Rank	Sum of Ranks
Score	Boys	8	8.25	66.00
	Girls	5	5.00	25.00
	Total	13		

Test Statistics[b]

	Score
Mann-Whitney U	10.000
Wilcoxon W	25.000
Z	−1.464
Asymp. Sig. (2-tailed)	.143
Exact Sig. [2 * (1-tailed Sig.)]	.171[a]

[a] Not corrected for ties.
[b] Grouping Variable: Sample

☞ **Remark.** Had we arbitrarily designated the boys as sample 2 and the girls as sample 1, the test would be right-tailed because a larger value of U in this case would suggest, as hypothesized, that girls score lower than boys. In this case, $R_1 = 25$ and U, from Equation 16.6, equals

$$U = (5)(8) + \frac{(5)(6)}{2} - 25 = 40 + 15 - 25 = 30.$$

The right-tail critical value from Table 7 in Appendix C for $N_1 = 5$ and $N_2 = 8$ is $U = 34$ and the rejection region is, therefore, $U \geq 34$. Notice that the sum of the left- and right-tail critical U-values equals the product of N_1 and N_2, or 5 and 8, or 40, in this case. Because $U = 30$ is not in the rejection region, we reach the same conclusion as before.

☞ **Remark.** We should note that a reassignment of boys to sample 2 and girls to sample 1 leaves the SPSS output unchanged ($U = 10$) because SPSS calculates U as the smaller of the two possible U-values. In particular, if $U > (N_1)(N_2)/2$, then the statistic used by SPSS is $U' = (N_1)(N_2) - U$. Clearly, special care must be taken when interpreting results using SPSS.

THE KRUSKAL – WALLIS ANALYSIS OF VARIANCE

The Kruskal – Wallis Analysis of Variance may be considered an extension of the Mann–Whitney U-test to three or more populations using unrelated samples. It tests the null hypothesis (that all population distributions are identical) against the nondirectional alternative that at least one of the population distributions is different from at least one of the others.

As with the Mann–Whitney U-test, the Kruskal – Wallis test is carried out using the ranks of the scores when they are all combined into a single group. To determine whether the differences among the samples are due to more than chance factors, we compare the obtained measure of separation, in this case referred to as H, against an appropriate sampling distribution. As long as the size of each group is at least five, the chi-square distribution with $K-1$ degrees of freedom is a good approximation to the appropriate sampling distribution, where K is the number of groups or samples. Because H is a measure of separation, H is compared to a right-tail rejection region. Like the Mann–Whitney test, H relies on the sum of the ranks in each of the K groups. H is given by Equation 16.10:

$$H = \frac{12}{N(N + 1)} \sum_{j=1}^{K} \frac{R_j^2}{N_j} - 3(N + 1), \qquad (16.10)$$

where K is the number of groups, N_j is the size of sample j, N is the total number of scores from all samples, and R_j is the sum of ranks for the scores in sample j.

For simplicity, we assume that all scores are unique and that there are no ties. For situations in which there are tie scores, the interested reader is referred to a more advanced book on this topic (e.g., Siegel, Sidney, & Castellan, 1988). We illustrate with an example.

•••

EXAMPLE 16.8. In a study to determine whether there is a relationship between age and time spent on the Internet, eight college students, ten adults between the ages of 35 and 45, and seven adults between the ages of 60 and 70 were randomly selected from their respective populations of known internet users. Participants were asked to indicate on a survey the average number of minutes they spent each day on the Internet. The data are given in the following table. Use the Kruskal-Wallis test to test the null hypothesis that the three population distributions of time are identical. Set $\alpha = .05$.

College students	Adults aged 35 to 45	Adults aged 60 to 70
48	28	15
42	33	19
40	26	20
46	34	25
35	29	18
39	36	27
32	31	16
41	22	
	21	
	17	

Solution. Grouping all 25 times together and rank ordering them, we obtain:

Times	15	16	17	18	19	20	21	22	25	26	27	28	29	31	32	33	34	35	36	39	40	41	42	46	48
Ranking	1	2	3	4	5	6	7	8	9	10	11	12	13	14	15	16	17	18	19	20	21	22	23	24	25
Group	3	3	2	3	3	3	2	2	3	2	3	2	2	2	1	2	2	1	2	1	1	1	1	1	1

$N_1 = 8$ $N_2 = 10$ $N_3 = 7$ $N = 25$
$R_1 = 168$ $R_2 = 119$ $R_3 = 38$ $K = 3$

Substituting these values into Equation 16.10, we obtain

$$H = \frac{12}{(25)(26)}\left[\frac{168^2}{8} + \frac{119^2}{10} + \frac{38^2}{7}\right] - 3(26)$$
$$= (0.01846)(5150.3857) = 95.08 - 78 = 17.08.$$

From Table 5 in Appendix C, we note that a chi-square value closest, but less than, 17.08 with $K - 1 = 2$ degrees of freedom is 13.82. This value marks off area .001 to its right, suggesting that the probability of observing 13.82 or higher is less than .001. Because .001 is less than .05, our conclusion is to reject the null hypothesis in favor of the alternative that the populations from which these samples were drawn do not have identical distributions in terms of average daily time spent on the Internet.

We may use SPSS to carry out the Kruskal – Wallis test. Once the data are entered as two variables GROUP (a trichotomous variable that distinguishes the three groups from one another) and TIME, select **Analyze** from the main menu bar, then **Nonparametric Tests**, then **K Independent Samples**. Move GROUP into the **Grouping Variable** box and Define Groups as coded 1 to 3. Click **Continue**. Move TIME into the **Test Variable** list box. Click **OK**.

Using SPSS, we obtain the following results, which corroborate those obtained earlier.

Test Statistics[a,b]

	Score
Chi-Square	17.084
df	2
Asymp. Sig.	.000

[a]Kruskal Wallis Test
[b]Grouping Variable: Sample

EXERCISES

Exercises 16.1 through 16.5 relate to the Learndis data set. For inferential purposes, we consider the children in the data set to be a random sample of all children attending public school in the urban area who have been diagnosed with learning disabilities. Use $\alpha = .05$ for all significance tests.

16.1. There are two different types of placement for these students diagnosed with learning disabilities: resource room for part of the day and full-time self-contained classroom (PLACEMEN). Perform a chi-square goodness-of-fit test to determine whether children attending public school in this urban area who have been diagnosed with learning disabilities are equally likely to be in either type of placement or whether one of the two placements is statistically significantly more prevalent than the other. Explain the results.

16.2. Are there gender differences in the type of placement assigned to public school children in this urban area who have been diagnosed with learning disabilities? Perform a chi-square test of independence to make the determination.
   a) According to the chi-square test of independence, are there gender differences in the type of placement assigned to public school children in this urban area who have been diagnosed with learning disabilities?
   b) What type of graph is appropriate to display these data?
   c) What other statistical significance test could we have performed to determine whether there are gender differences in the type of placement assigned to public school children in this urban area who have been diagnosed with learning disabilities?

16.3. In Exercise 11.22, we used a paired samples *t*-test to determine whether elementary school children in the city diagnosed with learning disabilities perform better in math comprehension or in reading comprehension. According to the descriptive statistics, the skewness ratio for math comprehension is 2.28 and the skewness ratio for reading comprehension is −3.46, indicating that both variables are statistically significantly skewed. Because the sample size was adequate, $N = 74$, we determined that the paired samples *t*-test was robust to the violation of the normality assumption. In this exercise, use an alternative approach, the sign test to answer the same question.
   a) According to the results of the sign test, do elementary school children in the city diagnosed with learning disabilities perform better in math comprehension or in reading comprehension? Explain.
   b) Do these results corroborate those obtained in Exercise 11.22?

16.4. Is there a statistically significant difference in reading achievement depending on type of placement?
   a) Why might someone question the appropriateness of the independent samples *t*-test, in this case?
   b) Conduct the Mann–Whitney *U*-test. Is there a statistically significant difference in reading achievement depending on type of placement? What is the nature of the difference?

16.5. Are there statistically significant differences in reading achievement by grade? Calculate relevant descriptive statistics and conduct the Kruskal – Wallis analysis of variance. Use your results to answer the following questions.

a) Why might one question the use of a one-way ANOVA to determine whether there is a statistically significant difference in reading achievement by grade?

b) Using the results of the Kruskal – Wallis test, is there a statistically significant difference in reading achievement by grade? Explain.

16.6. Data were gathered on a random sample of 200 people visiting the Museum of Natural History in New York City to understand the background of visitors to the museum. The variable descriptions of the various measures taken are contained in the following table.

Variable Name	What the Variable Measures	How the Variable Measures It
EDLEVEL	Highest educational level achieved	1 = Less than H. S. 2 = H.S. Graduate 3 = B.A. or more
MUSEUMS	Annual charitable contributions to museums	1 = $0 2 = $0.01–$100 3 = $100.01–$500 4 > $500
WILDLIFE	Annual charitable contributions to wildlife conservation	1 = $0 2 = $0.01–$100 3 = $100.01–$500 4 > $500
LOCATION		1 = Resident of NYC 2 = Tourist
MEMBER	Whether the person is a member of the Museum of Natural History	0 = No 1 = Yes

For each of the following questions based on this data set, select an appropriate statistical procedure from the following list to answer each of the following questions based on this data set. A nonparametric analysis is to be used. In some instances, more than one procedure may be appropriate. Also, procedures may be selected more than once. Note that you do not have to perform any analyses to complete this exercise, just specify the analyses that should be performed.

Procedures:
(1) Chi-square goodness-of-fit test
(2) Chi-square test of independence
(3) Sign test
(4) Mann–Whitney U-test
(5) Kruskal – Wallis analysis of variance

Questions:
a) Which is typically higher, charitable contributions to museums, or charitable contributions to wildlife preservation?

b) Is there a difference in charitable contributions to museums according to the highest educational level achieved?

c) Is the distribution of charitable contributions to museums between tourists and residents different from the distribution of charitable contributions to wildlife preservation between tourists and residents?

d) Is the amount of charitable contributions to museums higher among tourists or among residents?

e) Are visitors to the museum evenly divided between tourists and residents?

f) Is there a difference in the highest educational level attained between tourists and residents?

g) Is there a relationship between highest educational level attained and membership in the museum?

Exercises 16.7 through 16.11 relate to the NELS data set. For inferential purposes, we consider the students in the data set to be a random sample of the population of all college-bound students who have always been at grade level. Use $\alpha = .05$ for all significance tests.

16.7. Using cross-tabulation, introduced in Chapter 5, we may determine descriptively that there is a relationship between REGION and URBAN.

a) What nonparametric test is appropriate to determine whether this relationship is statistically significant?

b) Use this test to determine whether this relationship is statistically significant.

16.8. Is there a statistically significant difference in the frequency of classes cut by seniors (CUTS12) and the frequency of missed school by seniors (ABSENT12)? If so, which occurs more often?

a) What nonparametric test is appropriate to determine whether this difference is statistically significant?

b) Why is the test specified in your answer to part (a) more appropriate than a paired-samples *t*-test, in this case?

c) Is the nonparametric test statistically significant? What is the nature of the difference?

16.9. Is there a statistically significant difference in perceived teacher interest (TCHERINT) between those students taking a challenging curriculum and those taking a less challenging curriculum (ADVMATH8)?

a) What two nonparametric tests are appropriate to determine whether this difference is statistically significant?

b) Are these tests statistically significant? What is the nature of the difference in perceived teacher interest?

16.10. In the Marijuan data set, we see that, in 1992, 32.6 percent of high school seniors in the United States reported smoking marijuana at least once. The same information was measured for the college-bound students in the NELS data set when they were seniors in 1992. For those students, 92 reported that they had tried marijuana, whereas 408 reported that they never had. Do college-bound students report the same incidence of marijuana use as that of the population of all high school seniors?

a) What nonparametric test is appropriate to determine whether college-bound students report the same incidence of marijuana use as that of the population of all high school seniors?

b) Conduct the test specified in your answer to part (a). Use $\alpha = .05$.

16.11. Does time spent on homework outside school by high school seniors (HWKOUT12) vary by urbanicity (URBAN)?

a) Explain why a nonparametric test is appropriate, in this case.

b) Which nonparametric test would you use?

c) Conduct the test specified in your answer to part (b). Use $\alpha = .05$.

16.12. According to an article in the *New York Times* on June 1, 2000, the New York State health commissioner suspended the licenses of two doctors who were accused of falsifying mammogram test results for poor women. These radiologists, who screened approximately 10,000 women in the Bronx for breast cancer over the course of five years, were accused of providing faulty tests and billing for tests that they did not perform. The problem was detected by looking at the rate at which the two doctors reported abnormal mammogram results and comparing it to the average rate for all doctors in New York State. Of the 10,000 women evaluated by these doctors, only 13 screened positive for breast cancer, whereas the rate for the rest of the state is 52 positive screens per 10,000 patients. Conduct a hypothesis test at $\alpha = .05$ to determine whether the difference in rates is statistically significant.

16.13. According to data from the Department of Health and Human Services, there is an association between estrogen use and cardiovascular death rates. To corroborate these results, 1,500 people were randomly selected from the population of female Americans over 50; 750 took estrogen supplements and 750 did not. The results are summarized in the following table. Use them to conduct a nonparametric hypothesis test of the association between estrogen use and cardiovascular death rates. Use $\alpha = .05$.

		Status	
		Alive	Dead
Takes estrogen supplements?	Yes	746	4
	No	740	10

16.14. A researcher is studying whether the education level of first-born sons in a small rural community in the Midwest is higher than the education level of their fathers. Accordingly, the researcher randomly selects 15 adult males from this community who are first-born sons and asks them to indicate on a questionnaire the highest level of education attained by themselves and by their fathers. To measure the variable – highest level of education attained – the following scale is used:

1 = graduated from elementary school
2 = graduated from middle school
3 = graduated from high school
4 = graduated from two-year college
5 = graduated from four-year college
6 = at least some graduate training

The data are as follows:

Highest Level of Education Attained

Sons	3	3	3	5	6	4	3	5	2	4	4	1	4	3	6
Fathers	1	2	1	3	3	2	3	4	3	3	2	1	2	2	4

Run an appropriate nonparametric analysis on these data at $\alpha = .05$. Interpret your results within the context of the problem.

16.15. A researcher is interested in determining the degree of overall competitiveness between high school – aged siblings from two-child families. In particular, she is interested in determining whether siblings of the same sex are more competitive overall than siblings of the opposite sex. Accordingly, she selects at random 10 high school – aged students with younger siblings of the same sex in high school and 10 high school – aged students with younger siblings of the opposite sex in high school. Each student selected is asked to respond to a questionnaire in which degree of perceived competitiveness with younger siblings is sought in each of four areas (academic, athletic, personal appearance, and social). Each area is to be rated on a scale from 0 (no competition) to 10 (extreme competition). A total score of perceived overall competitiveness is obtained by summing the individual responses in each of the four areas. Assume that this competitiveness score is measured on an ordinal scale.

Same-sex siblings	15	23	38	35	29	22	31	26	39	36
Opposite-sex siblings	24	25	16	10	13	18	9	37	27	33

Perform an appropriate nonparametric analysis at $\alpha = .05$. Interpret your results within the context of the problem.

16.16. In a study to interpret the effects of music on mood, 12 adults are asked to spend 30 minutes in a room into which one of three different types of music is piped (slow classical, soft rock, or hard rock). At the end of the 30 minutes, participants are asked to complete a questionnaire designed to measure mood. Low scores on this test suggest a relaxed mood, whereas high scores suggest a relatively tense mood. Assume that these mood scores are measured at the ordinal level. The 12 participants are randomly assigned to one of the three music conditions. The data are as follows:

Slow Classical	1	3	4	2
Soft Rock	5	8	6	7
Hard Rock	9	12	11	10

Perform an appropriate nonparametric analysis at $\alpha = .05$ to determine whether mood differed depending on music type. Interpret your results within the context of the problem.

Data Set Descriptions

Anscombe

This data set is used to illustrate the importance of statistical display as an adjunct to summary statistics. Anscombe (1973) fabricated four different bivariate data sets such that, for all data sets, the respective X and Y means, X and Y standard deviations, and correlations, slopes, intercepts, and standard errors of estimate are equal. Accordingly, without a visual representation of these four panels, one might assume that the data values for all four data sets are the same. Scatterplots illustrate, however, the extent to which these data sets differ from one another.

Basket

The data set consists of the heights and weights of the 24 scoring leaders, 12 each from the U.S. Women's and Men's National Basketball Association, for the 1995–2006 season. These data are taken from the ESPN website.

Variable name	Variable label	Additional description
PLAYER	Player name	
GENDER		0 = Male; 1 = Female
HEIGHTIN	Height in inches	
WEIGHTLB	Weight in pounds	
GAMES	Games played	
MINUTESGAME	Minutes per game	
POINTS	Total points scored	

Blood

The data were collected to determine whether an increase in calcium intake reduces blood pressure among African-American adult males. The data are based on a sample of 21 African-American adult males selected randomly from the population of African-American adult males. These data come from the Data and Story Library (DASL) website. Ten of the 21 men were randomly assigned to a treatment condition that required them to take a calcium supplement for 12 weeks. The remaining 11 men received a placebo for the 12 weeks. At both the beginning and the end of this time period, systolic blood pressure readings of all men were recorded.

Variable name	Variable label	Additional description
ID		
SYSTOLC1	Initial blood pressure	
SYSTOLC2	Final blood pressure	
TREATMEN	Treatment	0 = Placebo; 1 = Calcium

Brainsz

The data set and description are taken from the DASL website. The data are based on a study by Willerman et al. (1991) of the relationships between brain size, gender, and intelligence. The research participants consisted of 40 right-handed introductory psychology students with no history of alcoholism, unconsciousness, brain damage, epilepsy, or heart disease who were selected from a larger pool of introductory psychology students with total Scholastic Aptitude Test scores higher than 1350 or lower than 940. The students in the study took four subtests (Vocabulary, Similarities, Block Design, and Picture Completion) of the Wechsler (1981) Adult Intelligence Scale-Revised (WAIS-R). Among the students with Wechsler full-scale IQs less than 103, 10 males and 10 females were randomly selected. Similarly, among the students with Wechsler full-scale IQs greater than 130, 10 males and 10 females were randomly selected, yielding a randomized blocks design. MRI scans were performed at the same facility for all 40 research participants to measure brain size. Each scan consisted of 18 horizontal MRI images. The computer counted all pixels with nonzero gray scale in each of the 18 images and the total count served as an index for brain size.

Variable name	Variable label	Additional description
ID		
GENDER		0 = Male; 1 = Female
FSIQ	Full-scale IQ score based on WAIS-R	
VIQ	Verbal IQ score	
PIQ	Performance IQ score	
MRI		
IQDI		0 = Lower IQ; 1 = Higher IQ

Currency

This data set contains, for the smaller bill denominations, the value of the bill and the total value in circulation. The source for these data is *The World Almanac and Book of Facts 2006*.

Variable name	Variable label
BILLVALU	Denomination
CIRC	Total currency in circulation

Framingham

The Framingham Heart Study is a long-term prospective study of the etiology of cardiovascular disease among a population of noninstitutionalized people in the community of Framingham, Massachusetts. The Framingham Heart Study was a landmark study in epidemiology in that it was the first prospective study of cardiovascular disease and identified the concept of risk factors and their joint effects. The study began in 1956 and 5,209 subjects were initially enrolled in the study. In our data set, we included variables from the first examination, in 1956, and the third examination, in 1968. Clinic examination data have included cardiovascular disease risk factors and markers of disease such as blood pressure, blood chemistry, lung function, smoking history, health behaviors, ECG tracings, echocardiography, and medication use. Through regular surveillance of area hospitals, participant contact, and death certificates, the Framingham Heart Study reviews and adjudicates events for the occurrence of any of the following types of coronary heart disease (CHD): angina pectoris, myocardial infarction, heart failure, and cerebrovascular disease.

The associated data set is a subset of the data collected as part of the Framingham study and includes laboratory, clinic, questionnaire, and adjudicated event data on 400 participants. The participants for the data set have been chosen so that, among all male participants, 100 smokers and 100 nonsmokers were selected at random. A similar procedure resulted in 100 female smokers and 100 female nonsmokers. This procedure resulted in an oversampling of smokers. The data for each participant is on one row. People who had any type of CHD in the initial examination period are not included in the data set.

Variable name	Variable label	Additional description
ID		
SEX	Sex	1 = Men; 2 = Women
TOTCHOL1	Serum cholesterol mg/dL (1)	
AGE1	Age (years) at examination (1)	
SYSBP1	Systolic BP mmHg (1)	
DIABP1	Diastolic BP mmHg (1)	
CURSMOKE1	Current cig smoker Y/N (1)	0 = No; 1 = Yes
CIGPDAY1	Cigarettes per day (1)	
BMI1	Body mass index kg/(M*M) (1)	
DIABETES1	Diabetic Y/N (1)	0 = Not a diabetic; 1 = Diabetic
BPMEDS1	Anti-hypertensive meds Y/N (1)	0 = Not currently used; 1 = Currently used
HEARTRTE1	Ventricular rate (beats/min) (1)	
GLUCOSE1	Casual glucose mg/dL (1)	
PREVCHD1	Prevalent CHD (MI,AP,CI) (1)	0 = Free of CHD; 1 = Prevalence of CHD
TIME1	Days since index exam (1)	
TIMECHD1	Days baseline-inc any CHD (1)	
TOTCHOL3	Serum cholesterol mg/dL (3)	
AGE3	Age (years) at examination (3)	
SYSBP3	Systolic BP mmHg (3)	
DIABP3	Diastolic BP mmHg (3)	
CURSMOKE3	Current cig smoker Y/N (3)	0 = No; 1 = Yes
CIGPDAY3	Cigarettes per day (3)	
BMI3	Body mass index (kg/(M*M) (3)	
DIABETES3	Diabetic Y/N (3)	0 = Not a diabetic; 1 = Diabetic
BPMEDS3	Anti-hypertensive meds Y/N (3)	0 = Not currently used; 1 = Currently used
HEARTRTE3	Ventricular rate (beats/min) (3)	
GLUCOSE3	Casual glucose mg/dL (3)	
PREVCHD3	Prevalent CHD (MI,AP,CI) (3)	0 = Free of CHD; 1 = Prevalence of CHD
TIME3	Days since index exam (3)	

Variable name	Variable label	Additional description
HDLC3	HDL cholesterol mg/dL (3)	
LDLC3	LDL cholesterol mg/dL (3)	
TIMECHD3	Days baseline-inc any CHD (3)	
ANYCHD4	Incident hosp MI, AP, CI, fatal CHD by the end of the study	0 = CHD event did not occur; 1 = CHD event did occur

Hamburg

This data set contains the fat grams and calories associated with the different types of hamburger sold by McDonald's. The data are from McDonald's Nutrition Information Center.

Variable name	Variable label	Additional description
CALORIES		
CHEESE	Cheese added?	0 = No; 1 = Yes
FAT	Grams of fat	
NAME	Type of burger	

Ice Cream

This data set contains fabricated data for the temperature, relative humidity, and ice cream sales for 30 days randomly selected between May 15th and September 6th.

Variable name	Variable label	Additional description
ID		
BARSOLD	Number of ice cream bars sold	
TEMP	Temperature in degrees Fahrenheit	
RELHUMID	Relative humidity	

Impeach

On February 12, 1999, for only the second time in the nation's history, the U.S. Senate voted on whether to remove a president, based on impeachment articles passed by the U.S. House. Professor Alan Reifman of Texas Tech University created the data set consisting of descriptions of each senator that can be used to understand some of the reasons that the senators voted the way they did. The data are taken from the *Journal of Statistics Education* [online].

Variable name	Variable label	Additional description
NAME	Senator's name	
STATE	State the senator represents	
REGION		1 = Northeast; 2 = Midwest; 3 = South; 4 = West
VOTE1	Vote on perjury	0 = Not guilty; 1 = Guilty
VOTE2	Vote on obstruction of justice	0 = Not guilty; 1 = Guilty

Variable name	Variable label	Additional description
GUILTY	Number of guilty votes	
PARTY		0 = Democrat; 1 = Republican
CONSERVA	Conservatism score	The senator's degree of ideological conservatism is based on 1997 voting records as judged by the American Conservative Union, where the scores ranged from 0 to 100 and 100 is most conservative
SUPPORTC	State voter support for Clinton	The percent of the vote Clinton received in the 1996 Presidential election in the senator's state
REELECT	Year the senator's seat is up for re-election	2000, 2002, or 2004
NEWBIE	First-term senator?	0 = No; 1 = Yes

Learndis

What is the profile of students classified as learning disabled? The questions on this exam relate to a subset of data from a study by Susan Tomasi and Sharon L. Weinberg (1999). According to Public Law 94.142, enacted in 1976, a team may determine that a child has a learning disability (LD) if a severe discrepancy exists between a child's actual achievement in, for example, math or reading, and his or her intellectual ability. The data set consists of six variables, described in the table that follows, on 105 elementary school children from an urban area who were classified as LD and who, as a result, had been receiving special education services for at least three years. Of the 105 children, 42 are female and 63 are male. There are two main types of placements for these students: part-time resource room placements in which the students get additional instruction to supplement regular classroom instruction and self-contained classroom placements in which students are segregated full time. In this data set 66 students are in resource room placements while 39 are in self-contained classroom placements. For inferential purposes, we consider the children in the data set to be a random sample of all children attending public elementary school in a certain city who have been diagnosed with LDs. Many students in the data set have missing values for math, reading comprehension, or both. Such omissions can lead to problems when generalizing results. There are statistical remedies for missing data that are beyond the scope of this text. In this case, we assume that there is no pattern to the missing values, so that our sample is representative of the population.

Variable name	Variable label	Additional description
GENDER	Gender	0 = Male; 1 = Female
GRADE	Grade level	1, 2, 3, 4, or 5
IQ	Intellectual ability	Higher scores ⟷ greater IQ Scores could range from 0 to 200

Variable name	Variable label	Additional description
MATHCOMP	Math comprehension	Higher scores $\leftrightarrow$ greater math comprehension Scores could range from 0 to 200
PLACEMEN	Type of placement	0 = Part-time in resource room; 1 = Full-time in self-contained classroom
READCOMP		Higher scores $\leftrightarrow$ greater reading comprehension Scores could range from 0 to 200

Mandex.sav

This fictional data set contains the treatment group number and the manual dexterity scores for 30 individuals selected by the director of a drug rehabilitation center. There are three treatments and the individuals are randomly assigned 10 to a treatment. After five weeks of treatment, a manual dexterity test is administered for which a higher score indicates greater manual dexterity.

Variable name	Variable label
SCORE	
TREATMEN	Manual dexterity score

Marijuan

The data set contains the year and percentage of twelfth graders who have ever used marijuana from 1987 to 2004. The source for these data is *The World Almanac and Book of Facts 2006*. The data for 1989 are not available.

Variable name	Variable label
YEAR	
MARIJ	Percentage of twelfth graders who reported that they have ever used marijuana

NELS

In response to pressure from federal and state agencies to monitor school effectiveness in the United States, the National Center of Education Statistics of the U.S. Department of Education conducted a survey in the spring of 1988. The participants consisted of a nationally representative sample of approximately 25,000 eighth graders to measure achievement outcomes in four core subject areas (English, history, mathematics, and science), in addition to personal, familial, social, institutional, and cultural factors that might relate to these outcomes. Details on the design and initial analysis of this survey may be referenced in Horn, Hafner, and Owings (1992). A follow-up of these students was conducted during tenth grade in the spring of 1990; a second follow-up was conducted during the twelfth grade in the spring of 1992; and, finally, a third follow-up was conducted in the spring of 1994.

For this book, we have selected a subsample of 500 cases and 50 variables. The cases were sampled randomly from the approximately 5,000 students who responded to all four administrations of the survey, who were always at grade level (neither repeated nor skipped a grade), and who pursued some form of post-secondary education. The particular variables were selected to explore the relationships between student and home background variables, self-concept, educational and income aspirations, academic motivation, risk-taking behavior, and academic achievement.

Variable name	Variable label	Additional description
ABSENT12	Number of times missed school	0 = Never; 1 = 1–2 Times; 2 = 3–6 Times; 3 = 7–9 Times; 4 = 10–15 Times; 5 = Over 15 Times
ACHMAT08	Math achievement in eighth grade	Similar to ACHRDG08
ACHMAT10	Math achievement in tenth grade	Similar to ACHRDG08
ACHMAT12	Math achievement in twelfth grade	Similar to ACHRDG08
ACHRDG08	Reading achievement in eighth grade	Gives a score for the student's performance in eighth grade on a standardized test of reading achievement. Actual values range from 36.61 to 77.2, from low to high achievement. 99.98 = Missing; 99.99 = Missing
ACHRDG10	Reading achievement in tenth grade	Similar to ACHRDG08
ACHRDG12	Reading achievement in twelfth grade	Similar to ACHRDG08
ACHSCI08	Science achievement in eighth grade	Similar to ACHRDG08
ACHSCI10	Science achievement in tenth grade	Similar to ACHRDG08
ACHSCI12	Science achievement in twelfth grade	Similar to ACHRDG08
ACHSLS08	Social studies achievement in eighth grade	Similar to ACHRDG08
ACHSLS10	Social studies achievement in tenth grade	Similar to ACHRDG08
ACHSLS12	Social studies achievement in twelfth grade	Similar to ACHRDG08
ADVMATH8	Advanced math taken in eighth grade	0 = No; 1 = Yes; 8 = Missing
ALCBINGE	Binged on alcohol ever?	0 = Never; 1 = Yes
ALGEBRA8	Algebra taken in eighth grade?	0 = No; 1 = Yes
APOFFER	Number of Advanced Placement courses offered by school	98 = Missing

Variable name	Variable label	Additional description
APPROG	Advanced Placement program taken?	0 = No; 1 = Yes; 6 = Missing; 8 = Missing
CIGARETT	Smoked cigarettes ever?	0 = Never; 1 = Yes
COMPUTER	Computer owned by family in eighth grade?	0 = No; 1 = Yes
CUTS12	Number of times skipped/cut classes in twelfth grade	0 = Never; 1 = 1–2 Times; 2 = 3–6 Times; 3 = 7–9 Times; 4 = 10–15 Times; 5 = Over 15 Times
EDEXPECT	Highest level of education expected	1 = Less than college degree; 2 = bachelor's degree; 3 = master's degree; 4 = Ph.D., M.D., J.D., etc.
EXCURR12	Time spent weekly on extracurricular activities in twelfth grade	0 = None; 1 = Less than 1 hour; 2 = 1–4 hours; 3 = 5–9 hours; 4 = 10–14 hours; 5 = 15–19 hours; 6 = 20–24 hours; 7 = 25 or more hours
EXPINC30	Expected income at age 30	−6 = Missing, −9 = Missing
FAMSIZE	Family size	98 = Missing
FINANAID	Received financial aid in college	0 = No; 1 = Yes; −9 = Missing; −8 = Missing; −7 = Missing; −6 = Missing
GENDER	Gender	0 = Male; 1 = Female
HOMELANG	Home language background	1 = Non-English only; 2 = Non-English dominant; 3 = English dominant; 4 = English only
HSPROG	Type of high school program	1 = Rigorous academic; 2 = Academic; 3 = Some vocational; 4 = Other
HWKIN12	Time spent on homework weekly in school per week in twelfth grade	0 = None; 1 = Less than1 hour; 2 = 1–3 hours; 3 = 4–6 hours; 4 = 7–9 hours; 5 = 10–12 hours; 6 = 13–15 hours; 7 = 16–20 hours; 8 = Over 20 hours; 98 = Missing
HWKOUT12	Time spent on homework out of school per week in twelfth grade	0 = None; 1 = Less than 1 hour; 2 = 1–3 hours; 3 = 4–6 hours; 4 = 7–9 hours; 5 = 10–12 hours; 6 = 13–15 hours; 7 = 16–20 hours; 8 = over 20 hours; 98 = Missing
ID	Case number	
IMPTEDUC	How important is a good education?	1 = Not important; 2 = Somewhat important; 3 = Very important
LATE12	Number times late for school in twelfth grade	0 = Never; 1 = 1–2 Times; 2 = 3–6 Times; 3 = 7–9 Times; 4 = 10–15 Times; 5 = Over 15 times

Variable name	Variable label	Additional description
MARIJUAN	Smoked marijuana ever?	0 = Never; 1 = Yes
NUMINST	Number post-secondary institutions attended	
NURSERY	Nursery school attended?	0 = No; 1 = Yes; 8 = Missing
PARMARL8	Parents' marital status in eighth grade	1 = Divorced; 2 = Widowed; 3 = Separated; 4 = Never married; 5 = Marriage-like relationship; 6 = Married; 98 = Missing
REGION	Geographic region of school	1 = Northeast; 2 = North Central; 3 = South; 4 = West
SCHATTRT	School average daily attendance rate	Gives the average daily attendance rate for the secondary school the student attends. 998 = Missing
SCHTYP8	School type in eighth grade	Classifies the type of school each student attended in eighth grade where 1 = Public; 2 = Private, religious; 3 = Private, Nonreligious
SES	Socioeconomic status	Gives a score representing the socioeconomic status (SES) of the student, a composite of father's education level, mother's education level, father's occupation, mother's education, and family income. Values range from 0 to 35, from low to high SES.
SLFCNC08	Self-concept in eighth grade	Similar to SLFCNC12
SLFCNC10	Self-concept in tenth grade	Similar to SLFCNC12
SLFCNC12	Self-concept in twelfth grade	Gives a score for student self-concept in twelfth grade. Values range from 0 to 43. Self-concept is defined as a person's self-perceptions, or how a person feels about himself or herself. Four items comprise the self-concept scale in the NELS questionnaire: I feel good about myself; I feel I am a person of worth, the equal of other people;

Variable name	Variable label	Additional description
		I am able to do things as well as most other people; and, on the whole, I am satisfied with myself. A self-concept score, based on the sum of scores on each of these items, is used to measure self-concept in the NELS study. Higher scores associate with higher self-concept and lower scores associate with lower self-concept.
TCHERINT	My teachers are interested in students	Classifies student agreement with the statement "My teachers are interested in students" using the Likert scale 1 = Strongly agree; 2 = Agree; 3 = Disagree; 4 = Strongly disagree
UNITCALC	Units in calculus (NAEP)	Number of years of calculus taken in high school
UNITENGL	Units in English (NAEP)	Number of years of English taken in high school
UNITMATH	Units in mathematics (NAEP)	Number of years of math taken in high school
URBAN	Urbanicity	Classifies the type of environment in which each student lives where 1 = Urban, 2 = Suburban, and 3 = Rural.
ABSENT12	Number of times missed school	

Skulls

Four size measurements are taken on 150 male skulls, 30 from each of 5 different time periods between 4000 b.c. and a.d. 150. The data include the time period and the four size measurements. These data come from the DASL website.

Variable name	Variable label	Additional description
BH	Basibregmatic height of skull	
BL	Basialveolar length of skull	
MB	Maximal breadth of skull	
NH	Nasal height of skull	
YEAR	Approximate year of skull formation	

States

This data set includes different measures of the 50 states and Washington, D.C. These data are from *The 2006 World Almanac and Book of Facts*.

Variable name	Variable label	Additional description
EDUCEXPE	Expenditure per pupil, on average, fall 2002	
ENROLLMT	Total public school enrollment, fall 2003	
GRADRATE	Graduates as percentage of fall 1998 ninth-grade enrollment	
PERTAK	Percentage of eligible students taking the SAT, 2005	
REGION	Region of the country in which the state is located	1 = Northeast; 2 = Midwest; 3 = South; 4 = West
SATM	Average SAT math in 2005	
SATV	Average SAT verbal in 2005	
STATE	Name of state	
STUTEACH	Pupils per teacher, on average, fall 2003	
TEACHPAY	Average annual salary for public school teachers, fall 2002	

Stepping

The data set and description are taken from the DASL website. Students at Ohio State University conducted an experiment in the fall of 1993 to explore the nature of the relationship between a person's heart rate and the frequency at which that person stepped up and down on steps of various heights. The response variable, heart rate, was measured in beats per minute. For each person, the resting heart rate was measured before a trial (RestHR) and after stepping (HR). There were two different step heights (HEIGHT): 5.75 inches (coded as 0), and 11.5 inches (coded as 1). There were three rates of stepping (FREQUENCY): 14 steps/min. (coded as 0), 21 steps/min. (coded as 1), and 28 steps/min. (coded as 2). This resulted in six possible height/frequency combinations. Each subject performed the activity for three minutes. Subjects were kept on pace by the beat of an electric metronome. One experimenter counted the subject's heart rate, in beats per minute, for 20 seconds before and after each trial. The subject always rested between trials until her or his heart rate returned to close to the beginning rate. Another experimenter kept track of the time spent stepping. Each subject was always measured and timed by the same pair of experimenters to reduce variability in the experiment.

Variable name	Variable label	Additional description
ORDER	Overall performance order of the trial	
BLOCK	Subject and experimenters' block number	
HEIGHT	Step height	0 = Low; 1 = High

Variable name	Variable label	Additional description
FREQ	Rate of stepping	0 = Slow; 1 = Medium; 2 = Fast
HRINIT	Resting heart rate of the subject before a trial, in beats per minute	
HRFINAL	Final heart rate of the subject after a trial, in beats per minute	

Temp

This data set gives the average monthly temperatures (in Fahrenheit) for Springfield, Missouri, and San Francisco, California. These data are from Burrill and Hopfensperger (1993).

Variable name	Variable label	Additional description
CITY		1 = Springfield, MO; 2 = San Francisco, CA
TEMP	Average monthly temperature	

Wages

This is a subsample of 100 males and 100 females randomly selected from the 534 cases that comprised the 1985 Current Population Survey in a way that controls for highest education level attained. The sample of 200 contains 20 males and 20 females with less than a high school diploma, 20 males and 20 females with a high school diploma, 20 males and 20 females with some college training, 20 males and 20 females with a college diploma, and 20 males and 20 females with some graduate school training. The data include information about gender, highest education level attained, and hourly wage.

Variable name	Variable label	Additional description
ED	Highest education level	1 = Less than a HS degree; 2 = HS degree; 3 = Some college; 4 = College degree; 5 = Graduate school
EDUC	Number of years of education	
EXPER	Number of years of work experience	
ID		
MARR	Marital status	0 = Not married; 1 = Married
OCCUP		1 = Management; 2 = Sales; 3 = Clerical; 4 = Service; 5 = Professional; 6 = Other
SEX		0 = Male; 1 = Female
SOUTH		0 = Does not live in South; 1 = Lives in South
WAGE	Wage (dollars per hour)	

Generating Distributions for Chapters 8 and 9 Using SPSS Syntax

In this appendix, we describe the output that is generated by executing each of four SPSS syntax programs used to generate figures in the text and give instructions for how to execute each of these programs.

1) **IDGENER.SPS** is a file that contains the syntax program to generate a new data set of ID values for 75 cases. If you would like a different number of IDs to be generated, simply change the value of 75 to that other number. This program is useful also as the first step in generating the binomial distributions of Chapter 8, because these distributions all require there to be data values in the data editor before applying the binomial distribution function.

2) **SAMPDIS.SPS** is a file that contains the syntax program to generate a sampling distribution of means. In particular, this program generates the sampling distribution of means illustrated in Figure 9.2 that is based on the small population of ten values given in the text. In this syntax program, the ten population values are included within the program itself and are accessed by the DATA LIST, BEGIN DATA, and END DATA commands.

3) **NORMDIS9_3.SPS** is a file that contains the syntax program to generate the normal distribution illustrated in Figure 9.3.

4) **NORMDIS9_4.SPS** is a file that contains the syntax program to generate the normal distribution illustrated in Figure 9.4.

5) **POSSKEWDIS9_5.SPS** is a file that contains the syntax program to generate the positively skewed distribution illustrated in Figure 9.5.

6) **SAMPDISVER2.SPS** is a file that contains another version (Version 2) of the syntax program **SAMPDIS.SPS**. Like the original version, Version 2 generates a sampling distribution of means, but, unlike the original version, Version 2 gets the population values from which it generates the sampling distribution from an external data file (using the GET FILE command) located on the CD accompanying the text. If your CD drive is designated as "a:" the file has address "a:\data\positively skewed population.sav". This external data file contains the 1,000 positively skewed values graphed in Figure 9.5. The histogram of the sampling distribution of means generated by this program is given in Figure 9.6.

(1) CREATING A NEW DATA SET FILE WITH ID VALUES FOR 75 CASES

Directions for use: Open the file labeled **IDGENER.SPS** in the SPSS syntax window from the CD that accompanies the text. Click **Run, All**. A new file containing 75 ID values will be generated.

The syntax file *IDGENER.SPS* appears below:

```
input program.
loop #i = 1 to 75.
compute id = #i.
end case.
end loop.
end file.
end input program.
execute.
```

(2) THE SPSS SYNTAX PROGRAM (CALLED, IN GENERAL, A MACRO) TO GENERATE THE SET OF 50,000 SAMPLE MEANS USED TO FORM THE SAMPLING DISTRIBUTION OF MEANS GRAPHED AS THE HISTOGRAM OF FIGURE 9.2

In this program, called **SAMPDIS.SPS**, the number of samples to be generated equals nsamp (which equals 50,000 in this version of the program); the size of the population is represented by the variable nsize (which equals 10 in this version of the program); each of the 50,000 samples generated is specified to be of size samsize (which equals 8 in this version of the program). Accordingly, in this version of the program, the sampling distribution of means is based on 50,000 samples, each of size $N = 8$, drawn randomly with replacement from the population: {0, 1, 3, 3, 5, 7, 7, 7, 8, 10}, found in Chapter 9. These ten population values are input directly into the syntax program between the BEGIN DATA and END DATA commands.

<u>Directions for use:</u> Open the file labeled *SAMPDIS.SPS* in the SPSS syntax window from the CD that accompanies the text. Click **Run, All**. The 50,000 sample means that are generated will appear in the data editor and will also be assigned the file name bootmean.sav. You may then construct a histogram of these data.

If you wish to adjust the population, change the set of data values between "begin data" and "end data." If you change the size of the population, make the appropriate adjustment to the value of nsize. If you wish to change the number of sample means generated, change the value nsamp. If you wish to change the size of each of the samples randomly selected, change the value of samsize.

The syntax file *SAMPDIS.SPS* appears below:

```
DEFINE bootmn (nsamp !tokens(1) / nsize !tokens(1) /samsize !tokens(1)
/ bootvar !tokens(1) / outfile !tokens(1)).
sort cases by !bootvar.
vector data (!nsize).
compute data ($casenum) = !bootvar.
compute nobreak = 1.
aggregate outfile*
  /break nobreak
  /data1 to !concat(data,!nsize) = max(data1 to !concat(data,!nsize)).
vector data = data1 to !concat(data,!nsize).
vector tmp(!nsize).
loop #p = 1 to !nsamp.
loop #q = 1 to !nsize.
compute tmp(#q) = 0.
end loop.
loop #I = 1 to !samsize.
compute id = trunc(uniform(!nsize) + 1).
```

```
compute tmp(id) = tmp(id) + 1.
end loop.
compute mean = 0.
loop #j = 1 to !nsize.
compute mean = mean + data(#j)*tmp(#j).
end loop.
compute mean = mean/!samsize.
*save to an outfile*.
xsave outfile !quote(!outfile)/keep mean.
end loop.
execute.
!ENDDEFINE.

data list /x 1-2.
begin data.
0
1
3
3
5
7
7
7
8
10
end data.
bootmn nsamp = 50000 nsize = 10 samsize = 8 bootvar = x outfile = bootmean.
get file "bootmean".
execute.
```

(3) THE SPSS SYNTAX PROGRAM TO GENERATE THE SET OF 1,000 NORMALLY DISTRIBUTED SCORES WITH MEAN = 15 AND SD = 3 AS ILLUSTRATED BY THE HISTOGRAM OF FIGURE 9.3

In this program, called ***NORMDIS9_3.SPS***, 1,000 probabilities are generated to be equally spaced on the interval from 0 to 1. The spacing is controlled by the statement compute prob = prob + 1/1000. These probabilities are then input into the idf.normal function to produce a set of 1,000 normally distributed scores with mean and SD values specified to be 15 and 3, respectively.

Directions for use: Open the file labeled *NORMDIS9_3.SPS* in the SPSS syntax window from the CD that accompanies the text. Click **Run**, **All**. The set of 1,000 normally distributed scores with mean = 15 and SD = 3 will appear in the Data View window of the SPSS data editor. You may then construct a histogram of these data in the usual way using Graphs/Histogram, placing SCORE in the **Variable** box, to obtain the histogram of Figure 9.3.

The syntax file *NORMDIS9_3.SPS* appears below:

```
new file.
input program.
compute prob = -(1/2000).
loop k = 1 to 1000.
compute mean = 15.
compute sd = 3.
compute prob = prob + 1/1000.
compute score = idf.normal(prob,mean,sd).
leave k, prob, score.
```

```
end case.
end loop.
end file.
end input program.
execute.
```

(4) THE SPSS SYNTAX PROGRAM TO GENERATE THE SET OF 1,000 NORMALLY DISTRIBUTED SCORES WITH MEAN = 15 AND SD = 3 AS ILLUSTRATED BY THE HISTOGRAM OF FIGURE 9.4

In this program, called *NORMDIS9_4.SPS*, 1,000 probabilities are generated to be equally spaced on the interval from 0 to 1. The spacing is controlled by the statement compute prob = prob + 1/1000. These probabilities are then input into the idf.normal function to produce a set of 1,000 normally distributed scores with mean and SD values specified to be 15 and 0.75, respectively.

<u>Directions for use:</u> Open the file labeled *NORMDIS9_4.SPS* in the SPSS syntax window from the CD that accompanies the text. Click **Run, All**. The set of 1,000 normally distributed scores with mean = 15 and SD = 0.75 will appear in the Data View window of the SPSS data editor. You may then construct a histogram of these data in the usual way using Graphs/Histogram, placing score in the **Variable** box, to obtain the histogram of Figure 9.4.

The syntax file *NORMDIS9_4.SPS* appears below:

```
new file.
input program.
compute prob = -(1/2000).
loop k = 1 to 1000.
compute mean = 15.
compute sd = 0.75.
compute prob = prob + 1/1000.
compute score = idf.normal(prob,mean,sd).
leave k, prob, score.
end case.
end loop.
end file.
end input program.
execute.
```

(5) THE SPSS SYNTAX PROGRAM TO GENERATE THE SET OF 1,000 POSITIVELY SKEWED DISTRIBUTED SCORES WITH MEAN = 8 AND SD = 4 AS ILLUSTRATED BY THE HISTOGRAM OF FIGURE 9.5

In this program, called *POSSKEWDIS9_5.SPS*, 1,000 probabilities are generated to be equally spaced on the interval from 0 to 1. The spacing is controlled by the statement compute prob = prob + 1/1000. These probabilities are then input into the idf.chisq function to produce a set of 1,000 positively skewed scores with mean specified to be 8.

If the mean of this distribution (called a chi-square distribution) equals 8, the SD will automatically be equal to 4 because the SD is a function of the mean (sqrt(2*mean) in this distribution. Accordingly, unlike for the normal distribution, which requires specification of both the mean and standard deviation, only the mean needs to be specified in the chi-square distribution. In this example, sqrt (2*mean) = sqrt(2*8) = sqrt(16) = 4.

Directions for use: Open the file labeled *POSSKEWDIS9_5.SPS* in the SPSS syntax window from the CD that accompanies the text. Click **Run, All**. The set of 1,000 normally distributed scores with mean = 8 and SD = 4 will appear in the Data View window of the SPSS data editor. You may then construct a histogram of these data in the usual way using Graphs/Histogram, placing score in the **Variable** box, to obtain the histogram of Figure 9.5.

The syntax file *POSSKEWDIS9_5.SPS* appears below:

```
new file.
input program.
compute prob = -(1/2000).
loop k = 1 to 1000.
compute mean = 8.
compute prob = prob + 1/1000.
compute score = idf.chisq(prob,mean).
leave k, prob, score.
end case.
end loop.
end file.
end input program.
execute.
```

(6) THE SPSS SYNTAX PROGRAM, *SAMPDISVER2.SPS,* TO GENERATE THE SET OF 5,000 SAMPLE MEANS USED TO FORM THE SAMPLING DISTRIBUTION OF MEANS GRAPHED AS THE HISTOGRAM OF FIGURE 9.6.

SAMPDISVER2.SPS reads the 1,000 data points as an external file using the GET FILE command. The 1,000 points originally were generated from the program *POSSKEWDIS9_5.SPS* and are graphed in Figure 9.5. The external file in which these points reside is located at "a:\data\positively skewed population.sav". Once read, this program, like *SAMPDIS.SPS,* generates a sampling distribution of means. In this case, we have chosen to compute means on 10,000 samples, each of size 100 and randomly selected from the positively skewed distribution. This program also incorporates the command for constructing the histogram given in Figure 9.6.

Directions for use: Open the file labeled *SAMPDISVER2.SPS* in the SPSS syntax window from the CD that accompanies the text. Click **Run, All**. The 10,000 sample means that are generated will appear in the data editor and will also be assigned the file name bootmean.sav. The histogram constructed on these data will appear in the Output window and correspond to the histogram of Figure 9.6.

If you wish to work with a different population of values, simply replace "a:\data\ positively skewed population.sav" with the location and name of the file in which this new population of values resides. If you change the size of the population, make the appropriate adjustment to the value of nsize. If you wish to change the number of sample means generated, change the value nsamp. If you wish to change the size of each of the samples randomly selected, change the value of samsize.

The syntax file *SAMPDISVER2.SPS* appears below:

```
DEFINE bootmn (nsamp !tokens(1) / nsize !tokens(1) /samsize !tokens(1)
  / bootvar !tokens(1) / outfile !tokens(1)).
Sort cases by !bootvar.
vector data (!nsize).
```

```
compute data ($casenum) = !bootvar.
compute nobreak = 1.
Aggregate outfile *
  /break nobreak
  /data1 to !concat(data,!nsize) = max(data1 to !concat(data,!nsize)).
Vector data = data1 to !concat(data,!nsize).
vector tmp(!nsize).
loop #p = 1 to !nsamp.
loop #q = 1 to !nsize.
compute tmp(#q) = 0.
End loop.
Loop #I = 1 to !samsize.
compute id =  runk(uniform(!nsize) + 1).
Compute tmp(id) = tmp(id) + 1.
End loop.
Compute mean = 0.
Loop #j = 1 to !nsize.
compute mean = mean + data(#j)*tmp(#j).
end loop.
Compute mean = mean/!samsize.
*save to an outfile*.
Xsave outfile !quote(!outfile)/keep mean.
End loop.
Execute.
!ENDDEFINE.

get file = 'D:\Data CD\positively skewed population.sav' /DROP= prob k mean
/KEEP=score.
Bootmn nsamp = 10000 nsize = 1000 samsize = 100 bootvar = x outfile = bootmean.
Get file "bootmean".
Graph /histogram=mean.
Execute.
```

Statistical Tables

Table 1. Areas under the standard normal curve (to the right of the z-score)

[For example, the area to the right of $z = 1.96$ is found by decomposing 1.96 as $1.9 + .06$ and referencing the entry in the row labeled 1.9 and the column labeled .06. This right-tailed area is .0250. To obtain the area to the left, calculate $1 - .0250$. The left-tailed area equals .9750. Because the normal curve is symmetric about its mean, the area to the left of $= -1.96$ is equal to the area to the right of $z = 1.96$.]

	0	0.01	0.02	0.03	0.04	0.05	0.06	0.07	0.08	0.09
0.0	.5000	.4960	.4920	.4880	.4840	.4801	.4761	.4721	.4681	.4641
0.1	.4602	.4562	.4522	.4483	.4443	.4404	.4364	.4325	.4286	.4247
0.2	.4207	.4168	.4129	.4090	.4052	.4013	.3974	.3936	.3897	.3859
0.3	.3821	.3783	.3745	.3707	.3669	.3632	.3594	.3557	.3520	.3483
0.4	.3446	.3409	.3372	.3336	.3300	.3264	.3228	.3192	.3156	.3121
0.5	.3085	.3050	.3015	.2981	.2946	.2912	.2877	.2843	.2810	.2776
0.6	.2743	.2709	.2676	.2643	.2611	.2578	.2546	.2514	.2483	.2451
0.7	.2420	.2389	.2358	.2327	.2296	.2266	.2236	.2206	.2177	.2148
0.8	.2119	.2090	.2061	.2033	.2005	.1977	.1949	.1922	.1894	.1867
0.9	.1841	.1814	.1788	.1762	.1736	.1711	.1685	.1660	.1635	.1611
1.0	.1587	.1562	.1539	.1515	.1492	.1469	.1446	.1423	.1401	.1379
1.1	.1357	.1335	.1314	.1292	.1271	.1251	.1230	.1210	.1190	.1170
1.2	.1151	.1131	.1112	.1093	.1075	.1056	.1038	.1020	.1003	.0985
1.3	.0968	.0951	.0934	.0918	.0901	.0885	.0869	.0853	.0838	.0823
1.4	.0808	.0793	.0778	.0764	.0749	.0735	.0721	.0708	.0694	.0681
1.5	.0668	.0655	.0643	.0630	.0618	.0606	.0594	.0582	.0571	.0559
1.6	.0548	.0537	.0526	.0516	.0505	.0495	.0485	.0475	.0465	.0455
1.7	.0446	.0436	.0427	.0418	.0409	.0401	.0392	.0384	.0375	.0367
1.8	.0359	.0351	.0344	.0336	.0329	.0322	.0314	.0307	.0301	.0294
1.9	.0287	.0281	.0274	.0268	.0262	.0256	.0250	.0244	.0239	.0233
2.0	.0228	.0222	.0217	.0212	.0207	.0202	.0197	.0192	.0188	.0183
2.1	.0179	.0174	.0170	.0166	.0162	.0158	.0154	.0150	.0146	.0143
2.2	.0139	.0136	.0132	.0129	.0125	.0122	.0119	.0116	.0113	.0110
2.3	.0107	.0104	.0102	.0099	.0096	.0094	.0091	.0089	.0087	.0084
2.4	.0082	.0080	.0078	.0075	.0073	.0071	.0069	.0068	.0066	.0064
2.5	.0062	.0060	.0059	.0057	.0055	.0054	.0052	.0051	.0049	.0048
2.6	.0047	.0045	.0044	.0043	.0041	.0040	.0039	.0038	.0037	.0036
2.7	.0035	.0034	.0033	.0032	.0031	.0030	.0029	.0028	.0027	.0026
2.8	.0026	.0025	.0024	.0023	.0023	.0022	.0021	.0021	.0020	.0019
2.9	.0019	.0018	.0018	.0017	.0016	.0016	.0015	.0015	.0014	.0014
3.0	.0013	.0013	.0013	.0012	.0012	.0011	.0011	.0011	.0010	.0010
3.1	.0010	.0009	.0009	.0009	.0008	.0008	.0008	.0008	.0007	.0007
3.2	.0007	.0007	.0006	.0006	.0006	.0006	.0006	.0005	.0005	.0005
3.3	.0005	.0005	.0005	.0004	.0004	.0004	.0004	.0004	.0004	.0003
3.4	.0003	.0003	.0003	.0003	.0003	.0003	.0003	.0003	.0003	.0002
3.5	.0002	.0002	.0002	.0002	.0002	.0002	.0002	.0002	.0002	.0002

Table 2. Distribution of *t*-values for right-tail areas

[For example, the *t*-value with 22 degrees of freedom that has to its right an area of .05 is found at the intersection of the row labeled *df* = 22 and the column labeled .05. The *t*-value is 1.717. Because the *t* curve is symmetric about its mean, the *t*-value with 22 degrees of freedom that has to its left an area of .05 is −1.717. The table also may be used to find approximate *p*-values corresponding to given *t*-values. For example, to estimate the *p*-value associated with a *t*-value of 8.42 with 83 degrees of freedom, we look at the line corresponding to the *df* value that is closest to and smaller than or equal to 83. In this case, we estimate the answer using 80 degrees of freedom. On the line corresponding to 80 degrees of freedom, we find the *t*-value that is closest to, but smaller than, 8.42. In this case, the value is 3.416. We conclude that *p* < .0005. If the *t*-value had been .5, with 83 degrees of freedom, we would see that there are no values smaller than or equal to .5 on the line and we would conclude that *p* > .25.]

df	.25	.20	.15	.10	.05	.025	.02	.01	.005	.001	.0005
1	1.000	1.376	1.963	3.078	6.314	12.706	15.894	31.821	63.656	318.289	636.578
2	0.816	1.061	1.386	1.886	2.920	4.303	4.849	6.965	9.925	22.328	31.600
3	0.765	0.978	1.250	1.638	2.353	3.182	3.482	4.541	5.841	10.214	12.924
4	0.741	0.941	1.190	1.533	2.132	2.776	2.999	3.747	4.604	7.173	8.610
5	0.727	0.920	1.156	1.476	2.015	2.571	2.757	3.365	4.032	5.894	6.869
6	0.718	0.906	1.134	1.440	1.943	2.447	2.612	3.143	3.707	5.208	5.959
7	0.711	0.896	1.119	1.415	1.895	2.365	2.517	2.998	3.499	4.785	5.408
8	0.706	0.889	1.108	1.397	1.860	2.306	2.449	2.896	3.355	4.501	5.041
9	0.703	0.883	1.100	1.383	1.833	2.262	2.398	2.821	3.250	4.297	4.781
10	0.700	0.879	1.093	1.372	1.812	2.228	2.359	2.764	3.169	4.144	4.587
11	0.697	0.876	1.088	1.363	1.796	2.201	2.328	2.718	3.106	4.025	4.437
12	0.695	0.873	1.083	1.356	1.782	2.179	2.303	2.681	3.055	3.930	4.318
13	0.694	0.870	1.079	1.350	1.771	2.160	2.282	2.650	3.012	3.852	4.221
14	0.692	0.868	1.076	1.345	1.761	2.145	2.264	2.624	2.977	3.787	4.140
15	0.691	0.866	1.074	1.341	1.753	2.131	2.249	2.602	2.947	3.733	4.073
16	0.690	0.865	1.071	1.337	1.746	2.120	2.235	2.583	2.921	3.686	4.015
17	0.689	0.863	1.069	1.333	1.740	2.110	2.224	2.567	2.898	3.646	3.965
18	0.688	0.862	1.067	1.330	1.734	2.101	2.214	2.552	2.878	3.610	3.922
19	0.688	0.861	1.066	1.328	1.729	2.093	2.205	2.539	2.861	3.579	3.883
20	0.687	0.860	1.064	1.325	1.725	2.086	2.197	2.528	2.845	3.552	3.850
21	0.686	0.859	1.063	1.323	1.721	2.080	2.189	2.518	2.831	3.527	3.819
22	0.686	0.858	1.061	1.321	1.717	2.074	2.183	2.508	2.819	3.505	3.792
23	0.685	0.858	1.060	1.319	1.714	2.069	2.177	2.500	2.807	3.485	3.768
24	0.685	0.857	1.059	1.318	1.711	2.064	2.172	2.492	2.797	3.467	3.745
25	0.684	0.856	1.058	1.316	1.708	2.060	2.167	2.485	2.787	3.450	3.725
26	0.684	0.856	1.058	1.315	1.706	2.056	2.162	2.479	2.779	3.435	3.707
27	0.684	0.855	1.057	1.314	1.703	2.052	2.158	2.473	2.771	3.421	3.689
28	0.683	0.855	1.056	1.313	1.701	2.048	2.154	2.467	2.763	3.408	3.674
29	0.683	0.854	1.055	1.311	1.699	2.045	2.150	2.462	2.756	3.396	3.660
30	0.683	0.854	1.055	1.310	1.697	2.042	2.147	2.457	2.750	3.385	3.646
35	0.682	0.852	1.052	1.306	1.690	2.030	2.133	2.438	2.724	3.340	3.591
40	0.681	0.851	1.050	1.303	1.684	2.021	2.123	2.423	2.704	3.307	3.551
50	0.679	0.849	1.047	1.299	1.676	2.009	2.109	2.403	2.678	3.261	3.496
60	0.679	0.848	1.045	1.296	1.671	2.000	2.099	2.390	2.660	3.232	3.460
70	0.678	0.847	1.044	1.294	1.667	1.994	2.093	2.381	2.648	3.211	3.435
80	0.678	0.846	1.043	1.292	1.664	1.990	2.088	2.374	2.639	3.195	3.416
90	0.677	0.846	1.042	1.291	1.662	1.987	2.084	2.368	2.632	3.183	3.402
100	0.677	0.845	1.042	1.290	1.660	1.984	2.081	2.364	2.626	3.174	3.390
500	0.675	0.842	1.038	1.283	1.648	1.965	2.059	2.334	2.586	3.107	3.310
1000	0.675	0.842	1.037	1.282	1.646	1.962	2.056	2.330	2.581	3.098	3.300
∞	0.674	0.841	1.036	1.282	1.645	1.960	2.054	2.326	2.576	3.091	3.291

Table 3. Distribution of F-values for right-tail areas

[For example, the F-value with numerator degrees of freedom 2 and denominator degrees of freedom 3 that has to its right an area of .05 is found at the intersection of the row with df FOR DENOM = 3 and the column with df FOR NUMERATOR = 2. The F-value is 9.55. The table may also be used to find approximate p-values corresponding to given F-values. For example, to find the p-value associated with F = 8.66 with numerator degrees of freedom = 2 and denominator degrees of freedom = 3, we find all of the values associated with df FOR DENOM = 3 and df FOR NUMERATOR = 2. We find that the F-values that are closest to F = 8.66 are F = 5.46 and F = 9.55. The area to the right of F = 5.46 is .10 and the area to the right of F = 9.55 is .05. The p-value, or the area to the right of F = 8.66, is less than .10 but larger than .05. We have the estimate .05 < p < .10. If, however, given the same degrees of freedom, we wished to find the p-value associated with F = 1.56, we find that the F-value that is closest to F = 1.56 is F = 2.28. The area to the right of F = 2.28 is .25. The p-value, or the area to the right of F = 1.56 is greater than .25. We have the estimate p > .25.]

df FOR DENOM	α	df FOR NUMERATOR																		
		1	2	3	4	5	6	7	8	9	10	12	15	20	24	30	40	60	120	10000
1	0.25	5.83	7.50	8.20	8.58	8.82	8.98	9.10	9.19	9.26	9.32	9.41	9.49	9.58	9.63	9.67	9.71	9.76	9.80	9.85
1	0.10	39.86	49.50	53.59	55.83	57.24	58.20	58.91	59.44	59.86	60.19	60.71	61.22	61.74	62.00	62.26	62.53	62.79	63.06	63.32
1	0.05	161.45	199.50	215.71	224.58	230.16	233.99	236.77	238.88	240.54	241.88	243.90	245.95	248.02	249.05	250.10	251.14	252.20	253.25	254.30
1	0.03	647.79	799.48	864.15	899.60	921.83	937.11	948.20	956.64	963.28	968.63	976.72	984.87	993.08	997.27	1.0E+03	1.0E+03	1.0E+03	1.0E+03	1.0E+03
1	0.01	4.E+03	5.E+03	5.E+03	6.E+03	6.E+03	6.E+03	6.E+03	6.E+03	6.E+03	6.E+03	6.E+03	6.E+03	6.E+03	6.E+03	6.E+03	6.E+03	6.E+03	6.E+03	6.E+03
1	0.001	4.E+05	5.E+05	5.E+05	6.E+05	6.E+05	6.E+05	6.E+05	6.E+05	6.E+05	6.E+05	6.E+05	6.E+05	6.E+05	6.E+05	6.E+05	6.E+05	6.E+05	6.E+05	6.E+05
2	0.25	2.57	3.00	3.15	3.23	3.28	3.31	3.34	3.35	3.37	3.38	3.39	3.41	3.43	3.43	3.44	3.45	3.46	3.47	3.48
2	0.10	8.53	9.00	9.16	9.24	9.29	9.33	9.35	9.37	9.38	9.39	9.41	9.42	9.44	9.45	9.46	9.47	9.47	9.48	9.49
2	0.05	18.51	19.00	19.16	19.25	19.30	19.33	19.35	19.37	19.38	19.40	19.41	19.43	19.45	19.45	19.46	19.47	19.48	19.49	19.50
2	0.03	38.51	39.00	39.17	39.25	39.30	39.33	39.36	39.37	39.39	39.40	39.41	39.43	39.45	39.46	39.46	39.47	39.48	39.49	39.50
2	0.01	98.50	99.00	99.16	99.25	99.30	99.33	99.36	99.37	99.39	99.40	99.42	99.43	99.45	99.45	99.46	99.47	99.48	99.49	99.50
2	0.001	998.38	998.84	999.31	999.31	999.31	999.31	999.31	999.31	999.31	999.31	999.31	999.31	999.31	999.31	999.31	999.31	999.31	999.31	999.31
3	0.25	2.02	2.28	2.36	2.39	2.41	2.42	2.43	2.44	2.44	2.44	2.45	2.46	2.46	2.46	2.47	2.47	2.47	2.47	2.47
3	0.10	5.54	5.46	5.39	5.34	5.31	5.28	5.27	5.25	5.24	5.23	5.22	5.20	5.18	5.18	5.17	5.16	5.15	5.14	5.13
3	0.05	10.13	9.55	9.28	9.12	9.01	8.94	8.89	8.85	8.81	8.79	8.74	8.70	8.66	8.64	8.62	8.59	8.57	8.55	8.53
3	0.03	17.44	16.04	15.44	15.10	14.88	14.73	14.62	14.54	14.47	14.42	14.34	14.25	14.17	14.12	14.08	14.04	13.99	13.95	13.90
3	0.01	34.12	30.82	29.46	28.71	28.24	27.91	27.67	27.49	27.34	27.23	27.05	26.87	26.69	26.60	26.50	26.41	26.32	26.22	26.13
3	0.001	167.06	148.49	141.10	137.08	134.58	132.83	131.61	130.62	129.86	129.22	128.32	127.36	126.43	125.93	125.44	124.97	124.45	123.98	123.46
4	0.25	1.81	2.00	2.05	2.06	2.07	2.08	2.08	2.08	2.08	2.08	2.08	2.08	2.08	2.08	2.08	2.08	2.08	2.08	2.08
4	0.10	4.54	4.32	4.19	4.11	4.05	4.01	3.98	3.95	3.94	3.92	3.90	3.87	3.84	3.83	3.82	3.80	3.79	3.78	3.76
4	0.05	7.71	6.94	6.59	6.39	6.26	6.16	6.09	6.04	6.00	5.96	5.91	5.86	5.80	5.77	5.75	5.72	5.69	5.66	5.63
4	0.03	12.22	10.65	9.98	9.60	9.36	9.20	9.07	8.98	8.90	8.84	8.75	8.66	8.56	8.51	8.46	8.41	8.36	8.31	8.26
4	0.01	21.20	18.00	16.69	15.98	15.52	15.21	14.98	14.80	14.66	14.55	14.37	14.20	14.02	13.93	13.84	13.75	13.65	13.56	13.46
4	0.001	74.13	61.25	56.17	53.43	51.72	50.52	49.65	49.00	48.47	48.05	47.41	46.76	46.10	45.77	45.43	45.08	44.75	44.40	44.05
5	0.25	1.69	1.85	1.88	1.89	1.89	1.89	1.89	1.89	1.89	1.89	1.89	1.89	1.88	1.88	1.88	1.88	1.87	1.87	1.87
5	0.10	4.06	3.78	3.62	3.52	3.45	3.40	3.37	3.34	3.32	3.30	3.27	3.24	3.21	3.19	3.17	3.16	3.14	3.12	3.11
5	0.05	6.61	5.79	5.41	5.19	5.05	4.95	4.88	4.82	4.77	4.74	4.68	4.62	4.56	4.53	4.50	4.46	4.43	4.40	4.37
5	0.03	10.01	8.43	7.76	7.39	7.15	6.98	6.85	6.76	6.68	6.62	6.52	6.43	6.33	6.28	6.23	6.18	6.12	6.07	6.02
5	0.01	16.26	13.27	12.06	11.39	10.97	10.67	10.46	10.29	10.16	10.05	9.89	9.72	9.55	9.47	9.38	9.29	9.20	9.11	9.02
5	0.001	47.18	37.12	33.20	31.08	29.75	28.83	28.17	27.65	27.24	26.91	26.42	25.91	25.39	25.13	24.87	24.60	24.33	24.06	23.79
6	0.25	1.62	1.76	1.78	1.79	1.79	1.78	1.78	1.78	1.77	1.77	1.77	1.77	1.76	1.76	1.75	1.75	1.74	1.74	1.74
6	0.10	3.78	3.46	3.29	3.18	3.11	3.05	3.01	2.98	2.96	2.94	2.90	2.87	2.84	2.82	2.80	2.78	2.76	2.74	2.72
6	0.05	5.99	5.14	4.76	4.53	4.39	4.28	4.21	4.15	4.10	4.06	4.00	3.94	3.87	3.84	3.81	3.77	3.74	3.70	3.67
6	0.03	8.81	7.26	6.60	6.23	5.99	5.82	5.70	5.60	5.52	5.46	5.37	5.27	5.17	5.12	5.07	5.01	4.96	4.90	4.85
6	0.01	13.75	10.92	9.78	9.15	8.75	8.47	8.26	8.10	7.98	7.87	7.72	7.56	7.40	7.31	7.23	7.14	7.06	6.97	6.88
6	0.001	35.51	27.00	23.71	21.92	20.80	20.03	19.46	19.03	18.69	18.41	17.99	17.56	17.12	16.90	16.67	16.44	16.21	15.98	15.75

(continued)

df FOR DENOM	α	df FOR NUMERATOR 1	2	3	4	5	6	7	8	9	10	12	15	20	24	30	40	60	120	10000
7	0.25	1.57	1.70	1.72	1.72	1.71	1.71	1.70	1.70	1.69	1.69	1.68	1.68	1.67	1.67	1.66	1.66	1.65	1.65	1.65
7	0.10	3.59	3.26	3.07	2.96	2.88	2.83	2.78	2.75	2.72	2.70	2.67	2.63	2.59	2.58	2.56	2.54	2.51	2.49	2.47
7	0.05	5.59	4.74	4.35	4.12	3.97	3.87	3.79	3.73	3.68	3.64	3.57	3.51	3.44	3.41	3.38	3.34	3.30	3.27	3.23
7	0.03	8.07	6.54	5.89	5.52	5.29	5.12	4.99	4.90	4.82	4.76	4.67	4.57	4.47	4.41	4.36	4.31	4.25	4.20	4.14
7	0.01	12.25	9.55	8.45	7.85	7.46	7.19	6.99	6.84	6.72	6.62	6.47	6.31	6.16	6.07	5.99	5.91	5.82	5.74	5.65
7	0.001	29.25	21.69	18.77	17.20	16.21	15.52	15.02	14.63	14.33	14.08	13.71	13.32	12.93	12.73	12.53	12.33	12.12	11.91	11.70
8	0.25	1.54	1.66	1.67	1.66	1.66	1.65	1.64	1.64	1.63	1.63	1.62	1.62	1.61	1.60	1.60	1.59	1.59	1.58	1.58
8	0.10	3.46	3.11	2.92	2.81	2.73	2.67	2.62	2.59	2.56	2.54	2.50	2.46	2.42	2.40	2.38	2.36	2.34	2.32	2.29
8	0.05	5.32	4.46	4.07	3.84	3.69	3.58	3.50	3.44	3.39	3.35	3.28	3.22	3.15	3.12	3.08	3.04	3.01	2.97	2.93
8	0.03	7.57	6.06	5.42	5.05	4.82	4.65	4.53	4.43	4.36	4.30	4.20	4.10	4.00	3.95	3.89	3.84	3.78	3.73	3.67
8	0.01	11.26	8.65	7.59	7.01	6.63	6.37	6.18	6.03	5.91	5.81	5.67	5.52	5.36	5.28	5.20	5.12	5.03	4.95	4.86
8	0.001	25.41	18.49	15.83	14.39	13.48	12.86	12.40	12.05	11.77	11.54	11.19	10.84	10.48	10.30	10.11	9.92	9.73	9.53	9.34
9	0.25	1.51	1.62	1.63	1.63	1.62	1.61	1.60	1.60	1.59	1.59	1.58	1.57	1.56	1.56	1.55	1.54	1.54	1.53	1.53
9	0.10	3.36	3.01	2.81	2.69	2.61	2.55	2.51	2.47	2.44	2.42	2.38	2.34	2.30	2.28	2.25	2.23	2.21	2.18	2.16
9	0.05	5.12	4.26	3.86	3.63	3.48	3.37	3.29	3.23	3.18	3.14	3.07	3.01	2.94	2.90	2.86	2.83	2.79	2.75	2.71
9	0.03	7.21	5.71	5.08	4.72	4.48	4.32	4.20	4.10	4.03	3.96	3.87	3.77	3.67	3.61	3.56	3.51	3.45	3.39	3.33
9	0.01	10.56	8.02	6.99	6.42	6.06	5.80	5.61	5.47	5.35	5.26	5.11	4.96	4.81	4.73	4.65	4.57	4.48	4.40	4.31
9	0.001	22.86	16.39	13.90	12.56	11.71	11.13	10.70	10.37	10.11	9.89	9.57	9.24	8.90	8.72	8.55	8.37	8.19	8.00	7.82
10	0.25	1.49	1.60	1.60	1.59	1.59	1.58	1.57	1.56	1.56	1.55	1.54	1.53	1.52	1.52	1.51	1.51	1.50	1.49	1.48
10	0.10	3.29	2.92	2.73	2.61	2.52	2.46	2.41	2.38	2.35	2.32	2.28	2.24	2.20	2.18	2.16	2.13	2.11	2.08	2.06
10	0.05	4.96	4.10	3.71	3.48	3.33	3.22	3.14	3.07	3.02	2.98	2.91	2.85	2.77	2.74	2.70	2.66	2.62	2.58	2.54
10	0.03	6.94	5.46	4.83	4.47	4.24	4.07	3.95	3.85	3.78	3.72	3.62	3.52	3.42	3.37	3.31	3.26	3.20	3.14	3.08
10	0.01	10.04	7.56	6.55	5.99	5.64	5.39	5.20	5.06	4.94	4.85	4.71	4.56	4.41	4.33	4.25	4.17	4.08	4.00	3.91
10	0.001	21.04	14.90	12.55	11.28	10.48	9.93	9.52	9.20	8.96	8.75	8.45	8.13	7.80	7.64	7.47	7.30	7.12	6.94	6.76
11	0.25	1.47	1.58	1.58	1.57	1.56	1.55	1.54	1.53	1.53	1.52	1.51	1.50	1.49	1.49	1.48	1.47	1.47	1.46	1.45
11	0.10	3.23	2.86	2.66	2.54	2.45	2.39	2.34	2.30	2.27	2.25	2.21	2.17	2.12	2.10	2.08	2.05	2.03	2.00	1.97
11	0.05	4.84	3.98	3.59	3.36	3.20	3.09	3.01	2.95	2.90	2.85	2.79	2.72	2.65	2.61	2.57	2.53	2.49	2.45	2.41
11	0.03	6.72	5.26	4.63	4.28	4.04	3.88	3.76	3.66	3.59	3.53	3.43	3.33	3.23	3.17	3.12	3.06	3.00	2.94	2.88
11	0.01	9.65	7.21	6.22	5.67	5.32	5.07	4.89	4.74	4.63	4.54	4.40	4.25	4.10	4.02	3.94	3.86	3.78	3.69	3.60
11	0.001	19.69	13.81	11.56	10.35	9.58	9.05	8.65	8.35	8.12	7.92	7.63	7.32	7.01	6.85	6.68	6.52	6.35	6.18	6.00
12	0.25	1.46	1.56	1.56	1.55	1.54	1.53	1.52	1.51	1.51	1.50	1.49	1.48	1.47	1.46	1.45	1.45	1.44	1.43	1.42
12	0.10	3.18	2.81	2.61	2.48	2.39	2.33	2.28	2.24	2.21	2.19	2.15	2.10	2.06	2.04	2.01	1.99	1.96	1.93	1.90
12	0.05	4.75	3.89	3.49	3.26	3.11	3.00	2.91	2.85	2.80	2.75	2.69	2.62	2.54	2.51	2.47	2.43	2.38	2.34	2.30
12	0.03	6.55	5.10	4.47	4.12	3.89	3.73	3.61	3.51	3.44	3.37	3.28	3.18	3.07	3.02	2.96	2.91	2.85	2.79	2.73
12	0.01	9.33	6.93	5.95	5.41	5.06	4.82	4.64	4.50	4.39	4.30	4.16	4.01	3.86	3.78	3.70	3.62	3.54	3.45	3.36
12	0.001	18.64	12.97	10.80	9.63	8.89	8.38	8.00	7.71	7.48	7.29	7.00	6.71	6.40	6.25	6.09	5.93	5.76	5.59	5.42
13	0.25	1.45	1.55	1.55	1.53	1.52	1.51	1.50	1.49	1.49	1.48	1.47	1.46	1.45	1.44	1.43	1.42	1.42	1.41	1.40
13	0.10	3.14	2.76	2.56	2.43	2.35	2.28	2.23	2.20	2.16	2.14	2.10	2.05	2.01	1.98	1.96	1.93	1.90	1.88	1.85
13	0.05	4.67	3.81	3.41	3.18	3.03	2.92	2.83	2.77	2.71	2.67	2.60	2.53	2.46	2.42	2.38	2.34	2.30	2.25	2.21
13	0.03	6.41	4.97	4.35	4.00	3.77	3.60	3.48	3.39	3.31	3.25	3.15	3.05	2.95	2.89	2.84	2.78	2.72	2.66	2.60
13	0.01	9.07	6.70	5.74	5.21	4.86	4.62	4.44	4.30	4.19	4.10	3.96	3.82	3.66	3.59	3.51	3.43	3.34	3.25	3.17
13	0.001	17.82	12.31	10.21	9.07	8.35	7.86	7.49	7.21	6.98	6.80	6.52	6.23	5.93	5.78	5.63	5.47	5.30	5.14	4.97
14	0.25	1.44	1.53	1.53	1.52	1.51	1.50	1.49	1.48	1.47	1.46	1.45	1.44	1.43	1.42	1.41	1.41	1.40	1.39	1.38
14	0.10	3.10	2.73	2.52	2.39	2.31	2.24	2.19	2.15	2.12	2.10	2.05	2.01	1.96	1.94	1.91	1.89	1.86	1.83	1.80
14	0.05	4.60	3.74	3.34	3.11	2.96	2.85	2.76	2.70	2.65	2.60	2.53	2.46	2.39	2.35	2.31	2.27	2.22	2.18	2.13

df FOR DENOM	α	1	2	3	4	5	6	7	8	9	10	12	15	20	24	30	40	60	120	10000
																				df FOR NUMERATOR
14	0.03	6.30	4.86	4.24	3.89	3.66	3.50	3.38	3.29	3.21	3.15	3.05	2.95	2.84	2.79	2.73	2.67	2.61	2.55	2.49
14	0.01	8.86	6.51	5.56	5.04	4.69	4.46	4.28	4.14	4.03	3.94	3.80	3.66	3.51	3.43	3.35	3.27	3.18	3.09	3.01
14	0.001	17.14	11.78	9.73	8.62	7.92	7.44	7.08	6.80	6.58	6.40	6.13	5.85	5.56	5.41	5.25	5.10	4.94	4.77	4.61
15	0.25	1.43	1.52	1.52	1.51	1.49	1.48	1.47	1.46	1.46	1.45	1.44	1.43	1.41	1.41	1.40	1.39	1.38	1.37	1.36
15	0.10	3.07	2.70	2.49	2.36	2.27	2.21	2.16	2.12	2.09	2.06	2.02	1.97	1.92	1.90	1.87	1.85	1.82	1.79	1.76
15	0.05	4.54	3.68	3.29	3.06	2.90	2.79	2.71	2.64	2.59	2.54	2.48	2.40	2.33	2.29	2.25	2.20	2.16	2.11	2.07
15	0.03	6.20	4.77	4.15	3.80	3.58	3.41	3.29	3.20	3.12	3.06	2.96	2.86	2.76	2.70	2.64	2.59	2.52	2.46	2.40
15	0.01	8.68	6.36	5.42	4.89	4.56	4.32	4.14	4.00	3.89	3.80	3.67	3.52	3.37	3.29	3.21	3.13	3.05	2.96	2.87
15	0.001	16.59	11.34	9.34	8.25	7.57	7.09	6.74	6.47	6.26	6.08	5.81	5.54	5.25	5.10	4.95	4.80	4.64	4.48	4.31
16	0.25	1.42	1.51	1.51	1.50	1.48	1.47	1.46	1.45	1.44	1.44	1.43	1.41	1.40	1.39	1.38	1.37	1.36	1.35	1.34
16	0.10	3.05	2.67	2.46	2.33	2.24	2.18	2.13	2.09	2.06	2.03	1.99	1.94	1.89	1.87	1.84	1.81	1.78	1.75	1.72
16	0.05	4.49	3.63	3.24	3.01	2.85	2.74	2.66	2.59	2.54	2.49	2.42	2.35	2.28	2.24	2.19	2.15	2.11	2.06	2.01
16	0.03	6.12	4.69	4.08	3.73	3.50	3.34	3.22	3.12	3.05	2.99	2.89	2.79	2.68	2.63	2.57	2.51	2.45	2.38	2.32
16	0.01	8.53	6.23	5.29	4.77	4.44	4.20	4.03	3.89	3.78	3.69	3.55	3.41	3.26	3.18	3.10	3.02	2.93	2.84	2.75
16	0.001	16.12	10.97	9.01	7.94	7.27	6.80	6.46	6.20	5.98	5.81	5.55	5.27	4.99	4.85	4.70	4.54	4.39	4.23	4.06
17	0.25	1.42	1.51	1.50	1.49	1.47	1.46	1.45	1.44	1.43	1.43	1.41	1.40	1.39	1.38	1.37	1.36	1.35	1.34	1.33
17	0.10	3.03	2.64	2.44	2.31	2.22	2.15	2.10	2.06	2.03	2.00	1.96	1.91	1.86	1.84	1.81	1.78	1.75	1.72	1.69
17	0.05	4.45	3.59	3.20	2.96	2.81	2.70	2.61	2.55	2.49	2.45	2.38	2.31	2.23	2.19	2.15	2.10	2.06	2.01	1.96
17	0.03	6.04	4.62	4.01	3.66	3.44	3.28	3.16	3.06	2.98	2.92	2.82	2.72	2.62	2.56	2.50	2.44	2.38	2.32	2.25
17	0.01	8.40	6.11	5.19	4.67	4.34	4.10	3.93	3.79	3.68	3.59	3.46	3.31	3.16	3.08	3.00	2.92	2.83	2.75	2.65
17	0.001	15.72	10.66	8.73	7.68	7.02	6.56	6.22	5.96	5.75	5.58	5.32	5.05	4.78	4.63	4.48	4.33	4.18	4.02	3.85
18	0.25	1.41	1.50	1.49	1.48	1.46	1.45	1.44	1.43	1.42	1.42	1.40	1.39	1.38	1.37	1.36	1.35	1.34	1.33	1.32
18	0.10	3.01	2.62	2.42	2.29	2.20	2.13	2.08	2.04	2.00	1.98	1.93	1.89	1.84	1.81	1.78	1.75	1.72	1.69	1.66
18	0.05	4.41	3.55	3.16	2.93	2.77	2.66	2.58	2.51	2.46	2.41	2.34	2.27	2.19	2.15	2.11	2.06	2.02	1.97	1.92
18	0.03	5.98	4.56	3.95	3.61	3.38	3.22	3.10	3.01	2.93	2.87	2.77	2.67	2.56	2.50	2.44	2.38	2.32	2.26	2.19
18	0.01	8.29	6.01	5.09	4.58	4.25	4.01	3.84	3.71	3.60	3.51	3.37	3.23	3.08	3.00	2.92	2.84	2.75	2.66	2.57
18	0.001	15.38	10.39	8.49	7.46	6.81	6.35	6.02	5.76	5.56	5.39	5.13	4.87	4.59	4.45	4.30	4.15	4.00	3.84	3.67
19	0.25	1.41	1.49	1.49	1.47	1.46	1.44	1.43	1.42	1.41	1.41	1.40	1.38	1.37	1.36	1.35	1.34	1.33	1.32	1.30
19	0.10	2.99	2.61	2.40	2.27	2.18	2.11	2.06	2.02	1.98	1.96	1.91	1.86	1.81	1.79	1.76	1.73	1.70	1.67	1.63
19	0.05	4.38	3.52	3.13	2.90	2.74	2.63	2.54	2.48	2.42	2.38	2.31	2.23	2.16	2.11	2.07	2.03	1.98	1.93	1.88
19	0.03	5.92	4.51	3.90	3.56	3.33	3.17	3.05	2.96	2.88	2.82	2.72	2.62	2.51	2.45	2.39	2.33	2.27	2.20	2.13
19	0.01	8.18	5.93	5.01	4.50	4.17	3.94	3.77	3.63	3.52	3.43	3.30	3.15	3.00	2.92	2.84	2.76	2.67	2.58	2.49
19	0.001	15.08	10.16	8.28	7.27	6.62	6.18	5.85	5.59	5.39	5.22	4.97	4.70	4.43	4.29	4.14	3.99	3.84	3.68	3.52
20	0.25	1.40	1.49	1.48	1.47	1.45	1.44	1.43	1.42	1.41	1.40	1.39	1.37	1.36	1.35	1.34	1.33	1.32	1.31	1.29
20	0.10	2.97	2.59	2.38	2.25	2.16	2.09	2.04	2.00	1.96	1.94	1.89	1.84	1.79	1.77	1.74	1.71	1.68	1.64	1.61
20	0.05	4.35	3.49	3.10	2.87	2.71	2.60	2.51	2.45	2.39	2.35	2.28	2.20	2.12	2.08	2.04	1.99	1.95	1.90	1.84
20	0.03	5.87	4.46	3.86	3.51	3.29	3.13	3.01	2.91	2.84	2.77	2.68	2.57	2.46	2.41	2.35	2.29	2.22	2.16	2.09
20	0.01	8.10	5.85	4.94	4.43	4.10	3.87	3.70	3.56	3.46	3.37	3.23	3.09	2.94	2.86	2.78	2.69	2.61	2.52	2.42
20	0.001	14.82	9.95	8.10	7.10	6.46	6.02	5.69	5.44	5.24	5.08	4.82	4.56	4.29	4.15	4.00	3.86	3.70	3.54	3.38
22	0.25	1.40	1.48	1.47	1.45	1.44	1.42	1.41	1.40	1.39	1.39	1.37	1.36	1.34	1.33	1.32	1.31	1.30	1.29	1.28
22	0.10	2.95	2.56	2.35	2.22	2.13	2.06	2.01	1.97	1.93	1.90	1.86	1.81	1.76	1.73	1.70	1.67	1.64	1.60	1.57
22	0.05	4.30	3.44	3.05	2.82	2.66	2.55	2.46	2.40	2.34	2.30	2.23	2.15	2.07	2.03	1.98	1.94	1.89	1.84	1.78
22	0.03	5.79	4.38	3.78	3.44	3.22	3.05	2.93	2.84	2.76	2.70	2.60	2.50	2.39	2.33	2.27	2.21	2.14	2.08	2.00
22	0.01	7.95	5.72	4.82	4.31	3.99	3.76	3.59	3.45	3.35	3.26	3.12	2.98	2.83	2.75	2.67	2.58	2.50	2.40	2.31
22	0.001	14.38	9.61	7.80	6.81	6.19	5.76	5.44	5.19	4.99	4.83	4.58	4.33	4.06	3.92	3.78	3.63	3.48	3.32	3.15

(continued)

df FOR DENOM	α	df FOR NUMERATOR																		
		1	2	3	4	5	6	7	8	9	10	12	15	20	24	30	40	60	120	10000
24	0.25	1.39	1.47	1.46	1.44	1.43	1.41	1.40	1.39	1.38	1.38	1.36	1.35	1.33	1.32	1.31	1.30	1.29	1.28	1.26
24	0.10	2.93	2.54	2.33	2.19	2.10	2.04	1.98	1.94	1.91	1.88	1.83	1.78	1.73	1.70	1.67	1.64	1.61	1.57	1.53
24	0.05	4.26	3.40	3.01	2.78	2.62	2.51	2.42	2.36	2.30	2.25	2.18	2.11	2.03	1.98	1.94	1.89	1.84	1.79	1.73
24	0.03	5.72	4.32	3.72	3.38	3.15	2.99	2.87	2.78	2.70	2.64	2.54	2.44	2.33	2.27	2.21	2.15	2.08	2.01	1.94
24	0.01	7.82	5.61	4.72	4.22	3.90	3.67	3.50	3.36	3.26	3.17	3.03	2.89	2.74	2.66	2.58	2.49	2.40	2.31	2.21
24	0.001	14.03	9.34	7.55	6.59	5.98	5.55	5.24	4.99	4.80	4.64	4.39	4.14	3.87	3.74	3.59	3.45	3.29	3.14	2.97
26	0.25	1.38	1.46	1.45	1.44	1.42	1.41	1.39	1.38	1.37	1.37	1.35	1.34	1.32	1.31	1.30	1.29	1.28	1.26	1.25
26	0.10	2.91	2.52	2.31	2.17	2.08	2.01	1.96	1.92	1.88	1.86	1.81	1.76	1.71	1.68	1.65	1.61	1.58	1.54	1.50
26	0.05	4.23	3.37	2.98	2.74	2.59	2.47	2.39	2.32	2.27	2.22	2.15	2.07	1.99	1.95	1.90	1.85	1.80	1.75	1.69
26	0.03	5.66	4.27	3.67	3.33	3.10	2.94	2.82	2.73	2.65	2.59	2.49	2.39	2.28	2.22	2.16	2.09	2.03	1.95	1.88
26	0.01	7.72	5.53	4.64	4.14	3.82	3.59	3.42	3.29	3.18	3.09	2.96	2.81	2.66	2.58	2.50	2.42	2.33	2.23	2.13
26	0.001	13.74	9.12	7.36	6.41	5.80	5.38	5.07	4.83	4.64	4.48	4.24	3.99	3.72	3.59	3.44	3.30	3.15	2.99	2.82
28	0.25	1.38	1.46	1.45	1.43	1.41	1.40	1.39	1.38	1.37	1.36	1.34	1.33	1.31	1.30	1.29	1.28	1.27	1.25	1.24
28	0.10	2.89	2.50	2.29	2.16	2.06	2.00	1.94	1.90	1.87	1.84	1.79	1.74	1.69	1.66	1.63	1.59	1.56	1.52	1.48
28	0.05	4.20	3.34	2.95	2.71	2.56	2.45	2.36	2.29	2.24	2.19	2.12	2.04	1.96	1.91	1.87	1.82	1.77	1.71	1.65
28	0.03	5.61	4.22	3.63	3.29	3.06	2.90	2.78	2.69	2.61	2.55	2.45	2.34	2.23	2.17	2.11	2.05	1.98	1.91	1.83
28	0.01	7.64	5.45	4.57	4.07	3.75	3.53	3.36	3.23	3.12	3.03	2.90	2.75	2.60	2.52	2.44	2.35	2.26	2.17	2.07
28	0.001	13.50	8.93	7.19	6.25	5.66	5.24	4.93	4.69	4.50	4.35	4.11	3.86	3.60	3.46	3.32	3.18	3.02	2.86	2.70
30	0.25	1.38	1.45	1.44	1.42	1.41	1.39	1.38	1.37	1.36	1.35	1.34	1.32	1.30	1.29	1.28	1.27	1.26	1.24	1.23
30	0.10	2.88	2.49	2.28	2.14	2.05	1.98	1.93	1.88	1.85	1.82	1.77	1.72	1.67	1.64	1.61	1.57	1.54	1.50	1.46
30	0.05	4.17	3.32	2.92	2.69	2.53	2.42	2.33	2.27	2.21	2.16	2.09	2.01	1.93	1.89	1.84	1.79	1.74	1.68	1.62
30	0.03	5.57	4.18	3.59	3.25	3.03	2.87	2.75	2.65	2.57	2.51	2.41	2.31	2.20	2.14	2.07	2.01	1.94	1.87	1.79
30	0.01	7.56	5.39	4.51	4.02	3.70	3.47	3.30	3.17	3.07	2.98	2.84	2.70	2.55	2.47	2.39	2.30	2.21	2.11	2.01
30	0.001	13.29	8.77	7.05	6.12	5.53	5.12	4.82	4.58	4.39	4.24	4.00	3.75	3.49	3.36	3.22	3.07	2.92	2.76	2.59
40	0.25	1.36	1.44	1.42	1.40	1.39	1.37	1.36	1.35	1.34	1.33	1.31	1.30	1.28	1.26	1.25	1.24	1.22	1.21	1.19
40	0.10	2.84	2.44	2.23	2.09	2.00	1.93	1.87	1.83	1.79	1.76	1.71	1.66	1.61	1.57	1.54	1.51	1.47	1.42	1.38
40	0.05	4.08	3.23	2.84	2.61	2.45	2.34	2.25	2.18	2.12	2.08	2.00	1.92	1.84	1.79	1.74	1.69	1.64	1.58	1.51
40	0.03	5.42	4.05	3.46	3.13	2.90	2.74	2.62	2.53	2.45	2.39	2.29	2.18	2.07	2.01	1.94	1.88	1.80	1.72	1.64
40	0.01	7.31	5.18	4.31	3.83	3.51	3.29	3.12	2.99	2.89	2.80	2.66	2.52	2.37	2.29	2.20	2.11	2.02	1.92	1.81
40	0.001	12.61	8.25	6.59	5.70	5.13	4.73	4.44	4.21	4.02	3.87	3.64	3.40	3.15	3.01	2.87	2.73	2.57	2.41	2.23
60	0.25	1.35	1.42	1.41	1.38	1.37	1.35	1.33	1.32	1.31	1.30	1.29	1.27	1.25	1.24	1.22	1.21	1.19	1.17	1.15
60	0.10	2.79	2.39	2.18	2.04	1.95	1.87	1.82	1.77	1.74	1.71	1.66	1.60	1.54	1.51	1.48	1.44	1.40	1.35	1.29
60	0.05	4.00	3.15	2.76	2.53	2.37	2.25	2.17	2.10	2.04	1.99	1.92	1.84	1.75	1.70	1.65	1.59	1.53	1.47	1.39
60	0.03	5.29	3.93	3.34	3.01	2.79	2.63	2.51	2.41	2.33	2.27	2.17	2.06	1.94	1.88	1.82	1.74	1.67	1.58	1.48
60	0.01	7.08	4.98	4.13	3.65	3.34	3.12	2.95	2.82	2.72	2.63	2.50	2.35	2.20	2.12	2.03	1.94	1.84	1.73	1.60
60	0.001	11.97	7.77	6.17	5.31	4.76	4.37	4.09	3.86	3.69	3.54	3.32	3.08	2.83	2.69	2.55	2.41	2.25	2.08	1.89
120	0.25	1.34	1.40	1.39	1.37	1.35	1.33	1.31	1.30	1.29	1.28	1.26	1.24	1.22	1.21	1.19	1.18	1.16	1.13	1.10
120	0.10	2.75	2.35	2.13	1.99	1.90	1.82	1.77	1.72	1.68	1.65	1.60	1.55	1.48	1.45	1.41	1.37	1.32	1.26	1.19
120	0.05	3.92	3.07	2.68	2.45	2.29	2.18	2.09	2.02	1.96	1.91	1.83	1.75	1.66	1.61	1.55	1.50	1.43	1.35	1.26
120	0.03	5.15	3.80	3.23	2.89	2.67	2.52	2.39	2.30	2.22	2.16	2.05	1.94	1.82	1.76	1.69	1.61	1.53	1.43	1.31
120	0.01	6.85	4.79	3.95	3.48	3.17	2.96	2.79	2.66	2.56	2.47	2.34	2.19	2.03	1.95	1.86	1.76	1.66	1.53	1.38
120	0.001	11.38	7.32	5.78	4.95	4.42	4.04	3.77	3.55	3.38	3.24	3.02	2.78	2.53	2.40	2.26	2.11	1.95	1.77	1.55
10000	0.25	1.32	1.39	1.37	1.35	1.33	1.31	1.29	1.28	1.27	1.26	1.24	1.22	1.19	1.18	1.16	1.14	1.12	1.08	1.01
10000	0.10	2.71	2.30	2.08	1.95	1.85	1.77	1.72	1.67	1.63	1.60	1.55	1.49	1.42	1.38	1.34	1.30	1.24	1.17	1.03
10000	0.05	3.84	3.00	2.61	2.37	2.21	2.10	2.01	1.94	1.88	1.83	1.75	1.67	1.57	1.52	1.46	1.40	1.32	1.22	1.03
10000	0.03	5.03	3.69	3.12	2.79	2.57	2.41	2.29	2.19	2.11	2.05	1.95	1.83	1.71	1.64	1.57	1.49	1.39	1.27	1.04
10000	0.01	6.64	4.61	3.78	3.32	3.02	2.80	2.64	2.51	2.41	2.32	2.19	2.04	1.88	1.79	1.70	1.59	1.48	1.33	1.05
10000	0.001	10.83	6.91	5.43	4.62	4.11	3.75	3.48	3.27	3.10	2.96	2.75	2.52	2.27	2.14	1.99	1.84	1.66	1.45	1.06

Table 4. Binomial distribution table

The entries in this table give the probability of k successes in N trials where p is the probability of success on a single trial. For example, to find the probability of obtaining 2 heads in 3 coin tosses, we have $N = 3$, $k = 23$, and $p = .5$. The probability of obtaining 2 heads in 3 coin tosses is .375.

N	k	p									
		0.05	0.10	0.15	0.20	0.25	0.30	0.35	0.40	0.45	0.50
2	0	0.9025	0.8100	0.7225	0.6400	0.5625	0.4900	0.4225	0.3600	0.3025	0.2500
	1	0.0950	0.1800	0.2550	0.3200	0.3750	0.4200	0.4550	0.4800	0.4950	0.5000
	2	0.0025	0.0100	0.0225	0.0400	0.0625	0.0900	0.1225	0.1600	0.2025	0.2500
3	0	0.8574	0.7290	0.6141	0.5120	0.4219	0.3430	0.2746	0.2160	0.1664	0.1250
	1	0.1354	0.2430	0.3251	0.3840	0.4219	0.4410	0.4436	0.4320	0.4084	0.3750
	2	0.0071	0.0270	0.0574	0.0960	0.1406	0.1890	0.2389	0.2880	0.3341	0.3750
	3	0.0001	0.0010	0.0034	0.0080	0.0156	0.0270	0.0429	0.0640	0.0911	0.1250
4	0	0.8145	0.6561	0.5220	0.4096	0.3164	0.2401	0.1785	0.1296	0.0915	0.0625
	1	0.1715	0.2916	0.3685	0.4096	0.4219	0.4116	0.3845	0.3456	0.2995	0.2500
	2	0.0135	0.0486	0.0975	0.1536	0.2109	0.2646	0.3105	0.3456	0.3675	0.3750
	3	0.0005	0.0036	0.0115	0.0256	0.0469	0.0756	0.1115	0.1536	0.2005	0.2500
	4	0.0000	0.0001	0.0005	0.0016	0.0039	0.0081	0.0150	0.0256	0.0410	0.0625
5	0	0.7738	0.5905	0.4437	0.3277	0.2373	0.1681	0.1160	0.0778	0.0503	0.0313
	1	0.2036	0.3281	0.3915	0.4096	0.3955	0.3602	0.3124	0.2592	0.2059	0.1563
	2	0.0214	0.0729	0.1382	0.2048	0.2637	0.3087	0.3364	0.3456	0.3369	0.3125
	3	0.0011	0.0081	0.0244	0.0512	0.0879	0.1323	0.1811	0.2304	0.2757	0.3125
	4	0.0000	0.0005	0.0022	0.0064	0.0146	0.0284	0.0488	0.0768	0.1128	0.1563
	5	0.0000	0.0000	0.0001	0.0003	0.0010	0.0024	0.0053	0.0102	0.0185	0.0313
6	0	0.7351	0.5314	0.3771	0.2621	0.1780	0.1176	0.0754	0.0467	0.0277	0.0156
	1	0.2321	0.3543	0.3993	0.3932	0.3560	0.3025	0.2437	0.1866	0.1359	0.0938
	2	0.0305	0.0984	0.1762	0.2458	0.2966	0.3241	0.3280	0.3110	0.2780	0.2344
	3	0.0021	0.0146	0.0415	0.0819	0.1318	0.1852	0.2355	0.2765	0.3032	0.3125
	4	0.0001	0.0012	0.0055	0.0154	0.0330	0.0595	0.0951	0.1382	0.1861	0.2344
	5	0.0000	0.0001	0.0004	0.0015	0.0044	0.0102	0.0205	0.0369	0.0609	0.0938
	6	0.0000	0.0000	0.0000	0.0001	0.0002	0.0007	0.0018	0.0041	0.0083	0.0156
7	0	0.6983	0.4783	0.3206	0.2097	0.1335	0.0824	0.0490	0.0280	0.0152	0.0078
	1	0.2573	0.3720	0.3960	0.3670	0.3115	0.2471	0.1848	0.1306	0.0872	0.0547
	2	0.0406	0.1240	0.2097	0.2753	0.3115	0.3177	0.2985	0.2613	0.2140	0.1641
	3	0.0036	0.0230	0.0617	0.1147	0.1730	0.2269	0.2679	0.2903	0.2918	0.2734
	4	0.0002	0.0026	0.0109	0.0287	0.0577	0.0972	0.1442	0.1935	0.2388	0.2734
	5	0.0000	0.0002	0.0012	0.0043	0.0115	0.0250	0.0466	0.0774	0.1172	0.1641
	6	0.0000	0.0000	0.0001	0.0004	0.0013	0.0036	0.0084	0.0172	0.0320	0.0547
	7	0.0000	0.0000	0.0000	0.0000	0.0001	0.0002	0.0006	0.0016	0.0037	0.0078
8	0	0.6634	0.4305	0.2725	0.1678	0.1001	0.0576	0.0319	0.0168	0.0084	0.0039
	1	0.2793	0.3826	0.3847	0.3355	0.2670	0.1977	0.1373	0.0896	0.0548	0.0313
	2	0.0515	0.1488	0.2376	0.2936	0.3115	0.2965	0.2587	0.2090	0.1569	0.1094
	3	0.0054	0.0331	0.0839	0.1468	0.2076	0.2541	0.2786	0.2787	0.2568	0.2188
	4	0.0004	0.0046	0.0185	0.0459	0.0865	0.1361	0.1875	0.2322	0.2627	0.2734
	5	0.0000	0.0004	0.0026	0.0092	0.0231	0.0467	0.0808	0.1239	0.1719	0.2188
	6	0.0000	0.0000	0.0002	0.0011	0.0038	0.0100	0.0217	0.0413	0.0703	0.1094
	7	0.0000	0.0000	0.0000	0.0001	0.0004	0.0012	0.0033	0.0079	0.0164	0.0313
	8	0.0000	0.0000	0.0000	0.0000	0.0000	0.0001	0.0002	0.0007	0.0017	0.0039

(*continued*)

N	k					p					
		0.05	0.10	0.15	0.20	0.25	0.30	0.35	0.40	0.45	0.50
9	0	0.6302	0.3874	0.2316	0.1342	0.0751	0.0404	0.0207	0.0101	0.0046	0.0020
	1	0.2985	0.3874	0.3679	0.3020	0.2253	0.1556	0.1004	0.0605	0.0339	0.0176
	2	0.0629	0.1722	0.2597	0.3020	0.3003	0.2668	0.2162	0.1612	0.1110	0.0703
	3	0.0077	0.0446	0.1069	0.1762	0.2336	0.2668	0.2716	0.2508	0.2119	0.1641
	4	0.0006	0.0074	0.0283	0.0661	0.1168	0.1715	0.2194	0.2508	0.2600	0.2461
	5	0.0000	0.0008	0.0050	0.0165	0.0389	0.0735	0.1181	0.1672	0.2128	0.2461
	6	0.0000	0.0001	0.0006	0.0028	0.0087	0.0210	0.0424	0.0743	0.1160	0.1641
	7	0.0000	0.0000	0.0000	0.0003	0.0012	0.0039	0.0098	0.0212	0.0407	0.0703
	8	0.0000	0.0000	0.0000	0.0000	0.0001	0.0004	0.0013	0.0035	0.0083	0.0176
	9	0.0000	0.0000	0.0000	0.0000	0.0000	0.0000	0.0001	0.0003	0.0008	0.0020
10	0	0.5987	0.3487	0.1969	0.1074	0.0563	0.0282	0.0135	0.0060	0.0025	0.0010
	1	0.3151	0.3874	0.3474	0.2684	0.1877	0.1211	0.0725	0.0403	0.0207	0.0098
	2	0.0746	0.1937	0.2759	0.3020	0.2816	0.2335	0.1757	0.1209	0.0763	0.0439
	3	0.0105	0.0574	0.1298	0.2013	0.2503	0.2668	0.2522	0.2150	0.1665	0.1172
	4	0.0010	0.0112	0.0401	0.0881	0.1460	0.2001	0.2377	0.2508	0.2384	0.2051
	5	0.0001	0.0015	0.0085	0.0264	0.0584	0.1029	0.1536	0.2007	0.2340	0.2461
	6	0.0000	0.0001	0.0012	0.0055	0.0162	0.0368	0.0689	0.1115	0.1596	0.2051
	7	0.0000	0.0000	0.0001	0.0008	0.0031	0.0090	0.0212	0.0425	0.0746	0.1172
	8	0.0000	0.0000	0.0000	0.0001	0.0004	0.0014	0.0043	0.0106	0.0229	0.0439
	9	0.0000	0.0000	0.0000	0.0000	0.0000	0.0001	0.0005	0.0016	0.0042	0.0098
	10	0.0000	0.0000	0.0000	0.0000	0.0000	0.0000	0.0000	0.0001	0.0003	0.0010
11	0	0.5688	0.3138	0.1673	0.0859	0.0422	0.0198	0.0088	0.0036	0.0014	0.0005
	1	0.3293	0.3835	0.3248	0.2362	0.1549	0.0932	0.0518	0.0266	0.0125	0.0054
	2	0.0867	0.2131	0.2866	0.2953	0.2581	0.1998	0.1395	0.0887	0.0513	0.0269
	3	0.0137	0.0710	0.1517	0.2215	0.2581	0.2568	0.2254	0.1774	0.1259	0.0806
	4	0.0014	0.0158	0.0536	0.1107	0.1721	0.2201	0.2428	0.2365	0.2060	0.1611
	5	0.0001	0.0025	0.0132	0.0388	0.0803	0.1321	0.1830	0.2207	0.2360	0.2256
	6	0.0000	0.0003	0.0023	0.0097	0.0268	0.0566	0.0985	0.1471	0.1931	0.2256
	7	0.0000	0.0000	0.0003	0.0017	0.0064	0.0173	0.0379	0.0701	0.1128	0.1611
	8	0.0000	0.0000	0.0000	0.0002	0.0011	0.0037	0.0102	0.0234	0.0462	0.0806
	9	0.0000	0.0000	0.0000	0.0000	0.0001	0.0005	0.0018	0.0052	0.0126	0.0269
	10	0.0000	0.0000	0.0000	0.0000	0.0000	0.0000	0.0002	0.0007	0.0021	0.0054
	11	0.0000	0.0000	0.0000	0.0000	0.0000	0.0000	0.0000	0.0000	0.0002	0.0005
12	0	0.5404	0.2824	0.1422	0.0687	0.0317	0.0138	0.0057	0.0022	0.0008	0.0002
	1	0.3413	0.3766	0.3012	0.2062	0.1267	0.0712	0.0368	0.0174	0.0075	0.0029
	2	0.0988	0.2301	0.2924	0.2835	0.2323	0.1678	0.1088	0.0639	0.0339	0.0161
	3	0.0173	0.0852	0.1720	0.2362	0.2581	0.2397	0.1954	0.1419	0.0923	0.0537
	4	0.0021	0.0213	0.0683	0.1329	0.1936	0.2311	0.2367	0.2128	0.1700	0.1208
	5	0.0002	0.0038	0.0193	0.0532	0.1032	0.1585	0.2039	0.2270	0.2225	0.1934
	6	0.0000	0.0005	0.0040	0.0155	0.0401	0.0792	0.1281	0.1766	0.2124	0.2256
	7	0.0000	0.0000	0.0006	0.0033	0.0115	0.0291	0.0591	0.1009	0.1489	0.1934
	8	0.0000	0.0000	0.0001	0.0005	0.0024	0.0078	0.0199	0.0420	0.0762	0.1208
	9	0.0000	0.0000	0.0000	0.0001	0.0004	0.0015	0.0048	0.0125	0.0277	0.0537
	10	0.0000	0.0000	0.0000	0.0000	0.0000	0.0002	0.0008	0.0025	0.0068	0.0161
	11	0.0000	0.0000	0.0000	0.0000	0.0000	0.0000	0.0001	0.0003	0.0010	0.0029
	12	0.0000	0.0000	0.0000	0.0000	0.0000	0.0000	0.0000	0.0000	0.0001	0.0002
13	0	0.5133	0.2542	0.1209	0.0550	0.0238	0.0097	0.0037	0.0013	0.0004	0.0001
	1	0.3512	0.3672	0.2774	0.1787	0.1029	0.0540	0.0259	0.0113	0.0045	0.0016
	2	0.1109	0.2448	0.2937	0.2680	0.2059	0.1388	0.0836	0.0453	0.0220	0.0095
	3	0.0214	0.0997	0.1900	0.2457	0.2517	0.2181	0.1651	0.1107	0.0660	0.0349
	4	0.0028	0.0277	0.0838	0.1535	0.2097	0.2337	0.2222	0.1845	0.1350	0.0873
	5	0.0003	0.0055	0.0266	0.0691	0.1258	0.1803	0.2154	0.2214	0.1989	0.1571

N	k	0.05	0.10	0.15	0.20	0.25	0.30	0.35	0.40	0.45	0.50
							p				
	6	0.0000	0.0008	0.0063	0.0230	0.0559	0.1030	0.1546	0.1968	0.2169	0.2095
	7	0.0000	0.0001	0.0011	0.0058	0.0186	0.0442	0.0833	0.1312	0.1775	0.2095
	8	0.0000	0.0000	0.0001	0.0011	0.0047	0.0142	0.0336	0.0656	0.1089	0.1571
	9	0.0000	0.0000	0.0000	0.0001	0.0009	0.0034	0.0101	0.0243	0.0495	0.0873
	10	0.0000	0.0000	0.0000	0.0000	0.0001	0.0006	0.0022	0.0065	0.0162	0.0349
	11	0.0000	0.0000	0.0000	0.0000	0.0000	0.0001	0.0003	0.0012	0.0036	0.0095
	12	0.0000	0.0000	0.0000	0.0000	0.0000	0.0000	0.0000	0.0001	0.0005	0.0016
	13	0.0000	0.0000	0.0000	0.0000	0.0000	0.0000	0.0000	0.0000	0.0000	0.0001
14	0	0.4877	0.2288	0.1028	0.0440	0.0178	0.0068	0.0024	0.0008	0.0002	0.0001
	1	0.3593	0.3559	0.2539	0.1539	0.0832	0.0407	0.0181	0.0073	0.0027	0.0009
	2	0.1229	0.2570	0.2912	0.2501	0.1802	0.1134	0.0634	0.0317	0.0141	0.0056
	3	0.0259	0.1142	0.2056	0.2501	0.2402	0.1943	0.1366	0.0845	0.0462	0.0222
	4	0.0037	0.0349	0.0998	0.1720	0.2202	0.2290	0.2022	0.1549	0.1040	0.0611
	5	0.0004	0.0078	0.0352	0.0860	0.1468	0.1963	0.2178	0.2066	0.1701	0.1222
	6	0.0000	0.0013	0.0093	0.0322	0.0734	0.1262	0.1759	0.2066	0.2088	0.1833
	7	0.0000	0.0002	0.0019	0.0092	0.0280	0.0618	0.1082	0.1574	0.1952	0.2095
	8	0.0000	0.0000	0.0003	0.0020	0.0082	0.0232	0.0510	0.0918	0.1398	0.1833
	9	0.0000	0.0000	0.0000	0.0003	0.0018	0.0066	0.0183	0.0408	0.0762	0.1222
	10	0.0000	0.0000	0.0000	0.0000	0.0003	0.0014	0.0049	0.0136	0.0312	0.0611
	11	0.0000	0.0000	0.0000	0.0000	0.0000	0.0002	0.0010	0.0033	0.0093	0.0222
	12	0.0000	0.0000	0.0000	0.0000	0.0000	0.0000	0.0001	0.0005	0.0019	0.0056
	13	0.0000	0.0000	0.0000	0.0000	0.0000	0.0000	0.0000	0.0001	0.0002	0.0009
	14	0.0000	0.0000	0.0000	0.0000	0.0000	0.0000	0.0000	0.0000	0.0000	0.0001
15	0	0.4633	0.2059	0.0874	0.0352	0.0134	0.0047	0.0016	0.0005	0.0001	0.0000
	1	0.3658	0.3432	0.2312	0.1319	0.0668	0.0305	0.0126	0.0047	0.0016	0.0005
	2	0.1348	0.2669	0.2856	0.2309	0.1559	0.0916	0.0476	0.0219	0.0090	0.0032
	3	0.0307	0.1285	0.2184	0.2501	0.2252	0.1700	0.1110	0.0634	0.0318	0.0139
	4	0.0049	0.0428	0.1156	0.1876	0.2252	0.2186	0.1792	0.1268	0.0780	0.0417
	5	0.0006	0.0105	0.0449	0.1032	0.1651	0.2061	0.2123	0.1859	0.1404	0.0916
	6	0.0000	0.0019	0.0132	0.0430	0.0917	0.1472	0.1906	0.2066	0.1914	0.1527
	7	0.0000	0.0003	0.0030	0.0138	0.0393	0.0811	0.1319	0.1771	0.2013	0.1964
	8	0.0000	0.0000	0.0005	0.0035	0.0131	0.0348	0.0710	0.1181	0.1647	0.1964
	9	0.0000	0.0000	0.0001	0.0007	0.0034	0.0116	0.0298	0.0612	0.1048	0.1527
	10	0.0000	0.0000	0.0000	0.0001	0.0007	0.0030	0.0096	0.0245	0.0515	0.0916
	11	0.0000	0.0000	0.0000	0.0000	0.0001	0.0006	0.0024	0.0074	0.0191	0.0417
	12	0.0000	0.0000	0.0000	0.0000	0.0000	0.0001	0.0004	0.0016	0.0052	0.0139
	13	0.0000	0.0000	0.0000	0.0000	0.0000	0.0000	0.0001	0.0003	0.0010	0.0032
	14	0.0000	0.0000	0.0000	0.0000	0.0000	0.0000	0.0000	0.0000	0.0001	0.0005
	15	0.0000	0.0000	0.0000	0.0000	0.0000	0.0000	0.0000	0.0000	0.0000	0.0000
16	0	0.4401	0.1853	0.0743	0.0281	0.0100	0.0033	0.0010	0.0003	0.0001	0.0000
	1	0.3706	0.3294	0.2097	0.1126	0.0535	0.0228	0.0087	0.0030	0.0009	0.0002
	2	0.1463	0.2745	0.2775	0.2111	0.1336	0.0732	0.0353	0.0150	0.0056	0.0018
	3	0.0359	0.1423	0.2285	0.2463	0.2079	0.1465	0.0888	0.0468	0.0215	0.0085
	4	0.0061	0.0514	0.1311	0.2001	0.2252	0.2040	0.1553	0.1014	0.0572	0.0278
	5	0.0008	0.0137	0.0555	0.1201	0.1802	0.2099	0.2008	0.1623	0.1123	0.0667
	6	0.0001	0.0028	0.0180	0.0550	0.1101	0.1649	0.1982	0.1983	0.1684	0.1222
	7	0.0000	0.0004	0.0045	0.0197	0.0524	0.1010	0.1524	0.1889	0.1969	0.1746
	8	0.0000	0.0001	0.0009	0.0055	0.0197	0.0487	0.0923	0.1417	0.1812	0.1964
	9	0.0000	0.0000	0.0001	0.0012	0.0058	0.0185	0.0442	0.0840	0.1318	0.1746
	10	0.0000	0.0000	0.0000	0.0002	0.0014	0.0056	0.0167	0.0392	0.0755	0.1222
	11	0.0000	0.0000	0.0000	0.0000	0.0002	0.0013	0.0049	0.0142	0.0337	0.0667
	12	0.0000	0.0000	0.0000	0.0000	0.0000	0.0002	0.0011	0.0040	0.0115	0.0278

(continued)

N	k	0.05	0.10	0.15	0.20	0.25	0.30	0.35	0.40	0.45	0.50
						p					
	13	0.0000	0.0000	0.0000	0.0000	0.0000	0.0000	0.0002	0.0008	0.0029	0.0085
	14	0.0000	0.0000	0.0000	0.0000	0.0000	0.0000	0.0000	0.0001	0.0005	0.0018
	15	0.0000	0.0000	0.0000	0.0000	0.0000	0.0000	0.0000	0.0000	0.0001	0.0002
	16	0.0000	0.0000	0.0000	0.0000	0.0000	0.0000	0.0000	0.0000	0.0000	0.0000
17	0	0.4181	0.1668	0.0631	0.0225	0.0075	0.0023	0.0007	0.0002	0.0000	0.0000
	1	0.3741	0.3150	0.1893	0.0957	0.0426	0.0169	0.0060	0.0019	0.0005	0.0001
	2	0.1575	0.2800	0.2673	0.1914	0.1136	0.0581	0.0260	0.0102	0.0035	0.0010
	3	0.0415	0.1556	0.2359	0.2393	0.1893	0.1245	0.0701	0.0341	0.0144	0.0052
	4	0.0076	0.0605	0.1457	0.2093	0.2209	0.1868	0.1320	0.0796	0.0411	0.0182
	5	0.0010	0.0175	0.0668	0.1361	0.1914	0.2081	0.1849	0.1379	0.0875	0.0472
	6	0.0001	0.0039	0.0236	0.0680	0.1276	0.1784	0.1991	0.1839	0.1432	0.0944
	7	0.0000	0.0007	0.0065	0.0267	0.0668	0.1201	0.1685	0.1927	0.1841	0.1484
	8	0.0000	0.0001	0.0014	0.0084	0.0279	0.0644	0.1134	0.1606	0.1883	0.1855
	9	0.0000	0.0000	0.0003	0.0021	0.0093	0.0276	0.0611	0.1070	0.1540	0.1855
	10	0.0000	0.0000	0.0000	0.0004	0.0025	0.0095	0.0263	0.0571	0.1008	0.1484
	11	0.0000	0.0000	0.0000	0.0001	0.0005	0.0026	0.0090	0.0242	0.0525	0.0944
	12	0.0000	0.0000	0.0000	0.0000	0.0001	0.0006	0.0024	0.0081	0.0215	0.0472
	13	0.0000	0.0000	0.0000	0.0000	0.0000	0.0001	0.0005	0.0021	0.0068	0.0182
	14	0.0000	0.0000	0.0000	0.0000	0.0000	0.0000	0.0001	0.0004	0.0016	0.0052
	15	0.0000	0.0000	0.0000	0.0000	0.0000	0.0000	0.0000	0.0001	0.0003	0.0010
	16	0.0000	0.0000	0.0000	0.0000	0.0000	0.0000	0.0000	0.0000	0.0000	0.0001
	17	0.0000	0.0000	0.0000	0.0000	0.0000	0.0000	0.0000	0.0000	0.0000	0.0000
18	0	0.3972	0.1501	0.0536	0.0180	0.0056	0.0016	0.0004	0.0001	0.0000	0.0000
	1	0.3763	0.3002	0.1704	0.0811	0.0338	0.0126	0.0042	0.0012	0.0003	0.0001
	2	0.1683	0.2835	0.2556	0.1723	0.0958	0.0458	0.0190	0.0069	0.0022	0.0006
	3	0.0473	0.1680	0.2406	0.2297	0.1704	0.1046	0.0547	0.0246	0.0095	0.0031
	4	0.0093	0.0700	0.1592	0.2153	0.2130	0.1681	0.1104	0.0614	0.0291	0.0117
	5	0.0014	0.0218	0.0787	0.1507	0.1988	0.2017	0.1664	0.1146	0.0666	0.0327
	6	0.0002	0.0052	0.0301	0.0816	0.1436	0.1873	0.1941	0.1655	0.1181	0.0708
	7	0.0000	0.0010	0.0091	0.0350	0.0820	0.1376	0.1792	0.1892	0.1657	0.1214
	8	0.0000	0.0002	0.0022	0.0120	0.0376	0.0811	0.1327	0.1734	0.1864	0.1669
	9	0.0000	0.0000	0.0004	0.0033	0.0139	0.0386	0.0794	0.1284	0.1694	0.1855
	10	0.0000	0.0000	0.0001	0.0008	0.0042	0.0149	0.0385	0.0771	0.1248	0.1669
	11	0.0000	0.0000	0.0000	0.0001	0.0010	0.0046	0.0151	0.0374	0.0742	0.1214
	12	0.0000	0.0000	0.0000	0.0000	0.0002	0.0012	0.0047	0.0145	0.0354	0.0708
	13	0.0000	0.0000	0.0000	0.0000	0.0000	0.0002	0.0012	0.0045	0.0134	0.0327
	14	0.0000	0.0000	0.0000	0.0000	0.0000	0.0000	0.0002	0.0011	0.0039	0.0117
	15	0.0000	0.0000	0.0000	0.0000	0.0000	0.0000	0.0000	0.0002	0.0009	0.0031
	16	0.0000	0.0000	0.0000	0.0000	0.0000	0.0000	0.0000	0.0000	0.0001	0.0006
	17	0.0000	0.0000	0.0000	0.0000	0.0000	0.0000	0.0000	0.0000	0.0000	0.0001
	18	0.0000	0.0000	0.0000	0.0000	0.0000	0.0000	0.0000	0.0000	0.0000	0.0000
19	0	0.3774	0.1351	0.0456	0.0144	0.0042	0.0011	0.0003	0.0001	0.0000	0.0000
	1	0.3774	0.2852	0.1529	0.0685	0.0268	0.0093	0.0029	0.0008	0.0002	0.0000
	2	0.1787	0.2852	0.2428	0.1540	0.0803	0.0358	0.0138	0.0046	0.0013	0.0003
	3	0.0533	0.1796	0.2428	0.2182	0.1517	0.0869	0.0422	0.0175	0.0062	0.0018
	4	0.0112	0.0798	0.1714	0.2182	0.2023	0.1491	0.0909	0.0467	0.0203	0.0074
	5	0.0018	0.0266	0.0907	0.1636	0.2023	0.1916	0.1468	0.0933	0.0497	0.0222
	6	0.0002	0.0069	0.0374	0.0955	0.1574	0.1916	0.1844	0.1451	0.0949	0.0518
	7	0.0000	0.0014	0.0122	0.0443	0.0974	0.1525	0.1844	0.1797	0.1443	0.0961
	8	0.0000	0.0002	0.0032	0.0166	0.0487	0.0981	0.1489	0.1797	0.1771	0.1442
	9	0.0000	0.0000	0.0007	0.0051	0.0198	0.0514	0.0980	0.1464	0.1771	0.1762
	10	0.0000	0.0000	0.0001	0.0013	0.0066	0.0220	0.0528	0.0976	0.1449	0.1762
	11	0.0000	0.0000	0.0000	0.0003	0.0018	0.0077	0.0233	0.0532	0.0970	0.1442

N	k	p									
		0.05	0.10	0.15	0.20	0.25	0.30	0.35	0.40	0.45	0.50
	12	0.0000	0.0000	0.0000	0.0000	0.0004	0.0022	0.0083	0.0237	0.0529	0.0961
	13	0.0000	0.0000	0.0000	0.0000	0.0001	0.0005	0.0024	0.0085	0.0233	0.0518
	14	0.0000	0.0000	0.0000	0.0000	0.0000	0.0001	0.0006	0.0024	0.0082	0.0222
	15	0.0000	0.0000	0.0000	0.0000	0.0000	0.0000	0.0001	0.0005	0.0022	0.0074
	16	0.0000	0.0000	0.0000	0.0000	0.0000	0.0000	0.0000	0.0001	0.0005	0.0018
	17	0.0000	0.0000	0.0000	0.0000	0.0000	0.0000	0.0000	0.0000	0.0001	0.0003
	18	0.0000	0.0000	0.0000	0.0000	0.0000	0.0000	0.0000	0.0000	0.0000	0.0000
	19	0.0000	0.0000	0.0000	0.0000	0.0000	0.0000	0.0000	0.0000	0.0000	0.0000
20	0	0.3585	0.1216	0.0388	0.0115	0.0032	0.0008	0.0002	0.0000	0.0000	0.0000
	1	0.3774	0.2702	0.1368	0.0576	0.0211	0.0068	0.0020	0.0005	0.0001	0.0000
	2	0.1887	0.2852	0.2293	0.1369	0.0669	0.0278	0.0100	0.0031	0.0008	0.0002
	3	0.0596	0.1901	0.2428	0.2054	0.1339	0.0716	0.0323	0.0123	0.0040	0.0011
	4	0.0133	0.0898	0.1821	0.2182	0.1897	0.1304	0.0738	0.0350	0.0139	0.0046
	5	0.0022	0.0319	0.1028	0.1746	0.2023	0.1789	0.1272	0.0746	0.0365	0.0148
	6	0.0003	0.0089	0.0454	0.1091	0.1686	0.1916	0.1712	0.1244	0.0746	0.0370
	7	0.0000	0.0020	0.0160	0.0545	0.1124	0.1643	0.1844	0.1659	0.1221	0.0739
	8	0.0000	0.0004	0.0046	0.0222	0.0609	0.1144	0.1614	0.1797	0.1623	0.1201
	9	0.0000	0.0001	0.0011	0.0074	0.0271	0.0654	0.1158	0.1597	0.1771	0.1602
	10	0.0000	0.0000	0.0002	0.0020	0.0099	0.0308	0.0686	0.1171	0.1593	0.1762
	11	0.0000	0.0000	0.0000	0.0005	0.0030	0.0120	0.0336	0.0710	0.1185	0.1602
	12	0.0000	0.0000	0.0000	0.0001	0.0008	0.0039	0.0136	0.0355	0.0727	0.1201
	13	0.0000	0.0000	0.0000	0.0000	0.0002	0.0010	0.0045	0.0146	0.0366	0.0739
	14	0.0000	0.0000	0.0000	0.0000	0.0000	0.0002	0.0012	0.0049	0.0150	0.0370
	15	0.0000	0.0000	0.0000	0.0000	0.0000	0.0000	0.0003	0.0013	0.0049	0.0148
	16	0.0000	0.0000	0.0000	0.0000	0.0000	0.0000	0.0000	0.0003	0.0013	0.0046
	17	0.0000	0.0000	0.0000	0.0000	0.0000	0.0000	0.0000	0.0000	0.0002	0.0011
	18	0.0000	0.0000	0.0000	0.0000	0.0000	0.0000	0.0000	0.0000	0.0002	0.0011
	19	0.0000	0.0000	0.0000	0.0000	0.0000	0.0000	0.0000	0.0000	0.0000	0.0000
	20	0.0000	0.0000	0.0000	0.0000	0.0000	0.0000	0.0000	0.0000	0.0000	0.0000

Table 5. Chi-square distribution values for right-tailed areas

[For example, the area to the right of $\chi^2 = 3.841$ with $df = 1$ is .05.]

df	0.10	0.05	0.025	0.01	0.001
1	2.706	3.841	5.024	6.635	10.83
2	4.605	5.991	7.378	9.210	13.82
3	6.251	7.815	9.348	11.34	16.27
4	7.779	9.488	11.14	13.28	18.47
5	9.236	11.07	12.83	15.09	20.51
6	10.64	12.59	14.45	16.81	22.46
7	12.02	14.07	16.01	18.48	24.32
8	13.36	15.51	17.53	20.09	26.12
9	14.68	16.92	19.02	21.67	27.88
10	15.99	18.31	20.48	23.21	29.59
11	17.28	19.68	21.92	24.73	31.26
12	18.55	21.03	23.34	26.22	32.91
13	19.81	22.36	24.74	27.69	34.53
14	21.06	23.68	26.12	29.14	36.12
15	22.31	25.00	27.49	30.58	37.70
16	23.54	26.30	28.85	32.00	39.25
17	24.77	27.59	30.19	33.41	40.79
18	25.99	28.87	31.53	34.81	42.31
19	27.20	30.14	32.85	36.19	43.82
20	28.41	31.41	34.17	37.57	45.31
21	29.62	32.67	35.48	38.93	46.80
22	30.81	33.92	36.78	40.29	48.27
23	32.01	35.17	38.08	41.64	49.73
24	33.20	36.42	39.36	42.98	51.18
25	34.38	37.65	40.65	44.31	52.62
26	35.56	38.89	41.92	45.64	54.05
27	36.74	40.11	43.19	46.96	55.48
28	37.92	41.34	44.46	48.28	56.89
29	39.09	42.56	45.72	49.59	58.30
30	40.26	43.77	46.98	50.89	59.70
32	42.58	46.19	49.48	53.49	62.49
34	44.90	48.60	51.97	56.06	65.25
36	47.21	51.00	54.44	58.62	67.98
38	49.51	53.38	56.90	61.16	70.70
40	51.81	55.76	59.34	63.69	73.40
50	63.17	67.50	71.42	76.15	86.66
60	74.40	79.08	83.30	88.38	99.61
70	85.53	90.53	95.02	100.4	112.3
80	96.58	101.9	106.6	112.3	124.8
90	107.6	113.1	118.1	124.1	137.2
100	118.5	124.3	129.6	135.8	149.4

Table 6. The critical q-values[a]

df_w	α	K (number of groups)									
		2	3	4	5	6	7	8	9	10	11
5	.05	3.64	4.60	5.22	5.67	6.03	6.33	6.58	6.80	6.99	7.17
	.01	5.70	6.98	7.80	8.42	8.91	9.32	9.67	9.97	10.24	10.48
6	.05	3.46	4.34	4.90	5.30	5.63	5.90	6.12	6.32	6.49	6.65
	.01	5.24	6.33	7.03	7.56	7.97	8.32	8.61	8.87	9.10	9.30
7	.05	3.34	4.16	4.68	5.06	5.36	5.61	5.82	6.00	6.16	6.30
	.01	4.95	5.92	6.54	7.01	7.37	7.68	7.94	8.17	8.37	8.55
8	.05	3.26	4.04	4.53	4.89	5.17	5.40	5.60	5.77	5.92	6.05
	.01	4.75	5.64	6.20	6.62	6.96	7.24	7.47	7.68	7.86	8.03
9	.05	3.20	3.95	4.41	4.76	5.02	5.24	5.43	5.59	5.74	5.87
	.01	4.60	5.43	5.96	6.35	6.66	6.91	7.13	7.33	7.49	7.65
10	.05	3.15	3.88	4.33	4.65	4.91	5.12	5.30	5.46	5.60	5.72
	.01	4.48	5.27	5.77	6.14	6.43	6.67	6.87	7.05	7.21	7.36
11	.05	3.11	3.82	4.26	4.57	4.82	5.03	5.20	5.35	5.49	5.61
	.01	4.39	5.15	5.62	5.97	6.25	6.48	6.67	6.84	6.99	7.13
12	.05	3.08	3.77	4.20	4.51	4.75	4.95	5.12	5.27	5.39	5.51
	.01	4.32	5.05	5.50	5.84	6.10	6.32	6.51	6.67	6.81	6.94
13	.05	3.06	3.73	4.15	4.45	4.69	4.88	5.05	5.19	5.32	5.43
	.01	4.26	4.96	5.40	5.73	5.98	6.19	6.37	6.53	6.67	6.79
14	.05	3.03	3.70	4.11	4.41	4.64	4.83	4.99	5.13	5.25	5.36
	.01	4.21	4.89	5.32	5.63	5.88	6.08	6.26	6.41	6.54	6.66
15	.05	3.01	3.67	4.08	4.37	4.59	4.78	4.94	5.08	5.20	5.31
	.01	4.17	4.84	5.25	5.56	5.80	5.99	6.16	6.31	6.44	6.55
16	.05	3.00	3.65	4.05	4.33	4.56	4.74	4.90	5.03	5.15	5.26
	.01	4.13	4.79	5.19	5.49	5.72	5.92	6.08	6.22	6.35	6.46
17	.05	2.98	3.63	4.02	4.30	4.52	4.70	4.86	4.99	5.11	5.21
	.01	4.10	4.74	5.14	5.43	5.66	5.85	6.01	6.15	6.27	6.38
18	.05	2.97	3.61	4.00	4.28	4.49	4.67	4.82	4.96	5.07	5.17
	.01	4.07	4.70	5.09	5.38	5.60	5.79	5.94	6.08	6.20	6.31
19	.05	2.96	3.59	3.98	4.25	4.47	4.65	4.79	4.92	5.04	5.14
	.01	4.05	4.67	5.05	5.33	5.55	5.73	5.89	6.02	6.14	6.25
20	.05	2.95	3.58	3.96	4.23	4.45	4.62	4.77	4.90	5.01	5.11
	.01	4.02	4.64	5.02	5.29	5.51	5.69	5.84	5.97	6.09	6.19
24	.05	2.92	3.53	3.90	4.17	4.37	4.54	4.68	4.81	4.92	5.01
	.01	3.96	4.55	4.91	5.17	5.37	5.54	5.69	5.81	5.92	6.02
30	.05	2.89	3.49	3.85	4.10	4.30	4.46	4.60	4.72	4.82	4.92
	.01	3.89	4.45	4.80	5.05	5.24	5.40	5.54	5.65	5.76	5.85
40	.05	2.86	3.44	3.79	4.04	4.23	4.39	4.52	4.63	4.73	4.82
	.01	3.82	4.37	4.70	4.93	5.11	5.26	5.39	5.50	5.60	5.69
60	.05	2.83	3.40	3.74	3.98	4.16	4.31	4.44	4.55	4.65	4.73
	.01	3.76	4.28	4.59	4.82	4.99	5.13	5.25	5.36	5.45	5.53
120	.05	2.80	3.36	3.68	3.92	4.10	4.24	4.36	4.47	4.56	4.64
	.01	3.70	4.20	4.50	4.71	4.87	5.01	5.12	5.21	5.30	5.37
∞	.05	2.77	3.31	3.63	3.86	4.03	4.17	4.29	4.39	4.47	4.55
	.01	3.64	4.12	4.40	4.60	4.76	4.88	4.99	5.08	5.16	5.23

[a]Adapted from E. S. Pearson and H. O. Hartley (eds.), *Biometrika Tables for Statisticians*. New York: Cambridge University Press, 1966, Vol. 1, Table 29. Used by permission.

Table 7. The critical U-values

Critical values of the U distribution (.01 level, two-tailed)[a]

n_2	1	2	3	4	5	6	7	8	9	10	11	12	13	14	15	16	17	18	19	20
	—	—	—	—	—	—	—	—	—	—	—	—	—	—	—	—	—	—	—	—
2	—	—	—	—	—	—	—	—	—	—	—	—	—	—	—	—	—	—	0	0
																			38	40
	—	—	—	—	—	—	—	—	0	0	0	1	1	1	2	2	2	2	3	3
									27	30	33	35	38	41	43	46	49	52	54	57
4	—	—	—	—	—	0	0	1	1	2	2	3	3	4	5	5	6	6	7	8
						24	28	31	35	38	42	45	49	52	55	59	62	66	69	72
5	—	—	—	—	0	1	1	2	3	4	5	6	7	7	8	9	10	11	12	13
					25	29	34	38	42	46	50	54	58	63	67	71	75	79	83	87
	—	—	—	0	1	2	3	4	5	6	7	9	10	11	12	13	15	16	17	18
				24	29	34	39	44	49	54	59	63	68	73	78	83	87	92	97	102
7	—	—	—	0	1	3	4	6	7	9	10	12	13	15	16	18	19	21	22	24
				28	34	39	45	50	56	61	67	72	78	83	89	94	100	105	111	116
	—	—	—	1	2	4	6	7	9	11	13	15	17	18	20	22	24	26	28	30
				31	38	44	50	57	63	69	75	81	87	94	100	106	112	118	124	130
	—	—	0	1	3	5	7	9	11	13	16	18	20	22	24	27	29	31	33	36
			27	35	42	49	56	63	70	77	83	90	97	104	111	117	124	131	138	144
10	—	—	0	2	4	6	9	11	13	16	18	21	24	26	29	31	34	37	39	42
			30	38	46	54	61	69	77	84	92	99	106	114	121	129	136	143	151	158
11	—	—	0	2	5	7	10	13	16	18	21	24	27	30	33	36	39	42	45	48
			33	42	50	59	67	75	83	92	100	108	116	124	132	140	148	156	164	172
	—	—	1	3	6	9	12	15	18	21	24	27	31	34	37	41	44	47	51	54
			35	45	54	63	72	81	90	99	108	117	125	134	143	151	160	169	177	186
13	—	—	1	3	7	10	13	17	20	24	27	31	34	38	42	45	49	53	56	60
			38	49	58	68	78	87	97	106	116	125	125	144	153	163	172	181	191	200
	—	—	1	4	7	11	15	18	22	26	30	34	38	42	46	50	54	58	63	67
			41	52	63	73	83	94	104	114	124	134	144	154	164	174	184	194	203	213
	=	—	2	5	8	12	16	20	24	29	33	37	42	46	51	55	60	64	69	73
			43	55	67	78	89	100	111	121	132	143	153	164	174	185	195	206	216	227
16	—	—	2	5	9	13	18	22	27	31	36	41	45	50	55	60	65	70	74	79
			46	59	71	83	94	106	117	129	140	151	163	174	185	196	207	218	230	241
	—	—	2	6	10	15	19	24	29	34	39	44	49	54	60	65	70	75	81	86
			49	62	75	87	100	112	124	136	148	160	172	184	195	207	219	231	242	254
18	—	—	2	6	11	16	21	26	31	37	42	47	53	58	64	70	75	81	87	92
			52	66	79	92	105	118	131	143	156	169	181	194	206	218	231	243	255	268
19	—	0	3	7	12	17	22	28	33	39	45	51	56	63	69	74	81	87	93	99
		38	54	69	83	97	111	124	138	151	164	177	191	203	216	230	242	255	268	281
	—	0	3	8	13	18	24	30	36	42	48	54	60	67	73	79	86	92	99	105
		40	57	72	87	102	116	130	144	158	172	186	200	213	227	241	254	268	281	295

[a] Adapted from D. V. Lindley and W. F. Scott, *New Cambridge Elementary Statistical Tables*. London: Cambridge University Press, 1984, Table 21. Used by permission.

Critical Values of the U distribution (.01 level, one-tailed) (continued)

1	2	3	4	5	6	7	8	9	10	11	12	13	14	15	16	17	18	19	20
—	—	—	—	—	—	—	—	—	—	—	—	—	—	—	—	—	—	—	—
—	—	—	—	—	—	—	—	—	—	—	—	0	0	0	0	0	0	1	1
												26	28	30	32	34	36	37	39
—	—	—	—	—	—	0	0	1	1	1	2	2	2	3	3	4	4	4	5
						21	24	26	29	32	34	37	40	42	45	47	50	52	55
—	—	—	—	0	1	1	2	3	3	4	5	5	6	7	7	8	9	9	10
				20	23	27	30	33	37	40	43	47	50	53	57	60	63	67	70
—	—	—	0	1	2	3	4	5	6	7	8	9	10	11	12	13	14	15	16
			20	24	28	32	36	40	44	48	52	56	60	64	68	72	76	80	84
—	—	—	1	2	3	4	6	7	8	9	11	12	13	15	16	18	19	20	22
			23	28	33	38	42	47	52	57	61	66	71	75	80	84	89	94	98
—	—	0	1	3	4	6	7	9	11	12	14	16	17	19	21	23	24	26	28
		21	27	32	38	43	49	54	59	65	70	75	81	86	91	96	102	107	112
—	—	0	2	4	6	7	9	11	13	15	17	20	22	24	26	28	30	32	34
		24	30	36	42	49	55	61	67	73	79	84	90	96	102	108	114	120	126
—	—	1	3	5	7	9	11	14	16	18	21	23	26	28	31	33	36	38	40
		26	33	40	47	54	61	67	74	81	87	94	100	107	113	120	126	133	140
—	—	1	3	6	8	11	13	16	19	22	24	27	30	33	36	38	41	44	47
		29	37	44	52	59	67	74	81	88	96	103	110	117	124	132	139	146	153
—	—	1	4	7	9	12	15	18	22	25	28	31	34	37	41	44	47	50	53
		32	40	48	57	65	73	81	88	96	104	112	120	128	135	143	151	159	167
—	—	2	5	8	11	14	17	21	24	28	31	35	38	42	46	49	53	56	60
		34	43	52	61	70	79	87	96	104	113	121	130	138	146	155	163	172	180
—	0	2	5	9	12	16	20	23	27	31	35	39	43	47	51	55	59	63	67
	26	37	47	56	66	75	84	94	103	112	121	130	139	148	157	166	175	184	193
—	0	2	6	10	13	17	22	26	30	34	38	43	47	51	56	60	65	69	73
	28	40	50	60	71	81	90	100	110	120	130	139	149	159	168	178	187	197	207
—	0	3	7	11	15	19	24	28	33	37	42	47	51	56	61	66	70	75	80
	30	42	53	64	75	86	96	107	117	128	138	148	159	169	179	189	200	210	220
—	0	3	7	12	16	21	26	31	36	41	46	51	56	61	66	71	76	82	87
	32	45	57	68	80	91	102	113	124	135	146	157	168	179	190	201	212	222	233
—	0	4	8	13	18	23	28	33	38	44	49	55	60	66	71	77	82	88	93
	34	47	60	72	84	96	108	120	132	143	155	166	178	189	201	212	224	234	247
—	0	4	9	14	19	24	30	36	41	47	53	59	65	70	76	82	88	94	100
	36	50	63	76	89	102	114	126	139	151	163	175	187	200	212	224	236	248	260
—	1	4	9	15	20	26	32	38	44	50	56	63	69	75	82	88	94	101	107
	37	53	67	80	94	107	120	133	146	159	172	184	197	210	222	235	248	260	273
—	1	5	10	16	22	28	34	40	47	53	60	67	73	80	87	93	100	107	114
	39	55	70	84	98	112	126	140	153	167	180	193	207	220	233	247	260	273	286

(continued)

Critical Values of the U distribution (.05 level, two-tailed) (continued)

	1	2	3	4	5	6	7	8	9	10	11	12	13	14	15	16	17	18	19	20
	—	—	—	—	—	—	—	—	—	—	—	—	—	—	—	—	—	—	—	—
2	—	—	—	—	—	—	—	0	0	0	0	1	1	1	1	1	2	2	2	2
								16	18	20	22	23	25	27	29	31	32	34	36	38
	—	—	—	—	0	1	1	2	2	3	3	4	4	5	5	6	6	7	7	8
					15	17	20	22	25	27	30	32	35	37	40	42	45	47	50	52
4	—	—	—	0	1	2	3	4	4	5	6	7	8	9	10	11	11	12	13	13
				16	19	22	25	28	32	35	38	41	44	47	50	53	57	60	63	67
5	—	—	0	1	2	3	5	6	7	8	9	11	12	13	14	15	17	18	19	20
			15	19	23	27	30	34	38	42	46	49	53	57	61	65	68	72	76	80
	—	—	1	2	3	5	6	8	10	11	13	14	16	17	19	21	22	24	25	27
			17	22	27	31	36	40	44	49	53	58	62	67	71	75	80	84	89	93
7	—	—	1	3	5	6	8	10	12	14	16	18	20	22	24	26	28	30	32	34
			20	25	30	36	41	46	51	56	61	66	71	76	81	86	91	96	101	106
	—	0	2	4	6	8	10	13	15	17	19	22	24	26	29	31	34	36	38	41
		16	22	28	34	40	46	51	57	63	69	74	80	86	91	97	102	108	111	119
	—	0	2	4	7	10	12	15	17	20	23	26	28	31	34	37	39	42	45	48
		18	25	32	38	44	51	57	64	70	76	82	89	95	101	107	114	120	126	132
10	—	0	3	5	8	11	14	17	20	23	26	29	33	36	39	42	45	48	52	55
		20	27	35	42	49	56	63	70	77	84	91	97	104	111	118	125	132	138	145
11	—	0	3	6	9	13	16	19	23	26	30	33	37	40	44	47	51	55	58	62
		22	30	38	46	53	61	69	76	84	91	99	106	114	121	129	136	143	151	158
	—	1	4	7	11	14	18	22	26	29	33	37	41	45	49	53	57	61	65	69
		23	32	41	49	58	66	74	82	91	99	107	115	123	131	139	147	155	163	171
13	—	1	4	8	12	16	20	24	28	33	37	41	45	50	54	59	63	67	72	76
		25	35	44	53	62	71	80	89	97	106	115	124	132	141	149	158	167	175	184
	—	1	5	9	13	17	22	26	31	36	40	45	50	55	59	64	67	74	78	83
		27	37	47	51	67	76	86	95	104	114	123	132	141	151	160	171	178	188	197
	—	1	5	10	14	19	24	29	34	39	44	49	54	59	64	70	75	80	85	90
		29	40	50	61	71	81	91	101	111	121	131	141	151	161	170	180	190	200	210
16	—	1	6	11	15	21	26	31	37	42	47	53	59	64	70	75	81	86	92	98
		31	42	53	65	75	86	97	107	118	129	139	149	160	170	181	191	202	212	222
	—	2	6	11	17	22	28	34	39	45	51	57	63	67	75	81	87	93	99	105
		32	45	57	68	80	91	102	114	125	136	147	158	171	180	191	202	213	224	235
	—	2	7	12	18	24	30	36	42	48	55	61	67	74	80	86	93	99	106	112
		34	47	60	72	84	96	108	120	132	143	155	167	178	190	202	213	225	236	248
19	—	2	7	13	19	25	32	38	45	52	58	65	72	78	85	92	99	106	113	119
		36	50	63	76	89	101	114	126	138	151	163	175	188	200	212	224	236	248	261
	—	2	8	13	20	27	34	41	48	55	62	69	76	83	90	98	105	112	119	127
		38	52	67	80	93	106	119	132	145	158	171	184	197	210	222	235	248	261	273

Critical Values of the U distribution (.05 level, one-tailed) (continued)

	1	2	3	4	5	6	7	8	9	10	11	12	13	14	15	16	17	18	19	20
1	–	–	–	–	–	–	–	–	–	–	–	–	–	–	–	–	–	–	0	0
																			19	20
2	–	–	–	–	0	0	0	1	1	1	1	2	2	2	3	3	3	4	4	4
					10	12	14	15	17	19	21	22	24	26	27	29	31	32	34	36
3	–	–	0	0	1	2	2	3	3	4	5	5	6	7	7	8	9	9	10	11
			9	12	14	16	19	21	24	26	28	31	33	35	38	40	42	45	47	49
4	–	–	0	1	2	3	4	5	6	7	8	9	10	11	12	14	15	16	17	18
			12	15	18	21	24	27	30	33	36	39	42	45	48	50	53	56	59	62
5	–	0	1	2	4	5	6	8	9	11	12	13	15	16	18	19	20	22	23	25
		10	14	18	21	25	29	32	36	39	43	47	50	54	57	61	65	68	72	75
6	–	0	2	3	5	7	8	10	12	14	16	17	19	21	23	25	26	28	30	32
		12	16	21	25	29	34	38	42	46	50	55	59	63	67	71	76	80	84	88
7	–	0	2	4	6	8	11	13	15	17	19	21	24	26	28	30	33	35	37	39
		14	19	24	29	34	38	43	48	53	58	63	67	72	77	82	86	91	96	101
8	–	1	3	5	8	10	13	15	18	20	23	26	28	31	33	36	39	41	44	47
		15	21	27	32	38	43	49	54	60	65	70	76	81	87	92	97	103	108	113
9	–	1	3	6	9	12	15	18	21	24	27	30	33	36	39	42	45	48	51	54
		17	24	30	36	42	48	54	60	66	72	78	84	90	96	102	108	114	120	126
10	–	1	4	7	11	14	17	20	24	27	31	34	37	41	44	48	51	55	58	62
		19	26	33	39	46	53	60	66	73	79	86	93	99	106	112	119	125	132	138
11	–	1	5	8	12	16	19	23	27	31	34	38	42	46	50	54	57	61	65	69
		21	28	36	43	50	58	65	72	79	87	94	101	108	115	122	130	137	144	151
12	–	2	5	9	13	17	21	26	30	34	38	42	47	51	55	60	64	68	72	77
		22	31	39	47	55	63	70	78	86	94	102	109	117	125	132	140	148	156	163
13	–	2	6	10	15	19	24	28	33	37	42	47	51	56	61	65	70	75	80	84
		24	33	42	50	59	67	76	84	93	101	109	118	126	134	143	151	159	167	176
14	–	2	7	11	16	21	26	31	36	41	46	51	56	61	66	71	77	82	87	92
		26	35	45	54	63	72	81	90	99	108	117	126	135	144	153	161	170	179	188
15	–	3	7	12	18	23	28	33	39	44	50	55	61	66	72	77	83	88	94	100
		27	38	48	57	67	77	87	96	106	115	125	134	144	153	163	172	182	191	200
16	–	3	8	14	19	25	30	36	42	48	54	60	65	71	77	83	89	95	101	107
		29	40	50	61	71	82	92	102	112	122	132	143	153	163	173	183	193	203	213
17	–	3	9	15	20	26	33	39	45	51	57	64	70	77	83	89	96	102	109	115
		31	42	53	65	76	86	97	108	119	130	140	151	161	172	183	193	204	214	225
18	–	4	9	16	22	28	35	41	48	55	61	68	75	82	88	95	102	109	116	123
		32	45	56	68	80	91	103	114	123	137	148	159	170	182	193	204	215	226	237
19	0	4	10	17	23	30	37	44	51	58	65	72	80	87	94	101	109	116	123	130
	19	34	47	59	72	84	96	108	120	132	144	156	167	179	191	203	214	226	238	250
20	0	4	11	18	25	32	39	47	54	62	69	77	84	92	100	107	115	123	130	138
	20	36	49	62	75	88	101	113	126	138	151	163	176	188	200	213	225	237	250	262

References

Aiken, L. S., & West, S. G. (1991). *Multiple regression: Testing and interpreting interactions.* Newbury Park, CA: Sage.

Anscombe, F. J., *Graphs in Statistical Analysis*, American Statistican, 27, 17–21.

Bakan, D. (1966). The test of significance in psychological research. *Psychological Bulletin, 66*(6), 423–437.

Becker, W., & Kennedy, P. (1992). A lesson in least squares and R squared. *The American Statistician, 46*(4), 282–283.

Bem, S. L. (1977). *Bem Sex-Role Inventory professional manual.* Mountain View, CA: Consulting Psychologists Press.

Burrill, G., & Hopfensperger, P. (1993). *Exploring statistics with the T1-81.* Reading, MA: Addison-Wesley.

Carver, R. P. (1978). The case against statistical significance testing. *Harvard Educational Review, 48*(3), 378–398.

Cohen, J. (1969). *Statistical power analysis for the behavioral sciences.* New York: Academic Press.

Cohen, J. (1988). *Statistical power analysis for the behavioral sciences* (2nd ed.). Hillsdale, NJ: Lawrence Erlbaum Associates.

Cohen, J. (1990). Things I have learned (so far). *American Psychologist, 45*, 1304–1312.

Cohen, J. (1994). The earth is round ($p < .05$). *American Psychologist, 49*(12), 997–1003.

Cohen, J., Cohen, P., West, S. G., & Aiken, L. S. (2003). *Applied multiple regression/correlation analysis for the behavioral sciences* (3rd ed.). Hillsdale, NJ: Lawrence Erlbaum Associates.

Cohen, R. J., & Swerdlik, M. (2005). *Psychological testing and assessment: An introduction to tests and measurement* (6th ed.). Boston: McGraw-Hill.

Darlington, R. B. (1990). *Regression and linear models.* New York: McGraw-Hill.

de Moivre, A. (1738). *The doctrine of chances* (2nd ed.). London: Woodfall.

Elmore, J., Barton, M. B., Moceri, V. M., Polk, S. Arena, P. J. & Fletcher, S. W. (1998). Ten-year risk of false positive screening mammograms and clinical breast examinations. *New England Journal of Medicine, 338*(16), 1089–1096.

Falk, R., & Greenbaum, C. W. (1995). Significance tests die hard. The amazing persistence of a probabilistic misconception. *Theory and Psychology, 5*(1), 75–98.

Fisher, R. A. (1934). *Statistical methods for research workers.* Edinburgh: Oliver & Boyd.

Fisher, R. A. (1959). *Statistical methods and scientific inference* (2nd ed.). Edinburgh: Oliver & Boyd.

Glass, G. V., Peckham, P. D., & Sanders, J. R. (1972). Consequences of failure to meet assumptions underlying the fixed effects analyses of variance and covariance. *Review of Educational Research, 42*(3), 237–288.

Hagen, R. L. (1997). In praise of the null hypothesis statistical test. *American Psychologist, 52*, 15–24.

Harlow, L. L., Mulaik, S. A., & Steiger, J. H. (Eds.). (1997). *What if there were no significance tests?* Mahwah, NJ: Lawrence Erlbaum Associates.

Hays, W. L. (1973). *Statistics for the social sciences* (2nd ed.). New York: Holt, Rinehart, and Winston.

Holcomb, Z. C. (1997). *Real data: A statistics workbook.* CA: Pyrczak Publishing.

Horn, L., Hafner, A. & Owings, J. (1992). *A profile of American eighth-grade mathematics and science instruction.* National Education Longitudinal Study of 1988. Statistical Analysis Report. ERIC Document (ERIC Document Reproduction Service No. ED337094).

Kaplan, A. (1964). *The conduct of inquiry: Methodology for behavioral science.* San Francisco: Chandler Publishing Company.

Keppel, G. (1991). *Design and analysis: A researcher's handbook.* Englewood, NJ: Prentice Hall.

Kirk, R. E. (1996). Practical significance: A concept whose time has come. *Educational and Psychological Measurement, 56*(5), 746–759.

Krugman, P. (2003). A Touch of Class. *New York Times* editorial, January 21st, Section A, 23.

Kruskal, W. H., & Wallis, W. A. (1952). Use of ranks in one-criterion variance analysis. *Journal of the American Statistical Association, 47*(260), 583–621.

Lykken, D. T. (1968). Statistical significance in psychological research. *Psychological Bulletin, 70*, 151–159.

Mann, H. B., & Whitney, D. R. (1947). On a test of whether one of two random variables is stochastically larger than the other. *Annals of Mathematical Statistics, 18*, 50–60.

Marascuilo, L. A., & Busk, P. L. (1987). Loglinear Models: A way to study main effects and interactions for multidimensional contingency tables with categorical data. *Journal of Counseling Psychology, 34*(4), 443–455.

Marascuilo L. A., & Serlin R. C. (1988). *Statistical Methods for the Social and Behavioral Sciences.* New York: Freeman.

Maxwell, S. E., & Delaney, H. D. (2004). *Designing experiments and analyzing data: A model comparison perspective.* Mahwah, NJ: Lawrence Erlbaum Associates.

Meehl, P. E. (1967). Theory testing in psychology and physics: A methodological paradox. *Philosophy of Science, 34*, 103–115.

Pearson, K. (1900). On the criterion that a given system of deviations from the probably in the case of a correlated system of variables is such that it can be reasonable supposed to have arisen from random sampling. *Philosophical Magazine 5*(50), 157–175. (Reprinted in Pearson, K. (1956), *Karl Pearson's Early Statistical Papers.* Cambridge: Cambridge University Press (first issued, 1948), pp. 339–357).

Riley, R. (1998). The state of mathematics education: Building a strong foundation for the 21st century. *Notices of the AMS, 45*(4), 487.

Rosnow, R. L., & Rosenthal, R. (1989). Statistical procedures and the justification of knowledge in psychological science. *American Psychologist, 44*, 1276–1284.

Rozeboom, W. W. (1960). The fallacy of the null hypothesis significance test. *Psychological Bulletin, 57*, 416–428.

Salsburg, D. (2001). *The lady tasting tea: How statistics revolutionized science in the twentieth century.* New York: A.W.H. Freeman/Owl Book.

Satterthwaite, F. W. (1946). An approximate distribution of estimates of variance components. *Biometrics Bulletin, 2*, 100–144.

Schau, C., Stevens, J., Dauphinee, T.L., & DelVecchio, A. (1995). The development and validation of the survey of attitudes toward statistics. *Educational and Psychological Measurement, 55*, 868–875.

Siegel, S., & Castellan, N. J., Jr. (1988). *Nonparametric statistics for the behavioral sciences.* New York: McGraw-Hill.

Stanton, J. (2001). Galton, Pearson, and the peas: A brief history of linear regression for statistics instructors. *Journal of Statistics Education, 9*(3).

Stevens, S. S. (1946). On the theory of scales of measurement. *Science, 103*, 677–680.

Stevens, S. S. (1951). Mathematics, measurement, and psychophysics. In S. S. Stevens (Ed.), *Handbook of experimental psychology.* New York: John Wiley & Sons.

Stigler, S. M. (1986). *The history of statistics: The measurement of uncertainty before 1900.* Cambridge: Harvard University Press.

Thompson, B. (1994). The concept of statistical significance testing. *ERIC/AE Digest.* ERIC Document (ERIC Document Reproduction Service No. ED366654).

Thompson, B. (1996). AERA editorial policies regarding statistical significance testing: Three suggested reforms. *Educational Researcher, 25*, 26–30.

Thorndike, R. L., & Hagen, E. P. (1977). *Measurement and evaluation in psychology and education.* 4th edition. New York: Wiley.

Tomasi, S., & Weinberg, S. L. (1999). Classifying children as learning disabled: An analysis of current practice in an urban setting. *Learning Disability Quarterly, 22*, 31–42.

Tukey, J. (1977). *Exploratory data analysis.* Reading, MA: Addison-Wesley.

Vogt, W. P. (1993). *Dictionary of statistics and methodology: A nontechnical guide for the social sciences.* Newbury Park, CA, Sage Publications.

Wechsler, D. (1981). *Manual for the Wechsler Adult Intelligence Scale-Revised.* New York: Psychological Corporation.

Weinberg, S. L., & Goldberg, K. P. (1990). *Statistics for the behavioral sciences.* Cambridge: Cambridge University Press.

Wilcoxon, F. (1945). Individual comparisons by ranking methods. *Biometrics Bulletin, 1,* 80–83.

Willerman, L., Schultz, R., Rutledge, J. N., & Bigler, E. (1991). In vivo brain size and intelligence. *Intelligence, 15,* 223–228.

The World Almanac and Book of Facts 2006. (2006). New York, NY: World Almanac Books.

Yates, F. (1943). Contingency tests involving small numbers and the χ^2 test. *Journal of the Royal Statistical Society Supplement, 1,* 217–235.

Solutions to Exercises

CHAPTER 1. **SOLUTIONS**

1.1.
a) Constant.
b) Variable; ratio.
c) Variable; nominal.
d) Constant.
e) Variable; ratio.

1.2.
a) Variable; ratio.
b) Constant.
c) Variable; ratio.
d) Variable; nominal.

1.3.
a) Discrete; ratio.
b) Continuous; ratio.
c) Discrete; ratio.
d) Continuous; ratio.
e) Continuous; interval. Given the care with which the SAT test has been developed, SAT scores are treated as though they are interval-leveled. What this means, of course, is that the higher the score, the greater the verbal aptitude, and that a constant difference in scores regardless of where that difference is measured along the SAT scale indicates a constant change in the underlying characteristic of aptitude. If equal discrepancies in scores do not correspond to equal verbal aptitude differences along the SAT scale then the level of measurement of the SAT would be considered ordinal. Because an absolute zero does not exist for the SAT test, this test, as well as other psychosocial tests, are not considered ratio.
f) Discrete; ratio.

1.4.
a) Discrete; ratio.
b) Continuous; ratio.
c) Continuous; ratio.
d) Discrete; ratio.
e) Continuous; interval (may be considered by some to be ordinal).
f) Continuous; interval.

1.5.
a) Discrete; nominal.
b) Discrete; ratio.
c) Continuous; usually treated as interval.
d) Discrete; ratio.
e) Continuous; interval.
f) Continuous; ordinal; although in some contexts it makes sense to treat this variable as nominal. It is useful to think of this variable as ordinal when the intent is to consider those who answer yes as having more confidence in their statistics ability than those who answer no. Typically, a yes response is coded 1 and a no response is coded 0.

1.6.
a) Ratio.
b) Nominal.
c) Ordinal.

1.7.
a) Ratio.
b) Nominal.
c) Ordinal. By definition, full-time students enroll for a greater number of credits than part-time students, and in this way the two categories may be ordered naturally.
d) Ordinal.
e) Ordinal.

1.8.

    a) Nominal if a simple distinction is to be made between those who smoked and those who did not in 1956. Ordinal if the variable is to be conceived in terms of an individual's degree of smoking in 1956, where degree is measured simply as a two-point dichotomous scale, yes or no.

    b) Ratio according to the classification hierarchy that we present. Scale according to the classification hierarchy that SPSS uses.

    c) Ratio. Within the SPSS program, this variable would be designated as scale.

    d) Ratio, because pressure has an absolute zero. Within the SPSS program, this variable would be designated as scale.

1.9.

    a) Discrete. Nominal if the intent is simply to distinguish between males and females; ordinal if the intent is to rank the categories according to degree of femaleness, for example. In the ordinal context, a higher score on this two-point dichotomous scale would imply greater femaleness.

    b) Continuous. Ordinal because the categories may be ranked according to how rural they are. Higher scores would imply greater ruralness on this three-point scale.

    c) Discrete; nominal.

    d) Continuous; interval. As noted in the text, Likert scales are often treated as interval, although some may wish to treat them as only ordinal.

    e) Discrete. Ratio because the value 0 meaningfully corresponds to "not any" institutions.

    f) Continuous; interval.

    g) Continuous; interval. SES can be considered to be an ordinal-leveled variable depending on the particular way it is measured.

    h) Continuous; interval. A variable defined by a sum of items measured on a Likert scale typically is treated as interval-leveled.

    i) Discrete; ratio. Because this scale has an absolute zero it is not simply interval-leveled.

    j) Discrete; ordinal. If the values had been the actual number of times the student was late, the variable would have been measured at the ratio level. Because broad categories of different lengths are used to classify the scores in this example, the variable is considered to be measured at the ordinal level.

1.10.

    a) ID.

    b) ADVMAT8. To find the variable label for this variable, click the white box in the column labeled "Label" in the row designated by ADVMAT8. The label is "Advanced Math Taken in Eighth Grade." Hence, this variable represents whether or not a student took advanced math in eighth grade.

    c) Click the white box in the column labeled "Values" in the row designated by ADVMAT8; then click the gray box labeled "…". We can see now that "no" is coded 0, "yes" is coded 1, and missing data are coded 8.

    d) The level of measurement has been entered as nominal, but the variable could have been entered as ordinal if the intent is to create a ranking in terms of whether or not a student took advanced math in eighth grade.

    e) Family Size.

    f) The variable gives the family size or the number of members in the person's household. This variable is naturally numeric, so it does not require value labels to explain what the numbers represent.

    g) The level of measurement is listed as scale. Although we have classified variables in this text as nominal, ordinal, interval, or ratio, as noted in earlier exercise solutions, SPSS does not distinguish between interval- and ratio-leveled variables and classifies them both as "scale."

    h) 48.

1.11.
a) 4.
b) Yes. The first student's score is a 1 on this variable, indicating that he did take advanced math in eighth grade.
c) We do not know. That student's score is 8 on this variable, which indicates that his or her information is missing from the data set.
d) 500.

1.12. Because of the grouping of values into six discrete categories with varied lengths, LATE12 is measured at the ordinal level. If grouping categories had not been used and instead the actual number of times late for school had been recorded, the variable would have been measured at the ratio level because zero times late is meaningful in terms of lateness.

1.13. EXPINC30 is at the ratio level because it is measured directly in dollars. If, instead, it had been measured in terms of grouped categories, as shown in the following list, for example, it would have been measured at the ordinal level.

1 = $0
2 = $1–$10,000
3 = $10,001–$20,000
4 = $20,001–$30,000
5 = $30,001–$40,000
6 = $40,001–$50,000
7 = >$50,000

1.14.
a) Numeric.
b) The South region of the country is coded with the value 3.
c) Variable labels are amplifications of the variable name. Whereas it is optional to enter variable labels, it is often a good idea to do so as a way to remember more fully what the variable name signifies. Value labels are used with categorical variables to indicate which values the researcher has chosen to code each of the categories of the variable. Whereas it is also optional to enter value labels, one should always do so as a way to remember the coding used for each categorical variable. As you will learn, the coding of a variable is critical for interpreting results.
d) Because the variable name REGION is itself sufficiently descriptive and needs no further amplification.
e) Arizona is in the West.

CHAPTER 2. SOLUTIONS

2.1.
a) 180

Number of Times Missed School in Twelfth Grade

		Frequency	Percent	Valid Percent	Cumulative Percent
Valid	Never	55	11.0	11.0	11.0
	1–2 Times	195	39.0	39.0	50.0
	3–6 Times	180	36.0	36.0	86.0
	7–9 Times	51	10.2	10.2	96.2
	10–15 Times	12	2.4	2.4	98.6
	Over 15 Times	7	1.4	1.4	100.0
	Total	500	100.0	100.0	

b) It is impossible to know the exact number. However, we can estimate the value by assuming that equal numbers of students were absent 3, 4, 5, and 6 times. Accordingly, the total number absent exactly 3 times in twelfth grade is estimated to be 180/4 = 45.

c) 36 percent.

d) 86 percent.

e) Positively skewed. The bulk of students have six or fewer absences, and there are only a few students with an unusually high number of absences.

2.2.

a) That the student's parents were separated at the time the student was in eighth grade.

Parents' Marital Status in Eighth Grade

		Frequency	Percent	Valid Percent	Cumulative Percent
Valid	Divorced	26	5.2	5.5	5.5
	Widowed	6	1.2	1.3	6.7
	Separated	8	1.6	1.7	8.4
	Never Married	5	1.0	1.0	9.4
	Marriage-Like Relationship	5	1.0	1.0	10.5
	Married	427	85.4	89.5	100.0
	Total	477	95.4	100.0	
Missing	98	23	4.6		
Total		500	100.0		

b) 8.

c) Of all students that reported their parents' marital status in eighth grade, 1.7 percent reported that their parents were separated. Of all students in the NELS data set, 1.6 percent reported that their parents were separated.

d) Because PARMARL8 is nominal, there is no intrinsic ordering to the categories; the numbers are arbitrarily assigned. As such, it does not make sense to consider the percent of people "below separated," for example.

e) Married.

2.3.

a) 9.

Family Size

		Frequency	Percent	Valid Percent	Cumulative Percent
Valid	2	9	1.8	1.8	1.8
	3	52	10.4	10.4	12.2
	4	199	39.8	39.8	52.0
	5	142	28.4	28.4	80.4
	6	55	11.0	11.0	91.4
	7	21	4.2	4.2	95.6
	8	9	1.8	1.8	97.4
	9	13	2.6	2.6	100.0
	Total	500	100.0	100.0	

b) 52.

c) 9 + 52 = 61.

d) 10.4 percent.

    e) 12.2 percent.

    f) Q_2 is approximately 4.

2.4.

    a) GENDER is a nominal variable.

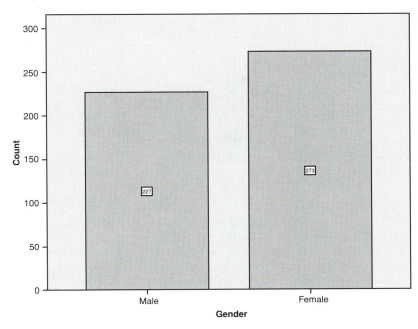

    b) There are more females. There are 273 females and 227 males.

    c) $\dfrac{273}{227 + 273} \times 100 = 54.6$ percent.

    d) Yes. Every person in the data set is classified as either male or female, so the categories are mutually exclusive and exhaustive.

2.5. For this solution, the graph was edited so that the bars are labeled with exact counts. If you do not do that, your answer will be an approximation of the answers given.

    a) For males the answer is $(66/227) \times 100$ or 29.1. For females the answer is $(42/273) \times 100$ or 15.4 percent.

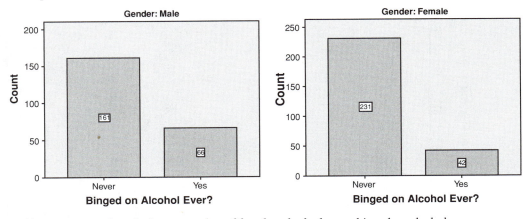

    b) To accommodate the larger number of females who had never binged on alcohol.

2.6.

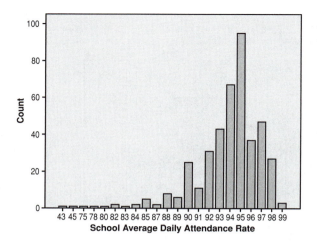

a) The values are not equally spaced, making it difficult to judge the shape of the distribution in general and the distance of the values in the lower tail from the bulk of the distribution in particular.

b) A stem-and-leaf plot, histogram, or interactive line graph.

c) The shape of the distribution is negatively skewed – even more negatively skewed than it appears to be, given the unequal spacing of values along the X-axis. Most schools have attendance rates above 90 percent; however, there are two schools with attendance rates below 50 percent.

2.7.

a)

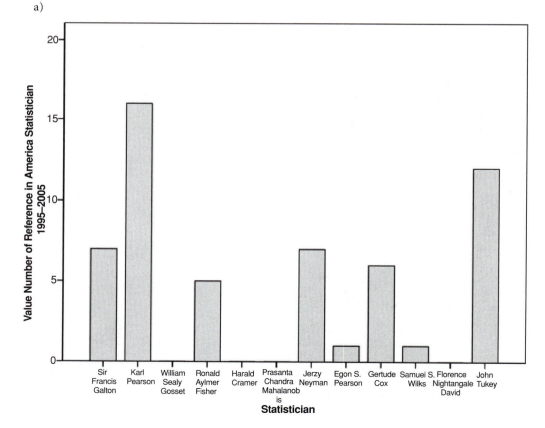

b) The ordering of categories along the *X*-axis corresponds to way in which the data were input into the data file.

c) 5.

d)

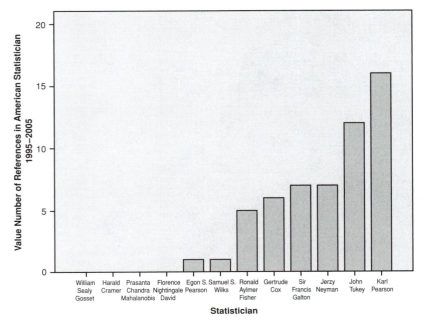

e) It is useful for ranking statisticians by their respective number of recent citations as recorded in *The American Statistician*.

f) He is sixth from the top.

g) The variable "number of recent citations/references" is represented by the *X*-axis in this graph. Because this variable is discrete, with a relatively small range of values, a bar graph would continue to be appropriate.

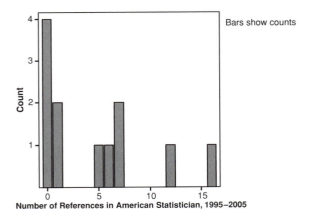

h) The distribution appears to be skewed positively, with a center at approximately 5 references (there are five values above 5 and six values below 5), and a spread from 0 to 16 references.

2.8.

a)

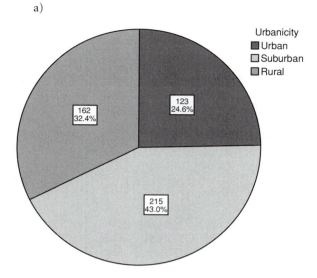

b) 123 students, or 24.6 percent, come from an urban area.

c)

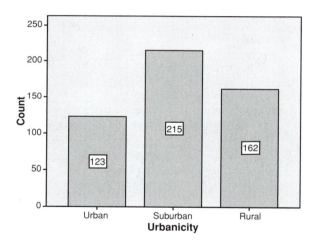

d) There is no "correct" answer to this question. It is a matter of preference.

e) Most students are from suburban areas, followed by rural, and the fewest are from urban areas.

2.9.

```
Math Comprehension Stem-and-Leaf Plot

Frequency     Stem    &    Leaf
      2.00      6      .    12
      7.00      6      .    6678999
      9.00      7      .    002223334
     19.00      7      .    5566777777888888889
     12.00      8      .    000122444444
      8.00      8      .    56667789
     12.00      9      .    011222333333
     10.00      9      .    5566777788
      6.00     10      .    001333
      1.00     10      .    8
      3.00     11      .    223
      4.00     11      .    5678
      1.00     12      .    1
Stem width:    10
Each leaf: 1 case(s)
```

a) The variable is interval, so a line graph, histogram, or boxplot could also be used.

b) $2 + 7 + 9 + 19 + 12 + 8 + 12 + 10 + 6 + 1 + 3 + 4 + 1 = 94$.

c) $9 + 19 = 28$.

d) No.

e) It is reasonably symmetric. The two tails are about equal in size and there are no outliers.

f) Because there is an even number of scores (94), the 50th percentile is the average of the two middle scores, which are in the 47th and 48th positions. Both of these values are 84, so the 50th percentile is 84.

g) 78; it occurs 8 times.   h) 121.   i) Yes.

2.10.

```
Year of Birth Stem-and-Leaf Plot

Frequency     Stem      &    Leaf
      1.00    Extremes         (=<1822)
      1.00         185    .    7
       .00         186    .
      1.00         187    .    6
       .00         188    .
      5.00         189    .    03345
      3.00         190    .    069
      1.00         191    .    5
Stem width:       10
Each leaf: 1 case(s)
```

a) 1.

b) Yes. One statistician was born on or before 1822.

c) The distribution is negatively skewed because of the low outlier.

d) Two statisticians were born in 1893. No other pair of statisticians was born in the same year.

e) 1915.

f) No. The exact value of the outlier cannot be determined from the display.

2.11.

```
┌─────────────────────────────────────────────────────────┐
│                                                         │
│  Number of References in American                       │
│  Statistician 1995-2005 Stem-and-Leaf Plot              │
│                                                         │
│  Frequency    Stem    &    Leaf                         │
│                                                         │
│        6.00     0    .    000011                        │
│        4.00     0    .    5677                          │
│        1.00     1    .    2                             │
│        1.00     1    .    6                             │
│                                                         │
│  Stem width:    10                                      │
│  Each leaf: 1 case(s)                                   │
│                                                         │
└─────────────────────────────────────────────────────────┘
```

a) 2.

b) The distribution is positively skewed despite the fact that there are no outliers. Most statisticians have fewer than 8 citations, but two have more than 10 citations.

c) The most frequently occurring number of citations is 0.

d) The 50th percentile is $(1 + 5)/2 = 3$.

2.12.

```
┌─────────────────────────────────────────────────────────────────────┐
│                                                                     │
│  Serum Cholesterol mg/dL (1) Stem-and-Leaf Plot                     │
│                                                                     │
│  Frequency    Stem        &    Leaf                                 │
│                                                                     │
│       1.00      1     .    &                                        │
│       4.00      1     .    55                                       │
│      24.00      1     .    66666677777                              │
│      52.00      1     .    888888888899999999999999999              │
│      62.00      2     .    000000000000011111111111111111           │
│      68.00      2     .    22222222222222222233333333333333333      │
│      74.00      2     .    444444444444444444455555555555555555555   │
│      46.00      2     .    6666666666666666777777777                │
│      31.00      2     .    888888899999999                          │
│      16.00      3     .    00001111                                 │
│       9.00      3     .    2233                                     │
│       3.00      3     .    4                                        │
│       2.00    Extremes     (>=353)                                  │
│                                                                     │
│  Stem width: 100                                                    │
│  Each leaf: 2 case(s)                                               │
│  & denotes fractional leaves.                                       │
│                                                                     │
└─────────────────────────────────────────────────────────────────────┘
```

a) The exact value of the lowest score cannot be determined because it has an ampersand (&), standing for a fractional value, as its leaf. All we know is that the exact value is between 120 and 130, inclusive.

b) Yes. There are two people with initial cholesterol levels that are greater or equal to 353.

c) Positively skewed due to the two high outliers.

d) Approximately 230. This stem-and-leaf plot reports values rounded to two significant digits, so that a value of 233, for example, is reported as 230. Given that there are 392 scores in this stem-and-leaf plot, the 50th percentile for these data, based on this stem-and-leaf plot, is estimated to be 230, which is the average of the 196th and 197th scores in this distribution. The 196th and 197th score each has a recorded value of 230.

e) The exact value of the highest score cannot be determined because it is recorded simply as an extreme value noted to be greater than or equal to 353.

f) No, for three reasons. First, the scores are rounded to two significant digits and so we would not know the actual units digit of each value (e.g., an original score of 253 would be represented in this stem-and-leaf as 250). Second, we do not know the value represented by the "&." Third, we do not know the values of the two outliers.

2.13.

```
Math Achievement in Eighth Grade Stem-and-Leaf Plot

Frequency    Stem   &   Leaf

    12.00      3    .   789&
    47.00      4    .   000112223334444
    73.00      4    .   5555566666777778888899999
   101.00      5    .   00000011111122222222233333444444444
    81.00      5    .   555556666667777778888888999
    77.00      6    .   00000011111222222333344444
    70.00      6    .   55555666666777777778888999
    28.00      7    .   001233444
    11.00      7    .   5577

Stem width:10.00
Each leaf: 3 case(s)
& denotes fractional leaves.
```

a) 37.

b) Approximately three, because there is a single leaf and each leaf is noted to represent three cases.

c) No.   d) Approximately symmetric.   e) 54.

f) For general questions about the shape, level, and spread of a distribution, a stem-and-leaf plot provides a better visual summary of the distribution. However, when exact frequencies and variable values are desired, the frequency distribution table often provides a greater level of detail.

2.14.

```
Systolic BP mmHg (1) Stem-and-Leaf Plot for
SEX= Men

Frequency    Stem       &   Leaf

     2.00        9      .   89
     3.00       10      .   012
    13.00       10      .   5555777788889
    24.00       11      .   000001111112222223333444444
    22.00       11      .   5555556666777889999999
    22.00       12      .   000111111222223444444
    20.00       12      .   55566677777777888999
    26.00       13      .   00000000011112222222333344
    16.00       13      .   5566677778888999
    14.00       14      .   00001111123444
     6.00       14      .   566789
     4.00       15      .   0023
     9.00       15      .   567899999
     4.00       16      .   0222
     2.00       16      .   78
     4.00       17      .   1234
     1.00       17      .   5
     8.00    Extremes        (>=179)

Stem width: 10
Each leaf: 1 case(s)
```

```
Systolic BP mmHg (1) Stem-and-Leaf Plot for
SEX= Women

Frequency    Stem      &    Leaf
       1.00        9    .    2
       5.00        9    .    56778
      13.00       10    .    0000002233334
      18.00       10    .    555567777778888999
      17.00       11    .    00001122233333444
      19.00       11    .    5555666666778888999
      20.00       12    .    00000012223333334444
      27.00       12    .    556666677777778888889999999
      21.00       13    .    000111222222222333344
      13.00       13    .    5566778899999
      10.00       14    .    0000111223
       4.00       14    .    6788
       5.00       15    .    02234
       4.00       15    .    5589
       3.00       16    .    001
       4.00       16    .    5558
       3.00       17    .    033
       2.00       17    .    66
      11.00    Extremes         (>=178)

Stem width: 10
Each leaf: 1 case(s)
```

a) Female. For males, the lowest systolic blood pressure value is 98, whereas for females it is 92.

b) Female. In the female distribution, the most frequently occurring systolic blood pressure is 132, whereas in the male distribution it is 130.

c) The distributions appear to be quite similar in spread.

d) The shapes of the distributions appear to be quite similar; they are both similarly positively skewed.

2.15.

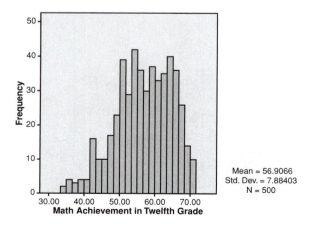

a) Estimating from the histogram, the lowest score is approximately 34 and it appears two times.

b) Between 54 and 55.

c) It is slightly negatively skewed. There is a longer tail on the left than on the right.

2.16.

a) The group that owned a computer in eighth grade.

b) Yes, it appears to be higher for the group that owns a computer because the distribution for this group begins and ends at a higher point along the SES scale and the bulk of the scores in that distribution is located higher up on the SES scale than for the other group.

c) No. The spread of the two distributions appears to be quite similar.

2.17.

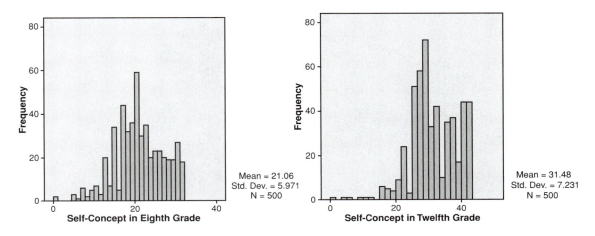

a) The level of self-concept is higher for the twelfth grade – the bulk of the scores in the histogram for twelfth grade is further to the right on the X-axis than for eighth grade.

b) In eighth grade the scores are more closely clustered.

c) The scores are more negatively skewed in twelfth grade – the tail is longer in the negative direction or to the left.

2.18.

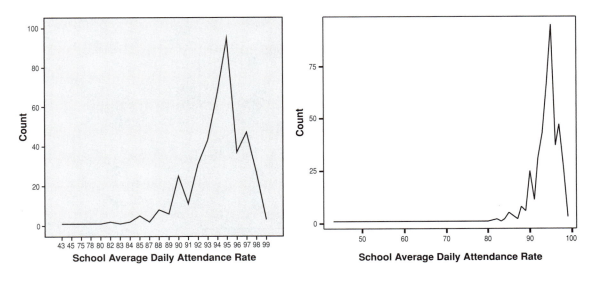

a) In the interactive line graph.

b) The interactive line graph. The regular line graph gives a distorted view due the way in which values are formatted along the *X*-axis. The distance between values on the *X*-axis shrinks toward the lower end of the tail.

2.19.

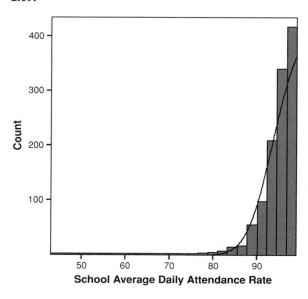

a) Approximately 75.

b) Negatively skewed.

2.20.

a)

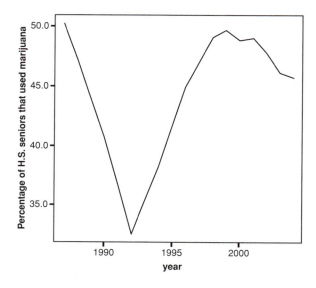

b) The compressed scale reduces the appearance of a change in the percentages of students who use marijuana over time. Said differently, student behavior with respect to smoking marijuana appears to be more consistent over time with the compressed scale.

c) The percentage of seniors who have tried marijuana increases rather dramatically from 1992 through 1999.

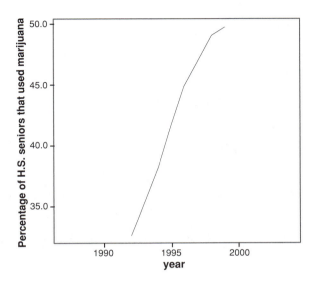

2.21.

   a) $30,000. This means that 15 percent of the students are expecting to be earning less than $30,000 at age 30.

   b) $40,000.

   c) 73.9.

2.22. Because PARMARL8 is only nominal. Variables must be at least ordinal-leveled for percentiles to be meaningfully calculated.

2.23.

   a) 102.

   b) 25.

   c) According to the frequency distribution table, the percentile rank of his eighth-grade self-concept score is 74.8 inclusive. While higher than almost three-fourths of the individuals in the data set, one might have expected this person's self-concept to be even higher.

   d) He was least self-confident in twelfth grade. In eighth grade, his self-concept score of 25 gave him a percentile rank of 74.8 percent. In tenth grade, his self-concept score of 32 gave him a percentile rank of 88 percent. In twelfth grade, his self-concept score of 22 gave him a percentile rank of 7.2 percent.

2.24.

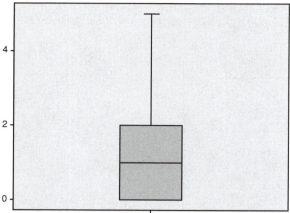

Number Times Late for School in Twelfth Grade

a) LATE12 is ordinal because a score of 0 represents no days late, a score of 1 represents one to two days late, a score of 2 represents three to six days late, and so on.

b) The value of the 50th percentile is 1. Because the value of 1 corresponds to being late one or two times, we know that half the students in the NELS study were late to school no more than only one or two times.

c) The graph is positively skewed because there is a long whisker above the box and no whisker at all below the box.

d) The minimum score is the same as the 25th percentile score. That is, at least 25 percent of students in the NELS data set were never late in twelfth grade.

2.25.

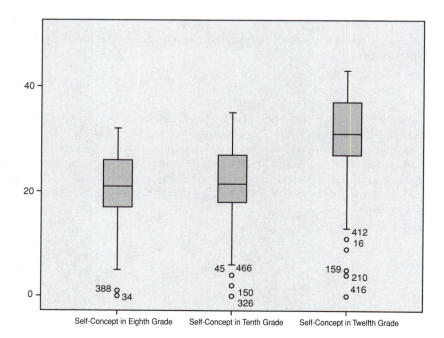

a) Negatively skewed. All of the outliers are on the more negative end of the scale.
b) Eighth grade.
c) Twelfth grade as measured by the 50th percentile.
d) The twelfth-grade distribution contains the highest self-concept score, which is approximately 43.
e) Twelfth grade.

2.26.

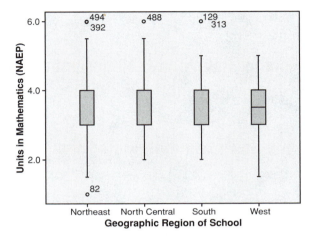

a) West.
b) West.
c) There is a student in the Northeast that took only one year of math in high school.
d) The distributions of all regions appear to be similar in spread according to the IQR.
e) Because 25 percent of the scores in any distribution fall between Q_1 and Q_2, the number of students in the Northeast whose scores fall between these two quartiles will be .25 × 106 or approximately 27 for those in the Northeast regardless of the variable in question.

2.27.

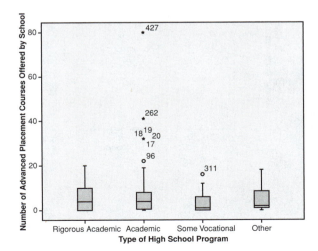

a) Schools that offer only rigorous high school academic programs are likely to be smaller in scale (e.g., they may be non–public schools) than those that offer academic programs, which could explain the relatively smaller number of AP course offerings overall.

b) By using the percentage of all course offerings per school.

2.28.

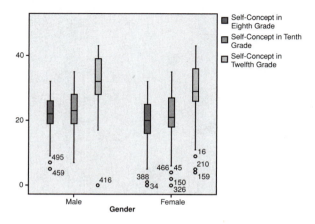

a) Yes.

b) The large presence of extremely low self-concept scores for females as compared to males.

c) Yes. Box and whiskers are themselves comparable for males and females.

2.29.

a) and b)

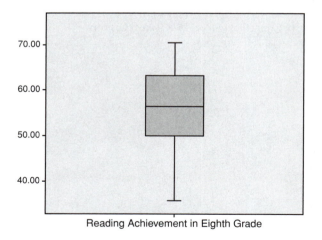

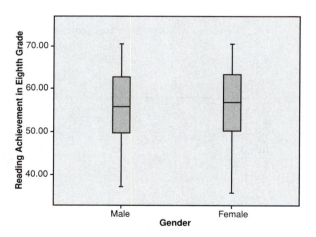

c)

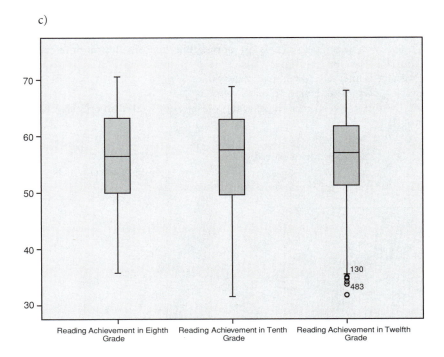

d)

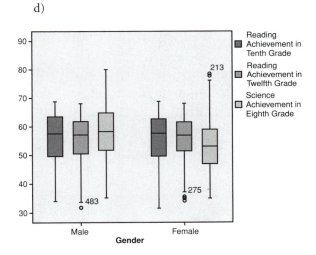

2.30.
   a) Positively skewed.   b) Negatively skewed.   c) Slightly positively skewed.
   d) Positively skewed.   e) Positively skewed.   f) Positively skewed.

2.31.
   a) South.   b) West.   c) Midwest.
   d) Northeast.

2.32.
   a) (1). The variable is nominal.
   b) (1). The variable is ordinal with only three categories.
   c) (1). The variable is nominal.

d) (1) or (2). The variable is interval, so (2) is appropriate, but it takes on only four values, so (1) is also appropriate.

e) (1) or (2). The variable is ratio, so (2) is appropriate, but there are only four categories, so (1) is also appropriate.

f) (2). The variable is interval and takes on many values.

g) (2). The variable is ratio and takes on many values.

h) (1) or (2). The variable is ordinal, so (2) is appropriate, but it takes on only six values, so (1) is also appropriate.

2.33.

a) 72.89.   b) 13 students scored 72.89.   c) 72.89.

d) 55.7.   e) 59.9.   f) 95.2 percent.

g) According to the histogram, it is reasonably symmetric.

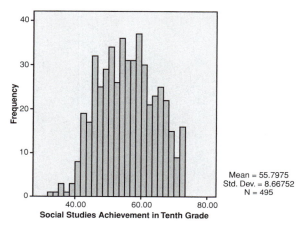

Mean = 55.7975
Std. Dev. = 8.66752
N = 495

Social Studies Achievement in Tenth Grade

2.34.

a) 1–4 hours were spent weekly on extracurricular activities in twelfth grade.

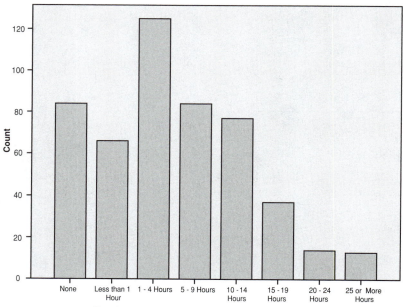

Time Spent Weekly on Extra-Curricular Activities in Twelfth Grade

b) 125.

c) 1–4 hours.

d) Slightly positively skewed. The bulk of the students spend less than 20 hours per week on extracurricular activities, but a few students spend quite a bit more than that.

2.35.

a) January.

b) March 2003.

c) September 2001 – 90 percent.

d) January or February 2002 – approximately $1.15 per gallon.

e) April 2006 – approximately 37 percent.

f) September or October 2005 – approximately $2.90 per gallon.

g) Yes. Beyond the specific reasonably associated highs and lows noted, the two lines cross in an X shape, indicating that, as gasoline prices have risen in his presidency, President Bush's approval ratings have decreased.

2.36.

a) Approximately $100,000,000.

b) $\dfrac{980000000}{3,919,680,000} = .25$ or 25 percent.

c) At the low end of the scale there is coffee, then household products, then personal products.

d) These products do not represent all of the products that Proctor & Gamble advertises. Several products, such as Mr. Clean, Febreze, and Pampers are omitted. Because there is no sense in which of these products represent 100 percent of Procter & Gamble's advertising budget, a pie graph could lead to an incorrect interpretation.

2.37.

a) 62 percent.

b) $.62 \times 1011 = 626.82$ or 627 people.

c) It is likely that a larger percentage of people would have responded that they would rather be "extremely attractive" than merely "good looking." The results could have been very different with a slight rephrasing, indicating the importance of the wording of a question.

2.38.

a) Time.

b) After Dogbert tells Dilbert that he sees two big dips (on day 6), the graph would probably look like:

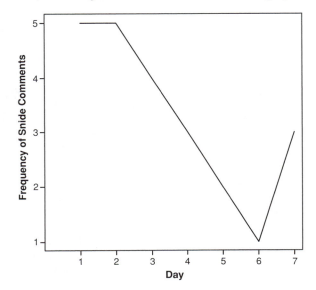

2.39.

a) In 1980, approximately .5 billion gallons of water. In 2005, approximately 7.5 billion gallons of water.

b) $(5 - 3)/3 = .67$, which equals a 67 percent increase.

c) $(26 - 17)/17 = .53$, which equals a 53 percent increase.

d) Decreasing in growth.

2.40. $C_4 D_1 Q_1 D_3 C_{50} Q_3$

2.41. The statement is wrong. For example, if everyone scores 10, then a raw score of 75 is not surpassed by any of the scores in the distribution. A raw score does not, in general, give information about percentages.

2.42. The statement is wrong. For example, if 100 people take the test, then the highest percentile rank possible is 99; that is, the highest score will have 99 percent of the scores falling below it, unless there is a tie.

2.43. The statement is wrong. This depends on the percentage of people below Alice's and Ellen's scores. For example, if there were 10 people taking the exam and eight people scored 40, Alice scored 50, and Ellen scored 100, then the percentile rank of Alice's score is 80, while the percentile rank of Ellen's score is 90, not twice that of Alice's score. Of course, a percentile rank can never be 100 or above.

2.44. The statement is wrong. Percentiles are not necessarily interval.

2.45. The statement is wrong. If the students at this student's school are exceptionally good in math, having a percentile rank of 85 in math relative to this school could be better than having a percentile rank of 95 in science relative to the entire city.

2.46 The statement is wrong. The validity of the conclusion depends on the number of people questioned. Whereas 5 out of 5 is 100 percent, 5 out of 100 is only 5 percent. A description in terms of relative frequency or percentage would probably be more appropriate in this situation than a description in terms of frequency.

2.47. They are all possible values for percentiles. Only 50 is a possible value for a percentile rank.

2.48. A distribution with outliers that are balanced in both the positive and negative directions can be symmetric.

2.49. A boxplot would have only one whisker, for example, if the 75th percentile was the same as the maximum score – that is, if the top 25 percent of the scores in the distribution were all the same value.

2.50.

a) and b)

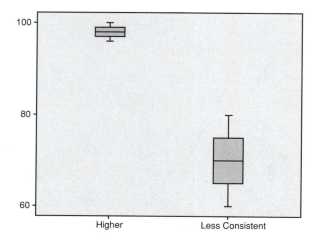
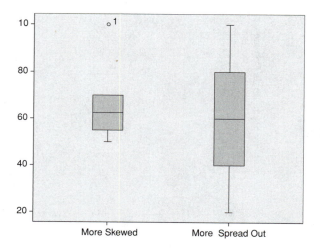

CHAPTER 3. **SOLUTIONS**

3.1.

a) It is appropriate to calculate the mode, median, and mode of GENDER. For the coding used (Male = 0; Female = 1), the mode, equal to 1, indicates that most students are female. The median, equal to 1, indicates that category 1 contains the 250th score (recall $N = 500$ in our NELS data set), which suggests, given that there are only two categories for this dichotomous variable, that at least 50 percent of the individuals in this data set are female. The mean, equal to .55, indicates, for the coding used, that 55 percent of the individuals in this data set are female.

b) If URBAN were considered to be an ordinal variable, it would be appropriate to calculate the mode and median of URBAN. If treated as a nominal variable, only the mode would be appropriate. The median, equal to 2, indicates that a typical student lives in a setting that may be described as having an intermediate level of urbanicity: a suburban setting. The mode, equal to 2, indicates that most of the individuals in this data set live in suburban settings, as opposed to rural or urban settings.

c) It is appropriate to calculate only the mode of SCHTYP8, a nominal variable. The mode, equal to 1, indicates that most individuals in this data set attend public school.

d) If TCHERINT, measured on a Likert scale, is considered to be interval-leveled, it would be appropriate to calculate the mode, median, and mean of TCHERINT. If considered only to be ordinal, then only the mode and median would be appropriate. The mean, equal to 1.96, and the median and mode equal to 2, all indicate that students agreed on average with the statement, "My teachers are interested in me." Here is an example where all three measures of central tendency are equal or reasonably so, yet the distribution itself is not symmetric. The mode provides meaningful information in this case because TCHERINT, while at least ordinal, has only four categories.

e) It is appropriate to calculate the mode, median, and mean of NUMINST, a ratio-leveled variable. The mode, equal to 1, indicates that most students attended one post-secondary institution. The median, also equal to 1, indicates that the typical student attended only one post-secondary institution. The mean, equal to 1.21, indicates that, on average, students attended 1.21 post-secondary institutions. With more than 80 percent of the respondents attending one post-secondary institution, and with only one respondent attending four post-secondary institutions–the maximum number recorded – the distribution is skewed in the positive direction. Unlike the mode and median, the mean is influenced more strongly by the few people who have attended three and four institutions.

f) While it is possible to calculate the mode, median, and mean of ACHRDG08, an interval-leveled variable, given the continuous nature of this variable and the fact that it is reasonably symmetric, the mean would be the most appropriate measure of central tendency in this case. The mean, equal to 56.05, indicates that, on average, students scored 56.05 on reading achievement in eighth grade.

g) While it is possible to calculate the mode, median, and mean of SCHATTRT, a ratio-leveled variable, given that SCHATTRT is many-valued, the median and mean would be more appropriate than the mode for assessing the location of this continuous variable. The median, equal to 95, indicates that the typical student attended schools with a daily attendance rate of 95. The mean, equal to 93.65, indicates that, on average, students attended schools with a daily attendance rate of 93.65. While the mean and median are not too dissimilar in value, relative to the median, the mean has been pulled in the direction of the tail of this negatively skewed variable.

h) It is appropriate to calculate the mode and median of ABSENT12, an ordinal variable with only six categories. Given the coding used, the mode, equal to 1, indicates that most students were absent from twelfth grade 1 or 2 times; and, the median, equal to 1.5, indicates that the typical student was absent from twelfth grade somewhere between 1 and 6 times.

3.2.

    a) 129.

    b) 7 to 9 times.

    c) One or two times, which is the value of both the mode and median, the appropriate measures to use with this ordinal variable.

3.3.

    a) (1).   b) (1) or (2).   c) (1).

    d) (3).   e) (3).   f) (4).

    g) (3).   h) (2).

3.4.

    a) The proportion that ever smoked is .142.

    b) The mean is .14, which equals the proportion found in part (a).

    c) A greater proportion of females (.161) report that they have ever smoked than males (.119).

Smoked Cigarettes Ever?

Gender			Frequency	Percent	Valid Percent	Cumulative Percent
Male	Valid	Never	200	88.1	88.1	88.1
		Yes	27	11.9	11.9	100.0
		Total	227	100.0	100.0	
Female	Valid	Never	229	83.9	83.9	83.9
		Yes	44	16.1	16.1	100.0
		Total	273	100.0	100.0	

3.5.

    a) Although both distributions are positively skewed, the male distribution has a more extreme outlier than the female distribution, suggesting that the male distribution is more positively skewed than the female distribution. The extreme case in the male distribution has case number 125. He smokes 60 cigarettes per day, far more than any other person in the data set.

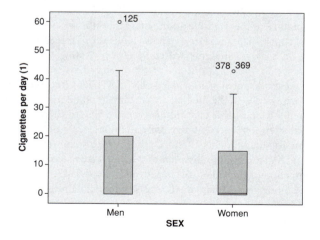

    b) Because the male distribution is far more positively skewed than the female distribution, a comparison of medians for the two distributions would be more appropriate than a comparison of means to control for this difference in skewness. According to the medians, we conclude that females (median = .50) typically smoke more than males (median = 0). However, if we chose to weight the presence of the extreme values more heavily in our analysis, we would base a comparison of smoking on the means. In this case, we would conclude that males (mean = 11.22), on average, smoke more than females (mean = 7.70).

3.6.

a) The distribution is positively skewed.

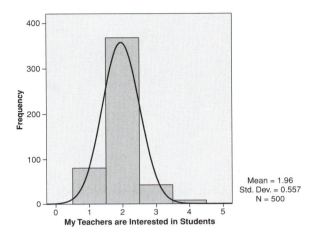

b) Contrary to the general rule of thumb, as it pertains particularly to the distribution of a many-valued unimodal continuous variable, in this example, the median of 2 is larger than the mean of 1.96.

3.7.

a) As a dichotomous variable, the variability of GENDER is best captured by the proportion of males and females in the distribution. In the NELS data set, there are 45.4 percent males and 54.6 percent females. The greatest variability (heterogeneity) occurs when there are half males and half females. The distribution would be symmetric in this case. The greater the departure from an even split, the more skewed the distribution may be said to be. Because the mean of a dichotomous variable has meaning (as the proportion of that group coded 1), the standard deviation is also often used for measuring the variability of a dichotomous variable. The standard deviation of GENDER is .50. For completeness, we can compute the skewness ratio for GENDER as a measure of the extent to which this variable is skewed. Given that the percent of females and males are each close to 50 percent, we would not expect the skewness ratio, in this case, to be large in absolute value. The skewness ratio is −1.70 (−.185/.109), indicating, as expected, a lack of skewness for this variable.

b) As only a three-valued variable (rural, suburban, urban), the variability of URBAN is also best captured by the proportion of cases within each of the three categories. In the NELS data set, 24.6 percent of the students come from an urban area, 43 percent come from a suburban area, and 32.5 percent come from a rural area. Greatest variability (or heterogeneity) occurs when there are an equal proportion of individuals in each category (in this case, 33.3 percent in each). Greatest homogeneity occurs when 100 percent of the cases are in only one category. Given the small number of possible values for this variable, the IQR would likely not be useful, even though this variable may be considered to be ordinal. The following frequency bar graph depicts well the spread and shape of this variable. According to this bar graph, the distribution is fairly symmetric, with approximately equal numbers of students in the urban and rural categories and most students in the suburban category. The extent of the skew cannot be quantified with the skewness ratio because it does not make sense to talk about distance from the mean for an ordinal-leveled variable.

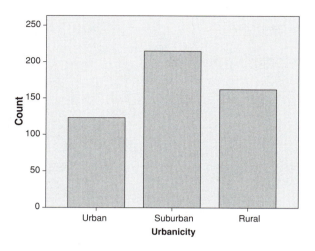

c) NUMINST, like the previous three variables in this exercise, takes on only a small number of values (four to be exact), and so much of what has been written in connection with the solutions for these other variables may be said in relation to this one. In particular, one may note that with more than 80 percent of the respondents attending one post-secondary institution, and with only one respondent attending four post-secondary institutions, the maximum number recorded, the distribution may be said to be skewed in the positive direction. Given the small number of values for this variable, the IQR would add little to measuring spread over and above a simple accounting of the proportion of responses to each of the four values noted. The standard deviation could be computed as this variable is ratio-leveled; but, given how skewed the variable is, the standard deviation may not be as useful as an accounting of the simple proportions.

d) Because ACHRDG08 is interval, many-valued, and reasonably symmetric, the standard deviation (or variance) offers an appropriate measure of spread. The value of the standard deviation is 8.83, indicating that students typically scored 8.83 points away from the mean of 56.05. The IQR would also be useful in documenting the range within which the middle 50 percent scored.

e) Because SCHATTRT is ratio, many-valued, and severely negatively skewed with skewness ratio equal to $-57.20 \left(\dfrac{-6.235}{.109} = -57.20 \right)$, the IQR, as opposed to the standard deviation, may be the most appropriate measure of spread. The value of the IQR is 3, indicating that the range of school attendance rate values for the middle 50 percent of the data is 3.

f) Because ABSENT12 is ordinal with a small number of discrete values, a bar graph may be used to show that the distribution is positively skewed, with most students being absent in twelfth grade fewer than 7 times, and only a few students absent more than 20 times. The extent of the skew cannot be quantified with say, a skewness statistic, because it does not make sense to talk about distance from the mean for an ordinal leveled variable. The IQR may be used to measure the spread of this variable. The value of the IQR is 1, indicating that the range of the middle 50 percent of the data is only 1 – that absences are highly clustered around the middle.

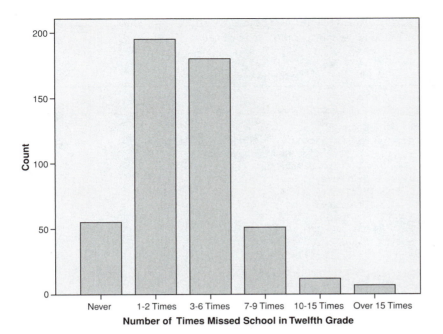

Number of Times Missed School in Twelfth Grade

3.8. There are several SPSS procedures that provide summary descriptive statistics and each procedure provides a slightly different subset of such statistics. The following statistics were obtained using the SPSS Frequencies procedure. Notice that the IQR is not among the statistics provided by Frequencies.

Statistics

Self-Concept in Eighth Grade

N	Valid	500
	Missing	0
Mean		21.06
Median		21.00
Mode		17
Std. Deviation		5.971
Variance		35.653
Skewness		−.286
Std. Error of Skewness		.109
Range		32
Minimum		0
Maximum		32
Percentiles	25	17.00
	40	19.00
	50	21.00
	75	26.00

The following statistics were obtained using the SPSS Explore procedure. Notice that the mode and percentiles are not among the statistics provided by Explore.

Descriptives

			Statistic	Std. Error
Self-Concept in Eighth Grade	Mean		21.06	.267
	95% Confidence Interval for Mean	Lower Bound	20.54	
		Upper Bound	21.59	
	5% Trimmed Mean		21.23	
	Median		21.00	
	Variance		35.653	
	Std. Deviation		5.971	
	Minimum		0	
	Maximum		32	
	Range		32	
	Interquartile Range		9	
	Skewness		−.286	.109
	Kurtosis		−.007	.218

a) 0. b) 32. c) 19.
d) 17. e) 21.06. f) 21.
g) 17. h) 32. i) 9.
j) 35.65. k) 5.97. l) −.286.
m) .109.

3.9.

a) The boxplots indicate that both distributions are similarly severely negatively skewed. The skewness ratios ($-.333/.15 = -2.22$ for those whose families did not own a computer and $-.37/.158 = -2.34$ for those whose families did) corroborate this visual impression.

b) Given the skewness of the two distributions, medians are used to answer this question. According to the respective medians, tenth-grade math achievement is higher for students whose families owned a computer when they were in eighth grade (median = 59.01) than for those whose families did not (median = 55.76). Because the distributions have similar shapes, the respective means lead to the same conclusion.

c) According to the IQR, tenth-grade math achievement is slightly more variable for students whose families owned a computer when they were in eighth grade ($IQR = 11.71$) than for those whose families did not ($IQR = 10.45$). Because the standard deviation is even more sensitive to outliers than the mean, the results from the respective standard deviations (for those whose families owned computers, $SD = 7.64$; for those whose families did not, $SD = 7.69$) leads to a different conclusion, Like the IQRs, however, the standard deviations are close in value.

3.10.

a) The skewness ratios for those from an urban, suburban, and rural environment are, respectively, -1.69, $-.67$, and $-.06$; we see that although all of the distributions have a degree of negative skew, none of the distributions are severely skewed.

b) Among students in the NELS data set, according to both the mean and the median, the typical SES of those from an urban environment ($M = 20.33$, median = 20) is higher than that of students from a suburban environment ($M = 19.23$, median = 19), which in turn is higher than that of students from a rural environment ($M = 15.94$, median = 16).

c) Among students in the NELS data set, according to the standard deviation, the SES of students from an urban environment is more dispersed ($SD = 6.92$) than that of students from a suburban environment ($SD = 6.73$), which in turn is more dispersed than that of students from a rural environment (($SD = 6.51$). According to the IQR, however, the SES of those from urban and suburban environments are equally dispersed ($IQR = 10$) and more dispersed than that of students from a rural environment ($IQR = 9$).

d) The person with the highest SES lives in a suburban environment. The maximum SES for the students from a suburban environment is 35, whereas for urban and suburban it is 32.

3.11.

a) The distribution of self-concept scores is severely negatively skewed in both eighth grade (skewness ratio $= -2.62$) and twelfth grade (skewness ratio $= -3.52$). The distribution is more severely skewed in twelfth grade.

b) According to both the mean and the median, students in the NELS typically have higher self-concept scores in twelfth grade ($M = 31.48$, median $= 31.00$) than in eighth grade ($M = 21.06$, median $= 21.00$).

c) According to both the standard deviation and the range, the self-concept scores of students in the NELS are more heterogeneous in twelfth grade ($SD = 7.23$, $IQR = 10.00$) than in eighth grade ($SD = 5.97$, $IQR = 9.00$).

3.12.

a) According to the two histograms, the male and female distributions are quite similar. The means for males and females, respectively, are 1.95 and 1.96, and their medians are identical at 2. Therefore, males and females perceive their teachers to show similar amounts of interest in them.

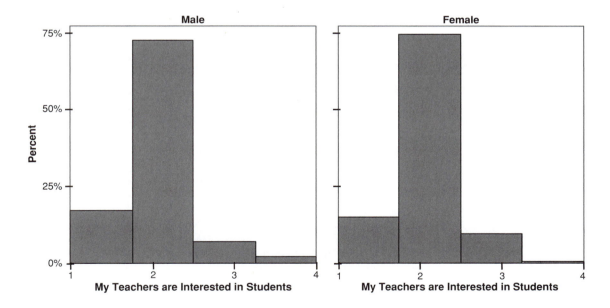

b) According to the boxplots, the distributions of reading achievement across the three grades are quite similar, indicating that males and females display similar changes in achievement in reading across eighth, tenth, and twelfth grades. There is an increase from eighth to tenth and then a slight decrease from tenth to twelfth. The means analysis shows a similar result to the boxplots, which are based on medians.

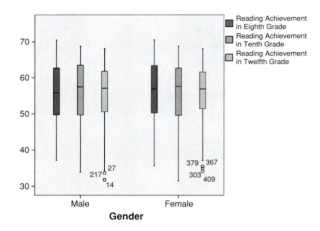

Report

Gender		Reading Achievement in Eighth Grade	Reading Achievement in Tenth Grade	Reading Achievement in Twelfth Grade
Male	Mean	55.5455	56.2570	55.3104
	N	227	227	227
	Std. Deviation	9.11576	8.60886	8.56015
Female	Mean	56.4678	55.9952	55.8443
	N	273	273	273
	Std. Deviation	8.57893	8.05658	7.48037
Total	Mean	56.0491	56.1140	55.6019
	N	500	500	500
	Std. Deviation	8.82973	8.30446	7.98492

c) According to the boxplots and follow-up descriptive statistics, the distributions for males and females are quite similar, in general, across all three measures of school attendance behavior. Differences may be noted in the following areas: The typical female reports being absent 3 to 6 times over the year (coded 2), whereas the typical male reports being absent only 1 to 2 times over the year (coded 1); also, females tend to be more variable than males with respect to being late as noted by the difference in their IQRs on LATE12.

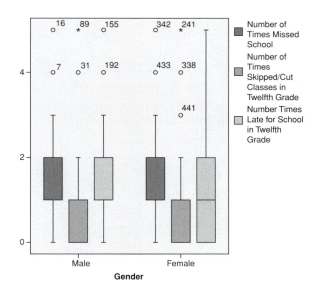

	ABSENT 12	CUTS12	LATE12
MALES	Median = 1.00 IQR = 1.00 Skewness = .58	Median = 0.00 IQR = 1.00 Skewness = 2.24	Median = 1.00 IQR = 1.00 Skewness = 1.03
FEMALES	Median = 2.00 IQR = 1.00 Skewness = .78	Median = 0.00 IQR = 1.00 Skewness = 2.31	Median = 1.00 IQR = 2.00 Skewness = 1.00

3.13.

a) According to these similarly shaped boxplots, the median time spent on homework outside of school for those who did take advanced math in eighth grade is higher than for those who did not. Follow-up analyses indicate that the medians are 3.50 and 3.00 for these two groups, respectively.

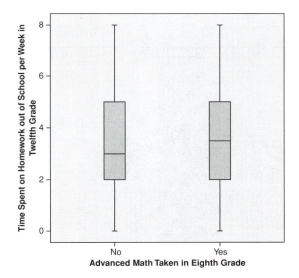

b) According to these similarly shaped boxplots, the median number of times of missed school in twelfth grade for those who did take advanced math in eighth grade is lower than for those who did not. Follow-up analyses indicate that the medians are 1.00 (1 to 2 times absent) and 2.00 (3 to 6 times absent) for these two groups, respectively.

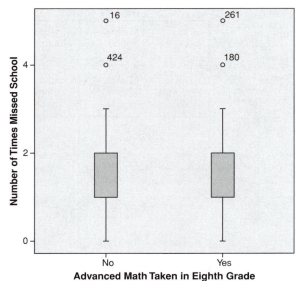

c) There is little difference in the shape of these two distributions – one for those who did and the other for those who did not take advanced math in eighth grade – although both distributions are severely positively skewed. The median and IQR for those who did not take advanced math in eighth grade are, respectively, 1 and 0; for those who did take advanced math in eighth grade, the median and IQR are, respectively, also 1 and 0.

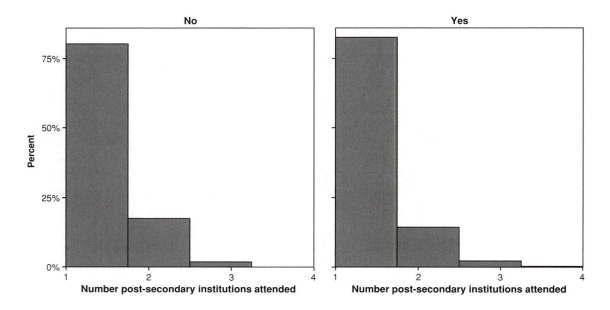

3.14.

```
Reading Comprehension Stem-and-Leaf Plot

Frequency      Stem        &      Leaf

     1.00     Extremes            (=<22)
     1.00        4         .      9
     1.00        5         .      1
     1.00        5         .      7
     4.00        6         .      1334
    11.00        6         .      55566779999
     7.00        7         .      0001222
    12.00        7         .      555666777888
    16.00        8         .      0000111112334444
    10.00        8         .      5555666788
     5.00        9         .      01111
     5.00        9         .      56689
     1.00       10         .      3
     1.00       10         .      7

Stem width:        10
Each leaf: 1 case(s)
```

a) Negatively skewed, there is one low outlier.

b) 81.   c) 107.

d) Probably the median. The mean is often pulled in the direction of the skew, which is negative.

e) IQR. A resistant statistic is selected because the distribution is skewed.

f) C.

3.15.

a) According to the boxplot, we see that the age distribution is similar for men and women. Both distributions are fairly symmetric. The IQRs are approximately equal, so the distributions are similarly spread out. The median age for men is slightly higher than it is for women. Descriptive statistics quantify these impressions. According to the skewness ratio, neither distribution is severely skewed. The skewness ratio for men is .148/.342 = .43 and for women it is .395/.172 = 2.29. The average age for men in the study at initial examination ($M = 49.26$) was slightly higher than for women ($M = 48.63$). The distribution of ages for men was slightly more dispersed ($SD = 8.67$) than it was for women ($SD = 8.18$). Men's ages ranged from 33 to 67 years, whereas women's ranged from 34 to 67 years.

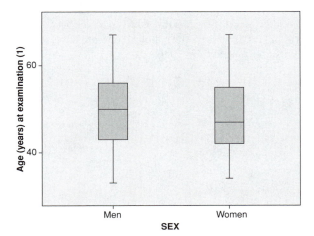

b) According to the boxplot, the cholesterol distribution is fairly symmetric for men, but positively skewed for women. The IQR for females is larger, so their cholesterol values are more heterogeneous. The median cholesterol for women is slightly higher than it is for men. Descriptive statistics quantify these impressions. According to the skewness ratio, the distribution is fairly symmetric for men (1.17) and severely positively skewed for women (4.34). The median cholesterol for men in the study at initial examination (median = 231.50) was slightly lower than for women (median = 239.00). The distribution of cholesterol for men was slightly more homogeneous (IQR = 54) than it was for women (IQR = 60). For men, the cholesterol levels ranged from 133 to 333, whereas for women they ranged from 152 to 464.

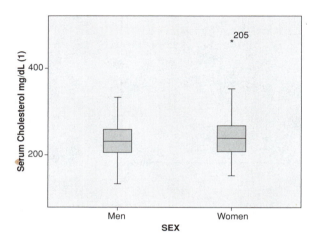

c) According to the boxplots, the blood pressure distributions are similar for men and women. All four distributions are positively skewed with outliers. The IQRs for systolic and diastolic blood pressure are approximately equal for the sexes, so there are no gender differences in the spread of these distributions. The median systolic and diastolic blood pressures are approximately equal for men and women. Descriptive statistics quantify these impressions. According to the skewness ratio, all four distributions are severely positively skewed. The skewness ratio for the systolic blood pressure for men is 6.73 and for women it is 6.84. The skewness ratio for the diastolic blood pressure for men is 2.09 and for women it is 3.13. The most severely skewed distribution is the systolic blood pressure for women. The median blood pressure is slightly higher for men (systolic = 127.75, diastolic = 81) than it is for women (systolic = 126.50, diastolic = 80). According to the values for the IQR, the blood pressure scores for men (systolic IQR = 24, diastolic IQR = 14) were slightly less spread out than they were for women (systolic IQR = 26, diastolic IQR = 15). For men, the systolic blood pressures ranged from 98 to 215 and the diastolic blood pressures ranged from 55 to 117. For women, the systolic blood pressures ranged from 93 to 213 and the diastolic blood pressures ranged from 50 to 118.

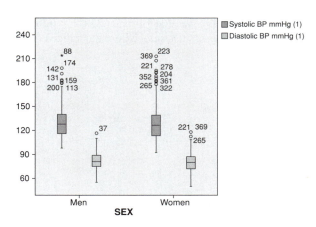

d) According to the boxplot, the BMI distributions for both men and women are positively skewed. Because the IQR is smaller, the BMI scores are more consistent for men than for women. The median BMI for men is higher than it is for women. Descriptive statistics quantify these impressions. According to the skewness ratio, the distribution for men is fairly symmetric (1.90) whereas for women it is severely positively skewed (6.55). The median BMI is higher for men in the study at initial examination (median = 26.31) than for women (median = 24.50). The BMI distribution was slightly more consistent for men (IQR = 3.95) than it was for women (IQR = 5.30). For men, BMI ranged from 16.98 to 38.14, whereas for women it ranged from 17.51 to 42.00.

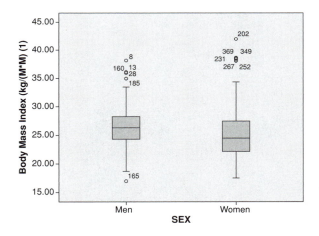

e) Because of the way the data were collected, of the 400 cases in the data set, 100 were nonsmoking men, 100 were nonsmoking women, 100 were men who smoked, and 100 were women who smoked.

f) According to the boxplot, the distributions of the number of cigarettes smoked per day for both men and women are positively skewed. Because the IQR is smaller, the distribution is more variable for men than for women. The median number of cigarettes smoked per day is very slightly higher for women than for men. Descriptive statistics quantify these impressions. According to the skewness ratio, the distribution of the number of cigarettes smoked per day is severely positively skewed for both men and women and more skewed for women (7.10) than for men (5.49). The median is slightly higher for women in the study at initial examination (median = .5) than for men (median = 0). The distribution was more variable for men (IQR = 20) than it was for women (IQR = 15). For men, the number of cigarettes smoked per day ranged from 0 to 60, whereas for women it ranged from 0 to 43.

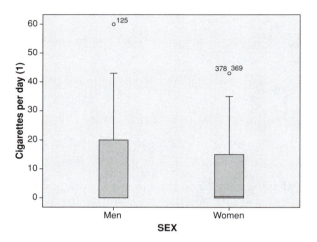

3.16.

a)

X	$X - \overline{X}$	$(X - \overline{X})^2$
7	2.42	5.856
16	11.42	130.42
0	−4.58	20.976
5	.42	.176
0	−4.58	20.976
0	−4.58	20.976
7	2.42	5.856
1	−3.58	12.816
6	1.42	2.016
1	−3.58	12.816
0	−4.58	20.976
12	7.42	55.056
Total: 55		**Total: 308.916**

$$\text{Mean} = \frac{\sum X}{N} = \frac{55}{12} = 4.58.$$

$$\text{Variance using Equation 3.4} = \frac{\sum (X - \overline{X})^2}{N} = \frac{308.916}{12} = 25.743.$$

$$\text{Variance as computed by SPSS} = \frac{\sum (X - \overline{X})^2}{N - 1} = \frac{308.916}{11} = 28.08.$$

$$\text{Standard deviation} = \sqrt{Variance} = \sqrt{25.743} = 5.07.$$

$$\text{Standard deviation as computed by SPSS} = \sqrt{Variance} = \sqrt{28.08} = 5.30.$$

It is because the data set is small (with only 12 cases) that the method used to compute the variance makes a difference.

To find the median, mode, range, and IQR, it is helpful to sort the data as follows:

0   0   0   0   1   1   5   6   7   7
12   16

The median is the average of the sixth and seventh scores or $(1 + 5)/2 = 3$.

The mode is 0.

The range is $16 - 0 = 16$.

To calculate the IQR, we need the 75th and 25th percentiles. The 25th percentile is 0 and the 75th is 7.

The IQR is $7 - 0 = 7$.

b)

Descriptives

			Statistic	Std. Error
Number of References in American Statistician 1995-2005	Mean		4.58	1.530
	95% Confidence Interval for Mean	Lower Bound	1.22	
		Upper Bound	7.95	
	5% Trimmed Mean		4.20	
	Median		3.00	
	Variance		28.083	
	Std. Deviation		5.299	
	Minimum		0	
	Maximum		16	
	Range		16	
	Interquartile Range		7	
	Skewness		1.063	.637
	Kurtosis		.399	1.232

c) $(0 - 4.58) + (0 - 4.58) + (0 - 4.58) + (0 - 4.58) + (1 - 4.58) + (1 - 4.58) +$
$(5 - 4.58) + (6 - 4.58) + (7 - 4.58) + (7 - 4.58) + (12 - 4.58) + (16 - 4.58) =$
$(-4.58 - 4.58 - 4.58 - 4.58 - 3.58 - 3.58 + .42 + 1.42 + 2.42 + 2.42 + 7.42 + 11.42 =$
$-25.48 + 25.52 =$
$.04 = 0$ within rounding error.

3.17.

a)

X	$X - \overline{X}$	$(X - \overline{X})^2$
107	−7	49
110	−4	16
123	9	81
129	15	225
112	−2	4
111	−3	9
107	−7	49
112	−2	4
135	21	441
102	−12	144
123	9	81
109	−5	25
112	−2	4
102	−12	144
98	−16	256
114	0	0
119	5	25
112	−2	4
110	−4	16
117	3	9
130	16	256
Total: 2394		**Total: 1842**

$$\text{Mean} = \frac{\sum X}{N} = \frac{2394}{21} = 114.$$

$$\text{Variance using Equation 3.4} = \frac{\sum (X - \overline{X})^2}{N} = \frac{1842}{21} = 87.71.$$

$$\text{Variance as computed by SPSS} = \frac{\sum (X - \overline{X})^2}{N - 1} = \frac{1842}{20} = 92.1.$$

$$\text{Standard deviation} = \sqrt{Variance} = \sqrt{87.71} = 9.37.$$

$$\text{Standard deviation as computed by SPSS} = \sqrt{Variance} = \sqrt{92.1} = 9.60.$$

It is because the data set is relatively small (with only 21 cases) that the method used to compute the variance makes a difference.

To find the median, mode, range, and IQR, it is helpful to sort the data as follows:

98	102	102	107	107	109	110	110	111	112
112	112	112	114	117	119	123	123	129	130
135									

The median is 112.

The mode is 112.

The range is $135 - 98 = 37$.

The IQR is $121 - 108 = 13$.

b) The following output, obtained using the SPSS Explore procedure, contains all of the required descriptive statistics.

Descriptives

				Statistic	Std. Error
Initial blood pressure	Mean			114.00	2.09
	95% Confidence	Lower Bound		109.63	
	Interval for Mean	Upper Bound		118.37	
	5% Trimmed Mean			113.72	
	Median			112.00	
	Variance			92.100	
	Std. Deviation			9.60	
	Minimum			98	
	Maximum			135	
	Range			37	
	Interquartile Range			13.00	
	Skewness			.612	.501
	Kurtosis			−.025	.972

3.18.

Age

		Frequency	Percent	Valid Percent	Cumulative Percent
Valid	6	22	21.0	21.0	21.0
	7	35	33.3	33.3	54.3
	8	26	24.8	24.8	79.0
	9	13	12.4	12.4	91.4
	10	9	8.6	8.6	100.0
	Total	105	100.0	100.0	

a) The 25th percentile, or Q_1 is approximately 7.
    The 50th percentile, or Q_2 is approximately 7.
    The 75th percentile, or Q_3 is approximately 8.
b) The IQR for this distribution is approximately $8 - 7 = 1$.
c) The mean decrease slightly, because the sum of all of the ages decreases by 2. The median does not change at all. The mode does not change at all.

3.19. Using Equation 3.1 for the mean, we see that, because the mean is 4 and the sample size is 12, the sum of the raw scores must be 48, not 36.

3.20. There are many possible answers. One is given for each case.
a) $\{0,0,0,0,0\}$.   b) $\{0,0,0,0,5\}$.   c) $\{1,2,3,5,5\}$.
d) $\{0,0,0,0,0\}$.   e) $\{5,5,5,5,5\}$.   f) $\{-5,0,0,0,0\}$.

3.21. If the distribution of wages is $5,000, $5,000, $7,000, $10,000, and $23,000, then the mean wage is $10,000, the median wage is $7,000, and the mode wage is $5,000.

3.22. In order for X to have a larger mean, its scores must be larger. In order for Y to have a larger standard deviation, its scores must be farther apart. One possible pair of distributions is $X = \{99, 100\}$ and $Y = \{1, 10\}$.

3.23. One possible pair of distributions is $X = \{10, 30, 50\}$ and $Y = \{10, 35, 40\}$.

3.24. One possible answer is $X = \{5, 5, 5, 5\}$ and $Y = \{1, 10\}$.

3.25. The majority means more than half. One possible distribution is $\{1, 2, 3, 4, 4\}$.

3.26. No. An algebraic explanation is given. We begin by noting that a distribution with only two extreme values, one on either side of the mean, and no intermediate values between those extremes, will have a standard deviation at least as large as a distribution with both extreme and intermediate values. We show that this distribution of two extreme values has a standard deviation equal to half the range, suggesting that any other distribution of values will have a standard deviation equal to no more than half the range. We assume, without loss of generality, that the distribution has the two values, a and b. The range of this distribution is, therefore, $b - a$ and half the range is, therefore, $(b - a)/2$. The mean of these two values equals $(b + a)/2$ and the standard deviation may be expressed as follows:

$$\sqrt{\frac{(X - \overline{X})^2}{N}} = \sqrt{\frac{\left(a - \left(\frac{a + b}{2}\right)\right)^2 + \left(b - \left(\frac{a + b}{2}\right)\right)^2}{2}}$$

$$= \sqrt{\frac{\left(\frac{2a - a - b}{2}\right)^2 + \left(\frac{2b - a - b}{2}\right)^2}{2}}$$

$$= \sqrt{\frac{\left(\frac{a - b}{2}\right)^2 + \left(\frac{b - a}{2}\right)^2}{2}} = \sqrt{\frac{a^2 - 2ab + b^2 + b^2 - 2ab + a^2}{8}}$$

$$= \sqrt{\frac{(b - a)^2}{4}} = \frac{b - a}{2}$$

which proves that it is not possible for the standard deviation of a distribution to be more than half the range.

3.27. In the distribution depicted in the following histogram, the mean is 4 and the modes are 3 and 5.

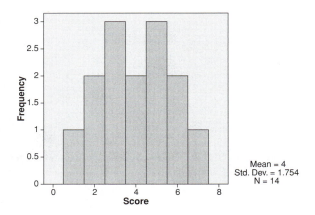

Mean = 4
Std. Dev. = 1.754
N = 14

3.28. One possible answer is depicted here.

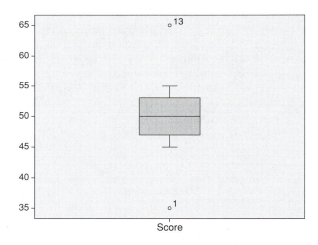

3.29. One possible answer is $X = \{0, 10\}$ and $Y = \{7, 9\}$.

3.30. One possible answer is $X = \{10, 50, 90\}$ and $Y = \{50, 89, 90\}$.

3.31. One possible answer is $X = \{10, 49, 50\}$ and $Y = \{60, 61, 62\}$.

3.32.
   a) The mean is higher. Because fewer than half of the players earn more than the average, the median is lower than the mean.
   b) We cannot be certain, but the distribution of salaries is probably positively skewed because the mean is higher than the median.

3.33. The standard deviation is closer to 5 months. Because almost all students enter kindergarten at age 5, they are within a year of each other's ages. The mean, however, is closer to 5 years.

3.34.

   a) It is probably true that the bulk of the students did fairly well, whereas there were a few students who did very poorly.

   b) Because the mean is probably lower than the median, it is preferable from a student perspective that the grade of B − be set to the mean, because a B − would then be easier to achieve.

3.35. They are probably due to differences in curricula and resources for different school systems.

3.36. A = X_5, B = X_1, C = X_3, D = X_4, E = X_2.

3.37.

   a) Positively skewed.

   b) Since "most" tax breaks were less than $500, the median must be $500 or less.

   c) The standard deviation will be larger than $500. Because most tax cuts are less than $500, the distance to the mean of $2,042 for most values in the distribution exceeds $1,500 ($2042 − $500 = $1542), thus creating a standard deviation greater than $500. The presence of a small number of "huge tax cuts" given to a small number of "very wealthy businessmen" produces the very large mean relative to the bulk of the tax break values, and, in turn, a large standard deviation, greater than $500.

3.38. We would expect the mean to be greater than the median. The distribution is likely to be severely positively skewed because one cannot have fewer than 0 children and most women probably have 0 − 4 children, but there are some positive outliers where women have an unusually large number of children. In the case of such positive skew, the mean is likely to be larger than the median.

CHAPTER 4. **SOLUTIONS**

4.1.

a) 15.	b) 15.	c) 1.14.	d) 11.
e) 5.	f) 1.14.	g) −10.	h) 10.
i) −1.14.	j) −1.	k) 5.	l) 1.14.

4.2.

   a) The average time for the fourth graders was 20 minutes. The average time for the sixth graders was 15 minutes. Thus, the sixth grade students were faster. The standard deviation for the fourth graders was 7 minutes. The standard deviation for the sixth graders was 5.4 minutes. Thus, the sixth-grade students were more similar to each other in the amount of time taken to complete the task.

   b) Adjusting the sixth-grade scores so that the time spent reading the instructions was not included in the calculation of the time to complete the task, the average time for the fourth graders was 20 minutes. The average time for the sixth-grade teacher was 18 minutes. Thus, the sixth-grade students were faster. The standard deviation for the fourth graders was 7 minutes. The standard deviation for the sixth graders was 5 minutes. Thus, the sixth-grade students were more similar to each other in the amount of time it took to complete the task.

4.3.

   a) CLASSES = CREDITS/3.

   b) 16.26/3 = 5.42.

   c) 2.40/3 = .8

   d) Skewness ratio = −12.05. The distribution of CLASSES is severely negatively skewed.

   e) Because of the presence of part-time students in the sample who could be taking only one credit during the semester. Full-time students typically take at least 15 credits during a semester.

4.4.

a)

Descriptives

		Statistic	Std. Error
School Average Daily Attendance Rate	Mean	93.65	.230
	95% Confidence Interval for Mean Lower Bound	93.20	
	Upper Bound	94.10	
	5% Trimmed Mean	94.14	
	Median	95.00	
	Variance	22.002	
	Std. Deviation	4.691	
	Minimum	43	
	Maximum	99	
	Range	56	
	Interquartile Range	3	
	Skewness	−6.235	.120
	Kurtosis	60.119	.238

b) SCHATTPP = SCHATTRT/100.

c) In this case, every data value in the distribution of SCHATTRT has been divided by 100, or multiplied by .01. Thus, we expect the mean, median, standard deviation, range, and IQR for SCHATTPP to be equal to the corresponding statistic for SCHATTRT divided by 100. We expect the variance for SCHATTPP to be equal to the variance for SCHATTRT divided by 100^2 or 10,000. Because the transformation is linear, we expect that it has no effect on the shape of the distribution so that the skew remains the same.

d) The following SPSS output corroborates our expectations. Note that the range is given as 1 because SPSS rounds .56 to 1.

Descriptives

		Statistic	Std. Error
schattpp	Mean	.94	.002
	95% Confidence Interval for Mean Lower Bound	.93	
	Upper Bound	.94	
	5% Trimmed Mean	.94	
	Median	.95	
	Variance	.002	
	Std. Deviation	.047	
	Minimum	0	
	Maximum	1	
	Range	1	
	Interquartile Range	0	
	Skewness	−6.235	.120
	Kurtosis	60.119	.238

4.5.

a)

Descriptives

			Statistic	Std. Error
Expected income at age 30	Mean		51574.73	2719.613
	95% Confidence Interval for Mean	Lower Bound	46230.26	
		Upper Bound	56919.20	
	5% Trimmed Mean		45168.24	
	Median		40000.00	
	Variance		3E+009	
	Std. Deviation		58265.758	
	Minimum		0	
	Maximum		1000000	
	Range		1000000	
	Interquartile Range		25000	
	Skewness		10.934	.114
	Kurtosis		161.570	.227

b) Compute EXPCENTS = EXPINC 30 *100.

c) The mean and median for EXPCENTS are equal, respectively, to the mean and median for EXPINC30 multiplied by 100. The standard deviation and IQR for EXPCENTS are equal, respectively, to the standard deviation and IQR for EXPINC30 multiplied by 100. The skew for EXPCENTS is equal to the skew for EXPINC30.

d)

Descriptives

			Statistic	Std. Error
expcents	Mean		5157473	271961.3
	95% Confidence Interval for Mean	Lower Bound	4623026	
		Upper Bound	5691920	
	5% Trimmed Mean		4516824	
	Median		4000000	
	Variance		3E+013	
	Std. Deviation		5826576	
	Minimum		0	
	Maximum		1E+008	
	Range		1E+008	
	Interquartile Range		2500000	
	Skewness		10.934	.114
	Kurtosis		161.570	.227

4.6.

a) .47.   b) The standard deviation is .50.

c) COMP1 = COMPUTER + 1.   d) COMP2 = (-1)* COMPUTER + 1.

e) For COMP1, the mean is 1.47 and the standard deviation is .50.
   For COMP2, the mean is .53 and the standard deviation is .50.

4.7.

a) $M = 9.44$, $SD = 12.37$, skewness ratio = 1.15/.122 = 9.42.

b) (-2)*9.44 + 3 = -15.88.

c) $(2)*12.37 = 24.74.$
d) $(-1)*9.42 = -9.42.$

4.8. The mean of SEX is 1.5. If 1 were subtracted from every score for the variable sex, the mean would be $1.5 - 1 = .5$ and the coding for the new variable would be 0 for Men and 1 for Women. Accordingly, the proportion of women in the *Framingham* data set is 50 percent.

4.9.
a) 3.   b) .99.   c) 31.

4.10.
a)

Descriptive Statistics

	N	Minimum	Maximum	Mean	Std. Deviation
Self-Concept in Eighth Grade	500	0	32	21.06	5.971
Valid N (listwise)	500				

b) ZSCORE = (SLFCNC08-21.06)/5.971.

c)

Descriptive Statistics

	N	Minimum	Maximum	Mean	Std. Deviation
ZSCORE	500	−3.53	1.83	.0003	1.00001
Zscore: Self-Concept in Eighth Grade	500	−3.52735	1.83184	.0000000	1.00000000
Valid N (listwise)	500				

d) The mean of this *z*-score distribution is 0, as it is for all *z*-score distributions. The standard deviation of this *z*-score distribution is 1, as it is for all *z*-score distributions. This is verified by using SPSS to calculate the mean and standard deviation of ZSCORE and ZSLFCNC0.

e) Mean: $21.06 + 5 = 26.06.$
Standard deviation $= 5.971.$

4.11.

a) $z = \dfrac{5.5 - 4.131}{.6605} = 2.07.$ b) $X = (.6605)(-1.71) + 4.132 = 3.00.$

c) 25. There are 7 *z*-scores below −2 and 18 above 2.

d) The cumulative percentage of the value 5.5 in English is 98.2. The cumulative percentage of the value 5.5 in math is 99.0. Accordingly, 5.5 represents a slightly more unusual number in math than in English because only 1 percent of the other students took more than 5.5 years of math, whereas 1.8 percent of the other students took more than 5.5 years of English.

e) The *z*-score of the value 5.5 in English is 2.07. The *z*-score of the value 5.5 in math is 2.31. Accordingly, 5.5 is slightly more unusual in math than in English because its *z*-score is higher.

4.12.

a) According to cumulative percentages, a score of 25 is relatively highest in eighth grade because the cumulative percentage in eighth grade is 74.8 percent, in tenth grade it is 67.2 percent, and in twelfth grade it is 20.6 percent.

b) According to *z*-scores, a score of 25 is highest in eighth grade because the *z*-score in eighth grade is .66, in tenth grade it is .35, and in twelfth grade it is −.90.

4.13.
  a) According to a cumulative percentage criterion, a self-concept score of 25 in eighth grade represents a higher level of self-concept for females than for males. For males, 70.9 percent of individuals have lower than or equal to a self-concept score of 25. That percentage for females is 78.0.
  b) According to a z-score criterion, a self-concept score of 25 in eighth grade represents a higher level of self-concept for females than males. The z-score for males is .52 and for females it is .78.

4.14.
  a) The female is slightly higher based on the cumulative percentage criterion. The percentage of females who scored at or below 58 is 70.0, whereas the percentage of males who scored at or below 63 is 68.6.
  b) The female is only slightly higher based on a z-score criterion. The z-score computed relative to females is $.51 \left(\dfrac{58 - 53.484}{8.8248} \right)$, whereas the z-score computed relative to males is $.50 \left(\dfrac{63 - 58.349}{9.381} \right)$.

4.15. $z = \dfrac{89 - 92}{2} = -1.5$. The score of 89 is 1.5 standard deviations below the mean.

4.16. $X = (10)(1.5) + 75 = 90$.

4.17. $Q_1 \le \overline{X} < z = +1$

4.18.
  a) $M = 2.54$, $SD = 1.20$.
  b) AGE = GRADE + 5.
  c) $2.54 + 5 = 7.54$.
  d) 1.20.
  e) The same as GRADE – approximately symmetric (or slightly positively skewed) – because the shape of a distribution does not change under translation.

4.19.
  a) The skewness ratio for the resource room placement is $\dfrac{-.477}{.327} = -1.46$, which indicates that the distribution is the skewed negatively, although not severely so. The skewness ratio for the self-contained classroom placement is $\dfrac{-2.301}{.481} = -4.78$, which indicates that the distribution is severely negatively skewed.
  b) According to both the mean and the median, the students have a higher overall level of reading comprehension in the resource room placement ($M = 81.43$, median = 83.00) than in the self-contained classroom placement ($M = 68.87$, median = 69.00).
  c) According to the IQR, the reading comprehension scores are more consistent for those in the self-contained classroom placement ($IQR = 12$) than for those in the resource room placement ($IQR = 12.50$). While the range and standard deviation lead to an opposite conclusion, they are not robust statistics and are influenced by the outliers present to varying degrees in these distributions.
  d) The maximum reading comprehension score for students in the resource room is 107, whereas for those in a self-contained classroom it is only 86.
  e) $z = \dfrac{75 - 81.43}{11.42} = -.56$.
  f) $X = sz + \overline{X} = (11.42)*2 + 81.43 = 104.27$.
  g) $z_{RR} = \dfrac{75 - 81.43}{11.42} = -.56$; $z_{SC} = \dfrac{75 - 68.87}{12.63} = .49$. A student with a reading comprehension score of 75 would be above the mean in the self-contained classroom and below the mean in the

resource room classroom. Furthermore, the student would be relatively farther below the mean in the self-contained classroom than above the mean in the resource room.

h) Yes. A percentile is a raw score in the distribution.

4.20.

a) 17.   b) 18.5 percent.

c) Below the median since the median has 50 percent of the distribution below it. Also, the median age is 48.

d) Below the mean by 1.07 standard deviations because $z = \dfrac{40 - 48.99}{8.425} = -1.07$.

e) 10 (all positive outliers).

f) There are five outliers among the men and five among the women.

g) BIRTHYR = 1956 − AGE1.

h) Given that the median for AGE1 is 48, the median for BIRTHYR must be 1956 − 48 = 1908.

i) The same as for AGE1, 8.425.

4.21.

Descriptive Statistics

	N	Minimum	Maximum	Mean	Std.	Skewness	
	Statistic	Statistic	Statistic	Statistic	Statistic	Statistic	Std. Error
Math Achievement in Tenth Grade	500	34.65	71.05	56.9897	7.83561	−.329	.109
Reading Achievement in Tenth Grade	500	31.53	68.80	56.1140	8.30446	−.558	.109
Science Achievement in Tenth Grade	497	33.13	72.48	55.7957	8.96852	−.188	.110
Social Studies Achievement in Tenth Grade	495	32.91	72.89	55.7975	8.66752	.015	.110
Valid N (listwise)	495						

Given that both math and reading achievement distributions have skewness ratios greater than 2 in absolute terms (for math it is −3.02 and for reading it is −5.12), we seek nonlinear transformations to reduce their skewness. The following transformations are explored:

$$ACHMATLG = LG10((-1)*ACHMAT10 + 72)$$
$$ACHMATSQ = SQRT((-1)*ACHMAT10 + 72)$$
$$ACHRDGLG = LG10((-1)*ACHRDG10 + 69)$$
$$ACHRDGSQ = SQRT((-1)*ACHRDG10 + 69)$$

These produce the following skewness results:

Descriptive Statistics

	N	Minimum	Maximum	Mean	Std.	Skewness	
	Statistic	Statistic	Statistic	Statistic	Statistic	Statistic	Std. Error
ACHMATLG	500	0	2	1.10	.302	−1.239	.109
ACHMATsq	500	1	6	3.72	1.086	−.319	.109
ACHrdglg	500	−1	2	.98	.386	−1.294	.109
ACHrdgsq	500	0	6	3.38	1.223	−.081	.109
Valid N (listwise)	500						

Based on these results, the square root transformations appear to be most appropriate.

4.22.

a) The following square root and log transformations were applied to APOFFER.

COMPUTE APOFFERSQ = SQRT(APOFFER+1).
COMPUTE APOFFERlg = LG10(APOFFER+1).

Based on the following skewness results, the square root transformation appears to be more appropriate in this case for symmetrizing the variable.

Descriptive Statistics

	N	Minimum	Maximum	Mean	Std.	Skewness	
	Statistic	Statistic	Statistic	Statistic	Statistic	Statistic	Std. Error
Number of Advanced Placement Courses Offered by School	473	0	80	5.42	6.664	4.093	.112
APOFFERlg	473	0	2	.61	.442	−.130	.112
APOFFERSQ	473	1	9	2.28	1.118	.939	.112
Valid N (listwise)	473						

b) The following square root and log transformations were applied to FAMSIZE:

COMPUTE FAMSIZEsq = SQRT(FAMSIZE).
COMPUTE FAMSIZElg = LG10(FAMSIZE).

Based on the following skewness results, the log transformation appears to be the more appropriate in this case for symmetrizing the variable

Descriptive Statistics

	N	Minimum	Maximum	Mean	Std.	Skewness	
	Statistic	Statistic	Statistic	Statistic	Statistic	Statistic	Std. Error
Family Size	500	2	9	4.69	1.319	1.101	.109
FAMSIZElg	500	0	1	.66	.118	.021	.109
FAMSIZEsq	500	1	3	2.15	.294	.584	.109
Valid N (listwise)	500						

c) The following square root and log transformations were applied to SCHATTRT:

COMPUTE SCHATTsq = sqrt(−1*SCHATTRT + 100).
COMPUTE SCHATTlg = lg10(−1*SCHATTRT + 100).

Based on the following skewness results, the square root transformation appears to be the more appropriate in this case for symmetrizing the variable

Descriptive Statistics

	N	Minimum	Maximum	Mean	Std.	Skewness	
	Statistic	Statistic	Statistic	Statistic	Statistic	Statistic	Std. Error
School Average Daily Attendance Rate	417	43	99	93.65	4.691	−6.235	.120
SCHATTlg	417	0	2	.74	.228	.144	.120
SCHATTsq	417	1	8	2.42	.692	2.282	.120
Valid N (listwise)	417						

d) No effect as shown in the following table.

Descriptive Statistics

	N	Minimum	Maximum	Mean	Std.	Skewness	
	Statistic	Statistic	Statistic	Statistic	Statistic	Statistic	Std. Error
Smoked Cigarettes Ever?	500	0	1	.14	.349	2.057	.109
CIGARETT1g	500	0	0	.04	.105	2.057	.109
CIGARETTsq	500	1	1	1.06	.145	2.057	.109
Valid N (listwise)	500						

4.23.

a) The following square root and log transformations were applied to GRADE:

COMPUTE GRADEsq = sqrt(GRADE).
COMPUTE GRADElg = lg10(GRADE).

Based on the following skewness results, the square root transformation appears to be the more appropriate in this case for symmetrizing the variable.

Descriptive Statistics

	N	Minimum	Maximum	Mean	Std.	Skewness	
	Statistic	Statistic	Statistic	Statistic	Statistic	Statistic	Std. Error
Grade Level	105	1	5	2.54	1.201	.508	.236
GRADElg	105	0	1	.35	.222	−.313	.236
GRADEsq	105	1	2	1.55	.380	.096	.236
Valid N (listwise)	105						

b) The following square root and log transformations were applied to MATHCOMP:

COMPUTE MATHCOMPsq = sqrt(MATHCOMP).
COMPUTE MATHCOMPlg = lg10(MATHCOMP).

Based on the following skewness results, the log transformation appears to be the more appropriate in this case for symmetrizing the variable.

Descriptive Statistics

	N	Minimum	Maximum	Mean	Std.	Skewness	
	Statistic	Statistic	Statistic	Statistic	Statistic	Statistic	Std. Error
Math Comprehension	94	61	121	86.28	13.754	.568	.249
mathcompsq	94	8	11	9.26	.731	.400	.249
mathcomplg	94	2	2	1.93	.068	.232	.249
Valid N (listwise)	94						

c) The following square root and log transformations were applied to READCOMP:

COMPUTE READCOMPsq = sqrt(−1*READCOMP + 108).
COMPUTE READCOMPlg = lg10(−1*READCOMP + 108).

Based on the following skewness results, the square root transformation appears to be the more appropriate in this case for symmetrizing the variable.

Descriptive Statistics

	N	Minimum	Maximum	Mean	Std.	Skewness	
	Statistic	Statistic	Statistic	Statistic	Statistic	Statistic	Std. Error
Reading Comprehension	76	22	107	77.63	13.078	−.956	.276
readcomplg	76	0	2	1.43	.257	−2.669	.276
readcompsq	76	1	9	5.37	1.242	−.414	.276
Valid N (listwise)	76						

4.24.

a) Construct a compute statement, as follows:

UNITMNC = UNITMATH − UNITCALC.

b) One student took 6 units (years) of noncalculus math.

4.25.

a) Construct a Compute statement, as follows:

ACHTOT12 = ACHMATH12 + ACHRDG12 + ACHSCI12 + ACHSLS12.

b) According to the histogram, the distribution is negatively skewed. This conclusion is corroborated by the skewness ratio of −3.7.

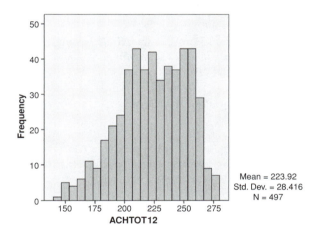

c) Among the students in the NELS data set, boys score higher than girls on the total achievement measure, because they have a higher mean as well as a higher median. The mean total achievement for boys is 230.14, whereas for girls it is 218.77. The median total achievement for boys is 234.19, whereas for girls it is 220.04.

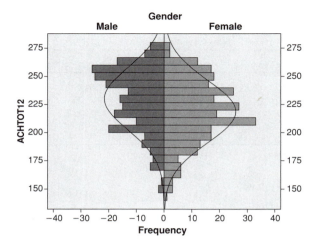

4.26.

   a) One way to create the variable is with the following sequence of old and new
       Values in the Recode procedure: $0 \to 0$, miss $\to$ sysmis, and else $\to 1$.

   b) 128.

   c) The mean of APOFFYN is .729, indicating that, not including those schools with a missing value
       on this variable, approximately 73 percent offer at least one AP course.

4.27.

   a) COMPUTE ALIVE = Death – Birth. At 92 years, Harald Cramer lived the longest.

   b) COMPUTE OLD = 2006 – Birth. If he were still alive today, John Tukey, at 91, would be the
       youngest of the statisticians in the data set.

4.28.

   a) 136 people ($.447 \times 304$) lost weight and 74 ($.243 \times 304$) reduced their cigarette smoking (those
       with negative values on the diff variables).

   b) For those who did not experience a CHD event, the mean change in BMI is .34, indicating an
       increase in BMI over this time period. For those who did experience a CHD event, the mean
       change in BMI is $-.28$, indicating a decrease in BMI over this time period. In short, those with-
       out a CHD event gained weight and those with such an event lost weight.

   c) Because the distribution of the difference in cigarettes smoked per day is severely positively
       skewed, we employ the median, a robust statistic, for the analysis. For both those who did and
       did not experience a CHD event, the median change in cigarettes smoked per day is 0, indicat-
       ing no change in cigarette use over time for either group. However, the means lead to a different
       conclusion. The mean change in cigarettes per day of those who did not experience a CHD event
       is –1.21, indicating a decrease in the average number of cigarettes smoked per day over this time
       period. For those who did not experience a CHD event, the mean change in CIGDAY is –3.01,
       indicating a decrease in the average number of cigarettes smoked per day over this time period.
       In short, although both groups smoked less, the decrease is greater by about two cigarettes per
       day for those who experienced a CHD event than for those who did not.

CHAPTER 5. **SOLUTIONS**

5.1. The relationship has a linear component, although from the look of the scatterplot, the relationship appears to be better described by a simple curve rather than a line.

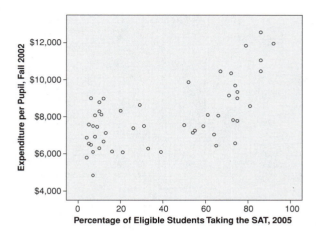

5.2. There appears to be little or no relationship (linear or nonlinear) between average teacher salary and graduation rate. In particular, it appears that states that pay their teachers better do not tend to have higher graduation rates.

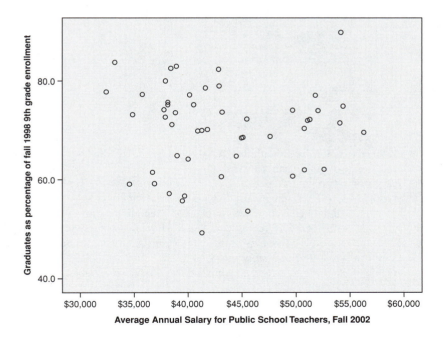

5.3.

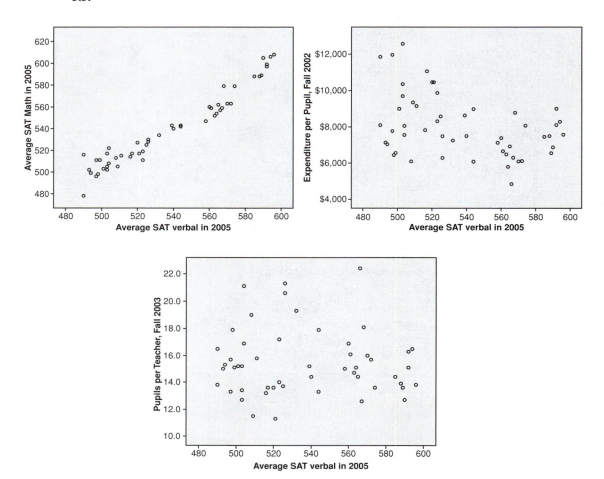

a) The strongest linear relationship is with SATM, followed by EDUCEXPEN, with STUTEACH having the weakest linear relationship to SATV.

b) It appears that states with higher average SAT verbal scores tend also to have higher SAT math scores; states with lower SAT verbal tend also to have lower SAT math.

c) It appears that states with higher average SAT verbal scores tend to have lower average expenditures per pupil; states with lower SAT verbal scores tend to have higher average expenditures per pupil. In this instance, a simple curve may fit the data better than a line, although the line does capture that part of the relationship that is linear.

d) There appears to be little or no linear relationship between these two variables.

5.4.

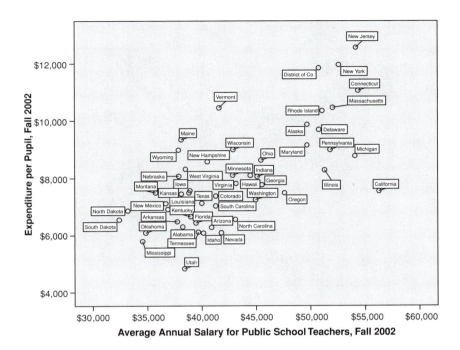

a) States with lower expenditures per pupil tend also to have lower teacher salaries and states with higher expenditures per pupil tend also to have higher teacher salaries.

b) California is an example of one state that is far from the linear trend. California spends less per pupil than what one would expect given what it pays teachers. Vermont is another example, but unlike California, Vermont spends more per pupil than what one would expect given what it pays teachers.

c) Yes. The Middle Atlantic states cluster together. Other geographical clusters are, for example, Vermont, Maine, and New Hampshire, states that all spend more money per pupil than expected given what these states pay their teachers.

5.5.

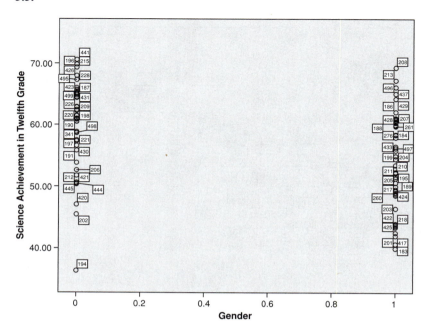

a) It appears as an outlier in the lower left of the scatterplot.

b) With all the cases in the data set, $r = .30$, indicating that adults with relatively high body mass index have relatively high total cholesterol levels as well.

c) The most unusual person in the data set has ID 205. For this person, the total cholesterol is a lot higher than one would expect given the body mass index. Looking at the data view, we see that this person is female and was 55 years old at the start of the study.

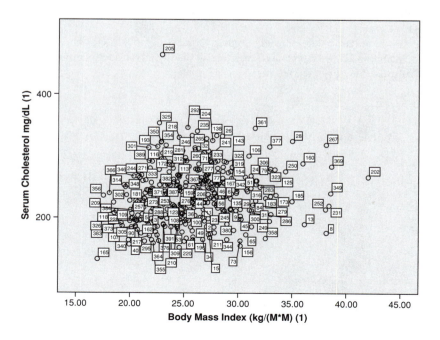

d) When omitting ID 205 the correlation is unchanged at $r = .30$. This is not unexpected because there are too many data points in this data set for this one outlier to affect the value of the correlation.

5.6.

a) A linear model appears to be the most appropriate way to represent these relationships in all cases.

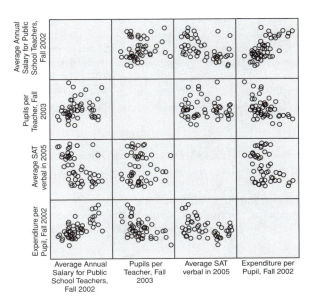

b)

Correlations

		Average Annual Salary for Public School Teachers, Fall 2002	Pupils per Teacher, Fall 2003	Average SAT verbal in 2005	Expenditure per Pupil, Fall 2002
Average Annual Salary for Public School Teachers, Fall 2002	Pearson Correlation	1	.162	−.501**	.688**
	Sig. (2-tailed)		.257	.000	.000
	N	51	51	51	51
Pupils per Teacher, Fall 2003	Pearson Correlation	.162	1	−.046	−.461**
	Sig. (2-tailed)	.257		.750	.001
	N	51	51	51	51
Average SAT verbal in 2005	Pearson Correlation	−.501**	−.046	1	−.408**
	Sig. (2-tailed)	.000	.750		.003
	N	51	51	51	51
Expenditure per Pupil, Fall 2002	Pearson Correlation	.688**	−.461**	−.408**	1
	Sig. (2-tailed)	.000	.001	.003	
	N	51	51	51	51

**Correlation is significant at the 0.01 level (2-tailed).

c) Yes, because the correlation between these two variables is $r = .688$.

d) No, because the correlation between these two variables is negative, $r = -.408$; states in which expenditures per pupil are higher tend to have lower verbal SAT scores, on average.

e) Yes, because the correlation between these two variables is negative: $r = -.461$.

f) Teacher salary.

5.7.

a) It is likely that students who have higher SES tend to have higher math achievement, and so one should expect a positive correlation between these two variables. Based on SPSS, the actual correlation is moderate and positive: $r = .32$.

b) It is likely that students who tend to have higher math achievement tend to perceive that their teachers are interested in them, and so one should expect a negative correlation between these two variables. Based on SPSS, the actual correlation is weak and negative: $r = -.18$.

c) There is likely to be no relationship between family size and math achievement, and so one should expect a near-zero correlation between these variables. Based on SPSS, the actual correlation is near zero: $r = .02$.

5.8.

a) The Pearson correlation between SCHATTRT and SLFCNC08 for the students in the NELS data set is $r = -.09$, indicating that for these data there is virtually no linear relationship between these two variables.

b) The correlation between SCHATTPP and SLFCNC08 remains at $r = -.09$ because, in converting from a percentage to a proportion, we multiply by the positive constant, .01. The linear transformation, in this case, does not involve reflection, thus keeping the sign of the correlation unchanged.

c) Without the most extreme value of expected income at age 30 of \$1,000,000, the pattern of points in the scatterplot indicates a slight positive correlation between SES and expected income. The extreme value at \$1,000,000, belonging to someone in the middle range of SES, serves to reduce the systematic positive orientation of points, as indicated by the correlation value, $r = .16$.

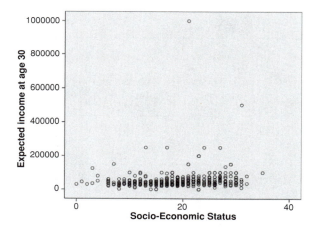

d) The new value of the correlation is now $r = .22$, suggesting that the influence of the extreme value of \$1,000,000 has been somewhat reduced by the square root transformation. Although weak, the correlation suggests that students with lower SES tend to have lower expected incomes whereas those with higher SES tend to have higher expected incomes.

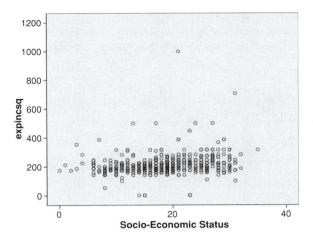

e) The correlation is .91, which is less than 1. The correlation would be equal to 1 in the case of a linear transformation (without reflection). A square root transformation is nonlinear and so we expect the correlation between the original and transformed variable to be less than 1.

f) $r(n = 97) = .21$.

g) $r(n = 97) = -.35$.

h) The correlation between the reflected variables is stronger than the one between the original variables. By transforming the variables in this case, they have each become more symmetric.

i) The signs are different because the self-esteem variable was reflected.

j) The interpretation remains the same because the self-esteem variable was reflected in the process of its being transformed.

5.9.

a) According to the scatterplot, the SES of students whose families owned a computer when they were in eighth grade appears to be higher overall than that of those who did not. That is, the mean SES for those families who owned a computer is higher than the mean of SES for those families who did not own a computer.

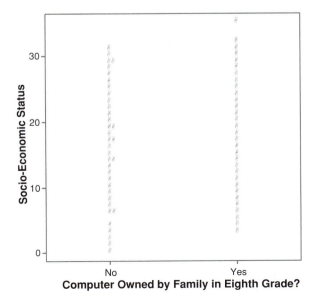

b) As shown by the scatterplot, the correlation between COMPUTER and SES is positive and moderate ($r = .35$), indicating that students whose families owned a computer when they were in eighth grade tend to have higher SES than those whose families did not own a computer when they were in eighth grade.

5.10.

Correlations

		Reading Comprehension	Grade Level	Intellectual Ability	Type of Placement
Reading Comprehension	Pearson Correlation	1	−.322**	.286*	−.444**
	Sig. (2-tailed)		.004	.012	.000
	N	76	76	76	76
Grade Level	Pearson Correlation	−.322**	1	−.272**	−.069
	Sig. (2-tailed)	.004		.005	.486
	N	76	105	105	105
Intellectual Ability	Pearson Correlation	.286*	−.272**	1	−.399**
	Sig. (2-tailed)	.012	.005		.000
	N	76	105	105	105
Type of Placement	Pearson Correlation	−.444**	−.069	−.399**	1
	Sig. (2-tailed)	.000	.486	.000	
	N	76	105	105	105

**Correlation is significant at the 0.01 level (2-tailed).
*Correlation is significant at the 0.05 level (2-tailed).

a) There is a small-to-moderate positive correlation between reading comprehension and intellectual ability, $r = .286$, suggesting that students with higher reading comprehension scores also tend to have higher intellectual ability and that students with lower reading comprehension scores also tend to have lower intellectual ability.

b) Because the correlation between these two variables is negative ($r = −.444$), and because resource room students are coded 0 and self-contained classroom students are coded 1, resource room students, on average, have the higher level of reading comprehension.

c) Because the correlation is so small, $r = −.07$, there is virtually no relationship between type of placement and grade level. That is, the typical grade level is about the same for the two placement types.

d) Because the correlation between grade level and reading comprehension is negative, $r = −.322$, the students in the higher grades tend to perform worse in reading comprehension relative to their peers than those in the lower grades. That is, as these learning-disabled students advance in grades, they appear to fall farther behind relative to their peers.

5.11.

a) $r = .18$. This relationship is positive, yet weak, suggesting preliminarily that adults taking blood pressure medication have slightly higher blood pressure, on average, than those who do not. The mean (81.00) and median (80.75) initial diastolic blood pressure of those not taking antihypertensive medication is in the normal range. The mean (91.54) and median (92.50) initial diastolic blood pressure of those taking antihypertensive medication is slightly above the normal range.

b) The point biserial correlation.

c) People with higher blood pressure often take such medication to lower their blood pressure. The positive relationship, however weak, suggests either that the medication is not wholly effective in lowering blood pressure to acceptable levels or that it has not yet been taken for long enough to be effective.

d) The correlation between SEX and ANYCHD4 is $r = -.18$. Because females are coded as higher on SEX and developing CHD is coded higher on ANYCHD4, females are somewhat less likely than males to develop CHD. A similar conclusion is reached using a cross-tabulation approach as noted below.

Incident Hosp MI, AP, CI, Fatal CHD by the end of the study*
SEX Crosstabulation

Count

		SEX		Total
		Men	Women	
Incident Hosp MI, AP, CI, Fatal CHD by the end of the study	CHD Event Did Not Occur	134	165	299
	CHD Event Did Occur	66	35	101
Total		200	200	400

Males are more likely to develop CHD ($66/200 \times 100 = 33$ percent) than females ($35/200 \times 100 = 17.5$ percent).

e) The phi coefficient.

f) Because the scatterplot indicates that the relationship is nonlinear. A simple curve would represent the relationship better than a line.

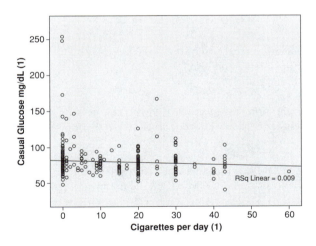

5.12. What evidence is there in these data to suggest that HDL is "good" cholesterol and LDL is "bad" cholesterol? [HINT: Compute the correlation between HDL3 and ANYCHD4 and between LDL3 and ANYCHD4.]

Correlations

		Incident Hosp MI, AP, CI, Fatal CHD by the end of the study	LDL Cholesterol mg/dL (3)	HDL Cholesterol mg/dL (3)
Incident Hosp MI, AP, CI, Fatal CHD by the end of the study	Pearson Correlation	1	.304**	−.249**
	Sig. (2-tailed)		.000	.000
	N	400	282	282
LDL Cholesterol mg/dL (3)	Pearson Correlation	.304**	1	−.199**
	Sig. (2-tailed)	.000		.001
	N	282	282	282
HDL Cholesterol mg/dL (3)	Pearson Correlation	−.249**	−.199**	1
	Sig. (2-tailed)	.000	.001	
	N	282	282	282

**Correlation is significant at the 0.01 level (2-tailed).

According to the correlations, those with high LDL cholesterol tend to be those who developed CHD during the course of the study ($r = .30$), whereas those with high HDL tend to be those who did not develop CHD during the course of the study ($r = −.25$).

5.13.

a) The Pearson Correlation between SES and COMPUTER for the students in the NELS data set is $r = 35$, suggesting that students who owned computers in eighth grade have higher SES, on average, than those who do not.

b) COMP1 = COMPUTER + 1.

The transformation does not include a reflection of the variable COMPUTER because a relatively low code score on COMP1 still represents "No."

c) $r = 1$.

d) COMP2 = COMPUTER + 1.

The transformation includes a reflection of the variable COMPUTER because we are multiplying COMPUTER by −1. As a result, a relatively low code score on COMP2 now represents "Yes" when it originally represented "No."

e) $r = −1$.

f) The correlation between SES and COMP1 is the same as the correlation between SES and COMPUTER because the (linear) transformation of COMPUTER did not involve reflection: $r = .35$. The correlation between SES and COMP2 is the negative of the correlation between SES and COMPUTER because the (linear) transformation of COMPUTER involved reflection: $r = −.35$.

5.14.

a) The Pearson correlation between SES and SLFCNC12 for the students in the NELS is $r = .11$. The interpretation is that students with a higher SES tend to have a higher self-concept whereas students with a lower SES tend to have a lower self-concept. However, the relationship is weak.

b) The Pearson Correlation between SESDI and SLFCNC12DI is $r = .001$, indicating a near-zero linear relationship between the two variables.

c) In this case, there was a reduction in the magnitude of the correlation based on the original continuous variables. The loss of information when transforming the multivalued continuous variables into two dichotomous variables, each split at its median, resulted in a near-zero correlation. As noted in Chapter 4, other types of nonlinear transformations that retain the multivalued nature of the continuous variable are to be preferred to the median split.

5.15.

Correlations

			Time Spent Weekly on Extra-Curricular Activities in Twelfth Grade	Smoked Cigarettes Ever?	Socio-Economic Status	Number of Times Missed School in Twelfth Grade
Spearman's rho	Time Spent Weekly on Extra-Curricular Activities in Twelfth Grade	Correlation Coefficient	1.000	−.197**	.120**	−.081
		Sig. (2-tailed)		.000	.007	.069
		N	500	500	500	500
	Smoked Cigarettes Ever?	Correlation Coefficient	−.197**	1.000	−.038	.108*
		Sig. (2-tailed)	.000		.397	.015
		N	500	500	500	500
	Socio-Economic Status	Correlation Coefficient	.120**	−.038	1.000	−.039
		Sig. (2-tailed)	.007	.397		.386
		N	500	500	500	500
	Number of Times Missed School in Twelfth Grade	Correlation Coefficient	−.081	.108*	−.039	1.000
		Sig. (2-tailed)	.069	.015	.386	
		N	500	500	500	500

**Correlation is significant at the 0.01 level (2-tailed).
*Correlation is significant at the 0.05 level (2-tailed).

a) According to the value of Spearman's rho (−.20), there is a weak negative relationship between cigarette smoking and participation in extracurricular activities in twelfth grade. In particular, students who had ever tried smoking were less likely to participate in extracurricular activities in twelfth grade.

b) According to the value of Spearman's rho (−.06), there is virtually no relationship between missing school and participation in extracurricular activities in twelfth grade.

c) According to the value of Spearman's rho (.12), there is a weak positive relationship between SES and participation in extracurricular activities in twelfth grade.

5.16.

Advanced Math Taken in Eighth Grade*
Urbanicity Crosstabulation

Count

		Urbanicity			Total
		Urban	Suburban	Rural	
Advanced Math Taken in Eighth Grade	No	59	112	94	265
	Yes	61	100	65	226
Total		120	212	159	491

a) Urban: 61/120 = .51; Suburban: 100/212 = .47; Rural: 65/159 = .41.

b) 226/491 = .47.

c) Urban with .51 advanced math takers.

d) There appears to be some relationship. If there were no relationship, each of the three environments would have the same proportion of students who took advanced math in eighth grade as the overall proportion (.47). Because the proportions given in part (c) are not all equal to .47, there appears to be a relationship. Namely, students from urban environments appear to be most likely to have taken advanced math in eighth grade, followed by those from suburban environments, and then finally those from rural environments.

5.17.

a) According to the contingency table, there is no relationship whatsoever between these two variables. The proportions of men and women who smoked at time 1 respectively equal the proportion of all individuals who smoked at time 1. Each proportion equals one-half. The sample for the data set was selected to have this property.

Current Cig Smoker Y/N (1) *
SEX Crosstabulation

Count

		SEX		Total
		Men	Women	
Current Cig Smoker Y/N(1)	No	100	100	200
	Yes	100	100	200
Total		200	200	400

b) According to the contingency table, at time 3, after being enrolled in the study for 12 years, females were more slightly more likely to smoke (40.3 percent) than males (32.2 percent). Overall, 36.4 percent were smokers at time 3. The patterns of difference from 36.4 percent is slight.

Current Cig Smoker Y/N (3) *
SEX Crosstabulation

Count

		SEX		Total
		Men	Women	
Current Cig Smoker Y/N (3)	No	101	95	196
	Yes	48	64	112
Total		149	159	308

c) The correlation between the two variables is $r = 0$, as expected.

d) The correlation between the two variables is quite small ($r = .08$), as expected.

5.18.

a) Of all men in the study that were initially measured on BMI, 52.76 percent were overweight and 13.07 percent were obese, totaling to approximately 66 percent who were either overweight or obese. Of all women in the study that were initially measured on BMI, 32.83 percent were overweight and 11.11 percent were obese, totaling to approximately 44 percent who were either overweight or obese.

SEX* Weight Category Crosstabulation

Count

| | | Weight Category | | | | Total |
		Under Weight	Normal Weight	Over Weight	Obese	
SEX	Men	1	67	105	26	199
	Women	3	108	65	22	198
Total		4	175	170	48	397

b) Yes, suggesting a relationship between weight category and sex. In particular, while there are basically an equal number of men and women who have BMI values recorded at time 1, the ratio of men to women in the normal weight category is approximately 1 to 1.5, and it is the reverse for the overweight category. There are too few underweight individuals to analyze this category, and there are about equal numbers of obese individuals by gender.

c) For men, approximately twice the number did not experience a CHD event compared to those who did. On the other hand, for women, approximately five times the number did not experience a CHD event compared to those who did. Said differently, the likelihood of having experienced a CHD event for this sample is far greater for men than for women.

SEX* Incident Hosp MI, AP, CI, Fatal CHD by the end of the study Crosstabulation

Count

| | | Incident Hosp MI, AP, CI, Fatal CHD by the end of the study | | Total |
		CHD Event Did Not Occur	CHD Event Did Occur	
SEX	Men	134	66	200
	Women	165	35	200
Total		299	101	400

d) By contrast to the ratios of 2:1 for men and 5:1 for women (no CHD vs. CHD), when we restrict to only those who are obese at time 1, the ratios remain at 2:1 for men, but they decrease to 2:1 for women. It appears that being obese as a woman greatly increases her chances of experiencing a CHD event, but not so for men.

SEX* Incident Hosp MI, AP, CI, Fatal CHD by the end of the study Crosstabulation

Count

| | | Incident Hosp MI, AP, CI, Fatal CHD by the end of the study | | Total |
		CHD Event Did Not Occur	CHD Event Did Occur	
SEX	Men	17	9	26
	Women	15	7	22
Total		32	16	48

5.19. There can be more than one correct analysis, although only one is given.

a) The correlation between years of math taken in high school and math achievement in twelfth grade is .42, which suggests that in general, students who take more math tend to score higher on math achievement.

b) According to Spearman's rho (.43), students who came to school late also had a tendency to cut or skip classes.

c) Using the cross-tabulation procedure, we find that 52 percent of public school students did not to take AP classes, whereas only 38 percent of private religious school students did not take AP classes and only 30 percent of private nonreligious school students did not take AP classes. Thus, public school students appear to be less likely to take AP classes than private school students.

d) The correlation between these two variables is $r = .02$, suggesting that there is virtually no linear relationship between family size and twelfth-grade self-concept.

e) The correlation between these two variables is $r = .32$, suggesting that among the students in the NELS data set, a higher SES is associated with a higher science achievement.

f) According to a contingency table analysis using cross-tabs, region appears to make a difference as to whether a student took advanced math in eighth grade. While 61 percent of students from the West took advanced math in eighth grade, so did 48 percent from the South, 41 percent from the Northeast, and 38 percent from the North Central region.

g) According to Spearman's Correlation (rho $= -.006$), there is virtually no relationship between the number of classes a student cut in twelfth grade and whether or not that student took advanced math in eighth grade.

h) According to a contingency table analysis using cross-tabs, there appears to be no relationship between URBAN and CIGARETTE among students in the NELS. Specifically, students overwhelmingly report that they have not smoked cigarettes, regardless of how urban the area is from which they come. In particular, 85 percent of urban students report not having smoked, 86 percent of suburban students report not having smoked, and 87 percent of the rural students report not having smoked. The uniformity of response across types of area suggests little relationship between these two variables.

i) According to the phi coefficient, $r = .27$, students that were enrolled in advanced math in eighth grade (ADVMATH8 = 1) tended also to take AP classes (APPROG = 1) in high school.

j) The scatterplot shows a curvilinear rather than a linear relationship, as further indicated by the Spearman Correlation Coefficient, rho $= .09$.

k) According to the scatterplot, and as corroborated by a Pearson Product Moment Correlation Coefficient of $r = .11$, there is a weak positive linear relationship between these two variables. In particular, students with higher self-concept tend to have higher SES, whereas those with lower self-concept tend to have lower SES.

l) According to the Point-Biserial Correlation Coefficient, $r = .38$ suggests that students who attended nursery school (NURSERY = 1) tend to have higher SES than those who did not (NURSERY = 0).

m) Because none of the three distributions of SES by urbanicity is severely skewed, this analysis is based on a comparison of means. On average, urban students have the highest SES ($M = 20.33$), followed by suburban students ($M = 19.23$), and then rural students ($M = 15.94$). Because the distributions are not skewed, a comparison of medians yields the same ordering.

5.20.

Correlations

		Vote on Perjury	Conservatism	State Voter Support for Clinton	First-Term senator?
Vote on Perjury	Pearson Correlation	1	.866**	−.429**	.203*
	Sig. (2-tailed)		.000	.000	.043
	N	100	100	100	100
Conservatism	Pearson Correlation	.866**	1	−.447**	.272**
	Sig. (2-tailed)	.000		.000	.006
	N	100	100	100	100
State Voter Support for Clinton	Pearson Correlation	−.429**	−.447**	1	−.012
	Sig. (2-tailed)	.000	.000		.906
	N	100	100	100	100
First-Term senator?	Pearson Correlation	.203*	.272**	−.012	1
	Sig. (2-tailed)	.043	.006	.906	
	N	100	100	100	100

**Correlation is significant at the 0.01 level (2-tailed).
*Correlation is significant at the 0.05 level (2-tailed).

a) Because the scatterplot can be described to have a linear pattern, it was appropriate to compute the correlation between the two variables.

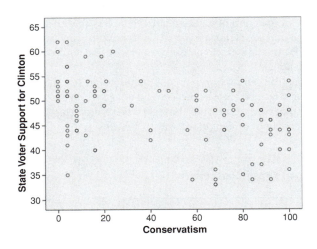

b) The correlation between these two variables is $r = -.45$, a moderate-to-strong negative correlation, indicating that conservative senators tended to come from states with little voter support for Clinton.

c) Conservative senators were much more likely to vote guilty on perjury. The value of r (.866) is positive and very strong, indicating that high scores on CONSERVA are associated with a high score on VOTE1, which represents a guilty vote.

d) Senators from states that supported Clinton in 1996 were more likely to vote not guilty on perjury. The value of r (−.429) is negative and moderate to strong, indicating that high scores on SUPPORTC are associated with a low score on VOTE1, which represents a not guilty vote.

e) First-term senators were slightly more likely to vote guilty on perjury. The value of r (.203) is positive, yet weak, indicating that a high score on NEWBIE (the senator is first-term) has a slight tendency to be associated with a high score on VOTE1 (guilty on perjury).

f) CONSERV. Its correlation with VOTE1 is the strongest of the three.

g) Because REGION is nominal with more than two categories, it has no inherent ordering, a requirement when computing a correlation. In this case, a more appropriate analysis would be based on a contingency table.

5.21.

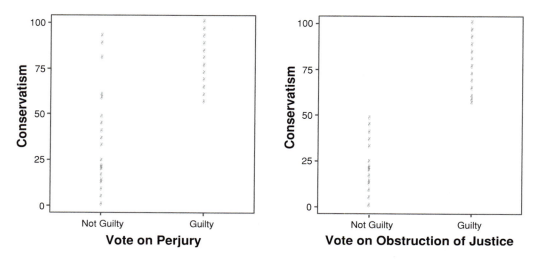

a) Those who voted not guilty on obstruction of justice tended to be less conservative and those who voted guilty on obstruction of justice tended to be more conservative, on average, $r = .94$.

b) The vote was along party lines. Democrats tend to be less conservative and tended to support the democratic president by voting not guilty.

c) The correlation between conservatism and the vote on obstruction of justice is the stronger of the two. Every senator with a conservatism score below 50 voted not guilty on obstruction of justice whereas every senator with a conservatism score above 50 voted guilty. This clear pattern of separation between voting groups is not evident in the vote on perjury.

5.22.

Vote on Perjury* region Crosstabulation

Count

		region				Total
		Northeast	Midwest	South	West	
Vote on Perjury	Not Guilty	15	12	16	12	55
	Guilty	3	12	16	14	45
	Total	18	24	32	26	100

a) 55.   b) 55 percent.

c) 29 percent.   d) 50 percent.

e) Yes. Senators from the Northeast had a great tendency to vote not guilty (83.33 percent voted not guilty) whereas those from the other regions were much more evenly split on guilty/not guilty.

In the Midwest, South, and West, 50, 50, and 53.85 percent of the senators, respectively, voted not guilty.

f) Clustered bar graph.

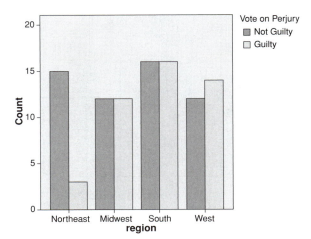

g) A contingency table is appropriate for variables with a small number of values. Although REGION is fine with only four categories, CONSERVA is not. A contingency table that included the variable CONSERVA would probably stretch over more than a page.

5.23.

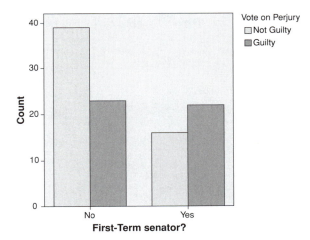

a) Yes. Not guilty votes tend to come from senior senators whereas guilty votes are evenly split between first-term and senior senators.

b) Positive. Low scores on VOTE1 (0 = not guilty) correspond to low scores on NEWBIE (1 = senior senator).

5.24.

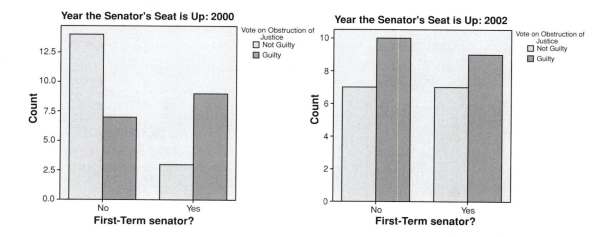

a) There is a relationship. First-term senators tended to vote guilty whereas more experienced, non-first-term senators tended to vote not guilty.

b) Positive. First-term senators scored 1 (relatively high) on NEWBIE and tended to score 1 (relatively high) on VOTE2. More experienced senators scored 0 (relatively low) on NEWBIE and tended to score 0 (relatively low) on VOTE2.

c) It is stronger for senators up for re-election in 2000. Among senators up for re-election in 2002, there is little or no relationship between whether or not the senator was first term and his or her vote on obstruction of justice because both first-term and experienced senators tended to vote guilty.

5.25.

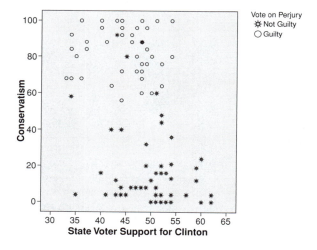

a) According to the cloud-like circular shape of the points on the scatterplot for the senators who voted guilty (given by the circles on the scatterplot), there appears to be little or no relationship between state voter support for Clinton and conservatism among those senators who voted guilty.

b) Because the points on the scatterplot for senators who voted not guilty (given by the starts on the scatterplot) may be described by a line with negative slope, it appears that senators from states with high voter support for Clinton who voted not guilty tended to be less conservative.

5.26. The relationship between manual dexterity and age is nonlinear.

5.27. The statement is false because the magnitude of the correlation measures the strength of a relationship on an ordinal, not ratio scale. A correct statement is "A Pearson Correlation Coefficient value of $r = 0.8$ represents a stronger linear relationship than a Pearson Correlation Coefficient value of $r = 0.4$."

5.28. Although there is a correlation between taking a challenging mathematics curriculum and college enrollment, this does not imply that there is a causal relationship between the two. A third variable, namely, general intelligence, may be the underlying cause of both taking a challenging mathematics curriculum and college enrollment.

5.29. Although there is a correlation between the incidence of smoking and the presence of Joe Camel, Joe Camel may not be the cause of the smoking increase. In fact, as we have seen, the incidence of other drug use, such as marijuana, was also on the rise during this time period. Both increases may be due to another factor, not Joe Camel.

5.30. The value of r ranges between -1 and 1 inclusive. The value $r = 1.05$ is impossible.

5.31. Region is a nominal-leveled variable with more than two categories. Correlation is not meaningful when at least one of the variables is nominal with more than two categories, as is the case for Region.

5.32. The statement is false because reflection, a type of linear transformation, of one of the variables (for example, multiplying the variable X by -1) will change the correlation to $r = -.50$.

5.33. The correlation does not provide information about the level of the two variables – how they compare, only about the relationship between them – how they are associated.

5.34. Nonlinear relationships are not measured well by the Pearson Product Moment Correlation Coefficient because this correlation coefficient is designed to measure linear relationships only. An example of such a scatterplot is the following:

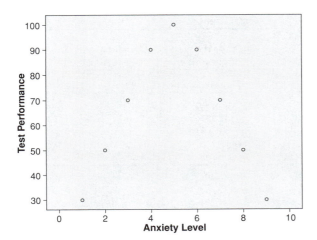

5.35.

Group 1 = c.
Group 2 = d.
Group 3 = e.
Group 4 = f.

CHAPTER 6. **SOLUTIONS**

6.1.

a) Because EDUCEXPE and TEACHPAY are both ratio-leveled variables, their level of measurement is appropriate. Furthermore, the scatterplot indicates that the pattern of points is effectively approximated by a line.

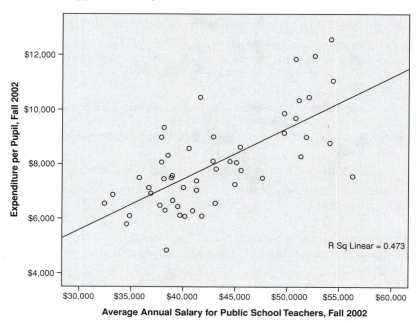

b) $\hat{Y} = .187(\text{TEACHPAY}) - 24.549$.

Coefficients[a]

Model	Unstandardized Coefficients		Standardized Coefficients		
	B	Std. Error	Beta	t	Sig.
1 (Constant)	−24.549	1226.989		.020	984
teachpay Average Annual Salary for Public School Teachers, Fall 2002	.187	.028	.688	6.630	.000

[a]Dependent Variable: educexpe Expenditure per Pupil. Fall 2002.

c) A one-dollar increase in the average annual salary for public school teachers corresponds to a .187 dollar (almost 19 cents) increase in the expenditure per pupil for the state, on average.

d) In this case the intercept is not meaningful because there are no states for which the average annual salary for teachers is close to $0.

e) $\hat{Y} = .187(40000) - 24.549 = \$7,455.45$.

f) No. The value 70,000 is well beyond the largest value of the data from which the model was created.

g) $R = .69$ indicating that the correlation between the actual and predicted educational expenditures is strong.

6.2.

a) Although the first two scatterplots are not exactly linear, there is not a simple curve that provides a better fit than the regression line. A line gives a good fit to the third scatterplot.

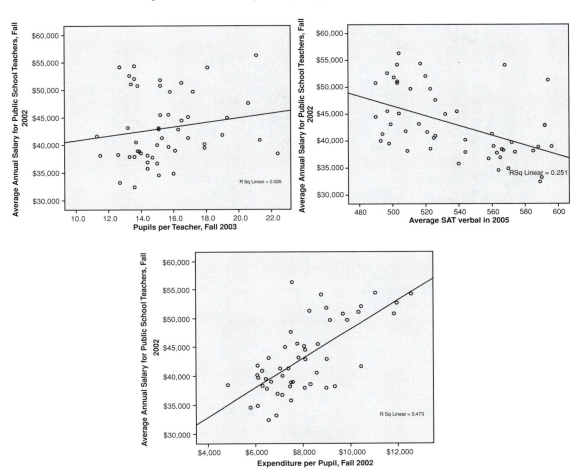

b) Educational expenditure per pupil. It is most strongly correlated with teacher salary.
c) No, because there is little or no correlation between the two variables.
d) Because REGION is nominal with more than two categories, there is no inherent ordering of the variable, as a linear model requires.

6.3.

a) Because both variables are interval the level of measure is appropriate. Furthermore, the pattern of points in the scatterplot is sufficiently modeled by a line.

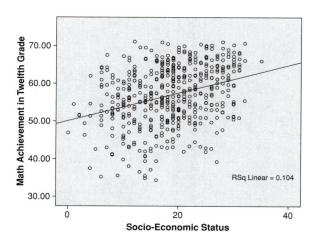

b) $\hat{Y} = .368(SES) + 50.123$.

c) Each one-point increase in SES is associated with a .368-point increase in twelfth-grade math achievement, on average.

d) A person with SES = 0 is predicted to score 50.123 in twelfth-grade math achievement.

e) 57.483.

f) 59.69.

g) 58.59.

6.4.

a) Although the shape of the data is not exactly linear, there is no other simple curve that does a better job of approximating the data.

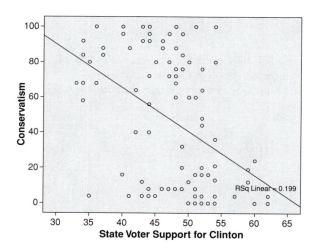

b) The value of the correlation, $r = -.447$, can be found using a correlation analysis, or using a simple regression analysis as the value of beta.

c) $R = .447$. That represents a moderate to strong goodness of fit.

d) $\hat{Y} = -2.488(\text{SUPPORC}) + 164.911$.

e) Each 1 percent increase in the state voter support for Clinton is associated with a 2.488-point decrease in that state's senator's conservatism rating, on average.

f) Because there were no states with no voter support for Clinton, there was no data collected near SUPPORTC = 0 (the lowest support level was larger than 30) and the value of the intercept is not meaningful.

g) $\hat{Y} = -2.488(50) + 164.911 = 40.51$.

6.5.

a) Yes. The variables are both ratio-leveled and the data in the scatterplot are effectively modeled by a line. There are a few outliers that warrant further investigation, however.

b) The slope of the regression line is positive, indicating that the correlation is, as well. Thus adults with relatively high BMI tend also to have relatively high diastolic blood pressure.

c) Approximately 75 mmHg.

d) Because 50 is above the highest value of BMI measured in the data set, it is inappropriate to extrapolate the model to that extreme.

6.6.

a)

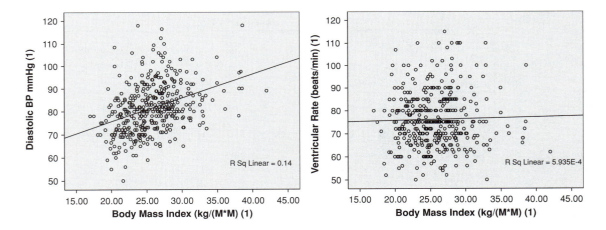

b) The relationship between body mass index and diastolic blood pressure will have the higher Pearsons r-value because the data points, overall, conform more closely to the regression line.

c) Because the slope of the regression line between BMI and blood pressure is steeper than that between BMI and heart rate, a one-unit increase in BMI is associated with a greater increase in diastolic blood pressure.

6.7.

a)

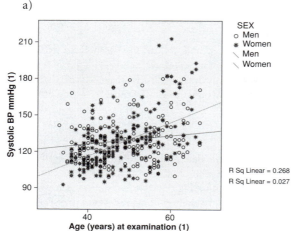

b) Select cases so that PBMEDS 1 = 0. Then, split the file by SEX and run the regression. The two regression equations are:

For men $\hat{Y}$ = .346(AGE1) + 112.431.

For women $\hat{Y}$ = 1.388(AGE1) + 60.841.

Coefficients^a

SEX SEX	Model		Unstandardized Coefficients		Standardized Coefficients		
			B	Std. Error	Beta	t	Sig.
1 Men	1	(Constant)	112.431	7.529		14.933	.000
		AGE1 Age (years) at examination (1)	.346	.151	.165	2.293	.023
2 Women	1	(Constant)	60.841	8.192		7.427	.000
		AGE1 Age (years) at examination (1)	1.388	.167	.518	8.295	.000

^{a}Dependent Variable: SYSBP1 Systolic BP mmHg (1).

c) For men, a one-year increase in age is associated with a .346-point increase in systolic blood pressure, on average. For women, a one-year increase in age is associated with a 1.39-point increase in systolic blood pressure, on average. Blood pressure is increasing faster with age for women than it is for men.

d) For men, R = .17, whereas for women, R = .52, indicating that the goodness of fit for the regression line for women is better than it is for men.

e) For men, $\hat{Y}$ = .346(50) + 112.431 = 129.73.

   For women, $\hat{Y}$ = 1.388(50) + 60.841 = 130.24.

6.8.

a) $7125.70.   b) $6300.

c) $-825.70.   d) Overpredicts.

e) The residual with the largest magnitude corresponds to California with value −2945.79.

f) The largest positive residual is $2700.70 and corresponds to Vermont. The model underpredicts the educational expenditure for Vermont.

g) It is larger in magnitude for the first. The value of the residual for the first is −825.70 and for the second is 605.74.

6.9.

a)

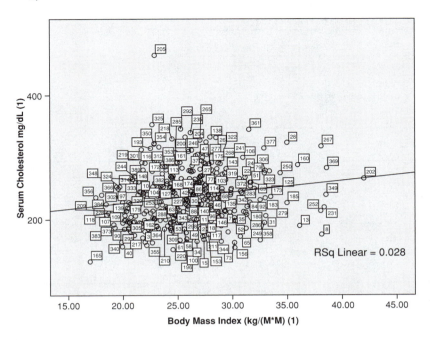

b) The data do follow an approximately linear trend, albeit not a strong one. There is a bivariate outlier (case 205) and its effects on the model should be investigated.

c) Approximately 220 mg/dL.

d) Approximately 130 mg/dL.

e) Approximately 90 mg/dL.

f) The most unusual person in the data set has ID 205. For this person, the total cholesterol is a lot higher than one would expect given the body mass index. Looking at the data view, we see that this person is female and is 55 years old at the start of the study.

g) 1.82.

h) When omitting ID 205 the slope of the regression line increases slightly to 1.93.

6.10.

a) $\hat{Y} = -3.345(\text{GRADE}) + 86.743$.

b) $\hat{Y} = -3.345(\text{AGE}) + 103.468$.

c) The slope of the regression equation is given by

$$b = (r_{\text{READCOMP,AGE}}) \frac{SD_{\text{READCOMP}}}{SD_{\text{AGE}}}$$

$r_{\text{READCOMP,AGE}} = r_{\text{READCOMP,GRADE}}$ because the linear transformation from grade to age does not involve reflection.

Also, $SD_{\text{AGE}} = SD_{\text{GRADE}}$ because the linear transformation from grade to age does not involve reflection. Thus, the slope does not change.

d) The intercept of the regression equation with GRADE as the independent variable is given by $a = \overline{Y} - b\overline{X}$.

The mean of AGE $= \overline{X} + 5$.

The intercept with AGE as the independent variable is

$a = \overline{Y} - b(\overline{X} + 5) = \overline{Y} - b\overline{X} - (-3.345)(5) = \overline{Y} - b\overline{X} + 16.725$.

6.11.

a) $\hat{Y} = -.113(\text{SCHATTRT}) + 31.816.$

Descriptive Statistics

	Mean	Std. Deviation	N
slfcnc08 Self-Concept in Eighth Grade	21.23	6.023	417
schattrt School Average Daily Attendance Rate	93.65	4.691	417

Coefficients[a]

Model		Unstandardized Coefficients		Standardized Coefficients		
		B	Std. Error	Beta	t	Sig.
1	(Constant)	31.816	5.887		5.405	.000
	schattrt School Average Daily Attendance Rate	−.113	.063	−.088	−1.801	.072

[a]Dependent Variable: slfcnc08 Self-Concept in Eighth Grade.

b) $\hat{Y} = -.11.3(\text{SCHATTRT}) + 31.816.$

6.12.

a) According to the boxplots, the distribution of SES is fairly symmetric whereas that of expected income at age 30 is severely positively skewed.

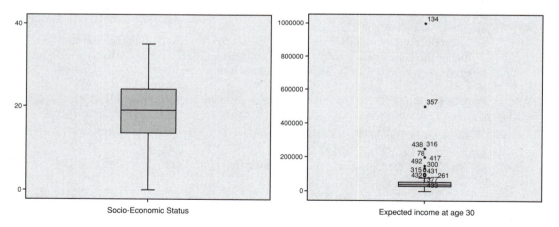

This visual impression is corroborated by the skewness ratios, which indicate that the distribution of SES is fairly symmetric (−1.02) and that of expected income is severely positively skewed (95.91).

The scatterplot shows that a linear model may not be the most appropriate due to the presence of several outliers.

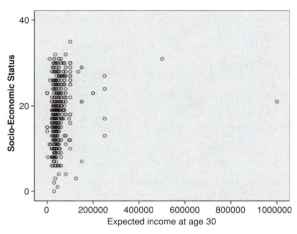

b) Prior to applying the nonlinear tranformations, the variable was translated by adding 1 to all values to avoid taking a log of a zero value. Although the transformed variable is still severely skewed, the square root transformation was the most effective at diminishing the severity of the positive skew. The log transformation overcorrected as it converted the positively skewed distribution to a negatively skewed distribution.

Descriptive Statistics

	N	Minimum	Maximum	Mean	Std.	Skewness	
	Statistic	Statistic	Statistic	Statistic	Statistic	Statistic	Std. Error
Expected income at age 30	459	0	1000000	51574.73	58265.758	10.934	.114
expinclg	459	0	6	4.59	.526	-6.889	.114
expincsq	459	1	1000	214.53	74.591	3.739	.114
Valid N (listwise)	459						

c) According to the correlation analysis, the strongest correlation is with the square root transformed variable.

Correlations

		ses Socio-Economic Status	expinc30 Expected income at age 30	expinclg	expincsq
ses Socio-Economic Status	Pearson Correlation	1	.157**	.120**	.221**
	Sig. (2-tailed)		.001	.010	.000
	N	500	459	459	459
expinc30 Expected income at age 30	Pearson Correlation	.157**	1	.399**	.905**
	Sig. (2-tailed)	.001		.000	.000
	N	459	459	459	459
expinclg	Pearson Correlation	.120**	.399**	1	.652**
	Sig. (2-tailed)	.010	.000		.000
	N	459	459	459	459
expincsq	Pearson Correlation	.221**	.905**	.652**	1
	Sig. (2-tailed)	.000	.000	.000	
	N	459	459	459	459

**Correlation is significant at the 0.01 level (2-tailed).

d) $\hat{SES} = 14.172 + .02(EXPINCSQ)$ OR

$\hat{SES} = 14.172 + .02(SQRT(EXPINC30 + 1))$.

Coefficients[a]

Model		Unstandardized Coefficients		Standardized Coefficients	t	Sig.
		B	Std. Error	Beta		
1	(Constant)	14.172	.949		14.934	.000
	expincsq	.020	.004	.221	4.846	.000

[a]Dependent Variable: ses Socio-Economic Status.

e) $\hat{SES} = 14.172 + .02(SQRT(75000 + 1))$

$\hat{SES} = 14.172 + .02(SQRT(75000 + 1))$

$\hat{SES} = 19.64$.

6.13.

a)

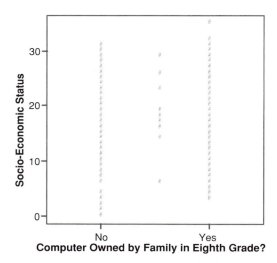

Computer Owned by Family in Eighth Grade?

b) $\hat{Y} = 4.83(COMPUTER) + 16.144$.

Coefficients[a]

Model		Unstandardized Coefficients		Standardized Coefficients	t	Sig.
		B	Std. Error	Beta		
1	(Constant)	16.144	.401		40.303	.000
	computer Computer Owned by Family in Eighth Grade?	4.830	.582	.349	8.302	.000

[a]Dependent Variable: ses Socio-Economic Status.

c) Students in the NELS data set who owned a computer in eighth grade have an average SES value that is 4.83 points higher than those who did not.

d) Students in the NELS data set who did not own a computer in eighth grade are predicted by the model to have a mean SES of 16.14.

e) $\hat{Y} = 4.83(1) + 16.144 = 20.97$.

f) $\hat{Y} = 4.83(0) + 16.144 = 16.14$.

g) One possibility is to use Means, Compare Means. That gives the following output:

Report

ses Socio-Economic Status

computer Computer	Mean	N	Std. Deviation
0 No	16.14	263	6.457
1 Yes	20.97	237	6.539
Total	18.43	500	6.924

h) $\hat{Y} = 4.83(COMP1) + 11.61$.

i) $\hat{Y} = -4.83(COMP2) + 20.97$.

j) Yes. The intercept is meaningful when one of the two levels of the dichotomous variable is coded as a 0. If neither is coded as 0, then the intercept is not meaningful.

6.14.

a) Positive, same as it is in the regression equation.

b) Females.

c) $\hat{Y} = .573(2) + 4.059 = 5.21$.

d) $\hat{Y} = .573(1) + 4.059 = 4.63$.

6.15. b)

6.16. a)

6.17. d)

6.18. b)

6.19. a)

6.20. b)

6.21. a)

6.22. a)

6.23. Among adults, there is a positive correlation between weight and height. That is, adults that weigh more tend to be taller, on average. Because of this, an adult's height may be predicted from his or her weight. However, increasing an adult's weight does not cause his or her height to increase, as it would if the relationship were causative.

6.24.

Group 1 = a.
Group 2 = b.
Group 3 = c.
Group 4 = d.

6.25.

a) $r_{XX} = 1$.

To see this by example, use the States data set with X = STUTEACH and Y = EDUCEXPE. The correlation between X and Y is $-.46$. The scatterplot follows:

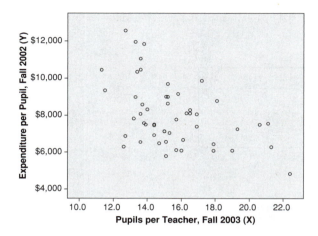

The scatterplot of X and X follows:

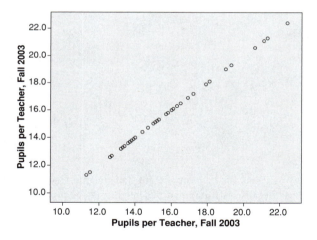

The pattern is a perfect line with positive slope, indicating that the correlation is 1. In general, the correlation of a variable with itself is always 1.

b) $r_{Y\hat{Y}} = .46$.

We have been calling $r_{Y\hat{Y}}$ the correlation between the actual and predicted values for Y, R. We know that $R = |r| = |-.46| = .46$. This relationship holds because $\hat{Y}$ is a linear transformation of X, which involves reflection in this case because the correlation between X and Y is negative. By reflecting X (or, said differently, by multiplying X by -1), the correlation between Y and $\hat{Y}$ retains the same magnitude as the correlation between Y and X, but has a positive (as opposed to negative) sign.

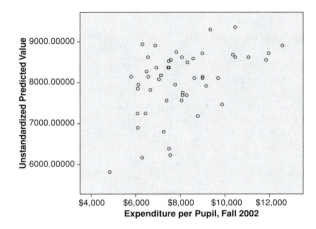

c) $r_{X\hat{Y}} = -1$.

Because $\hat{Y}$ is a linear transformation of X, one that involves reflection in this case, the correlation between X and $\hat{Y}$ has the same magnitude as the correlation between X and X, but with the opposite sign.

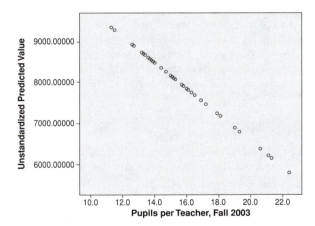

6.26. To show that the regression line always passes through the point $(\overline{X}, \overline{Y})$, we show that when the value $X = \overline{X}$ is substituted into the regression equation, $\hat{Y} = bX + a$, and we obtain $\hat{Y} = \overline{Y}$.

Substituting Equation 6.4 for a in $\hat{Y} = bX + a$, we obtain $\hat{Y} = b\overline{X} + \overline{Y} - b\overline{X}$.

Subtracting we obtain $\hat{Y} = \overline{Y}$, as desired.

6.27. According to Formula 6.3, $b = r\dfrac{S_Y}{S_X}$.

Substituting the expression for r given in Equation 5.5, we have

$$b = \frac{(\overline{Y}_1 - \overline{Y}_2)S_X}{S_Y}\frac{S_Y}{S_X}.$$

That expression is equivalent to $b = \overline{Y}_0 - \overline{Y}_1$.

6.28. The mean of the predicted values is given by $\dfrac{\sum \hat{Y}_i}{N}$. Thus, we need to show that $\dfrac{\sum \hat{Y}_i}{N} = \overline{Y}$.

Substituting Equation 6.2 for $\hat{Y}$, we have $\dfrac{\sum \hat{Y}_i}{N} = \dfrac{\sum bX_i + a}{N}$. Substituting Equation 6.4 for a, we have

$\dfrac{\sum \hat{Y}_i}{N} = \dfrac{\sum bX_i + \overline{Y} - b\overline{X}}{N}$. Using the formula for the mean and the rules for transforming the mean, we have

$\dfrac{\sum \hat{Y}_i}{N} = \dfrac{bN\overline{X} + N\overline{Y} - bN\overline{X}}{N}$. Simplifying yields the desired result: $\dfrac{\sum \hat{Y}_i}{N} = \overline{Y}$.

6.29. $\hat{Y} = bX + a$.

When r is positive, b is also positive, and $\hat{Y} = bX + a$ is a linear transformation of X that does not involve reflection. As we have seen, such a linear transformation preserves the sign and magnitude of the correlation. That is, the correlation between X and $\hat{Y}$ is the same as the correlation between X and Y ($R = r$).

On the other hand, when r is negative, b is also negative, and $\hat{Y} = bX + a$ is a linear transformation of X that does involve reflection. As we have seen, such a linear transformation changes the sign of the correlation. That is, the correlation between X and $\hat{Y}$ is the negative of the correlation between X and Y ($R = -r$).

6.30.

a) To use Equation 6.1, we need to find the residuals, or d_i.

To use SPSS to find the residuals we use the Regression procedure. Go to **Statistics** on the main menu bar, **Regression**, **Linear**. Put CALORIES in the box for the **Dependent variable** and FAT in the box for the **Independent variable**. Click **Save** and in the box labeled **Residuals**, click the box next to **Unstandardized**. Click **Continue** and **OK**. In the data window, you will see that a new variable, RES_1, has been created which gives the corresponding residual for each hamburger.

These values are provided in Table 6.2.

Table 6.2. Residuals for the McDonald's example.

Type	Fat	Calories	Res_1
Hamburger	10	270	−.67513
Cheeseburger	14	320	−5.51471
Quarter Pounder™	21	430	8.51604
Quarter Pounder with Cheese™	30	530	−14.87299
Big Mac™	28	530	12.54679

To calculate D using Equation 6.1, we may use one of two procedures:

1) Use the Descriptives procedure to calculate D as the standard deviation of the residuals. The value of SD_{RES} obtained through SPSS is 10.98. Recall that this value results from division by 4 instead of 5. We approximate D by $D = \sqrt{10.98^2 \frac{4}{5}} = 9.82$.

2) Use the SPSS Compute procedure to find the values of d_i^2, the squared residuals.

To use the Compute procedure to find the squared residuals, go to the SPSS Data Editor. Go to **Transform**, **Compute**. Type squares in the **Target Variable** box. Type res_1**2 in the **Numeric Expression** box (** means "to the power".) Click **OK**.

To find the sum of these squared residuals, use Options in the Descriptives procedure to obtain the value 482.02. Finally, to obtain D from the sum of squared residuals, use a calculator to divide the sum of squared residuals by N and take the square root. You should obtain the value $D = 9.82$.

b) To use formula 6.5 to calculate D, we use the SPSS Descriptives and Correlation. From Descriptives we obtain that the variance of $Y = S_Y^2 = (14180)\left(\frac{4}{5}\right) = 11344$ and from Correlation, we obtain that $r_{XY} = .996$. Substituting these values into formula 6.5 we obtain

$$D = \sqrt{S_Y^2(1 - r_{XY}^2)} = \sqrt{11344(1 - .996^2)} = 9.52.$$

c) To find D directly on the SPSS Regression output, perform the regression as in Example 6.1. The relevant SPSS output is reproduced below:

Model Summary[b]

Model	R	R Square	Adjusted R Square	Std. Error of the Estimate
1	.996[a]	.992	.989	−12.68

[a]Predictors: (Constant), FAT Grams of Fat.
[b]Dependent Variable: CALORIES.

The value of D is labeled "Std. Error of the Estimate" and equals 12.68. Again, for reasons that will become clear when we discuss inferential statistics, SPSS uses a different denominator. In particular, SPSS uses $N - 2$ instead of N. To adjust the value of the standard error of estimate to conform to our own descriptive measure, we take

$$D = \sqrt{12.68^2 \frac{3}{5}} = 9.82.$$

d) All obtained descriptive measures of D are equal, regardless of how they were obtained. Although in this small N example, the adjustments changed the value of D considerably, when N is large, the adjustments can be expected to make only minor changes in the value of D. Hence, when N is large, all methods can be expected to produce similar results without replacement.

CHAPTER 7. SOLUTIONS

7.1. The answers are rounded to the nearest hundredth.

Highest level of education expected

		Frequency	Percent	Valid Percent	Cumulative Percent
Valid	Less than College Degree	48	9.6	9.6	9.6
	Bachelor's Degree	159	31.8	31.8	41.4
	Master's Degree	190	38.0	38.0	79.4
	Ph.D., MD, JD, etc.	103	20.6	20.6	100.0
	Total	500	100.0	100.0	

a) $159/500 = .32.$ b) $190/500 = .38.$

c) $(159 + 190)/500 = .32 + .38 = .70.$

d) $1 - .32 = .68.$

Gender * Highest level of education expected Crosstabulation

Count

		Highest level of education expected				
		Less than College Degree	Bachelor's Degree	Master's Degree	Ph.D., MD, JD, etc.	Total
Gender	Male	20	75	81	51	227
	Female	28	84	109	52	273
Total		48	159	190	103	500

7.2.

a) $48/500 = .10.$

b) $273/500 = .55.$

c) $28/500 = .06.$

    d) $48/500 + 273/500 - 28/500 = 293/500 = .59$.
    e) $1 - .10 = .90$ or $(159 + 190 + 103)/500 = 452/500 = .90$.
    f) $28/48 = .58$.
    g) $28/273 = .10$.
    h) $273/(159 + 190 + 103) = 273/452 = .60$.

7.3.
    a) $159/500 = .32$.   b) $190/500 = .38$.   c) $.32 \times .38 = .12$.
    d) Yes. It can be used. Because the sampling is with replacement, the events are independent.

7.4.
    a) $159/500 = .32$.
    b) $(159/500) \times (190/499) = .32/.38 = .12$
    c) No. The Multiplicative Rule of Probability cannot be used because the events are not independent.

7.5.
    a) 320.
    b) 380.
    c) $320 + 380 = 700$.
    d) $1000 - 320 = 680$.

7.6.
    a) .5.   b) .5.   c) 1.
    d) .7.   e) .9.

7.7. The two events are not equally likely.

7.8. The statement is false. The fact that the urn contains equal numbers of black and white marbles is enough to conclude that the probability that one marble selected at random from this urn is white is .5.

7.9.
    a) They are not mutually exclusive because the outcome HH satisfies both E_1 and E_2.
    b) Step 1: The sample space is {HH, HT, TH, TT}, thus $P(E_2) = .5$. Step 2: The modified sample space is {HH, HT}, thus $P(E_2$ given that E_1 has occurred) $= .5$. Step 3: The modified sample space is {TH, TT}, thus $P(E_2$ given that E_1 has not occurred) $= .5$.

7.10.
    a) They are mutually exclusive because the sample space is {H, TH, TT}. None of these outcomes satisfies both E_1 and E_2.
    b) $P(E_2) = .33$. $P(E_2$ given that E_1 has occurred) $= 0$ because the modified sample space is {H}. $P(E_2$ given that E_1 has not occurred) $= .5$ because the modified sample space is {TH, TT}. Because these values are not the same, E_1 and E_2 are dependent.

7.11.
    a) They are not mutually exclusive because the outcome TT satisfies both E_1 and E_2.
    b) $P(E_2) = .25$. $P(E_2$ given that E_1 has occurred) $= .50$ because the modified sample space is {TH, TT}. $P(E_2$ given that E_1 has not occurred) $= 0$ because the modified sample space is {H}. Because these values are not the same, E_1 and E_2 are dependent.

CHAPTER 8. SOLUTIONS

8.1. The binomial probability model may not be used for this situation. Because the person studied, the probability of success from question to question will not be constant.

8.2. The binomial probability model may not be used for this situation. There are three, not two, possible outcomes.

8.3. The binomial probability model may be used for this situation. The probability of exactly 50 imperfections in 500 trials is .059.

8.4. The binomial probability model may be used for this situation. The probability of exactly one girl in three births is .375.

8.5. The binomial probability model may be used for this situation. Probabilities are given to 3 decimal places, where appropriate:
a) .056   b) .250   c) <.0005
d) <.0005   e) .922   f) .736

8.6. The binomial probability model may be used for this situation. The probability of selecting 5 schools from the Northeast out of 10 schools is .218.

8.7. The binomial probability model may not be used for this situation. The probability of correct installation is not constant from trial to trial.

8.8. The binomial probability model may be used for this situation. The probability of at least one false-positive result in 10 mammograms is .491.

8.9. Answers are given to two decimal places.
a) .25.   b) .43.   c) .68.
d) .75.   e) .99.   f) .08.
g) .10.   h) .99.

8.10. Answers have been rounded to three decimal places.
a) .001.   b) .246.

8.11. Solution 1 is incorrect because the outcomes listed are not equally likely. Solution 2 is correct.

8.12. False. The probability of obtaining 5 heads in 10 tosses of a fair coin is .2461, whereas the probability of obtaining 2 heads in 4 tosses is .375.

8.13.
a)

k	p
0	.016
1	.094
2	.234
3	.312
4	.234
5	.094
6	.016

b) The distribution is symmetric.
c) The mean is 3 and the standard deviation is 1.225.

8.14.
a) .09.   b) .98.   c) .91.
d) .02.   e) .89.   f) .26.
g) .26.   h) .69.

8.15.
a) .52.   b) −.39.   c) −.52.
d) .39.

8.16.
a) .023.   b) .023.   c) .045.
d) .955.

8.17.
a) .016.   b) .395.   c) .052.
d) .903.

8.18.
a) 1.2.   b) −.37.   c) −.42.

8.19.
a) .02.   b) .84.   c) .98.
d) .16.   e) .82.   f) .14.
g) .14.   h) .32.

8.20.
a) 62.8.   b) 37.2.   c) 62.8.
d) 37.2.

8.21.
a) 58.55   b) 91.45   c) .067
d) .067   e) .383   f) .006
g) .625

8.22.
a) $z = 1.645$.   b) $z = 1.960$.   c) $z = 2.576$.

8.23.
a) .175.   b) .309.   c) .841.

8.24.
Using SPSS: 130.81. Using Table 1: 130.75.

8.25.
a) 990 days.   b) Approximately 1 percent.

8.26.
a) 81 people.   b) 65.54 percent or .655.   c) 56.4.

8.27.
a) .933.   b) .933 or 93.3 percent.

8.28. Using the normal distribution, we estimate that the percentage of students in the NELS data set with eighth-grade math achievement scores greater than or equal to 72 is 95.1 percent. The actual percentile rank of 72 is 94.2 percent. The value based on the normal distribution (95.1) provides a reasonably good approximation of the one based on the actual distribution (94.2) and suggests, in this case, that the normal curve is reasonably appropriate for approximating the distribution of eighth-grade math achievement scores.

8.29. Using the normal probability model, we estimate that the number of students in the NELS data set with eighth-grade math achievement scores that are within one standard deviation of the mean is approximately 341 (approximately 68.26 percent). In fact, there are only actually 311 such students. Given the discrepancy between these two values (of approximately 10 percent), it appears that eighth-grade achievement scores are not as well approximated by a normal distribution as one might think from the previous exercise.

8.30. The z-score associated with offering 6 AP courses is .09. Using Table 1, we expect approximately 46.41 percent of the scores to have a z-score of .09 or more. Of the 473 students in the NELS data set for which the variable was measured, we would, therefore, expect approximately 220 to come from schools offering 6 or more AP courses. According to the frequency distribution table, only 186 students actually come from schools offering 6 or more AP courses. This discrepancy is probably because the distribution of APOFFER is severely positively skewed (skewness ratio = 36.54), so it is not well approximated by the normal distribution.

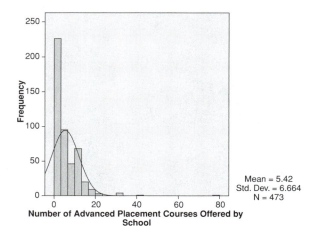

8.31.

a) The distribution of SUPPORTC is approximately normally distributed.

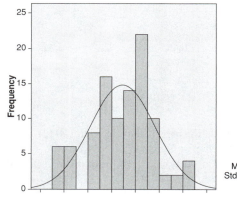

b) 56.049.   c) −1.83.   d) .033.

e) According to the cumulative percent column, it's 8 percent.

f) .033 or 3.3 percent.

g) .1271.   h) .8729.   i) .8393.

j) 43.80.   k) 58.37.   l) 47.3.

8.32.

a) .5823.

b) $np = (20)(.5) = 10$ and $nq = (20)(.5) = 10$. Both of these values are greater than 5, as required.

c) $\overline{X} = np = (20)(.5) = 10$ and $SD = \sqrt{npq} = \sqrt{(20)(.5)(.5)} = 2.24$.

d) .5802.

CHAPTER 9. **SOLUTIONS**

9.1.

a) The shape is uniform.

b) 00,01,02,03,04,05,06,07,08,09,10,11,12,13,14,15,16,17,18,19,20,21,22,23,24,25,26,27,28,29,30, 31,32,33,34,35,36,37,38,39,40,41,42,43,44,45,46,47,48,49,50,51,52,53,54,55,56,57,58,59,60,61,

62,63,64,65,66,67,68,69,70,71,72,73,74,75,76,77,78,79,80,81,82,83,84,85,86,87,88,89,90,91,92,
93,94,95,96,97,98,99

c) The frequency distribution is presented in the following table.

sampdis Sampling Distribution of the Mean

		Frequency	Percent	Valid Percent	Cumulative Percent
Valid	.0	1	1.0	1.0	1.0
	.5	2	2.0	2.0	3.0
	1.0	3	3.0	3.0	6.0
	1.5	4	4.0	4.0	10.0
	2.0	5	5.0	5.0	15.0
	2.5	6	6.0	6.0	21.0
	3.0	7	7.0	7.0	28.0
	3.5	8	8.0	8.0	36.0
	4.0	9	9.0	9.0	45.0
	4.5	10	10.0	10.0	55.0
	5.0	9	9.0	9.0	64.0
	5.5	8	8.0	8.0	72.0
	6.0	7	7.0	7.0	79.0
	6.5	6	6.0	6.0	85.0
	7.0	5	5.0	5.0	90.0
	7.5	4	4.0	4.0	94.0
	8.0	3	3.0	3.0	97.0
	8.5	2	2.0	2.0	99.0
	9.0	1	1.0	1.0	100.0
	Total	100	100.0	100.0	

d) Although the population was uniformly distributed, the sampling distribution of means is approximately normally distributed.

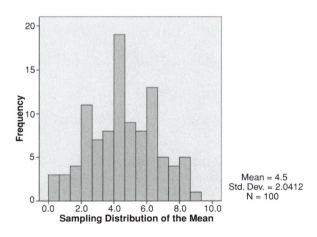

Mean = 4.5
Std. Dev. = 2.0412
N = 100

e) The values for the standard deviation are found using SPSS and are not adjusted. Although the mean of the sampling distribution is equal to the mean of the population, the standard error is not exactly equal to the standard deviation of the population divided by the square root of 2.

This result does not contradict the CLT because the conditions have not been met: given that the population is not normally distributed, the sample size should be at least 30.

Descriptive Statistics

	N	Minimum	Maximum	Mean	Std. Deviation
pop Population	10	0	9	4.50	3.028
sampdis Sampling Distribution of the Mean	100	.0	9.0	4.500	2.0412
Valid N (listwise)	10				

f) The probability of selecting a mean between 2.5 and 6.5 inclusive is 70/100 = .70.

9.2. The sampling distribution generated has mean 4.5 and standard deviation .479. The mean of the actual sampling distribution, as predicted from the CLT, is the mean of the population {0, 1, 2, 3, 4, 5, 6, 7, 8, 9}, which is 4.5, agreeing with the result we obtained by simulation. The mean of the actual sampling distribution, as predicted from the CLT, is the standard deviation of the population divided by the square root of 36. However, we need to adjust the value SPSS reports when it calculates the standard deviation of {0, 1, 2, 3, 4, 5, 6, 7, 8, 9}. SPSS reports the value 3.028. Adjusting so that we are dividing the variance by 10 and not 9 indicates that the population standard deviation is 2.873. Dividing the population standard deviation by the square root of the sample size, 6, yields .479, agreeing with the result we obtained by simulation.

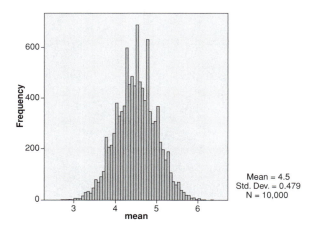

Mean = 4.5
Std. Dev. = 0.479
N = 10,000

9.3.

a) Empirically, one would find all equally likely samples of size 8, compute the mean of each, and the list of those means is the sampling distribution. However, for most populations, this would be too difficult and time-consuming to do without a computer. The SPSS macro provided with this text could be used to approximate that distribution.

b) For the sampling distribution, the mean is 70 and the standard deviation, or standard error, is .88 to two decimal places.

c) Increasing the sample size has no effect on the mean of the sampling distribution, but it would decrease the standard error.

d) .0116. Because the sampling distribution of the means is normally distributed with mean 70 and standard error .88, the probability of selecting a sample mean that is larger than 72 is the same as the probability of selecting a z-score that is higher than 2.27.

9.4.

  a) The distribution will be normally distributed.

  b) 500.

  c) 18.26.

  d) Approximately .046.

  e) It will be normally distributed with mean 500 and standard error approximately 33.33.

9.5.

  a) According to the CLT, it will be approximately normally distributed.

  b) 500.   c) 14.14.   d) Approximately .046.

  e) Given that the uniform distribution is symmetric, it is likely that the CLT applies and that the sampling distribution of means is approximately normally distributed with mean equal to 500 and standard deviation equal to 33.33.

9.6. One possible result is given here as a frequency distribution table:

RANDM

		Frequency	Percent	Valid Percent	Cumulative Percent
Valid	4	1	10.0	10.0	10.0
	16	1	10.0	10.0	20.0
	24	1	10.0	10.0	30.0
	24	1	10.0	10.0	40.0
	25	1	10.0	10.0	50.0
	30	1	10.0	10.0	60.0
	35	1	10.0	10.0	70.0
	38	1	10.0	10.0	80.0
	39	1	10.0	10.0	90.0
	49	1	10.0	10.0	100.0
	Total	10	100.0	100.0	

9.7. The sample is not random because not every person in New York City is equally likely to be a member of a statistics class at New York University.

9.8. The statement is false, because not all sampling distributions of means are normally distributed. For example, if the population is not normally distributed and the sample size is small, the sampling distribution of means may not be normally distributed.

9.9. In inferential statistics, one selects a single sample and bases the inferences on that. The sampling distribution of means is not empirically created when conducting an inferential analysis.

9.10. Using this procedure, the researchers will not obtain a simple random sample because the twin of any selected subject is also selected. Thus, it is not true that at each stage of the selection process all subjects remaining in the population have an equal chance of being selected.

9.11.

  a) Positively skewed.

  b) Approximately normal (from the CLT).

  c) Score or X.

  d) Sample mean or $\overline{X}$.

CHAPTER 10. **SOLUTIONS**

10.1.

a) Because $N = 100$ is greater than 30, the results of the CLT indicate that the normal curve gives a good approximation of the sampling distribution of means.

b) The 90 percent CI for the mean height of American males is $(67.51, 68.49)$.

c) The 90 percent refers to the process of constructing the CIs. That is, if the process of randomly selecting a sample of 100 American males and constructing the CI for the mean height based on each sample selected were repeated a large number of times, 90 percent of those times we would expect that the true population mean would be contained in the confidence interval.

d) Longer.

10.2.

a) The 99 percent CI for the mean IQ of all Americans is $(102.42, 107.58)$.

b) If we repeated the process of selecting samples of 225 Americans randomly from this population and computed the mean IQ for each such sample selected, 99 percent of all of the intervals we would construct about these sample means would contain μ.

10.3.

a) The 90 percent CI for the population mean is $(89.53, 94.47)$.

b) Because 96 falls above the 90 percent CI, we conclude that the population mean is statistically significantly lower than 96 at the $\alpha = .10$ level.

c) Because 91.5 falls within the 90 percent CI, we conclude that the population mean is not statistically significantly different from 91.5 at the $\alpha = .10$ level.

10.4. The 95 percent CI for the mean air-pollution index for Pittsburgh is $(14.02, 15.98)$. Because 14 falls below that CI, we conclude that the mean air-pollution index for Pittsburgh is statistically significantly higher than 14.

10.5.

a) $H_0: \mu = 600$ and $H_1: \mu > 600$.

b) According to the CLT, the sampling distribution of the mean for samples of size $N = 400$ is normally distributed.

c) $z = 3$.

d) One-tailed (right-tailed).

e) $p = .001$.

f) The employees who are given the training ($M = 603$, $SD = 20$) sort statistically significantly more mail, on average, than 600 letters, $z = 3$, $p = .001$.

g) The employees who are given the training sort only approximately .15 standard deviations more than 600 letters, a very small effect indicating that the training probably has little practical value.

h) The town should probably not pay for training that, while statistically significantly increasing performance does not practically significantly increase performance.

i) A CI would not be used to answer this one-tailed question.

10.6. Students in this district who participate in Project Advance ($M = 56$, $SD = 12$) do not score statistically significantly higher than 55 on the college-readiness test, $z = .5$, $p = .3085$.

10.7.

a) Adults following the diet ($M = 185$, $SD = 50$) had statistically significantly lower levels of cholesterol, $z = -2.12$, $p = .02$.

b) The cholesterol level of adults following the diet was approximately .3 standard deviations lower than 200 mg per dl, a small-to-moderate effect, supporting the results of the hypothesis test.

10.8.

a) The 95 percent CI for the mean scholastic aptitude test score for all current first-year students is $(99.54, 103.46)$.

b) Because 100 is contained in the CI, it is a plausible value of the mean, and no statistically significant difference is detected.

c) Not necessary. The result is not statistically significant.

d) Shorter.

e) Longer.

f) Longer.

10.9. The students at the university ($M = 106$, $SD = 15$) have a statistically significantly higher mean than 100 on the test of general intelligence because the 90 percent CI is (101.89, 110.11) and all of these values are larger than 100. Furthermore, the students at the university score .4 standard deviations higher than 100, a small-to-moderate effect that corroborates the results of the hypothesis test.

10.10. Eighth-grade students in Seattle taught using the new curriculum ($M = 95$, $SD = 10$) scored statistically significantly higher than 92 on the Stanford Secondary School Comprehension Test, $z = 6$, $p < .0005$. (Note that although SPSS reports p to 2 decimal places as .00, the real value of p is .000000000997. Because this value is so small, instead we write $p < .0005$. According to the table, the most precise estimate of p is $p < .0002$.) Furthermore, the students taught using the new curriculum score .3 standard deviations higher than those who are not, a small-to-moderate effect that corroborates the result of the hypothesis test. A 95 percent CI could not have been used to determine whether there would be an improvement in reading comprehension in general if the entire population of eighth graders in Seattle were taught using the new curriculum because the question is directional and CIs are nondirectional.

10.11. The mean price of all such textbooks ($M = \$76.40$, $SD = \$7.50$) is statistically significantly lower than \$79, $z = 2.19$, $p = .03$. The mean price of all such textbooks is approximately .35 standard deviations lower than \$79, a small-to-moderate effect.

10.12. The z_C is found by finding the score that has area .025 to its right, or area .975 to its left. One way to do that is to use the following numerical expression in the SPSS compute statement:

$$z = 1 - \text{IDF.NORMAL}(.975, 0, 1).$$

The result is $z = 1.96$ to two decimal places.

10.13. The power would have been greater for the one-tailed situation in which the research question was whether the students had a higher mean on this test, because the one-tailed hypothesis was in the correct direction. The smaller the p-value, the greater the power of the test. In the two-tailed version, the p-value was .02. In the one-tailed version it would be .01, which is more likely to be statistically significant.

CHAPTER 11. **SOLUTIONS**

11.1.

a) In this case, we perform a t-test instead of a z-test because σ is not assumed to be known and needs to be estimated from the sample.

b) The one-sample t-test is robust to violations of the normality assumption in this case because the sample size, $N = 105$, is large.

c) (79.38, 83.61).

One-Sample Test

	Test Value = 0	
	95% Confidence Interval of the Difference	
	Lower	Upper
Intellectual Ability	79.38	83.61

d) $H_0: \mu = 100$ and $H_1: \mu \neq 100$.

e) The null hypothesis can be rejected because, according to the 95 percent CI, 100 is not included in the CI, and as such is not a plausible value for the mean IQ of all children diagnosed with learning disabilities in this city.

f) Because all of the values in the CI are below 100, we may further conclude that children diagnosed with learning disabilities in this city have average IQ scores that are statistically significantly lower than 100.

11.2.

a) The one-sample t-test is robust to violations of the normality assumption in this case because the sample size, $N = 76$, is large.

b) $H_0: \mu = 75$ and $H_1: \mu \neq 75$.

c) $P = .083$.

One-Sample Statistics

	N	Mean	Std. Deviation	Std. Error Mean
Reading Comprehension	76	77.63	13.078	1.500

One-Sample Test

	Test Value = 75					
					95% Confidence Interval of the Difference	
	t	df	Sig. (2-tailed)	Mean Difference	Lower	Upper
Reading Comprehension	1.754	75	.083	2.632	−.36	5.62

d) We cannot reject the null hypothesis in favor of the alternative.

e) The mean reading comprehension score for children attending public elementary school in the city who are diagnosed with learning disabilities ($M = 77.63$, $SD = 13.08$) is not statistically significantly different from 75, $t(75) = 1.754$, $p = .083$.

f) (74.64, 80.62).

g) The null hypothesis cannot be rejected because, according to the 95 percent CI, 75 is included in the CI, and as such is a plausible value for the mean reading comprehension score of all children diagnosed with learning disabilities in this city.

h) More powerful because the standard error of the mean would have been smaller, producing a larger obtained t-value and a narrower CI.

11.3.

One-Sample Statistics

	N	Mean	Std. Deviation	Std. Error Mean
Body Mass Index (kg/(M*M)) (1)	400	25.7425	3.91174	.19559

One-Sample Test

	Test Value = 25					
					95% Confidence Interval of the Difference	
	t	df	Sig. (2-tailed)	Mean Difference	Lower	Upper
Body Mass Index (kg/(M*M)) (1)	3.796	399	.000	.74253	.3580	1.1270

a) The one-sample t-test is robust to violations of the normality assumption in this case, because the sample size, $N = 400$, is large.

b) $H_0: \mu = 25$ and $H_1: \mu < 25$.

c) Because the test is one-tailed, we first verify that the sample mean supports the direction of the alternative hypothesis. Because the sample mean ($M = 25.74$) is larger than 25, it does support the alternative hypothesis. We then conduct the t-test ($t(399) = 3.80$) and divide the obtained two-tailed p-value, $p < .0005$, in half. The p-value, $p < .00025$, suggests that the mean body mass index of population of noninstitutionalized adults as measured during the first examination is, in fact, greater than 25.

d) $d = \dfrac{25.7425 - 25}{3.91174} = .19$.

The mean body mass index is .19 standard deviations higher than 25, a small effect according to Cohen's rule-of-thumb guidelines.

e) CIs are not appropriate for conducting tests of directional hypotheses.

11.4.

a) $H_0: \mu = 120$ and $H_1: \mu < 120$.

b) Because the sample mean ($M = 130.36$) is larger than 120, we cannot reject the null in favor of the alternative hypothesis. The direction of difference alone is sufficient to determine that the mean systolic blood pressure of the population of noninstitutionalized adults as measured during the first examination is not less than 120 mmHg.

11.5.

a) The one-sample t-test is robust to violations of the normality assumption in this case, because the sample size, $N = 500$, is large.

b) (4.58, 4.81).

c) The average family size for this population is statistically significantly higher than 4.5.

d) $d = (4.69 - 4.5)/1.319 = .14$. The average family size is .14 standard deviations higher than 4.5, a negligible effect according to Cohen's rule-of-thumb guidelines. This is an example of a situation in which we have statistical significance but not practical significance.

11.6. According to the 95 percent CI, the average twelfth-grade self-concept score of the population of college-bound students who have always been at grade level is between 30.84 and 32.12. Because 32 is contained in the CI, 32 is a plausible self-concept average for this population. The population mean is therefore not statistically significantly different from 32.

11.7. According to the p-value derived from the results of a one-sample t-test ($t(499) = -1.61, p = .11$), the average twelfth-grade self-concept score of the population of college-bound students who have always been at grade level is not statistically significantly different from 32.

11.8. According to the p-value derived from the results of a one-sample t-test ($t(499) = 1.04, p = .15$), the population of college-bound students who have always been at grade level on average do not take a statistically significantly greater number of units of mathematics in high school than 3.6.

11.9.
  a)

To restrict the sample to students from the Northeast, click **Data**, **Select Cases**. Click the circle next to "If condition is satisfied" and click **If**. Type REGION $= 1$ in the box. Click **Continue**, **OK**.

---

  b) The one-sample t-test is robust to violations of the normality assumption in this case because the sample size, $N = 106$, is large.
  c) (3.957, 4.153).
  d) No, the estimate is greater than three.
  e) $d = 2.06$, indicating that the number of years of high school English taken by this population of college-bound students from the Northeast is approximately 2.06 standard deviations greater than 3 years. According to Cohen's rule-of-thumb guidelines, this is a very large effect.
  f)

To reset SPSS to include all students in the NELS in analyses, click **Data**, **Select Cases**. Click the circle next to **All cases**. Click **OK**.

11.10.

One-Sample Statistics

	N	Mean	Std. Deviation	Std. Error Mean
Social Studies Achievement in Twelfth Grade	149	57.3223	8.55524	.70087

One-Sample Test

	Test Value = 55			
	t	df	Sig. (2-tailed)	Mean Difference
Social Studies Achievement in Twelfth Grade	3.314	148	.001	2.32235

a) The one-sample t-test is robust to violations of the normality assumption in this case because the sample size, $N = 149$, is large.

b) $H_0: \mu = 55$ and $H_1: \mu < 55$.

c) Because the sample mean is 57.32, the direction of the alternative hypothesis is supported.

d) $p = .0005$ (.001/2). This value is derived from a one-sample t-test, $t(148) = 3.31$, $p = .0005$.

e) Yes, because the p-value is less than .05.

f) The mean social studies achievement score for this population ($M = 57.32$, $SD = 8.56$) is statistically significantly larger than 55, $t(148) = 3.31$, $p = .0005$.

g) The mean social studies achievement score for this population is .28 standard deviations larger than 55, a small-to-moderate effect, according to Cohen's rule-of-thumb guidelines.

h) The standard deviation value of 8.56 is an estimate of the population standard deviation, σ, which measures the spread in the population of the social studies achievement scores themselves. The standard error of the mean value of .70 is an estimate of $\sigma_{\bar{X}}$, which measures the spread of the social studies achievement means based on samples of size 149 randomly selected from this population.

i) Larger. The denominator of the t-statistic would have been larger, the t-value would have been smaller, and the area to its right would have been larger.

11.11.

a) The one-sample t-test is not robust to violations of the normality assumption in this case because the sample size, $N = 26$, is small. However, the skewness ratio is -1.62, which is less than 2 in magnitude, suggesting that the data are not skewed and the normality assumption is tenable.

b) (27.56, 34.13).

11.12.

Group Statistics

Gender		N	Mean	Std. Deviation	Std. Error Mean
Math Comprehension	Male	60	84.05	12.958	1.673
	Female	34	90.21	14.422	2.473

Independent Samples Test

		Levene's Test for Equality of Variances		t-test for Equality of Means						95% Confidence Interval of the Difference	
		F	Sig.	t	df	Sig. (2-tailed)	Mean Difference	Std. Error Difference	Lower	Upper
Math Comprehension	Equal variances assumed	.568	.453	−2.124	92	.036	−6.156	2.898	−11.912	−.400
	Equal variances not assumed			−2.062	62.754	.043	−6.156	2.986	−12.123	−.189

a) The independent samples t-test is robust to violations of the normality assumption in this case because the sample size is greater than 30 for both males and females.

b) Equal variances because Levene's test indicates the tenability of the equality of homogeneity-of-variances assumption in this case, $F(1, 92) = .57$ $p = .45$.

c) H_0: $\mu_{males} = \mu_{females}$ and H_1: $\mu_{males} \neq \mu_{females}$.

d) The results of the independent samples t-test indicate that for public elementary students with learning disabilities in this city females, on average ($M = 90.21$, $SD = 14.42$) have statistically significantly higher math comprehension scores than males ($M = 84.05$, $SD = 12.96$), $t(92) = -2.12$, $p = .04$.

e) For this population of learning disabled students, on average, females score approximately .46 standard deviations higher than males, which represents a moderate effect according to Cohen's rule-of-thumb guidelines.

11.13.

Group Statistics

	Type of Placement	N	Mean	Std. Deviation	Std. Error Mean
Intellectual Abilit	Part Time Resource Room	66	84.83	10.369	1.276
	Full Time Self Contained Classroom	39	75.85	9.568	1.532

Independent Samples Test

		Levene's Test for Equality of Variances		t-test for Equality of Means						95% Confidence Interval of the Difference	
		F	Sig.	t	df	Sig. (2-tailed)	Mean Difference	Std. Error Difference	Lower	Upper
Intellectual Ability	Equal variances assumed	1.298	.257	4.414	103	.000	8.987	2.036	4.949	13.025
	Equal variances not assumed			4.507	85.087	.000	8.987	1.994	5.022	12.952

a) The independent samples t-test is robust to violations of the normality assumption in this case because the sample size is greater than 30 for both those in a self-contained classroom and those in the resource room.

b) Equal variances because Levene's test indicates the tenability of the equality of homogeneity-of-variances assumption in this case, $F(1, 103) = 1.30$, $p = .26$.

c) The 95 percent CI of the difference is (4.95, 13.03), does not contain zero, and indicates that the difference is statistically significant. The average intellectual ability score of all public elementary school students diagnosed with learning disabilities in the city in the resource room ($M = 84.83$, $SD = 10.37$) was between 4.95 and 13.03 points higher than that of the students in the self-contained classroom ($M = 75.85$, $SD = 9.57$).

d) Public elementary students diagnosed with learning disabilities in the city with a resource room placement score approximately .89 standard deviations higher, on average, than students in a self-contained classroom from the same population. This represents a large effect according to Cohen's rule-of-thumb guidelines.

11.14.

Group Statistics

	SEX	N	Mean	Std. Deviation	Std. Error Mean
Age (years) at examination (1)	Men	200	49.36	8.672	.613
	Women	200	48.63	8.177	.578

Independent Samples Test

		Levene's Test for Equality of Variances		t-test for Equality of Means						
									95% Confidence Interval of the Difference	
		F	Sig.	t	df	Sig. (2-tailed)	Mean Difference	Std. Error Difference	Lower	Upper
Age (years) at examination (1)	Equal variances assumed	1.206	.273	.866	398	.387	.730	.843	−.927	2.387
	Equal variances not assumed			.866	396.631	.387	.730	.843	−.927	2.387

a)

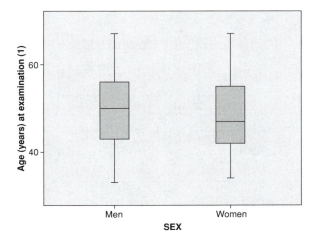

From the boxplot, it appears that the normality assumption is tenable because the distributions are fairly symmetric. The equality or homogeneity-of-variance assumption appears tenable as well because the IQRs are similar. Finally, the median for men is larger than it is for women, so given the reasonably symmetric nature of the distributions, a likely result of the independent samples *t*-test is that the mean age of men is statistically significantly higher than it is for women.

b) The independent samples t-test is robust to violations of the normality assumption in this case because the sample size is greater than 30 for both males and females.

c) Equal variances because Levene's test indicates the tenability of the equality of homogeneity-of-variances assumption in this case, $F(1, 396) = 1.21$ $p = .27$. Note that the t-values and CIs are the same regardless of whether equal variances are used to calculate them or not.

d) According to the p-value, the mean age of females at initial examination ($M = 48.63$, $SD = 8.18$) is not statistically significantly different from that of males ($M = 49.36$, $SD = 8.67$), $t(396) = .87$, $p = .37$.

e) According to the 95 percent CI, on average, the difference in age between males and females is $(-.93, 2.37)$, which includes zero, as expected from the answer to part (d).

f) Given a nondirectional alternative hypothesis, the independent groups t-test conducted at the α-level gives results with respect to statistical significance that are consistent with the $(1-\alpha)$ percent CI.

11.15.

Group Statistics

	Current Cig Smoker Y/N (3)	N	Mean	Std. Deviation	Std. Error Mean
Body Mass Index (kg/(M*M)) (3)	No	192	26.4535	3.98738	.28776
	Yes	112	25.2088	4.53045	.42809

Independent Samples Test

		Levene's Test for Equality of Variances		t-test for Equality of Means					95% Confidence Interval of the Difference	
		F	Sig.	t	df	Sig. (2-tailed)	Mean Difference	Std. Error Difference	Lower	Upper
Body Mass Index (kg/(M*M)) (3)	Equal variances assumed	1.637	.202	2.495	302	.013	1.24465	.49880	.26309	2.22621
	Equal variances not assumed			2.413	209.159	.017	1.24465	.51582	.22778	2.26152

a) According to the results of the independent samples t-test ($t(302) = .2.50$), the p-value of $(.013)/2 = .007$ indicates that on average, the body mass index of the smokers at the third examination ($M = 25.21$, $SD = 4.53$) is statistically significantly lower than that of nonsmokers ($M = 26.45$, $SD = 3.99$) for all noninstitutionalized adults.

b) Less powerful. In general, given that the direction for the sample is the same as the one that has been hypothesized, one-tailed tests are more powerful than corresponding two-tailed tests because the area of the tail for rejecting the null hypothesis is larger in a one-tailed test than in a two-tailed test.

11.16

Group Statistics

	SEX	N	Mean	Std. Deviation	Std. Error Mean
BMIDIFF	Men	147	−.13	1.911	.158
	Women	157	.50	2.342	.187

Independent Samples Test

		Levene's Test for Equality of Variances		t-test for Equality of Means							
										95% Confidence Interval of the Difference	
		F	Sig.	t	df	Sig. (2-tailed)	Mean Difference	Std. Error Difference	Lower	Upper
BMIDIFF	Equal variances assumed	1.960	.163	−2.569	302	.011	−.632	.246	−1.117	−.148
	Equal variances not assumed			−2.586	296.511	.010	−.632	.244	−1.113	−.151

a) Use **Transform**, **Compute** to create the new variable. The numeric expression should be BMI3 − BMI1. The score on BMIDIFF of the first person in the data set is −.64, indicating that the body mass index score for that person decreased by .64 BMI units from examination 1 (1956) to examination 3 (1968).

b) According to the boxplot, both distributions appear to be reasonably symmetric, although they each have several outliers. The female distribution appears to be more heterogeneous than that for males when one considers the outliers. According to the medians, the men appear to show a decrease in BMI whereas the women appear to show an increase.

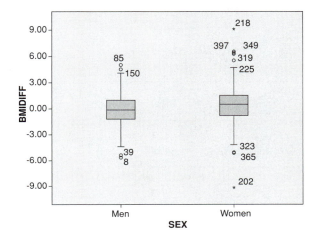

c) The independent samples *t*-test is robust to violations of the normality assumption in this case because the sample size is greater than 30 for both males and females.

d) Equal variances because Levene's test indicates the tenability of the equality of homogeneity-of-variances assumption in this case, $F(1, 302) = 1.96$ $p = .16$.

e) According to the *p*-value derived from an independent groups *t*-test on means, on average, the change in body mass index for women ($M = .50, SD = 2.34$) is statistically significantly different from that for men ($M = -.13, SD = 1.91$), $t(302) = -2.57, p = .01$. Whereas the body mass index for women increased from 1956 to 1968, it decreased for men.

f) According to the value of Cohen's *d*, the mean change in body mass index for women is .29 standard deviations higher than that for men. This represents a small-to-moderate effect.

11.17.

a) Because there are only 27 participants in the Framingham data set who used antihypertensive medication, the tenability of the normality assumption needs to be evaluated. In this case, it is not tenable because the distribution of systolic blood pressure scores at time 3 is severely skewed for those who were not taking blood pressure medication (skewness ratio = 4.68).

b) The log transformation is effective because it brings the skewness ratio into acceptable limits.

Descriptive Statistics

Anti-hypertensive meds Y/N (3)		N	Minimum	Maximum	Mean	Std.	Skewness	
		Statistic	Statistic	Statistic	Statistic	Statistic	Statistic	Std. Error
	Systolic BP mmHg (3)	50	108.00	200.00	137.9600	20.41304	1.081	.337
	sysbp3lg	50	2	2	2.14	.061	.755	.337
	sysbp3sq	50	10	14	11.72	.844	.917	.337
	Valid N (listwise)	50						
Not currently used	Systolic BP mmHg (3)	231	91.00	205.00	135.6277	21.59544	.748	.160
	Sysbp3lg	231	2	2	2.13	.067	.379	.160
	sysbp3sq	231	10	14	11.61	.909	.560	.160
	Valid N (listwise)	231						
currently used	Systolic BP mmHg (3)	27	128.00	205.00	158.2963	19.38589	.834	.448
	sysbp3lg	27	2	2	2.20	.052	.554	.448
	sysbp3sq	27	11	14	12.56	.757	.695	.448
	Valid N (listwise)	27						

c)

Group Statistics

	Anti-hypertensive meds Y/N (3)	N	Mean	Std. Deviation	Std. Error Mean
sysbp3lg	currently used	27	2.20	.052	.010
	Not currently used	231	2.13	.067	.004

Independent Samples Test

		Levene's Test for Equality of Variances		t-test for Equality of Means						
									95% Confidence Interval of the Difference	
		F	Sig.	t	df	Sig. (2-tailed)	Mean Difference	Std. Error Difference	Lower	Upper
sysbp3lg	Equal variances assumed	3.579	.060	5.200	256	.000	.069	.013	.043	.096
	Equal variances not assumed			6.393	37.130	.000	.069	.011	.047	.091

According to the results of the independent samples t-test, the mean of the logarithm of systolic blood pressure at time 3 of those currently taking anti-hypertensive medication ($M = 2.20$, $SD = .05$) is statistically significantly different from that for those not currently taking the medication ($M = 2.13$, $SD = .07$), $t(256) = 5.20$, $p < .0005$.

d) No. Because we do not know what their blood pressure readings were at time 1.

11.18.

Group Statistics

	SEX	N	Mean	Std. Deviation	Std. Error Mean
Serum Cholesterol mg/dL (3)	Men	142	226.70	42.306	3.550
	Women	144	245.57	48.305	4.025

Independent Samples Test

		Levene's Test for Equality of Variances		t-test for Equality of Means						
									95% Confidence Interval of the Difference	
		F	Sig.	t	df	Sig. (2-tailed)	Mean Difference	Std. Error Difference	Lower	Upper
Serum Cholesterol mg/dL (3)	Equal variances assumed	.499	.480	−3.513	284	.001	−18.872	5.372	−29.447	−8.298
	Equal variances not assumed			−3.516	280.104	.001	−18.872	5.367	−29.438	−8.307

An independent samples t-test was conducted to determine whether, among the population of noninstitutionalized adults, there are differences in total serum cholesterol by sex. Because the sample size for both men and women is greater than 30, the test results are robust to violations of the normality assumption. Furthermore, the result of Levene's test indicates the tenability of the equality of homogeneity-of-variances assumption in this case, $F(1, 284) = .50$, $p = .48$.

From the p-value derived from the independent groups t-test, we may note that the mean serum cholesterol for women ($M = 245.57$, $SD = 48.31$) is statistically significantly higher than that for men ($M = 226.70$, $SD = 42.31$), $t(284) = -3.51$, $p = .001$. Alternatively, using the CI, (-29.45, -8.30), which does not contain 0, we see that the mean serum cholesterol of women ($M = 245.57$, $SD = 48.31$) is statistically significantly higher than that for men ($M = 226.70$, $SD = 42.31$). According to the value of Cohen's d, the mean serum cholesterol of women is approximately .42 standard deviations higher than that for men, suggesting a moderate effect, according to Cohen's guidelines.

11.19.

Group Statistics

	Computer Owned by Family in Eighth Grade?	N	Mean	Std. Deviation	Std. Error Mean
Math Achievement in Twelfth Grade	No	263	55.5960	7.62416	.47013
	Yes	237	58.3610	7.92823	.51499

Independent Samples Test

		Levene's Test for Equality of Variances		t-test for Equality of Means						95% Confidence Interval of the Difference	
		F	Sig.	t	df	Sig. (2-tailed)	Mean Difference	Std. Error Difference	Lower	Upper
Math Achievement in Twelfth Grade	Equal variances assumed	2.207	.138	-3.973	498	.000	-2.76501	.69589	-4.13224	-1.39777
	Equal variances not assumed			-3.965	487.978	.000	-2.76501	.69731	-4.13510	-1.39491

a) An independent samples t-test is more appropriate than a one-sample t-test because the question relates to two population means: the twelfth-grade math achievement of those who owned a computer and the twelfth-grade math achievement of those who did not own a computer. An independent samples t-test is more appropriate than a paired samples t-test because each twelfth-grade math achievement score of a student who owned a computer is not paired with one from someone who did not own a computer. Another way to see that an independent samples t-test is more appropriate than a paired samples t-test is that the variable COMPUTER is dichotomous and the variable ACHMAT12 is interval. A paired samples t-test involves two variables that are at least interval.

b) Because there are 263 students whose parents did not own a computer when they were in eighth grade and 237 students whose parents did own a computer when they were in eighth grade, and both of these sample sizes are greater than 30, a violation of the normality assumption does not compromise the validity of the hypothesis test results in this case.

c) Levene's test indicates the tenability of the equality of homogeneity-of-variances assumption in this case, $F(1, 496) = 2.21$, $p = .14$.

d) H_0: $\mu_{\text{computer owned}} = \mu_{\text{no computer}}$ and H_1: $\mu_{\text{computer owned}} \neq \mu_{\text{no computer}}$.

e) $p < .0005$.

f) Among the population of college-bound students who have always been at grade level, students whose families owned a computer in eighth grade ($M = 58.36$, $SD = 7.93$) scored statistically significantly higher in twelfth-grade math achievement, on average, than those whose families did not own a computer ($M = 55.60$, $SD = 7.62$), $t(498) = -3.97$, $p < .0005$.

g) $(-4.13, -1.40)$ or $(1.40, 4.13)$.

h) Because 0 is not contained in the CI and because of the values of the sample means, among the population of college-bound students who have always been at grade level students whose families owned a computer in eighth grade ($M = 58.36$, $SD = 7.93$) scored statistically significantly higher in twelfth-grade math achievement, on average, than those whose families did not own a computer ($M = 55.60$, $SD = 7.62$).

i) Among the population of college-bound students who have always been at grade level, students whose families owned a computer in eighth grade scored approximately .36 standard deviations higher in twelfth-grade math achievement, on average, than those whose families did not own a computer, a small-to-moderate effect.

j) The 99 percent CI is longer. Whereas the 95 percent CI is $(-4.13, -1.40)$ or $(1.40, 4.13)$, the 99 percent CI is $(-4.56, -.97)$ or $(.97, 4.56)$.

11.20.

a) A two-tailed, independent samples t-test was performed to determine whether the average twelfth-grade self-concept score is different for smokers and nonsmokers. Prior to the analysis itself, an analysis of the underlying assumptions was conducted. Because there are 429 students who never smoked and 71 students who did and both of these sample sizes are greater than 30, a violation of the normality assumption would likely not compromise the validity of the results of the hypothesis test. Because $p = .27$ is greater than .05 for Levene's homogeneity-of-variances test, no statistically significant difference was detected in the population variances, so the homogeneity-of-variances assumption may be considered to have been met for these data. According to the results of the independent samples t-test, among the population of college-bound students who have always been at grade level, on average, nonsmokers ($M = 31.96$, $SD = 7.11$) score statistically significantly differently from smokers ($M = 28.58$, $SD = 7.31$) in twelfth-grade self-concept $t(498) = 3.70$, $p < .0005$. Nonsmokers score approximately .47 standard deviations higher in twelfth-grade self-concept, on average, than smokers, a moderate effect according to Cohen's rule-of-thumb guidelines.

b) A two-tailed, independent samples t-test was performed to determine whether students who take advanced math in eighth grade have different expectations for future income than students who do not. Prior to the analysis itself, an analysis of the underlying assumptions was conducted. Because there are 241 students who did not take advanced math in eighth grade and 209 who did and both of these sample sizes are greater than 30, a violation of the normality assumption would likely not compromise the validity of the results of the hypothesis test. Because $p = .44$ is greater than .05 for Levene's homogeneity-of-variances test, no statistically significant difference was detected in the population variances, so the homogeneity-of-variances assumption may be considered to have been met for these data. According to the results of the independent samples t-test, among the population of college-bound students who have always been at grade level, students who take advanced math in eighth grade ($M = \$52,191.39$, $SD = \$433,307.17$) do not have statistically significant differences in future income expectations than students who do not ($M = \$51,696.27$, $SD = \$69,560.29$), $t(448) = .09$, $p = .93$.

c) A one-tailed, independent samples t-test was performed to determine whether students who take advanced math in eighth grade have better eighth-grade self-concepts than students who do not. Prior to the analysis itself, an analysis of the underlying assumptions was conducted. Because there are 265 students who did not take advanced math in eighth grade and 226 who did and both of these sample sizes are greater than 30, a violation of the normality assumption would likely not compromise the validity of the results of the hypothesis test. Because $p = .78$ is greater than .05 for Levene's homogeneity-of-variances test, no statistically significant difference was detected in the population variances, so the homogeneity-of-variances assumption may be considered to have been met for these data. According to the results of the independent samples *t*-test, among the population of college-bound students who have always been at grade level, students who take advanced math in eighth grade ($M = 21.61$, $SD = 5.91$) have statistically significantly greater self-concept in eighth grade than students who do not ($M = 20.54$, $SD = 5.99$), $t(489) = -1.97$, $p = .02$. According to an effect size analysis, however, the magnitude of the effect is small according to Cohen's guidelines. Students who take advanced math in eighth grade score approximately only .18 standard deviations higher in eighth-grade self-concept than students who do not take advanced math in eighth grade.

d) An independent samples *t*-test was performed to determine whether females have better twelfth-grade self-concept than males. Prior to the analysis itself, an analysis of the underlying assumptions was conducted. Because there are 227 males and 273 females and both of these sample sizes are greater than 30, a violation of the normality assumption would probably not compromise the the validity of the results of the hypothesis test. An inspection of the sample means indicates that among the population of college-bound students who have always been at grade level, females ($M = 30.42$, $SD = 7.16$) do not have statistically significantly better twelfth-grade self-concept than males ($M = 32.75$, $SD = 7.13$). The boxplot indicates that there are only a small number of outliers and that the medians lead to the same conclusion about the direction of the difference.

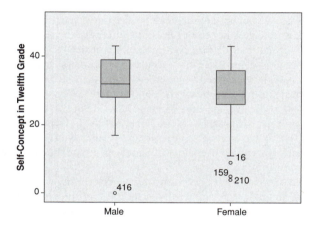

e) A one-tailed, independent samples *t*-test was performed to determine whether females do better on twelfth-grade reading achievement tests than males. Prior to the analysis itself, an analysis of the underlying assumptions was conducted. Because there are 227 males and 273 females and both of these sample sizes are greater than 30, a violation of the normality assumption would probably not compromise the validity of the results of the hypothesis test. Because $p = .04$ is less than .05 for Levene's homogeneity-of-variances test, a statistically significant difference was detected in the population variances, so the homogeneity-of-variances assumption is not met for these data. For this reason, the independent samples *t*-test with equal variances not assumed was used for the analysis. According to the results of the independent samples *t*-test for unequal variances, among the population of college-bound students who have always been at grade level, females ($M = 55.84$, $SD = 7.48$) do not have statistically significantly better twelfth-grade reading achievement scores than males ($M = 55.31$, $SD = 8.56$), $t(452.53) = -.74$, $p = .23$.

f) A one-tailed, independent samples *t*-test was performed to determine whether those who attended nursery school tend to have smaller families than those who did not. Prior to the analysis itself, an analysis of the underlying assumptions was conducted. Because there are 139 students who did not attend nursery school and 281 who did and both of these sample sizes are greater than 30, a violation of the normality assumption would likely not compromise the validity of the results of the hypothesis test. Because $p = .03$ is less than .05 for Levene's homogeneity-of-variances test, a statistically significant difference was detected in the population variances, so the homogeneity-of-variances assumption is not met for these data. For this reason, the independent samples t-test with equal variances not assumed was used for the analysis. According to the results of the independent samples t-test for unequal variances, among the population of college-bound students who have always been at grade level, students who attended nursery school ($M = 4.54$, $SD = 1.16$) have statistically significantly smaller families than those who did not ($M = 4.80$, $SD = 1.47$), $t(226.79) = 1.81$, $p = .04$. Among the population of college-bound students who have always been at grade level, students who attended nursery school have families that are only approximately .20 standard deviations smaller than those who did not, a small effect according to Cohen's guidelines.

g) A one-tailed, independent samples t-test was performed to determine whether students who live in the Northeast have mean SES that is higher than that of those who live in the West. Prior to the analysis itself, an analysis of the underlying assumptions was conducted. Because there are 106 students from the Northeast and 93 students from the West and both of these sample sizes are greater than 30, a violation of the normality assumption would probably not compromise the validity of the results of the hypothesis test. Because $p = .17$ is greater than .05 for Levene's homogeneity-of-variances test, no statistically significant difference was detected in the population variances, so the homogeneity-of-variances assumption may be considered to have been met for these data. According to the results of the independent samples t-test, among the population of college-bound students who have always been at grade level, the average SES of students from the Northeast ($M = 20.25$, $SD = 6.99$) is statistically significantly higher than the average SES of students from the West ($M = 18.38$, $SD = 6.68$), $t(197) = 1.93$, $p = .03$.

11.21. A two-tailed, independent samples t-test is performed to determine whether there is a difference in the average blood pressure reduction between the calcium and the placebo groups for African-American males. Prior to the t-test itself, an analysis of the underlying assumptions is performed. The normality assumption is found to be tenable by looking at the skewness ratios. For the placebo group, the ratio of the skewness to the standard error of the skew is $.616/.661 = .93$. For the calcium group it is $.37/.687 = .54$. Because for both the calcium and placebo group the skewness ratios for the blood pressure reduction distributions are less than 2 in magnitude, the normality assumption is tenable. The results of Levene's test indicate that the homogeneity-of-variances assumption is tenable ($p = .051$), although barely. The results of the independent samples t-test indicate that no statistically significant difference is detected in blood pressure reduction between the placebo ($M = -.64$, $SD = 5.87$) and calcium ($M = 4.90$, $SD = 8.67$) groups among African-American males, $t(19) = -1.78$, $p = .10$, regardless of whether the pooled equal variances or unequal variances are used in the calculation of the t-ratio.

Independent Samples Test

| | | Levene's Test for Equality of Variances | | t-test for Equality of Means | | | | | | |
| | | | | | | | | | 95% Confidence Interval of the Difference | |
		F	Sig.	t	df	Sig. (2-tailed)	Mean Difference	Std. Error Difference	Lower	Upper
Initial – final blood pressure	Equal variances assumed	4.327	.051	−1.728	19	.100	−5.536	3.204	−12.242	1.169
	Equal variances not assumed			−1.696	15.619	.110	−5.536	3.264	−12.469	1.397

11.22.

Paired Samples Statistics

		Mean	N	Std. Deviation	Std. Error Mean
Pair 1	Math Comprehension	86.41	74	14.592	1.696
	Reading Comprehension	77.78	74	13.138	1.527

Paired Samples Test

		Paired Differences							
------	--	-------	----------------	------------------	---				
					95% Confidence Interval of the Difference				
		Mean	Std. Deviation	Std Error Mean	Lower	Upper	t	df	Sig. (2-tailed)
Pair 1	Math Comprehension – Reading Comprehension	8.622	13.999	1.627	5.378	11.865	5.298	73	.000

a) The sample sizes are large enough so that failure to meet the normality assumption does not compromise the validity of the results of the t-test.

b) Because the sample sizes are equal in the paired samples t-test, failure to meet the homogeneity-of-variances assumption does not compromise the validity of test results in this case.

c) $H_0: \mu_{\text{mathcomp}} = \mu_{\text{readcomp}}$ and $H_1: \mu_{\text{mathcomp}} \neq \mu_{\text{readcomp}}$.

d) The results of the paired samples t-test indicate that students diagnosed with learning disabilities in the city scored statistically significantly higher in math comprehension, on average ($M = 86.41$, $SD = 14.59$), than they did in reading comprehension ($M = 77.78$, $SD = 13.14$), $t(73) = 5.298$, $p < .0005$.

e) Because zero is not contained in the CI (5.38, 11.87), we know that performance on the two tests is statistically significantly different. Looking at the sample means, we conclude that public elementary school students diagnosed with learning disabilities in the city score between 5.38 and 11.87 points higher in math comprehension, on average ($M = 86.41$, $SD = 14.59$), than they do in reading comprehension ($M = 77.78$, $SD = 13.14$).

f) Public elementary school children in the city score approximately .62 standard deviations (of the paired differences) higher in math comprehension, on average, than they do in reading comprehension – a moderate effect, supporting the result of the hypothesis test.

11.23.

Paired Samples Statistics

		Mean	N	Std. Deviation	Std. Error Mean
Pair 1	Systolic BP mmHg (1)	127.43	308	19.150	1.091
	Systolic BP mmHg (3)	137.9935	308	22.09507	1.25898

Paired Samples Test

	Paired Differences							
				95% Confidence Interval of the Difference				
	Mean	Std. Deviation	Std. Error Mean	Lower	Upper	t	df	Sig. (2-tailed)
Pair 1 Systolic BP mmHg (1) – Systolic BP mmHg (3)	−10.56169	19.49905	1.11106	−12.74795	−8.37543	−9.506	307	.000

a) $p < .00025$. The means are in the hypothesized direction. The p-value is calculated as .0005/2.

b) According to the p-value, the mean systolic blood pressure at time 3 (in 1968) ($M = 137.99$, $SD = 22.10$) is statistically significantly higher than at time 1 (in 1956) ($M = 127.43$, $SD = 19.15$), $t(307) = −9.51$, $p < .00025$.

c) According to the value of Cohen's d, the mean systolic blood pressure at time 3 (1968) is .54 standard deviations (of the paired differences) higher than at time 1 (1956), a moderate effect according to Cohen's guidelines.

11.24.

Paired Samples Statistics

		Mean	N	Std. Deviation	Std. Error Mean
Pair 1	Diastolic BP mmHg (1)	80.77	308	10.549	.601
	Diastolic BP mmHg (3)	81.6737	308	11.31241	.64458

The direction of the change in mean (from 80.77 in 1956 to 81.67 in 1968) suggests an increase rather than a decrease in diastolic blood pressure.

11.25.

a) According to the results of a paired samples t-test, the number of cigarettes smoked per day does decrease significantly from time 1 ($M = 8.94$, $SD = 12.28$) to time 3 ($M = 7.30$, $SD = 12.55$), $t(303) = 2.71$, $p < .007$.

b) During the time period in question, increased evidence was uncovered and publicized about the negative effects of smoking on health. One could only hope that such evidence served to convince people, at least to some extent, to either quit or cut back on smoking.

11.26.

Paired Samples Statistics

		Mean	N	Std. Deviation	Std. Error Mean
Pair 1	Science Achievement in Eighth Grade	55.6702	497	9.38704	.42107
	Science Achievement in Twelfth Grade	55.7777	497	8.56988	.38441

Paired Samples Test

| | Paired Differences | | | | | | | |
| | | | | 95% Confidence Interval of the Difference | | | | |
	Mean	Std. Deviation	Std. Error Mean	Lower	Upper	t	df	Sig. (2-tailed)
Pair 1 Science Achievement in Eighth Grade – Science Achievement in Twelfth Grade	−.10757	7.36274	.33026	−.75645	.54132	−.326	496	.745

a) A paired samples t-test is more appropriate than a one-sample t-test because the question relates to two population means: eighth-grade science achievement and twelfth-grade science achievement. A paired samples t-test is more appropriate than an independent samples t-test because each eighth-grade science achievement score is paired with the twelfth-grade science achievement score of the same person. The paired samples t-test may be viewed as equivalent to a one-sample t-test on the difference scores calculated as the difference between ACHSCI08 and ACHSCI12, two interval-leveled variables.

b) Because there are 497 scores for both eighth- and twelfth-grade science achievement and both of these numbers are larger than 30, a violation of the normality assumption would not compromise the validity of the results of the hypothesis test.

c) $H_0: \mu_{mathcomp} = \mu_{readcomp}$ and $H_1: \mu_{mathcomp} \neq \mu_{readcomp}$.

d) $p = .75$.

e) The p-value suggests that the change in science achievement from $M = 55.67$ $(SD = 9.39)$ in eighth grade to $M = 55.77$ $(SD = 8.57)$ in twelfth grade for this population of students is not statistically significantly different from zero, $t(496) = -.32, p = .75$.

f) The 95 percent CI for the mean difference in science achievement between eighth and twelfth grade is $(-.76, .54)$ or $(-.54, .76)$.

g) Because zero is contained in the 95 percent CI, zero is a plausible value for the mean difference in science achievement from eighth to twelfth grade for this population. Said differently, the level of science achievement in eighth grade relative to all students in the grade is not statistically significantly different from that in twelfth grade.

11.27.

Paired Samples Statistics

		Mean	N	Std. Deviation	Std. Error Mean
Pair 1	Self-Concept in Eighth Grade	21.06	500	5.971	.267
	Self-Concept in Twelfth Grade	31.48	500	7.231	.323

Paired Samples Test

| | Paired Differences | | | | | | | |
| | | | | 95% Confidence Interval of the Difference | | | | |
	Mean	Std. Deviation	Std. Error Mean	Lower	Upper	t	df	Sig. (2-tailed)
Pair 1 Self-Concept in Eighth Grade – Self-Concept in Twelfth Grade	−10.418	7.045	.315	−11.037	−9.799	−33.064	499	.000

A one-tailed, paired samples t-test was performed to determine whether among the population of college-bound students who have always been at grade level, the level of self-concept, relative to all students in the grade, increases from eighth (SLFCNC08) to twelfth grade (SLFCNC12). Prior to the analysis itself, an analysis of the underlying assumptions was conducted. Because all 500 students in the data set filled out the self-concept questionnaires in both eighth and twelfth grade, the paired sample size is greater than 30 and a violation of the normality assumption would not compromise the validity of the results of the hypothesis test. Because the sample sizes are equal, a violation of the homogeneity-of-variances assumption also would not compromise the validity of the results of the hypothesis test. According to the results of the paired samples t-test, among the population of college-bound students who have always been at grade level, the level of self-concept, relative to all students in the grade, increases statistically significantly from eighth ($M = 21.05$, $SD = 5.97$) to twelfth ($M = 31.48$, $SD = 7.23$) grade, $t(499) = -33.06$, $p < .00025$. Among the population of college-bound students who have always been at grade level, the level of self-concept, relative to all students in the grade, is 1.48 standard deviations (of the paired differences) higher in twelfth grade than in eighth grade, a large size effect according to Cohen's guidelines.

11.28.

   a) (6).   b) (5).   c) (2).

   d) (4).   e) (3).

11.29.

   a) A one-tailed, independent samples t-test was performed to determine whether among college-bound students who are always at grade level, those who attended nursery school tend to have higher SES than those who did not. Prior to the t-test itself, an analysis of the underlying assumptions was performed. The normality assumption was not an issue because the sample sizes were far greater than 30 for both nursery groups. The results of Levene's test indicated that the homogeneity-of-variances assumption was met ($p = .53$). The results of the independent samples t-test indicated that students who attended nursery school ($M = 20.74$, $SD = 6.51$) had a statistically significantly higher SES, on average, than those who did not ($M = 15.07$, $SD = 6.24$), $t(418) = 8.51$, $p < .0005$. Those who attended nursery school have SES scores that are approximately .88 standard deviations higher than those who did not, a large effect according to Cohen's guidelines.

   b) A two-tailed, paired samples t-test was performed to determine whether among college-bound students who are always at grade level, self-concept differed in eighth and tenth grades. Prior to the t-test itself, an analysis of the underlying assumptions was performed. The normality assumption was not an issue because the sample sizes were far greater than 30 for the eighth- and tenth-grade scores. The homogeneity-of-variances assumption was also not a concern because there were the same number of eighth- and tenth-grade scores. The results of the paired samples t-test indicated that students had statistically significantly higher self-concept scores, on average, in tenth grade ($M = 22.62$, $SD = 6.87$) than they did in eighth grade ($M = 21.06$, $SD = 5.97$), $t(418) = 8.51$, $p < .00025$. The tenth-grade self-concept scores were approximately .24 standard deviations higher than their eighth-grade self-concept scores, a relatively small effect according to Cohen's guidelines.

c) A two-tailed, independent samples t-test was performed to determine whether among college-bound students who are always at grade level, those who attended public school tend to perform differently in twelfth-grade math achievement from those who attended private school. Prior to the t-test itself, an analysis of the underlying assumptions was performed. The normality assumption was not an isssue because the sample sizes were far greater than 30 for both school groups. The results of Levene's test indicated that the homogeneity-of-variances assumption was met ($p = .32$). The results of the independent samples t-test indicated that students who attended private school ($M = 58.85$, $SD = 7.45$) had a statistically significantly higher twelfth-grade math achievement, on average, than those who did not ($M = 56.22$, $SD = 7.92$), $t(498) = 3.30$, $p = .001$. Students in private schools scored approximately .34 standard deviations higher in twelfth-grade math achievement than those in public schools, a small-to-moderate effect according to Cohen's guidelines.

d) A two-tailed, one-sample t-test was performed to determine whether among college-bound students who are always at grade level, families typically have four members. Prior to the t-test itself, an analysis of the normality assumption was performed. Because the sample size was far greater than 30, the normality assumption was not a concern. The results of the one-sample t-test indicated that families ($M = 4.69$, $SD = 1.32$) have statistically significantly more than four members, on average, $t(499) = 11.73$, $p < .0005$. The family size was approximately .52 standard deviations higher than 4, a moderate effect according to Cohen's guidelines.

e) A one-tailed, paired samples t-test was performed to determine whether college-bound students who are always at grade level take more years of English than math. Prior to the t-test itself, an analysis of the underlying assumptions was performed. The normality assumption was not a concern because the sample sizes were far greater than 30 for both subjects. The homogeneity-of-variances assumption was also not a concern because the two groups were paired and, therefore, the number in each group was the same. The results of the paired samples t-test indicates that students took statistically significantly more years of English ($M = 4.13$, $SD = .66$) than math ($M = 3.64$, $SD = .81$), on average, $t(499) = 11.39$, $p < .00025$. Students took approximately .67 standard deviations more years of English than math, a moderate-to-large effect according to Cohen's guidelines.

11.30.

a) Based on the boxplots, it appears as though the performance in math is slightly higher for the twelfth graders. A hypothesis test is necessary to determine whether the difference is statistically significant.

b) The results of the paired samples t-test indicate that among college-bound high school students who are always at grade level, there is not a statistically significant difference in math achievement between twelfth grade ($M = 56.91$, $SD = 7.88$) and eighth grade ($M = 56.59$, $SD = 9.34$), $t(499) = 1.25$, $p = .21$.

c) The results of the one-sample t-test indicate that among college-bound high school students who are always at grade level, the difference between math achievement in twelfth grade and eighth grade ($M = .32$, $SD = 5.67$) is not statistically significantly different from zero, $t(499) = 1.25$, $p = .21$. Thus, level of math achievement, on average, does not change from eighth to twelfth grades.

d) The t-ratios are identical. The two approaches are equivalent.

e) In general, the independent and paired t-tests yield different results, especially when the pairing of subjects across groups controls for extraneous factors related to the dependent variable. In this case, the paired sample t-test is more powerful than the independent samples t-test, thereby increasing the chance of obtaining statistical significance.

11.31. A one-sample *t*-test on means should not be used in this case because it is not appropriate to calculate the mean of an ordinal-leveled variable such as LATE12.

11.32.

  a) Because the focus here is on drawing a conclusion about the students in the NELS data set, this question requires the use of only descriptive statistics. Based on the higher mean value, students in the NELS data set who never smoked cigarettes ($M = 57.51$, $SD = 7.71$), on average, outperformed those who did ($M = 53.24$, $SD = 8.00$) in terms of twelfth-grade math achievement.

  b) Because the focus here is in drawing a conclusion about the population of college-bound students who are always at grade level, this question requires the use of inferential statistics. The question to be addressed is whether the observed difference in means is likely to be due to chance. Prior to performing the independent samples *t*-test, an analysis of the underlying assumptions was performed. Based on the results of the independent samples *t*-test, among college-bound students who are always at grade level, those who never smoked cigarettes ($M = 57.51$, $SD = 7.71$), on average, outperformed those who did ($M = 53.24$, $SD = 8.00$) in terms of twelfth-grade math achievement, $t(498) = 4.51, p < .0005$.

The p-values for Exercises 11.33 through 11.43 were estimated using Table 2 in Appendix C.

11.33.

  a) .02.

  b) Because the sample mean does not support the direction of the alternative hypothesis, the result is not statistically significant.

  c) .01.

11.34.

  a) .20.

  b) Because the sample means do not support the direction of the alternative hypothesis, the result is not statistically significant.

  c) .10.

11.35.

  a) $.20 < p < .30$.

  b) $.10 < p < .15$.

  c) Because the sample means do not support the direction of the alternative hypothesis, the result is not statistically significant.

11.36.

  a) $.05 < p < .10$.

  b) Because the sample mean does not support the direction of the alternative hypothesis, the result is not statistically significant.

  c) $.025 < p < .05$.

11.37.

Mean difference $= 81.50 - 85 = -3.5$

$$t = \frac{-3.5}{\dfrac{10.941}{\sqrt{105}}} = \frac{-3.5}{1.068} = -3.28$$

$df = 105 - 1 = 104$.
Using Table 2, using the approximation $df = 100$, $.001 < p < .005$.
Using SPSS Compute with $2*(1-CDF.T(3.28, 104))$, we obtain $p = .0014$.
The mean intellectual ability score for all children attending public elementary school in the city ($M = 81.5$, $SD = 10.94$) is statistically significantly lower than 85, $t(104) = -3.28$, $p = .001$.

11.38.

$df = 105 - 1 = 104.$

The standard error of the mean $= \dfrac{10.941}{\sqrt{105}} = \dfrac{10.941}{\dfrac{10.941}{\sqrt{105}}} = 1.068.$

Using Table 2, using the approximation $df = 100$, $t_c = 1.984$.
Using SPSS Compute with IDF.T(.975, 104), we obtain $t_c = 1.983$.
The 95 percent CI is $81.5 \pm 1.983*1.068$
$= 81.5 \pm 2.118$
$= (79.38, 83.62).$
The mean intellectual ability score for all children attending public elementary school in the city $(M = 81.5, SD = 10.94)$ is statistically significantly lower than 85 because the 95 percent CI is $(79.38, 83.62).$

11.39.

Mean difference $= 84.05 - 90.21 = -6.16$ or $90.21 - 84.05 = 6.16.$

$t = \dfrac{-6.16}{2.898} = -2.13.$

$df = 60 + 34 - 2 = 92.$
Using Table 2, using the approximation $df = 90$, $.02 < p < .04$.
Using SPSS Compute with $2*(1-\text{CDF.T}(2.13, 92))$, we obtain $p = .036$.
Using Table 2, using the approximation $df = 90$, $t_c = 1.987$.
Using SPSS Compute with IDF.T(.975, 104), we obtain $t_c = 1.986$.
The 95 percent CI is $-6.16 \pm 1.986*2.898$
$= -6.16 \pm 5.76$
$= (-11.92, -.40).$
With 6.16 as the mean difference, the CI is $(.40, 11.92).$
The results of the independent samples t-test indicate that female public elementary students with learning disabilities in the city $(M = 90.21, SD = 14.42)$ are statistically significantly different from males from the same population with respect to math comprehension $(M = 84.05, SD = 12.96)$, $t(92) = -2.13$, $p = .04$.

11.40.

Mean difference $= 86.41 - 77.78 = 8.63$ or $77.78 - 86.41 = -8.63.$

$t = \dfrac{8.63}{1.627} = 5.30.$

$df = 74 - 1 = 73.$
Using Table 2, using the approximation $df = 70$, $p < .001$.
Using SPSS Compute with $2*(1 - \text{CDF.T}(5.30, 73))$, we obtain $p = .0000018$.
Using Table 2, using the approximation $df = 70$, $t_c = 1.994$.
Using SPSS Compute with IDF.T(.975, 73), we obtain $t_c = 1.992$.
The 95 percent CI is $8.63 \pm 1.992*1.627$
$= 8.63 \pm 3.24 = (5.39, 11.87).$
With -8.63 as the mean difference, the CI is $(-11.87, 5.39).$
The results of the paired samples t-test indicate that students diagnosed with learning disabilities in the city, on average, score statistically significantly different in math $(M = 86.41, SD = 14.59)$ and reading comprehension $(M = 77.78, SD = 13.14)$, $t(73) = 5.30$, $p = .0000018$.

11.41.

a) The computation can be performed by hand. Alternatively it can be performed using SPSS. Using SPSS, we obtain the following output:

One-Sample Statistics

	N	Mean	Std. Deviation	Std. Error Mean
VAR00001	16	25.00	2.875	.719

One-Sample Test

	Test Value = 0	
	95% Confidence Interval of the Difference	
	Lower	Upper
VAR00001	23.47	26.53

The 95 percent CI for μ is (23.47, 26.53). Because 27 is not among these values, which are all below 27, we may conclude that 27 is not a plausible population mean value, and that in fact the mean of the population is likely to be lower than 27.

b) The computation can be performed by hand. Alternatively it can be performed using SPSS. Using SPSS, we obtain the following output:

One-Sample Test

	Test Value = 27			
	t	df	Sig. (2-tailed)	Mean Difference
VAR00001	−2.782	15	.014	−2.000

Because $p < .05$, we conclude that the mean in the population is statistically significantly different from 27, $t(15) = -2.78$, $p = .014$, and based on the previously given CI, likely to be lower than 27.

11.42.

The paired samples t-test can be performed by hand. Alternatively, it can be performed using SPSS. Using SPSS, we obtain the following output:

Paired Samples Statistics

		Mean	N	Std. Deviation	Std. Error Mean
Pair 1	After	7.92	12	4.502	1.300
	Before	9.08	12	5.452	1.574

Paired Samples Test

	Paired Differences							
	Mean	Std. Deviation	Std. Error Mean	95% Confidence Interval of the Difference		t	df	Sig. (2-tailed)
				Lower	Upper			
Pair 1 After – Before	−1.167	3.271	.944	−3.245	.911	−1.236	11	.242

The results of the paired samples *t*-test indicate that the mental alertness scores are not statistically different before (*M* = 9.08, *SD* = 5.45) and after (*M* = 7.92, *SD* = 4.50) taking the drug, *t*(11) = −1.24, *p* = .24.

11.43. The independent samples *t*-test can be performed by hand. Alternatively, it can be performed using SPSS. Using SPSS, we obtain the following output:

Group Statistics

Age		N	Mean	Std. Deviation	Std. Error Mean
Score	1	8	5.00	3.338	1.180
	2	8	9.00	3.703	1.309

Independent Samples Test

		Levene's Test for Equality of Variances		t-test for Equality of Means						
		F	Sig.	t	df	Sig. (2-tailed)	Mean Difference	Std. Error Difference	95% Confidence Interval of the Difference	
									Lower	Upper
Score	Equal variances assumed	.084	.776	−2.269	14	.040	−4.000	1.763	−7.781	−.219
	Equal variances not assumed			−2.269	13.852	.040	−4.000	1.763	−7.784	−.216

The results of the independent samples *t*-test indicate that the scores are statistically significantly different between 2-year-olds (*M* = 9.00, *SD* = 3.70) and 1-year-olds (*M* = 5.00, *SD* = 3.34), *t*(14) = −2.27, *p* = .04.

11.44. The *t*-distribution extends infinitely in both directions without crossing the horizontal axis; hence, there is always area under the curve beyond the observed *t*-value.

11.45. It decreases.

11.46. It decreases.

11.47. No. It would not be ethical to do so. If she conducts a more powerful one-tailed test but hypothesizes incorrectly about the direction of the mean difference, the penalty is that the results are not statistically significant. A one-tailed test is more powerful than a two-tailed test, as long as the mean differences are in the hypothesized direction. If she conducts a more powerful one-tailed test and hypothesizes correctly about the direction of the mean difference, but her results are not statistically significant, the results of the two-tailed test will also not be statistically significant.

11.48. No. Once statistical significance is established, the values of the sample means are used to determine the nature of the mean difference.

11.49. SPSS reports a statistically significant result whenever p is less than or equal to .05. However, in the case of a one-tailed test, the result is not statistically significant unless the direction of the difference according to the alternative hypothesis is the same as that indicated by the sample mean.

CHAPTER 12. **SOLUTIONS**

12.1.

a) One-way ANOVA is used to compare unrelated means of an at least interval-leveled variable for two or more independent groups. In this case, we are comparing the population mean math achievement for *four* different groups based on type of high school program. Assuming that the normality and homogeneity-of variances assumptions are tenable or that the test is robust to their violations (evaluated in later parts of this exercise), one-way ANOVA is an appropriate inferential test.

b) Based on the boxplot, the normality assumption appears to be tenable for all but possibly the some vocational program, because with the exception of one outlier, the distributions are fairly symmetric. The homogeneity-of-variance assumption appears tenable as well because the IQRs are similar. Finally, the results of the ANOVA are likely to mirror the pattern of the medians: the median eighth-grade math achievement for rigorous academic is the highest, followed by academic. The respective medians for some vocational and other program types appear to be approximately the same and lower than the other two program types.

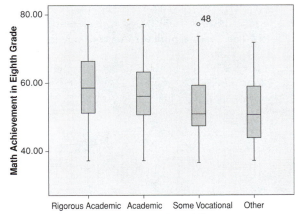

c) A test of the skewness must be performed to evaluate the normality assumption because not all of the groups have at least 30 students. To do that, we split the file and use the SPSS Descriptives procedure to calculate the skewness and the standard error of the skewness. The results appear in the following table.

Descriptive Statistics

hsprog Type of High School Program		N	Skewness	
		Statistic	Statistic	Std. Error
1 Rigorous Academic	achmat08 Math Achievement in Eighth Grade	149	.007	.199
	Valid N (listwise)	149		
2 Academic	achmat08 Math Achievement in Eighth Grade	279	.139	.146
	Valid N (listwise)	279		
3 Some Vocational	achmat08 Math Achievement in Eighth Grade	43	.470	.361
	Valid N (listwise)	43		
4 Other	achmat08 Math Achievement in Eighth Grade	29	.371	.434
	Valid N (listwise)	29		

For all types of high school program the skewness ratio (the skewness statistic divided by the standard error of the skewness) is less than 2 in magnitude, so we conclude that the normality assumption is tenable.

d) Levene's test must be performed to test the homogeneity-of-variance assumption because the sample sizes are not equal for the four groups. The results of Levene's test indicate that the homogeneity-of-variance assumption is tenable, $F(3, 496) = .78, p = .51$.

Test of Homogeneity of Variances
achmat08 Math Achievement in Eighth Grade

Levene Statistic	df1	df2	Sig.
.780	3	496	.505

e) $H_0: \mu_{RA} = \mu_A = \mu_{SV} = \mu_O$ and H_1: Not H_0.

f) $p < .0005$.

ANOVA

achmat08 Math Achievement in Eighth Grade

	Sum of Squares	df	Mean Square	F	Sig.
Between Groups	2064.673	3	688.224	8.233	.000
Within Groups	41462.234	496	83.593		
Total	43526.907	499			

g) We reject the null hypothesis in favor of the alternative.

h) According to the results of the one-way ANOVA, the average math achievement in eighth grade of college-bound students who have always been at grade level does vary as a function of their type of high school program, $F(3, 496) = 8.23, p < .0005$.

i) Approximately 4.74 percent $\left(\dfrac{2064.673}{43526.907} = .0474 \right)$ of the variance in eighth-grade math achievement can be explained by type of high school program, a relatively small effect, according to Cohen's rule-of-thumb guidelines.

j) Post-hoc tests are necessary, in this case, because the results of the ANOVA are statistically significant and more than two independent means are being compared. The following tables provide the summary statistics and the results of the two post-hoc tests. The results of the post-hoc analysis differ depending on the test selected.

Descriptives

achmat08 Math Achievement in Eighth Grade

	N	Mean	Std. Deviation	Std. Error	95% Confidence Interval for Mean		Minimum	Maximum
					Lower Bound	Upper Bound		
1 Rigorous Academic	149	58.7392	9.38950	.76922	57.2191	60.2593	37.24	77.20
2 Academic	279	56.5447	8.89065	.53227	55.4969	57.5925	37.20	77.20
3 Some Vocational	43	53.1116	9.46504	1.44341	50.1987	56.0245	36.61	77.20
4 Other	29	51.1583	9.77854	1.81583	47.4387	54.8778	37.14	71.85
Total	500	56.5910	9.33961	.41768	55.7704	57.4116	36.61	77.20

Multiple Comparisons

Dependent Variable: achmat08 Math Achievement in Eighth Grade

	(I) hsprog Type of High School Program	(J) hsprog Type of High School Program	Mean Difference (I-J)	Std. Error	Sig.	95% Confidence Interval for Mean	
						Lower Bound	Upper Bound
Tukey HSD	1 Rigorous Academic	2 Academic	2.19446	.92771	.085	−.1970	4.5859
		3 Some Vocational	5.62757*	1.58274	.002	1.5476	9.7075
		4 Other	7.58092*	1.85568	.000	2.7974	12.3644
	2 Academic	1 Rigorous Academic	−2.19446	.92771	.085	−4.5859	.1970
		3 Some Vocational	3.43310	1.49788	.101	−.4281	7.2943
		4 Other	5.38646*	1.78386	.014	.7881	9.9848
	3 Some Vocational	1 Rigorous Academic	−5.62757*	1.58274	.002	−9.7075	−1.5476
		2 Academic	−3.43310	1.49788	.101	−7.2943	.4281
		4 Other	1.95335	2.19694	.811	−3.7098	7.6165
	4 Other	1 Rigorous Academic	−7.58092*	1.85568	.000	−12.3644	−2.7974
		2 Academic	−5.38646*	1.78386	.014	−9.9848	−.7881
		3 Some Vocational	−1.95335	2.19694	.811	−7.6165	3.7098
LSD	1 Rigorous Academic	2 Academic	2.19446*	.92771	.018	.3717	4.0172
		3 Some Vocational	5.62757*	1.58274	.000	2.5179	8.7373
		4 Other	7.58092*	1.85568	.000	3.9350	11.2269
	2 Academic	1 Rigorous Academic	−2.19446*	.92771	.018	−4.0172	−.3717
		3 Some Vocational	3.43310*	1.49788	.022	.4901	6.3761
		4 Other	5.38646*	1.78386	.003	1.8816	8.8913
	3 Some Vocational	1 Rigorous Academic	−5.62757*	1.58274	.000	−8.7373	−2.5179
		2 Academic	−3.43310*	1.49788	.022	−6.3761	−.4901
		4 Other	1.95335	2.19694	.374	−2.3631	6.2698
	4 Other	1 Rigorous Academic	−7.58092*	1.85568	.000	−11.2269	−3.9350
		2 Academic	−5.38646*	1.78386	.003	−8.8913	−1.8816
		3 Some Vocational	−1.95335	2.19694	.374	−6.2698	2.3631

*The mean difference is significant at the .05 level.

According to the results of the LSD test, the students in the rigorous academic programs perform significantly better than those in all of the other programs. The students in the academic program perform significantly better than those in the vocational and other programs. There was no statistically significant difference between those in the vocational and those in the other programs. According to the results of the Tukey HSD test, the students in the rigorous academic program outperform those in the vocational and those in the other programs, but not those in the academic programs. The students in the academic program perform significantly better than those in the other programs, but not those in the vocational programs. Note that, as indicated in the chapter, the results based on the HSD test are more conservative than those based on the LSD test.

12.2.

a) In this case, we perform a one-way ANOVA over an independent samples *t*-test because there are three independent levels of urbanicity.

b) Based on the boxplot, the normality assumption appears to be tenable for those from an urban environment. Although those from a suburban and rural environment have one outlier each, the sample size in each of these groups is large enough to prevent these outliers from having an impact on the validity of the test results. The homogeneity-of-variance assumption appears tenable as well because the IQRs appear similar. Finally, the results of the ANOVA are likely to indicate that there are no statistically significant differences between the group means because the medians are all similar.

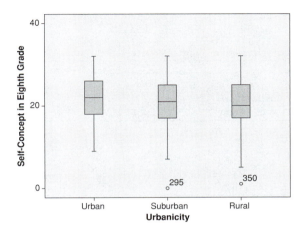

c) There are 123 students in the urban group, 215 in the suburban group, and 162 students in the rural group. Because all of these sample sizes are larger than 30, the ANOVA is robust to violations of the normality assumption, if it is violated. Levene's test must be performed to test the homogeneity-of-variances assumption because the sample sizes are not equal for the three types of environments. The results of Levene's test indicate that the homogeneity-of-variances assumption is tenable, $F(2, 497) = .45, p = .64$.

d) The results of the one-way ANOVA are summarized in the following table.

ANOVA

slfcnc08 Self-Concept in Eighth Grade

	Sum of Squares	df	Mean Square	F	Sig.
Between Groups	267.061	2	133.531	3.787	.023
Within Groups	17524.017	497	35.260		
Total	17791.078	499			

According to the results of the one-way ANOVA, the average self-concept score in eighth grade of college-bound students who have always been at grade level does vary as a function of the type of setting in which these are from, $F(2, 497) = 3.79, p = .02$.

e) Approximately 1.5 percent $\left(\dfrac{267.061}{17791.078} = .015 \right)$ of the variance in eighth-grade self-concept is explained by urbanicity, a small effect.

f) Post-hoc tests are necessary, in this case, because the results of the ANOVA are statistically significant and more than two independent means are being compared. The following tables provide the summary statistics and the results of the two post-hoc tests.

Descriptive

slfcnc08 Self-Concept in

	N	Mea	Std.	Std.	95% Confidence Mean		Minimum	Maximum
					Lower	Upper		
1	123	21.9	5.69	.51	20.9	23.0	9	32
2	215	21.2	5.80	.39	20.4	22.0	0	32
3	162	20.0	6.28	.49	19.1	21.0	1	32
Total	500	21.0	5.97	.26	20.5	21.5	0	32

Multiple Comparisons

Dependent Variable: slfcnc08 Self-Concept in Eighth Grade

	(I) urban Urbanicity	(J) urban Urbanicity	Mean Difference (I-J)	Std. Error	Sig.	95% Confidence Interval	
						Lower Bound	Upper Bound
Tukey HSD	1 Urban	2 Suburban	.731	.671	.521	−.85	2.31
		3 Rural	1.899*	.710	.021	.23	3.57
	2 Suburban	1 Urban	−.731	.671	.521	−2.31	.85
		3 Rural	1.168	.618	.142	−.28	2.62
	3 Rural	1 Urban	−1.899*	.710	.021	−3.57	−.23
		2 Suburban	−1.168	.618	.142	−2.62	.28
LSD	1 Urban	2 Suburban	.731	.671	.276	−.59	2.05
		3 Rural	1.899*	.710	.008	.50	3.29
	2 Suburban	1 Urban	−.731	.671	.276	−2.05	.59
		3 Rural	1.168	.618	.059	−.05	2.38
	3 Rural	1 Urban	−1.899*	.710	.008	−3.29	−.50
		2 Suburban	−1.168	.618	.059	−2.38	.05

*The mean difference is significant at the .05 level.

According to both the LSD and Tukey HSD post-hoc tests, the students from urban environments have statistically significantly higher eighth-grade self-concept scores than the students from rural environments. No other statistically significant differences are detected between the different environments.

g) We conduct a series of three independent samples t-tests, each with significance level $\alpha = \dfrac{.05}{3} = .017$. Comparing eighth-grade self-concept between those from urban and suburban environments, there is no statistically significant difference between the mean self-concept of those from an urban ($M = 21.99$, $SD = 5.70$) and those from a suburban environment ($M = 21.26$, $SD = 5.80$), $t(336) = 1.12$, $p = .26$. Comparing eighth-grade self-concept between those from suburban and rural environments, there is no statistically significant difference between the mean self-concept of those from a suburban environment ($M = 21.26$, $SD = 5.80$) and those from a rural environment ($M = 20.09$, $SD = 6.28$), $t(375) = 1.87$, $p = .06$. Comparing eighth-grade self-concept between those from urban and rural environments, the mean eighth-grade self-concept score of those from an urban environment ($M = 21.99$, $SD = 5.70$) is statistically significantly higher than that of those from a rural environment ($M = 20.09$, $SD = 6.28$), $t(283)$ = 2.63, $p = .009$. The results based on the *t*-test with the Bonferroni adjustment agree with those from the ANOVA.

12.3.

a) Based on the boxplot, the normality assumption appears to be tenable because both distributions are reasonably symmetric. The homogeneity-of-variance assumption appears tenable as well because the IQRs are similar. Finally, based on the medians of the two groups, the results of the ANOVA are likely to indicate that the twelfth-grade math achievement of those who never smoked cigarettes is higher.

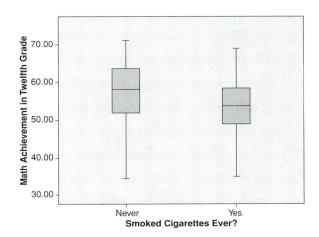

b) The sample sizes are large enough ($n = 429$ for those who have never smoked cigarettes and $n = 71$ for those who tried cigarettes at least once) to suggest that any deviations from normality that occur in the population for these two groups do not compromise the validity of the results of the ANOVA. The results of Levene's test indicate that the homogeneity-of-variance assumption is tenable, $F(1, 498) = .001$, $p = .98$.

c) According to the results of the one-way ANOVA, the average twelfth-grade math achievement score of college-bound students who have always been at grade level does differ depending on whether or not they smoked cigarettes in high school, $F(1, 498) = 18.53$, $p < .0005$.

d) According to the ratio of the sums of squares, approximately 3.59 percent of the variance in twelfth-grade math achievement scores can be explained by cigarette use, a relatively small effect.

e) It is not necessary to perform post-hoc testing in this case. Because there are only two groups, we may use the sample means to determine the nature of the mean difference. Students who never smoked cigarettes ($M = 57.51$, $SD = 7.71$) performed statistically significantly better, on average than those who did ($M = 53.24$, $SD = 8.00$).

f) According to the results of the independent samples *t*-test, students who never smoked cigarettes performed statistically significantly better, on average, than those who did, $t(498) = 4.31$, $p < .0005$. As expected, when there are only two groups, the results of the one-way ANOVA are consistent with those of the independent samples *t*-test.

g) Yes, but the *p*-value from the ANOVA must be divided in half because the one associated with the ANOVA is two-tailed and the question is one-tailed. The *p*-value associated with the one-tailed question is $p < .00025$.

12.4.

a) Based on the boxplot, the normality assumption appears to be tenable for those who expect to attain a Bachelor's degree or less. Although the distributions for those who expect to attain more than a Bachelor's degree have several outliers each, the samples are large enough in each of these distributions that these outliers are unlikely to impact the validity of the test results. The homogeneity-of-variance assumption appears tenable as well because the IQRs are similar. Finally, based on the medians, the results of the ANOVA are likely to indicate that those who expect to attain less than a college degree take statistically significantly fewer units of math than the other groups.

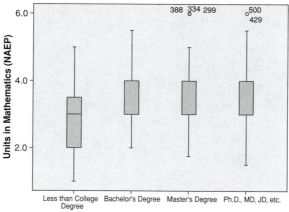

Highest level of education expected

b) There are 48 students who expect to attain less than a college degree, 159 who expect a Bachelor's degree, 190 a Master's degree, and 103 a terminal degree. Because all of these sample sizes are larger than 30, the ANOVA is robust to violations of the normality assumption, if it is violated. Levene's test must be performed to test the homogeneity-of-variance assumption because the sample sizes are not equal for the four expected levels of education. The results of Levene's test indicate that the homogeneity-of-variance assumption is tenable, $F(3, 496) = .37, p = .77$.

c) According to the results of the one-way ANOVA, the average number of years of mathematics taken by college-bound students who have always been at grade level does vary as a function of their expected educational attainment, $F(3, 496) = 15.70, p < .0005$.

d) Approximately 8.67 percent of the variance in units of math taken can be explained by the highest degree the student anticipates earning, a moderate effect.

e) Post-hoc tests are necessary, in this case, because the results of the ANOVA are statistically significant and more than two independent means are being compared. The following tables provide the summary statistics and the results of the two post-hoc tests.

Descriptives

unitmath Units in Mathematics (NAEP)

	N	Mean	Std. Deviation	Std. Error	95% Confidence Interval for Mean Lower Bound	95% Confidence Interval for Mean Upper Bound	Minimum	Maximum
1 Less than College Degree	48	2.984	.8728	.1260	2.731	3.238	1.0	5.0
2 Bachelor's Degree	159	3.565	.7497	.0595	3.448	3.682	2.0	5.5
3 Master's Degree	190	3.749	.7542	.0547	3.641	3.857	1.8	6.0
4 Ph.D., MD, JD, etc.	103	3.848	.7996	.0788	3.692	4.004	1.5	6.0
Total	500	3.637	.8077	.0361	3.566	3.708	1.0	6.0

Multiple Comparisons

Dependent Variable: unitmath Units in Mathematics (NAEP)

	(I) edexpect Highest level of education expected	(J) edexpect Highest level of education expected	Mean Difference (I-J)	Std. Error	Sig.	95% Confidence Interval	
						Lower Bound	Upper Bound
Tukey HSD	1 Less than College Degree	2 Bachelor's Degree	−.5807*	.1275	.000	−.909	−.252
		3 Master's Degree	−.7643*	.1251	.000	−1.087	−.442
		4 Ph.D., MD, JD, etc.	−.8638*	.1353	.000	−1.213	−.515
	2 Bachelor's Degree	1 Less than College Degree	.5807*	.1275	.000	.252	.909
		3 Master's Degree	−.1836	.0832	.123	−.398	.031
		4 Ph.D., MD, JD, etc.	−.2831*	.0979	.021	−.536	−.031
	3 Master's Degree	1 Less than College Degree	.7643*	.1251	.000	.442	1.087
		2 Bachelor's Degree	.1836	.0832	.123	−.031	.398
		4 Ph.D., MD, JD, etc.	−.0995	.0947	.720	−.344	.145
	4 Ph.D., MD, JD, etc.	1 Less than College Degree	.8638*	.1353	.000	.515	1.213
		2 Bachelor's Degree	.2831*	.0979	.021	.031	.536
		3 Master's Degree	.0995	.0947	.720	−.145	.344
LSD	1 Less than College Degree	2 Bachelor's Degree	−.5807*	.1275	.000	−.831	−.330
		3 Master's Degree	−.7643*	.1251	.000	−1.010	−.519
		4 Ph.D., MD, JD, etc.	−.8638*	.1353	.000	−1.130	−.598
	2 Bachelor's Degree	1 Less than College Degree	.5807*	.1275	.000	.330	.831
		3 Master's Degree	−.1836*	.0832	.028	−.347	−.020
		4 Ph.D., MD, JD, etc.	−.2831*	.0979	.004	−.476	−.091
	3 Master's Degree	1 Less than College Degree	.7643*	.1251	.000	.519	1.010
		2 Bachelor's Degree	.1836*	.0832	.028	.020	.347
		4 Ph.D., MD, JD, etc.	−.0995	.0947	.294	−.286	.087
	4 Ph.D., MD, JD, etc.	1 Less than College Degree	.8638*	.1353	.000	.598	1.130
		2 Bachelor's Degree	.2831*	.0979	.004	.091	.476
		3 Master's Degree	.0995	.0947	.294	−.087	.286

*The mean difference is significant at the .05 level.

According to both the LSD and HSD post-hoc tests, students who anticipate earning less than a college degree take statistically significantly fewer units of math than any other degree type. Also, students who anticipate earning a B.A. take statistically significantly fewer units of math than those in the Ph.D. group. According to the LSD, but not the HSD, students who anticipate earning a B.A. take statistically significantly fewer units of math than those who anticipate earning a Master's degree. No other statistically significant differences are detected.

12.5.

a) Based on the boxplot, the normality assumption does not appear to be tenable. However, the samples are large enough that these outliers are unlikely to impact the validity of the test results.

The homogeneity-of-variance assumption appears tenable as well because the IQRs are similar. Finally, based on the medians, the results of the ANOVA are likely to indicate that those who never smoked cigarettes attended schools with a similar school attendance rate than those who smoked cigarettes at least once.

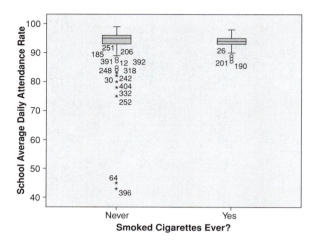

b) There are 359 students that reported that they have never smoked cigarettes whereas 58 reported that they had at least once. Because all of these sample sizes are larger than 30, the ANOVA is robust to any violation of the normality assumption. Levene's test must be performed to test the homogeneity-of-variance assumption because the sample sizes are not equal for the two groups. The results of Levene's test indicate that the homogeneity-of-variance assumption is tenable, $F(1, 415) = .37, p = .13$.

c) According to the results of the one-way ANOVA, among college-bound students who have always been at grade level, the average school attendance rate of those who ever smoked ($M = 94.12, SD = 2.43$) does not differ statistically significantly from that of those who never smoked ($M = 93.57, SD = 4.96$), $F(1, 415) = .68, p = .41$.

d) Post-hoc tests are not necessary, in this case, because the results of the ANOVA are not statistically significant.

e) No. Because the p-value at $.41/2 = .21$ still exceeds $.05$.

12.6.

a) According to the boxplots, the distributions are appropriate for use in one-way ANOVA. Further, for the sample, the median SES is higher for those who attended nursery school, confirming that the hypothesized direction of the difference is correct. Because there are more than 30 students who owned a computer ($n = 281$) or who did not own a computer ($n = 139$), the ANOVA is robust to violations of the normality assumption. The results of Levene's test indicate that the homogeneity-of-variance assumption is tenable, $F(1, 418) = .40, p = .53$. According to the results of the one-way ANOVA, among college-bound students who are always at grade level, SES does vary as a function of computer ownership, $F(1, 418) = 72.43, p < .00025$ (we halve the p-value because the question was directional). According to the sample means, the mean SES of students who owned a computer ($M = 20.74, SD = 6.51$) is statistically significantly higher than that of students who did not own a computer ($M = 15.07, SD = 6.24$). According to the value of R^2, approximately 14.77 percent of the variance in SES can be explained by computer ownership, a moderate effect according to Cohen's rule-of-thumb guidelines. Finally, because the alternative hypothesis is nondirectional, although there are only two groups, the ANOVA is appropriate to use in this case. The ANOVA is mathematically equivalent to a nondirectional t-test, and would, therefore, yield the same results as the t-test.

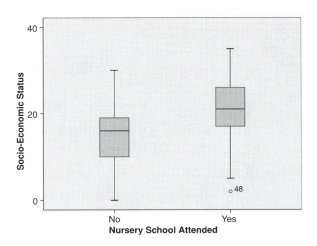

b) Because there are only 15 students in the NELS data set with a non-English-only background, the ANOVA is not robust to violations of the normality assumption and so this assumption needs to be tested. Because the skewness ratio of reading achievement in twelfth grade is less than negative 2 (skewness ratio = −3.69), the normality assumption is not tenable.

Descriptive Statistics

homelang Home Language Background		N	Skewness	
		Statistic	Statistic	Std. Error
1 Non-English Only	achrdg12 Reading Achievement in Twelfth Grade	15	−.103	.580
	Valid N (listwise)	15		
2 Non-English Dominant	achrdg12 Reading Achievement in Twelfth Grade	35	−.501	.398
	Valid N (listwise)	35		
3 English Dominant	achrdg12 Reading Achievement in Twelfth Grade	47	−1.279	.347
	Valid N (listwise)	47		
4 English Only	achrdg12 Reading Achievement in Twelfth Grade	403	−.660	.122
	Valid N (listwise)	403		

We may proceed by trying to use a nonlinear transformation to normalize the data prior to conducting the ANOVA or by using a nonparametric test described in Chapter 16, such as the Mann–Whitney U-Test. In this case, we attempt to find an appropriate nonlinear transformation.

ACHRDG12 is severely negatively skewed. Following the methods of Chapter 4, we reflect the variable, translate it so that it takes on positive values, and then take the log and square root transformations. The result is that the reflected square root transformation is most effective at reducing the skew.

Descriptive Statistics

	N	Minimum	Maximum	Mean	Std.	Skewness	
	Statistic	Statistic	Statistic	Statistic	Statistic	Statistic	Std. Error
achrdg12 Reading Achievement in Twelfth Grade	500	31.76	68.09	55.6019	7.98492	−.685	.109
ACHrdglg	500	−1	2	.98	.386	−1.294	.109
ACHrdgsq	500	0	6	3.38	1.223	−.081	.109
Valid N (listwise)	500						

Because the skewness ratios of twelfth-grade reading achievement are less than 2 in magnitude for all four types of home language backgrounds, the normality assumption is tenable with the transformed variable.

Descriptive Statistics

homelang Home Language Background		N	Skewness	
		Statistic	Statistic	Std. Error
1 Non-English Only	ACHrdgsq	15	−.320	.580
	Valid N (listwise)	15		
2 Non-English Dominant	ACHrdgsq	35	−.337	.398
	Valid N (listwise)	35		
3 English Dominant	ACHrdgsq	47	.069	.347
	Valid N (listwise)	47		
4 English Only	ACHrdgsq	403	−.064	.122
	Valid N (listwise)	403		

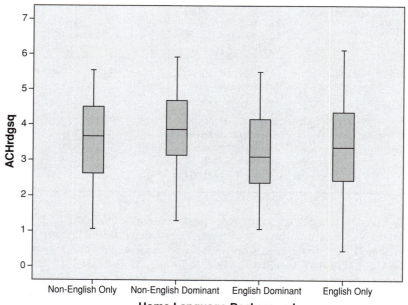

The results of Levene's test indicate that the homogeneity-of-variance assumption is tenable for the transformed data, $F(3, 496) = .53, p = .66$. According to the results of the one-way ANOVA, among college-bound students who are always at grade level, (the square root of) twelfth-grade reading achievement does not vary as a function of home language background, $F(3, 496) = 1.87, p = .13$.

c) One-way ANOVA is not appropriate. The scores are dependent. A paired samples t-test should be used instead.

d) One-way ANOVA is not the most natural choice because COMPUTER ownership (the dependent variable) in this example is dichotomous, not continuous. One may use a contingency table to analyze the relationship between these categorical variables, but also, because, in the long run with a large enough sample size, a binomial (0/1) variable approaches normality, one may use the ANOVA. Recall that the mean of COMPUTER is equal to the proportion of students with a computer in the household. Below are solutions using both approaches.

According to the results of the contingency table analysis, computer ownership does not vary much as a function of home language background. For all home language backgrounds, students were almost equally likely to own a computer as not. In the English-only households, 46.67 percent owned a computer, in non-English dominant, 42.86 percent owned, in English dominant, 48.94 percent owned, and in English only, 47.64 percent owned.

Prior to conducting the ANOVA, we conduct an analysis of the underlying assumptions. Because there are fewer than 30 students with a non-English-only home language background, we test the tenability of the normality assumption. The skewness ratio of computer ownership is not severely skewed for any of the different home language backgrounds. The results of Levene's test indicate that the homogeneity-of-variance assumption is tenable, $F(3, 496) = 1.09, p = .35$. According to the results of the one-way ANOVA, among college-bound students who are always at grade level, computer ownership does not vary as a function of home language background, $F(3, 496) = .12, p = .95$.

Descriptive Statistics

homelang Home Language Background		N	Mean	Std.	Skewness	
		Statistic	Statistic	Statistic	Statistic	Std. Error
1 Non-English Only	computer Computer Owned by Family in Eighth Grade?	15	.47	.516	.149	.580
	Valid N (listwise)	15				
2 Non-English Dominant	computer Computer Owned by Family in Eighth Grade?	35	.43	.502	.302	.398
	Valid N (listwise)	35				
3 English Dominant	computer Computer Owned by Family in Eighth Grade?	47	.49	.505	.044	.347
	Valid N (listwise)	47				
4 English Only	computer Computer Owned by Family in Eighth Grade?	403	.48	.500	.095	.122
	Valid N (listwise)	403				

e) One-way ANOVA is not appropriate because the variable ABSENT12 is ordinal. A nonparametric test as described in Chapter 16, such as the Mann–Whitney U-Test would be appropriate to use.

f) There are 106 students from the Northeast, 151 from the North Central, 150 from the South, and 93 from the West. Because these sample sizes are greater than 30, the ANOVA is robust to violations of the normality assumption. The results of Levene's test indicate that the homogeneity-of-variance assumption is tenable, $F(3, 496) = 1.52$, $p = .21$. According to the results of the one-way ANOVA, among college-bound students who are always at grade level, average family size does not vary by region, $F(3, 496) = 1.67$, $p = 17$.

g) Because there are more than 30 students from each level of urbanicity, 123 from an urban environment, 215 from a suburban environment, and 162 from a rural environment, the ANOVA is robust to violations of the normality assumption. The results of Levene's test indicate that the homogeneity-of-variance assumption is tenable, $F(2, 497) = .86$, $p = .42$. According to the results of the one-way ANOVA, among college-bound students who are always at grade level, twelfth-grade self-concept does vary as a function of urbanicity, $F(2, 497) = 5.47$, $p = .004$. According to the value of R^2, approximately 2.15 percent of the variance in twelfth-grade self-concept can be explained by urbanicity, a small effect according to Cohen's rule-of-thumb guidelines. According to Tukey's HSD post-hoc test, the mean twelfth-grade self-concept of students from an urban area ($M = 33.15$, $SD = 6.32$) is statistically significantly higher than that of students from a rural area ($M = 30.33$, $SD = 7.71$). No other statistically significant differences are detected by the Tukey HSD test. According to the LSD post-hoc test, the mean twelfth-grade self-concept of students from an urban area ($M = 33.15$, $SD = 6.32$) is statistically significantly higher than that of students from a rural area ($M = 30.33$, $SD = 7.71$) and higher than that of students from a suburban area ($M = 31.39$, $SD = 7.20$). No statistically significant difference between those from a suburban and rural environment is detected by the LSD test.

12.7. The sample sizes are large enough to suggest that the ANOVA is robust to violations of the normality assumption. However, the severity of the skew is a concern. The skewness ratio for males is 53.39 and for females it is 24.46. Furthermore, according to the results of Levene's test, the homogeneity-of-variance assumption is not tenable, $F(1, 457) = 9.48$, $p = .002$. Because of these violations, ANOVA on the data in their current form is not appropriate. Our options are to use a nonlinear transformation to normalize the data and stabilize the variances and proceed with the ANOVA or to use a nonparametric test such as the Kruskal–Wallis ANOVA described in Chapter 16.

12.8.   a) 3   b) 2   c) 6   d) 7   e) 5

12.9.

ANOVA	Sum of Squares	df	Mean Square	F	Sig.
Between groups	2,240	2	1120	5	$.001 < p < .01$
Within groups	26,208	117	224		
Total	28448	119			

The results of the one-way ANOVA indicate that there is at least one statistically significant difference in serotonin levels among bulimics, recovering bulimics, and the control group, $F(2, 117) = 5$, $p = .01$.

12.10.

a) The one-way ANOVA can be performed by hand. Alternatively, it can be performed using SPSS. Using SPSS, we obtain the following output:

Descriptive Statistics

Group		N	Skewness	
		Statistic	Statistic	Std. Error
1 Lecture-recitation	Score Score on Final Exam in French	5	1.118	.913
	Valid N (listwise)	5		
2 Programmed text	Score Score on Final Exam in French	5	−.565	.913
	Valid N (listwise)	5		
3 Tape-recorded lessons	Score Score on Final Exam in French	5	1.119	.913
	Valid N (listwise)	5		
4 Films	Score Score on Final Exam in French	5	−.584	.913
	Valid N (listwise)	5		

Descriptives

Score Score on Final Exam in French

	N	Mean	Std. Deviation	Std. Error	95% Confidence Interval for Mean		Minimum	Maximum
					Lower Bound	Upper Bound		
1 Lecture-recitation	5	78.00	7.583	3.391	68.58	87.42	70	90
2 Programmed text	5	67.20	4.970	2.223	61.03	73.37	60	73
3 Tape-recorded lessons	5	71.00	5.657	2.530	63.98	78.02	65	80
4 Films	5	83.40	5.941	2.657	76.02	90.78	75	90
Total	20	74.90	8.522	1.906	70.91	78.89	60	90

Test of Homogeneity of Variances

Score Score on Final Exam in French

Levene Statistic	df1	df2	Sig.
.306	3	16	.821

ANOVA

Score Score on Final Exam in French

	Sum of Squares	df	Mean Square	F	Sig.
Between groups	781.800	3	260.600	6.973	.003
Within groups	598.000	16	37.375		
Total	1379.800	19			

None of the distributions is statistically significantly skewed and the results of Levene's test indicate that the homogeneity-of-variance assumption is tenable, in this case, $F(3, 16) = .31$, $p = .82$. The results of the one-way ANOVA indicate that the mean score in the population is not the same across all four groups, $F(3, 16) = 6.97$, $p = .003$.

b) A post-hoc analysis should be conducted because the results of the ANOVA are statistically significant and there are more than two groups. The Tukey or LSD can be performed by hand. Alternatively, they can be performed using SPSS. Using SPSS, we obtain the following output:

Multiple Comparisons

Dependent Variable: Score Score on Final Exam in French

	(I) Group	(J) Group	Mean Difference (I-J)	Std. Error	Sig.	95% Confidence Interval Lower Bound	95% Confidence Interval Upper Bound
Tukey HSD	1 Lecture-recitation	2 Programmed text	10.800	3.867	.057	−.26	21.86
		3 Tape-recorded lessons	7.000	3.867	.305	−4.06	18.06
		4 Films	−5.400	3.867	.519	−16.46	5.66
	2 Programmed text	1 Lecture-recitation	−10.800	3.867	.057	−21.86	.26
		3 Tape-recorded lessons	−3.800	3.867	.761	−14.86	7.26
		4 Films	−16.200*	3.867	.003	−27.26	−5.14
	3 Tape-recorded lessons	1 Lecture-recitation	−7.000	3.867	.305	−18.06	4.06
		2 Programmed text	3.800	3.867	.761	−7.26	14.86
		4 Films	−12.400*	3.867	.025	−23.46	−1.34
	4 Films	1 Lecture-recitation	5.400	3.867	.519	−5.66	16.46
		2 Programmed text	16.200*	3.867	.003	5.14	27.26
		3 Tape-recorded lessons	12.400*	3.867	.025	1.34	23.46
LSD	1 Lecture-recitation	2 Programmed text	10.800*	3.867	.013	2.60	19.00
		3 Tape-recorded lessons	7.000	3.867	.089	−1.20	15.20
		4 Films	−5.400	3.867	.182	−13.60	2.80
	2 Programmed text	1 Lecture-recitation	−10.800*	3.867	.013	−19.00	−2.60
		3 Tape-recorded lessons	−3.800	3.867	.340	−12.00	4.40
		4 Films	−16.200*	3.867	.001	−24.40	−8.00
	3 Tape-recorded lessons	1 Lecture-recitation	−7.000	3.867	.089	−15.20	1.20
		2 Programmed text	3.800	3.867	.340	−4.40	12.00
		4 Films	−12.400*	3.867	.005	−20.60	−4.20
	4 Films	1 Lecture-recitation	5.400	3.867	.182	−2.80	13.60
		2 Programmed text	16.200*	3.867	.001	8.00	24.40
		3 Tape-recorded lessons	12.400*	3.867	.005	4.20	20.60

*The mean difference is significant at the .05 level.

The results of the Tukey test indicate that, on average, students in Group 4 score statistically significantly higher than students in both Group 2 and Group 3. There were no other statistically significant differences detected by the Tukey test. The results of the LSD test indicate that, on average, students in Group 4 score statistically significantly higher than students in both Group 2 and Group 3 and also that, on average, students in Group 1 score statistically significantly higher than students in Group 2. There were no other statistically significant differences detected by the LSD test.

CHAPTER 13. **SOLUTIONS**

13.1.

Graph (1)

a) There is a main effect due to gender. On average, males score higher in reading achievement ($M = 20$) than females ($M = 10$).

b) There is no main effect due to teaching method. On average, reading achievement for both males and females is the same under whole language ($M = 15$), synthetic phonics ($M = 15$), and analytic phonics ($M = 15$).

c) There is no interaction effect. The effectiveness of the different teaching methods does not differ by gender. Said differently, the difference between males and females in terms of their average reading achievement is the same ($M_{\text{Difference}} = 10$) under all three teaching methods.

d) In the absence of an interaction, the statistically significant main effects are used to summarize results. In this case, we may conclude that, on average, males outperform females by the same amount for all three teaching methods.

Graph (2)

a) There is no main effect due to gender. On average, reading achievement for males ($M = 20$) is the same as for females ($M = 20$).

b) There is no main effect due to teaching method. On average, reading achievement under whole language ($M = 20$) is the same as under synthetic phonics ($M = 20$) and analytic phonics ($M = 20$).

c) There is a disordinal interaction. Holding teaching method constant and comparing males with females we may note that, on average, males score 20 points higher than females on reading achievement under whole language – no differently than females under synthetic phonics – and 20 points lower than females under analytic phonics. Alternatively, we may characterize the interaction by holding gender constant and comparing the relative effectiveness of teaching methods. From this perspective, we note that males do relatively best under whole language, next best under synthetic phonics, and relatively worst under analytic phonics. By contrast, females do relatively best under analytic phonics, next best under synthetic phonics, and relatively worst under whole language.

d) Given the statistically significant interaction, the relative effectiveness of the three methods by gender is captured by the response to part (c) above.

Graph (3)

a) There is a main effect due to gender. On average, reading achievement for males ($M = 30$) exceeds that for females ($M = 16.67$).

b) There is a main effect due to teaching method. On average, reading achievement is highest under analytic phonics ($M = 30$), followed by synthetic phonics ($M = 25$), and worst under whole language ($M = 15$).

c) There is an ordinal interaction. Holding teaching method constant and comparing males with females we may note that, on average, males score 10 points higher than females on reading achievement under both whole language and synthetic phonics, and 20 points higher than females under analytic phonics. Holding gender constant and comparing the relative effectiveness of teaching methods, we may note that, on average, males perform relatively best under analytic phonics ($M = 40$), next best under synthetic phonics ($M = 30$), and worst under whole language ($M = 20$). We may also note that, on average, females perform equally under the two types of phonics instruction ($M = 20$), but relatively worse under whole language ($M = 10$).

d) Given the statistically significant interaction, the relative effectiveness of the three methods by gender is captured by the response to part (c) above.

Graph (4)

a) There is a main effect due to gender. On average, males ($M = 35$) score higher than females ($M = 15$) on reading achievement.

b) There is no main effect due to teaching method. On average, there is no difference on reading achievement ($M = 25$) across the three teaching methods.

c) There is an ordinal interaction in that, on average, males perform better than females under each teaching method by varying amounts of reading achievement. In particular, on average, males score 10 points higher than females under whole language, 20 points higher under synthetic phonics, and 30 points higher under analytic phonics. We may also characterize the interaction by comparing teaching methods for each gender. For males, the highest average reading achievement scores are associated with analytic phonics ($M = 40$), followed by synthetic phonics ($M = 35$), followed by whole language ($M = 30$). For females, the highest average reading achievement scores are associated with whole language ($M = 20$), followed by synthetic phonics ($M = 15$), followed by analytic phonics ($M = 10$).

d) Given the statistically significant interaction, the relative effectiveness of the three methods by gender is captured by the response to part (c) above.

Graph (5)

a) There is a main effect due to gender. On average, the reading achievement score for males ($M = 26.67$) is higher than it is for females ($M = 16.67$) across all teaching methods.

b) There is a main effect due to teaching method. On average, males and females both do better under whole language and analytic phonics ($M = 25$) than they do under synthetic phonics ($M = 15$).

c) There is no interaction effect. On average, males outperform females by the same amount under all three teaching methods. That is, the mean difference on reading achievement between males and females is the same ($M_{Difference} = 10$) under all three teaching methods.

d) In the absence of an interaction, as given in the responses to parts (a) and (b), the main effects characterize the results of this study. s are used to summarize the effects.

13.2.

a) For the main effect of SEX: H_0: $\mu_{male} = \mu_{female}$ and H_1: $\mu_{male} \neq \mu_{female}$. For the main effect of CURSMOKE1: H_0: $\mu_{smoker} = \mu_{nonsmoker}$ and H_1: $\mu_{smoker} \neq \mu_{nonsmoker}$. For the interaction effect: H_0: There is no interaction in the population between cigarette use and gender on body mass index. H_1: There is an interaction in the population between cigarette use and gender on body mass index.

b) Because the lines are approximately parallel, there does not appear to be an interaction between gender and cigarette use on BMI. Because the line for males is higher than that for females, on average, males have a higher BMI than females across both levels of CURSMOKE1, suggesting a main effect due to gender. Because both lines slope downward, and a higher BMI is associated with nonsmokers, there appears also to be a main effect due to cigarette use.

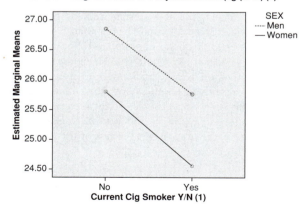

Estimated Marginal Means of Body Mass Index (kg/(M*M) (1)

c) The ANOVA is robust to possible violations of the normality assumption when each cell contains a large number of research participants, which is the case for these data because $N = 100$. Hence, the normality assumption is not an issue for these data.

d) The ANOVA is robust to violations of the homogeneity-of-variance assumption when cell sizes are equal and large, which is the case for these data. Hence, the homogeneity-of-variance assumption is not an issue for these data.

e) According to the ANOVA results, the interaction effect is not statistically significant, $F(1, 396) = .04$, $p = .85$. However, the main effect due to cigarette use is statistically significant, $F(1, 396) = 9.20$, $p = .003$, as is the main effect due to gender, $F(1, 396) = 8.59$, $p = .004$.

f) Because each statistically significant main effect only has two levels, post-hoc testing is not necessary. The sample means themselves are sufficient to indicate the direction of the difference.

   On average, males ($M = 26.31$, $SD = 3.48$) have a statistically significantly higher BMI than females ($M = 25.18$, $SD = 4.24$); and, on average, nonsmokers ($M = 26.32$, $SD = 3.80$) have a statistically significantly higher BMI than smokers ($M = 25.16$, $SD = 3.95$).

g) According to the value of R^2, approximately 2.22 percent (($135.664/105.39) \times 100$) of the variance in BMI is explained by cigarette use, and approximately 2.07 percent ($126.75/6105.39 \times 100$) of the variance in BMI is explained by gender. Collectively, both statistically significant main effects account for approximately 4.29 percent of BMI variance.

   In this example, the *partial eta squared* values are similar to the values of R^2. This is because each of the effects accounts for relatively little dependent variable variance as noted by the respective Sum of Squares values, and that, as a result, the Sum of Squares due to Error is nearly equal to the Sum of Squares due to the Corrected Total, the denominator used to compute R^2.

Tests of Between-Subjects Effects
Dependent Variable: Body Mass Index (kg/(M*M)) (1)

Source	Type III Sum of Squares	df	Mean Square	F	Sig.	Partial Eta Squared
Corrected Model	262.972[a]	3	87.657	5.941	.001	.043
Intercept	265071.037	1	265071.037	17966.550	.000	.978
CURSMOKE1	135.664	1	135.664	9.195	.003	.023
SEX	126.754	1	126.754	8.591	.004	.021
CURSMOKE1 * SEX	.554	1	.554	.038	.846	.000
Error	5842.420	396	14.754			
Total	271176.430	400				
Corrected Total	6105.392	399				

[a]R Squared = .043 (Adjusted R Squared = .036).

13.3.

a) Because the lines cross, there appears to be a disordinal interaction between gender and cigarette use on age. With respect to main effects, on average, females appear to be younger than males and, on average, smokers appear to be younger than nonsmokers.

Estimated Marginal Means of Age (years) at examination (1)

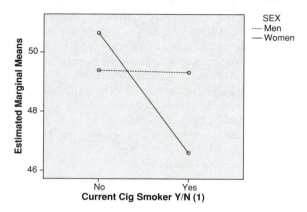

b) According to the ANOVA results, there is a statistically significant interaction, $F(1, 396) = 5.71$, $p = .02$, a statistically significant main effect due to cigarette use, $F(1, 396) = 6.12$, $p = .01$, but no statistically significant main effect due to gender, $F(1, 396) = .77$, $p = .38$.

c) Holding cigarette use constant: for nonsmokers, on average, males and females are not statistically significantly different in age. For smokers, however, males are statistically significantly older than females.

Holding gender constant: for males, smokers and nonsmokers are not statistically significantly different in age. For females, however, smokers are statistically significantly younger than nonsmokers.

Given that cigarette use and gender each have only two levels, additional post-hoc tests are not necessary.

Estimates

Dependent Variable: Age (years) at examination (1)

SEX	Current Cig Smoker Y/N(1)	Mean	Std. Error	95% Confidence Interval	
				Lower Bound	Upper Bound
Men	No	49.390	.833	47.753	51.027
	Yes	49.320	.833	47.683	50.957
Women	No	50.650	.833	49.013	52.287
	Yes	46.600	.833	44.963	48.237

Pairwise Comparisons

Dependent Variable: Age (years) at examination (1)

Current Cig Smoker Y/N(1)	(1) SEX	(J) SEX	Mean Difference (I-J)	Std. Error	Sig[a]	95% Confidence Interval for Difference[a]	
						Lower Bound	Upper Bound
No	Men	Women	−1.260	1.177	.285	−3.575	1.055
	Women	Men	1.260	1.177	.285	−1.055	3.575
Yes	Men	Women	2.720*	1.177	.021	.405	5.035
	Women	Men	−2.720*	1.177	.021	−5.035	−.405

Based on estimated marginal means.
*The mean difference is significant at the .05 level.
[a]Adjustment for multiple comparisons: Least Significant Difference (equivalent to no adjustments).

Pairwise Comparisons

Dependent Variable: Age (years) at examination (1)

SEX	(1) Current Cig Smoker Y/N(1)	(J) Current Cig Smoker Y/N(1)	Mean Difference (I-J)	Std. Error	Sig.[a]	95% Confidence Interval for Difference[a]	
						Lower Bound	Upper Bound
Men	No	Yes	.070	1.177	.953	−2.245	2.385
	Yes	No	−.070	1.177	.953	−2.385	2.245
Women	No	Yes	4.050*	1.177	.001	1.735	6.365
	Yes	No	−4.050*	1.177	.001	−6.365	−1.735

Based on estimated marginal means.
*The mean difference is significant at the .05 level.
[a]Adjustment for multiple comparisons: Least Significant Difference (equivalent to no adjustments).

d) According to the respective values of R^2, approximately 1.4 percent (($396.01/28323.96) \times 100$) of age variance is explained by the interaction of gender and cigarette use, and approximately 1.5 percent (($424.36/28323.96) \times 100$) of age variance is explained by cigarette use. Collectively, both statistically significant effects account for approximately 2.9 percent of age variance.

In this example, the values of the partial eta squared terms are similar to the respective values of R^2. This is because each of the effects accounts for relatively little dependent variable variance as noted by the respective Sum of Squares values, and that, as a result, the Sum of Squares due to Error is nearly equal to the Sum of Squares due to the Corrected Total, the denominator used to compute R^2.

Tests of Between-Subjects Effects

Dependent Variable: Age (years) at examination (1)

Source	Type III Sum of Squares	df	Mean Square	F	Sig.	Partial Eta Squared
Corrected Model	873.660[a]	3	291.220	4.201	.006	.031
Intercept	960008.040	1	960008.040	13849.145	.000	.972
SEX	53.290	1	53.290	.769	.381	.002
CURSMOKE1	424.360	1	424.360	6.122	.014	.015
SEX * CURSMOKE1	396.010	1	396.010	5.713	.017	.014
Error	27450.300	396	69.319			
Total	988332.000	400				
Corrected Total	28323.960	399				

[a]R Squared = .031 (Adjusted R Squared = .024).

13.4.

a) Because the lines cross several times, there appears to be a disordinal interaction between education level and gender on years of work experience. In particular, on average, the number of years of work experience appears to be greater for females than males when both have either less than a high school degree, some college, or a graduate degree, and greater for males than females when both have either a high school degree or a college degree. With respect to main effects, on average, the number of years of work experience for females appears to be approximately equal to that for males; and, on average, the number of years of work experience appears to be highest for those with less than a high school degree, next highest for those with a graduate school degree, and so on.

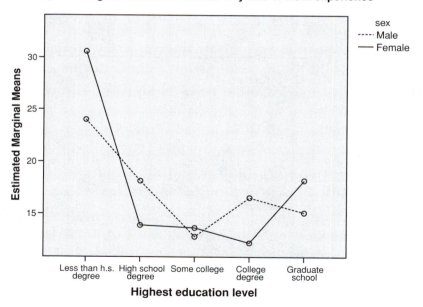

Estimated Marginal Means of Number of years of work experience

b) The ANOVA is robust to possible violations of the normality assumption when each cell contains a large number of research participants, which is the case for these data because $N = 40$. Hence, the normality assumption is not an issue for these data.

c) The ANOVA is robust to violations of the homogeneity-of-variance assumption when cell sizes are equal and large, which is the case for these data. Hence, the homogeneity-of-variance assumption is not an issue for these data.

d) According to the ANOVA results, there is a statistically significant interaction, $F(4, 390) = 4.11$, $p = .003$, a statistically significant main effect due to education level, $F(4, 390) = 23.15$, $p < .0005$, but not a statistically significant main effect due to gender, $F(1, 390) = .14$, $p = .71$.

Tests of Between-Subjects Effects
Dependent Variable: Number of years of work experience

Source	Type III Sum of Squares	df	Mean Square	F	Sig.	Partial Eta Squared
Corrected Model	11975.810[a]	9	1330.646	12.132	.000	.219
Intercept	122710.090	1	122710.090	1118.777	.000	.742
ed	10158.260	4	2539.565	23.154	.000	.192
sex	15.210	1	15.210	.139	.710	.000
ed* sex	1802.340	4	450.585	4.108	.003	.040
Error	42776.100	390	109.682			
Total	177462.000	400				
Corrected Total	54751.910	399				

[a]R Squared = .219 (Adjusted R Squared = .201).

e) Holding gender constant: for males, those with less than a high school degree have statistically significantly more years of work experience, on average, than those at other education levels, and those with a high school degree have statistically significantly more years of work experience, on average, than those with some college. For females, those with less than a high school degree, on average, have statistically significantly more years of work experience than those at other education levels, and those with a graduate degree have statistically significantly more years of work experience, on average, than those with a college degree.

Holding education level constant: for those with less than a high school degree, females have statistically significantly more years of experience, on average, than males. No other statistically significant differences are noted between males and females at any of the other education levels.

Estimates
Dependent Variable: Number of years of work experience

Highest education level	sex	Mean	Std. Error	95% Confidence Interval	
				Lower Bound	Upper Bound
Less than h.s. degree	Male	24.000	1.656	20.744	27.256
	Female	30.600	1.656	27.344	33.856
High school degree	Male	18.150	1.656	14.894	21.406
	Female	13.900	1.656	10.644	17.156
Some college	Male	12.800	1.656	9.544	16.056
	Female	13.650	1.656	10.394	16.906
College degree	Male	16.550	1.656	13.294	19.806
	Female	12.200	1.656	8.944	15.456
Graduate school	Male	15.100	1.656	11.844	18.356
	Female	18.200	1.656	14.944	21.456

Pairwise Comparisons

Dependent Variable: Number of years of work experience

sex	(I) Highest education level	(J) Highest education level	Mean Difference (I-J)	Std. Error	Sig.[a]	95% Confidence Interval for Difference[a]	
						Lower Bound	Upper Bound
Male	Less than h.s. degree	High school degree	5.850*	2.342	.013	1.246	10.454
		Some college	11.200*	2.342	.000	6.596	15.804
		College degree	7.450*	2.342	.002	2.846	12.054
		Graduate school	8.900*	2.342	.000	4.296	13.504
	High school degree	Less than h.s. degree	−5.850*	2.342	.013	−10.454	−1.246
		Some college	5.350*	2.342	.023	.746	9.954
		College degree	1.600	2.342	.495	−3.004	6.204
		Graduate school	3.050	2.342	.194	−1.554	7.654
	Some college	Less than h.s. degree	−11.200*	2.342	.000	−15.804	−6.596
		High school degree	−5.350*	2.342	.023	−9.954	−.746
		College degree	−3.750	2.342	.110	−8.354	.854
		Graduate school	−2.300	2.342	.327	−6.904	2.304
	College degree	Less than h.s. degree	−7.450*	2.342	.002	−12.054	−2.846
		High school degree	−1.600	2.342	.495	−6.204	3.004
		Some college	3.750	2.342	.110	−.854	8.354
		Graduate school	1.450	2.342	.536	−3.154	6.054
	Graduate school	Less than h.s. degree	−8.900*	2.342	.000	−13.504	−4.296
		High school degree	−3.050	2.342	.194	−7.654	1.554
		Some college	2.300	2.342	.327	−2.304	6.904
		College degree	−1.450	2.342	.536	−6.054	3.154
Female	Less than h.s. degree	High school degree	16.700*	2.342	.000	12.096	21.304
		Some college	16.950*	2.342	.000	12.346	21.554
		College degree	18.400*	2.342	.000	13.796	23.004
		Graduate school	12.400*	2.342	.000	7.796	17.004
	High school degree	Less than h.s. degree	−16.700*	2.342	.000	−21.304	−12.096
		Some college	.250	2.342	.915	−4.354	4.854
		College degree	1.700	2.342	.468	−2.904	6.304
		Graduate school	−4.300	2.342	.067	−8.904	.304
	Some college	Less than h.s. degree	−16.950*	2.342	.000	−21.554	−12.346
		High school degree	−.250	2.342	.915	−4.854	4.354
		College degree	1.450	2.342	.536	−3.154	6.054
		Graduate school	−4.550	2.342	.053	−9.154	.054
	College degree	Less than h.s. degree	−18.400*	2.342	.000	−23.004	−13.796
		High school degree	−1.700	2.342	.468	−6.304	2.904
		Some college	−1.450	2.342	.536	−6.054	3.154
		Graduate school	−6.000*	2.342	.011	−10.604	−1.396
	Graduate school	Less than h.s. degree	−12.400*	2.342	.000	−17.004	−7.796
		High school degree	4.300	2.342	.067	−.304	8.904
		Some college	4.550	2.342	.053	−.054	9.154
		College degree	6.000*	2.342	.011	1.396	10.604

Based on estimated marginal means.

* The mean difference is significant at the .05 level.

[a] Adjustment for multiple comparisons: Least Significant Difference (equivalent to no adjustments).

Pairwise Comparisons

Dependent Variable: Number of years of work experience

Highest education level	(I) sex	(J) sex	Mean Difference (I-J)	Std. Error	Sig.[a]	95% Confidence Interval for Difference[a]	
						Lower Bound	Upper Bound
Less than h.s. degree	Male	Female	−6.600*	2.342	.005	−11.204	−1.996
	Female	Male	6.600*	2.342	.005	1.996	11.204
High school degree	Male	Female	4.250	2.342	.070	−.354	8.854
	Female	Male	−4.250	2.342	.070	−8.854	.354
Some college	Male	Female	−.850	2.342	.717	−5.454	3.754
	Female	Male	.850	2.342	.717	−3.754	5.454
College degree	Male	Female	4.350	2.342	.064	−.254	8.954
	Female	Male	−4.350	2.342	.064	−8.954	.254
Graduate school	Male	Female	−3.100	2.342	.186	−7.704	1.504
	Female	Male	3.100	2.342	.186	−1.504	7.704

Based on estimated marginal means.

*The mean difference is significant at the .05 level.

[a]Adjustment for multiple comparisons: Least Significant Difference (equivalent to no adjustments).

f) According to the respective values of R^2, approximately 3.29 percent $((1802.34/54751.91) \times 100)$ of work experience variance is explained by the interaction of gender and education level, and approximately 18.56 percent $((10158.26/54751.91) \times 100)$ of work experience variance is explained by education level. Collectively, both statistically significant effects account for approximately 21.84 percent of work variance.

   In this example, the values of the partial eta squared terms are similar to the respective values of R^2. This is because each of the effects accounts for relatively little dependent variable variance as noted by the respective Sum of Squares values, and that, as a result, the Sum of Squares due to Error is nearly equal to the Sum of Squares due to the Corrected Total, the denominator used to compute R^2.

13.5.

a) Create

Descriptive Statistics

Dependent Variable: Final Exam Score

Time of Course	Academic Year	Mean	Std. Deviation	N
Morning	Freshman	75.00	5.000	5
	Sophomore	82.00	2.121	5
	Junior	89.20	2.490	5
	Senior	95.20	3.962	5
	Total	85.35	8.450	20
Afternoon	Freshman	65.00	5.000	5
	Sophomore	70.00	3.606	5
	Junior	78.80	6.058	5
	Senior	81.00	4.848	5
	Total	73.70	8.066	20
Total	Freshman	70.00	7.071	10
	Sophomore	76.00	6.912	10
	Junior	84.00	7.008	10
	Senior	88.10	8.569	10
	Total	79.53	10.064	40

b) Because there are only five students per cell we check the tenability of the normality assumption by computing the skewness ratio for each cell. Because the skewness ratio for each cell is less than 2 in absolute value, the data appear to be reasonably symmetric and the normality assumption may be considered to be tenable.

Descriptive Statistics

Time of Course	Academic Year		N	Skewness	
			Statistic	Statistic	Std. Error
Morning	Freshman	Final Exam Score	5	.000	.913
		Valid N (listwise)	5		
	Sophomore	Final Exam Score	5	.524	.913
		Valid N (listwise)	5		
	Junior	Final Exam Score	5	.920	.913
		Valid N (listwise)	5		
	Senior	Final Exam Score	5	−.125	.913
		Valid N (listwise)	5		
Afternoon	Freshman	Final Exam Score	5	.000	.913
		Valid N (listwise)	5		
	Sophomore	Final Exam Score	5	.000	.913
		Valid N (listwise)	5		
	Junior	Final Exam Score	5	−.242	.913
		Valid N (listwise)	5		
	Senior	Final Exam Score	5	.461	.913
		Valid N (listwise)	5		

According to the results of Levene's test, the homogeneity-of-variance assumption is tenable, $F(7, 32) = 1.60, p = .17$.

c) There is no statistically significant interaction effect, $F(3, 32) = .49$, $p = .69$. There is a statistically significant main effect due to time, $F(1, 32) = 72.58$, $p < .0005$, as well as a statistically significant main effect due to academic year, $F(3, 32) = 35.06$, $p < .0005$.

Tests of Between-Subjects Effects

Dependent Variable: Final Exam Score

Source	Type III Sum of Squares	df	Mean Square	F	Sig.	Partial Eta Squared
Corrected Model	3351.575[a]	7	478.796	25.604	.000	.849
Intercept	252969.025	1	252969.025	13527.755	.000	.998
FactorA	1357.225	1	1357.225	72.579	.000	.694
FactorB	1967.075	3	655.692	35.064	.000	.767
FactorA * FactorB	27.275	3	9.092	.486	.694	.044
Error	598.400	32	18.700			
Total	256919.000	40				
Corrected Total	3949.975	39				

[a] R Squared = .849 (Adjusted R Squared = .815).

d) According to the value of R^2, approximately 34.3 percent of the final exam variance is explained by time, and 49.8 percent by year. Alternatively, after controlling for the other effects in the model, the values of the partial eta squared terms indicate that approximately 69.4 percent of the final exam variance is explained by time and 76.7 percent by year.

e) According to the line graph, the nearly parallel line segments suggest the absence of an interaction. The difference in the heights of the two lines by academic year suggest a main effect due to time – in particular that students who take the course in the morning, on average, perform better on the final exam than those who take the course in the afternoon. There is a main effect due to academic year, as depicted by the positive slopes of the line segments depicting morning and afternoon times, suggest a main effect for academic year; in particular, that performance on the final exam increases with academic year.

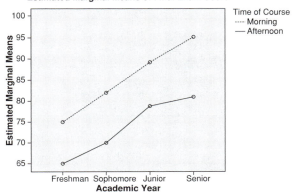

Estimated Marginal Means of Final Exam Score

f) Because time has only two levels (morning and afternoon), the sample means themselves are sufficient to indicate the nature of this main effect. We note that students taking the course in the morning, on average, perform better on the final exam than those taking the course in the afternoon.

g) Because academic year has more than two levels, we carry out a post-hoc test to understand the nature of the main effect due to academic year. According to the results of the Tukey HSD post-hoc test, on average, juniors and seniors perform best on the final exam, followed by sophomores, with freshmen performing statistically significantly worse than all other groups. No statistically significant difference in performance is observed between juniors and the seniors.

Descriptive Statistics

Dependent Variable: Final Exam Score

Time of Course	Academic Year	Mean	Std. Deviation	N
Morning	Freshman	75.00	5.000	5
	Sophomore	82.00	2.121	5
	Junior	89.20	2.490	5
	Senior	95.20	3.962	5
	Total	85.35	8.450	20
Afternoon	Freshman	65.00	5.000	5
	Sophomore	70.00	3.606	5
	Junior	78.80	6.058	5
	Senior	81.00	4.848	5
	Total	73.70	8.066	20
Total	Freshman	70.00	7.071	10
	Sophomore	76.00	6.912	10
	Junior	84.00	7.008	10
	Senior	88.10	8.569	10
	Total	79.53	10.064	40

Multiple Comparisons

Dependent Variable: Final Exam Score

Tukey HSD

(I) Academic Year	(J) Academic Year	Mean Difference (I-J)	Std. Error	Sig.	95% Confidence Interval	
					Lower Bound	Upper Bound
Freshman	Sophomore	−6.00*	1.934	.020	−11.24	−.76
	Junior	−14.00*	1.934	.000	−19.24	−8.76
	Senior	−18.10*	1.934	.000	−23.34	−12.86
Sophomore	Freshman	6.00*	1.934	.020	.76	11.24
	Junior	−8.00*	1.934	.001	−13.24	−2.76
	Senior	−12.10*	1.934	.000	−17.34	−6.86
Junior	Freshman	14.00*	1.934	.000	8.76	19.24
	Sophomore	8.00*	1.934	.001	2.76	13.24
	Senior	−4.10	1.934	.168	−9.34	1.14
Senior	Freshman	18.10*	1.934	.000	12.86	23.34
	Sophomore	12.10*	1.934	.000	6.86	17.34
	Junior	4.10	1.934	.168	−1.14	9.34

Based on observed means.

*The mean difference is significant at the .05 level.

13.6.

a) Because there are only five students per cell we check the tenability of the normality assumption by computing the skewness ratio for each cell. Because the skewness ratio for each cell is less than 2 in absolute value, the data appear to be reasonably symmetric and the normality assumption may be considered to be tenable.

Descriptive Statistics

Rate of stepping	Step Height		N Statistic	Skewness Statistic	Std. Error
Slow (14 steps/min)	Low (5.75")	The final heart rate of the subject after a trial, in beats per minute	5	−.226	.913
		Valid N (listwise)	5		
	High (11.5")	The final heart rate of the subject after a trial, in beats per minute	5	1.018	.913
		Valid N (listwise)	5		
Medium (21 steps/min)	Low (5.75")	The final heart rate of the subject after a trial, in beats per minute	5	.885	.913
		Valid N (listwise)	5		
	High (11.5")	The final heart rate of the subject after a trial, in beats per minute	5	.262	.913
		Valid N (listwise)	5		
Fast (28 steps/min)	Low (5.75")	The final heart rate of the subject after a trial, in beats per minute	5	.608	.913
		Valid N (listwise)	5		
	High (11.5")	The final heart rate of the subject after a trial, in beats per minute	5	.016	.913
		Valid N (listwise)	5		

The results of Levene's test indicate that the homogeneity-of-variance assumption is tenable, $F(5, 24) = 2.41$, $p = .07$.

b) The interaction is not statistically significant, $F(2, 24) = .54$, $p = .59$.

c) The main effect due to stepping rate is statistically significant, $F(2, 24) = 9.55$, $p < .0005$.

d) According to the Tukey HSD post-hoc test, the average heart rate is statistically significantly higher under fast stepping than it is under either slow or medium stepping. There is no statistically significant difference in heart rate between slow and medium stepping.

Multiple Comparisons

Dependent Variable: The final heart rate of the subject after a trial, in beats per minute
Tukey HSD

(I) Rate of stepping	(J) Rate of stepping	Mean Difference (I–J)	Std. Error	Sig.	95% Confidence Interval	
					Lower Bound	Upper Bound
Slow (14 steps/min)	Medium (21 steps/min)	−8.4000	6.24740	.385	−24.0016	7.2016
	Fast (28 steps/min)	−26.7000*	6.24740	.001	−42.3016	−11.0984
Medium (21 steps/min)	Slow (14 steps/min)	8.4000	6.24740	.385	−7.2016	24.0016
	Fast (28 steps/min)	−18.3000*	6.24740	.019	−33.9016	−2.6984
Fast (28 steps/min)	Slow (14 steps/min)	26.7000*	6.24740	.001	11.0984	42.3016
	Medium (21 steps/min)	18.3000*	6.24740	.019	2.6984	33.9016

Based on observed means.
*The mean difference is significant at the .05 level.

e) There is a statistically significant main effect due to step height, $F(1, 24) = 17.93$, $p < .0005$.

f) Based on the sample means, the average heart rate is statistically significantly higher when using the high step than when using the low step.

Descriptive Statistics

Dependent Variable: The final heart rate of the subject after a trial, in beats per minute

Rate of stepping	Step Height	Mean	Std. Deviation	N
Slow (14 steps/min)	Low (5.75")	87.6000	9.09945	5
	High (11.5")	103.8000	10.52141	5
	Total	95.7000	12.60555	10
Medium (21 steps/min)	Low (5.75")	94.2000	8.89944	5
	High (11.5")	114.0000	21.00000	5
	Total	104.1000	18.44180	10
Fast (28 steps/min)	Low (5.75")	108.0000	16.70329	5
	High (11.5")	136.8000	13.34916	5
	Total	122.4000	20.82306	10
Total	Low (5.75")	96.6000	14.26184	15
	High (11.5")	118.2000	20.30904	15
	Total	107.4000	20.44437	30

13.7.

a) The design is a 2 × 3 balanced ANOVA with five participants per cell.

b)

Weight Loss by Treatment

	Sum of Squares	df	Mean Square	F	Sig.
Between Groups	453.8	2	226.9	18.28	$p < .0005$
Within Groups	335	27	12.41		
Total	788.8	29			

c) Because the obtained F-statistic is larger for the two-way design ($F = 33.53$) than for the one-way design ($F = 18.28$), the two-way design provides a more powerful test of the treatment effect than the one-way design. By adding gender to the design as a second factor, we lose one degree of freedom but explain enough dependent variable variance to offset this loss. As a result, the MS_W (unexplained variance) associated with the two-way design is smaller than it is for the one-way design, producing a more powerful test of the treatment effect as noted by the larger F-test associated with the treatment effect in the two-way design.

13.8.

a) Yes. Nonsmokers weigh more, on average, than smokers.

b) No. People with no CHD have the same mean weight as those with CHD.

c) No. The lines are parallel.

d) (ii)

e)

Source of Variation	Sum of Squares	df	Mean Square	F	Sig.
CHD	0	1	0	0	1
Cigarette Use	41,000	1	41,000	463.88	$<.0005$
Interaction	0	1	0	0	1
Error	35,000	396	88.38		
Total	76,000	399			

13.9. No. In both cases, there are four sources of variance: two sources due to main effects, one due to an interaction effect, and the fourth due to remaining, unexplained error.

13.10. The two-way ANOVA is more powerful than the one-way ANOVA if there is a reduction in the MS_{error} term resulting from the addition of the second independent variable and if that reduction is large enough to compensate for the loss of degrees of freedom associated with adding that second independent variable. A reduction in the MS_{error} term comes about when the second independent variable is able to explain a large enough part of the dependent variable variance left unexplained by the first independent variable.

CHAPTER 14. **SOLUTIONS**

14.1.

a) Let ρ = the correlation between reading comprehension and intellectual ability in the population. Then $H_0: \rho = 0$ and $H_1: \rho \neq 0$.

b) There is a statistically significant, moderate, positive linear relationship between reading comprehension and intellectual ability among public school children in the urban area who have been diagnosed with learning disabilities, $r(N = 76) = .29$, $p = .01$. That is, such children who have relatively low intellectual ability tend to have relatively low reading comprehension and those with relatively high intellectual ability tend to have relatively high reading comprehension. The strength of the linear relationship is moderate, according to Cohen's rule-of-thumb guidelines.

c) There is a statistically significant moderate negative linear relationship between reading comprehension grade level among public school children in the urban area who have been diagnosed with learning disabilities, $r(N = 76) = -.322, p = .004$. That is, such children who have relatively low reading comprehension tend to be in the higher grades, whereas those with relatively high reading comprehension tend to be in the lower grades. Because the reading comprehension scores are relative to all students in the urban area, not just those with learning disabilities, these results indicate that the students with learning disabilities fall farther behind their peers as they get older. The strength of the linear relationship is moderate, according to Cohen's rule-of-thumb guidelines.

d) There is a statistically significant moderate correlation between reading comprehension and classroom placement among public school children in the urban area who have been diagnosed with learning disabilities, $r(N = 76) = -.44, p < .0005$. Students with the part-time resource placement have higher reading comprehension scores, on average, than those with the self-contained classroom placement. The strength of the linear relationship is moderate, according to Cohen's rule-of-thumb guidelines.

e) The elimination of the 29 students without reading comprehension scores could bias obtained results if their missing data were related systematically to reading comprehension or any of the variables studied in relation to reading comprehension. For example, if the 29 students who did not have reading comprehension scores missed the reading comprehension test because they were doing especially poorly in reading and were being tutored at the time the reading test was given, the obtained correlations of reading comprehension with intellectual ability, grade level, and class placement would likely be biased.

14.2.

a) $(.056, .435)$.   b) $(.067, .56)$.

c) Yes. Because zero is not contained in the 95 percent CI for b, it is not a plausible value for b, so that the model is statistically significant.

d) Because the range of values for both the CI of ρ and the population b are positive, the linear relationship between math comprehension and intellectual ability is positive. That is, public school children in the urban area who have been diagnosed with learning disabilities who have low math comprehension tend also to have low intellectual ability whereas those with high math comprehension tend also to have high reading comprehension. Because the slope in the population is likely to be between .067 and .56, a one-point increase in intellectual ability is likely to be associated with a .067- to .56-point increase in math comprehension in the population.

e) Because the value of ρ is thought to be between .06 and .44, we conclude that the strength of the correlation is anywhere from very weak to moderate.

14.3.

a) Because the points of the scatterplot do not follow a curve, and therefore, the relationship between these two variables appears to be linear, a correlation analysis is appropriate in this case.

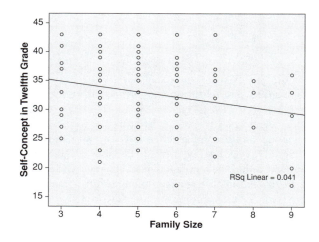

b) Among college-bound students who are always at grade level from urban areas, there is little or no linear relationship between family size and self-concept in eighth grade, $r(N = 123) = -.11$, $p = .23$.

c) The 95 percent CI for ρ is $(-.59, .43)$. Because zero is contained in the CI, we know that the correlation between family size and self-concept in eighth grade is not statistically significant.

d) Although, in this text, we have adopted the practice of not reporting effect sizes for results that are not statistically significant, it is worthwhile to note that the CI can be more useful than the sample correlation for estimating the size of the effect in the population. In this case, the sample correlation value is $r = -.11$, which is a small effect size. The CI shows just how imprecise the estimate is, in this case, because according to the CI, the correlation in the population could be anything from a strong negative correlation to a moderate-to-strong positive correlation. That it includes zero we know; most important in this case is that zero is a plausible value for the null hypothesis and, therefore, the null hypothesis cannot be rejected.

14.4.

a) The regression model is statistically significant. The results of the ANOVA $F(1,498) = 58.10$, $p < .0005$ and the test of the significance of the b-weight, $t(498) = 7.62$, $p < .0005$, both indicate equivalently that the model is significant.

b) $\hat{Y} = .368(X) + 50.123$.

c) The value of the slope of the regression equation indicates that for each one-point increase in SES there is, on average, a .368-point increase in twelfth-grade math achievement.

d) Given that an SES value of zero is meaningful on this scale used to measure SES in the NELS study, the value of the Y-intercept indicates that a person with an SES score of zero is predicted to have a twelfth-grade math achievement score of 50.123.

e) The value of $R^2 =$ adjusted $R^2 = .10$, which is an effect size measure indicating the proportion of twelfth-grade math achievement variance that can be explained by SES, a moderate effect.

14.5.

a) The regression model is not statistically significant. The result of the significance test associated with the b-weight, $t(103) = -.11$, $p = .92$, indicates that the model is not significant.

b) Because the regression model is not statistically significant, gender is not useful for predicting intellectual ability in the population.

14.6.

a) The regression model is statistically significant. The result of the significance test associated with the b-weight, $t(74) = -4.27$, $p < .0005$, indicates that the model is significant.

b) $\hat{Y} = -2.564(X) + 81.434$.

c) The slope is the difference between the average reading comprehension score of students in the full-time self-contained placement (PLACEMEN = 1) and those in the resource room part-time (PLACEMEN = 0). That is, according to this analysis, those in the self-contained classroom score 12.56 points lower, on average, than those in the resource room.

d) Because the value of zero on the placement variable is meaningful (PLACEMEN = 0 represents students in the part-time resource room), we may interpret the Y-intercept as the average reading comprehension score of resource room students.

e) The predicted reading comprehension score for a student with a resource room placement is $\hat{Y} = -12.564(0) + 81.434 = 81.434$. The predicted value is equal to the mean reading comprehension score for all students with a resource room placement.

f) The predicted reading comprehension score for a student with a self-contained classroom placement is $\hat{Y} = -12.564(1) + 81.434 = 68.87$.

g) A good approximation is given by R^2, which is equal, in the case of simple linear regression, to $beta^2$. Thus the proportion of the variance in reading comprehension scores that is explained by placement type is $(-.444)^2 = .20$, which may be considered a moderate effect.

h) Equivalently, an independent samples t-test or one-way ANOVA could have been used to determine whether reading comprehension may be predicted from type of placement.

14.7.

a) The regression model is statistically significant. The results of the ANOVA, $F(1,498) = 15.79$, $p < .0005$, and the test of the significance of the b-weight, $t(498) = 3.97$, $p < .0005$, both indicate equivalently that the model is significant.

b) $\hat{Y} = 2.765(X) + 55.596$.

c) Students whose families owned a computer when they were in eighth grade scored 2.765 points higher, on average, in twelfth-grade math achievement, than those whose families did not own a computer.

d) The value of the Y-intercept is obtained when the variable, computer ownership, equals zero, which represents those students whose families did not own a computer in eighth grade. Accordingly, we may interpret the Y-intercept of 55.596 as the average twelfth-grade math achievement of those students whose families did not own a computer in eighth grade.

e) The value $R^2 = .03$ (or equivalently, in this case, $adj\ R^2$) equals the proportion of twelfth-grade math achievement scores variance that can be explained by computer ownership, which may be described as a small-to-moderate effect. Because the relationship between twelfth-grade math achievement and computer ownership is a comparison of those who did and did not own computers in eighth grade in terms of average twelfth-grade math achievement, Cohen's d may be calculated as another measure of effect size. To perform the calculation, we need means and standard deviations of twelfth-grade math achievement for the two computer ownership groups, which may be obtained through the SPSS Means procedure. According to this calculation,

$$\frac{58.361 - 55.596}{\sqrt{\dfrac{262(7.6242)^2 + 23(7.9282)^2}{498}}},$$

students who owned a computer in eighth-grade performed approximately .36 standard deviations higher in twelfth-grade math achievement than those who did not own a computer in eighth grade, which may be considered a small-to-moderate effect.

14.8.

a) There is a statistically significant, moderate, positive correlation between intelligence and brain size, $r(N = 40) = .36$, $p = .02$. That is, among students with extremely high or extremely low intelligence, those with relatively low intelligence tend to have relatively small brain size and those with relatively high intelligence tend to have relatively large brain size.

b) The relationship between intelligence and gender among students with extremely high or extremely low intelligence, $r(N = 40) = -.07$, $p = .69$, is not statistically significantly different from zero.

c) Recall that in Chapter 5 it was mentioned that a correlation (calculated on a sample in which at least one of the variables contains only extreme values) tends to be inflated relative to the correlation value calculated on the entire distribution of values (i.e., including the middle values). Accordingly, one must take care not to generalize the finding in part (a) to all college students (those with low, middle, and high intelligence) because the correlation in that group is likely to be weaker than what was calculated in part (a).

d)

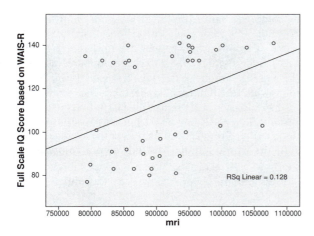

e) The two clouds of points represent the two extreme groups that form this sample of data – those with extremely low intelligence and those with extremely high intelligence. There are no points in the middle because there is no one in this sample with moderate intelligence.

f) The regression model, $\hat{Y} = .0001192(X) + 5.168$, is statistically significant. The results of the ANOVA, $F(1,38) = 5.57$, $p = .02$, and the test of the significance of the b-weight, $t(38) = 2.36$, $p = .02$, both indicate equivalently that the model is significant. The model fit as measured by R^2 equals .13, indicating that 13 percent of FSIQ variance is explained by brain size.

g) $R^2_{\text{single model}} = .13$. $R^2_{\text{low}} = .28$. $R^2_{\text{high}} = .30$.

The separate regression models provide a better overall fit to the data than the single regression equation fit to the entire sample. In short, we were able to take advantage of the existence of the two separate clouds of points in the scatterplot to produce two models that fit the data set better overall.

14.9.

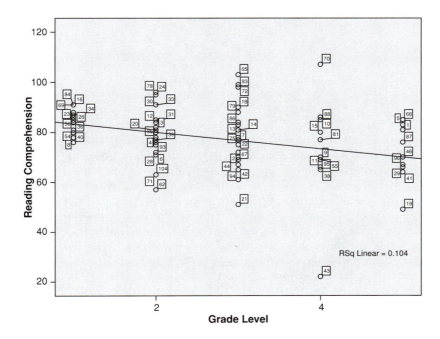

a) With the exception perhaps of the homoscedasticity assumption, the scatterplot does not appear to suggest a violation of any of these underlying assumptions. Although there appears to be a nonconstant variance of reading comprehension scores by grade (notice how tightly clustered the grade 1 distribution is relative to the grade 3 or grade 4 distributions, for example), the sample size is relatively small, and these variations simply may be due to chance. Nonetheless, reasons ought to be explored as to why grade 1 scores appear to cluster so much more tightly relative to the other grades. Once the regression model is developed, sensitivity analyses should be carried out to measure the extent to which the outliers in grade 4 influence results.

b) For case number 32 (in grade 4), the residual is negative and the case is overpredicted.

c) An extreme point in either the first or fifth grade would have relatively large leverage. One example is case number 19 in grade 5.

d) Case number 43 is farthest (in terms of vertical distance) from the regression line.

e) Case number 43 is farthest (in terms of vertical distance) from the regression line and because the person is in fourth grade, some distance from the mean of grade. Case number 70 is also relatively influential.

14.10.

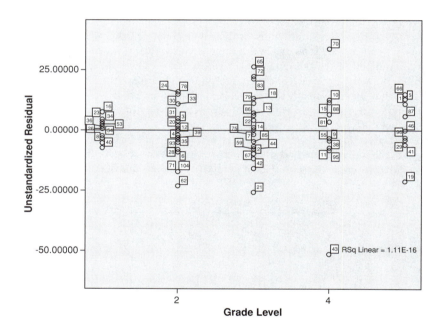

a) With the possible exception of homoscedasticity, all assumptions appear to be met. Reasons should be explored to explain the apparent nonconstant variance of reading comprehension residuals across grades and, in particular, the clustering of the residuals of grade 1 relative to the other grades. In general, with the exception of the low residual in grade 4, the residuals form a rectangular distribution, suggesting that, once the linear association between grade and reading comprehension has been accounted for, there appears to be no systematic association (e.g., quadratic) between grade and reading comprehension, and the assumption of linearity is met. The low residual in grade 4 should be examined more closely.

b) For case number 32, the residual is negative and the case is overpredicted.

c) An extreme point in either the first or fifth grade would have relatively large leverage. One example is case number 19 in grade 5.

d) Case number 43 has the largest standardized residual.

e) Case number 43 is farthest (in terms of vertical distance) from the regression line and because the person is in fourth grade, some distance from the mean of grade. Case number 70 is also relatively influential.

f) Although, in this case, both convey the same information, because two of the key assumptions underlying a regression analysis (normality and heteroscedasticity) involve the error (residual) term, the residual plot is, in general, preferred to the original scatterplot for analyzing violations of regression assumptions. Furthermore, by removing the linear association between the dependent and independent variables, the residual plot offers a more easily interpreted view of whether underlying assumptions appear to be met.

14.11.

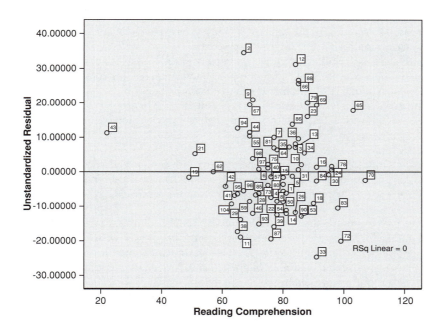

a) The residual plot does not depict an array of points scattered randomly in a rectangular band above and below the regression line that would characterize an absence of violations of assumptions. There is a suggestion of some curvilinearity, and it may be useful to test whether the square of reading comprehension improves the fit of the model. That is, to center reading comprehension and to include it in the equation along with a variable that equals the square of the centered reading comprehension variable. For more detail, the interested reader should reference Cohen, Cohen, West, and Aiken (2003).

b) The residual for case number 2 appears to have the largest magnitude. The residual is positive and the case is underpredicted by the model.

c) One possible answer is case number 43. Although the magnitude of its residual is not the most extreme in the model, given its position in the scatterplot, it has a lot of leverage.

14.12.

a) For the model without case number 43, $\hat{Y} = .616(X) + 38.258$.

For the model with all cases, $\hat{Y} = .549(X) + 43.691$.

Given where case number 43 sits in the scatterplot, one would expect that by excluding it the slope would increase, as it does, and yet the intercept would decrease, as it does. The differences in both slope and intercept that result when this case is excluded from the analysis are not dramatic but further indicate (beyond what is suggested by the residual plot) the extent to which this case is influential.

b) The regression model with case 43 is statistically significant (for the overall model, $F(1,72) = 23.30$, $p < .0005$; and equivalently in the case of simple regression, for the b-weight, $t(72) = 4.83$, $p < .0005$).

   The regression model without case 43 is also statistically significant (for the overall model, $F(1,71) = 22.01$, $p < .0005$; and equivalently in the case of simple regression, for the b-weight, $t(71) = 4.69$, $p < .0005$).

c) With case 43, according to the adjusted R^2, the model explains 22.6 percent of math comprehension variance.

   Without case 43, according to the adjusted R^2, the model explains 23.4 percent of math comprehension variance, a difference of less than 1 percent.

e) No, because the lowest reading comprehension score in the data set is 22, and not zero.

   According to the model with case 43, a one-point increase in reading comprehension is associated, on average, with a .55-point increase in math comprehension.

   According to the model without case 43, a one-point increase in reading comprehension is associated, on average, with a .62-point increase in math comprehension.

f) For model with case 43: $\hat{Y} = .549(75) + 43.691 = 84.87$.

   For model without case 43: $\hat{Y} = .616(75) + 32.258 = 84.46$.

g) Because both models, from a practical perspective, are similar and yield similar interpretations, unless one can make a strong argument as to why case 43 should be eliminated from the analysis, it would be preferable to report and use the results from the model based on all cases.

h) The formula for the total degrees of freedom in the ANOVA summary table is $N - 1$, where N is the total number of scores used in the analysis. Because $df_{total} = 74$, we see that $N = 76$.

i) The values of R^2 (.244) and adjusted R^2 (.234) are so similar because the ratio of the number of cases in the sample size to the number of predictors in the equation is very large at 76:1, way in excess of the 30:1 ratio suggested by the rule of thumb.

14.13. To evaluate the appropriateness of the fit of the simple linear regression model to the data and to explore possible violations of assumptions, a series of analyses was carried out using both the unstandardized and Studentized residuals. Given the difficulty of judging the normality of a dependent variable when the regressor is dichotomous (e.g., computer ownership groups) using a scatterplot (see following), boxplots of the residuals (both standardized and Studentized) were constructed. The boxplots of the residuals suggest that even with the outliers in the group that did not own a computer, both distributions appear to be only mildly negatively skewed. In addition to these residual analyses, an analysis of Cook's influence was carried out. Note that, although there are some outliers, all of Cook's scores are considerably less than one, suggesting that there were no individual points in the analysis that appeared to unduly influence the results and that the regression analysis was appropriate as reported.

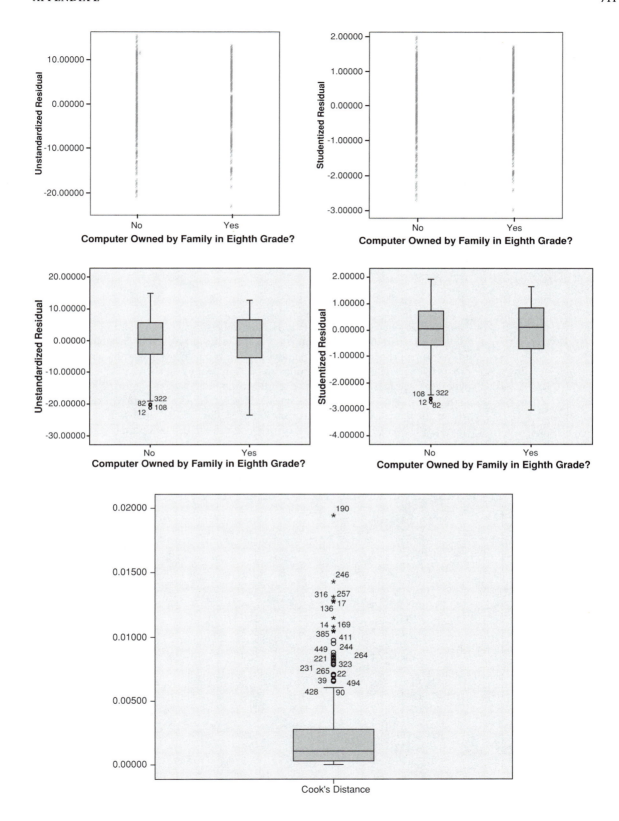

14.14.

a) Yes, the points of the scatterplot do not appear to violate the underlying assumptions of normality, homoscedasticity, and linearity.

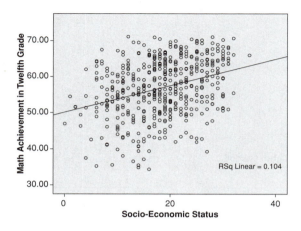

b) The residual plot (SES values versus Studentized residuals) is a random scatter of points organized in a rectangular fashion about a residual value of zero for each value of SES and suggests an overall appropriate fit of the model to these data. In particular, because the variability of points for each value of SES is similar, the data appear to satisfy homoscedasticity and, with no pattern of relationship between the residuals and SES, the assumption of linearity also appears to be met. To look more closely at specific residual values and particular cases that were not fit well by the model, a frequency distribution of Studentized residuals was obtained. There are 17 cases with studentized residual values that are greater than 2 or less than −2, indicating the presence of bivariate outliers to the model. Accordingly, we follow up by testing each point for its level of influence on the model.

SRE_1 Studentized Residual

		Frequency	Percent	Valid Percent	Cumulative Percent
Valid	−2.90228	1	5.9	5.9	5.9
	−2.78936	1	5.9	5.9	11.8
	−2.73470	1	5.9	5.9	17.6
	−2.65425	1	5.9	5.9	23.5
	−2.48060	1	5.9	5.9	29.4
	−2.45925	1	5.9	5.9	35.3
	−2.40028	1	5.9	5.9	41.2
	−2.33737	1	5.9	5.9	47.1
	−2.29682	1	5.9	5.9	52.9
	−2.27204	1	5.9	5.9	58.8
	−2.22802	1	5.9	5.9	64.7
	−2.19919	1	5.9	5.9	70.6
	−2.16053	1	5.9	5.9	76.5
	−2.13288	1	5.9	5.9	82.4
	−2.12862	1	5.9	5.9	88.2
	−2.10233	1	5.9	5.9	94.1
	2.22435	1	5.9	5.9	100.0
	Total	17	100.0	100.0	

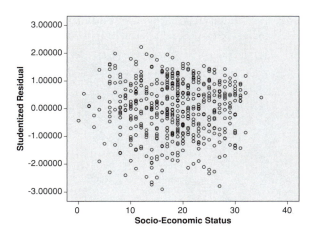

c) According to the boxplot of Cook's influence scores, all of the values are substantially less than 1, suggesting that no single point unduly influenced the result of the regression analysis and that the model is appropriate as obtained.

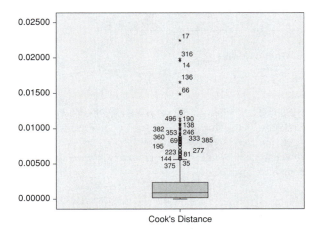

d) 58.59.

e) 1.10.

f) The value of the residual with the greatest magnitude is -21.65; it is associated with the person that has ID = 82. But, as shown in the plot of Cook's influence scores, even this person's data do not unduly influence the results of the analysis. That is, if this person's data were removed from the analysis, and a new model were fit to the data (without this person), results would not change by very much.

14.15.

a) The scatterplot was created with the case numbers included for each point. Because there are so few points, it is difficult to assess the normality and homoscedasticity assumptions. The data do appear linear, so the linearity assumption appears viable. Case number 8 is an outlier with a Studentized residual value of -2.04. Cook's influence scores were found for each point. The most influential point is case number 5. Although it is much more influential than the others, its Cook's influence value is much less than 1 (.51), so we do not need to be concerned about its undue influence on the analysis.

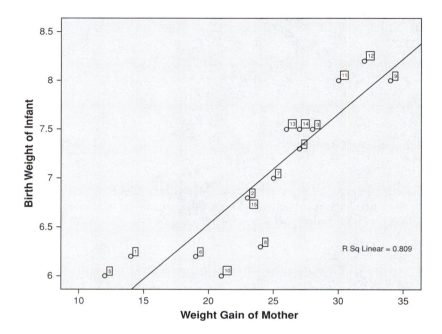

b) The 95 percent CI for Z_ρ is (.90, 2.03). The 95 percent CI for ρ is (.72, .97). There is a statistically significant, strong, positive correlation between the weight gain of the mother and the birth weight of the infant. That is, such mothers with a relatively high weight gain tended to have infants with relatively high birth weight and mothers with a relatively low weight gain tended to have infants with relatively low birth weight.

c) $\hat{Y} = .113(X) + 4.278$.

d) The regression model is statistically significant. The results of the ANOVA, $F(1,13) = 54.96$, $p < .0005$, and the test of the significance of the b-weight, $t(13) = 11.24$, $p < .0005$, both indicate equivalently that the model is significant.

e) 7.1 lbs.

f) .346.

g) The accuracy of predicting the weight gain of an infant given a particular weight gain for the mother is captured by the standard of estimate. That is, because the standard error of estimate is the standard deviation of scores about the regression line for given values of X, we know that, if normality and homoscedasticity are assumed to be true, then 68 percent of the predicted values of Y (the weight of the infant) for given values of X (the weight gain of the mother during pregnancy) will be within approximately one standard deviation (or .346) of the regression line. Likewise, 95 percent of predicted values of Y will fall approximately within two standard deviations of the regression line ($2 \times .346 = .692$) for all values of X. Said differently, we can predict with 95 percent accuracy the weight of an infant for a mother who gained 25 pounds during pregnancy to be $7.1 - .692$ to $7.1 + .692$ pounds, or approximately 6.4 to 7.8 pounds.

14.16. c)

14.17. a)

14.18. e)

14.19. b)

14.20. c)

14.21. c)

14.22. a)

14.23. b)

14.24. c)

14.25. a)

14.26. b)

14.27. c)

14.28. e)

14.29. e)

14.30. b)

14.31.

$$\frac{\sum (Y - \hat{Y})}{n} = \frac{\sum Y}{n} - \frac{\sum \hat{Y}}{n} = \frac{\sum Y}{n} - \frac{\sum (bX - a)}{n} =$$

$$\frac{\sum Y}{n} - \left(\frac{\sum bX}{n} - \frac{\sum a}{n} \right) = \overline{Y} - (b\overline{X} + a) = \overline{Y} - \overline{Y}$$

CHAPTER 15. **SOLUTIONS**

15.1.

a) Boxplots and skewness ratios of the two scale variables, ACHMAT12 and UNITMATH, indicate that these variables are negatively skewed with skewness values less than 1.00 in both cases. The skewness ratios for ACHMAT12 and UNITMATH are respectively $\frac{-.423}{.109} = -3.88$ and $\frac{-.247}{.109} = -2.48$. These values are moderately negative due to the large sample size of 500 and the corresponding relatively small standard error of skewness of .109. Given that the NELS data set contains approximately 45 percent females, we know that GENDER is not skewed and is, in fact, reasonably symmetric.

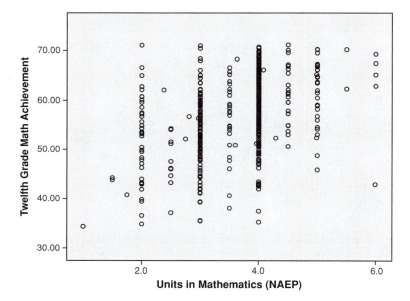

The scatterplot of the scale variables and the correlation values of each of the independent variables with ACHMAT12 ($r = .42$ with UNITMATH and $r = -.20$ with GENDER) are both statistically significant ($p < .0005$) and suggest the appropriateness of fitting these data with a regression model. According to the zero-order correlations with ACHMAT12, college-bound students who are always at grade level who take more math in high school tend to do better on twelfth-grade math achievement tests; and, among college-bound students who are always at grade level, males outperform females on twelfth-grade math achievement tests. Furthermore, because there is little or no relationship between the independent variables (the correlation between UNITMATH and GENDER is $r = -.07$, $p = .13$), there is little overlap in their proportion of shared variance and, therefore, both variables should contribute uniquely to the model.

Exercise 15.6 utilizes regression diagnostics to determine aspects of the model fit and whether underlying assumptions appear to be met.

b) According to the ANOVA summary table, the regression model with both first-order variables included in the equation is statistically significant, $F(2, 497) = 65.35$, $p < .005$.

c) According to the value of R^2, approximately 20.8 percent of the variance in twelfth-grade math achievement can be explained by gender and the NAEP units of math taken in high school. Because the ratio of sample size to independent variables is so large (500 to 2), the R^2 and adjusted R^2 values are quite similar.

d) Predicted ACHMAT12 = 43.793 − 2.719(GENDER) + 4.013(UNITMATH).

e) Predicted ACHMAT12 = 43.793 − 2.719(0) + 4.013(4) = 59.85.

f) Based on the relative magnitudes of the beta weights, UNITMATH is the more important variable in the equation. An analysis of the respective unique proportions of variance accounted for by each independent variable yields the same result. In particular, with UNITMATH in the equation by itself, R^2 is .179 and when GENDER is added to that equation, R^2 increases to .208, an increase of only .029. Alternatively, with GENDER in the equation by itself, R^2 is .04 and when UNITMATH is added to that equation, R^2 increases to .208, an increase of .204. Accordingly, the unique proportion of variance accounted for by GENDER is only 2.9 percent whereas for UNITMATH it is 20.4 percent, indicating that UNITMATH makes a greater unique contribution to explaining ACHMAT12 variance and is therefore the more important variable in the equation.

g) It would not be appropriate to interpret the value of the Y-intercept in this case because the smallest number of NAEP units of math taken in high school is 1 by those in our sample. We have no reason to believe that the model would generalize to values beyond those in our sample; namely, UNITMATH = 0.

h) Holding gender constant, each additional NAEP unit of math taken in high school corresponds to a 4.01-point increase in twelfth-grade math achievement, on average.

i) Holding NAEP units of math taken in high school constant, females perform 2.72 points lower in twelfth-grade math achievement, on average, than males.

j) Yes. The coefficient or slope associated with gender is statistically significant, $t(497) = -4.30$, $p < .0005$.

15.2.

a) Boxplots of the three variables indicate that all variables are negatively skewed with skewness values of $-.423$ for ACHMAT12, $-.247$ for UNITMATH, and $-.384$ for SLFCNC12. Because of the large sample size of 500, skewness ratios all exceed two standard deviations away from a skewness value of zero.

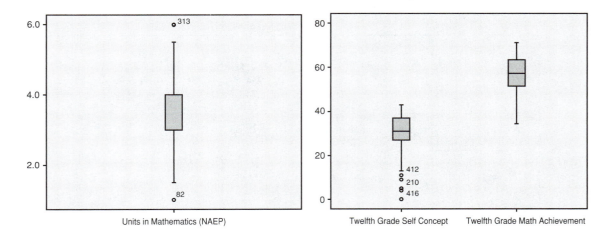

An investigation of the bivariate scatterplots between the dependent variable and each of the independent variables and between the two independent variables using a matrix scatterplot indicates that, even though at least one of the variables may be considered moderately negatively skewed, the relationships appear to be linear as opposed to curvilinear.

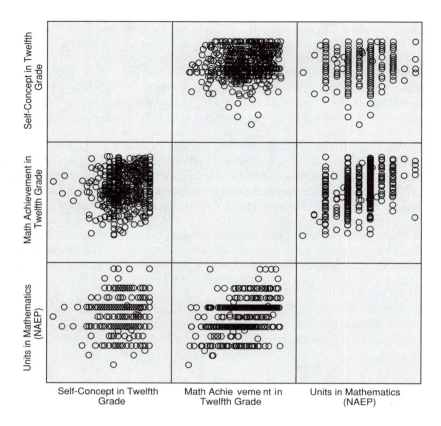

The bivariate correlations between pairs of independent and dependent variables and between the two independent variables are as follows:

Correlations

		slfcnc12 Self-Concept in Twelfth Grade	achmat12 Math Achievement in Twelfth Grade	unitmath Units in Mathematics (NAEP)
slfcnc12 Self-Concept in Twelfth Grade	Pearson Correlation Sig. (2-tailed) N	1 500	.146** .001 500	.128** .004 500
achmat12 Math Achievement in Twelfth Grade	Pearson Correlation Sig. (2-tailed) N	.146** .001 500	1 500	.423** .000 500
unitmath Units in Mathematics (NAEP)	Pearson Correlation Sig. (2-tailed) N	.128** .004 500	.423** .000 500	1 500

**Correlation is significant at the 0.01 level (2-tailed).

All correlations are statistically significant.

Exercise 15.7 utilizes regression diagnostics to determine aspects of model fit and whether underlying assumptions appear to be met.

b) According to the ANOVA summary table, the regression model is statistically significant, $F(2, 497) = 6.800$, $p < .005$, with both independent variables in the equation.

c) According to the value of R^2, approximately only 2.7 percent of the variance in twelfth-grade self-concept is explained by both achievement in math in twelfth grade and units of math taken in high school.

d) Only ACHMAT12 is statistically significant with $t = 2.287$, $p < .025$. That is, after controlling for units of math taken in high school, achievement in math in twelfth grade accounts for a statistically significant (albeit small) proportion of twelfth-grade self-concept variance. Notice that UNITMATH is not statistically significant in the equation although it was statistically significantly related to SLFCNC12 in the bivariate relationship. That it is not statistically significant in the equation suggests that, once ACHMAT12 is controlled, that part of UNITMATH that remains does not correlate significantly with SLFCNC12. That is, the part correlation between UNITMATH and SLFCNC12, after removing from UNITMATH that part related to ACHMAT12, is not statistically significantly related to SLFCNC12.

Coefficients^a

Model		Unstandardized Coefficients		Standardized Coefficients		
		B	Std. Error	Beta	t	Sig.
1	(Constant)	23.020	2.388		9.642	.000
	Twelfth Grade Math Achievement	.102	.045	.112	2.287	.023
	Units in Mathematics (NAEP)	.723	.437	.081	1.655	.099

^{a}Dependent Variable: Twelfth Grade Self Concept

e) According to the equation, the predicted twelfth-grade self-concept score of an individual who takes zero units of math in high school and who scores zero on twelfth-grade math achievement is 23.020, on average. However, because no one in the sample has taken zero units of math (the minimum number of units taken is 1) or scored zero on the math achievement test, we cannot interpret the Y-intercept meaningfully.

f) Holding the number of math units taken in high school constant, each additional one-point increase in twelfth-grade math achievement corresponds to a .1-point increase in twelfth-grade self-concept, on average.

15.3.

a) Boxplots suggest that MATHCOMP is fairly symmetric. The *Learndis* data set has approximately 63 percent in resource room placement; accordingly, the dichotomous variable PLACEMEN is also reasonably symmetric. READCOMP is less symmetric with a skewness value of $-.956$ and a skewness ratio of -3.46.

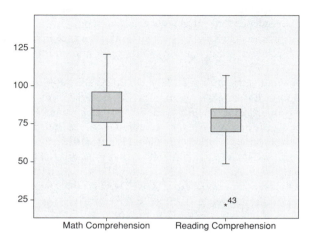

An investigation of the bivariate scatterplot between the scale variables indicates the presence of at least one bivariate outlier.

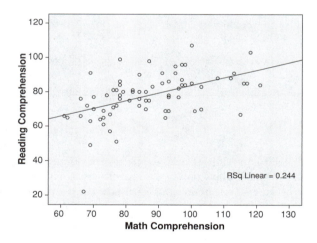

The two zero-order (bivariate) correlations of each independent variable with READCOMP are both statistically significant. The correlation with MATHCOMP is $r = .49$, $p < .0005$ and the correlation with PLACEMEN is $r = -.44$, $p < .0005$. Among children attending public school in the urban area who have been diagnosed with learning disabilities, higher reading comprehension is associated with higher math comprehension and placement in a resource room. The intercorrelation between PLACEMEN and MATHCOMP is $r = -.34$, $p = .001$.

Correlations

		Reading Comprehension	Math Comprehension	Type of Placement
Reading Comprehension	Pearson Correlation	1	.494**	−.444**
	Sig. (2-tailed)		.000	.000
	N	76	74	76
Math Comprehension	Pearson Correlation	.494**	1	−.337**
	Sig. (2-tailed)	.000		.001
	N	74	94	94
Type of Placement	Pearson Correlation	−.444**	−.337**	1
	Sig. (2-tailed)	.000	.001	
	N	76	94	105

**Correlation is significant at the 0.01 level (2-tailed).

In Exercise 15.9, we investigate the fit of the model and the appropriateness of underlying assumptions using regression diagnostics.

b) According to the ANOVA summary table, the regression model is statistically significant, $F(2, 71) = 16.65$, $p < .0005$. According to the coefficients table, PLACEMEN ($t(71) = -2.79$, $p = .007$) and MATHCOMP ($t(71) = 3.369$, $p = .001$) both make a statistically significant unique contribution to the model.

c) According to the value of adjusted R^2, approximately 30 percent of the variance in reading comprehension can be explained by type of placement and math comprehension.

d) R^2 (.319) and $R^2_{adjusted}$ (.30) are similar because the ratio of the number of subjects ($N = 76$) to independent variables ($k = 2$) is relatively large.

e) Predicted READCOMP = 52.043 + .329(MATHCOMP) − 8.533(PLACEMEN).

f) Because MATHCOMP does not take on scores near zero, it would not be meaningful to interpret the value of the intercept.

g) Controlling for PLACEMEN, children attending public school in the urban area who have been diagnosed with learning disabilities who have higher math comprehension scores tend also to have higher reading comprehension scores. The unique contribution of the variable MATHCOMP is statistically significant, ($t(71) = 3.37$, $p = .001$).

h) Holding PLACEMEN constant, a one-point increase in MATHCOMP is associated with a .329-point increase in READCOMP, on average.

i) Yes. Children attending public school in the urban area who have been diagnosed with learning disabilities who are full-time in a self-contained classroom (coded as 1) score statistically significantly lower, on average, than those in a resource room for part of the day (coded as 0). The unique contribution of the variable PLACEMEN is statistically significant, $t(73) = -3.48$, $p = .001$.

j) Holding MATHCOMP constant, children attending public school in the urban area who have been diagnosed with learning disabilities who are full-time in a self-contained classroom (coded as 1) score 8.533 points lower, on average, than those in a resource room for part of the day (coded as 0).

k) Predicted READCOMP = 52.043 + .329(84) − 8.533(0) = 79.68.

l) Because data have not been collected on students with MATHCOMP scores near 40, it would not be meaningful to make a prediction for those students based on this regression model.

15.4.

a) The correlation between READCOMP and IQ is statistically significant, $r = .29$, $p = .01$. Approximately 8.2 percent of the variance in READCOMP can be explained by IQ ($R^2 = .286^2 = .082$).

b) The correlation between READCOMP and MATHCOMP is statistically significant, $r = .49$, $p < .0005$. Approximately 49.4 percent of the variance in READCOMP can be explained by MATHCOMP ($R^2 = .494^2 = .244$).

c) The correlation between IQ and MATHCOMP is statistically significant ($r = .26, p = .01$).

d) Approximately 17.7 percent of the variance in READCOMP can be explained by MATHCOMP after controlling for intellectual ability ($R^2_{Change} = .177$), a statistically significant amount, $F_{Change}(1, 71) = 17.33, p < .0005$.

Model Summary

Model	R	R Square	Adjusted R Square	Std. Error of the Estimate	Change Statistics				
					R Square Change	F Change	df1	df2	Sig. F Change
1	.313[a]	.098	.085	12.564	.098	7.820	1	72	.007
2	.524[b]	.275	.255	11.343	.177	17.332	1	71	.000

[a]Predictors: (Constant), Intellectual ability.
[b]Predictors: (Constant), Intellectual ability, Math comprehension.

e) Approximately 3.1 percent of the variance in READCOMP can be explained by IQ controlling for MATHCOMP ($R^2_{Change} = .031$), which is not a statistically significant amount, $F_{Change}(1, 71) = 2.97, p < .09$.

Model Summary

Model	R	R Square	Adjusted R Square	Std. Error of the Estimate	Change Statistics				
					R Square Change	F Change	df1	df2	Sig. F Change
1	.494[a]	.244	.234	11.499	.244	23.296	1	72	.000
2	.524[b]	.275	.255	11.343	.031	2.988	1	71	.088

[a]Predictors: (Constant), Math comprehension.
[b]Predictors: (Constant), Math comprehension, Intellectual ability.

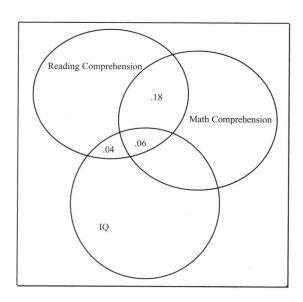

f) Using simultaneous multiple regression and placing both independent variables in the equation at the same time, we see that the proportion of variance in READCOMP that can be explained by IQ after controlling for MATHCOMP is not statistically significant $t(71) = 1.73, p = .09$.

Coefficients[a]

Model		Unstandardized Coefficients		Standardized Coefficients		
		B	Std. Error	Beta	t	Sig.
1	(Constant)	26.771	10.782		2.483	.015
	Math comprehension	.396	.095	.440	4.163	.000
	Intellectual ability	.207	.120	.183	1.728	.088

[a]Dependent Variable: Reading comprehension.

g) Approximately 8.2 percent of the variance in READCOMP can be explained by IQ, but only about 3.1 percent of the variance in READCOMP can be explained by IQ after controlling for MATHCOMP, a much smaller percentage. This is because MATHCOMP and IQ are intercorrelated, $r = .26, p = .01$.

h) R^2 for the model is .274 which is less than $r^2_{\text{Reading Comprehension,IQ}} + r^2_{\text{Reading Comprehension, Math Comprehension}} = .082 + .244 = .326$. That is because R^2 for the model only counts the overlap of approximately .06 between IQ and math comprehension (that is, the squared intercorrelation between IQ and math comprehension) once. See the Venn diagrams given in the answer to part (d) of this problem.

15.5.

a) An investigation of the univariate distributions indicates that all of the variables are significantly positively skewed. Boxplots of the variables all have outliers. The skewness ratio for TOTCHOL3, SYSBP1, and DIABP1 are 6.77, 9.45, and 3.63, respectively, indicating that the variables are significantly positively skewed.

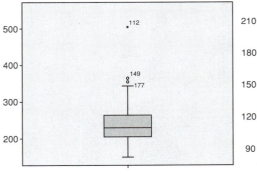

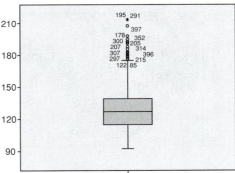

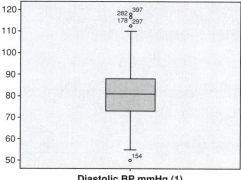

The bivariate scatterplots between the variables suggest that the relationships of the independent variables with the dependent variable are weak, and the intercorrelation between the two independent variables is strong.

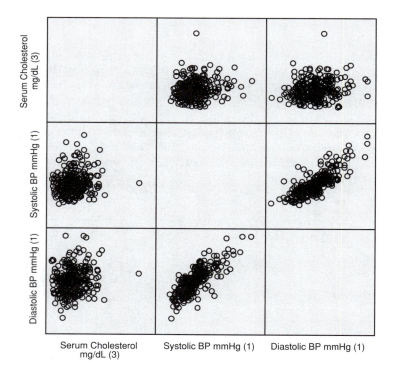

In particular, the zero-order correlations with TOTCHOL3 are given in the following table.

Correlations

		TOTCHOL3 Serum Cholesterol mg/dL (3)	SYSBP1 Systolic BP mmHg (1)	DIABP1 Diastolic BP mmHg (1)
TOTCHOL3 Serum Cholesterol mg/dL (3)	Pearson Correlation	1	.153**	.167**
	Sig. (2-tailed)		.010	.005
	N	286	286	286
SYSBP1 Systolic BP mmHg (1)	Pearson Correlation	.153**	1	.776**
	Sig. (2-tailed)	.010		.000
	N	286	400	400
DIABP1 Diastolic BP mmHg (1)	Pearson Correlation	.167**	.776**	1
	Sig. (2-tailed)	.005	.000	
	N	286	400	400

**Correlation is significant at the 0.01 level (2-tailed).

The bivariate correlations of SYSBP1 and DIABP1 with TOTCHOL3 are statistically significant. The intercorrelations between the independent variables is very strong ($r = .78, p < .0005$).

b) The regression model is statistically significant, $F(2, 283) = 4.20, p = .02$. However, none of the independent variables is statistically significant in the model.

Coefficients[a]

Model		Unstandardized Coefficients		Standardized Coefficients		
		B	Std. Error	Beta	t	Sig.
1	(Constant)	176.707	20.724		8.527	.000
	SYSBP1 Systolic BP mmHg (1)	.130	.237	.053	.546	.585
	DIABP1 Diastolic BP mmHg (1)	533	421	.124	1.265[a]	.207

[a]Dependent Variable: TOTCHOL3 Serum Cholesterol mg/dL (3).

c) Because the independent variables are highly intercorrelated and only moderately correlated with the dependent variable, each one does not make a unique contribution to the model. Because of the reasonably strong intercorrelation between independent variables in this case, the two variables may be considered to be multicollinear. Whereas individually each variable is not statistically significant, as a set of two taken together they explain a statistically significant amount of TOTCHOL3 variance.

d) With two highly overlapping independent variables, it would be better to eliminate one independent variable from the equation because they are tapping the same dependent variable variance and in that sense may be considered somewhat redundant of each other. In this case, the bivariate correlations indicate that DIAPB1 is a slightly better predictor of TOTCHOL3, so an appropriate regression equation is Predicted TOTCHOL3 = 178.33 + .717(DIABP1), which is still statistically significant.

e) According to the values of R^2, approximately 2.8 percent of the variance in TOTCHOL3 is explained by DIABP1 alone and 2.9 percent is explained by the combination of DIABP1 and SYSBP1. SYSBP1 does not contribute much explanatory power to the model over and above that explained by DIABP1.

15.6.

a) Given that the set of points in this residual scatterplot appears to be randomly scattered and to have a rectangular shape around the Studentized residual value of zero, there does not appear to be a curvilinear association between mathematics achievement in twelfth grade and the regressor, UNITMATH.

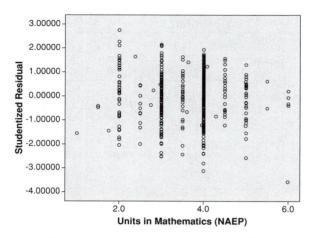

b) There are 22 cases that are bivariate outliers. Their case numbers and the values of their standardized residuals are given in the Case Summaries table. Any two of these with positive values and any two with negative values may be cited as examples of what is being asked by this question.

Case Summaries[a]

	Case Number	Standardized Residual
1	12	−3.11228
2	36	2.14910
3	39	−2.05863
4	45	−2.42565
5	105	−2.37945
6	108	−2.50864
7	118	−2.14919
8	120	−2.07237
9	137	−2.39367
10	192	2.73567
11	250	−2.02307
12	317	2.25748
13	322	−2.49726
14	333	−2.56058
15	352	−2.35480
16	358	2.10622
17	370	−2.02400
18	386	−2.04392
19	392	−3.54261
20	397	2.07512
21	426	2.09550
22	439	−2.79647
Total N		22

[a]Limited to first 100 cases.

A person would have a positive residual if his or her twelfth-grade math achievement were underpredicted by the model. That could occur, for example, when the person's math achievement was much better than would be expected based on the number of math classes taken. Likewise, a person would have a negative residual if his or her twelfth-grade math achievement were overpredicted by the model.

   c) These graphs suggest that no point or set of points is unduly influencing the results of the analysis and distorting the results obtained as all distance and leverage values cluster near zero.

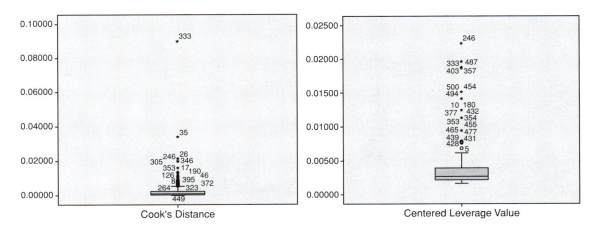

Cook's Distance   Centered Leverage Value

   d) It is appropriate as defined in Exercise 15.1.

15.7.

   a) Given that the sets of points in these residual scatterplots each appear to be randomly scattered and to have a reasonably rectangular shape around their respective Studentized residual value of zero, a curvilinear association between SLFNC12 and ACHMAT12 or between SLFNC12 and UNITMATH does not appear to exist.

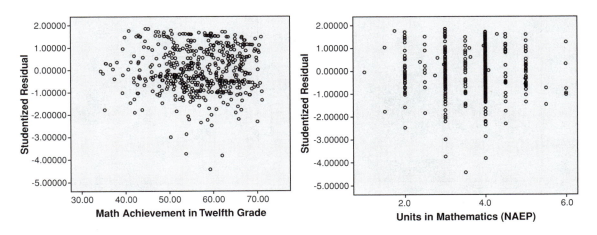

   b) There are 27 cases that are bivariate outliers. Their case numbers and the values of their standardized residuals are given in the Case Summaries table.

Case Summaries[a]

	Case Number	Standardized Residual
1	2	−2.04284
2	16	−3.23869
3	78	−2.04213
4	146	2.25305
5	157	−2.45115
6	159	−3.13915
7	180	−2.03980
8	210	−2.83462
9	221	2.03415
10	298	−2.60099
11	344	2.00261
12	373	−2.31821
13	412	−2.97563
14	416	−5.28624
15	477	−3.08413
16	482	2.07616
17	484	2.15910
Total N		17

[a]Limited to first 100 cases.

c) These graphs suggest that no point or set of points is unduly influencing the results of the analysis and distorting the results obtained as all distance and leverage values cluster near zero.

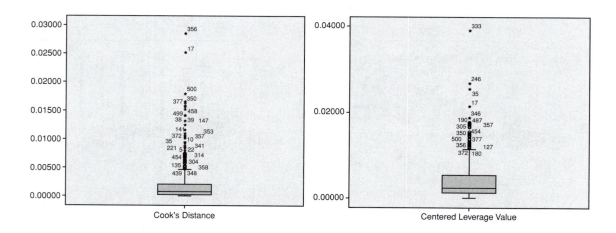

e) It is appropriate as defined in Exercise 15.2.

15.8.

a) Boxplots indicate that SES is fairly symmetric, but that EXPINC30 is severely positively skewed. The boxplot of EXPINC30 has many outliers, which create the severe positive skew (the skewness ratio for EXPINC30 is $\dfrac{10.934}{.114} = 95.91$).

GENDER is reasonably symmetric with approximately 45 percent females and 55 percent males.

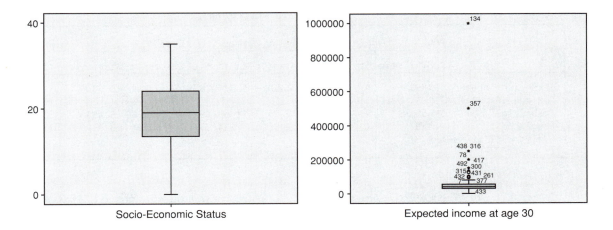

The outliers may also be observed clearly on the bivariate scatterplot between EXPINC30 and SES.

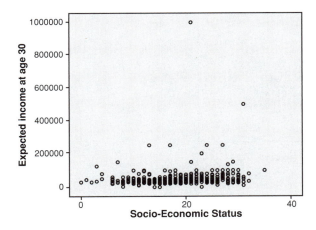

The bivariate correlations of SES with EXPINC30 ($r = .16$, $p = .001$) and GENDER with EXPINC30 ($r = -.15$, $p = .002$) are both statistically significant. College-bound students who are always at grade level who have higher SES tend to have higher income expectations. Among college-bound students who are always at grade level, males have higher income expectations than females, on average. There is a weak correlation between the two independent variables SES and GENDER ($r = -.09$, $p = .048$).

b) To avoid taking a log of zero, we add a small value ($+1$) to each variable prior to transforming the variables. Although the resulting transformed variables remain skewed, the square root transformation is more effective in creating a more symmetric variable.

Descriptive Statistics

	N	Minimum	Maximum	Mean	Std.	Skewness	
	Statistic	Statistic	Statistic	Statistic	Statistic	Statistic	Std. Error
Expected income at age 30	459	0	1000000	51574.73	58265.758	10.934	.114
expinclg	459	0	6	4.59	.526	−6.889	.114
expincsq	459	1	1000	214.53	74.591	3.739	.114
Valid N (listwise)	459						

c) With few exceptions, the scatterplot of points between the transformed EXPINC30 and SES is more regularly shaped.

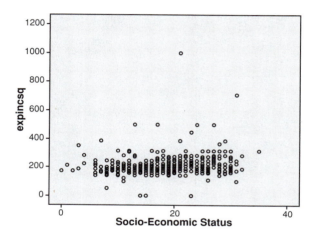

The bivariate correlations with the transformed EXPINC30 are each stronger than they were with the untransformed EXPINC30. The correlation of the square root of EXPINC30 with SES is $r = .22, p < .0005$ and with GENDER it is $r = −.20, p < .0005$.

d) According to the ANOVA summary table, the regression model is statistically significant, $F(2, 458) = 20.13, p < .0005$.

e) The percentage of variance in the untransformed EXPINC30 that is explained by SES and GENDER is 4.3 percent, but in the model using the transformed EXPINC30 it is 8.1 percent, suggesting that a better-fitting model is achieved through the transformation of the dependent variable in this case.

f) SQRT(EXPINC30 + 1) = 186.936 + 2.263(SES) − 26.899(GENDER).

g) SQRT(EXPINC30 + 1) = 186.936 + 2.263(15) − 26.899(0) = 186.936 + 33.945 = 220.881. Squaring both sides of the equation we have EXPINC30 + 1 = 48,788.42 and we determine that EXPINC30 = $48,787.42 for a male with an SES of 15.

15.9.

a) Given that the residuals for low values of math comprehension are largely negative, those with middle values of math comprehension are largely positive, and those with high values of math comprehension are largely negative, a curvilinear relationship is suggested between the residual READCOMP variance and MATHCOMP. In particular, the model would appear to be

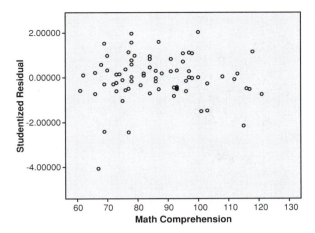

improved by the addition of the square of math comprehension, after math comprehension is centered.

b) MATHCOMPCTRDSQD = (MATHCOMP − 86.28)**2.

c) $\hat{Y} = 82.569 - 8.278(PLACEMEN) + .414(MATHCOMPCTRD) - .011(MATHCOMPCTRDSQD)$.

d) The model is statistically significant, $F(3, 70) = 13.03$, $p < .0005$. The squared term is statistically significant $t_{\text{MATHCOMPCTRDSQD}}(70) = -2.07$, $p = .043$.

e) According to the value of R^2_{Change}, approximately 3.9 percent of the variance in READCOMP is explained uniquely by the square term.

f) Given that the set of points in the residual scatterplot appears to be randomly scattered and to have a rectangular shape around the Studentized residual value of zero, the squared term appears to have captured the curvilinear association between READCOMP and MATHCOMP.

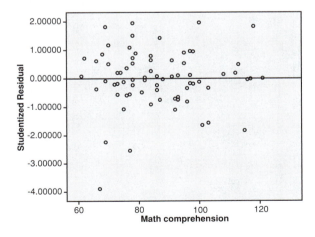

The boxplots suggest that no point or set of points is unduly influencing the results of the analysis and distorting the results obtained as all distance and leverage values cluster near zero.

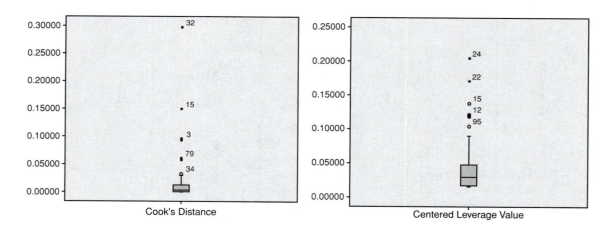

15.10.

a) Including religious and nonreligious: 130.

b) The lines are not parallel, so there appears to be an interaction, although tests of inference are needed to determine whether this appearance of an interaction is real or due to chance. According to the graph, students who took advanced math in eighth grade tended to do better than those who did not. Students who attended private schools tended to do better than those who did not. But, the interaction suggested by the nonparallel lines implies that the achievement gap between those who took and those who did not take advanced math in eighth grade is smaller for those in private schools.

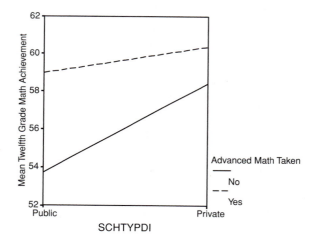

c) .56

d) According to the ANOVA summary table, the model including the two independent variables and their interaction is statistically significant, $F(3, 487) = 20.32, p < .0005$.

ANOVAc

Model		Sum of Squares	df	Mean Square	F	Sig.
1	Regression	3156.031	2	1578.016	28.130	.000a
	Residual	27375.044	488	56.096		
	Total	30531.076	490			
2	Regression	3396.411	3	1132.137	20.319	.000b
	Residual	27134.664	487	55.718		
	Total	30531.076	490			

a Predictors: (Constant), SCHTYPDI, ADVMATH8 Advanced Math Taken in Eighth Grade.
b Predictors: (Constant), SCHTYPDI, ADVMATH8 Advanced Math Taken in Eighth Grade, INTACHAD.
c Dependent Variable: ACHMAT12 Twelfth Grade Math Achievement.

e) There are two ways to tell if a single interaction term is statistically significant. According to the value of $F_{\text{Change}}(1, 487) = 4.31$, $p = .04$, the interaction is statistically significant. According to the t-test of the slope, $b = -3.29$, $p = .04$, the interaction is statistically significant.

Model Summary

					Change Statistics				
Model	R	R Square	Adjusted R Square	Std. Error of the Estimate	R Square Change	F Change	df1	df2	Sig. F Change
1	.322a	.103	.100	7.48975	.103	28.130	2	488	.000
2	.334b	.111	.106	7.46445	.008	4.314	1	487	.038

a Predictors: (Constant), SCHTYPDI, ADVMATH8 Advanced Math Taken in Eighth Grade.
b Predictors: (Constant), SCHTYPDI, ADVMATH8 Advanced Math Taken in Eighth Grade, INTACHAD.

Coefficientsa

Model		Unstandardized Coefficients		Standardized Coefficients	t	Sig.
		B	Std. Error	Beta		
1	(Constant)	50.749	1.109		45.754	.000
	ADVMATH8 Advanced Math Taken in Eighth Grade	4.450	.681	.281	6.530	.000
	SCHTYPDI	3.366	.780	.186	4.318	.000
2	(Constant)	49.031	1.381		35.513	.000
	ADVMATH8 Advanced Math Taken in Eighth Grade	8.539	2.082	.540	4.100	.000
	SCHTYPDI	4.694	1.006	.259	4.665	.000
	INTACHAD	−3.290	1.584	−.276	−2.077	.038

a Dependent Variable: ACHMAT12 Twelfth Grade Math Achievement.

f) According to the value of R^2, approximately 11.1 percent of the variance in twelfth-grade math achievement can be explained by the type of school, whether or not the student took advanced math in eighth grade, and their interaction. According to the value of R^2_{Change}, approximately .8 percent of the variance in twelfth-grade math achievement can be explained uniquely by the interaction.

g) $\hat{Y} = 49.031 + 8.539(ADVMATH8) + 4.694(SCHTYPDI) - 3.29(ADVMATH8)(SCHTYPDI)$.

h) For those who did not take advanced math in eighth grade, the equation is:
$\hat{Y} = 49.031 + 4.694(SCHTYPDI)$.
For those who did take advanced math in eighth grade, the equation is:
$\hat{Y} = 57.57 + 1.404(SCHTYPDI)$.

i) Based on the interpretation of the slopes of these equations, among those who did not take advanced math in eighth grade, those in private school score approximately 4.694 points higher in twelfth-grade math achievement, on average, than those in public school. Among those who did take advanced math in eighth grade, those in private school score approximately 1.404 points higher in twelfth-grade math achievement, on average, than those in public school. The difference in math achievement between public and private school students is less pronounced among those who do not take advanced math in eighth grade.

15.11.

a) The mean of the centered variable is 0.

b) .57.

c) Although the regression model with all three variables is statistically significant, $F(3, 496) = 44.39$, $p < .0005$, the interaction term is not statistically significant, $b = 1.146$, $p = .14$. or $F_{Change}(1, 496) = 21.58$, $p = .14$.

d) Because the interaction is not statistically significant, we may conclude that the relationship between twelfth-grade math achievement and the number of NAEP credits taken in math is not different for males and females.

15.12.

a) Because the two slopes appear to be approximately equal, there appears to be no statistically significant interaction between GENDER and SES.

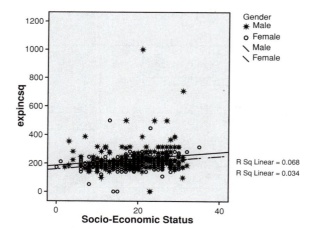

b) The interaction is not statistically significant. According to the value of $F_{Change}(1, 496) = 13$, $p = .72$, the interaction is not statistically significant. According to the t-test of the slope, $b = -.005$, $p = .72$, the interaction is not statistically significant.

15.13.

a) According to the histograms, EXPINC30 is severely positively skewed, SLFCNC08 is negatively skewed, and SES is symmetric.

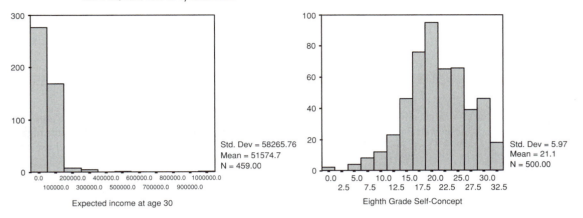

Expected income at age 30

Std. Dev = 58265.76
Mean = 51574.7
N = 459.00

Eighth Grade Self-Concept

Std. Dev = 5.97
Mean = 21.1
N = 500.00

According to the scatterplots, there are several bivariate outliers.

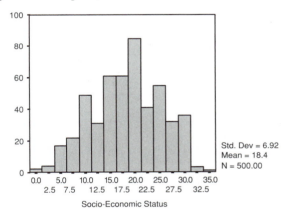

Std. Dev = 6.92
Mean = 18.4
N = 500.00

Socio-Economic Status

According to the first-order correlations, both eighth-grade self-concept and SES are significantly related to expected income at age 30.

Correlations

		Expected income at age 30	Eighth Grade Self-Concept	Socio-Economic Status
Expected income at age 30	Pearson Correlation	1.000	.097*	.157*
	Sig. (2-tailed)		.038	.001
	N	459	459	459
Eighth Grade Self-Concept	Pearson Correlation	.097*	1.000	.083
	Sig. (2-tailed)	.038		.064
	N	459	500	500
Socio-Economic Status	Pearson Correlation	.157**	.083	1.000
	Sig. (2-tailed)	.001	.064	
	N	459	500	500

*Correlation is significant at the 0.05 level (2-tailed).
**Correlation is significant at the 0.01 level (2-tailed).

b) According to both the F_{change}-statistic and the b-weight of the interaction term, the interaction is statistically significant, $F_{change}(1, 455) = 4.451, p = .04, t(455) = 2.11, p = .04$.

Model Summary

Model	R	R Square	Adjusted R Square	Std. Error of the Estimate	R Square Change	F Change	df1	df2	Sig. F Change
					Change Statistics				
1	.178ᵃ	.032	.027	57461.21	.032	7.458	2	456	.001
2	.203ᵇ	.041	.035	57245.02	.009	4.451	1	455	.035

ᵃPredictors: (Constant), SESC, SLFC8C.
ᵇPredictors: (Constant), SESC, SLFC8C, PRODUCT.

c) $\hat{Y} = 51123.759 + 902.28(SLFCNC08 - 20.94) + 1271.079(SES - 18.52) + 141.473(SLFCNC08 - 20.94)(SES - 18.52)$

OR

$\hat{Y} = 51123.76 + 902.28(SLFC8C) + 1271.079(SESC) + 141.473(PRODUCT)$.

Coefficientsᵃ

Model		Unstandardized Coefficients B	Std. Error	Standardized Coefficients Beta	t	Sig.
1	(Constant)	51576.564	2682.060		19.230	.000
	SLFC8C	846.475	461.069	.085	1.836	.067
	SESC	1277.154	394.267	.150	3.239	.001
2	(Constant)	51123.759	2680.576		19.072	.000
	SLFC8C	902.280	460.095	.090	1.961	.050
	SESC	1271.079	392.794	.149	3.236	.001
	PRODUCT	141.473	67.060	.097	2.110	.035

ᵃDependent Variable: Expected income at age 30.

d) According to the descriptive statistics available through the regression procedure, the standard deviation of SLFC8C is 5.8423 and of SESC is 6.8321. Thus, we say low SLFC8C $= -5.8423$, moderate SLFC8C $= 0$, and high SLFC8C $= 5.8423$. We say low SESC $= -6.8321$, moderate SESC $= 0$, and high SESC $= 6.8321$. Substituting each combination of low and high values for these variables into the regression equation produces the following 2×2 table of cell means that gives $\hat{Y}$ (predicted expected income at age 30) values at each of the four pairs of temperature and humidity values.

		SLFC8C	
		Low	High
SESC	Low	$42,815.15	$42,064.09
	High	$48,889.59	$70,726.21

e)

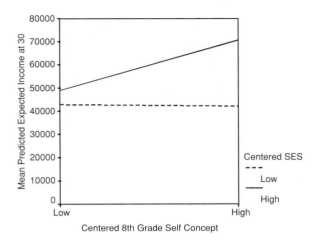

f) From the line graph, we understand the nature of the interaction. For students with low SES, there is little or no relationship between expected income at age 30 and eighth-grade self-concept, whereas for students with high SES, there is a positive relationship betweent these two variables; that is, for students with high SES, as eighth-grade self-concept increases, so does expected income at age 30.

15.14.

a) The full regression model is statistically significant, $F(3, 416) = 33.07$, $p < .0005$. The interaction term is statistically significant, $t(416) = 2.34$, $p = .02$.

ANOVA[c]

Model		Sum of Squares	df	Mean Square	F	Sig.
1	Regression	3675.796	2	1837.898	46.364	.000[a]
	Residual	16530.194	417	39.641		
	Total	20205.990	419			
2	Regression	3891.306	3	1297.102	33.074	.000[b]
	Residual	16314.684	416	39.218		
	Total	20205.990	419			

[a]Predictors: (Constant), Nursery School Attended?, unitmathctrd.
[b]Predictors: (Constant), Nursery School Attended?, unitmathctrd, prodmathnurctrd.
[c]Dependent Variable: Socio-Economic Status.

Coefficients[a]

Model		Unstandardized Coefficients		Standardized Coefficients		
		B	Std. Error	Beta	t	Sig.
1	(Constant)	15.191	.535		28.405	.000
	unitmathctrd	1.629	.390	.185	4.177	.000
	Nursery School Attended?	5.488	.654	.372	8.388	.000
2	(Constant)	15.101	.533		28.318	.000
	unitmathctrd	.405	.650	.046	.623	.533
	Nursery School Attended?	5.553	.651	.377	8.526	.000
	prodmathnurctrd	1.899	.810	.173	2.344	.020

[a]Dependent Variable: Socio-Economic Status.

b) $\hat{Y} = 15.101 + .405(UNITMATH - 3.653) + 5.553(NURSERY) + 1.899(UNITMATH - 3.653)(NURSERY)$.

c) $\hat{Y} = 20.65 + 2.304(UNITMATH - 3.653)$.

d) $\hat{Y} = 15.101 + .405(UNITMATH - 3.653)$.

e) The slopes are significantly different because the interaction is statistically significant.

f) For students who attended nursery school, taking one more unit of math is associated with a much larger increase in SES (2.3 points) than it is for students who did not attend nursery school (.41 points).

g)

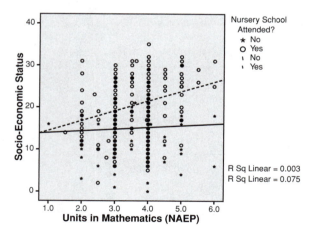

h) It means that although there is not a relationship between SES and the units of math taken in high school after controlling for nursery school attendance, the relationship between SES and the number of units of math taken in high school differs for those who did and those who did not attend nursery school.

15.15.

a) 77.78.

b) No. Centering is a translation in which the mean of the distribution is subtracted from every score. This type of linear transformation does not change the standard deviation.

c) The interaction is not statistically significant, $F_{change}(1, 70) = .56$, $p = .46$.
d) $\hat{Y} = 77.925 + .396(CENMATH) - 2.696(CENGRADE) + .05251(PRODUCT)$.
   Both main effects are statistically significant. The regression equation with mean effects only is a better model because it is more parsimonious; it contains only the variables that contribute to the model and no more.

Coefficients^a

Model		Unstandardized Coefficients		Standardized Coefficients		
		B	Std. Error	Beta	t	Sig.
1	(Constant)	77.795	1.280		60.775	.000
	Centered Math Comprehension	.412	.089	.458	4.621	.000
	Centered Grade	−2.804	1.023	−.271	−2.742	.008
2	(Constant)	77.925	1.296		60.131	.000
	Centered Math Comprehension	.396	.092	.439	4.299	.000
	Centered Grade	−2.696	1.036	−.261	−2.602	.011
	PRODUCT	5.251E-02	.070	.077	.746	.458

^aDependent Variable: reading comprehension.

e) Holding grade constant, each one-point increase in math comprehension score is associated with a .412-point increase in reading comprehension score, on average.
f) Holding math comprehension constant, each one-year increase in grade level is associated with a 2.696-point decrease in reading comprehension score, on average.
g) According to the value of R^2, approximately 32 percent of the variance in reading comprehension score is explained by the two independent variables. A more accurate estimate, given by the adjusted R^2 is approximately 29 percent of the variance is explained.
h) .227.
i) .095.
k) According to the change in R^2, if math comprehension were dropped from the equation, the proportion of variance explained would be only .322 − .227 or .095, whereas, if math comprehension were dropped from the equation, the proportion of variance explained would be .322-.095 or .227, indicating that math comprehension is more important. Furthermore, the beta-weight for math (.46) is larger in magnitude than that for grade (−.27).
l) The F-value of 11.09 is based on the proportion of dependent variable variance explained by the full model including the two main effects and their interaction. The F-value of .556 is based on the proportion of dependent variable variance explained by the interaction only.

15.16. As a first step, using the Ice Cream data set, a regression analysis was performed with RELHUMID as the dependent variable and TEMP as the independent variable. In this analysis, the unstandardized residuals were saved and the variable RES_1 was renamed X21. Then a regression analysis was used to show that b_2 (or the coefficient of RELHUMID in the multiple regression analysis on BARSOLD with RELHUMID and TEMP as independent variables, which was equal to .397) equals the b-weight in the simple regression equation that predicts ice cream sales (Y) from that part of humidity unrelated to temperature (X21).

Coefficients[a]

		Unstandardized Coefficients		Standardized Coefficients		
Model		B	Std. Error	Beta	t	Sig.
1	(Constant)	164.233	2.133		77.014	.000
	Unstandardized Residual	.397	.272	.266	1.461	.155

[a]Dependent Variable: Number of ice cream bars sold.

15.17.

a) According to the results of the hierarchical multiple regression analysis using the centered variables, the interaction term is statistically significant, $t(26) = -2.59$, $p = .016$. The proportion of variance explained by the model including the interaction term is approximately 87 percent, according to the value of adjusted R^2. These values are identical to those obtained in Example 15.4 based on the noncentered variables.

Model Summary

					Change Statistics				
Model	R	R Square	Adjusted R Square	Std. Error of the Estimate	R Square Change	F Change	df1	df2	Sig. F Change
1	.926[a]	.857	.847	4.66	.857	80.988	2	27	.000
2	.941[b]	.886	.873	4.24	.029	6.688	1	26	.016

[a]Predictors: (Constant), TEMPC, RELHC.
[b]Predictors: (Constant), TEMPC, RELHC, PRODUCT.

ANOVA[c]

Model		Sum of Squares	df	Mean Square	F	Sig.
1	Regression	3523.953	2	1761.976	80.988	.000[a]
	Residual	587.414	27	21.756		
	Total	4111.367	29			
2	Regression	3644.141	3	1214.714	67.596	.000[b]
	Residual	467.226	26	17.970		
	Total	4111.367	29			

[a]Predictors: (Constant), TEMPC, RELHC.
[b]Predictors: (Constant), TEMPC, RELHC, PRODUCT.
[c]Dependent Variable: number of ice cream bars sold.

Coefficients[a]

Model		Unstandardized Coefficients		Standardized Coefficients		
		B	Std. Error	Beta	t	Sig.
1	(Constant)	164.232	.852		192.853	.000
	RELHC	.397	.108	.350	3.659	.001
	TEMPC	.878	.127	.659	6.894	.000
2	(Constant)	165.838	.992		167.121	.000
	RELHC	.542	.114	.478	4.779	.000
	TEMPC	.852	.116	.640	7.337	.000
	PRODUCT	$-2.72E-02$	.011	$-.207$	-2.586	.016

[a]Dependent Variable: number of ice cream bars sold.

b) On a day with average relative humidity (RELHC = 0), a one-point increase in the temperature is associated with a .852 increase in ice cream sales, on average.

c) On a day with average temperature (TEMPC = 0), a one-point increase in the relative humidity is associated with a .542 increase in ice cream sales, on average.

d) Because although different values would be substituted into different regression equations, the resulting predicted number of ice cream bars sold would be the same.

15.18.

a) The smallest standardized residual is -1.609 and the largest is 1.946. None of these are outside our acceptable range. The largest value for Cook's distance is .521, which is also within our acceptable range.

Residuals Statistics[a]

	Minimum	Maximum	Mean	Std. Deviation	N
Predicted Value	140.34	181.23	164.23	11.21	30
Std. Predicted Value	-2.131	1.516	.000	1.000	30
Standard Error of Predicted Value	.89	2.92	1.46	.51	30
Adjusted Predicted Value	136.12	181.93	164.09	11.44	30
Residual	-6.82	8.25	2.65E-14	4.01	30
Std. Residual	-1.609	1.946	.000	.947	30
Stud. Residual	-1.748	2.015	.013	1.036	30
Deleted Residual	-8.25	9.50	.14	4.87	30
Stud. Deleted Residual	-1.824	2.151	.016	1.062	30
Mahal. Distance	.304	12.819	2.900	2.911	30
Cook's Distance	.000	.521	.060	.119	30
Centered Leverage Value	.010	.442	.100	.100	30

[a]Dependent Variable: number of ice cream bars sold.

b) Because both of the residual scatterplots have points in a circular, cloudlike shape, none of the assumptions (normality, homoscedasticity, and linearity) underlying the multiple regression analysis appear to be violated.

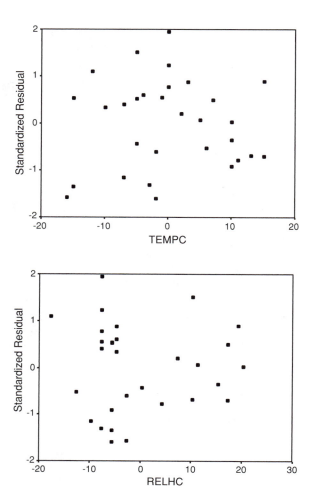

15.19. d)

15.20. b)

15.21. c)

15.22. c)

15.23. b)

15.24. There are two possible circumstances. First, X_3 could be statistically significantly correlated with Y but uncorrelated with both X_1 and X_2. Second, X_3 could be uncorrelated with Y.

CHAPTER 16. **SOLUTIONS**

16.1. According to the results of the chi-square goodness-of-fit test, students are not evenly divided into the two placement types, $\chi^2(df = 1, N = 105) = 6.94$, $p = .008$. Students are more likely to be placed in the resource room than in the self-contained classroom.

Type of Placement

	Observed N	Expected N	Residual
Part Time Resource Room	66	52.5	13.5
Full Time Self Contained Classroom	39	52.5	−13.5
Total	105		

Test Statistics

	Type of Placement
Chi-Square[a]	6.943
df	1
Asymp. Sig.	.008

[a]0 cells (.0%) have expected frequencies less than 5. The minimum expected cell frequency is 52.5.

16.2.

a) According to the chi-square test of independence, there are no gender differences in the type of placement assigned, $\chi^2(df = 1, N = 66) = 1.15$, $p = .28$. The same result obtains using the Fisher Exact Test ($p = .310$).

gender * Type of Placement Crosstabulation

Count

		Type of Placement		Total
		RR	MIS	
gender	male	37	26	63
	female	29	13	42
Total		66	39	105

Chi-Square Tests

	Value	df	Asymp. Sig. (2-sided)	Exact Sig. (2-sided)	Exact Sig. (1-sided)
Pearson Chi-Square	1.149[b]	1	.284		
Continuity Correction[a]	.750	1	.387		
Likelihood Ratio	1.161	1	.281		
Fisher's Exact Test				.310	.194
Linear-by-Linear Association	1.138	1	.286		
N of Valid Cases	105				

[a]Computed only for a 2 × 2 table.
[b]0 cells (.0%) have expected count less than 5. The minimum expected count is 15.60.

b) Clustered bar graph.

c) Correlation (in the case of two dichotomous variables, it is sometimes called the phi coefficient).

16.3.

a) According to the results of the sign test, such children perform better in math, $z = -3.852, p < .0005$.

Frequencies

		N
reading comprehension – math comprehension	Negative Differences[a]	51
	Positive Differences[b]	18
	Ties[c]	5
	Total	74

[a] reading comprehension < math comprehension.
[b] reading comprehension > math comprehension.
[c] math comprehension = reading comprehension.

Test Statistics[a]

	reading comprehension – math comprehension
z	−3.852
Asymp. Sig. (2-tailed)	.000

[a] Sign Test.

b) Yes.

16.4.

a) Because according to the skewness ratio, the distribution of reading comprehension scores is severely negatively skewed and the sample size is not adequately large to compensate.

b) According to the results of the Mann–Whitney U-test, students placed in the resource room perform statistically significantly better in reading comprehension than students placed in self-contained classrooms, $U = 236.5, p < .0005$.

Ranks

	Type of Placement	N	Mean Rank	Sum of Ranks
Reading Comprehension	Part Time Resource Room	53	45.54	2413.50
	Full Time Self Contained Classroom	23	22.28	512.50
	Total	76		

Test Statistics[a]

	Reading Comprehension
Mann–Whitney U	236.500
Wilcoxon W	512.500
Z	−4.221
Asymp. Sig. (2-tailed)	.000

[a]Grouping Variable: Type of Placement.

16.5.

a) Because the fourth-grade reading comprehension scores are significantly skewed and the sample size is not adequately large to compensate.

Descriptive Statistics

		N	Mean	Std.	Skewness	
GRADE		Statistic	Statistic	Statistic	Statistic	Std. Error
1	reading comprehension	14	84.64	4.88	−.239	.597
	Valid N (listwise)	14				
2	reading comprehension	22	78.77	10.42	−.115	.491
	Valid N (listwise)	22				
3	reading comprehension	20	77.45	13.45	.255	.512
	Valid N (listwise)	20				
4	reading comprehension	11	72.00	20.80	−1.053	.661
	Valid N (listwise)	11				
5	reading comprehension	9	71.22	11.40	−.681	.717
	Valid N (listwise)	9				

b) Yes, $\chi^2(df = 4, N = 76) = 11.01, p = .03$.

Ranks

	GRADE	N	Mean Rank
reading comprehension	1	14	53.96
	2	22	39.27
	3	20	36.38
	4	11	30.82
	5	9	26.67
	Total	76	

Test Statistics[a,b]

	reading comprehension
Chi-Square	11.009
df	4
Asymp. Sig.	.026

[a]Kruskal Wallis Test.
[b]Grouping Variable: GRADE.

16.6. The following answers are not necessarily the only correct choices.

a) iii.   b) v.   c) iii.

d) iv.   e) i.   f) ii.

g) ii.

16.7.

a) The chi-square test of independence.

b) According to the chi-square test of independence, there are differences in urbanicity by region, $\chi^2(df = 6, N = 500) = 45.49, p < .0005$.

Urbanicity * Geographic Region of School Crosstabulation

Count

		Geographic Region of School				
		Northeast	North Central	South	West	Total
Urbanicity	Urban	13	44	42	24	123
	Suburban	74	49	49	43	215
	Rural	19	58	59	26	162
Total		106	151	150	93	500

Chi-Square Tests

	Value	df	Asymp. Sig. (2-sided)
Pearson Chi-Square	45.493[a]	6	.000
Likelihood Ratio	45.874	6	.000
Linear-by-Linear Association	.029	1	.864
N of Valid Cases	500		

[a]0 cells (.0%) have expected count less than 5. The minimum expected count is 22.88.

16.8.

a) The sign test.

b) Because the variables are measured at the ordinal level.

c) According to the results of the sign test, there is a statistically significant difference in the frequency of classes cut by seniors and the frequency of missed school by seniors, $z = -13.63, p < .0005$. College-bound students who were always at grade level had a greater tendency to miss school than to cut classes.

Ranks

		N	Mean Rank	Sum of Ranks
Number of Times Skipped/Cut Classes in Twelfth Grade - Number of Times Missed School	Negative Ranks	347[a]	201.53	69932.00
	Positive Ranks	50[b]	181.42	9071.00
	Ties	103[c]		
	Total	500		

[a]Number of Times Skipped/Cut Classes in Twelfth Grade < Number of Times Missed School.

[b]Number of Times Skipped/Cut Classes in Twelfth Grade > Number of Times Missed School.

[c]Number of Times Missed School = Number of Times Skipped/Cut Classes in Twelfth Grade.

Test Statistics[b]

	Number of Times Skipped/Cut Classes in Twelfth Grade– Number of Times Missed School
z	−13.633[a]
Asymp. Sig. (2-tailed)	.000

[a]Based on positive ranks.

[b]Wilcoxon Signed Ranks Test.

16.9.

a) The chi-squared test of independence and the Mann–Whitney U-test.

b) According to the results of the chi-square test of independence, perceived teacher interest in students does not vary by whether or not the student took advanced math in eighth grade, $\chi^2(df = 3, N = 491) = 4.65$, $p = .20$. The results of the Mann–Whitney U-test lead to the same conclusion, $U = 27919$, $p = .10$.

Advanced Math Taken in Eighth Grade * My Teachers are Interested in Students Crosstabulation

Count

		My Teachers are Interested in Students				Total
		Strongly Agree	Agree	Disagree	Strongly Disagree	
Advanced Math Taken in Eighth Grade	No	41	190	29	5	265
	Yes	40	170	13	3	226
Total		81	360	42	8	491

Chi-Square Tests

	Value	df	Asymp. Sig. (2-sided)
Pearson Chi-Square	4.650[a]	3	.199
Likelihood Ratio	4.780	3	.189
Linear-by-Linear Association	2.830	1	.093
N of Valid Cases	491		

[a]2 cells (25.0%) have expected count less than 5.
The minimum expected count is 3.68.

Ranks

	Advanced Math Taken	N	Mean Rank	Sum of Ranks
My Teachers are Interested in Students	No	265	253.65	67216.00
	Yes	226	237.04	53570.00
	Total	491		

Test Statistics[a]

	My Teachers are Interested in Students
Mann-Whitney U	27919.000
Wilcoxon W	53570.000
Z	−1.668
Asymp. Sig. (2-tailed)	.095

[a]Grouping Variable: Advanced Math Taken in Eighth Grade

16.10.

a) The chi-square goodness-of-fit test.

b) According to the results of the chi-square goodness-of-fit test, college-bound students who are always at grade level report having ever smoked marijuana less often than the general population of high school seniors in the United States, $\chi^2(df = 1, N = 500) = 45.89, p < .0005$.

Smoked Marijuana Ever?

	Observed N	Expected N	Residual
Never	408	337.0	71.0
Yes	92	163.0	−71.0
Total	500		

Test Statistics

	Smoked Marijuana Ever?
Chi-Square[a]	45.885
df	1
Asymp. Sig.	.000

[a]0 cells (.0%) have expected frequencies less than 5. The minimum expected cell frequency is 163.0.

16.11.

a) A nonparametric test is appropriate in this case because HWKOUT12 is measured at the ordinal level.

b) The Kruskal–Wallis ANOVA.

c) According to the results of the Kruskal–Wallis test, time spent on homework outside school by high school seniors does vary by urbanicity, $\chi^2(df = 2, N = 500) = 15.17, p = .001$.

Ranks

	Urbanicity	N	Mean Rank
Time Spent on Homework out of School per Week in Twelfth Grade	Urban	123	282.67
	Suburban	215	256.63
	Rural	162	217.94
	Total	500	

Test Statistics[a,b]

	Time Spent on Homework out of School per Week in Twelfth Grade
Chi-Square	15.169
df	2
Asymp. Sig.	.001

[a]Kruskal Wallis Test.
[b]Grouping Variable: Urbanicity.

16.12. According to the results of the chi-square goodness-of-fit test, these doctors detected statistically significantly fewer positive results than the state average, $\chi^2(df = 1, N = 10000) = 29.40, p < .0005$.

RESULTS

	Observed N	Expected N	Residual
Negative	9987	9948.0	39.0
Positive	13	52.0	−39.0
Total	10000		

Test Statistics

	RESULTS
Chi-Square[a]	29.403
df	1
Asymp. Sig.	.000

[a]0 cells (.0%) have expected frequencies less than 5. The minimum expected cell frequency is 52.0.

16.13. According to the results of the chi-square test of independence, there is no association between estrogen use and cardiovascular death rates, $\chi^2(df = 1, N = 1500) = 2.60, p = .11$. The same conclusion results from using the Fisher Exact Test ($p = .18$).

X * Y Crosstabulation

Count

		Y		Total
		.00	1.00	
X	.00	746	4	750
	1.00	740	10	750
Total		1486	14	1500

Chi-Square Tests

	Value	df	Asymp. Sig. (2-sided)	Exact Sig. (2-sided)	Exact Sig. (1-sided)
Pearson Chi-Square	2.596[b]	1	.107		
Continuity Correction[a]	1.803	1	.179		
Likelihood Ratio	2.681	1	.102		
Fisher's Exact Test				.178	.089
Linear-by-Linear Association	2.594	1	.107		
N of Valid Cases	1500				

[a]Computed only for a 2×2 table.
[b]0 cells (.0%) have expected count less than 5. The minimum expected count is 7.00.

16.14. According to the results of the sign test, the education level of first-born sons in the small rural community in the Midwest is higher than the education level of their fathers, $Z = -3.04$, $p = .001$.

Ranks

		N	Mean Rank	Sum of Ranks
SONS – FATHERS	Negative Ranks	1[a]	3.00	3.00
	Positive Ranks	12[b]	7.33	88.00
	Ties	2[c]		
	Total	15		

[a]SONS < FATHERS
[b]SONS > FATHERS
[c]FATHERS = SONS

Test Statistics[b]

	SONS – FATHERS
z	−3.042[a]
Asymp. Sig. (2-tailed)	.002

[a]Based on negative ranks.
[b]Wilcoxon Signed Ranks Test.

16.15. According to the results of the Mann–Whitney U-test, siblings of the same sex are more competitive overall than siblings of the opposite sex, $U = 26.00$, $p = .04$.

Ranks

	Sex of Sibling	N	Mean Rank	Sum of Ranks
Competitiveness Score	Same	10	12.90	129.00
	Opposite	10	8.10	81.00
	Total	20		

Test Statistics[b]

	Competitiveness Score
Mann–Whitney U	26.000
Wilcoxon W	81.000
Z	−1.814
Asymp. Sig. (2-tailed)	.070
Exact Sig. [2*(1-tailed Sig.)]	.075[a]

[a]Not corrected for ties.
[b]Grouping Variable: Sex of Sibling.

16.16. According to the results of the Kruskal–Wallis test, there were differences in mood by type of music heard, $\chi^2(df = 2, N = 12) = 9.85$, $p = .007$.

Ranks

	Type of Music	N	Mean Rank
MOOD	Slow Classical	4	2.50
	Soft Rock	4	6.50
	Hard Rock	4	10.50
	Total	12	

Test Statistics[a,b]

	MOOD
Chi-Square	9.846
df	2
Asymp. Sig.	.007

[a]Kruskal Wallis Test.
[b]Grouping Variable: Type of Music.

Index